Human Sexuality

Self, Society, and Culture

Second Edition

Gilbert Herdt
San Francisco State University
Founder, National Sexuality Resource Center (NSRC)

Nicole C. Polen-Petit
National University

McGraw Hill

HUMAN SEXUALITY: SELF, SOCIETY AND CULTURE, SECOND EDITION

Published by McGraw Hill LLC, 1325 Avenue of the Americas, New York, NY 10121. Copyright © 2021 by McGraw Hill LLC. All rights reserved. Printed in the United States of America. Previous editions © 2014. No part of this publication may be reproduced or distributed in any form or by any means, or stored in a database or retrieval system, without the prior written consent of McGraw Hill LLC, including, but not limited to, in any network or other electronic storage or transmission, or broadcast for distance learning.

Some ancillaries, including electronic and print components, may not be available to customers outside the United States.

This book is printed on acid-free paper.

1 2 3 4 5 6 7 8 9 LWI 24 23 22 21 20

ISBN 978-1-260-57584-2
MHID 1-260-57584-5

Cover Image: *BUY THIS/Shutterstock*

All credits appearing on page are considered to be an extension of the copyright page.

The Internet addresses listed in the text were accurate at the time of publication. The inclusion of a website does not indicate an endorsement by the authors or McGraw Hill LLC, and McGraw Hill LLC does not guarantee the accuracy of the information presented at these sites.

mheducation.com/highered

About the Authors

Gilbert Herdt

Gilbert Herdt completed his undergraduate degree in anthropology, with significant coursework in psychology, at Sacramento State College, where he went on to get an MA in medical anthropology. He began his doctoral studies at the University of Washington in cultural anthropology, psychological anthropology, and Pacific studies. With support from a Fulbright scholarship to Australia in 1974, Gil enrolled as a doctoral student at the Australian National University. He received a PhD in 1978, following anthropological fieldwork in Papua New Guinea, and then studied adult psychiatry at UCLA's Neuropsychiatric Institute, where he received a postdoctoral certificate under the supervision of famed psychoanalyst Robert J. Stoller. While at UCLA, he published *Guardians of the Flutes* (McGraw-Hill, 1981), a study of ritualized homosexuality.

Gil has been an assistant professor at Stanford University (1979–1985), a professor of human development at the University of Chicago (1985–1997), and a professor and founder of the Department of Sexuality Studies at San Francisco State University, where he is emeritus professor. He has undertaken 15 field trips to Papua New Guinea and continues to do research with the Sambia people there. In addition to his research on sexual identity development, gender identity development, gender roles, sexual attitudes, sexual socialization, and male-female differences, Gil has taught large courses, as well as seminars, on many aspects of sexuality.

Gil has published 37 books and 104 scientific peer-reviewed journal articles, chapters, encyclopedia articles, and scholarly reports, and he is an expert in culture, HIV, and sexual risk behavior. With a National Institutes of Health (NIH) grant, he helped found the Center for Culture and Mental Health in Chicago, and he mentored many students who went on to work in these areas. In addition to long-term grants received from the NIH, Gil has also been funded through the Spencer Foundation, Wenner-Gren Foundation, Ford Foundation, Haas Foundation, and the Rockefeller Foundation to support his own research and that of his many students.

Gil has founded ongoing Summer Institutes on Sexuality and Society at the University of Amsterdam in the Netherlands and at San Francisco State. He founded and edited the *Journal of Sexuality and Social Policy* for many years, and he is emeritus founder of the Ford Foundation–funded National Sexuality Resource Center. At San Francisco State, Gil founded the first master of arts program in human sexuality at a public university in the United States. In 2014, Gil helped to found the first accredited PhD program in human sexuality studies on the West Coast at the California Institute of Integral Studies in San Francisco. Today he lives with his partner Agung Saryatmo in Bali, Indonesia, with his dogs.

Dedication

For Agung.

G. H.

About the Authors

Nicole C. Polen-Petit

Nicole Polen-Petit completed her undergraduate degree in psychology at Whitworth University. From there, she went to the University of California at Davis and completed her MS in child development and her PhD in human development in 2006. As a graduate student, Nicole began teaching large undergraduate courses in human sexuality.

After completing her doctoral degree, Nicole remained at UC–Davis as an adjunct faculty member in the Department of Human Ecology, where she has continuously taught human sexuality to large sections of students in various quarters. Nicole received the department's Instructor of the Year award in both 2008 and 2010.

Complementing her experience in the classroom, Nicole has also worked in a community mental health agency that serves children and adolescents in the Sacramento region. At this agency, she provided clinical training to staff on a variety of clinical and psychological issues. In this environment, she maintained a keen interest in the applied clinical and physical health aspects of sexuality.

In 2010, Nicole accepted a faculty position at National University in the Department of Psychology and served as an associate professor until 2019, when she accepted a position as interim associate dean for the College of Letters and Sciences at National University. She has taught a variety of courses to an incredibly diverse student body. Her research interests include sexual fluidity in women, sexual identity development in self-identified bisexual women, and intersections of faith and sexuality.

Nicole lives near Sacramento with her husband and three children. Her free time is often spent in the company of her extended family. She is a Gryffindor, scrapbook enthusiast, Disney-lover and amateur sommelier.

Dedication

For Damon: You have my whole heart forever. To Gracie, Presley, and Chandler: You are my world. Everything I do is for you always. To my students: thank you for teaching me and making me better. You inspire me.

N.P.-P.

Brief Contents

CHAPTER 1   The Study of Human Sexuality   1

CHAPTER 2   Contexts of Sexuality: Culture, History, and Religion   31

CHAPTER 3   Sexuality, Media, and the Internet   67

CHAPTER 4   Sexual Anatomy and Physiology   99

CHAPTER 5   Sexual Pleasure, Arousal, and Response   133

CHAPTER 6   Taking Care of the Sexual Body   167

CHAPTER 7   Contraception   215

CHAPTER 8   Reproduction: Conception, Pregnancy, and Childbirth   247

CHAPTER 9   Gender and Identity: Biology, Roles, and Culture   297

CHAPTER 10   Sexual Orientation   331

CHAPTER 11   Sexuality in Childhood and Adolescence   369

CHAPTER 12   Sexuality in Adulthood and Later Life   409

CHAPTER 13   Attraction, Love, and Communication   443

CHAPTER 14   Sexual Coercion and Resiliency   475

CHAPTER 15   Sexual Diagnoses: Sexual Dysfunction to Stigmatized & Normative Sexual Variations   511

Contents

CHAPTER 1 The Study of Human Sexuality 1

Sexual Literacy 3
Becoming Sexually Literate 3
Sexual Well-Being 5

Sexual Science—A Historical Perspective 8
The Medical Model of Sexuality 8
A New Approach to Sex Research 10
Sex Research Comes of Age 12
Sex and Social Justice Today 17

Methodology in the Study of Sexuality 19
Interdisciplinary Perspectives 19
Intersectionality and Social Justice 20
Ethics of Sexual Research 21
Research Designs 21
Participatory Action Research 25

Human Sexual Rights 26

CHAPTER 2 Contexts of Sexuality: Culture, History, and Religion 31

Human Sexual Nature in Context 32
The Sexual Triangle: Species, Culture, and Individual 33
Sexuality Among the Bonobo 34
Human Sexual Nature as Expressed Through Culture 34

Sex Since the Beginning of Time 37
Prehistoric Sex and Communication 38
A Brief History of Sex and Civilization 39

Sexual Cultures and Norms 48
Sexual Norms and Sexual Socialization 48
Sex-Approving and Sex-Disapproving Cultures 51
Sexual Unlearning 52

Sexuality and the Great World Religions 54
Sex, Religion, and Reality 55
Sex in the World Religions 56

Spirituality and Sexual Behavior in the United States 61

The Pursuit of Sexual Well-Being in Communities of Faith 63

CHAPTER 3 Sexuality, Media, and the Internet 67

Sex, Media, and Pop Culture 68
Sex in Pop Culture 68
Shared Sexual Images and Media 71
Sexual Images and Advertising 73
Popular Music and Sexual Attitudes 73
From Reality TV to Homemade Video 75

The Internet and Sexual Literacy 76
Snapchat, Facebook, YouTube, and Sexting 80
Online Sexual Socialization 82
Sexuality and Risk Online 85

Online Sexual Contexts 86
Online Boundaries 86
Online Romance, Dating, and Hooking Up 86
Sexual Avatars and Gaming 89

Adult Sexual Content 92
Pornography and Its Changing Meaning 92
Adult Sexual Entertainment Online 95

Online Communities, Rights, and Sexual Well-Being 96

Contents **vii**

CHAPTER 4 Sexual Anatomy and Physiology 99

Timothy A. Clary/AFP/Getty Images

Sexual Anatomy 100
Female Sexual Anatomy 101
External Female Sex Organs 102
Internal Female Sexual Organs 104
Breasts and Breast Development 108
Variability in the Female Body 109
Female Genital Mutilation 111

Female Sexual Physiology 112
The Endocrine System and Hormones 113
Pheromones and Their Role in Sexual Behavior 114
The Menstrual Cycle 114
Menopause 119

Male Sexual Anatomy 120
External Male Sex Organs 120
Internal Male Sex Organs 122
Erection and Ejaculation 122
Variability in the Male Body 125
Circumcision 125

Male Sexual Physiology 128
Bodily Integrity Rights and Sexual Well-Being 128

CHAPTER 5 Sexual Pleasure, Arousal, and Response 133

Doug Menuez/Getty Images

Pleasure, Culture, and Sexual Well-Being 134
Sexual Nature and Sexual Well-Being 135
Cultural Influences on Sexual Pleasure and Sexual Well-Being 135
Defining Your Personal Needs 136
Keeping a Sexual Journal 138

Sexual Arousal and Response 139
The Five Senses and Pleasure 140
Pheromones and Sexual Motivation 144
Sexual Excitement and Sexual Fantasy 144
Sexual Response Cycles 146
Orgasm 149

Sexual Techniques 150
Masturbation—Solitary and in Relationships 150
Kissing 153
Frequency of Sexual Activity 154
Other Intimate Behaviors 155

Sexual Pleasure as a Human Right 163

CHAPTER 6 Taking Care of the Sexual Body 167

nito500/123RF

Knowing Our Own Body 168
Taking Responsibility for Our Own Sexual Health 169
Female Sexual Health 171
Male Sexual Health 180

Sexually Transmitted Infections 184
Risks and Protective Factors for STIs 184
Sexual Risk Negotiation 187
Human Immunodeficiency Virus 188
Bacterial STIs 198
Parasitic STIs 205
Viral STIs 207

Sexual Well-Being and Innovation in STI Prevention 212

CHAPTER 7 Contraception 215

Fabio Cardoso/Getty Images

Contraception: History and Cultural Variations 216
Cross-Cultural Variations in Contraception 217
History of Contraceptives in the United States 219

Methods of Contraception 221
Choosing a Method of Contraception: What to Consider 221
Methods That Protect Against Pregnancy and STIs 231
Methods That Protect Against Pregnancy But Not Against STIs 235

Contraception and Sexual Well-Being 244

CHAPTER 8 Reproduction: Conception, Pregnancy, and Childbirth 247

Parenting and Reproductive Decisions 248
Pronatalism 251
Family Leave 252
Considering Parenthood 252

Ensuring a Healthy Pregnancy 253
Preparing the Body for Pregnancy 253
Nutrition and Exercise 255
Sex During Pregnancy 257

Conception and Pregnancy 258
Cross-Cultural Ideas About Conception 258
Trimesters: The Developing Fetus and Changes for Women and Partners 259
Potential Problems During Pregnancy 268
Detecting Problems in Pregnancy 271

Birth and the Postpartum Period: What to Expect 273
Options for Giving Birth 275
Birth Assistance and Interventions 275
Making a Birth Plan 280
After the Birth: The Postpartum Period 281

Infertility and Options 284
Assisted Reproductive Techniques 284
Other Options for Creating a Family 286

Abortion 287
Defining Abortion 289
Safe Methods of Abortion 289
Unsafe Methods of Abortion 291
After an Abortion 291

Sexual Well-Being and Reproductive Rights 292

CHAPTER 9 Gender and Identity: Biology, Roles, and Culture 297

Understanding Gender in Development and in Context 298
Gender and Sex 299
Biological Processes in the Development of Sex 300
Biological Sex Variations and Intersex People 302
Cultural Treatment of Intersex People 307

Gender Identity and Expression 307
Gender Identity—A Brief History 308
Biology and Gender Identity Development 309
Transgender and Cisgender Identities 311
Gender Confirmation 314
Androgyny (Gender Nonconforming/Non-Binary/Genderqueer) 317

Gender Roles 318
Gender Roles Across Time and Cultures 319
Social Institutions and Gender Role Development 319
Sexism, Inequality, and Gender Roles 323

Gender Norms and Variance 325
Factors of Gender Nonconformity 325

Gender Identity and Intersex Rights: Well-Being and Social Justice 326

CHAPTER 10 Sexual Orientation 331

Understanding Sexual Orientation 332
The Spectrum of Sexual Orientation 334
The Gap Between Sexual Attraction and Behavior 335
Development of Sexual Orientation 337
Sexual Socialization and Compulsory Heterosexuality 341
Sexual Individuality and Sexual Orientation 342

Variations in Sexual Orientation Across Time and Cultures 343
Same-Sex Behavior Variations Across Cultures 344
The Invention of Modern Western Identity 345
The Modern LGBTQ Movement 346
10% Are Gay: Myth or Sexual Geography? 348
Bisexuality 348
Men Who Have Sex with Men (MSM) 350
Female Sexual Fluidity 351
Queer and Questioning 352

LGBTQ Identity Discrimination and Stigma 353
  Sexual Prejudice, Homophobia, and Homonegativity 354
  Bullying and Internalized Homophobia 356
  Hate Crimes 357
Coming Out and Sexual Well-Being 360
  Social Acceptance and Being Out 360
  Being Out—Steps Toward Well-Being 361
  LGBTQ Family Formation 363
Coming Out, Sexual Well-Being, and Sexual Rights 365

CHAPTER 11 Sexuality in Childhood and Adolescence 369

Sexual Development in Childhood and Adolescence 370
  Biology, Family, and Culture 371
  Healthy Sexuality and Values in Childhood and Adolescence 372
  Emotional Literacy in Young People 373
Sexuality in Childhood 375
  Infants as Sensual Beings 375
  Childhood Curiosity, Masturbation, and Sexual Play 376
Sexuality in Adolescence 380
  The Magical Age of 10: Development of Desire 380
  The Biological Changes of Adolescence: Pubertal Development 380
  Romantic Relationships 385
  Fluidity in Adolescent Sexual Expression 385
  Sexual Identity 388
  Sexual Behaviors in Adolescence 389
  STIs, Pregnancy, and Contraception 391
Sexuality in Context: The Role of Institutions 392
  Families 392
  Peers 394
  Media Exposure: Television, Movies, Music, and the Internet 395
  Sexuality Education in Schools 396
  Sexual Health in Europe and the United States 402
Young People's Rights and Sexual Well-Being 404

CHAPTER 12 Sexuality in Adulthood and Later Life 409

Early Adulthood 411
  Single Living 412
  Casual Sex and What It Means 415
  Polyamory 417
  Cohabitation 418
  Early Cohabitation and Sexual Well-Being 424
Integrating Marriage and Sexual Well-Being 425
  Variations in Marriage 427
  Sex and Marriage 429
  Extramarital Relationships 430
  Divorce and Subsequent Marriages 431
  Same-Sex Marriage Equality 432
Sexuality in Midlife and Aging 434
  Sex and Well-Being at Midlife 434
  How Sex Shapes Men and Women as They Age 438
  Elderhood and Healthy Sexuality 438
Sexuality and Well-Being Late in Life 440

CHAPTER 13 Attraction, Love, and Communication 443

Sexual Attraction 444
  Theories of Sexual Desire and Attraction 445
  Physical Attractiveness 447
  Beauty and Sexiness 447
  Chemistry and Attraction 449
  Psychological Attraction 450
  Biological Attraction 451

Same-Sex Attraction 451
Sexual Scripts 452

Love 453
Theories of Love 454
Types of Attachment 459
When Love Ends: The Dissolution of Relationships 460

Communication 461
Emotional Literacy: Communicating Your Needs 461
Sexual Language 463
Nonverbal Sexual Communication and Flirting 464
Sexual Self-Disclosure: To Reveal or Not to Reveal? 466
Characteristics of Effective Communication 466
Styles of Communication 468
Characteristics of Ineffective Communication 469
Improving Communication Skills 471

Communication and Sexual Well-Being 472

CHAPTER 14 Sexual Coercion and Resiliency 475

Vassiliy Kochetkov/123RF

Sexual Coercion 477

Rape 477
Date Rape 479
Marital Rape 483
Prisoner Rape 484
Victim-Blame 486
Cultural Differences in Rape 486
Societies Prone to Rape 487
Perpetrators of Sexual Coercion 490
Survivors of Rape and Other Forms of Coercion 491

Childhood Sexual Coercion 493
Incest 497
Child Pornography 498

Teen and Adult Sexual Coercion 499
Sexual Harassment 499
Teen Dating Violence 502

Sex Work and Sex Trafficking 503
Different Types of Sex Work 504
Sex Work and Rights 504
Sex Trafficking 506

Recovery, Resiliency, and Sexual Well-Being 506

CHAPTER 15 Sexual Diagnoses: Sexual Dysfunction to Stigmatized & Normative Sexual Variations 511

Victor Moussa/Shutterstock

Understanding and Challenging Diagnostic Models of Human Sexuality 513

Medical and Physical Challenges to Normative Sexual Response 516
Desire Issues for Women 516
Arousal Issues for Men 518
The Challenges of Disability: Embracing New Possibilities 519

Diagnoses of Sexual Dysfunction and Behavior: The *DSM-5* and Paraphilic Disorders 521
The DSM *and Sexual Diagnosis* 521
Impulsive or Compulsive Sexual Behavior 522
Paraphilias 524
Theories of Origins of Paraphilias 533
Treatment of Paraphilic Disorders 534

From Normative to Extreme Sexual Behaviors 535
Cultural Extremes of Sexuality 536
Extreme Sexual Behaviors in Contemporary Society 538
Kinky Sex 539
Sex Tourism and Extreme Sexuality 541

Sexual Novelty and Healthy Sexuality 544

Achieving Sexual Well Being: Accepting Your Own Enjoyment 547

Glossary 551
References 563
Name Index 588
Subject Index 598

A Letter from the Authors

Dear Instructor,

Teaching human sexuality courses has been our passion for decades. There is no other subject that grips human beings in the way that sexuality does. Human sexuality courses can inspire incredible debate, reflection, and critical thinking, and the kind of personal application that is truly life-changing. For many years, prior to writing this text, we were increasingly frustrated by the overwhelming discussion of danger, risk, and dysfunction that seemed to cloud human sexuality texts. We wanted to teach with a silver lining of positivity that emphasized the beauty of the human sexual landscape. Rather than leaving classes frightened and paralyzed by sexual information, our aspiration is for students to emerge from the classroom enlightened, inspired, and equipped to successfully lead healthy and happy sexual lives. This kind of positivity is the framework from which we aim to teach so that students will gain the necessary knowledge and build skills that will enable them to practice sexual literacy in their own lives and serve as a model for those they are in relationship and community with.

We know from a deep body of research that when sexual information is presented in a positive way that speaks to holistic health, well-being, pleasure, and relationship formation that individuals are more likely to engage in behaviors that reflect and promote healthy sexual literacy. Further, we believe that understanding the full dignity of human sexual rights helps individuals, families, and communities to find themselves a part of the global community that supports the rights and well-being of all people.

We have also learned from our own years of teaching that the framework of sexual literacy is most successful when we can help students to *perform* sexual literacy. This means that we teach the **skill sets** (such as how to communicate sexual feelings and emotions) and **knowledge sets** (such as how to identify HIV or how to create better relationships) to help students narrate their experience as they actually put sexual literacy into practice in their lives.

Admittedly, the vast body of research and information that exists on the Internet and the immeasurable volume of sexual opinions that can be found through social media create certain challenges in today's human sexuality classroom. And yet helping students to navigate through the white noise and discern fact from opinion, and research from folklore, is a critical task in human sexuality instruction. We aim in this book to highlight current and relevant social movements, critical intersections such as social justice and sexuality, and discuss contemporary research and knowledge related to sexual controversies to give students better, more complete, and accurate information to inform their own views and refine their beliefs.

We are thrilled that you have chosen this text to accompany you as you walk into your sexuality course, whether onsite in a lecture hall on campus, or within a learning management system in an online course, or both. We have done both kinds of teaching for years, and we truly believe that our textbook equips you with the framework and tools to better reach students and enable them to become better human beings. It is our hope that in this text you will find all you need to create engaging and scientifically accurate lectures, thought-provoking content to help you frame discussions and assignments and, most importantly, the ways to narrate and teach through a framework of positive sexuality that emphasizes diversity, human sexual rights, and holistic well-being. We hope that this helps all of us to further the development of sexual literacy in classrooms, communities, and ultimately this earth of ours.

–Gil and Nicole

Preface

Human Sexuality: Self, Society, and Culture supports thinking critically about the contexts that shape sexuality and further highlights the role of sexuality in society and culture. With a thought-provoking appraisal of the human sexual experience, this approach enables readers to participate more fully and more knowledgeably as healthy sexual beings in the wider society and culture throughout their lifetimes. *Human Sexuality* fosters an atmosphere where students can safely ask questions about what they are learning or about their personal experiences. With *Human Sexuality*, we hope to empower students and inspire a lifelong appreciation of their own sexuality and the role of sexuality in their community, culture, and society.

Thinking Critically and Actively About Self and Sexuality

Students take the human sexuality course for many reasons. Some may simply be curious or are exploring different majors. Others may be taking the course to fulfill a major or general education requirement. Still others may be parents who want to be able to talk with their children about sexuality. Whatever their reasons for signing up for Human Sexuality, most students come to class eager to learn how they might have more satisfying sexual experiences.

The path to sexual well-being begins with knowledge, both factual knowledge and self-knowledge. In *Human Sexuality,* we introduce students to the wealth of information amassed through many years of sexuality research. Mastering the vocabulary and concepts of the discipline is essential to developing the skills to evaluate information and form thoughtful opinions, to develop self-awareness, and to nurture fulfilling intimate relationships. With this foundation, students can begin to take responsibility for their own sexual well-being.

Features supporting this journey include:

SmartBook 2.0

SmartBook 2.0, McGraw-Hill's adaptive learning system, helps students study more efficiently by highlighting what to focus on in the chapter, asking review questions, and directing them to resources until they understand. Over nine years ago, backed by the belief that we could unlock the potential of every student with the power of learning science, we embarked on a journey to create a unique educational experience. Spanning more than 90 disciplines and serving multiple education markets around the world, SmartBook has emerged as the leader in adaptive learning. Today, SmartBook 2.0 builds on our market-leading technology with enhanced capabilities that deliver a more personalized, efficient, and accessible learning experience for students and instructors. Some of the enhancements include:

- **Mobile and offline reading**—Just like McGraw-Hill's new eBook and Read Anywhere App, SmartBook 2.0 will be available for mobile use on smart devices, both online and off-line.

- **Greater flexibility**—With SmartBook 2.0, instructors can now assign readings down to the sub-topic level (rather than only to the topic level). This provides even greater control and alignment with their syllabus.
- **Accessibility**—SmartBook 2.0 was built from the ground up with accessibility in mind to account for appropriate color contrast, keyboard navigation, and screen reader usability, to support students with accessibility needs.

McGraw-Hill Education's Connect for Human Sexuality

In this digital age, students like to access information in multiple ways. Connect's assignments help students contextualize what they've learned through application, so they can better understand the material and think critically. Connect Human Sexuality includes assignable and assessable videos, along with quizzes, interactive Know Yourself assessments, concept clips, interactivities, and NewsFlash, all associated with learning objectives for this title. With Connect for Human Sexuality, students can study whenever and wherever they choose.

Know Yourself

Self-assessment content in every chapter enable students to develop personal awareness and relate their growing knowledge of human sexuality to themselves. For example, one such survey, in Chapter 4 ("Sexual Anatomy and Physiology"), asks about facts and myths regarding sexual anatomy. Correct answers to these true/false questions appear on a subsequent page in the chapter. These surveys and worksheets are assignable in Connect (as Application-Based Activities).

Communication Matters

Self-knowledge and openness, and the ability to express feelings and desires, typically make a huge difference in the quality of a relationship. The "Communication Matters" feature in each chapter presents ideas for communicating effectively about sexuality. Some of these sidebars include words to use in expressing feelings or desires, or words to listen for in conversations with family, friends, or intimate partners. For example, in Chapter 1 ("The Study of Human Sexuality"), the "Communication Matters" feature asks students to think about the words they would use with a partner to propose trying something new in their sexual relationship. Others offer tips for broaching a difficult topic, such as contraception (Chapter 7, "Contraception").

What's On Your Mind?

As instructors, we appreciate the questions students bring to the Human Sexuality course. They want to know how to enrich their intimate relationships, avoid risks, and protect themselves. Drawing on our own classroom experience, we present some of the questions students typically ask in short question/answer segments called "What's On Your Mind?" In each chapter, there are two or more "What's On Your Mind" questions, such as this one in Chapter 5 ("Sexual Pleasure, Arousal, and Response").

Developing Your Position/What's Your Position?

Open-ended questions at the beginning of the chapter encourage students to reflect on their own experiences and opinions, engaging them in the content. Chapter 10 ("Sexual Orientation"), for example, opens with "How did you come to realize your own sexual orientation?" By revisiting these questions at the end of the chapter, in the section called "What's Your Position?" students are prompted to reconsider their answers in light of what they learned in the chapter. At the end of Chapter 10, we pose the questions, "When did you first become aware of the direction of your orientation? Was this the result of your attractions or from things you observed on television or found on the Internet?" to encourage students to develop informed opinions about sexuality.

Thinking Critically About Society and Sexuality

What scientists know about human sexuality stems from research in a variety of disciplines, from biology and psychology to anthropology and sociology. By merging the findings of research in multiple fields, sexuality specialists have created a rich picture of sexuality and its place in culture and society. Thinking critically about research teaches us about the past, informs our understanding of the present, and better prepares us to apply this knowledge to develop our own sexual well-being. *Human Sexuality* not only highlights research throughout the main text, but also emphasizes research in three key features.

Research and Sexual Well-Being

Applying research to contemporary life and well-being is the focus of this feature. In Chapter 8 ("Reproduction"), for example, "Research and Sexual Well-Being: Understanding Birthing History in the U.S.: The Use of Interventions in 'Peak Hours'" explains how medical professionals might use more interventions while delivering a newborn during peak hours than during non-peak hours.

Controversies in Sexuality

Most fields of study include controversy, and sexuality is far from an exception. Controversies help to motivate research. They also illustrate the dynamic nature of the field. The "Controversies in Sexuality" feature presents both sides of the debate on a contentious topic and poses thought-provoking questions for student reflection. In Chapter 10 ("Sexual Orientation"), for example, the "Controversies in Sexuality" feature explores the issues surrounding parenting by same-sex couples.

Healthy Sexuality

Knowledge is a powerful tool for attaining healthy sexuality. By putting research into practice, we can enhance our own sexual well-being and potentially the sexual well-being of others. For example, knowing how to perform a breast or testicular self-exam, outlined in the "Healthy Sexuality" feature in Chapter 4 ("Sexual Anatomy and Physiology") and how to protect your privacy and your personal information on the Internet in Chapter 3 ("Sexuality, Media, and the Internet") enable students to take care of themselves so they can have positive sexual experiences.

Thinking Critically About Sexuality and Culture

Culture is intricately woven through our everyday life and sexuality. Together with biology and the influences of family, peers, and society, culture shapes our thinking and behavior in all domains of life, including gender identity and intimate sexual behavior. An important part of sexual literacy is understanding how these influences intersect and the dynamic role culture plays in sexual expression, both in the United States and in other cultures. We highlight culture in a number of ways in *Human Sexuality,* most notably in our distinctive introductory chapters.

Contexts of Sexuality: Culture, History, and Religion

Chapter 2 introduces students to the sexual triangle, in which culture intersects with other elements to shape our identity. In this chapter, we explain the concept of sexual culture as a means of regulating sexual practices, along with religion. We invite students to think critically about how their own cultural background and religious beliefs have influenced their sexuality and, more broadly, how the perspectives of different cultures and religious traditions may vary from their own.

Sexuality, Media, and the Internet

Chapter 3 explores changes in the way sexuality has been expressed over time in media and pop culture, starting with ancient cave art and concluding with the formation of global online communities advancing sexual rights for all individuals. It also shows how media not only reflect culture but also influence it. For example, in 1953, the first issue of *Playboy* magazine stirred controversy with its nude centerfold feature, but it paved the way for greater openness about sex in U.S. society.

Cross-Cultural Coverage

Comparisons and contrasts between the United States and other Western and non-Western countries are integrated throughout the main narrative of *Human Sexuality* and in the features. For example, in Chapter 9 ("Gender and Identity: Biology, Roles, and Culture"), the "Research and Well-Being" feature describes studies of so-called third sex individuals in the Dominican Republic and among the Sambia people of Papua New Guinea whose biological gender is unclear. In Chapter 8 ("Reproduction: Conception, Pregnancy, and Childbirth"), a "Healthy Sexuality" feature looks at variations in low birth weight across countries.

Teaching and learning are dynamic processes, filled with engaging opportunities to explore differences and similarities among individuals and groups. *Human Sexuality* establishes a foundation for understanding, evaluating, and acting within the ever-changing world of sexuality in the 21st century. We invite you to introduce your students to the many facets of sexuality and sexual well-being, using the full array of materials this program offers.

HEALTHY Sexuality

Variations in Low Birth Weight Across Countries

Not all babies are born within the same average birth weights, creating an interesting difference across countries. In some cultures, babies are born with lower average birth weights compared to the U.S. average, but they are in the normal range for their own country. Nutritional status and heritable factors are possible reasons for this. In fact, scientists believe the birth weight of a newborn largely depends on the health and nutritional status of the mother, and other factors such as the amount of weight the mother gains during pregnancy (Curtis & Schuler, 2008). In the United States, different maternal health factors correlate with low birth weights, such as chronic health problems, substance abuse, and placental problems. Low income and lack of education are associated with an increased risk for low birth weight, although researchers do not yet fully understand the reasons for this connection.

Instructional Resources from McGraw-Hill Education

McGraw-Hill Education's Connect offers comprehensive service, support, and training throughout every phase of your implementation. If you're looking for some guidance on how to use Connect, or want to learn tips and tricks from super users, you can find tutorials as you work. Our Digital Faculty Consultants and Student Ambassadors offer insight into how to achieve the results you want with Connect.

Tegrity: Lectures 24/7

Tegrity in Connect is a tool that makes class time available 24/7 by automatically capturing every lecture. With a simple one-click start-and-stop process, you capture all computer screens and corresponding audio in a format that is easy to search, frame by frame. Students can replay any part of any class with easy-to-use, browser-based viewing on a PC, Mac, iPod, or other mobile device.

Educators know that the more students can see, hear, and experience class resources, the better they learn. In fact, studies prove it. Tegrity's unique search feature helps students efficiently find what they need, when they need it, across an entire semester of class recordings. Help turn your students' study time into learning moments immediately supported by your lecture. With Tegrity, you also increase intent listening and class participation by easing students' concerns about note-taking. Using Tegrity in Connect will make it more likely you will see students' faces, not the tops of their heads.

Create

Easily rearrange chapters, combine material from other content sources, and quickly upload content you have written, such as your course syllabus or teaching notes, using McGraw-Hill Education's Create. Find the content you need by searching through thousands of leading McGraw-Hill Education textbooks. Arrange your book to fit your teaching style. Create even allows you to personalize your book's appearance by selecting the cover and adding your name, school, and course information. Order a Create book, and you will receive a complimentary print review copy in three to five business days or a complimentary electronic review copy via e-mail in about an hour. Experience how McGraw-Hill Education empowers you to teach *your* students *your* way.

> http://create.mheducation.com

Integration with Your Learning Management System

McGraw-Hill integrates your digital products from McGraw-Hill Education with your school LMS for quick and easy access to best-in-class content and learning tools. Build an effective digital course, enroll students with ease and discover how powerful digital teaching can be.

Available with Connect, integration is a pairing between an institution's learning management system (LMS) and Connect at the assignment level. It shares assignment information, grades, and calendar items from Connect into the LMS automatically, creating an easy to manage course for instructors and simple navigation for students. Our assignment-level integration is available with **Blackboard Learn, Canvas by Instructure,** and **Brightspace by D2L,** giving you access to registration, attendance, assignments, grades, and course resources in real time, in one location.

Instructor Supplements

Instructor's Manual The instructor's manual provides a wide variety of tools and resources for presenting the course, including learning objectives, ideas for lectures and discussions, and handouts.

Test Bank Organized by chapter, the test questions are designed to test factual, conceptual, and practice-based understanding. The test bank is available in Word and in Test Builder in Connect.

Available within Connect, Test Builder is a cloud-based tool that enables instructors to format tests that can be printed or administered within a LMS. Test Builder offers a modern, streamlined interface for easy content configuration that matches course needs, without requiring a download.

Test Builder allows you to:

- access all test bank content from a particular title.
- easily pinpoint the most relevant content through robust filtering options.
- manipulate the order of questions or scramble questions and/or answers.
- pin questions to a specific location within a test.
- determine your preferred treatment of algorithmic questions.
- choose the layout and spacing.
- add instructions and configure default settings.

Test Builder provides a secure interface for better protection of content and allows for just-in-time updates to flow directly into assessments.

PowerPoint Presentations These slides cover the key points of each chapter and include charts and graphs from the text. The PowerPoint presentations serve as an organization and navigation tool and include examples and activities from an expert instructor. The slides can be used "as is" or modified to meet your needs. The PowerPoints meet WCAG AA standards.

Image Gallery The Image Gallery features the complete set of downloadable figures and tables from the text. These can be easily embedded by instructors into their own PowerPoint slides.

Chapter-by-Chapter Changes

All chapters have been updated to include new research and data, when available. The following lists specific changes.

Chapter 1: The Study of Human Sexuality

- Updated example: "Self, Society, and Culture: Knowledge Is Empowering"
- Updated coverage: "Becoming Sexually Literate"
- New Figure 1.1
- Expanded coverage of social justice
- New section on "Intersectionality and Social Justice"

Chapter 2: Contexts of Sexuality: Culture, History, and Religion

- New section on "The Pursuit of Sexual Well-Being in Communities of Faith"

Chapter 3: Sexuality, Media, and the Internet

- New feature on "Sexual Images and Advertising"
- Expanded coverage of sexuality in music such as rap and hip-hop
- New figures on Internet use, social networking, and use by age
- New discussion of dating apps
- Updated coverage of social media sites and sexting
- Updated coverage of virtual sex and its contexts
- Updated coverage of online boundaries
- Updated coverage of online romance, dating, and hooking up
- New discussion of effects of pornography use
- New coverage of Internet censorship

Chapter 4: Sexual Anatomy and Physiology

- New coverage of sebum
- New figure (4.9) on female genital mutilation
- New figure (4.15) on circumcision

Chapter 5: Sexual Pleasure, Arousal, and Response

- New "Know Yourself" feature
- Expanded coverage of smell and its relation to orgasm
- Updated coverage of pheromones and sexual attraction
- Expanded coverage of sexual fantasy
- Expanded coverage of pornography and its effect on divorce
- New discussion of female sexual response as studied by Rosemary Basson
- New coverage of women's needs to achieve orgasm
- Updated coverage of female and male masturbation rates
- New Figure 5.3
- New Figure 5.6
- Updated coverage of frequency of sexual activity between partners

Chapter 6: Taking Care of the Sexual Body

- Updated data on breast cancer
- New figure labeling
- New coverage of PrEP to prevent the spreading of HIV
- Updated coverage of HIV/AIDS data
- Expanded coverage of HIV treatment research
- Updated coverage of HPV statistics
- Updated coverage of hepatitis A, B, and C statistics

Chapter 7: Contraception

- New figure labeling (7.4a, b, c)
- New "Did You Know?" feature
- Updated coverage of emergency contraception
- New coverage of the threat to abortion access

Chapter 8: Reproduction: Conception, Pregnancy, and Childbirth

- New figure (8.1) on age at birth of first child
- Updated coverage of birth data
- Updated coverage of stay-at-home fathers
- New discussion of oral and anal sex during pregnancy
- New section on "Racial and Ethnic Disparities in Pregnancy Complications"
- New Figure 8.10
- New discussion of postpartum depression in the partners of the pregnant person
- Updated coverage of abortion statistics

Chapter 9: Gender and Identity: Biology, Roles, and Culture

- Updated coverage of intersexuality
- New discussion of XYY and XXX syndromes
- Expanded coverage of Dr. Money and David Reimer
- Updated coverage of transgender, cisgender, non-binary, and gender nonconformity terminology
- Expanded coverage of transphobia and cis-sexism
- New coverage of transitioning mechanisms
- New figure of female earnings as a percent of male earnings
- Updated coverage of gender identity rights and well-being, especially those with differences of sexual development (DSD)

Chapter 10: Sexual Orientation

- Expanded coverage of LGBTQIA+ acronym to include more identities
- New discussion of determining sexual orientation and its culture meaning
- New coverage of pansexuality and asexuality
- New discussion of epigenetics and its explanation of sexual orientation
- New discussion of androgen exposure in prenatal development and its influence on sexual orientation
- New discussion of openly LGBTQIA+ people involved in politics
- Updated coverage of men who have sex with men (MSM)
- Expanded coverage of sexual fluidity, especially as demonstrated by women
- Expanded coverage of the more subtle forms of homophobia and microaggressions
- New discussion of legal same-gender marriage

Chapter 11: Sexuality in Childhood and Adolescence

- New "Know Yourself" feature
- Expanded coverage of child sexual play
- Expanded coverage of menarche, and theories of its earlier appearance
- Expanded coverage of religion's influence on adolescent sexual relationships
- New section on "Fluidity in Adolescent Sexual Expression"
- Expanded coverage of adolescent sexual relationship statistics
- New discussion of parental monitoring of adolescents
- New coverage of positive influences on sexuality from media sources

- Updated coverage of statistics on sexual intercourse among high school students and contraceptive use
- New figures 11.6 and 11.7

Chapter 12: Sexuality in Adulthood and Later Life

- Expanded coverage of changing adult relationships, including cohabitation before marriage or splitting
- Updated coverage of marriage and singlehood statistics
- New Figure 12.1
- New section on "Polyamory"
- Expanded coverage of cohabitation
- Updated coverage of same-sex marriage equality
- Expanded coverage of LGBTQ elderly sexuality

Chapter 13: Attraction, Love, and Communication

- Expanded coverage of sexual scripts and how they're learned from television
- Expanded coverage of types of attachments and their impact on sexual intimacy
- New "Communication Matters" feature on daily talk for your relationship's benefit

Chapter 14: Sexual Coercion and Resiliency

- New coverage of the #Me-Too Movement
- New Figure 14.1
- New table (14.2) on prison rape of random sample and transgender sample
- Expanded coverage of rape-prone societies
- Expanded coverage of sexual predators, the Internet, and grooming

Chapter 15: Sexual Diagnoses: Sexual Dysfunction to Stigmatized & Normative Sexual Variations

- Reconceptualized chapter that helps students navigate the complex area of sexual disease and sexual normality.
- Updated coverage of the DSM-5 and sexual diagnoses–the difference between paraphilia and paraphilic disorder
- Updated material on the importance of understanding and challenging diagnostic models of sexuality
- Integration of information regarding diagnoses related to aging, sexual desire and sexual functioning
- Integrated and expanded information regarding sexuality and disabilities, including the latest treatments
- Expanded coverage on extreme forms of sexuality in contemporary society and abroad; the role that culture plays; the role that sexual individuality plays.
- Critical discussion on sexual novelty, creativity, healthy sexuality and personal enjoyment; how sexual enjoyment is part of well-being.

McGraw Hill Connect®

FOR INSTRUCTORS

You're in the driver's seat.

Want to build your own course? No problem. Prefer to use our turnkey, prebuilt course? Easy. Want to make changes throughout the semester? Sure. And you'll save time with Connect's auto-grading too.

65%
Less Time Grading

They'll thank you for it.

Adaptive study resources like SmartBook® 2.0 help your students be better prepared in less time. You can transform your class time from dull definitions to dynamic debates. Find out more about the powerful personalized learning experience available in SmartBook 2.0 at **www.mheducation.com/highered/connect/smartbook**

Laptop: McGraw-Hill; Woman/dog: George Doyle/Getty Images

Make it simple, make it affordable.

Connect makes it easy with seamless integration using any of the major Learning Management Systems—Blackboard®, Canvas, and D2L, among others—to let you organize your course in one convenient location. Give your students access to digital materials at a discount with our inclusive access program. Ask your McGraw-Hill representative for more information.

Padlock: Jobalou/Getty Images

Solutions for your challenges.

A product isn't a solution. Real solutions are affordable, reliable, and come with training and ongoing support when you need it and how you want it. Our Customer Experience Group can also help you troubleshoot tech problems—although Connect's 99% uptime means you might not need to call them. See for yourself at **status.mheducation.com**

Checkmark: Jobalou/Getty Images

SUPPORT AT every step

FOR STUDENTS

Effective, efficient studying.

Connect helps you be more productive with your study time and get better grades using tools like SmartBook 2.0, which highlights key concepts and creates a personalized study plan. Connect sets you up for success, so you walk into class with confidence and walk out with better grades.

Study anytime, anywhere.

Download the free ReadAnywhere app and access your online eBook or SmartBook 2.0 assignments when it's convenient, even if you're off-line. And since the app automatically syncs with your eBook and SmartBook 2.0 assignments in Connect, all of your work is available every time you open it. Find out more at **www.mheducation.com/readanywhere**

> *"I really liked this app—it made it easy to study when you don't have your textbook in front of you."*
>
> - Jordan Cunningham, Eastern Washington University

No surprises.

The Connect Calendar and Reports tools keep you on track with the work you need to get done and your assignment scores. Life gets busy; Connect tools help you keep learning through it all.

Calendar: owattaphotos/Getty Images

Learning for everyone.

McGraw-Hill works directly with Accessibility Services Departments and faculty to meet the learning needs of all students. Please contact your Accessibility Services office and ask them to e-mail accessibility@mheducation.com, or visit **www.mheducation.com/about/accessibility** for more information.

Top: Jenner Images/Getty Images, Left: Hero Images/Getty Images, Right: Hero Images/Getty Images

Acknowledgments

Professional Acknowledgments

More than 100 human sexuality instructors have guided the development of this program. We are grateful to all who gave us feedback on the manuscript while it was in development. In particular, we want to acknowledge the hugely beneficial contributions of the instructors who provided detailed comments and edits that helped us shape the final draft.

Paul Abramson, *UCLA*
Gene Ano, *Mt. San Antonio College*
Cynthia Arem, *Pima Community College*
Amir Assadi-Rad, *San Joaquin Delta College*
Spike Babaian, *Mercy College*
Tracy C. Babcock, *Montana State University*
Michael Bailey, *Northwestern University*
Diana Lang Baltimore, *Iowa State University*
Alison Baren, *Temple University*
Kelly M. Bentley, *University of Maine, Farmington*
Shannon Bertha, *Middlesex County College*
Adrian Blow, *Michigan State University*
Saundra Y. Boyd, *Houston Community College, Southeast*
Tori Bovard, *American River College*
Kenneth Brownson, *American Public University System*
Elizabeth Calamidas, *Richard Stockton University of New Jersey*
Janell Campbell, *California State University, Chico*
Cathy Carey, *Salt Lake Community College*
Chwee Lye Chng, *University of North Texas*
Jane Cirillo, *Houston Community College*
Stephanie Coday, *Sierra College*
Katrina Cooper, *Bethany College, W. Virginia*
Ann Crawford, *Lynn University*
Nancy Daley, *University of Texas, Austin*
Jana Daniel, *South Plains College*
Lindsey Doe, *University of Montana*
Dale Doty, *Monroe Community College*
Rena Durr, *Christian Brothers University*
Kathy Erickson, *Pima Community College, East Campus*
Carole Espinosa, *El Paso Community College*

Samuel Fernandez-Carriba, *Georgia State University*
Paul Finnicum, *Arkansas State University*
Edward R. Fliss, *St. Louis Community College, Florissant Valley*
Tony Fowler, *Florence-Darlington Technical College*
Glen E. Fox, Jr., *Tidewater Community College*
Chris Furlow, *Santa Fe College*
Meghan Gillette, *Iowa State University*
George Gaither, *Ball State University*
Lois Goldblatt, *Arizona State University, Tempe*
Debra L. Golden, *Grossmont College*
Kathy Greaves, *Oregon State University*
Jerry Green, *Tarrant County College*
Melissa Grim, *Radford University*
Francoise Grossmann, *Tulane University*
Sarah Gulick, *Erie Community College, City Campus*
Gary Gute, *University of Northern Iowa*
David Hall, *University of the Pacific*
Diane Hamilton-Hancock, *Western Illinois University*
Michelle Haney, *Berry College*
Lena Hann, *Augustana College*
Pearl A. Hawe, *New Mexico State University*
Patrice Heller, *Temple University*
Sheri Hixon, *Truckee Meadows Community College*
Danelle Hodge, *California State University, San Bernardino*
Suzanne Hopf, *University of Louisville*
Simone Hopkins, *Ivy Tech Community College*
Suzy Horton, *Mesa Community College*
Shawn Hrncir, *University of New Mexico*
Robert Hunter, *Monroe Community College*

Frances Jackler, *De Anza College*
Susan Johnson, *Cypress College*
Jennifer Jones, *Arapahoe Community College*
Regina Kakhnovets, *Auburn University*
Jennifer Knapp, *Baton Rouge Community College*
Jessica Kruger, *Colorado Northwestern Community College*
Callista Lee, *Fullerton College*
Jennifer Lehmbeck, *Central Washington University*
James Leone, *Bridgewater State University*
Linette Liebling, *Wheaton College*
Martin Lobdell, *Tacoma Community College*
Don Lucas, *Northwest Vista College*
Kellie McCants-Price, *Anne Arundel Community College*
James McGowan, *Mercy College*
Davis Mannino, *Santa Rosa Community College*
Amy Marin, *Phoenix College*
Stacy Meier, *University of Houston*
Jennifer Mewes, *Pima Community College*
Richard Miller, *George Mason University*
Janet Minehan, *Santa Barbara City College*
Sarah Mitchell, *University of Nevada, Reno*
Tami Moore, *University of Nebraska*
Jennifer Musick, *Long Beach City College*
Peggy Oberstaller, *Lane Community College*
Diane Pisacreta, *St. Louis Community College*
Marilyn Pugh, *Texas Wesleyan University*
Anila Putcha-Bhagavatula, *California State University, Long Beach*

Brad Redburn, *Johnson County Community College*
Kathryn Redd, *New Mexico State University*
Daniel Rubin, *Valencia Community College*
Sonia Ruiz, *Palomar Community College*
Raymond Sacchi, *Washington State University, Pullman*
Jennifer Siciliani, *University of Missouri, St. Louis*
T.C. Sim, *Sam Houston State University*
Stephanie Sitnick, *Caldwell University*
Peggy Skinner, *South Plains College*
Brittany C. Slatton, *Texas Southern University*
Laurie Smith, *Washington State University*
Susan Sprecher, *Illinois State University*
Noelle Sullivan, *University of Florida*
Jana Tiefenworth, *Stephen F. Austin State University*
Tina Timm, *Michigan State University*
Terry Trepper, *Purdue University, Calumet*
Soni Verna, *Sierra College*
Nancy Voorhees, *Ivy Tech Community College*
Glenda Walden, *University of Colorado, Boulder*
Marie Wallace, *Pima Community College*
Matthew Webster, *Houston Community College*
Martin Weinberg, *Indiana University*
Glen Ellis Weisfeld, *Wayne State University*
Alyson Young, *University of Florida*
Judy Zimmerman, *Portland Community College, Rock Creek*

Personal Acknowledgments

Gil I would like to thank first of all Nicole Polen-Petit, for her long-term collegial support and collaboration in this textbook project. She has been an unending source of learning and teaching. Additionally, thanks to my long-term teaching assistant, Merlinda Cordasco, MPH, who was such a great source of learning and support, as well as Stefan Lutke, my PhD student, from whom I have learned and for whose support in this project I am so grateful. Additionally, for this second edition, we thank the following scholars who have provided very helpful input and advice: Professor Michelle Marzullo at CIIS; Ericka Burns, CIIS; Dr. Janna Dickenson, University of Minnesota; Dr. Angela Towne; Dr. Richard Sprott; and Professor Eli Coleman of the University of Minnesota; Mr. Alexander Farquhar-Leicester; and Dr. Lisa Rappalyea. We are especially grateful to Mr. Stefan Lucke, of the CIIS, for his generous help and assistance.

For their great help and support with the first edition of *Human Sexuality*, we are grateful to Mona Sagapouletele, at SFSU, a miracle woman; Sarah Miller, PhD; Marik Xavier-Brier, PhD; Peter Vielehr, PhD; Christine Buchheit, MA; Jennifer Brooke Clark, MA; Christopher Moffett, professor of biology at SFSU; Ivy Chen, MPH, instructor in sexuality studies, SFSU; and Professor Deborah Tolman at Hunter College.

Nicole I would like to express gratitude to some individuals without whom work on this project would not have been possible. To Gil, thank you for the opportunity to work with you. Over the years, I have learned so much from the rich work you have engaged in. I cherish our discussions and consider you one of the most critical mentors in my career. You could have chosen to work with anyone, and I am humbled to have done this work with you. It has been a genuine honor to collaborate with you on this beloved project.

To my amazing husband and partner, Damon, there is no one else I would ever want to do this life with. You have taught me so much about this thing we call "love." I adore you and hope that we only continue to grow in love and friendship together. Thank you for always supporting my aspirations and dreams.

To my extended family (Mom, Dad, Elizabeth, and Kirk), thank you for your endless support and for all the ways each of you contributes to my work. Whether through humorous conversations over a card game or serious discussions that stretch us, each of you has a special place in my heart . . . and in my course material.

To Brandt and Traci, my dearest friends. Thank you for the endless conversations, laughter, and the years of content you have given me. Your friendship and love mean more to me than you will ever know.

And finally, to National University and my colleagues, thank you for offering me an intellectual home among you. I cherish the work we do collectively and thank you for allowing me to be a part of an academic community I love and deeply respect.

We would like to extend our warm thanks to the McGraw-Hill team who enabled us to complete this second edition of *Human Sexuality*: portfolio manager Nancy Welcher, senior product developer Cara Labell, marketing managers A. J. Lafererra and Olivia Kaiser, content production managers Mary Powers and Jodi Banowetz, designer Beth Blech, content licensing specialist Jacob Sullivan, and copy editor Kevin Campbell.

While we acknowledge those whose work has been a critical addition to this edition of the text, we remain grateful to those individuals who supported this work from the very beginning. From the first edition of this book, we wish to say how fortunate we are to have worked with a stellar group of individuals. Every large project starts with a vision, and this one was supported and indeed inspired by early conversations with Mike Sugarman, director, Dawn Groundwater, our passionate senior director of development, and Mark Georgiev. Additionally, our team included wonderful editorial staff, and we are especially indebted to senior developmental editor Judith Kromm, whose keen eye and organizational talents kept us moving along, and to Sue Ewing, developmental editor par excellence, for her steadfast support and editing superpowers! We would also like to thank our first edition production team for their work and creativity, including content project manager Jennifer Gehl, designer Margarite Reynolds, copy editor Carey Lange, and photo researcher Emily Tietz. Finally, we would like to mention the important support we received from editorial coordinator Kevin Fitzpatrick, and Jason Kopeck.

The Study of Human Sexuality

Thomas Barwick/Photographer's Choice RF/Getty Images

Sexual Literacy
- Explain what sexual literacy means and how it relates to sexual well-being and emotional literacy.

Sexual Science—A Historical Perspective
- Describe the early scientific and clinical history of sexual science.
- Identify the positive contributions of Freud, Kinsey, Masters and Johnson, and others to sex research.
- Explain how sex research can improve the sexual well-being of individuals.
- Describe why sexual research has been disconnected from U.S. policy.
- Recall the meaning of social justice in social policy.

Methodology in the Study of Sexuality
- Explain the value of the interdisciplinary perspective in the study of sexuality.
- Distinguish between qualitative and quantitative methods in sexual research.
- Compare and contrast the key approaches to studying sexuality.
- Evaluate what it means to be a critical consumer of sex research.

Human Sexual Rights
- Explain what makes sexuality a human right, not a privilege.

Learning Objectives

Developing Your Position

1. What do the terms *sexual literacy* and *sexual well-being* mean to you?
2. How has sexuality changed from a negative to a more positive science?
3. What does sexuality as a human right mean to you?

Self, Society, and Culture: Knowledge Is Empowering

Clark Wilson was an eighth grader when his teacher in Colorado compared sex to a piece of tape. When you use a piece of tape for the first time, it sticks well. But once you peel the tape off and try to adhere it to something else, it loses its ability to stick. The lesson: "People are like tape, and once they have sex they're dirty and can't have meaningful relationships," said Clark, now 15 and a freshman at a public high school in the Denver suburbs. He and several other young people testified to the state legislature, which passed an important new bill authorizing sex education. Even though comprehensive sex education has been proven effective in supporting sexual literacy and sexual health, according to the Guttmacher Institute (2019), only 13 states in the United States require it. The percentage of schools that offered comprehensive sex education dropped significantly from 67% to 48% between 2000 and 2014, according to the Centers for Disease Control and Prevention (2015). The majority of states during those years actually withdrew knowledge and skills necessary to protect against unwanted pregnancy and sexually transmitted infections (STIs). It is no wonder the United States has the highest rate of STIs and indicators of poor reproductive health compared to other major industrial countries. When states such as California do implement scientifically accurate and honest sex ed, there is often conservative pushback, with some lawmakers arguing that sex education belongs at home, in the context of families and faith, though it has been widely documented that many families focus on abstinence only or teach their children nothing about sexuality through their silence (Levin, 2019). But Clark and other teens and young adults are taking the lead, and mobilizing discussions in their communities and classrooms about anatomy, birth control, sexual orientation, and gender identity. We think these young people are the front-runners, looking ahead to a time when everyone can pursue sexual literacy as a human right to achieve full sexual well-being.

Sexuality impacts all aspects of our lives—the mind, body, heart, and spirit. It can have holistic, healthy effects on both a physical and an emotional level. It also provides a truly important context to develop and understand more about our personal identities, relationships, and sexual selves. When sexual literacy is missing, people's decisions and actions can sometimes take very unfortunate directions. In fact, understanding more about ourselves through sexuality may change us and, in turn, change society.

In this chapter we begin our journey to sexual literacy. Here we will explore the meaning of sexual well-being and begin acquiring the knowledge and tools needed to develop healthy sexuality. We will examine the history of sexual science, and learn how sex research has improved people's lives and society. Then we will discuss the interdisciplinary nature of sex research and research methodology, to become better consumers of sex research and media depictions of sex acts. Finally, we will explore the wide diversity of human sexuality and see why the concept of sexuality as a human right is changing society.

SEXUAL LITERACY

Sexuality literacy is the knowledge, skills, and actions needed to achieve and protect sexual well-being. **Sexual well-being** is both a physical state, defined by positive health in your body, and a subjective or mental state, recognized by feeling positive or joyful about your sexual life (Laumann et al., 2006; Moore and Reynolds, 2018). As you develop sexual literacy, you enhance your own **holistic sexuality,** which means the integration of body, mind, feelings, and social life through sexuality. With the knowledge and skills you have from sexual literacy, you can go to the next step—achieving the kind of intimate love and sex that you aspire to through the kinds of relationships that will satisfy you. Having healthy relationships, being able to express pleasure and love in those relationships, being able to prevent disease, and understanding how sexual diversity can enrich society all contribute to holistic sexuality (Herdt & Howe, 2007; Moore & Reynolds, 2018).

> **DID YOU KNOW**
>
> People in the United States have changing views about what they consider to be "sex" acts. In the late 1990s, for instance, only about 40% said that oral–genital sex was "real sex." Ten years later, the number had increased to 70% (Saunders et al., 2010; Saunders & Reinisch, 1999). Today, 80% of people also say that anal sex is "real sex" (Saunders et al., 2010). The greater the diversity of a population, the fewer stereotypes by race, and the larger acceptance of diverse sexual behaviors (Hebernick et al., 2015).

sexuality literacy
The knowledge, skills, and actions needed to achieve and protect sexual well-being.

Becoming Sexually Literate

Sex is simply one of the most wonderful and complicated aspects of our lives. Sexual identity and gender experience are impacted by all the important parts of our lives—our age, race, family background, national origin, faith and friends, schooling, and sense of dignity and respect in society. When any of these factors are threatened or significantly change, our sexuality may be impacted. Sexual literacy is the dynamic intersection of all these experiences, especially the knowledge we acquire about sexuality, the skill sets that we learn that can improve us and our relationships, and the willingness to practice or apply what we have learned.

Sexual literacy is a thus never-ending process of gathering knowledge, improving skills, and being able to apply them to relationships. Not surprisingly, this actually begins before many people ever have their first sexual experience. We view sexual literacy as a way for people to promote the positive potential in their own sexuality and experiences, while also managing potential risk that affects their health and well-being. This action-based, contextual approach to sexual literacy is influenced by the comprehensive sex education model of Doug Kirby (2012), which supports people in improving the quality of their sexual experience. Our model is also influenced by the sex-positive model of Miriam Arbeit's (2014) work on adolescent developmental skills. In this skills-based approach, Arbeit combines the components of **sexual selfhood, sexual negotiation,** and **sexual empowerment** to demonstrate how people can achieve their aspirations. Translated into sexual literacy, we are especially focused on how these factors shape intimate relationships (sexual and nonsexual), and in particular how agency, intimacy, and social advocacy help people achieve sexual well-being. By seeing advocacy as part of the journey of sexual literacy, we hope to help young people to "skillfully engage their own sexuality [and] the world around them" (Arbeit, 2014: 260).

In short, to achieve sexual literacy is to get to know our bodies, our emotions, our sexual expressions, and our identities better, through knowledge + skills = practice—you will see this displayed in Figure 1.1. We can learn what pleases and displeases, what helps us to protect and support our sexual health, and how to function better within intimate relationships. However, sexual literacy is also about identifying ignorance, privilege, and prejudice and scoping out negative influences on people's decisions, including peers who hold prejudices, teachers who do not practice equality and respect, and the impact of false stories online. It includes surfacing old stereotypes that damage people, such as racial and social prejudices, and challenging toxic attitudes about body imagery. Becoming sexually literate means

sexual well-being
The condition of experiencing good health, pleasure, and satisfaction in intimate relationships.

holistic sexuality
The integration of body, mind, feelings, and social life through your sexuality.

Sexual selfhood
The totality of oneself as a sexual being, including positive and negative feelings.

Sexual negotiation
Discussion and interaction that lead to agreement about sexual relationships.

Sexual empowerment
Taking responsibility for one's own sexuality, making one's own choices, and respecting one's own needs, desires, and values.

HUMAN SEXUALITY

Understanding sexuality is a lifelong process.
(*top left*) Dreampictures/Image Source/Getty Images; (*top right*) Solid Porcupine/Getty Images; (*bottom left*) Jakob Helbig/Cultura RF/Getty Images; (*bottom right*) Hill Street Studios/Getty Images

learning positive skill sets, like how to communicate and negotiate better with the people we care about, how to empower our own emotions in demanding situations, and how to make positive and healthy choices in times when we dare to try new things and dare to be true to ourselves. Putting sexual literacy into practice in such ways enables us to create really important intimate friendships and relationships that reflect the best of who and what we are in society.

The most important sexual literacy goals for this course are:

- Knowing yourself as a whole person better, to enhance your own sexual well-being
- Being able to emotionally communicate about intimate sexual needs with partners

Figure 1.1

SEXUAL LITERACY

KNOWLEDGE + SKILLS LEADS TO PRACTICE

- Helping people understand each other better by first learning about your own body, desires, and behaviors, and how you might express them
- Knowing what science and research tell us about sexuality and being able to separate facts from myths about sex
- Helping to improve society by supporting diversity and dignity in the right of other people to have a full and satisfying sexual life
- Understanding how context, in terms of both nature and culture, contribute to sexuality
- Being able to talk about your own culture's sexual attitudes and how they contribute to your own holistic well-being
- Having the knowledge and skills to protect your sexual health throughout life
- Being able to implement the decisions and actions to protect and enact your sexual well-being when you need and want to

Before reading further, complete the short questionnaire about human sexuality titled "Know Yourself: Are You Sexually Literate?"

Sexual Well-Being

Sexual well-being refers to positive physical, mental, and social correlates of sexuality in your life, such as experiencing good health and pleasure, and satisfaction in intimate relationships. If sexual literacy is the journey, then sexual well-being may become the destination. We hope that as you progress through this course, holistic sexuality becomes more and more of a reality for you.

Four elements are fundamental to achieving sexual well-being: pleasure, protection, focus, and purpose in life. Let's consider each one briefly, knowing that we will refine our understanding as we progress through the course. Figure 1.2 shows schematically how the four elements intersect to bring about sexual well-being.

Pleasure is associated with joy and fun. As such, you may find pleasure when you are satisfied in your sexual life or your love life. Pleasure involves a basic acceptance of yourself, your body, and the role of pleasure in your own sexual selfhood. Research shows that people who know their bodies and accept their feelings, including pleasure, generally protect themselves better (Guzman et al., 2003; Tolman, 2005).

As Harry Potter grew up, a new generation discovered love and sex. (From *Harry Potter and the Deathly Hallows*.)
WARNER BROS PICTURES/Album/Alamy Stock Photo

Protection is keeping your body free of sexually transmitted infections, as well as knowing how to check your body for other medical conditions, such as skin, genital, and anal cancers. Protecting yourself also means knowing how to employ sexual negotiation in dealing with bullying, date rape, sexual coercion, and sexual harassment. To ensure that sexual functioning and health can continue throughout life, protection also means understanding sexual difficulties that people may experience along the way.

Focus is about total concentration on an activity, such as running, doing yoga, or playing a musical instrument. Focus increases your sense of being alive, of feeling connected to yourself, and integrating a sense of total contentment (Csikszentmihalyi, 1998; Seligman, 2002). In holistic sexuality, focus means being present and fully alert to what you feel sexually, what a prospective partner may say or do, and how your pleasure and self-protection create sexual empowerment. When you experience focus, you can create a relationship that can integrate your feelings and needs. Friendship can definitely provide focus

Know Yourself

Are You Sexually Literate?

Check your knowledge of sex in 5 minutes by answering these true/false questions.

1. ____ Anal sex can make you pregnant.
2. ____ Humans are the only species that have sexual pleasure and orgasms.
3. ____ In some cultures extramarital relationships are considered positive.
4. ____ You can become gay if you have close contact with gays.
5. ____ Too much sexual pleasure can make you mentally lazy.
6. ____ Kissing does not spread AIDS.
7. ____ In some cultures women may have multiple husbands at the same time.
8. ____ In some countries sexuality is becoming a human right in the 21st century.
9. ____ Religious people don't have fun in their sex lives.
10. ____ Homosexuality is legal in all countries.
11. ____ Condoms cannot prevent the spread of sexually transmitted infections.
12. ____ You can deliver a baby through your navel if really necessary.
13. ____ You can have good sex if you learn how to enjoy your sexual fantasies.
14. ____ One of the keys to a healthy life is to have a happy relationship.
15. ____ Masturbation started as a disease but is used as therapy for some people.
16. ____ Until sometime in the 20th century being fat was considered sexually attractive in women and men.
17. ____ People are having children and getting married younger than ever in the United States.
18. ____ Science has proved there is a gay brain.
19. ____ It is always better to live together before you get married to see if it works.
20. ____ In some cultures, a woman's crushed foot is considered intensely sexually attractive.

Answers appear on p. 7.

Figure 1.2
Four dimensions of sexual well-being.

Pleasure — Focus — Sexual Well-Being — Protection — Purpose in Life

ANSWERS to Are You Sexually Literate? *(p. 6)*

1. F	11. F
2. F	12. F
3. T	13. T
4. F	14. T
5. F	15. T
6. T	16. T
7. T	17. F
8. T	18. F
9. F	19. F
10. F	20. T

What is your degree of sexual literacy at this point? Grade yourself using this scale:

18–20 correct — You are a champion of sexual literacy!

14–17 correct — You are sexually literate to a high degree and are fairly comfortable with these issues.

10–13 correct — You may learn many enjoyable things in this course.

9 or less correct — Welcome to the human sexuality course. Like many people, you have a lot to learn about how to attain sexual well-being.

Know Yourself

and support across our lives (Amati et al., 2018). If you've ever fallen in love, you have experienced focus intensely.

Purpose in life strengthens our basic sense of identity and validates our existence in the world, including our love and romantic relationships. The chapter-opening story of 15-year-old Clark Wilson illustrates how purpose in life can help people and make the world a better place for people and their diverse sexuality. It is through purpose that we extend our sense of pleasure, protection, and well-being.

Sexual well-being is a spectrum that goes from less to more as we practice sexual literacy and work toward the integration of all of these positive things with our sexual selfhood. The goal of sexual literacy is to achieve greater sexual well-being by expressing more of what you feel, who you are, what you need, and how you would like your community to support that. When applied to close relationships, this expression of emotion can make a huge difference in the quality of your life, as you can read in "Communication Matters: Emotional Literacy and Close Relationships."

WHAT'S ON YOUR MIND?

Q: My girlfriend is younger than I am—she's only in her first year of college. How do I tell her that now is the right time to have sex?

ANSWER: We suggest you approach this issue with significant caution. It may be true that *you* feel it is the right time to become sexually involved, but that may not be what your girlfriend feels. We encourage you to tell her about how you are feeling and ask her to talk with you about what she is feeling. Understanding how you feel *and* learning about how another person feels are essential for sexual literacy. The decision to have sex needs be made by both of you when you are both ready to make it.

COMMUNICATION Matters

Emotional Literacy and Close Relationships

Strong, supportive, close relationships have a positive influence on sexual well-being throughout life. Research shows that being close to other people and having empathy for them increases our overall health and well-being, because social relationships are a source of positive emotion, and long-term satisfaction in life; and being close is the basis of sound social policy (Bradburn, 1969; Amati et al., 2018); Diener & Seligman, 2004; Forgeard, Jayawickreme, Kern, & Seligman, 2011; Seligman, 2011). In fact, researchers apply terms such as *happiness, wellness, quality of life,* and *life satisfaction* to the general concept of well-being (Argyle, 2001; Diener & Diener, 2008; Seligman, 2011) and to subjective sexual well-being (Das, Waite, & Laumann, 2012; Laumann et al., 2006).

Attaining sexual well-being in close relationships requires emotional literacy. **Emotional literacy** is the capacity to perceive and to express feelings, especially as they surround intimate relationships (Mayer, Salovey, & Caruso, 2000; Moore and Reynolds, 2018, p. 208). Although this is an important skill set for developing close relationships, people are typically expected to learn emotional communication on their own (Matthews, 2006; Pascoe, 2011; Tolman, 2006). When you are emotionally literate, you are able to talk freely about your sexual feelings, your body, sexual needs, and behaviors to friends, families, and intimate partners.

Emotional literacy also means being able to achieve sexual selfhood like this, combining negotiation and empowerment (Arbeit, 2014) so that you are not being caught off guard in a vulnerable moment when you need to express your feelings. It means having sexual empowerment to achieve your own needs and goals. How would you discuss your feelings about particular sexual practices with your partner? Do you both use the same terms for the same sexual experiences, such as oral sex? If one of you proposes doing something novel or sexually creative in your relationship, what words would you use to describe it? Try writing them down, and then reflect on how you would feel about saying them. This exercise in emotional literacy may help you to focus on what it is you most enjoy and love about your own body and to share it with your partner (Moore and Reynolds, 2018).

SEXUAL SCIENCE—A HISTORICAL PERSPECTIVE

Sexual science is the study of sexual behavior across the human species, all cultures, and individuals. Few fields of science have such a provocative, fascinating history as sexual science. The systematic study of sexual interests, functions, and behaviors began in the 19th century as an extension of medicine and psychiatry and was dubbed **sexology.** Sexology was quite negative in its treatment of sexuality as a set of symptoms and diseases and in the way it influenced the norms and values of the late 19th century (Oosterhuis, 2000). In time, researchers in other sciences, including psychology, sociology, and sexual anthropology, and in a variety of newer fields, including endocrinology, behavioral genetics, public health, and evolutionary psychology, began their studies of sexual behavior. Today, this interdisciplinary field looks at the positive aspects of sexuality, such as sexual health and wellness, social and cultural influences, and the relationship between marriage and sexual intimacy. But in the beginning, sexology was much more about the study of what was considered abnormal behavior than about sexual diversity (Oosterhuis, 2000).

The Medical Model of Sexuality

The roots of sexual knowledge began with psychiatrists and medical doctors who typically saw most sex acts in terms of negative or bizarre symptoms that they couldn't explain (D'Emilio & Freedman, 1998; Irvine, 2000; Jordan-Young, 2010; Maier, 2009; Robinson, 1976). These symptoms were extremely diverse and included interests such as a desire for sex with animals (bestiality) and a sexual attraction to dead bodies (necrophilia).

---

emotional literacy
The capacity to perceive and to express feelings, especially as they surround intimate relationships.

sexual science
The study of sexual behavior across the human species, all cultures, and individuals.

sexology
Systematic study of sexual interests, functions, and behaviors.

Additionally, physicians noted an interest in sex for pleasure and not for reproduction, a practice that was generally frowned upon. For example, bisexuality was considered a disease in the 19th century, and doctors could see no possible reason for having sex with people of both genders other than for pathological reasons. There was a fear that humans would stop reproducing if people pursued only pleasurable sex and the species would become extinct (Foucault, 1980).

Sexual behaviors that deviated from reproduction came to be thought of as **sexual degeneracy,** meaning impairment or decline of sexual function. For example, all homosexuality was labeled as degenerate and identified with mental illness and physical impairment (Robinson, 2000). As society changed, so did attitudes about a lot of these sexual behaviors, including homosexuality, possibly because sexual taboos changed over time (Stoller, 1985; Weeks, 2010).

sexual degeneracy
Impairment or decline of sexual function.

Nineteenth-century doctors also considered masturbation a serious sexual disease that could lead to degeneracy and death. They believed that it could be spread like the common cold, and people brought children to medical clinics looking for a cure. Early on, doctors used primitive, cruel treatments, such as submerging patients for hours in freezing cold water, to try to stop this behavior.

With little research or knowledge of sexuality outside their clinics, 19th-century physicians—who were universally male—applied their own ideas to classifying and treating sexual diseases and atypical sexual behavior. Some of their attitudes were biased against women and children. For example, they believed that female sexuality should be directed toward reproduction and mothering, and not toward sexual desires or sexual pleasure, because they believed that women were too fragile and innocent but also had uncontrollable sexual urges. Such ideas created a way for society to control women, especially women of color and immigrants new to the country (Collins, 2005; Espiritu, 2012; Groneman, 2001) and even allowed for the abuse of women. Some advocates of the #Me-Too Movement believe that the roots of abusive attitudes come from this original bias against women.

Some doctors were also prudish, ignorant about sex, and focused on highly puritanical theories of sex (Money, 1985). One such physician was John Harvey Kellogg (1852–1943), an American who is probably best known as the inventor of Kellogg's Corn Flakes. Though married, Kellogg did not engage in sex. He firmly believed that all sex, including marital intercourse, was bad and debilitating. He invented graham crackers, granola cereal, and peanut butter because he believed these foods would cure sexual problems. Kellogg also ran a sanitarium for the insane that included people incarcerated for masturbation. Read his prescription for curing children of masturbation (Money, 1985):

> A remedy [for masturbation] which is almost always successful in small boys is circumcision. . . . The operation should be performed by a surgeon without administering an anesthetic, as the brief pain attending the operation will have a salutary effect upon the mind. . . . In females, the author has found the application of pure carbolic acid to the clitoris an excellent means of allaying the abnormal excitement.

In other words, doctors in the 19th century, and well into the 20th century, tended to view sex as a disease to be cured or a problem to be fixed, seldom as something positive. But consider this: Doctors saw only patients with unusual sexual behaviors who came to their clinics. They did not observe "normal" people because they never came to the clinics. Because Doctors worked only with people who sought treatment, they saw their sexual symptoms as the norm, not the exception. The doctors' treatments became a self-fulfilling prophecy of their theories (Oosterhuis, 2000).

From these negative beginnings, sexual science struggled for decades with the perception that sex was mostly diseased and abnormal (Herdt, 2009a; Irvine, 2000; Laumann et al., 1994; Weeks, 2010). Doctors never asked questions like: Could the range of human sexual behavior be a lot greater than we previously thought? Could these diverse behaviors have some positive function? or Is it possible that experiencing sexual pleasure helps people to feel closer to each other? In time, sex researchers began to address and answer such questions.

A New Approach to Sex Research

Sexuality research was built on a new approach to science in the late 1800s. This approach used scientific investigation to explain reality instead of using magic, faith, folklore, personal beliefs, or tradition. The new advocates for scientific investigation believed that the scientific study of sexuality could improve people's sexual health, and society at large, by breaking away from the old idea that sex was a disease (Irvine, 2000). This trend started in Europe and later spread to the United States (Parker and Gagnon, 1995; Weeks, 2010).

An important cornerstone of the new approach was Charles Darwin's theory of evolution. **Evolution** is the general idea that change occurs in all life-forms over time by the process of one generation of species passing inherited characteristics on to the next. Darwin (1809–1882) was a British naturalist who used evolutionary theory to explain how sexuality contributes to the diversity of life. He built this theory of natural selection on the widely held scientific view that through the individual's sexual development, the history and development of a species and its process of replication was actually a biological design of remarkable orderliness in nature (Pinker, 2018).

A number of Darwin's contemporaries in a variety of fields, including chemistry and physics, anthropology, and psychiatry, adopted a systematic approach to the study of sexuality that followed this view and laid the foundation of modern sex research in Europe. Foremost among them were Richard von Krafft-Ebing, Magnus Hirschfeld, Havelock Ellis, and Sigmund Freud. When something went wrong in evolution or human development, it could cause sexual symptoms.

evolution
The general idea that change occurs in all life-forms over time.

fetishism
The attraction to physical objects, such as boots, or to human appendages.

Richard von Krafft-Ebing Among the pioneers of early clinical research on sexual behavior was the German psychiatrist Richard von Krafft-Ebing (1840–1902). Krafft-Ebing published a highly successful series of dramatic case studies of sexual diseases, titled *Psychopathia Sexualis* (1886), in which he named and classified some of the most unusual sexual behaviors of his day (Oosterhuis, 2000). For example, he coined the term **fetishism** to describe the sexual attraction to physical objects, such as boots, or to human appendages, such as feet or toes. By suggesting treatment instead of incarceration and holding empathy for people who had never been treated kindly, Dr. Krafft-Ebing revealed himself to be progressive.

Krafft-Ebing was particularly known for treating masturbation in a more humane way. Some of his patients truly felt that they were subhuman "monsters" because they could not control their sexual urges, some of which, including masturbation, are today considered normal. They readily accepted treatment because their lives were often tragic and sad. Other patients were proud of their sexual urges and resisted treatment (Oosterhuis, 2000). Krafft-Ebing collected their histories and differentiated between what he called "normal" and "abnormal" sexuality. He called the abnormal sexual symptoms **perversions,** by which he meant unusual or extreme sexual urges or acts.

Richard von Krafft-Ebing pioneered sexual case studies.
Josef Loewy/ullstein bild/Getty Images

perversions
Sexual urges or acts considered unusual or extreme in a specific culture.

Magnus Hirschfeld A medical doctor, Magnus Hirschfeld (1868–1935) was influential in two ways: He was the first to use surveys to study sexual behavior scientifically in groups of people, and privately he helped found the homosexual rights movement in Germany. He also worked with early feminists to improve women's sexual and reproductive lives and create a more humane community of support for sexuality. In addition, Hirschfeld founded the Institute for Sexual Research in Berlin. The first of its kind, this treatment center housed tens of thousands of books on sex and was linked with the effort to create social and scientific support for homosexual rights. During their rise to power, the Nazis raided the Institute in 1927 and burned its library to the ground. Hirschfeld died a broken man while in exile in France (Robinson, 2000).

Havelock Ellis Over many decades the great British medical doctor and psychologist Havelock Ellis (1859–1939) saw thousands of patients, traveled the world, wrote dozens of books, and became one of the foremost authorities in the treatment of sexual problems. He had few equals in his time, and his advice was widely sought. Like Krafft-Ebing, however, Ellis typically studied what went wrong with people's sexuality, including heterosexuals' marriages.

Ellis's clinical studies of individual patients continue to fascinate today's scientists because of his meticulous observations and objectivity. At age 32, he married an early feminist. He and his wife famously had an open marriage and kept separate houses. This arrangement was controversial but not unknown in the late 19th century, as a "free love movement" began taking hold among upper-class people in England and the United States.

Sigmund Freud Perhaps the best known of the early medical sex researchers was Sigmund Freud (1856–1939), an Austrian neurologist who revolutionized the study of the human mind as applied to personality, sexuality, and symbolism. Freud invented psychoanalysis and through it theorized a more complex sexuality built upon family dynamics and the question of frustrated pleasure. His approach dominated sexual science until the late 1960s in sexual and social science.

Freud treated sexuality from infancy onward as a fundamental part of human nature, largely the result of irrational and nonconscious factors. But he also treated sex as a symptom of an underlying mental disorder. In Freud's view, people's earliest sexual desires and fantasies revolved around deep conflicted sexual attraction to the opposite-sex parent involving incest. He believed that children had sexual feelings and had to **repress** their incestuous feelings, because they were unacceptable to society and led to fetishism and madness (Freud, 1905). He also believed that deep sexual motives unconsciously influenced all other behaviors and were causes of mental distress.

Freud developed a new way to treat mental distress. This treatment approach, called **psychoanalysis,** focused on using dreams and free association from the unconscious mind and "talking therapy." According to Freud, the unconscious part of the mind is hidden from awareness. It acts as a repository of hidden feelings, thoughts, drives, and memories that can motivate sexual behavior. He believed that talking about feelings and desires and early childhood memories could cure all sexual symptoms and mental illness. Freud examined the sexual thoughts and the unconscious mind of his patients, including their sexual fantasies. He used hypnosis as a tool for helping his patients uncover their unconscious motives, including their incestuous fantasies, which Freud believed to be the normal expression of early childhood sexual attraction of a boy toward his mother and a girl toward her father.

Many researchers today criticize Freud's psychiatric methodology. They say Freud's practices were flawed because people could not really remember their childhood fantasies, and he observed only adults, not children, and only in his office (Gagnon & Simon, 1973). These and many other important criticisms of Freud's approach led later scientists, including Alfred Kinsey, to create new methodologies for studying sex (Kinsey et al., 1948; Robinson, 1976). For decades, Freud's emphasis on childhood led to the assumption that sexual development ceases after childhood (Boxer & Cohler, 1989). And if patients talked about sexual abuse or incest in their families, Freud tended to treat these revelations as childhood fantasies, not as reality (Foucault, 1980). Today, researchers believe that sexual development and sexual well-being continue into old age (Valliant, 2002). And we now know that sexual abuse within families and communities is a reality.

Nonetheless, Freud's contributions to the study of personality and human sexuality remain important. He helped to develop the idea of **biological bisexuality,** the idea that people may be naturally attracted to both sexes. Freud also recognized that the body has **erogenous zones,** major areas of the body—especially the mouth, genitals, and anus—that are highly sensitive to sexual stimulation.

---

repress
In Freudian terms, to suppress upsetting sexual feelings or memories to keep them from causing mental distress or motivating unacceptable behavior.

Sigmund Freud accepted sexuality as a fundamental part of human nature that begins in infancy.
Time Life Pictures/Mansell/The LIFE Picture Collection/Getty Images

psychoanalysis
Treatment approach, known as talking therapy, developed by Freud to uncover feelings and memories hidden in the unconscious mind.

biological bisexuality
The idea that people may be naturally attracted to both sexes.

erogenous zones
Major areas of the body, especially the mouth, genitals, and anus, that are highly sensitive to sexual stimulation and excitement.

In the 20th century, sex researchers came to reject many of Freud's ideas and methodology. They rejected the huge emphasis on the unconscious, as well as the disease model of sexuality, and began to see themselves as part of a positive movement to reform society's understanding of sexuality and to make people healthier (Irvine, 2000). They saw sex as a measure of social progress and compared acceptance of sexual diversity to inventions such as the telephone and radio (Irvine, 2000; Robinson, 1976). For example, progressive sex researchers, including psychologists, sociologists, anthropologists, nurses, and a new generation of doctors and theologians, accepted the radical new idea that marriage should be based on love and mutual attraction between equals, not on power or arranged marriages, as was common in earlier times (Cott, 2002).

Two early anthropologists were part of this critical movement. They introduced the notion that sexuality is always part of culture and is adaptive to the context of behavior. First, Bronislaw Malinowski (1884–1942), a physicist who became the first anthropologist to study a culture through its own language and institutions, was the first scientist to study human sexual behavior in a non-Western society. To do this, he invented participant-observation **field study,** a research method in which the researcher observes behavior outside a clinical setting in its own cultural and linguistic context. The second researcher was Margaret Mead, the famed cultural anthropologist and feminist who helped to pioneer field studies of child and adolescent sexual development in other cultures.

field study
A research method in which the researcher observes behavior outside a clinical setting in its own cultural and linguistic context.

Margaret Mead Margaret Mead (1901–1978) was perhaps the first notable female sex researcher in the United States. Her first book, *Coming of Age in Samoa* (1927), became instantly famous, because Mead reacted to Freud and showed that culture was more important than personality or biology in the development of sexual behavior, especially among teenagers. Mead observed that adolescence was a time of great turbulence for youth in the United States, including conflict with their parents, as they asserted their independence. For the Samoans, however, adolescence was filled with positive feelings about sex, love, and sexual experimentation. Samoan youth experienced far less conflict with society. Mead's thesis was later challenged, but many of her basic discoveries have held up, including the notion that both culture and biology contribute to sexual well-being (Herdt & Leavitt, 1998). Mead (1935, 1949) went on to show that cultures vary widely by gender roles and sexual expression in adults.

Sex Research Comes of Age

As the influence of physicians and clinicians declined and social and behavioral scientists took up the study of sexuality in the 20th century, increasingly more people challenged the moralistic idea that all sex was a symptom of disease, an expression of sin, or the product of abnormal personality. And so began the first large scientific empirical studies of sexual behavior in the heart of small-town America. Researchers most influential during this time include Alfred Kinsey, Mary Calderone, William Masters and Virginia Johnson, and later, Michel Foucault, William Simon, and John Gagnon.

Alfred Kinsey In the late 1930s, Alfred Kinsey (1894–1956) also rejected Freud's methods and focused on people's sexual behavior in the real world. Kinsey changed the perspective of sex research that began in Europe and placed an American stamp upon it. Though he came from a strong religious background and grew up believing that all sex was intrinsically wrong, Kinsey developed an unshakable faith in science and in the notion that sex was a good thing (Gagnon, 2004; Jones, 1998). Trained as a zoologist, Kinsey had a keen interest in all nature, including reproductive sexuality, spurred by his own sexual curiosity and by the knowledge that the young adult students who came to his class on marriage and the family were afraid of sex (Jones, 1998).

Alfred Kinsey (left), pictured with his research assistants, was the first American to study the sexual behavior of large numbers of typical adults. His research changed the way people act and think about sex. In the 2004 movie *Kinsey,* Liam Neeson (right) portrayed the title character.
(*left*) Keystone Features/Hulton Archive/Getty Images; (*right*) AF archive/Alamy Stock Photo

Inspired by his own bisexuality and an interest in helping people who were scared of sex, Kinsey applied scientific methodology to eliminate superstition and harmful stereotypes. Rather than treating abnormal patients on a one-to-one basis or probing unconscious desires, as Freud had done, Kinsey studied the actual behaviors of large populations of normal people, including for the first time women, ethnic minorities, and homosexuals. His studies of human sexual behavior convinced him that there was wide natural variation in sexuality in human populations and that bisexuality was normal. These findings led him to reject traditional thinking about homosexuality and heterosexuality and about normal versus abnormal sexual behavior, and to accept the concept of a continuum of sexual behavior that ranged from being exclusively attracted to the opposite sex, to being exclusively attracted to the same sex, with bisexuality in between.

Kinsey began his research in 1937, when most Americans lived in small towns. For this undertaking, he pioneered the scientific **survey study,** using a questionnaire to reveal the attitudes and behaviors of a large number of people. The Kinsey study included more than 5,300 males and 5,940 females, thousands of whom Kinsey himself interviewed. In addition to ordinary people, there were also many famous people whose identities had to be kept secret, such as President Franklin D. Roosevelt. With funding from the Rockefeller Foundation, Kinsey and two colleagues, psychologist Wardell Pomeroy and sociologist Clyde Martin, expanded the study to include **representative samples,** individuals who represent diverse segments of the population of interest. They interviewed young and old, male and female, people from different social classes, and residents from cities and small towns (Kinsey et al., 1948). However, the studies generally ignored ethnic diversity, a major problem that later studies corrected (Herbenick et al., 2015; Herdt, 2004; Laumann et al., 1994; Das et al., 2012).

What Kinsey and his colleagues discovered shattered social stereotypes: People in the United States were engaging in far more types of sexual behaviors than previously believed, including masturbation, premarital sex, and homosexuality. In effect, Kinsey revealed what was going on in people's private sexual lives and uncovered contradictions between their beliefs and practices.

But the explosive findings that made media headlines came from Kinsey's second study, of female sexuality (Kinsey et al., 1953). Surveys of women found that, like men, they masturbated, had homosexual relations, and engaged in premarital and extramarital sexual relationships. In the 1950s, these findings were considered a moral outrage (Gagnon, 2004; Robinson, 1976).

Some researchers have argued that Kinsey's empirical data were more important than the theory, methodology, and other underpinnings of the study. One significant finding was that 37% of the U.S. males surveyed had had some homosexual experience. Critics complained that such findings were disruptive of traditional values about marriage and the family. As a result of heated

survey study
Investigations of different kinds of sexuality employing representative samples of people from different populations to establish norms of some kind, such as sexual health norms.

representative samples
Components of the natural population that represent diverse segments of the population of interest.

political attacks, Kinsey lost his funding and was hounded by the press. Yet newspapers widely reported on the results of the Kinsey studies, and continued to do so for decades. That coverage influenced how people perceived sex in their daily lives (Gagnon, 2004; Parker & Gagnon, 1995). Because of Kinsey's work, sex research and attitudes about sex would never be the same.

Mary Calderone Mary Calderone (1904–1998) became the first female doctor to promote contraceptives and adopt a more positive view of human sexuality. After marrying, having children, and divorcing, Calderone went to medical school. In time, she became one of the early leaders of Planned Parenthood, an organization devoted to family planning. She believed that women had a right to sexual pleasure and was a strong advocate of marriage and mutual pleasure of spouses in marital relations. She was not supportive of sex outside of marriage, however.

Calderone opposed the medical establishment for blocking distribution of birth control information to all people in the United States who went into doctors' offices in the 1950s and 1960s (Irvine, 2002). She felt that everyone had a right to family planning information and birth control, though many male doctors disagreed with her. She took her views to the media and was influential in changing the stance of the medical establishment. In 1964, along with Wardell Pomeroy, a protégé of Kinsey, she founded the Sexuality Information and Education Council of the United States (SIECUS), a group that pioneered teen sex education. In the 1970s, this organization became a focus of political reaction by sexual conservatives, who opposed Calderone (Irvine, 2002). Though Calderone lost influence, sex education continued to be a huge and growing concern to Americans.

William Masters and Virginia Johnson Between 1957 and 1965, a research team in St. Louis, Missouri, began an 8-year study, during which time they observed in their laboratory more than 10,000 complete cycles of orgasm in 382 women and 312 men. William H. Masters (1915–2001), a gynecologist, and Virginia E. Johnson (1925–2013), a psychologist, worked together to understand how people became aroused and what went wrong when they couldn't have an orgasm. They capitalized on Kinsey's more naturalistic and positive line of sex research and the public's mutual interest.

Like Kinsey, the Masters and Johnson team were critical of Freud's emphasis on verbal reports; and so they implemented a new clinical method for the study of orgasm and sexual functioning in large numbers of participants in a laboratory. But unlike other sex researchers who came before them, Masters and Johnson believed that only observed sexual behavior in the laboratory behind a two-way mirror was scientifically accurate.

Before Masters and Johnson began their research, Masters worked with couples to help them conceive. Later, he broadened his efforts to help people have more enjoyment and satisfaction in their sexual lives. He worked with heterosexuals and homosexuals and put orgasm in the spotlight for the first time (Maier, 2009; Robinson, 1976).

Imagine this scene in the Masters and Johnson clinic: a nude man with a paper bag over his head enters a lab and is greeted by a nude woman with a paper bag over her head! This is how Masters and Johnson arranged their sex research to allow participants to remain anonymous. Some of the participants admitted that they felt nervous, but others felt that it didn't matter because they said, "This was for science" (Maier, 2009). Some married males had strong sexual responses to their anonymous female partners, but felt they were relatively inexperienced in sexual technique. Johnson would coach the participants from the sidelines, giving suggestions about what to do physically.

Virginia Johnson and William Masters observed the sexual behavior of individuals and couples in a laboratory setting to better understand normal sexuality.
Bettmann/Getty Images

Masters and Johnson developed a technique to help couples deal with **sexual dysfunctions,** broadly defined negatively as problems that interfere with enjoyment of sexual intercourse or with orgasm. By talking with the couple over a two-week period, they helped to make people more comfortable with sex, so that they could relax and enjoy their sensual feelings. This method had a success rate of 80%—far better than psychoanalysis. However, as we will later see in Chapter 15, treating sexual problems with the diagnosis of dysfunction stigmatized women and men, particularly in later adulthood and aging.

Masters and Johnson's work was both fascinating and controversial, because they created the context for direct observation of sex in the lab. Critics still wonder if their observations actually changed people's sexual functioning in the lab (Maier, 2009). Nevertheless, Masters and Johnson made important discoveries about the physiological responses of sexual intercourse. One is that women generally can have multiple orgasms. Another is that there is a period after intercourse, known as the **refractory period,** when men cannot ejaculate. They also disproved Freud's belief that the only real orgasm for women is in the vagina. We discuss the findings of Masters and Johnson's research in more detail in Chapter 5.

Michel Foucault A French philosopher and historian of sexual ideas, Michel Foucault (1926–1984) did more than anyone in the social sciences to challenge Freud's ideas about the unconscious and sexual repression and to advance the social evaluation of sexuality. Building on decades of social and cultural studies by historians and sociologists, Foucault wrote a series of books and papers describing how history, context, institutions, roles, and ideas shape all human sexuality. He also showed how the language surrounding sexuality in laws and societal concepts powerfully regulates sexual emotions and human sexual behavior, including individual sexual expression and reproduction (Foucault, 1980). Unfortunately subsequent research has shown that Foucault was focused more on language than actual social behavior and he tended to draw his examples more from western society rather than the cross-cultural record.

In the 1980s, gay and lesbian scholars, and feminists, extended Foucault's approach to study how sexual movements were helping to advance people's identities and rights. Tragically, Foucault, a gay man, died of AIDS in 1984. This was a time when the whole notion of positive sexuality again began to be challenged, this time by the AIDS epidemic. As we will see later, within a few years, this terrible epidemic also coincided with a global movement toward the recognition of sexuality as a human right.

National Health and Social Life Survey Society changes and so does sexual behavior. Toward the end of the 20th century, researchers realized that Kinsey's studies from the mid-20th century were outdated. It was time for a new and more representative survey in the United States, one that would include ethnic diversity, identify how sexuality was changing, and study the role of pleasure in sexual behavior.

In the early 1990s, a team from the University of Chicago undertook a new study of sexual behavior using the latest scientific sampling and interview techniques. Led by sociologist Edward O. Laumann, the research team sampled 3,432 men and women from all ethnic groups to rectify the problem of the earlier Kinsey surveys that neglected diversity (Laumann et al., 1994). This effort included a new way of creating a true large **random sample**—that is, a sample in which every element in the population has an equal chance of being selected. In this case, the technique involved dialing random telephone numbers to find people for the study.

The 1994 survey, known as the National Health and Social Life Survey (NHSLS), uncovered some surprises about how sexuality had changed since Kinsey's work. For example, oral

---

DID YOU KNOW

Masters and Johnson tackled the fundamental challenge of all sex research: Researchers usually do not see people having sex (Herdt, 1999b). Using a two-way mirror seemed to solve this scientific problem, at least for a time, but this approach created a whole new scientific and ethical problem. Critics pointed out that some subjects were aware that they were being watched and changed how they engaged in sex—possibly having more sex or more orgasms than they normally would. This dilemma is now called the *Masters and Johnson's conundrum* because, in solving one problem with the two-way mirror, they inadvertently created another problem. Since then, researchers have been careful to consider such effects.

sexual dysfunction
The inability to enjoy sexual intercourse or achieve orgasm.

refractory period
The normal response immediately after ejaculation, when men cannot ejaculate.

random sample
A sample in which every element in the population has an equal chance of being selected.

Table 1.1 Oral and anal sex practices in diverse ethnic groups

	WHITE		AFRICAN AMERICAN		HISPANIC	
SEX PRACTICE	MEN	WOMEN	MEN	WOMEN	MEN	WOMEN
Giving oral sex	81.4%	75.3%	50.3%	34.4%	70.7%	59.7%
Receiving oral sex	81.4	74.9	66.3	48.9	73.2	63.7
Anal sex—any experience	25.8	23.2	23.4	9.6	34.2	17.0

Source: Laumann et al., 1994.

and anal sex were found to be far more common. As a result of including diverse ethnic groups too, the researchers discovered some large and important differences, including the fact that oral and anal sexual practices vary considerably among Whites, African Americans, and Hispanics, as shown in Table 1.1. As you will see later in the book, the percentage of the general population that engage in oral and anal sex has continued to increase.

The NHSLS also found important differences in who was or was not faithful (practicing sexual fidelity) in marriage (Figure 1.3). Husbands said they had sex more frequently than their wives reported. Also, 94% of married men and women had only one sex partner (their spouse), but 4% had two to four partners and 1% had more than five partners.

The NHSLS sparked controversy by reporting that homosexuality occurs less frequently in the population than reported by Kinsey and colleagues in 1948. The 1994 study reported that about 2.8% of men and 1.4% of women said they thought of themselves as homosexual or bisexual. The 1948 Kinsey study reported that 4% of men and 1-3% of women were exclusively homosexual. The findings seemed counterintuitive, though, because wasn't homosexuality more accepted? Critics have pointed out that the NHSLS may have underrepresented the number of homosexuals sampled in its survey, and one of its own authors agreed (Michaels, 1996). In Chapter 10 we will study why and how the LGBTQ population has changed and the expression of sexual orientation has become more widely accepted in society.

In addition, the NHSLS raised an old and controversial question: Is sexual behavior the consequence of nature or nurture? Politicians attacked the study for even raising such a question (Laumann et al., 1994). The historic controversy stems from the fact that most people assume others are heterosexual—and that nature, or biology, makes them that way. This controversy has long intrigued the public and researchers alike. Generally, a large body of research in sexual science suggests that both nature and nurture contribute to sexuality (Bailey et al., 2016).

Figure 1.3
Percent of Americans reporting sexual fidelity in the National Health and Social Life Survey (NHSLS).
Source: Laumann et al., 1994.

Married Females: 85
Married Males: 75.5
Homosexual Males (current relationship): 4.5

> **WHAT'S ON YOUR MIND?**
>
> **Q:** *My buddy says that guys always want to have sex and a lot of women don't want sex as much as men. He says it's what evolution is all about—that men have more sex drive than women. Is that true?*
>
> **ANSWER:** Men appear to think about sex more and pursue sex more strongly than many women. How much of that comes from evolution and how much from what people's culture teaches them about sex and the emotions that go along with it is uncertain, but it may be a combination of both factors. The majority of men who are 60 and under think about sex once a day, while only about 25% of all women do. Also, women do not fantasize about sex as frequently as men do (Laumann et al., 1994). But don't forget, there is huge variation between how individuals respond to these things, with some individual women having more sex drive than men and some women wanting to have sex more often or for longer periods of time than their partners.

Nevertheless, it is still a controversial topic, as outlined in "Controversies in Sexuality: What Makes People Heterosexual—Nature or Nurture?"

As the NHSLS indicates, people's sexual attitudes and behaviors have evolved, and there now appears to be greater tolerance and acceptance of diversity (Cott, 2002; Floyd & Bakeman, 2006; Herbenik, et al., 2015; Herek, 2009; Marzullo & Herdt, 2011). Tolerance in general and teaching sexual diversity in particular are aims of sexual literacy. When we support individuals to engage with a "sexually oppressive, alienating and exploitative world" (Moore & Reynolds, 2018, p. 202) we move closer to the idea that sexuality can become an important part of social justice in society.

Sex and Social Justice Today

For decades, progress occurred in the application of sexual science in U.S. society, but in recent years, a combination of political reactions, social movements, and political stalemate has truly challenged our view that progress is possible. Sometimes researchers are caught in the middle, trying to do their best to apply science to the very real problems of society. Only part of this reaction can be attributed to sexual illiteracy. For example, the sudden and extremely important rise of the #Me-Too Movement to oppose sexual harassment, abuse, and intimidation has caused huge reactions in Hollywood, government, industry, and now society in general. Sexual ethics and social justice require a new attitude that places people in positions to achieve their own well-being, negotiate and empower themselves, and make policies and actions transparent whenever possible. **Social justice**, defined as the fair distribution of wealth, opportunities, and privileges in society, implies respect, dignity, and the application of human rights in people's daily lives. Today, not only are we learning that social justice that provides for the well-being of diverse people is good for our society and our economy (Forgeard, Jayawickreme, et al., 2011; Herbenik et al., 2015; Moore & Reynolds, 2018) but we are also coming to realize that creating norms, attitudes, and policies that foster social justice and sexual well-being is good for protection of sexual health and for the increase in positive relationships and family functioning throughout our society (Diener & Seligman, 2004; Das et al., 2012). For example, sexuality policies that foster comprehensive sexual education can contribute to students' focus, protection, and, possibly, performance in school (Fields, 2008; Kirby, 2008). Unfortunately, a variety of recent research studies reveal that some politicians oppose rational planning and good public health care when it comes to family planning (DiMauro & Joffe, 2009; Epstein, 1996; Herdt & Howe, 2007). As a result, sex research has not been part of broad public planning in the United States, even when it comes to preventing sexually transmitted diseases (CDC, 2011a; Epstein, 2003).

Consider the findings of a blue-ribbon panel convened by U.S. Surgeon General David Satcher regarding sexual health. Satcher assembled a group of 100 experts in sexuality,

social justice
The fair distribution of wealth, opportunities, and privileges in society that imply respect, dignity, and the application of human rights in the daily lives of people.

CONTROVERSIES in Sexuality

What Makes People Heterosexual—Nature or Nurture?

In the 19th century, sexologists tried to show that medical symptoms or physical factors caused sexual behavior, especially the abnormal side of it (Irvine, 2000; Robinson, 1976). They considered sex drives and sexual desire as primarily determined by nature, especially for men. By the mid-20th century, this view began to change. First, Alfred Kinsey suggested that sexual expression existed on a continuum from heterosexual to homosexual, influenced by a combination of biology (nature) and culture (nurture). Then Foucault showed that particular forms of sexual behavior occurred only in certain historical societies. In the 1970s and 1980s, many social scientists followed this change and argued that sexuality was influenced more by society and culture than by biology. They studied what was called the **social construction** of sexual behavior, meaning that social, cultural, political, economic, and other institutional forces shape sexual behavior. However, in taking this view, scientists never explained why most people are heterosexual. Are people born with heterosexual drives and desires, or is it constructed and nurtured into them by society? Or is it both?

What makes people heterosexual: Is it all nature?

Yes:

- Males and females report feeling that they are attracted only to the opposite sex and they say it feels "natural" for them.
- Some males and females experiment with same-sex practices but drift back to the opposite sex because they say it feels "right" to them (Diamond, 2008; Bailey et al., 2016).
- Some straight males report that by 9 years of age they knew they were straight and never felt differently (Bailey & Oberschneider, 1997). They are likely to say that they have never been attracted sexually to another male.
- Males, in particular, have a likelihood of feeling that their sexuality is totally the result of nature (Herdt & Boxer, 1993).

No:

- Heterosexuality is something that is learned, just like learning to be a man or a woman in society, and so it has to be both nurture and nature, no matter what drives it.
- Some people are heterosexual because they want to have a family and children, and they think they can only do that by being heterosexual (Hirsch et al., 2009).
- Some people act heterosexual, but then have relations with the same gender. For example, some people may be attracted to both genders, but their family and community make them afraid or ashamed to express their attractions (Herdt & McClintock, 2000).
- When a culture requires heterosexual marriage as a condition of being accepted in the community, people will adapt and conform to it, even when it is not their first choice (Badgett, 2009).

What's Your Perspective?

1. Are sex drives all biology or nature, or do they get shaped to some extent or expressed due to societal forces?
2. Do males and females differ with respect to what makes them heterosexual? Why or why not?
3. Do the same arguments apply to what makes people gay? Why or why not?

---

social construction
The social, cultural, political, economic, and other institutional forces that shape sexual behavior.

including researchers, policymakers, doctors, professionals, and teachers, who met over many months to open a "mature national dialogue on issues of sexuality, sexual health, and responsible sexual behavior." Based on their recommendations, Surgeon General Satcher issued the *Call to Action to Promote Sexual Health and Responsible Sexual Behavior* in 2001 (Surgeon General's Report, 2001). The vision of forward-looking policy was threefold:

1. To increase awareness through education and media
2. To implement and strengthen interventions that can help prevent HIV/AIDS, unintended pregnancy, and other problems
3. To expand the research base through a variety of positive projects that could help people understand sexual decision making, such as a study of adolescent sexual behavior

What happened to these recommendations? Nothing. Politicians intervened, and the effort to have a rational, scientific, and humane discussion to support the full spectrum of sexual health and well-being did not succeed. Far ahead of its time, Satcher's call to action, the most important policy guidelines on sexuality in years, revealed that sexual literacy in the United States is weak, and because it is weak, the recommendations were blocked (Surgeon General's Report, 2001). Nevertheless, they remain a strong call to action for sexual literacy (Coleman, 2010; Herdt & Howe, 2007; Klein, 2006).

When sex research is applied correctly, it can provide benefits, as revealed by experiences in some Western European nations (Badgett, 2009; DiMauro & Joffe, 2009). Some of these nations have lower rates of sexually transmitted infections (STIs), lower rates of unintended pregnancy, better mental and physical health correlates of sexual behavior, and generally a higher level of sexual well-being than the United States (Correa et al., 2008; Petchesky, 2003). In the United States, there exists a "code of silence" surrounding sexual health and sex education, rather than sound public policy, particularly with respect to issues such as teen pregnancy, homosexuality, and reproductive decisions (Institute of Medicine, 2000). Increased sexual literacy could help change this situation if the next generation supports proactive policies.

In the next section we discuss the basic research methods that scientists use in sex research, the kind of research that can help the U.S. government form strong policies about sexuality.

METHODOLOGY IN THE STUDY OF SEXUALITY

Have you ever wondered how researchers study human sexuality? Think about all of the possible questions about sex and sexuality that you would like to have answered. Could you ask people directly, or would you have to study it indirectly? How would you know if you were changing people's sexuality even as you studied it? And how would you go about finding answers without violating anyone's privacy? Freud, Kinsey, Margaret Mead, Masters and Johnson, and other researchers have long struggled with this major challenge to sex research.

Like other sciences, the study of sexuality uses a broad range of standard methods of research, as we have examined in this chapter, including but not limited to individual clinical studies, field studies, surveys, and laboratory experiments. Also, like other scientists, sex researchers must abide by a code of ethics as they gather information about people's intimate behavior. What might surprise you is that sex research cuts across several scientific and social scientific disciplines. Let's look first at the interdisciplinary nature of human sexuality research.

Interdisciplinary Perspectives

Because human sexuality holistically involves all aspects of the body, mind, heart, and experience, the study of sexuality involves biological, social, psychological, and health sciences. These disciplines provide an **interdisciplinary perspective** that helps to integrate all aspects of the field of human sexuality. Their contributions complement each other (Diamond, 1997; Herdt & Howe, 2007; Tolman & Diamond, 2002; Jordan-Young, 2010).

The body and its biological functioning are part of this interdisciplinary knowledge. For example, think about why females have a clitoris. Is this highly sensitive external genital structure an ancient evolutionary equivalent of the male penis, as some biologists suspect (Symonds, 1979)? Or is the clitoris a human adaptation that enhances pleasure and motivates males and females to bond as a long-term couple? Historically, this nature–nurture debate pitted biological explanations against cultural explanations. However, these biological and evolutionary perspectives on sexuality supplement, rather than contradict, perspectives from other disciplines about why females have a clitoris and enjoy orgasm (Sherman, 1988). Either way, the clitoris actually enhances successful reproduction and thus human society.

interdisciplinary perspective
The holistic integration of research in different disciplines to describe and explain all of human sexuality.

DID YOU KNOW

Researchers have made great strides in protecting people who participate in sexuality studies. In general, researchers are guided by the principle of never doing harm to research participants. Three important things can be done to achieve this goal:

1. Anticipate any possible risks of participation, and then take care to address all of these.
2. Be open and honest about what the research entails, to avoid *deception in research*—that is, intentionally misleading participants or withholding information about the study to achieve some scientific result—which is a risk in sexuality studies.
3. Provide support and follow-up to ensure that participants had a positive experience or get needed support if they had a negative emotional reaction to their participation in the study.

Intersectionality
Research methodology that addresses the combination of all kinds of social identities and social inequality.

In studying sexuality, interdisciplinary research has three primary goals:

1. *To better understand human sexual behavior.* For example, if researchers gain an accurate understanding of the kind of sexual behaviors teenagers (ages 13 to 19) engage in, they can use that information to develop educational programs and policies to promote sexual well-being through better sexual decision-making skills.
2. *To help predict the sexual behavior of others.* For example, research that examines childhood sexual abuse can help predict the behavior of other victims (Gibson & Leitenberg, 2001; Marx & Sloan, 2003). With this knowledge, people may more effectively pinpoint prevention and intervention efforts. Additionally, predicting the sexual behaviors of others can help to encourage family, friends, schools, churches, and child welfare agencies to intervene early when signs of abuse occur, thus enabling the survivors to pursue sexual well-being in their lives (Widom & Kuhns, 1996).
3. *To influence laws and policies regarding sexual behavior.* Examples include policies promoting tolerance in high schools for diverse sexual and gender expressions, preventing bullying, and reducing trauma and suicide that may result from antigay prejudice (Fields, 2008; Pascoe, 2007).

Intersectionality and Social Justice

While interdisciplinary research is critical in examining sexuality within the lens of multiple schools of thought, researchers must also engage in research that closely examines the intersection and interdependence of social and sexual identities (Bowleg, 2008). **Intersectionality** in research refers to a methodological approach that addresses social identities and social inequality that is based on the combination of ethnicity, sexual orientation, gender identity, class, disability status, etc. and stresses areas of interdependence (Collins, 1998). When engaging in research around issues of sexuality, it is critical that researchers understand issues of power and privilege and, in particular, how people's sexuality is impacted by systems of status, power, and privilege embedded in race, gender, social class, national origin, and religion. For example, this means that the experiences of a White middle-class lesbian cannot automatically be compared to or regarded as the same as the experiences of a Black middle-class lesbian unless the researcher closely examines the difference of racism in its multiple forms. In addition, factors such as heterosexism and misogyny may have an impact on the lived experience of the person in this example.

As a major illustration, consider how in Chapter 8 we will discuss the high infant and maternal mortality rates of women of color in the United States. By comparison, the same mortality rates are lower for White women (Amnesty International, 2010). Intersectional research suggests that we cannot achieve a full understanding of this issue until we examine pregnancy complications within the context of unequal health care and the intersection of race, gender, and socioeconomic status. Consequently, when we examine the issue of infant and maternal mortality within the intersection of these important identities, researchers can more clearly understand how pregnant women of color in the United States are impacted by multiple forms of racism every day. Racism is correlated with higher stress levels (Meyer, 1995, 2007), which in turn can have a negative impact on a developing fetus. Thus, when we fail to examine the intersection of race, gender, socioeconomic status, and pregnancy, we ultimately risk not fully understanding the contexts and situations that threaten the health and well-being of women of color and their babies. And without this understanding we can never hope to improve the health and well-being of the mother and child.

Ethics of Sexual Research

As you might expect, sex research raises issues regarding ethics and personal rights. Researchers must protect people who participate in sex research. Additionally, researchers must strive to include all segments of society in sexuality studies because, historically, ethnic minorities were left out (Epstein, 2007; Herdt, 2004).

When research is conducted with people, it is mandatory to include certain measures to protect the participants, to enable them to understand what the research is about, and to know how it may affect them. These protections include the following (Epstein, Klinkenberg, Wiley, & McKinley, 2001):

1. Ensuring that data collection is done anonymously and confidentially
2. Ensuring that participants are of legal age
3. Authenticating that the participants' attitudes, experiences, and behaviors are truthful as reported in terms of their age, ethnicity, and gender
4. Ensuring that no harm is done to research participants

The last two points are especially important because data increasingly are collected via the Internet, where it's hard to be sure who the participants really are and how the research might affect them (Buchanan & Ess, 2009).

Now we examine some of the methods used in sex research and consider the advantages and disadvantages of each method.

Research Designs

Sexual science employs a variety of **research designs,** which are scientific models that lay out the aims, methods, and analysis of data. In general, every kind of research method can be categorized as either a quantitative research method or a qualitative research method. **Quantitative research** focuses on gathering numeric information or nonnumeric information that is easily encoded into a numeric form, such as a survey. **Qualitative research,** in contrast, involves the collection and analysis of qualitative (i.e., nonnumerical) data to search for patterns, themes, and holistic features. Each category has strengths and weaknesses. Most researchers typically fall into one of the two camps (Ponterotto, 2005; Tolman & Diamond, 2002) as befits a field that is highly interdisciplinary like human sexuality.

Quantitative methods are designed to ensure objectivity, make it possible to generalize the results, and ensure validity and reliability. **Objectivity** refers to the absence of personal bias. Research attempts to confirm or support a question of interest or **hypothesis,** which is a proposition set forth to explain some observation, method, or data analysis. **Generalizability** means the extent to which research findings and conclusions from a study conducted on a sample population can be applied, or *generalized,* to the population at large. **Reliability** refers to the extent to which a measure, procedure, or instrument yields the same result on repeated trials. **Validity** is the extent to which a test measures what it claims to measure. It is vital for a test to be valid in order for the results to be accurately applied and interpreted.

Quantitative research is concerned with studying how one variable impacts another. A **variable** is something that can be changed, such as a characteristic or value. Variables are generally used in research to determine if changes to one thing result in changes to another. In research there are two different kinds of variables. An **independent variable** is the variable being manipulated to test its effect on the **dependent variable**—that is, the variable being measured. For example, a researcher who wants to determine if room temperature affects sexual desire could manipulate the temperature (independent variable) by increasing or decreasing it and then measuring its impact on sexual desire (dependent variable). The relationship between the independent and dependent variable

---

research designs
Scientific models that lay out the aims, methods, and analysis of data in research.

quantitative research method
A type of study that focuses on sample design and on large representative or random samples.

qualitative research method
A type of study that focuses on meaning and context, with small or nonrandom samples, or both.

objectivity
The absence of personal bias in research.

hypothesis
A proposition set forth to explain some observation, method, or data analysis.

generalizability
The extent to which research findings and conclusions from a study conducted on a sample population can be applied, or *generalized,* to the population at large.

reliability
The extent to which a measure, procedure, or instrument yields the same result on repeated trials.

validity
The extent to which a test measures what it claims to measure.

variable
Something that can be changed, such as a characteristic or value.

independent variable
A variable that is manipulated to test its effect on other variables in a research study.

WHAT'S ON YOUR MIND?

Q: *In my psychology class, I was asked to participate in a research project about sexual behaviors. We were invited to take a survey that asked a lot of personal questions about sexuality and my personal sexual preferences in relationships. I walked out without taking it because I was really nervous about revealing some of these details. Are researchers required to protect anonymity when asking about sexuality?*

ANSWER: Your question is a really good one and I am sure many others have wondered the same thing. At universities, an Institutional Review Board (IRB) governs research projects. Part of the IRB's responsibility is to review safeguards for participants. The study probably went through an intensive review process where the researchers had to ensure that participants' identity and their responses would remain anonymous. It is really important that researchers help us to understand sexuality better. But it is also important for researchers to make sure that participants feel comfortable with this level of personal disclosure. To double check, you can ask the instructor about the privacy of your responses to make sure that you are comfortable answering the survey questions.

---

dependent variable
The variable that is being measured in a research study.

correlation
The statistical measurement of the strength of a relationship between variables, such as dating and marriage.

is called a **correlation,** a statistical measurement of the strength of the relationship between two variables. Here, researchers might correlate room temperature with sexual desire to discover if desire rises or falls with temperature (a positive correlation), if desire falls as temperature rises or vice versa (a negative correlation), or if room temperature has no observable effect on desire (no correlation). Note that a correlation between variables does not mean that a change in one *causes* a change in the other, only that they are related somehow. In other words, an increase in room temperature may be associated with a rise in sexual desire, but that doesn't mean higher temperatures are the cause of increased sexual desire. It might be that a hot room causes the body to produce hormones that increase desire. Remembering this limitation of correlation will help you become a sexually literate consumer of research.

From the interdisciplinary perspective, researchers can study individuals, communities, or whole societies. To do so, they employ one or more different research designs. Here we briefly examine some common approaches to data collection used in sexuality research: case study, surveys and interviews, direct observation, and experiments.

case study
A research method that professionals in clinical psychology, medicine, and sexuality use to study a single individual or very small group in depth.

Case Study The **case study** is a popular research method used by professionals in clinical psychology, medicine, and sexuality that dates back to 19th-century sexology. In case studies, researchers use direct observation, questionnaires, and testing to collect information. A researcher studies a single individual or very small group in depth. Usually the researcher follows this individual or small group closely over time. Freud (1905) relied heavily on individual case studies of his patients in formulating his theory about sexuality in infancy and childhood. Researchers may also gather information by analyzing medical records, journals, diaries, or other historical records of the individual or small group being studied.

retrospective self-report
An account of a memory of an event in one's life.

retrospective bias
The tendency for people to not remember certain aspects of their lives clearly or to misremember certain aspects.

The main disadvantage of case study research in sexuality is that it is hard to generalize the results to a larger population (Laumann et al., 1994). Because the research focuses on an individual or a small number of people, it is difficult to argue that their experiences can be generalized to very large groups of people. Another disadvantage is that case studies are often based on the **retrospective self-report,** which is an account of a memory of an event in one's life. Although people may have great knowledge about their own lives, they may not remember certain aspects of it clearly and may misremember other aspects. This distortion of recalled events is the **retrospective bias** (Boxer & Cohler, 1989; Laumann et al., 1994). In addition, people may avoid divulging information for personal reasons, either intentionally or accidentally, such as whether they masturbate (Wyatt, Peters, & Guthrie, 1988) or whether they seek sex online (Pascoe, 2011). Given this concern, case studies are often unsuitable for many research questions.

Surveys and Interviews Researchers use surveys to identify the knowledge, attitudes, or behaviors of a large group of people. Types of surveys include self-administered written questionnaires, face-to-face interviews, telephone surveys, and Internet-based surveys. Deciding which survey method to use depends on which kind of survey will yield the most honest and complete answers. Each method has advantages and disadvantages (Catania et al., 1995). For one thing, basic literacy, including computer literacy, is required to participate in some of these survey methods, limiting the use of the methodology to literate populations.

An advantage of face-to-face interviews is that they allow researchers to build a rapport with each participant to draw out authentic answers and information. An interviewer can also vary the sequence of questions depending on how a person responds to previous questions (Laumann et al., 1994, 2004). For example, if a person answers positively to a question about having been sexually abused in childhood, the next series of questions could be about that experience; the researcher could eliminate those questions if that person did not report previous sexual abuse. In addition, an interviewer can ask a person in an interview to clarify information in order to increase understanding of the answer. Printed surveys and questionnaires do not offer this type of flexibility. The downside to face-to-face interviews is that they can be costly to conduct, as they require a significant time investment. Also, the personal nature of the interview may overwhelm some individuals, which can lead to dishonest responses or purposeful omissions of information.

Questionnaires are much less costly than face-to-face interviews because they can be administered to large groups of people at one time. Another advantage of questionnaires is that they can ensure anonymity, which means the responses may be honest. Increasingly, this issue is addressed when subjects use laptops or tablets to answer questions by themselves, rather than in a direct question-and-answer mode such as Kinsey used.

Internet questionnaires are increasing in popularity in sex research. Internet surveys offer the possibility of even greater numbers of respondents from a wide geographic area over a relatively short period of time. This method is also very popular with students because it is relatively inexpensive or free and allows access to populations that may otherwise be difficult to reach, such as transgender youth in rural communities. However, researchers agree that while Internet-based research offers real advantages, it also raises serious methodological problems (Buchanan & Ess, 2009). Consider that every day hundreds of items in our lives and the media pertain to sexuality. Being able to sift out what is real or fake, helpful or just nonsense, from this sea of information can be a great bonus to your own sexual literacy. You can read more in "Research and Sexual Well-Being: Becoming a Critical Consumer of Sex Research in the 21st Century."

Internet surveys have the potential to reach more people over a wide geographic area than other research designs and they are inexpensive to conduct. One limitation is that this method of data collection rules out people who don't have access to a computer.
Sam Edwards/Caia Image/Glow Images

Direct Observation Another way to collect data is through **direct observation,** which provides an opportunity to observe natural behaviors in context as they occur. A great deal of information can be collected about people by watching them in person, as researchers have learned from field studies (Fields, 2008; Hirsch et al., 2009; Pascoe, 2007). Researchers conduct direct observation studies in small to moderate-size samples of people and record their behaviors or responses. Reliability of data increases with more representative samples and the accuracy of tape recordings and videotaped studies. Another advantage of direct observation studies is that the observation by researchers eliminates the possibility of falsification because they are observing behavior as it occurs.

direct observation
A data collection method that provides the researcher an opportunity to observe natural behaviors in context as they occur.

RESEARCH and Sexual Well-Being

Becoming a Critical Consumer of Sex Research in the 21st Century

How does having an understanding of research methods help support your sexual well-being? When you learn to interpret and apply research, you are in a better position to stay healthy, because studies have consistently shown that active engagement in your own quality health produces better care, understanding, interventions, and outcomes (WHO, 2018).

The difficulty is that even professionals may face problems in separating research that is well done from research that is flawed with respect to the sample, methods, or conclusions. In fact, every piece of research is potentially flawed in some way, because research is an imperfect reflection of the real world. Even though research provides us with immense knowledge, we must be able to see its weaknesses to improve our understanding of a given issue. Nowhere is this truer than in sex research, because inaccurate research studies may lead to faulty interpretation of results, which in turn may become like myths that mainstream media report as fact. How many of you have seen or heard on television or the Internet an expert make a claim about sex, only to hear another expert dispute it later? When people rely on mainstream media, including popular magazines, for information about sex, these issues prevail.

Cosmopolitan and *Maxim* are well known for regularly publishing survey results about various sexual issues, often about sexual attraction, beauty, or performance. One popular magazine, for example, publishes the results of an annual Internet poll about what men most desire in the bedroom. But how do you know if what these popular magazines are reporting accurately reflects research or reflects the general population? While the article offers responses to all kinds of questions, it is important to understand the weaknesses of the survey so you can read the results with a critical eye.

Consider what is said in a recent article about sample size: 6,000 men between the ages of 18 and 35 were polled. Albeit good information, it is only partial information about the sample. Consider some things that were not stated about the sample:

- What is the relationship status of the men surveyed?
- What is the race/ethnicity breakdown of the sample size?
- What is the educational level of those surveyed?

It may be as important to have answers for each of these questions as it is to know how many men were surveyed and how old they were. For example, knowing the relationship status of the men in the survey may explain relationship stability and frequency of sexual interaction. Ethnicity and education are critical factors because sexual norms vary greatly across communities. What may be typical for one culture may be completely atypical for another.

Understanding flaws in methodology is another critical skill to have when reading research findings. The magazine's survey methodology has the following issues:

- Could the men log on more than once to take the survey?
- How were the men recruited to answer the survey?
- Are the survey questions valid and reliable?

This particular poll was conducted through an online men's magazine. The issue of whether or not men could take the survey more than once is critical. If men took the survey more than once, results may not represent 6,000 *different* men. Recruitment of subjects may be influenced by *self-selection bias*. For example, men who have had a lot of sexual experience may have been more inclined to take this survey than men who have limited experience, and men who lack access to a computer would not be represented in the results.

The survey consisted of multiple-choice questions, which limit the possible answers in a way that raises concerns about reliability and validity. For example, one question asked: "When you meet a woman for the first time, what grabs your attention?" The answer options were:

A. A hot body
B. Seductive eyes
C. Gorgeous hair
D. A sexy voice

Although the choices are quite interesting, the four characteristics do not represent the full spectrum of what men find most attractive in women. The men were not allowed to include other things that they might like more in women, such as intelligence or being a good companion. What if all these answers represent what grabs their attention? What if none of these answers represents what grabs their attention? A more reliable study question might have offered characteristics that represent different traits, such as having a sense of humor, being intelligent, being physically healthy, being educated, or enjoying sex.

Even though the article is fun to read and reveals a few interesting details about a relatively small group of men, as a piece of research, this survey is significantly flawed in almost all areas. For this reason, call it entertainment, not research. Learning to discriminate between information that is important and applicable to your sexual well-being, and separating out facts from myths, is vitally important.

One disadvantage of this kind of research is that sexual behavior in a laboratory setting may not perfectly imitate behavior that occurs in private. Also, observers may influence the behavior they are observing. Another disadvantage of direct observation is *self-selection:* One could argue that it takes people who are extremely comfortable with themselves, their body, and their sexual performance to agree to engage in such private behaviors in front of others. This skews the sample, then, because people who are uncomfortable in this situation will not agree to be part of the study.

Experiments Another method, called **experimental research,** involves researchers putting more limitations into place, to examine or predict how changes in independent variables (e.g., age, medication, emotions, attraction, behavior) influence dependent variables (e.g., disease, behavior, response). Correlation studies, which are a subtype of experiments, look for relationships across a broad range of variables (e.g., sexual activity and rates of sexually transmitted infections), but as noted earlier, do not determine if one variable causes another.

Sexuality research that is experimental often focuses on physiological responses to various stimuli, such as sexual imagery that arouses a response in the brain or genitals, or both. The response is measured by instruments attached to the genitals that monitor physiological or sexual arousal responses, such as heart rate, pupil dilation, and brain activity.

The benefit of experimental methods is that the influence of external variables can be controlled somewhat. In addition, experimental studies allow researchers to draw conclusions about cause-and-effect relationships among the variables of interest.

The drawback to experimental research is that the laboratory setting can also influence the behavior of participants. In addition, depending on the kinds of equipment necessary to conduct the research, experimental research can be very costly.

Participatory Action Research

Participatory action research (PAR) is a relatively new social method of gathering and using information that involves strong community participation. Rather than a set of procedures for collecting information, PAR involves the people who are affected most directly by issues in the community in the effort to apply the research to their benefit. This approach to sex research also helps to motivate greater community participation in the study, whether it concerns sex education, date rape, coming out as homosexual, or being sexually active in a community that discourages sex outside of marriage. PAR studies in human sexuality have encompassed a huge range of concerns from classroom sex education, sexual identity formation, and homelessness in youth to access to sexual partners for prison inmates. PAR often involves a research alliance between the subjects and the scientist for the purpose of improving society—for example, by reducing police brutality against women and transgender people of color, or by supporting young women's self-esteem in dating relationships (Fields, 2008; Teunis & Herdt, 2006; Tolman, 2005).

PAR is a way to build and strengthen sexual well-being in communities by increasing people's understandings of each other's sexual lives, their relationships, and themselves (Urban Justice Center, 2005).

Methods for gathering information in PAR include:

- Community-based surveys
- Group discussions
- Individual interviews
- Community art projects to represent experiences through visual art, poetry, spoken word, theater, or music
- Photo or video documentation
- Storytelling and oral history

experimental research
A data collection method that involves researchers putting more limitations into place, to examine or predict how changes in independent variables influence dependent variables.

participatory action research (PAR)
Collecting information that honors, centers, and reflects the experiences of people most directly affected by issues in their communities.

Employing this approach enables the researchers to create an action plan with the community to help ensure that the research and community realize complementary goals.

HUMAN SEXUAL RIGHTS

As you grew up, you may not have heard much about sexuality as a human right. This is understandable, partly because it is a relatively new perspective, but also because human sexual rights are becoming increasingly necessary. In this section, we examine the current status of human sexual rights for the achievement of sexual literacy and well-being. In the coming chapters we'll continue to examine rights issues as they apply to sexual, gender, and reproductive topics, because research now shows that without sexual rights, people cannot hope to secure a positive and respectful approach to sexuality, pleasure, and relationships free of coercion and violence, and focused on sexual, gender, and reproductive well-being (Correa, Petchesky, & Parker, 2008; Petchetsky, Correa, & Parker, 2010; WHO, 2019).

Universal human rights are rights to which all humans are entitled, such as the freedoms of speech and religion, freedom from violence or intimidation, and the most basic right of all, to life. Researchers and advocates of human rights believe that these rights are inherent qualities of life, especially equality, freedom, and dignity (Farmer, 2008; WHO, 2019). When deprived of these rights, people may suffer a wide range of physical, mental, emotional, and social abuses. They may even be killed. The World Health Organization understands that there is a growing consensus that "sexual health cannot be achieved and maintained without respect for, and protection of, certain human rights."

How did the focus on rights evolve? In the past, some societies did not respect diversity and violated basic human rights. But it was the experiences of World War II, including the genocide of millions of Jewish people and other groups, that led to a call for human rights as a global perspective. As information about mass killings, rape, sexual torture, sexual abuse, and the violation of people's bodies through medical experiments and forced sterilization during World War II came to light, a new world order of universal human rights emerged. The United Nations (UN) Charter, signed in 1945 by 50 countries, stated as one of its goals: "To promote . . . universal respect for, and observance of, human rights and fundamental freedoms for all without discrimination as to race, sex, language, or religion." By 1948, members of the UN adopted *The Universal Declaration of Human Rights* (UDHR), the first international document to delineate human rights. Many nations, led by the United States and Great Britain, wanted to ensure that never again would human rights be so horribly violated as they had been during World War II. The UN Charter includes the word *human* in the title of the document to rule out any ambiguity that might have resulted if the word *man* had been used. The rights of women, children, the disabled, and other vulnerable populations were protected for the first time in this document (Hunt, 2007; Petchesky, Correa, & Parker, 2010).

It was many years before research and positive changes in the world revealed that human sexuality rights were largely left out of this document. The emergence of the AIDS pandemic exposed this weakness in policies and rights worldwide (Farmer, 2006). Today there is a growing consensus among scientists, policy experts, and sex educators about the need to protect reproductive, sexual, and gender rights. That's because decades of study have revealed that when people feel *safe and secure* in their right to pursue their individual sexual pleasure, reproductive potential, and expression of sexual and gender identity, they are healthier in general and are better able to attain their full potential as human beings (Aggleton & Parker, 2002, 2010; Coleman, 2010; Correa, Mcintyre, Rodriguez, Paiva, & Marks, 2005; Correa, Petchesky, & Parker, 2008; Miller, 2000; Petchesky, 2003).

universal human rights
Rights to which all humans are entitled, such as equality and nondiscrimination, freedom of speech and religion, and the most basic right of all, to life.

Human sexual rights violations can destroy sexual, gender, and reproductive health and well-being, and possibly life itself. These violations may include forcing people to have sex, to have abortions, or to be sterilized, thus denying people the right to contraceptives, executing or imprisoning people because of their sexual or gender orientations, and forcing people to have their genitals altered as well as being raped and sexually coerced (Correa et al., 2008; Hunt, 2007; Joffe, 2009). The United States has led the way in some areas of sexuality rights, but in other areas, such as reproductive and transgender rights, it has fallen behind.

Globally, human rights policies increasingly include sexual health and well-being among their stated goals. Countries as diverse as Australia, Brazil, Costa Rica, India, the Netherlands, and Sweden consider sexual well-being to be critical to their public health policies. Not only have some nations passed laws to support these rights, but they have also aligned themselves through international organizations and treaties, especially the United Nations, to advance sexual well-being (Correa et al., 2008).

Although sexuality as a human right is laden with the politics and controversies of individual countries, research surrounding these rights is more generally helping to reveal the extent of the most vulnerable sexual populations globally. This research helps to create more humane discussions about how rights interact with such factors as poverty in challenging sexual health and well-being (Coleman, 2010; Correa et al., 2008; Merry, 2006; Petchesky, 2003). In the country of South Africa, for example, by understanding these dynamics, researchers were able to improve the sexual health of poor young women and their families.

Over the past 30 years many organizations have used research to link sexual health and reproductive, sexual, and gender orientation rights. The World Health Organization (WHO) has played the most critical role in championing this new era of rights. In 1975, WHO released a history-making document titled "Education and Treatment in Human Sexuality: The Training of Health Professionals." It called on all societies to create sexuality education, counseling, and therapy to promote "[s]exual health [as] the integration of the somatic, emotional, intellectual, and social aspects of sexual being, in ways that are positively enriching and that enhance personality, communication, and love" (WHO, 1975, p. 6). The document also made it clear that the right to sexual information is linked to the right of sexual pleasure. It has taken decades, but many nations are coming to accept this view (Petchesky, Correa, & Parker, 2010).

Sexuality rights have been added to the human rights that were already recognized (Aggleton & Parker, 2010; Correa et al., 2008; Miller, 2000). Notably, these rights include:

- The right to equality and nondiscrimination
- The right to teach and learn about sex
- The right to respect people's bodies
- The right to be sexually active or not
- The right to choose when and how to have children or not
- The right to pursue sexual pleasure in a safe and satisfying way

As you will learn throughout this book, a variety of rights support sexual well-being, including reproductive rights, gender identity (the sense of being a man or woman), and sexual rights related to the expression of desires, feelings, needs, and intimate relationships. Helping to protect people against all kinds of challenges to their sexual well-being, including gender and sexual violence, is one of the great outcomes of the sexual literacy approach. By understanding more about how rights are connected to cultures and provide a space for critical thinking and change when it comes to holistic sexuality, you move so much closer not only to advancing your own sexual well-being, but to helping society improve as well.

Chapter Review Summary

Sexual Literacy

- Sexual literacy is defined as the knowledge, skills, and action or empowerment needed to achieve and protect sexual well-being. Sexual literacy involves the sexual self, sexual negotiation, and sexual empowerment.
- Sexual well-being is the condition of experiencing good health, pleasure, and satisfaction in intimate relationships, and is part of the purpose in life.
- Emotional literacy can help people achieve better sexual health by knowing what to say, how to name body parts, and how to protect themselves.
- When people are informed about sexual well-being, they tend to be more tolerant and respectful of the sexuality of other individuals and cultures.

Sexual Science—A Historical Perspective

- Sexual science is the study of sexual behavior.
- Sexology originated in medical clinics in the 19th century and was dominated by physicians, who promoted a medical model of sexuality.
- Early sexual scientists in the late 19th and early 20th centuries tended to equate being different with being abnormal in terms of sexual development and expression.
- Research by Freud, Kinsey, Masters and Johnson, and others advanced the scientific study of sexuality as a normal part of life.
- Sexual science has gradually changed from studying negative outcomes to researching more positive human behaviors, such as well-being.
- Science and society are disconnected when it comes to sexuality policy because politics sometimes interferes with rational research and planning.

Methodology in the Study of Sexuality

- The interdisciplinary perspective is the holistic integration of different sciences in describing and explaining human sexuality.
- Many protections are in place to help sex research participants understand what the research is about and how it may affect them.
- There are two general categories of research design: quantitative and qualitative research methods.
- The types of research designs used in the study of sexuality include case studies, surveys and interviews, direct observation, experiments, field studies, and participatory action research.
- Intersectional research methodology provides a new critical lens on how inequality undermines sexuality and social justice in society.
- Being a critical consumer of sex research means having the skills to evaluate research and apply the findings to improve life.

Human Sexual Rights

- Human rights emerged as a social issue after World War II and in recognition of the need to support diversity and self-expression of all people.
- The AIDS epidemic raised awareness of sexuality as a human right.
- Sexual and gender identity rights are only now becoming part of the recognized global order by the United Nations, other agencies, and individual countries.

What's Your Position?

1. **What do the terms *sexual literacy* and *sexual well-being* mean to you?**
   - How would you define sexual literacy and its desired outcome, sexual well-being?
   - What does sexual negotiation mean to you?
   - What emotions would you like to articulate when it comes to your sexual experiences and expression?
   - How do you feel about participating in sexual research? Is this part of being sexually literate?
   - How do you understand diversity when it comes to sexual well-being?
   - How would you define healthy sexuality in your own life? Does it involve sexual negotiation and sexual empowerment for you?

2. **How has sexuality changed from a negative to a more positive science?**
   - Can you explain why researchers viewed sex as a disease or symptom, rather than a positive function of human life?
   - Can you identify changes in the behaviors and beliefs that people expressed about sexuality as society became more tolerant?
   - How do you see sex research in relation to societal policies today?

3. **What does sexuality as a human right mean to you?**
   - How did our society change historically when it comes to sexual rights?
   - How might big societal forces, such as poverty, affect sexuality as a human right?
   - How would you relate sexual literacy to human sexual rights?

Design elements: Controversies in Sexuality: HBRH/Shutterstock; Research and Sexual Well Being: verity jane smith/Getty Images; Healthy Sexuality: Sergey Furtaev/Shutterstock; Communication Matters: PeopleImages/Getty Images; Know Yourself: Plush Studios/Blend Images LLC; What's Your Position: Luis Molinero/Shutterstock; Healthy Sexuality: A. Minde/PhotoAlto; Did You Know icon: McGraw-Hill Education; Page corner icon: McGraw-Hill Education.

Contexts of Sexuality: Culture, History, and Religion

2

Richard Baker/In Pictures/Getty Images

Human Sexual Nature in Context
- Describe the sexual triangle model of human sexuality.
- Relate the sexual behavior of the bonobo chimps to human sexual behavior.
- Identify unique traits of human sexuality and how culture influences them.

Sex Since the Beginning of Time
- Explain how sex, history, and religion are intertwined.
- Outline the changes in human sexuality over the past century, including the concept of sexual identity.

Sexual Cultures and Norms
- Explain what sexual culture means and how it organizes sexual behavior.
- Recognize how sexual norms influence group acceptance of individuals.
- Compare and contrast cultural relativism, cultural chauvinism, and sexual chauvinism.
- Describe the continuum of approving and disapproving cultures around the world.
- Define sexual unlearning.

Sexuality and the Great World Religions
- Define religious identity in relation to sexual behavior.
- Compare and contrast how the great world religions view sexuality.

Spirituality and Sexual Behavior in the United States
- Explain how different religions shape sexual attitudes in the United States through symbolic boundaries.

The Pursuit of Sexual Well-Being in Communities of Faith
- Explain how spirituality and sexual individuality can be compatible.

- **Learning**
- **Objectives**

Developing Your Position

1. How do you define your own human sexual nature?
2. What has your culture taught you about sex?
3. How have your religious beliefs influenced your sexual well-being?

Self, Culture, and History: Understanding Influences on Human Sexual Nature

The Sambia people of Papua New Guinea have a radically different culture than we do in the United States. When I (Gil) first arrived to do fieldwork in 1974, they had a male secret society and their lives revolved around hunting, gardening, and defending themselves against attack from their neighbors who lived on the other side of the ridge. Their traditional rituals were a powerful support for their gender and sexual beliefs and practices. They believed that masculinity had to be produced by rituals to grow boys into strong warriors. They believed that semen was the key life force. What's more, they thought that semen did not naturally occur in the boys and had to be introduced from an external source. Their secret male rituals, which you will read about in the chapter, involved same-sex practices between older and younger boys and a form of domination over girls and women. They truly believed that their bodily fluids, their social lives, and their spiritual development were deeply integrated as a vital part of nature and culture. By the early 1990s, evangelical Christianity had completely overwhelmed their traditional culture, and the secret society and rituals were gone.

I took many field trips before I understood all the Sambia sexual meanings and practices surrounding families, puberty, and the development of sexuality. Looking back, I realize that I had never really understood how my own culture influences sexuality until I went to Papua New Guinea, where I discovered both how we differ from them and how our common human nature links us together.

In this chapter, we discuss the contexts of holistic sexuality through history, culture, and religion to understand how such forces have shaped human sexuality over eons. People all over the world experience religion as a vital force, even when they may not worship daily or attend church, or even believe in God. Nevertheless religion has the power to influence society and human sexuality mightily, as we will see in this chapter. We explore the continuing influence of the great world religions on people's beliefs and behaviors surrounding sexuality across cultures. For some people who are deeply religious, their beliefs are actually more important to them than their culture's general attitudes regarding sexuality, as we will see. And so we will consider questions such as: How am I like all other human beings? How am I different from others in the world? How is my sexuality shaped by my culture? How do my religious beliefs influence my sexuality?

HUMAN SEXUAL NATURE IN CONTEXT

Why do humans enjoy sex so much and why does it occupy such a large place in our lives? Anthropologists and human paleontologists think that part of the answer lies in our incredible genetic history and DNA, as we learn below. Historians and sociologists and scholars of comparative religion also stress the vital roles played by history and religion in shaping our sexuality. Indeed, great thinkers throughout history, from the time of the ancient Greek philosophers Socrates and Plato to Freud and right up to the present-day evolutionary psychologists and feminists, have theorized about the role of sexuality in human existence. In this section we look at sex in the context of human evolution and culture to understand the part individuals play in this pageant of events and to see why sex is such a vital part of understanding so many areas of human experience.

The Sexual Triangle: Species, Culture, and Individual

There is general agreement that sexuality is a common denominator among all humans and that the human sexual experience has unique aspects (Symonds, 1987). First, our species *Homo sapiens* is distinguished in its intellectual abilities from all other animals (Sherwood, Subiaul, & Zawidzki, 2008). For example, only humans developed rules and beliefs around sex that have become the foundation of culture, individuality, and religion (Diamond, 1997; Herdt, 1997a; Thornhill & Gangestad, 2008). Secondly, emotional bonding, which may occur when people look into each other's faces during sexual intercourse, leading to lifelong adult relationships, is yet another distinctive aspect of human sexuality (Diamond, 1997). These unique traits come from the combination of three elements: our species, culture, and individuality, as represented in Figure 2.1.

How did we get to be human? A growing consensus of scientists working with human evolution theorize that across millions of years our species refined and adapted right up to 40,000 years ago when *Homo sapiens* outcompeted other species, such as Neanderthals. The essence of our species is in the genes, hormones, brains, and culture of every individual and can be passed on through evolution and procreation (Buss, 1994, 2008; Coolidge & Wynn, 2009; Geertz, 1973). These factors influence every human being's growth and development. Additionally, our culture specifically defines the context of our behavior, including sexual behavior; culture influences what we learn and how we create sexual relationships. But each of us is a one in a billion combination of these traits, which shape our sexual well-being.

Humans are one of two species believed to pursue sex for fun and pleasure, as well as for **procreation,** the conception of offspring. Indeed, it is estimated that 95% of all human sex is for recreation, not procreation (Efstathiou, 2006). The other species that seems to enjoy sex almost as much as humans do is our close relative, the bonobo chimpanzee.

procreation
Conception of offspring.

Figure 2.1

Each element of the sexual triangle contributes to human sexuality. The three elements intersect with each other as a result of millions of years of evolution of our species, hundreds of generations of the development of culture, and the uniqueness of each individual.

Species
You are like all others of your species.

Sexuality

Culture/Religion
You share similar things with some others.

Individuality
You are like no others.

Sexuality Among the Bonobo

As a way to better understand how human sexuality evolved, and the nature of early human sexuality, let's briefly consider sexual expression in the bonobo chimpanzee. Chimpanzees are the species most like humans, sharing more than 98% of our genes, and scientists believe that the sexual behavior of the bonobo chimps is most like human sexual behavior (de Waal, 1995; Dixon, 2015; Wallen & Parsons, 1997). Bonobo are peaceable and they are **matriarchal,** meaning that females dominate and organize the group, controlling males to share food resources and cooperating to protect the group, one of the many traits of the bonobo that make them unusual. Remarkably, adolescent female bonobo leave the group to find mates and to create new matriarchal groups (unlike most other primate groups), a sign of high female social status. This is almost unheard of in nature, because usually the males leave to form new groups.

Unlike other lower primate species as well, the female bonobo is sexually active and attractive to mates *year round,* but she conceives and bears only one offspring every 5 or 6 years. Research reveals then, that sexual pleasure is a larger motivator for sex among the bonobo than is procreation. In fact, 75% of all bonobo sexual behavior is nonreproductive (de Waal & Landing, 1998).

Sexuality among the bonobo creates intense social bonding and greater diversity of sexual behaviors compared to other species (de Waal, 1987). These chimps appear to have a lot of sex and a lot of different kinds of sex, and they seem to enjoy it more (Dixon, 2015; Wallen, 1995). Their species' emphasis upon pleasure and bonding, how they form social groups, and the ways in which individual bonobo differ from one another and assert their individuality are highly suggestive of human sexuality.

Some bonobo sexual behaviors strongly resemble those of humans more than other primate species. For example, bonobo females appear to have emotional and physiological responses that closely resemble human orgasm. The peak of sexual desire in females and males does not differ so much as how consistently and frequently males and females experience intense sexual desire (Wallen, 1995). Bonobo sexual behaviors include the only nonhuman examples of face-to-face genital sex, tongue kissing, and oral sex known in the wild. They also engage in manual sex, rubbing genitals, grinning and squealing as if in delight; and sexual behavior between individuals of the same sex is common. However, the average bonobo sexual episode lasts only 13 seconds!

For the bonobo, the nature of their species, the social context, and the unique characteristics of the individual all shape their sexual expression in ways that parallel important aspects of human sexuality (Hess, 2008). But there are critical differences, too, and these make human sexuality distinct (Darwin, 1879). For example, humans differ from the bonobo in the absence of an estrus period among females, commonly known as "being in heat." **Estrus** is the recurring time when a female ovulates and is most receptive to becoming pregnant. In the bonobo, more sex occurs when a female is in estrus, which is physically obvious because of red genital swelling. In humans, estrus is concealed, and so it is both possible and necessary for humans to have sex frequently to ensure reproduction (Meston & Buss, 2009).

Human Sexual Nature as Expressed Through Culture

As we saw in Chapter 1, culture is such a distinctly human creation that it gives people a sense of group cohesion, shared meaning and identity, and also establishes standards for acceptable behavior, called **norms.** Sex is an integral part of culture because it, too, connects people—to their bodies, to institutions such as the family, to nature, and to the past. Human nature for our species is at least 200,000 years old and is a living legacy, including our procreation and parenting as expressed through culture (Hydy, 2009). Culture accounts for much of the adaptive success of human groups as expressed through the traits that

---

matriarchal
Type of social system in which females are dominant.

estrus
The recurring time when a female ovulates and is most receptive to becoming pregnant.

norms
Cultural rules about acceptable behavior.

humans have developed over 6 million years, including language and culture (Coolidge & Wynn, 2009). Among the characteristics that make us uniquely human, all of the following are especially important for a discussion of sexuality:

- At birth, our brains are not fully developed; they develop quickly in the first 3 years of life, as our local culture shapes us.
- We have larger brains in terms of body weight than other species at maturity.
- We learn verbal language and symbols in context to represent the language of our group.
- Through language we culture.
- We create and use tools that allow human groups to adapt to diverse environments.
- We each have a unique sense of self within the context of our culture.
- We have a sense of finite time and thus have knowledge of our own mortality.
- We have deeply held beliefs about ultimate concerns, especially the meaning of life, death, and immortality, which are the basis of culture, history, and religion.

What makes this list of traits so powerful when it comes to human sexual expression is what we might call the distinct *human package for evolution:* the human brain, language, and culture. This evolutionary package made possible human sexual expression and reproduction and adaption to all environments (Paabo, 2014), an important facet for the survival of any species. In terms of sexuality, these unique traits also allowed for the development of new centers of sexual pleasure in the brain, and for the communication of this pleasure linguistically and emotionally to sexual partners. Human sexuality is unique in such ways, because it is a combination of what is biological and what is learned. This blend of biology (nature) and culture (nurture) working together to produce sexual behavior is **human sexual nature.**

As our brains evolved to enable us to connect emotionally with other humans, especially lovers, human sexuality enhanced **pair bonding,** the sexual and romantic association between two people (Birkhead, 2000; Fisher, 2004; Meston & Buss, 2009). Pair bonding provided great adaptive advantages to individuals and groups who would band together and cooperate, especially for reproduction, and also for protection, sharing food and water resources, and for the location of mates. Language and culture also increased our thinking and reasoning abilities and allowed us to pass on the shared meanings and knowledge to the next generation, making human adaptation more successful and efficient. Sometimes that knowledge made the difference between life and death in different surroundings as, for example, when the group learned where to find water in the desert (Shostak, 1980). Culture made it possible for early human groups to avoid some aspects of sexual competition that other species experience. For example, having norms regarding sex and marriage prevented fighting among males inside the group and competition over females (Meston & Buss, 2009), and thus enabled people to live in stable groups over generations.

To test your emerging knowledge of human sexuality and adaptation, consider the questions in "Know Yourself: Where Do You Need Sexual Knowledge, Skills and/or Practice?"

Emotional bonding, pleasure, and communication, along with reproduction and power, are all attributes of human sexual nature and, as such, are regulated to some extent by the group (Herdt, 2009b; Lyons & Lyons, 2011; Mead, 1961). Consider how the following characteristics have evolved out of culture to uniquely express our human sexual nature:

- We engage in sex not only for reproduction, but also for pair bonding and pleasure.
- We reach puberty and develop sexual maturity very slowly, in the context of cultures.
- We form *nuclear families,* composed of parents and offspring, and multigenerational *extended families,* including grandparents, aunts, uncles, and cousins.

human sexual nature
The combination of human culture and human nature working together to produce sexual behavior.

pair bonding
The sexual and romantic association between two individuals.

Know Yourself

Where Do You Need Sexual Knowledge, Skills and/or Practice?

Think about human sexuality as described within the sexual triangle described in Figure 2.1: species, culture, and individuality and in the discussion in chapter 1 on the development of sexual literacy: knowledge + skills → practice (p. X).

For each of the following statements below, decide if you feel you have acquired the knowledge, and/or skills, and/or ability to practice each. Then, utilize this as a road map to personalize your own goals for sexual learning and the furthering of your sexual literacy.

	KNOWLEDGE	SKILLS	PRACTICE
Species			
I recognize that sexual pleasure is a part of the Great Apes and Hominids.			
I understand that sexual intercourse is the basic foundation for reproduction for all animal life.			
I recognize that biological sex is different than gender identity in humans.			
I realize that although sexual cultures differ, humans as a species share many sexual traits in common.			
I understand that mating for humans is more than just sex but may include elements such as love, commitment, family formation and community norms.			
I realize masturbation is condemned by some faiths but is probably universal in the human species			
Culture			
I realize that non-monogamy is common in many areas of the world			
I recognize that for some people sex is deeply part of their faith and I accept that			
I realize that for some people, casual sex is enjoyable and fulfilling			
I recognize that the family unit varies across cultures and history.			
Sexual and gender prejudice are part of some cultures, but these attitudes may also cause trauma and harm people			
LGBTQ+ people may not behave according to the standards of my faith or community, but they are individuals who deserve human rights and dignity			
Sexual aggression and violence may be widespread but that does not make it right or acceptable behavior			
I understand that social structures exist which create imbalances of interpersonal power and that they can be harmful and oppressive in sexual relationships			
Individual			
I understand that effective contraception is part of responsible sexuality			
I understand that being able to communicate about sexuality is a critical skill needed for sexual literacy			
I understand sex is most enjoyable when individuals feel safe and secure			
I understand that some individuals do not desire sexual relationships and that choice should be respected			
I realize sex is more equal when individuals are able to openly communicate desires and needs			
I understand that the spectrum of normative and acceptable sexual behaviors is wide and includes behaviors I am unfamiliar or not comfortable with			
I realize that sexual pleasure can be experienced by all people regardless of physical ability			

- We forbid sex within family units, through the **incest taboo,** a cultural and/or social prohibition against sexual relations between relatives.

- We form social institutions, including government, family, and religion, to affirm our sense of group norms, membership, and sexual regulation (Armstrong, 1999).

incest taboo

Social or cultural prohibition against sex between close family members.

These traits expressed through culture are critical to human survival because of how frail and helpless infants are at birth compared to other species, and how much brain development and learning occurs after birth. Family members exercise so many years of influence over child and adolescent development compared to other species through emotional bonding, taboos, and how late and prolonged puberty is in human nature. And so children have time to develop their thinking and communication skills, and to learn their culture's sexual rules and roles before they reach sexual maturity (Herdt, 2009a; Mead, 1961, Waal; 2018). By the time individuals reach reproduction and pair bonding, they have adapted to their cultures and learned who are regarded as the best potential mates, and whether they will make good providers and parents (Fisher, 2004; Mead, 1961).

It is so uniquely human for two people to express mutual sexual pleasure and love by communicating *emotional satisfaction* with their intimate partners. Some researchers believe that emotional satisfaction may allow for the creation of lifelong bonds through attraction, as well as nesting (Buss, 1994; Meston & Buss, 2009). *Nesting* here means that females do not just want to procreate; they want to mate with the person who will provide strong genes for their offspring (Thornhill & Gangestad, 2008). Human nesting thus allows people to also fall in love, create pleasure and mate, and choose to live together or marry, and possibly stay together for life.

SEX SINCE THE BEGINNING OF TIME

There is mounting evidence that human nature evolved historically and biologically to integrate culture and religion into our sexual well-being; discoveries have helped us understand how prehistoric humans may have experienced culture and sex together in ways that led to our present-day existence (Coolidge & Wynn, 2009). Archaeologists in Europe have found evidence that humans began to communicate through art, ritual, music, and perhaps dance and religious ceremonies between 30,000 and 40,000 years ago (Bahn, 1998; Sosis & Alcorta, 2003). They made sex a part of these cultural experiences. Cave paintings, carvings, statues, and tools from this period give us a glimpse into just how long sexual pleasure has been part of human sexual nature.

WHAT'S ON YOUR MIND?

Q: The other night, I was talking with my three roommates about sex and it seems that my sex drive is much higher than theirs. Am I normal, and what causes someone to have more of a desire for sex than someone else?

ANSWER: Isn't it interesting we are all so different? Even in the realm of sexual drive and desire, each person is distinct and unique. To answer your first question, yes, you are normal. There are countless reasons why each of us has a different level of desire for sex. Physical contributors such as hormones play a role in our individual differences but it is also important to look at environmental contributions. Have you been raised in a sexually positive environment that teaches what a wonderful thing your sexuality is? People who have been brought up in cultures or families that have a negative view of sex often feel like they have to stifle their desire. Consider your own environment and think about what may contribute to your desire for sex.

History of Sexuality

35,000 BCE
First cave paintings and statues representing human sexuality/ritual/human individuality

3150 BCE
Ancient Egyptian civilization and divine kingship/incest marriage

500 BCE
Rise of Buddhism and new ideas about sexual being

500–1500
Rise of Roman Catholic Church

1200–1834
Holy Inquisition trials for witchcraft, sodomy, and adultery

1600
Age of Enlightenment, science opens way for new medical ideas about sex

5000 BCE   1000 BCE   500 CE   1200   1500   1600

5000 BCE
Rise of Hinduism and positive approach to sexuality

3000 BCE
Rise of Judaism, monotheism, and sexual culture attitudes

800 BCE
Ancient Greek sexuality and religion depicting same-sex relationships and sexual anatomy

5BC–30CE
Life of Christ, rise of Christianity, and new sexual code

574–632
Life of Muhammad and rise of Islam, new sexual code embraces sexual pleasure between husband and wife

1500s
Protestant Reformation divides Roman Catholic Church

---

spirituality
An individual's inner sense of having deep values, a spiritual path, or belief in an ultimate reality.

Prehistoric Sex and Communication

A spectacular example of prehistoric cave art was discovered inside Chauvet-Pont-d'Arc Cave in France in 1994. The remarkable paintings, many of them at least 32,000 years old, appear to be the efforts of prehistoric humans to capture on the cave walls the essence and movement of animals such as bears, horses, and rhinos, as well as human sexuality. Recent carbon dating in 2016 established that the paintings may date back as far as 37,000 years ago and are characteristic of early humans living in that area of France. A painting of human female genitals found in the cave is probably the earliest known representation of female sexual fertility.

Cave paintings in other parts of the world also depict prehistoric humans' keen interest in sex and hunting, ritual, and animal behaviors, including mating (Coolidge & Wynn, 2009). Some paintings depict reproduction and population expansion linked to early contraception. Sexual variations are also represented in how the prehistoric cave paintings depict human same-sex activities, sexual interactions with animals, payment for sex, and the combination of pain and pleasure in diverse human sexual interactions.

Scientists believe that these same prehistoric people drew on their experiences to communicate with each other in ritual and to connect with the realm of spirits (Bahn, 1998; Sosis & Alcorta, 2003). Their art directly connects sex with **spirituality,** a person's

These animals were painted on the walls of Chauvet-Pont-d'Arc Cave thousands of years ago. The artists also left representations of human fertility along with many other images of animals in the cave.
Hemis/Superstock

38

1800s
Rise of public health system and sexology in Europe and United States

1837–1901
Victorian era and invention of modern sexuality

1873
U.S. Congress passes Comstock Act making contraceptives illegal

1890s–1920s
Free love movement

1920s
First wave of feminism in the United States

1800 — 1890 — 1920

1650
Tokugawa Japan era brings sex into new qualities of objects and actions

1811
Europe bans execution of homosexuals

1869
Kertbeny coins the term *homosexuality*

1889
Krafft-Ebing coins term *heterosexuality*

1905
Sigmund Freud introduces notion of childhood sexuality in *Three Essays on the Theory of Sexuality*

1916
Margaret Sanger fights Comstock Law and coins term *birth control*

---

inner sense of deep belief in an ultimate reality (Sheldrake, 2007). Their paintings portray rituals and religious practices that may have celebrated hunting, connection to the earth and animals, procreation, and death (Taylor, 1997). Prehistoric paintings also suggest that ancient people thus had a notion of mortality and a spirit world, concepts that separate humans from all other species and are reflected in our diverse religions. In this ancient art researchers see the religious motivation that connects culture, spirituality, sex, and human awareness, the contexts that support the survival of a group's offspring (Armstrong, 1999; Becker, 1973; deVries, 1967; Rossano, 2010).

Some prehistoric images also seem to suggest a burning desire to capture the power or miracle of sex, including the power to procreate, as seen in the painting of female genitals in Chauvet Cave. Additionally, numerous prehistoric Venus-type statues have been found in Europe that seem to inspire and capture the power of female fertility.

The *Venus of Willendorf* is one of a number of prehistoric so-called Venus statuettes symbolizing female fertility.
Iberfoto/SuperStock

A Brief History of Sex and Civilization

Since ancient times, as we have just seen, human sexual nature has been expressed in diverse ways. In fact, civilization itself has been shaped by **sexual culture,** which encompasses the distinct shared sexual meanings and practices of a group (Herdt, 1999a, 2006; Hirsch et al., 2009). Through the ages, each human group developed its own sexual culture to regulate morality and sex, passion, including sexual jealousy and rape, love, family, and procreation. The expressions of these meanings and practices are contained in social institutions,

sexual culture
Distinct shared sexual meanings and sexual practices of a group.

39

History of Sexuality (continued)

1942 Planned Parenthood Federation of America founded

1948 Alfred Kinsey publishes *Sexual Behavior and the Human Male*

1948 United Nations Charter on Human Rights invokes new era of sexual and gender global rights

1953 First issue of *Playboy* published

1960 Second wave of feminism movement

1962 First birth control pill

1965 Supreme Court strikes down Comstock Act, making contraceptive information legal in the United States

1969 Stonewall riots (New York) and LGBT movement founded

1973 American Psychiatric Association declares homosexuality normal

1973 *Roe v. Wade* legalizes abortion in the United States

---

including the family, morals, religion, education, government, law, and later the media, all of which have shaped sexual expression.

Organized religion, in particular, has helped to create and reinforce the reality of human spirituality and the sense of existence and meaning, including transcendeance and immortality (Armstrong, 1999; Geertz, 1966; Machacek & Wilcox, 2003; Mead, 1961; Weber, 2002). The rise of civilization and diverse forms of sexuality are thus linked to the **great world religions** of Hinduism, Judaism, Buddhism, Christianity, and Islam, among others, all of which have many followers, are global, have roots in traditional holy texts, and in the eyes of experts such as Stephen Prothero (2010) also "run the world" (Armstrong, 1999; Smith, 1991). Each of these ancient traditions of faith provides a deep identity with specific sexual customs and attitudes, as we will examine in this section.

great world religions Religions that have huge followings around the world, have roots in traditional holy texts and moral principles, and have changed the course of history.

Asian Civilization Beginning several thousand years ago, Asian civilizations evolved complex sexual cultures that celebrated fertility and pleasure, as well as procreation through marriage. Ancient myths, ritual, and social hierarchy were part of these sexual patterns (Basham, 1999; Fuller, 2004). Hinduism, the religion on which much of Asian civilization is based, spread from India and South Asia between 3,000 and 5,000 years ago (Armstrong, 1999). In India especially, female fertility and mutual sexual satisfaction for both men and women took on greater meaning than elsewhere in Asia where Hinduism took hold.

The tradition of Buddhism also originated in India and South Asia thousands of years ago. It began with Gautama Buddha, an Indian prince who was born about 563 BCE in Nepal on the Indian border (Armstrong, 2001a). As an adult, Buddha, which means "enlightened one," renounced his position and title, wealth, and family and traveled all over India, founding an order

1990
Transgender concept goes viral

1998
Viagra approved for male erectile dysfunction

2003
U.S. Supreme Court strikes down sodomy laws *(Lawrence v. Texas)*

2004
President George W. Bush calls for constitutional ban on gay marriage

2011
Secretary of State Hillary Clinton declares "gay rights are human rights" at UN

1980　　1990　　　　　2000　　　　　　　　2010

1981
Worldwide AIDS epidemic

1998
White House sex scandal and impeachment trial of President Clinton

2001
The Netherlands becomes first country to make gay marriage legal

2004
Same-sex marriage legalized in Massachusetts

2007
Research reveals failure of "abstinence only" sex education

---

of monks and nuns, challenging the caste system that divided Indian society into rigid social classes, and exhorting his followers to help the sick and poor (Smith, 1991). Known for his cool mind and warm heart, Buddha recognized diverse spiritual beliefs, different forms of worship,

Erotic Art from Ancient Japan—love and lust in the premodern period.
Historical Views/age fotostock/ Alamy Stock Photo

History of Sexuality (continued)

2016
#Me-Too Movement begins from exposure of extensive sexual abuse cases in Hollywood.

2018
President Trump reverses policy regarding transgender persons serving openly in military.

2015
Obergefell v. Hodges, Supreme Court rules in favor of LGBTQ right to marry.

2019
Rowe v. Wade protections jeopardized.

2020

2017
Late-term abortion challenged.

2018
Supreme Court Justice Brett Kavanaugh challenged during confirmation proceedings regarding his sexual behavior as a young college student.

(*Left to right*) Iberfoto/SuperStock; blickwinkel/Alamy Stock Photo; Photodisc/Getty Images; Bilderbuch/Design Pics; Pixtal/age fotostock; Historical Views/age fotostock/Alamy Stock Photo; Visual Language Illustration/Veer; Ingram Publishing; Ingram Publishing/Alamy Stock Photo; Library of Congress, Prints and Photographs Division [LC-USZ62-29808]; Keystone Features/Hulton Archive/Getty Images; Ken Cavanagh/McGraw-Hill Education; Stockbyte/Punchstock/Getty Images; Stockbyte/Punchstock/Getty Images; Comstock Images/Getty Images; Eric Draper, photographer, courtesy of the George Bush Presidential Library; Anton Havelaar/Alamy Stock Photo; Evan Agostini/Getty Images; Noam Galai/WireImage/Getty Images

---

and many deities. Buddhism came to be identified ideally with abstinence among its priests and nuns, but tolerance for a broad spectrum of sexual expression, so long as it was not excessive.

After the 5th century BCE, the spread of Hinduism and Buddhism to China, Korea, and Japan led to even more diverse belief systems, including varied notions of sex and love, among the cultures that blossomed there. In later centuries, same-sex relationships became common among noble Japanese warlords and in some Buddhist monasteries up to the 19th century.

China's traditional culture, Taoist philosophy, ritual practice, and ancestral worship, attributed to Lao Tzu (500 BCE), included Tao sexual practices designed to heal the body and infuse energy and strength into the organs. This complements the dualistic *yin-yang* powers of men and women. Japanese beliefs included elaborate traditions centering on a male warrior class and masculine warfare, discipline, and male and female beauty. The Japanese practiced gender segregation with separate living, eating, and sleeping spaces for men and women. They also cultivated the *geisha,* beautiful female companions for men.

Ancient Greece, Rome, and Christianity Ancient Greek civilization dates from 800 BCE until 197 CE when it was incorporated into the Roman Empire. The Greeks practiced a complex form of sexuality and love that included sexual pleasure but tempered it with restraint. Their sexual culture was ideally democratic, but male power was a significant element of their tradition, and the role of women in public life was often limited. Too much sex was considered bad for health, but in general, sex was a natural, positive function of human life in ancient Greece.

The Greeks believed in many gods, a concept they borrowed from ancient Egypt, a civilization dating back to about 3100 BCE. Greek religion included the important idea that the gods, including their ruler Zeus, were believed to be highly sexual and engaged in all kinds of sexual exploits. Zeus could take human or animal form, he engaged in sexual interactions with women and boys, and he produced human offspring.

Not surprisingly, then, the Greeks accepted same-sex relations, but because all Greeks had to marry, homosexuality was not an exclusive sexual practice for them. Young men in their late teens had sexual relations with older males to achieve social status, masculinity, and honor as well as to cultivate self-discipline and citizenship as free men. Married men could have extramarital relationships with younger males who were in their late teens. Typically, these relationships involved sex, love, and mentoring to make the youths into proud free citizens (O'Donnell, 2015).

The Roman Empire kept many of the Greek traditions, including its gods and religious beliefs and sexual practices, at least at first. As the power of Rome declined, however, same-sex relationships eventually were discouraged. At the time of Emperor Augustus (63 BCE to 14 CE), all sex with slaves and prostitutes, especially same-sex relationships, were outlawed to ensure that Rome's powerful families did not become "weakened" by disputes over property from offspring of "inferiors." The emergence of Christianity further eroded freedom of sexual expression in the Roman Empire.

Ancient Greek mythology is full of supermen such as Achilles, hero of the Trojan War, who was the offspring of a goddess and a human king.
Fine Art Images/Heritage Image Partnership Ltd/Alamy Stock Photo

Christianity dates from the 1st century after the birth of Jesus Christ, who was a Jew by birth and who is believed to have lived from about 5 BCE to 30 CE (Ehrman, 2008, p. 57). Jesus was born in the reign of the Roman Emperor Augustus, and we learn from the study of his disciples such as St. Paul that the early Christians were "beaten down" and hungry and sick of hard labor under the imperial Roman predation (Armstrong, 2015, p. 5). In the Christian tradition, Christ is the Messiah, whose coming was foretold in the Old Testament. In contrast to the Romans, Christians believed in one God (Armstrong, 1999). They also considered Christ to be the Son of God, whose birth and death created the possibility of salvation and reconciliation with God. And, as we will see later, Christians had definite ideas about sexual relations and marriage that conflicted with Roman views. Despite attempts by the Romans to stamp it out, Christianity flourished and eventually extended westward into Europe, carrying its sexual beliefs along with it.

From 500 to 1500 CE, early Christianity strongly shaped Western civilization and marital and sexual practice. During this period, the Roman Empire slowly disintegrated, and the Roman Catholic Church rose to become powerful, implementing laws and sexual beliefs that were previously unknown or not emphasized. For example, certain sex-negative ideas were introduced during this time, such as views about sin and the dangers of the female body, including female pollution. During this time women were thus excluded from Church leadership. Also, some sexual behaviors were regarded as sinful and worthy of severe punishment. Oral and anal sex, sex with animals, and sex between people of different cultures were all labeled as *sodomy,* meaning "unnatural sex," but in actuality the label was applied to any sexual act that went against the norm (Hull, 1997). Homosexuality came to be regarded as unnatural, even though it was tolerated in some communities and was a part of the experience of some monks and church leaders into the modern period.

Islamic Civilization Islam, Judaism, and Christianity are referred to as the "Abrahamic" religions, because they share a common geography and history (Armstrong, 1999, 2001b;

Smith, 1991). Muhammad, the founding prophet of Islam, was born about 570 CE in Mecca, in what is now Saudi Arabia. As an adult, Muhammad had a spiritual revelation that convinced him that the one god is Allah. He began sharing his beliefs and acquired many followers in Mecca and far beyond during his lifetime. His revelations are recorded in the Quran, the holy book of Islam. By the time of his death in 632 CE, when "he died in the arms of his beloved wife Aisha," virtually all of the Arabian tribes had joined in what would become Islamic Civilization (Armstrong, 2001b, p. 20). Islam spread throughout the Middle East and into Africa and Spain during the 7th and 8th centuries, and into Asia and as far east as Indonesia in the 12th century, as armies of believers sought to spread their faith and extend Islamic civilization.

The ultimate values of early Islamic civilization were marriage and family and gaining entrance to Heaven, but followers of Islam, called Muslims, also had ideals of sexual virtue. Muslims professed values of male sexual honor, female virginity before marriage, gender segregation, and the sexual purity of children. In some early Islamic groups, such as the famous Sufi dancers, there was also a sexual practice not unlike the ancient Greeks of older males having relationships with younger males to inspire masculinity and honor. The famous Sufi poet Rumi was led to write poems and idealize his love for a man in the 13th century.

One area where the Muslim East diverged from the religion of the Christian West was in beliefs about sexual pleasure. Muslims believed that it was a husband's duty to pleasure his wife sexually, but in European sexual relationships, sexual pleasure centered on the man. Today, however, it is hard to generalize. For example, Turkey, Indonesia, and Iran are all Islamic countries, but they have greatly different beliefs about sex and gender. Turkey allows divorce and does not require women to wear the veil, which is related to the sexual parts of women that need to be covered. In Iran, however, divorce is difficult for women, and the veil is worn universally.

Western Europe from the Crusades to the 19th Century In the 12th century CE, Christians from western Europe fought a number of crusades with Muslims in the Middle East, in an effort to recapture Jerusalem and Palestine, where Christianity began, and to extend Western civilization. Muslims believed that they had a mandate from Allah to protect the Holy Land, where their religion and society were also born, and in the end managed to repel the crusaders. As this history suggests, both Christianity and Islam had become major influences in Europe and the Middle East. In Europe, Christianity was powerful enough to organize a fighting force for centuries of religious crusades.

The Christian knights associated with the Crusades evolved a new sexual and romantic code called **chivalry,** which focused on purity of heart and body, chastity for females, and honor in war. Sexual virtue was of supreme importance during the Middle Ages. Men had valor, which was the male form of sexual virtue, and women were virgins before marriage, which was the female form of virtue. Echoes of these sexual values live on today.

Between 500 and 1500 CE, the period known as the Middle Ages, Christianity became a state institution throughout the known world, and the Roman Catholic Church was at its core. Kings and popes were believed to be appointed by God. Women and sexuality were ideally controlled through religious institutions, and women continued for centuries to be excluded from all religious leadership. Chastity and notions of sexual purity for women and men alike were the rule, but more onerous for women, who were closely associated with marriage and property transmission.

Around 1200 CE, the Church formalized penalties for sodomy and other violations of its teachings through the creation of the Holy Inquisition, a religious court that could arrest and try people for heresy, sometimes as a result of gossip or rumor and jealousy within a community. The Inquisition did try and execute countless men, women, and children on charges of devil worship, witchcraft, and sodomy in Spain, England, the Netherlands, Germany, France, and elsewhere during the Middle Ages. Torture was used nearly always to extract confessions, and the whole religious climate advanced extremely negative attitudes about sexual relationships between men and women and between same-sex couples. Fear of the devil became a tool to suppress childhood sexuality, promiscuity, and homosexuality for centuries to come.

chivalry
A code of Christian knights that focused on purity of heart and body, chastity for females, and honor in war.

With the dawn of the Renaissance in the 14th century, new forms of secular art and discoveries in nature, science, and astronomy challenged the Church and the power of clerics (Foucault, 1973; Greenberg, 1988). Nevertheless, the Inquisition continued to punish people who defied it, holding onto dogmas such as belief in the Earth being flat. When the Italian physicist Galileo Galilei (1564–1642) published his observations of the planets confirming that the Earth rotates around the sun, for example, he was tried by the Inquisition and imprisoned for contradicting the Church's view of the heavens as unchanging. Eventually, Galileo was compelled to renounce his discovery. In 1992, the Church apologized to Galileo, 350 years after his persecution.

By the 18th century, reason and science were being applied to the study of nature, human society, art, government, and even sexuality (Foucault, 1973; Kuhn, 1970) in ways that broke through the narrow thinking of the Middle Ages. This was the era of the Enlightenment. It ushered in science and medicine as lines of reasoning in human sexuality and rational planning, based on observation and evidence that remain intact today, though science was continuously challenged by politics and religion. And the French Revolution challenged the divine right of kings and the power of the Church, ushering in democracy in Europe.

As sexual mores and laws began to evolve into the modern period, there also emerged a flowering of sexual expression and sexual diversity (D'Emilio & Freedman, 1988). For example, the first two communities of homosexuals secretly began in the Netherlands and England during this period of time (Trumbach, 1998; Van der Meer, 1994). In Europe after 1811, homosexuality was changed from a crime carrying a punishment of execution to one punishable by imprisonment.

At the time of the American Revolution, sexual pleasure and sexual expression were very much a part of people's lives. Benjamin Franklin, for example, was known to openly court other men's wives. Thomas Jefferson secretly fathered several children with his slave Sally Hemings. Abigail Adams reminded her husband, John Adams, who became the second president of the United States, not to forget the "ladies" voices, needs, and political position as he and others created the U.S. Constitution. These founding fathers lived within a web of terrible contradictions, however. Slavery, repression of women's rights, and the genocide of American Indians shaped their attitudes about sexuality, but did not inhibit their expressions of sexual pleasure in their own intimate lives. It would take a Civil War and a hundred years of social unrest to achieve fuller human and sexual rights for African Americans and women by the 1960s.

In the United States and Europe, the public health systems as we now know them came into existence during the 19th century. Doctors led the effort to set up clinics and establish mechanisms to control disease, including sexual "diseases" such as masturbation by children (Foucault, 1980). Sanitation systems were established on scientific principles in the cities. The introduction of modern sewers and pure water systems improved public hygiene and health. Many of the old laws against sexual crimes, including prostitution, adultery, and homosexuality, remained on the books, however. During this period, scientists began to understand that microbes cause disease. The start of public health clinics made it possible to monitor the population and to better control people's sexual behavior (Foucault, 1980). Unfortunately, folklore and myth found their way into sexual science at this time, including some deep-seated prejudices about gender and sexuality. Hygiene became a way for the state to control people's sexual and gender roles.

The Victorian Era and Sexual Identity We think of the Victorian era (1837–1901) as prudish, but it was really the beginning of the modern period. During the Victorian era, the accepted view was that sex should be private, hidden from and emotionally suppressed in children, and never mentioned in polite society. The genders were set in highly rigid roles, and the higher up in society, the more polarized the imagery and mythology that limited how men and women could be intimate and even seek a meaningful life.

DID YOU KNOW

Between 1940 and 1945 more than 20 million women joined the workforce, more than a 50% increase from pre–World War II levels (Porter, 1980). Women became factory workers, bank tellers, and airplane mechanics. Some of the women never went back to being housewives when the war ended, and they instilled in their daughters the notion that they, too, could compete in a man's world—possibly motivating a new wave of feminism in the 1960s.

sexual identity

Self-identification as heterosexual, bisexual, or homosexual.

To conform to the Victorian standard a nd gender roles, one's body had to be fully covered, and for a woman, coverage was from neck to toes. Victorian-era women were expected to be submissive, motherly, and asexual. They did this by wearing corsets, staying at home, remaining relatively uneducated, being spiritually and morally pure, using good hygiene, and being passive and religious, all to express Christian norms of the times. In the sexual culture, it was said that women lacked sex drives but had "mothering drives." And so, women were not allowed to express sexual pleasure, and they were even considered abnormal if they enjoyed sex. Toward the end of the 19th century, as the first women's emancipation movement gathered momentum as a reaction in the rising middle class to these ideals, women began to search for a more holistic, meaningful sense of social power and sexual well-being that would also include pleasure and a larger role in society. Children, once deemed in an earlier era to be sexual creatures in their own right, were recategorized as pure and without any sexual drives, essentially as sexually innocent and in need of protection to keep them that way.

But men were expected to be worldly and if of higher social class, educated, active, manly, sexually aggressive, breadwinners, and stronger than the "fair sex," and to express what people called very natural and innate "sex drives." Such modern attitudes motivated potential conflicts between men and women and between adults and children for human sexual nature. For example, women and children had to deny all sexuality, and men's sexuality was believed to be a conflict between good and evil, a struggle between the pure or good side and the lustful, animal-like male sexual side. One of the most popular novels of the day, *Dr. Jekyll and Mr. Hyde* by Robert Louis Stevenson, expressed this dualistic conflict through the story of a good doctor who used drugs that changed his personality: Sometimes he would degenerate into the villainous and animal-like Jack Hyde, who behaved like a sex fiend, while at other times he was the good Dr. Jekyll, who was kind and served society. As sexuality advanced into the 20th century, this kind of conflicted sexual motive was one of the conditions commonly treated by doctors and psychiatrists, such as Freud. And Freud through psychoanalysis became the new "priest" for the confession of sexual feelings (Foucault, 1980).

As explained in Chapter 1, many new forms of sexuality unfolded in the 19th century, including sexual degeneration (identified with homosexuality) and perversion (associated with medical conditions such as fetishism). But there were also positive ideas that began to emerge from all these medical forms. The most important new concept during this time was **sexual identity,** defined as the self-identification by an individual as heterosexual, bisexual, or homosexual. The concept of *homosexuality* as a distinctive sexual orientation of individuals attracted to others of the same gender emerged first, followed in 1889 by the concept of *heterosexuality* as an identity. Some scholars believe homosexuality emerged first because people noticed what was different before they actually recognized what was typical in society (heterosexuality).

But the rise of women's demands for equality and the increasing visibility of homosexuals threatened masculinity. In reaction to these developments, men increasingly went to pubs or joined secret male societies or Christian purity movements in droves, seeking the solidarity of other men and a sense of haven away from home. In areas such as the former slave states of the South, masculinity in White men sometimes took the form of reacting to and oppressing African Americans. During this time, too, the Boy Scouts organization began and spread throughout Europe and the United States as a way to bring boys back to nature and to their masculine ideals. These late 19th-century developments became the basis of sexuality movements in Europe and the United States over the next hundred years.

Also during the Victorian era, a new norm redefined the concepts of production and consumption: the *heterosexual couple.* Prior to this time, marriage was largely a political contract, and husband and wife lived with the extended family of the man, typically in small villages. The idea of an individualized long-term romantic sexual partnership in marriage began taking shape as society industrialized and people moved to the cities. New concepts of companionship and gender equality for women grew popular and controversial. Romantic love between couples and the concept of individual choice in sex and marriage became increasingly popular in novels, magazines, and the media. In other words, sexuality was being modernized.

20th-Century Sexuality By the beginning of the 20th century, sexuality was shaping up as a whole new area of expanded concern, including the emergence of sexual freedom for women, new choices to enhance sexual expression, and changes in intimate and family relationships—new forms of sexuality not previously seen for centuries in Western civilization. In 1919, the U.S. Congress passed the 19th Amendment, which upon ratification the following year granted American women the right to vote. By the 1920s, the first wave of feminism became prominent in the United States, encouraging sexual freedom and greater rights for women. Through many hard battles, American women also won the right to own property, hold public office, go to university, and generally exert some power in society.

Egalitarian gender roles and **companionate marriage**—the cultural idea that a man and woman are not just sex partners but also social and intellectual companions and equals for life—increasingly became the middle-class ideal, though the reality was far different because of how hard it was for women to exit negative relationships (Ramsey, 2013). Gradually the ideal expanded to all social classes and ethnic groups, and would later include gay and lesbian couples. Religious control over marriage and sex was declining but still highly influential. For example, it was still common for religions to oppose marriage outside of their own groups, and in some countries it remained illegal to marry someone of another religion, just as it remained illegal to marry someone of another race in the United States. But new public spaces, such as "dance halls," gave men and women open places where they could gather socially, and African American clubs became semisecret venues for jazz, dancing, interracial intimacy, and sexual encounters (Heap, 2009). The opening of public high schools further expanded how boys and girls could mingle, and the family automobile created a private space where romance and sex could—and did—take place. Casual sex, including premarital sex, began to increase during this era of the Roaring Twenties.

In the 1930s and 1940s, massive migrations due to the Great Depression and then war impacted heavily on sexual behavior. In the United States, people from the South moved to northern cities such as Chicago where they could get better jobs, and poor farmers who went bust in the Depression relocated to California and Florida, disrupting family ties and cultural control over sexuality. The two world wars, especially World War II, disrupted people's lives: Men went off to war and often formed new romantic and sexual unions, and women took men's places in factories and managerial jobs. Migration from villages and towns into cities dramatically increased after the war, as did the kinds of sexual behavior that Alfred Kinsey later documented in small-town America.

After World War II, intense compression of gender stereotypes of masculinity and femininity in some ways reversed the progress from before and dampened some of the sexual and gender freedom that prevailed in the war years. Movies and popular music were filled with romance, love, and sexual innuendos that revealed conflict with tradition. Also, increasingly the middle class perceived adolescents as sexual beings (Mead, 1927). Homosexual men who had secretly joined the armed services during the war discovered others like themselves, and upon their discharge remained in cities such as San Francisco and New York and began the gay communities that exist today, rather than returning to the small towns of their birth. With all the sexual changes, early medical contraceptives became more prevalent, as did an increase in sexually transmitted infections, such as gonorrhea.

The 1960s ushered in the second wave of feminism, as well as the sexual revolution that is identified with the baby boomers, the generation born between 1946 and 1963. Contraceptives, especially the birth control pill, became readily available in 1963, followed

This "Rosie the Riveter" poster symbolized the new role of working women during World War II, when U.S. women held jobs that were once filled by the men who went to war. It was the first time many women went to work outside the home.
John Parrot/Stocktrek Images/Getty Images

companionate marriage
The cultural idea that a man and woman are not just sex partners but also social and intellectual companions and equals for life.

During the post–World War II era, gender norms were compressed into stereotyped masculine and feminine behaviors.
H. ARMSTRONG ROBERTS/ClassicStock/Alamy Stock Photo; Bob Aylott/Keystone/Getty Images

by an increase in recreational sex (Laumann, Gagnon, Michael, & Michaels, 1994). More women began to choose to delay or to avoid having children. And variations in sexual behavior, such as oral and anal sex, became more common (Laumann et al., 1994).

In the 1970s, the gay liberation movement, an organized effort to end the criminalization of homosexual behavior in the United States, gained momentum. Now there were more casual same-sex activities than ever before, later followed by notions of social and legal recognition of same-sex relationships. Lesbians became more visible and present than ever, and bisexuality became a focus of public discussion unlike before. But in 1981, a deadly new sexually transmitted disease, AIDS (acquired immunodeficiency syndrome), began to take its toll, claiming the lives of thousands of gay men. Government and medical authorities ignored the epidemic for years—a consequence of the shame and stigma of homosexuality in the United States. During this time there was a renewed push toward sexual abstinence as the only sure way to stop the transmission of HIV (human immunodeficiency virus), which can lead to AIDS. A new wave of religious conservatism generated moral campaigns against all homosexuality, abortion, and comprehensive sex education. This reaction also fed countertrends of increased social activism to support groups stigmatized by religious conservatives, such as transgender men and transgender women, sex workers, and people living with HIV. And so sexual literacy arose in the 1990s along with the concept that sexuality is a human right, an idea that very slowly spread with the help of Internet access. The World Wide Web opened the door to all kinds of sexual communities, most notably transgender communities, around the globe.

History reveals how attitudes toward sexuality have been profoundly shaped by social institutions, including marriage, family, and religion. In turn, these institutions have all been shaped by sexuality. In the next section we discuss the key role culture plays in teaching and learning about negative and positive sexual attitudes.

SEXUAL CULTURES AND NORMS

In general, different societies have been shown to have opposing attitudes about whether sex is a good thing or a bad thing, whether sexual intercourse should be frequent or rare, and whether people ought to pursue pleasure or avoid it. It makes sense, then, that sexual norms vary across these societies.

Sexual Norms and Sexual Socialization

All cultures have built into their roles and institutions specific expectations for sexual behavior, which we have called sexual culture. These sexual cultures function today as a way of both helping people to adapt to their environments and controlling their behavior and social relationships, including regulation of morality, women's and men's power, sexual practices, and sexual health and well-being (Herdt, 1999a; Lyons & Lyons, 2011; Moore & Reynolds, 2018).

People's expectations form the ideal blueprint of a sexual culture and are put into practice through sexual norms. A **sexual norm** is the standard of sexual behavior expected of people in a particular role, relationship, and situation. Sexual norms may be very general or context specific, which means that you may do one thing in a certain context, such as in the bedroom, but must behave very differently in another setting, such as at a shopping mall. The sexual culture also determines who has the power to initiate sex, approve of sex, and control sex (Lyons & Lyons, 2011; Schippers, 2016). Within a particular culture, there can be different sexual norms for different types of people, such as males versus females, children versus adults. An example would be the sexual norm governing who can kiss or hold hands in public, who is allowed to date, who is allowed to have premarital sex, and who is forbidden to have sex of any kind. In many cultures around the world men often have more freedom when it comes to sexual norms than women.

Training people from infancy to adulthood to follow these expectations is the process of **sexual socialization,** the application of the culture's blueprints to sexual feelings, thoughts, meanings, and behaviors as people grow up. As discussed, humans take a lot longer to mature than other species and are under the guidance of their families for many years, and so sexual socialization can strongly influence all areas of sexuality, from babies to elders. In general, children are subject to sexual socialization and parental control of their sexual norms till they reach adolescence, and sometimes beyond.

Differences in sexual norms increase diversity in sexual behavior and account for dramatic variations in sexuality across cultures. One culture might allow childhood sexual play and another forbid it (Ford & Beach, 1951; Giddens, 1992; Herdt, 2009a; Moore & Reynolds, 2018). One sexual norm that is common in cultures other than the United States is **polygamy,** a practice that allows men to have multiple wives (Hirsch et al., 2009). In years past, sexual scientists focused on sexual norms as being either abnormal or normal. Today, scientists seek to explain how sexual norms differ across societies, in addition to studying the positive functions of sexual well-being (Fisher, 2004; Grauvogl, Peters, Evers, & van Lankveld, 2015).

Placing behavior in context is known as **cultural relativism.** For example, kissing someone in a particular way may mean one thing in one context and something different in another context, according to the cultural blueprint. You may see a parent kiss a child on the head and recognize it as a symbol of love. You may also see two people entwined in a deeply romantic kiss and recognize that as an erotic type of love. People from another culture may view kissing in general as disgusting because they do not share bodily fluids. **Cultural chauvinism,** by contrast, is when one group judges another's behaviors against its own standards, and usually finds them inferior. Chauvinism may be responsible for some of history's greatest conflicts, when nations have gone to war over hatred, greed, differences in religious or national belief or creed, and then have been able to impose their own sexual norms on the conquered people (Herdt, 1997b, 2004).

Sexual chauvinism, the belief that one's sexual culture is superior to others, continues to be a global problem when it comes to sexual well-being (Herdt, 2010a). For example, in some cultures, adolescents may be regarded as sexually mature and given the benefits of comprehensive sexual education, while in other cultures they may be denied sex education, contraceptives, and even effective information about sexually transmitted disease prevention (Impett, Schooler, & Tolman, 2006; Moore & Reynolds, 2018; Santelli et al., 2006). Learning how to communicate your own sexual culture and norms without being a sexual chauvinist is a key to better personal, societal, and professional relationships in today's highly diverse, global environment. You can read more about these issues in "Communication Matters: Sexual Culture Differences, Respect, and Chauvinism."

Of all the forms of sexual chauvinism, one of the most severe is when someone breaks the sexual norm and is labeled "abnormal," meaning that the person's behavior is

---

sexual norm
A cultural standard of sexual behavior expected of people in a particular role, relationship, and situation.

sexual socialization
The application of a culture's blueprints to sexual feelings, thoughts, and behaviors.

polygamy
Marriage between one man and more than one woman at the same time.

cultural relativism
The viewing of people's attitudes and behavior in the context of their own culture.

cultural chauvinism
The belief that one's cultural norms are superior to the norms of another's group.

sexual chauvinism
The belief that one's sexual culture is superior to others.

COMMUNICATION Matters

Sexual Culture Differences, Respect, and Chauvinism

Have you ever found yourself in a situation where you wanted to communicate that you recognized or respected another's sexual culture or norms, but you were not comfortable doing so? Today's world is filled with different sexual cultures, as you are likely discovering in this course, and learning to recognize these differences, to understand and tolerate them, represents a significant step toward achieving sexual literacy. Note, however, that showing respect does not mean that you have to engage in such behaviors, in person or online. As former president Bill Clinton's political advisor James Carville once joked, "I was against gay marriage until they told me I didn't have to have one!"

Consider the following simple rules of engagement that you can apply to your own relationships with people from diverse sexual cultures.

Communicating respect *does* mean:

- Being able to ask respectful questions about someone's culture, sexual norms, and their beliefs
- Being able to continually learn about others' sexual cultures
- Being able to describe your own sexual norms and cultures to others respectfully
- Being willing to learn enough about another person to work together comfortably on a professional level
- Being able to adapt your own personal sexual style, beliefs, and behavior to situations where others are very different

Communicating respect *does not* mean:

- That you know or have to know everything there is about different sexual cultures throughout the world
- That you are required to engage in their sexual norms or practices
- That you cannot disagree with certain aspects of their sexual culture
- That you assume a person has certain sexual norms or beliefs if they belong to a specific ethnic or cultural group

Following these simple guidelines can improve your communication and help you avoid the trap of sexual chauvinism. In today's world, having these communication skills can make a difference at school, at work, in the community, and when traveling.

---

dysfunctional compared to "normal" people, who uphold the culture's norms (Stoller, 1985). The label "abnormal" has a specific meaning in psychology, but also has been applied through the modern period to refer to sexual deviants, moral outlaws, or revolutionaries (D'Emilio & Freedman, 1988; Foucault, 1980). For example, divorce was once considered abnormal in the United States, and premarital sexual relationships may still be regarded as

WHAT'S ON YOUR MIND?

Q: I am seeing this guy in my dorm from another culture and he says that it is normal where he comes from for men to flirt with lots of women. He even says that having sex with multiple women is OK so long as you are careful about it. Could this be true?

ANSWER: Well, there is tremendous variation between cultures, some of which allow for men to have multiple sexual relationships. But how this is done in the context of relationships is very important. If it is disrespectful, then that's different from being coy and discreet about such flirting. Also, having multiple sexual relationships at the same time is something else altogether, when it comes to our own society. Consider asking him whether he feels close enough to you to explore these issues in conversation, and then see how you feel about how he relates his experience to you and your own sexual culture. That could make a huge difference, too. Also, consider that as he adapts to American society, he may learn and adjust to new sexual norms.

tabooed or even abnormal in some communities (Ramsey, 2013). In addition, until recently, people in the United States referred to homosexuality as abnormal; but today, experts in the field of mental health agree that homosexuality is psychologically normal. Yet other cultures in Asia and Africa, by comparison, still strongly condemn such behaviors and consider the offenders to be sick criminals or even crazy and dangerous, a view exemplified by the execution of a gay teenager in Iran in 2016, in violation of international law (Amnesty International, 2016 (https://www.amnesty.org.uk/press-releases/iran-hangs-teenage-student-first-child-offender-execution-year). Being normal, then, means that you fit the norms and behaviors of your culture, even if you may not agree with them or like them; behaving abnormally means you may become an outcast.

Sex-Approving and Sex-Disapproving Cultures

Sexual attitudes vary across a spectrum of human cultures, ranging from totally approving to totally disapproving in terms of sexual norms, values, attitudes, and institutions (Ford & Beach, 1951; Hirsch et al., 2009; Mead, 1961; Lyons & Lyons, 2011). In reality, many groups fall between these extremes, and some cultures are actually positive about sex (Herdt, 1997a, 2009a; Kinsey, Pomeroy, Martin, & Gebhard, 1948; Moore & Reynolds, 2018). The culture of the Kwoma people of New Guinea, for example, allows a woman to hit a boy's penis with a stick if he gets an erection (Whiting, 1941). Similar examples are found worldwide. In contrast, sexual play is supported in some sexual cultures (Mead, 1961). As a result, researchers have categorized a *spectrum of cultures* into societies that range from being **sex-approving** to **sex-disapproving** when it comes to sexual attitudes and behavior.

sex-approving Culturally supportive of positive attitudes toward sexual expression and behavior.

Consider how this spectrum can be seen in four different types of cultures that exist around the globe, as shown in Table 2.1 (Ford & Beach, 1951; Herdt, 1997a, 2010a). They vary according to how sex-approving or sex-disapproving their attitudes and behaviors are, especially when considering the culture's degree of regulation of sexuality in childhood, adolescence, and adulthood.

sex-disapproving Generally negative cultural attitudes toward sexual expression and behavior.

Table **2.1** Four types of sexual cultures around the world

TYPE OF SOCIETY	ACCEPTANCE OF SEX	CHILDHOOD SEXUAL EXPLORATION	MASTURBATION	PREMARITAL SEXUALITY	SAME-SEX RELATIONSHIPS	EXTRA-MARITAL RELATIONSHIPS	MARRIAGE
Encouraging	All human development related to sexual well-being	Encouraged	Normal behavior	Positive attitude; cohabitation common before marriage	Regarded as normal behavior for some people	Accepts extramarital relations in some contexts	Based on mutual respect, joy, and rights
Approving	Accepted as normal most of the time	Generally allowed	Accepted	Sexual pleasure approved of in premarital relationships	Accepted in adolescence with same-aged peers	May be tolerated	Gives choice to women and men
Disapproving		Disapproved of but not condemned	Warned against	Virginity expected before marriage	Denies existence of homosexuality or calls it bad	Does not allow this	Assigns marriage without choice
Oppressive	Is risky and dangerous	Condemned	Sinful, diseased	Condemned	Abnormal	Condemned	Single people are abnormal

Sambia boys are initiated as warriors and a new phase of their sexual life begins.
Gilbert Herdt

sexual individuality
The unique expression of an individual's most basic sexual needs and attractions, based on the individual's body and anatomy, DNA, hormones, orientations, fantasies, feelings, behaviors, and relationships.

sexual unlearning
The process of unlearning something about sexuality that may have been learned at a very young age.

Where would you place your own sexual culture on the spectrum of sex-approving and sex-disapproving societies? A classic cross-cultural study found that societies vary in being approving or disapproving in the degree to which they "deny young children any form of sexual expression" (Ford & Beach, 1951, p. 180; Kinsey et al., 1948). The study concluded that such a level of denial of sexual expression by children "is the prevailing attitude in American society." Another classic study found that children in the United States were less knowledgeable about sexuality than children in Australia, Sweden, and England (Goldman & Goldman, 1982). And advanced industrial societies that have extensive sexuality education programs, such as Denmark, tend to have more accepting attitudes about having sex before marriage or casual sex (Herdt, 1997a; Moore & Reynolds, 2018; Schalet, 2000). Parents in the United States generally tend to respond negatively to childhood sexual exploration (Waites, 2005; Weiss, 2004).

Such variations in attitudes may shape the context of sexuality in any culture, whether those attitudes are toward the body, masturbation, premarital sex, childhood sexual expression, same-sex practices, or extramarital sex, to name a few (Herdt, 1997a, 2009a; Jankowiak, 2008; Laumann et al., 1994; Waites, 2005). In turn, cultural context influences **sexual individuality,** defined as the expression of the self's most basic sexual needs and attractions, and based in our body and anatomy, DNA, hormones, orientations, fantasies, feelings, behaviors, and relationships. Sexual individuality is as unique as each person's fingerprints. Consider how the people of one tribal culture view sexuality in "Research and Sexual Well-Being: Sex and Culture in Papua New Guinea."

Sexual Unlearning

In sex-approving cultures, young people tend to learn about sexuality by observation and then exploration. In sex-disapproving cultures, another pattern exists, often connected to the kinds of taboos you have read about. Children may learn at an early age that certain behaviors, such as running around nude, are OK, only to find out when they're older that those behaviors are now tabooed for them, and so they must unlearn them. This pattern of sexual socialization is called **sexual unlearning** (Herdt, 1990; Herdt & McClintock, 2000). In the traditional culture of the Sambia of Papua New Guinea, boys needed to unlearn what they had learned about females when they were growing up with their mothers (Herdt, 1990). They experienced taboos and painful rituals to make them avoid what is forbidden and motivate unlearning. In some cultures, people may be forced to stop engaging in certain behaviors, such as sexual play, touching or holding hands, or touching their genitals (Ford & Beach, 1951; Waites, 2005). Read "Healthy Sexuality: How Unlearning Influences Sexual Individuality" to see if such a process may have influenced your sexual socialization in the past, or may continue to influence your present behavior.

Sexual unlearning is common, especially in societies that are sex-negative or that are undergoing rapid change (Benedict, 1938; Carrillo, 2007; Herdt, 1990, 2006; Laumann et al., 1994). The reason is that sexual behaviors that were once considered unacceptable may change in value in the next generation (Gagnon, 2004). People who have grown up in a sex-disapproving culture may have been taught that menstruation or masturbation were disgusting. Yet menstruation is a normal part of being female and masturbation is now common. A girl thinking that menstruation is disgusting may develop negative self-esteem. What if people grow up being taught that only heterosexuals are normal and healthy and then discover that they are gay? These examples are relevant to the United States, because masturbation,

RESEARCH and Sexual Well-Being

Sex and Culture in Papua New Guinea

How much do sexual taboos really influence a culture? Across the Pacific Islands sexual cultures range from highly sex-approving to those, such as the Sambia culture of Papua New Guinea, that are sex-disapproving, but have same-sex rituals as part of their traditional religion. Since 1974, Gil has studied and continues to do anthropological fieldwork in the Sambia culture (Herdt, 2006). He found that the men and women's sexuality was highly influenced by rituals and taboos. To gain a strong understanding of these taboos in the sexual culture, he has interviewed more than 400 individuals from diverse villages and age groups since 1974, some as many as 50 times over a 7-year period (Herdt & Stoller, 1990). His fieldwork since 2010 has showed how much the sexual culture has really changed.

Traditionally, the Sambia people of Papua New Guinea were a warrior culture of 2,000 people who were gender segregated by their institutions and sexual socialization. Generally, they had a sex-disapproving attitude that restricted childhood sexual exploration and sexual individuality. Their sexual culture involved secret same-sex rituals that resembled those of the ancient Greeks but are typically forbidden in many cultures. Boys grew up close to their mothers, but between ages 7 and 10, they were taken away to live in a house restricted to boys and men. To ward off attack from their enemies, they were trained to be fierce warriors, capable of killing in combat. To be entitled to join the men's secret society, boys had to *unlearn everything* about their mothers and the women's social world. In fact, they were taught to fear everything about women.

Sambia women were the focus of many anxieties and fears among the men. They especially feared menstruation and menstrual blood, which they believed could kill men and stunt the growth of boys. This was the greatest cause of sexual antagonism between the genders. In fact, men avoided their wives and other women during menstruation and spontaneously spit whenever they said their word for *menstruation*. Their culture tabooed sex during this time. Women had to go to the menstrual hut during their periods and when they gave birth. These spaces were taboo to men. Not too many years ago, all kinds of foods, especially red foods, which were identified with women's menstrual blood, were tabooed to all men to eat. And boys and men had the belief that, just by living in the same house as women, they somehow absorbed their tabooed menstrual blood and then had to be nose-bled violently in order to expel it (Herdt, 1982). Men feared each sexual interaction with their wives in the belief that their penis might absorb menstrual blood. All their lives men had to nose-bleed themselves through painful rituals for this reason.

Like the ancient Greeks, the Sambia initiated boys into "ritualized homosexuality" as part of their sexual socialization into the men's house and warrior ways (Herdt, 1984). Many cultures in the Pacific Islands also practiced this ritual custom, with older and younger males required to be sexually intimate after they were initiated and before they married. They engaged in oral sex in which the younger boy sucked an older boy's penis to ejaculation. The young boys were taught that semen was a substitute for mother's milk and that the semen would make them big and strong, since they were no longer permitted to drink their mother's milk. The Sambia also believed that the male body did not naturally produce semen but that swallowing it made them produce it. As part of this ritual, the Sambia used secret bamboo flutes that they said were the voice of female spirits, as they taught the boys—linking their sexuality to their religion. Insemination became a powerful metaphor for the relationships between the younger and older boys, because men told the younger boys that they were married to the female spirits of the men's house, and their older sexual partners impersonated these spirits. When the older boys married women, they stopped these practices. When their own sons were old enough, they sent them to the men's secret house for initiation.

Today, as a result of the end of warfare, and missionization, the Sambia men's society has disappeared into history. The last initiation ritual of boys, which was performed in the early 1990s, is documented in the film *Guardians of the Flutes*. A new order of more equal gender relations and sexual behavior is emerging that is focused on family formation and romantic marriage in the context of the Seventh Day Adventist church, with young women selecting their own husbands (Herdt, 2019).

menstruation, and homosexuality were all traditionally tabooed, but as social attitudes and religious beliefs have changed, these behaviors have become more broadly accepted (Institute of Medicine, 2012; Regnerus, 2007).

HEALTHY Sexuality

How Unlearning Influences Sexual Individuality

Being taught something at one time and then something almost totally the opposite later can be confusing and cause conflict. It's not exactly a double standard, because different sexual norms are applied at different points in the life cycle. It is tempting to think that such conflicts are the result of dysfunctional families or defective parents, but long ago, anthropologist Ruth Benedict (1938) pointed out that such processes are common in sexual cultures, and may lead to great difficulties when it comes to sexual individuality. Problems of this kind are common in sex-disapproving cultures. Benedict noted, for example, that people who are taught not to be aggressive when they are young are expected to act aggressive as adults. More to the point, she noted that people in countries such as the United States regard children as sexually innocent; then, without the benefit of any further familial or community sex education, they expect adolescents to be competent sexual actors almost overnight (Schalet, 2000). Such contradictory expectations can confuse and produce conflict in sexual development (Herdt & Boxer, 1993).

Think about the following sexual behaviors that you might have engaged in as a child. Have you had to unlearn any of them as you matured?

- Masturbation
- Sexual play (playing "doctor and nurse") in childhood
- Freedom to be nude when you were a child
- Same-sex sexual play with your same-aged peers
- Kissing considered inappropriate as you mature
- Expression of sexual desire that may not conform to the sexual norm

Did your family or sexual culture or religion consider these behaviors taboo? If they did, how did they communicate these taboos? Who might have communicated the need for you to unlearn any of these behaviors? Parents? Ministers? Teachers? Or did you find out via the media or the Internet? Can you now say, "I'm an adult so I can make decisions for myself about what is best for my own sexual well-being"?

In fact, in rapidly developing countries, such as Mexico, it has been found that what was once considered very negative or tabooed, such as abortion and homosexuality, may actually become symbolic of people's tolerance, since they believe that to accept these behaviors is to be modern (Carrillo, 2007). Such changes may be especially challenging to older generations that may need to unlearn the old taboos and integrate new, progressive attitudes (Herdt, 2019). Sexual literacy, then, may involve *unlearning* norms acquired in a disapproving or oppressive culture if the norms change and allow individuals greater freedom to satisfy their desires or pursue sexual well-being.

As we discuss in the next section, religion appears to be one of the forces that may contribute to sexual taboos and how much a culture may approve or disapprove of sex or have to unlearn things, in the United States.

SEXUALITY AND THE GREAT WORLD RELIGIONS

Hinduism, Buddhism, Judaism, Islam, and Christianity are great world religions that, as we have seen, have figured prominently in the history of culture and civilization. Researchers now are learning that religion also plays a very large role in sexual socialization (Prothero, 2007; Regnerus, 2007; Smith, 1991). One of the reasons why these great world religions are important to sexuality is they influence guidelines for behaviors that people consider wrong or immoral within their own group or other groups. Often these behaviors are considered taboos. Many cultures' most deeply held guidelines and sexual taboos stem from their spirituality or religions and provide for how they cope with the life crises that occur throughout the human life cycle—birth, puberty, marriage, childbirth, and death (Armstrong, 1999; Herdt, 1997, 2009a; Turner, 1967). Researchers have found that when it comes to these taboos, some individuals' beliefs are so powerful that they can actually outweigh what their culture says about sexuality (Regnerus, 2007). Appreciating how people's religious beliefs influence their holistic sexuality is critical to sexual well-being, as we will see.

Traditionally, a number of religious groups have primarily communicated *negative* sexual attitudes, norms, and taboos, rather than discussing the *positive* elements of sexual well-being with their followers. Because of this negative approach, many people have never learned how to be sexual, to become sexually literate, or to pursue sexual well-being in the context of their particular faith. In part because of this failure to approach sexuality in a positive, supportive way, many people stereotype religious groups as being either sexually progressive or conservative (Luker, 2006). As you will read, the truth is far more complex and interesting than these stereotypes suggest (Machacek & Wilcox, 2003; Prothero, 2010).

Think about your own experience. How do you react if there is a difference between your own sexual culture and what your religious upbringing says? Whether the issue is masturbation, premarital sex, or something else, religious training may contradict how people actually behave in society (Regnerus, 2007). How do you negotiate the contradictions between such religious and cultural or societal meanings or sexual relationships? Without challenging your own religious beliefs, let's consider how the world's largest faith communities have influenced sexuality. Later, we'll discuss spirituality and sexual behavior in the United States.

DID YOU KNOW

In 2010, the world's total population was approximately 6.5 billion people. Figure 2.2 shows how people describe their religious affiliation.

- Christians 31.4%
- Muslims 23.2%
- Hindus 15%
- Buddhists 7.1%
- Folk religions 5.9%
- Jews 0.2%
- Other religions 0.8%
- Unaffiliated 16.4%

Figure 2.2
How people worldwide describe their religious affiliation.
Source: CIA, 2019.

Sex, Religion, and Reality

A core belief of many world religions is that human sexuality is divinely inspired and created, rather than a product of human design, such as family planning or social attitudes (Prothero, 2010; Smith, 1991). Philosophers and scientists question this assumption (Dawkins, 2006). But sexual scientists are coming to see just how much religion can influence social and cultural systems of beliefs, norms, and rules that are the blueprint for people's social behavior in general and their sexuality in particular (Ellington, 2004; Parrinder, 1996; Prothero, 2007; Regnerus, 2007). In short, religion helps shape how we perceive reality and, in turn, sex.

When it comes to reality beliefs and sex, one thing that differentiates religions and cultures is whether they believe in a single god or in many gods (Armstrong, 1999; Bellah, 2006; Smith, 1991). As we learned earlier, the ancient Greeks and Romans believed in multiple gods, as did many non-Western cultures, such as the Sambia. Some of these cultures had more sex-approving attitudes, such as the ancient Greeks, and a few had more sex-disapproving attitudes. The worship of many gods is called **polytheism.** Hinduism and

polytheism
Belief in multiple gods and spirits.

monotheism
Belief in one God.

organized religion
Sharing practices of worship with others and belonging to a group that is based on shared beliefs and practices.

religious identity
The social expression of an individual's faith in the context of community and nation.

Buddhism are generally regarded as polytheistic religions (Armstrong, 2001a). Generally they are more sex-approving than sex-disapproving. By contrast, a belief in one God is called **monotheism.** Christianity, Judaism, and Islam are monotheistic religions that go back thousands of years (Armstrong, 1999). Whether a culture is polytheistic or monotheistic is important in shaping people's sense of reality as a community, and probably their sense of approving or disapproving sex, at least to some extent.

While spirituality is the inner sense of an individual, **organized religion** means sharing practices of worship with others and belonging to a faith-based group, both of which create collective social experiences (Durkheim, 1915). Belonging to a church can provide some people with a social community of economic, social, and psychological support, especially in times of need, and this may outweigh their beliefs and many other social connections, whether it is gender, age, ethnicity, or social class (Regnerus, 2007). This is why some evolutionary scholars view the emergence of religion in the advance of civilization as an early form of social networking and a safety net of support (Rossano, 2010). For some people, this safety net is so important that it may outweigh other elements of their societal support, even their own immediate community (Bellah, Madisen, Sullivan, Swindler, & Tipton, 1985). Because members of an organized religion tend to share beliefs, however, they also exert social and psychological pressure on each other to conform to their religion's blueprint of how to behave, including how to behave sexually (Machacek & Wilcox, 2003). These shared beliefs and behaviors create a **religious identity,** which is the social expression of an individual's faith in the context of one's community and nation.

Sometimes a religious identity, such as Catholic or Protestant, may actually influence how people vote in elections, raise their families, and follow sexual taboos or beliefs (Bellah et al., 1985; Regnerus, 2007). For example, young children's sense of whether nudity is "natural" or "unnatural" and something to fear or be ashamed of can influence their sexual expression and well-being (Fisher, 1986; Kinsey et al., 1948). In fact, sex-negative attitudes toward nudity and sexual shame may reflect what their culture teaches (Laumann et al., 1994; Moore & Reynolds, 2018; Weiss, 2004).

Sexual behavior can actually define the basic sense of whether someone is a person and a citizen-member of a particular country or state (Laumann, Ellington, Mahay, Paik, & Youm, 2004; Prothero, 2010; Richardson, 2000). For example, in some Islamic communities in the Middle East, a person who occupies a social or professional position, such as being a teacher, government employee, or doctor, is expected to be an upstanding member of the local mosque or risk losing that position, and women may be automatically excluded from occupying these important social roles. And in some Christian communities, living up to sexual taboos and norms can become such a profound pressure that people will even devise ways to hide or shield what they actually do in private, such as hiding the fact that they may use pornography (Regnerus, 2007).

Sex in the World Religions

Religious belief and practice continue to be among the most powerful forces that shape sexuality globally. Belonging to a religion can actually influence sexual practices and relationships and even go so far as to exclude people from their religion because of their sexuality (Regnerus, 2007). Why does sex remain a largely tabooed and negative topic in many world religions, even in the United States (Ellington, 2004; Parrinder, 1996; Prothero, 2007; Regnerus, 2007)? While people may expect religious leaders to provide moral education and support when it comes to basic areas of family formation, marriage, and children's development, sex complicates the situation hugely.

Let's consider two key questions about each of the great world religions: How do they view sexuality in general, and how are their sexual norms similar or different as expressed in beliefs, attitudes, and behaviors? Table 2.2 condenses seven points of comparison among the great world religions, to highlight the similarities and differences.

Hinduism Hinduism, perhaps the most ancient religion, includes a complex philosophy and ritual practices and taboos that affect people's everyday lives. Hinduism is highly diverse with many spiritual practices, including yoga. Its teachings include many things about sex, pleasure, relationship formation, and sex education. Through its ancient holy text, the *Kama Sutra*, Hinduism directs men and women to pleasure each other and shows them how to do it with remarkable illustrations of real sexual techniques and positions (Daniélou, 1994). Hindu tradition is exceptional in its acceptance of pleasure and sexuality. There are numerous Hindu festivals and pilgrimages throughout the year, some of which involve sexual imagery and open sexual expression. The Hindu god Krishna, who sometimes takes physical forms, is thought to have sung the *Bhagavad Gita,* a beautiful epic poem, to teach his followers how to live life by seeking joy, knowledge, and awakening, even through sex (Basham, 1999; Fuller, 2004; Smith, 1991).

Hindu philosophy is based on the sex-approving view that it is natural for people to want pleasure (Smith, 1991). As long as basic rules of morality are obeyed, such as not to harm

Table 2.2 Sexuality and sexual norms of the great world religions

RELIGION	SEX	PREMARITAL SEX	DIVORCE	HOMOSEXUALITY	ADULTERY	CONTRACEPTION	ABORTION
Hinduism	Not openly discussed Pleasure is valued, with restraint	Disapproved of and virginity expected for marriage	Disapproved and may stigmatize divorced women	Tabooed topic; same-sex behavior known of in Indian history	Double standard Women: tolerate to save marriages Men: may have a mistress	Accepted but not widely used	Not accepted, though attitude about it may be changing
Buddhism	Positively viewed, in moderation; mutual pleasure between spouses	Disapproved	Not prohibited; viewed as causing pain	Not tabooed but not encouraged	Avoid because it causes disharmony	Accepted	Not accepted; it disrupts harmony and causes guilt
Judaism	Joyful; for procreation; masturbation condemned	Disapproved	Negatively viewed; allowed in certain situations	Forbidden; some Jews are more open to it than in the past	Forbidden	More accepted now than in traditional Judaism	Mandatory when the mother's life is in jeopardy
Islam	Taboo topic; mutual pleasure between spouses	Disapproved and virginity is prized	Allowed under extreme conditions	Condemned	Forbidden; the Koran allows men to have four wives	Negatively viewed	Not accepted
Christianity	Supported in marriage to some extent; masturbation sinful in some groups and tolerated in others	Disapproved of in many Christian groups; a sin in Catholicism and some Protestant groups	Disapproved of but tolerated in most Christian groups, with some exceptions	Treated differently among all Christian groups	Forbidden	Many groups allow it; some do not	Generally not accepted; a sin in Catholicism

or kill others, people are free to seek all the pleasure they want. Hindus believe that mental and spiritual values multiply when they are shared. Money and power, however, do not multiply when they are shared, and ultimately Hindus regard them as toys to be set aside. So they may renounce material things as part of their search for enlightenment, especially later in life (Armstrong, 1999; Smith, 1991).

Hinduism also carries some negative attitudes about sex, noted in the following general guidelines. First, pleasure with restraint is valued. Sex is not taboo, but it is not discussed openly in the home. Women are expected to be virgins when they marry. Hinduism disapproves of divorce and may stigmatize divorced women, causing them to live as widows. Homosexuality goes against the Hindu tradition of marriage and having children, yet same-sex sexual desire is not considered immoral and same-sex sexual behavior is known throughout Indian history (Vanita & Kidwai, 2001). The Hindu faith appears to have a double standard about extramarital relations. Women are encouraged to tolerate adultery to save their marriage, and some men may have a mistress. The punishments for extramarital relations range from penance to death but are not necessarily enforced (Parashar, 2008). Contraception is acceptable, but not widely used, because large families are customary. Abortion is not acceptable in the Hindu faith, although as the middle-class expands in India, this attitude may be changing (Bowker, 1998; Bowker & Holm, 1994).

This statue of the Hindu deity Krishna depicts him as a young boy playing the flute.
blickwinkel/Alamy Stock Photo

Buddhism Buddhism advocates intense self-effort toward greater consciousness, and is generally tolerant of many forms of sexuality. It combines qualities of being practical, scientific, psychological, and egalitarian that are reflected in its sexual norms. Buddha was opposed to formality and ritual, was mistrustful of power, tried not to create traditions, and worked against negative views in favor of realistic or natural observations (Smith, 1991). Following these beliefs opens a path toward greater enlightenment, focused on having "right views, right intent, right speech, and right conduct." Buddha also believed that it is wrong to kill humans or other animals and so encouraged vegetarianism.

In the Buddhist faith, sex is viewed positively, in moderation, like everything else in life. Mutual pleasures between spouses are expected. Premarital sex is discouraged because it falls outside the context of doing no harm to the self or others, including the possibility of unintended pregnancy. It can also create false promises to others and represents loss of self-control (Armstrong, 2001a; Stevens, 1990). Divorce is regarded as a secular matter and is not prohibited, but because divorce disrupts families, people are expected to marry for life. Among Buddhist monks, same-sex relationships are tolerated (Herdt, 1997a). In the general population, homosexuality is not tabooed, but it is not encouraged. Engaging in same-sex sexual practices does not excuse someone from the social obligation to have children. However, adultery is regarded as immature and self-indulgent. It also shows a lack of loving kindness and compassion for one's spouse or intimate partner. Further, committing adultery may create a lack of harmony, and since harmony is such an extremely positive goal, adultery should be avoided. In general, contraception is acceptable, but abortion is opposed because it disturbs harmony and makes the individual feel guilty (Stevens, 1990).

Children become monks at a very young age to pursue the Buddhist path, a path that does not necessarily preclude sexuality.
Katie Garrod/AWL Images/Getty Images

Judaism Judaism is an ancient religion as well, with complex attitudes toward sexuality. Jews believe that God made an eternal agreement with them, promising a land "flowing with milk and honey" (Exodus 33:3), and in return they promised to honor him and follow his commandments. The image of this land, which is Israel today, is deeply enmeshed in Jewish religious and social identity (Bowker, 1998; Boyarin, 1994). This compact with God also anchored their culture in their religious identity, and taboos and beliefs regarding marriage, family, and sex (Armstrong, 1999). For this reason, experts regard being Jewish as having a religious identity that connects all people of Jewish heritage through a common tradition of cultural norms, such as what foods to eat (Boyarin, 1994). In other words, it's possible to be socially Jewish without living in Israel or following the religion.

In the Torah, Judaism's most holy text, the word used for sex between husband and wife comes from an ancient term meaning "to know." It signifies that sexuality involves the heart and mind, as well as the body. In this cultural blueprint, the sole purpose of sex is procreation. For this reason, masturbation was taboo. Judaic law makes it clear a husband and wife must control and channel sexual desire and fulfill it in the morally correct time and place. When a husband and wife satisfy sexual desire at the proper time, out of mutual love and desire, they are fulfilling tradition (Judaism 101, 2010). Ritual marks entry into puberty, because at age 13 for boys and age 12 for girls, Jewish people partake in a coming-of-age ceremony, called a *bar mitzvah* for boys and a *bat mitzvah* for girls. After this ceremony, the adolescents are of age to follow the commandments of Jewish law. This ceremony roughly marks the time of entering into adulthood with the expectation of acting responsibly in all things, including sex. Traditionally, this ritual was a form of sexual socialization into Jewish culture, too (Armstrong, 1999).

Though tolerant in some ways, early Judaism considered certain forms of sexual behavior, including homosexuality, wrong and tabooed. As Judaism adapted to changing times, some of its earlier norms also changed. For example, one branch of Judaism has become more accepting of diverse sexual techniques, such as oral sex, and also of equality for women.

As the Jewish tradition has evolved, differences in religious practices have created three main branches: Orthodox, Conservative, and Reform or Liberal. The former group conforms to the Torah more strictly than the other two groups. Reform Judaism has implemented reforms, including less stringent dietary rules, recognition of women as rabbis, and greater acceptance of sexual pleasure.

Although the Torah forbids homosexuality, today there is a distinction between having a homosexual orientation, which is accepted, and homosexual behaviors. Reform Judaism is becoming more open to same-sex relationships, and some Reform congregations welcome all people regardless of sexual orientation (Abrams, 2008; Broyde & Ausubel, 2005; Ruttenberg, 2009). Orthodox Judaism and, for the most part, Conservative Judaism remain opposed to homosexuality. Traditionally, Judaism opposed birth control, but permitted abstinence; now there is greater acceptance of contraceptives by many Jews. Jewish law requires abortion in some circumstances, for example, when birth would harm the mother or the unborn child.

Traditional Jewish scholars studying the Torah in ancient times.
Maria Taglienti-Molinari/Getty Images

Islam The religion of Islam lays out a clear blueprint for sexuality that outweighs local social and cultural traditions around the globe. Embraced by more than 1.5 billion people, Islam is the second largest religion and perhaps the fastest growing religion in the world (Nasr, 2009). It is also the newest of the great world religions. Muslims live in all parts of the world, with significant concentrations in the Middle East and Indonesia

Wearing the head scarf, or *hijab,* in Islamic tradition has become controversial in the athletics world. The sports hijab is one answer that allows Muslim women to compete. It is a tight-fitting hood attached to a T-shirt with a high collar and is made of stretchy, fast-drying fabric.
Torsten Blackwood/AFP/Getty Images

(Geertz, 1968). Because Muslims worship one God, Islam is a monotheistic faith. Among the three interconnected faiths of Judaism, Christianity, and Islam, some experts believe that Islam is the most positive and supportive of sexuality (Armstrong, 2001b; Smith, 1991). Within marriage, Islam strongly endorses sexual pleasure as a right of both spouses.

The Quran, which Muslims regard as God's word, is their blueprint for behavior, including sexual behavior. Some Islamic beliefs and practices create gender and sexual differences between men and women (Mahdavi, 1978). In the context of marriage, the Quran specifies that procreation is of central importance. Though men are allowed to have up to four wives, the Quran tells spouses to pleasure each other, and if a man fails in this duty, his wife may divorce him. Also, marriage is the only lawful context for sexual relations between men and women, and a woman can be put to death for adultery or for engaging in premarital sex. The Quran also gives women the right to inherit property from their family (Smith, 1991).

One Islamic tradition that many women follow is to wear a head covering. One type of covering is a *hijab,* which covers the head and neck. Another is a veil that covers the head and face except for the eyes. In some cultures, women wear a long cloak called a *burqa,* which covers them from head to toe, when they go out in public. These styles of dress are part of a thousand-year-old tradition that encompasses gender and sexual issues of faith for Islam, including the public demonstration of a woman's virtue and piety, and before marriage, virginity (Ahmed, 1992; Bloom & Blair, 2002). Today, some Muslim women have moved away from head covering. In Turkey, a secular republic where the people are predominantly Muslim, women have stopped covering their heads. This change reflects broader trends across Islam toward greater equality for women (Mahdavi, 1978).

In some Muslim countries, people can support sexual individuality and also meet their responsibility to uphold societal and Islamic law. In addition to treating women and men equally, Turkey, Morocco, and a few other countries with large Muslim populations tolerate discreetly expressed homosexuality. While it is still frowned upon as a way of life, a tradition of same-sex romantic ideas and sex between younger and older males existed in earlier times (El-Rouayher, 2005). In strict Muslim countries, however, extreme punishments, including execution, can be inflicted on people who violate religious laws, including taboos against homosexuality. Table 2.2 summarizes the views of Islam on sexuality.

Christianity Over the course of 2,000 years, Christianity has emerged from being a tiny sect of Judaism to the largest family of religious denominations (Johnson & Grim, 2013). Christianity, another ancient religion, is embraced throughout many parts of the world, although there are important variations in its practices. In general, Christianity has long reflected deep concerns about sexuality. Genesis, the first book of the Bible, tells about the loss of innocence after eating forbidden fruit and the recognition of nudity as a moment of sexual awakening. Thus, attitudes and beliefs about sexuality have always been part of Christian tradition.

Early on in Christianity (1st to 5th century CE), some sex-negative attitudes developed (Brown, 1988). These attitudes were associated with prayer, sacrifice, and the notion that giving in to sexual pleasure was sinful. One way to understand how these ideas developed is to understand the powerful role that the practice of abstinence played in early Christianity. Christians were expected to remain celibate or virginal for life, to resist sin and temptation. Some men even castrated themselves, cutting off their testes to avoid sinning. These practices, known as *sexual renunciation,* were so widespread that the pope at the time, as head of the Roman Catholic Church, forbade self-castration out of fear that too many men would not reproduce and Christianity would vanish (Greenberg, 1988).

A contemporary image of Adam and Eve, key figures in Christianity.
Alina555/Getty Images

The teachings of Jesus Christ are recorded in the New Testament. Though these books reveal very little about how Christ viewed sexuality in the broad sense, it appears that he was generally tolerant of diverse sexual and gender practices. For example, Christ never specifically mentioned homosexuality, but he tended to defend people he saw as downtrodden or oppressed, such as the poor. He may have departed from some earlier Judaic beliefs of the times, as shown in his defense of a woman accused of adultery (Jansen, 2000). According to some scholars, Christ espoused positive views when it came to women, sexuality, and mutual joy or pleasure in marriage (Phipps, 1996). Later, Saint Augustine (354–430 CE), a philosopher and theologian who had negative views about sex, became influential in Christianity (Soble, 2002). The role of sexuality in Christianity derives in part from Saint Augustine's writing. Even today there are many Christian groups that oppose premarital sex, adultery, homosexuality, and abortion (Regnerus, 2007). However, there are other Christian groups that are pressing for greater tolerance and acceptance of sexuality, including in the United States.

Now let's see how these patterns of sexual culture and religion have played out in the United States from the beginning to today.

WHAT'S ON YOUR MIND?

Q: I was raised in a fairly conservative Christian home. I do not want to have sex until I get married, but my friends all say that I am being foolish because I could marry someone who I don't end up meshing with sexually. Should I wait to have sex, which is what my faith and belief system says, or should I be more open to sex before marriage to make sure I am fulfilled in that part of my life?

ANSWER: If you believe that you should wait to have sex until you get married, that is the decision you should pursue. Because this is your desire, you may also meet and marry someone who shares your belief and respects your decision. About meshing with someone sexually: A couple's sexual life is very much about learning how to please one another. This process is lifelong because we can always work at improving our sexual lives. As long as you openly communicate with your spouse and you are open to suggestions, you will most likely have a very fulfilling sexual life. So, if you want to remain true to your faith and belief system and wait to have sex until you are married, you can expect to have a great sex life as long as you and your spouse both are open to change.

SPIRITUALITY AND SEXUAL BEHAVIOR IN THE UNITED STATES

Christianity has been the dominant religion and a key source of attitudes toward sexuality in the United States from the time Europeans, the Puritans, first settled here.

The Puritans were a Christian sect renowned for having very prudish sexual practices. They established the original colonies of New England. Persecuted in England for trying to "purify" the Church of England, the Puritans fled to America "to worship God as they saw fit" (Prothero, 2007). Although they were a positive influence on colonial economics, literature, and politics, the Puritans are widely believed to have made the United States into a prudish, uptight, and sex-disapproving society (Prothero, 2007). But although they held such beliefs and taboos, they also appeared to have enjoyed mutual sexual pleasure in their intimate relationships and marriages (D'Emilio & Freedman, 1988).

Puritanism, the morally upright and socially strict beliefs and practices of the Puritans, certainly has been a factor in how American society has framed the discussion about such topics as nudity, premarital sex, extramarital sex, virginity, and pornography. But other factors have also played a significant role in keeping U.S. society conservative about sexuality, with sexual cultures that have a variety of taboos that were intolerant of diversity, until the past few years (Regnerus, 2007).

puritanism
The morally upright and socially strict beliefs and practices of the Puritans.

symbolic boundary

Divides people according to their religious beliefs about what are "good" and "bad" sexual behaviors.

Yet there has long been tension in the United States between identifying itself as a Christian country and priding itself on the separation of church and state, with the right to worship any religion freely. The tension is expressed as a **symbolic boundary** that divides people with respect to "good" versus "bad" attitudes and behaviors. The different ways in which different religious groups in the United States regard sex have resulted in a number of symbolic boundaries (Regnerus, 2007). Divorce, for example, was once a widely shared symbolic boundary that was condemned all across Christian churches. If you were divorced in the old days you were a "bad" person. Today divorce is widely tolerated in many sexual cultures and also accepted in many Christian groups, including Roman Catholics, for whom divorce at one time meant being cast out of the church and condemned to hell (Regnerus, 2007).

Another symbolic boundary that continues to divide the culture and Christian groups dramatically is homosexuality. Many Christian groups continue to disapprove or even condemn gay and lesbian people, though U.S. public opinion has increasingly supported same-sex marriage, for example, and it is no longer illegal, as it once was, to engage in adult same-sex relationships. Between 1996 and 2009, public opinion polls showed that youth and young adults in general trended between 11 and 21 percentage points higher than their adult counterparts in approving of same-sex marriage (Marzullo & Herdt, 2011). For example, a 2009 Pew report comparing polls from 2004 and 2008 reveals clear generational difference for support of marriage rights: Youth and young adults ages 18 to 29 provide the highest levels of support at 46% in 2004 and 52% in 2008, although few people age 65 supported it then at 20% and 24%, respectively (Marzullo & Herdt, 2011). In short, people born since 1992 have experienced, and lived through, nothing short of a revolution in attitudes about gays and lesbians, and yet there remain strong symbolic boundaries about this issue among religious groups.

Equally problematic is the fact that today, women can occupy virtually all roles and offices in the United States, but consistent with centuries of sexual history, many Christian groups and other religions continue to prohibit women from being clergy, and this may determine whether people affiliate with those particular religions (Prothero, 2007). Likewise, gays and lesbians serving as clergy have split some Christian groups that do not allow gays, lesbians, or transgender people to join their religion. In short, sexuality divides people of different religious affiliations in the United States (Laumann et al., 1994; Smith, Emerson, Gallagher, Kennedy, & Sikkink, 1998), and defines who is considered to be a person, in terms of gender and sexuality (Herdt, 2009a; Regnerus, 2007).

To understand how sex symbolically divides people, researchers interviewed 3,370 U.S. adolescents age 15 to 19 from different religious groups, including various Christian denominations (Evangelical Protestants, mainline Protestants, African American Protestants, Roman Catholics, and Mormons) and Jews (Regnerus, 2007). The study found that parents vary greatly in how much they talk to their children about sex education, birth control, and sexual morality in general. Some don't discuss sex with their children at all. Parents who attend religious services often or feel that religion is either fairly important or very important are more likely to talk with their children about sexual morality. Of the parents who attend services weekly, 48.2% talk with their children about sex, compared to 28.6% who never attend services. In families who go to services regularly, children are far more likely to pledge abstinence (50%) if parents talk to them a lot about sex and morality. Among different groups, African American Protestant parents (54%) followed by Mormons (52%) are more likely to talk to their children about sexual morality, whereas Roman Catholics (33%) and Jews (17%) are much less likely to have this discussion.

Other attitudes reflect this symbolic boundary, too, but also reveal that attitudes are changing. For example, 15- to 19-year-olds who are less religious or not religious at all are twice as likely to say that they have had same-sex relations as are those who attend religious services more than once a week (Regnerus, 2007). Attitudes about premarital sex in general are often negative, but when people are asked about their views regarding premarital sex between unmarried adults who are in committed relationships, they are less negative (Regnerus, 2007).

Another long-standing symbolic barrier regarding religion and sex in the United States concerns the use of contraception. The issue goes right to the heart of sexual well-being and really has served to divide society and different religious groups over the central question of whether women should have access to reproductive health care and especially contraceptives. Furthermore, the question of who should pay for this health care is of concern to these groups. You can read more about these issues in "Controversies in Sexuality: Women's Right to Birth Control and Access to Reproductive Health Care."

As symbolic boundaries shift, old attitudes and taboos are dropped, and new ones are added. For example, masturbation was once condemned by all faiths in the United States, but now the culture widely accepts this practice, and most religious groups either ignore it or accept it as normal. And some Christian groups now tolerate premarital sex, once totally tabooed. Adultery, however, remains almost universally condemned among all religious groups (Regnerus, 2007).

> **DID YOU KNOW**
>
> Research reveals important differences in attitudes regarding oral sex in the United States. Jewish people are the most positive when it comes to *cunnilingus* (oral stimulation of the female genitals) and probably practice it more frequently than people of other faiths (Laumann et al., 1994). Catholic young men are the most positive about having their girlfriends perform *fellatio* (oral stimulation of the male genitals) (Regnerus, 2007).

THE PURSUIT OF SEXUAL WELL-BEING IN COMMUNITIES OF FAITH

History reveals, as we have seen, very large differences among religions when it comes to their attitudes, beliefs, and practices surrounding human sexuality. Many of the great world religions tend to discuss sexuality only as it pertains to marriage while ignoring many other critical aspects of sexuality that impact people's lives, relationships, and identity. Unfortunately, some religious leaders seem to be more concerned with dogma than with cultivating and supporting sexual literacy in their faith communities. For example, a taboo on premarital sexual intercourse has been a stronghold for many religious communities, yet fewer faith communities openly discuss the human desire and gift of physical intimacy and how single people can nurture sexual intimacy and love in their own lives. However, there are other religious leaders who do believe it is important to approach spirituality, intimate sexual feelings, and love in positive and inclusive ways and to help people integrate their own sexuality and identity into all parts of their lives, including their spirituality or faith, if they have a religious identity.

Today in the United States we can find almost all of the religions of the world practiced among its citizens. Some are extremely conservative and focus on doctrine and a more literal interpretation of scripture or other religious texts. Their faith and morality tend toward the more traditional conservative moral rules of gender, sexuality, and marriage. Our society in recent decades has witnessed huge controversy over how churches and faith communities treat divergent sexual expressions, such as being LGBTQ people, often expressing disapproval, rejection, and even condemnation of diverse nonheterosexual orientations and alternative gender expressions such as transgender people. When these individuals are excluded and treated as inferior, they are further stigmatized in society, and if they also happen to be people of color, they experience a **double stigma**, which means exclusion from their own community as well as the larger society. Stigma can damage people for life by creating a sense of being inferior, leading to stress and shame and permanent inequality, as we will see in later chapters. Sadly, rarely, if ever, do church leaders discuss how to support and enhance the sexual well-being, health, and rights of the members of their church and the stigmatized in society (Klein, 2018).

Today, within the Christian religion, we see major differences in this attitude between more traditional and more progressive denominations and communities of faith, which has split Catholic and Protestant denominations into opposing sides. Progressive communities of faith suggest that sexual well-being and religious faith do not have to be in conflict any longer. Despite these controversies, progressives argue that to continue the exclusionary

double stigma
Experienced by individuals when they are excluded from their own community as well as from the larger society.

CONTROVERSIES in Sexuality

Women's Right to Birth Control and Access to Reproductive Health Care

Over the past 40 years there has been an ongoing controversy in the United States about women's use of contraception that stems from a single question: Can society dictate whether or not women should have access to contraception despite marital status? Actually, as you will discover in later chapters, contraception was illegal from 1873 until the 1960s, as a result of the Comstock Law that banned the distribution of any information about contraception. When oral contraceptives, commonly known as "the pill," became available in the 1960s, many people believed the days of restrictive access to contraception were over.

Today, however, a new, more general controversy reigns, because socially conservative religious groups and some politicians objected to a government mandate requiring all health insurers to cover reproductive health care costs. Some churches, notably the Roman Catholic Church, oppose coverage for contraception out of a conviction that contraceptives promote promiscuity. Oral contraceptives can cost as much as $3,000 a year for a woman whose health plan does not cover it.

The controversy erupted when a Georgetown University law student was called a "slut" and "prostitute" by a nationally prominent radio commentator because she testified in Congress about the need for insurance coverage of contraception. She was inspired to testify by a friend who suffered from polycystic ovary syndrome, a disease that results in an imbalance of a woman's sex hormones and is best treated by taking oral contraceptives. Her insurance company refused to cover the cost of the treatment prescribed by her doctor on grounds that the treatment was really for birth control. Such denials of coverage are not that rare, the law student said.

Should women have access to contraceptives?

Yes:

- Just because a woman is taking birth control doesn't mean she's having sex.
- All women should have the right to sexual pleasure with their intimate partners in the privacy of their bedroom.
- Some medical conditions actually require contraception as a form of treatment, even for young children, which has nothing to do with being promiscuous.
- This just goes to show that some men really don't understand women and their bodies, and they need sexual literacy to bring them up to date.

No:

- Women who take contraceptives are just preparing for having fast sex.
- Society should not have to pay for these women to enjoy their own private sexual adventures.
- Women who choose to have sex should shoulder the responsibility of their own contraception.
- Insurance companies need to make a profit, and coverage of things like this is just not that important.
- I'm sympathetic to women needing contraceptives but just don't feel that this is something the government should pay for. It's a private need, not a public concern.

What's Your Perspective?

1. Should women have legal access to contraceptives?
2. Should insurance companies pay for contraception when medically prescribed?
3. If a woman is taking oral contraceptives, does it mean that she is horny and wants sex?

traditional attitudes promotes deep social and sexual inequality in the United States and serves to deeply divide faith communities.

Some churches, such as the United Church of Christ (UCC), have been dealing with these issues already for years, and they adopted a progressive approach they call "radical inclusion." Radical inclusion means accepting everyone regardless of sexual and gender preferences; color or gender or sexual identity; or country of origin. Bishop Yvette Flunder, an ordained minister of the UCC, founded such a church decades ago in the San Francisco Bay Area.

A more recent and hopeful example and sign of change can be seen from the center of the country, Oklahoma, where a 55-year-old woman has been moved toward acceptance and love for LGBTQ people. In 2017, Sara Cunningham posted on *Facebook* that she would stand in as the

"Mom" at LGBTQ wedding ceremonies (Free, 2019). The message went viral, and eventually she created a movement, "Free Mom Hugs." It all started some years before when Sara's youngest son, Parker Cunningham, came out to her in 2011. With the knowledge of his sexual identity, Sara had to make a decision how she would process her faith, which held to doctrine that conflicted with accepting her son's identity. She chose acceptance and affirmation of her son but did not dismiss her faith. This has led her into a journey in which her faith would ultimately integrate with her decision to affirm her son. Sara's personal and familial journey is not unlike those of many other people who are actively working to integrate their own religious identity with a desire to accept and affirm people regardless of their sexual or gender identity.

There are many ways to express faith and spirituality. People can be spiritual and even deeply religious and still enjoy a satisfying sex life. That enjoyment translates into different things for different people. For some, it is about waiting until marriage to have sex. For others, it is about feeling comfortable and safe enough with their intimate partner to express their sexuality in mutually accepting ways and to affirm each other's dignity. When it comes to our sexual individuality, recognizing the role culture and religion play in sexual well-being is not only critical but can also be affirming of life and loving relationships. Moving toward sexual literacy means understanding that religious faith and practice can not only coexist with sexual desires, behavior, and identity, but faith and religious communities have the capacity to actually further acceptance, sexual pleasure and joy, ultimately contributing to holistic and healthy sexual individuality.

Sara Cunningham, Hero of Hope
Rich Fury/Getty Images

Chapter Review

SUMMARY

Human Sexual Nature in Context

- Human sexuality is the result of our species, our culture, and the diversity of individuals.
- The human species has unique traits of sexuality, and these influence culture.
- The sexual triangle shows how we are like all other people, like some other people, and like no one else.
- Bonobo chimps are thought to be the only species other than humans to have sex for both pleasure and procreation.
- Humans are unique among species by virtue of our large brains, language, and formation of sexual pleasure relationships.

Sex Since the Beginning of Time

- Prehistoric cave art reveals that ancient humans were interested in sex and may have connected it to their spirituality.
- Ancient China, India, and Japan had diverse sexualities that tended to allow greater expression of pleasure, but not as much for women as for men.
- The ancient Greeks viewed sexual pleasure as important, in moderation, and approved of same-sex relationships between older men and young men.
- Sex in the Middle Ages was dominated by religious beliefs and reproductive concerns.
- Colonial and Victorian sexual culture focused on being morally proper and pure, and tolerated a double standard for men and women.

- Gender relations became companionate and more equal in the 20th century.
- Sex in the 20th century became more public and political.

Sexual Cultures and Norms

- Sexual chauvinism, the belief that one's own sexual culture is superior to others, is a barrier to sexual well-being around the world.
- There is a continuum of sex-approving and sex-disapproving cultures around the world.
- Sexual unlearning means changing something we learned in the past in order to change or grow sexually.

Sexuality and the Great World Religions

- The five great world religions are Hinduism, Buddhism, Judaism, Islam, and Christianity.
- The great world religions have defined civilization and sexual norms for centuries.
- For some people, religion is more influential than culture in their view of sexuality.
- There are significant similarities and differences in the teachings of the great world religions regarding sexuality.

Spirituality and Sexual Behavior in the United States

- Sex is a symbolic barrier that separates people according to their sexual attitudes and behaviors.
- The United States continues to be highly religious as a society even as it struggles to accept sexual and gender diversity in the context of religious faith.

The Pursuit of Sexual Well-Being in Communities of Faith

- Faith communities may support or undermine sexual literacy.
- Radical inclusion means acceptance of people's gender identity and sexuality into their religion.
- One can be spiritual or religious and still be a sexual person.

What's Your Position?

1. **How do you define your own human sexual nature?**
   - What has sexuality meant in your development?

2. **What has your culture taught you about sex?**
   - Is your culture more sex-approving or sex-disapproving?

3. **How have your beliefs about faith influenced your sexual well-being?**
   - Is there a symbolic boundary regarding sex in your faith?

Design elements: Controversies in Sexuality: HBRH/Shutterstock; Research and Sexual Well Being: verity jane smith/Getty Images; Healthy Sexuality: Sergey Furtaev/Shutterstock; Communication Matters: PeopleImages/Getty Images; Know Yourself: Plush Studios/Blend Images LLC; What's Your Position: Luis Molinero/Shutterstock; Healthy Sexuality: A. Minde/PhotoAlto; Did You Know icon: McGraw-Hill Education; Page corner icon: McGraw-Hill Education.

Sexuality, Media, and the Internet

3

Oleksiy Maksymenko Photography/Alamy Stock Photo

Sex, Media, and Pop Culture
- Describe how the media can blur the boundary between private and shared sexual imagery.
- Examine how diverse media have influenced sexual norms and expression.

The Internet and Sexual Literacy
- Explain the role that the Internet has played in revolutionizing human society and how it impacts our social connection to one another.
- Describe norms and boundaries as they occur online.
- Explain how technological advancement has altered the frequency and methods of communication between people.

Online Sexual Contexts
- Explain how the Internet allows for sexual self-exploration and has changed the ways in which people interact with their sexuality online.
- Explain the real-world consequences of online romance, hooking up, and sex.

Adult Sexual Content
- Describe how pornography has changed the role of media in our personal sexual lives.
- Describe the process of pornification and its effect on sexual conduct on- and offline.

Online Communities, Rights, and Sexual Well-Being
- Explain how sexual expression online may contribute to people's sexual well-being.

• Learning
• Objectives

Developing Your Position

1. How has the media impacted your attitudes about sexuality, including the way you express your desires, romance, dating, and sex?
2. What aspects of your individual sexuality, including sexual images or photos, would you make public on the web?
3. Why would you or wouldn't you choose to present an identity that is true and authentic online when expressing your sexuality?

Self, Society, and Culture: Expanding Your Boundaries Online

Online connectivity is revolutionizing people's sexual expression, love, and relationships. Gil learned from a close friend and her husband that their 18-year-old son is having an online sexual relationship with his same-aged girlfriend from the United States who is studying abroad. He's in the United States right now and she's in Asia. They connect daily through Skype and a webcam. They have sexual interactions online by revealing their bodies and masturbating so the other can see as they talk erotically with each other. Gil's friends' son is pretty open with his family and friends about having online sex. At first it shocked his parents, but they are sexually progressive in terms of their values and socialization. They are proud of their son and want the young couple to stay connected during this time apart. Yet they are not entirely comfortable about this kind of sexual expression because they had never done anything like it and are unsure how the norms from the virtual world apply to this situation. The young couple, however, view their real-time online sex and this segment of their relationship as perfectly normal.

How have the Internet and other media affected your sexuality? In their various forms, the media play a large role in how society regards and handles sexuality. This chapter explores the impact of the media on sexuality, including the pleasures and pitfalls of sexual expression online.

SEX, MEDIA, AND POP CULTURE

One of the most powerful tools that we humans have in adapting to the global world today is the means to communicate to a large number of people at one time: the media. Whether print, music, movies, television, radio, cell phone, or the Internet, all media play a large role in how society regards and handles sexuality. According to the PEW Foundation (2018), 78% of Americans in their 20s use Snapchat, many of them multiple times per day. We are still just learning the potential impacts that social media and applications have on our lives and our journey towards sexual literacy. In this section we consider the historic role of media in shaping pop culture and how media contribute to the way we view sexuality. Figure 3.1 provides a historical overview of sex and the media.

Sex in Pop Culture

As discussed in Chapter 2, people have been communicating and learning about sexuality through stories, culture, and art for thousands of years. But in the 20th century, media and globalization expanded communications rapidly to a mass market, through print, then radio and television, movies and music, and most recently, the Internet and handheld portable phones or other devices. Words such as "selfie" have become literal new additions to dictionaries, and social media enables people to broadcast their thoughts, ideas, and personal photographs to billions of people around the world. The content of this media became more sexual, too. As access to the Internet has spread around the world, pop culture and social networking have created a global media market that is sexually savvy.

Sexual content, as expressed in the media, has changed our culture in four fundamental ways: (1) private sexual imagery has become public, (2) more explicit sexual images are being shared in public, (3) explicit sex talk has become acceptable in diverse conversations, and (4) all this sex in pop culture has transformed public attitudes about sexuality in society as a whole. Let's consider each change.

1. Private sexual imagery has become public. The media changed what was once very private and hidden sexually into something more public and visible. One of the earliest examples is the "personal" ad or column that may date from as early as the 18th century but became more widespread in the 1920s (Cocks, 2009). Mass production of pornography in the form of *Playboy* magazine began in 1953, as explained later, but personal sexual messages, such as ads that sought companionship, sex, or love, became much more common after the rise of the Internet. Generally, the media have published more information about sex, especially about the sex lives of famous people. Consider, for example, the media attention given to the sexual antics of politicians (to be studied later), movie stars, and rock stars, such as the naked photos of Justin Bieber during a vacation, or Donald Trump's multiple sex scandals that rose to attention in 2016, and in 2018, the royal wedding of Prince Harry and Meghan Markle in Great Britain. In reality, due to social media, nude photos of celebrities and details about their private sexual lives, either leaked or published with permission, have become a medium of public sexual consumption in a very different way than they used to be.

Sex and the City changed the way people thought about sex in pop culture.
HBO FILMS/HOME BOX OFFICE/NEW LINE CINEMA/VILLAGE ROADSHOW/Album/Alamy Stock Photo

2. More explicit sexual images are being shared in public. Advertisers have long used sexual imagery to sell products. Perhaps the first success was a soap jingle dreamed up by a woman in 1911 to promote the beauty product with the words: "The skin you like to touch." Personal ads became a discreet way for people to connect soon after World War I, when gay men, single women, servicemen, and others who were unable to directly seek sexual and romantic partners used newspaper ads for sexual expression (Cocks, 2009). But it was "swingers," especially in the 1960s, seeking others to join a couple in sex, that greatly expanded this medium to hook up sexually. Meanwhile, Madison Avenue began to use sex to sell everything from makeup and swimsuits to new cars, and the famous Marlboro "cowboy"—a sex symbol in his own right—was born, to sell cigarettes.

Today sexual imagery is explicit and far more "in your face" than before. Sexual images of bodies and genitals, of people making love, of diverse forms of sexual expression, and of people in scant underwear are everywhere—in magazines, on billboards, on television, and online—selling products that range from dental floss to luxury vacations. Online pornography is another source of public sexual images. Is it any wonder that advertisers use explicit sexual imagery to sell products that appeal to an individual's most intimate needs, desires, and vanity?

3. Explicit sex talk has become acceptable in diverse conversations. Tabloids such as the *National Enquirer* and magazines such as *Vanity Fair*, cable television, online venues such as

History of Sexuality in Media

35,000 BCE
Cave paintings and Venus statues depict first prehistoric images of human sexuality

1895
Oscar Wilde is tried in London for sodomy, and newspapers carry the story worldwide

1932
Bessie Smith is sex symbol of soul

1940
Pinup girls popular during World War II

1948
Alfred Kinsey publishes *Sexuality in the Human Male*, the first large survey study of sexual behavior in the United States

79 CE
Roman graffiti

1895–1915
Gibson Girls used in advertising feminine beauty

1938
Sinatra is sex symbol for teenage girls

1942
Planned Parenthood founded

Figure **3.1**
Historical overview of sex and the media

DID YOU KNOW

Sex sells products, and has for a hundred years in the United States. From lingerie and coffee to cigarettes and toilet paper, studies have shown that nothing sells like sex (Reichert, 2002). The use of sexuality to market and sell products to consumers is called **sexual consumerism**. One of the perks of being a celebrity is the ability to sell products through sexual consumerism.

sexual consumerism
The use of sexuality to market and sell products to consumers.

YouTube, and other social media exploit romantic and sexual images, celebrity romances, and sexual scandals by mainstreaming even very raw sex talk to diverse audiences as never before. What was once whispered about sex is now shouted in widely acceptable media, including talk shows on radio and television, which have made sex a regular topic of conversation (Gamson, 1998). Viewers of reality shows such as *The Bachelor* wait with intense curiosity to see whether couples will opt to take advantage of the "dream suite" and engage in sexual behavior behind somewhat closed doors.

4. **Sex in pop culture has transformed public attitudes about sexuality in society as a whole.** After World War II and the advent of mass television, sex became increasingly common in the public content of TV shows and what was expected of the movies and other media. Sex became an effective marketing tool used to change popular tastes, fashions, and attitudes, especially through television (Reichert, 2002). New media campaigns related to HIV and safer sex became so explicitly sexual that, in the 1980s and 1990s, politicians condemned some of them (Herdt, 2009a). In politics, just the hint of a sex scandal can still threaten the career of a public figure, from the local mayor to the president of the United States, yet in so many circumstances sex has indeed factored into political campaigns. Consider, for example, the notion of a presidential candidate or politician being a sex symbol, from the image of John F. Kennedy to today's Alexandria Ocasio-Cortez. The huge amount of media attention to these issues sometimes increases public awareness of sexual literacy, as when the sex scandal involving then-President Bill Clinton and a White House intern in the 1990s made *oral sex* a household term (Herdt, 2009a). Consider, also, how the #Me-Too

1953 Alfred Kinsey publishes *Sexuality in the Human Female*, causing a firestorm of media reaction

1956 Elvis appears on TV, but is censored from the waist down

1962 SIECUS founded

1995 Online adult sexual entertainment begins

2004 Facebook launched

1960 1970 1990 2000 2005

1953 Hugh Hefner publishes first issue of *Playboy*

1950–1970 TV sitcoms are censored for sexual and intimate scenes

1973 American Psychiatric Association declassifies homosexuality as a disease

1991 Transgender online movement begins

1998 Clinton impeachment scandal tests new norms of sexuality in the United States

2004 Online dating sites begin

2006 Twitter launched

Movement was sparked and went instantly viral, illustrating how quickly public discourse on social media platforms such as Twitter, Instagram, and Facebook can have incredible impacts within minutes.

Shared Sexual Images and Media

As we have seen, human nature is closely linked to learned culture and language. Sexual culture and communication in all societies involve **shared sexual imagery,** whether real or imagined, visual or auditory, the content of which contains explicit or hidden sexual messages. As we saw in Chapter 2, such images can be ancient, and they have the power to shape how individuals behave in their own cultures. In traditional cultures, for example, shared sexual imagery may be communicated through ritual or ceremony, or myth and folktales, whereas in complex modern societies it may flow from pop culture, art, mass social media, and the Internet (Altman, 2001; Becker, 1973; Boellstorff, 2008; Levi-Strauss, 1971; Smith, 1991).

Shared sexual images can range from the sublime to the ridiculous, as when Freud said that a cigar could represent a penis, or when Bill Clinton used a cigar tube to sexually tease his White House intern in the affair that brought the nation to a halt. They can be funny, sarcastic, angry, political, and even religious—all at the same time. Consider, for example, how sexual images may be purely symbolic, like the American flag, or implicitly sexual, such as Michelangelo's iconic statue *David,* or even blatantly sexual, such as penis and vagina symbols that occur widely in many cultures, as we saw in Chapter 2. However, with the advent of movies in the early 20th century, the media have included increasingly explicit sex symbols, beginning with Marilyn Monroe and Cary Grant up to Angelina Jolie and Channing Tatum.

shared sexual imagery Content that contains explicit or hidden sexual messages, whether real or imagined, visual or auditory.

History of Sexuality in Media (continued)

2011
Snapchat launches and revolutionizes the "selfie" and photos that are shared and then automatically deleted

2015   2020

2017
The #Me-Too Movement goes viral as a hashtag on social media and begins a massive cultural shift in discourse around sexual harassment and abuse

2012
Tinder launches, and the world begins to find partners by "swiping"

Alfredo e Pio Foglia/Mondadori Portfolio/age fotostock; Ingram Publishing; Popperfoto/Getty Images; Everett Collection/Alamy Stock Photo; David Crausby/Alamy Stock Photo; Library of Congress [LC-USZ6-2067]; Comstock/Stockbyte/Getty Images; Library of Congress [LC-USZ62-107700]; PhotoEdit/Alamy Stock Photo; tanuha2001/Shutterstock

---

Gibson Girls (left) were the standard of feminine beauty from about 1895 to 1915. Pinup girls (right) were the female sex symbols during World War II. Images like these promoted new public talk about sex.
(*left*) Popperfoto/Getty Images; (*right*) Bettmann/Getty Images

Sex symbols also include sports celebrities and rock stars from Elvis to Justin Bieber, who has thousands of girls screaming his name at his concerts (Weisman, 2012).

In the past hundred years, the media have helped to break down taboos and have created new shared visual imagery. Whether it pertains to 20th-century thrillers and spy icons such as James Bond, new future worlds like those in *Star Wars,* cuddly aliens (E.T.), or young wizards (Harry Potter), the visual media have combined adventure with love and sex. Some of the visual images from early media have also been transformed from something very negative to something positive, as in certain movies about vampires. Based on ancient superstitions about death, vampires were considered to be horrific figures, and have been a subject of popular fiction since the late 19th century. Now, however, vampires have come to symbolize shared sexual and romantic fantasies.

Bram Stoker's novel *Dracula* was published in 1897. Since then, the story has been made into at least 70 films and plays, some of them sexual, some funny or monstrous. Today in the United States, vampires are often portrayed as beautiful, intelligent, protective, loyal, wealthy, wise, and extremely erotic—generally positive traits. Edward, the vampire of the *Twilight* series, has these characteristics, and many fans, especially teenage females, perceive him to be a nearly "perfect" man because of his imagined masculinity. In a twist on the original theme of vampires being corpses, Edward can have sex, orgasms, and children. In some ways, Edward and other modern vampires are perfect sexual creatures with immortal sexual well-being. These shared vampire images possess what many people wish for in a partner: ageless, sexy, strong bodies; manly and womanly perfection; wealth, beauty, intelligence, wisdom, and virginity—and possibly immortality. But they are not real, and this raises the question of how sexual culture can influence people's attitudes.

Images such as these have become commonplace in public spaces to sell products or associate sexuality with various companies.
CHROMORANGE/Ralph Peters/Alamy Stock Photo

Sexual Images and Advertising

It should not be a surprise that human sexuality is seen as one of the most potent tools of advertising. For years, sexuality and sexual appeal has been used to sell everything from tennis shoes to cars. Work in sexology, social psychology, and even medicine confirms that sexual information elicits a sexual response. So when advertisers use sexual imagery in their campaigns, they are doing so because they understand that sexual imagery or content has the potential to produce very strong physiological reactions, such as changes in heart rate, pupil dilation, and sweating, in addition to eliciting emotional reactions and even imaginative ones where people are able to fantasize or imagine themselves in the narrative being presented to them (Reicher, 2018). In other words, it is clear that viewers of sexually focused advertising tend to be favorably energized by sexual information.

Popular Music and Sexual Attitudes

Of all the media in pop culture that may truly transform sexual attitudes, none is more potentially powerful, holistic, and personal than popular music. Music has the impact, as does touch and smell, to arouse deep feelings and desires—even years later. Music can bring about these feelings in ceremonies and rituals that mark birth, death, and other great transformative events from Africa and Asia to the United States and Europe (Geertz, 1973; Levi-Strauss, 1971). It can tap into our deepest expressions of shared experience—the attitudes, emotions, identities, and passions for the people we are attracted to and/or love. It is the auditory way in which a culture fashions what is beautiful or ugly and significant of sexual love. In the United States, sex and love have been the most enduring themes of popular music and pop culture since the modern period, as described in Chapter 2.

Many of us associate specific songs with a particular time in life, such as when we were falling in love, enjoying an intense sexual relationship, getting to know a special someone, or possibly breaking up with someone. Music erases the boundary between what is outside and public in the culture and what is private and inside the individual. A song can evoke raw and deep emotional reactions, making us happy or sad. We often associate that mood with someone we like or love or lost, and it may leave a lasting impression on our memory. Music is so entwined with sex that pop singers themselves become sex symbols. From Sinatra to Elvis to

Know Yourself

Musical Genres and Sex Symbols

Music often has romantic and sexual associations for people. Consider how music from the following musical genres might remind people about romance and sex. Note that some of the singers listed either were or are sex symbols in the United States.

Blues	Bessie Smith 1920–1930s
Big Band	Frank Sinatra 1930–1940s
Jukebox	Johnson Sisters 1940s (wartime)
Samba/Chic	Carmen Miranda 1940–1950s
Jazz	Miles Davis 1950s
Rock and Roll	Elvis Presley 1950–1970s
Pop	The Beatles 1960–1970s; NKOTB 1980s, 2000s; NSync 1990s; Katy Perry 2000s; Justin Bieber 2000s–2010s
Swing/Classic	Frank Sinatra 1960–1970s
Disco/Soul	Gloria Gaynor 1970–1980s
Soul	Marvin Gaye 1970s
Early Country	Patsy Cline 1950–1960s; Johnny Cash 1950–2000s
Rap	Eminem 1990s; Wiz Kalifa 2012
R&B	Rhianna 2000s; SoMo 2018
New Country	Carrie Underwood 2000s; Taylor Swift 2000s–2010s
Adult Rock	Lady Gaga 2011

Now think about how your favorite music links to your own sexuality.

- Is there one song that blends your desires, identity, and sexual behavior together?
- How does your current choice of music relate to your own sexuality?
- Has this music ever put you into a romantic mood?
- Have you ever gotten sexual to the sound of this music?
- Do these lyrics come back to you when you are being intimate with someone?
- Do you associate a particular song with someone you care for deeply, perhaps from when you first met?
- Have you wanted someone to share a song that is dear to your heart?
- Do the songs you love communicate what you feel or do they just provide you with a ready-made line or lyric when you need it?

Whatever your answers to these questions, music can play a large role in how we experience sexuality.

Lady Gaga, pop singers not only define some of the key trends of appearance and behaviors but also set the standards of what we consider sexy, beautiful or handsome, and attractive. Many of these celebrities make the most of their mass appeal to sell products.

A tour of popular music in the United States, from the 1920s when pop music became more accessible through records and radio to become a major theme of culture to the present, reveals changing trends in sexual passion along with frustrations in the search for sexual individuality. The icons of each musical era projected sex appeal in their performances. For example, in the 1940s, Frank Sinatra's crooning regularly caused huge crowds of teenage girls to faint. The effect was quite different as the culture moved into the sexual revolution of the 1960s and beyond. From Elvis and the Beatles, to Mick Jagger of the Rolling Stones, Madonna, Jennifer Lopez, Lady Gaga, Kanye West, Justin Bieber, and Wiz Kalifa, singers and musicians have forged new sexual attitudes and erased the line between real sexual love and fantasy for many fans. This happens through the creation of "fan clubs," websites dedicated to these celebrities and their sexual and romantic lives, where the stars sell their personal products, promote books, meet fans, appear in concerts, and perform in highly suggestive sexual ways (as Madonna has done numerous times). You can read more about these issues and how you feel about them in your own life in "Know Yourself: Musical Genres and Sex Symbols." Each musical genre is associated with musicians who became sex symbols in their own right.

An examination of musical history shows us that popular music has become more explicitly sexual as time marches forward (Montemayor, 2019). The increase in overt sexuality has been almost entirely attributed to the rise of hip-hop and rap music, which has a solid tradition of including more explicit sexual themes and lyrics not as commonly found in other types of music (Hall, West, & Hills, 2012). The availability of music videos has also increased exponentially with the rise in consumption of streaming services such as YouTube and iTunes. Content analysis shows that implied sexual themes and even overt sexual content are now staples of music videos (Vandenbosch, Vervloessem, & Eggermont, 2013).

Music may influence people's sexual well-being in a variety of ways, including how they feel about their own body, their sexual feelings, and an intimate partner. But visual imagery like movies and television have also come to have great influence on sexuality.

From Reality TV to Homemade Video

As media transformed people's sexual attitudes and their own sexual individuality, the images also changed. From generalized shared and idealized imagery in the movies, films began to encroach on private sexual behavior, with an increased tendency to challenge the sexual norms of each generation. Movies and then television have always depicted idealized versions of romance and sex, desire and pleasure, and life itself. At first, sex could only be hinted at in films, and even deep kissing was considered highly risky; nudity was taboo. Because people realized the influence movies could have on sexuality, they started censoring and rating films in 1934. Censors often read scripts and barred steamy romantic scenes, as well as imagery of couples seen simply sharing a bed.

Classic movies such as *Gone with the Wind* (1939), *Casablanca* (1942), and *The Graduate* (1967) have shattered the shared idealized images by depicting new notions of love, sex, and romance (Table 3.1). Some films explicitly challenged taboos about homosexuality

Table 3.1 Groundbreaking movies in shared sexual imagery

MOVIE	YEAR	HOW IT BROKE NEW GROUND
Gone with the Wind	1939	Depiction of Southernism, Blacks and Whites, and sexual seduction
Casablanca	1942	Extramarital affair challenged norms
The King and I	1956	Sexual dominance and interracial issues
Some Like It Hot	1959	Sexual flirting, prostitution, cross-dressing, and homosexuality
Breakfast at Tiffany's	1961	Sexual passions, dancing, and love-making
My Fair Lady	1964	Intergenerational romance and mixing social classes
Grease	1978	New images of sexual love in dance and film
Raiders of the Lost Ark	1981	Steamy sex scenes between unmarried singles
Titanic	1997	Soaring passions and shipboard romance
Avatar	2009	Sexual passion of animated characters/human and otherworldly
Fifty Shades of Grey Trilogy	2015–2018	A film series created from the works of EL James that documents a volatile couple who engages in more extreme sexual variations.

(*Brokeback Mountain,* 2005) and marriage (*The Kids Are All Right,* 2010), for example. *Fifty Shades of Grey* (2015), a trio of books written by EL James, were made into movies and opened up the world of BDSM to millions of people who never really exposed themselves to these sexual behaviors.

TV shows made between 1950 and 1970 were subject to heavy censorship because of the rigid sexual and gender norms of the times, as well as other social and cultural taboos. For example, when Elvis Presley first appeared on *The Ed Sullivan Show* in 1956, the cameras were allowed to film him only from the waist up, because the way he swiveled his hips was considered highly sexual!

Even in TV sitcoms in the 1950s and 1960s, network censors sanitized sexuality. Masculinity and femininity were highly stereotyped on television as well, due to strict gender and sexual norms, when men were thought of as "warriors" and women as mothers and wives (Corber, 1997; Levine, 2007). The gender roles portrayed on television were very traditional: wives were perfect stay-at-home, beautiful moms; husbands were out-in-the-rough-business-world dads. Sitcoms such as *I Love Lucy, The Dick Van Dyke Show,* and *Father Knows Best* focused on happily married heterosexual couples. They did not explicitly mention sexual love, and the couples had separate beds to avoid any hint of sex in the bedroom. By the 1970s and on, television had evolved to include explicit discussion of premarital sex, extramarital affairs, recreational sex, out of wedlock birth, gay relationships, and other themes. Breakthrough sitcoms focused on new sexual themes previously regarded as private: in *Three's Company* (1974-1984), *Seinfeld* (1989-1998), *Friends* (1994-2004), *Sex and the City* (1998-2004), and *Modern Family* (2009-2020), the great diversity of sexual lives, attitudes, behaviors, and relationships became a regular part of television viewing and impacted all the conversation that results from investing our time into the shows and story lines we view.

Reality TV today has increased the raw imagery with real people who are not actors and real-life situations that involve all kinds of arrangements that challenge sexual norms, such as two guys sharing a girlfriend or a mother sharing a boyfriend with her daughter. Cable television has also broken taboos, such as a restriction on showing genitals, and it has blurred the line between shared imagery of sex and pornography. Cable porn channels show raw sex. Other programs, including some on MTV, have been a huge force for change, largely in a positive way, because they promote sexuality education and healthy sexuality. Physician Drew Pinsky's show, *Sex—with Mom and Dad,* helped a wide audience of teens negotiate the pleasures and dangers of their sexuality while still living at home with their parents. And the popular Netflix series *Thirteen Reasons Why* features story lines about previously tabooed sexual topics, including high school sex, both consensual and rape, same-sex desire, sexual bullying, and suicide.

Such shows provide new shared images about bodies, romance, attraction, and dating for this age group. But all these images, however transformative, cannot match the impact of the Internet on sexuality. By allowing people to upload personal images and home videos to social media websites such as YouTube, Snapchat, TikTok, and Facebook, the Internet has virtually erased the boundary between public and private.

THE INTERNET AND SEXUAL LITERACY

The Internet is one of the greatest advances in media technology because it enables us to learn, teach, enrich, connect, and extend ourselves directly and emotionally with others on a global scale, anytime, anywhere. It began with research on artificial intelligence decades ago and transformed our society through the "Age of Information" (Castells, 2001). Evolving from simple e-mail into a radical new form of social connection, online communications enable many people to keep up with news, politics, family, friends, and cultural developments. For example, astute political observers believe that President Obama's 2008 campaign demonstrated the power of democracy and ordinary people's work on the Internet in winning elections and forging online social movements. Even in the presidential election of Donald Trump in 2016, we saw incredible ways in which people all around the world had a major impact on campaigns and the election process in the United States.

Young people who have never known life without computers have embraced the Internet and social media to connect with existing friends and make new ones (Figure 3.2). Approximately, 88% of teenagers in the United States between the ages of 13 and 17 have access to a desktop or laptop computer. Youths between the ages of 12 and 17 spend an average of almost 7 hours a month accessing the Internet via *computer*. During 2017, it was found that online users aged 18–24 spent an average of nearly 25 hours online via PC per month (Pew Foundation, 2018). These numbers do not even reflect access to online content via smartphone. Estimates of smartphone ownership suggest that over 90% of individuals aged 12–24 own at least one smartphone and use it at least once per month (eMarketer, 2016). It has been reported that nearly 98% of young adults report regular and daily use of at least one social media platform in 2016 (Villanti et al., 2017). YouTube, Instagram, and Snapchat have grown to become regular outlets for young people to post photos, document snippets of their lives, and vlog (video blog) about every topic imaginable from makeup and fashion to simply talking about the day's activities (Yockey, King, Vidourek, Burbage, & Merianos, 2019) (Figure 3.3).

Due to the public nature of these websites, people can express their opinions openly on many intimate subjects, including things we once discussed with only our family or a few friends (Hine, 2000). These opinions and reactions are public and are open to response, but because of the openness of the Internet, it's easy for people to misrepresent themselves. This makes it our responsibility to scrutinize anything we read on the Internet, especially about sex.

Right now, how would you define your own sexual individuality online? Recall from Chapter 2 that sexual individuality refers to a person's unique sexual personality, desires, and expressions. Has the Internet changed your sexual boundaries? Before moving on to the larger discussion of sexuality and the Internet, take a few minutes to consider your own sexual individuality and boundaries in "Know Yourself: How Personal Are You Willing to Get Online?"

Although we need to scrutinize everything we find on the Internet, we can use it in many positive ways. The Internet may actually provide a safer, more neutral area for people to try things out than in their actual communities (Boyd, 2008; Fox & Ralston, 2016; Pascoe, 2011; Polen-Petit, 2016). For example, the Internet allows individuals to locate others who share the same sexual desires, thus allowing them to avoid local laws and rules that prevent certain forms of sexual expression and to create, among other things, more sexual communities online. LGBTQ youth, for example, who live in communities where it may be difficult to find people with similar identities, can form community in online spaces, which allows them to be known in ways that may be unsafe within the community in which they live (Polen-Petit, 2016). In addition, the Internet has definitely expanded

DID YOU KNOW

A national survey by Pew Research Center conducted in 2015 among 2,001 adults found that 12% of American adults had ever used an online dating site (up from 13% in 2013). In addition, nearly 10% of American adults used a dating app on their cell phone. This growth has been highest for those who have not historically used online dating sites and apps in previous years—the youngest adults, as well as those in their late 50s and early 60s. Today, 27% of 18- to 24-year-olds report having used online dating, triple the amount of people in this age group reported in the two years prior.

Source: Smith, A. (2016). 15% of American adults have used online dating sites or mobile dating apps. Retrieved October 6, 2016, from: http://www.pewinternet.org/2016/02/11/15-percent-of-american-adults-have-used-online-dating-sites-or-mobile-dating-apps/.

Teenagers who have a smartphone and use it at least one a month

92.9% of 12- to 17-year-olds
99.4% of 18- to 24-year-olds

Figure **3.2**

Percent of teenagers with smartphones.

DGLimages/Shutterstock

Figure 3.3
Social networks most frequently used by U.S. teenagers and young adults.

Social Networks Most Frequently Used by Teenagers:
- Snapchat 35%
- YouTube 32%
- Instagram 15%
- Facebook 10%
- Twitter 3%
- None of the above 3%
- Reddit 1%
- Tumblr 1%

Social Networks Most Frequently Used by those 18+ (Mobile reach):
- Facebook 90.6%
- Instagram 62.8%
- Facebook Messenger 59.6%
- Twitter 37.7%
- Pinterest 31.3%
- Snapchat 28%
- Reddit 18%
- Tumblr 12.5%
- WhatsApp 11.2%
- Google Hangouts 8.2%
- GroupMe 5.8%
- Discord 5.2%
- Kik 4.5%
- Skype 4.2%
- Periscope 2.5%

virtual sex
Sexual activity through online communication.

ordinary people's access to the knowledge, skills, and behaviors that lead to healthy sexuality (Pascoe, 2011). For example, a study by the Kaiser Foundation (2009) discovered that the elderly in the United States are comfortable obtaining health information through the Internet.

The Internet has become a practical social tool in a time when so many pressures compete for our attention. As mentioned previously, individuals who have little social support in their local communities for expressing variations in sexual attraction may find identity, support, and sexual relationships online. The Internet allows millions of people who participate in following current events and celebrity news via Twitter, or playing online interactive games, to sometimes become involved sexually. These games encourage exploration and experimentation because they allow people to create virtual or "pretend" identities different from what they have in everyday life. Another positive way to use the Internet is to learn how to protect ourselves both online and in the real world (Levine, 1998). Experts believe that in terms of society and sexuality, the Internet has both positive and negative features that create new opportunities (Boyd, 2014; DiMaggio, Hargittai, Celeste, & Shafer, 2004; Gray & Klein, 2006). In terms of sexuality, it has opened a whole new chapter: a world of online dating, virtual relationships, virtual love, **virtual sex**, and that most radical of ideas, a virtual human (Boellstorff, 2008; Gershon, 2010; Giddons, 1992; Lenhart, Madden, & Hitlin, 2005). As the opening story of this chapter relates, people are able to connect online to maintain love and closeness across long distances, which has deepened and enriched our communication. It has also created worldwide instant access to pornography, accelerating the trend toward the infusion of pornography into pop culture. Perhaps this is why research reveals that people are still trying to figure out what role the Internet plays in their sexual relationships and well-being (Pascoe, 2011).

Know Yourself

How Personal Are You Willing to Get Online?

Use this scale to rate how you feel you would express yourself for each question:

1. Very unlikely
2. Somewhat unlikely
3. Unsure
4. Somewhat likely
5. Very likely

1. You will post the news of a breakup with your intimate partner on Facebook, Instagram, or Snapchat.
2. You will discuss your friends' sexual behaviors and relationships online.
3. You will review a movie that has sexually explicit information and attach your name to it.
4. You will post graphic photos of yourself online.
5. You will post your actual birth date online.
6. You will post a photo of yourself kissing your current romantic partner online.
7. You will go out on a date with someone you met online.
8. You will reveal your personal sexual feelings online.
9. You will reveal religious or spiritual feelings online.
10. You will chat or text about your parents and post this online.
11. You will talk about your use of contraceptives or condoms online.
12. You will discuss the sexual features and attraction of TV characters online.
13. You will actually share your sexual fantasies with people online.
14. You will discuss your sexual health online.
15. You will talk about masturbating online.
16. You will criticize other people's Facebook pages for their sexual content.
17. You will consider marrying someone you would meet online.
18. You will check out the background of someone who connects to you online.
19. You will travel to another country to meet someone sexually you have been hooking up with online.
20. You will try new sexual techniques in your relationship you saw online.

Score

Over 40: You are very willing to reveal your personal self online, without boundaries.

31–40: You are willing and are fairly comfortable with revealing your personal self online.

26–30: You have set boundaries on how much of yourself you will reveal online.

20–25: You are very personal and have set tight boundaries on how much you are willing to express about yourself online.

Now, considering how you answered these questions, would you change how much of your intimate life you might be willing to publicize online?

microcelebrities
A term coined by Theresa Senft to describe Internet users who gain a cult or mainstream following online.

strange familiarity
People's ability to feel like they know someone intimately without the other person knowing who they are.

social media
A collective term referring to online communication channels devoted to user-based input, interaction, collaboration, and sharing of content.

social networking sites (SNSs)
Sites that allow people to form online relationships, for business and pleasure, creating networks that encompass friends and sexual and romantic interests.

Of course, abuses occur every day on the Internet. Celebrities, politicians, and everyday people get caught violating sexual norms and rules on the Internet. Other negative influences, including cyberbullying, fake information, and online predators, suggest that sexual illiteracy is widespread on the Internet. These issues join the continuing controversy about whether live, adult sexual entertainment that goes further than commercial pornography should be so easily accessible online. These pitfalls aside, the Internet is reshaping sexual individuality (Holloway & Valentine, 2003; Livingstone, 2002; Thurlow & McKay, 2003; Turkle, 1996; Yockey et al., 2019).

Snapchat, Facebook, YouTube, and Sexting

The Internet has also become the single largest force for sexual literacy in young people's lives (Levine, 2011; Pascoe, 2011). Let's review the evidence that we currently have and you can decide how the Internet revolution has influenced your own sexuality and sexual well-being.

YouTube launched in 2005 and currently houses millions of videos. If one wants to watch Barack Obama's acceptance speech after he won the 2008 presidential election, or if you want to watch a clip from the television show *Friends*, you will more than likely be able to find anything you are seeking on YouTube. There is also a whole genre of **microcelebrities** who make a living by creating videos and posting them online on sites such as YouTube (Johnston, 2017). These microcelebrities discuss everything from makeup (consider James Charles) to food preparation, and now they are even becoming famous for the creation and dissemination of sexual education content. Laci Green, for example, began posting videos on YouTube in 2010 on her channel titled *Sex Plus*, which proudly boasts over 1.4 million subscribers. She is young and entertaining, while also communicating valuable educational content such as how people with vaginas can reach orgasm on their own or with others. It appears that the reason these microcelebrities and their YouTube channels are so effective in garnering attention and communicating a message is because of a social concept called **strange familiarity** (Senft, 2013). This term refers to people's ability to feel like they know someone intimately without the other person knowing who they are (Senft, 2013). The fact that viewers can directly respond to YouTube figures through comments and then also follow them on other platforms such as Instagram or Facebook increases the felt-familiarity that a viewer has with a figure, creating an illusion of a reciprocal relationship or face-to-face friendship (Boyd, 2008). For educational channels, this kind of personal engagement has the effect of being able to fully integrate informative content into their viewers' lives (Johnston, 2017). The field of sexual research and sexual health are both coming to acknowledge the critical role these people take on in the sexual education of young people (Johnston, 2017).

Social media is a collective term referring to online communication channels devoted to user-based input, interaction, collaboration, and sharing of content (Eleuteri, Saladino, & Verrastro, 2017). **Social networking sites (SNSs)** have greatly expanded since their origin in the 1990s, and they have increased our ability to connect emotionally and even physically to other people all over the world at any time of the day or night (Ryan, Allen, DeLeon, & McInerney, 2017). SNSs have three main characteristics centered around connectivity with other users: (1) they allow people to construct a public or semipublic profile; (2) they offer a list of other users with whom people share a connection; and (3) they allow people to view other people's networks (Boyd, 2008; Levine, 2011). On the personal level, SNSs have increased communication dramatically, but they can have some associated risks, including loneliness, depression, and suicide (Esposito, 2011; Ryan et al., 2017). On the professional level, they have opened new opportunities for work and

James Charles, a microcelebrity, mostly known for his make-up style and techniques, became famous through his presence on YouTube
Taylor Hill/FilmMagic/Getty Images

career development. And on the political level, they have exposed backroom politics and revealed closed nations to outside scrutiny. In fact, media commentators routinely refer to the movements that toppled the governments of Tunisia in 2010 and Egypt and Libya in 2011 as "Twitter revolutions."

Add to these SNSs the powerful connectivity of cell phones and smartphones that give portable Internet access anywhere, anytime, and the potential for sexual connectivity increases dramatically. Social networking sites also have grown in importance for sexual connectivity with each passing year. They simplify the experience of meeting someone and forming online relationships, for business and pleasure, with networks that encompass friends, romantic interests, and virtual or actual lovers. This is especially striking in dense urban areas, where individuals who would never have otherwise met in person can now relate, connect to, and hook up with one other.

Social media platforms and apps provide not only the opportunities for sexual connectivity but also the means for new and faster ways of expressing sexual individuality. For example, an Australian study has found that many young gay and lesbian people use the Internet to develop six areas of their lives: identity, friendship, coming out, intimate relationships, sex, and community (Hillier, Mitchell, & Ybarra, 2012; Hillier & Harrison, 2007). Many LGBT (lesbian, gay, bisexual, and transgender) people who grow up and live in rural areas find support online for the meaning and expression of their emotions and their identity development (Pascoe, 2011). Another study showed that women who may never have been comfortable with masturbation could find support online, especially through Facebook and Twitter.

Twitter postings often reveal a huge amount of spontaneous information about people's moods, tastes, and preferences, as well as rants and reactions that can be highly emotional and situational. For celebrities, Twitter postings can actually move public opinion. High-profile celebrities or political personalities may have tens of thousands of Twitter followers. Sometimes their messages, or *tweets,* can lead to positive outcomes, such as drawing attention to the need to support human sexual rights in Afghanistan. But sometimes they can backfire, as in 2011 when actor Russell Crowe ranted against circumcision. He had to retract some of his statements because they went against what is known as best science and medical practice (Child, 2011).

Online dating provides another way for people to connect sexually and romantically, one that feels more comfortable to some people. Likewise, using the Internet, men and women may locate a broader array of potential partners, potential sexual expressions, and sexual communities than previously imagined.

Sharing highly explicit sexual images of oneself through the Internet, a practice known as **sexting,** is another easy way for people to express their sexual individuality. It has been suggested that age is a decent predictor of the level of engagement in sexting. Previous research indicates that sexting is more common among older adolescents and young adults than children or young adolescents (Dake et al., 2012; Klettke et al., 2014; Lenhart, 2009; Ybarra & Mitchell, 2014). In one major study of 23,000 high school students, 13% reported that they had received "sext" messages, and 1 in 10 had forwarded, sent, or posted sexually suggestive, explicit, or nude photos or videos of people they knew by cell phone or online (Esposito, 2011). Attitudes toward sexting among teens has been well documented (Dake et al., 2012). Research indicates teens had both positive and negative views about sexting. Some viewed it as flirty (61%), hot (46%), and exciting (49%). Despite the positive attributions, many young people also viewed sexting as dangerous (67%), stupid (57%), and immoral (40%) (NCPTUP, 2008). Sexting should not be confused with pornography, which involves sexual images being sold for personal titillation, but it comes close if the images are transmitted to a third party. When you share a sexual image beyond a personal relationship, it may be passed around among strangers in a manner not unlike commercial pornography.

sexting
Sharing highly explicit sexual images of oneself through the Internet.

Consider what can happen if an image that one person thinks is completely private goes to someone besides the intended recipient. Margarite, age 14, posed nude in front of a mirror, photographed herself in different poses, and sent the images to her new boyfriend, Isaiah (Hoffman, 2011). They broke up soon afterward. Isaiah then sent the photos to another eighth-grade girl, an ex-friend of Margarite's. This girl then sent the photos to her network of friends with a message that referred to Margarite as a "whore." Within 24 hours, hundreds, if not thousands, had seen Margarite's photo, and her life was nearly ruined. It was as if she had committed some horrible crime. In fact, technically, the people who shared her sexual images did commit a crime: promotion of child pornography, according to the law in that state. The humiliation and turmoil for all the kids involved and their families could have been avoided if the original images had not been sent.

Who takes more risks online, females or males? Recent media coverage suggests that men may take more sexual risks than women on the Internet. Do you agree? Read "Controversies in Sexuality: Why Do Men Do It?" and then decide how you feel.

People are still figuring out how to use social media in their actual relationships (Gershon, 2010). There are positive aspects of sexting that may involve a couple texting each other, for instance, or friends who want to explore some aspects of their sexuality. It does appear that sexting is a common component of the technological communication among young adult romantic partners (Weisskirch, Drouin, & Delevi, 2017) Yet the act of sexting continues to provoke controversy due to some of the associated negative outcomes such as sexual risk taking, including an increase in the number of partners and engaging in unprotected sex, consuming drugs and alcohol prior to sex and a greater likelihood of being diagnosed with an STI, and daring use of social media to attain personal goals (Weisskirch, Drouin, & Delevi, 2017). Let's look at how all these changes are influencing sexual socialization.

Online Sexual Socialization

Historically, sexual socialization was intensely private, largely restricted to the family, and generally considered the province of personal morality (Gagnon, 2004; Irvine, 2000, 2002; Kinsey et al., 1948; Laumann et al., 1994; Regnerus, 2007). Religion has also played a huge role in sexual socialization (see Chapter 2).

Research suggests that just as there was a decline in comprehensive school-based sex education in the United States, adolescents' use of the Internet became nearly universal (Jones & Biddlecom, 2011). Now the Internet is changing sexual socialization in a largely unacknowledged way, especially for teens and young adults (Boyd, 2008, 2014; Carlsson, 2006;

WHAT'S ON YOUR MIND?

Q: I am in a committed long-term relationship, but I enjoy engaging in online sex with others. Am I cheating on my partner?

ANSWER: First, you need to distinguish between the physical sex act and the emotional side of a relationship. Is one more important than the other to you and your partner? Are they equally important? For many people, whether the sex is physically or emotionally driven, sex outside the partnership would be cheating, and they would not like it. For some, however, an emotional betrayal might be worse than engaging in the physical sex act with someone else. Second, are you having online sex one time or multiple times with the same person? If you are having sex repeatedly with the same person, you may have become emotionally involved with that virtual personality. Third, does your partner know or suspect that you are having online sex with others? You and your partner have to decide what constitutes infidelity in your relationship and communicate that with each other.

CONTROVERSIES in Sexuality

Why Do Men Do It?

In 2011, then U.S. Representative Anthony Weiner was caught sending sexual and lewd images of himself to admirers. He resigned after he was caught. In 2017, he pled guilty to a different sexting charge and was sentenced to 21 months in prison.
BRENDAN MCDERMID/REUTERS/Newscom

Boys are particularly fond of using digital communication technologies for romance, meeting new girls, and flirting (Lenhart & Madden, 2007). Some males even say that they don't text their male friends much—just their girlfriends. Maybe this is because they find it easier or safer to text than to talk in person (Gershon, 2010). Or maybe it's because some online venues allow males to engage in more sexual risk taking and that's what they really want to do.

Just look at all the sexual scandals that involve male politicians, as one example. Over the past few years, there have been many scandals involving male politicians of both political parties. "I'm telling you," said Representative Candice Miller (R-Mich), "every time one of these sex scandals goes, we just look at each other, like, 'What is it with these guys? Don't they think they're going to get caught?'"

The scandals range from former New Jersey Governor Jim McGreevey having an affair with a man who served as his aide to former South Carolina Governor Mark Sanford saying he was going hiking in the mountains when he was really in Argentina with his female lover. These incidents occurred in the real world.

But online sex scandals are now becoming common. Former New York Representative Anthony Weiner was caught using Twitter to send sexual photos of his genitals to young women. His sudden exposure brought a huge public reaction, to the effect that he lacked mature judgment and was not suitable to be a legislator. He was compelled to resign from Congress in disgrace. Was that consequence too extreme? Whatever your opinion, the outcome of this scandal reveals how our online actions can have real-world consequences.

Compare these examples with President Donald Trump who, right before he was elected in 2016, was featured in a leaked tape where he was recorded in 2005 talking to *Access Hollywood's* host Billy Bush and states, "I just start kissing them. It's like a magnet. Just kiss. I don't even wait. And when you're a star, they let you do it. You can do anything. . . . Grab 'em by the pussy. You can do anything."

Does power motivate these guys? Maybe it's just that males are more romantic online than in reality. Or maybe it's that men's nature is to take more risks sexually, even when it could cost them their job and family. Can it be the convergence of men who naturally take more sexual risks and the Internet providing a perfect outlet for it?

Yes:

- Boys and men prefer the Internet and cell phones because it is easier for them to be more romantic in virtual time than in real time.
- Men have always taken more sexual risks than women.
- Men just have to assert their power: It's a dominance thing.

No:

- Men and boys are just using the new technology; their sexual risk taking is not that different from when the technology was unavailable.
- Males aren't that much more sexually aggressive online than females; some women and girls can be aggressive sexually too, and they are also aggressive online.
- Just because men have an aggressive sexual nature doesn't make it right to send such images over the Internet. They should control themselves better and keep their sexual images off the Internet.

What's Your Perspective?

1. Why might boys be more romantic online than face-to-face?
2. Why might men be willing to take more sexual risks than women?
3. Why might the Internet motivate some men to be more sexual than in person by sending sexually explicit messages and pictures of themselves?

> **DID YOU KNOW**
>
> Facebook, with 800 million users, is the most successful social networking site in the world. It was the brainchild of Mark Zuckerberg and fellow students at Harvard University in 2004. *The Social Network* (2010) dramatized the story of its founders.

Ybarra & Mitchell, 2005; Owens et al., 2012). Perhaps the risk is increased for young children whose parents may depend upon handheld devices to focus the attention of young children and who increasingly are online before they enter elementary school (Freitas, 2017; Levine, 2011). They are using computers or smartphones and may thus be exposed to an array of overtly sexual materials, including pornography. In fact, according to Bryant Paul, an associate professor and author of multiple studies of consumption of porn content by adolescents and adults, it is estimated that boys are around age 13 and girls are around age 14 when they first see pornography (Jones, 2019). Further, it is estimated that 93% of male college students and 62% of female students report viewing online porn before the age of 18 (Jones, 2019).

And so children's online access has changed sexual socialization in terms of its potential psychological and social effects (Carlsson, 2006; Holloway & Valentine, 2003; Livingstone, 2002; Osgerby, 2004; Thurlow & McKay, 2003). We don't know exactly what effects this exposure has on psychological and sexual development, but research suggests that children below age 12 rarely search for sexually explicit images online (Wolak, Finkelhor, Mitchell, & Ybarra, 2008). But whether they are searching for them or not, children may well encounter sexual images that are harmful to their sexual development and well-being (Holloway & Valentine, 2003; Levine, 2011; Livingstone, 2002; Osgerby, 2004; Pew Foundation, 2018; Thurlow & McKay, 2003).

Because preschool children go online and a majority of older children surf the web daily, it is quite likely they will encounter online pornography early in development, too. It also means that a high percentage of young people may somehow relate what they see online to their own feelings and experiences. This is a challenge to healthy sexuality, because they may pick up ideas about sex that may be grossly inaccurate (e.g., seeing images of anatomy or bodies in sexual ways that are weird or abnormal for their age group or forms of sexual practice that are atypical), or disconnect sex from emotions in ways that may set them up for false notions or expectations about what happens later in intimate sexual relations (Levine, 2011; Pascoe, 2011; Jones, 2019).

A positive gain is that people are using the Internet to find out about sex in ways that may enhance their sexual individuality. They can find information about what sexual behavior is perceived as normal, and what is quirky. And they can do this anonymously, sometimes avoiding the censure of parents or peers (Pascoe, 2011). Some experts believe that anonymity has made the Internet a safer, more neutral area for people to learn about sex and try out new things sexually (Boyd, 2008), though other experts disagree (Freitas, 2017). In particular, they can anonymously find answers to questions they may be too embarrassed to ask others, even in their human sexuality course.

Others may anonymously search the Internet to satisfy desires, especially if they do not have the opportunity or are afraid to take it in their own local community. Research shows, for example, that people may try out new sexual identities online first, because they are deprived of social support for expressing variations in sexual attraction where they live (Hillier & Harrison, 2007). On the Internet, these individuals can locate others who have similar sexual desires and create their own online sexual communities (Klein, 2006), such as couples who use sadism and masochism (S/M) in their sexual relationships (Califia, 2002). A study of women and their sexual expressions suggests that when women can explore their sexual desires and feelings, they may develop a keener understanding of who they really are emotionally and what they want in sexual relationships (Bogle, 2008; Gray, Klein, Noyce, Sesselberg, & Cantrill, 2005). Similar online patterns are found for men who explore their sexual desires with cybersex partners and develop relationships that enhance sexual well-being (Pryce, 2007).

One force that may be motivating these new patterns of sexual socialization is the reluctance or even resistance of parents and schools to openly teach about sexual well-being

HEALTHY Sexuality

Personal Safety Online

What you place on the Internet may become an identity tag for an employer and work colleagues; for your family, friends, lovers, and partners; and for your future. There are many horror stories about how people e-mailed or texted someone and discovered that their words went viral and could be seen all over the world. To help protect yourself and your information online, a report from the U.S. Office of the Attorney General offers key rules to follow when using the Internet (Wolak et al., 2008):

- Be aware of what you are doing.
- Remain as anonymous as possible online.
- Keep all your private information PRIVATE.
- Create an e-mail or Twitter address that does not reveal any private information.
  - Consider creating separate account names for websites such as Twitter and Facebook that do not reveal your real identity to strangers.
- If you get a message that looks suspicious, trash it, don't respond; someone may be baiting you.
- Be more careful than usual if you agree to meet an online friend in the actual world.
- Never post anything online that you wouldn't want to see on the front page of your newspaper, because it could wind up there.
- Computers and the Internet never forget, so don't post something you might not like to see about yourself five years from now.

Be careful what you put on the Internet. It is likely to outlive you.

(Regnerus, 2007; Kirby, 2012). Also, revelations about sexual scandals involving clergy make it awkward, at best, for clergy to get into sexual education issues (Terry, 2011). It appears, then, that the Internet may have become the default institution of sexual socialization. That may be one reason why the topic of sex is searched on the Internet with greater frequency than other topics (Pascoe, 2011). But then it raises the question: Who is watching out for such risk online?

Sexuality and Risk Online

The risks of being sexual online are real (Esposito, 2011; Peter & Valkenburg, 2016). The problem is more acute on the Internet than in real-world places because the norms for online behavior are still developing quite rapidly (Boyd, 2014). These risks include distorting personal boundaries, online pornography, the factuality of online sexual information, the authenticity of people online, and the ability to detect fakery. False information provided by others makes many parents worry about younger people meeting sexual predators or pedophiles online.

Another online risk is that information you post is available for everyone to see. It may reveal too much or it may end up attached to another website that makes you cringe with embarrassment because you never imagined it would show up there. Though online risk does exist, with some caution, you can minimize it. Consider some basic rules to follow to reduce online risk in "Healthy Sexuality: Personal Safety Online."

Without norms and personal boundaries to guide us in deciding what to share, what to make public, and what to keep private, people sometimes fall prey to fads, seduction, and shared images, such as pictures of porn stars. People may find themselves acting in ways that don't reflect who they want to be, and these actions may lead to unhealthy sexual development. In the next section, we will explore how the Internet has affected all sexual relationships between adults, especially online.

ONLINE SEXUAL CONTEXTS

The Internet has made a variety of sexual expressions available globally 24/7. Millions of people appear to be exploring some aspect of their sexuality on any given day of the year online. Whether one is learning about sexual health, seeking to find a romantic partner, reading an erotic story, viewing pornographic videos, or playing games where one can virtually engage in sex, it is clear that the ways in which humans can interact with their sexuality online are endless. As we continue to integrate technology into nearly every facet of our lives, it is critical to remain aware of how these online contexts can affect our lives, our relationships, and multiple facets of our sexual and emotional health and well-being.

Online Boundaries

Boundaries are important in relationships between people. As social networking sites and smartphones have grown technologically more sophisticated, the boundary between virtual and actual reality has blurred. Beginning in 2004, huge numbers of preteens and teens began to join social networking websites with no defined boundaries or norms for social and sexual connection. Without established boundaries on Instagram, Snapchat, Facebook, and other venues, young people were placed in unknown territory (Jones & Biddlecom, 2011). Some posted personal information that attracted unwanted attention. Soon social and sexual interactions between adults and teens were causing concern, and people demanded tighter control over the content posted on these websites. Many individuals found their lives suddenly altered by material posted online. College admissions teams and HR departments have become well-known for looking up applicants' social media profiles and making admissions and hiring decisions dependent on what is found in those profiles. Because of these kinds of issues and the sometimes-unintended consequences of having a highly public life online, the establishing of boundaries around how one uses social media and publicizes aspects of their lives is critically important.

Boundaries enable each of us to establish a set of self-imposed rules around what we are comfortable with posting online. Some may feel perfectly comfortable with having multiple pictures posted of themselves in little to no clothing, while others may not be comfortable with a public posting of their bodies. Boundaries also help people to know what is unique about their own sexual individuality, to support sexual well-being. These limits can range from being very rigid and even malicious to being flexible, nurturing, and negotiable. You may say to a friend, "You really stepped over the line when you said that," or to your partner, "I can be flexible about your online relationships, as long as you are honest in communicating with me."

Boundaries help us all to keep our own attitudes and tastes in perspective. For example, if something has become an online fad, people who are comfortable with their own boundaries may recognize that it is only a fad, and not something worth imitating.

How much of your sexual individuality do you want to explore or reveal online? To help you think through your own boundaries, complete the assessment in "Know Yourself: Your Sexual Individuality Online."

Some individuals have greater comfort with their bodies being posted online than others. Kim Kardashian has been well known for publicly displaying selfies and photos of her body on Instagram. Online boundaries are useful in making personal decisions about what each of us is comfortable with others viewing about ourselves in online spaces.
Cindy Ord/Getty Images Entertainment/Getty Images

Online Romance, Dating, and Hooking Up

The Internet has allowed millions of adults in the United States to turn online dates into long-term relationships or marriages. For example, many young people now meet friends and prospective partners online (Pascoe, 2011). So it is not surprising that the sexual norm is changing to accept online relationships

Your Sexual Individuality Online

In terms of your own sexual literacy, what does it mean to you that the Internet is a virtual experience? As you think about these questions, consider how you would respond to these online experiences:

- Creating personal blogs
- Sending personal Twitter messages
- Accepting online information as fact
- Having a lack of control online
- Expressing things online that would be completely private offline
- Trying out risky sexual things online

Now circle the numbers to answer the following questions to rate yourself and your sense of virtual reality and sexuality today. Use the numbers to mean the following:

1 Never
2 Hardly ever
3 Some of the time
4 Most of the time
5 Always

1. I tend to believe that what I read online is fact.
  1   2   3   4   5

2. I reveal personal things to strangers in blogs and web pages.
  1   2   3   4   5

3. I am willing to engage in online sex.
  1   2   3   4   5

4. I think that I may find and meet my mate online.
  1   2   3   4   5

5. I am willing to pretend I am someone or something else sexually online.
  1   2   3   4   5

6. I let my sexual feelings get carried away online.
  1   2   3   4   5

7. I have a feeling of total control online.
  1   2   3   4   5

8. For some reason there is a huge difference between how I am in real life and online.
  1   2   3   4   5

9. My friends think that I am out of control when it comes to what I say and do online.
  1   2   3   4   5

10. I have done something sexually online I would never do in real life.
  1   2   3   4   5

We encourage you to return to the questions after you've finished reading the chapter to see if you would answer them differently.

Know Yourself

WHAT'S ON YOUR MIND?

Q: My boyfriend tells me that he sometimes pretends to play the part of being a teenage girl when he engages in online sex. Is that normal?

ANSWER: Many people like to dress up in costumes or pretend from time to time that they are someone or something else, but when it comes to pretending that you are a different gender online or virtual gender impersonation, our society has a definite code. Basically, it is wrong. Your boyfriend may want to explore why he chooses to change his gender online. He may be just playing online or he may be wondering if he is gay or transgender. If he is wondering about other identities, he could explore other online communities. For example, he could visit Advocates for Youth at www.advocatesforyouth.org, a transgender website.

hooking up
Meeting a partner online or in a physical setting for a casual sexual encounter outside of a romantic or committed relationship.

as real dating in real time (Bogle, 2008). The Internet allows people to find romance and sex online, whether to find a potential mate or for the purpose of **hooking up,** defined as casually engaging in a sexual encounter with someone outside of a romantic or committed relationship, instead of seeking potential mates only in physical settings. The availability of online dating sites (i.e., Match, Zoosk, OurTime) and web applications has changed the way romantic relationships and even more casual sex encounters (i.e., Tinder, Grindr, Blendr, FriendFinder-X) are pursued and developed (Silva et al., 2019). Online dating and app usage gives people access to an unparalleled number of potential partners than conventional offline dating provides. People can share personal information with others and even communicate without ever having to meet face-to-face. Complex algorithms will even pair one with potential partners based on the information provided in profiles and a calculation of romantic compatibility (Silva et al., 2019).

Early on, there seemed to be some stigma in regard to finding romantic partners online. The perception of online daters was often that they were "desperate" or that they were individuals who needed to lie about something whether it was their marital status or even body type. Deceit was often documented as a chief concern among people who were gaining experience in the online dating world. Figure 3.4 shows that more recent studies indicate attitudes toward online dating have significantly improved, with a majority of Internet users believing it is a good and reliable way to meet people and find a better match due to the sheer number of people one can potentially meet in online spaces (Smith, 2016).

Figure 3.4
Positive attitudes and digital dating.

Percentage of people believing the following are reliable ways to meet others.

Statement	Have used online dating	Have not used online dating
Online dating is a good way to meet people	80	55
Online dating helps people find a better match for themselves	62	50
Online dating is easier and more efficient than other ways	61	44
Online dating is more dangerous than other ways of meeting	45	60
Online dating keeps people from settling down	31	32
People who use online dating are desperate	16	24

Does initiating an online dating relationship appeal to you? What would it take for you to attempt it? Are you concerned about the impact of virtual relationships on your real-life relationships in your community? Use the information in "Communication Matters: Establishing an Online Dating Relationship" to consider your own strategies.

While using the Internet for dating poses challenges, and is not for everyone, the majority of research suggests that virtual relationships can be beneficial for some people (Bogle, 2008; Ryan, Allen, DeLeon, & McInerney, 2017). Of those who first met on the Internet, a majority of people reported forming a close relationship (McKenna, Gree, & Gleason, 2002). Additionally, 50% and more of these participants had moved from an Internet relationship to one in real life, and nearly a quarter of them became engaged, married, or lived together. Other studies have discovered that people who met on the Internet liked each other more than those who met face-to-face first (Bargh et al., 2002; McKenna, Gree, & Gleason, 2002). In short, people who like developing online relationships also feel that they can truly express themselves and their sexual individuality openly but cautiously on the Internet (Pascoe, 2011).

Sexual Avatars and Gaming

At one time, imaginary games were generally perceived to be a place of fantasy play for children or adolescents, with few equivalent games for adults who wanted to create shared imaginary worlds, but the Internet ushered in all kinds of adult games (Williams, Yee, & Caplan, 2008). Unlike parlor games such as cards or chess, which have rigid rules and do not require players to take imaginary roles, Internet games draw upon fantasy and science fiction themes and content.

Literally hundreds of thousands of people simultaneously play these games together as they socialize, market products, create friendships, and find potential sex partners. One study revealed that people may spend as much as 8 hours per day, 7 days a week online, often with an online romantic partner whom they have never met before in real life. Their shared time ultimately led to intense sexual relationships in the actual world for some of them who spent a huge amount of time online getting to know each other's minds, hearts, and interests (Wholeslagle, 2006). In one study, EverQuest players stated that their virtual relationships were more meaningful than their actual relationships. In some games, players can even pimp and sell cybersex favors through exchanges of online things—virtual gold or currency, furniture, clothes, and more (Brathwaite, 2006). These kinds of exchanges move the virtual worlds further away from being "just a game" of shared images into virtual social interactions that feel as real as what happens in the physical world. These types of games have sparked a whole new discussion about sexual individuality and what are authentic/real identities, and the definitions of sexual cultures (Boellstorff, 2008; Ryan et al., 2017).

In 1992, science fiction writer Neal Stephenson popularized a new way of thinking and talking about online personalities and collective images, using the term *avatar*. An **avatar** is an online representation or alter ego (literally "another self") for someone playing a computer game. It's been popularized in multiple different media contexts (Ryan et al., 2017) and connects virtual sexuality to nature, spirituality, and falling in love. Avatars are a radical manifestation of how sexual individuality can influence virtual reality. Millions of people have avatars today through online games, though very little is known about how these shared sexual images change sexual personality or self-awareness.

The Second Life world is a leading interactive virtual experience. It allows people to have imaginary bodies and sex lives in dreamlike places so different from the actual world. And thus, people can create virtual sexual interactions, including kissing and facial gestures, holding hands, genital movement, and even more subtle cues such as agreed-upon unique sexual signals (Bardzell, 2006). You can read more about this virtual world in "Research and Sexual Well-Being: The Sexual Life of Avatars in Second Life."

avatar
An online representation or alter ego for someone playing a computer game.

COMMUNICATION Matters

Establishing an Online Dating Relationship

Every relationship is different, and there is no right or wrong way to form one. What is important is to establish a relationship that is mutually beneficial and built on respect of the people within that relationship. The lack of boundaries for meeting people online, and possibly falling in love, suggests that people need a sense of their own sexuality. Consider the following issues when establishing online relationships:

1. **Trust your intuition.** Your intuition is a powerful medium. As you read profiles and responses to e-mails, have phone conversations, and meet an online friend in real life, your instincts can help tell you if something is right or not. Trust your intuition because it's one of the most powerful tools you have.

2. **Don't provide personal information too soon.** Your home phone number and full name provide easy ways to track who you are and where you live. Armed with just your home phone number, a person can easily gain access to your income information, home address, and other personal information. So in the initial stages of communication, guard your personal information.

3. **Use a free e-mail account.** If you decide to move your communication from the anonymous e-mail feature provided by the majority of online dating services, provide an e-mail address that isn't your regular one. Also, don't use your full name in the field—use only your first name or other words that will not give away your full name. This protects you from a person being able to search your normal e-mail address to find out more information about you.

4. **Use a cell phone or anonymous phone service to chat.** When it's time to move your communication to the next level, which is usually speaking, provide a cell phone number, use Skype to communicate, or use an anonymous phone service. It's just an added barrier until you get to know the person better.

5. **Beware of individuals who are married.** It's unfortunate, but a lot of married people do use online dating services. They'll even go as far as to meet people. It has been suggested that a significant number of people using online dating services are married! (Bogle, 2008).

6. **Look for questionable characteristics in any communication.** As you chat via e-mail and on the phone, you may be able to pick out characteristics of the other person. Is he controlling? Does she seem to anger easily? Does he avoid some of your questions? Unfavorable answers to these types of questions may tell you that it is time to move on.

7. **Ask for a recent photo.** There's nothing wrong in asking someone if photos are recent or requesting recent ones. It's important to get a good look at the person you may eventually meet. Plus, if someone lies about a photo or profile, that may be reason enough not to pursue a relationship.

8. **Stick with paid online dating services.** Free online dating services may attract potentially dangerous individuals because people do not have to provide a credit card or other information that identifies them.

9. **Don't develop a false sense of security.** Some online dating services claim to offer background checks. If you sign up with such services you may find it easier to let your guard down. Beware of this statement because laws differ from state to state about background checks; several states have laws where checks cannot be effectively performed. Because of the inconsistency, questionable people can become part of online dating services that do so-called background checks.

10. **Meet in a public place for your first meeting.** For that first exciting face-to-face encounter, meet in a public place and provide your own transportation. Never accept an offer to be picked up at your house. Your initial meeting will tell you a lot, including whether or not the person lied in his or her profile. Your gut instincts will kick in. Make sure a friend knows where you are and who you are with.

RESEARCH and Sexual Well-Being

The Sexual Life of Avatars in Second Life

Imagine being an explorer in a strange culture, but instead of exploring the Amazon or the Moon, say, you are discovering a whole dimension of virtual culture and sexuality online. What will you see, what will your own identity be, and what will be your role in this virtual culture? These are questions that anthropologist Tom Boellstorff (2008) investigated for 2 years, as reported in his book, *Coming of Age in Second Life*. The research and shared images that include films, such as *Avatar*, support the notion that sexual connectivity and animated online activity are changing how we perceive sexual individuality.

Most people who log on to Second Life seek nonsexual friendships, so this cyber world is much more than a sex stop (Boellstorff, 2008). Yet many people say that Second Life is more important to their sexuality than anything else, including their jobs, families, and real sexual relationships. What kind of sex is this virtual sex? It seems mysterious until we remember that people can create multiple identities online, and these identities enrich gender and sexuality and allow them to explore sexuality. The people who play the Second Life game often report that their avatar experiences and relationships are more immediate, exciting, and intense than they would be in the real world, where they have to be more cautious (Boellstorff, 2008; Ryan, et al., 2017).

Second Life reveals sexual situations, characters, and spaces where, for example, virtual bars and discos cater to particular sexual tastes. Many residents who participate in intimate, virtual sex say it's "like licking honey through the glass" (Boellstorff, 2008, p. 160). Through various animations, avatars "engage in a wide range of sexual practices, from embracing and kissing to oral, vaginal, and anal sex" (Boellstorff, 2008, p. 161). Residents often like to have "sex undisturbed," which is sex in private away from other avatars, apparently because it becomes more meaningful and real to them. Yet sex cannot be completely private because Second Life is a public venue, followed by tens of thousands of fans.

Sexual individuality may motivate people to use avatars to extend their sexual attractions and relationships online. This online venue may provide a "safe" space to try out new desires or roles and figure out what feels "right" to them. Their desire is not always achieved, however (Boellstorff, 2008). Their virtual avatar may be younger or older, have a different gender, have a different body type, and have a different personality from who they are in the real world.

Avatars can connect to others who share in their arousal or pleasure associated with parts of the body, such as a penis or breasts, in fantasy and reality. A whole sexual community can form around such shared interest, which may be defined as a form of **kinky sex,** a form of sexual interaction that may involve pain and ritual rules, pushing sexuality to the extreme. Such relationships may then be carried over to the actual world where having norms and boundaries in place will help people know what is safe and comfortable for them and whether the partners they meet online are really who they seem to be.

Avatars and virtual worlds like Second Life are potentially liberating for people (Turkle, 1996), but they also pose ethical issues about such basic matters as how we think about ourselves as human. In fact, some individuals assign such deep meaning to androids, avatars, and their avatars' words and actions that they may no longer seem human (Turkle, 2006). Also, it's impossible to know if these emotions are integrated into an individual's actual self. *Coming of Age in Second Life* reports that some residents found the gap between the actual and virtual identities uncomfortable, even painful at times, and some talked about it as a "shared hallucination" between the actual person and virtual avatar (Boellstorff, 2008, p. 171). Ethical issues arise because some residents like to engage in a form of virtual pedophilia that is disturbing to others and may challenge legal norms (Boellstorff, 2008, p. 164). Such ethical dilemmas may be resolved as the Internet and its shared imagery continue to evolve.

As people experiment with new games and media, they are becoming more sexual, but they are still trying to figure out how their virtual sexuality impacts their actual relationships. There is a gap that has opened up between all this online content and what young people are *not* learning in school or from families (Jones & Biddlecom 2011; Kantor, Rolleri, & Kolios, 2014). Sometimes that gap can be filled with experiences that transition youth into adulthood, including emergent online adult sexual content.

kinky sex
A form of sexual interaction that may involve pain and ritual rules, pushing sexuality to the extreme.

WHAT'S ON YOUR MIND?

Q: I like to videotape myself masturbating and engaging in sexual acts. Why?

ANSWER: We are not sure why. Maybe you do it because you like what you see on the monitor. Now that people have access to a lot of video equipment, recording sexual activities appears to be increasing in popularity. It is less expensive than renting a video and watching strangers. Just be careful about who gets their hands on your videos and always be sure that any partner(s) you have consent to be recorded.

ADULT SEXUAL CONTENT

As sex on the Internet has evolved, a whole group of websites has been identified with a label known from prior decades of censorship and regulation: adult sexual content (ASC). Like certain movies, many sexually explicit websites are legally required to use this label and, in turn, require users to indicate that they are at least 18 years old, the age of legal adulthood in many U.S. states. In this section, we consider the category of adult sexual content and briefly survey its evolution and history.

Pornography and Its Changing Meaning

Adult sexual content takes many diverse forms, but it is probably best identified with the general category of **pornography.** This is any form of media created to explicitly sexually arouse the user, especially for commercial purposes. Pornography may be as old as civilization, and it exists in many cultures of the world. In the words of pornography researcher Robert Stoller (1991), it serves as "the myth of modern times"—that is, it serves as a collective fantasy of huge importance in Western society. Today, the global pornography industry is estimated to be worth $100 billion or more.

Although pornography has been around for thousands of years, it was first mass-produced in print in the late 1800s, when French pornographers began to market inexpensive sexual material featuring "artistic" poses of women. Mass-produced **soft pornography,** which features nude images but no actual penetrative sex scenes, began with *Playboy* magazine in 1953. It is hard to imagine the sexual panic set off by the first issues of *Playboy*. Consider that in 1953, television was in its infancy, and exposing any part of the sexual anatomy was unthinkable. This was the same year that Kinsey published his study about female sexuality, revealing that masturbation, homosexuality, and premarital sex occurred in mainstream society (Kinsey, Pomeroy, & Martin, 1953).

When Hugh Hefner created *Playboy* and featured Marilyn Monroe as its first centerfold, he was accused of being a pornographer and an exploiter of women. The mass commercial marketing of high-quality glossy nudes of the female body prompted many people, including politicians, community leaders, and religious clergy, to suggest that the United States was undergoing serious moral decay. *Playboy* was regarded as the worst form of smut imaginable, not only in our country, but around the world. In fact, it was officially banned in Thailand and Singapore, for example, and the U.S. government repeatedly tried to prosecute the owners of *Playboy* for obscenity. Opposition to *Playboy* continued for years, as it broke taboo after taboo—for instance, by publishing the first model showing pubic hair in the late 1960s. Meanwhile its sales soared, along with the growth

---

pornography
Sexual images sold for personal titillation; any form of media used to create sexual arousal, especially for commercial purposes.

soft pornography
Nude images that do not depict penetrative sex scenes.

The first issue of *Playboy* with Marilyn Monroe as its cover girl and its centerfold caused quite a scandal. Looking at this cover today, you might wonder what all the fuss was about.
Photo 12/Universal Images Group/Getty Images

of men's lifestyle magazines (Benwell, 2003), especially in conservative parts of the United States. The money reaped from this magazine and similar enterprises is phenomenal and has encouraged many imitators.

It seems hard to understand such an extreme reaction to a magazine that many people now regard as iconic of mainstream American culture. However, there were serious critiques of the male sexual objectification of women, as exemplified by *Playboy*. The criticism probably increased the appeal of these publications to American boys who over the years purchased and masturbated to pornography in the course of growing up. For this reason and due to its status as an icon, movies and television sitcoms often use *Playboy* as a prop for male characters who need to give a sperm sample for medical purposes.

Hard-core pornography, which depicts penetrative sex and aggressive, raw sexual interactions between adults, followed the first issue of *Playboy* by about 10 years. *Hustler,* the iconic magazine of hard-core pornography, was produced for heterosexual men who wanted more explicit sexual material than was offered in *Playboy*. It became the focus of (1) highly publicized censorship battles and lawsuits to prevent it from being sold, (2) a government commission on pornography, and (3) court decisions that upheld the right to publish hard-core porn under the First Amendment of the Constitution protecting free speech (Abramson, Pinkerton, & Huppin, 2003). Similar censorship efforts and lawsuits have been brought against strip clubs that feature topless and bottomless dancers or lap dancers, which are still banned in some parts of the United States. In these cases, the local community standards of what people consider "obscene" come into play, though the Internet may be having an effect on this process, too (Peter & Valkenburg, 2016). As sexual norms began to change in the United States, and attitudes became more permissive, people began to produce more diverse soft and hard-core pornography for women, gays, and couples. These forms include X-rated movies, numerous porn magazines, and websites designed for heterosexual women and for gay men.

Moving away from the magazines and videos, pornography has migrated to a digital format—in a thousand different forms—serving the straight and the gay, and all in between. Self-produced home videos of people having sex are common, often free to view, and downloadable. Highly sexualized forms of animated pornography have also become part of this new format, further erasing the line between actual and virtual collective sexual fantasy, as seen in the anime and manga comics, which were predominantly from Asia but are now global in pornographic representations, virtual or actual, of comic book characters having sex. As discussed, people can easily acquire sexually explicit content online, both privately and anonymously, as they seek to fulfill their sexual and personal wants (Fisher & Barak, 2001a, 2001b; Owens et al., 2012).

Every second 28,258 Internet users are viewing pornography of some kind (Ropelato, 2009). In addition, controversial websites such as Ice TV and XTube (restricted to people over the age of 18) have reinvented the shape and feel of pornography by taking it from the slick and ultra-commercial format to more familiar imagery that is homemade, self-produced sexual entertainment. This homegrown pornography is another revolutionary and democratic feature of the Internet because it is freely available to everyone and is being produced in culturally contextual ways that allow understanding in multiple languages and communities. These sites are changing the so-called face of "slick" pornography with ordinary individuals engaging in sexual acts alone or with others (Owen et al., 2012). Today, people still access pornography through magazines and videos, but now also through millions of websites and peer-to-peer (p2p) sites called *torrents* (CBS News, 2007).

DID YOU KNOW

Once widespread Internet access became available, commercial pornography companies quickly moved to exploit the medium. Many people are unaware that major media companies, such as Time Warner, make $10 billion a year selling sexually explicit materials, including pornography, to the public. The companies that distribute pornography and adult entertainment reap the financial rewards. These include the big cable companies and Internet browsers such as AOL, Time Warner, Google, and Microsoft. The numbers reflect just how large the pornography industry is:

- $3,075.64 is spent on pornography every second.
- 4.2 million porn websites (12% of the total websites) are available.
- 420 million pornographic web pages are on the Internet.
- 68 million search engine requests for pornography (25% of total search engine requests) occur daily.

hard-core pornography
Nude images that depict penetrative sex and aggressive, raw sexual interactions between adults.

Though some consider it racy, people videotaping their own sexual intercourse is nothing new. But what about using the Internet to broadcast personal video sexual encounters for the rest of the world to see? Would you define this as pornography if it were free on the Internet? What about *child pornography,* erotic images or videos featuring children too young to consent to being photographed in sexually suggestive ways? Child pornography greatly complicates the issues surrounding pornography on the Internet (see Chapter 14). Yet, at least for adults, any individual's relationship to shared sexual imagery is more vital, intentional, and under his or her own individual control than ever before because of the Internet.

Not only can people post their homemade pornographic videos to websites for partners to view, but they can also tag their online address or phone number in order to solicit sex or sell it. Some people might consider such videos to be a positive expression of their sexual freedom and a way to achieve sexual well-being, but others are offended by such highly personal images. Likewise, on the Internet, sexual minorities may find videos of people engaging in some of the sexual behaviors that they enjoy. So online sexual images can be advertisements for sex or be a means of connecting sexually to others in one's own country or globally, involving tremendous challenges for sex trafficking and sex tourism explored in later chapters.

What has been the impact of pornography on popular culture? Sexual behavior in commercially distributed movies resembles soft pornography now more than it did a few years ago. For example, today it is more common in movies for the female partner to be shown on top thrusting with her male partner in a position that filmmakers never used a generation ago. With the pervasiveness of Internet sex and pornography, people may be exposed to an array of different sexualities, including stereotypes that are not necessarily positive for young people (Peter & Valkenburg, 2016). For example, women in their early 20s complained to a professor about having painful, rough anal sex with their boyfriends. When the professor inquired why they were doing it, they reported that their boyfriends had shown them online videos of pornography stars engaging in raw sex to prove that this practice was "normal," to get them to try it. They agreed to try it but did not have the necessary lubricant or experience for this kind of sex, and they regretted the experience.

Access to pornography and the meaning that it has for people has greatly changed in recent years in large part due to the Internet, with positive (increases in knowledge and attitudes about sex) and negative (increases in distress) results reported from research (Short, Black, Smith, & Wetterneck, 2012). Historically, people have worried about whether it was healthy, safe, or good for people to watch people engage in explicit sexual activity on the computer or television (Barak & King, 2000; Cooper, Putnam, Planchon, & Boies, 1999; Freeman-Longo & Blanchard, 1998; Peter & Volkenburg, 2016). Making everyday sexual images available to anyone, even when the material is not for sale or is not strictly pornographic, is known as **pornification.** Sex education film expert Mark Schoen (personal communication) believes that the trend toward pornification in mainstream films really started

pornification
The use of sexual images from popular culture as pornography even when they are not pornographic.

WHAT'S ON YOUR MIND?

Q: I have a friend who spends quite a lot of money visiting online adult sexual entertainment websites, and he has actually developed a kind of fixation on one female entertainer in Las Vegas. Is this normal?

ANSWER: More guys than ever have experimented with or sampled these adult websites, and to that extent it is becoming more common. The companies behind the websites may have restrictions to ensure that when someone is racking up bills to pay for this online through their credit cards they don't go bankrupt. Some guys develop regular appointments and "dates" with particular adult entertainers and may develop fixations, too. When it reaches that level, no, it is not normal in the usual sense of people having relationships or dating, because it moves closer to commercial sex. Your friend's motivation matters. Is this his only sexual outlet or just a supplement? If he uses it as a substitute for real-life relationships, consider asking him how he feels about that, and whether it is something he sees himself doing temporarily or for the rest of his life.

in 1989, when video stores began renting mass-market pornographic videos. Pubic shaving, another practice evident in pornography, also became increasingly common among ordinary people after this time. Could it be that the pervasiveness of pornography does affect how we fashion our bodies, through shaving, buffing, waxing, and so on? It is important that people not fall into the trap of trying to mimic what they view online, especially as portrayed by highly experienced porn stars who are athletic and well paid for what they do. Just because something is online does not make it normal.

Pornography should not set the standards for your own sexual individuality, any more than it should determine society's norms or sexual practices. Some experts have warned that some individuals may be more vulnerable than others, and pornography use may be contraindicated (Owens et al., 2012). In addition, we do not really understand the long-term effects of people watching particular kinds of pornography, soft or hard-core, over their lifetime, and more research is needed. However, when repeated online viewing of pornography causes distress and/or disrupts people's lives, and especially when this is linked to issues of aggression, violence, or uncontrollable behavior (Owens et al., 2012; Peter & Volkenburg, 2016), as we shall see in Chapter 15, then we pass into the realm of concern and professional counseling. Finally, it is important to respect the diversity of different kinds of communities' values and standards when it comes to online shared sexual imagery. There is no cookie-cutter recipe for how to correlate sexual well-being with pornography in people's development and societal expressions, as we will learn in Chapter 15.

Adult Sexual Entertainment Online

In the 1990s, as the online pornography revolution was underway, a whole new form of the sex industry emerged: online live adult sexual entertainment. Some people confuse this live, pay-for interactive type of sexual interaction between individuals with pornography in general, but they are quite different. Pornography is static, mass-produced images or videos, and the commercial product is not made for or connected to individuals. In other words, you would never expect to actually meet a porn star. With adult sexual entertainment, clients actually pay females and males, some of whom are porn stars of these websites (by the minute), to have online sexual communications and interactions, to satisfy their own sexual individuality. TV cable channels featuring adult porn shows, such as *SexTV: The Channel,* also developed during this time. Utah consumes the most online adult entertainment in the United States, and the San Fernando Valley is the world leader in adult content production (Patil, 2015).

Paid adult sexual entertainment online is live and done in private via webcams, one performer for one client. It is to some extent a relationship between two individuals, and some clients appear to become "regulars" of certain sexual performers. Women are the highest paid in the adult entertainment industry, with stars such as Jenna Jameson making $30 million without having starred in a porn movie (Patil, 2015). The entire performance is a display of provocative language and live body customized for the tastes, fantasies, and self-awareness of the client. Most of the performing is by heterosexual women for heterosexual men. Some performances may appeal to gays, lesbians, or transgenders, however. Rarely, if ever, do these entertainers meet their clients in person; it is all performed online. Some of these venues actually forbid any actual sexual contact or socializing between the performers and clients. Many of the performers appear to be from developing countries. Women entertainers are paid nearly twice as much as male performers, and they typically begin their careers in their early 20s (Patil, 2015).

In the United States, all the performers and clients of sex-for-sale websites must be at least 18 years of age, by law, and all the sex must be consensual. Both requirements are difficult to enforce, though professional companies may require a driver's license or passport data. Many companies, especially in the developing world, do not conform to these standards. Experts also worry about whether child pornography may be part of some of the businesses, though opinions are divided on what to do about it. The Association of Sites Advocating Child Protection (ASACP) provides more information about these issues on its website.

Some online venues become so popular that they receive awards—sort of like Academy Awards for the adult sexual entertainment industry. The Fans of Adult Media and Entertainment (F.A.M.E.) Awards were created in 2006 so that people could vote for their favorites. Some female stars become wealthy and relatively famous. This industry reached $2.8 billion in revenue in 2006 (Edelman, 2009). It is a little-known fact that these venues actually pioneered online payment via credit cards, which then spread into mainstream Internet shopping.

Online adult sexual entertainment provides a sexual outlet for people throughout the United States, though its use is not equally distributed across the 50 states (Edelman, 2009). Utah has the largest number of people who use online adult sexual entertainment, and research has suggested it is because the state is largely rural, agricultural, and is among the more conservative states in terms of its values and voting patterns (Edelman, 2009). However, recent research questions the basis of this correlation (Gmeiner, Price, & Worley, 2015). Remember, correlation is not causation! People who live in rural or sexually conservative areas might seek some form of online sexual expression or adult sexual entertainment due to its accessibility or the restrictive nature of their actual communities. By contrast, people living in California, which is at the bottom of the list of online adult sexual entertainment users, have very high accessibility to the Internet and pornography and are "left-leaning ultra-progressive" (Edelman, 2009, p. 2019). It will be interesting to see if this correlation continues as online venues become more accessible to everyone. As social media become more global, some of these differences may thin out or even disappear in time (Friedman, 2005).

ONLINE COMMUNITIES, RIGHTS, AND SEXUAL WELL-BEING

At the beginning of the 21st century, some experts worried that global connectivity might homogenize the world and destroy the uniqueness of individual cultures (Altman, 2001; Freidman, 2005; Gilbert, Masucci, Homko, & Bove, 2008; Hargittai, 2007). That fear seems exaggerated now; in fact, some of the most savvy observers suggest that connectivity is a prime force of progress and globalization the world over (Friedman, 2005). Not only has the Internet made health care and sexual literacy more accessible (Levine, 2011), it has also opened new kinds of communities and made transparent who has rights and who is denied them (Boyd, 2014). Of course, this has also produced some political backlash (Herdt, 2009b), some risk to mental health (Esposito, 2011), and the need for new norms to govern the morality of online relationships (Freitas, 2017). That's because just as the Internet has brought new sexual boundaries, roles, and norms for individuals, it has also created controversy about the political control of these boundaries through regulation of online sexual communities (Boellstorff, 2008; Braman, 2011)). Let's look at how these new communities' search for respect and existence online has created greater sexual health and well-being (Pascoe, 2011).

Censorship of sexual expression is as old as civilization, but the censorship of online sexuality is relatively new (Warf, 2011). More than 60 countries engage in some form of state-sponsored censorship, often involving online sexuality (Khattak, 2016). Increasingly, countries such as China employ mass surveillance through social media and other online platforms to regulate politics and religion, control academic speech, and generally control the mass media (Human Rights Watch, 2018). Such censorship is actually common in countries that are generally considered to be authoritarian or hostile to democracy, such as Russia, China, North Korea, Syria, and Cuba, but it also occurs in countries that are allies of the United States, including Saudi Arabia, Indonesia, and Vietnam. These nations use Internet censorship of "morality" and "antisocial" content, including political action communities, reproductive health rights and sexual rights advocates, and pornography, as justification for the censorship. Of most concern for sexual literacy are those countries that ban sexual education and reproductive health information online, such as Indonesia. Other countries restrict or ban minority sexual and gender or reproductive expression. Although the People's

Republic of China has long had a hostile relationship with major search engines such as Google (Shanker, 2011), in 2018 some Chinese women took the courageous step of publicly saying that they had been sexually harassed, but government censorship quickly put down this expression of the #Me-Too Movement (Human Rights Watch, 2018).

In spite of such barriers, however, online sexual communities have flourished elsewhere, as in the United States, and some have gone global. Of all of these developments, what has happened to the online **transgender** movement suggests a huge historic change. Transgender people express gender behavior and relationships that may depart from the norms in their own communities (IOM Report, 2011). Before the Internet, many lived in isolation, feeling alone and disconnected from other transgender people. Transgender people, however, can be found in most if not all societies, and the Internet has enabled them to join online communities to meet and strengthen their identities and their common cause (Soriano, 2014). Experts believe that without the Internet, the transgender community would not exist in the same way today (Currah, Juang, & Minter, 2006; IOM Report, 2011). Experts also speculate that sexual specializations, such as kinky sex, have become more prominent through online community formation, as we will see later. It would be difficult, if not impossible, to find like-minded individuals in the actual world, simply because there aren't that many living in proximity to one another. No one really knows how many hundreds or thousands of such communities exist online, but the number is growing (Pascoe, 2011). These online communities are now part of the diversity of all human sexuality. Although not for everyone, these communities do provide support for the growth of sexual individuality and sexual well-being for people all over the world.

transgender
A person who expresses gender behaviors that vary from the norm.

Chapter Review

SUMMARY

Sex, Media, and Pop Culture

- Pop culture is connected to major cultural attitudes in sexuality and shared sexual images.
- Four changes brought about by the media include making private sexual imagery more public, having explicit sexual images in public media, making conversations about sex more acceptable, and changing public attitudes about sex.
- Popular music influences our sexual emotions and attitudes, and performers sometimes become sex symbols.
- For a century, advertisers have seized upon shared sexual images to market products and bodies.
- Shared imagery is basic to all human cultures, and as the media have become more pervasive, these images have been extended to all media.
- Movies, television, and home videos have changed notions of sexuality in the United States and also altered public and private boundaries.

The Internet and Sexual Literacy

- Diverse media have played a role in shaping our reality and communications.
- Shared sexual imagery is increasing due to the Internet and new online forms of sexual expression.
- Sexual socialization increasingly occurs online, especially among teens and young adults.
- The Internet has revolutionized human society by providing a wealth of opportunities for social connections to one another worldwide.
- The Internet has radically changed the way we think about friendship, romance, dating, and sexuality.

Online Sexual Contexts

- Sexual individuality is how you experience your own sexual uniqueness in needs, feelings, desires, communications, and behaviors, especially online.
- Norms for sexual behavior online are still evolving, so it is important to set clear personal boundaries for your online sexuality.
- The Internet allows people to locate a large number of other people who share their interests and perhaps even find a mate.
- Online relationship formation, whether long-term romantic relationships or casual sexual hook-ups, are growing in importance in our culture.
- Online games and avatars are part of the virtual sexual landscape.

Adult Sexual Content

- The label "adult sexual content (ASC)" has long been applied to sexually explicit materials, and it is now applied to online pornography.
- Pornography has reshaped how some people imagine their bodies and sexual expression.
- The Internet allows individuals to explore and express their own sexuality, privately and anonymously.
- The pornification of our culture and sexuality in films and online should not be taken to mean that what is shown is normal.
- Adult sexual entertainment is a live, online form of paid sexual interaction.

Online Communities, Rights, and Sexual Well-Being

- Newly forming global sexual communities might not have come together without the Internet.
- Governments can use the Internet to censor sexual expression, as the People's Republic of China has tried to do.
- The right of free expression online has advanced reproductive and sexual rights in cultures.
- The Internet has made possible the creation of a global transgender community.

What's Your Position?

1. **How has the Internet changed your sexuality, including expression of your desires, romance, dating, and sex?**
   - Is the Internet helping you to define your sexual individuality?
   - Do you regularly engage in online sexual communications, and are these helpful or not helpful to you?

2. **What aspects of your individual sexuality, including sexual images or photos, would you make public on the web?**
   - Can you define your own boundaries?
   - Where do you set the limits of what you will share in sexual images—your own or someone else's?

3. **Why would you choose or not choose to present an identity that is true and authentic online when expressing your sexuality?**

Design elements: Controversies in Sexuality: HBRH/Shutterstock; Research and Sexual Well Being: verity jane smith/Getty Images; Healthy Sexuality: Sergey Furtaev/Shutterstock; Communication Matters: PeopleImages/Getty Images; Know Yourself: Plush Studios/Blend Images LLC; What's Your Position: Luis Molinero/Shutterstock; Healthy Sexuality: A. Minde/PhotoAlto; Did You Know icon: McGraw-Hill Education; Page corner icon: McGraw-Hill Education.

Sexual Anatomy and Physiology

Timothy A. Clary/AFP/Getty Images

Sexual Anatomy
- Explain why it is important to know about the sexual body.

Female Sexual Anatomy
- Identify the structures of the female reproductive system and those related to arousal.
- Describe the variability in appearance of female genital structures.
- Describe what female genital mutilation is and why it is performed in certain cultures.

Female Sexual Physiology
- Describe the role of the endocrine system in sexual physiology.
- Identify the major hormones that play a role in the functioning of the reproductive system.
- Describe the role pheromones play in sexual behavior and menstrual synchrony.
- Describe the process of menstruation and what happens in menopause.

Male Sexual Anatomy
- Identify the structures of the male reproductive system and understand how the male reproductive system functions.
- Describe the variability in appearance of male genital structures.
- Describe the process of circumcision and how it affects the physical structure of the penis and the male sexual experience.
- Explain why individuals circumcise their own or their children's genitals.

Male Sexual Physiology
- Compare the hormonal cycle of men to the female menstrual cycle and menopause.

Bodily Integrity Rights and Sexual Well-Being
- Apply the concept of bodily integrity rights to female genital mutilation and male circumcision.

• Learning
• Objectives

Developing Your Position

1. Have you ever examined your own genitals? If yes, how did you feel when looking at them?
2. What do you believe influenced your reactions?
3. What words do you use to identify your reproductive and sexual organs?
4. How do you feel about the practice of circumcision?

Self, Society, and Culture: The Perfect Genitals?

The perfect penis. Do you think it actually exists? My (Nicole) brother-in-law seems to think it does. Though he doesn't believe he possesses it, he believes he has part of the "perfect penis." Let me explain. When my brother-in-law, Kirk, was in college, he and his friends decided among the four of them that together they possessed the perfect penis. One person's penis had the perfect girth; one the perfect length, one the perfectly shaped head, and one had the perfect testicles in size and shape. It is fascinating that these young men had such a well-defined interest in the male genitals. Their interest is actually not unusual, though.

Art, writings, and practices going back thousands of years illuminate the great interest humans have in genitals. Even today, our media are filled with articles about the perfect genitals and ads for products and pills claiming to help create them. We have creams and pills claiming to enhance penis size; articles on the right length for pubic hair; and surgical procedures that claim to enlarge the controversial G-spot or decrease the size of the labia. It is incredible that the size, shape, and appearance of genital and reproductive body parts is the focus of so much economic activity.

In this chapter, we will examine female and male genital and reproductive structures to develop a more complete understanding of how these parts of our bodies work together to procreate and to bring us sexual pleasure. We will also look at variations in cultural practices and standards of beauty and how they relate to the issue of bodily integrity rights.

SEXUAL ANATOMY

This chapter is devoted to our bodies, how they work to help us reproduce and how they help us experience incredible pleasure. Part of the journey toward sexual literacy involves becoming aware of our anatomy and being able to refer to it correctly as we engage in discussions about bodies and their relationship to sexuality, sexual behavior, gender and sexual identity, and reproduction. Essentially, **anatomy** is the study of the physical structure of our bodies and the intricate design of the systems that live within the structures, for example, the respiratory, circulatory, nervous, endocrine, and reproductive systems. **Physiology** is the study of how all these internal systems and structures function. In this chapter, we introduce the structures and functions of the female and male reproductive and genital systems to learn how to care for them. Having accurate knowledge about human sexual anatomy and physiology can help you increase your sexual well-being and your comfort level and ability to talk with loved ones and professionals about what is going on with your body at any one moment. It is critical to understand the physiological and hormonal influences of the body and how they affect males and females in order to examine other social and psychological aspects of our sexuality.

How well do you know the inner workings of your sexual anatomy? Take the quiz in "Know Yourself: Sexual Anatomy Facts and Myths" to check your understanding of sexual anatomy and physiology.

anatomy
The study of the physical structure and systems of the body.

physiology
The study of how bodily structures and systems function.

Know Yourself

Sexual Anatomy Facts and Myths

Answer the following true/false questions to gauge your own knowledge of sexual anatomy and to learn whether you have bought into society's most common myths about the structure and function of our sexual bodies.

1. Men have only male hormones and women have only female hormones.
2. The anus has an erotic capacity for both men and women irrespective of sexual orientation.
3. The correct name for the female genitals is the vagina.
4. The clitoris is the only organ in the human body with the sole function of giving sexual pleasure.
5. The ovaries and testes are formed from the same embryonic tissue.
6. Men who have a larger penis can give their partners more orgasms.
7. If you hit it hard enough, a man's penis can "break."
8. A vaginal, or G-spot, orgasm is more powerful than an orgasm from clitoral stimulation.
9. Women can ejaculate.
10. All men should be circumcised for hygienic reasons.

For the correct answers, see page 103.

Being able to label the sexual parts of the body and knowing how the body sexually functions are not the only reasons for studying sexual anatomy and physiology. Thinking about how you *feel* about your own body will increase your emotional literacy. If you have knowledge of how your body is built and how it functions, you are much less likely to have inaccurate or even false beliefs about sexuality and your body. Time and again research has shown that when people are comfortable with their own bodies and at ease talking about them, they generally do better in communicating their needs, and typically feel better about their own body image (Aggleton, Wood, Malcolm, & Parker, 2005; Tepper & Owens, 2007; Tovar, 2012).

In addition, the more comfortable you are with your own body, the better able you are to have important conversations about your body and the body of your sexual partner(s) and to make good health decisions. This factual and emotional communication is critical for creating and maintaining personal relationships over time. It also becomes a starting point for passing positive knowledge along to children, friends, family members, and other important people in your life.

We suggest personalizing the information in this chapter to yourself. We invite you to sit down, pull out a mirror, and explore your own body as we discuss sexual anatomy and physiology. If you have an intimate partner with whom you feel comfortable sharing this journey or a friend who is interested in comparing notes with you, then begin the dialogue.

FEMALE SEXUAL ANATOMY

Our understanding of our genitals begins with what we can see on our own bodies and the bodies of others. Because they are visible to us, we tend to know something about how they look and perhaps what they do. Part of learning about sexual anatomy is learning how the

vulva
The external female genitals; often incorrectly referred to as the vagina.

mons pubis
Also called the *mons veneris*, the female pubic mound of fatty tissue that covers the pubic bone.

pubic bone
Part of the pelvis, the pubic bone is covered by a layer of fat known as the mons pubis.

appearance of our external genitals corresponds with our internal organs and the physiological processes associated with them (Fausto-Sterling, 2000). While we understand that there is a spectrum of physical and sexual differentiation and that the terms *male* and *female* seem to reinforce the binary view of sex and gender, we believe it is important to have a good understanding of male and female bodies to then better understand the wider spectrum of anatomical and physiological possibilities within human bodies. We discuss this spectrum in much more detail in Chapter 9.

External Female Sex Organs

The term for the female external genital region is the **vulva,** though it is often mistakenly called the vagina. (The vagina is an internal organ that lies just inside the vulva.) Figure 4.1 shows the structures of the vulva. Figure 4.2 shows variations of the vulva. The **mons pubis** (aka *mons veneris*) is the fatty tissue overlying the **pubic bone.** After the onset of puberty, this region is generally covered with pubic hair. Part of the vulva is the **labia majora** (Latin for "large lips"). The labia majora are vertical, outer liplike structures of skin folds that cover the **labia minora;** and like the mons pubis, the outside of the labia majora is generally covered with hair after puberty. The labia minora (Latin for "small lips") are also liplike structures that comprise smaller and more delicate skin folds. Unlike the labia majora, the labia minora are hairless, although they contain numerous **sebaceous glands** that resemble small bumplike structures. **Sebum,** or **oil,** produced by the sebaceous glands coats the surface of the labia minora to lubricate and protect the underlying

Figure 4.1
The structures of the vulva, the external female genitals.

(a) Superficial structures of external genitalia
- Glans of clitoris
- Mons pubis
- Clitoral hood
- Urethral opening
- Vestibule
- Vaginal opening
- Opening for Bartholin's glands
- Labia minora
- Labia majora
- Perineum
- Anus

(b) Closeup of clitoris, Skene's glands, and Bartholin's glands
- Clitoris
- Labia minora
- Urethra
- Skene's glands
- Vagina
- Bartholin's glands

(c) Deep structures of external genitalia
- Pubic symphysis
- Body of clitoris
- Crus of clitoris
- Bulb of the vestibule
- Bartholin's gland

(d) Scan of internal structures of clitoris

From Clinical Anatomy, Christine M. Vaccaro © 2015 Wiley Periodicals, Inc. Reproduced with permission of John Wiley & Sons Inc.

ANSWERS to Sexual Anatomy Facts and Myths *(p. 101)*

1. False: Men and women have the same hormones; but hormone levels differ. Furthermore, hormone levels differ from one man to another and from one woman to another.

2. True: The anus has an erotic capacity for all humans, regardless of sex or gender. As the genitals and anus share a lot of the same musculature and nerve endings, the anus can provide as much pleasure and arousal as other parts of the body. In addition, sexual orientation has no bearing on erotic capacity of the anus.

3. False: The vagina is the birth canal and the pathway to the cervix, uterus, and fallopian tubes. The collective term for the external female genitals is the "vulva."

4. True: The clitoris is the only organ in the human body with the sole function of giving sexual pleasure.

5. True: The ovaries and testes are formed from the same embryonic tissue. All embryos have the same genital and reproductive structures before sexual differentiation begins.

6. False: Solid scientific evidence has consistently shown that there is no relationship between penis size and sexual desire or response for either men or women. Most partners state that it is not the size but how one engages in sexual behavior that is important.

7. True and False: While the penis does not have any kind of skeletal structure or bone that can be broken, the penis can experience damage to its tissue if it is hit hard enough or bent in such a way as to cause damage to its internal structure.

8. False: The reality is that there is much controversy over the existence of the G-spot. What we know about female orgasms is that the clitoris is the primary mode of orgasmic experience for women. The question of whether vaginal orgasms exist independently of clitoral stimulation is quite controversial.

9. True: Some researchers and some women say that there is a female ejaculation that can occur when sensitive areas within the vagina are stimulated to the point of climax. The Skene's glands are located in this area and drain into the urethral opening—this is what is thought to produce the emission, which has been shown to be similar to the secretions produced by the prostate gland in men.

10. False: Circumcision was once thought to be necessary for male hygiene. Some research still shows that uncircumcised men can be at higher risk for STIs due to the fact that bacteria and viruses can conceal themselves under the foreskin, but there is no research to support the idea that uncircumcised men have difficulties maintaining hygiene with an intact foreskin.

Know Yourself

labia majora
The outer lips of the vulva.

labia minora
The inner lips of the vulva, one on each side of the vaginal opening.

sebaceous glands
Glands that produce oil.

sebum
Oil produced by sebaceous glands that coats and protects the surface of tissue the glands are on.

tumescence
The state of being swollen or engorged with blood.

clitoral hood
The fold of skin that surrounds and protects the clitoral glans.

clitoris
A highly sensitive structure of the female external genitals.

clitoral glans
The small external portion of the clitoris.

clitoral crura
The internal portion of the clitoris.

---

tissues (Barclay, 2017). During sexual arousal, blood rushes into the vascular tissue of the labia in a phenomenon known as **tumescence.**

The folds of the labia minora connect at the top of the vulva to the **clitoral hood,** which covers the **clitoris.** Unlike the male penis, which serves as the organ of sexual pleasure, reproduction, and urination, these functions are all separate in the female. The sole function of the clitoris is to produce pleasure, and thus it contains numerous nerve endings that render it the most sexually sensitive organ in the female body (Levin, 2015). In comparison to the male penis, the clitoris contains more nerve endings in its pea-shaped glans than are found in the entire head or glans of the penis. In its unaroused state, the clitoris is retracted under the clitoral hood. However, during sexual arousal and tumescence, the clitoris becomes stiff and erect, causing the clitoral hood to pull back. The clitoris is primarily an internal structure with only a small area, the **clitoral glans,** being visible. The internal part of the clitoris is shaped like an inverted V, forming two legs that extend from the clitoral glands along both sides of the labia. These legs are called the **clitoral crura** (singular, *crus*). The crura are made up of spongy tissue that will engorge with blood during sexual arousal.

103

urethral opening
Opening between the clitoris and the vaginal opening that allows urine to be expelled from the bladder.

vaginal opening
Opening between the urethral opening and the perineum; a tubular tract that leads to the uterus.

anus
The opening of the digestive tract for the expulsion of feces.

tenting effect
The vaginal wall's increase in size during sexual arousal.

mucous membrane
The inner wall of the vagina made up of moist, soft tissue.

Bartholin's glands
Glands located on each side of the vaginal opening.

vaginal lubrication
Fluid produced by the Bartholin's glands in the vagina to aid in penetration during sexual activity.

vagina
An elastic, muscular canal that extends from the vulva inward to the cervix.

cervix
The neck of the uterus, connecting the uterus with the vagina.

uterus
Also called the womb, the structure connected at one end to the cervix and at both sides to the fallopian tubes.

fallopian tubes
Ducts that hover over the ovaries to the uterus.

introitus
The opening of the vagina.

hymen
The fold of tissue that partially covers the introitus.

Figure 4.2
The appearance of the vulva varies from woman to woman.
(*left*) John R. Foster/Science Source; (*right*) Medicshots/Alamy Stock Photo

Below the clitoris is the **urethral opening** where women expel urine from the bladder. The **vaginal opening,** found between the urethra and the **anus,** extends into the vagina. The vagina is an elastic canal, which, with sexual arousal, will increase in length and width. In an unaroused state, the vaginal opening is about 1 centimeter (0.4 inch) wide and 7 centimeters (2.8 inches) long. As the woman becomes sexually aroused the vaginal opening may increase to about 2 cm (0.8 inch) and the length of the vagina will increase to about 9 cm (3.5 inches). The vaginal wall's increase in size during sexual arousal is called the **tenting effect.** The inner wall of the vagina is made up of moist, soft tissue called **mucous membrane.** Mucous secretions help to keep the vagina clean by producing a balanced solution of acid-alkaline. During sexual arousal these secretions will increase and the **Bartholin's glands,** located on each side of the vaginal opening, will begin to produce **vaginal lubrication.** The inner vagina is also the location of the highly debated G-spot. See "Controversies in Sexuality: The Elusive G-Spot" to engage in the discussion around this interesting anatomical debate.

Internal Female Sexual Organs

The internal female sexual organs, illustrated in Figure 4.4, include the **vagina,** the cervix, the uterus, and the fallopian tubes, as well as the introitus and hymen. The vagina is a potential space for different forms of sexual penetration. It is also the birth canal and the place where the menstrual blood leaves the body. The inner part of the vagina is connected to the **cervix,** which opens into the **uterus.** Also called the *womb,* the uterus is connected at one end to the cervix and on both sides to the fallopian tubes. The conelike cervix (from Latin for "neck of the uterus") rests on the top of the vagina. During heterosexual intercourse, semen may be delivered right into the entrance to the cervix, increasing the likelihood for sperm to travel up through the cervix and into the uterus and the **fallopian tubes** (also called *uterine tubes*), where fertilization may take place.

The opening of the vagina, called the **introitus,** is located between the urinary opening and the anus. The **hymen** is a fold of tissue that, in most women, partially covers the introitus. The hymen is typically present at birth, although some females have no hymen at birth, and it stays intact until penetration by the penis or some other object, or is torn in some other way. The hymen, like other sexual structures, varies in shape and size among females, as you can see in Figure 4.5. The tissues of the vulva are generally thin and delicate prior to puberty, and many girls and teens tear or stretch the hymen while participating in sports like bicycling, horseback riding, or gymnastics, or while inserting tampons. Therefore, contrary to many cultural and

CONTROVERSIES in Sexuality

The Elusive G-Spot

Is there a place on the female body that may really arouse a woman? You may have seen stories in magazines like *Cosmopolitan* that discuss how women can experience greater orgasmic potential by locating their G-spot. Some sexual scientists dispute its existence or importance, but still, many women endorse the G-spot as their source of potential pleasure and orgasm.

How do we know that the G-spot even exists? The G-spot, or Grafenberg spot, is theorized to be located approximately 2 inches up the anterior vaginal canal (Figure 4.3). When sexually stimulated, this dime-size area will protrude and can be felt. During sexual arousal, vasocongestion, or increasing blood flow to erectile tissues in the genitals and nipples, occurs and the nerve endings surrounding the G-spot allegedly can be stimulated enough to produce an orgasm.

While anecdotal evidence suggests that some women have had their G-spot surgically enlarged to intensify orgasm, to the benefit of plastic surgeons, the evidence for the existence of a G-spot remains sketchy. So, the real question is, does this structure really exist?

Figure 4.3
Many women attest that stimulation of the G-spot can produce orgasm, but its existence is not well established by research.

Yes:

- Dr. Ernst Grafenberg described the existence of an allegedly highly sensitive area on the anterior wall of the vagina. Subsequent research suggested that stimulation of this particular area results in high levels of sexual arousal and powerful orgasms (Addiego, Belzer et al., 1981; Belzer, Whipple, & Mosher, 1984).
- Many women identify with this pleasure zone and attest to its existence (Ladas, Whipple, & Perry, 2005).
- Several studies in the anatomy, behavior, and biochemical fields have tried to prove the existence of the G-spot by demonstrating that orgasm can occur as a response to stimulation to specific zones felt through the anterior wall of the vagina (Alzate & Hoch, 1986).
- One study published in 2013 conducted ultrasound imaging during coitus and proposed that the penis appears to stimulate the base of the clitoris. Thus, the G-spot may actually refer to the internal base of the clitoris, rather than to a separate structure (Buisson & Jannini, 2013).

No:

Many scientists and experts are skeptical.

- A recent identical twin study from researchers in the United Kingdom found no detectable genetic basis for the G-spot. Only 56% of women in their study reported having a G-spot, and the prevalence steadily decreased with age (Burri, Cherkas, & Spector, 2010).
- Most historical studies of the G-spot have been inconclusive. The sample sizes are small, and there have been significant difficulties in replicating the results (Burri, Cherkas, & Spector, 2010).
- Sexual scientists wonder why it took so long for the G-spot to emerge in the public consciousness and are suspicious that it has been exploited by plastic surgeons for profit.

For now, it appears that women must rely on their own feelings and experiences to determine whether this pleasure zone exists. Do you think the G-spot is real?

Figure 4.4
Side view of the female reproductive system.

imperforate hymen
Occurs when the tissue of the hymen completely closes the vaginal opening causing menstrual fluid to accumulate.

perimetrium
The outer layer of the uterus.

myometrium
The middle layer of the uterus, which comprises smooth muscle and vascular tissue.

endometrium
The inner membrane of the uterus; the lining of which is shed during menstruation.

religious beliefs, an intact hymen is not a good indicator of virginity. Because there may be little or no blood or pain involved when the hymen is torn, a girl may not even know about it. Remnants of the hymen usually remain until a woman delivers a baby vaginally. Occasionally, the tissue of the hymen is too thick to break easily during intercourse. In these cases, a medical practitioner might have to make a small incision to open it further. In the rare case of an **imperforate hymen,** the tissue of the hymen completely closes the vaginal opening, causing menstrual fluid to accumulate. This condition, too, requires a small incision to open the hymen. For more information on the hymen, see "Healthy Sexuality: The Hymen and Virginity."

The uterus is a muscular, pear-shaped organ that connects to the fallopian tubes, one on each side. Three layers comprise the uterine walls: the **perimetrium,** which is the outermost part; the **myometrium,** or the muscular middle layer; and the **endometrium,** or the

Figure 4.5
The hymen, like other sexual structures, varies in shape and size among females. Imperforate hymens are rare and can be corrected with minor surgery. A microperforate hymen has a very small opening, and a septate hymen is divided in two by a band of tissue. Microperforate and septate hymens also can be corrected with minor surgery.

HEALTHY Sexuality

The Hymen and Virginity

In many cultures the hymen is traditionally the physical marker of a woman's virginity (Blank, 2007). In fact, many of the phrases we use to describe a woman losing her virginity illustrate how we think of the role of the hymen. For example, the phrase "popping the cherry" describes the loss of virginity as marked by the breaking of the hymen. In many societies, if a husband finds that his wife's hymen is already broken on their wedding night, he and her community may humiliate, shame, ridicule, or stone her to death for being immoral (Scarleteen, 2009; Yalom, 2002).

Today, some women turn to reconstructive plastic surgery to replace their hymen. A woman may do this for many reasons. For example, she may be nervous that her future spouse might think she was promiscuous or she may want her husband to experience tighter penetration during intercourse. Some women report requesting this surgery on their twenty-fifth wedding anniversary to enjoy this milestone as a "re-virgin" (Prakash, 2009). Whatever the reasons, the surgery is drastic and invasive.

Discussing the hymen brings up some interesting questions to consider. Because we may have misconceptions about certain issues, thinking about the following questions may help to identify your own feelings. Additionally, the exercise may help us realize the value that we place on the symbols of virginity.

- Do you think people should consider that an intact hymen truly represents a woman's virginity?
- What other ways could people think of a woman's virginity?
- What about male virginity? Is there a way to check if males have engaged in sexual intercourse?
- Is virginity still an important concept? Why or why not?
- For women, if your hymen breaks before you engage in sex, would you have your hymen surgically reconstructed to assure your spouse or partner that you are a virgin?
- Would you want your intended spouse or lifetime partner to be examined to see if her hymen was intact to prove her virginity?
- Does sexual assault, in your mind, result in a "loss of virginity"?

WHAT'S ON YOUR MIND?

Q: It is really easy for me to have an orgasm when I masturbate or when my partner stimulates my clitoris, but I cannot orgasm during intercourse. My friends have said there is a difference between a clitoral orgasm and an orgasm produced during intercourse. Is there really a difference?

ANSWER: People often get confused as to the definition of an orgasm, which contributes to these statements. An **orgasm** is defined as the peak of sexual excitement, characterized by strong feelings of pleasure and by a series of involuntary contractions of the muscles of the genitals and other areas of the body. The idea that a clitoral orgasm is less pleasurable than an orgasm achieved through intercourse goes back to the days of Sigmund Freud in the early 1900s. Freud believed that a clitoral orgasm was emotionally immature. Pop culture has largely played into this idea through various articles and products that tout the power of the orgasm achieved during intercourse, known as the **G-spot** or vaginal **orgasm**. The reality is that an orgasm is an orgasm no matter how it is achieved, though women do differ in their sexual individuality and their experience of orgasm. Each orgasm may also differ in strength and duration depending on a variety of factors.

If you reach an orgasm more easily through clitoral stimulation (like the majority of women), focus on that area in order to climax. Most importantly, relax and enjoy yourself.

orgasm

The peak of sexual excitement, characterized by strong feelings of pleasure and by a series of involuntary contractions of the muscles of the genitals and other areas of the body.

G-spot orgasm

An orgasm achieved during intercourse that occurs from stimulation to the G-spot rather than the clitoris.

107

fimbria
The fringe tissue near the ovary leading to the fallopian tube.

ovulation
The phase of a woman's menstrual cycle in which an egg is released.

ovary
Houses both gonads and endocrine glands; attaches to the fimbria of each fallopian tube to allow release of ovum into the uterus.

follicle
Part of the ovary; each contains a hollow ball of cells with an immature egg in the center.

mammary glands
Internal breast; its principal function is to produce milk to nourish an infant after childbirth.

areola
The dark visible center of the breast.

nipple
The raised bud at the center of the areola.

Figure 4.6
Internal front view of the ovary, fallopian tube, and layers of the uterus.

innermost layer, into which a fertilized ovum will implant. The fallopian tubes are approximately 7 to 14 cm (2.76 to 5.5 inches) long. Each one ends in a fringe of tissue called the **fimbria** (plural, *fimbriae*), which sweeps over the ovaries during **ovulation** (the phase of a woman's menstrual cycle in which an egg is released), picks up the ovum, and, with the help of tail-like projections inside the walls of the fallopian tubes, guides the ovum down to the uterus.

Figure 4.6 shows the structure of the ovary and other parts of the reproductive system. The **ovary** resembles an almond in size and shape and has two main functions: to release ova (eggs) and to produce hormones. Most females have two ovaries in the pelvic cavity on each side of the uterus. Every month during ovulation, either the right or left ovary produces a single mature egg for fertilization. When a baby girl is born, she already has about 1 million **ovarian follicles,** each containing a hollow ball of cells with an immature ovum (egg) in the center. During childhood, approximately half of ovarian follicles are absorbed by the body. By the time a girl reaches puberty and her menstrual cycle begins, about 400,000 ovarian follicles are left.

Unlike men who produce sperm throughout most of their lifetime, women are born with all the ova they will ever have. During the reproductive years, the time between puberty and menopause, the ovaries may release 300 to 500 mature ova, which is less than 0.1% of the remaining ovarian follicles.

Breasts and Breast Development

Though the breasts are often sexualized, they are not part of the female genitalia. Rather, they are secondary sex characteristics that develop during puberty, as a girl matures. The **mammary glands** and fat deposits primarily comprise the internal breast, whose principal function is to produce milk to nourish an infant after childbirth. Externally, the **areola** is the dark center of the breast and the **nipple** is the raised bud at the center of the areola. Figure 4.7 shows the structure of the breasts. (The development of female and male secondary sex characteristics during puberty is discussed in detail in Chapter 11.)

Breast development is often the first thing that young girls experience in puberty and is also the first thing those around young girls notice. Thus, it can be an awkward milestone for girls. It outwardly portrays the psychological changes that occur during puberty and forces friends and family to notice a young girl's maturation as

Breast development is one of the earliest signs of pubertal development in females.
Fancy Collection/SuperStock

Figure 4.7 Internal and external structures of the female breast.

(a) Front view
(b) Side view

she copes with it herself. **Thelarche** is the name for the first stage of breast development, characterized by a small lump that forms beneath the areola. In puberty the ovaries begin to produce greater amounts of **estrogen,** a hormone that produces female reproductive and secondary sex characteristics and influences the menstrual cycle. At this time, fat begins to accumulate in the breast and the ducts develop. At **menarche,** or a female's first menstrual period, secretory glands form at the ends of the milk ducts, and they continue to mature.

Maintaining breast health is an important part of health care. One of the ways to do this is to self-examine the breasts monthly for changes, lumps, or secretions from the nipples. All of these could be signs of cancer, which is why monthly breast examinations should become a routine part of self-care. See "Healthy Sexuality: How to Examine Your Own Breasts" for instructions on how to do this important exam.

Variability in the Female Body

Though the descriptions of female sexual anatomy and secondary sex characteristics have been very general, it's important to note that not all female bodies look the same. In fact, all bodies vary in some way. These variations are most evident in the size, shape, and color of our bodies. But bodies often differ anatomically. For example, some women are born with only one ovary; some women have very large clitorises. These variations are not visible to the whole world, but may cause stress to those who perceive themselves to be different. Generally, these variations do not indicate problems or dysfunctions, but rather are evidence that each body develops in a different way (Martin, 2013). This is perfectly natural. Figure 4.8 shows variation of female breasts.

Now that we know that there is a wide range of variability, what is the standard for beauty? Most cultures have standards of female beauty to which many women aspire. In some West African cultures, such as Nigeria, large buttocks, breasts, and curvaceous hips are the epitome of female beauty (Oloruntoba-Oju, 2007). In the contemporary United States, many people think that female beauty is a slender body with large breasts.

The size, shape, and weight of our bodies are sources of anxiety for many people in the United States. In the movie *Phat Girlz* (2006), comedienne Mo'Nique battles feelings of self-doubt because of her weight. Everywhere around her are thin women who wear the most stylish clothes and get the attention of men. Hoping to change her body, Mo'Nique struggles with dieting, but to no avail. Then, she meets the handsome Dr. Tunde, visiting from Nigeria. They fall in love and Dr. Tunde explains to Mo'Nique that he finds her beautiful exactly as she is, because in Nigeria larger women are considered more beautiful. *Phat Girlz* illustrates how variations in the appearance of the body are treated differently in different cultures.

Chances are, your body looks different in some ways from the people you know. In other ways it looks similar. Recognizing the natural variability in bodies helps in understanding that,

thelarche
The first stage of breast development.

estrogen
Hormones that produce female reproductive and secondary sex characteristics and impact the functioning of the menstrual cycle.

menarche
A female's first menstrual period.

HEALTHY Sexuality

How to Examine Your Own Breasts

Women should examine their breasts at least once a month.
David Parker/Science Source

It's important to be aware of the benefits and limitations of breast self-exams (BSE). Please take note: If you find a change in your breasts, it does not necessarily mean cancer is present.

To examine your breasts, be aware of how your breasts normally look, and feel your breasts for changes. Or, use BSE with its step-by-step approach and its specific schedule. The best time to conduct BSE is when your breasts are not tender or swollen. This may be about 3 to 5 days after your menstrual period. Conduct a BSE at relatively the same point in your monthly cycle so that you can more accurately assess any possible changes in your breasts. Also, have your health care professional review your BSE technique during your periodic health exams.

If you have breast implants, you can also perform BSE. Have your surgeon help identify the edges of the implant so that you know what you are feeling. There is some thought that the implants push out the breast tissue and may actually make it easier to examine. If you are pregnant or breastfeeding, you can also examine your breasts regularly.

While breast cancer is about 100 times less common in men than in women, it is estimated that the lifetime risk of a man developing breast cancer is 1 in 1,000. About 2,000 new cases of breast cancer are diagnosed in men every year in the United States. While the risk is small, it is not a bad idea for men to do checks of their breast tissue as well in order to check for any lumps or changes that seem unusual.

Steps in a Breast Self-Exam

1. Conduct the BSE lying down so the breast tissue spreads evenly over the chest wall and is as thin as possible, making it much easier to feel all the breast tissue.
2. With your right arm behind your head, use the finger pads of the three middle fingers on your left hand to feel for lumps in the right breast. Use overlapping dime-sized circular motions of the finger pads to feel the breast tissue.
3. Use three different levels of pressure to feel all the breast tissue. Light pressure is needed to feel the tissue closest to the skin; medium pressure to feel a little deeper; and firm pressure to feel the tissue closest to the chest and ribs. A firm ridge in the lower curve of each breast is normal. If you're not sure how hard to press, talk with your doctor or nurse. Use each pressure level to feel the breast tissue before moving on to the next spot.
4. Move around the breast in an up-and-down pattern starting at an imaginary line drawn straight down your side from the underarm and moving across the breast to the middle of the chest bone (sternum). Be sure to check the entire breast area going down until you feel only ribs and up to the neck or collar bone (clavicle).
5. Some evidence suggests that the up-and-down pattern (sometimes called the vertical pattern) is the most effective pattern for covering the entire breast, without missing any breast tissue.
6. Repeat the exam on your left breast, using the finger pads of the right hand with your left arm behind your head.
7. While standing in front of a mirror with your hands pressing firmly down on your hips, look at your breasts for any changes of size, shape, contour, dimpling, redness, or scaliness of the nipple or breast skin. (Pressing down on the hips with your hands contracts the chest wall muscles to help enhance any breast changes.)
8. Examine each underarm while sitting up or standing and with your arm only slightly raised so you can easily feel in this area. Raising your arm straight up tightens the tissue in this area and makes it harder to examine.

For more information on breast cancer, including risk factors, see Chapter 6.

Source: Adapted from American Cancer Society. (2008). How to Perform a Breast Self-Exam. Retrieved online from http://www.cancer.org/Cancer/BreastCancer-early-detection-acs-recs-bse

Sexual Anatomy and Physiology 111

Figure 4.8

The size and shape of female breasts vary from woman to woman, just like other parts of the body.

(*top left*) Tetra Images/Corbis; (*top right*) Jeane Ellroy/Photononstop/Getty Images; (*bottom left*) Ken Weingart/Alamy Stock Photo; (*bottom right*) Morris Huberland/Science Source

despite what might be narrow standards of beauty, each of us has the right to know about our bodies, to keep them healthy and to seek pleasure in safe and satisfying ways. Many individuals feel so uncomfortable with a part of their body that they elect to modify it with plastic surgery to feel more beautiful (Frederick et al., 2007). For a discussion about surgical modification, see "Healthy Sexuality: What Do You Think About Plastic Surgery and Body Modification?"

In the United States, we consider body modification to be an elective procedure; however, in many areas of the world, genital modification is a cultural practice. Rituals such as female circumcision, or female genital mutilation, have critical and important consequences to the sexual health and well-being of those who are subjected to them. In the next section, we discuss female genital mutilation.

Female Genital Mutilation

Female circumcision is a cultural practice most often associated with African and Middle Eastern cultures, and the Islamic religion in particular. Some cultures believe that removal of the clitoris enhances the beauty and desirability of the female body, and others are also taught that unless the clitoris (the major source of sexual pleasure for women) is removed, women may become promiscuous or unfaithful to their partners (Blank, 2007; DeMeo, 1986).

There is much variation in the kinds of procedures performed on the genitals from one culture to another (DeMeo, 1986). In one culture, a woman may have her clitoris lightly cut, enough to cause bleeding but not to cause excessive damage. In another, her clitoris may be shortened. The most severe degree of female circumcision involves completely removing the clitoris and labia minora and scraping the labia majora. Any remaining tissues are then sewn together, leaving only a very small hole to allow the menstrual blood and urine to pass. This may also prevent a female from having sexual intercourse or having her hymen ruptured. When she marries, the stitches are either removed before her first night with her husband or broken apart when she and her husband have intercourse for the first time. Rates of female genital mutilation among girls under 14 have fallen sharply in most regions of Africa over the last three decades, but there are other areas in African and in the Middle East where it remains widespread (Galey, 2018). Because this procedure is often performed without antiseptic or anesthesia, some people refer to it as **female genital mutilation (FGM)**. According to the

female circumcision
The removal or shortening of the clitoris. It may include sewing the labia together to prevent sexual intercourse or the rupture of the hymen.

female genital mutilation (FGM)
Performing female circumcision without antiseptic or anesthesia.

HEALTHY Sexuality

What Do You Think About Plastic Surgery and Body Modification?

In the United States and countries around the world, elective plastic surgery is more popular today than ever. It has become more affordable and more acceptable. Saturated in a media culture that offers airbrushed perfect photos, women and men alter many parts of their face and body to feel more beautiful. Breast implants, facelifts, botox injections to eliminate wrinkles, and tummy tucks are all popular ways to change appearance.

Women today express concern about differences in the appearance of their breasts and have reconstructive surgery to make their breasts more "even" or "equal" in mass or shape. Doctors say that the key aesthetic elements of the ideal breast are nipple position and the proportions of the upper and lower halves of the breast. One doctor reported, "The ideal is a 45 to 55 percent proportion—that is, the nipple sits not at the half-way mark down the breast, but at about 45 percent from the top."

Think about your personal body image. Is there a part of your body (male or female) that you are so unhappy with that you would consider plastic surgery as a treatment option? What's your opinion about plastic surgery? Would you elect surgery? Under what circumstances? Do you believe that plastic surgery would increase your feelings of sexual attractiveness? In what ways?

Before and after breast augmentation surgery.
Steve Percival/Science Source

World Health Organization (WHO) (2019), FGM is most common in Central and Northern Islamic Africa, in parts of the Middle East, and among migrants from these areas. Approximately 3 million women a year, primarily under the age of 15, experience female genital mutilation. Figure 4.9 shows the distribution of the practice, primarily across African countries.

Today, FGM is a highly controversial cultural practice. This traditional procedure is associated with the transition from girlhood to womanhood. In addition to believing that the procedure enhances a girl's chance to marry, some people believe that it delays the onset of sexual desire, which they believe may enable a woman to control the urge to have premarital sex (Van Rossem & Gage, 2009). Some research has led experts to question this assumption. For example, a study of 6,753 females in the African country of Guinea revealed that FGM was not significantly associated with preventing premarital sexual relations, the age of first sex, or other claims that have been used to justify the practice (Van Rossem & Gage, 2009). In short, for their physical and sexual well-being, many women are better off without FGM.

FEMALE SEXUAL PHYSIOLOGY

Sexual physiology refers to the way that anatomical structures work during sexual development and sexual response. It's worth noting that although we focus on processes that occur inside the body, complex external processes also influence our sexual development and response. In other words, sexual physiology happens in tandem with our interactions in the social world, rather than in isolation and in response only to biological influences.

endocrine system
The system of glands that regulates body functions and processes, including puberty, metabolism, and mood, by releasing hormones.

hormone
A chemical substance produced in the body that controls and regulates the activity of certain cells or organs.

hypothalamus
The area of the brain that secretes substances that influence pituitary and other gland function and is involved in the control of body temperature, hunger, thirst, and other processes that regulate body equilibrium.

Figure 4.9

Distribution of female genital mutilation (FGM) in Africa. This map illustrates the distribution of FGM: the percentage of the female population that is subject to FGM and by country.

The Endocrine System and Hormones

In all human beings, the **endocrine system** is the system of glands that regulates body functions and processes, including puberty, metabolism, and mood, by releasing chemical substances called **hormones.** The endocrine system includes the **hypothalamus,** the area of the brain that secretes substances that influence the function of the pituitary and other endocrine glands and is involved in the control of body temperature, hunger, thirst, and other processes that regulate body homeostasis. The **pituitary gland** is a pea-sized gland located at the base of skull that is sometimes referred to as the "master gland," because it controls the hormone functions mentioned above. The endocrine system also regulates important parts of sexual development and arousal, pregnancy and menstruation, and sperm production.

Although it's fairly common to hear people refer to "female sex hormones" and "male sex hormones," there is no such thing (Nehm & Young, 2008). Men and women produce the same hormones, but in varying quantities (Jordan-Young, 2010). The two primary groups or categories of hormones regulating sexual development and arousal are androgens and estrogens, which belong to a class of hormones called **steroid hormones.** The **gonads,** or glands that produce sex hormones and reproductive cells (i.e., ovaries in women and testes in men), and the adrenal glands located on top of the kidneys secrete the steroid hormones. Though females produce greater amounts of estrogens, they also produce androgens, and though male bodies produce greater amounts of androgens, they also produce estrogens.

Testosterone is a steroid hormone from the androgen group that has been shown through research to have a greater effect on male sexual desire than on sexual function (Crenshaw & Goldberg, 1996). This means that low testosterone levels will not necessarily impair male sexual functions. However, testosterone has been shown to affect genital

pituitary gland
A small oval endocrine gland that lies at the base of the brain. It is sometimes called the master gland of the body because all the other endocrine glands depend on its secretions for stimulation.

steroid hormones
A group of hormones that include androgens and estrogens.

gonad
Glands that make sex hormones and reproductive cells; called testes in the male, ovaries in the female.

testosterone
A steroid hormone that helps organize male reproduction and produces secondary sex characteristics in males, and impacts sexual functioning in both sexes.

DID YOU KNOW

What role does smell play in sexual attraction? People in the United States use a range of deodorant and perfume products each day, including so-called *feminine hygiene products*. Often these products are marketed in a way that plays to consumer anxiety about embarrassing body odor or to the desire to smell pleasant to attract mates. In the United States, the heavy emphasis placed on masking the body's natural smells means that we often don't know what our bodies smell like or that we find the odors of our body unpleasant. In other parts of the world, the smells of the body, and specifically the scents that the genitals produce, are considered highly erotic. People in Europe and elsewhere do not rely as heavily on deodorants, antiperspirants, and perfumes as we do in the United States. Rather they let the natural odors of their bodies convey messages to others about attraction.

What do you think about body odors? Are they disgusting or neutral or sexy? Do you use products to mask them? Why?

oxytocin
Produced in the hypothalamus, is one of the most important neuropeptides.

pheromones
Chemical signals or odors that bodies release to effect a behavioral or psychological response in another body.

menstrual synchrony
Alignment of the menstrual cycles of women who live together (such as in homes, prisons, convents, bordellos, dormitories, or barracks) that reportedly occurs over time.

menstruation
The shedding of the uterine lining.

sensitivity and higher levels may result in more sexual pleasure. Testosterone is also known to play a primary role in female sexual drive and is thought to affect energy and feelings of well-being.

Estrogens and their roles in female sexual behavior are less clear. Research has shown that estrogens contribute to vaginal lubrication, to maintenance of the thickness and elasticity of the vaginal walls, and to a general sense of well-being (Kingsberg, 2002; Martin, 2013).

Another class of hormones, the *neuropeptide hormones*, influences the emotional aspects of sexuality, including attraction and arousal. Unlike steroid hormones produced in the gonads and adrenal glands, the brain produces neuropeptide hormones. **Oxytocin** is one of the most important neuropeptides. It may influence our feelings of erotic attraction and love. Oxytocin serves many purposes, including facilitating the flow of milk during breastfeeding, elevating our feelings of love and attraction while we cuddle, and helping us form strong emotional bonds with those to whom we're close (Kendrick, 2004).

Pheromones and Their Role in Sexual Behavior

Pheromones, from the Greek *pherein* (to transport) and *hormone* (to stimulate), are chemical signals that are not readily noticed by human senses, but are released by organisms to effect a behavioral or psychological response in another body. Females in many animal species release pheromones during the fertile period of their menstrual cycles to signal their availability for reproduction. Males may secrete pheromones that convey information about their genes, perhaps indicating health status or longevity or some other characteristic necessary for the survival of that particular species (Thornhill & Gangestad, 1999).

Research on the presence of pheromones in humans is inconclusive, though some studies suggest that certain scents can activate or inhibit sexual attraction and arousal (Levin, 2004). The classic study suggests that women who live together may menstruate at the same time, a phenomenon known as **menstrual synchrony,** based on odor cues (McClintock, 1971). In the study, women were exposed to sweat collected from other women. Depending on when the sweat was collected during a woman's menstrual cycle (before, during, or after ovulation), the woman's menstrual cycle sped up or slowed down. As a result, the researcher proposed the existence of two types of pheromones, one produced before ovulation that shortens the cycles, and one produced just at ovulation that lengthens it (McClintock, 1971). Some researchers have questioned the validity of these results, and so our understanding of pheromones is still developing (Yang & Schank, 2006; Martin, 2013).

Although our understanding of pheromones in humans is incomplete, knowing about them may be helpful in evaluating some of the claims proffered by deodorant and perfume companies claiming that their products include synthetic pheromones or similar substances developed to increase sexual attractiveness.

The Menstrual Cycle

Menstruation, the shedding of the uterine lining, is one of the most significant physiological processes of the female body. During each menstrual cycle, the lining of the uterus is prepared to nourish a fertilized ovum. If conception occurs, the ovum will implant in the uterus and the uterine lining will not be shed. If conception does not occur, the uterine lining is shed and exits the body through the vagina. This shedding process is what is referred to as a woman's *period*. The menstrual period generally lasts 2 to 6 days and may produce up to 8 ounces of menstrual flow. The menstrual cycle is measured from the first day of the period to the day before the next period begins, usually anywhere from 24 to 42 days. In the United States, menstruation usually begins around 12 years of age. This age has declined significantly throughout history. In Europe in the early 1800s, the average age of a girl's first period was 17 (Steingraber, 2007; Martin, 2013). In 1900, the average age of a first period among girls in the U.S. was 14.2 and now, the average age for girls beginning menstruation is about 12.4 years and still declining (Fuhrman, 2011). There are several theories that address this dramatic drop in the age of pubertal development. See "Research and Sexual Well-Being: Girls' Early Pubertal Development" for a more detailed examination of this trend and what may be causing it.

Throughout the cycle, the uterus passes through three phases in preparation for the implantation of a fertilized ovum (Figure 4.10). The first phase begins during ovulation and is called the **proliferative phase** (*pro*, "in support of; life"). During this phase, the endometrium of the uterus thickens and the ovum matures. In the next stage, the **secretory phase**,

proliferative phase
The first phase of ovulation.

secretory phase
The second phase of ovulation.

Figure 4.10

The three phases of the menstrual cycle. FSH stimulates the maturation of an ovum, and LH triggers the release of the ovum. If the ovum isn't fertilized and implanted in the uterine wall, it dissolves and the endometrium is shed during menstruation.

RESEARCH and Sexual Well-Being

Girls' Early Pubertal Development

In recent years, there has been much discussion about the declining age of pubertal development in girls in the United States. The concern is with girls who are achieving pubertal development at very early ages—sometimes as early as 7 or 8 years of age. In the United States today, approximately 16 percent of girls enter puberty by age 7 and almost one-third of girls enter puberty by 8 years of age (Fuhrman, 2011).

Early pubertal development (aka precocious puberty) is considered to be problematic for a variety of reasons. First, on an emotional and psychological level, few young girls are able to fully comprehend the biological processes their bodies are going through, and they have a difficult time understanding and adjusting to the events of puberty, such as menstruation and breast development. In addition, early puberty presents behavioral risks, as studies show that girls who enter puberty early tend to engage in more sexual risk taking (Ge, Conger, & Elder, 1996; Weir, 2016).

Early puberty is considered risky on a biological and physical level as well. Studies have shown that girls who begin menstruation at young ages are at increased risk for breast cancer (Leung et al., 2008; Pike, Pearce, & Wu, 2004). This increased risk is due to the extended exposure to ovarian hormones.

What are the possible reasons that girls are entering puberty at younger and younger ages? There are a few theories that address this.

- *Increasing epidemic of childhood obesity:* There have been many studies documenting the link between earlier pubertal development in girls and obesity (Aksglaede et al., 2009; Steingraber, 2007). When girls carry around excess body fat, their levels of certain hormones such as estrogen, leptin, and insulin are altered. These alterations accelerate pubertal timing.

- *Diet and nutrition:* A few studies have documented that girls ages 3–7 who consume large amounts of animal protein are more likely to experience early menstruation (Günther et al., 2010). Higher protein intake elevates a hormone called IGF-1, which is very similar to insulin. This increase promotes growth and is thought to accelerate the onset of pubertal development (Steingraber, 2007). In addition, children who eat large amounts of processed foods, dairy, processed meats, and fast food show pubertal development at early ages (Cheng et al., 2010).

- *Exposure to certain chemicals:* Some chemicals commonly found in products we use daily have been shown to accelerate puberty. These chemicals are called endocrine-disrupting chemicals or EDCs. They are known to mimic, inhibit, or alter natural hormones in the body. One of the most common EDCs that is causing the most concern is BPA. BPA is used in the production of plastics and can be found in water bottles and food storage containers. BPA can leach from containers into food and drinks, particularly if microwaved, heated, or washed. BPA exposure is associated with early menstruation in girls (Roy, Chakraborty, & Chakraborty, 2006). Due to this finding, many manufacturers are removing BPA from food containers.

A growing consensus of researchers is that obesity is not the cause of this early puberty, at least not the only cause (Aksglaede, et al., 2009). It is more likely that the environment is now stimulating hormone production. It is always important to be aware of these risk factors in order to make the best health and nutritional decisions for children.

---

corpus luteum
The tissue formed from a ruptured ovarian follicle.

progesterone
A steroid hormone produced in the ovary; prepares and maintains the uterus for pregnancy.

menstrual phase
The third and final phase of ovulation.

the endometrium further thickens and the **corpus luteum** develops. This is the tissue formed from a ruptured ovarian follicle after the release of the ovum. The corpus luteum produces important hormones, including **progesterone,** which prepares and maintains the uterus for pregnancy. In the third and final phase, the **menstrual phase,** the ovum has passed through the fallopian tube and into the uterus. Unfertilized, it dissolves and the uterus sheds the endometrium through the cervix as menstrual flow.

What causes the menstrual cycle each month? A delicate dance of hormones and brain signals lie behind menstrual physiology. During puberty the ovaries begin to produce greater amounts of estrogens. This increase in estrogens signals the hypothalamus to release **gonadotropin-releasing hormone (GnRH).** GnRH then stimulates the pituitary gland

Table 4.1 Sexual and reproductive hormones of males and females

HORMONE	SOURCE	FUNCTION
Estrogen	Ovaries, adrenal glands	Promotes maturation of reproductive organ development during puberty. Regulates menstrual cycle.
Progesterone	Ovaries, adrenal glands	Promotes breast development, maintains uterine lining in women. Helps to regulate menstrual cycle and assists in sustaining pregnancy.
Gonadotropin-releasing hormone (GnRH)	Hypothalamus	Stimulates pituitary gland to secrete FSH and LH in order to promote the maturation of gonads in both sexes. Also assists in the regulation of the menstrual cycle.
Follicle stimulating hormone (FSH)	Pituitary gland	In females, regulates ovarian function and maturation of ovum. In men it stimulates spermatogenic cells in the seminiferous tubules to produce sperm.
Testosterone	Ovaries, testes, and adrenal glands	Stimulates development of male primary and secondary sexual characteristics and affects sexual libido for both males and females.
Luteinizing hormone (LH)	Pituitary gland	Assists in the production of estrogen and progesterone. Helps regulate maturation of ovum and triggers ovulation in females. In men, it stimulates cells in the testes to produce testosterone.
Human chorionic gonadotropin (HCG)	Embryo and placenta	Helps sustain pregnancy.
Oxytocin	Hypothalamus	Stimulates uterine contractions in childbirth. Produces feelings of fondness and attachment in partners as well as between caregiver and child.
Prolactin	Pituitary gland	Stimulates milk production in women after childbirth.
Prostaglandins	All body cells	Mediates hormonal response and stimulates muscular contractions.

to release two hormones called **luteinizing hormone (LH)** and **follicle stimulating hormone (FSH),** which trigger menstruation. When LH is released into the body, the body produces greater amounts of progesterone to suppress LH. If fertilization does *not* occur (which is usually the case), the rising level of progesterone inhibits the release of GnRH which, in turn, inhibits further production of progesterone. As the progesterone level drops, the corpus luteum begins to degenerate; the endometrium begins to break down, the inhibition of uterine contractions is lifted, and the bleeding and cramps of menstruation begin. See Table 4.1 for descriptions of these important hormones and their roles in our sexual and reproductive lives.

Because the menstrual process is a complex interplay of hormones that have secondary effects on the body, a number of complications may arise during the phases of a woman's menstrual cycle. One of them, **premenstrual syndrome (PMS),** is well known and has been the source of endless laments. However, not all females experience PMS.

All too often the media represent women in the days leading up to and including their menstrual periods as raging, frenzied, teary-eyed women who complain of bloating and who appear out of control. These PMS stories refer to a collection of symptoms that affect women before or during menstruation. Thinking of PMS symptoms in this way, however, oversimplifies what happens hormonally during the menstrual cycle. Because the range of symptoms is so broad—from cramps, to nausea, to pain, to depression, to cravings—the exact causes of the wide variation of PMS symptoms are unknown. Several

gonadotropin-releasing hormone (GnRH)
Pituitary hormone that stimulates activity in the gonads (testes and ovaries).

luteinizing hormone (LH)
A hormone secreted by the pituitary gland that helps stimulate ovulation in the female. In males it stimulates the production of androgens in the testes.

follicle stimulating hormone (FSH)
A hormone secreted by the pituitary gland that helps regulate ovulation in females. In males, it stimulates sperm production.

premenstrual syndrome (PMS)
A collection of physical and emotional symptoms that may affect a woman before or during menstruation.

neurotransmitters
Chemical messengers in the brain.

premenstrual dysphoric disorder (PMDD)
A condition in which a woman has severe depression symptoms, irritability, and tension before menstruation. The symptoms of PMDD are more severe than those seen with premenstrual syndrome (PMS).

dysmenorrhea
Severe uterine pain during menstruation.

amenorrhea
The absence of menstrual periods.

toxic shock syndrome (TSS)
A severe disease that produces fever, shock, and problems with the function of several body organs.

factors, primarily hormonal fluctuations and interactions with **neurotransmitters** (chemical messengers in the brain) are suspected. Current findings suggest that fluctuations in hormones during menstruation cause the neurotransmitter serotonin to fluctuate, disrupting mood and causing other symptoms of PMS (Office on Women's Health, 2018).

How common is PMS within the general population? Estimates of the number of women who suffer from PMS vary widely. For example, the American Congress of Obstetricians and Gynecologists estimates that over 90% of menstruating women have one or more PMS symptoms during their monthly cycle (Office on Women's Health, 2018). Most women's symptoms are mild and do not require medical treatment. However, about 3–8% of women endure more severe symptoms and have a condition called **premenstrual dysphoric disorder (PMDD).** Symptoms of this condition are severe enough to seriously impair a woman's ability to function normally in daily life (Office on Women's Health, 2018). Women with PMDD often report that they feel "out of control" during the time right before their period begins. Symptoms include markedly depressed mood, increases in anxiety, and significantly decreased interest in activities. These symptoms appear during the week prior to the start of the menstrual period and tend to disappear in the week following the completion of the menstrual period (Office on Women's Health, 2018). There is a variety of treatment options for PMDD, including medication and therapy.

Another complication that may arise during menstruation is **dysmenorrhea,** severe uterine pain during menstruation. Compounds called *prostaglandins* are released during menstruation and cause inflammation in the uterus, making it contract to shed the endometrium. The uterine contractions and the oxygen deprivation of nearby tissues cause the painful cramps of dysmenorrhea. In some cases, dysmenorrhea may signify the presence of uterine fibroids or endometriosis. Treatment of dysmenorrhea largely depends on what is causing the pain.

Another condition, **amenorrhea,** refers to the absence of menstrual periods. States of amenorrhea are completely natural in many women's lives, particularly during pregnancy and after menopause. Primary amenorrhea is the term used when a young woman has never had a period, usually by the age of 16 in the United States. Secondary amenorrhea describes a disruption in a previously normal menstrual cycle, often because of disturbances in the hypothalamus or pituitary gland. Other causes of secondary amenorrhea are extreme weight loss caused by eating disorders, excessive stress or exercising, and some secondary weight gain as a result of a serious illness.

One last menstrual concern is **toxic shock syndrome (TSS).** Toxic shock syndrome is a rare but severe infection that involves fever, shock, and problems with the function of several body organs. TSS can be fatal if not treated promptly. TSS is caused by a toxin produced by certain types of bacteria. TSS used to be associated with women who used tampons on a regular basis during their menstrual cycle, but today less than half of current cases are associated with the use of tampons (Mayo Clinic, 2017; Martin, 2013). Risk factors for developing TSS include:

- Childbirth
- Presence of a staph infection
- Menstruation
- Surgery of any type
- Tampon use (particularly if they are left in the vagina for an extended period of time)
- Using barrier contraceptives such as a diaphragm

Symptoms of TSS include confusion, diarrhea, headaches, high fever, low blood pressure, muscle aches, nausea and vomiting, organ failure, and a widespread rash that looks like sunburn particularly on the palms of the hand or the bottom of the feet.

Any menstrual problems that are unusual or concerning should be brought to the attention of a health care provider. It is always better to err on the side of safety. Specifically, if a woman experiences one of the following menstrual problems, she should contact a health care provider:

- Menarche has not occurred by the age of 16
- The menstrual period has suddenly stopped
- Menstrual bleeding is excessive
- Severe pain occurs during menstruation

Menopause

Human females are unique in living beyond and enjoying sexual pleasure long after their menstrual periods cease. As women live longer, it is likely that menopause will become common throughout all human groups. Not only does this trend indicate that reproduction is just one aspect of sexuality, but because sexual pleasure and desire continue after menopause for most women, it also suggests some unique aspects of female sexual pleasure as well (Meston & Buss, 2009; Martin, 2013).

Menopause is a time in a woman's life when menstruation eventually stops and the body goes through changes that no longer allow her to get pregnant. The word *menopause* comes from the Greek meaning "end of monthly cycles" (*meno,* "month"; *pausis,* "cessation"). It generally occurs when women are in their mid-40s to early 50s. While the term *menopause* actually refers to a specific date—the last menstruation—the time around menopause when the female body is undergoing changes associated with menopause is known as **perimenopause.** What's happening inside the female body that causes this change?

During perimenopause, the amounts of estrogen, progesterone, and testosterone that the body produces begin to diminish. Once the ovaries have stopped releasing ova each month, the levels of follicle stimulating hormone (FSH) and luteinizing hormone (LH) in the body increase. This fluctuation in hormones leads to changes in the body, the most notable of which is the *hot flash,* during which the body's temperature rapidly increases and then returns to normal. Hot flashes are often the first signals to women that they are near menopause, and they can last 4 to 5 years or longer for some women. Other symptoms may be present during menopause, including a feeling of depression. These feelings can be a result of the biological process involved in menopause as well as the social and environmental change that women experience during this period of their life span. If the culture highly values youthfulness, fertility, and beauty, women in menopause may feel sad about getting older. Partners can help cope with menopause in a variety of ways. See "Communication Matters: Coping with Menopause" for some helpful tips in coping with menopause in a positive way.

When a woman goes 12 months without ovulation, she has reached menopause. Many women elect **hormone replacement therapy (HRT)** to offset some of the effects of decreased natural levels of hormones associated with menopause. There are various types of hormone replacement therapies that target certain effects of menopause, one particular concern being **osteoporosis,** or abnormal bone loss. A woman should discuss HRT with a doctor to make sure that she understands the advantages and disadvantages, because it does have some risks. For example, while estrogen can help to maintain the thickness and elasticity of the vaginal walls, it can increase the incidence of endometrial, ovarian, and breast cancer (Speroff & Fritz, 2005). Women can even incorporate testosterone in the HRT to help maintain or increase sexual drive, but one side effect can be an increase in facial hair growth and acne (Martin, 2013).

For some women, menopause is just the beginning of a new phase of sexual satisfaction and intimate relationships (Schwartz, 2007a). The reason is that sexuality depends in part on brain, in part on body, and in part on personality and context or circumstances.

menopause
The time in a woman's life when menstruation eventually stops and the body goes through changes that no longer allow her to get pregnant. It is a natural event that normally occurs in women age 45 to 55.

perimenopause
The time when the female body is undergoing changes associated with menopause.

hormone replacement therapy (HRT)
Treatment that can offset some of the effects of decreased natural levels of hormones associated with menopause.

osteoporosis
Abnormal bone loss, a potential risk for menopausal women.

COMMUNICATION Matters

Coping with Menopause

How can you communicate about menopause? Women can experience a lot of physical and emotional symptoms with the onset of their menstrual period, and as they age and their menstrual period stops, women once again experience a variety of symptoms that accompany this life milestone. While physical symptoms are often easier to understand, the emotional symptoms of menopause can be confusing for women and particularly confusing for their partners and families (Megge, 2006). Unfortunately, many partners respond to the hormonal imbalances of menopause in ways that aren't always effective or welcome.

Some partners will simply try to ignore the problem and hope it will go away and others can become overbearing and treat their partner as if she is fragile and incapable of dealing with life. The reality is that the relationship issues that many couples experience during midlife and menopause really stem from a lack of communication and a misunderstanding of the hormonal changes and decline in fertility in premenopausal and menopausal women.

Here are some suggestions from a health and fitness expert whose career centers on helping women and partners navigate through this time in life:

1. Be aware that women going through menopause often feel less attractive than they once did.
2. Listen to the concerns and emotions that are expressed. Even if they seem irrational, it is important for a woman to feel validated and to have an opportunity to communicate.
3. Have open communication regarding sex. Often women going through menopause experience a decrease in their usual level of desire for sex. Additionally, they may experience decreasing or different sensations, reduction in lubrication, and even some pain associated with sexual intimacy. This is often confusing and scary for women, so open communication about these changes can create an environment in which women and their partners can work together to overcome these challenges and pursue an active and healthy sex life.
4. Take time to laugh.
5. Express your love for each other often and acknowledge and understand that this time of life can be rough but that working together can pave the road for a smoother transition into menopause.

Based on S. Megge, 2006.

ericsphotography/iStockphoto.com

MALE SEXUAL ANATOMY

penis
The primary male organ of sexual pleasure that transports semen as well as urine.

The primary male organ for sexual pleasure, the **penis,** takes its name from the Latin word *phallus.* The penis has long been celebrated as an object of power, fertility, and good luck in many cultures throughout history. In Greek mythology, Priapus, famous for his exaggerated and always erect penis, was a god of fertility. Among other things, he protected the male genitalia. In Thai culture and various Native American cultures, phallic symbols in the shape of lucky charms or amulets were worn as a sign of masculine power and thought to bring good fortune. Despite the focus on the penis as the symbol of male sexual function, however, other male sexual organs help it to fully function.

External Male Sex Organs

root
The base of the penis.

erection
The firm and enlarged condition of a body organ or part when the erectile tissue surrounding it becomes filled with blood.

As the primary organ for male sexual pleasure, the penis contains many sensitive nerve endings. As an organ that is used for both urinating and reproducing, the penis transports both urine and semen, though not at the same time. Contrary to popular belief, the penis is not a muscle. However, the base of the penis, called the **root,** connects to several muscles and pelvic structures. During an **erection**—the firm and enlarged condition of a body organ or part when the erectile tissue surrounding it becomes filled with blood, especially such a condition of the penis or clitoris—the penis is stabilized by the muscles at the base of the penis.

Sexual Anatomy and Physiology 121

Besides the root, the penis contains a number of other structures (Figure 4.11). The **penile shaft** contains three tubular cylinders, which are made out of smooth spongy tissue. The inside, hollow tissue of the penis is called the **corpus cavernosa** and the erectile tissue surrounding the urethra is known as the **corpus spongiosum.** During sexual arousal, this spongy tissue becomes engorged with blood, making the penis erect. The urethra, which transports urine and semen, runs through the corpus spongiosum and ends at the **penile glans** found at the very top of the penis. The glans of the penis is a very sensitive area containing many nerve endings. The rounded base of the penile glans is called the **corona,** which is the most sexually sensitive part of the penis.

On an uncircumcised penis, the **foreskin** covers the penile glans. If uncared for, the glans of an uncircumcised penis produces secretions that accumulate beneath the foreskin, forming a smelly and cheesy substance called **smegma**. Regular washing, however,

Priapus, a fertility god in Greek mythology, was typically represented as a virile figure with an erect penis.
VPC Travel Photo/Alamy Stock Photo

Figure 4.11
Side view of the internal structures of the male genitals.

- Urinary bladder
- Vas deferens
- Corpus cavernosa
- Urethra
- Corpus spongiosum
- Penis
- Penile glans
- Ureters
- Seminal vesicle
- Ejaculatory duct
- Prostate gland
- Cowper's glands
- Anus
- Epididymis
- Testis
- Scrotum

Figure 4.12
The external structure of the penis.

- Urethral opening
- Penile glans
- Frenulum
- Corona
- Foreskin
- Penile shaft

penile shaft
The part of the penis between the penile glans and the body.

corpus cavernosa
Two paired tubular cylinders in the penis that fill with blood during sexual arousal causing an erection.

corpus spongiosum
The underlying spongy tissue that surrounds the urethra inside the penis.

penile glans
A sexually sensitive area at the very top of the penis that contains numerous nerve endings.

corona
The rounded area at the base of the penile glans.

foreskin
A thin, sensitive layer of skin that covers part of the shaft, the corona, and the glans of the penis.

smegma
Smelly, cheesy substance formed by penis secretions that accumulate beneath the foreskin. This substance has also been found under the clitoral hood in female anatomy

Figure 4.13
Internal view of the testicles inside the scrotum.

frenulum
Sensitive tissue on the backside of the penis that connects the penile glans with the shaft and the foreskin of the penis.

scrotum
An extension of the abdomen located between the penis and the anus.

scrotal sac
Holds the testicles.

testicles
Also known as testes or male gonads; are part of the reproductive system that produces sperm and the sex hormone testosterone.

cremaster muscle
A muscle in the scrotum that helps to maintain the ideal temperature for sperm production.

spermatogenesis
The process of sperm production.

seminiferous tubule
A thin, coiled structure in the testes where sperm is produced.

tunica albuginea
The capsule that holds the tightly coiled seminiferous tubules.

epididymis
A tightly coiled tubular structure that is located on top of each testicle.

vas deferens
Ducts that help to move sperm from the epididymis to the ejaculatory ducts.

penile columns or erectile tissues
Spongy tissue within the penis that becomes engorged with blood during an erection.

keeps the area under the foreskin clean and healthy. The **frenulum** is an elastic fold of tissue connecting the penile glans with the foreskin and the shaft of the penis (Figure 4.12). This area is also highly sensitive.

The **scrotum** is located between the penis and the anus and is an extension of the abdomen. The **scrotal sac,** which holds the **testicles** or testes, is a delicate layer of skin that contains numerous sweat glands and hair follicles. During puberty, pubic hair appears in this area and the surrounding area of the penile root. Figure 4.13 shows the location and structure of the testicles. Testicular cancer, discussed in detail in Chapter 6, affects more young men than any other type of cancer. For this reason, it is important for men to perform a testicular self-exam regularly. Learn how to do this procedure in "Healthy Sexuality: Performing a Testicular Self-Exam."

Internal Male Sex Organs

The testicles, or testes, are the male gonads and have two primary functions: the production of the hormone testosterone and of sperm. The testes need to be kept 1 to 2 degrees below the normal body temperature of 98.6°F for sperm production, which is why they are external structures (unlike their ovarian counterpart). The **cremaster muscle** in the scrotum helps to maintain the ideal temperature for sperm production no matter the climate. In hot climates, it lowers the testes away from the body to reduce their temperature; in cold climates, it pulls them up closer to the body to increase their temperature. The process of sperm production, known as **spermatogenesis,** takes place inside the testicle in a tubular structure called the **seminiferous tubule** (Figure 4.14). The seminiferous tubules are tightly coiled into a capsule called **tunica albuginea,** giving the structure the appearance of a cross section of a grapefruit.

The entire process of producing fully mature sperm takes about 72 days. However, sperm production is constant, and the human male may produce up to 200 million sperm each day. Upon leaving the seminiferous tubules, the sperm enter the **epididymis.** The epididymis is also a tightly coiled tubular structure that connects the testes with the **vas deferens,** a duct connecting the testicles with the urethra.

Erection and Ejaculation

During sexual arousal, nerve impulses from the brain travel down to the erection centers on the spinal cord. The production of nitric oxide signals the smooth muscle tissue in

WHAT'S ON YOUR MIND?

Q: I am concerned about the size of my penis and its ability to please my partner, sexually. Can you tell me if it is better to have a longer penis or a wider penis?

ANSWER: We understand that penis size can create some insecurity in men who may believe that their penis is smaller than it should be. Heterosexual women often report that penis size is not really important to them in their sexual relationships. Rather, it is how their partner approaches sex and his total response to her in their sexual encounters and in their relationship that matters most. Pleasurable encounters do not require a minimum penis length or girth—a hand or mouth can often provide equal or more stimulation for a partner. Relax a little bit and enjoy pleasuring your partner in a variety of ways and don't worry about something that seems more important in the locker room than it really is in the bedroom.

---

the penis to relax, which allows blood to enter the **penile columns** or **erectile tissues.** This smooth muscle tissue in the corpus cavernosa and corpus spongiosum engorges with blood and an erection occurs, a phenomenon called *tumescence*. With penile erection, the muscles just below the surface of the **perineum,** the area of skin between the scrotum and the anus, contract and help to stabilize the penis. During **ejaculation,** an autonomic nervous system reaction, the sperm leave the epididymis, move through the vas deferens, and are expelled from the body through the urethra. This constitutes an orgasm for the male.

As the sperm leave the vas deferens and enter the urethra, secretions from the **seminal vesicles** and the **prostate gland** are added to the sperm. The resulting fluid mixture is called **semen.** The prostate gland, located just beneath the bladder (see Figure 4.11), surrounds the urethra and is responsible for the creation and storage of semen. About 70-75% of semen is made up of secretions from the seminal vesicles, about 20-25% comes from the prostate gland, and 1% consists of sperm. One ejaculate, which is between 0.1 and 10 milliliters of semen, contains a maximum of about 500 million sperm (Rehan, Sobrero, & Fertig, 1975; Martin, 2013). During the earlier stages of sexual arousal there is a small secretion of clear fluid from **Cowper's glands** (also known as the *bulbourethral* glands; see Figure 4.11),

perineum
A sexually sensitive and arousing area in both men and women. In women it extends from the vulva to anus and in men between the scrotum and anus.

ejaculation
The ejection of semen (usually carrying sperm) from the male reproductive tract that is usually accompanied by orgasm.

seminal vesicles
A pair of tubular glands that produce seminal fluid, which makes up the majority of semen.

prostate gland
A gland that produces prostatic secretions.

semen
Sexual fluid ejaculated through the penis that contains sperm and fluid from the prostate gland, seminal vesicles, and Cowper's glands.

Cowper's gland
During sexual arousal, this structure secretes a clear mucuslike fluid; also called the *bulbourethral gland*.

Figure 4.14

Testicles and seminiferous tubules. (a) Cutaway view of a testicle. (b) Greatly enlarged photomicrograph of a seminiferous tubule in cross section. An unfolded seminiferous tubule would stretch over one mile.

Al Telser/McGraw-Hill Education

(a) Testicle

- Spermatic cord
- Blood vessels and nerves
- Head of epididymis
- Duct of epididymis
- Seminiferous tubule
- Vas deferens
- Body of epididymis
- Tunica albuginea
- Tail of epididymis

(b) Seminiferous tubule, cross section

- Seminiferous tubule
- Sperm

LM 250x

HEALTHY Sexuality

Performing a Testicular Self-Exam

Testicular cancer is most common in men ages 20 to 35, but it can occur at any age. In the United States, between 7,500 and 8,000 diagnoses of testicular cancer are made each year. Over a man's lifetime, he has approximately a 1 in 250 chance of developing testicular cancer. Beginning at age 15, it's a good idea to do a monthly testicular self-exam to improve your chances of finding a tumor early. Testicular cancer is highly treatable when found early. Over time, testicular cancer can spread and become more dangerous and difficult to treat. Lumps or other changes found during a testicular self-exam may not be signs of cancer, but a doctor still needs to check them.

By regularly doing a testicular self-exam, you'll learn to recognize what's normal, and what's not, with your testicles. If you aren't sure whether something is normal, ask your doctor to check your testicles, even if it feels odd. In fact, have a doctor check your testicles whenever you have a physical exam.

Steps in a Testicular Self-Exam

Examine your testicles monthly after a warm bath or shower. The heat from the water relaxes your scrotum, making it easier to check for anything unusual. To do a testicular self-exam, follow these steps:

1. Stand in front of a mirror. Look for any swelling on the skin of the scrotum.
2. Examine each testicle with both hands. Place the index and middle fingers under the testicle while placing your thumbs on the top.
3. Gently roll the testicle between the thumbs and fingers. Feel for lumps and bumps. Remember that the testicles are usually smooth, oval shaped, and somewhat firm.
4. If you find a lump, call your doctor as soon as possible.

Is What I'm Finding Normal or Not?

You may notice a few things about your testicles that seem unusual, but the following things are usually normal:

- One of your testicles is larger than the other. It's normal for one testicle to be slightly larger—it's a cause for concern only if there's a significant difference or change in the size of one of your testicles.
- You have bumps on the skin of your scrotum. Ingrown hairs, a rash, or other skin problems may be the cause.
- You feel a soft, ropy cord leading upward from the top of the back part of each testicle. This is a normal part of the scrotum called the epididymis. It may be tender when you press on it.

Lumps, swelling, testicular pain, or other changes can be caused by something other than cancer, such as inflammation, enlargement of scrotal veins, fluid around the testicle, or a hernia. Even so, a doctor needs to examine these symptoms, and you may still need treatment.

For more information, including risk factors for testicular cancer, see Chapter 6 or visit the website of the Testicular Cancer Resource Center (TCRC) at tcrc.acor.org.

DID YOU KNOW

An important study on penis size with more than 3,000 men found that most men who sought penis enhancement because they were dissatisfied with their penises were within the normal size range and greatly overestimated the size of an average penis (Dillon et al., 2008). These men thought the average flaccid size was about 5 inches, although some thought it was as long as 6.5 inches. Men get their ideas about penis size mostly from porn, where male performers have penises that are longer than average. In reality, a 7-inch erect penis would place you in the 99th percentile (Dillon et al., 2008). For more on the dissatisfaction of penile size, see "Healthy Sexuality: Penile Enhancement Techniques."

which helps to clear out and lubricate the urethra in preparation for ejaculation.

The process of ejaculation occurs in two stages: the **emission phase** and the **expulsion phase.** During the emission phase, the cremaster muscle pulls the testes up close to the body preparing to release sperm. Semen is prepared for secretion and the man feels that he is about to ejaculate or "come." This part of the ejaculation process is known as **ejaculatory inevitability.** As the expulsion phase begins, rhythmic contractions of smooth muscles and tissue in the epididymis, vas deferens, seminal vesicles, **ejaculatory ducts,** prostate gland, and urethra force semen out of the body. After the semen has been ejaculated, the penis becomes soft and loses its erection, a state called **detumescence.** For a period of time after resolution, regardless of further sexual stimulation, the penis will not become erect. This unresponsive time is called a **refractory period.** In younger men this period may be less than 1 hour. With age the refractory period becomes longer, and in older men it may last several hours or as long as a day (Scarleteen, 2009).

Variability in the Male Body

Like the female body, the male body varies in shape, size, color, and function. For example, some men are born with one testicle; other men may develop large, pronounced breasts. Both occur naturally and do not necessarily indicate a problem.

As standards of female beauty differ by culture, so do standards of male beauty. Many cultures value men for their physical stature and equate power and influence with men who are tall and muscular. For example, research shows some cultural differences in body shape preferences. While American and Asian cultures tend to value leaner and thinner body types, heavier figures are often preferred in Middle Eastern and African countries (Davidson, Thill, & Lash, 2002). In the contemporary United States, we recognize the most handsome men as having sharp facial features and lean, fit bodies (Grogan, 2006). Many men elect to spend a lot of time exercising and weight-lifting to develop a muscular physique since we often equate muscularity with power and sex appeal (Duggan & McCready, 2004; Morrison, 2006). Even penis size has been a marker of male beauty or masculinity, and men often experience emotions of pride, concern, or anxiety over the appearance and size of their penis. Unfortunately, a few men who desire a larger penis may go for undergoing potentially risky penile enhancement techniques, which are not recommended medically in almost all cases, as you can read about in "Healthy Sexuality: Penile Enhancement Techniques."

Do penis sizes vary? Yes, but when penises are erect, they are all about the same size (Kinsey, et al, 1948; Martin, 2013). The biggest difference in size is in the **flaccid,** or unaroused, penis. It averages about 3 inches in length and varies between 1 and 4 inches for most men, as measured in many scientific studies from locations as diverse as the United States, Germany, Nigeria, Iran, and South Korea (Tiefer, 2004). The small, flaccid penis appears to be at the root of men's insecurity about penis size, the so-called *locker-room syndrome.* Flaccid length does not predict erect length, however, and most of the variation disappears in an erect penis. Most penises measure between 5 and 6 inches in length when erect, regardless of the size of the flaccid penis.

Experts have repeatedly shown that size is not the critical variable in sexual pleasure and fulfillment (Perel, 2006). After all, compared to our chimpanzee cousins, human genitalia are small (Martin, 2013). For heterosexual intercourse, an erect penis longer than 4 inches is usually big enough to stimulate erogenous tissue in a woman's vagina. Most of the nerve endings relating to sexual pleasure in a woman's vagina are located within the first one-third of the length of the vagina. This means that most penises are capable of stimulating these nerves and providing pleasure during coital activities. A penis that is too big can actually cause difficulties: one that is longer than 8 inches can hit a woman's cervix and cause her discomfort. Having a positive attitude, positive acceptance of your own body, and regard for your partner's body and joy in the mutual pleasure are far and away the critical issues in sexual satisfaction (Perel, 2006).

Circumcision

Another issue affecting the appearance of the penis is whether or not a man has been circumcised. Figure 4.15 shows the difference between an uncircumcised penis and a circumcised penis. **Male circumcision,** usually performed on infant boys, involves entirely or

emission phase
The first of two stages of the ejaculation process.

expulsion phase
The second stage of the ejaculation process.

ejaculatory inevitability
During intercourse, the point when semen is about to be secreted and a male feels that he is "about to come."

ejaculatory ducts
Two short ducts located within the prostate gland that transport sperm to the urethra prior to ejaculation.

detumescence
The soft state of the penis after the semen has been ejaculated.

refractory period
The unresponsive time after resolution when a man cannot get a new erection.

flaccid
The state of a penis being limp or soft.

male circumcision
A common genital modification in the United States and other places in which the foreskin is removed from the penis.

HEALTHY Sexuality

Penile Enhancement Techniques

Throughout history and across cultures people have clung to fascinating attitudes about what makes the perfect penis, and especially what makes for greater sex appeal and pleasure (Hull & Budiharsana, 2001). There has been attention in the media, medicine, and popular culture paid to penis modification, the counterpart to plastic surgery in women used to enhance sex appeal (Tiefer, 1986). Because of medical advances, what we once thought was fixed for life can now be surgically altered. The penis is no different, and in fact, there is evidence that all kinds of new procedures, such as **penile implants,** which are objects or substances inserted into the penis to increase size and pleasure, are increasing (Fischer, Hauser, Brede, Fisang, & Müller, 2010). The implants include plastic beads, metal ball-bearings, palm oil, soft plastic, metal clasps, and other more exotic items. With enough money and desire, men can try to attain this mythical ideal organ. In other words, the collective fantasy, with enough money, can become reality. Many men do report subjectively that they and their sexual partners experience greater sexual pleasure following these operations, but there may be significant medical complications and possible side effects (Fisher et al., 2010). Potential side effects include having a permanent erection (depending on the type of procedure or implant), which can be bothersome, create an abnormal feel and appearance of the penis, and cause possible deterioration and thinning of the penile flesh over time, or even permanently lose sexual functioning.

You may have seen TV advertisements and e-mails for products that make the penis bigger. All those penis enhancement ads are a complete waste of money—whether it is pills, pumps, or exercises. In fact, pills do nothing, and exercises are futile and potentially harmful. Experts say that devices like penile pumps simply simulate an erection and have no long-term effect on size. Exercises can even lead to nerve damage. One exercise called *jelqing* entails stroking a semi-erect penis in a certain way for about 30 minutes a day for months to enlarge the penile cavities that fill with blood, supposedly making for larger erections. This exercise makes no sense biologically, however, and it could cause blood vessels to tear or cause the penis to lose sensitivity if the tugging is too hard. There are some physical exercises, such as kegel exercises, that do have benefits in strengthening underlying musculature, stamina, and endurance.

Penile surgery has helped men who truly need it (Barrell, 2018). Men who are born with a congenital abnormality, who have suffered an injury, or who have severe difficulties achieving erections may seek and receive surgery. In all these scenarios, men essentially have a nonfunctioning penis for sexual purposes, which means the benefits greatly outweigh the risk. This is not the case for most already sexually healthy men seeking penile enhancement.

Penis enlargement surgery is risky enough that a man may lose sensation or the ability to have an erection (Barrell, 2018). Doctors do try to dissuade men from these procedures through counseling and a frank discussion of the facts. In fact, few urologists will attempt surgery on a man whose erect penis is larger than 3 inches. One surgical method to enlarge a penis is to transfer fat to add to girth. This often leads to lumping and a distorted penis shape over time. Another technique involves the release of the suspensory ligament, the ligament that helps retract and release the penis into the body, often resulting in infection, loss of sensitivity, and **erectile dysfunction,** the inability to gain or sustain an erection. "The surgeries to perform elective penile enhancement that are advertised to enlarge a normal, functional penis do not work and shouldn't be performed," says Dr. Karen Boyle (2007).

penile implants
Objects or substances inserted into the penis to increase size and pleasure.

erectile dysfunction
The inability to gain or sustain an erection.

partially removing the foreskin (Figure 4.16). In the United States and other countries, circumcision is a common type of genital modification. It is an ancient practice known in many cultures, although in recent years, people have begun to question the procedure, and it has been the focus of increasing controversy.

Though normal male genitals are fully functional just as they are, some cultures have developed rituals for modifying genitals to express religious conviction, to make a moral statement, or to improve hygiene (DeMeo, 1986; Hull & Budiharsana, 2001). Thousands of years ago, the ancient Egyptians are known to have performed circumcision. Today ritual

Figure 4.15
The size and shape of the penis vary from one man to another. Note that the penis on the left is uncircumcised.

circumcision continues to be practiced in many cultures around the world. In the Jewish tradition, a biblical story relates God's command that the Hebrews circumcise all Hebrew men to set themselves apart from other tribes at the time. In tribal societies, circumcision was traditionally performed on young boys or adolescents as part of an initiation ritual (Murdock, 1981; Vincent, 2008). In South Africa, many males believe that circumcision may enhance the sexual pleasure of vaginal intercourse for themselves and their female partners (United Nations, 2007). In other cultures, circumcision is regarded as a way to enhance the beauty and sexual attractiveness of the male body (Greenberg, 1986; Vincent, 2008).

In the 21st century, male circumcision is very unusual in Western Europe and increasingly questioned by pediatricians in the United States, although it continues to be practiced. In 2012, the American Academy of Pediatrics released a medical research review that suggested that the benefits of circumcision to newborns outweigh the risks, but that the benefits are not great. Thus, male circumcision provided benefits in the prevention of urinary tract infections, acquisition of HIV and some other STIs, and potential reduced rates of penile cancer (American Academy of Pediatrics, 2012). Parents and families are advised to make the decision about circumcision in the context of their culture, faith, and own convictions.

An increasing number of public health advocates have campaigned to make male circumcision widespread in developing countries with high HIV and STI rates, particularly in Africa (Newell & Bärnighausen, 2009). In fact, recent research in Malawi, Africa, suggests that male circumcision provides strong perceived protection against HIV infection (Kapumba & King, 2019). According to this recommendation, removing the foreskin

Figure 4.16
The steps involved in the male circumcision procedure.

decreases the likelihood that bacteria will accumulate under the foreskin, thereby reducing the spread of bacteria and viruses to sexual partners. Compelling findings suggest that male circumcision reduces the risk of heterosexually acquired HIV infection in men by approximately 60% (WHO, 2018). Male circumcision is recommended by WHO and UNAIDS as an additional HIV prevention intervention in settings of high HIV prevalence. Two global HIV prevention goals for 2020 focus on the provision of safe male circumcision to achieve maximum impact on HIV incidence (WHO, 2018). Circumcision decreases risk for heterosexual males, not for female partners in vaginal sex, and anal sex risk protection is unknown (Kaiser Foundation, 2009). In favor of bodily rights and genital integrity, the preferred recommendation from many human rights advocacy groups is to let males decide what they would like to do with their foreskin.

MALE SEXUAL PHYSIOLOGY

Males generally go through hormonal cycles during their lives, though they aren't comparable to the female menstrual cycle. During adolescence, the testes begin to produce greater amounts of testosterone, which promotes the maturation of the male sex organs and secondary sex characteristics, such as the growth of body hair. In later life, a process similar to menopause, called **andropause,** occurs in some men, as decreasing levels of testosterone slow the desire for sex and reduce the depth of sensation in the genitals. These changes sometimes contribute to erectile dysfunction. While the circulating levels of testosterone decrease in most men, not all men experience the same effects.

andropause
A process similar to menopause that occurs in some men.

BODILY INTEGRITY RIGHTS AND SEXUAL WELL-BEING

bodily integrity
The idea of the inviolability of the physical body and the importance of personal autonomy and the self-determination of individuals over their own bodies.

The topics of female genital mutilation and male circumcision relate directly to the issue of bodily integrity rights. Many experts regard bodily integrity as a basic human privacy right. The concept of **bodily integrity** refers to the inviolability of the physical body. It emphasizes the importance of personal autonomy and the self-determination of individuals over their own bodies. It considers the violation of bodily integrity as an unethical infringement, intrusive, and possibly criminal (Fenwick & Kerrigan, 2011).

Experts say that decisions involving bodily integrity rights should be an individual choice, and if it pertains to a child, the family should wait until the child is old enough to make his or her own decision (Fausto-Sterling, 2000). Bodily integrity rights cover circumcision, genital surgery, genital cutting, cosmetic surgery, and all aspects of how people present themselves to the public.

Because cultures vary widely in values about personal appearance and taboos about the body, it is not surprising that bodily integrity raises many controversies (Correa et al., 2008; United Nations, 2007; W-PATH Standards of Care, 2012). Throughout the global community today there is increasing concern about how cultures tamper with human anatomy, both female and male. As we have seen in this chapter, there's much controversy surrounding whether female genital cutting should occur at all, because it appears to be medically risky, abusive, and anti-female (Correa, Petchesky, & Parker, 2008; W-PATH Standards of Care, 2012). Some advocates for women in

Evidence that circumcision was performed in ancient egypt as far back as about 2300 BCE comes from tomb art, such as this carving, and also from written accounts.
DeAgostini/Getty Images

developing countries, particularly human rights groups, have countered that such criticisms are colonial and patronizing, and fail to account for the fact that Western women undergo body modifications as well, such as breast implants, plastic facial surgery, and botox injections (Aggleton & Parker, 2010; Petchetsky, 2003).

Some people, including experts on the topic, feel that the genitals are so basic to our sense of who we are as men and women that any alteration to them through surgery or hormones or other means is a direct assault (Stoller, 1975). One form of bodily integrity is **genital integrity,** the idea that someone's genitals ought to be left intact and not be interfered with by anyone. Genital integrity would leave the choice to modify the genitals to the individual woman or man (Bailey et al, 2016).

It is important to understand that female genital mutilation is not a universal procedure—it is certainly not as widely practiced as male circumcision (DeMeo, 1986). Additionally, female genital mutilation is often practiced for reasons having to do with particular families and individual circumstances and does not necessarily reflect the attitude or recommendation of an entire locale, culture, or religious tradition (Ball, 2008).

In the United States, some laws prohibit the genital modification of female minors, unless medically necessary. However, as mentioned, many countries, especially some Islamic states, favor female genital mutilation. This practice continues, even in places where the government has banned it, because some women feel that traditional feminine honor and their reputations depend on having FGM to demonstrate to their families and communities that they are moral and virtuous. As long as this value holds within the context of these cultures, the controversy will continue because human rights advocates come from a different point of view (Petchesky, 2003).

Opponents of male circumcision assert that laws against genital modification of minors should apply equally to males and females. Many anticircumcision groups have joined the International Coalition for Genital Integrity, a coalition that advocates preserving the integrity of the penis. This issue has become more complicated because of the finding that circumcision may help prevent HIV, as we also mentioned earlier.

Many authorities believe that male circumcision and female genital mutilation are very different and should not be lumped together. As UNICEF explains: "When the practice first came to be known beyond the societies in which it was traditionally carried out, it was generally referred to as female circumcision. This term, however, draws a direct parallel with male circumcision and, as a result, creates confusion between these two distinct practices" (UNICEF, 2005).

This conversation will likely continue for a long period of time, and it is important to be informed, no matter what position you take. Before making a decision, particularly regarding circumcision for a male child, understand the process, the risks, potential benefits, and other issues involved. Sexual well-being requires taking the time to acquire information in order to make the best decision possible. This concept doesn't just apply to the issue of circumcision or genital modification. It applies to a variety of issues including sexual health, as we will discover in future chapters.

genital integrity
The idea that someone's genitals ought to be left intact and not be interfered with by anyone.

Chapter Review

SUMMARY

Sexual Anatomy

- Understanding our sexual anatomy and physiology is essential for sexual well-being, including the ability to communicate what you're feeling and what your needs are.
- Anatomy is the study of the physical structures of our bodies.
- Physiology is the study of how our organs and systems work.
- If we have knowledge about our bodies, we are much less likely to have inaccurate beliefs about our bodies.

Female Sexual Anatomy

- Female external genitalia vary in size, shape, and color.
- The clitoris is the external structure most responsible for sexual pleasure in females.
- Major internal sexual and reproductive structures in women are the vagina, cervix, uterus, fallopian tubes, and ovaries.
- Breast development is an important event in female development. Breast augmentation is the most common cosmetic surgical procedure performed in the United States.
- Female circumcision involves sewing the labia or vaginal opening or removing or slicing the clitoris or a combination of these procedures.
- Female circumcision is also referred to as female genital mutilation because of the conditions under which these procedures are often performed.

Female Sexual Physiology

- The endocrine system is the body's system for releasing hormones that regulate important body processes.
- Both men and women produce the same kinds of hormones, but the amounts produced depend on the sex of the individual.
- Ovaries and adrenal glands are responsible for the production of steroid hormones in women.
- Pheromones are chemical signals that our bodies release and that may have a behavioral or psychological response in another body.
- Menstruation, the cyclical process of shedding the uterine lining, consists of three phases: proliferative, secretory, and menstrual.
- Menopause occurs when a woman in midlife has not ovulated for 12 months.
- Hormone replacement therapy (HRT) during menopause can offset some of the effects that the decrease in hormone production causes.

Male Sexual Anatomy

- The penis is an important symbol of power, fertility, and good luck in many cultures and societies.
- The penis is the primary organ for male sexual pleasure.
- The testicles are the male gonads and serve two primary functions: the production of testosterone and sperm.
- The process of ejaculation occurs in two stages: emission and expulsion.
- Men, like women, express varied emotions regarding the appearance of their genitalia. There is considerable difference in the size of flaccid penises and much less variation among erect penises.
- Male circumcision is a surgical procedure that removes the foreskin of the penis.
- Male circumcision may be beneficial for newborns and older men, for different reasons, but the final decision rests with the family and individual in the context of their faith, culture, and convictions.

Male Sexual Physiology

- The testes and adrenal glands are responsible for the production of steroid hormones.
- Testosterone is an important hormone for sexual desire and behavior.
- Men go through testosterone cycles during their lives in which they produce varying amounts of testosterone.

Bodily Integrity Rights and Sexual Well-Being

- There is much controversy surrounding the issue of circumcision for men and female genital mutilation because these procedures are done without consent of the individuals on whom they are performed.
- Many experts regard the concept of bodily integrity as a basic human right. Bodily integrity is the right to determine what is done to one's own body—whether by a person or any kind of medical procedure.

What's Your Position?

1. **Have you ever examined your own genitals? If yes, how did you feel when looking at them?**
   - Do you feel comfortable touching or examining your own genitals?
   - What early messages did you receive as a child about the sexual parts of your body?

2. **What names do you use to identify your own reproductive and sexual organs?**
   - What kind of language are you most comfortable using to talk about your sexual organs (i.e., slang or medical terms)?
   - Why do you think people in the United States are uncomfortable talking about the sexual structures and functions of our bodies?
   - Do you believe your genital structures are attractive? Do you feel self-conscious about them?

3. **How do you feel about the practice of circumcision in the United States and around the world?**
   - Do you feel that we should tell other cultures that it is inhumane to practice female circumcision?
   - What about male circumcision? Is it objectionable to you? Do you feel differently about male circumcision than you do about female circumcision? Why?

Design elements: Controversies in Sexuality: HBRH/Shutterstock; Research and Sexual Well Being: verity jane smith/Getty Images; Healthy Sexuality: Sergey Furtaev/Shutterstock; Communication Matters: PeopleImages/Getty Images; Know Yourself: Plush Studios/Blend Images LLC; What's Your Position: Luis Molinero/Shutterstock; Healthy Sexuality: A. Minde/PhotoAlto; Did You Know icon: McGraw-Hill Education; Page corner icon: McGraw-Hill Education.

Sexual Pleasure, Arousal, and Response

5

Doug Menuez/Getty Images

Pleasure, Culture, and Sexual Well-Being
- Describe what is distinctive about human sex and love.
- Describe how personal sexual needs influence sexual well-being.
- Explain how to create a sexual journal and the benefits of keeping one.

Sexual Arousal and Response
- Describe how the five senses shape and express sexuality.
- Explain the connection between pheromones and sexual attraction and arousal.
- Describe how sexual fantasy shapes sexual motivation and behavior.
- Compare Masters and Johnson's EPOR model of sexual response with the one proposed by Kaplan.
- Outline what happens in the body during orgasm.

Sexual Techniques
- Identify the various sexual positions.
- Describe the benefits and drawbacks of each sexual position on performance and sexual enjoyment.

Sexual Pleasure as a Human Right
- State why the right to sexual pleasure is considered essential for sexual well-being.
- Explain why the power structure in many cultures prevents women from realizing their right to sexual pleasure.

• Learning
• Objectives

Developing Your Position

1. How did you come to realize your own sexual and emotional needs when it comes to sexual activity and behavior?
2. What do you focus on in your sexual thoughts and fantasies?
3. What gives you the highest levels of sexual pleasure?

Self, Society, and Culture: Satisfying the Desire for Pleasure

Sexual pleasure. We rarely see these two words together. Instead, we see sex associated with risk and disease so often in our society. We hear stories of people affected by unintended pregnancies. We read about people battling HIV and AIDS. In the political arena, we debate critical issues such as abortion and reproductive health care. But we rarely see a healthy, positive discussion of the pleasure sex may bring us throughout our lives. The media portray sex as pleasurable, but they also tell us that our bodies should be flawless or behave like a porn star to enjoy our sexuality.

As an undergraduate taking a course in biological psychology, I (Nicole) remember the professor simply said, "There is no greater motivator of human behavior than sex." Although we could debate the truth of this concise statement, it conveys the power that sex has in our lives. Why is it so powerful? Because it makes us feel good, and it can bring pleasure to those we truly care about and love. Sex is fun; it can bring us closer to our partner(s) emotionally as well as physically. It can relieve the stresses of the day and it can cause the body to react in a way that no other stimulus can. Sexual pleasure is also a lifelong journey. Throughout life, we get to discover what gives our partner(s) and ourselves the most satisfaction. Arguably, there is no other learning experience that is more fun. To be sure, sex can have negative and destructive consequences, and it's important to understand them, but here we pay respect to the wonders of sexual pleasure.

When experiencing sexual pleasure—the goal of our personal enjoyment of sex—we want to feel the pleasurable aspects of our sexual behavior. This is a difficult topic to discuss because there is so much variation in what people find pleasurable in their sexual interactions. Thanks to our imagination and the body's sensuality, the ways in which we find pleasure in sexual interaction is practically limitless. Think about the first time you experienced sexual pleasure: You may have thought, "Oh, I need to learn more about this!" In this chapter, we explore sexual pleasure, physical sexual arousal and response, as well as some sexual techniques that can help maximize pleasure in intimate relationships.

PLEASURE, CULTURE, AND SEXUAL WELL-BEING

Pleasure is a basic life function, like eating and sleeping. Some researchers see pleasure as such a powerful motivation that it can sometimes override social rules and norms of culture (Freud, 1905; Herdt & McClintock, 2000; Kinsey et al, 1948, 1953; Martin, 2013). As described in Chapter 2, sexual pleasure may have emerged in human evolution as one of the most important ways for people to create and maintain intimate attachments. This means that people can connect sexual pleasure with long and important relationships in ways that most other species of animals cannot. Humans can enjoy sex and orgasm at any time, and sexual pleasure is not exclusively controlled by reproduction.

Humans have depicted sexual pleasure in incredibly diverse ways for thousands of years. Though not as ancient as the cave art pictured in Chapter 2, the *Kama Sutra* is the world's oldest sex manual. Dating back to 600 BCE, the *Kama Sutra* depicts at least 64 sexual positions that give pleasure to each partner. Here are descriptions of just some of those options:

- *Kaurma* (The Tortoise): Seated, mouth-to-mouth, arms against arms, thighs against thighs.
- *Paravartita* (Turning): The lovers' thighs, still joined, are raised.
- *Markata* (The Monkey): The man sits rotating his hips like a black bee within the cave of her thighs.
- *Marditaka* (Crushing Spices): In the monkey pose, partners turn away from each other.
- *Kshudgaga* (Striking): The woman sits with raised thighs, her feet placed either side of the man's waist; linga (penis) enters yoni (vagina); the man rains hard blows upon the woman's body.

The *Kaurma* (Tortoise) position depicted in the *Kama Sutra*.
Werner Forman/Universal Images Group/Getty Images

These positions are also enshrined in beautiful temple sculptures that communicate a pleasure principle for living. The *Kama Sutra,* European cave art from around 35,000 BCE, and Japanese erotic art from the 17th century (see Chapter 2) are striking examples of the sexual nature of humans and the high regard different cultures have had for sexual pleasure.

Sexual Nature and Sexual Well-Being

The human species is distinctive from other species in that we combine sexual activity and interaction with the emotion of love. How strongly one feels love and the expression of sexual pleasure often go hand in hand (Jankowiak, 2008). When humans combine attraction, romantic love, and sexual pleasure to shape long-term relationships, sexual well-being may be fulfilled. This does not mean that all sexual relationships involve love, that casual sex may not be fulfilling, or that long-term commitment or marriage always includes sexual fulfillment. Rather, it means that for many individuals, attraction, sexual pleasure, and love combine in ways that can be deeply meaningful. For many people, then, sexual pleasure is associated strongly with sexual well-being, that sense of feeling sexual joy and pleasure in our bodies and expressing it appropriately throughout our life cycle (Abramson, 1996; Jankowiak, 2008; Martin, 2013).

Cultural Influences on Sexual Pleasure and Sexual Well-Being

In many cultures, sexual pleasure and love are part of a package that allows people to experience sexual well-being. In other cultures, these attributes may be separated. For example, in cultures with arranged marriages, romantic love may not be considered (Gonzaga, Turner, Keltner, Campos, & Altemus, 2006; Herdt, 2019; Lepani, 2012). If two people enter a marriage to procreate and to secure an inheritance of property, then the couple may experience great commitment and companionship but little passion. In other situations, such as extreme poverty, achieving sexual well-being may be difficult (Hirsch et al., 2009).

Sexual interaction is one of life's greatest pleasures.
Cavan Images/Getty Images

Some cultural groups believe that delaying the enjoyment of sexual pleasure until marriage is ultimately the best way to pursue sexual well-being.
Vespasian/Alamy Stock Photo

Unfortunately, some cultures define sexual nature to exclude sexual pleasure, and this may have a very serious impact on an individual's development of sexual well-being. For example, in some cultures in East Africa and the Middle East, same-sex partners may be condemned and belittled by their family, friends, and community, and their relationship will never be accepted. This lack of acceptance denies the couple any possibility of openly expressing their feelings. In other cultures, society may so negatively influence the expression of sexual pleasure for girls that they actually fear revealing their attractions, desires, and attachments to boys (Tolman, 2006). Some cultures include messages about channeling sexual energy in ways that influence how we form relationships, seek pleasure, and come to understand sexual well-being (Carpenter, 2005; Carpenter & Delamater, 2012). One example of this type of message is to "save yourself" sexually for marriage.

Some communities' norms inhibit particular forms of sexual expression for pleasure. Sex-positive cultures tend to accept a broader range of the expression of sexual well-being and pleasure than sex-negative cultures. Sex-negative communities are more restrictive when it comes to certain practices, such as heterosexual anal sex (Laumann et al., 1994; Correa, Petchesky, & Parker, 2008).

Another powerful example of how culture affects sexual pleasure is the way it views masturbation, which is the self-stimulation of the genitals with one's hand or with an object, such as a vibrator. As stated in Chapter 2, many cultures historically disapproved of masturbation. Some cultures still condemn it. Historically, if a culture causes people to feel abnormal or stigmatized about it, those who do engage in it may not develop a strong sense of sexual well-being (Kinsey et al 1948; Lacquer, 2003).

Because culture exerts such a strong influence on sexual expression, there are large variations in how sexual pleasure is experienced and expressed around the globe and over time (Gagnon, 2004; Kinsey et al., 1948; Laumann et al., 1994). Even within U.S. society, a major change has occurred in recent decades in the way sexual pleasure is depicted in the media, from music and movies to the Internet, as seen in Chapter 3.

Defining Your Personal Needs

An important task in the pursuit of sexual well-being is to understand what you need to be comfortable in relationships so you can enjoy your own sexuality. Are you a person who feels sexual pleasure is best enjoyed in the context of a loving and committed relationship, or are you comfortable with the idea that sex can occur simply because it is pleasurable?

Sexual desire and love appear to be normal for all human beings (Fisher, 2004; Jankowiak, 2008; Martin, 2013; Das et al., 2012). Nevertheless, people may experience these feelings differently, some leaning more toward sex, others leaning more toward love. Still others may choose to remain single and abstain from sex. It depends, in part, on sexual motivation, background, culture, gender roles, and interpersonal cues from other people. For many individuals, there can be a huge gulf between sex and love, between what they desire and cultural expectations about gender roles (Diamond, 2008; Tolman, 2006). Desire and love also influence the expression or inhibition of sexual behaviors. Individual differences, someone's mood, and even the time of day can

Pleasure, love, and marriage go together in many cultures.
Purestock/SuperStock

Understanding Your Sexual Needs

Know Yourself

Steven Ing (2015), a therapist, designed this questionnaire to help individuals understand their own perception of how well their sexual needs are being met and where there is an opportunity for continued growth in taking responsibility for meeting their sexual needs. It is meant to be taken by both individuals who are not in a relationship as well as those who are. A range of numbers (from 1 to 5) follows each of these statements; 1 indicates "poorly" and 5 indicates "superior." Where one answers less than 5, it can be understood that there's room for improvement and practice in order to continue moving toward personal sexual fulfillment.

1. I give myself permission to simply have my sexual thoughts rather than repressing them. I encourage myself to think deeply about what I am thinking and how I came to think that way.

    1   2   3   4   5

2. I acknowledge to myself, at least, that I engage in sexual fantasy and that being aware of my sexual fantasies is a normal part of intelligent management of my sexuality.

    1   2   3   4   5

3. I know that, as an adult, I have a need for sexual touch. I may not be getting that need met, but I have my need instead of my need having me.

    1   2   3   4   5

4. I love sexual pleasure and am comfortable with loving it.

    1   2   3   4   5

5. I understand that the need for sexual release (orgasm) is normal and that, whether single or in a relationship, I need to take care of this matter.

    1   2   3   4   5

6. I need to feel safe to simply be the best sexual being I am and, if in a relationship, I have negotiated my way to getting this need met.

    1   2   3   4   5

7. I know I have a need to be desired, and I have built a life that enables me to proceed mindfully and intentionally.

    1   2   3   4   5

8. I enjoy my sexual desires. They are a vital part of a healthy sexuality; nevertheless, I have evolved to the point that I have my sexual desires rather than their having me.

    1   2   3   4   5

9. My sexual identity is an important facet of my life. I am who and what I am, and I like myself.

    1   2   3   4   5

10. I have intentionally pruned away those who cannot accept me for who I am, and I have just as intentionally surrounded myself with those who can accept me.

    1   2   3   4   5

11. Those who are a part of my inner circle offer me the same level of approval that I give myself; I do not have to fake being someone different in order to achieve an illusion of approval.

    1   2   3   4   5

(Continued)

12. I surround myself with those people, books, and influences that help further my sexual development and understanding.

    1   2   3   4   5

13. I allow myself adventure; I even pursue it in a manner consonant with who I really am and who I want to be. I take appropriate risks in a manner pleasing to myself.

    1   2   3   4   5

14. I am intentional about integrating my sexuality into my romantic pursuits, especially in my primary relationship. I am assertive about pursuing my sexual happiness.

    1   2   3   4   5

15. Sexually speaking, I am less concerned about rules than about the more important guiding principles of my spiritual path. My spirituality provides context and meaning to my sexuality, and my sexuality grounds my spirituality in a helpful way. I have found an honorable way to be me.

    1   2   3   4   5

Source: Ing, S. (2015). *We're All Like This: Learning to Talk About Our Human Sexual Needs.* Tuscon, AZ: Giant Publishing.

also affect the expression of sexual desire and behavior (Masters & Johnson, 1966; Van Anders, 2015). Consider your own sexual needs by taking the self-assessment quiz in "Know Yourself: Understanding Your Sexual Needs."

Keeping a Sexual Journal

Researchers from several disciplines, including psychology, sociology, anthropology, and gerontology, are learning that people's life stories can add deeper meaning to their sexual relationships and their feelings of positive sexuality (Hammack & Cohler, 2009; Herdt & Stoller, 1990; Plummer, 1995). Our sexual needs often overlap with other needs; our needs for safety, for play, for dignity, and for connection run together and support one another (Ing, 2015). Therapists recommend keeping a sexual journal to help individuals and couples explore their sexual fantasies and sexual needs, but recording personal sexual thoughts and experiences in a sexual journal can enhance everyone's sexual well-being.

Another reason to keep a journal is that our sexuality changes as much as our personality, and relationships with peers, friends, and family. Keeping a journal helps us to look back and reflect on how much we've changed. Research has shown that a sexual journal can help people understand how and why they express their attractions and pleasure in their sexual

WHAT'S ON YOUR MIND?

Q: My mom once mentioned that she couldn't imagine having casual sex just to have sex. I see people all the time who enjoy sex without being in a committed relationship. Is casual sex a bad thing? Do people enjoy sex more when they are in a committed relationship?

ANSWER: The generational change that has occurred about casual sex is huge. Two generations ago this behavior was considered so "bad" that someone could be ostracized from his or her family, community, and even society. Today many more people than ever live together before marriage, and this practice is far more widely accepted (Dougherty, 2010). Yet studies show that commitment does enrich the meaning of sexual relations. You may not feel comfortable having casual sex or sex with an exclusive partner before you actually live together or make a deeper commitment. Decisions such as these are part of your journey toward sexual literacy. According to the morals you have adopted for your own personhood, you decide how you feel about these issues, and no one else.

experience. People can reflect on their thoughts and what time of day and settings they occur, the partners they have, and the kinds of feelings and desires that they associate with their partner (Coxon, 1988).

Knowing that there is such great variability in the process of connecting sexual motivations, emotions, and love, you may want to begin keeping a sexual journal while you're learning about sexuality. Though many people write in a daily journal, try writing down your sexual motivations and desires, fantasies, and the expression of your pleasure. Use a notebook or your laptop to identify all your sexual thoughts and feelings as they come to you. Write whatever you feel or think that seems sexual to you. Keep your journal in a secure place, because it is for your eyes only (unless *you* decide to share it with someone).

Journaling is your own experience, no one else's. For this reason, try not to be judgmental or critical of your own sexual thoughts and feelings. Especially, try not to censor yourself, because the point is to reflect back on what you are feeling. Try to accept everything that you experience in self-awareness, to begin to see how all the pieces of your sexual self-awareness fit together. For example, you may want to write about how sexual attractions define your sexual awareness. Try to accept your own attractions even if they surprise you. As a result, you may find ways to express your attractions and sexual response to particular people. You may also discover whether your culture provides subtle cues that you might not have recognized.

In the context of this chapter, keeping a journal may reveal aspects of your pleasure seeking and patterns of attraction that you have not yet noticed. What you personally experience and define as "sexual" can be very different from what someone else thinks of as sexual. What excites you is as unique as your fingerprints.

In your journal consider including details such as these:

- Erotica—books, magazines, or websites of interest
- Sexual thoughts you had in different places, such as in the shower, at lunch, in bed
- Dreams that led to wet dreams or physical arousal
- Sexual daydreams
- Thoughts during masturbation
- Thoughts about sexual play with your partner
- How you touched and caressed someone playfully or sexually
- Positive and negative thoughts about your relationship(s)
- Sexual fantasies

These are just a few examples. The point is not to censor yourself.

Many people report an interactive effect of keeping a journal after several days: The more they write down what they are feeling or desiring, the more they are able to understand their own sexual feelings, and perhaps accept these feelings as part of their whole sexuality. This insight is helpful on the journey toward personal sexual well-being.

SEXUAL AROUSAL AND RESPONSE

Turning to a discussion of arousal and response, we now examine how our minds and bodies respond to sexual stimulation. Human sexual motivation is a powerful, unusual incentive for behavior. In lower animals we talk about sexual motivation as a "drive," an innate force that directs animals to engage in reproductive behavior. In humans, our desires and responses are conditioned by a variety of issues, including the bodily desire and subsequent arousal and even emotional needs that may push us to be closer to others or to express love to our mate.

Human motivation to engage in sexual behavior arises from several physiological and psychological factors, as we know from a huge body of research and observation. For example, we would place hormones, which are part of sexual motivation, in the physiological category.

People in all cultures around the world have their own ways of flirting and expressing a desire for interaction.
Paul Bradbury/Alamy Stock Photo

But the desire for physical pleasure, another element of sexual motivation, can be placed in both categories (Abramson & Pinkerton, 1995). Pleasure is influenced both by our thoughts or cognitions and by our physiological functioning.

We can become sexually aroused for many reasons, from flirting, to having fantasies, to wanting to reproduce. These possibilities all appear to be part of our human sexual nature, which inclines us to express pleasure in relationships. Sexual motivations are the mechanisms for this expression. Other components of sexual arousal and response include our senses, pheromones, and sexual fantasy, which we discuss next.

The Five Senses and Pleasure

We experience and communicate sexuality through our senses—touch, taste, smell, sound, and sight. From the day we are born until we die, these organs allow us to see and touch beauty; taste the world's wonderful foods; enjoy the sounds of nature, laughter, and music; and breathe in the scent of forests and all the smells that connect us to other people. These sensory stimulations are so invigorating that many poets and artists have written or represented them, including the sensuality of sexuality. In fact, research shows that these sensual senses are basic to human sexual nature (Ryan & Jetha, 2010).

People's experiences of the senses vary by culture. In the United States, for example, we tend to deodorize our bodies with perfumes, aftershave colognes, and commercial deodorants. In other parts of the world such as Europe, Africa, and Asia, there is not as much emphasis placed on covering natural body odors. In fact, people in the United States are considered to be hypersensitive to such odors because of the great measures we take to mask them (MacPhee, 1992). It is almost as if people in our culture want to downplay natural odors associated with sexuality (Gagnon, 2004). Additionally, the media in this country have developed our visual sense of sexual images. By comparison, people living in societies with little or no access to electronic media do not have this visual sense of sexuality and do not have the cultural understanding of being aroused by a picture or an image of a sexual body. They experience sexual arousal when they see an actual human being (Herdt & Stoller, 1990). How might this change people's sense of visual sensory stimulation? In countries with a lot of visual images, people may become somewhat desensitized to them. Consequently, their intimate interactions with partners may not be as visually arousing as for those who are flooded with erotic images.

Let's consider how our senses affect sexual arousal regardless of culture. Start by imagining how losing one of your senses, such as sight, hearing, or touch, might affect your sexual pleasure. Although the senses are easily taken for granted, they are as precious as our bodies and selves. Now, as we explore each sense, think about how they enhance sexual motivation and sexual pleasure.

Erogenous zones can be found all over the human body. The primary erogenous zones are highlighted.

Touch Touch is a sense that is not only dominant in human sexuality, but it is actually a necessity for sustaining life. From birth to death, the need for humans to experience touch is widely documented and universally accepted (Ing, 2015). Human beings cannot physically or emotionally thrive in a life where they are never touched in a loving way. In human sexuality, touch is the sense that often leads to the highest levels of arousal and response to sexual stimulation. Pleasure, sexual or otherwise, is enhanced by touch—that is, the gentle holding of hands, the leaning of one's body into another, the caress and intimacy of a body massage, or the deepest passion of sexual interaction. It is hard to overestimate touch. Many people believe that without touch they cannot have sexual pleasure or achieve sexual connection. Take a moment to think about how you use touch to extend your pleasure, either to your own body or to your partner's.

When looking at the role touch plays in our experience of sexual pleasure, it is important to consider **erogenous zones.** Erogenous zones are areas on the body that provide a lot of pleasure when touched, caressed, licked, or kissed. **Primary erogenous zones** are the areas of the body that are most associated with sexual touch and pleasure. They include the genitals, butt, anus, perineum, breasts, and inner surface of the thighs, armpits, navel, neck, ears, and mouth. **Secondary erogenous zones** are other areas of the body where we feel sexual sensations. Due to individual variation in people's preferences for touch, virtually any other area of the body can be a secondary erogenous zone.

Sight Sight is the next dominant sense in the realm of sexual pleasure. This is no surprise, considering the great emphasis that we in the United States place on physical appearance. Clothing, makeup, and personal grooming habits all support this idea. People do vary, however, in the degree to which they can be sexually aroused by what they see (Kinsey et al., 1948; Masters & Johnson, 1966). Men and women are both physically stimulated by erotic images or visual cues that they find attractive, but men often tend to be more open in reporting their preference for visual images (Koukounas & McCabe, 1997). In fact, it is widely believed that generally men and women experience quite different sexual arousal sequences on the basis of visual cues, with men tending to be aroused more easily than women (Diamond, 2008; Schwartz, 2007b). Women may respond more to facial cues and the sense of seeing their partner in a particular context whereas men may respond more to overt sexual gestures.

Researchers speculate that this gender difference may help to explain the arousal response of men to pornography, in which sight influences sexual motivation and arousal more in comparison to women. For example, a study of 688 heterosexual Danish adult men and women found large gender differences in the use of pornography, because men were exposed to pornography at a younger age, consumed more pornography as adults, and tended to use pornography on their own (Hald, 2006). You can read more about how men and women respond to pornography in "Research and Sexual Well-Being: Viewing Pornography and Sexual Excitement."

Smell Some people feel that smell is our most powerful sense and that it is not an accident that we may associate certain fragrances with particular people. Many people feel that their partner's smell is so distinctive that they can enter a room and know whether their partner is present or absent. A scent may linger in the partner's hair and clothes and remind them of that person's touch and smile. Someone who has been working hard outdoors or exercising may exude that special scent of musk and dry cedar.

Smells are known to both stimulate and offend with regard to sexual arousal. One interesting study looked at penile engorgement and vaginal blood flow in response to certain smells during sexual arousal (Hirsch, 1998). The study showed sex differences in the kinds of odors that both aroused and offended men and women. Men responded positively to aromas of lavender, pumpkin pie, and doughnuts, while women responded positively to the scents of licorice, cucumbers, and banana nut bread. Women were most turned off by the smells of barbecued meat, cherries, and, interestingly, men's cologne. There were no smells that inhibited arousal on the part of men.

---

erogenous zones
Areas on the body that provide great pleasure when stimulated by touch.

primary erogenous zones
Areas of the body that are most commonly associated with sexual touch and pleasure, including the genitals, butt, anus, perineum, breasts, inner surface of the thighs, armpits, navel, neck, ears, and mouth.

secondary erogenous zones
Areas of the body that, when touched in a sensual way, can trigger arousal in the primary erogenous zones. These areas may include the back and the feet and virtually any other area of the body.

RESEARCH and Sexual Well-Being

Viewing Pornography and Sexual Excitement

Have you ever thought about how viewing pornography may influence sexual excitement? One study examined such a question as it relates to men. It looked at how male participants responded to different kinds of sexual stimuli to see if their arousal would sort heterosexual men from men who say they are bisexual (Rieger, Chivers, & Bailey, 2005). The results suggested that all the men showed genital arousal to pornography regardless of their sexual orientation. The results also indicated that men became much more sexually aroused when they viewed stimuli they were really interested in than if they viewed material they were less interested in and were even less aroused by neutral stimuli. For example, when heterosexual men viewed pornography featuring women, they were much more aroused than when they viewed pornography that did not feature women. They also found that the men who said they were bisexual were generally not that different in arousal from heterosexual men and showed nothing that was distinctive in their arousal by visual images.

It is interesting that men and women report their arousal to visual sexual stimuli differently. Historically, men have always reported that they are highly aroused by visual representations of sexuality. Women historically have reported lower levels of sexual arousal to visual stimulation. However, when researchers have studied biological indicators of sexual arousal in male and female response to visual stimulation, such as erection and vaginal lubrication, it appears that women and men are stimulated equally on a physiological level. Recent studies have reported that women have discussed and admitted their arousal from viewing pornography but had hesitated to admit it due to a perception about those who view pornography (Ashton, McDonald, & Kirkman, 2018). So it appears that visual preference and sexual arousal occurs for women as well as men even though women have less of a tendency to admit their arousal. Why do you think that women do not "own up" to their arousal from viewing explicit images? How might women communicate this interest to their partners?

Some researchers have hypothesized a potential relationship between orgasm and smell. Specifically, one study showed that the strength or depth of an orgasm experienced by women was related to the attractiveness of smell of their male sexual partner (King & Belsky, 2012). Deep orgasms were defined as those that produced full-body sensations, more internal sucking sensations, and a higher likelihood of sensations such as "loss of self" and "loss of clarity" during the orgasm, whereas surface orgasms were defined as producing feelings of relaxation and were more localized in intensity (King & Belsky, 2012). In this study, females who experienced deep orgasms compared to surface orgasms described their partners as having a more attractive smell (King & Belsky, 2012).

Theorists have also considered the roles of pheromones in studying smell and sexual arousal in humans. As you may remember, pheromones are odorless chemical signals that are not readily noticed by the nose but are detected in the environment. Later we consider some studies on pheromones, even though studying human pheromones is difficult because soaps and perfumes may mask these signals.

Taste We have a storehouse of taste sensations, and using our taste buds to savor the experience of one's partner can deepen the sexual experience. Culture plays a part in the tasting of bodily fluids, including semen and vaginal fluid. When people kiss on the lips, particularly deep kissing with the tongue, they exchange saliva. In cultures with strong taboos against the exchange of body fluids between men and women, kissing may be taboo as well.

The sources of different taste sensations in people's fluids are not known but they may reflect the foods that people eat and individual differences in the sensory modalities. For example, drinking a lot of pineapple juice or eating bananas can sweeten semen and vaginal

COMMUNICATION Matters

Time to Taste: Exploring One of the Senses in a Sexual Experience

Have you ever stopped to think that communication does not always mean using words to convey meaning? We can communicate nonverbally in a variety of ways. We can even use our mouths to convey messages without speaking. Consider the kiss or tasting a partner with your lips and tongue. Many people have differing feelings regarding the taste of their partner's body. Some people enjoy the idea of tasting their partner's lips, saliva, and even fluids associated with the genital region. In the *Twilight* series about vampires, author Stephanie Meyer describes the sweet taste that Bella (the heroine) enjoys when kissing Edward (the main vampire character). For some people the most intimate and vulnerable activities are those that involve the mouth and the mouth or body of someone else.

Can you think of elements in your own sexual experience that you enjoy or hope to enjoy regarding the sense of taste? Here are some suggestions:

- As you are touching, first kiss your partner on the lips and then slowly kiss all over the body. Place your lips right up to your partner's, probing inside the mouth. Think about what kind of message this action communicates to your partner. Switch places to take turns.
- How does your partner taste when you kiss? Pause to file away this memory and then share this feeling—it can connect the two of you at a deep level.
- Now, alternating and taking turns, allow your mouth and tongue to move over other parts of your partner's body. How does he or she taste to you? What are you saying when you are engaged in this intimate activity? What messages do you think your partner is receiving?
- While tasting your lover, you can use different tongue techniques. First use the tip of your tongue to taste, and then introduce your entire tongue. Does it offer a different taste? How? Explain to your lover.

---

fluids. Consider this list of foods or chemicals that can impact the taste of bodily fluids (Ingraham, 2009):

- Bitter: Red meat, fish, alcohol, coffee, smoking, asparagus
- Mild: vegetables, fruits
- Sweet: pineapple juice, bananas, papaya, and foods high in sugar

A person who is diabetic may also have very sweet tasting bodily fluids due to the elevated levels of sugar in the bloodstream.

If you'd like to experience how taste can enhance a sexual experience and communication of desire, read "Communication Matters: Time to Taste: Exploring One of the Senses in a Sexual Experience."

Sound During lovemaking and intimacy, sounds may play a critical part, enhancing the sensations of touch and taste. For example, some people may enjoy having music playing in the background. Like the other senses, what people enjoy regarding sound is highly individual and variable. When it comes to moans and groans in the bedroom or other noises prompted by sexual arousal, people have varied feelings. Some people are highly turned on by the sounds of their partner in the bedroom and others find noises to be a distraction.

In this section we have reflected upon how the five senses can enhance sexual pleasure. Consider how these experiences may infuse sexuality with more meaning and connect partners even more deeply.

Although we may not be aware of it, a person's natural scent may be a big factor in attracting potential partners.
Ingram Publishing

Pheromones and Sexual Motivation

From the discussion of the senses, it is clear that smell plays a big role in sexuality. According to the evolutionary psychologist David Buss (1994), the first requirement of finding a mate is that "they smell right." But what does that mean? In mammals, smell plays a role in sexual response and perhaps in mate selection, but as with many other matters in evolution and social development, humans are more complicated (Verhaeghe, Gheysen, & Enzlin, 2013). Smell appears to have evolved to support sexuality in many species. In certain species, sex pheromones also appear to communicate either the availability of females for mating and/or the presence of males in the females' territory. For example, the wild boar sprays its pheromones and female sows appear to respond with sexual arousal that may lead to mating. Do humans have a similar sexual motivation? Let's consider some research related to this controversial question.

An early and very important study about human menstrual synchrony offers a key to understanding the role human pheromones may play in mating and reproduction. Menstrual synchrony refers to the effect of women living in such ways that their menstrual periods time together. This remarkable synchrony is named the *McClintock effect* after renowned biological psychologist Martha McClintock (1971), who discovered this human pattern. While an undergraduate living in a female dorm, she noticed that her peers began to have their menstrual cycles at the same time. She wondered what could produce such a reaction. Pheromones are now believed to be the cause (Bancroft, Graham, & Jenssen, 2009).

A review of the science reveals several key points to keep in mind about the link between pheromones and sexual attraction. First, there is great individual variability in the effect of smell on attraction; second, context seems to play an overly large role in response; and third, mate selection may be the evolutionary effect of such a response mechanism (Verhaeghe, Gheysen, & Enzlin, 2013). Other research has suggested that pheromones may be part of the sexual attraction between people of the same sex, but there is no evidence yet to support this hypothesis (Ryan & Jetha, 2010). Researchers have concluded that of the pheromones known as 16-androstenes, there is one in particular, androstadienone, that is fairly well documented to be a pheromone for women (Verhaeghe, Gheysen, & Enzlin, 2013).

Thus, sexual motivation and scent are potentially connected in some individuals and couples, but how general is this response in the human population? We do not know the answers yet, and further research is needed before we'll even be sure if pheromones play a significant role in how most humans experience sexual motivation and arousal (Ryan & Jetha, 2010). But for now, just be alert to colognes and perfumes that claim they have "added" pheromones that will attract a partner. They may bring you enhanced confidence but probably not the love of your life.

Sexual Excitement and Sexual Fantasy

sexual excitement
The subjective experience of sexual arousal.

sexual fantasy
Private mental imagery associated with explicitly erotic feelings, possibly accompanied by sexual arousal.

As we have seen, people absorb a great deal from their own experiences and motivations, and from their cultures in making sex an exciting part of their daily lives. Sexual fantasy is perhaps the most powerful internal tool of human sexual nature and it supports sexual excitement at all ages (Stoller, 1979).

Sexual excitement is the subjective experience of sexual arousal, especially but not limited to genital arousal. It is the feeling of excitement a man may feel in his penis or a woman may feel in her vagina and clitoris or surrounding tissue. A **sexual fantasy** is the imaginary roles and parts that people may play out in their minds relating to sexual expression. People may engage in

WHAT'S ON YOUR MIND?

Q: So many of my straight men friends talk about their sexual fantasies either involving two women having sex or having sex with two women at the same time. Why are these particular fantasies such a turn-on for some men?

ANSWER: A good deal of male heterosexual porn expresses the fantasy of a man having sex with more than one woman or the image of two women sexually interacting. One fantasy may be about men wanting to dominate women. The second fantasy may arouse a man to want to "have his way with women." This implies a deeper feeling that the women, whom the man thinks may be lesbians, may need a "real man" to make them into "honest women." Others suggest that many men like to see a woman masturbating, and other men get aroused, as do some women, watching two men enjoying gay sex. Sexual fantasies take many twists and turns, some of which may be based on power differences between the sexes.

sexually fantasy to achieve orgasm, although this is not always the case. Sexual fantasies combine arousal, desire, and sexual interaction (Freud, 1905; Kinsey et al., 1948; Leitenberg & Henning, 1995; Money & Ehrhardt, 1972; Stoller, 1979). Also, sexual fantasies may be more common than daydreams (Wilson, 1978). Engaging in fantasy about our sexuality and desires has many positive aspects we can consider. For example, in our fantasies we are not risking rejection, getting emotionally or physically hurt, or experiencing embarrassment because our fantasies are internal and personal; we don't have to share them with anyone unless we choose to (Ing, 2015).

Some experts speculate that highly sexualized contexts online may be changing our sexual fantasies or how we express them. For example, the wide availability of online pornography or websites devoted to erotica and sexual storytelling can expose us to a wide range of content to add to our repertoire of sexual fantasy. Researchers do not know if this is positive or negative for people's spontaneous and creative use of sexual fantasy in their intimate relationships. It does seem paradoxical that in the United States people's most intensely private activity, sexual fantasy, may now be played out in virtual public settings on the Internet instead of in the bedroom.

Sexual excitement appears to be as unique in each person as fingerprints (Stoller, 1979; Herdt & Stoller, 1990). In his studies of sexual excitement, Stoller was fascinated by how people would weave their sexual fantasies into a **fantasy system** that expressed their deepest sexual motivations, pleasures, fears, and yearnings for emotional connection with others. Stoller believes these fantasy systems combine rapidly moving images with feelings that switch between danger and pleasure. These fantasy systems are unique to each person.

Humans are fortunate because we have this ability to create sexual fantasies. In fact, sexual fantasy is an innate characteristic of humans, just as is the capacity for language or the ability to make tools. This unique capacity contributes to our ability to enjoy sexual pleasure in a way that other animals cannot. Through sexual fantasy, humans connect to others as individuals, as sexual beings, and as sources of pleasure. Everything that we have learned about sexual fantasy as a human capacity suggests that it has a positive and significant role in stable, mature relationships.

Women and men may experience sexual fantasies differently (Buss, 1994; Diamond, 2008, 2014). Men have twice as many fantasies as women and emphasize the visual stimuli of body parts. Women tend to emphasize emotion and context. When men fantasize and then engage in sex with a partner, they may be only partially aware of their body and experiences (Fisher, 1989). For a further look into the effects of pornography on sexual well-being, see "Controversies in Sexuality: Does Pornography Enhance or Damage Sexual Relationships?"

fantasy system

Interwoven sexual fantasies that express individuals' deepest sexual motivations, pleasures, fears, and yearnings for emotional connections with others.

Sexual fantasies can take a variety of forms and are often experienced differently by men and women.
1001nights/Getty Images

CONTROVERSIES in Sexuality

Does Pornography Enhance or Damage Sexual Relationships?

One of the most controversial issues in sexuality and human relationships is pornography. Psychologists, sociologists, therapists, clergy, and politicians all seem to quibble about the impact that pornography has on people and their intimate relationships. Pornography, which at one time was not very accessible, is now easily found on the Internet and on adult cable channels and on-demand services. Researchers now study whether easy access to pornography affects relationships and reshapes expectations about sex (Kraus, Voon, & Potenza, 2016; Paul, 2004). In other words, does pornography damage sexual relationships?

Yes:

- Some psychologists and sociologists argue that men who frequently view porn may develop unrealistic expectations about how women should look and behave.
- Due to these unrealistic expectations, men may have a more difficult time forming and sustaining relationships and feeling sexually satisfied.
- Sometimes pornography can tear couples apart. At a 2003 meeting of the American Academy of Matrimonial Lawyers, two-thirds of the 350 divorce lawyers who attended said that the Internet played a significant role in divorces in the previous year, with excessive interest in online porn contributing to more than half of such cases (Paul, 2004).
- One recent longitudinal study showed an association of beginning pornography use and rates of divorce among younger Americans (Perry & Schleifer, 2018). This same study showed that women who discontinued pornography consumption saw their likelihood of divorce decrease by nearly 60%. Interestingly, for men, there was no reduction in the likelihood of divorce upon stopping pornography consumption (Perry & Schleifer, 2018).

No:

- Most consumers of online pornography say that sex online is nothing more than good fun. According to a 2001 online survey of more than 7,000 adults, two-thirds of those who visited pornographic websites said their online activities did not affect their level of sexual activity with their partners (Paul, 2004).
- Some therapists believe that pornography is a healthy way to refresh relationships or spark desire. The key is for consumption of porn to be mutual and seductive to the partners. The partners need to find the material to be "erotic" rather than "pornographic." The difference is that porn can be objectifying and derogatory while erotica depicts mutually satisfying sex between equal partners.

What Is Your Perspective?

1. Do you think pornography is a healthy way to enhance or spice up intimacy?
2. Do you believe that it presents an element of danger to personal and intimate aspects of a relationship?

Sexual Response Cycles

You may remember the mention of William Masters and Virginia Johnson in Chapter 1. When it comes to the research concerning sexual arousal and response, we can credit much of our current understanding to their work. While their work is important to the field of human sexuality, not all of their observations and conclusions are universally accepted. Both Helen Singer Kaplan and Rosemary Basson have proposed alternative models to Masters and Johnson, which we'll study as well.

To more fully understand how the body responds sexually, Masters and Johnson (1966) initially observed more than 10,000 episodes of sexual activity in 382 women and 312 men. Their initial studies included only heterosexual individuals, though they did study the sexual behavior of gay men and lesbians at a later time. As described in Chapter 1, Masters and Johnson observed volunteers who did not know their sexual partner. Based on their results, they described the human sexual response as a cycle with four phases: excitement, plateau, orgasm, and resolution. This model is often called the **EPOR model.** Though it describes the sexual response cycle for many people, not every person may progress through each phase or progress at the same pace. For example, some people may have spontaneous orgasms or may reach plateau and never orgasm. Masters and Johnson never intended for these four phases to be seen as four separate and distinct events. The reality is that sexual response is a much more seamless process than this model suggests. However, the four-phase model was simple for people to understand, and it helps us to conceptualize the physiological changes and responses that occur during sexual activity. In addition, it should be noted that while this model is widely used and accepted, there is some variation in how people experience sexual activity. For example, it is quite common for women not to experience orgasm during sexual interaction. Just because they do not experience one phase does not mean that there is something wrong with them.

The phases of the response cycle follow the same pattern regardless of the kind of sexual activity that one is engaged in. Masturbation, manual or oral stimulation, same-sex interaction, penile-vaginal intercourse, and engagement in fantasy can all result in a similar sexual response cycle. The cycle is pictured in Figure 5.1 and is slightly different for men and for women.

Excitement phase is the first phase in the body's sexual response. Arousal happens when the body reacts to a specific stimulus. Perhaps it's an attractive person or sexually explicit material. The brain sends signals to the rest of the body to prepare it for possible sexual activity. For both women and men, one change in the body during the excitement phase is vasocongestion. This is when erection occurs in the clitoris and the penis. In women, the labia also become swollen and the vagina loosens and secretions begin to lubricate it. If the vagina feels tight and dry, the woman may not yet be aroused sexually.

Plateau phase is the second phase in the body's sexual response. Once the body and the mind have become sexually aroused, individuals may start to stimulate partners or themselves. As arousal increases, sensitivity to touch increases, and the sensation of touching the genitals is often heightened and more pleasurable. As the genitals are stimulated more, the chest area may turn pink or red with what is called **sex flush,** blood pressure increases, and the heartbeat grows stronger. During this phase, people often feel like they are on edge or ready to explode. The name of this stage—that is, plateau—can be confusing because the term typically suggests a leveling off, which is not the case.

Orgasm, the third phase of the body's sexual response, occurs at the peak of the plateau phase, and typically lasts for only a few seconds, though it may feel much longer. An orgasm is simply a series of rhythmic muscle contractions. In men, orgasm involves rapid contractions of the prostate gland, the seminal vesicles, and the vas deferens, which generally produce an

EPOR model
Four stages of the human sexual response, including excitement, plateau, orgasm, and resolution.

excitement phase
The first stage of the body's sexual response, marked by vasocongestion and erection in the clitoris and the penis.

plateau phase
The second stage of the human sexual response, according to the EPOR model, in which sensitivity to touch increases and becomes more pleasurable.

sex flush
During the plateau phase, as the genitals are stimulated more, the chest area flushes to pink or red.

Figure 5.1
Masters and Johnson's EPOR model of the human sexual response.

Male Sexual Response Cycle

Female Sexual Response Cycle

orgasm
The third phase of the human sexual response, at the peak of the plateau phase; for both women and men, orgasm involves increased muscle tension throughout the body and then relaxation, especially in the pelvic area.

endorphins
Chemicals produced in the brain during strenuous exercise, excitement, pain, and orgasm that may alter our emotions in the period after orgasm; work as "natural pain relievers" to produce a sense of well-being.

resolution
The fourth phase of the human sexual response, involving the relaxation of the body and a feeling of psychological wellness, as the extra blood in the genitals that caused erection drains out and the genitals return to their normal state.

DID YOU KNOW

Where in the world does orgasm happen most often? A poll of 26,000 people in 26 countries revealed considerable variation by country in the percentage who said they achieved orgasms every time they had sex (Durex, 2007/2008):

- 66% from Italy, Spain, and Mexico
- 48% from France, the global average
- 24% from China and Hong Kong

The Japanese were the least satisfied with the intensity of the orgasm. Mexicans and Brazilians were the most satisfied. Factors that enhanced an orgasm included delaying climax, longer foreplay time, and a strong emotional relationship between partners.

Source: Reuters Life! India, April 29, 2008.

---

ejaculation of semen. Some men may orgasm without ejaculation; some men may ejaculate without orgasm. Women experience rapid contractions around the vagina that may or may not produce a vaginal secretion or ejaculate. Orgasm may also involve the uterus. For both women and men, orgasm involves increased muscle tension throughout the body and then relaxation, especially in the pelvic area. The brain also releases certain chemicals during orgasm, primarily **endorphins,** which may alter emotions in the period after orgasm. Endorphins are produced by the pituitary gland and the hypothalamus in humans during strenuous exercise, excitement, pain, and orgasm, and they resemble the opiates in their ability to produce a sense of well-being. Essentially, endorphins work as "natural pain relievers." For most people, orgasm is the desired phase, but it may not occur every time they engage in sexual intercourse.

Resolution is the last phase of sexual response, in which the body experiences relaxation and a feeling of psychological wellness. During resolution, everything returns to its normal state: The extra blood in the genitals that caused erection drains out and the genitals return to their normal state. Men's penises lose their erections and women's clitorises and labia return to their normal size. If we stop being sexually aroused, resolution can also happen without orgasm. Women may complete their resolution phase very soon after orgasm and be ready to begin the response cycle all over again. This makes multiple orgasms much more common in women than men. Men's resolution phases are typically longer and during this time men cannot get erections even if they do feel sexually aroused. This phase between orgasm and a subsequent erection is called the **refractory period.**

Between the sexes, the refractory period in the male cycle is one, if not the major, difference in sexual response. Men typically find that a minimum period of time must elapse after an orgasm before they can experience an erection and a subsequent orgasm. Most women do not have a similar physiological barrier that prevents physical arousal and response. In fact, women are more likely than men to experience repeated orgasms (Masters & Johnson, 1966; Meston, Hull, Levin, & Sipski, 2004b). The interesting thing about the refractory period is that we really have no idea why it occurs or what function it serves. What we do know is that the human male is *not* the only species to experience a refractory period. Male rats, dogs, and chimpanzees, for example, experience this physically imposed shutdown phase.

Another sexual response cycle, proposed by sex therapist Helen Singer Kaplan (1979), has similarities to the EPOR model of Masters and Johnson as well as some important distinctions. Kaplan's model of sexual response includes three stages: desire, excitement, and orgasm (Figure 5.2). The most distinct difference in Kaplan's model is the desire phase, which she describes as a prelude to physical response. While many appreciate this inclusion, the reality is that desire is not necessary for sexual interaction or response. One study noted that as much as 30% of sexually experienced women with the capacity for orgasm rarely or never experience spontaneous sexual desire (Levin, 2002). This shows that not all sexual expression is preceded by desire. For example, a woman might agree to have sexual intercourse to please her partner even though she may not have a real desire to engage in it herself. She may find that her body begins to respond during sex despite her initial lack of desire.

A more recent model of female sexual response was introduced by Rosemary Basson (2000) that addresses specific nuances of women's psychophysiology that are not acknowledged in older, linear models of sexual response. Basson (2000) acknowledged that even with Kaplan's (1979) introduction of sexual desire into Masters and Johnson's model, these models were still insufficient for addressing women's sexual response. What was missing from these models were important documented components of women's sexual satisfaction, including: trust, intimacy, the ability to be vulnerable, respect, communication, affection, and pleasure resulting from sensual touching. As you can see in Figure 5.3, Basson's female sexual response

Figure **5.2**

Kaplan's model of sexual response includes the element of desire, which Masters and Johnson's EPOR model did not.

cycle is cyclical rather than linear and incorporates elements of desire, physical responses to sexual stimuli and emotional and relational aspects of sexual satisfaction (Basson, 2001).

Orgasm

A colorful collection of euphemisms describes orgasm, one of the most pleasurable physiological processes humans experience. People sometimes refer to orgasm as *getting-off, cumming, climaxing,* or *ecstasy.* Whatever you call it, it is one of the most pleasurable parts of sexuality.

What's actually happening in the body during orgasm? Orgasm is an autonomic nervous response, meaning that it is involuntary because the brain's limbic system controls it. During orgasm, the lower pelvic muscles go through a series of quick contractions around the genitals and the anus. Orgasm may involve involuntary muscle spasms in other parts of the body including vocal spasms that we express in moans, gasps, or screams.

As you may recall from Chapter 4, orgasm for men is a common result of masturbation or sexual penetration via vagina, mouth, or anus. For women, however, there is variation in terms of what kinds of interactions are necessary for orgasm. In one study, 1,055 women aged 18–94 completed a web-based survey about how they best achieved orgasm (Herbenick, Fu, Arter, Sanders, & Dodge, 2018). Over one-third of women reported that clitoral stimulation was necessary for orgasm during intercourse, while 18.4% of women reported that vaginal intercourse alone was sufficient to achieve orgasm. Interestingly, an additional one-third (36%)

refractory period
The period following orgasm during which a man cannot have another erection.

Figure **5.3**

Basson's female sexual response cycle.

reported that clitoral stimulation wasn't necessary for them to achieve orgasm, but their orgasms were perceived to be better if the clitoris was stimulated during intercourse (Herbenick et al., 2018). It is also not surprising to learn that women reported incredibly diverse preferences for how and where they were touched in their genitals (Herbenick et al., 2018).

Before we leave the topic of sexual arousal and response, we need to acknowledge that each person is unique and what may be satisfying and arousing to you may not be for your partner(s). Sexual pleasure is ultimately a lifelong journey, and the first step in attaining great levels of pleasure is understanding yourself. In the next section, we will look into specific sexual techniques that can increase pleasure in sexual relationships.

SEXUAL TECHNIQUES

Engaging in sexual intimacy is one of the most pleasurable experiences in life for many people. When sexual activity is approached responsibly—that is, with accurate knowledge, adequate protection, and mutual respect—sex can be one of the most satisfying forms of self-expression available to humans.

Sexual activity or intimacy can produce a wide range of emotional responses from people. Most often, the feelings people have are positive such as desire, excitement, and happiness. Others may experience different feelings, especially when they've suffered sexual trauma or abuse. These people may be fearful, embarrassed, and anxious at the thought of engaging in sexual behaviors. It is possible for people to overcome these negative feelings. Through therapeutic techniques and a responsive, respectful, and caring partner, they can begin to enjoy their sexuality and move toward having a sexual life that supports sexual well-being.

Many people assume that sexual behaviors come their way naturally. After all, sexuality is a foundational piece of what it means to be human. While the drive to engage in sexual activities may very well be a human instinctual behavior, sexual technique is not easy to perfect. People's knowledge of and experience in sexual activities vary greatly depending on many factors such as family background, culture, religious heritage, childhood experiences, and sexual orientation. In this section, we discuss various sexual behaviors, techniques, and positions to help you understand the variety of sexual activities that are possible for personal enjoyment and sexual well-being. We will discuss both **noncoital behaviors** (sexual behaviors without vaginal penetration by a penis) and **coital positions.** Coital positions are the placement of bodies during sexual intercourse involving penile-vaginal penetration. The techniques we discuss are not exhaustive. People find thousands of variations to increase their enjoyment of sex. This section should be seen as an introduction to possibilities rather than a list of approved techniques. Each person will discover through time and experience his or her own personal preferences and desires. Table 5.1 details the best and most widely acknowledged population-based study in the United States showing how common certain sexual behaviors are among men and women of diverse age groups throughout the life span.

noncoital behaviors
Sexual behaviors that do not involve penetration of a vagina by a penis.

coital positions
The placement of bodies during sexual intercourse involving penile-vaginal penetration.

Masturbation—Solitary and in Relationships

We know that the history of masturbation has been relatively controversial with respect to how people feel about it on social, moral, and religious levels. Despite the history of strongly held beliefs, research shows that the great majority of boys actually have their first sexual experience alone, masturbating to fantasy (Gagnon, 2004). In an important national study, Herbenick et al. (2018) found that: "64% of men and 40.8% of women had masturbated in the last month, and 8.2% of men and 21.8% of women reported having never masturbated in their lifetime." Among those who reported masturbating, men reported masturbating approximately 12 times a month and women reported an average of over 4 times a month (Pinkerton, Bogart, Cecil, & Abramson, 2002). Given the results of these studies, it appears

Table **5.1** Percentage of Americans performing certain sexual behaviors in the past year

SEXUAL BEHAVIORS	AGE GROUPS									
	14–15		16–17		18–19		20–24		25–29	
	MEN	WOMEN	MEN	WOMEN	MEN	WOMEN	MEN	WOMEN	MEN	WOMEN
Masturbated Alone	62%	40%	75%	45%	81%	60%	83%	64%	84%	72%
Masturbated with Partner	5%	8%	16%	19%	42%	36%	44%	36%	49%	48%
Received Oral from Women	12%	1%	31%	5%	54%	4%	63%	9%	77%	3%
Received Oral from Men	1%	10%	3%	24%	6%	58%	6%	70%	5%	72%
Gave Oral to Women	8%	2%	18%	7%	51%	2%	55%	9%	74%	3%
Gave Oral to Men	1%	12%	2%	22%	4%	59%	7%	74%	5%	76%
Vaginal Intercourse	9%	11%	30%	30%	53%	62%	63%	80%	86%	87%
Received Penis in Anus	1%	4%	1%	5%	4%	18%	5%	23%	4%	21%
Inserted Penis into Anus	3%		6%		6%		11%		27%	

SEXUAL BEHAVIORS	AGE GROUPS									
	30–39		40–49		50–59		60–69		70+	
	MEN	WOMEN	MEN	WOMEN	MEN	WOMEN	MEN	WOMEN	MEN	WOMEN
Masturbated Alone	80%	63%	76%	65%	72%	54%	61%	47%	46%	33%
Masturbated with Partner	45%	43%	38%	35%	28%	18%	17%	13%	13%	5%
Received Oral from Women	78%	5%	62%	2%	49%	1%	38%	1%	19%	2%
Received Oral from Men	6%	59%	6%	52%	8%	34%	3%	25%	2%	8%
Gave Oral to Women	69%	4%	57%	3%	44%	1%	34%	1%	24%	2%
Gave Oral to Men	5%	59%	7%	53%	8%	36%	3%	23%	3%	7%
Vaginal Intercourse	85%	74%	74%	70%	58%	51%	54%	42%	43%	22%
Received Penis in Anus	3%	22%	4%	12%	5%	6%	1%	4%	2%	1%
Inserted Penis into Anus	24%		21%		11%		6%		2%	

Source: National Survey of Sexual Health and Behavior (NSSHB). "Findings from the National Survey of Sexual Health and Behavior, Center for Sexual Health Promotion, Indiana University." *Journal of Sexual Medicine* 7, suppl 5 (2010).

that masturbation is accepted by some segments of society as basic to sexual liberation (Lacquer, 2003).

Sexual scientists now understand that masturbation is an activity in which many but not all people engage. And why not? It is a great way to learn about one's body and what sexually excites

Figure 5.4
Male masturbation.

and arouses. For some who haven't engaged in it, though, the prospect of pleasing oneself can be daunting. Here are a few things to consider about masturbation and sexual self-discovery.

- **Make time.** Allow plenty of time so that there is not a feeling of being rushed or pressured as this could prevent full enjoyment of the experience.
- **Ensure privacy.** Masturbation as a solitary activity is meant to be done privately. Turn off the phone, lock the doors, and do what you can to create a private and comfortable environment.
- **Pay attention to feeling.** As you touch yourself pay attention to how your body feels. Notice your breathing and how your muscles feel. Is there tension in some areas of your body and relaxation in others? Consider how it feels prior to orgasm and then how your body feels after orgasm.
- **Experiment with technique.**
  Men: Vigorous up and down stroking on the shaft of the penis usually ends in orgasm. Other types of strokes can bring different sensations and different orgasms, though. Experiment with different movements, pressures, and speeds. Rolling your penis in between your hands, moving your hands up and down your shaft may feel good. Long twisting strokes instead of just up and down may work. For many men the scrotum is a very sensitive area that responds well to feelings of touch and pressure. Use your forefinger and thumb and circle the top of your scrotum. Gently tug on your scrotum as you masturbate. This may prevent you from ejaculating and extend the sexual feelings in your body. Experiment with other kinds of touch, including tickling, scratching, and rubbing (Figure 5.4).

  Women: Run your hands along parts of your body, lingering along areas that are more responsive to touch than others. Look at your genitals in a mirror (especially if you're unfamiliar with them) and caress the different parts to see what feels especially good. Find and touch your inner and outer labia, clitoris, vagina, and perineum. Using one or two fingers, rhythmically stroke the different parts of your vulva, paying particular attention to your clitoris and labia. Experiment with different types of pressure, speed, and motion. Try placing a finger on either side of the clitoris and stroking up and

Figure 5.5
Female masturbation.

down, or placing two fingers on the clitoral hood and rubbing in a circular motion. Try different types of touch: stroke, tickle, knead, pinch, or lightly pull your genitals. Try using one or several fingers, the palm of your hand, your knuckles (Figure 5.5).

- **Experiment with positions.** Your personal experiences masturbating are a great time to try new things. Changing positions can be a great way to bring some new excitement to your sexual experiences. If you normally masturbate while lying in bed, try it standing up or sitting in a chair. You might feel strange at first but may find that different positions bring different sensations.
- **Touch other places.** The genital regions are not the only areas of the body where sensual pleasure can be felt. Try rubbing and touching other areas of the body such as your chest, inner thighs, and abdomen. You might find erogenous zones that you did not know would bring you pleasure.
- **Experiment with toys.** Sex toys can add a completely new kind of stimulation, and accentuate the manual stimulation you're doing. In addition if you are contemplating using a toy with a partner, you may want to use it on yourself first so that you can better communicate your preferences about it to your partner.

Kissing

While masturbation and solo-sexual activities can bring about a great amount of pleasure as well as a good deal of self-awareness, sexual interaction with another person is typically the goal we people strive to attain. As we discussed in the section on the senses and sexual arousal, touch is the chief way in which the process of arousal begins. Kissing with the lips is one form of sexual interaction.

A kiss can mean a variety of things. It can be sweet and soft on the forehead indicating a gesture of support, encouragement, and care. It can be open and intense, using the lips and tongue to communicate sexual passion and desire. It can be the symbol of two people joining their lives together in committed marriage or union as done in some wedding ceremonies. A kiss triggers a cascade of neural messages in the body and the release of chemicals that lead to physical sensations, feelings of sexual excitement and closeness, and even euphoria (Walter, 2008).

Kinsey and colleagues (1948) found that almost all couples in the United States included deep (or French) kissing in their sexual interaction. Today, kissing continues to be a favorite activity. In fact, among college students, kissing is reported to be one of the most popular sexual behaviors and something that a majority of students fantasize about (Hsu et al., 1994).

As wonderful as kisses can be, they can also be powerful markers of the future of a relationship (Walter, 2008). In one survey, 59% of men and 66% of women admitted there had been times when they were attracted to someone only to find that interest fizzle after a first kiss that did not go so well. These "bad kisses" did not have any specific flaw—it was reported that they just didn't feel right and that was enough motivation to end the relationship (Gallup, Hughes, & Harrison, 2007).

Frequency of Sexual Activity

It's no surprise that people often compare themselves to others. It is not surprising, then, that many people and couples wonder if they have as much sex and if they enjoy it as much as their friends, co-workers, and neighbors. Figure 5.6 presents the estimated number of times American adults had sex.

The Global Study of Sexual Attitudes and Behaviors (GSSAB) polled over 27,000 men and women from 29 different countries regarding their sexual behaviors and attitudes (Das et al., 2012; Laumann et al., 2006). Worldwide, women reported a lower degree of sexual satisfaction, which is consistent with the findings in the United States (Erber & Erber, 2011). The issues associated with decreased sexual satisfaction for women were a lack of interest in sex (31%), an inability to reach orgasm (22%), an inability to enjoy sex (21%), physical difficulties with lubrication (20%), and painful intercourse (14%) (Laumann et al., 2006). Interestingly, sexual satisfaction findings were also associated with a variety of social and gender-related dimensions. For example, men and women from countries where gender equality is more pronounced reported higher sexual satisfaction. These countries included the United States, Canada, Mexico, Australia, New Zealand, South Africa, and the

Figure **5.6**
Estimated times per year American adults had sex, 1989–2014.

countries of Western Europe. Sexual satisfaction was lower in countries that are more male-dominated, including Morocco, Egypt, Israel, Italy, Turkey, Malaysia, and Thailand (Laumann et al., 2006). The lowest levels of sexual satisfaction were found among collectivist cultures, including Taiwan, Japan, China, and Indonesia. It might be that the collectivist nature leads to a belief that individual gratification in sexual relationships is not important (Erber & Erber, 2011). As mentioned previously, there seems to be some data indicating that sexual frequency may be on the decline, particularly among younger people in the United States (Twenge, Sherman, & Wells, 2017). American adults had sex about nine fewer times per year in the early 2010s compared to the late 1990s. The average American born in the 1990s—also known as Millennials—has sex about six times a year less often than the average American born in the 1930s. Researchers hypothesize that this decline, which is consistent across gender, race, and religion, could be attributed to the fact that there is a reduction in the number of people who are married. This study reaffirmed the knowledge that married people tend to have more sex than unmarried people (Twenge, Sherman, & Wells, 2017). However, it appears that even marriage has not protected individuals from this decline in sexual activity. More research will need to be done to more fully understand why we are seeing declines in sexual connection between individuals, both single and married, and what this might mean for sexual well-being and relational health.

Other Intimate Behaviors

Questions to consider while reading this section include, "Would my partner enjoy this?" and "How would my partner like to be touched, kissed, caressed?" If you are comfortable with an activity, focus on what your partner enjoys. Pay attention to nonverbal cues such as body movements, breathing, facial expressions, and vocalizations. In addition, an excellent way to find out if you have the right touch is simply to *ask*.

Oral Sex **Oral sex,** the stimulation of a partner's genitals by mouth, has gained popularity in recent decades, though many people are still uncomfortable openly discussing it or admitting that they enjoy it. The majority of men and women who engage in this intimate behavior say they enjoy it (Laumann et al., 1994). Recent studies show that half or more of women ages 18 to 39 reported giving or receiving oral sex in the past 90 days (NSSHB, 2010). Receptive oral sex is reported by more than half of women between the ages of 18 and 69 who are in a cohabitating relationship and more than half of married women ages 30 to 39 (NSSHB, 2010). Couples often feel that giving and receiving oral sex deepens the intimacy in their relationship more than any other behavior including intercourse. Perhaps this is due to the vulnerability that individuals feel in both giving and receiving it. Some individuals report that their orgasms are strongest when they come via oral sexual activity.

Oral sex involves two behaviors depending on who the recipient is. **Fellatio** is oral sex performed on a man, and **cunnilingus** is oral sex performed on a woman. Figure 5.7 illustrates these behaviors.

The English noun *fellatio* comes from the Latin verb *fellāre,* meaning "to suck." A person may perform fellatio to induce male orgasm and ejaculation of semen or it may be used as foreplay prior to sexual intercourse. Men vary in how they like to receive oral sex. Techniques can include kissing or licking the shaft of the penis as well as the head (or glans). Often the partner puts the entire penis inside the mouth and stimulates it by moving it in and out while using a hand to hold and stimulate the penis. Some men also like manual or oral stimulation of the scrotum during oral sex.

The person performing fellatio can decide whether to ingest semen. Some individuals like it a great deal while others are not fond of the taste and do not like to orally stimulate their partner to orgasm and ejaculation into their mouth. Some pregnant couples use fellatio to replace vaginal sex because vaginal intercourse during the later stages of pregnancy can

oral sex
The stimulation of a partner's genitals by mouth.

fellatio
Oral sex performed on a man.

cunnilingus
Oral sex performed on a woman.

Figure 5.7
Fellatio.

be difficult. Interestingly, as late as 1976, some doctors advised women in the eighth and ninth months of pregnancy not to swallow semen lest it induce premature labor, even though it is now known to be safe.

Oral sex may not be universal but in some cultures, semen has a kind of "nutritional value" or "growth" potential that becomes a sexual motivation. As described in Chapter 2, for example, the Sambia of Papua New Guinea historically believed that regular ingestion by prepubescent boys of an older boy's semen helped the younger boys to achieve sexual maturity and masculinity. As soon as the younger boys begin to develop facial hair or muscles, the older males typically lose interest in them. Women also "drink" semen to strengthen their bodies and create babies, according to the Sambia belief system (Herdt & McClintock, 2000). Today, however, due to rapid social change and modernization in the past three generations, the Sambia have adopted vaginal sex as their preferred sexual technique (Herdt, 2019).

Sexual Pleasure, Arousal, and Response **157**

Figure **5.8**
Cunnilingus.

As illustrated in Figure 5.8, cunnilingus, the stimulation of the female genitals using the mouth, lips, and tongue, comes from the Latin words *cunnus* for vulva and *lingua* for tongue. While it seems relatively simple, a wide variety of activities can occur besides simply licking the genital area. In general, the woman's partner stimulates the vulva by licking, kissing, or sucking on the inner and outer labia, clitoris, and clitoral hood. Some women even enjoy having the tongue inserted into the outer part of the vagina. Movements can range from slow and soft to more fierce and vigorous. Many women also enjoy simultaneous manual stimulation of the vagina, perineum, anus, breasts, or nipples during oral sex.

Figure 5.9
Anal intercourse.

anal intercourse
A form of sexual expression in which the anus is penetrated by a penis.

anilingus
Oral-anal stimulation.

Anal Sex Anal stimulation, which includes **anal intercourse** and manual stimulation of the anal area during sexual activity, is an activity that divides many people. Some people see the anus as dirty and unappealing while others enjoy the stimulation to the anus due to the extraordinarily sensitive tissues surrounding it and the rectum. Anal activities may include touching or massaging the anal area, insertion of a finger or penis into the anus, and kissing or licking the anal area (Figure 5.9).

Heterosexual anal sex has been present in sexual fantasy and behavior for hundreds, if not thousands, of years (McBride & Fortenberry, 2010). A popular belief among heterosexuals is that only gay men practice anal intercourse and oral-anal stimulation, called **anilingus.** Part of this belief is also that all gay men engage in anal intercourse as part of their sexual activities. The reality is that while anal intercourse is the least common of sexual activities discussed here, it is rising in popularity among heterosexuals. In recent years, anal sex among heterosexuals has risen in frequency so much so that the news media has suggested that anal sex is the "new oral sex" (McBride & Fortenberry, 2010). While there hasn't been a formal study of public interest or opinion of heterosexual anal sex, the vast materials

WHAT'S ON YOUR MIND?

Q: My partner would like to try anal sex. I am kind of shocked and not really interested, but I don't want to hurt any feelings. What do I do?

ANSWER: You need to be open and honest about your feelings. We encourage you to discuss it to explore why you are opposed to it. Is your opposition due to a social stigma? Do you think this is something you might be able to work through or is this crossing a boundary for you? Even if you ultimately decide not to engage in this intimate behavior with your partner, make sure you clearly communicate that this is a boundary for you. Then suggest an alternative activity that might be interesting and sexually arousing!

Sexual Pleasure, Arousal, and Response

available in addition to the references in popular culture suggest that we might be seeing a shift in cultural norms.

Regarding the prevalence of anal intercourse, research has shown that it is not an uncommon behavior, with 36% of women and 44% of men aged 25-44 reporting ever having engaged in heterosexual anal intercourse in their lifetime (Chandra et al., 2011). It appears that the prevalence of heterosexual anal intercourse is increasing, which may be due to an actual increase in the behavior, or simply that it has become less taboo and more acceptable for people to report having anal sex (Hess et al., 2016). Anal sex among gay and bisexual men is a bit more complicated by the fact that they may be inserters or recipients or both. Anal sex is not universal among these men, and it is sensitive to context and issues of STIs, of course, but it is likely that at least a third or more of gay and bisexual men engage in anal sex (National Survey of Sexual Health and Behavior, 2010). While it is hard to generalize due to the sensitive nature of the LGBTQ population, it appears that oral sex is more frequent than anal sex among gay men, though a large recent study showed for example that 68% of men had engaged in anal sex in the last month (Vansintejan, Vandevoorde, & Devroey, 2013).

There are some significant cautions regarding anal sex. Because the tissues surrounding the anus can tear easily, unprotected anal intercourse is considered to be the highest-risk sexual behavior for the transmission of HIV and certain sexually transmitted infections. Because of the high levels of bacteria present in this orifice of the body, the fragility of the tissue, and the fact that it does not produce a natural lubricant as does the vagina, much care needs to be taken when engaging in anal sex. Condoms and lubricant should be used to prevent the transmission of infections and to minimize possible tearing of anal tissue during anal intercourse. Some evidence suggests that frequent anal intercourse over time can lead to painful breaks in the skin, called **fissures,** and hemorrhoids, and may cause more permanent weakness of the sphincter muscles surrounding the anus.

Noncoital and Coital Positions Up to this point, all the sexual behaviors we have discussed—masturbation, sexual touching, oral, and anal sexual activities—are enjoyed and engaged in by people of any sexual orientation. In this section we discuss the one exception to this, namely coitus. **Coitus** specifically refers to penile-vaginal intercourse and so, by definition, is engaged in by heterosexual couples.

The topic of coital positions has been a topic of interest for people throughout time. Today we often see discussions of the benefits and drawbacks of various positions. People often wonder how many coital positions exist. There are hundreds of, if not more, possibilities for positions. The number is limited only by people's imaginations. In fact, it would be impossible to try to discuss or illustrate all the possibilities.

Part of increasing sexual pleasure in our lives is using our imaginations to come up with new and exciting ways to enjoy each other during sexual intercourse. As mentioned

fissure

A small break in the anal tissue that may result from anal intercourse without proper lubrication.

coitus

Penile-vaginal intercourse.

> ### WHAT'S ON YOUR MIND?
>
> *Q: My partner really wants us to experience simultaneous orgasms, but it hasn't happened yet. Are simultaneous orgasms more powerful or do they bring you more sexual pleasure?*
>
> **ANSWER:** Many couples desire the experience of simultaneous orgasm believing that it will amplify their pleasure or connection to one another. But simultaneous orgasms are not necessarily more powerful. The benefit of simultaneous orgasms is that both partners reach climax at the same time, so that one partner is not winding down while the other is still trying to achieve an orgasm. The reality, though, is that this does not happen all that often. In heterosexual couples, the time from arousal to orgasm for men is consistently shorter than the time from arousal to orgasm in women. Try to see the benefits of not attaining orgasm at the same time. When one partner reaches orgasm at a different time than the other, partners are able to take in the sights and sounds of their partner's pleasure more fully as they are not engrossed in their own feelings and sensations.

Figure 5.10
Missionary position.

previously, this is another area in sexual pleasure where individual variability and preference play a large role. Not everyone enjoys the same positions, and every person and couple are different in their preferences.

missionary position
Position in which the man lies on top of the woman during sexual intercourse.

Missionary Position: Man on Top The **missionary position,** in which the man lies on top of the woman during sexual intercourse, is the most common position for sexual intercourse in Western cultures (Figure 5.10). The missionary position was named after Christian missionaries who introduced this position to the people of the Polynesian Islands. Before their arrival, people of these islands engaged in sexual intercourse with the woman on top.

Benefits of the missionary position:

- Maximizes eye contact during intercourse
- Good position for kissing
- Penis can be easily inserted into the vagina
- Either partner can help guide penis into vagina
- There are several possibilities for leg positions for the woman which can lead to more comfort or to control depth of penetration
- Man feels dominant, which may be preferable for both partners

Drawbacks of this position:

- Difficult for man to touch or caress woman's body because his arms and hands are used to support his weight
- More difficult to stimulate the clitoris
- Due to the high level of stimulation for the man, he may have less control over his orgasm and ejaculation
- The man's weight may be too much for the woman to be comfortable
- Can be exhausting for man to support weight on arms and legs for an extended period of time
- Woman may feel too passive or dominated

Cowgirl Position: Woman on Top In many areas of the world, the female-on-top position is the most common position for coitus. There are many variations of this position; a women can kneel or squat over the man or lie down on him (Figure 5.11).

Benefits of this position:

- Can be a better position for woman's orgasm due to her ability to control angle of penetration, movement, and speed of thrusting

Sexual Pleasure, Arousal, and Response   **161**

Figure 5.11
Cowgirl position.

- Both partners are able to touch each other's body
- Either partner is able to manually stimulate the clitoris during intercourse, increasing the possibility for woman to achieve an orgasm
- For men who carry more weight in the abdominal area, this position may allow for deeper penetration than the man-on-top position
- For men who have difficulty controlling ejaculation, this position is less stimulating which may help them delay orgasm and ejaculation
- Woman is in a more dominant position, which may be preferable for both partners

Drawbacks of this position:

- This position makes thrusting for the male more difficult
- For men with difficulties reaching orgasm, this position is less stimulating
- Men and women may both feel that this position is too passive for the man

Side Lying Position (Face-to-Face)   In the side lying position (Figure 5.12), both partners lie on their sides facing one another with their legs intertwined. As penile insertion can be difficult in this position, many couples begin with either the missionary or cowgirl position and then roll over onto their sides.

Benefits of this position:

- Neither partner is required to support the weight of the other
- Not as physically demanding as other positions
- Penetration of the penis is shallower
- Partners are able to touch each other's bodies easily

Drawbacks of this position:

- Much more difficult to insert penis into vagina
- Not an easy position for partners who are overweight
- Penetration of the penis is shallower

Figure 5.12
Side lying position, face-to-face.

- More difficult to stimulate the clitoris
- Increased chance of penis slipping out of the vagina during intercourse due to angle
- Lower arms and legs may fall asleep due to the weight resting on them

Doggy Style: Rear Entry In the rear-entry position (Figures 5.13 and 5.14), the man inserts his penis into the woman's vagina from behind her. While there are many variations

Figure 5.13
Doggy style, rear entry.

Figure **5.14**
Rear entry, front-to-rear.

of the rear entry position, the most common is a woman kneeling with the man behind her. Variations of rear entry might include lying side-by-side, front-to-rear (also called "spooning"), or the woman sitting in the man's lap facing away from him.

Benefits of this position:

- Deep penetration into the vagina is possible
- Man's hands are free to reach around to caress the breasts or manually stimulate the clitoris
- Very good position during pregnancy as no pressure is exerted on the woman's belly
- Some men and women report different feelings of stimulation

Drawbacks of this position:

- Penetration may be uncomfortably deep for woman
- No real possibility for eye contact or kissing
- May feel too impersonal due to the lack of face-to-face contact

SEXUAL PLEASURE AS A HUMAN RIGHT

You may be wondering what sexual pleasure, arousal, and response have to do with human rights? This question is answered by many international organizations. For example, in 1975, the World Health Organization (WHO) recognized that the right to pursue sexual pleasure in a safe and satisfying way can lead to better overall health. In recent years, women activists have sugggested that there is a triangle involved—health, rights, and pleasure—all of which are necessary for sexuality (Merelli, 2018). In fact, research shows that when people feel *safe and secure* in their right to pursue their individual sexual pleasure as part of their holistic sexuality, they are better able to attain sexual well-being and are healthier in general (Aggleton & Parker, 2002; Coleman, 2010; Correa, Mcintyre, Rodriguez, Paiva, & Marks, 2005; Correa, Petchesky, & Parker, 2008; Herdt, 2004; Miller, 2000; Parker & Aggleton, 2002; Petchesky, 2003). However, the whole notion of pleasure is sometimes very male-oriented, and so it always requires a context and consent.

Since 1983, researchers have worked with WHO to define the concepts of sexuality and sexual health. This work culminated in 2000 at a meeting with the Pan American Health Organization (PAHO) that led to WHO endorsing the World Association for Sexology's "Declaration of Sexual Rights." This declaration states that sexual rights are fundamental to human rights, and the right to sexual pleasure is one of 11 core principles.

Another international organization, named Health, Empowerment, Rights and Accountability (HERA), drafted this statement in the mid-1990s:

> Sexual rights are a fundamental element of human rights. They encompass the right to experience pleasurable sexuality, which is essential in and of itself, and, at the same time, is a fundamental vehicle of communication and love between people. Sexual rights include the right to liberty and autonomy in the responsible exercise of sexuality (HERA, 1995, p. 27).

Though statements such as these support human sexual rights, some professionals remain concerned about the incredible amount of inequity and male control of pleasure across cultures with regard to roles of women and their relationship to men (Oriel, 2005). While these statements present sexual pleasure as gender-neutral, research reveals that these statements do not reflect what, in fact, really occurs for women (Oriel, 2005). Research and theory indicate that male sexual pleasure often reinforces male sexual dominance over women through prostitution, rape, and compulsory marital coitus (Oriel, 2005). In this context, activists suggest a focus on pleasure and consent, and not just for sex but for all intimacies, such as holding hands and kissing—ensuring the highest level of empathy, support, and care between partners (Merelli, 2018).

The authors of these declarations state that coercion, violence, and exploitation are unacceptable, but they fail to acknowledge the power differential that exists in many cultures. This power difference often results in sexual subordination and exploitation of women as a man's "right" and at the very least, a form of male sexual pleasure, a problem that has been thrown into dramatic relief in the #Me-Too Movement.

We highlight this issue because many times in our culture we fail to understand how some groups—women and LGBTQ people and especially communities of color—are oppressed. The stated idea of sexual pleasure being a fundamental right is a huge step toward sexual equality, but with strings attached. All people should be able to engage in forms of sexual behavior that bring them happiness and fulfillment as long as these forms are consensual and allow their partner(s) to experience dignity, power, and well-being. As powerful as declarations of sexual rights are, alternative declarations of sexual rights with sexual equality at the core are also necessary (Ilkkaracan, 2000; Oriel, 2005; Correa, Petchesky, & Parker, 2009).

Sexual pleasure is much more than just "feeling good." A lot goes into our enjoyment of sexuality. Understanding the many influences of sexual pleasure such as societal standards for beauty and attraction are just as important as knowing our own preferences for sexual enjoyment, such as what excites our senses. Sexual pleasure is a lifelong pursuit for many of us because it takes significant time to learn how to make our intimate lives more fulfilling for our partners and ourselves.

Chapter Review Summary

Pleasure, Culture, and Sexual Well-Being

- Sexual pleasure allows people to create intimate attachments that connect sex, love, and relationships but it always requires care and consent.
- For many individuals, sexual pleasure is associated strongly with sexual well-being, taking care of themselves, and ensuring good health as well as intimate understanding. All world cultures accept being attracted to someone, falling in love, and wanting to give and receive pleasure as natural human attributes.
- Cultures differ in whether they include or exclude sexual pleasure (and consent to have pleasure) in their definition of sexual nature.

- Sex-negative cultures tend to be more restrictive toward certain sexual practices and sex-positive cultures tend to accept a broader range of sexual expression and pleasure.
- Keeping a sexual journal can reveal changes in an individual's sexuality and identify patterns in personal sexual experiences, expressions, and behaviors that may increase understanding of how pleasure connects to culture, context, and moods.

Sexual Arousal and Response
- Human sexual motivation is a complex set of relationships that are both emotional and physical in nature.
- We experience and communicate sexuality through our senses—touch, taste, smell, sound, and sight.
- Erogenous zones are areas of the body that are most associated with sexual touch and pleasure. Primary erogenous zones include the genitals, butt, anus, perineum, breasts, and inner surface of the thighs, armpits, navel, neck, ears, and mouth. Secondary erogenous zones are other areas of the body where we feel sexual sensation.
- Men tend to self-report higher levels of arousal in response to visual stimuli than women, but physiological measures show that they respond similarly.
- Pheromones may play a significant role in human sexual motivation, but research suggests that there is individual variability and sensitivity to context.
- Sexual fantasies combine sexual desire and interaction, contribute to sexual excitement, and are thought to be unique to humans.
- Men have more sexual fantasies than women and tend to focus on visual images of the body, while women tend to emphasize emotion and the context of romantic and sexual situations.
- Masters and Johnson described the human sexual response as a cycle with four phases: excitement, plateau, orgasm, and resolution. Known as the EPOR model, this pattern is typical, but some individuals may not experience all its phases.
- Basson introduced a new cyclical model of sexual response directed more toward women that addresses elements of physical, psychological, and relational enjoyment in sexual interaction.
- Orgasm, one of the most pleasurable physiological processes humans experience, is an involuntary physiological response.

Sexual Techniques
- Sexual intimacy can be one of the most satisfying forms of self-expression.
- People's knowledge and experience of sexual activities depend on many factors, including culture, religious heritage, childhood experiences, and sexual orientation.
- Masturbation is one way to get to know one's own body and enhance sexual pleasure, although it is still controversial in some cultures and societal groups.
- Oral sex has gained in popularity over recent years.
- In recent years, anal sex has become more popular with heterosexuals, and while it is not universal, it is a fairly important practice among gay and bisexual men.
- A variety of sexual positions make it possible to enjoy sexual expression.

Sexual Pleasure as a Human Right
- Many sexual researchers and advocacy groups have declared that sexual pleasure is a human right because it contributes to our health and sexual well-being.
- Male sexual pleasure often reinforces male sexual dominance. Therefore, in addition to statements about the rights of human sexual pleasure, declarations of sexual rights and sexual equality require that consent from one's partner be vital at all times.

HUMAN SEXUALITY

What's Your Position?

1. **How did you come to realize your own sexual and emotional needs when it comes to sexual activity and behavior?**
   - Do you consider the pursuit of sexual pleasure a human right? If so, how do we best act on that right in connection with our partner(s)?
   - Where have you gathered information relating to your own sexual needs and desires (books, Internet, experience, etc.)?

2. **What do you focus on in your sexual thoughts and fantasies?**
   - Is there anything that surprises you about your own fantasies?
   - Would you consider communicating your fantasies to a sexual partner? If so, how do you imagine doing so?

3. **What gives you the highest level of sexual pleasure?**
   - What sexual positions do you enjoy the most and why? If you are not sexually active, what sexual positions do you hope to try in your life?
   - What kinds of sights, smells, touches, and sounds arouse your interest in sex or intimacy?

Design elements: Controversies in Sexuality: HBRH/Shutterstock; Research and Sexual Well Being: verity jane smith/Getty Images; Healthy Sexuality: Sergey Furtaev/Shutterstock; Communication Matters: PeopleImages/Getty Images; Know Yourself: Plush Studios/Blend Images LLC; What's Your Position: Luis Molinero/Shutterstock; Healthy Sexuality: A. Minde/PhotoAlto; Did You Know icon: McGraw-Hill Education; Page corner icon: McGraw-Hill Education.

Taking Care of the Sexual Body

6

Knowing Our Own Body
- Explain what it means to be proactive in one's own health care.
- Identify gynecological and reproductive health concerns for both women and men.

Sexually Transmitted Infections
- Identify the risks and protective factors for STIs.
- Summarize the prevalence, symptoms, transmission, testing, and treatments for bacterial, parasitic, and viral STIs.
- Describe how sexual risk among intimate partners in a couple can be reduced.
- Exemplify how to engage in sexual risk negotiation with partners.
- Summarize the biological, cultural, social, and historical factors associated with the HIV/AIDS pandemic in the United States and around the world.

Sexual Well-Being and Innovation in STI Prevention
- Explain why protecting oneself from STIs is considered by experts to be a human right.

● Learning
● Objectives

nito500/123RF

Developing Your Position

1. How comfortable are you in discussing sex with your doctor?
2. How comfortable are you with examining your own genitals?
3. How do you and your sexual partner(s) discuss having sex and issues related to the risks of STIs?

Self, Society, and Culture: A Lesson for the Professor

It is amazing how much professors learn from students. I (Nicole) learned this lesson the hard way. When I first started teaching Human Sexuality courses, I mistakenly believed that if I scared my students with statistics and horrifying pictures of genitals marked with sores and warts, they would be motivated to make decisions in favor of protecting their bodies. My thinking was that if I frightened them enough about STIs, they would make wise decisions. After the class ended, a student e-mailed politely questioning my method of instruction. She had contracted an STI prior to taking my class. Her feedback was that my class did not encourage her to make healthy choices—instead, it frightened her, embarrassed her, and then made her angry. I thought a lot about her words. I had not thought about what my class would be like for individuals who already had an STI. Was I focusing too much on the danger and not enough on the pleasure and the positive aspects of sexuality? The answer was "yes." My motives were good—I wanted to see an increase in healthy behaviors and decisions—but my methods needed improvement. Making room for the pleasure also means knowing how to protect our bodies from the risk of infections.

We can't ignore the fact that STIs are a very large and growing problem in the United States. We can, however, discuss the dangers of unprotected intercourse and encourage people to follow safe practices when having sex. We can also focus on healthy sexuality as an amazing part of our lives. We can maximize our pleasure and at the same time protect our intimate partners and ourselves. To this end, it is the goal of this chapter to present accurate information, not to scare you about sexuality.

KNOWING OUR OWN BODY

Taking care of our own sexual body always involves both *pleasure* and *danger*. These two terms define the extreme ends of what's at stake during the sexual encounters we have in our lives. Experts have long stated that pleasure and danger help explain the excitement and appeal of sex (McClelland et al., 2017; Money, 1986; Stoller, 1979). As we explore in Chapter 15, the extremes of sexuality can result in danger becoming pleasure. However, there can be conflict and contradiction in how pleasure and risk mingle (McClelland & Fahs, 2018). Too often, the risks of sex are emphasized so much that we feel there is nothing we can do proactively to enjoy sex and still protect ourselves. Preserving good health means knowing one's body and understanding the real-world sexual risks involved. In emphasizing sexual well-being, we aim to weight this sexual "teeter-totter" in favor of pleasure, because by taking the positive steps to protect our own body and pleasure, we can arm ourselves against the risks of sexually transmitted infections (STIs).

Carefully examining our bodies, too, on a regular basis and understanding how the parts typically feel and respond to touch not only helps maximize sexual pleasure, but also helps us to maintain our own sexual health. If we don't know how our bodies regularly look

Common Misconceptions About Sexually Transmitted Infections

Know Yourself

Good information about STIs is widely available, but there are also a lot of myths about this sensitive topic (STD Express, 2011). Are you aware of some of the most common myths and misconceptions regarding STIs? Take the true/false quiz below and find out. Consider sharing this questionnaire with your friends or intimate partner.

1. Heterosexual men can actually become infected with the human immunodeficiency virus (HIV) from other men.
2. Two condoms are better than one and provide double protection.
3. You can get some STIs from skin-to-skin contact.
4. Knowing your intimate partner and communicating about the need to protect your bodies against STIs can lower your risk of disease.
5. The birth control pill provides protection from STIs.
6. Chlamydia and gonorrhea will go away on their own without treatment.
7. If condoms aren't available, you can use plastic wrap as a substitute.
8. If you have sex in a pool or hot tub, chlorine will kill everything so there is no need to wear a condom.
9. If your partner has herpes, you can contract it only when he or she is having an outbreak.
10. The greatest risk of STI transmission is from anal sex.
11. Deep French kissing can infect you with HIV/AIDS.

Answers can be found on page 170.

---

and feel, it is difficult to gauge a change that may signal a problem. In this chapter we explore female and male sexual health by looking at common sexual and reproductive health concerns for women and men. To check how much you know about your own sexual body, see "Know Yourself: Common Misconceptions About Sexually Transmitted Infections."

Taking Responsibility for Our Own Sexual Health

The United States continues to have the highest rates of certain STIs in the industrial world. In fact, with certain STIs, such as chlamydia and syphilis, the numbers of infected people have reached record levels (CDC, 2018). Reasons include inadequate sex education and sexual health education, and the absence of honest dialogue about sexual pleasure and risk among young people today (IOM, 2011; Irvine, 2002; Pascoe, 2011; Schalet, 2000, 2011). Former U.S. surgeon general Joycelyn Elders (2008) says that "sexual healing" starts with all of us being well informed, having sound government programs that support comprehensive sexual health, and urging individuals to take responsibility for their own well-being and to care about the well-being of others.

Teens and young adults have a disproportionately higher rate of certain STIs than other age groups in our society. Because an STI sometimes leads to serious illness and costly treatment needs, it is essential for this group to take steps to maintain good health. Positive health means being

DID YOU KNOW

- Many STIs have no apparent symptoms, and for most STIs, you cannot tell by looking at your partner(s) that he or she might have an STI.
- You can contract an STI from unprotected oral sex. Many people don't protect themselves during oral sex with contraception because it is not possible to get pregnant by giving or receiving oral sex. However, the mouth often has small cuts and sores, and those points of entry can allow for the passage of sexually transmitted viruses and bacteria to the bloodstream. It is important to choose a contraceptive method that will protect against STIs during oral sex.

Know Yourself

ANSWERS to Know Yourself Quiz (p. 169)

1. **True:** HIV does not discriminate based on sexual orientation. Gay or straight men and women can contract the virus if they engage in unprotected sexual behavior with infected individuals regardless of sex.

2. **False:** Currently, it is considered a bad idea to use two condoms at one time. While there does not yet seem to be any scientific literature to support this stance, it comes from the advice of professionals (including the Centers for Disease Control and Prevention (CDC), OB/GYN doctors and nurse practitioners, and condom manufacturers). Their explanation is that during sex, an excessive amount of friction will occur between the two condoms and increase the likelihood of either, or both, condoms breaking.

3. **True:** Some STIs, such as pubic lice and scabies, can be passed to a partner by engaging in skin-to-skin contact. It is important to be aware of the modes of transmission of STIs so you can best protect yourself.

4. **True:** We know that communicating with partners about sexual histories and risk can be an uncomfortable discussion, but research shows that when people take the time to communicate honestly about histories and potential risk, they tend to make positive sexual health decisions to protect themselves and enjoy a more fulfilling sexual relationship.

5. **False:** The birth control pill only protects against pregnancy. Because the birth control pill does not prevent the sharing of bodily fluids during intercourse, it does not protect against any form of STI.

6. **False:** Gonorrhea and chlamydia are bacterial STIs and need to be treated with antibiotic medications.

7. **False:** Plastic wrap, baggies, and other household materials are not good substitutes for a condom. They don't fit well, can easily be torn, and can get displaced during sex. Condoms are specifically made to provide a good fit and good protection during sex, and they are thoroughly tested for maximum effectiveness. When it comes to condoms, there's no substitute for the real thing.

8. **False:** The idea behind this method of avoiding pregnancy is, if you and your partner have sex in chlorinated water, the chemical will kill the sperm. The truth is, while chlorine can act as a spermicide, its effectiveness depends on how heavily the water is chlorinated. More importantly, this chemical would have to reach deep inside a woman's vagina and reproductive organs in order to kill the sperm that have been ejaculated into them.

9. **False:** During inactive periods, the virus cannot be transmitted to another person. However, at some point, it often begins to multiply again without causing symptoms (called *asymptomatic shedding*). During shedding, the virus can infect other people through exchange of bodily fluids.

10. **True:** Unprotected anal sex is considered, by the CDC and many health professionals, to be among the riskiest behaviors for STI transmission. The reason is, the tissues around the anus are very fragile, and small tears (called *fissures*) are common after engaging in anal intercourse or even using sexual toys and inserting them into the anus. The best way to proceed with caution is to always use condoms; and if you are using sex toys, be sure they are sanitized and not shared with others.

11. **False:** There is an extremely low chance (actually, the risk is considered to be nonexistent) of transmitting the virus by French kissing, although it is theoretically possible because of the potential for blood contact.

our own best advocate and communicating effectively and honesty with health care professionals about our sexual body and needs. For steps you can take to communicate with health care professionals, see "Communication Matters: Being Proactive With Your Sexual Health Care."

COMMUNICATION Matters

Being Proactive With Your Sexual Health Care

The following steps can help you to protect your sexual body, become a better consumer of health care, and make informed decisions about your own health.

- **Know your primary care doctor.** Having a consistent primary care doctor allows both you and your doctor to know your sexual body together. This ensures continuity in your treatment. If a doctor delivers a personal or moral bias, consider finding a new one who is objective when dispensing patient care.
- **Meet and greet your doctor (while dressed).** Instead of booking your first appointment as an exam, arrange a "meet and greet" to get to know the doctor and see if you are comfortable talking about your sexual body.
- **Know your family history.** Tell your primary physician about your entire family health history including such medical issues as diabetes, high blood pressure, and cancer, to create a full picture of potential medical issues.
- **Convey your sexual history.** If you feel comfortable, try to communicate about your own vital sexual issues, including values, sexual relationships, history of sexual abuse or coercion, and your sexual orientation.
- **Have a health care buddy.** A health care buddy, who could be a good friend, can remind you to see a doctor and can be your extra eyes and ears if you need them.
- **Ask questions.** When a doctor proposes tests or a course of treatment, always ask about the risks, any alternatives, and what happens if you do nothing. Doctors and nurses converse in medical terms; if you don't understand these terms, ask what they mean.
- **Always ask if you need a referral to see a specialist.** If you do not inquire, a specialist may refuse to see you or your insurance company may send you a huge bill.
- **Set a date for preventive screenings.** Book these appointments well in advance, especially for routine but potentially lifesaving screenings such as mammograms, Pap smears, or a colonoscopy.
- **Become familiar with your insurance coverage.** Use your insurance company's website and toll-free number to find out exactly what your plan covers.
- **Carry your emergency health information and insurance card at all times.** This list should include your doctors, medications, herbs and vitamins you take, allergies, immunizations, family history, emergency-contact information, and blood type.
- **Use the Internet wisely.** The Internet can be a valuable tool, but it should never replace a consultation with your doctor. Print articles and take them to your health care provider for help sifting through the information.

ericsphotography/iStockphoto.com

Female Sexual Health

It is a rare experience to find an individual who has NOT been touched by breast cancer in some form or fashion. I (Nicole) have been affected by breast cancer because both my grandmothers had breast cancer. My maternal grandmother lost her life when I was a young girl as a result of her breast cancer diagnosis. My paternal grandmother was diagnosed when I was in college, and I was frightened that she would also die. What I found was that treatment had improved immensely in the years that separated the two diagnoses. My paternal grandmother has been cancer-free for over 20 years. She is an encouragement to me and represents so many millions of women who have this disease.

Because a woman's sexual anatomy is partly internal, understanding and becoming familiar with the sexual body is more challenging for females than it is for males. A woman's breasts,

> ### WHAT'S ON YOUR MIND?
>
> **Q:** *I know it is really important that I take the time to examine my body to ensure my own sexual health, but I have to admit that I hate the way my vagina looks and I don't want to look at it. What do I do?*
>
> **ANSWER:** Your feelings about your body are not uncommon ones. Many women are a bit uncomfortable with the way their vulva/vagina looks. Unfortunately, many young women are given negative messages about their genitals in childhood. Little girls are taught that touching their genitals is "dirty" or "not nice," so they absorb the message that their genitals are ugly. We would encourage you to think about the messages you've received and grab a mirror. Take time to look at yourself and become familiar with this specific part of your body. In time we think you will learn to see the beauty of every part of your body.

vagina, and surrounding tissue all play a role in both sexual health and pleasure. For discussion regarding a woman's perspective on the female body and the ability to reach orgasm, see "Healthy Sexuality: What Does Orgasm Have to Do With It?"

In the next section, we will discuss sexual and reproductive health concerns common to women. Having an understanding of these health issues is important, to ensure people have the right information so they can take care of their bodies.

Breast Cancer   Every year, approximately 1 in 8 women, or 268,000 in the United States, are diagnosed with breast cancer, and more than 40,000 women die from the disease (American Cancer Society, 2019). In the United States, breast cancer is the fifth leading cause of death for women. Worldwide, breast cancer comprises 23% of all cancers (excluding non-melanoma skin cancers) in women and has caused more than 521,000 deaths worldwide (GLOBOCAN, 2012). The older a woman is, the more likely she is to develop breast cancer. Globally, breast cancer is the greatest cause of death to all women, and education is the best all-around way to avoid it (Ghoncheh, Poumamdar, & Salehiniya, 2016). Non-Hispanic White women have the highest incidence of breast cancer. Figure 6.1 shows how the incidence of breast cancer varies by race and ethnicity in the United States.

The chances of dying from breast cancer increase as a woman ages, but dying from breast cancer is much less common than being diagnosed with it. For Hispanic women, it is the most common cause of cancer-related death. For White, Black, Asian, Pacific-Islander, and Native American women, it is the second most common form of cancer-related death; the most common is lung cancer (U.S. Cancer Statistics Working Group, 2012). Men can get breast cancer as well, but it is much less common.

A diagnosis of breast cancer is frightening, but if caught early, people with breast cancer now have a much better outlook than they did 20 to 30 years ago. Treatment options have improved, and researchers continue to look for a cure for this disease.

Risks associated with the development of breast cancer in women include (American Cancer Society, 2015):

- Not having children or having a first child later in life (i.e., 30s and 40s)
- Reaching menarche at an early age
- Beginning menopause at a late age
- Having a personal history of breast diseases
- Having close family relatives (mother, sister, father, daughter) who have had breast cancer

The National Football League (NFL) adds an interesting addition to players' uniforms every October: pink. For a stereotypical group of "macho" men, pink may seem flamboyant, but by wearing it, they are showing support for the millions of women who have been diagnosed with breast cancer.

Andrew Dieb/Icon Sportswire/Getty Images

HEALTHY Sexuality

What Does Orgasm Have to Do With It?

Current research has revealed that women who feel more positive about female genitalia are more likely to engage in behaviors that promote sexual health. For example, they may have regular gynecologic exams or perform self-exams on a regular basis (Herbenick et al., 2009). An even bigger bonus for women who feel good about their genitals is that these women also tend to reach orgasm more easily.

This type of research suggests that there is a critical connection between our attitudes about our own sexual bodies and good sexual health. We know that the mind and body are inextricably linked to sex. When we feel that our bodies are beautiful, we take pleasure in them and are motivated to take care of them.

Our culture today often portrays women's genitals as dirty and in need of constant cleaning and grooming (e.g., the popularity of shaving or waxing pubic hair). These negative messages can have a large impact on how women feel about their own bodies. People who have had negative experiences with relationships and difficulty reaching orgasm tend to have more health problems and lower sexual well-being (Laumann, Paik, & Rosen, 1999). Changing our culture's sex-negative views into positive messages can help women of all ages take pride in their bodies (Tolman, 2006).

- Having a genetic condition or genetic mutations that can lead to breast cancer
- Having been treated with radiation therapy to the chest area or breasts
- Being overweight, particularly after menopause
- Using hormone replacement therapy for an extended time
- Using oral contraceptives recently
- Drinking alcohol
- Being age 65 or older

As numerous as these risk factors are, women can lessen the chances of getting breast cancer by maintaining a healthy weight, avoiding the use of hormone replacement therapy (HRT), and limiting alcohol consumption. Also, every woman should conduct a monthly breast

Figure 6.1

Incidence of female breast cancer by race and ethnicity (2012–2016).

Rate per 100,000:
- Non-Hispanic White: 130.5
- African American: 124
- Hispanic/Latina†: 97.2
- American Indian/Alaska Native: 79.5
- Asian American/Pacific Islander: 100.1

*Rates are age adjusted to the 2000 US standard population.
†Persons of Hispanic origin may be any race.

self-exam. These exams ought to be considered a regular part of how they maintain their sexual body. (Refer to Chapter 4 to learn how to perform breast self-exams.) In addition to performing self-exams, it is important to receive regular medical checkups.

Every woman should become familiar with her own breasts so she can readily notice even slight changes. Most women commonly experience lumpy breasts, particularly around their menstrual period. If a lump doesn't disappear or if it feels abnormal, the woman should consult a physician. When breast cancer starts, it is often too small to feel and may not cause any noticeable signs or symptoms. As the cancer grows, it can change how the breast appears or feels. Some symptoms include:

- A new lump in the breast or a change in a current breast lump
- A change in the size or shape of the breast
- Pain in the breast or nipple that does not go away (Breast pain or tenderness can be common for women, which is often associated with the menstrual cycle or pregnancy. Pain that does not go away or is unusual should be checked.)
- Flaky, red, or swollen skin anywhere on the breast
- A dimpled appearance to the breast when the arm is raised over the head
- A nipple that is extremely tender or suddenly turns inward
- Blood or any other fluid coming from the nipple, and is not milk when nursing a baby

Researchers are continuously assessing preventive measures for both women and men due to their potential negative side effects, cost, and effectiveness. At one time, women were advised to begin having yearly mammograms at age 20 to detect breast abnormalities that might be cancerous. However, the U.S. Preventive Services Task Force (2009) published new guidelines for preventive mammograms. These guidelines have been reaffirmed by various professional groups (CDC, 2015a). The new guidelines have caused some controversy among health care professionals and women. For a discussion of this issue, see "Controversies in Sexuality: Breast Cancer Screening."

mammogram
Low-dose X-ray of the breast used to detect growths and cancer in breast tissue.

lumpectomy
Removal of the cancerous tumor in the breast while leaving the breast intact.

mastectomy
Removal of one or both breasts, and possibly other tissue around the breast, to eradicate cancer from that area.

Having a mammogram, especially for a woman with risk factors for breast cancer, is the best screening technique for early detection of the disease.
Image Point Fr/Shutterstock

CONTROVERSIES in Sexuality

Breast Cancer Screening

Recommendations for breast cancer screening from the U.S. Preventive Services Task Force of the CDC (2015a) suggest that women begin routine screenings at age 50, as opposed to age 40—as long recommended by the American Cancer Society. Additionally, the group recommends that women between the ages of 50 and 74 get mammograms every 2 years, as opposed to annually, as previously recommended. In keeping with earlier research that questioned the value of physical breast exams, the task force suggests that doctors should no longer encourage their patients to conduct breast self-exams, because the practice hasn't been proven to significantly reduce breast cancer deaths, and it may cause unnecessary alarm and anguish (O'Callaghan, 2009). These recommendations were intended to be for women who were at average risk for breast cancer rather than high risk. However, there was a large outcry against the change, especially from women who credit self-exams with saving their own lives. Women have been left confused, and the only official response has been to "ask your doctor." The question on many people's minds then is, "Should we adopt these new guidelines for women's breast health care?"

YES:

The members of the professional panel suggest that women in their 40s do not need to be screened unless they are at high risk. They argue that the harm from mammograms outweighs the benefits, especially if a woman is not at risk. Mammograms can turn up many small abnormalities that are not cancerous or cancers that grow far too slowly to lead to death. The panel members also cited the stress and anxiety that many women experience when a mammogram shows these types of abnormalities and stated that it is unnecessary to put women through such anguish.

NO:

Opponents of these guidelines cite evidence that mammography has saved the lives of many women in their 40s. Without this routine screening, small lumps and abnormalities that women cannot feel during a self-exam would go undetected. These abnormalities could lead to an aggressive cancer, which could compromise a woman's life. In fact, some analyses suggest that mammography reduces the risk of dying from breast cancer by 15% among women ages 39 to 49 years (O'Callaghan, 2009). In addition, opponents of the health care reform bills in the United States cite these recommendations as evidence that the government is seeking to put bureaucrats between women and their doctors or argue that these reforms would eventually ration this kind of care by denying coverage for mammograms that are now routinely covered.

This issue highlights the importance of self-advocacy in health care. Women need to research and be in contact with their doctors, to be proactive with their health care, and to advocate for screenings and exams they feel are necessary.

For more information about breast health care, visit "the breast site" at www.thebreastsite.com.

What Is Your Perspective?

1. What is your opinion regarding the new guidelines on mammograms and breast self-exams? Do you believe that we should adopt these guidelines and end mammograms for women in their 40s who are not at high risk? Why or why not?
2. Do you know someone who was diagnosed with breast cancer in her 40s or earlier due to a routine mammogram? If so, does this influence your opinion of the new guidelines?

A **mammogram** is a low-dose X-ray of the breast used to detect growths and cancer in breast tissue. Figure 6.2 shows the results of breast imaging. These X-rays allow physicians to look for early signs of breast cancer, which can sometimes be detected as early as 3 years before a breast cancer lump can be felt. Treatment depends largely on how advanced the cancer is at the time of detection and its location in the body. Chemotherapy, radiation, lumpectomy, and mastectomy (single or double) are all possible treatments for breast cancer. A **lumpectomy** removes the cancerous tumor in the breast while leaving the breast intact. A **mastectomy** is the removal of one or both breasts, and possibly other tissue around the breast, to eradicate cancer from that area.

speculum
An instrument used to open the vagina during vaginal exams performed by a physician.

Figure 6.2

Mammogram images showing normal breast (left) and cancerous breast (right).
Southern Illinois University/Science Source

---

bimanual exam

An exam in which the doctor inserts two fingers in the vagina while placing the other hand on top of the lower part of the abdomen in order to feel for any abnormalities and to check the size, shape, and mobility of the uterus.

DID YOU KNOW

- The majority of women diagnosed with cervical cancer have not had a Pap smear within the last 5 years.
- The best time to schedule an annual pelvic exam and Pap smear is 1 to 2 weeks after a woman's menstrual period stops.
- Women should refrain from sexual intercourse for 24 hours prior to their exam.
- 24% of women report that their OB/GYN is the only doctor they see on a regular basis.

Source: USDHHS, Office on Women's Health, 2009.

Gynecologic Exams Although seeing a gynecologist for a pelvic exam is probably not on a woman's list of desirable activities, it is one of the most important things that a woman can do to maintain positive sexual health. It is recommended that teenage girls begin to see a gynecologist between the ages of 13 and 15 (Cornforth, 2009). A pelvic exam is rare at this age, but an initial visit helps to establish good rapport with the doctor and review pertinent medical and sexual histories, even if the girl has not yet had sexual intercourse.

Currently, the American College of Obstetricians and Gynecologists (ACOG, 2019) recommends that Pap smears begin within 3 years of first engaging in sexual intercourse, or by age 21 if the woman has not yet had sexual intercourse. Women should have Pap smears every 2 years until age 30, when healthy women who have had at least three consecutive normal Pap smears may begin to have the test done every 3 years, or as often as their doctor recommends.

This does not mean that women should still not have yearly pelvic exams to check for changes or infections that may have occurred since the last exam.

The procedures for a pelvic exam and Pap smear are quite simple and the exam is usually quite short, although most women might not agree. After an initial consultation with a nurse, women will be directed to remove all of their clothing and put on a hospital gown. With a nurse present, the doctor will do a breast examination and then ask the woman to lie down on the table and put her feet into the stirrups. A **speculum,** an instrument used to open the vagina, is inserted as illustrated in Figure 6.3, so the physician is able to view the vagina, the vaginal walls, and the cervix. The physician will collect a small sample of cervical tissue for a Pap test.

The last part of the pelvic exam is called a **bimanual exam.** This exam requires that the doctor insert two fingers in the vagina while placing the other hand on top of the lower part of the abdomen. This allows a doctor to feel for any abnormalities and to check the size, shape, and mobility of the uterus. Ovarian changes, such as the growth of cysts, can also be detected during this exam.

Urinary Tract Infections A **urinary tract infection (UTI)** begins in the urinary system, which is composed of the kidneys, ureters, bladder, and urethra. Men also get urinary tract infections, but women are more susceptible to developing them. UTIs typically develop when bacteria enter the urinary tract through the urethra and multiply in the bladder. While the urinary system is designed to keep out these kinds of bacteria, sometimes the defenses fail or are compromised. Steps to reduce the risk of getting a UTI include:

- Drink plenty of fluids, particularly water.
- Empty the bladder as soon as possible after intercourse. In addition, drink a full glass of water to help flush out bacteria.

For women specifically:

- Wipe from front to back after going to the bathroom. Doing so after urinating and after a bowel movement helps to prevent bacteria from spreading from the anal region to the vagina and urethra.
- Avoid using irritating feminine products. Using vaginal deodorant sprays, douches, or powders can irritate the urethra (Mayo Clinic, 2019).

If you contract a UTI, you may experience these common symptoms:

- A strong, persistent urge to urinate
- A burning sensation while urinating
- Passing frequent but very small amounts of urine
- Detecting blood in the urine or cloudy, strong-smelling urine (Mayo Clinic, 2019)

Without treatment, UTIs can spread to the kidneys. The good news is that despite the inconvenience and sometimes pain they cause, UTIs are very treatable with antibiotics.

Vaginitis **Vaginitis** is an inflammation of the vagina that can result in some unpleasant symptoms including discharge, itching, and pain. Women may experience vaginitis

Figure 6.3
(a) During a pelvic exam a speculum is inserted into the cervix and a spatula is used to withdraw a small sample of cervical tissue for the Pap test. (b) The bimanual exam allows the doctor to check for abnormalities in the uterus and changes in the ovaries.

urinary tract infection (UTI)
An infection of the urethra, bladder, or other urinary structure, usually caused by bacteria.

vaginitis
Inflammation of the vagina that can result in some unpleasant symptoms including discharge, itching, and pain.

bacterial vaginosis
A type of vaginitis that results from overgrowth of one or more of several organisms typically present in the vagina.

yeast infection
A type of vaginitis that occurs when a naturally occurring fungus changes the normal environment in the vagina, mouth, skinfolds, or fingernail beds.

trichomoniasis
A common sexually transmitted protozoan parasite causing symptoms in women, but typically not in infected men.

atrophic vaginitis
This type of vaginitis is due to reduced estrogen levels resulting from menopause and can cause vaginal tissues to become thinner and drier.

gynecologic cancer
A group of five different cancers affecting a woman's reproductive system. Includes vaginal, vulvar, uterine, ovarian, and cervical cancers.

vaginal cancer
A gynecologic cancer that begins in the vagina.

vulvar cancer
A gynecologic cancer that forms in the vulva.

uterine cancer
A gynecologic cancer that begins in the uterus.

ovarian cancer
A gynecologic cancer that begins in one of the two ovaries.

cervical cancer
A gynecologic cancer that begins in the cervix.

due to changes in the normal balance of bacteria in the vagina. It can also be caused by an infection elsewhere in the body and can result from reduced estrogen levels after menopause (Mashburn, 2006). The most common types of vaginitis are treatable and include the following:

- **Bacterial vaginosis.** This type results from overgrowth of one or more of several organisms typically present in the vagina, upsetting the natural balance of vaginal bacteria. It can be spread during sexual intercourse but also occurs in people who are not sexually active. Bacterial vaginosis is treated with an antibiotic and requires a prescription from a health care provider.
- **Yeast infection.** This type of vaginitis is so common that it is estimated that three of four women will have a yeast infection in their lifetime (Mashburn, 2006). A naturally occurring fungus changes the normal environment in the vagina. Yeast infections can also occur in the mouth, skinfolds, and fingernail beds. It is also thought to be one of the causes of diaper rash in babies. Yeast infections are usually treated with an anti-yeast cream or suppository placed in the vagina. Some products are available over the counter, others by prescription only.
- **Trichomoniasis.** This is caused by a parasite that is spread during sex with someone who already has the infection. It usually infects the urinary tract in women, but may not cause any symptoms in men. Symptoms in women include genital irritation, burning or pain during urination, and a foul-smelling discharge. Trichomoniasis is treated with an antibiotic and requires a prescription from a health care provider.
- **Atrophic vaginitis.** This vaginitis is due to reduced estrogen levels resulting from menopause. The vaginal tissue becomes thinner and drier, which can lead to itching, burning, and pain particularly as a result of intercourse. Using water-based lubricants can prevent inflammation and help women to enjoy intercourse.

Cancers of the Female Reproductive System Five main types of cancer affect a woman's reproductive system: vaginal, vulvar, uterine, ovarian, and cervical cancers. As a group they are referred to as **gynecologic cancer.** Each year, approximately 100,000 women, or 1 in 78 women in the United States, get ovarian cancer. Among U.S. women, ovarian cancer is the eighth most common cancer and the fifth leading cause of cancer death (Centers for Disease Control and Prevention [CDC], 2010d). See Table 6.1 for descriptions of known risk factors, common symptoms, and prevention efforts that women can take to reduce the risk of contracting one of these gynecologic cancers.

Cancer that originates in the vagina is called **vaginal cancer.** Cancer that first forms in the vulva is called **vulvar cancer.** Although these two kinds of cancer are quite rare, all women are at some risk to develop them; the greatest risk is to older women. Of all gynecologic cancers, vaginal and vulvar cancers account for 6% to 7% (CDC, 2012d).

Uterine cancer begins in a woman's uterus. The most common type of uterine cancer, *endometrial cancer,* often forms in the endometrial lining of the uterus. The risk for getting this cancer typically increases with age. The majority of uterine cancers are found in women who are going through or have already gone through menopause. In the United States, uterine cancer is the fourth most common cancer in women (CDC, 2012c).

Ovarian cancer usually begins in one of the two ovaries. Similar to uterine cancer, ovarian cancer is not as common in younger women. Approximately 90% of women who get ovarian cancer are older than 40, with the greatest number being 55 or older. Of all the gynecologic cancers, ovarian cancer is the deadliest, but it accounts for only about 3% of all cancers in women (CDC, 2010d).

Cervical cancer begins in the cervix, and is the easiest female cancer to prevent with regular screening tests. When found and treated early, it is also the most curable. Cervical cancer occurs most often in women over the age of 30. The **human papillomavirus (HPV)**

Table 6.1 Cancers of the Female Reproductive System

TYPE	RISK FACTORS	SYMPTOMS	PREVENTION
Vaginal/vulvar	• Have a history of human papillomavirus (HPV) • Smoking • Have a condition that weakens the immune system such as HIV • Have had cervical precancer or cervical cancer	• Persistent itching of the vulva (mostly on the labia) • Changes in the color of the skin of the vulva, so that it looks redder or whiter than normal • Skin changes in the vulva, including what looks like a rash or warts • A sore on the vulva that does not go away • Pain in the pelvis, especially during intercourse or urination	• Get the HPV vaccine • Stop smoking • Reduce risk of contracting STIs
Uterine	• Older than 50 years of age • Obesity • Take estrogen by itself (without taking progesterone with it) for birth control or as a part of hormone replacement therapy (HRT) • Have had trouble getting pregnant, or have had fewer than five periods in a year prior to the start of menopause • Take tamoxifen (a drug used to treat/prevent certain types of breast cancer) • Have a family history of uterine, colon, or ovarian cancer	• Abnormal vaginal bleeding or unusual bleeding between periods • Pain or pressure in pelvis	• Use birth control pills • Maintain a healthy weight and physical activity • Take progesterone if taking estrogen in HRT • Communicate with physician to determine frequency of checkups, especially if there are many risk factors present
Ovarian	• Middle-aged or older • Have a family history of ovarian cancer • Have had breast, uterine, or colorectal cancer • Have an Eastern European (Ashkenazi) Jewish background • Have endometriosis	• Pain in the pelvis, abdomen, or back • Extreme fatigue • Bloating, when the stomach swells or feels full • A change in bathroom habits, such as having to pass urine very badly or very often • An upset stomach or heartburn • Abnormal discharge from the vagina	• Using birth control pills for more than 5 years • Having a tubal ligation (getting tubes tied), both ovaries removed, or hysterectomy • Giving birth
Cervical	• Not having regular Pap tests • Not following up with doctor after an abnormal Pap test result • Having a condition that weakens the immune system such as HIV • Smoking	• Early on, cervical cancer usually does not cause signs or symptoms • Advanced cervical cancer may cause abnormal vaginal bleeding	• Get the HPV vaccine • Get regular Pap tests • Do not smoke • Use condoms during sex • Limit the number of sexual partners

Source: CDC, n.d.

is the main cause of cervical cancer. Two HPV types, type 16 and type 18, cause 70% of cervical cancers and cervical lesions (WHO, 2019). Even though HPV is quite common, most women who get HPV will not develop cervical cancer (CDC, 2015b).

Discussing topics such as cancer can be frightening, but most of these conditions are treatable when detected in the early stages. With the wealth of accurate and helpful information available, most women are able to face these life struggles with a strong, positive attitude. This information may empower women to become their own best advocate when it comes to their sexual body and well-being, so they may enjoy the benefits of healthful living.

In the next section we discuss male sexual health care, understanding that there are some important differences, along with similarities, between male and female sexual health.

human papillomavirus (HPV)
A sexually transmitted infection; a primary cause of cervical cancer.

Male Sexual Health

Many men would agree with Woody Allen's quip that their penis is their favorite organ. After all, a man's penis can bring him intense pleasure throughout his lifetime. It makes sense, then, that men would desire to optimize the health of this important organ (Gregoire, 1999). Yet, like women, men can experience warning signs that something may be wrong with their sexual body. It is important that men, too, take an active role to ensure the health of their own reproductive organs and to understand common problems associated with their reproductive health.

Penis Health Care Some men routinely groom, trim, or wax their pubic hair. Some of the benefits of regular grooming are that it improves cleanliness and reduces moisture, it can be sexually stimulating, it may increase sensitivity during sex, and it can be an enjoyable partner experience. A significant health benefit of regular grooming is that it causes men to become more aware of any changes in their penis (Franek, 2006).

With regard to washing and cleansing the penis, it is important to remember that the penis is a sensitive organ. It is not necessary to vigorously scrub the penis with powerful soaps or disinfectants. Simply washing with warm water and a mild soap will ensure cleanliness. Men who are uncircumcised should slide back the foreskin to wash the head of the penis with warm water, then dry the entire pubic area well.

Taking care of the penis on a regular basis also helps men to notice any changes in their testicles that might raise health concerns. Testicular self-exams, described in Chapter 4, and testicular exams by a doctor are also practices that all men should engage in on a regular basis.

Testicular Cancer We often do not hear about cancers affecting young people because the media tend to emphasize cancers that affect older people, but young people are certainly not out of the realm of possibility when it comes to getting cancer. **Testicular cancer,** in particular, tends to occur among younger men. As shown in Figure 6.4, testicular cancer is most common in U.S. males between 15 and 34 years of age (Moynihan, 2009). Testicular cancer generally affects only one testicle. It occurs when healthy cells in the testicle become altered in some way. Nearly all testicular cancers are thought to begin in the **germ cells,** the cells in the testicles that produce sperm. What exactly causes these germ cells to become abnormal and develop into cancer is still unknown, but some risk factors include (Mayo Clinic, 2011c):

- An undescended testicle—One or both testicles may not descend in infancy, a condition called **cryptorchidism.** The risk remains even for men who had surgery to have the testicles descend.
- Abnormal testicle development—Conditions that cause testicles to develop abnormally (e.g., Klinefelter's syndrome, a genetic condition that results in anatomical variations) may increase the risk of contracting testicular cancer.
- Family history—As with many forms of cancer, having a family history of testicular cancer may put an individual at risk.
- Age—It is most common among younger men between the ages of 15 and 34, but it can occur at any age.
- Ethnicity—Testicular cancer is more common in Whites than in Blacks or Hispanics.

Testicular self-exams, performed on a regular basis, are the best way to detect changes in the testicles. Some doctors recommend that men between the ages of 15 and 40 perform self-exams monthly. Signs and symptoms of testicular cancer include:

- A lump or enlargement in either testicle
- A feeling of heaviness in the scrotum

---

testicular cancer
A cancer that begins in one of the testicles; tends to occur among younger men.

germ cells
Cells in the testicles that produce immature sperm.

cryptorchidism
A condition that occurs in infancy in which one or both of the testicles do not descend.

Figure 6.4 Testicular cancer is the most common form of cancer among young men between the ages of 15 and 34, but it also can occur in older men.

- A dull ache in the abdomen or groin
- A sudden collection of fluid in the scrotum
- Pain or discomfort in the testicle or scrotum
- Unexplained fatigue or a general feeling of being ill

Testicular cancer is highly treatable, even when it has spread beyond the testicle. Treatment options depend on several factors, including a man's overall health and preferences. These options include surgery to remove the cancerous testicle, radiation therapy, and chemotherapy.

Prostate Cancer Prostate cancer affects the prostate gland, which produces seminal fluid. Affecting approximately one in six men in the United States, prostate cancer is one of the most common types of cancer in men. One of the misconceptions about prostate cancer is that it is an old man's disease. Prostate cancer does occur in young men, although it is rare before age 40, and about two-thirds of all prostate cancer cases occur in men over age 65 (U.S. Cancer Statistics Group, 2009). There are a number of myths about prostate cancer. Read "Healthy Sexuality: Ten Myths About Prostate Cancer" to learn more about them.

As Figure 6.5 shows, Blacks experience higher rates of prostate cancer than Whites, and the disease occurs less frequently among Asian/Pacific Islanders and American Indian/Alaska Natives. The incidence of prostate cancer in the United States significantly decreased in the early 1990s, but since 1995 it has remained level (Espey et al., 2007).

Knowing the risk factors of prostate cancer can help men determine when to begin regular prostate screening. The main risk factors include:

- Age—After 50, the chance of having prostate cancer increases.
- Family history—If an immediate family member (brother or father) has had prostate cancer, the risk increases.
- Race/ethnicity—Blacks have a higher risk of both developing and dying of prostate cancer.

Ben Stiller brought the issue of prostate cancer to the public eye when he was diagnosed in 2014.
Lucky Team Studio/Shutterstock

HEALTHY Sexuality

Ten Myths About Prostate Cancer

Myth #1: Prostate cancer is an old man's disease.
Fact: Many men get prostate cancer. It is rarely fatal, and it can occur even in young men.
Myth #2: If you don't have any symptoms, you don't have prostate cancer.
Fact: Prostate cancer is one of the most asymptomatic cancers. Symptoms can be mistaken for or attributed to something else.
Myth #3: Prostate cancer is a slow-growing cancer I don't need to worry about.
Fact: Sometimes this is true. Researchers have discovered 25 types of prostate cancer, some of which a man may die *with* but not *of,* while others are very aggressive.
Myth #4: Prostate cancer doesn't run in my family, so the odds aren't great that I will get it.
Fact: Although a family history of prostate cancer doubles a man's odds of being diagnosed to one in three, the fact is that one of every six U.S. men will be diagnosed with prostate cancer in their lifetime.
Myth #5: The PSA test is a cancer test.
Fact: The PSA test measures levels of prostate-specific antigen in the prostate, not cancer. Experts believe the PSA test saves the lives of approximately 1 in every 39 men who are tested.

Myth #6: A high PSA level means that you have prostate cancer and a low PSA means you do not have prostate cancer.
Fact: Although prostate cancer is a common cause of elevated PSA levels, some men with prostate cancer may even have low levels of PSA.
Myth #7: Vasectomies cause prostate cancer.
Fact: Having a vasectomy (a surgical procedure that prevents the release of sperm during ejaculation) was once thought to increase a man's risk, but careful research has not uncovered a link between vasectomy and a higher risk of prostate cancer.
Myth #8: Treatment for prostate cancer always causes impotence or incontinence.
Fact: Erectile dysfunction (ED) is a possibility following surgery or radiation therapy for prostate cancer, but it is not true that all men experience these effects.
Myth #9: Sexual activity increases the risk of developing prostate cancer.
Fact: Some studies show that men who reported more frequent ejaculations had a lower risk of developing prostate cancer.
Myth #10: You can pass prostate cancer on to others.
Fact: Prostate cancer is not infectious or communicable. There is no way to pass it on to someone else.

Adapted from: Dan Zenka, Ten Myths and Misconceptions about Prostate Cancer. (2011). www.pcf.org/site/c.leJRIROrEpH/b.7425707/k.7A02/10_Myths_and_Misconceptions_About_Prostate_Cancer.htm

Figure 6.5
U.S. prostate cancer incidence rates by race and ethnicity, 1999–2016.
Source: CDC, 2016.
*Hispanic origin is not mutually exclusive from race categories (White, Black, Asian/Pacific Islander, American Indian/Alaska Native).

WHAT'S ON YOUR MIND?

Q: I haven't had sex with anyone yet, but I really feel that I am ready to experience it. I have been trying to prepare myself and make good decisions, but the more I read about sex, the more scared I get about STIs. How do I enjoy sex with all the STIs out there?

ANSWER: Great question! We know that so many people associate sex with danger rather than pleasure. The truth is, though, that if you take some simple precautions like consistently using condoms and communicating effectively with your sexual partners, there is no reason that you cannot enjoy your sex life.

- Diet—A high-fat diet may increase the risk because fat increases the production of testosterone, which may promote growth and development of prostate cancer cells.
- High testosterone levels—Testosterone naturally stimulates growth of the prostate gland. Men who use testosterone therapy are more likely to develop prostate cancer than are men who have lower levels of testosterone.

Prostate cancer usually does not produce any noticeable symptoms in its early stages, so many cases are not detected until the cancer has spread beyond the prostate. If symptoms do appear, they can include urinary problems caused by the tumor pressing on the bladder or the urethra. For most men, prostate cancer is first detected during a routine screening procedure called the **prostate-specific antigen (PSA) test** or during a **digital rectal exam** (Figure 6.6).

The PSA blood test is primarily used to screen and detect high levels of early-stage prostate cancer. Recent studies show that the PSA is not perfect and cannot detect all cancers (Mayo Clinic, 2019). We know that treatment is more effective the earlier the condition is diagnosed. The problem is the PSA tests are known to result in many false positives, and because it cannot indicate how aggressive a cancer might be, doctors will often recommend a biopsy after a positive PSA test. Biopsies in this area of the body are problematic because

prostate-specific antigen (PSA) test
A routine screening used to detect prostate cancer.

digital rectal exam
An exam during which the physician inserts the fingers into the rectum in order to feel the size of the prostate gland.

Figure 6.6

Having a routine rectal exam performed by a physician is the best way to detect prostate cancer.

there are many concerns and possible side effects, including incontinence and impotence. It is best to discuss the advantages and disadvantages with your doctor and keep current on how your body changes.

Having discussed some general reproductive health concerns, next we will discuss the risks, protective factors, symptoms, and treatment of STIs. This information is helpful when making informed decisions to promote excellent sexual health and well-being.

SEXUALLY TRANSMITTED INFECTIONS

The United States today is in the midst of a long-term epidemic of sexually transmitted infections (STIs). Each year we seem to break new records when it comes to diagnosed cases of STIs, and in 2018 the CDC reported that there were 2.3 million new cases. Of all industrialized countries in the world, the United States has the highest rate of STIs, and the three major infections, chlamydia, gonorrhea, and syphilis, are now at unprecedented levels. Approximately 20 million Americans a year contract an STI. Researchers suggest that one in two people will contract an STI by age 25, and 80% of Americans will have an STI in their lifetime (Chesson, Dunne, Hariri, & Markowitz, 2014). What's going on? With education, prevention, and treatment, many of these negative outcomes can be avoided. We strongly believe that understanding how to communicate about these issues and then taking the steps to protect and ensure prevention with our intimate partners ensures that we protect them and ourselves against STIs. In this section we will discuss various STIs and their transmission, symptoms, prevention, and how to obtain the best treatment.

Risks and Protective Factors for STIs

As we have discussed, sexuality involves a balance of pleasure and excitement with risk and danger. Sex and love are exciting because of this balancing act. There is always a risk and potential for getting an STI. Such infections do not discriminate among individuals, but young people are the most likely to get STIs. Knowing some of the risk factors can help us to avoid them and maximize pleasure in our sexuality (Mayo Clinic, 2012; American Sexual Health Association, 2019). Consider these as your risk factors (adapted from Mayo Clinic, 2012, and the American Sexual Health Association, 2019):

- Unprotected sex—For sexually active individuals, consistent, effective condom use is the best protection against a possible STI. Consistent, effective condom use means using a condom *every single time* you have sex with a partner and ensuring that the condom is used properly. Although using a condom does not guarantee that you won't get an STI, it is the best way to help ensure healthy sexual encounters.
- Multiple partners—This is a pretty simple fact to understand, but the logic goes like this: The more partners you have, the more likely you are to be exposed to an STI at some point.
- Engaging in sex from an early age—Youths, particularly teenagers, are more likely to contract an STI than older people (Guttmacher Institute, 2009; American Sexual Health Association, 2019). Young people are more likely not to use condoms and to engage in sexual risk taking, perhaps because of shame or not being able to ask a partner to use one, or because condoms are not readily available to teens. In addition, young people who engage in sex early on are more likely to have more partners over their lifetimes, thereby increasing their risk.
- Alcohol and drug use—These are problematic for sexual health in many ways. We know that using injectable drugs is a high-risk behavior for the transmission of HIV, hepatitis, and other viruses due to the high incidence of sharing needles. In addition, people who are intoxicated or in an altered state of mind may be less discriminating

about whom they choose to have sex with. Alcohol and drugs are also known to lower inhibitions, and people may make a decision while intoxicated that they would not make when sober. Finally, in addition to compromised judgment, being intoxicated may make it more difficult to negotiate condom use or to use them correctly with your partner.

- Having an STI—A person with one STI is more susceptible to getting other STIs. For example, it is easier for a different pathogen to infect skin that is already irritated, inflamed, or blistered.

- Using the pill as the sole form of contraception—While this may be surprising, for many people the biggest concern over having sex isn't STIs. It is pregnancy. When protected from pregnancy, many couples are reluctant to use condoms as part of their sexual routine. The combination of using birth control pills and condoms is a better option than the pill alone or a condom alone, particularly since the pill can reduce the risk of **pelvic inflammatory disease (PID)**, a disease that commonly results from STIs.

- Being female—The cells of the cervix constantly change in teenage girls and young women, and so their cervix is more vulnerable to certain sexually transmitted organisms, especially HPV. In addition, women at any age are more likely to have more severe and long-lasting complications from STIs than men, particularly infertility and including HIV, since almost three times as many heterosexual women as men are diagnosed with HIV (CDC, 2017a).

STI awareness campaigns today promote protection, pleasure, and controversy.
Chung Sung-Jun/Getty Images News/Getty Images

Many public health agencies have devised routine self-assessments that enable people to determine their own risk for STIs. Take a few minutes to review the level of your own risk in "Know Yourself: What Is Your Personal STI Risk?"

Being proactive to protect yourself and your loved ones is not only smart but will also ensure a greater likelihood of life success. Consider applying the following measures (Kirby, 2007):

- Talk about sex—Communication is key. Greater adult-child communication, particularly between parents and children, about sex and condoms or contraception should occur before a young person engages in sex. In addition, individuals who discuss sexual risk, STIs, and pregnancy prevention with their partners often are more successful in remaining free from STIs.

- Create a positive peer culture—Find a peer group that really supports and uses condoms and contraception and promotes protective norms, behaviors, and relationships (Johns et al., 2017).

- Keep a positive attitude—Value partners who consistently use condoms, have a positive attitude toward condoms and contraception, and know the benefits of condom and contraception use (Johns et al., 2017).

- Consistently use effective protection—People who have previously used condoms or contraception often have greater motivation, intent, and confidence in using effective and protective means of contraception.

- Be informed—Individuals who are older at the time of first voluntary sexual intercourse are more likely to use condoms and contraception and to use them correctly.

pelvic inflammatory disease (PID)

A painful condition in women marked by inflammation of the uterus, fallopian tubes, and ovaries; typically caused by the presence of one or more untreated STIs.

Know Yourself

What Is Your Personal STI Risk?

Have you ever wondered what kinds of questions a health care practitioner asks when a person seeks testing for STIs? Naturally, people wonder and sometimes worry about the kind of information that is gathered on an STI risk assessment. The following questionnaire is commonly used by health care providers to assess risk for STIs. Answers to questions of this type allow the health care providers to assist clients with STI testing and to provide information about contraceptive and sexual health decisions.

Have you been seen in this STI clinic before? _____Yes _____No

If yes, when? _____

1. What is the reason for your visit? *(Check all that apply.)*
   _____You think you could be at risk for an STI.
   _____You think you could be at risk for HIV/AIDS.
   _____Other: _____

2. If you have symptoms, please check all that apply:
   _____Bleeding _____Pain _____Rash _____Warts _____Itching
   _____Problems with urination _____Other: _____

3. Have you had sexual interactions with anyone in the last 6 months?
   _____Yes _____No With how many people?
   1 2 3 4 5 6 7 8 9 10 more than 10

4. How many people have you had sexual interactions with in your lifetime?
   0 1 2 3 4 5 10 15 25 30 50 75 more than 100

5. When with new or non-steady partners, do you use a condom or barrier?
   _____Always _____Most of the time _____Sometimes _____Rarely _____Never

6. Have you had sexual interactions with: _____A man _____A woman
   _____Both _____Other

7. Check all that apply: _____Oral sex _____Vaginal sex
   _____Anal sex: _____Top (Insertive) _____Bottom (Receptive) _____Both

8. Please list any medication(s) you are currently taking: _____
   _____

9. Please list any allergies to medication(s): _____

10. Have you ever exchanged drugs or money for sex? _____Yes _____No

11. Have you had sex with someone you know injects drugs? _____Yes _____No

12. Have you ever used a needle to inject drugs? _____Yes _____No

13. Have you had sexual interactions with someone you know has HIV/AIDS?
    _____Yes _____No

14. Have you used meth, speed, crank, crystal, cocaine, or crack in the last year?
    _____Yes _____No

15. Do you smoke cigarettes? _____Yes _____No

16. Have you ever been in jail or prison? _____Yes _____No

17. Do you have any tattoos? _____Yes _____No

18. Have you had the hepatitis B vaccine? _____Yes _____No

19. How many HIV/AIDS tests have you had before today? _____

20. Have you ever been diagnosed with an STI? *(Check all that apply below and indicate when.)*

_____Have symptoms   _____Have no symptoms – STI testing/screening only

_____Referred by another doctor or clinic

_____Discharge _____   _____Sores/Blisters _____

_____Chlamydia _____   _____Gonorrhea _____

_____Genital Warts _____   _____Herpes _____

_____Syphilis _____   _____Trichomonas (trich) _____

_____HIV _____   _____Other: _____

_____**Never** been diagnosed with an STI

21. Do your female sex partners use birth control?   _____Yes   _____No   _____Not sure

22. If so, what birth control method(s) are used: _____

23. Would you like more information on contraceptive methods? _____Yes _____No

Source: Questionnaire adapted from: Marin County Department of Health and Human Services, STD Risk Self-Assessment Questionnaire 2010.

It might feel a little personal and invasive to fill out a questionnaire such as this, but it is important that you have this information readily available, particularly for health care providers so they can work with you in making important sexual health decisions.

Of course, just knowing about the risk or protective factors does not mean that persons will either avoid or contract an STI. Other considerations come into play, including sexual risk negotiation between partners.

Sexual Risk Negotiation

When was the last time you and your partner talked about steps to take to protect yourselves during your sexual moments together? How has that conversation affected your relationship? Or does the thought of having such a discussion make you scared or uncomfortable? If the answer is "yes," you are not alone. Whether you are in a heterosexual relationship or a gay relationship, the issue of trust, respect, risk, and prevention of STIs is one that couples should acknowledge openly and talk about today.

WHAT'S ON YOUR MIND?

Q: I just recently found out that I have an STI and I informed my partner, but my partner is refusing to get tested. What do I do?

ANSWER: This is a pretty serious situation. Have you tried talking to your partner about why she won't get tested? It could be because she is afraid or feeling shame or guilt. Are there issues of infidelity in the relationship or questions of who gave the STI to whom? If your partner will not get tested, then it will probably make it difficult to remain in the sexual relationship due to the risks of reinfection. I am sure this has had a huge impact on your relationship, and while you cannot force your partner to be tested, you can make the decision of whether or not you want to continue in this relationship. You need to give serious thought to this dilemma and stand firm in your decision to take care of your own sexual health. Good luck!

Because many people in the United States are socialized to view sex as negative and a taboo, generally avoiding the topic in all conversations, they lack the understanding that being upfront about sexual desire and risk and helping to protect each other can lead to better and healthier relationships. Conversely, mistrust and lack of communication can place people at risk, including risk of infection (Johns et al., 2017; UNAIDS, 2009). It is vital for sex partners to talk to each other about STIs, contraception, and pregnancy prevention and to try to set aside old stereotypes about who should do what (Herbenick et al., 2017).

Sex partners must talk about STIs *before* having sex (Sowadsky, 2009). If they wait until after having sex, it may be more difficult, and they may have already exposed the other person to an STI. Partners should consider talking about STIs in a quiet face-to-face setting, perhaps while taking a walk or on a quiet date together. The conversation should be in person, however, not by way of texting and e-mail, because of the depth of conversation and the details that need to be discussed. If the couple is unsure about how to bring up the subject, one of them could mention that he heard about STIs on a TV program, or that she read about the subject in a magazine.

In addition to setting up the right time and place to have this important conversation, sex partners need to have some knowledge about STIs. Books like this one or a credible website (e.g., Mayo Clinic, at mayoclinic.com; or CDC, at www.cdc.gov) provide the right language to speak about STIs, to ease the flow of conversation.

Partners should also prepare themselves emotionally. One may be either defensive or uncomfortable with the discussion, so both need to express their feelings toward each other clearly, which is why the conversation is necessary. To minimize a partner's defensiveness, the supporting partner can offer her own risk factors first and refrain from interrogation tactics. The couple should consider going together if they're being tested for STIs. Getting tested together may remove some of the pressure both are feeling at this time.

Finally, when sex partners start having sex and one notices a symptom of an STI, he or she must tell the other partner immediately. This will be an upsetting time, but by gently pointing out the symptom(s) and discussing their concerns about health and well-being, the partners are paving the way to a healthy and enjoyable sexual relationship. And who knows—they just might find that this discussion will lead to other more pleasurable sexual discussions that will lead to even more satisfying sexual relations.

Research on both gay and straight couples has found that when people gain trust with their partners, their risk goes down (Cusick & Rhodes, 2000; Hoff et al., 2010). However, there may be other barriers to communication, such as culture, language, and power. Power differences in couples can prevent open communication and risk prevention. Today the United Nations and similar organizations refer to the most sensitive of these relationships as "intimate partner relationships" in which a man may infect a woman with an STI without her knowing about it due to his sexual behavior or drug use (UNAIDS, 2009). Some of the most important characteristics of these relationships concern how, when, and why partners communicate with each other about risk taking, as you will see in "Healthy Sexuality: Negotiating Intimate Partner Risk."

Next we will explore the signs and symptoms of the common sexually transmitted infections and consider the best treatment options for each. Table 6.2 summarizes the different types of STIs, specifically bacterial, parasitic, and viral infections. We also will examine at length the viral infection called HIV/AIDS, because it is the most common STI but the most difficult to treat.

Human Immunodeficiency Virus

Globally, the risk of becoming infected with the **human immunodeficiency virus (HIV)** is one of the clearest dangers of unprotected sex. Untreated HIV leads to the destruction of the immune system through a variety of illnesses known as the **acquired immunodeficiency syndrome (AIDS).** What people once considered a mysterious and exotic disease that infected

human immunodeficiency virus (HIV)
A virus that leads to the destruction of the immune system through a variety of illnesses known as AIDS.

acquired immunodeficiency syndrome (AIDS)
A late-stage infection with HIV.

HEALTHY Sexuality

Negotiating Intimate Partner Risk

There are many ways for people to reduce risk with their intimate partners in ongoing relationships (El-Bassel et al., 2003; Hoff et al., 2010). In addition to the tips provided in this chapter, couples can learn about better ways to recognize risk, commit themselves to change, and act on strategies of mutual love and respect by working with a professional facilitator.

Using techniques from family therapy and problem solving, partners who are at least 18 years old and are committed to staying together each get to determine whether the sexual partnership is "safe" or "not safe." The couple then attends five sessions together in a private office with the facilitator. The intervention serves to enhance the couple's relationship by exploring their gender and power dynamics and focuses on the links between the couple's communication skills, HIV/STI risk, intentions, and behaviors. They learn communication, problem-solving, and negotiation skills. Condom use skills are demonstrated, and condoms are given out at each session. The couple also identifies social supports to help them maintain safer sex behaviors, which could include having individuals or other couples who practice safe sex as friends, and sharing what they have learned with family, peers, and community. Each partner focuses on:

- Emphasizing the relationship as the target of change: redefining sexual risk reduction from individual protection to protecting and preserving the relationship between two intimate partners—that is, "protecting us."
- Discussing ideas about relationship fidelity and the need to reduce HIV/STI risk among couples.
- Identifying how gender differences, stereotypes, and power imbalances influence safe-sex decision-making and behaviors.
- Using video-based scenarios to model good communication and negotiation of safer sex to stimulate discussions and role-plays.
- Using modeling, role-play, and feedback to teach, practice, and promote mastery in communication, negotiation, and problem solving, and the increase of the couple's social and community support, including attending events or social functions that feature protection and risk reduction.

How would you feel about engaging in this kind of process with a partner? In what aspects of your relationship might this kind of process be beneficial to you and/or your partner?

Haitian immigrants, sex workers, hemophiliacs, homosexuals, and sexual tourists has become a **global pandemic,** meaning there is no corner of the earth that HIV/AIDS has not reached.

At the end of 2017, 37 million people worldwide were infected by and living with HIV (see Figure 6.7) (WHO, 2017). The World Health Organization confirms that since the beginning of the epidemic, more than 70 million people have been infected with the HIV virus, and about 35 million people have died of HIV. Countries where the people are poor and underprivileged, where education is weak and health care is absent, have had the most difficulty controlling the spread of HIV. Africa has been especially ravaged by HIV; cases in the sub-Saharan African countries alone accounted for over two-thirds of all new HIV infections in 2007.

HIV is a disease that has benefited from gender, social, and economic inequality, and the epidemic reveals the fault lines of poverty the world over (Farmer, 2003; Parker, 2002; Richardson et al., 2014). A cure remains close, but more effective treatments have enabled millions, including children born with HIV, to look forward to the possibility of a long life living with HIV/AIDS as a chronic disease. While some countries have made impressive gains, others have lagged behind in improving HIV rates. Clearly social inequality is a key factor. The decline in new HIV infections among adults has slowed in the past decade, which indicates the need for increased funding and scale-up of services (AVERT, 2019).

Most experts agree that nothing has altered the sexual landscape of the world and the United States as much as the HIV epidemic has. The shape of the HIV epidemic has

global pandemic
Worldwide epidemic.

Table 6.2 Summary of sexually transmitted infections

STI	SYMPTOMS	TRANSMISSION AND PREVENTION	TREATMENT	POSSIBLE COMPLICATIONS
BACTERIAL STIs				
Gonorrhea	Men: Burning sensation during urination or bowel movement, and/or a cloudy discharge from the penis or anus. Women: Often no noticeable symptoms. Cloudy vaginal discharge, irritation during urination, or vaginal bleeding between periods. Rare symptoms: lower abdominal pain or pain during intercourse.	Vaginal, anal, or oral sexual contact. Transmission to newborns can cause eye infections. Condoms can help prevent the transmission of gonorrhea infection.	Oral antibiotics cure most cases. Some strains are becoming antibiotic-resistant. All sexual partners must be treated concurrently to prevent reinfection. No vaccine available but research is ongoing.	Untreated may lead to infections of reproductive system, pelvic inflammatory disease, and possible infertility in women, and epididymitis or prostatitis in men.
Chlamydia	Thick, cloudy discharge from the vagina or penis occurring 1 to 3 weeks after exposure; less common: pelvic pain, irregular periods, increased pain during menstrual periods, discomfort during urination, or irritation of the vaginal and/or anal area; often asymptomatic.	Oral, vaginal, or anal sex. Extremely contagious bacterium; may be transmitted during a single sexual encounter with an infected partner. Condoms can help prevent the transmission of chlamydia infection.	Oral antibiotics cure most cases. All sexual partners must be treated concurrently to prevent reinfection. No vaccine available but research is ongoing.	Untreated may lead to infections of reproductive system and pelvic inflammatory disease in women and epididymitis in men, a major cause of infertility.
Nongonococcal urethritis (NGU)	Similar to gonorrhea: discharge from the urethra; burning and itching at the end of the urethra or upon urination.	Vaginal, anal, or oral sexual contact. Condoms can help prevent the transmission of NGU.	Oral antibiotics cure most cases. All sexual partners must be treated concurrently to prevent reinfection. No vaccine available.	Untreated may lead to infections of reproductive system and pelvic inflammatory disease and possible infertility in women and epididymitis or prostatitis in men.
Syphilis	Primary stage: Sore called a chancre appears at the point of infection. Usually heals within a few weeks. Secondary stage: Occurs within weeks or months; symptoms include low-grade fever, sore throat, fatigue, headache, hair loss, and skin rashes, typically on hands or feet. Late stage: Spread of the bacterium leads to organ and neurologic damage, paralysis, mental illness, and death.	Sexual contact including vaginal, anal, and oral sexual practices. Condoms can help prevent the transmission of syphilis.	Antibiotics, primarily penicillin, cure the infection. All sexual partners must be treated concurrently to prevent reinfection. No vaccine available but research is ongoing.	Untreated, bacterium spreads to all bodily systems, causing new symptoms and eventual destruction of organs and brain tissue and death.
Pelvic inflammatory disease (PID)	Not an STI but results from several STIs. Lower abdominal sensitivity and pain, pain during intercourse, irregular periods, cervical discharge and tenderness, fever, nausea, and vomiting.	Direct result of various STIs transmitted through sexual contact. Condoms can help prevent the transmission of STIs that can lead to PID.	Various oral or injected antibiotics. Vaccines that will prevent STIs such as chlamydia and gonorrhea will have the effect of preventing millions of PID cases.	PID can affect the uterus, ovaries, fallopian tubes, or related structures. Untreated, PID can lead to infertility, tubal pregnancy, chronic pelvic pain, and other serious consequences.

Taking Care of the Sexual Body

Table 6.2 (continued)

STI	SYMPTOMS	TRANSMISSION AND PREVENTION	TREATMENT	POSSIBLE COMPLICATIONS
PARASITIC STIs				
Trichomoniasis	Men: Usually asymptomatic. Possibly: irritation of the urethra, slight discharge, and pain after urination or ejaculation. Women: Yellow or greenish vaginal discharge accompanied by an unpleasant odor, genital irritation, and pain upon urination.	Sexual contact, including vaginal, anal, and oral sexual practices. Condoms can help prevent the transmission of trichomoniasis.	Oral antibiotics will cure most cases. All sexual partners must be treated concurrently to prevent reinfection. No available vaccine.	Without proper treatment, may cause PID among women and NGU among men.
Scabies	Irritation and rash in genital or anal area or on hands or feet.	Sexual activities as well as nonsexual skin-to-skin contact. Refraining from sexual contact during infection can protect self or partner from transmission. Decontaminating clothing and bedding can also help prevent reinfection.	Prescription lotions (pyrethrum, lindane, crotamiton) applied to all areas of the body from the neck down and washed off after 8 to 14 hours. Decontamination of all clothing and bedding. No available vaccine.	No serious complications. Difficult to cure and easily spread.
Pubic lice	Genital irritation and extreme itching, often said to be the most intense itching imaginable, caused by lice biting the skin to feed on blood.	Sexual contact, sharing bedding, sharing clothing. Refraining from sexual contact during infection can protect self or partner from transmission. Decontaminating clothing and bedding can also help prevent reinfection.	Prescription shampoos, creams, and ointments containing chemicals that are toxic to the lice. Wash all bedding and clothes in hot water. No available vaccine.	No serious complications. Difficult to cure and easily spread.
VIRAL STIs				
Herpes simplex virus (HSV), types 1 and 2	Often asymptomatic. Clusters of small, painful blisters in genital and anal areas or around mouth. General flulike symptoms: mild fever, fatigue, and tenderness in lymph nodes, perhaps urinary pain.	Oral, vaginal, or anal sexual activities; kissing. Condoms can help prevent transmission of HSV. Avoid unprotected oral sex during the time when blisters are present either orally or in the genital region.	No cure. Treated with antiherpetic drugs (acyclovir, famciclovir, valacyclovir). No vaccine available though research is underway.	Sores create route of transmissions for other STIs. May be passed from pregnant mother to child during birth.
Human papillomavirus (HPV): Genital warts	Warts on the penis, opening to the vagina, cervix, labia minora, or anal area. Warts may also appear inside the vagina or anus and may not be noticed at all. Warts are flat or lumpy; they may be single or in groups and vary in size. Sometimes the warts may be too small or flat to be seen or felt.	Skin-to-skin contact; vaginal, oral, or anal sexual activities. Transmission possible with or without visible warts. Condoms can help prevent the transmission of HPV. Gardasil, a vaccination, prevents acquisition of some types of HPV and is currently offered to both young men and women.	No cure. Removal of warts through cryosurgery (freezing), laser therapy, surgery, and topical medications applied by the patient. Removing warts does not cure infection.	Major cause of cervical and anal cancers.

(continued)

Table 6.2 (continued)

STI	SYMPTOMS	TRANSMISSION AND PREVENTION	TREATMENT	POSSIBLE COMPLICATIONS
VIRAL STIs				
Hepatitis B (HBV)	Usually no symptoms unless virus becomes active. Jaundice, a deep yellowing of the skin and eyes. Loss of appetite, fatigue, abdominal pain, nausea, vomiting, darkening of the urine, rash, and joint pain.	Contact with blood, serum, semen, vaginal fluids, and in rare instances, saliva. Routes of transmissions are sharing needles, sexual contact, and sometimes tattooing and body piercing. Condoms can help prevent the transmission of hepatitis B.	No cure. Acute infection: bed rest, increased fluid intake, good nutrition, and avoiding alcohol (which may exacerbate liver inflammation). Chronic infection: Alpha interferon boosts the body's immune system; lamivudine, antiviral medication, slows liver infection. A series of three injections over 6 months prevents infection for life.	In small percentage of chronic cases: serious liver disease, including cirrhosis and liver cancer, which may lead to liver failure and either a liver transplant or death.
HIV/AIDS	HIV: Initially no symptoms or mild fever, headache, fatigue, and rash. As virus progresses: loss of energy; unexplained weight loss; frequent fevers and night sweats; frequent yeast infections; enlarged lymph glands; persistent skin rashes; short-term memory loss; mouth, genital, or anal sores; and blurred vision. AIDS is diagnosed when CD4 + T-cell count dips to below 200 or when the person becomes infected with one or more opportunistic infections.	Transmission requires that semen, vaginal fluids, or blood from an infected person enter the bloodstream of an uninfected person. The most common routes of HIV are through sexual contact, primarily vaginal and anal intercourse and, less commonly, oral sex. Condoms can help prevent the transmission of HIV. PrEP medicines can stop HIV from taking hold and spreading throughout your body. It is very effective but must be taken consistently and daily. Daily PrEP reduces the risk of getting HIV from sex by more than 90%. Among people who inject drugs, it reduces the risk by more than 70%. HIV sexual risk can be even lower when combined with PrEP and condoms and other prevention methods.	The treatment of HIV has rapidly improved and now offers a great deal of hope in an eventual cure. In addition to PrEP, new HIV medicine identified as PEP can be highly effective to prevent becoming infected when one is potentially exposed to HIV. PEP should be used only in emergency situations and must begin within 72 hours after possible exposure to HIV. When exposed to HIV during sex, through the sharing of needles, or if you've been sexually assaulted, talk to your health care provider or an emergency room doctor about immediate use of PEP.	With proper treatment, life expectancy of HIV-infected individuals is rapidly increasing (approaching 25 years in the United States). Survival following diagnosis with AIDS is approaching 10 years.

Source: CDC, 2012g.

followed the inequalities (gender, sexual, and economic) of society, striking where poverty, illiteracy, racism, homophobia, and other social factors have created vulnerability to the disease. Consequently, there is a huge disparity between racial groups when it comes to who actually gets HIV. According to the Kaiser Foundation (2019), although Blacks are only 12% of the population. Blacks account for a much larger share of HIV diagnoses (43%), people estimated to be living with HIV disease (42%), and deaths among people with HIV (43%) compared to all other racial groups in the United States. You can see these trends for the United States displayed in Figure 6.8, and you may read more about this disparity and HIV in "Research and Sexual Well-Being: HIV in the African American Community."

Figure 6.7

Worldwide, the number of people living with HIV rose from around 8 million in 1990 to 37 million by the end of 2017, including almost 2 million children and 18 million women. Approximately 25% of all of these people were unaware that they actually had HIV (AVERT, 2018).

Today, with good medical interventions, people can expect to live out their lives with HIV. In time, it is possible that HIV will have a place only in history books.

History of HIV/AIDS The first documented cases of AIDS appeared in the United States in 1980, but research suggests that HIV may have been present in human beings for decades, perhaps even before 1900. Recent discoveries suggest that a virus in primates crossed to humans in the late 1800s. The virus did not sicken the primate population, but it converted to HIV (Worobey et al., 2008).

Figure 6.8

New HIV infections by race and transmission group, U.S. 2010 vs. 2016 (from U.S. government statistics).

Group	2010	2016
Black gay and bisexual men	9,800	9,800
Latino gay and bisexual men	6,400	8,300
White gay and bisexual men	8,000	6,700
Black heterosexual women	4,700	4,000
People who inject drugs	2,700	1,900
Black heterosexual men	2,300	1,800
White heterosexual women	1,000	1,000
Latino heterosexual women	1,200	980

RESEARCH and Sexual Well-Being

HIV in the African American Community

Early on in the HIV epidemic, the disease began to attack people who were the most vulnerable and least able to cope well with its effects, including poor African Americans in the United States. African Americans were not the first victims of HIV, but HIV has claimed a hugely disproportionate number of its victims from the African American community. Among all U.S. ethnic groups, African Americans have the highest risk of contracting HIV/AIDS (Sutton et al., 2009).

By 2011, over 230,000 African Americans had died of HIV/AIDS. Of the 1 million people living with HIV/AIDS in the United States today, almost half are African American. In addition, AIDS is now affecting African American women in very high numbers. How did this happen? According to researchers, a complex of environmental, social, and individual factors is responsible for the increase among African Americans (Fullilove, 2006).

Poverty and unstable housing conditions, risk of incarceration, poor health care, and lack of treatment are the forces that produce marginalized communities and populations, and thus fuel the epidemic among African Americans (Fullilove, 2006). In study after study, research has tended to confirm that being socially and economically marginal has made the African American community highly vulnerable to HIV/AIDS (Kaiser Foundation, 2019). It is especially noteworthy that although the HIV rate has been much lower among U.S. females than among males, this is not true of African American women, who now have the highest risk. African American MSM (men-who-have-sex-with-men), who have a high rate of HIV, may be the key to understanding the spread of HIV/AIDS. African American MSM are less likely to be tested for HIV and are less likely to disclose their sexual identity to their intimate partners, potentially spreading HIV to African American women and young gay African American men. As one MSM told researchers: "Gays to me were white men. The brothers that I hung out with, we never called ourselves gay. We just liked men."

In response to their findings, the National Minority AIDS Council made the following policy recommendations (Fullilove, 2006) for curbing the HIV epidemic in the African American community:

1. Strengthen stable African American communities by providing more affordable housing
2. Reduce the impact of incarceration as a driver of new HIV infections within the African American community by:
   - Providing voluntary, routine HIV testing to prisoners on entry and release
   - Making HIV prevention education and condoms available in prison facilities
   - Expanding reentry programs to help formerly incarcerated persons successfully transition back into society
3. Stop marginalizing homosexuality and reduce stigma and discrimination against all MSM, including those of African American descent

The U.S. government has endorsed these policy recommendations, some of which have become part of public health policy (CDC, 2011c). Perhaps in the coming years we will see a real decline in HIV among African Americans as knowledge and awareness about these issues increase.

The first recognized cases of AIDS in the United States occurred among gay men, hemophiliacs, sex workers, and Haitian immigrants in the early 1980s. The early cases in New York and California were mysterious and highly resistant to any kind of known treatment. While AIDS lacked a name at this point, it became apparent that the symptoms of these individuals belonged to a common syndrome (AVERT, 2009). In 1981, the CDC released a report of a rare form of pneumonia (CDC, 1981). Other mysterious diseases, including a rare form of skin cancer called Kaposi's sarcoma, also surfaced and puzzled doctors and medical researchers.

The medical community could not stop the progression of diseases that were quickly taking the lives of those who had them. Symptoms of AIDS at this time were unexplained weight loss, rare forms of pneumonia, and rare cancers and infections not found in healthy human populations. Within 1 year of the CDC's 1981 report, 452 cases of AIDS from 23 states had been reported to the CDC.

At the beginning of the AIDS crisis in the United States, most of the illnesses and deaths were occurring among gay men—and so they were mistakenly referred to as the "gay cancer." This early trend is primarily responsible for the stigma HIV and AIDS still have today, despite the fact that both occur in every community in the world. In December 1982, a 20-month-old child who had received multiple transfusions of blood and blood products died from infections related to AIDS (*MMWR Weekly*, 1982). This case provided the first clear evidence that an infectious agent caused AIDS. It also raised serious concerns about the safety of the world's blood supply. In that same month, the CDC reported the first cases of possible transmission of AIDS from mother to child. Following this discovery, it was reported that increasing numbers of women were contracting HIV through heterosexual sex. Today heterosexual sex is one of the most common ways of transmitting HIV (see Figure 6.9).

In late 1983, American and French researchers discovered that the organism responsible for AIDS is a **retrovirus**, a virus that destroys the cells of the body's immune system as it reproduces. Only a small number of human retroviruses are known, including HIV.

HIV has now been around for so long and is so deeply embedded in some countries that it is woven into the very fabric of their culture. For example, in Tanzania, popular culture reflects how people's knowledge of what is accurate and true about the disease is changing their perceptions of the body, sexuality, and intercourse. Traditionally, their perceptions of the sexual body, love, and even gender were governed by rituals to protect well-being. The rituals functioned effectively until HIV/AIDS came along and the rituals did not protect people from this deadly disease. Pastors admonished young people to stop going to the disco and to "change your ways, or you will die of AIDS . . . leave the Disco behind . . . it is a European thing. Why do you need such noise?" (Setel, 2000, p. 173). Today even the popular music of Tanzania is laced with lyrics about HIV.

HIV/AIDS continues to affect people of all genders, races, ethnicities, and communities in American society, including gay and bisexual men and injecting drug users.

DID YOU KNOW

Sex is safer when you:

- Don't have sex in any way that puts you and your partner in direct contact with each other's blood, semen, or other body fluids.
- Avoid vaginal and anal intercourse with new partners until you have both been tested for STIs.
- Use a latex condom every time you have sex.
- Never use an oil-based lubricant with a latex condom. Oil-based lubricants break down the latex material and can lead to breakage.
- Don't drink or do drugs and then have sex. Our inhibitions are lowered and decision-making is compromised when under the influence. Sobriety helps to ensure we are having consensual sex and that we are in a mind-frame to make good health decisions.

retrovirus

A virus that survives and multiplies by invading and destroying the DNA of normal body cells and then replicating its own DNA into the host cell's chromosomes.

Figure 6.9

Estimated adult and adolescent new HIV diagnoses in 2009 by transmission route and gender.

Male:
- Black male to male sexual contact: 10,233
- Hispanic / Latino male to male sexual contact: 7,425
- White male to male sexual contact: 7,390
- Black men, heterosexual contact: 1,926

Female:
- Black women, heterosexual contact: 4,189
- White women, heterosexual contact: 1,032
- Hispanic, Latina women, heterosexual contact: 1,025

In addition, HIV/AIDS has become a serious problem among heterosexual women, especially in African American and Hispanic/Latino populations (Kaiser Foundation, 2019).

By age group, between 2010-2016, the annual number of HIV infections went down for young people 13-24 and adults 45-54 but increased among persons aged 25-34. Among older adults over age 55 the infections remained stable (HIV Gov, 2019).

Transmission of HIV   HIV can be detected in several fluids and human body tissues. It is important to understand, however, that finding a small amount of HIV in a body fluid or tissue does not mean that HIV is transmitted by that body fluid or tissue. Only specific fluids (blood, semen, vaginal secretions, and breast milk) from an HIV-infected person can transmit HIV. These specific fluids must come in contact with a mucous membrane or damaged tissue or be directly injected into the bloodstream (from a needle or syringe) for transmission to possibly occur (CDC, 2010c).

In the United States, HIV is most commonly transmitted through specific unprotected sexual behaviors (anal or vaginal sex) or sharing of needles with an infected person. It is less common for HIV to be transmitted through oral sex or for an HIV-infected woman to pass the virus to her baby before or during childbirth or after birth through breastfeeding her infant. Although the risk is extremely small due to rigorous testing of the U.S. blood supply and donated organs, it is also possible to acquire HIV through exposure to infected blood, transfusions of infected blood, blood products, or organ transplantation (CDC, 2010c).

It is not possible to transmit HIV by hugging someone, or sharing food or eating utensils. In addition, close-mouthed kissing is considered to be completely safe. Deep or French kissing carries a slight risk of viral transmission but only if there are open sores in the mouth and infected blood is exchanged (CDC, 2010c).

Symptoms of HIV   HIV infects cells in the immune system, called *T-cells,* and the central nervous system in the body. T-cells play a critical role in our immune systems by coordinating the actions of other immune system cells. When HIV infects and reduces the number of available T-cells, the immune system can become seriously threatened. Over time, usually years, HIV infection will lead to a significant decrease in these cells.

HIV infection can be broken down into four distinct stages: (1) primary infection, (2) clinically asymptomatic stage, (3) symptomatic HIV infection, and (4) progression from HIV to AIDS.

Stage 1: Primary HIV Infection. This stage of infection lasts for a few weeks and is often accompanied by a short flulike illness (see Figure 6.10). In up to 20% of people, HIV symptoms can be serious enough to consult a doctor, but the diagnosis of HIV is often missed (AVERT, 2009). During this stage, there is a large amount of HIV in the bloodstream, and the immune system responds by producing HIV antibodies—substances that detect HIV particles and disable them. This process is known as *seroconversion.* If an HIV antibody test is done before the completion of seroconversion, it may show as a false-negative result.

Stage 2: Clinically Asymptomatic Stage. This stage lasts on average about 10 years, though we know that with some of the new advances of treatment, this stage can last up to 20 years or longer in individuals. As the name suggests, this stage is often free of major symptoms. The levels of HIV in the bloodstream drop to lower levels, but HIV antibodies are still detectable in the blood.

Stage 3: Symptomatic HIV Infection. Over time, the immune system will become severely damaged by the human immunodeficiency virus. As the immune system fails, symptoms will begin to appear. Initially, many of these symptoms are mild, but as the immune system deteriorates, the symptoms can get worse. Symptomatic HIV infection is mainly caused by the emergence of **opportunistic infections** and cancers that a normal immune system would fight off and prevent. This stage of HIV infection is

opportunistic infections
Infections that establish themselves in the human body as a result of a weakened immune system due to HIV infection.

Systemic:
- Fever
- Weight loss

Pharyngitis

Esophagus:
- Sores

Muscles:
- Myalgia

Liver and spleen:
- Enlargement

Central nervous system:
- Malaise
- Headache
- Neuropathy

Mouth:
- Sores
- Thrush

Lymph nodes:
- Lymphadenopathy

Skin:
- Rash

Gastric system:
- Nausea
- Vomiting

Figure 6.10
Some of these symptoms of primary HIV infection may occur within days or weeks of exposure to the virus, but some people don't experience any symptoms at all.

characterized by multisystem disease and infections, which can occur in almost every bodily system.

Stage 4: Progression from HIV to AIDS. A diagnosis of AIDS is made after a positive test for HIV and after two criteria are met: The T-cell count must dip below 200 (half the normal amount), and the person must be infected with one or more of 20 opportunistic infections. In the United States, the most common AIDS-defining opportunistic infection is *Pneumocystis carinii* pneumonia (PCP). Research reveals that young people now have near-normal life expectancy because of improvements in treatments. For example, 20-year-olds who started antiretroviral therapy in 2010 are projected to live 10 years longer than those first using it in 1996 (Becker, 2018).

Testing and Treatment There are simple, accurate, and minimally invasive techniques for HIV testing. The tests are all designed to detect antibodies that the body produces in response to HIV infection. Because a number of antibodies must be present in order to signal a positive result on a test for HIV, a conclusive negative result cannot usually be obtained until 3 to 6 months after the time of possible infection. A person planning on being tested for HIV should refrain from all risky sexual activities for several months prior to the test. After a positive HIV antibody test, a follow-up test is usually conducted to ensure the reliability of the result.

Testing methods include taking a blood sample or saliva sample. Many sites around the country offer anonymous and confidential testing. Anyone who has a concern about HIV should be tested as soon as possible. A negative result can provide a deep sense of relief and can provide motivation to take precautions to remain free from HIV. A positive result, while emotionally difficult, can allow for early medical intervention, as well as the emotional and psychological support necessary for a healthy and satisfying quality of life while living with HIV.

In the past decade, we have seen significant advances in the development of *antiretroviral therapy* (ART) made up of a combination of medications that work together to reduce the replication of the human immunodeficiency virus. The latest medications have successfully reduced the levels of the virus in the bloodstream of HIV-infected persons to undetectable levels, lengthening the time it takes for the virus to cause further symptoms and develop into AIDS. See "Health Sexuality: New Advances in PrEP." Although these medications do not eliminate the possibility of viral transmission to an uninfected partner, they do greatly reduce the risk of transmission (AVERT, 2011b).

The important thing to understand is that research is still continuing with the goal of finding a cure for HIV. In early 2019, it was reported that a man in London appeared to be free of HIV after a stem cell transplant. This is the second known case of an apparent "cure" for the virus following a stem cell transplant. The first known is the case of Timothy Ray Brown, an American man treated in Germany 12 years ago with a stem cell transplant. To date, he is still free from HIV and is thought to have been cured from the HIV infection.

Prevention Condoms can also greatly reduce the risk of transmission of HIV. If HIV infection has already occurred, the new HIV medications available through health care practitioners can reduce the viral load in the human body and prevent HIV from escalating to AIDS. The medications can also aid in preventing HIV transmission. We can look forward to the possibility of a cure for HIV in the future, but until that time, taking care of the sexual body is our best insurance.

Bacterial STIs

Single-cell organisms called bacteria cause bacterial STIs. These organisms are found in various bodily fluids, including saliva, mucous membranes, semen, vaginal secretions, and blood. Bacteria that cause STIs are spread primarily via sexual contact, including oral, vaginal, and anal sex, or when contact with bodily fluids occurs. The good news about bacterial STIs is that they can be treated successfully with antibiotics, especially when they are detected early. Seeking medical attention at the first sign of infection with a bacterial STI is key to successful treatment.

Once treatment has begun, it is important to let any sexual partners know that they may have been infected. This may be a daunting task given the stigma that surrounds STIs.

In this section, we will discuss gonorrhea, chlamydia, syphilis, and pelvic inflammatory disease (PID), a nonbacterial condition that is associated with bacterial STIs. For each of these problems, we will look at its general description, incidence and prevalence, signs and symptoms, routes of transmission, diagnostic tests, and treatment options.

Gonorrhea Watch a movie from the 1960s or 1970s and you might hear about something called "the clap." This slang term has been used as an alternative name for gonorrhea. **Gonorrhea** is caused by the bacterium *Neisseria gonorrhea,* which grows in the warm, moist areas of the reproductive tract, including the cervix, uterus, and fallopian tubes in women, and in the urethra in both men and women. The bacteria also grow in the anus, mouth, and throat (SIECUS, 2003).

Prevalence. Gonorrhea is a common bacterial STI. Along with chlamydia and syphilis, gonorrhea infections have skyrocketed in the United States and are now at epidemic levels. In 2018, 555,000 new

In sub-Saharan Africa, the number of people living with HIV/AIDS continues to rise, possibly due in part to a decrease in AIDS-related deaths. For these children living with AIDS in Togo, Africa, there is hope that they will have a normal life span, unlike the generation of their parents.
Pascal Deloche/Godong/Photononstop/Getty Images

gonorrhea
A common STI caused by the bacterium *Neisseria gonorrhea.*

Timothy Ray Brown, also known as the "Berlin Patient" is the only person to date that is known to have been cured of HIV/AIDS.
T.J. Kirkpatrick/Getty Images

HEALTHY Sexuality

New Advances in PrEP

Long-acting pre-exposure prophylaxis, or PrEP, refers to newer, longer-lasting forms of HIV prevention that researchers are studying that could provide a better and more convenient alternative to taking a daily pill, which is the current process by which PrEP works. Studies show that among those at most risk from sexual transmission of HIV, PrEP reduces the risk of transmissions by more than 90% when it is used consistently. For those who are at risk from IV drug usage, consistent use results in a reduced risk of over 70%. But as many of us know, remembering to take a pill every day can be challenging. Currently, the NIH National Institute of Allergy and Infectious Diseases is working to design and test four different forms of long-acting PrEP, including intravaginal rings, injectable drugs, implants, and antibodies. While it may be a while before long-acting PrEP is widely available to the public, the best forms of prevention against sexual transmission of HIV continue to be:

- HIV testing—so that you know your own HIV status and your partner's, too.
- Antiretroviral therapy for people who have HIV, to protect their health and to prevent their transmitting the virus to their sexual partners.
- Daily oral PrEP for people who do not have HIV but are at very high risk of getting it.
- Using condoms consistently and correctly.
- Choosing less risky sexual behaviors.
- Reducing the number of people you have sex with.
- Post-exposure prophylaxis, or PEP, meaning taking antiretroviral medicines very soon after being potentially exposed to HIV to avoid becoming infected.

Source: HIV.gov (2019). *What is long-acting PrEP and why is it needed?* Retrieved from https://www.hiv.gov/hiv-basics/hiv-prevention/potential-future-options/long-acting-prep.

---

cases were reported, up 16% in three years (CDC, 2019). The CDC estimates that more than 700,000 people in the United States contract new gonorrheal infections each year (CDC, 2012h). In the period from 1975 to 1997, the United States implemented a national gonorrhea control program that resulted in a decline in infections. In the United States, the highest reported rates of infection are among sexually active teenagers, young adults, and African Americans (CDC, 2019d).

Symptoms. One of the reasons gonorrhea can go undetected for a long period of time is that many individuals who have gonorrhea have no symptoms. If symptoms do appear, they usually surface anywhere from 2 to 5 days after infection, but they can take up to 1 month to appear (Figure 6.11).

For men, common symptoms may include:

- Burning sensation when urinating
- White, yellow, or green discharge from penis
- Presence of painful or swollen testicles

For women, common symptoms may include:

- Painful or burning sensation when urinating
- Symptoms often mistaken for a bladder or vaginal infection
- Increased vaginal discharge
- Vaginal bleeding between periods

Symptoms of rectal infection in both men and women may include discharge and itching, soreness, bleeding, or painful bowel movements. An individual with a rectal infection

199

Figure 6.11

Gonorrhea symptoms in the penis (left), showing a cloudy discharge, and in an inflamed cervix (right), with a visible discharge. Women may not notice any symptoms of a gonorrhea infection.

(*left*) Dr. P. Marazzi/Science Source; (*right*) Centers for Disease Control and Prevention

may also not show any symptoms. Gonorrhea infection in the throat may cause a sore throat, but it usually causes no symptoms.

Transmission, Testing, and Treatment. Gonorrhea is spread through contact with the penis, vagina, mouth, or anus. Ejaculation does not have to occur for gonorrhea to be transmitted or acquired. Gonorrhea can also be spread from a mother to her baby during childbirth. This mode of transmission can cause blindness, joint infection, or a life-threatening blood infection in the baby. Treatment of gonorrhea should begin as soon as it is detected in pregnant women in order to reduce the risk of these complications.

Laboratory tests are available to diagnose gonorrhea. A doctor or nurse can obtain a sample for testing from the parts of the body most likely to be infected, including the cervix, urethra, rectum, or throat. If gonorrhea is present in the cervix or urethra, diagnosis is as simple as providing a urine sample for analysis.

There are several antibiotics that can cure gonorrhea in both adolescents and adults. However, at a time when the medical field is being challenged with several conditions that are drug-resistant, gonorrhea has its own subset of drug-resistant strains that make treatment more complicated. It is important to note that while gonorrhea can be treated successfully with medication, its persistence can have other effects, such as pelvic inflammatory disease, causing swelling and pain.

Prevention. Gonorrhea can be prevented by using latex condoms. Condoms and dental dams can help protect against transmission during oral sex. Health care practitioners will do comprehensive STI screening during pregnancy to ensure a pregnant woman is free from infection.

Possible Complications. If gonorrhea is left untreated in men, the infection can cause *epididymitis,* which is a painful condition of the ducts attached to the testicles. This condition is known to lead to infertility in men. Women are also at risk of developing serious complications, such as pelvic inflammatory disease, from a gonorrhea infection, regardless of the presence or severity of symptoms.

Gonorrhea can also spread to the blood or bone joints, which can be life threatening. Those who have gonorrhea also are more prone to contract HIV. Individuals with both HIV and gonorrhea are also known to transmit HIV more easily to others than if they did not have gonorrhea (CDC, 2012h).

chlamydia

A common STI caused by the bacterium *Chlamydia trachomatis.*

Chlamydia Chlamydia is another very common STI caused by the bacterium *chlamydia trachomatis.* Even though symptoms of chlamydia are usually mild or nonexistent, serious complications can result that have the potential to cause permanent damage including infertility. Chlamydia can also cause discharge from the penis of an infected man.

Prevalence. In the United States, chlamydia is the most frequently reported bacterial STI. More than 1.8 million people in the U.S. have chlamydia (CDC, 2019). The CDC suspects that the number of actual infections in the United States is much higher due to the fact that most people are unaware that they are infected and so do not seek testing.

Figure 6.12

Chlamydia symptoms: testicular swelling (left) and vaginal discharge (right). Chlamydia infections often are asymptomatic.
(*left*) Dr. M.A. Ansary/Science Source; (*right*) Dr. Lourdes Fraw; Jim Pledger/CDC

Symptoms. As stated, chlamydia is known as a "silent" infection because approximately 75% of infected women and 50% of infected men have no symptoms. If symptoms do occur, they usually surface within 1 to 3 weeks after exposure (CDC, 2012i) (Figure 6.12).

Common symptoms for men may include:

- Discharge from penis
- Burning sensation when urinating
- Burning or itching around the opening of the penis
- Swelling and pain in the testicles (much less common)

Common symptoms for women may include:

- Abnormal vaginal discharge
- Burning sensation when urinating

If the infection spreads from the cervix to the fallopian tubes, some women will still exhibit no symptoms; others may report the following:

- Lower abdominal pain
- Low back pain
- Nausea
- Fever
- Pain during intercourse
- Bleeding between menstrual periods

Men and women who have receptive anal intercourse may acquire the chlamydia infection in the rectum, which can result in rectal pain, discharge, or bleeding. Chlamydia can also be found in the throats of men and women who have had oral sex with an infected partner.

Transmission, Testing, and Treatment. Any sexually active individual can be infected with chlamydia. It can be transmitted during vaginal, anal, or oral sex. Due to the immature development of the cervix in teenage girls and young women, it is thought that they are more susceptible to this infection (CDC, 2012i). It can also be passed from an infected mother to her baby during childbirth. In pregnant women, there is evidence suggesting that chlamydia infections that are left untreated can lead to premature delivery (CDC, 2012i). Babies born to infected mothers can get chlamydia infections in their eyes and respiratory tracts. Chlamydia is a leading cause of early infant pneumonia and conjunctivitis (pink eye) in newborns.

Chlamydia can be diagnosed through laboratory testing. Some tests can be performed on urine samples. Other tests require collecting a specimen from the penis or cervix. The CDC recommends yearly chlamydia testing of all sexually active women age 25 and younger, older women who have a new sex partner or multiple sexual partners, and all pregnant women.

As with gonorrhea, chlamydia is easily treated and cured with antibiotics. A single dose of azithromycin or a week of doxycycline is the most common treatment. Individuals who are being treated for chlamydia are advised to abstain from sexual intercourse until they and their sexual partners have completed treatment in order to prevent reinfection.

Prevention. Latex male condoms, when used correctly and consistently, can greatly reduce the risk of transmission of chlamydia.

Potential Complications. Untreated chlamydia may lead to infections of the reproductive system and pelvic inflammatory disease in women and epididymitis in men, a major cause of infertility.

Syphilis **Syphilis** is an STI caused by the bacterium *Treponema pallidum*. It has often been referred to as the "great imitator," because so many of its symptoms are indistinguishable from those of other infections. Contrary to myth, syphilis cannot be spread through contact with toilet seats, doorknobs, swimming pools, hot tubs, bathtubs, shared clothing, or eating utensils. It is transmitted by direct contact with a syphilis sore or prenatal exposure through an infected mother (CDC, 2012k).

syphilis
An STI caused by a bacterium and characterized by a chancre, or sore, at the point of infection.

Prevalence. The rates of syphilis infection reported in the United States decreased during the 1990s, and in 2000 the United States enjoyed the lowest rates of syphilis infections since reporting began in 1941. Between 2001 and 2008, however, the rate of infection increased again. In 2018, there were 26,000 cases of syphilis reported in the United States, approximately 8.6 cases per 100,000 (CDC, 2019).

Symptoms. Syphilis develops in stages, defined by the symptoms present, which range from the primary stage to the secondary and then latent and late stages (CDC, 2012k). Many people who are infected with syphilis remain symptom-free for many years. However, even without symptoms, people are at risk for late complications if they are not treated.

chancre
A sore that typically appears at the site of infection with syphilis.

Primary stage. The primary stage of syphilis is usually marked by the appearance of a single sore called a **chancre** (Figure 6.13). The chancre is usually firm, round, and small, but painless. The chancre will appear at the spot where syphilis entered the body. It will last for 3 to 6 weeks and will heal without treatment. The time between infection with syphilis and the start of the first symptoms can range anywhere from 10 to 90 days with an average of 21 days. If adequate treatment is not given at this time, the infection will progress to the secondary stage.

Secondary stage. In this stage, common symptoms include a skin rash and mucous membrane lesions. The rash will appear on one or more areas of the body and can appear as the chancre is healing or several weeks after the chancre has healed. The rash appears as rough, red or brownish spots that are most commonly found on the palms of the hands or the bottoms of the feet. In addition to the rashes, symptoms of secondary syphilis may include:

- Fever
- Swollen lymph glands
- Sore throat
- Patchy hair loss
- Headaches
- Weight loss

- Muscle aches
- Fatigue

As in the primary stage, symptoms of the secondary stage will resolve without treatment. However, without treatment, the infection will progress to the latent and possibly the late stages of the disease.

Latent and late stages. Syphilis has a hidden stage, called the *latent stage,* when the symptoms of the primary and secondary stages begin to disappear. Without treatment, an infected person will continue to have syphilis even though there are no signs or symptoms. This latent stage can last for several years. The late stage of syphilis can develop in approximately 15% of people who have gone untreated for the infection. This stage can appear 10 to 20 years after the infection was first acquired. Common symptoms of the late stage of syphilis are:

- Significant damage to internal organs including the brain, nerves, eyes, heart, blood vessels, liver, bones, and joints
- Difficulty coordinating muscle movements
- Paralysis
- Numbness
- Gradual blindness
- Dementia
- Potentially death

Figure 6.13
Primary stage syphilis chancre.
Clinical Photography, Central Manchester University Hospitals NHS Foundation Trust, UK/Science Source

Transmission, Testing, and Treatment. Transmission of syphilis can occur during vaginal, anal, or oral sex. Syphilis is passed from person to person through direct contact with a chancre. The chancres are mainly found on the external genitals, vagina, and anus or in the rectum. They can also be found on the lips and in the mouth.

Syphilis can also be passed from pregnant women to their babies. Depending on how long a pregnant woman has been infected, she may have a high risk of having a stillbirth. Untreated early syphilis in women results in prenatal death in up to 40% of cases and, if acquired during the 4 years preceding pregnancy, leads to infection of the fetus in 80% of cases (CDC, 2010a). An infected baby may be born without signs or symptoms of syphilis. However, if left untreated, a baby could develop serious problems within a few weeks and ultimately experience developmental delays, frequent seizures, or death.

A blood test is the most common way to detect syphilis. Shortly after an infection occurs, the body produces antibodies that will produce a positive result on a blood test. In addition to blood tests, some health care providers will diagnose syphilis by examining material from chancres with a microscope. If the syphilis bacteria are present in the sore, they will be visible through the microscope.

In its early stages, syphilis is relatively easy to cure. A single intramuscular injection of penicillin (a common antibiotic) will cure a person who has had the infection for less than 1 year. Additional doses will be required for people who have had syphilis longer than 1 year. Treatment will kill the syphilis bacteria and prevent further damage, but it will not repair damage that has already occurred. It is recommended that individuals who receive syphilis treatment abstain from sexual contact until the sores are completely healed.

Prevention. Condoms can help prevent the transmission of the syphilis bacterium. Dental dams and condoms can help prevent transmission from oral sex.

Potential Complications. Untreated, the syphilis bacteria invade all bodily systems, causing new symptoms, eventually destroying organs and brain tissue, and resulting in death.

Pelvic Inflammatory Disease Pelvic inflammatory disease (PID) confuses many people because, although it is most always associated with STIs, it is really a general term that refers to infection of the uterus, fallopian tubes, and other female reproductive organs. In fact, PID is a common and serious complication of some STIs, particularly gonorrhea and chlamydia (CDC, 2011f). PID can cause significant damage to the fallopian tubes and tissues in and near the uterus and ovaries. PID is also known to lead to serious health concerns such as infertility, a higher incidence of ectopic pregnancy (pregnancy that occurs outside the womb), formation of abscesses in reproductive structures, and chronic pelvic pain.

Prevalence. Every year in the United States, it is estimated that more than 1 million women experience acute PID requiring treatment (CDC, 2015b). As a result of PID, more than 75,000 women become infertile each year, and a large proportion of ectopic pregnancies that occur each year are due to PID.

Sexually active women in their childbearing years are at most risk for developing PID and those under the age of 25 are at higher risk than women older than 25. As with chlamydia, younger women are at an increased risk due to the immaturity of their cervical structures (CDC, 2011f).

Symptoms. Symptoms of PID can vary from none to severe. When PID is caused by a chlamydia infection, women may experience mild or even no symptoms. Even when there are no symptoms, PID often causes significant damage to the reproductive system. The CDC estimates that due to the vagueness of symptoms, PID is unrecognized by health care providers in approximately two-thirds of reported cases. Among the women who have symptoms, the following are the most common:

- Lower abdominal pain
- Fever
- Unusual vaginal discharge that may have a foul odor
- Painful intercourse
- Painful urination
- Irregular menstrual bleeding

Transmission, Testing, and Treatment. PID occurs when bacteria move upward from a woman's vagina or cervix into her reproductive organs. Although many different organisms can cause PID, it is most commonly associated with gonorrhea or chlamydia. A woman who has had PID has an increased risk of experiencing further episodes.

Women who douche may have a higher risk of developing PID than women who do not douche (Mayo Clinic, 2011a). Research shows that douching changes the balance of the organisms that normally live in the vagina in harmful ways and can actually force bacteria into the upper reproductive organs.

There are no precise tests for PID. Usually a diagnosis of PID is brought about by clinical findings or a patient describing symptoms and the health care provider conducting a physical examination to look for evidence of infection. Pelvic ultrasounds are also useful in diagnosing PID. An ultrasound procedure can reveal infections or enlargements of the fallopian tubes or surrounding reproductive structures. In some cases, laparoscopy may be necessary to confirm a diagnosis. Laparoscopy is a surgical procedure in which a thin, rigid tube with a lighted end and camera is inserted through a small abdominal incision. This procedure enables the doctor to view the internal pelvic organs and to take tissue samples for analysis.

PID can be cured with a variety of antibiotics, but any damage cannot be reversed. If a woman is experiencing symptoms, prompt antibiotic treatment can prevent severe damage to her reproductive organs. The longer a woman delays treatment, the more likely she is to become infertile or have a future ectopic pregnancy.

Prevention. Women can effectively prevent PID by not acquiring STIs. Condoms can help reduce the risk of transmission of STIs that could lead to PID. In addition, women should refrain from douching, as it upsets the delicate balance of bacteria in the vagina. It is also important to pay attention to hygiene habits. Women should wipe from front to back after urinating or having a bowel movement to avoid introducing bacteria from the colon into the vagina, to help protect vaginal and reproductive structures (Mayo Clinic, 2011b).

Potential Complications. Women who contract PID are at higher risk for further reproductive problems. PID can affect the uterus, ovaries, fallopian tubes, and related structures. Untreated, PID can lead to infertility, ectopic pregnancy, chronic pelvic pain, and other serious consequences.

Parasitic STIs

Some forms of STIs are not really infections at all but are body infestations. Infestations differ from infections, in that infections get into the bloodstream whereas parasites infest generally on top of the body or just under the skin. The two most common body infestations caused by parasites are scabies and pubic lice.

Scabies Human **scabies** is caused by an infestation of the skin by the human itch mite (*Sarcoptes scabiei* var. *hominis*). The microscopic scabies mite (Figure 6.14) burrows into the upper layer of the skin where it lives and lays its eggs. Scabies occurs worldwide and affects people of all races and social classes (CDC, 2010f). Scabies can spread rapidly under crowded conditions where close body contact is frequent. Institutions such as nursing homes, extended care facilities, and prisons are often sites of scabies outbreaks.

Symptoms. If a person has never had scabies, symptoms can take as long as 4 to 6 weeks to develop. It is important to know that infected persons can spread scabies during this time even if they are not experiencing symptoms. The most common symptoms of scabies are intense itching and a pimple-like skin rash. The itching is most commonly felt at night. The itching and rash may affect much of the body or be limited to common sites such as the wrist, elbow, armpit, webbing between the fingers, nipple, penis, waist, belt line, and buttocks. The rash can also include small blisters and scales.

Transmission, Testing, and Treatment. The scabies mite usually is spread by direct, prolonged, skin-to-skin contact with a person who has scabies. For this reason, scabies can be spread via sexual contact, though that is not the only way it can be transmitted. Contact generally must be prolonged; a quick handshake or a hug is not likely to cause a spread of scabies from one person to another. Scabies can contaminate clothing, bedding, and furniture, and people can acquire scabies by contact with these items as well. The life span of a scabies mite can be 1 to 2 months on the body of a person. Off a person, scabies mites usually do not live longer than 48 to 72 hours.

Diagnosis of a scabies infestation is usually based on the customary appearance and distribution of the rash and presence of burrows. Whenever possible, the diagnosis of scabies should be confirmed by identifying the mite, mite eggs, or mite fecal matter. This process is done by

scabies
A skin infestation caused by a microscopic mite that burrows under the skin and causes a very itchy rash.

Figure 6.14

The scabies mite (left) is a microscopic organism that burrows beneath the skin and causes a rash (right).
(*left*) Natural History Museum, London/Science Source; (*right*) Dr. P. Marazzi/Science Source

carefully removing a mite from the end of its burrow using the tip of a needle or by obtaining a skin scraping in order to examine it underneath a microscope. Even though the mite may not be found, it is still possible for a person to be infested; it is common for fewer than 10 to 15 mites to be present on the entire body of an infested person who is otherwise quite healthy.

Scabies is quite treatable with a *scabicide,* a product that kills the scabies mites as well as the eggs they produce. Scabicides are available only with a physician's prescription. No over-the-counter products have been tested and approved for humans as yet.

In addition to the person who has been infested with scabies, it is recommended that all people in the household and all possible sexual contacts receive treatment as well. All persons should be treated at the same time to prevent reinfestation. One important caution is to refrain from using a scabicide intended for animals because that can be quite dangerous (CDC, 2010f).

Prevention. Refraining from sexual contact during infection can protect against transmission. Decontaminating clothing and bedding can help prevent infestation.

Potential Complications. There are no serious complications from a scabies infestation, but it can be difficult to cure and can easily spread.

pubic lice (crabs)
Very small parasitic insects that attach themselves to hair shafts and cause itching.

Pubic Lice   **Pubic lice** or **crabs** are parasitic insects (Figure 6.15) that are found primarily in the pubic or genital area of individuals. Pubic lice have different forms including the egg, the nymph, and the adult. Lice eggs, or *nits,* are tiny and can be hard to see. They are found firmly attached to the hair shaft. They are oval and usually yellow to white in color. Pubic lice nits take about 6 to 10 days to hatch.

The nymph is an immature louse that hatches from the nit. A nymph looks like an adult pubic louse, but smaller. Pubic lice nymphs take approximately 2 to 3 weeks after hatching to mature into adults capable of reproducing. A nymph must feed on blood in order to survive.

The adult pubic louse resembles a small crab when viewed through a strong magnification lens. Pubic lice have six legs. Their two front legs are very large and look like the pincher claws of a crab, hence the nickname "crabs." Pubic lice are tan to grayish-white in color. Females are usually somewhat larger than males. Like nymphs, lice must feed on blood in order to survive. If a louse falls off a person, it will usually die within 1 to 2 days.

Symptoms. These include itching in the genital area and seeing nits or crawling lice on the body.

Transmission, Testing, and Treatment. Pubic lice are usually spread through sexual contact and are most commonly found in adults. Pubic lice found on children may be a possible sign of sexual exposure or sexual abuse. Occasionally, pubic lice can be spread by close personal contact or contact with clothing, bed linens, towels, or other articles that have been used by a person infested with pubic lice. A common misunderstanding is that we get pubic lice by sitting on a toilet seat. We know that this is extraordinarily rare due to the fact that pubic lice cannot live very long away from a warm body, and their feet are not designed to hold onto or walk on smooth surfaces such as toilet seats (CDC, 2010e).

Pubic lice infestation is diagnosed by finding a "crab" louse or nit on the hair in the pubic region or elsewhere on the body. Pubic lice may be difficult to find because there may be only a few. Pubic lice often attach themselves to more than one hair and generally they do not crawl as quickly as head and body lice are known to do.

A lice-killing shampoo (also called a *pediculicide*) is recommended to treat pubic lice. These products are available without a prescription at drug stores. Medication is generally very effective if applied exactly as directed on the bottle. A prescription medication called Lindane (1%) is

Figure 6.15
Pubic lice (crabs) attach themselves to pubic hair, but can spread to the upper thighs, abdominal area, armpits, chest, beard, and even eyelashes.
Eye of Science/Science Source

available through health care providers. Lindane is not recommended for pregnant or nursing women, or for children younger than 2 years old.

Prevention. Refraining from sexual contact during infection can prevent transmission. Decontaminating clothing and bedding can also help prevent infestation.

Potential Complications. While there are no serious complications possible from a pubic lice infestation, it can be difficult to cure and can easily spread.

Viral STIs

We have now come to what most people view as the scariest subset of sexually transmitted infections. Different viruses contracted through high-risk sexual behaviors, such as unprotected vaginal, anal, and oral intercourse, cause viral STIs. Viral STIs include the four Hs: HIV, HPV (genital warts), herpes, and hepatitis. These viruses have no cure, but many of their symptoms can be alleviated with treatment. In addition, it is important to remember that safer sexual practices can assist in the prevention of every one of these STIs. There are vaccines available to help prevent both HPV and hepatitis. Individuals should consult with their health care provider about whether to be vaccinated for either of these infections. The following information about these four viruses may help when making safe choices in pursuit of sexual health and happiness.

Herpes Simplex Virus Genital **herpes** is an STI caused by two types of viruses. The viruses are called herpes simplex virus type 1 (HSV-1) and herpes simplex virus type 2 (HSV-2) (Figure 6.16). While HSV-1 mostly causes cold sores or fever blisters on the mouth or face and HSV-2 mostly causes sores on the penis or vulva, the viruses are identical under a microscope, and either type can infect the mouth or genital region.

herpes
A recurrent skin condition characterized by sores on the mouth or genitals; caused by the herpes simplex virus.

Prevalence. Genital herpes infections are quite common in the United States. One in six people between the ages of 14 and 49 have genital herpes. The good news is that if you use a condom in the right way and are in a long-term relationship with a partner who is not infected by the virus, you may remain clear of the virus.

Genital HSV-2 infections are more common in women. Currently, approximately one in four women and one in eight men have HSV-2 infections (CDC, 2012j).

Symptoms. HSV-1 and HSV-2 can be found in the sores that the viruses cause, but they are also released between outbreaks from skin that does not appear to have a sore. Most people infected with HSV-2 are not aware of the infection. If signs and symptoms do appear, they usually occur within 2 weeks after the virus is transmitted, and the sores typically will heal within 2 to 4 weeks. Other symptoms may include a second set of sores and flulike symptoms, including fever and swollen glands.

Transmission, Testing, and Treatment. Generally, a person can acquire an HSV-2 infection only during sexual contact with someone who has a genital HSV-2 infection. Transmission

Figure 6.16
Cold sore HSV-I (left) and genital herpes HSV-II (right).
(*left*) Dr. Hermann/CDC; (*right*) Biophoto Associates/Science Source

can occur from an infected partner who does not have a visible sore and may not know that he or she is infected. HSV-1 can be passed from mouth to mouth by kissing. For example, it is thought that many children with HSV-1 acquired it from kissing infected relatives and friends (Whitley & Roizman, 2001). HSV-1 can cause genital herpes, but it more commonly causes infections around the mouth and on the face. HSV-1 infection of the genitals can be caused by oral–genital or genital–genital contact with a person who has HSV-1 infection.

Genital HSV also can be passed from mother to infant during pregnancy. This kind of infection can lead to potentially fatal infections in babies. A newly acquired infection during late pregnancy poses a greater risk of transmission to the infant. If a woman has an active outbreak of genital herpes at delivery, a cesarean is usually performed (Corey & Handsfield, 2000).

Herpes is also known to play a role indirectly in the spread of HIV. Herpes can make people more susceptible to HIV infection through sores and can make those with HIV more infectious to others (CDC, 2012j).

Health care providers can diagnose genital herpes by visual inspection of the active outbreak. They can also take a sample from the sore(s) and test it for the virus. Between outbreaks, HSV-1 and HSV-2 can be detected with blood tests for antibodies to the viruses.

There is no cure for herpes, but there are antiviral medications that can shorten and prevent outbreaks while an individual is taking the medication. In addition, daily medication therapy designed to suppress the viral concentration in symptomatic herpes can reduce the possibility of transmission to partners.

Individuals with herpes should abstain from sexual activity with uninfected partners when lesions or other symptoms of herpes are present. It is also important to know that even if a person does not have symptoms, he or she can still infect sexual partners (CDC, 2012j).

Prevention. Condoms can reduce the risk of transmission (CDC, 2012j).

Potential Complications. One possible complication of HSV is that the sores provide a more direct connection to the bloodstream and can create a route of transmission for other STIs.

Human Papillomavirus The human papillomavirus (HPV) is a condition contracted from one of a group of more than 100 related viruses. Thirty of these different types of HPV are known to be genital strains. Each type of HPV has the potential to cause an abnormal growth on a particular part of the body—genital warts and other lesions on or near the genitals or anus are the most common symptoms of genital HPV infections (Figure 6.17). The HPV is also the leading cause of cervical cancer in women, and is associated with anal cancer in men (Grce & Davies, 2008).

Nearly all cases of cervical cancers are caused by HPV infections. Worldwide, cervical cancer is very common due to the fact that many women lack access to Pap test screening.

Prevalence. About 79 million people are infected with HPV in the United States, making it so common as to be pervasive, and about 14 million people become newly infected each year (CDC, 2019). The CDC estimates that at least 80% of women and men will be infected at some point in their lives, often without knowing it.

Symptoms. HPV infections are often undetected because most of the strains do not cause warts or lesions. Even if no signs are exhibited, it is still possible to transmit the infection to sexual partners.

When symptoms are present, they vary according to the type of HPV infection one may have. Common symptoms of genital HPV strains are:

- **Genital warts.** These are noncancerous and appear as a flat lesion, a small cauliflower-like bump, or a stemlike protrusion. In women these warts most commonly appear on the vulva, but they may be found near the anus, on the cervix, or in the vagina. In men, the

Figure **6.17**
Genital warts.
Clinical Photography, Central Manchester University Hospitals NHS Foundation Trust, UK/Science Source

warts may appear on the penis and scrotum or around the anus. Genital warts are not known to cause pain or discomfort.

- **Precancerous genital lesions.** Certain HPV infections can cause cellular changes that result in precancerous lesions in women. A Pap test most often detects these abnormalities. Persistent infections (those that last more than 2 years) create a greater risk for cancer. Abnormal vaginal bleeding is a common symptom of cervical cancer.

Transmission, Testing, and Treatment. Genital HPV infections are contracted through vaginal and anal sex, as well as through other skin-to-skin contact in the genital region. HPV may affect males and females and lead to various cancers. Some HPV infections that result in oral or upper respiratory lesions are contracted through unprotected oral sex.

It is also possible, though more rare, that a woman with HPV can transmit the virus to her infant during delivery. The exposure can cause HPV infection in the infant's genitals or upper respiratory system.

Diagnosis of an HPV infection may include the following tests:

- Visual inspection of any warts or lesions
- Pap test
- DNA test, to detect DNA of 13 strains of high-risk HPVs

There is no cure for HPV infection. In most cases, the immune system will rid the body of the virus and warts will often disappear without treatment. There are a number of treatments available to remove warts and these treatments appear to reduce the concentration of HPV but they will not eliminate the virus.

There has been some controversy associated with the vaccine, especially when the idea of mandating its use is discussed. Some socially conservative advocacy groups argue that the HPV vaccine does not meet historical criteria necessary for it to be a requirement for children attending school. Many of these groups also stand by abstinence-only education and suggest that while the vaccine is a positive step, they will strenuously oppose any effort to require it for school enrollment (Dailard, 2006).

Prevention. It is possible to reduce the risk of developing genital warts and other HPV infections by being in a mutually monogamous sexual relationship, reducing the number of sexual partners, and consistently using a latex condom, which may prevent some but not all of HPV transmission.

Vaccination against HPV can help reduce the risk of transmission and infection for both males and females. The CDC now recommends HPV vaccination for all boys and girls age 11 to 12. Vaccines that include Gardasil and Cervarix prevent HPV infections most often linked to cervical cancer. These vaccines are available for females between the ages of 9 and 26. Either vaccine is recommended as a part of the regular immunization regimen for girls age 11 to 12. Gardasil is recommended for boys age 11 to 12 and helps protect against throat and anal cancer (CDC, 2011d).

Potential Complications. HPV is the major cause of cervical and anal cancers.

Hepatitis The word **hepatitis** means "inflammation of the liver." A virus most often causes hepatitis. In the United States, the most common types are hepatitis A, hepatitis B, and hepatitis C, though there are now cases of hepatitis D and E. Hepatitis D requires an infection of hepatitis B. Hepatitis B is the hepatitis virus that is associated with sexual contact. It causes chronic infection, cirrhosis (scarring), and cancer of the liver. The virus is present in blood, semen, vaginal secretions, and breast milk. A blood test is used to diagnose hepatitis. Table 6.3 gives a comparison of the prevalence, symptoms, transmission, and treatment of the most common forms of hepatitis.

hepatitis
A chronic viral infection of the liver.

Table **6.3** Hepatitis facts

	HEPATITIS A (HAV)	**HEPATITIS B (HBV)**	**HEPATITIS C (HCV)**
STATISTICS	• Hepatitis A rates in the U.S. have declined by more than 95% since the hepatitis A vaccine first became available in 1995. • In 2016, there was a significant increase in acute cases thought to be linked to imported foods.	• In 2016, a total of 3,218 cases of acute hepatitis B were reported to the CDC from 48 states. The actual acute cases were estimated to be nearly 21,000 for 2016. • The rate of new HBV infections declined from 1990 to 2014, with the greatest decline among children born since 1991 when routine vaccination of children was first recommended. • Estimated between 847,000 and 2.2 million people with chronic HBV infection.	• In 2016, a total of 2,967 cases of hepatitis C were reported to the CDC from 42 states. The actual acute cases are estimated to be nearly 14 times the number of reported cases in any year. • An estimated 2.4 million people in the U.S. are living with the HCV infection.
ROUTES OF TRANSMISSION	Ingestion of fecal matter, even in microscopic amounts, from: • Close person-to-person contact with an infected person • Sexual contact with an infected person • Ingestion of contaminated food or drinks	Contact with infectious blood, semen, and other body fluids, primarily through: • Birth to an infected mother • Sexual contact with an infected person • Sharing of contaminated needles, syringes or other injection drug equipment • Needlesticks or other sharp instrument injuries	Contact with blood of an infected person, primarily through: • Sharing of contaminated needles, syringes, or other injection drug equipment Less commonly through: • Sexual contact with an infected person • Birth to an infected mother • Needlestick or other sharp instrument injuries
PERSONS AT RISK	• Travelers to regions with intermediate or high rates of hepatitis A • Sex contacts of infected persons • Household members or caregivers of infected persons • Men who have sex with men • Users of certain illegal drugs (injection and non-injection) • Persons with clotting-factor disorders	• Infants born to infected mothers • Sex partners of infected persons • Persons with multiple sex partners • Persons with a sexually transmitted disease (STD) • Men who have sex with men • Injection drug users • Household contacts of infected persons • Health care and public safety workers exposed to blood on the job • Hemodialysis patients • Residents and staff of facilities for developmentally disabled persons • Travelers to regions with intermediate or high rates of hepatitis B (HBsAg prevalence of ≥2%)	• Current or former injection drug users • Recipients of clotting factor concentrates before 1987 • Recipients of blood transfusions or donated organs before July 1992 • Long-term hemodialysis patients • Persons with known exposures to HCV (e.g., health care workers after needlesticks, recipients of blood or organs from a donor who later tested positive for HCV) • HIV-infected persons • Infants born to infected mothers
INCUBATION PERIOD	15 to 50 days (average: 28 days)	45 to 160 days (average: 120 days)	14 to 180 days (average: 45 days)
SYMPTOMS OF ACUTE INFECTION (all types of viral hepatitis)	• Fever • Fatigue • Loss of appetite • Nausea • Vomiting • Abdominal pain • Clay-colored bowel movements • Joint pain • Jaundice		
LIKELIHOOD OF SYMPTOMATIC ACUTE INFECTION	• <10% of children <6 years have jaundice • 40%–50% of children age 6–14 years have jaundice • 70%–80% of persons >14 years have jaundice	• <1% of infants <1 year develop symptoms • 5%–15% of children age 1–5 years develop symptoms • 30%–50% of persons >5 years develop symptoms **Note:** Symptoms appear in 5%–15% of newly infected adults who are immunosuppressed	• 20%–30% of newly infected persons develop symptoms of acute disease

Table 6.3 (continued)

	HEPATITIS A (HAV)	**HEPATITIS B (HBV)**	**HEPATITIS C (HCV)**
POTENTIAL FOR CHRONIC INFECTION	None	• Among unimmunized persons, chronic infection occurs in >90% of infants, 25%–50% of children aged 1–5 years, and 6%–10% of older children and adults	• 75%–85% of newly infected persons develop chronic infection • 15%–20% of newly infected persons clear the virus
SEVERITY	Most persons with acute disease recover with no lasting liver damage; rarely fatal	• Most persons with acute disease recover with no lasting liver damage; acute illness is rarely fatal • 15%–25% of chronically infected persons develop chronic liver disease, including cirrhosis, liver failure, or liver cancer • Estimated 2,000–4,000 persons in the United States die from HCV-related illness per year	• Acute illness is uncommon. Those who do develop acute illness recover with no lasting liver damage • 60%–70% of chronically infected persons develop chronic liver disease • 5%–20% develop cirrhosis over a period of 20–30 years • 1%–5% will die from cirrhosis or liver cancer • Estimated 8,000–10,000 persons in the United States die from HCV-related illness per year
TREATMENT	• No medication available • Best addressed through supportive treatment	• Acute: No medication available; best addressed through supportive treatment • Chronic: Regular monitoring for signs of liver disease progression; some patients are treated with antiviral drugs	• Acute: Antivirals and supportive treatment • Chronic: Regular monitoring for signs of liver disease progression; some patients are treated with antiviral drugs
VACCINATION RECOMMENDATIONS	Hepatitis A vaccine is recommended for: • All children at age 1 year • Travelers to regions with intermediate or high rates of hepatitis A • Men who have sex with men • Users of certain illegal drugs (injection and non-injection) • Persons with clotting-factor disorders • Persons who work with HAV-infected primates or with HAV in a research laboratory • Persons with chronic liver disease, including HBV- and HCV-infected persons with chronic liver disease • Anyone else seeking long-term protection	Hepatitis B vaccine is recommended for: • All infants within 12 hours of birth • Older children who have not previously been vaccinated • Sex partners of infected persons • Persons with multiple sex partners • Persons seeking evaluation or treatment for an STD • Men who have sex with men • Injection drug users • Household contacts of infected persons • Health care and public safety workers exposed to blood on the job • Persons with chronic liver disease, including HCV-infected persons with chronic liver disease • Persons with HIV infection • Persons with end-stage renal disease, including predialysis, hemodialysis, peritoneal dialysis, and home dialysis patients • Residents and staff of facilities for developmentally disabled persons • Travelers to regions with intermediate or high rates of hepatitis B (HBsAg prevalence of ≥2%) • Anyone else seeking long-term protection	There is no hepatitis C vaccine.

Source: CDC, 2018; 2019.

SEXUAL WELL-BEING AND INNOVATION IN STI PREVENTION

There is a growing vulnerability among the poor in the United States and in Third World countries caused by the lack of access to health care and awareness about STIs and how to prevent them. There are many ways for societies to improve conditions and control the spread of STIs. All over the world, education is a key to prevention, and when new resources are injected by governments or foundations, the effect can be really dramatic. For example, providing antiretroviral treatment in sub-Saharan Africa has been an incredible achievement and a lifesaver for many, reducing death and disease (Renju, 2017). More than anything, such measures would equip people with the knowledge, skills, and motivation to fight HIV in their own backyards. However, societies do not uniformly provide such support or engage in the fight against HIV. In fact, until recently, one of the countries with the highest rates of HIV, South Africa, suffered from leadership that claimed HIV did not exist. Research has consistently shown that when the leaders of a country actively talk about HIV and publicly stress the importance of sexual literacy regarding HIV and sexual protection, that country does much better at combating the spread of HIV and protecting its people (Lamptey, Johnson, & Khan, 2006; Moran, Butcher, Curtis, & Laurence, 2003).

But research shows that HIV infections are actually increasing in some populations globally and in the United States. This is the result of poverty, poor health care, and lack of education about HIV, as well as high-risk unprotected sexual behavior. Researchers have concluded that poverty exerts a huge negative effect on sexual well-being and human rights. There appears to be a strong correlation between poverty and being sexually exploited, being the victim of gender violence, and being susceptible to sexually transmitted infection (Karim et al., 2010). Paul Farmer (2008), a medical doctor who pioneered health care for the poor in Haiti, has stated that poverty is the worst crime against humanity, and therefore it creates the greatest infringement upon human rights—including sexuality and sexual health. If we are going to end AIDS by 2030, the goal of the UNAIDS and Bill and Melinda Gates Foundations, we are going to need new ideas and new approaches to ending bottlenecks in care and treatment (Renju, 2017).

A powerful example of both the profound effect of poverty on STIs and the power that innovative thought can have on prevention can be found among women in South Africa. For almost 2 years, researchers conducted a study in South Africa that showed the dramatic effect of poverty on sexual choices. Funded by the World Bank, this important study asked what results might occur if someone was paid an allowance to delay having sex in their life.

The study was conducted among 3,800 girls and women, ages 13 to 22, whose families were poor and who were quite vulnerable to HIV/AIDS (Karim et al., 2010).

In the study, the researchers provided one group of girls with a very small cash allowance ($2 or $3 a day or less) to delay having sex. It worked. The girls who received the cash actually delayed having sex. When they did have sex, they had less of it, and they tended to have fewer sexual partners compared to girls who did not receive the allowance.

Furthermore, the researchers found that the greater the allowance, the less likely the girls were to agree to have sex for money. Because they had less sex, they were also less likely to be infected with HIV or the herpes virus compared to girls who did not receive the allowance. The prevalence of HIV was 60% lower among the girls receiving allowances in this study than among those who received no allowance. In short, it appears that money can make a difference in

Volunteers who participated in a study on reducing the risk of HIV infection in women listened as the test results were announced during a meeting in South Africa.
Joao Silva/The New York Times/Redux Pictures

determining whether or not girls from poor families contract HIV and possibly die from AIDS. The girls also experienced less sexual and gender-related violence. Here is the kind of courageous example that can lead to ending AIDS by 2030.

Chapter Review

SUMMARY

Knowing Our Own Body

- Taking responsibility for our own sexual health and well-being means understanding the risks as well as the pleasures of sexual encounters.
- One of the most serious health concerns for women is breast cancer, the fifth leading cause of death for women in the United States. New treatments are helping millions of women successfully fight breast cancer.
- Regular pelvic exams and Pap smears are important screening procedures for women when they turn 21 or begin to engage in sexual intercourse.
- For men, testicular and penile self-exams are a good way to monitor health and look for potential changes that might signal a medical condition.
- Testicular cancer is a common cancer among younger men, typically affecting those between the ages of 15 and 34.
- Prostate cancer is one of the most common cancers in men in the United States and often does not produce any noticeable early symptoms.

Sexually Transmitted Infections

- The United States has the highest rate of STIs of any industrialized nation in the world.
- Every year, approximately 20 million Americans contract an STI.
- A variety of risks and protective factors affect the rate of transmission of STIs.
- When sexual partners discuss STI risk and pertinent sexual history information prior to engaging in sexual acts that might pose a risk for STI transmission, they can take precautions to protect themselves and each other.
- STIs caused by a variety of bacteria, viruses, and parasites can be transmitted through high-risk sexual behaviors, such as unprotected anal, oral, and vaginal intercourse. Using condoms reduces the risk of transmission.
- The human immunodeficiency virus (HIV) is a global pandemic. If left untreated, HIV will eventually develop into AIDS, which is potentially fatal. Recent improvements in medical treatment have enabled many HIV-positive individuals to greatly improve their health and live a long time with this condition. Bacterial STIs, including gonorrhea, chlamydia, and syphilis, are spread primarily via sexual contact. Early diagnosis is important for successful treatment with antibiotics.
- Pelvic inflammatory disease (PID) can result when bacteria move from a woman's cervix or vagina into the upper reproductive organs. It is associated mainly with gonorrhea and chlamydia and can permanently damage the reproductive system unless treated early with antibiotics.
- Parasitic STIs are external infestations by parasites such as scabies and pubic lice and can be spread by sexual contact. Both can be effectively treated with prescription medication, or in the case of pubic lice, with a special over-the-counter shampoo.
- Viral STIs, including the four Hs (HIV, HPV, herpes, and hepatitis), are contracted by high-risk sexual behaviors, such as unprotected intercourse. The symptoms of these STIs can be treated, but they cannot be cured. Vaccines are available to help prevent HPV and hepatitis.

Sexual Well-Being and Innovation in STI Prevention

- Experts suggest that providing equal access to quality health care can make all the difference in protecting sexual well-being.
- Self-protection from STIs is considered by some to be a human right.
- Poverty worldwide has a profound effect on STI risk and transmission, thus putting people at heightened risk.
- Innovative programs like the one funded by the World Bank for women in South Africa can help to decrease STI transmission and increase positive sexual health decision-making by directly focusing on reducing the impact of poverty.

What's Your Position?

1. **How comfortable are you in discussing sex with your care provider?**
   - How assertive are you with your health care practitioners?
   - Do you feel comfortable asking questions when it comes to your own health and well-being?

2. **How comfortable are you with examining your own genitals?**
   - What emotions do you feel when purposely examining yourself?
   - Where do you think those feelings come from?
   - What can you do to increase your own comfort level so that you can engage in self-exams to help protect your own sexual health and well-being?

3. **How do you and your sexual partner(s) talk about having sex and about STI risk?**
   - If you have had a conversation about STIs, how did it go?
   - If you have not had a conversation about STIs, why not?
   - How might you work to overcome potential discomfort with bringing this subject up with partners?
     - How does knowledge of STIs affect your own attitudes toward sexuality?
   - Do you believe it's possible to have an enjoyable sexual life while still taking active measures to protect yourself and your partners against STI transmission?
   - What is one thing you can do to engage in safer sex?

Design elements: Controversies in Sexuality: HBRH/Shutterstock; Research and Sexual Well Being: verity jane smith/Getty Images; Healthy Sexuality: Sergey Furtaev/Shutterstock; Communication Matters: PeopleImages/Getty Images; Know Yourself: Plush Studios/Blend Images LLC; What's Your Position: Luis Molinero/Shutterstock; Healthy Sexuality: A. Minde/PhotoAlto; Did You Know icon: McGraw-Hill Education; Page corner icon: McGraw-Hill Education.

Contraception

fabio cardoso/Getty Images

Contraception: History and Cultural Variations
- Identify methods of contraception that were commonly used in ancient times.
- Describe the political and social controversies surrounding birth control in U.S. history.
- Outline contraceptive history and development in the United States.

Methods of Contraception
- Explain the things to consider when choosing a contraceptive method.
- Identify, describe, and understand the function and effectiveness of contraceptive methods that protect against pregnancy and STIs.
- Identify, describe, and understand the function and effectiveness of contraceptive methods that protect against pregnancy but not STIs.
- Describe the connection between sexual health, positive decision-making, and communication skills.

Contraception and Sexual Well-Being
- Identify new forms of contraception that might be available in the future.

• **Learning**
• **Objectives**

Developing Your Position

1. How do you see the history of contraception in the United States affecting how we think about contraception today?
2. What kind of contraceptive method would best fit your lifestyle, sexual needs, and desires?
3. In what ways do you see contraception and sexual health care changing in the future?

Self, Society, and Culture: Taking Responsibility for Contraception

When you think of contraceptive decisions, do you usually think of men or women? The reality about contraception is that most methods are developed for women to use (the pill, patch, ring, diaphragm, cervical cap, implant, sponge, and so on). Current methods available to men are only condoms and vasectomies. What if there were other options for male birth control? Consider this: Two forms of male hormonal contraceptives, one pill and the other injected, are currently under study. In fact, several products are expected to become commercially available in the future. It is now believed that a male hormonal contraceptive (MHC) in the form of a daily pill could be available on the market. Men may soon have the options of taking a daily pill, applying a patch or gel to the skin, receiving an injection regularly or having an implant placed under the skin every 12 months. Given the possibility of all of this wonderful and ground-breaking technology, there is one question that remains: Will men use these methods? Some say yes; some say only if their partners make them; and others say they would never even consider them.

In this chapter, we will consider not only the available methods of contraception and their effectiveness in preventing pregnancy, but also the history of contraception, cultural variations in the use of contraception, and the role of contraception in sexual well-being.

CONTRACEPTION: HISTORY AND CULTURAL VARIATIONS

Pleasure and danger—these two words come up again and again in discussions of sexuality. Chapter 6 describes some of the risks of engaging in sex, including STIs. Unintended pregnancy and STIs certainly qualify as potential dangers of sexuality. The positive aspects of taking care of the sexual body come into play with respect to preventing pregnancy. Although the practice of preventing pregnancy is as old as human existence, the technology today is becoming more advanced than ever, and yet the culture has lagged in knowing how to handle these advances in contraception. In this section, we consider how contraception differs among cultures and the history of its acceptance in the United States.

Contraception is any method that we use to prevent conception and unintended pregnancy. Additionally, many contraceptive methods prevent the transmission of STIs. Because contraception is used to prevent pregnancy, abortion does not fit the definition of contraception. Read why this is the case in "Healthy Sexuality: Abortion Is Not Contraception."

contraception
Any process or method used to prevent conception or pregnancy. Some contraceptive methods may also prevent the transmission of STIs.

HEALTHY Sexuality

Abortion Is Not Contraception

It may seem obvious but it is important to underline that only after conception has occurred can abortion take place. The purpose of contraception is to *prevent* conception. Abortion is among the biggest and longest-running controversies in all of sexuality in the United States (Joffe, 2006), and it is considered fully in Chapter 8. Abortion is a difficult and personal decision, and none of the groups in the debate over abortion recommend it as a birth control method. Abortion decisions sometimes come into play later in the process of pregnancy, and may result from a true lack of sexual literacy, including the absence of positive resources, such as quality health care, that might have resulted in the use of contraceptives in the first place. Healthy sexuality and sexual well-being depend on understanding these processes.

Cross-Cultural Variations in Contraception

Across cultures and throughout history, humans have used many different methods to prevent pregnancy. For example, Egyptian records dating back to 1850 BCE describe a form of contraception that involved placing a device in a woman's vagina made of crocodile dung and fermented dough. Such an unlikely combination was certainly meant to create a hostile environment for sperm. The Egyptians also placed plugs of gum, honey, and acacia in the vagina. The ancient Romans used a highly acidic concoction of fruit and nuts in the vagina. In fact, they may have been the first society to invent a *barrier method* in which wool was placed over the cervix to stop the movement of sperm to the fallopian tubes. Society and medicine have come a long way in the effort to invent and apply effective contraception since that time.

Throughout history, belief systems surrounding notions of birth, conception, and contraception have varied across cultures (Engelman, 2011; Joffe, 2006; Lewis, 2000; Russell & Thompson, 2000). Let's consider some methods of contraception used in different cultures. Most of these methods are not effective.

1. *Coitus interruptus,* or withdrawal of the penis from the vagina before ejaculation, is a technique practiced in many cultures around the world.
2. *Coitus obstructus* is the general category of putting pressure on the testicles, a method from ancient India, which was thought to cause sperm to be ejaculated into the bladder (Gordon, 1976).
3. *Coitus reservatus* is a method from Hindu medicine in which the male totally avoids ejaculation. In the United States in the 19th century, some groups used this method. For example, some of the Shaker communities, whose members believed in free love and generally opposed marriage, used this method (Passet, 2003).
4. **Douching**, a method of washing out the vagina or washing the penis, has been used since the ancient Greeks. American cookbooks of the 19th century commonly had recipes for douching that often listed cider vinegar as an ingredient.
5. A suppository, object, or elixir placed in the vagina is known as a *pessary*. It either kills or blocks the passage of sperm into the cervix. Widely used since ancient times, pessaries have been made from a range of substances including crocodile dung, as we mentioned earlier, grass, and cloth. Japanese prostitutes perfected balls made from bamboo. Greek and Middle Eastern women used wool or linen (Gordon, 1976). Elixirs made of medicinal plants and substances were also common pessaries in ancient societies (Russell & Thompson, 2000).

douching
A method of washing out the vagina or washing the penis.

217

HEALTHY Sexuality

How Effective Is Breastfeeding as a Contraceptive?

The American Academy of Pediatrics (2011) states that under certain conditions breastfeeding can be effective in preventing pregnancy. Here are the conditions:

Breastfeeding is a reliable form of contraception if you are exclusively breastfeeding, if your menstrual periods have not resumed, and if your baby is less than 6 months old. Once your baby is 6 months old and has begun sampling solid foods, breastfeeding is no longer a reliable form of birth control. If you do not want to become pregnant, you will need to consider what kind of contraception you will use. It's best to consult your gynecologist for advice on which types to use while breastfeeding, but in general, condoms, a diaphragm, a cervical cap, and spermicides are considered the most preferable forms of birth control for a breastfeeding mother because they are least likely to interfere with milk supply. Low-dose birth control pills should not have a significant impact on your milk supply when begun at this age.

condom
Popular barrier contraceptive device worn by either the male or the female.

6. *Sea sponges* were used by the ancient Jews and other peoples to block the sperm from entering the cervix. This method was considered highly effective until the invention of the diaphragm in the late 1800s.

7. **Condoms** are known from 3,000 years ago and have been made from such diverse materials as fish bladders, animal intestines, and cloth. The ancient Egyptians used condoms to protect against disease. Ancient Romans used them as well (Langley, 2000; Lewis, 2000). In the 1500s, people used condoms to prevent the spread of syphilis. Condoms have been produced in the United States since 1840 and have been second in popularity of contraceptive methods only to the fairly ineffective withdrawal method (Engelman, 2011; Gordon, 1976).

8. *Breastfeeding* in many cultures is used as a form of contraception. For example, the !Kung Bushmen of Southern Africa believe that breastfeeding delays conception. In their culture, the space between the birth of siblings is about every 4 years, which tends to support this belief (Shostak, 1991). The Sambia of Papua New Guinea likewise believe that breastfeeding delays pregnancy. Also like other groups, they have a postpartum taboo of sexual activity that lasts for the first 2 years of a child's life as well as during nursing (Herdt, 2006).

See "Healthy Sexuality: How Effective Is Breastfeeding as a Contraceptive?" for a discussion concerning what we currently understand about the effectiveness of this method.

When we look closely at cultural beliefs and practices, we find many variations in contraception. These variations depend greatly on the cultural context in which contraception occurs, as well as on how people of the culture perceive pregnancy and birth. Chapter 8 examines the differences in detail, but we introduce some of them here.

Of all of the different contraceptive methods, tribal societies appear to practice the pessary method most commonly using traditional elixirs. Native American tribes, for example, have employed traditional medicines for thousands of years (Josephy, 1991; Ortiz de Montellayano, 1990; Vogel, 1977). The elixirs they used for contraception were made primarily from local plants, including leaves, bark, berries, and other parts that they boil for teas, which women would drink for contraception. The Potawatomie Indians of the northeastern United States made tea from the plant named Dogbane, a relative of the milkweed that is common in many parts of the Americas and all over the world. Teas made from snakeroot or other substances were strongly believed to protect temporarily against conception. Pennyroyal tea was also believed to induce menstruation and prevent pregnancy, if consumed several times a day. Shoshone Indians of Nevada and Utah used a plant called stoneseed *(Lithospermum ruderale)* as a contraceptive. Scientists confirmed in the 1950s that this plant works as an effective oral contraceptive. Now it is suspected that at least some of these Indian medicines contain substances that function like modern synthetic hormones (Josephy, 1991; Ortiz de Montellayano, 1990; Vogel, 1977).

In addition to understanding how some cultures used contraception, it is interesting to read about the history of contraception in the United States. For an item that many rely on today for family planning and to protect against STIs, contraception has a complicated history.

History of Contraceptives in the United States

Early condoms were made from a variety of materials. The condom pictured here in its case is made of silk.
Science & Society Picture Library/Getty Images

The history of contraceptives in the United States is riddled with political controversy and sexual morality (Beisel, 1997; Engelman, 2011; Joffe, 2006; Langley, 1973; Tone, 2001). In the 19th and early 20th centuries, those who opposed the use of contraceptives passed federal laws making it illegal even to distribute information about them. Some people were brave enough to oppose this law despite the threat of being imprisoned, but believe it or not, that law was not repealed until 1965.

Anthony Comstock (1844–1915), a Connecticut social reformer, was instrumental in the passage of the Comstock Act (1873), officially titled "Act for the Suppression of Trade in, and Circulation of, Obscene Literature and Articles for Immoral Use." Part of this law made it illegal to distribute information about contraception and devices because they were considered immoral and obscene. The Comstock Act passed through Congress with wide support from very powerful individuals, political parties, and religious institutions. Even President Theodore Roosevelt in 1905 attacked birth control and condemned the trend toward smaller families as a sign of "moral disease" (Gordon, 1976).

In contrast to Comstock, Margaret Sanger (1879–1966) believed in free love and sexual rights. A mother of three, an active feminist, and the person generally credited with coining the term *birth control,* Sanger was motivated not only by her compassion for people struggling with issues of contraception, but also by personal experience (Baker, 2011). Her mother had 18 pregnancies in 22 years and was dead by age 45 of cervical cancer and tuberculosis.

Sanger actively campaigned to decriminalize contraception. She decided to fight the contraceptive part of the Comstock Act and advance the sexual literacy of women through contraceptive education, counseling, and clinical services. In 1914, she published *The Woman Rebel,* a periodical that advocated women's rights, including the right to contraception. To avoid arrest, she went to Europe; while there, she observed much more tolerant and humane laws and visited clinics that distributed information about contraception to families. After returning to the United States, she opened the first birth control clinic in 1916. She was arrested and later sentenced to jail, but this short-lived clinic started a movement in favor of birth control, which ultimately allowed doctors to prescribe contraception to patients in 1938.

Other Comstock laws about birth control remained on the books until 1965, when the U.S. Supreme Court ruled them unconstitutional. Since then, contraceptive information and devices have been legally available to anyone seeking them, including minors.

Anthony Comstock was a primary figure in early attempts to limit the use of contraceptive methods in the United States.
Bettmann/Getty Images

Sanger's efforts to remake public policy regarding contraception continued throughout her lifetime. As a pioneer, Margaret Sanger was to create a sense of how her gender and women leaders might shape the contraceptive movement in the United States (McCann, 2010). She lived to see birth control pills become a reality and contraception sanctioned by the U.S. Supreme Court. Consider her contributions to these milestones in the history of contraception (Our Bodies, Ourselves, 2012):

- 1916—Margaret Sanger opens first birth control clinic in the United States. The next year she was arrested, found guilty of "maintaining a public nuisance," and sentenced to jail for 30 days. Once released, she reopened her clinic and continued to persevere through more arrests and prosecutions.
- 1938—In a case involving Margaret Sanger, a judge lifted the part of the Comstock Act that banned distributing birth control information and devices. Diaphragms became a popular method of birth control.
- 1950—While in her 80s, Sanger raised $150,000 for the research necessary to develop the first birth control pill.
- 1960—The first oral contraceptive, Enovid, was approved by the FDA as a form of birth control. It had already been on the market for 2 years and prescribed for menstrual irregularities.
- 1960s—The first intrauterine devices (IUDs) were manufactured and marketed in the United States.
- 1963—The number of women using birth control pills doubled to 2.3 million, and by 1973 they totaled 10 million.
- 1965—The Supreme Court (in *Griswold v. Connecticut*) established the right of married couples to use birth control as protected in the Constitution as a "right to privacy." However, millions of unmarried women in 26 states were still denied birth control.
- Late 1960s—Women challenged the safety of the birth control pill as a result of confirmed health risks associated with it. Successful efforts led by feminist and consumer activist groups, along with hearings in the U.S. Congress, led to its modifications.
- 1972— The Supreme Court (in *Baird v. Eisenstadt*) legalized birth control for all citizens of this country, irrespective of marital status.
- 1975—The Dalkon Shield, a popular IUD, was recalled after charges that it caused infertility in thousands of users. Although other IUD designs were not implicated, all IUDs were then taken off the market under fear of litigation. They are available now after research led to improved safety.
- 1980s and 1990s—Hormonal birth control methods expanded to include the internal condom, implants, and injectables. Low-dose pills were also introduced.
- 1992—Emergency contraception became more widely available as a result of public awareness campaigns.

Today we continue to see a rapid expansion in available methods as well as in improvements in safety and effectiveness of contraceptives. Some newer methods include the hormonal patch, the vaginal ring, injectable hormones, single rod implants, and transcervical female sterilization. More research is needed in woman-controlled methods that also protect against STIs. Also, worldwide, not all women have access to reliable contraception (Our Bodies, Ourselves, 2012).

Activist Margaret Sanger coined the term "birth control," opened the first birth control clinic in Brownsville, Brooklyn, and started the American Birth Control League, the precursor to Planned Parenthood.
Bettmann/Getty Images

Birth Control Myths

Know Yourself

Have you ever felt caught in a whirlwind of misinformation about birth control methods, such as knowing which ones are effective and which ones don't work? To help you understand which ones do not work, let's consider the following statements. Decide whether each statement is true or false.

1. You can't get pregnant if you are breastfeeding.
2. Pregnancy is not possible if a woman doesn't have an orgasm.
3. If a woman douches after sex, she won't get pregnant.
4. A woman is only fertile one day a month, so there's no need for contraception if sex happens only during the "safe time."
5. A woman can't get pregnant if she has sex while on top or standing up.
6. If you don't have a condom, you can use a balloon or plastic wrap.
7. If a man withdraws his penis from the woman's vagina before he ejaculates, neither pregnancy nor an STI is possible.
8. You can't get pregnant when having sex for the first time.
9. You can't get pregnant if you shower, bathe, or urinate right after sex.
10. The birth control pill is effective as soon you begin taking it.

Answers appear on p. 222.

METHODS OF CONTRACEPTION

People often associate sex with reproduction, though it doesn't accurately reflect the role of sexual behavior in many people's lives. In fact, most people engage in sexual activities not to conceive offspring, but to experience sexual pleasure as we discussed in Chapter 5. Many heterosexual couples of childbearing age want to enjoy sex and to prevent unplanned pregnancy. In addition, the prevention of STIs is critical for people in intimate relationships who engage in sexual activity regardless of sexual orientation and age. Thus, contraception is an important concern for most people.

The sad truth is that most sexually active teens, college students, and adults in the United States are not using reliable contraceptive methods, and among those who do use it, most tend to use it inconsistently (Gerrard, 1987; Sheeder, Tocce, & Sturns-Simon, 2009; Welti, Wildsmith, & Manlove, 2011). Equipping yourself with contraceptive knowledge can help you understand which methods are reliable. It can also help you understand why using it consistently helps to prevent both unintended pregnancies and STIs and helps to increase your ability to find pleasure in your sexual encounters.

In this section, we discuss how to choose a contraceptive method. We address some common myths about contraception and provide enough information so that you will feel confident to make important decisions about contraception.

Choosing a Method of Contraception: What to Consider

Knowing the facts about birth control options is as important as knowing what options exist. Read "Know Yourself: Birth Control Myths" to learn about some common myths about contraception.

DID YOU KNOW

The former Soviet Union (now Russia) was committed to being a global superpower, and its domestic policy reflected that in its total lack of support for contraceptives. Many Russian women during the Soviet era had five or more abortions as a functional way to cope with the lack of access to condoms and other forms of contraception (Kon, 1995). Since the fall of the Soviet regime in 1991, abortions have fallen, but the abortion rate in Russia remains very high (Deschner & Cohen, 2003).

Know Yourself

ANSWERS to Birth Control Myths *(p. 221)*

1. False: As we previously noted, breastfeeding tends to postpone ovulation, but breastfeeding alone is not a guarantee, because ovulation can still occur. A nursing mother should use birth control if she does not want to get pregnant.

2. False: Pregnancy occurs when a sperm and an egg unite, regardless of whether a woman has an orgasm during sex.

3. False: Douching is not an effective method of contraception. After ejaculation, the sperm enter the cervix and are out of reach of any douching solution. In addition, douching can irritate the vagina and is not a recommended practice.

4. False: Myths such as this may stem from not fully understanding the menstrual cycle. Certain hormones need to work together for ovulation to occur. While a woman's cycle is more or less regular, various factors can disrupt this delicate balance of hormones, such as age, stress, or medications. Therefore, pinpointing the exact time of ovulation and predicting "safe days" can be difficult.

5. False: Some people falsely believe that having sex in certain positions will force sperm out of the woman's vagina via gravity. Sexual positions have nothing to do with whether or not fertilization occurs. When a man ejaculates into a woman's vagina, the sperm begin to move up through the cervix immediately.

6. False: While the ingenuity of these ideas is interesting, they are not good substitutes for condoms. They do not fit well and can be easily torn during sex. Condoms are made specifically to provide a good fit and therefore good protection during sex.

7. False: Pulling out before a man ejaculates, known as the **withdrawal method,** is not a foolproof method for contraception. Some ejaculate (fluid that may contain sperm, viruses, or bacteria that cause STIs) may be released before a man actually begins to climax. In addition, some men may not have the willpower or be able to withdraw in time.

8. False: A woman can get pregnant any time ovulation occurs, even if it is her first time having sex.

9. False: Washing or urinating after sex will not stop sperm that have already entered the uterus through the cervix.

10. False: In some women, one complete menstrual cycle is needed for the hormones in the pill to work with their naturally produced hormones to prevent ovulation. To make sure you do not get pregnant, use a backup method of contraception during the first month of taking the birth control pill.

Did you previously believe any of these myths? Which ones did you have incorrect information about? Myths about birth control are common, and it is easy to believe something that we hear from media or from peers. It is important to make sure that we use trusted resources when considering any form of contraception to make sure we understand the method fully so we can use it correctly.

Source: Adapted from The National Women's Health Information Center, (2012).

---

withdrawal method
An unreliable method of contraception involving removing the penis from the vagina just prior to ejaculation.

It can be overwhelming to consider all the options for contraception. You might be asking yourself, "How do I choose the best method for me and my partner(s)?" That is the perfect question for this discussion. We encourage you to think about the many issues that may pertain to your life, so that you can decide which method of contraception best fits you. Before making a decision, you may want to consider the following points:

- **Do you one day want to have a child or children?**

    One of your first considerations might be to determine whether you want a temporary or permanent method of birth control. If you know that you will never want to conceive a pregnancy, a **tubal ligation** (for women) or a **vasectomy** (for men) might be a reasonable option to consider. (We explain and illustrate these methods later in the chapter.) If you are not sure about this part of your future, a temporary method is a better choice. If you choose a tubal ligation or a vasectomy because a partner wants it or thinks it may solve money or relationship issues, consider whether you might be setting yourself up for regret or disappointment later in life.

- **What is the effectiveness of different birth control methods?**

  The effectiveness of any given contraceptive method is best evaluated by examining the **failure rate,** which is the number of women out of 100 who will become pregnant within the first year of using a particular method. Every method of contraception has a failure rate. In fact, most contraceptives have two known failure rates: **typical failure rate** and **perfect-use failure rate.** Typical failure rate is the typical number of people who become pregnant accidentally with a particular method, while the perfect-use failure rate is the failure rate of a contraceptive method that is used regularly and correctly.

  Hormonal injections are highly effective methods because fewer than 3 of 100 women using these methods become pregnant in a year (Trussell, 2004). Barrier methods are only moderately successful in preventing pregnancy. See Figure 7.1 to learn more about contraceptive effectiveness.

  Human error is the most important variable when evaluating effectiveness. In fact, one startling finding is that approximately half of all unintended pregnancies occur among women who use contraception (Speroff & Fritz, 2005). But when individuals do not understand a particular method or feel negative about it, they tend to use contraception ineffectively. Other issues that influence the effectiveness of available contraception include the user's motivation, lack of partner involvement, forgetfulness, accessibility, and the inability to follow directions. Individuals should consider these issues as well as effectiveness ratings when deciding on a particular method.

- **The prevention of STI transmission.** As we saw in previous chapters, protecting oneself from STIs is a critical step in sexual literacy, one not to be forgotten in efforts to prevent pregnancy. Many people often focus on the prevention of pregnancy and may leave themselves at risk for an STI. Unless you are really sure that your partner has no other sex partners and is free from STIs, you are at risk for contracting an STI. If you are at risk, protecting yourself from an STI means using a condom in addition to any method of contraception every time you have sex. You can choose between an external or internal condom to reduce your risk for STIs.

- **Your own health.** If you have health problems or other risk factors, some contraceptive methods may not be right for you. One such risk factor is smoking. If you smoke more than 15 cigarettes a day and are 35 or older or if you have a history of high blood pressure, stroke, blood clots, liver disease, or heart disease, you may not want to consider combined hormonal methods. If you have latex allergies, latex condoms or other latex barrier methods may not be an option. In addition, if a woman is breastfeeding, the estrogen found in combined hormonal methods is known to lower the milk supply. Progestin-only pills, IUDs, or injections do not affect milk supply and may be a good option.

- **Your comfort level.** It is important to be honest with yourself, particularly if you are a woman. Do you feel comfortable touching your body? There are many contraceptive methods that require you to insert and remove them from your vagina. Women who are uncomfortable touching their bodies in this way need to gauge whether these methods would work for them.

- **Your own sexual behavior.** Understanding your own sexual behavior is important because most contraceptives will not protect you against STIs or HIV. In a committed

tubal ligation
A form of permanent, surgical contraception in which the fallopian tubes are tied, cut, or blocked to prevent egg and sperm from uniting.

vasectomy
A form of permanent, surgical contraception where sperm are prevented from mixing with semen in ejaculate by cutting or tying off the vas deferens.

failure rate
The number of women out of 100 who will become pregnant within the first year of using a particular method.

typical failure rate
The typical number of people who become pregnant accidentally utilizing a particular method.

perfect-use failure rate
The failure rate of a contraceptive method used by people who utilize it regularly and correctly.

Comparing Effectiveness of Family Planning Methods

More effective
Less than 1 pregnancy per 100 women in 1 year

- Implants
- IUD
- Female sterilization
- Vasectomy

How to make your method more effective

Implants, IUD, female sterilization: After procedure, little or nothing to do or remember

Vasectomy: Use another method for first 3 months

- Injectables
- Regular breastfeeding
- Pills
- Patch
- Vaginal ring

Injectables: Get repeat injections on time

Regular breastfeeding (for 6 months): Breastfeed often, day and night

Pills: Take a pill each day

Patch, ring: Keep in place, change on time

- External condoms
- Diaphragm
- Internal condoms
- Fertility awareness methods

Condoms, diaphragm: Use correctly every time you have sex

Fertility awareness methods: Abstain or use condoms on fertile days. Newest methods (Standard Days Method and TwoDay Method) may be easier to use.

Less effective
About 30 pregnancies per 100 women in 1 year

- Withdrawal
- Spermicides

Withdrawal, spermicides: Use correctly every time you have sex

Figure 7.1 The effectiveness of different contraception methods varies from most effective (highest in the figure) to the least effective (lowest in the figure).

Sources: Steiner, M. J., Trussell, J., Mehta, N., Condon, S., Subramaniam, S., & Bourne, D. (2006). Communicating contraceptive effectiveness: A randomized controlled trial to inform a World Health Organization family planning handbook. *Am J Obstet Gynecol*, 195(1), 85–91; World Health Organization/Department of Reproductive Health and Research (WHO/RHR), Johns Hopkins Bloomberg School of Public Health (JHSPH)/Center for Communication Programs (CCP). (2007). *Family planning: A global handbook for providers*. Baltimore, MD, and Geneva: CCP and WHO; Trussell, J. Choosing a contraceptive: Efficacy, safety, and personal considerations. In R. A. Hatcher, J. Trussell, F. Stewart, A. L. Nelson, W. Cates Jr., F. Guest, & D. Kowal (Eds.), *Contraceptive Technology* (19th Rev. ed.). New York: Ardent Media, Inc.

heterosexual relationship, you may want to use a method that prevents pregnancy but does not prevent STIs. In a same-sex committed relationship, you may not need to consider any method. If you are not in a committed relationship, however, and have multiple sexual partners, you will want to consider methods that prevent pregnancy or that prevent STIs, or both. Condoms typically offer the greatest protection from contracting many potential infections. When they are used with spermicides, they offer additional protection from unintended pregnancy.

As we've seen, there are many things to consider in choosing a contraception method. Table 7.1 summarizes the different types according to their ability to prevent STIs and pregnancy, the method's effectiveness, cost, and the pros and cons of each. Being able to talk with a partner about which method to use is a key part of the decision-making process. For some tips about how to have this conversation, see "Communication Matters: Discussing Contraception With Your Partner."

Table 7.1 Overview of contraceptive methods

METHOD	ACTION REQUIRED	TYPICAL FAILURE RATE (%)*	PERFECT-USE FAILURE RATE (%)**	COST***	PROS	CONS AND POTENTIAL SIDE EFFECTS
No method (intercourse without contraception)	n/a	85	85	Average cost of full-term pregnancy delivered vaginally in the United States: $1,500–$4,000 (with insurance); $5,000–$10,000 (without insurance)	Best method if trying to conceive	No protection against pregnancy or STIs; high probability of pregnancy or transmission of STIs
METHODS THAT PROTECT AGAINST PREGNANCY AND STIs							
Abstinence	No sexual behavior or behaviors that can transmit STIs or cause pregnancy	Not known	0	Free	No cost; no risk of pregnancy; protection from STI transmission with committed, consistent use	Requires self-discipline; partner agreement; strong commitment; risk of unprotected intercourse if commitment wanes
Fluid-free sexual behaviors	Sexual behaviors that do not allow for the possibility of exchanging bodily fluids	Not known	0	Free	No cost; no risk of pregnancy; protection from STI transmission with committed, consistent use	Requires self-discipline; partner agreement; strong commitment; risk of unprotected intercourse if commitment wanes
Barrier Methods							
External Condom	Placed on erect penis. Must use for every act of intercourse	12	3	$0.50–$1.00 each	Accessible, portable, inexpensive; usable with many other methods; help protect against transmission of STIs and pelvic inflammatory disease (PID)	Possible reduced male sensitivity; possible interruption of sexual "moment"; latex may cause irritation (less likely with polyurethane condoms). May not protect against scabies or pubic lice as condom doesn't cover all areas where parasites exist
Internal Condom	Vaginal insertion of condom. Must use for every act of intercourse	21	5	$2.50–$3.00 each	Does not require male involvement in decision; may be inserted up to 8 hours before intercourse	Potentially less interruption in sexual activity; some irritation and allergic reactions reported; can be noisy and distracting during intercourse; may be a "turn-off" to some partners
METHODS THAT PROTECT AGAINST PREGNANCY BUT NOT STIs							
Cervical Barrier Methods							
Diaphragm with spermicide	Vaginal insertion. Must use for every act of intercourse	20	6	$50–$150 including medical visit and fitting	Does not require male involvement in decision; need not interrupt intercourse (may be inserted up to 6 hours in advance); may protect against cervical abnormalities and cancer	Possible skin irritation from spermicide or latex; may cause increased risk of female urinary tract infections; additional spermicide must be used for repeated intercourse

(continued)

Table 7.1 (continued)

METHOD	ACTION REQUIRED	TYPICAL FAILURE RATE (%)*	PERFECT-USE FAILURE RATE (%)**	COST***	PROS	CONS AND POTENTIAL SIDE EFFECTS
Cervical Barrier Methods (continued)						
Cervical cap with spermicide Women who have never given birth Women who have previously given birth	Vaginal insertion Must use for every act of intercourse	 18 36	 9 26	$50–$150 including medical visit and fitting	Does not require male involvement in decision; need not interrupt intercourse; protects for 48 hours	Low effectiveness; increase risk of urinary tract infections; should not be used during menstruation or left in place longer than 48 hours to avoid possible toxic shock syndrome; possible skin irritation from spermicide or latex; low effectiveness for women who have previously given birth
Lea's Shield	Vaginal insertion Must use for every act of intercourse	20	6 with spermicide; 15 without	Approx. $65; no medical visit or fitting necessary	No fitting or prescription needed; one-size-fits-all; allows cervical secretions to escape through one-way valve; may be left in place for 48 hours; no interruption of sexual activities; silicone construction avoids latex reactions; additional spermicide not required for repeated intercourse	Must be used with spermicide for full protection; relatively expensive; must be replaced every 6 months; not recommended for women with abnormal cervical cells in Pap test
Contraceptive sponges Women who have never given birth Women who have previously given birth	Vaginal insertion Must use for every act of intercourse	 20 40	 9 20	$2.50–$3.00 each	Controlled by woman; can be inserted ahead of time; provides 24 hours of protection	Possible temporary skin irritation due to spermicide; low effectiveness for women who have previously given birth
Vaginal spermicides	Vaginal insertion Must use for every act of intercourse	21	6	$0.50–$1.50 per use	Simple to use; available over the counter; provides increased effectiveness when used with other methods; provides extra lubrication for intercourse	Possible temporary skin irritation due to spermicides
Hormonal Methods						
Combination pills (estrogen and progestin)	Oral medication for women Must take daily at the same time	2	0.1	$100–$300 per year	Very effective when taken consistently and correctly; reversible; safe for most healthy women under 35; decrease in menstrual cramps and pain; regulates periods; may reduce premenstrual symptoms; acne improvement; may	Some forms may be associated with missed periods; possible breakthrough bleeding or spotting between periods; weight gain; increased breast size; nausea; headaches; depression; possible rare complications of cardiovascular disease;

Table 7.1 *(continued)*

METHOD	ACTION REQUIRED	TYPICAL FAILURE RATE (%)*	PERFECT-USE FAILURE RATE (%)**	COST***	PROS	CONS AND POTENTIAL SIDE EFFECTS
Hormonal Methods *(continued)*						
					decrease risk of developing ovarian cancer, endometrial cancer, ectopic pregnancy, PID	most minor side effects decrease after first couple of months of use. Not recommended for women over 35 who smoke as it increases potential for fatal blood clots
Minipills (progestin-only)	Oral medication for women. Must take daily at the same time	2	0.5	$100–$300 per year	Fewer health risks overall than combination pills; reversible; decreased menstrual cramps or pain; less heavy bleeding; shorter periods; decreased PMS symptoms and breast tenderness; breastfeeding women can use them	Similar cons and side effects as combination pills
90-day pills (Seasonale)	Oral medication for women. Must take daily at the same time	2	0.1	$300–$400 per year	Four periods per year instead of 12; fewer menstruation-related problems including migraine headaches, cramping, mood swings, bloating; may reduce uterine fibroids and endometriosis symptoms	Similar cons and side effects as combined hormone pills
Implants	Subdermal implant—usually placed in the upper arm. Must be replaced every 3–5 years	0.05	0.05	Approx. $190–$270 per year of protection	Long-term, effective contraception; reversible; light or no periods; decreased menstrual cramps and pain; decreased risk of developing endometrial cancer, ovarian cancer, and PID	Higher initial costs; headaches; menstrual irregularities (breakthrough bleeding or cessation of periods); breast tenderness; rare cases of prolonged periods
Injectable (Depo-Provera)	Injection. Must be repeated every 3 months	0.3	0.3	Approx. $65 per injection (four needed per year)	Very high contraceptive efficacy; each injection provides 3 months of contraception; light or no periods; decreased menstrual cramps and pain; decreased risk of developing endometrial cancer, ovarian cancer, and PID	Return of fertility may take up to a year; discomfort of injections for some; return visits every 3 months; menstrual irregularities (breakthrough bleeding or cessation of periods); significant weight gain; breast tenderness; possible loss of bone mass (recovers when discontinued); cannot use for extended periods of time
Contraceptive patch (Ortho Evra)	Transdermal patch is placed on the skin of	1.0–2.0	1.0	Approx. $60–$80 per three-pack (one pack needed per month)	Continuous, consistent dose of hormones; one patch per week eliminates need to	Breast tenderness and enlargement; headache; nausea; spotting

(continued)

Table 7.1 (continued)

METHOD	ACTION REQUIRED	TYPICAL FAILURE RATE (%)*	PERFECT-USE FAILURE RATE (%)**	COST***	PROS	CONS AND POTENTIAL SIDE EFFECTS
Hormonal Methods (continued)						
	the buttocks, thighs, or abdomen for 1 week before changing Removed completely for the week 4				remember daily pill; no interruption of sexual activity; helps regulate periods; less abdominal side effects than pill (hormones do not pass through digestive tract)	or breakthrough bleeding; abdominal cramps and bloating; vaginal discharge; may expose women to level of hormones 60% higher than most oral contraceptives; serious risks include blood clots, stroke, or heart attack especially for women over 35 who smoke; may not be as effective for overweight women
Contraceptive ring (NuvaRing)	Vaginal insertion of ring that is left in place for 3 weeks and removed for week 4	1.5	0.7	Approx. $30 per ring (one per month)	Convenient once-a-month insertion; no medical fitting required; no interruption in sexual activity; lowest dose of hormones due to release directly into mucous membranes	Headaches; vaginal irritation and discharge; may slip out during sexual intercourse (rare); weight gain; headache; nausea; serious risks include blood clots, stroke, or heart attack especially for women over 35 who smoke
Emergency contraceptive pills (Ella, Plan B, My Way, Take Action)	One pill taken within 72 hours after unprotected intercourse; Ella can be taken up to 5 days (120 hours) after unprotected sex	5–25****	5 ****	$15–$70 depending on which type of emergency contraception is used.	Provides protection from pregnancy after unprotected intercourse or failure of primary method; highly effective in reducing risk of pregnancy after unprotected intercourse; provides backup method for emergency situations; most effective when taken as closely to episode of unprotected intercourse as possible	Should not be used if woman is already pregnant; nausea; vomiting; lower abdominal pain; fatigue; headache; dizziness; breast tenderness; and menstrual timing changes in month of use (side effects may last several days)
Intrauterine Devices (IUDs)						
Progestin IUDs (Mirena, Kyleena, Liletta, and Skyla)	Intrauterine device placed by a physician Can be left in place from 3–10 years depending on the type	2.0	1.5	$300–$500 insertion cost; $40–$80 per month over 5 years continuous use	Highly effective; safe; long-acting; hassle-free	Increased risk of PID; may cause menstrual problems; more risk for women who have never had children; requires trained personnel for insertion and withdrawal
Copper (Paragard T380A)		0.8	0.6			
Progestin IUDs (Mirena, Kyleena, Liletta, and Skyla)		0.1	0.1			
Surgical Methods						
sterilization (tubal ligation)	Surgical procedure	0.4	0.4	$1,500–$2,500	Highly effective; permanent; cost effective over time	Surgical procedure; expensive at time of surgery; permanent; reversibility difficult

Table 7.1 (continued)

METHOD	ACTION REQUIRED	TYPICAL FAILURE RATE (%)*	PERFECT-USE FAILURE RATE (%)**	COST***	PROS	CONS AND POTENTIAL SIDE EFFECTS
Surgical Methods *(continued)*						
						and expensive; usual risks that accompany surgery (anesthesia, hemorrhage, organ damage)
sterilization (vasectomy)	Surgical procedure	0.15	0.10	$500–$1,000	Highly effective; inexpensive in the long run; very safe; considered permanent, but successful reversals are common	Permanent; minor surgical procedure; expensive at time of surgery
FERTILITY AWARENESS METHODS						
Calendar ("rhythm")	Calendar-based; tracks a woman's menstrual cycle to predict when ovulation occurs and when to avoid intercourse to reduce the likelihood of pregnancy; requires daily action	20	9	Either no cost or one-time thermometer purchase, $5–$80; ovulation prediction kit, $20–$50	Inexpensive; may be effective when used perfectly; no serious side effects; increases knowledge of reproductive physiology; enhances self-reliance	Requires careful record keeping; unforgiving of imperfect use; irregular menstrual cycles makes use more difficult
Cervical mucus	Monitor changes in mucus; requires daily action	9	3			
Basal body temperature	Monitor changes in body temperature; requires daily action	20	9			
Postovulation	Engage in intercourse only after ovulation has occurred; must monitor ovulation with a fertility monitor or other method (i.e., cervical mucus method)	20	1			

* Percent of people who become pregnant using this method.
** Percent of people who become pregnant while using this method correctly and consistently.
*** Many costs are significantly lower (or zero) at public health clinics and campus health services.
**** Reduces chance of pregnancy by 75 percent in women who use early contraceptive pills following unprotected intercourse during the two midcycle weeks when ovulation is most common.

Source: Office on Women's Health (2017); Peragallo Urrutia, Polis, Jensen, Greene, Kennedy, & Stanford (2018); Trussell, Aiken, Micks, & Guthrie (2018).

COMMUNICATION Matters

Discussing Contraception With Your Partner

Contraceptive discussions can be just plain uncomfortable to have. They can be so anxiety-provoking that the mere thought of bringing up the topic can cause a multitude of unpleasant physical and mental symptoms. It is incredibly important, though, to discuss contraception with your sex partners.

After you have fully evaluated all the contraceptive options, it is time to talk with your partner about what you are considering. It is important that people in sexual relationships discuss and make contraceptive decisions together because when both people are informed and invested in a particular method, they tend to use it more effectively (Tschann & Adler, 1997). If you feel that you cannot discuss contraception, STIs, and sexual histories with your partner, you may want to reevaluate whether or not you are ready to engage in a sexual relationship with this person.

When you are ready to converse about contraception with your partner, these tips may help make the discussion productive and less anxiety-provoking.

1. **Prepare yourself ahead of time.** By reading this chapter, you are already completing this step. Understanding the available methods of contraception is an important first step in communication. Try to figure out which method is best for you as it will be easier to have this discussion if you feel informed and confident in your decision.

2. **Familiarize yourself with what the contraceptive looks like.** If you have already chosen a method and have access to it (such as an internal condom), it may help to ease fears and embarrassment if you are familiar with how the method looks and feels.

3. **Plan a time and place that is comfortable for both of you.** Don't have this conversation in text messages or in a lecture hall while waiting for class to begin. Pick a time and place to ensure that you will have privacy and plenty of time. Consider taking a walk, where you both can enjoy some physical contact like holding hands, which can provide some comfort. In addition, by walking side-by-side you reduce direct eye contact, which can make the conversation less stressful.

4. **Discuss sexual histories and your relationship.** In any sexual relationship, both partners have a right to know if they could potentially be exposed to an STI. Discuss your sexual histories and whether either of you has been exposed to an STI. In addition, discussing exclusivity in a relationship is important. Will you have sex with others or will you be monogamous? As you've read, your type of relationship may dictate the kind of contraception to use because some are more effective in protecting against STIs than others.

5. **Talk about pleasure.** Using a contraceptive method doesn't necessarily mean that the sexual pleasure you experience will be reduced. You can explain to your partner that when you both feel adequately protected, sex between you will be more relaxed and pleasurable. You can even discuss ways to include contraception in your sexual interaction. For example, putting on condoms during foreplay can be fun and exciting when both partners are involved.

6. **Talk about the "what ifs."** If you are in a heterosexual relationship, you certainly should discuss what will happen if the contraceptive method fails and an unintended pregnancy occurs. You both need to be clear on what will happen in the event a contraceptive fails.

7. **Discuss the different contraceptive options.** Share the information you have gathered about particular methods and discuss the ease of use, effectiveness, and pros and cons of each method. Try to agree on a method that suits you both.

8. **Agree to disagree . . . for awhile.** If you cannot come to an agreement right away, promise to do further research and set a time and place to discuss what else you found to make a decision. It really is valuable if both of you agree.

9. **Make it clear you will not have sex without contraception.** Sexual literacy involves making choices that promote your own sexual health and that of your partner. Talking about contraception and then using it shows that you value your health and the health and sexual well-being of your partner. If your partner shows an unwillingness to discuss or use contraception, you need to be clear that you will not have sex until you've both discussed it and have made a decision. You can tell your partner that you do not want to have sex with someone who does not respect you or himself or herself enough to use contraception.

Source: Adapted from Stacey, D. (2009). How to talk to your partner about birth control and sex. *About.com Contraception.* Copyright © 2012 Dawn Stacey. Used with permission. Retrieved January 24, 2012, from http://contraception.about.com/od/talkingaboutbirthcontrol/ht/TalktoPartner.htm

Methods That Protect Against Pregnancy and STIs

For many individuals, contraception needs to protect against both unplanned pregnancy and STIs. It is important to remember that unless you know for sure that your partner has no other sexual partners and is free from STIs, you are at risk for an infection. To protect yourself completely from that possibility, using one of the following methods described is highly advisable.

Abstinence and Fluid-Free Sexual Behaviors Completely refraining from sexual intercourse in order to prevent pregnancy is called **continuous abstinence.** Religious groups, among others, endorse this method, particularly for unmarried individuals. It is 100% effective in preventing pregnancy and STIs and causes no hormonal side effects. There is no cost to abstinence, but it may be difficult for some couples to maintain.

As we discuss throughout this book, though, sexuality involves much more than intercourse. People may choose to express physical intimacy in many ways without engaging in intercourse. **Selective abstinence** means engaging in sexual behaviors that will not cause pregnancy or transmission of STIs and that do not involve vaginal, anal, or oral intercourse. These kinds of behaviors can include deep kissing, touching, and mutual masturbation with a partner. Adolescents and teenagers often engage in these behaviors as they are experimenting and engaging in their own sexual discovery. Due to the fact that these behaviors are quite arousing and inhibitions can be lowered when in a heightened state of sexual arousal, it is important to talk about contraceptive measures with young people as they increase their sexual involvement with partners. For a discussion about the issue of providing contraceptives to minors without parental knowledge, see "Controversies in Sexuality: Access to Contraception and Abortion Services for Adolescents."

One type of selective abstinence, **fluid-free sexual behavior,** means engaging in sexual behaviors that avoid the sharing or mixing of bodily fluids. In other words, fluid-free sexual behavior excludes unprotected vaginal, anal, or oral intercourse. People who think of sexual behavior in terms of intercourse alone may want to expand their view to include a variety of methods of sexual expression and pleasure that provide intense feelings of satisfaction and intimacy without any risk of pregnancy or STIs (Hatcher et al., 2008). Fluid-free sexual behaviors include activities such as mutual masturbation or pleasuring one another with toys (as long as they are not shared).

It can be very difficult to rely on either continuous or selective abstinence as methods of contraception because passion can cloud a person's judgment. Therefore, use of these methods takes a strong commitment combined with clear communication between partners.

Barrier Methods Barrier methods generally work by preventing sperm from reaching an egg in the female reproductive tract. It is important to understand that condoms are the only barrier method that protects against STIs, including HIV.

External Condom. The **external condom** is a thin sheath made of latex, natural animal membrane, polyurethane, silicone, or other material that fits over the erect penis. During ejaculation, the condom catches semen and prevents it from entering the vagina, cervix, anus, or mouth. Latex and polyurethane condoms will protect against STIs, including HIV.

Condoms come rolled up in a package and are either lubricated or nonlubricated. Lubricated condoms are less likely to break. The rolled-up condom is placed at the tip of the erect penis. A small pouch at the tip of the condom will hold ejaculated semen. To use correctly, grasp it with one hand and unroll it over the erect penis with the other. Figure 7.2 illustrates how to use one. Immediately after ejaculation, grasp the condom at the base of the penis before withdrawal to avoid leakage. Use a new condom every time an act of sexual intercourse occurs.

continuous abstinence
A form of contraception that involves completely refraining from sexual intercourse.

selective abstinence
A form of contraception in which individuals avoid certain sexual behaviors that could lead to pregnancy or the transmission of STIs, such as vaginal, anal, or oral intercourse.

fluid-free sexual behavior
Sexual behaviors that avoid the sharing or mixing of bodily fluids, including unprotected vaginal, anal, or oral intercourse.

external condom
A thin sheath made of latex, natural animal membrane, polyurethane, silicone, or other synthetic material that fits over the erect penis prior to intercourse.

CONTROVERSIES in Sexuality

Access to Contraception and Abortion Services for Adolescents

The question of whether contraception should be freely available to adolescents without parental consent has been a hot topic for years for parents, teachers, health practitioners, and health educators. In fact, many states allow adolescents to acquire contraceptive care without parental consent. However, many states do not allow minor adolescents to undergo an abortion without the consent of a parent or legal guardian. It appears that even though many lawmakers agree that minors should have privacy for contraceptive care, they want parents involved in an adolescent's decision about abortion. The question we consider, then, is this:

Should minor adolescents have access to contraceptive and abortion services without parental consent?

YES:

- Allowing minor teenagers access to contraception may help decrease the number of unintended pregnancies that occur every year in the United States.
- Granting access to contraception allows teens to be proactive in their sexual health and can have the effect of preventing abortions.
  - Minors may not seek health services if they are required to inform their parents (Dailard & Richardson, 2005).
  - Allowing minor teenagers the right to have an abortion without parental consent may mean they can have an abortion earlier in the pregnancy, which poses less serious risks to their reproductive health, for two reasons:
    - They may detect pregnancy earlier than they currently do.
- They may face fewer legal obstacles earlier in the pregnancy.
- Forcing minor teens to inform parents that they are seeking an abortion may place some at risk of physical violence or abuse (Dailard & Richardson, 2005).

NO:

- Teens with access to birth control think they have a ticket for sexual freedom.
- Many parents believe that they need to retain the legal authority to make medical decisions for their minor teens because teens often lack the maturity and judgment to make fully informed decisions (Dailard & Richardson, 2005).
- Laws requiring parental consent or knowledge reduce abortion and pregnancy rates among teenagers for two reasons:
  - If parents are able to guide their pregnant teens, more would choose childbirth (and potentially adoption) over abortion.
  - Teenagers who have to inform parents about a pregnancy to obtain an abortion will think twice before having sex in the first place (Dailard & Richardson, 2005).

What Is Your Perspective?

1. Do you believe that teenagers should have access to contraceptive care without parental consent? What about access to abortion services?
2. Do you believe that granting teenagers confidential contraceptive and reproductive care encourages sexual activity and promiscuity?
3. How might we strike a balance between parents' desires to be involved in their minor teen's health care while ensuring safe options for sexual health care for them?

Condoms are widely available in the United States without prescription. Unused condoms have a life span of about 5 years if they are stored in a cool, dry place. Latex condoms should not be stored in hot places such as a car glove box or a wallet because heat can cause a latex condom to deteriorate over time. Check for expiration dates on condoms; if they have expired, throw them away and get fresh ones. In addition, do not use oil-based lubricants with condoms. For a discussion of different types of lubricants, see "Healthy Sexuality: Lubricants for Sex."

① Carefully tear open the foil

② Pinch tip of condom to remove any air

③ Fit condom on before anal, vaginal, or oral penetration

④ Roll on condom down to the base

⑤ After ejaculation remove condom

⑥ Tie off condom and dispose of in bin

Figure 7.2
How to put on an external condom effectively.

WHAT'S ON YOUR MIND?

Q: In my shopping and looking for condoms, I have never come across a formal size chart. I have been told that I am "endowed" and that I need to look for larger sized models, but I don't ever see a size chart. How big is big? Do you know of a size chart?

ANSWER: There does seem to be a lack of information about the sizes of condoms, but don't fear, you too can find a condom that fits. Consider this chart about different sizes of condoms available:

Size of Condom	CLOSE FIT*	STANDARD*	LARGER*
Length of condom (inches)	7 to 7.8	7.25 to 7.8	7.25 to 8.1
Diameter of condom	1.75	1.75 to 2	2 to 2.25

*Every condom manufacturer has different labels for the sizes they provide. The important thing is to use their size charts and your measurements to find the most appropriate fit.

To find out where you fall along the size continuum, you can measure your erect penis. Or for even more fun, have a partner do it! Measure the length from the tip of the head along the upper side of the shaft to the point where the penis joins the body. For girth, measure the penis circumference at the widest point using a tape measure. With this information, you'll find a condom that fits well, that will protect you and your partner, and that will allow you to enjoy all the pleasures of sex. Enjoy and good luck.

HEALTHY Sexuality

Lubricants for Sex

Lubricants are used in sexual activity for a variety of reasons. They can increase pleasure when used with sex toys or when a little extra lubrication is warranted (e.g., when a woman's vagina is a little too dry). However, knowing what kinds of lubricant are available is important because some can be used with contraceptive devices such as condoms and others cannot. Virtually all lubricants on the market today fall into one of three categories:

1. Water-based
2. Silicone-based
3. Oil-based

Water-based lubricants are just that: water-based. They tend to be fairly thin and are easily removed from the skin with a little water and soap. Because they are water-based, they tend to be absorbed into the skin and mucous membranes easily, and if intimate behavior continues for a significant time, reapplication may be necessary. The main advantage of water-based lubricants is that they are completely compatible with condoms.

Silicone-based lubricants are similar to water-based lubricants, but they are generally a lot greasier and last much longer than water-based products. Their main advantage is that there is virtually no need for reapplication because they do not dry out as quickly as a water-based lubricant. The main disadvantage is that the cleanup takes more time because they are water resistant.

Oil-based lubricants should be considered only for sexual activities of a solo nature, for which penetration or use with a condom is not a consideration. Oil-based lubricants corrode latex so they should not be used with condoms. In addition, they are bad for vaginal health in a variety of ways and so should not be used in intercourse with a woman. Finally, they tend to be very slimy, messy, and difficult to clean up.

Adapted from Hauck, T. (n.d.). Lubricants for sex. *AskMen.com*. Retrieved June 9, 2012, from http://www.askmen.com/feeder/askmenRSS_article_print_2006.php?ID=910171

---

internal condom
A thin sheath made of latex or polyurethane that is worn internally by a woman during intercourse.

Internal condom. The **internal condom,** like the external condom, is made of latex or polyurethane. It resembles the external condom in appearance, but it is worn internally within the vagina (Figure 7.3). It is a sheath with a closed flexible ring on one end and an open-ended ring on the other. Internal condoms are coated inside and out with a silicone-based lubricant. During ejaculation, the condom prevents semen from entering the vagina and cervix.

To use an internal condom, insert the closed end into the vagina and position against the cervix much like a diaphragm. The open end lies outside of the vaginal opening. The internal condom fits the contours of the vagina, allowing the penis to move freely inside the sheath.

Figure 7.3
How to insert an internal condom.

Internal condoms can be inserted up to 8 hours before intercourse and should be removed and thrown away immediately after intercourse. An internal condom should not be used with an external condom because the two materials can adhere to one another and cause slippage or breakage to one or both devices. Used correctly, internal condoms can substantially reduce the risk of pregnancy and STIs.

Methods That Protect Against Pregnancy But Not Against STIs

For individuals who are in monogamous or committed relationships, who have a clear understanding of their partner's sexual history, and who are certain they are free from any STIs, the main contraceptive concern may be to prevent pregnancy. A variety of methods are available for this situation. These include cervical barrier methods, vaginal spermicides, hormonal methods, intrauterine methods, surgical methods, and fertility awareness.

Cervical Barrier Methods Cervical barrier contraception methods use an object in combination with a vaginal spermicide to cover the opening to the cervix to prevent sperm from joining an egg. In the United States, four types of cervical barriers are available: diaphragm, cervical cap, Lea's Shield, and FemCap (Figure 7.4). These devices are dome-shaped, with a rim around the open side. The diaphragm covers the upper vaginal wall from behind the cervix to underneath the pubic bone. The cervical cap is smaller and fits over the cervix only (Figure 7.5). FemCap and Lea's Shield have rims that rest on the vaginal wall surrounding the cervix and have removal straps. Unlike the other devices, Lea's Shield allows a one-way flow of fluid from the cervix to the vagina but prevents semen from contact with the cervix. A physician must fit individuals with the diaphragm and cervical cap. FemCap and Lea's Shield do not need to be fitted but require a prescription in the United States.

To use any one of these devices, first place spermicide on the side that goes against the cervix. Then squeeze the sides of the rim together with one hand. While using the other hand to open the lips of the vulva, push the device into the vagina, spermicide side up. After it has been inserted, check to ensure that the dome covers the cervix. Leave the device in the vagina for at least 8 hours after intercourse to allow time for the spermicide to kill sperm. If intercourse happens again before 8 hours lapses, leave the device in place and apply additional spermicide inside the vagina. Recommendations for the length of time to insert it before intercourse and to remove it after intercourse vary by method. See Table 7.2 for these recommendations.

Caring for the cervical barrier methods after removal is fairly simple. Wash them clean with mild soap and warm water. The diaphragm and cervical cap can last for several years. Check them regularly for possible holes. Also have your physician regularly evaluate the fit. If you gain more than 10 pounds or experience a pregnancy, you need to be refitted for a new device. FemCap and Lea's Shield are usable for up to 1 year before they need to be replaced.

Figure **7.4** Types of cervical barrier methods of contraception in use in the United States (from left to right): diaphragm, cervical cap, and FemCap.
(*left and right*) Jill Braaten/McGraw-Hill Education; (*center*) Science & Society Picture Library/SSPL/Getty Images

Figure 7.5
Properly placed, the cervical cap fits over the opening of the cervix.

spermicides
Substances that kill sperm cells. They can be used alone or together with a barrier method of contraception.

oral contraceptives
Pills containing female hormones that are taken every day by women to prevent pregnancy; also known as birth control pills.

Vaginal Spermicides Spermicides are creams, foams, gels, suppositories, and films that contain a chemical that is lethal to sperm. They can be used alone or together with another barrier method. Creams, foams, and gels are placed high up in the vagina, near the cervix, with a plastic applicator. Spermicidal suppositories and films inserted into the vagina take approximately 15 to 20 minutes to dissolve and become effective. Spermicides can be applied up to 1 hour before intercourse and must be reapplied with every act of intercourse. With spermicides, women should not rinse the vagina or douche for at least 6 hours after intercourse.

While spermicides can be used alone, they are most effective when used with barrier methods. Spermicides do not protect against STIs. For example, the widely known spermicides containing nonoxynol-9 do not protect against infection with HIV and may in fact increase risk if used frequently (WHO, 2019). If used frequently, they can also increase the risk of vulva and vaginal irritation, which could also lead to an increase in susceptibility to HIV if exposed to the virus.

Hormonal Methods Female hormonal methods of contraception alter specific characteristics of a woman's ovulation cycle or reproductive tract. Hormonal methods prevent ovulation, thicken cervical mucus to prevent sperm from joining the egg, or alter the lining

Table 7.2 Recommendations for effective use of cervical barrier methods of contraception

	HOURS BEFORE INTERCOURSE	HOURS AFTER INTERCOURSE
Diaphragm	up to 6	at least 8; no more than 24
Cervical cap	up to 6	at least 8; no more than 24
FemCap	up to 8	at least 8; no more than 48
Lea's Shield	up to 8	at least 8; no more than 48

of the uterus to prevent implantation of a fertilized egg. These methods differ mainly in the specific hormonal formulation and the method used to deliver those hormones to the body.

Currently, all available methods of hormonal contraception are designed for women, but there are some new research projects targeting male populations. The goal is to use hormones to reduce the production of sperm to levels that would be unlikely to cause pregnancy.

Oral contraceptives. As we said earlier, the first **oral contraceptive,** or birth control pill, was introduced in 1960 (Engelman, 2011). It revolutionized contraception because for the first time in history, women could control their own reproductive cycles. Today's birth control pill differs quite a bit from the original version. The single biggest difference is that it contains much lower doses of estrogen, which means potential side effects are substantially reduced. There are two basic types of birth control pills: *combination pills,* named this because they combine estrogen and progestin, and the *minipill,* which contains progestin only.

Over 30 different combinations of birth control pills are currently available in the United States. The majority of them have 21 hormonally active pills followed by 7 pills containing no hormones. A woman begins taking a pill on the first day of her period or the first Sunday after her period has begun. Birth control pills work in three ways:

- They prevent ovulation from occurring by changing a woman's hormone levels.
- They thicken the cervical mucus to prevent sperm from joining the egg.
- They change the uterine lining to prevent implantation of a fertilized egg.

There are three basic types of pills; they differ because of the levels of hormones in each type: the *monophasic pill,* the *biphasic pill,* and the *triphasic pill.* The monophasic pill contains 21 active pills that all contain the same level of hormones. The biphasic pill contains 21 active pills with two different levels of estrogen and progestin. The triphasic pill contains 21 active pills with three different hormone dosages. The dose changes every 7 days. In terms of safety and effectiveness, the three combination pills are primarily interchangeable.

The progestin-only minipill contains no estrogen and is designed specifically for women who are breastfeeding, because the estrogen in combination birth control pills can reduce milk production. The minipills are also designed for women who have health conditions that prevent them from taking estrogen, including women who have a history of blood clots. Minipills and combination pills work in exactly the same way.

Women need to be vigilant about taking their oral contraceptives at the same time every day. When pills are not taken consistently, the effectiveness of this contraceptive method declines. In addition, prescription antibiotics reduce the effectiveness of oral contraceptives. Because they are not 100% foolproof, women should use a backup method to make sure they will not get pregnant. Read more about when to use a backup method when on the pill in "Healthy Sexuality: Ensuring Contraceptive Success While on the Pill."

Hormonal implants. The **hormonal implant** is a small tube of progestin that is inserted under the skin of a woman's upper arm. Implanon is a single-rod hormonal implant that is inserted in about 1 minute and prevents pregnancy for 3 years. It can be removed at any time to allow fertility to return.

Spermicidal creams, foams, and gels are placed high up in the vagina, near the cervix, with a plastic applicator.
Christopher Kerrigan/McGraw-Hill Education

hormonal implants
Small tubes of progestin that are inserted under the skin of a woman's upper arm. These implants can provide continuous protection against pregnancy.

There are many kinds of birth control pills on the market today that are available to meet a variety of women's needs.
Science & Society Picture Library/Getty Images

HEALTHY Sexuality

Ensuring Contraceptive Success While on the Pill

Despite the popularity of the birth control pill, it is important to have detailed knowledge of how to use it and to know when to use a backup method to prevent pregnancy. If the birth control pill is your contraceptive choice, read this information for guidelines to help ensure its effectiveness.

1. Use a backup method (foam, condoms, sponge) with the pills for the first month.
2. Take a pill every day until you finish a pack; then start a new pack. Do not skip any days between packs.
3. Take your pills every day at the same time. If you miss or take any pills late, you may spot or bleed and should use a backup method until you start the next pack of pills.
4. IF YOU ARE LATE taking a pill by 4 hours or more, use a backup method until you start the next pack of pills.
5. IF YOU MISS ONE PILL, take it as soon as you remember it, then take today's pill at the regular time. Use a backup method until you start the next pack of pills.
6. IF YOU MISS TWO PILLS IN A ROW, take 2 pills as soon as you remember and 2 pills the next day. For example, if you forget pills on Monday and Tuesday, take 2 pills on Wednesday and 2 pills on Thursday to catch up. Use a backup method until you start the next pack of pills.
7. IF YOU MISS THREE PILLS IN A ROW, start using a backup method right away. Start a new pack of pills on the next Sunday after the last pill you took. Use your backup method until you finish the new pack of pills. If you have been sexually active before starting your new pack of pills, you must wait for your next period before starting a new pack. Use your backup method for the month and for the next cycle of pills.
8. MISSED PERIODS
   - IF YOU HAVE TAKEN ALL PILLS CORRECTLY and have a very light period or miss a period, keep taking your pills.
   - IF YOU MISS TWO PERIODS in a row, call your health care provider.
   - IF YOU MISS ANY PILLS AND MISS A PERIOD, call your health care provider. You may need a pregnancy test.
9. If you are sick and experience diarrhea or vomiting within 2 hours of taking the pill, use a backup method until you start your next pack of pills. Keep taking your pills.

Additionally, any time you see doctors or nurses, tell them you are on birth control pills, especially if you may be hospitalized. Certain medicines, such as antibiotics, may cause your pills to be less effective. If you are prescribed any medications, ask your health care provider if they will interfere with the effectiveness of birth control pills and if you need to use a backup method.

Source: University of Iowa Hospitals and Clinics. (2004). *Birth control pill fact sheet*. http://www.uihealthcare.com/depts/med/obgyn/patedu/birthcontrol/pillfacts.html

---

Implanon is a small rodlike device that is implanted into the upper arm.
Hattie Young/Science Source

These implants work by slowly releasing hormones into the body to prevent pregnancy by inhibiting ovulation or thickening cervical mucus.

Injectable contraceptives. Another method of administering contraceptives is through an injection of Depo-Provera to the hip or upper arm. The liquid contains a form of progestin called DPMA (medroxyprogesterone acetate), which prevents pregnancy in a manner similar to hormonal implants. A single shot of Depo-Provera provides contraceptive protection for up to 14 weeks before another injection is required (Web MD, 2017). While this is a reversible method of birth control, fertility can take up to a year to return after discontinuing the injections (Hatcher et al., 2008).

The Patch. Also available in the United States is a patch worn on the skin of the arm, buttocks, or abdomen that releases estrogen and progestin directly into the skin (brand name of Ortho Evra). Each patch contains a 1-week supply of hormones and releases a daily dose of hormones equivalent to a low-dose oral contraceptive. A woman applies a new patch every week for 3 weeks and then does not wear a patch during the fourth week when the menstrual period occurs. This method loses effectiveness for women who weigh more than 198 pounds.

The Vaginal Ring. The contraceptive or vaginal ring (brand name of Nuva-Ring) is a flexible, transparent ring that is placed in the vagina. It delivers hormones similar to a combination oral contraceptive every day over a 3-week period. One ring remains in place for 3 weeks followed by a week of not using it. Most couples are unaware of the ring's presence during intercourse, but if it does present a problem, it can be removed during intercourse and then reinserted within 3 hours. If the ring is removed for more than 3 hours, an additional form of barrier contraception should be used until the ring has been back in the vagina for 7 days.

Depo-Provera is a shot of progestin that is given every 3 months in order to prevent pregnancy.
Kumar Sriskandan/Alamy Stock Photo

Emergency Contraception. **Emergency contraception (EC)** can prevent up to 95% of pregnancies when taken within 5 days of intercourse (WHO, 2018). Plan B is the most common form of EC and contains levonorgestrel. Other levonorgestrel pills include Take Action, My Way, and AfterPill. Ella is another form of EC and contains ulipristal acetate. They should be taken as soon after unprotected intercourse as possible but within 72 hours for the best results. If taken before ovulation, EC may prevent an egg from developing and releasing; if taken after ovulation it may prevent implantation of a fertilized egg. A menstrual period and fertility return with the next menstrual cycle. While EC is 75–95% effective in preventing pregnancy, this method of contraception should be used in case of *emergency only*. EC should not be used as a regular form of contraception due to the high dosage of hormones it contains, which can impact a woman's normal menstrual cycle.

emergency contraception (EC)
Concentrated hormonal pills that can interrupt a woman's normal hormonal patterns to protect against an unplanned pregnancy in the event of unprotected intercourse.

intrauterine device (IUD)
A small T-shaped plastic device containing hormones or copper that is placed in the uterus to prevent pregnancy.

EC has been available over-the-counter without age restriction for some time. Ella requires a doctor visit and a prescription but is also considered to be the most effective type of emergency contraception in pill form (Planned Parenthood, 2019b). Even though it is widely available, research shows that college-age females may not be well informed about all the options for it, as explained in "Research and Sexual Well-Being: Female College Students and Emergency Contraception."

Intrauterine Methods An **intrauterine device (IUD)** is a small, T-shaped plastic device that a medical professional places in the uterus to prevent pregnancy. Approximately 2% of women who use birth control in the United States use IUDs (Sonfield, 2007). Figure 7.6 shows the correct placement of an IUD. A plastic string attached to the end of the device ensures correct placement and allows it to be removed. In the United States, two types of IUDs are available: hormonal and copper (ParaGard T-380A). There are currently four different types of hormonal IUDs that have received FDA approval: Mirena, Kyleena, Liletta, and Skyla. All four of these IUDs use the hormone progestin to prevent pregnancy.

With a copper IUD, a small amount of copper is released into the uterus. This type of IUD does not affect ovulation or a woman's menstrual cycle. Copper IUDs prevent sperm from reaching the egg by immobilizing the sperm on the way to the fallopian tubes. If an egg does become fertilized, it cannot implant on the wall of the uterus because the copper changes the uterine lining.

The patch (Ortho Evra) should be placed on one of four designated areas on the body: buttocks, upper torso (excluding breasts), abdomen, or upper outer arm.
moodboard/Corbis

RESEARCH and Sexual Well-Being

Female College Students and Emergency Contraception

The World Health Organization recommends EC in cases of unprotected intercourse, risk of possible contraceptive failure, incorrect use of contraceptives, and sexual assault if without contraception coverage (WHO, 2018). Despite the wide availability of emergency contraception (EC), many women know little about it. This may help explain why the incidence of unintended pregnancies in the United States is so high compared to other nations. Recent studies found that 60–80% of pregnancies in women aged 18–24 were unplanned (Vahratian, Patel, Wolff, & Xu, 2008). It has been nearly two decades since the FDA approved emergency contraception, and for several years there have been no restrictions based on age or the need for a prescription to obtain it.

In fact, women have only a general awareness about the existence of EC and approve of it as a means to prevent unintended pregnancies. They do not know about its effectiveness, safety, availability, and side effects, however. Also, in findings from previous research, it is clear that many women don't know the difference between emergency contraception and mifepristone, an oral medication that can induce spontaneous abortion in the first trimester of pregnancy (Hickey, 2009).

It is also clear from these studies that health care providers have not received adequate information and counseling about EC. Many women reported that their information about EC came from friends, peers, or the Internet and that they would be more likely to use EC if a health care provider had informed them about it.

Women's knowledge, perceptions, and use of EC have not been adequately investigated since it became available over the counter in 2006 (Hickey, 2009). The research done on EC highlights both the need for health care professionals to share their knowledge of available resources and the need for women to be proactive about their own health care.

DID YOU KNOW

The Paragard (copper) IUD works really well as emergency contraception! In fact, it is the MOST effective way to prevent pregnancy after unprotected sex. When placed in the uterus within 120 hours (5 days) after unprotected sex, it is more than 99% effective in preventing pregnancy (Planned Parenthood, 2019a).

With hormonal IUDs, a small amount of progestin is released into the uterus. These hormones thicken cervical mucus to make it difficult for sperm to enter the cervix. Hormonal IUDs also work by slowing down the growth of the uterine lining, making it uninhabitable for fertilized eggs.

A woman using an IUD is always protected against pregnancy. IUDs begin working right away and can be removed at any time. In addition, they can be inserted 6 weeks after the delivery of a baby or an abortion. Over time, they are relatively inexpensive as they can remain in place for an extended period of time. The copper IUD can remain in place for 10 years. Mirena and Liletta work for up to 7 years, Kyleena works for up to 5 years, and Skyla works for up to 3 years (Planned Parenthood, 2019a).

Figure **7.6**
An IUD is a small T-shaped plastic device that a medical professional places in the uterus to prevent pregnancy.

IUDs do not protect against STIs, and women are at an increased risk for an STI during the first 4 months after insertion. IUDs are recommended mainly for women in monogamous relationships. See Table 7.1 for more information about the effectiveness of these devices.

Surgical Methods—Sterilization One of the most widely chosen methods of contraception in the United States is **sterilization,** also referred to as **voluntary surgical contraception (VSC).** There are three methods of sterilization available for women and men today. For women, tubal ligation and a small metallic implant (called Essure) are two VSC methods. For men, it's the vasectomy. While VSC is considered a permanent method of birth control, reversal (particularly vasectomies) is becoming increasingly common and successful. In general, vasectomy reversal leads to overall pregnancy rates of greater than 50%, and has the greatest chance of success within 3 years of the vasectomy (Speroff & Fritz, 2005). In fact, a vasectomy reversal leads to pregnancy only about 30% of the time if the reversal is done 10 years after vasectomy.

Those individuals who choose VSC are typically in their 30s and 40s, have had at least one child, and do not desire more. Some doctors will not perform a VSC if they believe the patient is too young or has not yet had a child. Additionally, most individuals who seek out VSCs are in stable, long-term relationships. None of these methods prevents exposure to or transmission of STIs. A disadvantage for some is that they later regret their decision in choosing sterilization as their contraceptive method, so we recommend careful consideration about whether VSC is the right option (Walling, 2002).

In women, surgical sterilization is typically done by **laparoscopy** (Figure 7.7). Two small incisions are made in the abdomen in which a viewing scope and surgical instruments are inserted. For a tubal ligation, the fallopian tubes are cut, tied, or blocked using a variety of techniques. This prevents fertilization by interrupting the passage of sperm or egg through the fallopian tubes. The procedure is usually done on an outpatient basis and women can resume their normal activities very shortly after the procedure.

Note that an older product named ESSURE is no longer available on the market. Bayer (the manufacturer) pulled it from the market in late 2018, so it is not a currently available option.

NuvaRing is a small ring that is inserted in the vagina for 1 week at a time to release hormones to prevent pregnancy.
Phanie/Alamy Stock Photo

sterilization, or **voluntary surgical contraception (VSC)**
A surgical alteration of the internal reproductive system of either male or female that permanently blocks sperm cells from fertilizing an ovum.

Figure 7.7

Tubal ligation can be done by one of three different methods: pinching off the fallopian tube in a loop with a band, cutting and cauterizing (burning) the tube ends, and cutting and tying off the tube ends.

Figure 7.8
Vasectomy involves cutting the vas deferens and tying off the ends. This surgery is usually done under local anesthesia in an outpatient setting.

laparoscopy
A surgical procedure whereby small incisions are made in the abdomen in which a viewing scope and surgical instruments are inserted to perform surgery.

For men, a vasectomy involves making a small incision in the scrotal sac to reach the vas deferens, which are cut and then blocked at both ends (Figure 7.8). The blocked vas deferens prevents the passage of sperm into seminal fluid. Vasectomies are usually performed under local anesthesia in an outpatient setting. They tend to be faster, less invasive, safer, and less expensive than VSC procedures for women (Himmerick, 2005). After the vasectomy, some sperm may remain in the ducts, and a man is not considered sterile until he has produced sperm-free ejaculations. Semen is tested in the lab several weeks and then again a few months after the procedure is complete to ensure that all sperm are gone. This usually requires 15 to 20 ejaculations, so a couple should use another form of birth control during this period.

fertility awareness methods or **natural methods**
Contraceptive methods based on ovulation prediction and the viability of sperm; intercourse is timed to avoid fertile days in a woman's reproductive cycle.

Fertility Awareness Methods Of all the contraceptive methods available, **fertility awareness methods,** or **natural methods,** are the least successful ways to prevent pregnancy. These methods are based on abstaining from intercourse when a woman is fertile. One reason for their higher failure rate is that trying to determine when a woman is fertile depends on many factors. Usually, a woman is only fertile for about 1 day every month after an egg is released during ovulation. Sperm, however, can survive for 3 to 7 days in a woman's reproductive tract. The idea of fertility awareness methods is to learn when a woman ovulates and then to agree to abstain from intercourse for 7 days prior to and 1 day after ovulation to reduce the risk of pregnancy. Logically, this makes sense. The problem, however, is that knowing when a woman will ovulate is a complicated learning process that involves self-discipline, time, organization, and a willingness to become intimately familiar with one's body and bodily fluids. In addition, these methods provide no protection from STIs. The names of three common fertility awareness methods are the Standard Days Method (SDM), the TwoDay Method, and the Basal Body Temperature Method.

The Standard Days Method is based on reproductive physiology. A woman's fertile "window," which are the days in the menstrual cycle when she can get pregnant, begins approximately 5 days prior to ovulation and lasts up to 24 hours after ovulation. Most ovulations occur around the midpoint of the menstrual cycle, which includes 3 days on either side of it.

Researchers at the Institute for Reproductive Health at Georgetown University (2019) have identified the fertile window in the woman's menstrual cycle, using a computer simulation that takes into account the probability of pregnancy, probability of ovulation occurring on different cycle days, and variability in cycle length from woman to woman and from cycle to cycle. Their analysis found that avoiding unprotected sex on days 8 through 19 of the cycle provided maximum protection from pregnancy while minimizing the number of days to avoid intercourse. Women with menstrual cycles between 26 and 32 days long can use the

Figure 7.9
The TwoDay Method of fertility awareness uses cervical secretions to indicate when a woman is likely to be fertile.
Source: Institute of Reproductive Health, Georgetown University (2012).

SDM to try to prevent pregnancy by avoiding unprotected intercourse during the 12 fertile days identified by the method.

The TwoDay Method, illustrated in Figure 7.9, is a fertility awareness-based method that uses cervical secretions as the indicator of fertility. This method instructs women to monitor daily the presence of secretions to know when pregnancy is most likely. If a woman notices any secretions today or yesterday, she should consider herself fertile today. A user of the TwoDay Methods asks herself two questions every day:

- Did I note any secretions today?
- Did I note any secretions yesterday?

If she noticed any secretions today *or* yesterday, she is potentially fertile today and should avoid unprotected intercourse today to prevent pregnancy. If she did not notice any secretions today *and* yesterday (two consecutive dry days), pregnancy is very unlikely today.

The Basal Body Temperature Method is another form of fertility awareness. To use this method, a woman must take her **basal body temperature (BBT)** each morning before getting out of bed using a BBT thermometer that measures to tenths of a degree and record it on a temperature graph like the one in Figure 7.10. Basal body temperature is the lowest temperature attained by the body during rest (usually during sleep). After 3 to 4 months a woman should be able to predict when she is ovulating based on the fact that the temperature drops just prior to ovulation and rises and remains elevated for several days after. The temperature rises in response to increased progesterone levels that occur in the second half of the menstrual cycle. Couples must avoid intercourse on the day that the temperature rises and for 3 days after. Because the temperature rise does not occur until after ovulation, sex just prior to the rise increases the risk of pregnancy. Some couples abstain for several days before the anticipated time of ovulation and for 3 days after.

Understanding common sexual and reproductive health issues; knowing about STIs and how they are transmitted, tested for, and treated; and having the knowledge necessary to

basal body temperature (BBT)
The lowest temperature attained by the body during rest (usually during sleep).

Figure 7.10

The basal body temperature (BBT) method requires a woman to chart her temperature every morning to predict and track ovulation. Typically a woman's temperature (taken orally) is lower right before ovulation, and raises immediately after. The orange line represents normal body temperature first thing in the morning.
Source: JustMommies.com.

make wise contraceptive decisions are at the heart of how we ensure our own sexual health. This knowledge informs our decisions so that we can take another positive step toward sexual health, sexual well-being, and sexual literacy. Having this knowledge, though, is just a piece of that step. Another important piece is clearly communicating our decisions and our desires with our partners.

CONTRACEPTION AND SEXUAL WELL-BEING

Contraception has always been hugely controversial in the United States since the 19th century, as politics blocked people's access to sound pregnancy planning and sexual well-being (Engelman, 2011; Tone, 2001). Politics has thus long impacted almost everything about how and why people participate in and receive sound reproductive decision-making information (DiMauro & Joffe, 2009; Kirby, 2012). But research has consistently shown that better sexual literacy and access to preventive health care for family planning is associated with a reduction in abortion (Engelman, 2011; Joffe, 2006). For example, the Guttmacher Institute (Frost & Lindberg, 2012) has shown that when sound contraception information is available about sexual health and contraception, unwanted pregnancies and, therefore, abortions tend to decline. And the reverse is now more true than ever: When abortion rights become endangered in the political environment, the need becomes greater for sound contraceptive information and the sexual literacy to apply it.

However, at no time in the 45 years since *Roe v. Wade* became the law of the land in the United States, allowing all women access to abortion, has the threat to reproductive rights and especially a woman's access to reproductive choice been more at risk. Articles routinely appear with such titles as "Punishing Pregnant Women" (Goodwin, 2019), and "Nearly Forced to Give Birth" (Levin, 2019). New draconian laws such as those in the state of Alabama, among others, indicate that states are unwilling to understand the full impact that removing choice has on both women and children; they will potentially cause an actual increase in the rates of unintended pregnancy and abortion. This is a devastating trend that makes poor pregnant women, who are dependent upon public health medicine, extremely vulnerable and even liable to criminal penalties and imprisonment, along with the doctors and other health professionals who care for them.

Advocates for contraception as a tool for public health and sexual well-being have two clear goals: greater access and more choice (O'Callaghan, 2011). What new options for contraception are on the horizon? Several new methods are currently being studied in the United States through the Contraceptive Clinical Trial Network (CCTN). The CCTN was formed in 1996 and has conducted clinical trials of oral, injectable, implantable, and topical contraceptive drugs and devices (Jensen, 2011). New forms of contraception being developed and tested include barrier methods, oral hormonal contraceptives, permanent contraception, and emergency contraception.

Due to the fact that so many of the available contraceptive methods are utilized by women (e.g., the pill, the patch, diaphragms), many wonder what is on the horizon for men. Currently, scientists are researching hormones like testosterone, progestin, and androgen to inhibit sperm production, and the University of Washington has successfully tested a male contraceptive pill (Blair, 2019). The patch, the pill, injections, and implants are all being considered as possible hormonal methods of birth control for men.

Whatever the approach, providing greater access to contraception and increasing the effectiveness of existing methods requires continued research and development. Contraceptive decisions have a powerful impact on our sexual well-being because they help to ensure that we can protect our sexual health and maximize the pleasure we get from sex. We can enjoy the pleasure of sexual interaction more when we feel confident that we are protected from STIs and unintended pregnancy.

Chapter Review

SUMMARY

Contraception: History and Cultural Variations

- Contraception is any method we use to prevent pregnancy. Several contraception methods also work to prevent the transmission of STIs.
- The practice of preventing pregnancy is as old as human existence.
- Cultures around the world have different methods of contraception. The beliefs underlying these various methods vary by virtue of the cultural context and belief system regarding the issues of birth, conception, and contraception.
- The history of contraception in the United States is riddled with political controversies that directly reflect people's beliefs about sexual morality and conception of human life.
- Anthony Comstock and Margaret Sanger are two historical individuals who were quite opposite in their stance on contraception and access to it, but both were critical players in the history of contraception in the United States.

Methods of Contraception

- Choosing a contraceptive method is a decision that should be made with the input of each partner.
- It is important to have knowledge of the availability and methods of various forms of contraception when choosing a contraceptive method. Individuals must also consider effectiveness, pros and cons of usage, and cost.
- The three most effective methods to protect against both unplanned pregnancy and transmission of STIs are abstinence, fluid-free sexual behaviors, and barrier methods such as condoms.
- Hormonal methods to prevent pregnancy offer no prevention of STIs. These methods are oral contraceptives, the hormonal IUD, the contraceptive patch, hormonal

implants, the vaginal ring, and injections. The differences among these methods relate to how hormones are delivered to the female body.
- Cervical barrier methods used to prevent pregnancy include the diaphragm, cervical cap, Femcap, and Lea's Shield. All are used with spermicides.
- Surgical sterilization is a relatively permanent method of contraception. In females this method is tubal ligation; in men, the vasectomy.
- Fertility awareness methods of contraception may be effective for some couples who are very careful in predicting ovulation via a calendar method, monitoring body temperature or vaginal mucus.

Contraception and Sexual Well-Being
- Access to quality sexual health care is associated with several positive outcomes, such as lower numbers of unintended pregnancies and abortions and lower STI rates.

What's Your Position?

1. **How do you see the history of contraception in the United States affecting how we think about contraception today?**
   - What does history tell you about the debate over sexual health care and contraception in the United States?
   - Think about your own family. Do you know if your family's beliefs about contraception changed or evolved from generation to generation? In what ways?

2. **What kind of contraceptive method would best fit your lifestyle, sexual needs, and desires?**
   - What personal needs or habits might indicate whether one type of contraception would work better for you than another?
   - What else would you consider when choosing a contraceptive method?

3. **In what ways do you see contraception and sexual health care changing in the future?**
   - Do you see access to sexual health care becoming more widespread or more limited in the United States? Why or why not?
   - How do you think that we, as citizens, can impact the need for and access to quality sexual health care in the United States?

Design elements: Controversies in Sexuality: HBRH/Shutterstock; Research and Sexual Well Being: verity jane smith/Getty Images; Healthy Sexuality: Sergey Furtaev/Shutterstock; Communication Matters: PeopleImages/Getty Images; Know Yourself: Plush Studios/Blend Images LLC; What's Your Position: Luis Molinero/Shutterstock; Healthy Sexuality: A. Minde/PhotoAlto; Did You Know icon: McGraw-Hill Education; Page corner icon: McGraw-Hill Education.

Reproduction: Conception, Pregnancy, and Childbirth

8

ballyscanlon/Getty Images

Parenting and Reproductive Decisions
- Define pronatalism and describe its impact on the decision to have children.

Ensuring a Healthy Pregnancy
- Describe how to prepare the body for a healthy pregnancy.

Conception and Pregnancy
- Identify the stages of pregnancy and the processes of prenatal development.
- Describe how pregnancy affects both pregnant women and their partners in biological, social, and interpersonal ways.

Birth and the Postpartum Period: What to Expect
- Identify the available birthing options in the United States.
- Identify the features of postpartum depression and available treatment options.
- Recall when it is healthy to resume sex after birth.

Infertility and Options
- Identify the options available for those who face infertility and for those who desire alternative methods of becoming parents.

Abortion
- Describe the medical techniques of abortion available in the United States.
- Explain how the decision to have an abortion involves the holistic issues of body, individuality, and community participation.

Sexual Well-Being and Reproductive Rights
- Identify how changes in policies and laws have affected reproductive decisions.

● Learning
● Objectives

Developing Your Position

1. Do you want to have children in your lifetime?
2. What do you envision as the ideal birth experience?
3. What is your position on abortion?

Self, Society, and Culture: Unexpected Parenthood

My sister Elizabeth was 20 years old and newly married when she received the shock of a lifetime. Having enjoyed only a month of her newlywed life, she found out one summer morning that she and her husband would be expecting their first child. For some individuals, this news would be welcome, and exciting. For my sister, who always vehemently stated that she would not have children until she was well into her 30s, the reaction was one of "shock and awe." She and her husband had utilized a contraceptive method (incorrectly, as it turns out) and so they assumed they were protected and would be able to decide when they wanted to conceive. Elizabeth spent the early part of her pregnancy contemplating how this event would change her life. From dealing with the physical changes and sickness that her pregnancy brought, to contemplating the changes a new baby would bring to her life, marriage, education, and career, my sister realized how this unintended turn of events would dramatically change the course of her life. Retrospectively, she sees the birth of her first child, Dani, as the most amazing "surprise" of her life. Yet it changed all her plans. What would her life have been like had she not gotten pregnant so soon after she was married and at such a young age?

Planning for parenthood and adjusting to the physical and psychological changes involved in becoming parents are the focus of our discussion on reproduction. To help with this decision-making process, in this chapter we provide knowledge, tools, and resources about reproduction and birth, such as how to ensure a healthy pregnancy and how to create a birth plan. We also discuss conception, the development of a fetus, and the changes that a pregnant woman and her nonpregnant partner experience in each phase of pregnancy. (We use the term *partner* to refer to husbands, spouses, same-sex life partners, or nontraditional cohabitating relations.) Additionally, we discuss some reproductive techniques that assist in either becoming pregnant or terminating an unintended pregnancy.

PARENTING AND REPRODUCTIVE DECISIONS

Everyone makes the decision about becoming a parent in light of their own experience and their particular values, attitudes, desires, and interests. Becoming aware of all of these factors and how they shape your decisions related to having children provides the context for this chapter. Even if you choose not to become a parent, it is valuable to understand this process, because you may have siblings, other relatives, close friends, or colleagues who will become parents.

The reproductive process and the myths surrounding it are fascinating. Learn about some of the myths now by completing "Know Yourself: Reproduction and Sex—Myth or Truth?"

Know Yourself

Reproduction and Sex—Myth or Truth?

Test your knowledge of sex and reproduction by answering these true/false questions.

1. Oral sex can make you pregnant.
2. Too much sex during pregnancy can cause birth defects.
3. A lesbian cannot become pregnant.
4. A mother can spread HIV to her fetus if precautions are not taken.
5. Natural at-home childbirth is a lot more dangerous than hospital birth.
6. Delaying birth decisions into your 30s can make conception more difficult.
7. In some cultures the fathers (or partners) also act out the pregnancy at the time of birth.
8. Some countries pay families not to have children.
9. The rate of abortion is actually in decline in the United States.
10. Abortion can cause legal problems in many countries.

Answers appear on page 250.

To appreciate the power of parenthood as a role in one's life, ask a parent what was the best day of their life. Many people may tell you it was the day that each of their children was born. These may be the most memorable days of their lives because reproduction integrates everything about our lives—our human sexual nature, culture, relationships, and individuality.

Because infants must rely completely on caregivers early in life for all their needs, we humans experience bonding and parenting differently in some ways from other species (Hrdy, 2009; Weisner, 2009). Because humans spend so many years raising children, parents tend to learn a great deal about themselves as they teach children how to navigate through society (Weisner, 2009).

The processes of conception and fetal development result in physical and hormonal changes for the pregnant woman. Additionally, the experiences she has in the time after pregnancy and birth all produce enormous changes within her body and possibly her mind. For women who experience fertility challenges, too, biology or physiological processes are also important as they consider the many fertility interventions or other options for conceiving a child.

Many psychological changes occur for those who choose to become parents. One such change impacts an individual's identity. For example, when people become parents, they may think about social and political events, future planning, and many other issues quite differently. Parents may dramatically shift their own priorities as they put the needs, desires, and dreams of their children before their own (Lerner & Steinberg, 2004).

Additionally, parents often find that experiencing pregnancy and the birth of their child brings about emotions and thoughts they had never considered before (Weisner, 2009). For example, many women experience a newfound sense of empowerment as they realize the amazing capacities their bodies have in bringing forth new life (Spock & Needleman, 2004). Those who become parents using the reproductive technologies or other options such as adoption or surrogacy may also experience certain emotions and feelings.

Society and cultural norms also influence our decision-making processes when considering parenthood. For example, in the United States, it is more common for women today to bear children in their late 20s and early 30s than it was in the 1950s and 1960s, when women were more likely to have children in their late teens and early 20s. As of 2016, it was reported that the average age of U.S. women at the birth of a first child was 26.3 years

Know Yourself

ANSWERS to Reproduction and Sex—Myth or Truth? *(p. 249).*

1. False
2. False
3. False
4. True
5. True
6. True
7. True
8. True
9. True
10. True

How many of these questions did you answer correctly? If you learned something new from this quiz, you are not alone. In this chapter, the important discussions surround decisions to procreate, what happens during conception and pregnancy, and what options are available for those who are not ready for parenthood.

(Bui & Miller, 2018). See Figure 8.1 to understand better the shifting age in women at the birth of their first child. What, then, may be the social effect about women and men in their teens that bear children today? Do children of teen parents face some kind of stigma (Russell, Crockett, Shen, & Lee, 2008)? What about the challenges women in their 50s face in bearing a child at an age that some may believe is "too old"? For single women who do

Figure 8.1
The age of women at the birth of their first children has increased with more women having their first child later in life.

Ages of first-time mothers in 1980

Ages of first-time mothers in 2016

250

not have a partner, what social challenges might they face if they decide to get pregnant and raise a child on their own? There is a myriad of social considerations to examine as each person thinks about the appropriateness and timeliness of parenthood in their own lives.

Pronatalism

Becoming a parent is one of society's most pervasive social expectations (Meyers, 2001). This is partly due to the fact that in the United States we have a cultural bias called **pronatalism,** which is the belief system that promotes childbearing. This set of beliefs, attitudes, and practices is so ingrained that many individuals do not recognize it, much less question it. We simply accept that all typical adults want to and *should* have children. The whole notion of motherhood is part of this. In fact, motherhood is such a core part of current gender expectations that a woman who decides not to have children is often seen as deviant and is stigmatized (McQuillan, Greil, Shreffler, & Tichenor, 2008).

DID YOU KNOW

The following birth data provide a snapshot of the United States in 2015:

- Number of births: 3,978,497
- The preterm birth rate (infants born earlier than 37 weeks gestation): 9.63% (an increase from earlier years)
- Percentage of babies born via cesarean: 32.0%
- Percentage of low-birth-weight infants: 8.07%
- Percentage of infants born to unmarried women: 40.3%
- Birth rate of infants born to teen mothers (15–19 years): 22.3 births per 1,000 females
- Mean age of women at first birth: 26

Source: Martin, A. J., Brady, E. H., Michelle, J. K., Osterman, A. K. D., & Mathews, T. J. *Division of vital statistics reports. Births: Final data for 2015.* Centers for Disease Control and Prevention. Retrieved July 30, 2019, from https://www.cdc.gov/nchs/data/nvsr/nvsr66/nvsr66_01.pdf

In traditional societies throughout much of history as well, parenting and having children was regarded as natural and even required to be a member of the group (Hrdy, 2009). Motherhood is held in such high esteem in some societies that women who did not bear children were viewed as not having achieved the meaning and full power of their lives (Bledsoe, 2002). In some other societies, females are regarded as girls until they become mothers. If they do not bear children, they may be viewed negatively or even treated with shame and stigma (Ford & Beach, 1951; Herdt, 1997a; Mead, 1961; Weisner, Bradley, & Kilbride, 1997). These attitudes are expressions of pronatalism.

pronatalism
A belief system that promotes childbearing.

There is some debate about the origin of this belief system: Some see it as stemming from biological and natural drives and others view it as a learned expectation. Few individuals, however, question the notion that they will one day conceive and raise a child or multiple children (Parmely, 2001). People who accept this belief often do not think critically about how this expectation impacts their decision making in regard to the idea of parenthood. Few consider alternatives for their adult lives, such as choosing to be child-free either to pursue careers or possibly to use the resources they work hard for to travel rather than to save for a child's education (Burns, Futch, & Tolman, 2011). Think how this might apply directly to you: If you decide not to have children, you may find others disregard your opinions about parenting styles because they think you lack the actual experience. This exclusion may be painful, and make you feel shame, guilt, or anger (Parmely, 2001).

Today, in the United States, women experience increasing cultural tension between valuing motherhood and valuing career success. Why do some people continue to see this as a duality of either motherhood or career? The answer today for many women, but not all, is to do *both.* That women can juggle such demands and stay on top of everything is quite a challenge and does worry some experts (Tolman, 2006). People tend to think that this tension is about competing passions or commitments between family and career, and this may contribute to an idea that women must choose between the two (McQuillan et al., 2008). The reality, however, is that women are doing both. In 2015, over two-thirds (64.2%) of women with children under the age of 6 years were working (U.S. Bureau of Labor Statistics, 2016).

Many in the United States might view a couple as selfish for choosing to remain child free. Is it selfish to make a conscious decision not to become a parent?
Cavan Images/Getty Images

But this talk of the tension between motherhood and career totally leaves fathers out of the equation. How do fathers face this tension between career and family? Perhaps some men shrug off the duality by thinking that their wives or partners will do the domestic work, leaving them to pursue their careers (Tannen, 2001). That traditional attitude is breaking down.

More and more men are making critical decisions regarding career and family that favor more time and commitment to their families and children. For example, men who have high-pressure jobs that require 60- or 80-hour workweeks or more may choose to scale down to lesser positions. Or men who work in high-risk jobs may consider a safer occupation when they have children, or men who travel extensively may choose a job that keeps them closer to home. Interestingly, the number of men who are stay-at-home dads continues to rise. As of 2012, approximately 16% of stay-at-home parents in the United States are fathers (Livingston, 2014). It appears that many families make the decision for the fathers to stay home with children when the partner brings home a heftier paycheck than the father. A substantial number of men also report becoming stay-at-home fathers for various employment reasons, such as losing a job or inflexible work hours. There is a smaller proportion that report they decided to stay at home because they wanted to directly care for their children in that capacity (Lee & Lee, 2018). Regardless of the reason, stay-at-home dads are becoming more common in the United States. Organizations such as the National At-Home Dad Network (www.athomedad.org) and social groups are popping up at rapid rates to support dads at home taking care of children.

It is unfortunate that many in our society believe that, for women especially, career and family cannot coexist. Clearly, people can devote time and attention to both of these huge areas of life (Tannen, 2001). We need to reinforce our efforts to restructure organizations, institutions, and policies to support holistic work–life integration for both women and men (McQuillan et al., 2008). The provisions for health care and family leave for parents are among the kinds of policies we need in our society, government, and institutions for families to be adequately supported.

Family Leave

family leave
An absence from work, either paid or unpaid, granted so that an employee can give care to a family member, such as a new baby.

Having a family these days can have tremendous effects on finances and income. For this reason, **family leave**—the amount of paid or unpaid leave allowed for the parents—is an important issue for those who are considering parenthood. In fact, the United States is one of the few industrialized nations that do *not* provide paid family leave for new parents. The Netherlands, by contrast, provides 16 weeks paid leave for the mother, 8 weeks for the father, and a total of 26 additional weeks unpaid leave. In the United States, parents are covered only by the Family and Medical Leave Act of 1993, which guarantees that employees in companies or organizations with more than 50 employees can take 12 weeks of unpaid leave to care for a newborn, adopted child, or family member with an illness. In 2002, California became the first state to institute a paid family leave act that entitles any employee to 55% of their salary for 6 weeks to take care of a newborn, adopted child, or family member with a significant illness. When family leave is available, it seems to enhance family life and career development (Slater & Uniat, 2019). When society supports family leave, it appears not only to ensure better prospects for the mother and child, but also helps ensure the financial security and support of the whole family.

Considering Parenthood

Couples often wonder how having children will affect their relationship. They often view the transition to parenthood as creating a large, persistent change (Pancer, Pratt, Hunsberger, & Gallant, 2000). One study has shown that husbands and wives, in particular, who become parents within the first 5 years of marriage, were more satisfied with their marital relationships when they were newlyweds than when they became parents. In the same study, people associated a decline in marital satisfaction with the transition to parenthood as compared to

COMMUNICATION Matters

To Have or Not to Have Children?

What are your attitudes about having children? Communication matters here because research suggests that becoming parents changes how we view ourselves as sexual individuals and also changes our relationships (Klernan, 2004). The following questions may help you and your partner talk about whether or not to have children:

- *Do you really want children or is becoming a parent something you feel forced into?* As we discussed, in a pronatalistic society people may feel pressure to have children. Examine your own desires for children separate from the pressures of society, family, and peers that might impact on your decision.
- *How do you and your partner plan to divide child-rearing tasks, household work, and discipline?* Discuss who will perform these tasks. It could be valuable to talk about which parent from your own childhood home handled which tasks because it could provide perspective about what each person thinks or expects. If you decide to rear children alone, consider whether you know anyone who would help with any of these tasks.
- *Are you prepared economically to handle the costs of having a child now?* Discuss with your partner where these expenses would come from and how the anticipated bills could be met.
- *What is the health history of you and your partner?* It is important to discuss your health histories as well as pertinent family histories of chronic diseases such as diabetes, heart disease, and cancers.
- *What faith or cultural traditions will you teach your child?* While you may have had little reason to discuss these issues with your partner before, they may surface when you discuss whether to have children.
- *Are family members, friends, or the community eager for you to have children?* Would they step in and play roles that would support your decision? The choice to have one or more children is one of the most important and exciting decisions a person or couple can make. Ideally, you get to make this decision voluntarily after thoughtful consideration of these questions and with careful planning (Klernan, 2004).

ericsphotography/iStockphoto.com

couples that were not parents. This difference suggests that the transition to parenthood does affect the quality of a couple's relationship (Lawrence, Rothman, Cobb, Rothman, & Bradbury, 2008; Waite & Joyner, 2001). Consider this important topic further in "Communication Matters: To Have or Not to Have Children?"

ENSURING A HEALTHY PREGNANCY

Once the choice has been made to have a child and the timing has been decided, there are things a woman can do to ensure a healthy pregnancy. A healthy pregnancy begins long before a woman gets pregnant. Good nutrition, exercise, and regular prenatal care can have positive effects for both the woman and her fetus.

Preparing the Body for Pregnancy

Because so much prenatal development occurs even before a woman knows she is pregnant, it is important that she prepares her body before getting pregnant. The CDC (2018) offers the following five steps to aid in the preparation for a healthy pregnancy:

1. Take 400 micrograms (mcg) of folic acid every day for at least 3 months before getting pregnant to help prevent birth defects.
2. Stop smoking and drinking alcohol.

3. Make sure that any preexisting medical conditions are under control. These include asthma, diabetes, obesity, epilepsy, and oral health. Ensure that your vaccinations are up-to-date.
4. Talk with your health care provider about any over-the-counter medication or prescription medication you are taking. This includes any dietary or herbal supplements.
5. Avoid toxic substances or material that can cause infection. Stay away from chemicals and feces from cats and rodents.

Some factors can have serious negative effects before and during pregnancy, including legal and illegal drugs, alcohol, and nicotine. Many medications can have a negative impact on a pregnancy. A woman using a prescribed medication should tell the doctor who prescribed it that she may become pregnant, or that she is pregnant, to make sure that the drug will harm neither her health nor the health of the developing fetus. Table 8.1 summarizes the possible effects of prescription and over-the-counter drugs on fetal development. For example, if a woman ingests high levels of alcohol during pregnancy, her infant may be born with **fetal alcohol syndrome (FAS).** Figure 8.2 depicts some physical characteristics of children born with FAS. Note that FAS represents one of the **fetal alcohol spectrum disorders (FASDs),** which form a group of conditions that can occur in a person whose mother ingested alcohol during pregnancy (CDC, 2011b). Fetal alcohol syndrome represents the severe end of the spectrum. In addition to a variety of physical characteristics, children with FAS can have problems with learning, memory, attention span, communication, vision, or hearing. Children with FAS may also display behavioral difficulties, thus making social interaction difficult (CDC, 2011b).

fetal alcohol syndrome (FAS)
A pattern of mental and physical defects that can develop in a fetus in association with high levels of alcohol consumption during pregnancy.

fetal alcohol spectrum disorders (FASDs)
A group of conditions (including FAS) that can occur in a person whose mother ingested alcohol during pregnancy.

Table 8.1 Effects of drug use during pregnancy

PRESCRIPTION DRUG TYPE	EFFECTS ON DEVELOPING FETUS
Barbiturates	Associated with newborn addiction to substance. Infants may have tremors, restlessness, and irritability after birth.
Tranquilizers	Associated with cleft palate or other congenital malformations when taken during the first trimester of pregnancy.
NONPRESCRIPTION DRUG TYPE	**EFFECTS ON DEVELOPING FETUS**
Alcohol	Small amounts—increased risk of spontaneous abortion. Moderate amounts (1–2 drinks a day)—associated with poor attention in infancy. Heavy drinking—may lead to fetal alcohol syndrome (FAS). Some experts suggest that even low to moderate amounts of alcohol ingested in the first trimester of pregnancy can increase the risk of FAS.
Amphetamines	Associated with heart defects and cleft palate and low-birth-weight newborns. When addicted at birth, infants can exhibit drowsiness, jitteriness, and respiratory distress.
Cocaine	May cause withdrawal symptoms at birth and physical and mental problems, especially if mother used it in first trimester. Infants experience higher risks for hypertension, heart problems, developmental retardation, and learning difficulties.
Marijuana	May cause a variety of birth defects and is associated with low weight and under-length newborns.
Nicotine	Associated with low-birth-weight newborns, which may indicate that they will experience a higher likelihood of health problems than other infants. Smoking may be especially harmful in the second half of pregnancy when fetal lungs develop.

Eyes
Extra skin folds on eyelids
Drooping eyelids
Downward slant of eyes
Unusually small eyes and/or eye openings
Short-sightedness
Inability to focus ("wandering eyes")

Ears
Uneven in placement and size
Poorly formed outer ear
Backward curve

Lips
Absence of groove in upper lip; flat upper lip
Thin upper lip

Head
Small head size

Forehead
Narrow, receding forehead

Nose
Short, upturned nose
Flattened nose bridge

Jaw
Underdeveloped jaw
Receding chin
Receding or flattened upper jaw

Figure 8.2
Physical characteristics of a child with fetal alcohol syndrome (FAS). Other signs of FAS may include mental retardation and delayed development, learning disorders, behavioral problems, and heart defects.

Sexually transmitted infections (STIs) can also have a negative impact on pregnancy and the developing fetus. Untreated genital herpes, for example, can lead to spontaneous abortion, preterm birth, or birth defects. Chlamydia can also lead to premature birth as well as neonatal eye infections. Some pregnancy-related problems or complications women cannot prevent occur, such as chromosomal disorders. Many of these issues are related to maternal age as can be seen in the box "Healthy Sexuality: Getting Pregnant Later in Life." Despite these occurrences, women can take steps to ensure the best possible health for themselves and optimal development for their unborn child.

Nutrition and Exercise

We have all heard it before, whether it be from a pregnant character on television or a pregnant friend or relative: "I can eat anything I want because I am eating for two!" Many pregnant women would love for this to be the case, but unfortunately it is not. Although pregnant women do require an increase in calories, it is excessive to double the amount of calories eaten unless they were undereating prior to becoming pregnant.

A balanced and nutritious diet is key to a healthy pregnancy. A balance of carbohydrates, fat, and protein is vital to help support the development of the fetus. Folate, vitamin D, and calcium are important as they help to ensure healthy development of the fetus's neural and skeletal structures (Blount, 2005).

A pregnant woman also needs a healthy level of exercise. Research shows that regular exercise contributes to a healthier pregnancy. Walking and swimming are considered healthy activities to engage in during pregnancy (American Pregnancy Association, 2011). In addition, women who exercise are thought to have shorter labors and less time pushing during delivery, as their muscles

Pregnant women need to take care to wash raw fruits and vegetables carefully to remove any bacteria or parasites that may contaminate them. In addition, meats and eggs must be cooked well to prevent salmonella poisoning.
Maike Jessen/Getty Images

HEALTHY Sexuality

Getting Pregnant Later in Life

As a woman ages, so do her eggs. A woman who is 27, for example, which is close to the average age of first birth in the United States, is twice as likely to conceive as a woman who is over 35 (Dunson, Colombo, & Baird, 2002). While it is common today for a woman to conceive after 35, some fertility risks are associated with conception later in life:

- A decrease in the number of eggs to be ovulated makes it harder to conceive.
- Changes in hormone production can alter timing and regularity of ovulation.
- Possible presence of other gynecologic issues such as **endometriosis,** a condition in which tissue similar to the uterine lining grows outside of the uterus, makes conception difficult.

If an older woman does get pregnant, she is at higher risk for miscarriage, increased labor time, and cesarean birth. She may also give birth to a newborn that is under typical weight. Age also increases the risk of conceiving a fetus with chromosomal abnormalities, especially Down syndrome, as shown in Figure 8.3 (Hook, 1981).

Figure 8.3
Increased risk for Down syndrome based on maternal age.

endometriosis

A potentially painful and dangerous medical condition caused when endometrial cells grow outside of the uterus into the abdominal cavity.

are more toned and efficient due to their fitness level. If exercise was a regular part of a woman's daily routine prior to getting pregnant, she should continue in her exercise regimen. Women who did not exercise regularly should consult a health care professional to see what kind of physical activities are beneficial during pregnancy.

Consider the following guidelines for engaging in healthy exercise during pregnancy (American Pregnancy Association, 2009):

- Be aware of any signs that it is time to reduce your level of exercise.
- Never exercise to the point of exhaustion or breathlessness. A pregnant body needs oxygen supply for both the mother and the fetus.
- Wear comfortable exercise footwear with strong ankle and arch support.
- Take frequent breaks, and drink plenty of fluids during exercise.
- Avoid exercise in extremely hot weather.
- Avoid rocky or unstable ground when running or cycling because joints are more lax in pregnancy, and ankle sprains and other injuries may occur.

- Avoid contact sports during pregnancy.
- Avoid lifting weights above the head and using weights that strain the lower back muscles. Weight training should emphasize improved tone, especially in the upper body and abdominal area.
- During the second and third trimesters, avoid exercise that involves lying flat on the back as this decreases blood flow to the womb.

Sex During Pregnancy

Individuals often wonder if it is safe to engage in sexual behavior and/or have sex while pregnant. The reality is pregnancy can coexist with passionate sexual relationships and pleasure, and it can be an exciting time to feel intimate with your partner. In fact, people in some cultures encourage sex during pregnancy because they believe that the father's semen is necessary for fetal development or completion of the personality (Dunham, Myers, McDougall, & Barnden, 1992; Lepani, 2012).

Biologically, changes during pregnancy may cause an increase in the desire for sexual interaction. Interestingly, some pregnant women report a decrease in libido. Every woman's body reacts somewhat differently to the hormone increase and to bodily changes that pregnancy brings. Regarding sexual activity, an increase in hormones may create a new kind of connection between the partner and the pregnant woman (Brott & Ash, 2001; Martin, 2013). Unless a health care provider advises against it, sex to orgasm is a healthy activity for a pregnant woman, at least until the start of labor (Schaffir, 2006). Many partners absolutely revel in the sex they have with their pregnant partner. Couples may need to discover alternative positions, as a woman's growing belly may impede certain positions. In addition, they may need to accommodate changes in the woman's sex drive resulting from hormone changes, breast tenderness, and fatigue.

Despite the benefits of an active sex life during pregnancy, women and their partners often worry about whether intercourse can harm the developing baby. One of the fears most often stated, particularly in popular culture, is that the penis will invade the baby's space during intercourse and cause subsequent physical or emotional trauma. In reality, we understand that a penis cannot invade the space of a developing fetus because the cervix acts as a barrier between the fetus and the vagina. The cervix remains tightly closed throughout pregnancy and only opens during labor and delivery when the baby is on the way down the birth canal. Regardless, as the pregnancy progresses, many couples may feel that continuing to engage in sex can begin to feel inappropriate. In fact, different cultures have varying beliefs about how long a couple should engage in sex prior to the time of delivery. Some impose taboos meant to protect the pregnancy or fetus (Liamputtong, 2007). In Thailand, for example, many women decrease or stop their sexual activity during pregnancy, particularly in the third trimester (Morris, 1975).

Many expecting parents are also concerned about whether or not it is safe to engage in oral and/or anal sex during pregnancy as well. Oral sex is considered to be "likely safe" during pregnancy if both partners are in a mutually monogamous relationship where both have tested negative for STIs. During pregnancy it is important that if a pregnant person is receiving oral sex, their partner does not blow into the vaginal opening or cause any air to be trapped inside the vagina because a bubble of air can travel and enter the placenta, which could potentially cause problems with fetal development. In addition, spotting or bleeding may be caused by the rupture of blood vessels as a result of air trapped in the vagina (American Pregnancy Association, 2018).

Regarding anal sex, this is a practice that is generally not recommended, mostly due to the potential for anal sex to exacerbate common issues experienced during pregnancy. For example, hemorrhoids are a common occurrence in pregnant bodies. Engaging in anal sex where hemorrhoids are present can make the experience painful and may inflame or cause them to rupture, leading to serious anal bleeding (American Pregnancy Association, 2018).

Each culture has unique ideas and beliefs about conception, pregnancy, and childbirth.
MIXA/Getty Images

If a pregnant person does engage in anal sex, it is critical that nothing that has entered the anus then be inserted into the vagina without making sure it is completely clean first. Bacteria found in the anus can infect the infant if transmitted to the vagina.

CONCEPTION AND PREGNANCY

In this section, we will venture into the exciting world of pregnancy as experienced by the woman and her partner. First, we will examine some cross-cultural beliefs about how we conceive babies. Then, we will look at the biological processes of conception and prenatal development.

Cross-Cultural Ideas About Conception

Beliefs about conception are often at the heart of a culture's vision of life and death, the afterworld, and family formation. These beliefs help shape a culture's understanding of society (Squire, 2003; Weisner, Bradley, & Kilbride, 1997). For example, the people of the Trobriand Islands in Papua New Guinea have a **matrilineal society,** meaning that descent and inheritance come through the mother's kinship line. They believe that a spirit causes conception. While bathing in a lagoon, a woman may become pregnant when a spirit enters her womb. Because the resulting pregnancy apparently has no connection to her husband, it connects her to her mother's people rather than to her husband's (Malinowski, 1948; Lepani, 2012).

For many years, Asian cultures have believed that either a pregnant woman or some other close family member will have a conception dream for each of their children before the baby is born. This belief originated in China and has influenced Korea, Japan, Vietnam, and other Asian countries. Specifically, people believe that the birth dream predicts pregnancy for the person having the dream or a close friend or family member (Seligson, 2002). Dreams are also thought to predict the gender of the baby, and the future of the baby. According to Seligson (1989), conception dreams are gradually disappearing due to modern lifestyles, Western psychology, religious beliefs, and communism. However, conception dreams are still taken seriously by many Korean people, as numerous individuals still report having them.

More commonly, however, attitudes about conception and birth focus on the social and psychological states of the parents, and whether they are being properly moral in their conduct toward each other and toward their society. As such, they believe that immoral acts, especially extramarital relationships, may cause birth defects. Typically, the mother is blamed, but sometimes the father is blamed as well (Herdt, 1981). In **patriarchal societies,** where men assume primary responsibilities for families and community, infertility may be blamed on women (Sanday, 1981a; Weisner, Bradley, & Kilbride, 1997). Some societies deny the possibility that men could be infertile because that possibility would undermine the patriarchy that governs inheritance and power (Herdt, 1997a). Beliefs about conception, in summary, take shape in the context of social relationships, conventional morality, and the transmission of property and power from one generation to the next. Though people in different cultures have beliefs about how babies are conceived, we know a lot about the biological processes involved in conception, which we discuss in the next section.

matrilineal society
A society in which descent and inheritance come through the mother's kinship line.

patriarchal society
A society in which descent and inheritance come through the father's kinship line.

HEALTHY Sexuality

The Developing Fetus's Chances for Survival

The millions to one chances of fertilization based on these numbers alone are incredible:

- Depending on the volume of ejaculate, the typical man has 40–400 million sperm cells contained in his ejaculate.
- Only 1% of sperm deposited in the vagina will make it to the top of the fallopian tubes potentially to fertilize a waiting ovum (Pinon, 2002).

Then, only 31% of all conceptions survive prenatal development to become living newborn babies (Pinon, 2002):

- During the **germinal period,** from the moment of conception through the fourteenth day, 58% of all fertilized ova will not survive due to gross abnormalities in one or more areas of physical development.
- During the **embryonic period,** from day 14 through day 56, approximately 20% of all embryos are spontaneously aborted, most often due to chromosomal abnormalities.
- During the **fetal period,** from the ninth week through birth, approximately 5% of fetuses are either spontaneously aborted before 20 weeks or are stillborn after 20 weeks of gestation. **Gestation** is the period of time between conception and birth; it is usually referred to in terms of weeks.

Trimesters: The Developing Fetus and Changes for Women and Partners

Pregnancy is an amazing time of growth and change. The changes that pregnancy leads to for women, men, and families are astonishing, both psychologically and socially. It could be argued that there is no other period in one's lifetime that brings so many large-scale changes. Read "Healthy Sexuality: The Developing Fetus's Chances for Survival" to learn how amazing it is that any of us sit here today.

Pregnancy is divided into 3-month blocks of time, commonly known as **trimesters.** Each of these trimesters includes significant development to the fertilized ovum, embryo, or fetus as well as accompanying changes for the pregnant woman and for nonpregnant partners.

Conception and the First Trimester The first trimester of pregnancy includes weeks 0–12 and begins after the first day of the last menstrual period. Fertilization takes place about 2 weeks after the first day of the last menstrual period. During ovulation, a woman's body releases an ovum, which is fertilized when one sperm cell breaks through the **zona pellucida,** the thick, protective layer on the outer part of the ovum. Fertilization happens typically in the upper third of one of the fallopian tubes. From there, the fertilized ovum, known as a **zygote,** begins to divide as it moves down the fallopian tube toward the uterus where, about 6 to 7 days after fertilization, it implants into the endometrium, the lining of the uterus. We call this attached mass of cells a **blastocyst.** Once attached, significant changes begin to occur in the tissue surrounding the blastocyst, which continues to develop into an **embryo.** In humans, an embryo is the product of conception from the time of implantation until the eighth week of development at which time it is considered a **fetus.** A developing baby is called a fetus from the eighth week of pregnancy until birth. Figure 8.4 illustrates the process of cell division and implantation of the fertilized ovum.

The embryo begins to release human chorionic gonadotropin (hCG), the hormone that signals the corpus luteum to release progesterone, a hormone that helps to sustain the

germinal period
The first phase of prenatal development, from conception through day 14.

embryonic period
The second phase of prenatal development, from day 14 through day 56 after conception.

fetal period
The third phase of prenatal development, from the ninth week through birth.

gestation
The period of time between conception and birth.

trimester
One of three periods of approximately 3 months each that make up full-term pregnancy.

zona pellucida
The thick, protective layer on the outer part of the ovum.

259

Figure 8.4

In the first 7 to 10 days after conception the fertilized egg travels through the fallopian tube to the uterus where it will implant and develop for the next 9 months.

(*top right*) David M. Phillips/Science Source

---

zygote
The product of the fusion of an egg and a sperm.

blastocyst
The developing zygote prior to implantation in the uterine wall.

embryo
A blastocyst that has implanted in the uterine wall.

fetus
A developing baby from the eighth week of pregnancy until birth.

amniotic sac (amnion)
The sac in which the fetus develops.

chorion
A membrane that separates the fetus from the mother.

---

pregnancy. This hormone release continues throughout the first trimester. It is important to note that when a woman takes a pregnancy test, whether it is an at-home urine test or in a doctor's office with a blood sample, a positive result is dependent upon the presence of hCG in the mother's body. Generally, levels can first be detected by a blood test about 11 days after conception and about 12 to 14 days after conception by a urine test (American Pregnancy Association, 2007). In general, hCG levels will double every 72 hours peaking in the first 8 to 11 weeks of pregnancy after which the levels will decline and level off for the remainder of the pregnancy (American Pregnancy Association, 2007).

The embryo cells are quickly differentiated into outside and internal cells. The outside cells develop into membranes that nourish and protect the embryo. These membranes include the **amniotic sac** or **amnion**, the **chorion**, the **placenta**, and the **umbilical cord** (Figure 8.5). The placenta is extraordinarily important; it nourishes the embryo and fetus as well as helps to remove waste. It is a semipermeable membrane, which means that some substances can pass through but others cannot. Nutrients and oxygen pass from the mother to the embryo through the placenta, and the embryo passes waste through the placenta to the mother to be expelled. Some dangerous substances (e.g., alcohol, nicotine) that women may ingest can pass through the semipermeable membrane to the developing embryo as well, endangering its sensitive development.

The internal cells of the embryo actually become the embryo itself. These cells develop into three distinct cellular layers and separate into the major organ systems in the body. The *ectoderm* becomes the nervous system, skin, endocrine glands, and sensory receptors; the *endoderm* becomes the respiratory and digestive system; and the *mesoderm*

Figure 8.5
The membranes that nourish and protect the embryo are the amnion, the chorion, the umbilical cord, and most important, the placenta.

becomes the reproductive, circulatory, and skeletal systems. During each month in each trimester, these internal cells develop in specific ways. Let's consider the first 3 months of development.

Month 1. By the end of week 4, the embryo is approximately 1/100 of an inch long. The ectoderm, endoderm, and mesoderm have developed and the embryo has developed a spinal cord.

Month 2. By the end of this month, all of the major body organs and systems have begun to develop. The limb buds of arms and legs are beginning to develop. Blood is being pumped and a heartbeat can be detected via ultrasound. The embryo at this point is approximately 1 inch long and weighs less than 1 ounce.

Month 3. The embryo is now considered a fetus. By the end of the month, all major organ systems and human characteristics are fully formed though highly immature. The fetus can move its hands and legs as well as open and close its mouth. Fingers and toes are becoming distinct and hair is forming on the head. At the end of this month, the fetus is approximately 4 inches long and weighs a little more than 1 ounce. Figure 8.6 summarizes the stages of prenatal growth from conception through birth.

Changes in Pregnant Women. By the time a woman finds out that she is pregnant, usually because she has missed her regular menstrual period, she may have experienced some symptoms of pregnancy. These may include sensitive or swollen breasts or both, nausea, fatigue, backaches, headaches, frequent urination, darkening of the areolas, and food cravings and aversions. Hormone production often influences these symptoms, which are usually most severe in the first trimester. One of the most common challenges more than half of all women face in the first trimester is morning sickness. It can range from mild to quite severe. Morning sickness is the nauseated feeling a pregnant woman gets and it does not always occur in the morning. It is quite common for morning sickness to occur at various points in the day and may or may not be accompanied with vomiting. The nausea is often a result of

placenta
An organ attached to the uterine wall that joins the embryo to the mother's bodily systems to transfer nutrients, oxygen, and waste products between the fetus and the mother.

umbilical cord
A structure that transports oxygen, waste, and nutrients between the fetus and the placenta.

Figure 8.6

Important milestones of fetal development.

(top) Biophoto Associates/Science Source; (center) Neil Bromhall/Science Source; (bottom) Steve Allen/Brand X Pictures/Getty Images

First trimester (first 3 months)

Conception to 4 weeks
- Is less than 1/10 inch long
- Beginning development of spinal cord, nervous system, gastrointestinal system, heart, and lungs
- Amniotic sac envelops the preliminary tissues of entire body
- Is called a "zygote"

8 weeks
- Is just over 1 inch long
- Face is forming with rudimentary eyes, ears, mouth, and tooth buds
- Arms and legs are moving
- Brain is forming
- Fetal heartbeat is detectable with ultrasound
- Is called an "embryo"

12 weeks
- Is about 3 inches long and weighs about 1 ounce
- Can move arms, legs, fingers, and toes
- Fingerprints are present
- Can smile, frown, suck, and swallow
- Sex is distinguishable
- Can urinate
- Is called a "fetus"

Second trimester (middle 3 months)

16 weeks
- Is about 6 inches long and weighs about 4 to 7 ounces
- Heartbeat is strong
- Skin is thin, transparent
- Downy hair (lanugo) covers body
- Fingernails and toenails are forming
- Has coordinated movements; is able to roll over in amniotic fluid

20 weeks
- Is about 12 inches long and weighs close to 1 pound
- Heartbeat is audible with ordinary stethoscope
- Sucks thumb
- Hiccups
- Hair, eyelashes, eyebrows are present

24 weeks
- Is about 14 inches long and weighs 1 to 1 1/2 pounds
- Skin is wrinkled and covered with protective coating (vernix caseosa)
- Eyes are open
- Waste matter is collected in bowel
- Has strong grip

Third trimester (last 3 months)

28 weeks
- Is about 16 inches long and weighs about 3 pounds
- Is adding body fat
- Is very active
- Rudimentary breathing movements are present

32 weeks
- Is 16 1/2 to 18 inches long and weighs 4 to 5 pounds
- Has periods of sleep and wakefulness
- Responds to sounds
- May assume the birth position
- Bones of head are soft and flexible
- Iron is being stored in liver

36 to 38 weeks
- Is 19 to 20 inches long and weighs 6 to 7 1/2 pounds
- Skin is less wrinkled
- Vernix caseosa is thick
- Lanugo is mostly gone
- Is less active
- Is gaining immunities from mother

ultrasound
A form of screening used to monitor development of the fetus throughout a pregnancy.

the increased hormones in the body. Many health care providers actually believe that morning sickness is a positive sign because it indicates the placenta is developing well (American Pregnancy Association, 2007). Normally, it eases as women near the second trimester (American Pregnancy Association, n.d.). For other common symptoms and signs of pregnancy, please see Figure 8.7.

Many parents are anxious to find out when their baby is due. Currently, there are several due date calculators online that can help women pinpoint their due date, but many people are curious as to how this calculation is done. The due date is typically calculated based on the first day of the mother's last menstrual period (LMP). Delivery of a baby is about 266 days from conception, or about 280 from your LMP. This is 40 weeks or 9 months (give or take a few weeks). If women do not remember the exact date of their LMP or when they might have conceived, doctors are able to pinpoint fetal development through the use of an **ultrasound**. Ultrasound is a very common form of screening and is used often to monitor the development of the fetus throughout the pregnancy. We will discuss it in detail a little further in the chapter.

Reproduction: Conception, Pregnancy, and Childbirth

THE FIRST SIGNS OF PREGNANCY

According to research by the American Pregnancy Association, a missed period tops the list as the first sign of pregnancy. Nausea and tender or changing breasts are number two and three respectively, occurring right on the heels of a missed period.

Food Related
2% report either a change in appetite, aversion to foods, or feeling hungrier.

FREQUENTLY SUSPECTED AS A FIRST SIGN BUT:
Headaches, increased urination, and cramps are considered early signs of pregnancy, however each only accounts for 1.5% of first signs.

OTHER SYMPTOMS
- Sensitivity to smell
- Gas
- Mood change
- Weight change
- Heartburn
- Cold Symptoms
- Constipation
- Backaches
- Gagging reflex

Most commonly reported first signs of pregnancy

- Fatigue
- Implantation bleeding
- Missed Period
- Tender or Changing Breasts
- Nausea

% of Reported signs: 3%, 8%, 29%, 17%, 25%

Figure 8.7

The first signs of pregnancy can vary widely. Described here are the most commonly reported signs and symptoms of pregnancy.

Women may not notice changes to their bellies during the first trimester, particularly if they are pregnant for this first time. This may be disappointing, as many women want to see the actual physical manifestations of a developing child growing within them. Others may feel stress because the impending bodily changes may make them worry about whether their partner will still find them attractive or desirable while they are pregnant.

The main physical changes during the first trimester are to the breasts. They increase in size and the nipples and areolas darken. The typical weight gain in the first trimester is about 5 pounds, though many women may notice a slight weight loss, particularly if they have been plagued with morning sickness. In some cultures, this weight gain enhances attractiveness significantly, and communicates to the family and community that the mother and fetus are healthy (Bledsoe, 2002).

Cognitively, women may begin to notice changes such as decreases in attention span and increased difficulties with decision-making, planning, and memory (Kumari, 2019). For example, 50–80% of women report lapses in their memories and thinking during the first trimester. Researchers have called this the "baby brain phenomenon." Interestingly, the female brain actually shrinks a bit during pregnancy (DeAngelis, 2008). This research suggests that on a biological and cognitive level, pregnancy and a short period after the baby's birth are "downtimes" for women. These downtimes can translate into some interesting experiences for women. For example, pregnant women may forget where they put their car keys or walk into a room and forget why they went there in the first place.

Emotionally, women can experience a vast array of feelings during the first trimester. The rapid increase in hormone production at unparalleled levels may contribute to women being irritable or tearful. Hormones, however, are not the only plausible correlation to their increased emotionality. Pregnancy brings many social changes, too. Families, friends, and possibly partners may treat pregnant women differently in their own excitement and expectation of a newborn baby. In addition, women and their partners may begin to ponder the responsibilities and expectations of parenthood. Such factors can be confusing, and women and their partners often find themselves overwhelmed with information, advice, and opinions. Women also experience a variety of feelings regarding the pregnancy itself. Fear, anxiety, excitement, and joy are all common emotions they feel during this first trimester.

Changes in Nonpregnant Partners. Partners also experience hopes, anxieties, fears, and questions similar to those of their pregnant partner. Finding out that their partner is pregnant may trigger feelings of responsibility, excitement, relief, and even some irrational fears (Brott & Ash, 2001). One study found that approximately 60% of men whose partners were pregnant had fleeting thoughts about whether they were actually the biological father of the child despite knowing that their partner was not engaging in sexual relations outside of their relationship. This suspiciousness may stem from the idea that men believe that they are not capable of accomplishing something as amazing as the creation of new life (Shapiro, 1992).

Partners also experience a connection with the growing child inhabiting *their partner's* body. Studies show that pregnant women "connect" with their pregnancies sooner than the partners (Brott & Ash, 2001). Pregnancy can feel more abstract or distant for partners. They may reflect on what it will mean for them to connect to the pregnancy and their partner in new ways as they go through this experience together.

Second Trimester The second trimester, between weeks 13 and 24, brings a whole host of new experiences. Because they often feel better and more energized with the lessening of morning sickness, pregnant women may find this the most exciting time during pregnancy. In fact, many people say women have a "pregnant glow" during this trimester. Women may revel in their bodies, as their bellies begin to display their pregnancy. They may begin to feel the first movements of the fetus, described as "flutters" or "bubbles." Planning for the birth and the new addition to the family are activities that women may engage in during this time. Let's consider how the fetus is developing during these 3 months.

Month 4. Facial development continues as the outer ear begins to take shape. The fetus moves a lot, which women begin to feel. By the end of this month, the fetus is about 8 to 9 inches long and weighs about 6 ounces.

Month 5. During this time of rapid growth, the fetus develops muscle, grows fat under its skin, and grows hair on top of it. Internal organs continue to develop with the exception of the lungs, which fully develop in the last month of the pregnancy. The male genitals begin to form, making it easier to detect the sex of the baby via ultrasound. The fetus sleeps and wakes at regular intervals. Often lulled to sleep by the woman's movement during the day, the fetus may move around a lot when she lies down at night being awoken by the woman's stillness. At the end of this month, the fetus weighs about 1 pound and is 10 to 12 inches in length.

Month 6. Brain development continues during this month. Eggs will develop in the ovaries of female fetuses and the fetus's skin will be covered with a fine, soft hair called **lanugo** as well as a protective, waxy substance called **vernix**. Fingerprints will develop in this month. By the end of this trimester, the fetus is 11 to 14 inches in length and weighs approximately 1 to 1.5 pounds.

Feeling the baby move is one of the highlights for pregnant women and their partners in the second trimester.
Auremar/123RF

For a summary of the changes that occur during the second trimester, refer back to Figure 8.6.

Changes in Pregnant Women. Women begin to "feel" pregnant at this time because their regular clothes no longer fit. They begin to feel the fetus's movements and often report that the pregnancy feels more real, which is perhaps a psychological sign that they are accepting this new presence as separate from themselves.

Physical symptoms of the second trimester vary. Some women experience little or no physical symptoms; others experience changes in skin coloration, swelling in the extremities, clumsiness, backaches, nosebleeds, heartburn, and hemorrhoids. Weight gain in this trimester is approximately 1 pound per week. The amount of weight gained during an entire pregnancy depends on many factors, such as whether a woman was overweight or underweight before pregnancy. Every woman should talk with her health care providers about the optimal amount of weight she should gain during her pregnancy. Figure 8.8 shows how the woman's body adapts to the presence of the growing fetus during pregnancy.

Changes in Nonpregnant Partners. The pregnancy may begin to feel more real or concrete for partners, too. Partners who have attended prenatal appointments most likely have heard the heartbeat or have seen the developing fetus through ultrasound. As the pregnant woman's bodily changes become more obvious, nonpregnant partners may begin to feel more "left out" (Brott & Ash, 2001). For a more detailed discussion on how partners can be involved in the experience of pregnancy, see "Healthy Sexuality: Tips for Nonpregnant Partners."

Some cultures have a ceremonial practice that allows the fathers-to-be to act out their own pregnancy. In native North and South American tribes, some husbands experience a sympathetic pregnancy during their wife's pregnancy, labor, and delivery (Lang & Vantine, 1998). These symptomatic experiences are referred to as **couvade**. Some men actually "go into labor" in a place separate from their wife when she is delivering. Men may experience these symptoms as social and psychological reactions to stress and a change in social status within their relationship and outside in the community. This experience is regarded as normal and natural for the men.

Third Trimester The exciting third trimester, weeks 25 to 40, is a time of rapid fetal growth and great emotion for the partners as they prepare for the day a new life will enter their world. *Finalizing* aptly describes the activities of the woman, her partner, and her family, as well as those of the developing fetus.

lanugo
A fine, soft hair that covers a fetus's body.

vernix
A protective waxy substance on a fetus's body.

couvade
A syndrome in which male partners experience pregnancy symptoms similar to those of their pregnant partners.

HEALTHY Sexuality

Tips for Nonpregnant Partners

Despite the fact that partners do not go through the same physical, psychological, hormonal, and social changes of pregnancy, they do experience unique challenges and have questions. For example, they may wonder how they can best help their pregnant partner through the valleys and peaks of pregnancy and childbirth. Here are a few tips on how to be involved in this experience.

- Attend prenatal care appointments. These visits are a wonderful way to ask questions and learn more about the pregnancy and developing fetus.
- Attend prenatal classes such as Lamaze birth classes and parenting courses. These offer a wide array of tips, advice, and tools for preparing for this new life event. They also give you an opportunity for further communication with your partner.
- Ask questions to share in the excitement. Ask your partner about the pregnancy such as how she is feeling or what concerns she has.

Source: Sutter Health, n.d.

Month 7. The fetus may begin to feel cramped in the uterus as it gains length and weight. Despite this restricted area, it kicks and moves often. It can open and close its eyes and can see light changes outside of the uterus. It can make grasping motions with its hands and may suck its thumbs or fingers. At the conclusion of this month, it is about 15 inches long and weighs about 2 to 2.5 pounds. If a woman experiences premature labor and gives birth to the fetus during this month, its chance for survival is high, especially if hospitalization is an option. It may need hospital care, particularly due to the immaturity of the lungs.

Figure 8.8
During pregnancy, a woman's body goes through dramatic change. Most notable are the enlargement of the uterus and the increase in breast size as the body prepares for milk production.

(a) Before conception
(b) 4 months
(c) 7 months
(d) 9 months

266

Month 8. The fetus gains a lot of weight during this month, as it gets ready to enter the world. The skeletal system gains strength and the brain begins to differentiate the various regions that are synonymous with adult brain structure. The brain now directs the bodily functions of the fetus. Taste buds develop, which means a fetus can show preferences for different tastes, such as salty, bitter, sweet, and sour. At the end of this month, the fetus is approximately 16 to 18 inches long and weighs between 4 and 5 pounds.

Month 9. Lung development finalizes during this month, preparing the fetus to breathe when it is born. In addition, the fetus gains approximately 0.5 pound per week. The fetus turns to a head-down position to prepare for birth. A fetus that does not turn is in a **breech** position. If health care providers cannot get the fetus to rotate into the head-down position, they may schedule a **cesarean (or C-section) birth,** a surgical birth of the baby via incision in the mother's abdomen. This intervention minimizes the health risks to both baby and mother if the baby is not in the right position. Figure 8.9 illustrates a fetus in the breech position and a fetus with its head down ready for a vaginal birth. By their birthday, most babies weigh between 6 and 9 pounds and are between 18 and 22 inches long. Interestingly, some cross-cultural differences occur with birth weight. In the United States, low birth weight is anything less than 5.8 pounds. Other places, however, define low birth weight differently, as discussed in "Healthy Sexuality: Variations in Low Birth Weight Across Countries."

breech
Position of a fetus that is emerging with buttocks or legs first rather than head first.

cesarean (C-section) birth
Surgical removal of a fetus from the mother's uterus through an incision in the abdomen.

Changes in Pregnant Women. By the end of the third trimester, most women are ready to birth their babies. Many second trimester symptoms continue into the third. Additionally, women begin to feel achy or tired because of the pressure and weight of the growing fetus. Pressure symptoms include varicose veins, hemorrhoids, swelling in the legs and ankles, leg cramps, backaches, and shortness of the breath as the large fetus pushes against women's diaphragm. Many women experience *Braxton-Hicks contractions,* which are likened to a dress rehearsal for the big day. These contractions can be quite uncomfortable but rarely do anything to enhance the labor process.

Emotionally, women begin to feel tired of being pregnant. As their due date approaches, they become more anxious and apprehensive about the baby's health and the processes of labor and delivery. It is also common for women and their partners to be nervous about their parenting skills.

Typical weight gain in the third trimester is about 1 pound per week. Total weight gain for a pregnancy should be approximately 25 to 35 pounds depending on a woman's prepregnancy weight.

WHAT'S ON YOUR MIND?

Q: I am pregnant in my third trimester and I would really like to know if having one glass of wine will really hurt my baby?

ANSWER: The effects of small-to-moderate amounts of alcohol consumption on pregnancy are unclear, but heavy drinking and binge drinking present serious risks to a developing fetus. Researchers are still trying to understand the effects of how much and when alcohol is ingested on an embryo and fetus. Currently, the consensus seems to be that any alcohol consumption is unsafe and should be strongly cautioned against (Curtis & Schuler, 2008). Many people find this statement to be extreme. Some physicians state that enjoying a small glass of wine in the third trimester is completely safe. Some midwives suggest that a small glass of wine may help relax a woman who is highly anxious about her child's impending birth. Regardless of your stance on this issue, alcohol can pose risks to a developing child, and it's advisable to be highly cautious in alcohol consumption during pregnancy. After all, is alcohol really worth the risk of your child's health?

HEALTHY Sexuality

Variations in Low Birth Weight Across Countries

Not all babies are born within the same average birth weights, creating an interesting difference across countries. In some cultures, babies are born with lower average birth weights compared to the U.S. average, but they are in the normal range for their own country. Nutritional status and heritable factors are possible reasons for this. In fact, scientists believe the birth weight of a newborn largely depends on the health and nutritional status of the mother, and other factors such as the amount of weight the mother gains during pregnancy (Curtis & Schuler, 2008). In the United States, different maternal health factors correlate with low birth weights, such as chronic health problems, substance abuse, and placental problems. Low income and lack of education are associated with an increased risk for low birth weight, although researchers do not yet fully understand the reasons for this connection.

Changes in Nonpregnant Partners. Partners experience thoughts and questions similar to pregnant women: Am I ready for this? Will I be a good parent? What will my child look like? Social and identity shifts can occur at this time, and partners begin to notice other parents in their own social circles and environments. They may seek out other parents' advice about their new life experience.

Potential Problems During Pregnancy

Occasionally, complications arise during pregnancy. In the United States, there are approximately 6 million pregnancies every year with just under 4 million resulting in live births. Out of those, approximately 875,000 women experience one or more pregnancy complications (American Pregnancy Association, n.d.; CDC, 2012c). Let's consider the following pregnancy-related complications.

Figure 8.9

Typically, at birth the baby is in a head-down position in the mother's womb (left, at 40 weeks) and emerges from the birth canal head first. A breech presentation (right) usually results in a cesarean delivery unless the baby turns to a head-down position by delivery.

Uterus
Fetus
Cervix
Plug of mucous
Vagina
Bladder

Racial and Ethnic Disparities in Pregnancy Complications There is a critical issue currently plaguing pregnancy and childbirth in the United States that must be highlighted and discussed. The issue surrounds the high incidence of pregnancy complications and maternal and infant injury and death as a result of being pregnant and giving birth in the United States. It is important to understand that the increased risk exists for all women who give birth and infants born (see Figure 8.10), but there is great disparity for women of color compared to white women. Poor women are especially at risk.

We know from recent statistics that approximately 700 women die each year in the United States from pregnancy-related complications (Petersen et al., 2019). The risk of death related to childbirth is three times higher for women of color than for White women, even when they receive the same level of prenatal medical care. The issue is complex, and truly understanding the causes of this gross disparity requires innovation in thought and research extending beyond medical lines of research (Mkandawire-Valhmu et al., 2018). What we are beginning to understand is that the experience of racism, sexism, poverty, and a lack of good health care, social support, resources, and safe neighborhoods endured by women may be significant contributors to decreased health and well-being of pregnant women and their babies. One study, for example, detailed how the lack of social support and resulting stress and isolation felt by black women leave them to face complicated life challenges that can contribute to a wide variety of poor birth outcomes (Mkandawire-Valhmu et al., 2018). This is one more area where we see communities and healthy sexuality negatively impacted by continued racism, sexism, and a lack of attention and resources paid to women and children of color. In moving toward sexual literacy, we must bring these critical issues to the forefront and work to reduce the incredible social, economic, and health disparities that continue to bring harm to these communities.

Infant mortality per 1,000 live births, 2014

Country	Rate
United States	5.8
Canada	4.8
Switzerland	3.9
United Kingdom	3.9
Netherlands	3.6
France	3.5
Comparable Country Average	3.4
Australia	3.4
Belgium	3.4
Germany	3.2
Austria	3
Sweden	2.2
Japan	2.1

Figure **8.10**

Infant mortality in the United States.

Comparable countries are defined as those with above median GDP and above median GDP per capita in at least one of the past 10 years. Canada data estimated from 2012.

ectopic pregnancy

A complication in which a fertilized ovum grows outside the uterus, most commonly in the fallopian tubes.

Ectopic Pregnancy If a fertilized ovum implants outside of the uterus, usually in a fallopian tube, it is called an **ectopic pregnancy.** A variety of factors may cause this complication to occur, including previous STIs or other conditions that may have caused scar tissue to develop, which then prevents a fertilized ovum to move through a fallopian tube to the uterus. Ectopic pregnancies are extraordinarily dangerous and can cause significant pain and internal bleeding if not detected early. They are a significant health risk to women. They are not viable, meaning that fetal development and survival is impossible because they have no nutrients to help them continue to grow.

miscarriage (spontaneous abortion)

The unintentional loss of an embryo or fetus during the first 20 weeks of pregnancy.

Miscarriage A **miscarriage,** also known as **spontaneous abortion,** is the premature end of pregnancy usually before 20 weeks of gestation. When a miscarriage occurs, especially in the early part of pregnancy, it is difficult if not impossible to discern the cause. Many factors can cause miscarriage, including the following (Curtis & Schuler, 2008):

- Chromosomal abnormalities: Scientists speculate that when abnormal genetic chromosomes are present in either the egg or the sperm, the pregnancy is susceptible to miscarriage.
- Structural problems with the uterus: Factors may affect the uterus, such as uterine scar tissue, possibly resulting from an STI or from a second trimester abortion, and may make it difficult for an embryo to adhere to the uterine wall.
- Chronic maternal health conditions.
- High fever early in the pregnancy.
- Certain autoimmune disorders, such as type I diabetes or lupus.
- Unusual infections: Toxoplasmosis, a condition caused by contact with feline feces, has caused some women to miscarry. If you have a cat box and suspect you are pregnant, arrange for someone else to clean it. The STI syphilis can also cause a miscarriage.
- Substance use: Alcohol, cigarettes, and other chemical substances early in a pregnancy may cause miscarriage.
- Trauma from an accident or major surgery: Trauma to the abdomen whether from a fall, car accident, or surgery can cause the placenta to detach from the uterine wall, cutting off the fetus's access to oxygen and nutrients.

stillbirth

The unintentional loss of a pregnancy after 20 weeks of gestation.

preterm (premature)

Birth of an infant less than 37 weeks after conception.

The loss of a viable pregnancy after 20 weeks of gestation is called a **stillbirth.** No matter when it occurs, the loss of a pregnancy can be devastating for the mother and her partner. They experience this event as a loss of their baby, their hopes and wishes for their future (Swanson et al., 2007). People can experience grief and anxiety from days to years after a miscarriage or stillbirth. In addition, people may feel stress when they decide to try to conceive again as they worry about whether they will miscarry again. Additionally, women who do not conceive or who experience another miscarriage within a year of their loss may require more extensive support and assessments of their physical and emotional health (Swanson, Connor, Jolley, Pettinato, & Wang, 2007).

Preterm Birth A baby born before 37 weeks of gestation is considered to be **preterm.** Many often refer to these babies as "preemies." Another term often used in this context is **premature,** although premature

A preterm or premature baby is born before 37 weeks of gestation.
Alvis Upitis/Getty Images

birth most often describes infants whose lungs are immature at the time of birth (Curtis & Schuler, 2008). As with miscarriage, preterm birth can evoke a host of emotions, particularly anxiety, as parents and doctors work together for the health and survival of the infant. The cause of preterm birth is often difficult for medical professionals to discern. Doctors may attempt to understand the cause of preterm labor to stop it or to prevent it from occurring in a subsequent pregnancy. Some risk factors for preterm birth are as follows (Curtis & Schuler, 2008; March of Dimes, 2018).

- Having experienced preterm labor or delivery, or both, in a previous pregnancy
- Using chemical substances, specifically cigarettes and cocaine
- Carrying twins or multiple fetuses
- Having a cervix or uterus that is structurally abnormal
- Having abdominal surgical procedures during pregnancy
- Experiencing infections in either the urinary tract or the roots of the teeth
- Having had or currently having STIs
- Being underweight prior to or during pregnancy
- Carrying a fetus with chromosomal disorders
- Experiencing increased levels of **estriol,** a chemical found in women's saliva. (If a woman tests for high levels of estriol, she is seven times more likely to deliver a preterm baby.)

estriol
A chemical found in women's saliva that may indicate preterm birth.

Treatment of premature labor often requires partial or continuous bed rest and some medications. Nearly 1 million women are prescribed bed rest every year due to complications in their pregnancies. Not all medical professionals agree with the practice of bed rest as it can lead to other complications due to lack of movement (Curtis & Schuler, 2008).

Gestational Diabetes **Gestational diabetes,** intolerance of glucose during pregnancy, is a fairly common complication of pregnancy. It occurs when a woman's body does not produce enough insulin or when her pregnant body does not use insulin properly. According to the CDC (2019a), every year between 2% and 10% of pregnancies in the United States are affected by gestational diabetes. The biological reasons for gestational diabetes are largely still a mystery. One hypothesis is that the hormones involved in pregnancy interfere with how the body uses insulin, often leading to insulin resistance. Once the woman gives birth, the gestational diabetes usually disappears. If she gets pregnant again, however, she has about a 90% chance of experiencing the condition again (Curtis & Schuler, 2008). Risk factors for developing gestational diabetes include the following:

gestational diabetes
A condition of glucose intolerance that may occur during pregnancy.

- Age 30 or older
- Obesity
- A family history of type I or II diabetes
- Gestational diabetes in a previous pregnancy
- A previous baby weighing over 9.5 pounds
- Mother's own birth weight in the bottom 10th percentile

Detecting Problems in Pregnancy

Pregnant women may receive a variety of tests to monitor both their health and the development of the fetus. Historically, health care professionals checked the pregnant woman's blood pressure, weight, and urine throughout the pregnancy (Simonds, 2007). Urine tests can reveal gestational diabetes, a kidney problem, or a poor diet. Now a multitude of

amniocentesis

A procedure done between 16 and 20 weeks of gestation in which a doctor removes a small amount of amniotic fluid via a needle in the abdomen to test for genetic abnormalities.

chorionic villus sampling (CVS)

A procedure in which a small amount of tissue from the placenta is analyzed for genetic abnormalities.

prenatal tests are routinely used—a practice that is debatable. Part of the debate surrounds tests that might return a *false-positive* result, meaning that the test seems to show an abnormality that does not actually exist. For example, doctors might see what appears to be an abnormality on an ultrasound only to find out later that there was a glitch in the equipment or that what they thought they originally saw is no longer present. Receiving a false-positive result, only to find out later that the result was inaccurate, can be devastating, or at least cause unnecessary worry for a pregnant woman and her partner. As a consequence, some women question the practice of prenatal testing, or at least too much of it. Let's consider some common prenatal tests.

Amniocentesis An **amniocentesis** is a procedure done usually between 16 and 20 weeks of gestation. A doctor removes a small amount of amniotic fluid via a needle in the mother's abdomen (Figure 8.11). Genetic studies are done on the cells contained in the fluid to test for conditions such as Down syndrome and cystic fibrosis. Amniotic fluid can also give doctors information regarding the presence of defects such as spina bifida. Due to the higher rates of genetic abnormalities more common among older mothers, doctors recommend this test for women over the age of 35.

Some women are concerned about the risks of an amniocentesis, particularly the risk of miscarriage. One study documented the risk of miscarriage to be about 0.06%, or 1 in 1,600 (Edelman et al., 2006). Another study estimated the risk to be between 0.13% and 0.97% for women who had an amniocentesis prior to week 24 of pregnancy, which is still quite low (Odibo et al., 2008).

Chorionic Villus Sampling **Chorionic villus sampling (CVS)** is another screening procedure in which a doctor obtains a small amount of tissue from the placenta by inserting a thin, hollow tube into the vagina and through the cervix to reach the placenta (see Figure 8.11). The tissue is analyzed for chromosomal disorders and specific genetic diseases. This procedure can be performed as early as 10 weeks of gestation.

Ultrasound Ultrasound is a very common form of screening and is used often to monitor the development of the fetus throughout the pregnancy. In an ultrasound procedure, a device known as a transducer is placed on the abdomen. This device directs high-frequency

Figure **8.11**

Two common procedures for detecting abnormalities in pregnancy are (a) amniocentesis and (b) chorionic villus sampling (CVS).

(a) Amniocentesis

(b) Chorionic villus sampling

Figure 8.12
Ultrasound is a safe way to monitor a baby's growth and development throughout pregnancy. (a) 3-D ultrasound image; (b) traditional ultrasound image.
(a) whitetherock photo/Shutterstock; (b) UHB Trust/Stone/Getty Images

(a) 3-D ultrasound image

(b) Traditional ultrasound image

sound waves toward the fetus. The echoes created from the sound waves are then turned into visual images of the fetus. Details such as arms, legs, fingers, toes, and internal organs can be seen on a computer monitor. An ultrasound can detect several different kinds of birth defects and is the primary way parents find out the sex of their fetus. An amniocentesis and CVS can provide this information as well. Other information parents and doctors can detect from an ultrasound includes:

- Number of fetuses present
- Fetal growth
- Confirmation of due date
- Position of placenta

A three-dimensional ultrasound provides a more detailed picture of the fetus. Figure 8.12 shows examples of both a traditional and a three-dimensional ultrasound.

BIRTH AND THE POSTPARTUM PERIOD: WHAT TO EXPECT

"It's time!" These two exciting words may be spoken at approximately 40 weeks of pregnancy, the culmination of a long period of change, development, and preparation. The average length of a pregnancy is 40 weeks, but a normal birth can occur anywhere from 37 to 42 weeks. Only 3–5% of babies are actually born on their due date (Dunham et al., 1992; McCulloch, 2018). It is a time of increased anxiety, excitement, and anticipation of the coming birth. Health care professionals are not exactly sure why labor starts. It most likely has something to do with a chemical message from the fetus that alerts the woman's body to begin preparing for its journey through the birth canal. Labor and childbirth occur in three distinct stages (Figure 8.13).

Stage 1 prepares the cervix for delivery of the baby. Propelled by intense contractions of the uterine walls, the cervix will undergo a process of **dilation,** which expands the cervical opening to approximately 10 cm in diameter. **Effacement,** the thinning of the cervical tissue to a paperlike thickness, allows for dilation and the passage of the fetus into the vaginal canal. During this stage of labor, women begin to feel the pain of childbirth as **contractions** do their job. In the childbirth process, the work of labor is done through a series of contractions. These contractions cause the upper part of the uterus (fundus) to

dilation
The expansion of the cervical opening (to approximately 10 cm) in preparation for birth.

effacement
Thinning of cervical tissue that occurs in preparation for birth.

contractions
Muscular movement that causes the upper part of the uterus to tighten and thicken while the cervix and lower portion of the uterus stretch and relax, helping the baby pass from the uterus into the birth canal for delivery.

(a) First stage of birth: Cervix dilates.

(b) Second stage of birth: Baby emerges.

(c) Baby has arrived.

(d) Third stage of birth: expelling afterbirth.

Figure 8.13
Childbirth occurs in three stages.
(c) Rune Hellestad/Corbis/Getty Images

tighten and thicken while the cervix and lower portion of the uterus stretch and relax, helping the baby pass from inside the uterus and into the birth canal for delivery. Contractions are often described as a cramping or tightening sensation that starts in the back and moves around to the front in a wavelike manner. Others say the contraction feels like pressure in the back. During a contraction, the abdomen becomes hard to the touch.

Stage 2 involves the actual birth of the fetus. As contractions get closer together and more intense, the laboring woman will begin to feel the urge to push as the fetus moves down through the birth canal to the vaginal opening. The end result of stage 2 is the birth of the child.

Stage 3 involves the birth of the placenta. Once the child is born, the woman will continue to feel contractions as her uterus releases the placenta. Like the infant, the placenta will pass through the birth canal and vagina. The doctor or midwife will inspect it closely to ensure that the entire placenta is present as infection can occur if any part of it remains inside the woman's body.

In the United States, the placenta is usually seen as nothing more than medical waste—a by-product of childbirth that is most often simply discarded. Consequently, most people don't spend much time contemplating its life-sustaining powers.

The placenta is an incredible, life-sustaining organ that is treated with respect in many cultures. For example, the Ibo people of Nigeria regard the placenta as the newborn infant's twin or double. They believe that it must be recognized and celebrated (Birdsong, 1998).

The Hmong people of Southeast Asia believe it is the father's responsibility to bury the placenta. Where the father buries it depends on the child's gender. If the child is female, the placenta is buried in the ground underneath the parents' bed. If the child is male, the placenta is usually buried near the strongest base or structural support of the family home, a place of honor for the family. This burial site defines the ancestral home for the family (Birdsong, 1998). By comparison, the Sambia people of Papua New Guinea and their neighboring tribes believe that the placenta is polluting to men. But it may help women get pregnant. Women, then, bury the placentas in the floor of the menstrual hut, which is not only off limits to men but is also outside of the village (Herdt, 2006).

Some cultural groups in Vietnam and China prepare the placenta for the newborn's mother to eat. Considered a source of protein and nutrition, it is thought that the placenta aids in the production and quality of the new mother's breast milk.

Options for Giving Birth

The act of birthing a child brings on a wealth of emotions. People use anxiety, fear, elation, and joy, among other words, to describe this event. In addition to experiencing the multitude of emotions, women have choices to consider when it comes to their child's birth. Over the years in the United States, childbirth has become a medical procedure that takes place in a hospital. In contrast, many other countries combine indigenous childbirth practices with holistic medicine and, when needed, with hospital delivery (Floyd & Sargent, 1997).

Because childbirth has become so medicalized in the United States, many women may not realize they have choices, and they may not realize that they have authority over their childbirth experiences. Learning about all the options for childbirth allows women to make decisions that reflect their desires for pain management, movement while laboring, birthing environment, partner involvement, and medical interventions if they are needed. Knowing about the options helps women and their partners take an active, authoritative role in their birthing experience or in helping someone else. Consider some of these options described in "Controversies in Sexuality: Hospital Birth Versus Home Birth: Is One Safer Than the Other?"

Birth Assistance and Interventions

Preparing for the birth of a child requires that parents make many important decisions. Some decisions revolve around what kind of birth assistance might be helpful in the labor process. It is also important to know about medical interventions should any complication arise during labor and delivery. Understanding this information helps people remain empowered to make decisions even when they are in the vulnerable position of labor and delivery.

Some women and their partners have found one type of birth assistance, the Lamaze method, helpful during labor. Learn how it may assist women when you read "Healthy Sexuality: Lamaze Method—Try This."

Midwives and Doulas While some women prefer the presence of a physician at the birth of their child, others prefer the more involved and hands-on orientation of a midwife, doula, or trained labor coach. The profession of midwifery is quite old. Prior to the 1920s, in the United States, **midwives** attended and assisted in births but were not considered to be trained medical

midwife
A person who has been trained in most aspects of pregnancy, labor, and delivery but who is not a physician.

Consistent fetal monitoring is a regular part of maternal care when delivering in a hospital.

Jason Edwards/National Geographic/Getty Images

CONTROVERSIES in Sexuality

Hospital Birth Versus Home Birth: Is One Safer Than the Other?

Around the world, childbirth happens in a variety of settings. In many countries, it is actually more typical to find that childbirth happens within the home accompanied by a midwife or individual trained in assisting women through the process of birth. Women in the U.S. can decide whether to give birth in a hospital or at home. Part of their decision relates to which place they perceive to be safer to give birth. Part of their decision relates to which place may provide a more comfortable and natural environment to give birth.

Hospital birthing has some real advantages, and many families prefer this method. One advantage is that modern medical technology is at the fingertips of medical personnel should something unforeseen happen during childbirth. Advocates of hospital birth argue that there is no substitute for these modern medical advances, such as fetal monitoring. Women with high-risk pregnancies due to blood pressure, gestational diabetes, multiple fetuses, or other medical conditions are better off with hospital birth. In addition, many women prefer to give birth in a hospital, where they can receive pain management drugs to minimize the pain of childbirth.

Many hospitals have private labor, delivery, and recovery rooms. They allow women to make more decisions about their birth experiences, including choosing a labor coach, keeping lights turned down, and asking for softer sound levels. Partners and spouses may stay overnight to aid in the care of the newborn and the mother.

While many agree that hospitals provide the most medical technology to support childbirth, a growing movement encourages home birth. Many women in other cultures give birth at home, a practice that has been going on for centuries. Part of the reason that the home birth movement is growing is because hospitals make childbirth overly technological and institutionalized and may even utilize interventions that actually put mothers and babies at risk for complications (Rothman, 2007). Parents often feel that their personal comfort, desires, and wishes for childbirth are not placed at a high priority by medical staff seeking to do their job. For example, directly after birth, a newborn may be whisked off to undergo a long list of medical procedures that involve weighing, measuring, bathing, and testing. These procedures may override the mother and her partner's desires to spend the first moments of life bonding with their newborn, unless they know to address this beforehand with their obstetrician, pediatrician, and nursery staff.

Women who give birth at home may labor in bed, outside, on the couch, or in a bathtub. In addition, they are free to decide who should be present during the birth. Home births can empower women to create a birth experience where they have some authority.

The question, then, is this: Is giving birth in a hospital safer than giving birth at home in the United States for mothers and newborns?

Yes

- Medical technology has made huge gains in helping to deal with real life risks to either the mother or a newborn, or both (Curtis & Schuler, 2008).
- Women with high-risk pregnancies may need the help that a hospital staff provides.
- Constant fetal monitoring during labor can help medical personnel foresee problems that may arise.
- Drugs for pain management are easily administered in hospitals.

No

- Hospitals make childbirth overly technological and institutionalized (Rothman, 2007).
- Doctors and hospitals routinely use interventions that are shown to actually increase the cesarean birth rate.
- Hospital workers need to enforce hospital policies that may be unnecessary in routine childbirth.
- To circumvent the possibility of being sued, doctors may choose to deliver a baby by C-section even prior to it becoming a medical necessity (Simonds, Rothman, & Norman, 2007).
- Because a home birth is more free of typical hospital routines practiced during labor and delivery, families may experience a very different beginning from the first moment that labor starts.

What's your perspective?

1. What do you see as advantages to having a baby born in a hospital?
2. What do you see as advantages to having a baby born at home?
3. In what way(s) can you take an active, authoritative stance in the health care of yourself, your partner, and your baby during pregnancy and childbirth, to ensure both safety and personal choice?

HEALTHY Sexuality

Lamaze Method—Try This

The Lamaze method of childbirth was designed to help women manage the pain of childbirth. It helps them maintain their focus and calm. It is a series of breathing exercises that vary from slow, deep breaths during the early parts of labor to quick short breaths during the latter parts of labor. Individuals are often curious if Lamaze really works. Try this exercise to see how Lamaze works. Then decide if you think Lamaze would be a useful tool.

Materials:

1. Two ice cubes
2. An object of focus, such as a picture on a wall
3. Stopwatch or timer

Procedure:

1. Hold on tightly to one ice cube in your right hand.
2. Time how long you can hold onto it before it becomes too uncomfortable. Write down that time.
3. Now, hold on tightly to the other ice cube with your left hand.
4. Look at your focus object while inhaling and exhaling slowly. Be aware of your breathing and concentrate.
5. Time how long you are able to hold onto the ice cube before it becomes too uncomfortable. Write down that time.
6. Compare the two times. You should have been able to hold onto the ice cube in your left hand longer than the one in your right because of your concentration and breathing exercises.

Lamaze breathing works on two levels in the laboring woman—that is, cognitive and physiological. Cognitively, the attention required to do Lamaze breathing correctly necessarily steers the laboring woman's attention away from the pain her body is experiencing, to her breath: how it feels (cool going in, warm coming out), how deep it is (upper lungs? lower lungs/diaphragm? deep belly?), how long it stays in her lungs before the exhalation (a slow pace or a faster one?), all of which can significantly affect her perception of the pain.

With Lamaze breathing, the mind quite literally begins to "steer" the body toward a more comfortable labor. As the breathing techniques start to work on the mind and body, circulation and oxygenation of the body increase. This is good for labor progress as opposed to the constricted blood flow and restricted breathing that occurs when our bodies naturally react to stressful situations.

---

practitioners. Today, midwives are typically registered nurses with additional training and certification in nurse-midwifery. Like doctors, midwives provide prenatal care. While the prenatal care provided by doctors and midwives is quite similar, many women report greater satisfaction with midwives (Turnbull et al., 1996). In addition, many midwives provide care to mothers after the birth of their babies in order to monitor and assist with issues such as recovery, prevention of postpartum depression, and breastfeeding.

Doulas are trained labor coaches who have extensive training to assist a pregnant woman and her partner in the labor and delivery process. In fact, many of them are certified through educational programs as childbirth assistants. They often assist midwives or doctors in birth-related activities and provide a constant presence during labor. Doulas can act as a woman's advocate as their knowledge is often extensive due to their training and certification. They may even be able to provide another perspective if a question of using an intervention arises during the childbirth process.

doula
A person trained in the process of labor and delivery and assists a midwife in childbirth.

Pain Management: Hydrotherapy and Pain Medication Labor can be painful for the birthing mother. Different ways to help ease the pain include hydrotherapy and pain medication. **Hydrotherapy,** immersion in a tub of warm water, may help the mother relax her muscles. Some women opt to deliver their babies in water as well. This method of delivery may create a better transition from the warm, insulated environment of the womb to the cold, harsh

hydrotherapy
The use of a warm tub of water in the birth process to encourage relaxation.

277

Delivering a baby in a tub is a great way to lessen contractions and create a more calm entrance into the world.
Ian Hooton/Getty Images

epidural
A form of pain management in which a doctor passes pain medication through a small tube that has been inserted at the base of a woman's spine.

environment of the outside world. If a bath is not available, many women find that a shower can provide similar pain relief and relaxing effects during their labor.

Pain medication is an option for women who want to ease the pain of childbirth. Sedatives and a variety of anesthesia may help relieve labor pains. A doctor may prescribe sedatives or antianxiety medications to help calm a woman who has become anxious as a result of the pain she is experiencing. They may use a local or a regional anesthesia to numb a woman's pelvic area to lessen the feeling of the pain. The **epidural** is a common form of pain management. With an epidural a doctor inserts a small tube at the base of a woman's spine. A woman can then receive pain medication through this tube as needed throughout the labor and delivery process. All these pain management techniques may allow a woman to experience labor and delivery in relative comfort. In addition, they allow her to be awake and alert so that she can actively push the baby out during delivery.

Interventions The medical field has many available interventions should they be needed to assist in the birth of a child. Unfortunately, women in labor often feel ill-equipped to assert their wishes or concerns when a medical professional urges them to approve the use of an intervention. Doctors gain more control over the birth experience if they convince women and their partners that what they are doing reduces risk and is in the baby and mother's best interests. For example, fetal monitoring during labor can solely dictate the need for a C-section birth if the *monitor* indicates fetal distress. The implication of this is a scary one: It means that a machine may determine whether or not a doctor performs surgery. This example supports the argument that the United States has created a culture of fear surrounding childbirth (Simonds, Rothman, & Norman, 2007).

As we become more literate about sexuality, we become more critical consumers of information about all things sexual. By gathering information from many sources, we can make informed decisions about our health and question routine health care practices when appropriate. This information may help us recognize the difference between the need for an intervention and fear-based rhetoric. In this spirit then, let's discuss four interventions widely used in hospital births today: forceps delivery, vacuum extraction, episiotomy, and cesarean section.

forceps
Metal instruments placed around the baby's head inside the birth canal to aid in the birth of the child.

Forceps and Vacuum Extraction. **Forceps** are metal instruments placed around the baby's head inside the birth canal to aid in the birth of the child. These instruments, which look like large salad tongs, are placed on either side of the baby's head. Slight force is then applied to pull the infant further down into the birth canal. Figure 8.14a depicts the position of forceps around the baby's head. Forceps are used in about 3% of births in the United States (Martin, Hamilton, Osterman, et al., 2015). This rate of forceps deliveries has fallen dramatically over the years for at least three reasons: adverse complications for both the baby and mother, and women's hesitation to allow their use. Most doctors will only use forceps in extreme emergencies when quick delivery of the infant is the highest priority.

Complications may result from a forceps delivery for both the baby and the mother. Complications for the baby include:

- Temporary, though possible permanent, facial marking, bruising, and lacerations
- Injuries to infant facial nerves
- Skull fractures or intracranial hemorrhage

Know Yourself

What Do You Want in a Birth Plan?

These sample questions may help you create a birth plan.

- Who do you want to be present? Will they be present during labor and the birth? Just labor? Just the birth?
- Do you want a doula present to assist in the labor process?
- Do you want children/siblings present?
- What activities or positions do you want to use during labor, such as walking, standing, or squatting?
- Would you prefer a certain position to give birth?
- What will you do for pain relief, such as massage, hot and cold packs, positions, Lamaze, and hydrotherapy?
- Do you want pain medications or do you want to avoid them? What kind of pain medication do you want?
- How do you feel about fetal monitoring?
- How do you want to stay hydrated, such as taking sips of drinks, sucking on ice chips, or being given fluids through an IV?
- Do you want an episiotomy or do you want to avoid one using other measures?
- Do you want to listen to music and have focal points?
- Do you want to use a tub or shower?
- If you need a cesarean, do you have any special requests?
- Do you want skin-to-skin contact with your newborn? How long do you want to hold your child before weighing, measuring, bathing, and testing?
- What are your preferences for your baby's care, such as when and how to feed it, where it should sleep?
- Do you want to wear your own clothing?
- For home and birth center births, what are your plans if you or your baby needs to get to a hospital?
- If your baby is a boy, do you want him to be circumcised? If so, who would you prefer to do that?

their needs and desires for the birth of their child. Devising the plan takes time because there are many issues to discuss with partners and health care professionals (Simkin, Whalley, & Keppler, 2001). See "Know Yourself: What Do You Want in a Birth Plan?"

Because most health care providers and hospitals follow a set of policies and procedures, discuss your birth plan with all individuals who will be involved during the birth and the care of the baby at the hospital. Try to match your desires with the policies of the doctors, nurses, and staff at the hospital (Simkin et al., 2001). It may take a few attempts to create a plan that satisfies everyone. Staying flexible is important because deviations to any plan may be necessary for safety or medical necessity.

After the Birth: The Postpartum Period

The changes of the **postpartum period** after birth last for about 6 weeks and create flux for the entire family as everyone gets used to new routines, including older siblings. These changes require patience, understanding, and sensitivity from parents, family, friends, and the surrounding community. Parents may have questions that range from wondering if their

postpartum period
Literally meaning "following birth," this term refers to the months or first year following the birth of a child.

newborn is healthy to examining their own parenting skills. New parents, for example, may need to adjust the baby's sleeping schedule because he or she may sleep when they are awake and may want to play or eat when they typically sleep. During this time, family and friends can assist with preparing meals or helping with older children.

As parents adjust to life with their newest family member, they may need to deal with two major issues in this postpartum period: depression and resumption of sexual activity. It is important to have accurate information about both issues because opinions abound.

Depression   Following the birth of a child, many women experience **postpartum depression,** also called *postpartum blues.* This is a critical issue in women's health care, because studies show that high levels of maternal depression are associated with compromised parenting, unhealthy infant attachment, poorer infant cognitive development, and higher rates of infant behavior problems. Additionally, it negatively affects the quality of life and functioning of new mothers (Howell, Mora, & Leventhal, 2006; Martin, 2013). Different studies show that postpartum depression may occur in as many as 10–50% of women. Some studies cite that approximately 70% of all new mothers experience some sort of postpartum depression (Brott & Ash, 2001).

It is also important to be aware that new fathers or partners of new moms can experience postpartum depression as well. Fathers who are young, have a history of depression, and are experiencing challenges in relationships or are struggling financially are at the highest risk of postpartum depression (Mayo Clinic, 2018b). Postpartum depression in fathers—sometimes referred to as paternal postpartum depression—can impact the health and well-being of new fathers in much the same ways as postpartum depression impacts mothers (Mayo Clinic, 2018b).

Many factors cause postpartum depression. Medical doctors cite the vast decrease in hormone production as the most likely cause of postpartum depression. It is clear, however, that other issues are correlated, including all the responsibilities of caring for a newborn. It is important that women who experience higher than normal levels of depressive symptoms seek help from a health care provider.

Symptoms of postpartum depression include the following:

- Feelings of sadness, doubt, guilt, hopelessness, or anger that get worse with each passing week and cause disruptions in one's daily life
- Inability to sleep even when tired
- Sleeping most of the time even when the baby is awake
- Constant worry and anxiety about the baby
- Lack of interest in or feelings for the baby and family
- Panic attacks
- Thoughts of harm to the baby or to self
- Changes in appetite including reduced appetite or overeating

Several methods of coping are available for new mothers. Support groups, therapy, and medications are some of the approaches that may lessen the symptoms.

Resuming Sexual Activities   Many women are excited at the thought of resuming sexual activity because they want to reclaim their own personal space and to reconnect on a physically intimate level with a partner. Other women may be hesitant to engage in sexual activity

Postpartum depression is a serious condition that affects many women after the birth of their babies. Treatment options include support groups, therapy, and medication.
Jamie Grill/Getty Images

postpartum depression
A psychological depressive disorder that may occur within 4 weeks following the birth of a child.

HEALTHY Sexuality

Pelvic Pain After Childbirth?

Visit a variety of blogs on the Internet from new mothers who have just experienced childbirth and it is not unusual to see postings such as "Extreme pelvic pain: please help!" These women are highlighting an issue that is starting to become known in the medical community.

An article in the *Los Angeles Times* in 2009 suggested that the mode of delivery during childbirth has an impact on the quality of sexual satisfaction after birth for women. The research findings discussed in the article suggested that women who experienced planned cesarean sections had the lowest rate of long-term maternal and paternal sexual dysfunction while those who had vaginal deliveries experienced much higher rates of sexual dysfunction (Safarinejad, Kolahi, & Hosseini, 2009).

Some physicians suggest that it could take up to 2 years for a woman's body to recover from pregnancy and childbirth, yet very few in the medical community are open to discussing sexual pleasure after childbirth with their patients. Perhaps one advantage of Internet communities and blogs is that they shed light on issues that affect many but that few openly acknowledge or discuss. Sexual literacy advances when people tell their stories and help one another, particularly when the medical and scientific fields have not yet investigated a problem adequately.

---

due to fears of pain or injury. Immediately after delivery, some women report a decreased level of arousability and excitement because of decreased vaginal lubrication. Typically, though, about 3 months after delivery, most women report that their normal level of sexual desire and excitement has returned (Masters & Johnson, 1966). For some women, however, it takes longer due to the added stress and responsibilities of the new infant, which can be all-consuming in the first days, months, or even the first year.

The consensus is that women can resume having vaginal intercourse approximately 6 weeks after giving birth. By this time the uterus has shrunk back to its prepregnancy size and the **lochia,** the menstrual-period like fluid that is expelled following birth has stopped flowing. At this time, women should also begin doing regular **Kegel exercises,** which involve the contraction and relaxation of pelvic floor muscles, to strengthen this area. Stronger pelvic floor muscles help to prevent urinary incontinence and uterine prolapse, and may increase pleasure during sex. If a woman had a cesarean, episiotomy, or other invasive intervention, physicians may recommend postponing vaginal intercourse for a longer period. Even though a doctor may advise against vaginal intercourse for various medical reasons, partners can still be intimate. In fact, this postponement may encourage a couple to discover new sexual activities they might not have thought about before, as discussed in the "Healthy Sexuality: Pelvic Pain After Childbirth?"

lochia
Fluid that is expelled following the birth of a child.

Kegel exercises
The voluntary contraction and relaxation of pelvic floor muscles to help prevent urinary incontinence and slippage of the uterus following childbirth.

WHAT'S ON YOUR MIND?

Q: I am currently pregnant and I am a little concerned about whether my vagina will return to its normal size after I give birth. Will it go back to its normal size or will it not feel as tight when I have sex?

ANSWER: After giving birth vaginally, it's normal for the vagina to be larger than it was before. The new size depends on a number of factors, such as the size of your baby, the number of children you've had, and whether you do Kegel exercises regularly. If you do not already do these exercises, begin now. After birth, the muscles of the pelvic floor relax and lose tone. You can identify the muscle to tone while urinating — if you can stop the flow of urine when tightening, you're toning the correct muscle. If you do these Kegel exercises regularly, your vagina will get back into shape relatively quickly.

In many cultures, postpartum taboos are among the most important ways to regulate marital sex and the establishment of family units (Mabilia, 2006; Murdock, 1949). The Sambia of Papua New Guinea, for example, prohibit the resumption of vaginal sex for up to 2 years, fearing that the baby will be harmed if the mother's milk dries up. New mothers can have sex, though, in the form of the wife fellating her husband (Herdt, 1981). Consider how not having vaginal sex for 2 years postpartum creates an age span between siblings in their society.

INFERTILITY AND OPTIONS

For those who want to raise children but either have been unsuccessful conceiving, do not have a partner, or are in a same-sex relationship, not all is lost. They can explore other options such as assisted reproductive techniques, surrogacy, and adoption. First we'll consider infertility and its causes. Then we'll look at options that people can explore.

Infertility is often a difficult challenge to face. Most people, unless they know someone who has experienced it, do not think about their ability to conceive. Often, infertility is not something that could have been predicted. Despite whether or not a couple knew in advance that they may have difficulty conceiving, facing infertility is a mourning process of not being able to conceive a child without outside medical assistance. Generally, health care professionals consider that a heterosexual couple has fertility problems when they have had unprotected sexual intercourse at least twice a week for a 12-month span and have not conceived.

Many factors can cause infertility, including problems with the woman, the man, or both (Martin, 2013). Possible causes of infertility among women age 35 years and younger include the following problems (CDC, 2012l; Mayo Clinic, 2018a):

- Fallopian tube blockage or abnormality: Endometriosis or scar tissue from STIs, pelvic inflammatory disease (PID), or a second trimester abortion may cause the blockage. The blockage may not allow sperm to reach the egg or may not allow the fertilized ovum to reach the uterus, which may lead to an ectopic pregnancy.
- Ovulatory disruptions: Many factors may cause these disruptions, including hormone imbalances, benign pituitary growths, amenorrhea due to a lower or higher than normal body weight, or conditions such as polycystic ovarian syndrome, a disorder in which numerous small cysts develop on the ovaries and prevent ovulation of mature ova.
- Endometriosis.

Women are not the only ones with conditions leading to infertility. Main issues for male infertility are abnormally low sperm count and low movement of sperm. Causes of low sperm count can be either biological or environmental. Evidence shows that toxic substances, alcohol, tobacco, and certain prescription medications can affect the volume of sperm. Low sperm movement, or **motility,** means that sperm do not move through the female reproductive tract quickly enough and die before they reach the ovum as it moves down the fallopian tube. Men can also have high levels of **malformed sperm,** which are sperm with structural abnormalities or deficiencies, that do not live very long and have difficulty reaching and penetrating the ovum. Causes of sperm malformation may be biological or environmental.

Assisted Reproductive Techniques

A variety of fertility technologies, called **assisted reproductive techniques,** have been developed to assist people in their efforts to conceive. Before we discuss how the different techniques work biologically, however, it is important to understand some sociological implications about these techniques:

- Not everyone may have access to them, including single women, lesbians, poor women, women with disabilities, and older women (Peterson, 2005).

motility
Ability of sperm to move when ejaculated.

malformed sperm
Sperm that are abnormally formed.

assisted reproductive techniques
Fertility technologies that assist people in their efforts to conceive.

- Individuals may not be covered by health insurance, which makes them more available to the more affluent people in society.
- Physicians who perform these techniques may impose their own biases and may discriminate based on age, socioeconomic status, or marital status.

None of the techniques we will discuss are available equally. It is important to be aware that many infertile individuals or couples face a multitude of challenges in order to have a child. It is not as simple as taking a drug or undergoing a medical process. Many couples have to face the extreme financial and emotional stress that can come with infertility.

Egg Donors "Attention all young, attractive, intelligent and healthy women! Did you know that you could make around $10,000 for donating your eggs?" This kind of teaser ad makes its way onto college campuses and websites on a regular basis. While eggs have been traded since the fertility industry began in the 1970s, new technologies tied to the Internet have made it possible for massive levels of advertising to help balloon a booming business of egg merchants into a $3 billion a year industry (Hopkins, 2006).

To donate her eggs, a woman must be in the age range of 18 to early 30s and pass a variety of medical and psychological exams. Once they are chosen to donate, donors begin taking hormone shots that boost their egg production for about 30 days. Ten to 15 eggs are extracted via needle from the sedated donor. These eggs are then combined with sperm to create embryos, which may later be inserted into the uterus of a would-be mother to possibly become a child.

While it seems like an easy procedure and an easy way to make money, many lawmakers are saying that young women may not fully understand the consequences of their decision to donate eggs. The reality is that long-term studies of the impact on fertility and health of egg donors has really not been studied closely (Elton, 2009). When women donate eggs, they are given hormones and medications, which help bring numerous eggs to maturity. Some believe that this treatment can have long-term effects on later fertility, age at menopause, and increased risk for some cancers (Elton, 2009). Young college women with student loans are often attracted to the high price that some are willing to pay for their eggs. Other women, regardless of the amount of money they may receive, sell their eggs because they want to help others to become parents.

Next time you see an ad for egg donation in your school newspaper, on the bulletin board in the campus coffee house, or on the web, think about it. How do you feel about egg donation? Are you willing to do it? Why or why not? How about sperm donation? Do you believe that men who donate sperm should be compensated to the same extent as women? Why or why not?

With each of the following techniques described, the goal is to provide the best possible chance of a healthy egg to be fertilized by healthy sperm and to correctly implant the embryo into the uterus to pave the way for a healthy pregnancy. For those facing infertility, a doctor will assist in the decision-making process and identify which procedures will maximize the possibility of success. These different procedures are designed to address the specific cause of prior pregnancy loss or inability to conceive and hopefully make it possible for healthy fertilization, viable pregnancy, and birth.

With **in-vitro fertilization (IVF)**, mature eggs are removed from a woman's ovaries and are fertilized by sperm in a laboratory dish. Once the eggs appear to be fertilized, a doctor inserts them in the woman's uterus, where they may implant. They usually insert several fertilized eggs to maximize the chances for at least one to implant into the uterine lining and begin growing.

Gamete intrafallopian transfer (GIFT) is a procedure in which a doctor places the sperm and egg directly into the fallopian tube

in-vitro fertilization (IVF)
Fertilization of eggs by sperm in a lab dish for implantation in a woman's uterus.

gamete intrafallopian transfer (GIFT)
Procedure in which sperm and egg are placed directly into the fallopian tube to aid in fertilization.

Assisted reproductive techniques have helped thousands of people attain their dreams of parenthood. Here a doctor is preparing embryos for implantation into the uterus.
Science Photo Library/Getty Images

In vitro fertilization and other ARTs more often result in multiple births than does conception by natural means.
digitalskillet/Shutterstock

zygote intrafallopian transfer (ZIFT)
Implantation of a fertilized ovum in the mother's fallopian tube.

artificial insemination (AI)
A procedure that artificially introduces semen into a female for the purpose of fertilization.

surrogacy
A woman becomes pregnant for another individual or couple and then gives the child to them to raise.

open adoption
A form of adoption in which birth parents remain connected to the adoptive family through periodic updates and other communication.

in the hope that their proximity will aid in the process of fertilization. The possible benefit of GIFT over IVF and ZIFT (explained next) is that it more closely follows the journey of a typical fertilized ovum as it travels from the fallopian tubes into the uterus where it will hopefully implant.

Zygote intrafallopian transfer (ZIFT) is similar to GIFT, but in this case the ovum is fertilized in a laboratory dish and then a doctor places the fertilized egg in the fallopian tube for it to travel to the uterus for possible implantation.

Artificial insemination, or intrauterine insemination, is a means for a woman to conceive when she does not have a male partner, when she does not want a male partner, or when a male partner's sexual inhibition or physical limitation impedes his ability to impregnate her. **Artificial insemination (AI)** is the deliberate introduction of semen into a female for the purpose of fertilization, by means other than ejaculation directly into the vagina or uterus. Usually sperm is taken from a partner or donor and placed either in the vagina or deeper into the uterus during the time at which a woman is thought to be ovulating.

In the United States, there are many sperm banks where men have donated sperm for use in assisting a woman in conceiving a child. Sperm banks are a good source for lesbian couples looking to conceive a child, single women wishing to conceive a child without a partner, and heterosexual couples where the man has challenges with fertility. The cost is usually less expensive than procedures like IVF or ZIFT.

Other Options for Creating a Family

For individuals struggling with infertility or for same-sex couples who desire to build their families, other nonmedical options are available. They include using a surrogate to grow and birth the baby and adoption.

Parenthood Through Surrogacy For women who are unable to carry children, or for gay men who want to raise children, parenthood through **surrogacy** is an option. With surrogacy, a woman outside of the pair bond carries the fetus to term, delivers the baby, and then turns it over to the parents to adopt and raise. The options for creating a zygote for the surrogate mother to carry include using donor sperm, using a donor egg from the surrogate or from another woman, or using sperm or egg from one partner or the other. The surrogate may be impregnated either with artificial insemination with sperm or via one of the assisted reproductive techniques. Gay men have increased their use of surrogate mothers to have children in recent years. This option is expensive, however: Couples may pay tens of thousands of dollars for surrogacy.

Adoption Adoption is another option for people who desire to start a family or to add a child or children to their existing family. Earlier in the chapter, we discussed adoption as an option for a birth mother who wants to give her baby to others to raise. Here, we discuss the other part of adoption: the parents who want to raise a child that a birth mother is willing to give up. Adoptions can be done privately where the biological mother chooses the people whom she wishes to parent her unborn child. Some agencies specialize in **open adoption,** which means that the adoptive parents will update the birth parents on how their child is doing. It is common for adoptive parents to assume the health care costs for the birth mother's prenatal care and the birth of the child. Adoptions can also occur when parents adopt children whose biological parents have had their parental rights legally removed. Often referred to as foster adoption, the child in this situation is placed in a foster home and may be eventually adopted by that family once the biological parents have had their rights legally terminated. Kinship adoption is also a possibility whereby adoptive parents adopt children who are biologically related to them in some form (e.g., grandchild, niece, nephew). In each of these cases, agencies often require adoptive parents to participate in extensive interviews, attend classes, and prepare their homes adequately before a child is placed in their care.

Private adoption is expensive as adoptive families often cover the cost of the biological mother's prenatal care and hospitalization for the birth of the child. In addition, adoptive parents must assume the expensive court and attorney costs that are necessary to finalize the adoption. Some states, such as Florida and Arkansas, still prohibit single individuals and lesbian and gay couples from adopting children in an effort to thwart nontraditional family arrangements. In addition, some countries, such as China, do not allow gay and lesbian couples and single individuals to adopt a child from their countries. In recent years the whole issue of adopting children from another country has become increasingly complicated and controversial as well.

Adoption is one choice for people who want a family or want to add children to their existing family. Here actress Sandra Bullock holds her adoptive son.
Marcel Thomas/FilmMagic/Getty Images

Public adoption is a much more cost-effective way to start a family. Some states and counties in the United States cover the legal costs of adoption and even subsidize the cost of caring for the child until age 18 years. In most cases, these public adoptions involve caring for "special needs" children. Many children who are put up for adoption by a county court have been removed from the home due to biological parents' inability to care for them. Many of these children have experienced extreme trauma due to stressors like violence, parental substance abuse, and poverty. Adoptive parents are required to take parenting courses to learn the best way to care for these special children.

Regarding the decision of birth mothers to offer their child for adoption, it is an option for women who do not want to terminate a pregnancy but do not wish to parent their child. In the United States, agencies are available to assist pregnant women (and sometimes their partner) in finding adoptive parents for their unborn child.

Though adoption may seem like a selfless choice, it's important to consider several important emotional issues. During nine months of pregnancy a woman may create a bond with her unborn child and the unborn with its mother. Terminating that bond can create feelings of sadness and anxiety. Many women find it distressing to think about having a child and then giving it to perfect strangers to raise. If they elect to do this, it is common for them to think about how their birth child is doing and if the adoptive parents are doing a good job rearing their child.

ABORTION

People in the United States are at a critical crossroads. More than at any other time since the Supreme Court handed down its *Roe v. Wade* decision in 1973, women's reproductive health care and their ability to make decisions about reproduction, contraception, and abortion are imperiled by lawmakers. In 2019, the U.S. saw an unprecedented surge of abortion bans across the country. The first 6 months of 2019 saw 26 abortion bans enacted in 12 states, with more to come (Nash, 2019). See Figure 8.15 to better understand the climate regarding abortion rights among the individual states.

Figure 8.15

This map of the U.S. provides a general overview of the attitudes of citizens regarding abortion rights.

No professional in the field of sexual health wishes to see abortion rates increase. The problem is that enacting bans and restrictions on women's reproductive choices and tying the hands of doctors and nurses does not decrease abortion rates. Historically we have seen how such changes result in terrible human costs (Engelman, 2011). We know that the best way to decrease abortion rates is to provide good comprehensive sexuality education for all young people, open access to health care, contraceptive choice, and family planning services (Kirby, 2012). What is so disturbing about the current state of affairs is that many of the states enacting these bans are the same states that are cutting funding for the services that support women's sexual health, well-being, and choice (Nash, 2019).

Many states have enacted laws protecting the right to abortion up to the point of fetal viability and at any time during pregnancy if the patient's life or health is at risk (Nash, 2019). The best hope for our society is that a woman's right to maintain bodily autonomy and dignity will be a priority and will continue to be the prevailing law of the land rather than the exception.

Defining Abortion

Of all the areas of human sexuality that spark controversy and strong emotional reactions, ending a pregnancy may be the most conflict-laden. Even though abortion is actually in decline in the United States, there are many misconceptions about it. And as we have stated, at this writing abortion rights are in a state of peril in many states in the United States.

Abortion, the elective termination of a pregnancy, is one of the most difficult topics when it comes to reproductive and family life and sexual health and well-being (Guttmacher Institute, 2018), and it has become a hugely important social problem in the United States today (DiMauro & Joffe, 2009; Engelman, 2011). Many women believe for a variety of reasons, including moral and religious ones, that abortion is their best possible option to end a pregnancy, especially in tragic cases of rape, incest, and life-threatening medical risk to the fetus or mother. They may seek an abortion for many reasons, but chief among them are that they feel too young or unprepared to have children or that they are pregnant because of sexual violence, such as rape or incest. These are important factors in considering abortion and its safety for a woman and her family (Joffe, 2009). But there are very real risks in abortion and safe and unsafe methods involved. Here we consider these questions in more depth and discuss clinically safe methods to terminate a pregnancy.

Deciding to terminate a pregnancy can be quite difficult. Those who consider abortion may want to think about the following issues:

- Do you have any reason to be concerned about your safety during this procedure?
- How far along in the pregnancy are you and what abortion options are available?
- Is a partner involved in the decision and will you consult with that person?
- How will your decision fit with your faith or cultural traditions?
- Do you anticipate any emotional reactions to an abortion that you should investigate or be prepared for in advance?
- Do you have a solid support system in place through partner, friends, family, church, or community groups?

Women choose to have an abortion for many different reasons. One study by Jones and colleagues (2008) reported that some women choose abortion because the cost of raising a child and providing an education is beyond them. Other women cite parenting characteristics such as the desire to create a "good home," which means wanting the child to grow up in a stable family environment with financial security. One-quarter of the women claimed they had considered the option of adoption, but felt that the emotional consequences would be too distressing (Jones, Frohwirth, & Moore, 2008; Guttmacher Institute, 2018).

Research shows that women do much better after an abortion when they have good social support—especially when the support comes from their partners (Cozzarelli, Sumer, & Major, 1998). Evidence also shows that women who make this decision independently, versus feeling coerced or pressured into the decision by a partner or family, tend to cope better (Patterson, Hill, & Maloy, 1995).

Safe Methods of Abortion

Given the heightened emotion around abortion, accurate information about how they are performed in the United States can be hard to find. In fact, some information is inaccurate or distorted because it's designed to gather support for one political, social, or religious

---

DID YOU KNOW

- Nearly half of pregnancies among U.S. women are unintended, and about 4 in 10 of these are terminated by abortion.
- Of all pregnancies annually in the United States, 19% end in abortion (excluding miscarriages).
- In 2014, White patients accounted for 39% of abortion procedures, Blacks for 28%, Hispanic for 25%, and other races and ethnicities 9%.
- In 2014, approximately 926,100 abortions were performed in the United States. This rate is 12% lower than what was reported in 2011 (1.06 million).
- In 2014, the United States saw the lowest abortion rate ever observed: 1.5% of women aged 15-44 had an abortion. Under half (45%) of these women reported having a previous abortion.
- Reasons women gave for having an abortion were concern for or responsibility to other individuals; the inability to afford raising a child; and the belief that having a baby would interfere with work, school, or the ability to care for dependents. Half of these women said they did not want to be a single parent or were having problems with their husband or partner.

Source: Guttmacher Institute, 2018.

abortion
Elective termination of a pregnancy.

Figure 8.16
Vacuum aspiration is the most common abortion method used in clinics. After inserting the speculum into the vagina, the doctor dilates the cervix and inserts a suction tube to empty the uterus.

Labels: Uterus; Amniotic sac; Vaginal canal; Speculum; Suction curette

aspiration
An abortion procedure using suction to remove an embryo or fetus from the uterus.

dilation and evacuation (D&E)
An abortion procedure used after the first trimester in which medication is administered to ensure fetal death prior to removing it from the uterus.

abortifacients
Medications used to prevent the progression of pregnancy and induce uterine contractions to remove embryonic or fetal tissue.

stance or another. Being sexually literate, however, is about knowing how safe abortions are conducted. With accurate information, you are best able to make informed decisions.

When a woman chooses to terminate a pregnancy in the United States, it is done before she has reached 24 weeks of gestation. The latest statistics show that two-thirds of abortions occur at 8 weeks of pregnancy or earlier, with a total of 89% occurring within the first 12 weeks or first trimester of pregnancy (Guttmacher Institute, 2018). If an abortion is performed after 24 weeks, it is usually only done for serious threats to the mother's health or life or the discovery of a serious fetal anomaly (National Abortion Federation, 2009).

Women may opt to have an in-clinic abortion or to take an abortion pill. The most common form of in-clinic abortion is **aspiration.** Doctors often use the aspiration method until 16 weeks after a woman's last menstrual period. A health care provider inserts a speculum into the vagina to gain access to the cervix. The opening of the cervix is stretched with dilators. A tube is then inserted through the cervix into the uterus. A suction device is used to empty the uterus. Illustrated in Figure 8.16, this procedure usually takes 5 to 10 minutes, but more time may be necessary to prepare the cervix.

Less than 10% of in-clinic abortions in the United States are performed using the method of **dilation and evacuation (D&E).** This procedure is usually performed once a woman has passed the first 16 weeks after her last menstrual period, but before 24 weeks. It is similar to aspiration, except that in this procedure, a medication is given through the abdomen to ensure that the fetus dies and the doctor may use forceps to assist in the abortion procedure. This procedure usually takes between 10 and 20 minutes and is normally done under general anesthesia in a hospital setting.

Other options for a medical abortion in the United States are abortion pills. These pills are known as **abortifacients.** They can be used up to 9 weeks after a woman's last menstrual period. Mifepristone, also known as RU486, is most common in the United States and in Europe. Using mifepristone is a two-step process. First, a woman takes it to block progesterone, the hormone that maintains a pregnancy. Without progesterone, the endometrium breaks down and a pregnancy cannot continue. Then a woman takes a second medication, misoprostol, which causes severe cramping and bleeding. It is reported that more than

HEALTHY Sexuality

When an Abortion Becomes Dangerous

In developing nations where abortion is not legal or is considered unsafe, women who want an abortion may opt for methods that pose significant risks to their health and lives. Complications due to unsafe abortion procedures account for an estimated 13% of maternal deaths worldwide (approximately 67,000) every year. Some of these methods include:

- Drinking bleach, turpentine, or tea made with livestock manure
- Inserting herbal concoctions into the vagina or cervix
- Placing foreign bodies, such as a coat hanger, chicken bone, or stick in the uterus
- Jumping from the tops of roofs or staircases

In addition to the health risks and consequences such as death, long-term health problems, and infertility, unsafe abortions lead to increases in economic burdens on public health systems (Guttmacher Institute, 2008). When a woman is given an unsafe abortion, there is a high likelihood that she will experience health complications. These complications can cost thousands of dollars in further medical care, many of which can be avoided with proper medical care and a safe abortive method.

50% of women abort within 4 to 5 hours after taking the second medication. Most women who take it will abort within a few days. Women who choose this method of abortion must follow up with their health care providers within 2 weeks to ensure that the abortion is complete and that the woman is healthy.

Unsafe Methods of Abortion

Unsafe abortion procedures are common especially in countries where abortion is illegal. The World Health Organization (WHO) defines an unsafe abortion as a procedure for terminating an unintended pregnancy carried out by someone who lacks the necessary skills or in an environment that does not conform to minimal medical standards, or both (Abdullaeva, 2008). Using WHO's standards, an estimated 48% of all induced abortions are unsafe. In developed regions, however, over 92% of abortions are considered safe (Guttmacher Institute, 2008). The information in "Healthy Sexuality: When an Abortion Becomes Dangerous" offers more detail about unsafe abortion procedures.

After an Abortion

Women experience a variety of emotions after they elect to terminate a pregnancy. Most women experience relief but others also report feeling anger, regret, guilt, or sadness for a period of time (Russo & Dabul, 1997). The sense of relief is a result of feeling such high anxiety about an unintended pregnancy and then resolving it with an abortion. Occasionally, some women experience emotional problems after having an abortion. Long-term emotional problems after abortion are about as common as they are after women give birth (Russo & Dabul, 1997). Some women who experience them may have a history of emotional problems prior to the abortion (Russo & Dabul, 1997). Also, women with an unsupportive partner, family, or friends, and women who have to terminate a wanted pregnancy because of health reasons for either themselves or their fetus may also experience long-term emotional problems (Planned Parenthood, 2008). Today, women struggling with emotions after having an abortion can find many websites, blogs, and support groups within communities to help them.

Do women who are minors experience emotional problems after an abortion that older women do not? This question is valid to consider because over the past few years, U.S. citizens have voted for or against propositions that require parental notification and permission for a pregnant minor to receive an abortion (Quinton, Major, & Richards, 2001). Proponents of these propositions have stated that abortion brings unique risks to adolescents due to their cognitive and emotional immaturity compared to older adults. As a result of the controversial nature of these laws, the U.S. Supreme Court has heard many cases regarding parental involvement. Some Supreme Court justices have even asserted that "abortion has potentially grave emotional and psychological consequences" for minors (Quinton et al., 2001, p. 492). However, studies show that minors are not at higher risk for depression or adverse consequences as compared to older women (Quinton et al., 2001).

Specifically, research shows that at 1 month after an abortion, minors were somewhat less satisfied with their decision than adult women. This dissatisfaction was primarily because the coping skills of adolescents are underdeveloped or less mature than adults. Parental conflict was an important part of this finding (Quinton et al., 2001). The pressure parents can purposely or inadvertently place on their pregnant teenager can be overwhelming for a young woman who is already experiencing a lot of stress, worry, and anxiety. This pressure likely impedes her ability to make a difficult decision on her own. Despite this finding at 1 month after an abortion, research also shows that at 2 years after an abortion, adolescents reported similar levels of satisfaction with their decision as adult women and were no more likely than adult women to experience postabortive depression.

Regardless of age, making the decision to terminate a pregnancy is terribly difficult. If a woman is having trouble coping with her decision to have an abortion, professional counseling may help to ensure her emotional health and well-being in the short and longer term.

As we have seen, the decision to become a parent is life changing. Some individuals decide in advance when and how they want to become parents. Others find that parenthood finds them, either through an unintended pregnancy or some other unexpected route. Understanding the role parenthood plays in our lives and in the larger context of our social environment can help us make critical life decisions.

SEXUAL WELL-BEING AND REPRODUCTIVE RIGHTS

No topic in human sexuality is more controversial and loaded with all of the issues of being human than giving birth or having an abortion. And so it will come as no surprise that pursuit of sexual well-being in the context of reproductive rights and justice in the United States has been difficult, political, and hard—perhaps more challenging than in any other major industrial country in the world (DiMauro & Joffe, 2009). Poverty is a large factor, because people in rural areas tend to be poorer and have less access to quality health care compared to urban areas, including good sexual health and maternal or reproductive health care (Galambos, 2005). However, as we are currently experiencing in the United States, there is political opposition to providing for sound medical decisions regarding contraception and abortion as reproductive rights, and some states prohibit any abortion supported by public or private funds, which has a negative effect on poor women and women of color (Joffe, 2009). The reasons for this political opposition, especially among conservative males, are complex, but they tend to be reinforced by traditional gender role attitudes (Joffe, 2009). In addition to gender roles, some people think that women should just not have abortions, they should stay at home and not work, and they may believe that women who have abortions are sexually promiscuous (DiMauro & Joffe, 2009; Petchesky, 2003). For example, many Mexican and Mexican American girls grow up with the fear that sex could lead to pregnancy, the loss of reputation, and dishonor to their families and guilt to themselves, which limit their sexuality (Gonzales-Lopez, 2005).

Some of this attitude may also influence people's reaction to the 1973 Supreme Court decision in the case of *Roe v. Wade* (DiMauro & Joffe, 2009). With this decision, the United States affirmed the right of a woman to have an abortion under certain conditions. Over the years there have been many legal challenges to this policy, but it has endured as the policy of the land while being undermined in some more sexually conservative states such as Alabama. As time went along, though, some limitations emerged in the law, as shown in the following list (Guttmacher Institute, 2019):

- *Physician and hospital requirements:* A licensed physician must perform the abortion procedure in 41 states. Abortions must be performed within a hospital after a certain gestational age in 19 states, and a second physician must be present after a certain gestational age in 18 states.
- *Gestational limits to abortion:* In 43 states, once a fetus passes the age of fetal viability, abortion is prohibited. This may only change if the woman's life or health is in danger.
- *"Partial Birth" abortion:* laws impacting "partial birth" abortion are in effect within 20 states.
- *Public funding of abortion counseling or procedures:* 16 states employ their own state funds to pay for nearly all medically necessary abortions for Medicaid enrollees; 33 states and the District of Columbia prohibit the use of any state funds for abortion except in cases of rape or incest or when a woman's life is in danger. South Dakota stands in defiance of federal requirements and provides state funding for abortion only in the case of life endangerment of a pregnant individual.
- *Coverage by private insurance:* Restrictions around private insurance coverage of abortion, except for life endangerment of the pregnant individual,exist in 11 states.
- *Refusal:* Health care providers are allowed to refuse to provide abortion procedures in 45 states. 42 states allow entire institutions to opt out of performing abortion procedures, and of these 42 states, 16 states allow only private or religiously-affiliated institutions to refuse to perform abortion procedures.
- *State-mandated counseling:* 18 states require pregnant individuals to be given counseling services before pregnancy termination. Content included in counseling must include at least one of the following pieces of information: the link between abortion and breast cancer rates (5 states), the ability of a fetus to experience pain or sensation after a certain gestational age (13 states), and the potential long-term mental health outcomes of abortion for women (8 states).
- *Waiting periods:* women are required to wait for 24 hours (on average) in 27 states between receiving counseling and being able to get an abortion. Of these states, 14 require women to make separate trips to the clinic to obtain the procedure.
- *Parental Involvement:* Parental notification or involvement is required for a minor seeking an abortion in 37 states. One or both parent's consent is required in 26 states and 11 states require notification to one or both parents.

There is no simple explanation for all of these many perplexing and tragic challenges to reproductive health and rights (Joffe, 2009; Merry, 2006), but helping to protect women's and families' rights, and helping to ensure the very best quality health care, and helping women to determine their own destiny is really vital to protecting and advancing sexual literacy in the United States and abroad.

Chapter Review

SUMMARY

Parenting and Reproductive Decisions
- The decision to have children is affected by biological, social, and personal factors.
- Personal emotions and identity can shift and fluctuate for individuals who are preparing to become parents.
- The average age for women to give birth to their first child in the United States is currently 25.
- The belief system of pronatalism promotes childbearing as an expectation for people in their lifetime.
- Becoming a parent is one of society's most pervasive expectations.
- For women, tension exists between valuing motherhood and valuing career success.

Ensuring a Healthy Pregnancy
- Taking proper care of the body is important to ensure as healthy a pregnancy as possible.
- Good nutrition, exercise, and regular prenatal care are critical factors for a healthy pregnancy.

Conception and Pregnancy
- A variety of cultural beliefs surround conception.
- Each trimester includes significant development and changes for the developing fetus, the pregnant woman, and her partner.
- Some medical technologies that help identify potential complications in pregnancy include amniocentesis, chorionic villus sampling, and ultrasound.

Birth and the Postpartum Period
- Birth is divided into three stages: (1) dilation and effacement, (2) birth of the fetus, and (3) birth of the placenta.
- Hospital births and home births are both common in the United States. It is critical for individuals to understand the benefits and drawbacks of both in order to decide on a birth method that best fits their desires and needs.
- If necessary, interventions available to assist in a birth include forceps, vacuum extraction, episiotomy, and C-section.
- Postpartum blues or depression occurs in as many as 10–50% of women.

Infertility and Options
- For individuals who face fertility challenges, assisted reproductive techniques include IVF, GIFT, and ZIFT.
- Surrogate parenthood and adoption are nonmedical options available to assist individuals and couples in becoming parents.

Abortion
- If women experience an unintended pregnancy, they have the option to abort the fetus, to carry the pregnancy to term and give the baby up for adoption, or to raise the child.
- However, currently the challenges to the right to have an abortion in the United States are significant and seem to be increasing.

- Among the most common reasons women choose to abort an unintended pregnancy are feeling too young to have children and conceiving as a result of rape or incest.
- Women cope better with abortion when they have positive social support and are able to make the decision independently without coercion.
- The most common techniques of safe abortion in the United States are aspiration, dilation and evacuation (D&E), and the abortion pill for very early pregnancies.
- The World Health Organization (WHO) defines unsafe abortions as procedures carried out by persons who lack the necessary skills or that occur in an environment that does not conform to minimal medical standards.
- The emotional health of adolescents and older women following an abortion varies and depends on the availability of social supports.

Sexual Well-Being and Reproductive Rights

- The laws and mores surrounding sexual well-being and reproduction vary significantly across the United States, though currently the challenges to access abortion are increasing.
- Reproductive rights define the ability of women and their families to make their own decisions regarding birth and family formation.

What's Your Position?

1. **Do you want to have children in your lifetime?**
   - What have you thought about having children and becoming a parent?
   - In what ways have you thought about taking on the role of parent?
   - What kind of parent do you aspire to be?
   - What do you think about stay-at-home dads? What kinds of assumptions or stereotypes enter your mind when you consider a man giving up or putting his career on hold to engage in full-time child rearing?

2. **What do you envision as the ideal birth experience?**
   - For women who may want to have children: What information might be valuable in a birth plan? Refer to the questions posed in the chapter and document the type of birth experience you desire for your future child(ren).
   - For partners of women who may give birth: What kind of involvement do you hope to have in the experience of pregnancy, prenatal care, and the birth of your child(ren)?
   - For people who already have children: What would you want to do differently if you were to have more children?

3. **What is your position on abortion?**
   - How do you feel about the abortive techniques discussed in this chapter?
   - Think and write about what you might do if you experienced an unintended pregnancy.
   - Do you consider the decision to have an abortion a reproductive right? Why or why not?

Design elements: Controversies in Sexuality: HBRH/Shutterstock; Research and Sexual Well Being: verity jane smith/Getty Images; Healthy Sexuality: Sergey Furtaev/Shutterstock; Communication Matters: PeopleImages/Getty Images; Know Yourself: Plush Studios/Blend Images LLC; What's Your Position: Luis Molinero/Shutterstock; Healthy Sexuality: A. Minde/PhotoAlto; Did You Know icon: McGraw-Hill Education; Page corner icon: McGraw-Hill Education.

Gender and Identity: Biology, Roles, and Culture

9

Adam Hester/Getty Images

Understanding Sex and Gender in Development and in Context
- Define the difference in the use of the words *sex* and *gender*.
- Explain the spectrum of gender based on masculinity and on femininity.
- Describe five genetic intersex variations.

Gender Identity and Expression
- Explain the difference between gender identity and expression.
- Explain the difference between androgyny as gender expression and cisgender as identity.
- Describe variations in the spectrum of gender identity.
- Describe the spectrum of gender expression.
- Explain the difference between gender identity and sexual orientation.

Gender Roles
- Explain how culture influences gender roles and how they vary across cultures.
- Define the term cisgender.
- Define genderqueer, gender binary, and non-binary.
- Explain the role of power, stereotypes, and control in gender roles.
- Identify the five major social institutions that influence gender roles.

Gender Norms and Variance
- Describe how norms influence conformity to traditional masculine and feminine behavior.
- Define gender congruence.

Gender Identity and Intersex Rights: Well-Being and Social Justice
- Describe gender identity rights for individuals who do not conform to gender norms.

● **Learning**
● **Objectives**

Developing Your Position

1. Do you see gender and sexual differentiation as being based on biology or culture, or both?
2. How did society's gender expectations help shape your attitudes and socialization in growing up, or did they play a part at all?
3. In what ways were you socialized to be the gender you are now?

Self, Society, and Culture: Sex and Gender Ambiguity

I (Nicole) will never forget the day when I realized how critical the concept of gender is to our human and Western identity. My sister had some close friends who were expecting their first child. This couple decided to wait until the baby was born to find out if they were having a "boy" or a "girl." When the father called to tell us about the birth, our first question was, "Is it a boy or a girl?" After a long pause, the father responded, "We don't know." In the coming days, the parents began unlocking the mystery of their child's biological sex. Chromosomally, their child was a male. Physically, however, the baby's genitals did not look like those of either male or female. They were left with a difficult decision to identify their child as male or female on the birth certificate. They ultimately decided to go with the DNA results and register the baby as male. The parents would better understand their child's sex and gender in a few years when the child would develop an identity and when, later on, their child's body would develop more in puberty. They have raised the child as a "boy" with an understanding that as he grows up and uncovers his own gender, he may need or want to change.

Take some time to consider what you would do as a parent in this situation. Consider how much sex and gender contribute to who we are as individuals and what is expected of us in our families and culture. Consider how easily our society convolutes sex with gender. In this chapter we shall make clear how a different or ambiguous gender identity can also occur without any intersex variations.

UNDERSTANDING GENDER IN DEVELOPMENT AND IN CONTEXT

Someone's gender seems obvious at first glance, or does it? If you encounter someone whose gender is not clear, do you find yourself intensely curious about whether that person is a man or a woman? Why do you think that we are so intent on needing to know the answer? The reality is that the concepts of sex and gender are so deeply ingrained in our Western identity that it is difficult to think about anything else without knowing that contextual piece of information.

Today, we seem to recognize how gender ambiguity and changes in gender are more common than ever before (Germon, 2009). "With many terms and definitions used for gender identity, sensitivity and uncertainty may arise regarding the appropriate terminology," two United Nations directors of population policy have recently written (Chamie & Mirkin, 2019). Society is now adjusting to these huge changes. This is reflected in how we talk about biology, gender, and identity expressions, and in how science is learning that biological and social variation in nature is far greater than ever imagined. Nevertheless, people may be surprised by such revelations because many continue to think that gender is fixed and unchangeable. In this section, then, we explore the biological basis of gender.

HEALTHY Sexuality

Sex and Gender Terminology

When it comes to the discussion of sex and gender, the terminology can be confusing. To increase your understanding and to reduce any confusion, refer to the definitions of these terms:

sex—the biological differentiation into male or female, based upon genes, hormones, and other internal developmental factors. With the term *sex*, the focus is on:

- Biological structures and development
- Hormones and endocrine processes
- Genes, chromosomes, and DNA

gender—the social differentiation into masculine or feminine, based upon institutions, roles, and meanings of a particular culture. With gender, the focus is on:

- Social roles defined by society
- Gender meaning as defined by culture
- Institutions and roles as defined by society

gender identity—the sense that one is a boy/man or a girl/woman, inside of someone's own experiences of growing up. The term *gender identity* focuses on:

- Individual self-awareness and subjectivity
- One's sense of being a boy/man or girl/woman, or something different
- Development in the context of family and peers

gender role—the culturally patterned and expected expression of masculinity or femininity that is identified with particular tasks, knowledge, and power. Sometimes gender roles are referred to as sex roles. The term *gender roles* focuses on:

- Social categories of men and women
- Cultural codes of masculinity and femininity
- Power and who gets to use it in society

Gender and Sex

Have you ever wondered how you became the sex and gender you are? The answer to that question is not as easy as you may think. The process of gender and sexual differentiation is an intricate constellation of chromosomes, hormones, and body tissues in the context of culture and socialization. These elements often work together to determine two things: sex and gender.

Sex is based on biological elements, whereas gender is based primarily on external social, cultural, and environmental elements. To help you learn the differences in these terms, read "Healthy Sexuality: Sex and Gender Terminology."

For the most part (98.3%), a person's biological sex matches (or is compatible with) the socially assumed corresponding gender identity (Chamie & Mirkin, 2019), which is referred to as **cisgender**. A cisgender person may include a man with a masculine gender identity or a woman with a feminine identity. But it is not that way for all people; 131 million people globally (1.7%) fall outside of these categories.

As we shall learn in this chapter, there are a variety of biopsychosocial factors that influence gender identity (Bailey et al, 2016; Herdt & McClintock, 2000; McClintock & Herdt, 1996; Money, 1991; Sterling, 2001; Tolman & Diamond, 2002). We can no longer view gender as being determined either entirely by biology or entirely by social learning and culture; instead, many researchers understand gender (as well as sexuality) is an interaction of all these factors (Connell, 1995; Fausto-Sterling, 2000; Ford & Beach, 1951; Freud, 1905; Herdt, 1997b; Irvine, 2002; Kinsey et al., 1948; Laumann et al., 1994; Money & Ehrhardt, 1972; Tolman, 2005; Ruble, Martin, & Berenbaum, 2007; Brettell & Sargent, 2017).

sex
The genes and biological development that determine whether we are male or female.

gender
The social differentiation into masculine or feminine, based in a historical culture.

gender identity
The sense of being a boy/man or girl/woman.

gender role
The socialization of people in masculinity and femininity in society.

299

Table 9.1 Sex differentiation as a biological process—prenatal differentiation

CHARACTERISTIC	FEMALE	MALE
Chromosomal sex	XX	XY
Gonadal sex	Ovaries	Testes
Hormonal sex	Estrogens Pregestational compounds	Androgens
Internal reproductive structures	Fallopian tubes Uterus Cervix Inner portions of vagina	Vas deferens Seminal vesicles Ejaculatory ducts Prostate
External genitals	Vulva, which includes the clitoris, inner labia (labia minora), vaginal opening (introitus) and outer labia (labia majora)	Penis Scrotum
Sex differentiation of the brain	Hypothalamus becomes estrogen sensitive, influencing cyclic release of hormones. Two hypothalamic areas are smaller in the female brain. Cerebral cortex of right hemisphere is thinner in the female brain. Corpus callosum is thicker in the female brain. Less lateralization of function in the female brain compared to the male brain.	Estrogen-sensitive male hypothalamus directs steady production of hormones. Two hypothalamic areas are larger in the male brain. Cerebral cortex of right hemisphere is thicker in the male brain. Corpus callosum is thinner in the male brain. More lateralization of function in the male brain compared to the female brain.

Biological Processes in the Development of Sex

cisgender
A person whose behaviors and identity are congruent with more traditional gender roles, and which may include a man with a masculine gender identity or a woman with a feminine identity.

sexual differentiation
The process of developing into a male or female that begins before conception and continues during fetal development.

The biological process of **sexual differentiation**—that is, developing into a male, female, or intersex—begins at conception and continues during fetal development and through puberty. At conception, chromosomes that determine genetic sex for being male or female are fixed. This process continues as the fetus develops gonads, produces hormones, develops internal and external sex organs, and then culminates with the sex differentiation of the brain. Exploring the sexual differentiation process helps us understand the typical and exceptional development of sex. As shown in Table 9.1, a number of important differences unfold in early development.

A person's biological sex is determined at the moment of conception. Both the ovum and sperm cells carry sex chromosomes. Each ovum normally carries an X chromosome. Each sperm cell normally carries either an X or a Y chromosome. An XY chromosomal combination will typically produce a male child and an XX combination will typically produce a female child. At birth, then, they also have anatomy and physiology that is either male or female. However, some people's chromosomes do not fall easily into one of two categories, and there are exceptions in sex development, which we will discuss. Figure 9.1 shows colorful micrographs of XX chromosomes and XY chromosomes.

Figure 9.1
Micrographs of the sex chromosomes: XY is male and XX is female.
Biophoto Associates/Science Source

In a developing fetus, the external genitals of typical male and female humans emerge from the same tissues. Early on in a pregnancy, the genitals are indistinguishable. The default condition is to develop into a female, unless a genetic or hormonal signal activates male development (Meyer-Bahlburg, 1984; Money & Lewis, 1990; Stoller, 1974). Both the genetic male and genetic female fetuses possess Müllerian and Wolffian ducts, which will differentiate or degenerate and become the female or male sex and reproductive organs. The Müllerian ducts will form the female reproductive system and the Wolffian ducts will form the male reproductive system given the presence of androgens (male hormones) (Stoller, 1974). The Müllerian ducts begin to differentiate in the human embryo at around 2 months. The Müllerian ducts differentiate into fallopian tubes, the uterus, and the upper part of the vagina. If androgens are present, the Müllerian ducts degenerate. In the male fetus, the Wolffian ducts are dependent on the presence of androgens (testosterone) and become the vas deferens system and seminal vesicles, which are involved in sperm production and ejaculation. In the female fetus, the Wolffian ducts degenerate. Figure 9.2 shows the sex differentiation process related to male and female genitalia.

Figure 9.2

The process of sexual differentiation during prenatal development.

Mader, S. (2011). *Human biology.* New York: McGraw-Hill.

Hijras are a "third sex" subculture recognized in India and Pakistan as well as other countries in Southeast Asia.
Bruno Morandi/Photonica World/Getty Images

sexual dimorphism
Being either female or male.

intersexuality
The condition of someone being biologically between a male and a female.

virilization
The masculinization of the human body and genital structures.

An intersex child born with ambiguous external genitals.

Biological Sex Variations and Intersex People

As mentioned, not all fetuses go through these multiple processes of sexual differentiation. Though we often discuss anatomy as it relates to male or female bodies, **sexual dimorphism**—developing characteristics that are either female or male—does not account for all of the variation among human bodies. In fact, some children are born with an extra sex chromosome or a missing sex chromosome. They may be born as female with XY chromosomes or male with XX chromosomes. In addition, some fetuses do not develop a clear set of male or female genitals, as you read in the opening story. When the process of sexual differentiation follows an exceptional path, intersexuality may result. **Intersexuality** in humans refers to biological sexes that are not easily categorized as either male or female (Money & Erhardt, 1972; Stoller, 1974).

People with intersex conditions are those whose anatomy or genes do not fit typical biological definitions of male and female (Chamie & Mirkin, 2019). Such variations are chromosomal, genital, and gonadal in sexual nature. People who are intersex may have biological characteristics of both the male and female sexes (Dreger, 1999; Karkazis, 2008). Thus, an individual might be born appearing to be female but with mostly male-typical anatomy on the inside (Chamie & Mirkin, 2019).

Several rare genetic variations in sex appear with enough frequency that they have specific genetic and physical structures. Both female XX and male XY are subject to these variations. Research generally suggests that XY cells are more susceptible to genetic issues, perhaps because both X and Y are single and not paired.

Congenital Adrenal Hyperplasia The most common cause of sexual ambiguity in XX individuals with XX sex chromosomes is congenital adrenal hyperplasia (CAH), which occurs in 1 in 10,000 to 18,000 people (White, 2011). Individuals with XY sex chromosomes can also have CAH. In this endocrine variation, the adrenal glands produce abnormally high levels of hormones that masculinize the female body, retarding breast development and pubic hair growth.

Researchers who study the effects of gender identity as a result of CAH have found that those who are assigned as males typically develop sex-typical behaviors, identity, and preferences similar to their male peers. Those who are assigned as females tend to engage in many sex-atypical behaviors. Some research shows that the female assigned gender identity with CAH shows higher levels of aggression as well as increased preference for toys considered to be more "masculine" (Berenbaum & Resnick, 1997; Hines & Kaufman, 1994). From these examples, it is apparent that there is some kind of influence of biological processes on the later process of gender development. We discuss this interaction in more detail later in the chapter.

Progestin-Induced Virilization Another condition of individuals with XX sex chromosomes is caused by the mother's use of progestin during pregnancy. In the United States, mothers were given this drug in the 1950s and 1960s to prevent miscarriage. If the timing is right, **virilization** occurs, which means the fetal genitals are masculinized. The genitals may include, however, an enlarged clitoris or a penis with an attached urethra and corpus spongiosum with labia that are fused. In all cases, the ovaries and uterus or uterine tract are present. In extreme cases there is no vagina or cervix, and the uterine tract is connected to the upper portion of the urethra internally. Because of functioning ovaries, the adolescent will develop female sex characteristics.

Occasionally a female infant will be so genitally virilized that she is assigned a male gender identity at birth and raised as a boy. After the onset of puberty, such a child may want to explore the option of genital surgery to allow expression of either female or male sexuality.

Androgen Insensitivity Syndrome Androgen insensitivity syndrome (AIS) is an inherited genetic condition in approximately 1 in 20,000 individuals (Medline Plus, 2010). (It can be a spontaneous mutation, but this is rare.) It occurs when a fetus with XY sex chromosomes is unable to respond to androgens. This insensitivity ranges from mild to extreme and results in the newborn having female genitalia. In its mild form there may be some variation in the appearance of the genitals, including a larger clitoris or small penis. Individuals who have the extreme form (complete androgen insensitivity syndrome, or CAIS) do not have a vagina, uterus, cervix, or ovaries, and they are infertile. Instead of having female internal reproductive organs, people with CAIS have undescended or partially descended testes, and they might not even know it. At puberty, the insensitivity to the hormone testosterone continues, and the testosterone is converted to estrogen. The estrogen produced by the testes produces breast growth and other female secondary sex characteristics. Due to the absence of ovaries and the uterus, menstruation will not occur. It is often at this point—the lack of menstruation—that findings prompt the diagnosis.

For many years, doctors advised that the internal testicles should be removed and hormone therapy prescribed. Vaginoplasty surgery, where surgical procedures and skin grafts reshape the small or absent vagina, was frequently performed on those with AIS, to create a larger functional vagina. Today, many intersex activists oppose this treatment and advocate a critical discussion about the person's options (Human Rights Watch, 2017).

Klinefelter Syndrome In the condition known as Klinefelter syndrome (Figure 9.3), people inherit an extra X chromosome from either parent. The typical result, then, is XXY sex chromosomes. This intersex syndrome is the most common sex chromosomal aneuploidy (the presence of an abnormal number of chromosomes in a cell) occurring at a rate between 1 in 448 to 1 in 917 male births (Davis, Howell, Wilson et al., 2016). This syndrome produces effects such as an absence of sperm in the ejaculate, causing infertility; small testes; and the lack of a masculine body with facial and body hair, muscles, larger penis, and testes (Eunice Kennedy Shriver National Institute of Child Health and Human Development, 1997). Physicians often recommend that these persons be given testosterone at puberty, which addresses many of these challenges.

XYY Syndrome XYY syndrome is a rare chromosomal disorder that affects males in about 1 in 1,000 births. It is caused by the presence of an extra Y chromosome. Males normally have one X and one Y chromosome. But individuals with this syndrome have one X and two Y chromosomes. The affected individuals are typically very tall. Many experience severe acne during adolescence (Nord, 2019).

XXX (aka Triple X) Triple X syndrome, also called trisomy X or 47,XXX, is characterized by the presence of an additional X chromosome in each of a female's cells. Although females with this condition may be taller than average, this chromosomal change typically causes no unusual physical features. Most females with triple X syndrome have normal sexual development and are able to conceive children.

Figure 9.3
Common characteristics of individuals with Klinefelter syndrome.

Labels: Tall stature; Lack of facial hair; Tendency to lose chest hairs; Breast development; Osteoporosis; Female pubic hair pattern; Testicular atrophy

Turner Syndrome In Turner syndrome (Figure 9.4), which occurs only in females, the cells are missing all or part of an X chromosome. Most commonly, then, the female has only one X chromosome. Some may have two X chromosomes, but one of them is incomplete. Sometimes a person has some cells with two X chromosomes and others with only one. This genetic condition is known as a mosaic, or mosaicism, to refer to the fact that two different genotypes developed from a single fertilized egg. Turner syndrome occurs in about 1 in 2,000 live births in the United States (Morgan, 2007).

Turner syndrome can be diagnosed at any stage of life. It may be diagnosed before birth if a chromosome analysis is done during prenatal testing. The doctor will perform a physical exam and look for signs of poor development because infants with Turner syndrome often have more potentially major harmful health problems than infants with Klinefelter syndrome, although a wide range of symptoms exists. Infants with Turner syndrome often have swollen hands and feet. Other common symptoms or developmental indicators are absent or incomplete pubertal development, a broad, flat chest, short

Figure 9.4
Common characteristics of individuals with Turner syndrome.

Labels: Short stature; Hearing problems; Minimal breast development; Extra folds of skin; Heart abnormalities; Kidney malformations; Underdeveloped ovaries; No menstruation; Puffy hands; Puffy feet.

height, a lack of menstrual periods, or a wide, webbed neck. Estrogen replacement therapy starting at around age 12 may greatly help the child's development through puberty.

5-Alpha-Reductase Deficiency The rare condition 5-alpha-reductase deficiency occurs in genetic males. In developed societies such as the United States, this biological condition occurs at the rate of 1 in 200,000 individuals, but in communities that experience inbreeding, it can be as high as 1 in 200 (Imperato-McGinley et al., 1979). This condition does not allow a fetus to convert testosterone to dihydrotestosterone (DHT), which is necessary for the development of male genitalia. The absence of DHT tends to result in ambiguous genitalia at birth; there may be a small or microscopic penis with testes and a vagina and labia. The small penis is capable of ejaculation, but it looks like a clitoris at birth. This results in many of these genetic males being raised as girls. When additional sex hormones are released during puberty at around age 11 or 12, the genitals of these genetic males that were assigned

RESEARCH and Sexual Well-Being

Studies of 5-Alpha-Reductase Deficiency

Since ancient times, there have been reports of individuals changing their sex because of the confusion they have over their own body and genitals. For example, among the ancient Greeks was Tiresias, their most famous prophet, who was blind and was said to have first been born a boy, later lived as a woman for 7 years, and then went back to being a man. Did these changes occur because he had the genitals of both sexes at different times in his life? Though we may not have the answer about the case of Tiresias, anthropological research has examined more recent incidences of 5-alpha-reductase deficiency. Individuals with this deficiency help us to understand the influences of culture, anatomy, and biology in sexual development. This research also suggests that in some cultures there may be at least three sex categories of humans (Herdt, 1994; Money, 1991; Sterling, 2001).

Medical doctors conducted studies in the Dominican Republic because people with 5-alpha-reductase deficiency have been born there with regularity over generations. In fact, the local culture created a term for a third-sex category for these newborns. They were called guevedoche, roughly translated as "testicles at 12," meaning they will develop testicles when they are about 12 years old (Herdt, 1994; Imperato-McGinley et al., 1981). Among five villages this condition has occurred frequently, perhaps the result of long-term inbreeding.

Researchers noted that 38 individuals (out of several hundred people in the five villages) were seen as guevedoche. Many were reared as girls. In time, however, 33 of them underwent a sex change. Seventeen changed to male gender identity because they felt more like men and developed the awareness that they had a male gender identity. Sixteen reported changing to a male gender role because by age 16 they no longer felt like girls. As men, these former girls assumed such male gender roles as farmers and woodsmen, and some married women. The researchers decided that it was the biology and hormones that caused these individuals to change from female to male (Imperato-McGinley et al., 1979). The researchers did not explain what happened to the individuals who did not change to male gender identity or roles.

But what is the role of culture and context here? The term guevedoche is about both biology and culture, because part of it refers to anatomy (nature) and part of it refers to what people in their culture expect regarding how a male or a female will act (nurture).

The Sambia people of Papua New Guinea have a similar intersex condition known as kwolu-aatwul, colloquially known as "turnem man" or "changing into a man." Fieldwork revealed that 12 individuals were born with this condition over a period of several generations (Herdt & Davidson, 1988). From birth, they were reared as "turnem man" and grew up expecting to be men but probably not marrying. Or at birth they were mistaken as female and reared as girls. Late in adolescence some of those who were raised as girls tried to become men and to marry. This did not work in their own villages, perhaps because people could not "change" their perception to think of them as male, not female. In this situation, culture created perceptions that were as powerful as the biology. So, the turnem men raised as girls had to move to towns far away, where they could be seen as male.

One intersex individual was Sakulambei, who had a tiny penis and an odd-looking scrotum at birth (Herdt & Stoller, 1990). He was treated as a turnem man because people knew that the appearance of his genitals would change around puberty. His father rejected him in childhood, and his mother died when he was 5 years old. His mother's brother, a powerful shaman, loved and reared him as a son in another village. Sakulambei married, against great odds and with some stigma, which he overcame in part because he also became a powerful shaman (Herdt & Stoller, 1990). It is clear that contrary to the received wisdom, these people were not confused about their feeling of who they were, but rather about how to express their identities in traditional society.

female develop to look more like an adult male penis and testes, though smaller. To read about this condition in two areas of the world, see "Research and Sexual Well-Being: Studies of 5-Alpha-Reductase Deficiency." Additionally, see Table 9.2 for a summary of the intersex conditions just discussed.

Table **9.2** Summary of biological intersex variations

CHROMOSOMES	BIOLOGICAL INTERSEX VARIATION	DESCRIPTION
XX	Congenital adrenal hyperplasia (CAH)	The most common cause of sexual ambiguity in individuals with XX sex chromosomes.
XX	Progestin-induced virilization	This condition of individuals with XX sex chromosomes is caused by the mother's use of progestin, a drug used in the 1950s and 1960s to prevent miscarriage.
XY	Androgen insensitivity syndrome (AIS)	This occurs in approximately 1 in 20,000 individuals when the cells of the body are unable to respond to androgen, so they have a Y chromosome (typically XY) but their body is unable to masculinize, which results in them having female appearance and genitalia.
XXY	Klinefelter syndrome	A condition in which a person inherits an extra X chromosome from either the father or mother. It occurs in about 1 in 500, or approximately 550,000 people in the United States.
	XXY syndrome	
	XXX (AKA triple X)	A condition characterized by the presence of an additional X chromosome in each of a female's cells. AKA trisomy X or 47,XXX syndrome.
XO	Turner syndrome	A rare condition in which a female does not have the usual XX sex chromosomes.
XY	5-alpha-reductase deficiency	A rare condition that occurs in genetic males. It occurs in much higher incidence in inbreeding communities.

Cultural Treatment of Intersex People

It is interesting to note how different cultures react to intersex people. Navaho Indians, for example, regard intersex people as powerful in having special healing or shamanic qualities (Edgerton, 1964). In 19th-century Western society, we have learned through the personal diaries of how a remarkable person, Herculine Barbin, who may have had 5-alpha-reductase deficiency, was mistreated in French society. She was assigned to the female sex and grew up as a French girl, but she always felt like she was a boy. In puberty, her male genitals were discovered, and she developed sexual interest in other girls (Foucault & Barbin, 1980). She sought help from doctors but felt shunned. Herculine killed herself because she thought she was unique and condemned to suffer her fate utterly alone (Herdt, 1994; Dreger 1999; Karkazis, 2008).

The biological process of fetal sexual differentiation is critical for setting the stage in society for how parents, caretakers, and community respond in deciding how to gender socialize children. There are many controversies in this process, and intersex activists do not agree with the medical doctors regarding treatment and socialization issues (Viloria, 2016). For example, a very powerful documentary film, *Intersexion: Gender Ambiguity Unveiled* (2012), provides a very detailed but critical understanding of the issues. Once children are born, though, they enter a world in which they are bombarded with gendered expectations and environments (Fausto-Sterling et al., 2015). These expectations play a large role in how people define their own gender identity throughout life.

How do these biological and cultural factors influence the internal experience of identity? That is the focus of the next section.

GENDER IDENTITY AND EXPRESSION

Gender identity is the sense of feeling that one is a boy/man or girl/woman or, for some individuals, neither one nor the other. Some people might identify as genderqueer or non-binary, and some people do not subscribe to or identify with conventional gender categories at all.

COMMUNICATION Matters

The Trouble with Labels

You know by now just how important words are in life, especially words used as labels for someone's identity. Even the pronouns we use in reference to an individual's gender can be either affirming or offensive. One such historical label related to gender is hermaphrodite. Though it is now considered offensive, it is still used in some books to refer to people who are intersex. The word *hermaphrodite* comes from the Greek god Hermaphroditus, who was both fully male and fully female. A true hermaphrodite, therefore, would be someone who has fully functioning male and female sex organs. Because such a condition does not occur in humans, the term is inaccurate. In fact, the terminology is changing rapidly.

Later in the chapter, we discuss the topics of transgender people and intersex identities. Many people also misuse the term *transgender* to include everyone who is gender-variant, gender nonconforming, or non-binary, genderqueer, or who is transitioning from one gender to another (Davidson, 2007; Viloria, 2016)—lumping too much together. As we will learn later, transgender people often feel that the requirement to live according to this binary of being either male or female is too restrictive, because culture and society have so many ideals and expectations for what it means to be either male or female. They believe that it may even prevent adequate access to medical treatment and legal status.

The problem with seeing sex and gender as binary is that **gender binary** assumes that there are only two genders, which are completely different and separate. Consider these situations: A person could identify as genderqueer or non-binary, or could be transitioning in **gender expression** or role in order to match their identity. Concerning one's body, a person could elect gender-affirming treatment or surgeries, or have been born as an intersex individual. In any of these situations, a person could be in a quandary as to whether to use a men's restroom or a women's restroom, or be legally forced to use one or the other. This is just one issue that most people take for granted, but for some, it can be quite stressful.

So, then, what terms and pronouns do we use? The answer is, better to ask. When introducing yourself to people, tell them your name and disclose your gender identity or the pronouns that you prefer to use and then ask what they prefer to be called or what pronouns they use. Some may look at you strangely, but one day you will find someone who is grateful that you took the time to ask their preference rather than just assume based on external appearances and gender expectations.

gender binary
The illusionary but common perception that sex and gender are either male or female. In actuality, sex and gender exist on a spectrum.

Even when gender identity is expressed as masculine and feminine, there can be a spectrum of meanings. Different people express different degrees of masculinity or femininity in their behavior, dress, attitudes, and personality. Consider how important gender identity is to you: Are you able to imagine what it might feel like to be another gender? What about genderqueer? What about not having a gender identity at all? What about having a gender identity that is different from your sex? For more on this topic, see "Communication Matters: The Trouble with Labels."

Gender Identity—A Brief History

Scientific theorists whose work centers on gender identity, most of them from Western countries, historically have argued that gender is the rock of our self-awareness and, equally as important, that it cannot be changed, no matter what (Bailey, 2003; Stoller, 1974; Zucker & Bradley, 1995). Some contemporary theorists question this perspective (Diamond, 2014b; Dreger, 1999).

There is an early, well-known story that highlights just how critical gender identity is to our sense of who we are and how we interact with the world around us. In the late 1950s, psychologists and medical doctors created the clear concept of "gender identity." At that time there were reports of individuals seeking to change their sex from being male to female. One was Christine Jorgensen. Jorgensen's transition was the object of much medical and media attention. She was born George William Jorgensen, Jr., in New York City. As a male, George served in the army but later went to Denmark to have a vagina created and socially transitioned her gender identity to publicly identify as the woman she knew herself to be. She went on to develop a successful nightclub act, appeared numerous times on television, and wrote a best-selling autobiography that was made into a movie in the 1970s (Meyerowitz, 2006). Some pundits (Lieberman, 2017) have referred to Christine as the Caitlyn Jenner of the 1950s. Taking such drastic steps to reconcile the body with the gender identity is a testament to how critical and powerful gender is to our identity.

During Christine's era, all cases of gender affirmation surgeries were male to female. Today, we see a dramatic shift, as females now also transition into a male sex in order to affirm their gender identity (Olyslager & Conway, 2007). The reasons for this shift remain complex, but part of it may be due to the greater power of women and the societal acceptance of transitions to confirm gender identity. Christine Jorgensen led the way for this acceptance.

Many psychological and behavioral cues are built into our cultural blueprint to affect the perception of gender identity. These range from socialization to prefer either pink (girls) or blue (boys), to the association of superhero comic book characters with having a penis, to whether a child likes to climb trees or to play with dolls, to whether someone prefers to sit down or to stand up when peeing. Later, it may involve to what sex the person is attracted. When these characteristics, preferences, or behaviors are grouped together as a set of dynamic socializations, we better understand the connections between gender identity, body image, and societal attitudes and expectations about gendered behaviors (Stoller, 1974).

In fact, many people may perceive these characteristics as so basic and unchangeable in terms of masculinity and femininity that they never question them, unless something goes wrong or seems unusual. For example, as an anecdotal experiment, a male student wore "feminine" clothes to work one day. He also used more "feminine" language, using terms that reflected feelings that expressed subordination, such as being different. Throughout the day, many of his co-workers asked him if he was OK. He reported that the change in his external appearance and behavior appeared to create discomfort in his co-workers, which they, in turn, experienced as something being wrong within him. You may begin to understand how this student felt as you read "Know Yourself: Being True to Yourself: Imagine Being the Other Gender—for 5 Minutes."

Christine Jorgensen was the first well-publicized individual who transitioned from male to female. Her case created public interest in gender identity.
Photo Researchers/Science Source

gender expression
The way people express their gender by behavior, clothes, hair, voice, gait. A person's gender expression might adhere to or violate culturally expected gender roles or norms. Usually, people prefer to feel that their gender expression agrees with their gender identity, but nonconforming gender expressions could be difficult to embody in society. As opposed to gender roles that are produced by culture as a whole, gender expression is performed by a person.

Biology and Gender Identity Development

Our gender identity responds to development, much like our brain, skeleton, and our ability to learn behaviors that allow for adaptation. The development of the sense of feeling male, female, or something different may interact with internal cues, as from the brain, and external environmental forces, such as parents, peers, and media sources. It is complicated to understand to what extent biology plays a role in gender identity. For years, however, many have argued whether it's the biological or the environmental forces that drive gender identity development.

In trying to understand biology's effects on gender identity, some scientists have looked at the role of hormones. While many scientists believe that hormones are part of gender identity development, it is difficult to study this in human beings. It would be unethical to subject people to hormonal changes to study how they affect gender identity. This means we rely on studying individuals with hormonal disorders to gain insight into how hormones may affect gender identity.

Know Yourself

Being True to Yourself: Imagine Being the Other Gender—for 5 Minutes

Let yourself relax in your favorite comfortable chair in a quiet room. Close your eyes and allow yourself to be fully focused on your body and feelings. For 5 minutes, imagine that you are changing gender. Imagine that you are changing your cisgender body image and that, from head to toe, you begin to see yourself as the other gender. As you imagine the change, notice whether your appearance changes. What kind of clothes are you wearing? Is your body the same or has it changed? Do you have on makeup? Now allow yourself to come back to your real body and identity and gradually open your eyes. Once you feel fully in the present, do this self-assessment to see what is true for you:

- How did you feel being in the body of the other gender? Was it pleasant or unpleasant, exciting or fearful, or all of this?
- On a scale of 1 to 5, with 1 being the lowest and 5 being the highest, how would you rate your sense of being the other gender?
- What did you feel about your body image as the other gender?
- Did you feel that your self-awareness changed?
- Did you experience any sexual changes, such as a different sense of desire or possibly attraction?
- How did you feel when you returned to your present body and gender identity? Happy, sad, relieved, anxious?

Were you able to experience another gender, if only for 5 minutes? Some cisgender may be unable to imagine the change—and there is nothing wrong with that. In our experience cisgender men have considerably more difficulty with this exercise than cisgender women, although times are changing, and more young adult men are able to imagine the change.

WHAT'S ON YOUR MIND?

Q: My 3-year-old son loves to play with dolls, and he keeps saying that he wants to be a girl. His father is getting very concerned about this behavior, and it is starting to worry me as well. What do we do?

ANSWER: We can imagine this may be a difficult issue to cope with, especially for your son's father because he may be feeling a loss of his dreams for his son. Your child may simply be trying on different identities or may be dealing with deeper, enduring feelings of his body not matching his developing gender identity. When the right time comes later on, talk openly with your son to try and understand how they are feeling. Keep the conversation open with his dad as well and encourage him to be patient as you both wait to see the development of your son's gender identity. We would caution you, though: Allow your son to explore various play habits or desires. Let your son know of your continued love and support.

DID YOU KNOW

"It is so funny when people ask me how I know that I am a boy. I just ask them; how do you know you are a boy? You just know those things. I have known all my life!"

—Tommy, 7-year-old transgender boy

Source: Brill & Pepper, 2008.

Many cases of changes in gender identity during a person's lifetime have been reported in medicine and science during the 20th century, such as the famous story of Lili Elbe, depicted in the book and movie, *The Danish Girl*. However, in sexology, the significant work in this area began with Dr. John Money in the mid-1950s, who founded a gender identity clinic at Johns Hopkins University Hospital in Baltimore. This was a time of strict gender roles, due to Cold War pressures to ensure that men were very masculine and fit for war, while women were prepared to be homemakers and mothers (Corber, 1997; D'Emilio & Freedman, 1988; Herman, 1997). This clinic began to receive increases in parents' requests to examine and possibly treat their children who seemed to be different than expected in terms of gender identity.

Among the most famous of these cases was that of a Canadian boy named David Reimer, which is described in the book *As Nature Made Him* (Colapinto, 2000). David was born a genetic male. At about 8 months old, his penis was accidentally destroyed when he was circumcised. Dr. Money suggested that he be assigned to the female sex, given the name "Brenda," and reared as a girl. Doctors created a vagina for him and later gave her hormone treatments to promote breast development and other female secondary sex characteristics. This history was hidden from her until she was 13. Brenda, however, never felt like a girl; she had always said that she felt like a boy and seemed to express the interests and behaviors of a stereotypical boy. In fact, she experienced bouts of depression and feelings of alienation and worthlessness, which are symptoms known to occur when someone is struggling to transition to the other gender (Stoller, 1974). At age 14, Brenda had surgery and hormonal treatment to change her back to a man, and he chose the name David. All throughout the issues in his life and treatment, it appears that Dr. Money denied that David was depressed and needed help, and in other ways Dr. Money did not appropriately support David's life-course transition (Colapinto, 2000). David attempted to live a normal life and even married a woman and became a stepfather. Unfortunately, at age 38, David succumbed to deepening depression and died by suicide in 2004.

David Reimer, pictured as an adult man, was raised as a female, despite being genetically male.
STR/REUTERS/Newscom

While very controversial, the exposure of these facts suggests that Reimer's treatment was associated with flawed methods used by Dr. Money, including dishonesty in data reporting and questionable ethics of sex reassignment surgeries on infants and children (Gaetano, 2017). All of this, as well as other controversies, significantly tarnished Dr. Money's and his clinic's reputation. Because of the difficulties David faced in his life, critics say that physicians should not try to surgically treat problems in infancy that involve genitalia. David's remarkable life has also challenged theories of plasticity of gender identity and whether people can change their innate sense of being male or female. In addition, such cases have ignited the passion of activists who criticize traditional medical approaches that regard conditions that cause problems with infants' genitalia as abnormal and the parents or professionals who are overly eager to "correct" what they perceive as "natural mistakes." Often these procedures have resulted in shame and harm for individuals (Dreger, 1999, 1998; Karkazis, 2008; Kessler, 1998).

Transgender and Cisgender Identities

Transgender people have been the focus of increasing societal attention in the classroom and in social media. A controversial film entitled *Girl*, made in Belgium but released on Netflix, reveals some of the challenges of portraying the lives of transgender people in order for people to understand them better. Some have questioned the rarity of transgender people in the general population. A new probability-based statistical model has revealed that within the current U.S. population, transgender people number 390 adults per 100,000, or almost 1 million adults nationally (Meerwijk & Sevelius, 2017). Researchers believe that this statistic is more indicative for younger adults right now.

In the United States, people who identify with the sex they were assigned at birth and the assumed corresponding gender as well can be referred to as cisgender (Killermann, 2017, p. 41). However, some individuals appear to depart from traditional gender identities; today they are called transgender people.

Jazz Jennings is notable for being one of the youngest publicly documented people to be identified as transgender.
Noam Galai/WireImage/Getty Images

Transgender
Someone whose self-identification and behavior do not match the traditional gender role for their assigned sex.

Since the early 1990s, **transgender** has been used as an umbrella term to describe two different areas of meaning: first, gender diversity (Feinberg, 1992), and second, people who do not resonate with the gender they were assigned at birth and who instead identify through the gender binary as trans women and trans men. Thus, a variety of different people may refer to themselves as gender-variant, gender or sex-changing, gender-expansive, gender nonconforming, agender, gender-blending, genderqueer, and gender-bending, (Cover, 2018; Davidson, 2007). It appears that cultural, biological, and psychological factors are involved in how individuals identify their gender.

Regarding sexual orientation and its relationship to transgender people, the term *transgender* does not imply any specific form of sexual orientation such as same-sex attraction. Transgender people may identify by conventional sexual orientation labels such as heterosexual or bisexual, or they may feel that these are inadequate or inapplicable to them. A transgender individual may have characteristics that are normally associated with a particular gender, yet feel most comfortable identifying with the other gender available in the gender binary. Such transgender individuals may apply terms such as *transman, transwoman, other, agender, third gender,* or *genderqueer* (Viloria, 2016). Transgender people may also reject all these labels or use *they or zie* as the neutral pronouns. This ambiguity of presenting themselves without using *he* or *she* pronouns, and presenting themselves as different than a man or woman, seems basic to non-binary gender identity today (Killermann, 2017). Thus, being transgender identified is a creative and highly individual process.

Unlike people who are intersex, transgender people have typical genitals at birth, and they do not require reassignment (Cromwell, 1999). For example, some genetic females who are transgender do wish to have their female breasts removed to give the appearance of a flat chest, but they wish to retain their female genitals. In short, they want to change their outward identity and body presentation to make it true and more complete as an expression of their self-awareness.

Many young people who have a transgender identity appear to be both invisible and extremely vulnerable to issues of aggression, bullying, assault, and suicide (James et al., 2016). One study reveals that 60% of transgender people are out to their families, who are generally supportive. However, there are many factors related to their negative perception and treatment in society, and among those transgender people who had unsupportive relationships with their families, fully 37% had attempted suicide. One in 10 transgender people who were out to their families reported that a family member was violent toward them.

Transgender individuals often experience challenges related to their identity. Certainly, there is a lot of prejudice and discrimination. Previously invisible and neglected in health and family care, transgender children and adolescents often fail to receive good health care (James et al., 2016). Transgendered children have difficulty adjusting to many aspects of daily life. They are generally discouraged by their families and bullied at school (Higdon, 2011). Parents are often confused, even frightened, by the behavior of the child. *The Transgender Child* (Brill & Pepper, 2008) and *The Gender Creative Child* (Ehrensaft, 2016) are

Transgender or gender fluid children are vulnerable to relational and mental health risks. Resources are necessary to help these children thrive.
Matt Short/Barcroft Images/Getty Images

HEALTHY Sexuality

Transgender Day of Visibility

The more visible transgender people are, the more likely it is that they will be harassed. To address this issue, a new national day has been created to celebrate being transgender and being open about transgender identity. The Transgender Day of Visibility (March 31) was created by Rachel Crandall for people to celebrate and express their unique gender qualities as transgender people. The topics to think about and discuss with others on this day include the following:

- What is gender? Why is gender so essential in this society?
- Is gender limitless, or limiting?
  - What do you identify as your gender? How did your self-discovery occur?
- What steps or changes can we make on a local, national, and global level to become more inclusive of transgender individuals?
- How have the media influenced the visibility and progress of members of the transgender community?
- Discuss pioneers of the transgender movement for equality and visibility.

By discussing these topics, we can help families, peers, and professionals to support transgender people in positive ways that create safety, self-awareness, and acceptance.

---

handbooks that help families, teachers, and medical practitioners to understand what is happening in the child's self-definition and experience. The organization Gender Spectrum, based in California, aims to support families, schools, and professionals in addressing the needs of gender-expansive and transgender kids and teens. It hosts a growing annual conference that currently attracts participants in the thousands. Other avenues also offer hope, as explained in "Healthy Sexuality: Transgender Day of Visibility."

One form of prejudice is **transphobia**, a term that describes the fear and hatred of transgender people, or cis-sexism, a term that describes gender binary privilege and the oppression of transgender people. Transphobia and cis-sexism can result in violence or other forms of oppression, such as job discrimination, microaggressions, or intentional misgendering directed toward transgender people (Valentine, 2007; Nadal et al., 2016). In fact, many cases of transgender murder in the United States have occurred. Brandon Teena was assigned female at birth, transitioned into the masculine, and expressed himself as a man. Brandon was killed in Nebraska. This story is depicted in the film *Boys Don't Cry*. In California, Gwen Araujo was assigned male at birth and expressed her feminine gender identity and was killed.

The facts show that there is a disproportionately higher number of Black transgender women who were killed in the United States in 2018 (Human Rights Campaign, 2019). It does not look random, because in 2018, 26 transgender people were killed in violent homicides, most of whom were trans women of color. The data show that they were killed by acquaintances, partners, and strangers; some have been arrested, while others have yet to be identified. Here we see the effects once again of racial and social inequality in the United States. Although the details differ a bit, the fatal violence has a greater impact on these trans women due to the intersection of racism, sexism, homophobia, biophobia, and transphobia. This sexual and gender prejudice has the effect of denying these women necessary housing and health care, and other necessities that make them vulnerable to poverty, homelessness, and survival sex work (Human Rights Campaign, 2019). Unfortunately, the legislation that was needed to ensure that people who oppress trans individuals in any way are brought to justice was opposed by the administration of President Donald Trump, which instead rolled back some protections already in place (Salam, 2018).

transphobia
Fear and hatred of transgender people.

Brandon Teena, a female to male transgender, was murdered when peers discovered his transgender identity.
AP Images

Gender Confirmation

Many transgender people would like to confirm their gender identities by changing their biological sex. The history of transsexualism reveals how difficult this process has been (Bailey et al., 2016; Cromwell, 1999; Oosterhuis, 2000). Pioneers like Christine Jorgensen sought medical treatment outside the United States because there was greater understanding in other countries of their desire to change their sex. These individuals went to great lengths to locate doctors who would perform surgical procedures that gave them the appearance and body that better reflected their true sex and gender identity. This process of "re-becoming" is known as hormonal and/or surgical gender confirmation or gender affirmation. Those who seek gender confirmation or gender affirmation surgeries are estimated to occur at the rate of roughly 1 in 30,000 males and 1 in 100,000 females in the United States who seek sexual reassignment (APA, 2000). Some researchers believe it is more common than these statistics reflect, but reports are affected by the stigma involved, the problem of maintaining confidentiality, and the economic disadvantages faced by some patients (Olyslager & Conway, 2007).

The American Psychiatric Association (APA) currently has a diagnostic category for people feeling distress because of a discrepancy between their gender identity and their assigned sex at birth (2013).

It is important to recognize that gender nonconformity is not the same as gender dysphoria. According to W-PATH (2012), an important and respected scientific organization dealing with these issues, gender nonconformity refers to how a person's gender identity, role, or expression differs from the cultural norms prescribed for people of a particular sex. **Gender dysphoria** refers to discomfort or distress that is caused by a discrepancy between a person's gender identity and that person's sex assigned at birth (and the associated gender role and/or primary and secondary sex characteristics) (W-PATH, 2012). Not everyone who experiences gender nonconformity experiences discomfort or distress.

When we talk of "transitioning" for transgender individuals, it is important to be aware of several different mechanisms that affect this process, including social, hormonal, surgical, and legal measures of transition and affirmation. Hormonal puberty blockers, for example, are not used to alter appearance, but to prevent undesired development of certain primary and secondary sex characteristics. W-PATH (2012, p. 19) has developed significant minimal criteria for advising doctors when to provide adolescents with puberty-suppressing hormones, such as the presence of long-term gender non-conforming behavior and gender dysphoria worsened by the onset of puberty. Some people may also undergo surgical procedures to change their bodies and appearance. They often refer to these surgeries as "top surgery," which is modification of breast tissue, and "bottom surgery," which is the modification of the genital structures.

Male-to-Female (MTF) Procedures Male-to-female (MTF) hormone therapy with estrogen results in significant changes to the body. Estrogen therapy can create permanent or temporary effects. Permanent effects include breast development, enlargement of the nipples, loss of ejaculation, loss of erection, shrinkage of the testicles, and sterility. Temporary effects include a decrease in acne, a decrease in facial and body hair, a decrease in muscle mass and strength, softening of the skin, slowing of balding patterns, decreased sexual interest, suppression of testosterone production, and redistribution of fat from the abdominal area to the hips and buttocks (Vázquez, 2008). These temporary effects reverse when a person stops using estrogen.

gender dysphoria
Refers to discomfort or distress that is caused by a discrepancy between a person's gender identity and that person's sex assigned at birth (and the associated gender role and/or primary and secondary sex characteristics).

Photo of completed genital surgery for a male to female transsexual.
Courtesy of Dr. Daniel Greenwald, Tampa, Florida.

MTF transitioning individuals may opt for the following surgical procedures (Center of Excellence for Transgender Health, 2011):

- Orchiectomy—Removal of the testes.
- Vaginoplasty—Construction of a vagina, clitoris, and vulva, enabling female sexual function using tissue from the penis or a colon graft.
- Breast augmentation—If the estrogen therapy is not successful in stimulating enough breast growth, individuals may opt for augmentation of the breasts to be able to function socially as women.
- Reduction thyroid chrondroplasty—This procedure reduces prominent thyroid cartilage, which alters the appearance of the Adam's apple.
- Voice surgery—This evolving procedure is designed to raise the pitch of the speaking voice. Speech therapy is often recommended prior to seeking this surgical solution.
- Facial feminization—This includes a variety of aesthetic plastic surgeries and removal of facial hair follicles (beard) via electrolysis or laser treatment; these are arduous and expensive procedures that facilitate social functioning as a woman.

Female-to-Male (FTM) Procedures Female-to-male (FTM) hormonal therapy and surgical procedures are also available. The hormone for FTM transitions is testosterone. Similar to MTF hormonal therapy, some effects are permanent and some are temporary if the hormone is discontinued. Permanent effects of testosterone include atrophy of the uterus and ovaries, which results in sterility; baldness and hair loss, especially at the temples and crown of the head; beard and mustache growth; deepening of the voice; enlargement of the clitoris; and increased growth of body hair (Vázquez, 2008). Temporary testosterone effects include behavioral changes such as increased aggression as well as an increase in sexual interest. Other potential side effects include the development of acne, increased muscle mass and strength, an increase in number of red blood cells, and redistribution of fat from breast, hips, and thighs to the abdominal area (Vasquez, 2008).

Genital surgical procedures, or "bottom surgeries," available to FTM transitioning individuals are more complicated than the MTF procedures (Morrison, Perez, Nedelman, & Crane, 2015). It is medically easier to create a vagina and have it respond sexually than it is to create a penis that responds sexually. The technology for these surgeries is not as advanced as many individuals would like. Because of these complications, many FTM transitioning individuals have put off "bottom surgeries" until technology can create full physical and sexual functioning. The surgeries today include the following (Center of Excellence for Transgender Health, 2011):

- Chest reconstruction/bilateral mastectomy—Removal of breast tissue. FTM individuals request this procedure more often than other ones.
- Hysterectomy/oophorectomy—Removal of the uterus, fallopian tubes, and ovaries.
- Metoidioplasty—The ligament that connects the clitoris to the pubic bone is cut to create more length for the testosterone-enlarged clitoris as the erectile phallus along with a urethroplasty. The benefit is that the erectile tissue and sensation are preserved for the purpose of sexual enjoyment.
- Phalloplasty—The construction of a phallus that is larger in size than what is available through metoidioplasty. In this surgery, size and appearance are prioritized over erectile capacity and sensation. This surgery requires penile implants for erection.

For some transgender individuals, Genital Confirmation Surgeries may be considered a critical step in affirming one's gender identity.
MediaforMedical/Andrea Aubert/Alamy Stock Photo

- Scrotoplasty—The construction of a scrotum using labia majora tissue and optional testicular implants (similar to breast implants).
- Urethroplasty—The creation of a urethral canal through the created penis in order to facilitate urination when standing. This is usually, though not always, done in conjunction with the phallic reconstruction.
- Vaginectomy—The removal of the vagina. This is required if the vaginal opening is going to be closed.

The procedures presented here are all major surgeries, which means the choice to undergo surgical reconstruction or modification is a serious decision. In fact, many surgeons require patients to undergo extensive therapy before they agree to perform these surgeries, a requirement that is perceived as onerous gatekeeping by many in the transgender community. Additionally, these gender-affirming surgeries must usually be performed in several stages. The good news is that most people who do undergo these procedures are satisfied and feel better adjusted in their own bodies (DeCuypere et al., 2005; James et al., 2016).

Even in the face of controversy there is increasing acceptance of transgender people in the United States, as best indicated by the appearance of transgender characters in television since the 1970s. Historically, TV series, such as *Law & Order, Nip/Tuck, Glee, Orange Is the New Black, Sense8,* and *Transparent* have included transgender characters. Movies also include transgender characters. Some popular movies include *Transamerica,* made in 2005, with Felicity Huffman playing a transsexual woman prior to undergoing surgery. In 2011, Chaz Bono, who was born Chastity Bono to pop stars Cher and Sonny Bono, aired a documentary entitled *Becoming Chaz*. In the film, Chaz explains how he transitioned biologically and socially to better express who he knew himself to be from as young as he could remember.

As discussions of gender identity variations become more common, individuals may become more self-conscious of their gender identity expressions and related masculinity, femininity, or—a different gender topic—androgyny.

Chaz Bono (left), formerly known as Chastity Bono (right), is a famous individual who has openly shared his story of the female to male transition.

(*left*) Jason LaVeris/FilmMagic/Getty Images; (*right*) Paul Harris/Hulton Archive/Getty Images

Androgyny (Gender Nonconforming/Non-Binary/Genderqueer)

Some people do not seem to lean toward either masculinity or femininity. Rather, they express a high degree of both masculine and feminine traits in their personality and behavior, a phenomenon historically referred to as **androgyny**. In today's terminology, gender nonconforming and non-binary or genderqueer have similar meanings. Androgyny, to some degree, may also involve a person's appearance. In psychological terms an androgynous person is a female or male who has a high degree of both feminine and masculine traits (Bem, 1974). Feminine traits are considered expressive and male traits are instrumental. A feminine person may rate high on expressive traits and low on instrumental ones. A masculine person is high on instrumental traits and low on expressive ones. The category of an undifferentiated person is low on both expressive and instrumental traits. In psychological terms an androgynous person is a female, male, or intersex person who has a high degree of both feminine and masculine traits.

In individuals who are considered androgynous, the degree of feeling both male and female components is not great enough to lead them to change their gender identity or body. Some well-known musicians who have presented themselves as androgynous are David Bowie, Michael Jackson, Prince, and Annie Lennox.

In the view of an expert on this issue, Dr. Sandra Bem (1993), being androgynous is a good thing and may mean that you are psychologically healthy and creative. She believes that androgynous men and women seem to be both more flexible and mentally healthier than those who are either more strictly masculine or feminine.

In close relationships, a feminine or androgynous gender role may be more desirable because personal expression helps people to be intimate in relationships. A masculine or androgynous gender role may be more desirable, however, in work settings because of their demands for action and assertiveness (Choi, 2004).

Skeptics argue that androgyny is a culture-bound issue, meaning it is relative to the historical period and society in which one grows up. For example, consider one of the behaviors used to create the Bem Inventory in the 1970s. Women were scored as typical if they preferred a bath, and men as typical if they preferred a shower. In fact, if a woman preferred to shower, she was considered atypical (Bem, 1974). At the time, these traits were considered accurate based on societal perceptions of bathing habits (i.e., women took baths and men took showers). Now, these kinds of gender stereotypes are outdated. By comparison, the term *metrosexual* from the early 2000s has some of the same androgynous qualities and is a bit dated already. **Gender stereotypes** are simplistic generalizations about the gender attributes, differences, and roles of individuals and/or groups. It will be interesting to learn which current cultural gender traits will be considered outdated in about 40 or 50 years, just as these bathing habits are now considered outdated.

The word "unisex" once described a growing cultural gender concept that quickly went out of style. In the United States we see it in reference to haircuts, perfumes, clothes, cars, and restrooms, for example. The degendering of college dormitories is another sign of such cultural transformations.

Cultural variations in androgyny are also important because what appears masculine for one society may be defined as feminine in another. For example, in some cultures, a woman who wears pants or jeans is considered masculine, whereas in the United States, pants are common attire for women.

Actress Tilda Swinton is one of a number of celebrities who present themselves as androgynous.
Fernando Leon/Getty Images

androgyny
Characteristics of a male or female who has a high degree of both feminine (expressive) and masculine (instrumental) characteristics.

gender stereotypes
Traditional notions about being masculine or feminine.

WHAT'S ON YOUR MIND?

Q: *I am a heterosexual woman, though I am not what people would define as "girlie" or "feminine." I despise dresses, high heels, and makeup and I am very active in sports. People keep questioning my sexual orientation. How do I address these people who don't believe that I am attracted to men, despite my appearance and hobbies?*

ANSWER: Unfortunately, many people stereotype and begin to question sexual orientation when others do not follow the typical cultural male or female ideals in dress, mannerisms, behavior, and hobbies. Androgyny has been part of human experience for thousands of years and is nothing to be ashamed of. Explain to people that androgyny is different from sexual orientation, and because you are different in your gender identity or expression, it does not mean that your sexual orientation is same-sex oriented. You get to decide who you are sexually attracted to, not them.

Androgyny affects our life span development as well as culture. In fact, as people age, many become more androgynous than when they were younger. One researcher used the Bem Inventory with people as they aged across time. The studies suggest that both females and males may become more feminine with age, definitely indicating that males in the second half of life become more androgynous (Hyde et al., 1991; Das, Waite, & Laumann, 2012).

It appears that as transgender identities have increased in visibility, sexism has declined, and vice versa—and this may not be a coincidence. As women in the United States have moved into the main institutions and roles of society, and as society is not as rigid as it once was in gender categories and stereotypes, variations in gender identity expression have definitely increased. Intolerance does exist, but society appears to be accepting gender and its variations with greater respect. We discuss these issues in the next section on gender roles.

GENDER ROLES

Gender roles are the behaviors, attitudes, and characteristics that any given society expects of males and females. These gender roles are the bedrock of many societies' systems of power relations due to the economic, political, religious, familial, and even military attitudes that are directed toward men and women in the roles expected of them (Chodorow, 1978; Connell, 1995; Friedl, 1975; Hirsch et al., 2009). In many societies gender roles are the foundation for the ideas of what constitutes masculinity and femininity (Barth, 1974; Godelier, 1985; Herdt, 1981; Mead, 1949; Stimpson & Herdt, 2014).

WHAT'S ON YOUR MIND?

Q: *I am pregnant with my first child (a boy) and my partner and I disagree about the kinds of toys to put in our child's bedroom. I would like to have a variety of both boy and girl toys and my partner wants only more masculine ones. If we expose our son to more feminine toys, will this disrupt his gender development in any way?*

ANSWER: Exposing your child to both male and female toys will not disrupt his gender identity. We think it is great that you want to expand his playtime opportunities. Your son will decide on his own what he likes to play with and what he doesn't enjoy. Give him the freedom and know that he will be well rounded because you have given him options.

Gender Roles Across Time and Cultures

Every society has cultural meanings that surround gender roles, and these meanings may change over time (Cott, 2002; Ensler, 2001; Maccoby & Jacklin, 1974; Mead, 1935; Whiting & Edwards, 1988). Gender roles connect individuals' behaviors and lives to the history, culture, and context in which they grow up and learn to express their sexuality (Martin & Ruble, 2004; Ruble et al., 2007; Bhana, 2016). This means that the societal standards have changed, and the meaning of gender identity expression is still changing, as we learned.

Because most cultures are concerned with issues of security, reproduction, and economic production, it follows, then, that gender roles revolve around them and that the roles are divided between masculine roles and feminine roles. For example, child rearing is central to the reproduction of these societies and may influence many of the differences stressed in a society (Chodorow, 1978; Whiting & Edwards, 1988). Many societies entrust the care of children to women because many child-rearing tasks, such as caring and nurturing, have been associated mostly with women.

As we saw in Chapter 3, the great world religions also provide a sort of blueprint for gender and sexuality. In Western civilization, for example, the ancient biblical story of Adam and Eve has long shaped both positive and negative perceptions of being male and female. These expressed roles provided a foundation for the ancient societies of the time, and later in history, a point of reaction for social movements that advanced feminism and sought equal rights for women (Woodhead, 2004). Through these foundations people understand and communicate the stereotyped psychosocial meanings that surround male and female as selves, persons, and roles in intimate relationships (Connell, 1995; Friedl, 1975; Giddens, 1992; Rosaldo & Lamphere, 1974). These ideas and expectations of gender have a direct impact on how generations of people perceive their society's expectations of them as male or female. Gender socialization is the primary way in which we assign meaning, attitudes, and behaviors to our understanding of who we are as men and women.

Social Institutions and Gender Role Development

How do we learn what each society considers to be appropriate gender roles? In each sphere of society, be it home, school, or work, forces are at work that shape gender roles and behaviors. These forces help to define gender roles, which may help make people competent members of their society (Banner, 1984; Giddens, 1992; Mead, 1949; Tolman, 2005). In fact, expectations of masculine and feminine behaviors begin in very early childhood (Jacobson, 2011; Fausto-Sterling et al., 2015). The experiences of children in growing up sexually can vary greatly within a complex society like the United States (Kinsey et al., 1948), and as we will study in Chapter 10, when rapid change occurs, people unlearn things and may develop new knowledge and skills in achieving sexual literacy (Moore & Reynolds, 2018).

However, to anchor our understanding of gender roles, norms, and stereotypes, we will here examine the most important agents that socialize us—parents and caregivers, peers, school, the media, and religion.

Parents and Caregivers Parents and caregivers are the first to influence gender roles. In some ways they may be the most significant influence until late childhood. They teach children the ways of society and how to behave in it. This is reflected in everything from the toys that children receive, to parental responses to their apparent masculinity or femininity, to the way that parents model their own gender roles for children (Bem, 1974; Maccoby, 2002).

From the moment we come into the world, gender expectations are placed upon us.
Dasha Muller/Shutterstock

The power of societal expectations regarding gender development and roles is so strong that it appears from the beginning of life. As the fetus emerges in the womb, the doctor can typically tell whether it is male or female. Many parents are eager to know what sex their infant will be, and they dream up gender-appropriate names long before birth, demonstrating how much this issue is part of society. In fact, at birth, most infants are assigned either to the male or the female category in all societies.

Almost immediately after birth the baby may be handled in gender-distinct ways and be dressed in gender-distinct colors, such as pink for girls and blue for boys. Studies have shown for decades that even in the hospital nursery from a distance, fathers tend to respond to the look and actions of their newborn in gender-distinct ways, even when they have incorrectly guessed the "wrong" infant or "wrong" sex. For example, the father of a girl would describe her as "soft" and of a boy as "strong" or "active," even though the infants were similar in body weight, musculature, and behavior (Rubin et al., 1974). A restudy of this classic experiment with 40 pairs of parents showed that 20 years later parents still stereotype infants, and that no difference exists between fathers and mothers when stereotyping infants (Karraker et al., 1995).

Gender expectations are also conveyed through the toys that parents give their children. Although an increasing number of parents appear to be more open to allowing their children to play with whatever pleases them, many parents still encourage their children to play with toys that reinforce the gender roles and stereotypes society holds. Little girls are often given dolls, stuffed animals, tea sets, dress-up clothes, and miniature kitchen appliances. These toys certainly reflect the stereotype of females as being nurturing caregivers whose primary responsibilities lie within the home. Boys are often offered sports equipment, action figures, and play weapons, which reinforce the male stereotypes of athlete, aggressor, and protector. Some studies have shown toy preference to be somewhat innate and established early in life (Tavros, 2004). Others, however, believe that social learning also impacts children's preferences and behaviors (Wong & Hines, 2015).

Parents also may teach a moral code that affects how their children perceive gender roles. For example, girls may be taught to be submissive or less active when it comes to initiating sexual relationships because that is what a "good girl" does. Boys may be taught to be more independent or aggressive and active in initiating sexual relationships because these behaviors are acceptable for them; but if a girl acts this way, she may be called a "bad girl" or worse (Tolman, 2005).

Peers Children are among the most powerful teachers of gender roles to each other. Studies show that both the emotional and cognitive sides of peer group learning help the process of becoming a boy or becoming a girl along (Gelman, Collman, & Maccoby, 1986; Maccoby, 2002; Whiting & Edwards, 1988; Martin & Ruble, 2004).

In many cultures, there appears to be a consistent pattern of gender behavior in early peer groups (Whiting & Edwards, 1988). Girls appear to be more emotionally expressive. They also appear to enjoy cuddling and soothing as a regular part of interaction. Girls tend to develop their verbal skills earlier in development than boys, and these verbal skills become a way of connecting to other children and adults. Boys tend to engage in more aggressive behaviors, playing such games as "war" or "king of the mountain." In fact, in some cultures they are reinforced for this kind of play, including forming hierarchies (Herdt, 2006). These early gender patterns may reflect both biological and social differences between the genders (Diamond, 2008; Maccoby, 2002; Moore & Reynolds, 2018).

As children mature, they tend to play in groups that are either all male or all female. In play, girls appear to use their verbal skills and to learn cues that help them understand societal rules. Their play reinforces the relational and emotional skills exhibited by their mothers, teachers, and other adult women. For example, girls use storytelling to understand things that happen to them. They find stories from a variety of sources, whether traditional

HEALTHY Sexuality

Are the Genders More Different or More Similar?

Gender studies traditionally look at the differences between males and females, but psychologist Janet Hyde (2005) suggests that far too often we look for differences, rather than similarities, between genders. In reviewing a huge number of studies that assessed such things as cognition, communication, personality, well-being, and motor coordination, Hyde found strong and consistent similarities between males and females. Surprisingly, in 78% of the individual studies, the differences were either small or nonexistent. In fact, in the 40 studies she reviewed, gender similarities were more compelling and consistent than gender differences. In short, differences may have been exaggerated. This does not mean that there are no differences; only that males and females are a lot more alike than people know.

myths or television to help them develop their understanding. Boys may engage in more aggressive behaviors, using physical aggression as a basic mechanism to reach their goals. Girls, by contrast, may display more covert aggression or hostility, including the use of gossip as a tool to use against someone. Forming intimate bonds with the same gender is part of how peers mutually identify gender roles and expected behaviors that they teach to each other (Herdt & McClintock, 2000).

Socialization in later childhood appears to reinforce these original perceptions (Gelman et al., 1986; Maccoby, 1999). In fact, decades of studies primarily in Western societies provide support for some important gender role differences in boys and girls. For example, in same-sex play groups from ages 3 to 9, the themes of boys' fantasies are very different from girls' fantasies: Boys express danger, conflict, and destruction, and they play-act masculine superheroes with superhuman strength. Girls, on the other hand, typically express domestic and romantic themes, with characters and relationships that depict safety and order. Girls' friendships are more intimate than boys', and their relationships involve sharing knowledge and details of their concerns and lives. Boys share less about their concerns with other boys and instead focus on shared activities (Maccoby, 2002).

The influence of peers during adolescence becomes even more important (Hyde, 2005). Conformity in the social sphere is important to many adolescents, and adhering to traditional gender roles tends to promote social acceptance by peers. Individuals who behave in ways contrary to the typical behavior of their gender pay some form of social consequence for their differences, such as being ostracized (Pascoe, 2011). The social pressure to conform to these typical gender behaviors can significantly impact a person's gender socialization. Explore this idea further in "Healthy Sexuality: Are the Genders More Different or More Similar?"

School One function of school is to teach societal standards and institutional expectations, and gender roles are very powerful parts of such expected learning. Most studies show that, on average, girls do better in school than boys. Girls get higher grades and complete high school at a higher rate compared to boys (Jacob, 2002). Standardized achievement tests also show that girls are better at spelling and perform better on tests of literacy, writing, and general knowledge (National Center for Education Statistics, 2003). Girls continue to exhibit higher verbal ability throughout high school, but they do not achieve as much as boys after fourth grade on tests of both mathematical and science ability.

In late elementary school, girls tend to outperform boys on several verbal skills tasks, including verbal reasoning, fluency, comprehension, and understanding logical relations (Hedges & Nowell, 1995). Boys, on the other hand, outperform girls on a variety of spatial skills tasks (Voyer, Voyer, & Bryden, 1995). Boys also perform better on mathematical achievement tests than girls. However, gender differences do not apply to all aspects of mathematical skill. Boys and girls do equally well in basic math knowledge, and girls have better computational skills. Interestingly, boys display greater confidence in their math skills, and this type of confidence is a strong predictor of math performance (Casey, Nuttall, & Pezaris, 2001).

For years, researchers have wondered if these gender differences in ability in school subjects were more a product of biological differences or of social impact. Parents, as socializing agents, may tip the scale in this nature versus nurture balance. Some parents tend to view math as more important for sons and language arts and social studies as more important for daughters (Andre, Whigham, Hendrickson, & Chambers, 1999). In fact, parents are likely to encourage their sons more than their daughters to take advanced high school courses in chemistry, mathematics, and physics (Wigfield, Battle, Keller, & Eccles, 2002). This socialization to underline cisgender roles is now associated with **genderism**, the belief that gender nonconformity is unacceptable (Hill & Willoughby, 2005).

genderism
The belief that people need to be cisgender and that all gender nonconformity is bad or unacceptable (Hill & Willoughby, 2005).

Teacher characteristics and the classroom environment may also contribute to gender differences in school. For example, many girls report being passed over in classroom discussions, not encouraged by the teacher, and made to feel stupid (Sadker & Sadker, 1994). In addition, teachers tend to call on and be more encouraging of boys than girls; they tend to reprimand girls for inappropriate behavior more often than they do boys; and boys tend to receive more praise, attention, and remedial help.

The Media Children early on begin to learn gender roles on television and the Internet. Today, they grow up with a sense that these media are a natural extension of the self and imitate dress, makeup, behavioral and emotional expression, and games they see in the media. Then they apply what they learn from these sources to interactions with family and peers.

In terms of media, children learn gender roles from characters in books, music, and computer games. In the 1970s, characters that were boys and men outnumbered characters that were girls and women (Saario et al., 1973), but by 1990 they were more evenly distributed in these media. In television and computer games, however, gender roles are becoming more "masculine" and aggressive, with themes of conflict, violence, and domination common in them.

Some experts believe that the media have contributed to our understanding of diversity but also have instilled harmful stereotypes about race and gender roles (Alexander, 2010; Cohen, 2009; Collins, 2005). Since the early 20th century, some African American men were portrayed as sexually aggressive, hungry, dangerous, and prone to sexual assault, especially on White women. African American women were portrayed as sexually wild and out of control. These stereotypes, expressed in film, magazines, books, and television, became ways of racially restricting African Americans in the United States, revealing the power of gender to control bodies and minds.

Religion Religion influences gender socialization, especially regarding attitudes about morality, masculinity/femininity, and sexual expression (Regnerus, 2007). In fact, historically, most clergy were men, and this male role has had an important effect on how the imagery of religious teaching works (Prothero, 2007). In fact, research has revealed several key areas in which gender differences by socialization into religious orientations have proved significant for men and women, and the same research provides support for religious orientation being a function of gender orientation (Francis, 1997). One area of difference is that women are more religious than men as evidenced by women attending church more often than men. Is being more religious an essential difference between genders or an extension of a woman's perceived gender role as homemaker and mother? The answer may be a little of both. Women, more than men, are likely to report mystical and deep religious experiences, to watch television programs with religious themes, and to assert that God is important in their lives.

Sexism, Inequality, and Gender Roles

For many women, part of that historical reality of power is the continuing prejudice of **sexism** that holds them back from achieving their fullest human potential and full equality. Enduring sexism in our society is defined in a number of ways, but the #Me-Too Movement in recent years has drawn critical attention to the legacy of how sexism allowed abuse and harassment to dominate Hollywood and corporate America, as we will examine in Chapter 14. It is considered one form of systematic oppression based on biological sex. It is a belief system that assumes a hierarchy of human worth based on the social construction of the differences between the sexes. In the United States, sexism is an ideology of male supremacy, superiority, and authority.

Let's consider for example the glass ceiling faced by women in wage inequality (Figure 9.5). Since the United States passed the *Equal Pay Act*, American women face a substantial gender wage gap. On average, a woman working full time earns 80.7 cents for every dollar a man working full time earns. Additionally, women's median annual earnings are $9,909 less than men's (U.S. Census Bureau, 2017). Currently the Institute for Women's Policy Research estimates that we will not reach gender equity in pay until 2059. See "Controversies in Sexuality: Sexism in the Workplace" for more on how gender may play a defining role in one's career.

Sexism may also bring hatred of, or prejudice toward, either sex, as conveyed through gender violence. In many parts of the world, such as Pacific Island societies, gender stereotypes and sexism perpetuate systematic domestic violence (Jolly, Stewart, & Brewer, 2012). In fact, domestic violence, including rape, is a common means of "keeping women in their place" (Ford & Beach, 1951; Herdt, 2006; Odem & Clay-Warner, 1998). One out of four men will hit their partners in the United States (Tjaden & Thoennes, 2000), a disturbing issue that we will examine further in Chapter 14.

sexism
Prejudice directed toward women.

Figure 9.5

A map of US states and the inequity of female earnings compared to those of men.

Female earnings as a percent of male earnings, 2017
68% (Worse) — 90% (Better)

CONTROVERSIES in Sexuality

Sexism in the Workplace

Women in the United States reached a new level of status during the campaign season for the 2008 presidential election. For the first time in history, both major political parties had female candidates in the presidential election. Sarah Palin was the Republican vice-presidential candidate. During the primary, Hillary Clinton gave other Democratic hopefuls a run for their money in the bid for their party's nomination as the candidate for president. Both women ignited a controversy that has been smoldering for years regarding certain occupations and whether women are as qualified as men to hold them and whether the pay should be equal.

During her bid for the presidential nomination, Clinton spoke of the glass ceiling in today's workplace. This glass ceiling is an invisible barrier that can determine the level to which women or other minorities can rise in a business organization. The imagery is that women can see through the glass to the ceiling, but many are unable to break through it to reach the top, especially in positions that are typically dominated by men. Consider the occupation of policeman. To change the perception that this occupation is only for men, the title has been changed to police officer because the use of "man" seemed to exclude women. Today, many people still struggle with the notion of whether or not women are capable of this work due to the perceived differences in abilities. For example, a police officer requires a certain level of assertiveness and physical ability to ward off criminal behavior in addition to taking someone's life when a situation requires it. Many believe that these requirements are contrary to stereotypes of the female gender role of being nurturing, being weak, and wanting to avoid confrontation. Yet many women are employed as police officers in the United States.

The question for this controversy, then, is this:

Do barriers exist that prevent women from taking on certain careers or from being promoted within their chosen careers?

Yes:

- In the political arena, only 16.8% of the members of the U.S. Congress are women (90 seats out of 535). In the Senate, women hold 17 of the 100 seats. In the House of Representatives, only 73 out of 435 members are women.

- According to a British survey of 3,000 members of the Institute of Leadership and Management, 73% of female respondents felt barriers exist for women seeking senior-level management and board-level positions. Only 38% of men believe that this glass ceiling exists in the business world (Snowdon, 2011).

- Men are promoted more quickly than women with equivalent qualifications, even in traditionally female-dominated occupations of nursing and education (Quast, 2011).

No:

- Some argue that women are allowed to assume certain careers, but they must face obstacles to succeed in certain positions of great leadership such as a CEO or an elected politician. These obstacles include the following:

  - Leadership style issues: Many female leaders struggle to reconcile qualities people prefer in women (compassion for others) with qualities people think leaders need to succeed (assertion and control) (Quast, 2011).

  - Family demands: Women are often the ones who interrupt their careers to balance work and family issues. When overloaded by family demands, they often lack the time to engage in the social networking that is essential for advancement at work. Children often take women away—mentally and physically—from a competitive work environment (Quast, 2011; Schroeder, 2011).

What Is Your Perspective?

1. Do you believe a glass ceiling exists for women in the workplace?
2. Do you believe that there are positions better suited for one sex than for the other?
3. How do you think we can level the playing field for men and women in the workplace?

GENDER NORMS AND VARIANCE

Society sets up the standards for being full and morally acceptable men and women according to their gender roles and standards of masculinity and femininity, but not everyone is able to live up to these standards—or wants to. People who manifest gender behaviors that go beyond or against the norms of their community may be referred to as **gender nonconforming**. A gender nonconformist is "someone who adopts gendered traits that are stereotypically associated with members of the opposite sex" (Lester, 2002, p. 4). Researchers treat gender nonconformity as being motivated by biological forces such as genes and hormones (Money & Ehrhardt, 1972; Stoller, 1974). **Gender variance** is different from the physical forms of biological development, although in popular culture and in the public mind they are often confused. The causes of gender variance are probably complex and may be thought of in terms of the interaction of biology, culture, and individual characteristics such as personality and temperament.

gender nonconforming
Individuals who manifest gender behaviors that go beyond or against the norms of their community.

gender variance
Nonconforming gender behavior that may result from the interaction of biology, culture, and individual characteristics, such as personality and temperament.

Factors of Gender Nonconformity

Is a girl who plays with boy's toys gender nonconforming? In 1950 in the United States, the answer would have been yes; by the 1980s it was still frowned upon. By the early 2000s gender fluidity was more accepted but still not the norm. Today, children of both genders and especially in the urban middle class who play with all types of toys are more tolerated, accepted, and in some households celebrated (Bailey et al., 2016). Of course, the critical difference is the parents and community (Floyd & Bekman, 2007; Price, 2017).

Many children were once punished for exhibiting gender-variant behaviors, and in some conservative communities they still are. Why? Parents may fear that their child's actions may become permanent expressions of gender variance in adulthood. They may also recognize that these expressions are clearly frowned upon by their culture. The labels of "tomboy" for a girl and "sissy" or "fag" for a boy are powerful gender stereotypes that are laden with strong feelings of shame, humiliation, fear, anxiety, and sometimes disgust, loathing, or rage. Parents may want to protect their children from such hurt. Of course, adults in their roles as parents and grandparents may try to enforce these standards in children, along with teachers, family, friends, and others. Additionally, there is the strong fear of some parents that gender nonconformity could be taken as a sign of homosexuality in their community. Thus, it is hard to disentangle sexual orientation here in the common cultural perceptions of nonconforming gender.

Some things do change with time, though. What was once believed to be gender nonconforming behavior is now regarded by many people as less so, or perhaps even normal, especially for girls. Girls who like to climb trees or play with guns or like rough-and-tumble play were, at one time, all regarded as weird, gender nonconforming. Now the whole discussion about gun violence and violent video games has blurred the gender boundary and opened a wider question: Should the culture support this level of violence? Today in the United States, girls have much more freedom to engage in a wide range of activities without being stigmatized or labeled as gender nonconforming. It does seem, however, that boys who engage in gender nonconforming behaviors still provoke strong reactions of disapproval (Landolt et al., 2004; Price, 2017).

Children are often encouraged by parents to conform to play practices and behaviors that are considered gender appropriate.
Ingram Publishing/SuperStock

HEALTHY Sexuality

Proving Your Masculinity

A consistent finding of gender studies in the United States is that boys as early as second and third grades begin to use the term *fag* to say what is "bad" about things, including their peers' behavior (Cahill, 2008). Sociologist C. J. Pascoe discovered what happens in high school to boys who grew up this way. She discusses in her book, *Dude, You're a Fag: Masculinity and Sexuality in High School*, that boys were very cruel in stigmatizing other males whom they perceived to be even slightly gender nonconforming. The conforming boys used strict standards for gender. If a boy was too expressive or artistic, they would identify that behavior as "fag." She also found that these boys had strict views about what was and was not "manly": For example, if someone was not being rough enough in team sports, that person was not manly.

Having sex with a girl definitely influenced the perception that a boy was not a "fag." Some of the "coolest guys" in the high school believe that "if a guy wasn't having sex, he's no one. He's nobody" (Pascoe, 2007, p. 88). In fact, some of the boys felt that having a girlfriend "served as proof of heterosexuality" (Pascoe, 2007, p. 89). Some boys chose to remain virgins, but they felt that they had to hide this fact, to preserve their masculinity. Their ultimate way of getting each other to stick to a masculine gender role norm was to call anyone a "fag" who failed to act masculine. The gay and bisexual boys in the school were picked on and bullied, sometimes mercilessly. Also, some heterosexual boys who were not very aggressive were also called "fags" and bullied.

Gender variance appears to be a big challenge to young males who are trying to prove themselves in our society.

Adolescent peers, young men especially, are sensitive to gender nonconformity and may react against it with bullying, aggression, hazing, and sexual coercion (Pascoe, 2011). Studies of masculinity reveal how insecure boys may use bullying as a way to mask weakness or fear in their own sense of self (Connell, 1995). Bullying and gender nonconformity have long been regarded as major ways for suppressing homosexuality and differentiating straight from gay boys (Herdt & Boxer, 1992; Herek, 2004). One study found that straight boys who were nonconforming in appearance or in their choice of activity were rated less acceptable than gay men who conformed to gender norms (Horn, 2007). These issues of bullying dovetail because sometimes people are attacked because they are ambiguous in gender and/or sexual orientation. This is now open to new scrutiny and critical thinking, especially when it comes to bullying that targets lesbians and gay men, transgender people, and gender nonconforming or fluid boys and girls in school. Even heterosexual boys who are perceived to be "softer" than athletes on campus may be subject to hazing, bullying, and other forms of stigma and exclusion (Pascoe, 2007). We explore this issue further in "Healthy Sexuality: Proving Your Masculinity."

GENDER IDENTITY AND INTERSEX RIGHTS: WELL-BEING AND SOCIAL JUSTICE

DSD
An identity label used by some transgender people to refer to "differences in sex development" rather than the old-fashioned and negative language of "disorders of disease."

The human rights for intersex and transgender people are more controversial than almost any other kinds of rights in countries. Traditionally, most societies divided human populations into two sex categories: male and female. But as we have seen, it is estimated that there are 131 million people in the world who do not fit this old schema (Chamie & Mirkin, 2019). Today we are seeing huge controversy in sports and society surrounding women athletes whose **DSD** (differences of sexual development) exposes them to medical or political intervention. In short, these individuals have been regarded as stigmatized and misfits by virtue of how their bodies and behaviors challenged the traditional gender roles, religious beliefs, and notions of masculinity and femininity. Discrimination or worse—some societies execute people for being like this—can be the result unless society takes heed of the need for protection of human rights for all people. Today, as gender identity is a key part of human rights and well-being, we can be clear that difference does not equal disorder.

In the history of intersex research treatment and education, society has often treated these differences as if there was something wrong or abnormal about intersex people, the kind of discriminatory history we have seen with regard to many other communities, including people of color and LGBTQ people. Interestingly, some intersex people now use the language of DSD as an identity label to refer to "differences in sex development" rather than the old-fashioned language of "disorders of disease" to make it clear how intersex people are perceived by mainstream society. As we have seen, there are large numbers of intersex people who continue to suffer from stigma and shame in the United States and throughout the world, but through no fault of their own. Like all of us, they seek social justice and freedom, which is so basic to sexual literacy that we are seeing a new perspective emerge to reflect the critical changes. Here are some elements of the new perspective:

- Intersex and transgender people often experience stigma, abuse, discrimination, and systematic oppression because they challenge sex and gender norms.
- Intersex activists and allies are working to stop pathologizing identity labels, such as the use of the terms "conditions" and "disorders of sex development" to justify this mistreatment, as well as ending medically unnecessary genital surgeries done to force people into binary sex categories (LaHood & Keir, 2012; Viloria, 2016).
- So far Australia is the only country that has civil rights protections for intersex people, and these were achieved by rejecting pathology models and labels (Viloria, 2016).
- Transgender activists and allies are working to create a safer and more accepting and tolerant society for all gender and gender nonconforming expressions and embodiment; this will likely reduce rates of negative mental health issues, especially suicide attempts and violence against transgender people.
- As violence and suicide rates decrease, more transgender people will likely come out socially.

While challenging, these new attitudes, policies, and calls for the protections of rights can have a very positive effect in supporting the well-being of everyone, especially transgender and intersex people. Judging from the appearance of new articles and research venues, websites, media coverage, and innovative policies (Chamie & Mirkin, 2019; Herman et al., 2017; Wilson et al., 2017), there is an important and growing awareness of these issues. This is an area wherein biology and gender and sexual literacy can really help us to make a significant leap ahead in improving society in the years to come.

Chapter Review

SUMMARY

Understanding Sex and Gender in Development and in Context

- Sex is defined as the biological differentiation into male or female, based upon genes, hormones, genital assignment based on appearance, and other internal developmental factors.
- Gender is defined as the social differentiation into masculine or feminine, based upon institutions, roles, and meanings of a particular culture.

- There is a diverse spectrum of gender based on masculinity and femininity.
- Sexual differentiation is the biological process of creating male or female sexual structures during conception and in fetal development.
- Human intersexuality is the condition of someone being biologically between a male and a female, with intermediate or atypical combinations of physical features that usually differentiate one sex from the other.
- Biological sex variations are conditions that cause people to become intersex.
  - The results of these genetic or hormonal conditions create a body and feeling of maleness or femaleness that are atypical.
  - Intersex refers to someone being biologically between a male and a female, with intermediate or exceptional combinations of physical features that usually differentiate one sex from the other.
- The condition of 5-alpha-reductase occurs so often in some communities that the culture has created a system of sex assignment and socialization especially for it.

Gender Identity and Expression

- Cisgender means having your sex assigned at birth correspond to your gender identity.
- Transgender is an identity used in two different ways: first, gender diversity (Feinberg, 1992), and second, people who do not resonate with the gender they were assigned to at birth and who instead identify through the gender binary as trans women and trans men.
- Individuals seeking genital confirmation or affirmation procedures are those who feel the need to transition from one sex to another in order to feel correct or complete, where surgery and hormonal and related treatments may be requested.
- Androgyny is the condition of having traits of both masculinity and femininity in a personality.

Gender Roles

- Gender roles are the culturally patterned expressions of masculinity or femininity that are identified with particular tasks, knowledge, and power.
- Large variations in masculinity and femininity occur across cultures that result in different gender roles.
- Five major socializers influence gender roles: parents and caregivers, peers, school, the media, and religion.

Gender Norms and Variance

- Gender norms are social forces that encourage people to conform to what is perceived to be traditional masculinity and femininity.
- In gender nonconformity, people depart from the norms of masculinity and femininity in their society.

Gender Identity and Intersex Rights: Well-Being and Social Justice

- The legal right of people to self-identify as transgender or as neither male nor female is beginning to be recognized in some parts of the world.

What's Your Position?

1. **Do you see gender and sexual differentiation stemming more from biology or from culture, or both?**
   - Is maleness and femaleness part of gender or culture, or both?
   - Does gender appear to be a range based upon the degree of sexual differentiation that occurs in people?
   - Can you define intersexuality? Is this a product of culture or nature?
   - Do people with the 5-alpha-reductase condition in the Dominican Republic and New Guinea appear to have something different about their biology, their culture, or both?

2. **How have power and control played a part, if any, in shaping your attitudes and socialization in growing up?**
   - How is power related to gender role differences between males and females?
   - How do gender stereotypes continue to play a role in social life?

3. **In what ways were you socialized to be the gender you are now?**
   - Did your parents direct your social/play activities toward one gender or another? How did they do this?
   - What are two major social institutions that socialize people into gender roles?
   - How have the media influenced your gender identification?
   - Do you believe men and women should hold different roles in society and family? Why or why not?

Design elements: Controversies in Sexuality: HBRH/Shutterstock; Research and Sexual Well Being: verity jane smith/Getty Images; Healthy Sexuality: Sergey Furtaev/Shutterstock; Communication Matters: PeopleImages/Getty Images; Know Yourself: Plush Studios/Blend Images LLC; What's Your Position: Luis Molinero/Shutterstock; Healthy Sexuality: A. Minde/PhotoAlto; Did You Know icon: McGraw-Hill Education; Page corner icon: McGraw-Hill Education.

Sexual Orientation

10

Understanding Sexual Orientation
- Identify the different expressions of sexual orientation.
- Explain the factors that contribute to sexual orientation.
- Describe compulsory heterosexuality and how society may influence the expression of sexual orientation.

Variations in Sexual Orientation Across Time and Cultures
- Identify same-sex relationships across cultures as structured by differences in age, gender, and roles.
- Describe the social and political context of the LGBTQ movement in the United States.
- Describe bisexuality, sexual fluidity, and queer or questioning.

LGBTQ Identity Discrimination and Stigma
- Describe the nature of sexual prejudice and homophobia.
- Explain how bullying may lead to terrible outcomes.
- Identify the factors that contribute to hate crimes.

Coming Out and Sexual Well-Being
- List various steps in deciding to be out socially.
- Describe the social and psychological pressures of keeping sexual orientation hidden.
- Identify the dynamics of LGBTQ family formation in the United States.

Coming Out, Sexual Well-Being, and Sexual Rights
- Explain how the United Nations' stance came about.
- Describe gay rights as human rights.

Stockbyte/Getty Images

● Learning
● Objectives

Developing Your Position

1. How did you come to realize your sexual orientation?
2. What has culture taught you about different sexual orientations?
3. Have you ever experienced or witnessed homophobia?
4. What is your view about sexual orientation as a human right?

sexual orientation
The structure of a person's sexual or romantic attractions or both to people of the same or the other sex, or toward both sexes.

heterosexual/straight
People who are attracted to the other sex.

lesbian
A woman who is attracted to other women.

gay/homosexual
A man who is attracted only or primarily to other men.

bisexual
A person who is sometimes attracted to men or women or both, although not necessarily to the same degree or at the same point in time.

LGBTQIA+ (lesbian, gay, bisexual, transgender, queer, questioning, intersex and asexual)
The collective name for the social movement supporting sexual minority rights in the United States and similar Western nations.

queer or questioning
A person who does not wish to be classified as heterosexual and who may be questioning an attraction to people of the same sex.

Self, Society, and Culture: Self-Awareness and Sexual Orientation

"A boy reports that he was sitting in the family room with his parents watching the original *Star Trek* television series. The boy is 10 years old and he has not yet come into the obvious signs of puberty. He reports an absence of attractions of any kind by around age 5, and even by age 8 he remembers that he had not experienced overt awareness of sexual attraction. Suddenly "Captain Kirk" peels off his shirt and the 10-year-old boy is titillated. This is his first experience of same-gender attraction and he intuitively knows he should not be feeling this according to the norms of his parents and society" (Herdt & Boxer, 1993; McClintock & Herdt, 1996). By age 18, he came out as gay.

"I've kind of been surprised at how intense [my attraction to women] is. I mean, when it's happening. Whoa,. . . I don't know.. . . I'll sit down and talk with my friends, and be like, 'I don't understand . . . it's got to be biological, because I don't have any control over this!' It's so strong, and then it just reminds me, 'Wow! I'm so gay!'"
—30-year-old woman (L. Diamond, 2008, p. 251)

"This is elementary stuff, but if she smiles at you a lot or if she does more nice things than she usually does—if you start seeing that, you might want to ask her if she likes you."
—9-year-old Alec Greven (*How to Talk to Girls,* 2008)

Without exception, from early in their lives, these three people became aware of their sexual orientations. Thinking about the boy watching *Star Trek,* do you remember when you recognized your own sexual orientation? This chapter includes information that will help to answer this and other questions about sexual orientation.

UNDERSTANDING SEXUAL ORIENTATION

Sexual orientation is the combination of a person's structure of sexual and/or romantic attractions, arousal, identity, and behavior that is targeted toward people of the same or other genders. People who identify as **heterosexual**, or **straight**, report attractions and engage in romantic and sexual behavior with the other gender. Women who are attracted to other women may refer to themselves as gay or **lesbian**, whereas men who are attracted to other men may refer to themselves as **gay** or **homosexual**. Some individuals are known as **bisexual** because they are attracted to both sexes, though not necessarily at the same time or to the same degree. Some individuals prefer to call themselves **queer**, which is an umbrella term for all sexual and gender identities that are specifically included in the LGBTQIA+ acronym. Collectively, these sexual orientations are often referred to as the constellation **LGBTQIA+** for short. For some, the "Q" also means **questioning**, which refers to people who are considering if they might be LGBTQIA+ or at least do not wish to identify as heterosexual. The "T" in LGBTQIA+ stands for *transgender,* which is not a sexual orientation, as discussed in Chapter 9. The "I" represents intersex individuals, and that is not a sexual orientation, but rather a gender identification, as discussed in Chapter 9. The "A" stands for asexual individuals—those who do not experience sexual attraction—they are not drawn to people sexually, and they do not wish to act upon attraction to others in a sexual way (AVERT, 2019). The "+" is an indicator of inclusivity and allowance for others to be identified who may define their sexual and/or gender identity in different ways. Besides attraction, sexual orientation also encompasses the actual sexual behavior and the sexual identity of a person (Institute of Medicine, 2011). Identity, behavior, and attraction may not always align perfectly, which some people can experience as problematic, for reasons that we will discuss.

Generally, in the United States and advanced industrialized countries, as well as many developing countries, all nonheterosexual orientations are stigmatized to some degree. Part of the stigma has to do with the perception of a mismatch between gender and sexuality. Think of it this way: Heterosexual behaviors and intimate relationships provide a cultural blueprint that drives expectations of masculinity and femininity and family formation, whereas same-gender behaviors depart from such cultural expectations. As the society advances and integrates new norms, such as same-gender marriage and same-gender families into their vision and goals, the stigma may defuse or fade, allowing greater equality for everyone.

Determining one's sexual orientation is an iterative process, that is, something that develops prior to adulthood but for some people continues to change in later life (Bailey et al., 2016; Diamond, 2014; Floyd & Bakeman, 2006; Mustanski, Kuper, & Greene, 2014; Rosario & Scrimshaw, 2014; Van Anders, 2015). Biology and culture probably both play roles in this developmental process of discovery (Money, 1998). Because people are typically socialized into heterosexual roles and rules of their sexual cultures from infancy on, they may never be asked whether their sexual orientation matches their sexual socialization (Bhana, 2013; Renold, 2005; Robinson & Davies, 2015). As people mature and come to understand their own sexual needs and emotional feelings, they become more aware of their own sexual desires and romantic attractions (Calzo, Antonucci, Mays, & Cochran, 2011; Hammack & Cohler, 2009; Herdt & McClintock, 2000).

Recent research has called into question whether the concept of sexual orientation, which commonly means to orient one's sexual desires toward people in terms of their perceived biological sex, may actually be more correctly conceived as alternatively orienting perception to other factors, such as cultural meanings of gender, or the relationship between sex and gender (van Anders, 2015). Given information on physical sexual variation reviewed in Chapter 9, we understand that the definition of sex is based on biological elements in which differentiation may result in more sexes than just the two, male and female. This means that although many people commonly understand the human condition as only having two sexes (what is commonly referred to as a binary), actually more sexes exist. Therefore, what is frequently referred to as an attraction to the "sex" of a person is many times actually an attraction to the gender of a person in combination with their sex.

Most experts agree that the roots of sexual orientation are in childhood, but increasingly we understand that it continues to develop across the life span. Research in the United States and across cultures shows that by age 9 or 10, most individuals begin to become aware of attractions and interest (McClintock & Herdt, 1996; Savin-Williams, 2005). Middle childhood is considered to be a sensitive period for sexual development, as it co-occurs with maturation of the adrenal glands, which begin releasing androgens into the bloodstream. Biological men regardless of orientation may develop these feelings earlier than women (Bailey & Oberschneider, 1997; Herdt & Boxer, 1993; Katz-Wise et al., 2017). Like the two boys in the opening story, people may become aware of their orientations through subjective responses to their peers, things they see on television or the Internet, and their personal fantasies (Morin, 1995).

DID YOU KNOW

The word *gay* probably got its specific homosexual meanings in the 1920s (Chauncey, 1995). It found its way quickly into popular literature and then through Hollywood films, such as *Bringing Up Baby*, in the 1930s and 1940s. By then, gay, fairy, fag, or queer were all explicit terms for LGBTQIA+ individuals, generally negative. The drag balls in New York City's Harlem historic neighborhood were a hidden part of African American culture at that time, so vividly depicted in the film *Paris Is Burning*. By the 1960s, gay had become the official term designated by the gay men's movement to advance homosexual rights, while other terms were shunned as derogatory. In the 1980s, however, the term *queer* was resurrected as an "in your face" gender-bending identity term.

habitualization
Actions repeated frequently enough to be cast into a pattern so that they seem natural.

Over time, most individuals experience these attractions as so routine that they hardly think about them, a phenomenon that is called **habitualization**. These feelings and behaviors recur frequently enough to become a pattern. Remarkably, people come to feel that their attractions are spontaneous, automatic, and beyond their control (Diamond & Savin-Williams, 2000; Herdt & McClintock, 2000). Psychologist Jerome Kagan once referred to such deep-seated habits as "our second nature," meaning that, in time, most people's sexual attractions feel so spontaneous that they simply do what seems natural. This pattern of attractions becomes automatic and makes sexual orientation resistant to change. However, change can occur, but the changes occur outside of individuals' control, and attempting to change sexual orientation is therefore difficult or impossible and has devastating consequences (Bailey et al., 2016; Diamond, 2016; Katz-Wise, 2015).

The Spectrum of Sexual Orientation

Researchers have found that sexual orientations rarely fit into a defined set of categories but rather appear to exist on a continuum ranging from being exclusively heterosexual to being exclusively homosexual. Variations of nonexclusive orientations exist between the two ends of the spectrum (Diamond, 2008; Money, 1998; Mustanski et al., 2014). Newer research has updated these early studies, revealing an even greater spectrum of sexual orientation than previously known, as well as its causes and expressions (Cover, 2018; Diamond, 2014; Floyd & Bakeman, 2006; Rosario & Scrimshaw, 2014; Saewyc, 2011; Vrangalova & Savin-Williams, 2010, 2012).

pansexual
Refers to a person who is attracted sexually, emotionally, romantically, or spiritually to others regardless of their biological sex, gender, or orientation.

In recent years, emerging sexual orientations such as **pansexuality** and omnisexuality have begun to highlight the importance of gender in some people's sexual attractions (Greaves, Sibley, Fraser, & Barlow, 2019; Morandini, Blaszczynski, & Dar-Nimrod, 2017; Rice, 2015). Pansexuality refers to a person who is attracted sexually, emotionally, romantically, or spiritually to others regardless of their biological sex, gender, or orientation (Rice, 2015). Because of the flexibility in pansexuality, someone may not feel they have to limit themselves to the binary, and they may fall anywhere on the spectrum.

Viewing sexual orientation as a spectrum thus allows us to understand sexual diversity, whether heterosexual, bisexual, gay/lesbian, or something else (Klein, 1978; Laumann et al., 1994). Seeing sexual orientation as a spectrum also captures the complexity of many people's attractions and desires, which may change over time and vary in different contexts (Diamond, 2008, 2016; Kinnish, Strassberg, & Turner, 2005; Rosario, Scrimshaw, Hunter, & Braun, 2006; Rosario & Scrimshaw, 2014).

Historically, the famous Kinsey scale (1948) of sexual orientation measured the spectrum of orientation (Figure 10.1). Through systematic interviews with more than 10,000 people, Kinsey found that "pure" LGBTQ individuals and "pure" heterosexuals are the exception, not the rule, in the United States. In fact, only about 4% of the males in his historic sample were exclusively homosexual, while about 12% were bisexual, and the remainder were heterosexual (84%). At the time, a smaller percentage of women reported being gay/lesbian or bisexual. Most people tend toward one end of the spectrum or the other and have had a smattering of experiences in between. Kinsey also found that 37% of men from his interviews had experienced an orgasm in a same-gender sexual behavior while growing up, but many of these men also had sexual experiences with the other gender, and most of them went on to marry and have children. He concluded that human sexual nature allows for a lot of flexibility of sexual expression as conditioned by gender, age, experience, and cultural context. His studies also revealed significant individual differences in sexual behavior across entire populations. Subsequent research has confirmed Kinsey's

Gay Pride Day celebrates sexual diversity.
Andy Newman/Florida Keys News Bureau/Getty Images

conclusion that the human species is highly adaptive, and populations display significant individual differences in sexuality (Ford & Beach, 1951; Gagnon, 2004; Savin-Williams & Ream, 2007).

From the perspective of current sexual variations, Kinsey's scale seems a bit too monodimensional, and other researchers have tried to better measure the full range and fluidity of sexual orientation diversity, beginning with psychologist Fritz Klein (1978), who created the Klein scale. The scale significantly refined the Kinsey scale by including questions to measure sexual feelings, fantasies, and identities, in addition to sexual behavior. Klein also included questions about community identification, in terms of belonging to a sexual community, such as the LGBTQ community. Klein, who identified as bisexual, also believed that people's desires and orientations are complex and may change over time. To test this idea, he added three distinct time periods: the present, defined as the most recent 12 months; the past, defined as more than 12 months ago; and the ideal, which represents the future. In fact, Klein's early research and newer studies revealed more bisexual orientation in the United States (Diamond, 2008).

To understand Klein's research better, consider how constant your own sexual orientation is. Read and answer the questions in "Know Yourself: Assessing the Change or Constancy of Your Sexual Orientation."

Even though Kinsey et al. (1948, 1953) had already noticed that some people could not be located anywhere on his orientation scale (Walton, Lykins, & Bhullar, 2016), **asexuality** is an orientation that only recently has been given full attention by research. Asexual people do not feel any noteworthy sexual attraction to other people, but some might have romantic relationships. A large British study of more than 18,000 people found that 1% of the respondents had never experienced sexual attraction to another person (Wellings, 1994). Asexuality should not be confused with celibacy or abstinence, as discussed later in Chapter 12. There are strong indicators that asexuality should be regarded as a sexual orientation that is not to be confused with clinically diagnosable issues such as low sexual desire (Bogaert, 2015, 2017; Brotto & Yule, 2017; Gressgård, 2013; Van Houdenhove, Gijs, T'Sjoen, & Enzlin, 2014; Yule, Brotto, & Gorzalka, 2017). Since the advance of the World Wide Web, asexuality has become the basis for community formation (Bogaert, 2012).

The Gap Between Sexual Attraction and Behavior

Research reveals that some individuals experience a gap between their sexual attractions and their expressed sexual behavior. For example, a man may be attracted to other men, but date or have sex only with women. Or a woman who is attracted to men might have had sexual experiences with other women, and thus she questions if she is heterosexual or bisexual. Though both Kinsey and Klein noted this gap, they did not study it. Researchers have now

Figure 10.1
The Kinsey scale emphasizes sexual behavior and attraction as expressions of sexual orientation. It is split into three ranges: 0–1 indicates exclusive or predominant heterosexuality, 2–4 indicates equal or "more than incidental" homosexuality and heterosexuality, and 5–6 indicates "exclusive or predominant homosexuality."
Source: Kinsey, C. A., Wardell, B. P., Clyde E. M., & Paul, H. G. (1953). *Sexual behavior in the human female.* Philadelphia, PA: W. B. Saunders.

asexuality
Asexual people do not feel any noteworthy sexual attraction to other people, but some might have romantic relationships.

Know Yourself

Assessing the Change or Constancy of Your Sexual Orientation

Consider the following questions about your sexual orientation. Use the three time dimensions that Klein described in his research to answer the questions to help you determine if your sexual orientation has changed or has remained steady over time. This means that you will have three responses for each of the following seven questions.

> **Past:** Your life up to 12 months ago.
>
> **Present:** The most recent 12 months.
>
> **Ideal:** Your prediction for the future.

1. **Sexual Attraction:** Who turns you on? Who do you find attractive as a real or potential partner?

    MALE ____ FEMALE ____ ANDROGYNOUS ____

2. **Sexual Behavior:** Who are your sexual contacts or partners?

    MALE ____ FEMALE ____ ANDROGYNOUS ____

3. **Sexual Fantasies:** Whom do you enjoy fantasizing about in erotic daydreams?

    MALE ____ FEMALE ____ ANDROGYNOUS ____

4. **Emotional Preference:** With whom do you prefer to establish strong emotional bonds?

    MALE ____ FEMALE ____ ANDROGYNOUS ____

5. **Social Preference:** Which sex do you prefer to spend your leisure time with, and with which sex do you feel most comfortable?

    MALE ____ FEMALE ____ ANDROGYNOUS ____

6. **Hetero/Gay Lifestyle:** What is the sexual orientation of the people with whom you socialize?

    GAY ____ STRAIGHT ____ BI ____ TRANS ____ QUEER ____ OTHER ____

7. **Self-identification:** How do you think of yourself?

    GAY ____ STRAIGHT ____ BI ____ TRANS ____ QUEER ____ OTHER ____

Did you find change or continuity over time in your own sexual orientation? Remember, there are no right or wrong answers, only what is true for your own individual sexuality.

Source: Based on Klein, F. (1978). *The bisexual option: A concept of one hundred percent intimacy*. New York: Arbor House.

---

developed ways to measure it that were previously unavailable (Diamond, 2008; Herdt, 1990; Mustanski, Kuper, & Greene, 2014).

One way to describe the gap between sexual attraction and behavior is to consider statistics that surround same-gender sexuality as an exclusive adult sexual orientation. For decades, the incidence of same-gender sexuality has been measured at between 2% and 15% in different populations in the United States, with the average being about 5% (Binson et al., 1995; Laumann et al., 1994; Savin-Williams & Ream, 2007). However, the percentage of people who express any kind of LGBTQ attraction or experience is greater: 8.6% for women and about 10.1% for men (Laumann et al., 1994). In short, more people experience attraction to the same gender than there are people who actually express their attractions and engage in sexual behavior with the same gender.

How have researchers explained this gap? They compared three dimensions of same-gender sexuality—behavior, desire, and identity—to see how they are interrelated. They measured each dimension using two samples: 150 women and 143 men.

Figure 10.2
The gap between desire, behavior and identity in men and women.

As shown in Figure 10.2, women experience attractions for women more often than men experience attractions for men: 59% for women compared to 44% for men. Women do not necessarily express their attraction in their behavior, however. Men tend to act on their attractions more often than women: 22% for men compared to 13% for women. Additionally, notice that more men than women fully integrated all of the attraction/behavior/identity dimensions in their social lives: 24% of men and 15% of women. In terms of sexual identity, none of the women and only 2% of the men said that they were exclusively lesbian or gay. In short, for both men and women in varying degrees, there is a sizable gap between people feeling sexual attractions and then acting on those feelings or integrating their orientations into their identities and their real lives. The researchers concluded that sexual orientation is multidimensional, and its meaning depends on context and purpose (Laumann et al., 1994, p. 300).

Development of Sexual Orientation

Despite the difficulties in studying issues of sexual orientation, researchers continue to work on refining its sources. They have determined four potential sources of its structure to be genetic, prenatal, postnatal, and interactive biopsychosocial. Some combination of these sources may one day lead to the origin of sexual orientation and how attraction and sexual behavior are consistent or changing (Buss, 2008; McClintock & Herdt, 1996; Money & Ehrhardt, 1972; Mustanski, Chivers, & Bailey, 2002; Tolman & Diamond, 2002; Bailey et al. 2016; Savin-Williams, 2016).

Genetic Sources The genome (genetic code) is set at the time of conception and influences fetal development. Although this influence is believed to continue throughout a person's lifetime regardless of the culture in which the individual grows up (Ellis & Blanchard, 2001; LeVay, 2016), evidence now suggests that the environment can change the expression of genes, and this environmental influence on genes can be inherited across generations (Martin, 2013; Mustanski, Kuper, & Greene, 2014).

This process, called epigenetics, has led to understanding that genetic and environmental influences are not always easy to tease apart. Epigenetics is the way a gene changes in the environmental context; this is a growing branch of biological research that offers potentially new ways for explaining how genes can become active or remain inactive in interaction with environmental and social factors over time. Epigenetics thus plays a role in prenatal and postnatal development. While research on the sources of sexual orientation has gotten out of favor in general, epigenetics could soon provide new knowledge on the complexities that arise when trying to explain a person's sexual orientation in regard to the human genome (Ngun & Vilain, 2014).

WHAT'S ON YOUR MIND?

Q: My cousin claims that research proves that the brain can be hardwired to be gay or straight and that explains why people act the way that they do. What do you think?

ANSWER: There is so much individual and gender variation in sexual attraction and behavior, even within families, and there is enough evidence from studies of identical twins to suggest that internal mechanisms do influence sexual orientation. Identical twins share 100% of their genes. Research with identical and fraternal twins suggests that identical twins are more likely than fraternal twins to have the same sexual orientation. But researchers don't have evidence yet to say that a brain mechanism produces sexual orientation. Society plays a role, too, and perhaps in time we will see how nature and nurture both contribute.

Historically, researchers were interested in understanding the causes of sexual orientation. Before knowing about epigenetics, researchers believed that if DNA causes sexual orientation, then that orientation may be present prior to birth. It is almost scientifically impossible, however, to establish cause and effect from DNA to behavioral traits, including sexual orientation. Genetic inheritance often cannot necessarily explain variation within a family or differences among individuals (Buss, 2008). As with many other traits, such as height and eye color, sexual orientation likely involves many genes acting together to produce the effect of attraction to one gender or others.

Additionally, just because someone may have the genes to produce a specific effect, a person may not necessarily ever express a trait. This is crucial to understand about humans. For example, we have the genes that create speech centers in the brain, but it takes parental love, active learning, and the cultural environment for us to know how to express speech. Remove these elements and we do not develop speech properly. In fact, if these elements are not present during a certain point in our development, our speech and intelligence are forever stunted. It takes having the genes present and having the genes triggered at the correct time during maturation for humans to develop speech fully. This kind of precise timing may also be true of many of our behavioral traits, including sexual orientation, and this is why genetic research on sexual orientation presents problems (Murphy, 1997; Savin-Williams, 2005). Recent epigenetic studies have shown that some of these environmental effects can directly affect genetic expression, which can then be passed down from parent to child (Bailey et al., 2016). Because epigenetics is only beginning to be understood, its influence on sexual orientation is probable but remains to be replicated more thoroughly (for an interactive guide on epigenetics, see https://learn.genetics.utah.edu/content/epigenetics/).

Studying the genetic basis of sexual orientation is unusually complex, which is something popular media often ignore when discussing the development of sexual orientation (Byrne & Parsons, 1993; Diamond, 2005). Scientists, in contrast, look for ways to work with such complexity. They have found that studies of twins are an important way to research the complex effect of genes on behavior. **Twin studies** compare twins to see what part of nature or nurture may influence behavior. There are two types of twins: monozygotic (MZ), or "identical," twins share 100% of their genes. This means, then, that the variation that occurs in the traits of MZ twins, whether they be in weight, intelligence, depression, or sexual orientation, is the result of their individual life experiences, or the influence of nurture. Dizygotic (DZ), or "fraternal," twins share only 50% of their genes, which is the same as siblings who are not twins. Because MZ twins are more similar than DZ twins, it is possible to tease out the effects of genes, culture, and unique experiences when it comes to sexual orientation (Bailey & Pilliard, 1991).

Research shows that if one identical twin is gay, the other is most likely to be gay, too; or if one is straight, the other is most likely to be straight (Blanchard & Bogaert, 2001). This research may allow us to see the likelihood that MZ brothers have the same sexual

twin studies
Research that compares twins to determine what part of nature or nurture may have influenced behavior.

orientation compared to DZ brothers or non-twin brothers. The largest twin studies have determined that 30% of identical twins share a gay/lesbian or bisexual orientation, as compared to 8% of fraternal twins. Note that this 30% linkage is not even close to 100%, though identical twins share 100% of their DNA. This means that 70% of the individuals' source of sexual orientation is social. The social factors may include social learning experiences, family environment, and culture.

A twin study is an excellent example of how the combination of genetics and interactive biopsychosocial sources may explain sexual orientation: It is believed that a genetic predisposition toward LGB orientation may exist and that this predisposition is reinforced in the social context of growing up in the same family.

The adage of "correlation is not causation," however, applies here. Consider this example: Basketball players are tall, so their height correlates with playing basketball, and yet there is no "basketball-playing gene." Height does not cause the ability to play basketball well. It may correlate with being able to play basketball. This is why some experts are skeptical that they will ever identify a gene that causes sexual orientation (Jordan-Young, 2010). This doesn't make genes irrelevant as a possible source, but science is still not adequate to answer such questions (Jordan-Young, 2010). Researchers do continue to learn how culture affects the expression of sexual orientation through sexual norms, taboos, and marriage, as you will read in the section "Men Who Have Sex with Men."

Identical twins share 100% of their genes. Research with identical and fraternal twins suggests that identical twins are more likely than fraternal twins to have the same sexual orientation.
golf9c9333/Getty Images

Prenatal Development The leading theory on the biological development of sexual orientation suggests that hormones in the prenatal environment contribute to sex differentiation, and the brain's sensitivity to exposure to certain hormones makes a person more or less susceptible to being attracted to female or male bodies later in life. Researchers who study prenatal sources of sexual orientation typically consider two factors. The first is hormones. They look for a patterned link between a hormonal trait in the mother's biology and the expression of sexual orientation in her offspring. For example, what if the mother's body cannot produce enough male sex hormones to start the process of sexual differentiation in the fetal brain? Some researchers hypothesize that prenatal androgen hormones circulating in the mother's body may correlate with the tendency for one of her offspring to be LGB (Williams et al., 2000).

In line with this hypothesis, researchers have found that birth order can affect sexual orientation. Some studies (Blanchard, 2018) suggest that each older brother increases a younger brother's odds of developing a same-gender orientation by 28–48% (Savin-Williams & Ream, 2007). The specific biological mechanism is still being investigated, but some scientists believe that lower levels of androgens in the prenatal environment are caused by development of the mother's antibodies with each pregnancy with a male fetus (Blanchard et al., 1998; Ellis & Blanchard, 2001). Remember, though, that correlation is not causation. In short, hormonal sources can establish a tendency in sexual orientation development, but we cannot predict if that tendency will actually be manifest in adulthood.

What about exposure of the prenatal brain as a source of sexual orientation? Animal research indicates that the preference of sexual partners can be changed by manipulating these animals' androgen exposure (Alexander, 2011). In humans, researchers have found that women with congenital adrenal hyperplasia, who have been exposed to high levels of androgens, are more likely to develop same-gender attraction (Meyer-Bahlburg et al., 2008). Whether these studies inform the typical development of sexual orientation is unknown. However, scientists hypothesize that a portion of the hypothalamus (a brain region that is involved in regulation of metabolic processes that play a role in sexual behavior, and which is sensitive to circulating hormones in the prenatal regulation environments) differs among people who vary in their sexual orientation. A classic study examining the brains of people who had died from AIDS indicated important differences between the brains of heterosexual men and those of gay men (LeVay, 1991). In fact, LeVay found that the medial preoptic area of the hypothalamus (called the INAH3) was more than twice as large in heterosexual men as in gay men, with the size in homosexual men being closer to the size in heterosexual women. Other studies find differences between gay and heterosexual people, including the function of the inner ear, the first-finger-to-third-finger digit ratio, and eye-blink reflexes (LeVay, 2017). Later researchers criticized the accuracy of the methods of the classic LeVay study and how the sample was composed of corpses, whose brains may differ from those of living people (Jordan-Young, 2010). Such studies remain controversial but of continuing importance.

Postnatal Development **Imprinting** is an early learning process when newborns establish a behavior pattern of recognition and attraction to another animal of its own kind or to an object identified as the parent. Researchers consider imprinting to be one of the major behavioral and cognitive mechanisms that may influence sexual orientation (Money et al., 1957). It is akin to exposure to human touch, love, or neglect as well as the ability to bond or attach to people (Bowlby, 1973). It is essential for human infants to develop a deep and secure attachment to an adult during the sensitive period from about 6 months to 2 years of age. Generally psychological studies have found correlations between poor or insecure attachment and later life relationship difficulties (Perel, 2006). John Money famously suggested that during the early imprinting period, adults could implicitly communicate sexual feelings or implant sexual scripts, called "love maps," into children's development of sexual orientation (Money, 1988). For example, a child may develop a love map that projects the ideal traits of a lover in adulthood, such as gender, anatomy, body size, skin color, or even personality characteristics, such as being timid or aggressive. Unfortunately, there is little empirical evidence to support this theory. Moreover, subsequent theories of this kind, such as Bem's "Exotic Becomes Erotic" theory (Bem, 1996), though similarly interesting in matching early and later sexual orientation outcomes, has been extensively critiqued and found to be focused more on men than women (Peplau et al., 1998). Generally, then, it remains unclear the extent to which imprinting may contribute to sexual orientation in humans, though it is a factor in the development of other mammals' sexual orientation (Roughgarden, 2004).

Interactive Biopsychosocial Sources This is a more comprehensive explanation of sexual orientation than the first three. The **interactive biopsychosocial approach** suggests that, starting in early life, biological, psychological, and social factors interact to produce sexual attractions and sexual orientation (Money & Ehrhardt, 1972; Tolman & Diamond, 2002). In this explanation, sexuality is viewed as a biological process that is later reinforced by culture and behavioral experiences such as pleasure (Fausto-Sterling, 2000). For example, an individual may have a predisposition to be attracted to the same gender, and this tendency will be expressed or inhibited based on the environmental demands, social experiences, and ongoing biological and social development (Diamond, 2008; Savin-Williams, 2005).

For reasons that remain unknown, the link between genes and sexual orientation among women is less clear than it is for men (Savin-Williams & Ream, 2007). For example, the evidence linking female siblings by sexual orientation is much weaker than for men. As you can see in Figure 10.2, men more than women tend to express their same-gender attractions in behavior, which might explain this sibling difference. Another possible effect of this genetic difference for women comes from recent studies showing how women more than men show nonexclusive patterns of attraction. One study of 767 people who ranged in age from 18 to 74 was conducted; 47% of the participants were women. The results showed that women have a greater likelihood of expressing bisexual behavior, regardless of the influences from their family background or culture (Floyd & Bakeman, 2006). As we discuss later in the chapter, this type of change in sexual expression is more common among women than men in a variety of studies.

---

imprinting
A rapid early learning process by which a newborn establishes a behavior pattern of recognition and attraction to another animal of its own kind or to an object identified as the parent.

interactive biopsychosocial approach
A theory that suggests that biological, psychological, and social factors work together to produce sexual attractions and feelings, and perhaps sexual orientation.

There is no scientific consensus on which of these four explanations is accurate or whether they are mutually exclusive. Today researchers in psychology and biology and other social sciences lean toward integration of biological and environmental approaches. These approaches imply that orientation is, to a certain extent, hardwired in human development, especially during the prenatal stage (Kirk, Bailey, Dunne, & Martin, 2000; Rahman & Wilson, 2003), but that such wiring naturally depends on social and cultural factors (Herdt, 2010b; Money & Ehrhardt, 1972; Tolman & Diamond, 2002). However, today many researchers prefer to understand the interaction between all of these factors and their moderators, including how human nature and nurture might fit together (Van Anders, 2015).

Sexual Socialization and Compulsory Heterosexuality

Across all cultures, most individuals conform to what their culture, family, and community expect them to do in growing up, especially when it comes to getting married and having children. In a manner similar to how they unconsciously learn the speech patterns required to be competent in the language of their culture, children "learn" how to express their attractions and sexual orientation according to the expressed rules of their culture (Bhana, 2016; Herdt, 1999, 2010b). When such expectations are reinforced in school, in church, and in the media, years of social learning can influence the expression of sexual orientation. By late childhood or early adolescence, when most children understand what sexual orientation means, it is not surprising that they have been sexually socialized into their community's heterosexual norms (Carver, Egan, & Perry, 2004). In fact, for more than a hundred years, heterosexuality has been the longstanding and effective cultural norm and expectation in the United States. Being heterosexual or straight has been an expression of gender roles as well as a commitment to having a heterosexual identity (D'Emilio & Freedman, 1988).

What happens, however, when people do not conform to the community expectation of being heterosexual? Later we will consider many examples of sexual variations, but let's consider a few examples of variations of heterosexuality now. For example, consider a man identified as straight who dates women but prefers not to marry. Do people think that he is "really" gay? Some clergy members such as priests or nuns renounce sexuality. Are they heterosexual or something else? Consider a man who has spent years behind bars in prison without a female sexual partner. Some people would assume that he would have had sex with other men to satisfy his sexual desires. When he gets out, has that behavior compromised his heterosexuality? In each of these situations, being heterosexual is a powerful sexual orientation that outweighs many other considerations of life experiences, as well as gender, age, race, social class, and culture (Katz, 2007).

Currently, 75 countries legally proscribe same-gender sexual behavior. Eleven countries—all in Africa, Asia, or the Middle East—retain the death penalty as a possible sanction for same-gender behavior (Human Dignity Trust, 2019; Stewart, 2014). What this means is that expressing nonheterosexual behavior in these countries is not only potentially ruinous to someone's reputation and their family's standing in their community, but also dangerous and even lethal. It is no wonder people in such countries go to great lengths to keep their sexual orientations secret.

By contrast today, the United States and Western European countries are more tolerant and permissive of the expression of nonheterosexual behaviors. Through changes in the law allowing same-gender marriage and family formation, the norms and surrounding values have changed in these countries (Badgett, 2009; Marzullo & Herdt, 2011).

When countries continue to expect people to be heterosexual and to marry and have children together, researchers refer to this concept as **compulsory heterosexuality**. Coined by feminist writer Adrienne Rich (1994), compulsory heterosexuality describes the condition of women's being socially compelled to have sexual relationships with and marry men, regardless of the women's sexual orientation. By default, women have to adopt heterosexuality as their preferred mode, even if they are lesbian (Tolman, 2005). Feminists view compulsory heterosexuality as a basic tool to control women and their bodies, especially in

compulsory heterosexuality
The condition of being socially compelled to have sexual relationships with the other gender, be married, and have children, regardless of sexual orientation.

male-dominated societies. These social mandates are so powerful that many people internalize them (Diamond, 2008). The concept is now extended to both genders and enables us to understand how certain individuals and groups may have to hide, disguise, or otherwise alter their sexual attractions and relationships to conform to society (Laumann et al., 1994). Compulsory heterosexuality can also be termed heteronormativity, that is, treating heterosexuality as normal and natural. Carried to its extremes in discrimination and prejudice, this becomes heterosexism. These forms of prejudice all share the idea that being heterosexual is superior to all other orientations.

For some people, conforming to heterosexuality seems natural, but those with diverse attractions and orientations may experience compulsory heterosexuality as a mechanism of power that coerces them into living a secret life, or makes them feel like failures because they cannot live up to the sexual norm. Accordingly, researchers have argued that compulsory heterosexuality may be socially and sexually oppressive to all people: women and men, heterosexuals and homosexuals, people of color, and so on (Butler, 1990; Halperin, 1995; Striepe & Tolman, 2003). In this view, compulsory heterosexuality prevents the free expression of sexual individuality among some women, men, and minorities, including LGBTQ people. It may also result in other disastrous side effects, such as increased exposure to HIV/AIDS, as noted later in the chapter.

In some cultures and religions, such as Islam, heterosexuality is compulsory. Regardless of sexual orientation, Muslim men and women are expected to marry and have children.
NAZRUL NAIM BIN NAZMI/Shutterstock

Some individuals may experience a shift in their attractions or behaviors long after they have socially adapted to living up to the heterosexual norm (Floyd & Bakeman, 2006; Laumann et al., 1994). How does this shift occur? Some individuals may not become totally aware of all their sexual attractions when they were experiencing sexual socialization early in life, perhaps because of compulsory heterosexuality (Diamond, 2008; Herdt & DeVries, 2003; Tolman, 2005). Consider the following example: A man's spouse died when he was in middle age. He then met a man and fell in love, discovering feelings he had never before felt (Herdt, Beeler, & Rawls, 1997). This new situation offered him new opportunities for the expression of what may have been a long dormant or even unconscious desire.

It appears that people really do experience this kind of change in their sexual orientation more often than was once believed as they learn new things or experience new opportunities for sexual individuality later on in life (Floyd & Bakeman, 2006). As we learned in Chapter 3, our information society and online dating apps have been a big factor in enabling such new opportunities or explorations. Some women say that their sense of attraction is to another person's idealized or real traits—such as their energy, love of life, personality, shared values, or interests—regardless of that person's gender or orientation (Diamond, 2008, 2014; Hammack & Cohler, 2009). In short, it is not that they "learn" a new sexual orientation but that over time new opportunities for sexual expression and love may emerge to allow for expansion of individual sexuality.

Sexual Individuality and Sexual Orientation

The integration of sexual individuality with sexual orientation is vital to sexual well-being. Sexual individuality may be an acquired expression of self that is grounded in very basic experiences of our own body and biology: our DNA, prenatal hormones, genitals, attractions, attachments, and early feelings about other people's bodies. Surely families and sexual socialization into norms influence sexual individuality to some extent.

Consider how this influence is similar to the way people experience liking or disliking certain foods from childhood on, and later how they acquire the taste for foods beyond their communities of origin. In many cultures, people eat certain foods at social gatherings, such as roast turkey at Thanksgiving in the United States, or the brains and other organs of certain animals at marriage ceremonies in the Pacific Islands. Most people adapt to these food preferences, but some cannot, despite social pressure to conform to the traditional foods. There are a few who from the start have great difficulty conforming to traditional food tastes, whether from personal taste, allergies, or natural aversion. As people grow up, however, their tastes may change as they learn to expand what they were required or taught to eat in childhood. This may be the result of new tastes they acquire through travel and other opportunities to try different cuisines, including exotic foods from other cultures. The expression of changing food tastes through life may be not unlike the development of sexual individuality.

Sexual individuality, also developed through our senses, gives us signals about our attractions and bodily arousal. As we saw earlier, some people may experience a gap between their physical attractions and their expressed sexual behavior. That may be partly due to compulsory heterosexuality, or to the lack of integration of their orientation with their sexual individuality, including their awareness of their bodily attractions (Herdt & McClintock, 2000). As people mature, they become aware of a larger range of sexual feelings, attractions, and expressions. Additionally, over time, they may choose to integrate this awareness or not into their unique sexual individuality to support holistic sexual health and well-being (Hensel & Fortenberry, 2014).

According to the American Academy of Child and Adolescent Psychiatry (AACAP, 2011) literally millions of children in the United States and Western Europe have LGBTQ parents. Research shows that these children are no more likely to be gay than children with heterosexual parents.
Dinis Tolipov/123RF

Sexual individuality leads to this question: Will children brought up in a household headed by a gay or lesbian couple become gay or lesbian (Erzen, 2006; Savin-Williams, 2005; Vrangalova & Savin-Williams, 2012)? Considerable controversy exists over whether someone can actually be socialized as LGBTQ or whether someone can teach someone else to be gay (Badgett, 2009; Stacey & Biblarz, 2001). There is much evidence to the contrary (Patterson, 2006; Patterson & Riskind, 2010). No evidence supports the idea that parental sexual orientation influences that of their children (Herdt & Kertzner, 2006; Patterson, 2006; Patterson & Riskind, 2010; Stacey & Biblarz, 2001). In fact, studies of the children of LGBTQ people prove the point, as studied later in the chapter.

We have explored sources of sexual orientation, among other issues. Let's now examine how some cultures have channeled the expression of same-gender attractions across history. When we consider how past cultures practiced the integration of sexual expression, we may be better able to understand the full spectrum of sexual orientation across time and space.

VARIATIONS IN SEXUAL ORIENTATION ACROSS TIME AND CULTURES

Try this thought experiment: Imagine growing up in a society that has no categories of sexual orientation. In this imaginary society, you would be categorized not by your internal attractions or external identity. Rather, you would be an individual involved in the rich web of social life and institutions into which you were born: gender, economy, extended family, religious community, and other social or military groups. That was the situation in ancient and traditional societies and even in modern society in the United States until the 20th century (Greenberg, 1988). It also remains common in many non-Western societies even today. In fact, some societies still do not include the category same-gender sexuality in their language or culture (Aggleton & Parker, 2010).

As you have read, different terms are used in the United States to refer to distinct sexual orientations. Globally, however, there is a much richer range of concepts and meanings used in other cultures to describe these and other orientations (Herdt, 2010b). It is still not clear whether all these terms refer to the same or different kinds of sexual orientations. What is clear, though, is that in certain cultures some sexual behaviors occur without identities attached to them. For example, people may engage in same-sex behavior for months or years, but still think of themselves as being no different from other heterosexuals when it comes to getting married and producing a family (Padilla, 2008).

Same-Sex Behavior Variations Across Cultures

Sexual orientation can be understood as a phenomenon that can actually be oriented across multiple social and cultural dimensions such as gender and also in combination with age or the kind of relationship a person is already in that provides clues or guides to others as to their sexual orientation (van Anders, 2015). Because of this lack of globally shared sexual orientation categories across cultures, some researchers focus on three areas of sexual behavior expression to link people: age difference, gender difference, and role difference (Greenberg, 1986; Herdt, 1997a; Trumbach, 1977).

Cultures Defined by Age Difference In some cultures, age is the primary difference for structuring the expression of same-gender relationships. Ancient Greece is an example of a culture that for centuries used age to define how males engaged in same-gender relations. These relationships were allowed between older married men and younger men in their late teens and early 20s. This was a social demonstration of virility, honor, courage, and nobility and helped to create warrior cultures (Dover, 1978). In ancient Greek and Roman cultures, men who were equal in age were forbidden to engage in same-gender relations. Those who broke this taboo were stigmatized and sometimes punished. Similar forms of age-defined same-gender behavior between older and younger men occurred in ancient Arabia, Korea, China, and Japan (Pflugfeltder, 1999).

As we saw in Chapter 2, some Pacific Islands cultures that emphasized age difference practiced boy-inseminating rituals. In these religious rituals, boys had to be inseminated orally or anally for their society to consider them masculine and strong. Later in their lives, marriages were arranged for them (Herdt, 1991). Historically, the Sambia of Papua New Guinea had a sexual norm by which older Sambia men were attracted only to prepubertal boys ages 7 to 13; the moment a boy showed the first signs of manhood, especially facial hair, they were no longer attracted to him, and he went on to a higher level of initiation that allowed him to inseminate younger boys. Interestingly, this is the opposite pattern from that of the ancient Greeks, who were attracted to young men with facial hair (Herdt, 2006). Other examples of this age difference existed in areas of Africa, Asia, and South America.

Native American Indian two-spirit people today.
Brian Brainerd/The Denver Post/Getty Images

Cultural Variation in Sexual Orientation Based on Gender Many cultures in Asia and the Pacific, North and South America, and Africa permitted the expression of same-sex behaviors by a male who would actually take on the gender role of women (Herdt, 1994; Williams, 1992). Less frequently but still importantly, some of these cultures had women who also took on the gender role and expression of men. The indigenous people of the Great Plains, North America, on precolonial Turtle Island is a critical example of this gender-role difference. Today, this orientation is referred to as the two-spirit role in these living traditions (Jacobs, Thomas, & Lang, 1997). For example, the Mohave tribe believed that even very small children could express their orientation toward being two-spirit. During a ceremony for the baby, they placed a basket to represent women on one side of the baby and a bow and arrows to represent men on the other side. Whichever tool the baby selected for its play object was an indication from the individual and the spirits that the child would become defined as two-spirit (Herdt, 1991).

Today, numerous examples of gender-defined sexual expressions exist, such as the Polynesian Fafafina role among biological men who express the female role, which occurs widely across the Asian Pacific region (Greenberg, 1986).

Cultures defined by gender roles tend to be a bit more tolerant of same-gender relationships. The men who had same-gender attractions were socialized into women's roles and lived as women. Likewise, certain women were socialized into men's roles and lived as men (Herdt, 1993; Roscoe, 1991; Williams, 1992).

Cultural Variations in Sexual Orientation Based on Gender Role In some complex societies, such as in ancient Japan and Korea, as well as in England during the period of Shakespeare, same-gender relationships were allowed for men who performed as actors in plays or on stage, as well as in certain religious institutions, such as monks in the Buddhist tradition or shamans in some traditional cultures (Herdt, 1997a).

But the best-known examples come from the stage traditions, such as the plays of ancient Japan, in which men played every role. In Shakespeare's plays, most of the time men or boys played all the roles, which may have facilitated same-gender sexual expression off-stage as well (Trumbach, 1998). In fact, in some London pubs of those times, referred to as Mollys after the name of one of the popular pubs, individual men would dress and act sexually as women (Trumbach, 1994).

In the Netherlands, too, the variety of role-defined same-sex practices seemed to explode in the modern period; for example, women dressed in men's clothes to gain position and status (Dekker & van der Pol, 1989). This practice was historically known as cross-dressing, but this term is no longer used due to the fact that gender now represents a spectrum rather than a binary (see Chapter 9). In 19th-century sexology, the focus was on being a **transvestite**, someone with a sexual interest in cross-dressing. Women also began to pass as men in certain contexts in the United States during this era. In England some cross-dressing women were called Sapphists, after the ancient Greek woman poet, Sappho, who is believed to have been lesbian. Until at least the 1960s, this kind of role-defined difference sometimes accompanied by cross-dressing in male–male and female–female relationships remained common, and was referred to in what LGBTQ people called "butch" (masculine) and "fem" (feminine) roles in LGBTQ circles (Newton, 1993).

The Invention of Modern Western Identity

As discussed in Chapter 2, the concept of sexual identity emerged in the modern period to organize a new social movement focused on social and political rights, rather than as determined by disease or biology. As a defined social and political position in society, sexual identity does require the underlying sexual orientation, as we have seen with compulsory heterosexuality.

As noted in Chapters 1 and 2, a defined LGBTQ movement began in the later 19th century that was pivotal in making sexual identities the focus of political activism for LGBTQ rights. For the first time, researchers began to think that sexual attractions were located within an individual, rather than as part of a category or cultural norm (Foucault, 1980; Robinson, 1976). In fact, prior to this time researchers had not studied the concepts of homosexuality or of heterosexuality simply because they did not exist as such.

Before the use of sexual identity as a concept, American and Western European LGBTQ people thought of themselves as not fitting into the prevalent binary gender system, and so they felt immoral and were treated as abnormal (Oosterhuis, 2000). Freud (1905) referred to LGBTQ individuals as "psychic hermaphrodites," meaning such a person was a woman in a man's body or a man in a woman's body. Doctors believed that homosexual men were attracted to only

DID YOU KNOW

In the late 1800s, when the term heterosexuality was introduced, famed American psychologist William James considered heterosexuality to be "abnormal." James stated in his lectures at Harvard University that heterosexuality must be a perversion because it restricted desire to only one gender (the opposite gender), not two. Like Freud, James believed that "normal sex" development ought to include desire for both genders, even if society dictated that normal relationships are between men and women.

transvestite
Someone with an interest in wearing clothing typical of the other gender.

The late 1960s were a time of huge social unrest. Not surprisingly, in view of the political and social oppression of gay men and lesbian women at the time, gay men fought back one hot summer night in New York City. The Stonewall Tavern riot started a new movement that now stands for the broadest political rights for all LGBTQ people.
Barbara Alper/Archive Photos/Getty Images

heterosexual men, an idea that today strikes researchers as implausible (Chauncey, 1995). The medical and cultural ideal was that "opposites attract." Some women engaged in "Boston marriages" or "Wellesley marriages," which were friendships among women who lived and slept together, but the belief was that they did not necessarily have sex (Horowitz, 2002).

In 1969, the Stonewall Tavern riot in New York City started the modern LGBTQ movement. After experiencing so much oppression for so long, LGBTQ individuals, transgender people, and their allies fought back against police harassment, blackmail, and jail time (Duberman, 1993). Similar riots occurred in San Francisco and elsewhere. These events mark the beginning of homosexuals insisting on the right to live openly with dignity (D'Emilio, 1998; Stryker & Buskirk, 1996).

The Modern LGBTQ Movement

LGBTQ activists began to base their advocacy for rights in terms of sexual identity in the context of same-gender sexuality being illegal throughout the United States. Police harassment just for being gay was routine. In fact, it was legal to arrest two men or two women for dancing together or for holding hands. They could be imprisoned, or worse, if they were caught having sex (D'Emilio, 1998). Additionally, many LGBTQ people who wanted to keep their same-gender sexuality feelings and behaviors secret worried that blackmailers could threaten them with exposure and loss of everything, even citizenship (Corber, 1997; Terry, 1999).

In the medical arena, doctors considered same-gender sexual feelings and behaviors to be indicative of a physical and mental disease, while among the clergy, LGBTQ people were considered morally degenerate (Bayer, 1987; D'Emilio, 1998). Many LGBTQ people were even referred to psychiatrists for treatment or placed in mental hospitals against their will (Murphy, 1997). Electric shock treatment to "change" their sexual orientation was common (Cohler & Galatzer-Levy, 2000; Duberman, 1993). However, attempts to change sexual orientation only incurred more physical and mental harm to LGBTQ individuals.

In the late 1950s and early 1960s, however, some courageous doctors and researchers began working with LGBTQ advocates to reform the mental health view of same-gender sexuality as a disease in favor of the current view that it is part of the vast expression of sexual diversity. Notable among these pioneers was Dr. Evelyn Hooker, a psychologist from UCLA who employed standard psychological personality tests comparing LGBTQ individuals and heterosexuals. She discovered that there was no difference between them (Bayer, 1987). Thus began the long, difficult challenge of changing the status of homosexuality in medicine from that of mental illness to normality, as you can read in "Healthy Sexuality: Being Gay Is Normal!"

Fortunately, there are many positive role models of people who are openly LGBTQ now. Science, medicine, media, and popular culture depict LGBTQ sexuality as normal more than at any other point in history (Terry, 1999). President Obama's expressed support for the legalization of same-gender marriage and the Supreme Court decision of 2015 legalizing same-gender marriage are strong indications of these winds of change. Hollywood's growing recognition of the normalcy of LGBTQIA+ people includes the stunning performance by Sean Penn of gay activist Harvey Milk in the film *Milk*. Television shows such as *Modern Family, Brothers and Sisters, Will and Grace, Grey's Anatomy, Orange Is the New Black, Queer Eye,* and *Chilling Adventures of Sabrina* feature attractive, successful, humane LGBTQIA+ characters. Openly gay television celebrities such as Ellen DeGeneres, Tracy Chapman, Ricky Martin, newsman Anderson Cooper, Olympic diver Matthew Mitcham,

HEALTHY Sexuality

Being Gay Is Normal!

In 1957, Dr. Evelyn Hooker, a psychologist at UCLA and a married heterosexual woman, examined the personality tests of 60 individuals; one group was heterosexual and the other homosexual. She had a panel of three distinguished doctors and researchers analyze the tests without knowing the sexual orientation of the subjects. They all declared that in terms of the psychological adjustment of these 60 people, they were equal. To her shock, however, when she reported these findings, many of her scientific colleagues did not believe her.

Together with psychiatrists and other researchers, she began new studies that eventually led to the creation of the blue-ribbon task force of the National Institute of Mental Health to reconsider all the scientific evidence regarding homosexuality as a mental disease (Bayer, 1987; Hooker, 1957). As a result of the final recommendations by this task force, the American Psychiatric Association declassified homosexuality as a mental disorder in 1973. At the time, this change was regarded as highly controversial and was opposed by many in society. Three decades later, however, the doctors, such as psychiatrist Robert L. Spitzer, who argued that gay men could be "cured" through treatment, have now found that they were wrong and that sexual orientation cannot be changed. Dr. Spitzer later apologized to homosexual people for how these flawed views harmed LGBTQ people (Carey, 2012).

Years later, an award-winning film about Dr. Hooker's work appeared, called *Changing Our Minds,* which celebrated this landmark in the rights of LGBTQ people and the achievements of the heterosexual psychologists who served as allies in the search for truth and equal treatment for LGBTQ people (http://www.imdb.com/title/tt0103938/). Today the American Psychological Association also views LGBTQ orientations as normal variations of human development (see APA policy statement: http://www.apa.org/topics/sorientation.html).

and singer Ari Gold are just a few people who serve as positive role models. Also, consider that famous cultural icon of macho heterosexuality, James Bond, in the 2012 film *Skyfall*, as played by actor Daniel Craig, who when sexually taunted by the manly villain, responds by saying, "What makes you think this is my first time [having sex with a man]?" surprising everyone.

Politics too is reflecting this sea change. Where once there were no openly LGBTQIA+ people in the U.S. Congress, there are now several senators and 10 members of the House of Representatives. Others are joining them at the levels of local, state, and federal government offices, such as Lori Lightfoot, mayor of Chicago, and Jared Polis, governor of Colorado. And history was made again in 2019 when Pete Buttigieg, the openly gay mayor of South Bend, Indiana, began his run for president, with his husband joining him at times on the campaign trail.

Laverne Cox, a transgender woman, played a critical role in the Netflix Drama, "Orange is the New Black" and increased visibility in television for transgender people.
Netflix/Photofest

WHAT'S ON YOUR MIND?

Q: My college roommate says that gay and lesbian people make up about 10% of the population, but in the small town in North Dakota where I grew up, hardly anybody was gay, and there were no gay people out in my high school. Is he right or wrong?

ANSWER: The actual number of people who are openly gay or lesbian in the United States is not precisely known, but studies measure it between 1% and 15%, depending on whether bisexual, queer, and other sexual orientations are also included in the figure. It may be 10% or higher in some large cities.

10% Are Gay: Myth or Sexual Geography?

As the modern LGBTQ movement got going, the press began to report the number of gay people as being around 10% of the general population. In fact, critics and advocacy groups of LGBTQ alike have used this 10% number to claim different things (Michaels, 1996). Earlier research studies, however, reported the percentages of homosexual people as smaller. The true percentage is hard to determine because some people will not state their sexual orientation, or surveys might ask differently about sexual attraction, identity, or behavior. A good estimate is 4–5% of the general population—about 9 million Americans (Badgett & Herman, 2011). When separating by gender, fewer women (83%) than men (94%) are exclusively attracted to the other sex (Rosario & Schrimshaw, 2014).

Researchers use statistical methods to estimate the probable percentage of LGBTQ individuals in the larger society (Laumann et al., 1994). The best national random sample available shows that 2.4% of all men and 1.3% of all women are LGBTQ (Laumann et al., 1994; Vrangralova & Savin-Williams, 2012). There are always fewer lesbian women than gay men in these surveys (Michaels, 1996). What effects produce the apparent gap between the small percentage found in random samples and the larger percentage that some people use?

One explanation for the difference may be **sexual geography**, the idea that people with different sexual orientations live in particular cities and even distinct neighborhoods or social spaces that are "safe" and gay-friendlier (Laumann et al., 2004). In fact, many LGBTQ people believe that large cities are the safest spaces to live because of their diverse, tolerant, and anonymous populations (Badgett, 2009; Chauncey, 1995; D'Emilio, 1998).

Estimates for same-gender behavior in the largest 12 cities in the United States range between 8% and 12%, with the median being 10%. Compare that number to the smallest rural counties that have less than 1% LGBTQ (Binson et al., 1995). Thus, the LGBTQ population averages 10% in big cities and a lot less in small towns. The distribution of LGBTQ populations is not equal even among the largest 10 cities, however. For example, the number of LGBTQ people in San Francisco and New York is much denser than in Dallas.

How did LGBTQ people come to live in cities in the first place? During World War II, gay men and lesbian women were mobilized along with millions of other Americans to fight against the enemy. At this time, people generally hid their sexual orientation, but for the first time, many soldiers realized that they were not alone in the world in having same-gender attractions (Berube, 1990). At the end of the war, when they were discharged in big city ports such as New York, San Francisco, Chicago, and Miami, many of them never went back to their small hometowns. This core of people formed the basis for LGBTQ communities in these cities (Berube, 1990; D'Emilio, 1998). As these early gay communities began, they attracted other gay men and lesbian women from surrounding small towns. For example, people in the northwestern area of the United States relocated to Seattle and Portland. Not every gay man or lesbian woman has left the rural areas, though; there is a Gay Hog Farmers Association of Wisconsin, and many stories tell of the continuing hidden life of people in the rural South (Sears, 1990).

Whatever the true number of sexual minorities in the United States, they have become more visible, active, and out, and as we will see in the closing section of this chapter, along with LGBTQ people from other places around the world, they seek the dignity of being regarded with full human rights.

Bisexuality

Although bisexuality has begun to be viewed in a positive way, for decades it was viewed mostly in negative cultural terms (Diamond, 2008; Eliason, 1997; Weinberg, Williams, & Pryor, 1995). This negative view was partly because, in the 19th century, medical sexologists saw bisexuality as another form of mental and physical disease. Moreover, both heterosexuals and LGBTQ individuals were suspicious of people who stated that they had dual

---

sexual geography

Cities and neighborhoods to which sexual minorities migrate as safe places to live.

attractions to more than one gender, because they saw this as lying or fence-sitting—or even being disloyal (Diamond, 2008; Weinberg et al., 1995).

Many bisexual people felt they had to pretend to be either heterosexual, or, in the case of homosexuals, that they had to pretend to be gay in order to be accepted by either group. Some gay men and lesbian women were sometimes resentful toward bisexuals because they felt that bisexuals who passed as straight "got to have their cake and eat it, too" (Herdt & Boxer, 1993).

Individuals who were bisexual were often thought to be emotionally immature, socially and psychologically inadequate, or unbalanced, perhaps because they did not conform to the cultural expectations of getting married, settling down, and having children (Klein, 1978). Today, however, we understand that there is much more variation in the expression of orientation and attractions than was ever discussed in the past (Kinsey et al., 1948; Laumann et al., 1994; Savin-Williams & Ream, 2007; Vrangalova & Savin-Williams, 2012). In other words, research points toward a greater prevalence of bisexual patterns than previously thought, and this holds for the whole spectrum of sexual communities in the United States (Garofalo, Wolf, Wissow, Woods, & Goodman, 1999; Kirk et al., 2000; Mosher, Chandra, & Jones, 2005; Weinberg et al., 1995).

Gay, straight, or in-between?
Jo Hale/Getty Images

Bisexuality, similar to same-gender sexuality, is especially regulated by cultural and sexual norms. If people have attractions to both sexes, but their culture erects strong barriers against expressing these feelings, they may live their entire life only living one side of their sexual feelings, heterosexuality (Herdt & Boxer, 1993). In fact, the taboos may be so strong against expressing their same-gender sexual attractions that they may not even be aware of what those feelings mean or how deep and powerful they could be (Floyd & Bakeman, 2007). These barriers can be built through marriage, religion, and social values. They may especially regulate women, who are expected to marry and have children, but also to men living in poor and disempowered communities (Johnson, 2008). This also happened in the lives of older gay men and lesbian women, who came of sexual age when homosexual orientation in the United States was so taboo and viewed as sinful and horrible that many of them married, women especially, and suppressed their same-gender attractions and behaviors, in order to avoid severe punishment or ostracism (Diamond, 2008; Herdt & DeVries, 2003).

Being bisexual in Mexican and Hispanic communities is sometimes associated with the cultural pattern of machismo, or "being macho," a concept about demonstrating hypermasculinity in Spanish-speaking cultures (Carrier, 1995; Diaz, 1998; Munoz-Laboy, 2008). Young Hispanic men who grow up in traditional Hispanic communities learn that being macho and being sexually active and aggressive are part of traditional sexual culture. They also learn that same-gender sexuality means to be sexually receptive, more like a woman than a man, and this feminine sexual role is morally bad. This may lead them to deny their same-sex desires (Diaz, 1998). Such attitudes may lead some people to despise gay men as being *puta* (which means "bitch" or "whore" in Spanish). Popular culture also explores the concept of machismo and breaking the boundaries of the binary, as for example in the film, *Hazlo Como Hombre*.

Consider the story of a middle-aged Hispanic man from Chicago, named Johnnie. The following happened to him at age 21 (Herdt et al., 1997): "My Daddy said to me, 'You are going to get married! You are going to have kids! That's just how it is going to be.'" As a child, he was quiet, sensitive, mildly gender atypical, which is what may have made his father wonder if his son was gay. Johnnie did get married and have children just as his father directed. Like many bisexual men, he clearly loved his children. He claims to have been happily married for 20 years. After his children grew up, he and his wife grew apart. Johnnie waited to express his same-sex sexual desires until after his parents died, and he was more established in the community. He now lives as an openly gay man in his community, but it took great effort to get to that point of overcoming social taboos.

Women may express their bisexual attractions and sexual individuality differently from men (Fine & McClelland, 2007; Meston, Hull, Levin, & Sipski, 2004b; Tolman, 2005). In one study, young women between the ages of 13 and 20 reported that their sequence of sexual attraction and sexual behavior began with opposite-sex relationships and then shifted over several years' time to same-gender relationships (Herdt & Boxer, 1993). Gay men had the opposite experience; they tended to start with same-gender relationships and then experimented with opposite-sex encounters, and almost always went back to having sex with men.

Bisexual expression is influenced by cultural norms in ways that are both very modern but also the results of inequality and prejudice left over from the past, as we will see in the next section.

Men Who Have Sex with Men (MSM)

In a variety of cultures, including some communities within the United States, there are men who historically could not express their sexual or romantic feelings for other men due to discrimination, prejudice, inequality, and threats of violence and death. Their concept of being masculine did not allow them to express multiple desires or behaviors, but rather forced them into a binary situation. In a very broad way, these men were given an identity by health workers battling the HIV epidemic in the 1980s: **Men who have sex with men (MSM)**. The World Health Organization adopted the term out of necessity because the bisexual men could not identify with being gay or bisexual and indeed sometimes were extremely hostile or even violent to nonheterosexual men and women. Thus, MSM is a cultural tag or label, not an orientation, although there are places where men have grown up learning to refer to themselves as MSM. In this sense, MSM represents bisexual desires, sexual emotions, and behaviors. Among the various factors that influence this labeling are history, economics, culture, and faith.

For example, LGBTQ sexual identities in the African American community remain deeply controversial in the United States. **Being on the down low (BODL)** is a perplexing and controversial African American term that refers to a man who hides his sexual orientation (Johnson, 2008). While not exactly the same as MSM, some African American men who are attracted to other men are recognized socially as important heterosexual role models who are married with children. The idea that an African American man could have sexual relations with women publicly and with men secretly remains controversial in their community. Some African American literature touches on this theme, as for example in Alice Walker's *The Color Purple* (1982), or in academic accounts, such as E. Patrick Johnson's *Sweet Tea* (2008), which describes the "open secret" of being an African American gay male "church sissy." Historically, African American clergy downplayed or have been openly hostile toward LGBTQ individuals among their church members, and same-gender sexuality is rejected in some African American churches (Cohen, 1999, 2010). Another contributing factor is the African American community's cultural rule requiring marriage and children to carry on their heritage.

Unfortunately, this form of sexual expression is also correlated with HIV and definitely helps to explain part of the reason that HIV is higher among young men of color in some

men who have sex with men (MSM)
Men who are married or date women and also have sex with other men.

being on the down low (BODL)
An African American term that refers to a man who hides his sexual orientation.

African American men who love other men may not necessarily be out about their sexual orientation.
Stockbyte/Getty Images

parts of the United States. In fact, some of these people keep such a low profile that it has been possible for one person to contract HIV and eventually die of AIDS without it becoming known in his own church. Today, a radically inclusive faith movement actually celebrates the faith of African American gay men and lesbians within the African American church, as discussed in Chapter 2. This theme of hidden bisexual orientation is not unique to African American males. Certain White pastors, deacons, or other church members are perceived to be heterosexual but have secret same-gender relationships until their exposure (White, 1995).

Historically, younger African American gay and bisexual males have had the highest rate of infection of HIV in the United States, especially because of the strong correlation between unprotected bisexual behavior and HIV infection (Binson et al., 1995; Diaz, 1998; Mays & Cochran, 1994). Today Black/African American gay and bisexual men are more affected by HIV than any other group in the United States (CDC, 2019). By 2017, Black/African American gay and bisexual men accounted for 26% of the new HIV diagnoses and more than a third of all cases of gay and bisexual men with HIV in the nation.

There are various forms of MSM globally in which some men are married or date women and also have sex with other men on occasion or even regularly. MSM are like LGBTQ individuals, but they live socially as heterosexuals and are married. They definitely do not identify as gay or homosexual or LGBTQ. Some younger MSM have started to use the term "heteroflexible" to describe their sexual identity (Carrillo & Hoffmann, 2016, 2018). Many of their same-gender relationships are not only secret but are regarded as morally wrong or illegal, and if they are married, these extramarital relationships may violate the norms of their society (Caceres & Race, 2010; Hirsch et al., 2009; Munoz-Laboy, 2008; Stewart, 2014).

Thus, the category of MSM emerged from the devastating HIV epidemic of the 1980s and the education and prevention effort because same-gender sexuality was illegal in so many countries, and men who were having sex with men could not identify with the gay or LGBTQ categories and were getting infected with the HIV/AIDS virus (Aggleton, Wood, Malcolm, & Parker, 2005; Munoz-Laboy, 2004, 2008). As a result of these global HIV efforts, some men in certain countries, such as Fiji where same-gender sexual behavior was previously illegal and unknown as an identity, may now refer to themselves as being MSM (Hammar, 2011; Stewart, 2014). Today, males who are considered MSM or bisexual and are lumped together as MSM exist in many societies, including the United States, Mexico, India, Kenya, and Brazil, among others (Hirsch et al., 2009).

Once again, the tragedy is that some of these MSM are prominent leaders in their communities who actually speak out against homosexuality while still carrying on secret sexual relationships with male lovers (Herdt, 2009; Stewart, 2014). They may even have multiple wives or girlfriends (e.g., in the Middle East) and serve as sex workers (Padilla, 2008). Unfortunately, this contradiction stems from the fact that same-gender sexuality in these countries is illegal, and exposure would mean public humiliation, loss of jobs, family, imprisonment, or even death, as noted above. Let us hope that as societies strive to achieve greater equality and sexual literacy, these conditions will improve and allow for greater sexual individuality.

Female Sexual Fluidity

Having studied various forms of bisexuality prominent in men, let's examine relatively new research that has found greater sexual plasticity among women. Researchers have come to see female sexuality as generally being more socially flexible and responsive than male sexuality (Baumeister, 2000). **Stig** is the capacity for some individuals to have context-dependent changes in their erotic response (Diamond, 2008; 2014; 2016). Sexual fluidity is distinct from bisexuality, in that it is not a sexual orientation. Whereas bisexuality reflects a tendency to be attracted to more than one gender, **sexual fluidity** marks deviations in one's overall pattern of attractions, behaviors, and desires and is thought to operate alongside sexual orientation. For example, you can be a sexually fluid bisexual person, which would suggest that you tend

stig
The capacity for some individuals to have context-dependent changes in their erotic response, in Lisa Diamond's research.

sexual fluidity
A form of sexual expression that is more situation-dependent and perhaps more open to the characteristics of the individual, rather than focusing so much on a person's anatomy.

to experience attractions to various genders (e.g., bisexuality), but your relative attractions, behaviors, and identity toward a specific gender might vary across time and situation (sexual fluidity) or a nonfluid bisexual person, which would suggest you tend to experience attractions to various genders and the specific pattern of attraction is stable over time and across situations (Diamond, Dickenson, & Blair, 2017).

Psychologist Lisa Diamond conducted the first major study of sexual fluidity of 100 women that she has followed over a 10-year period. This makes her research very important because it allows us to see change, continuity, and even reversal of sexual orientation over time. She discovered how women in their 20s and 30s feel strong attractions to other women and begin to express these attractions, fall in love, and have sex, but not necessarily change their sexual orientation (Diamond, 2008). In Diamond's study, some women have the capacity to experience context-dependent changes in their pattern of attractions, desires, and behaviors (i.e., sexual fluidity). Her research challenges the historical notion that people's sexual orientation develops in adolescence, at which point it becomes stable. From this perspective, people who come out later in life have "always" been gay and were hiding it from themselves or others. However, the problem with this narrative is that it does not map onto many people's experiences, and it negates the real romantic and sexual feelings of people's past. For example, Diamond's research pointed out that some women who established long-term heterosexual relationships and had children may spontaneously fall in love with a woman later in life. Sometimes the change in attractions is lasting, and people may come to identify with a nonheterosexual sexual orientation, or sometimes the change in attractions was specific to the context. Researchers also believe that this context-dependent change is not under a person's control. For example, the women in Diamond's study reported that these changes felt surprising and unexpected, and they sometimes actively tried to resist the change. She found that two-thirds of the women changed their sexual labels at least once over that decade. They would sometimes say that they had two sexual expressions, lesbian and heterosexual (Diamond, 2008).

In another study, young women between the ages of 13 and 20 reported a sequence of attraction and sexual behavior that would begin with opposite-sex relationships with males, then shift to same-gender relationships with women over the course of a few years (Herdt & Boxer, 1993).

During the Diamond study, one important point was the direction of the sexual orientation change: At the start of the study, many women who started out as lesbian or bisexual in sexual attraction, sexual behavior, or sexual identity had changed to heterosexuality. This is consistent with a national population study by Laumann and colleagues (1994) that indicates how "a greater number of women found same-gender contact 'appealing' than indicated being attracted to women" (Diamond, 2008, p. 5). This evidence points to a trend that may allow for more sexual fluidity in women than men. This finding is also consistent with the fact that older lesbians have a fairly high level of prior heterosexual relationships with men, although the percentage appears to be decreasing, because lesbians can now more openly express their identities beginning in adolescence (Floyd & Bakeman, 2006). This evidence points to a trend that may allow for more sexual fluidity in women than men. However, recent research indicates that men also have the capacity for sexual fluidity and that gender differences in sexual fluidity depend on the time scale assessed (Diamond et al., 2017). Whatever the case, sexual fluidity among women definitely reveals how culture and gender and sexual expression are changing.

Queer and Questioning

When a young person says "it is cool to be queer," what does this statement mean? For older LGBTQ people, the term *queer* was historically offensive. With the advent of the LGBTQ movement and increasing change in how young people have grown more accepting and tolerant of sexual variation, a larger number of young people now use queer as an alternative to calling themselves gay, lesbian, bisexual, or straight. From the context of their expression of sexual attractions and identity labels, they may also be exploring or questioning their orientation (Herdt, 2000).

How did this notion evolve? Think about the dilemma of a boy who realizes that he would like to kiss another boy or even have sex with him, but he cannot accept that he is gay (Savin-Williams, 2005). If his family and friends perceive him to be heterosexual, he may try to hide his attractions because he doesn't want to be ostracized. He may not yet have thought about his sexual orientation. He may even be questioning just what his sexual orientation is—maybe he just wants to experiment with something. If he acts on these attractions, however, he may have to deal with the disapproval of some of his male and female peers, because they will regard his behavior as "queer" and stigmatize him (Gagnon, 2004). Here questioning suggests that someone wants to explore his or her sexual attractions and feelings for the same gender, without abandoning the social identity as being heterosexual or bisexual. It is important to understand how sexual orientation, sexual attractions, and gender conformity intersect in such a person's experience.

Early research stated that youths who engaged in same-gender sexual behavior were simply confused and in transition to heterosexuality. Subsequent research concluded something very different: The youths were not confused about their LGBTQ orientation. Rather, they were confused about how to express their same-gender attractions in a society defined by compulsory heterosexism (Herdt & Boxer, 1993).

People who are queer or questioning "or fluid" are also challenging how sexual attraction, sexual orientation, and gender go together (Cover, 2018; Kaufman & Powell, 2014). For example, more than half of all youth occasionally engage in sexual behaviors with the same sex, such as kissing or sexual intercourse, as found in a sample of about 20,000 youths from the public schools in Massachusetts and Minnesota. Yet, these individuals still identified themselves as heterosexual (Garofalo et al., 1999; Remafedi et al., 1992). Labels such as homoflexible, pseudo-bisexual, tri-sexual or plainly stating that "I love who I love" is sufficient as a sexual identity (Kaufman & Powell, 2014). One youth, who identifies as pansexual, stated that she likes "gender benders, the mixtures, the people that look like both boys and girls. Then it's a 'special surprise inside' when you discover them in a sexual situation" (Kaufman & Powell, 2014, p. 11). Even for mostly straight youth, the "heterosexual label and gender norms feel reductive, constraining, and outdated and unnecessary burdens imposed on heterosexist societal standards" (Kaufman & Powell, 2014, p. 13).

LGBTQ IDENTITY DISCRIMINATION AND STIGMA

Discrimination against LGBTQ people may profoundly shape the development and expression of their orientation in much the same way that racism affects how people of color grow up, develop self-awareness, and behave in their lives (Herek, 2004; Meyer, 1995). Many in society have an irrational fear and hatred of same-gender sexuality and LGBTQ individuals; this attitude can have a negative impact on the real-world experiences of LGBTQ individuals. The majority of LGBTQ people grow up having experienced harassment and discrimination in one form or another (Cianciotto & Cahill, 2010).

Accumulating research evidence, however, supports the idea that positive acceptance of sexual diversity makes a difference in how people feel about their lives and opportunities to develop sexual well-being (Diamond, 2008; Vrangalova & Savin-Williams, 2012). Until the U.S. Supreme Court struck down "sodomy" laws prohibiting sexual acts between individuals of the same gender in the landmark case of *Lawrence v. Texas* in 2003, homosexuality was

stigma
Extreme disapproval attached to someone who deviates from socially and culturally acceptable standards of behavior, turning the person into a social outcast.

sexual prejudice
Irrational hatred directed toward people because of their sexual orientation or sexual behavior.

homophobia
Irrational fear of or discrimination against same-gender sexuality or LGBTQIA+ individuals.

homonegativity
Subtle negative social perceptions and behaviors against LGBTQIA+ people or those suspected of same-gender sexuality.

minority stress
Chronic health effects of homophobia, such as high blood pressure and depression.

illegal in 23 states. The negative effects of these old laws on the lives of LGBTQ people is hard to calculate, but some believe that they have left a lifelong sense of silence, shame, fear, and stress (Meyer, 2007).

Stigma, which is a sign of all this social unacceptability, is a huge effect of this process for LGBTQ people. Stigma spoils a person's identity and turns him or her into a social outcast. Stigma influences people's health and sexual well-being because their family and friends may avoid them, and they may be deprived of basic services such as health care as a result (Epstein, 1999; Meyer et al., 2008). In fact, stigma is such a huge thing in some cultures that people will go to extreme lengths to avoid having their identity discredited by being associated with same-gender sexuality, as we have seen in the studies of MSM. The media have indirectly helped create this stigma for LGBTQ people by stereotyping (Badgett, 2009). Now, many media outlets are upsetting those stereotypes to foster more tolerant attitudes about LGBTQ people (Diamond, 2005; Gross, 2001). Some experts also believe that improving attitudes regarding same-gender marriage, especially among young people, are generally lifting up LGBTQ people (Badgett & Herman, 2011; Marzullo & Herdt, 2011). However, despite these positive changes, stigma, harassment, and discrimination remain all too common in the United States and similar countries (Aggleton & Parker, 2010; Badgett & Herman, 2011).

Sexual Prejudice, Homophobia, and Homonegativity

Sexual prejudice is the general intolerance and hostility directed toward people because of their sexual orientation or sexual behavior. Sexual prejudice, like racism, is learned during childhood and adolescence (Herek, 2004). It is also reinforced by major institutions of society, including well-known businesses, enforcement of laws, religious organizations and community influences, neighborhood cultures, family, and peers. Being taught such attitudes in the course of growing up affects the social and personal perception of and response toward LGBTQ people (Boswell, 1980; Herek, 2009).

Sexual prejudice directed toward LGBTQIA+ people or people perceived to be gay or lesbian is **homophobia**, the specific fear and hate projected toward same-gender sexuality in general and LGBTQ people in particular. Researchers have found that homophobia is a lot more common than previously known, and it has a lot more effects than previously known (Erzen, 2006; Herek, 2004; Meyer, Schwartz, & Frost, 2008). Carried to its extreme, homophobia may lead to aggression or even violence directed at LGBTQIA+ people, including cases of people who assaulted or murdered LGBTQ individuals. There are, however, more subtle forms of homophobia experienced in micro-settings, and in the negative treatment of people called **homonegativity**, the encompassing negative perceptions of people just because they are thought to be LGBTQIA+. These mild but hurtful forms of prejudice, as we have previously seen, occur across many situations in society, such as being less likely to be hired due to an implicit bias of gender presentation, or suspicion of same-gender relationships that leads to people being turned down for a loan to buy a house. Tragically, the truly horrible expressions of homophobia lead to everyday occurrences of robbery, rape, assault, and murder, sometimes even against people who were perceived to be LGBTQ but were actually straight (Rivers & D'Augelli, 2001). To think more about the issue of homophobia, see "Know Yourself: Understanding Internalized Homophobia."

Learning about sexual prejudice and internalizing homophobia can start early in life.
ZUMA Press/Newscom

Understanding Internalized Homophobia

Know Yourself

In some communities, homophobic attitudes may be part of regular sexual socialization, although these attitudes may be unintentionally or intentionally taught (Herek, 2004). While homophobia may be common in some communities today, **internalized homophobia**, which is a feeling that a person may absorb from societal hostility toward LGBTQ people, can motivate this behavior. If people grow up in a community that actively teaches homophobic prejudice, it would not be surprising if they internalized such hostile feelings or attitudes about homosexuality. For example, they may have learned that all homosexuals engage in childhood sexual abuse or carry the HIV/AIDS virus. It is really no different than learning negative stereotypes about someone's skin color or race.

Consider the following questions in terms of how you feel about homosexuality:

1. Do you believe gay men and lesbian women can influence others to become homosexual?
2. Do you think someone could influence you to change your sexual preference?
3. If you are a parent (straight or gay), how do you feel about having a gay child? (Consider this question even if you are not yet a parent but think that you might be one in the future.)
4. How do you think you would feel if you discovered that one of your parents, parent figures, or siblings were gay or lesbian?
5. Are there any jobs, positions, or professions that you think lesbian women or gay men should be barred from holding? If yes, which ones and why?
6. If someone you care about says to you, "I think I'm gay," would you suggest that person try to hide or resist the feeling or perhaps see a therapist?
7. Would you ever consider going to a gay or lesbian bar, social club, party, or march? If no, why?
8. Would you wear a button that says, "How dare you assume I'm heterosexual"?
9. Can you think of three positive aspects of being gay? Three negative things?
10. Have you ever laughed at a joke about being gay or lesbian or queer?

Reflecting on these questions and your answers can be helpful for your own experience and to society as a whole. Consider reading further about internalized homophobia in books and papers cited in this chapter. Consider going online to check organizations such as Advocates for Youth (advocatesforyouth.org) and Gay Straight Alliances (GSAs) (glsen.org). GSAs may be on high school or college campuses and may help young people to integrate their sexual orientation and help family and friends learn about minority sexual orientations (Herdt, Russell, Sweat, & Marzullo, 2006). Or consider visiting a LGBTQIA+ support group on your campus or in your city. These organizations can help challenge antigay attitudes and support the rights of LGBTQIA+ people.

Source: Adapted from Moses, A. E., & Hawkins Jr., R. O. (1986). *Counseling lesbian women and gay men: A lifeissues approach.* St. Louis, MO: Merrill.

Victims of homophobia and homonegativity face discrimination or are denied a job, military service, housing, or health care. They tend to develop feelings of distress, poor self-esteem, and alienation from society. As a consequence, their health and well-being may suffer greatly, a condition known as **minority stress**, associated with chronic physical and mental health stress and disease (Meyer, 1995; Meyer, Schwartz, & Frost, 2008). The chronic physical effects include high blood pressure, heart disease, and incidence of cancer, while the chronic mental health effects include depression, anxiety, and tendency toward

internalized homophobia
Negative stereotypes or beliefs about LGBTQIA+ people that a person may absorb from societal hostility toward LGBTQIA+ people.

WHAT'S ON YOUR MIND?

Q: *At Thanksgiving last year I was really upset when my uncle referred to gay people as "faggots" and claimed that they were dirty good-for-nothings who sexually abuse children. I was so shocked and angry at his tirade that I didn't know what to say. What's the best way to respond to someone in your family saying that?*

ANSWER: Your uncle may have grown up learning homophobic attitudes and falsehoods, such as the common one that all gay men sexually abuse children. If the topic should come up again, you could respectfully talk about sexual orientation using terminology from this class. You may even want to offer the names of some well-known people who are gay or lesbian and are doing great things for society—that may give your uncle reason to rethink his position.

suicidal thoughts. Some researchers suggest that prejudice against bisexual people, also known as biphobia, is even greater (Dodge et al., 2016).

Growing up in a homophobic society does not necessarily mean that people have to be homophobic; they may learn that sexual prejudice is unfair and irrational, and change their behavior to be tolerant. This is where cultural belief comes in. Once people meet or get to know someone who is gay or lesbian, their homophobic attitude may be challenged.

Bullying and Internalized Homophobia

Homophobia can also fuel aggressive antisocial behavior, especially bullying in the classroom, which in turn can lead to violence or extreme risk taking, such as daring individuals to do something against their will to prove they are not gay. Such was the situation that led a Rutgers University student named Tyler Clementi to commit suicide. Clementi's roommate Dhuran Ravi secretly videotaped his sexual interaction with a male friend and then broadcasted it through social media. Ravi was convicted of invading Clementi's privacy and was sentenced to 30 days in the county jail, 3 years of probation, and 300 hours of community service. See "Healthy Sexuality: Online Bullying: Cyberspace Is the New 'Bathroom Wall'" for tips about how to prevent cyberbullying.

Other tragic incidents connect bullying and internalized homophobia. Horrible shootings, such as one that occurred in 1999 at Columbine (Colorado) High School that took the lives of 12 people, have been linked to homophobia. The boys who opened fire and then killed themselves were often the victims of merciless bullying. These boys' extreme emotional reaction was to retaliate with guns against threats to their manhood, ultimately ending in suicide. Research shows that males who may become violent are most likely to be White and insecure about their sexual and gender expression, which establishes a link between compulsive heterosexuality, internalized homophobia, and violence (Kimmel & Mahler, 2003).

Internalized homophobia can also harm LGBTQ individuals, as they may turn to bullying and inflict harm on themselves. Most commonly the result of negative attitudes toward same-gender sexuality on the part of family and peers, internalized homophobia may stem from the fear that their family will reject them if they knew about their sexual orientation (Ryan, Huebern, Diaz, & Sanchez, 2009). Sometimes this may actually happen, but other times, families can be supportive when a child comes out (Herdt & Koff, 2000; LaSala, 2010).

Microaggressions are another, less overt and often unintentional or unconscious form of bullying and hostility. These behaviors and statements convey derogatory messages to a sexual minority group and have detrimental effects on their mental health. Microaggressions manifest in language such as calling

Tyler Clementi was a victim of sexual bullying by his Rutgers University roommate.
Splash News/Newscom

HEALTHY Sexuality

Online Bullying: Cyberspace Is the New "Bathroom Wall"

For decades, homophobic bullying has been a serious problem in many places, including schools, playgrounds, fraternity houses, military academies, and the armed services. Social media and technology have made cyberspace the new "bathroom wall" for microaggressions of writing cruel and often false statements. No one is immune from homonegativity or cyberbullying, and LGBTQIA+ people are especially vulnerable.

To help put a stop to cyberbullying, consider these tips:

Tips to prevent cyberbullying:

- Be careful to whom you provide your email address, cell phone number, etc. Do not friend people on social networking sites you do not know personally.
- Set privacy settings on social networking sites so only friends can see your information.
- Do not send anything on the Internet or cell phone that you would not want to be public. Remember that once you post something, it is out of your control.
- Be familiar with the policies in your school or workplace that relate to cyberbullying.

Tips for targets of cyberbullying:

- Preserve the evidence by saving the email, text message, chat history, or offensive website post.
- You might respond with one clear message saying you do not want to be contacted again by this person, but do not retaliate. Save your email to show you have clearly told the person to stop.
- Report the incident to the appropriate officials at your school or workplace.
- Use technology to prevent further attacks. Block the sender of emails or text messages or un-friend cyberbullies from your social networking accounts and remove them from IM buddy lists.
- Report offenders to the Internet service provider, cellular service provider, or website owner. Follow up if your complaint is not handled promptly.
- Report credible threats to the police.

Source: Sheri Bauman, University of Arizona (http:// uanews.org/node/33847, downloaded 4/10/12). Copyright © Sheri Bauman. Used with permission.

---

something "gay" in order to devalue, or propagating stereotypes, clichés, and jokes about LGBTQ people (Nadal, Whitman, Davis, Erazo, & Davidoff, 2016).

When people's ability to express their sexual orientation is stunted by fear of rejection by religion or family, stigma, bullying, or discrimination, their mental distress and anxiety may increase significantly (Barker, Herdt, & DeVries, 2006; Regnerus, 2007). They may engage in self-destructive behaviors, such as drug use, risky sex, or suicide (Paul et al., 2002), and these effects may extend into midlife and aging for LGBTQ people (DeVries & Herdt, 2012).

Public health officials have long feared that stigma, internalized homophobia, and family exclusion may lead to a higher suicide rate among LGBTQ people, compared to heterosexuals, especially among teens (Makadon et al., 2008). You can read more about this risk of suicide in "Research and Sexual Well-Being: Gay and Lesbian Suicide Risk—The Tragic Cost of Internalized Homophobia."

Hate Crimes

The most severe form of homophobia can lead to **hate crimes**, where people inflict violence on LGBTQ men and women. It is tempting to think that hate crimes are rare, but sadly they are all too common (Herek, Gillis, Cogan, & Glunt, 1997). Studies reveal that between one-quarter

hate crime
An act of aggression or hatred targeted toward someone because of religion, race, or sexual orientation.

RESEARCH and Sexual Well-Being

Gay and Lesbian Suicide Risk—The Tragic Cost of Internalized Homophobia

Suicide risk is one of the great tragedies of internalized homophobia in our society, but it is a lot less well known among LGBTQ people. However, researchers have gradually shown how LGBTQ people have higher rates of suicide compared to the general population (Paul et al., 2002). According to one national study, at least 15% of LGBTQ youth thought about suicide (Russell & Joyner, 2001). The consensus today is that there is a greater suicide risk as a result of being LGBTQ and dealing with the stressors that society imposes. Today the Trevor Project (2019) states that suicide is the second leading cause of death among LGBTQ youth ages 10 to 24.

A comprehensive analysis of 214,344 heterosexual and 11,971 nonheterosexual people in hundreds of studies between 1966 and 2005 found that gay people are at a higher risk of mental disorders, thoughts of suicide, drug misuse, and deliberate self-harm than heterosexuals (King et al., 2008). Other research has consistently shown that gay men are many times more likely to attempt suicide in the military than their heterosexual military peers (Herrell et al., 1999).

Suicide is a difficult problem to study when it involves teenagers who are in a sexual orientation minority (Gibson, 1989; Herdt & Boxer, 1993). One reason is that researchers may find it hard to correlate sexual orientation and suicides or suicide attempts accurately because the family may either hide the sexual orientation of a family member or hide that person's suicide attempt to avoid social stigma. Additionally, more people consider committing suicide than attempt it (American Academy of Pediatrics, 2001), and those who consider it may never report it. Researchers do find, though, that among LGBTQ people, including different races, genders, and social classes, there appears to be a greater incidence of suicide attempts (King et al., 2008; Paul et al., 2002).

What contributes to such a high suicide risk among gay men and lesbian women? Perhaps the single most important factor has to do with being bullied or otherwise victimized. Many studies have shown that gay and lesbian people are assaulted and bullied, especially in schools (Rivers & D'Augelli, 2001). Many research studies have linked this bullying to risk behaviors, especially suicide (D'Augelli, Hershberger, & Pilkington, 1998; Herdt & Boxer, 1993; Rivers & D'Augelli, 2001). The suicide of Tyler Clementi because of cyberbullying is, sadly, one such example.

In a nonrandom study of 388 subjects, some surprising correlations between sexual orientation and suicide were discovered (Meyer, 2007). These New York residents identified themselves as lesbian, gay, or bisexual; male or female; and Black, White, or Latino. Of this sample, 44% were aged 18–29, 44% were 30–44, and 12% were 45–59. Researchers studied mental health disorders such as depression and discovered that younger LGBTQ people have fewer mental health disorders than older ones. The researchers theorized that the reason is that older LGBTQ people suffer from the effects of discrimination over a longer period than the younger people (DeVries & Herdt, 2012). They also hypothesized that as society has become more liberal and attitudes have become more positive, there is less stigma and stress for younger White people. Also, they found that more Blacks and Latinos than Whites have a history of attempting suicide. This may result in a sense of hopelessness and lack of a future correlated with internalized homophobia in certain communities where homophobia is more open and the fear of family rejection is greater (Ryan et al., 2009).

Having family members and loved ones who really care about someone regardless of their orientation can make all the difference in the world and can give young people hope that they can be successful in life and need not consider suicide as an option (Herdt & Koff, 2000). They can give young people hope and courage to deal with daily challenges that may include harassment, bullying, and rejection due to their sexual orientation (Herdt, 2001; Herek, 2004; LaSala, 2010; Savin-Williams, 2005).

and one-half of LGBTQ individuals have been threatened or physically attacked because of their sexual orientation. Gay men are more likely to be victimized than gay/lesbian women (22%) and bisexual men and women (20%), with 4–5% experiencing violence in the past year (Huebner, Rebchook, & Kegeles, 2004; Pew Research Center, 2013). While some aspects of LGBTQ life are improving, such as the positive role models on television, hate crimes have actually increased in some parts of the United States, especially in classroom settings (Cianciotto & Cahill, 2010). As recently as 2003, 55% of Americans continued to view gay sex as a sin, whereas straight sex is seen more as a blessing (Pew Foundation, 2003).

Hate crimes are not uniformly distributed across the United States, either. In more rural or conservative areas, their very real threat keeps LGBTQ people hidden for fear they will be harassed, assaulted, raped, or even murdered. One of the most tragic hate crimes occurred in November 1998, when a young gay man, Matthew Shepard, left a bar in Laramie, Wyoming. Two men robbed, pistol whipped, and crucified him; they literally hung him up on a barbwire fence in the form of a crucifixion. Eighteen hours later the person who cut him down, at first glance, believed that his body was a scarecrow. Matthew's beating destroyed his brain, and the only clear areas on his face were streaks where his tears had washed away the bloodstains. He died a few hours after being found. So terrible was the brutality that even the murderers' own girlfriends testified against them. One of them was alleged to be bisexual and in deep denial of his sexual attraction to homosexual men such as Matthew. The two young men who murdered him were found guilty of premeditated crimes; one was sentenced to life in prison and the other was sentenced to death. They were not, however, convicted of a hate crime, which became a recognized category of crime as a result of Matthew's murder. In fact, in 2009, Congress passed the Matthew Shepard and James Byrd, Jr., Hate Crimes Prevention Act to help protect people from hate crimes that are based on sexual orientation, gender, or disability. (This law expanded an earlier one that applied to attacks based on race, religion, or national origin.) *The Laramie Project,* both a film and a play, shows how this brutal hate crime changed attitudes of homophobia in a small conservative town. See Figure 10.3 that shows the incidence of hate crimes in the major cities of the United States and how in recent years the incidence of such crimes has actually gone up.

Matthew Shepard of Wyoming was killed in a hate crime that changed the law and some people's minds about LGBTQ people.
Patsy Lynch/Shutterstock

Figure 10.3

Incidence of hate crimes in major cities of the U.S. is still common.
Source: FBI

COMING OUT AND SEXUAL WELL-BEING

After reading about heterosexism, sexual prejudice, and internalized homophobia, you may better understand the compromises that some people need to make just to survive. Integrating sexuality and self-awareness in the context of social disapproval can be a difficult task for people. Their fear, shame, and silence may stop them dead in their tracks. The truth is that being open and out with a nonheterosexual sexual orientation can be a frightening, exciting, and momentous step (Dodge, et al, 2016; LaSala, 2010).

Social Acceptance and Being Out

In 2015, the United States Supreme Court ruled that same-gender marriage was legal, thus ending decades of legal argument about whether LGBTQ individuals may marry, have a home together, raise families, and pursue their lives with dignity and respect. Since that time, polls indicate that 62% of the public support same-gender marriage rights (Pew Foundation, 2017). This is a generational change of huge proportions. Such changes have made it possible for young people growing up now to imagine being socially accepted and being out in ways impossible not so long ago.

In spite of much progress surrounding the human rights and sexual orientation rights of LGBTQ people in the United States, stigma, discrimination, bullying, violence, and outright expulsion continue to occur in schools. Also, as we have seen, online bullying is a very serious problem for LGBTQ youth (Pascoe, 2011). Bullying and sexual orientation–related hate crimes might begin early in childhood and continue into college. Consider the following conversation reported by a parent of a young child in a public school (Safe Schools Coalition, 1999):

"Daddy, do you know what a 'faggot' is?"

"Why do you ask?"

"(My friend) called me one at recess."

One meta-study examined hundreds of school studies in the United States and discovered that violation of sexual orientation rights continues today. The 2007 National School Climate Survey of 6,209 LGBT youths found that 86% were verbally harassed due to their sexual orientation and 67% were bullied, harassed, or assaulted because of their gender identity expression. Researchers also found that when principals, teachers, parents, and community members speak out in support of LGBTQ people in the classroom, things get better (Cianciotto & Cahill, 2010).

WHAT'S ON YOUR MIND?

Q: My gay partner is from Mexico. He is not as comfortable as I am in identifying as gay—in fact, he sometimes tells people that we are "friends" and it really hurts me. Is this problem from him or his family or what?

ANSWER: Many cultures have very traditional values when it comes to expressing sexual orientation. Also, family and faith figure prominently in how people think about themselves. Though your partner may live in the United States, he may be more comfortable with what he learned as a child in Mexico. See if you two can discuss what being gay or closeted is like where he grew up. Help him understand your need to be true to your own self and cultural background. Also, listen as he expresses his needs and cultural background, because he may not be at the same place as you in expressing his orientation, and you can show respect for his views in this way. A relationship is about compromise, and so we hope these suggestions help you find one.

Does social acceptance increase the likelihood that people will openly express their sexual orientation? The answer from decades of research is clearly yes. Additionally, research suggests that when we know someone who is openly gay or lesbian, our positive regard for gay men and lesbian women increases (Cianciotto & Cahill, 2010; Herek, 2004; Meyer et al., 2008). This reaction makes sense: It is easier for people to project their fears and hates onto an unknown person who is unlike oneself. In fact, one study found that 18% of students who spoke regularly with people who are gay were comfortable around them, while 61% of students who lacked the opportunity to interact with gays were nervous in their company (Lance, 1987). These findings suggest that the positive effect of being out is "greater when the exchange is between people who share greater emotional closeness" (Swank, Faulkner, & Hesterberg, 2008, p. 261).

Consider this study on being out. Researchers asked openly gay and lesbian adolescents, who averaged about 18 years old, about the future. They could chart a future only to about age 33 with goals, such as going to college, serving in the military, getting a job, and living with an intimate partner. By contrast, their same-aged straight peers could project their own futures up to age 55, listing life goals that included college, career, plus being married and having children, and becoming grandparents (Herdt & Boxer, 1993; Herdt & Koff, 2000). The researchers speculated that this 22-year difference resulted from stigma, discrimination, and the lack of positive role models to help inspire young gay and lesbian people. A subsequent study about LGBTQ youth today confirms that they have a greater sense of a future, and some of that feeling of well-being comes from the possibility of same-gender marriage in the United States (Marzullo & Herdt, 2011).

Polls reveal how important it is for LGBTQ people to actually be visible and out in society to increase social acceptance (Herek, 2004, 2009). One survey was conducted with a representative national sample of more than 2,100 adults who were identified as heterosexual (Herek, 2009). Along with questions about the nature and extent of their personal relationships with lesbian and gay individuals, people were surveyed about general feelings toward gay men and lesbian women, their comfort or discomfort level around both, and their general attitudes toward them. The researcher found that many people did not know about the impact of stigma and discrimination on the lives of gay and lesbian people. This study underlines the importance of LGBTQ people having conversations with their heterosexual friends and family about their lives and issues such as being denied jobs, health insurance, or marriage.

Being out, then, may help people with nonnormative sexual orientations to be socially accepted. Much as people may want to be out and are encouraged to do so by accepting and tolerant peers, parents, and teachers, that first step can be scary and hard to take, and it requires all the courage and resources they can muster.

Being Out—Steps Toward Well-Being

Being out, in this context, means disclosing a sexual orientation to the people who truly matter, whether that be friends and family, peers or grandparents, a favorite teacher, and others. Being out is not an "all or nothing" gamble with life. The process is a bit different

DID YOU KNOW

To give hope and respect to young LGBTQ people, noted gay writer Dan Savage created an important online project, titled It Gets Better. The project allows hundreds of thousands of people to post their personal testimonies in support of these identity rights and has enlisted more than a half million people online to pledge support of LGBTQ rights. Celebrities have also uploaded many videos on YouTube, ranging from politicians such as Secretary of State Hillary Clinton and President Obama, to movie stars, clergy, members of the military, and many ordinary people. You can also view these at http://www.itgetsbetter.org/.

Hip-hop artist Frank Ocean came out in 2012. His announcement was significant because many hip-hop and rap lyrics express homophobic sentiments, and yet a number of Ocean's fellow artists supported his decision to come out.
FilmMagic/Getty Images

COMMUNICATION Matters

Coming Out

What are steps that people can take to communicate to others about their sexual orientation? We encourage you to be cautious and think about your safety if you decide to come out. Consider these tips while you are deciding to come out:

- Use the Internet to find resources that are available in your area and to find websites that are helpful.
- Consider talking through issues by first confiding in a dear friend or trusted family member.
- If you use online resources to start the process of coming out, be cautious about revealing your identity if you do not want to be out completely.
- Consider what information you will be comfortable sharing with other people.
- Keep a sexual diary to reflect on your experience regularly and to practice what you are going to say to let people know about yourself.
- Think about what might be the best time and place to tell others about your orientation.
- Talk to others who have come out to their family members before coming out to your own.
- Go to a campus counseling center or community agency that offers ethical and anonymous psychological services if you are distressed.

As you move forward in the process of telling others about your sexual orientation, every day ask yourself questions similar to these:

- Am I feeling good about myself? Are these communications helping or upsetting me? How am I coping with all the emotion?
- How do I feel about my own self-awareness and body today?
- Am I protecting myself from harm, such as bullying or homophobia?
- Am I sexually protecting myself from getting or passing on an STI?

If others are pressuring you to take a course of action, listen to your own heart and mind about what you think is best for you; be guided by your own sense of what is right and true for you. Seek help and support from the people who really care about you. Remember to keep your own best interest uppermost in your mind by staying true to yourself.

---

depending on whether someone is a young teen or a young adult, as being younger may require thinking about the impact of being out and living at home or being out at school (Cianciotto & Cahill, 2010). This is why some youth today prefer to engage in their first sexual explorations anonymously online, as discussed in Chapter 3. It can be a gradual process, set up on a time schedule according to people's own needs. In fact, studies confirm that the context, time, and the people to whom others talk with about coming out are critical issues to consider in making the experience comfortable and successful (Herdt & Koff, 2000; LaSala, 2010).

One way to begin this process may be to gather support materials from organizations such as online projects like It Gets Better, GSAs, LBGTQ centers on campuses and in communities, and student counseling centers. The organization Parents, Families, and Friends of Lesbians and Gays (PFLAG) often counsels people to take their time in expressing sexual orientation. Online organizations can also be helpful. For example, websites such as YouthResource.com and AdvocatesforYouth.org offer quality, ethical information about being open and out. (The Spanish language website for AdvocatesforYouth.org is AmbienteJoven.org.) Some people may begin this process of coming out online where they can create a virtual community of support. To read more about the process of coming out, see "Communication Matters: Coming Out."

Dignity and respect are essential to the whole process of being out. Some individuals who are unsure of their orientation, and are not sure enough of the support of their friends and family, may want to postpone this process or think about who in the context of their culture they can trust in and come out to. They may not even feel comfortable going to an LGBTQ support organization. They may want to wait until they are older and have more independence from family, or they may want to have more social support from peers and friends. Research shows that a number of people postpone being out until they have entered college (Savin-Williams, 2005). Some people of color may postpone their sexual orientation expression until later because of social pressures in their communities (Munoz-Laboy, 2008). Today, people's abilities to integrate their sexuality into their self-awareness vary by individual, race, family of origin, faith, social class, and geographic region (Cianciotto & Cahill, 2010; Teunis, 2006).

LGBTQ Family Formation

Historically, LGBTQ people were forced to live in secretive ways that did not allow them to love each other or even to treat other gay men or lesbian women with dignity, respect, or equality (D'Emilio, 1998). In fact, until sometime in the 1960s, gay men felt that they could only love or have sex with heterosexual men, not other gay men, and the same was true for lesbian women. Today, it is possible to find love and to create family with other LGBTQ people. Forming their own family is now considered an act of sexual orientation expression for many people in the world (Badgett, 2009; LaSala, 2010). Research reveals that when LGBTQ people can integrate sexual orientation into their families and familial relationships, they experience a greater likelihood of sexual well-being (Badgett & Herman, 2011; Herdt & Koff, 2000; Ryan et al., 2009). Without doubt the landmark Supreme Court ruling (*Obergefell v. Hodges*) has strongly influenced attitudes in this area in the support of same-gender marriage rights.

However, this dramatic and historic change has not automatically translated into acceptance of LGBTQ families. With many LGBTQ people being rejected by their biological families, they invented the idea of creating a "family of choice" (LaSala, 2010). A **family of choice** is composed of intimate partners or spouses, close friends, and neighbors and other loved ones who feel so close to each other that they celebrate holidays and birthdays together as if they were a biological family (Barker et al., 2006). Like other positive changes regarding LGBTQ people, the concept of family of choice draws attention to the many creative forms of family occurring within our society (Badgett & Herman, 2011; LaSala, 2010; Lewin, 1999). This includes families headed by lesbian mothers or by gay fathers and includes adopted children or biological children (Badgett, 2009).

In the 1990s a new trend began that some call the lesbian "baby boom." At that time lesbian couples began to form families and to rear children in ways that challenged social norms (Badgett & Herman, 2011; Lewin, 1999). Some couples chose adoption and others chose to have their own biological offspring through artificial insemination. Social acceptance of lesbian families has grown since then, but support structures that may include helpful neighbors and babysitters are not the same as they are for heterosexual couples (Stein, 2001). Today, however, lesbian and gay couples rear children, pay taxes, and grapple with the same basic issues that straight couples face (Badgett & Herman, 2011).

While it is difficult to pin point the exact number of gay and lesbian parents due to the fact that some people do not disclose sexual orientation, the best research reveals a surprisingly large number. According to UCLA's Williams' Institute, as many as 3.7 million U.S. children under age 18 may have a lesbian, gay, bisexual or transgender parent. Today, 200,000 or more children are being raised by couples (Gates, 2015). You can read more about the issue of whether LGBTQ people should be parents in "Controversies in Sexuality: Can Same-Sex Couples Raise Well-Adjusted Children?"

family of choice
A group composed of those intimate partners or legally married spouses, close friends, and neighbors who feel so close to each other that they celebrate holidays and birthdays.

Gay parents today
Jon Kopaloff/FilmMagic/Getty Images

CONTROVERSIES in Sexuality

Can Same-Sex Couples Raise Well-Adjusted Children?

Some political and social commentators believe that people can learn to be gay, and so allowing gay parents to raise children can make them gay (Irvine, 2002; Stacey & Biblarz, 2001). For example, in 2008 when voters in California were to vote about legalizing same-sex marriage, a television commercial strongly hinted that young children would "learn" to be gay if same-sex marriage was made legal. No empirical evidence supports the notion that sexual attractions can be taught or learned in this way (Cianciotto & Cahill, 2010). In fact, researchers have found that this belief that people can teach others to be gay is a form of prejudice against sexual minorities (Herek, 2004). The 2015 Supreme Court ruling that made same-gender marriage legal in all states and territories is probably influencing these attitudes in a positive direction, but the prejudice remains in traditional areas.

One meta-analysis of 21 studies of LGBTQ parents did show small differences between straight and gay parenting, but these differences appear to be generally positive in nature, not negative (Stacey & Biblarz, 2001). For example, daughters of lesbian couples aspire to occupations more traditionally filled by men compared to their heterosexual peers (Stacey & Biblarz, 2001). The researchers also found gender differences in the behavior of the offspring of gay and lesbian families. Boys raised by lesbian mothers, for example, tended to be less assertive than traditionally raised males. There was, however, no statistical difference showing that children are more likely to be gay, lesbian, bisexual, or transgender.

Another study in the Netherlands looked at 100 heterosexual couples and 100 lesbian couples with children ages 4 to 8 who were raised by these couples since birth (Bos, van Balen, & van den Boom, 2007). Data were collected using questionnaires, observations, and a diary of activities to understand if there were differences in child adjustment, parental characteristics, and child rearing. The researchers found that lesbian mothers who were not the biological mothers differ from heterosexual fathers in certain parental characteristics: The mothers experienced more satisfaction with their partner as a co-parent and in child rearing; they also expressed more parental concern and less power assertion over the child. Another group of researchers confirmed these patterns and found that 17-year-olds raised from birth by lesbian mothers were as happy as their peers, and the mothers' quality of life was equal to or better than matched heterosexual parents (van Gelderen, Bos, Gartrell, Hermanns, & Perrin, 2012).

In general, the American Academy of Child and Adolescent Psychiatry (AACAP, 2011) has found that children who have LGBTQ parents:

- Are not more likely to be gay than children with heterosexual parents.
- Are not more likely to be sexually abused.
- Do not show differences in whether they think of themselves as male or female (gender identity).
- Do not show differences in their male and female behaviors (gender role behavior).

In simple terms, people do not learn to be LGBTQ, any more than they learn to be straight.

Given all of this research, you might ask yourself what controversy remains? The key issue is what the long-term effects will be on these children. We simply do not know yet how the children will do when they are grown adults. This is an example of how research can help you form an opinion and increase your sexual literacy. Do you believe that LGBTQ parents are effective in raising well-adjusted children, and have each child's well-being in mind?

Yes:

- The meta-study suggests that while there are some gender differences with the LGBTQ offspring, overall the children seem to do pretty well.
- LGBTQ families don't seem to produce more sexual minority children compared to other heterosexual families—that seems to be a myth.
- The Dutch study showed that the children of the LGBTQ families are as happy as the children of the straight families (van Gelderen, Bos, Gartrell, Hermanns, & Perrin, 2012).
- Even if the girls do have more nontraditional occupations when they grow up from the lesbian households, so what? That could be a positive thing.

No:

- The meta-analysis did find small differences in gender, such as boys raised by mothers who are lesbian being somewhat less masculine, and that could affect them when they are adults.

- Children of LGBTQ parents may get teased or bullied in school, which could be hurtful.
- Women entering occupations that are more traditionally filled by men such as firefighters or police officers suggest that their lesbian mothers may be less effective in terms of traditional parental styles.
- We just don't know yet what the long-term effects of LGBTQ parents will be on their children's adjustment.

What's Your Perspective?

1. Do you believe that LGBTQ parents can be effective in raising their offspring? Why or why not?
2. Are the gender differences in offspring of LGBTQ parents a positive or negative influence? Please explain your answer.
3. If you know any children of LGBTQ people, what is your view of their family compared to families with heterosexual parents?

COMING OUT, SEXUAL WELL-BEING, AND SEXUAL RIGHTS

"Gay rights are human rights, and human rights are gay rights." This is how the then Secretary of State Hillary Clinton changed the U.S. government policy in a speech to the United Nations in 2011. By 2015, the president of the United States, Barack Obama, would go further to include sexual orientations and rights: "As Americans, we respect human dignity," he said. "That's why we defend free speech, and advocate for political prisoners, and condemn the persecution of women, or religious minorities, or people who are lesbian, gay, bisexual, or transgender."

Globally, a sea change is occurring with new laws and policies about sexual rights, but the change confronts important political resistance in corners of the world, as well as in the United States. The idea of achieving sexual well-being for all sexual minorities is at the heart of the World Health Organization's definition of sexual health. This has provided growing support for LGBTQIA+ human rights by the United Nations and many countries, including the United States. However, as we have seen, more than 75 countries still define same-gender sexuality as illegal, and some impose extreme punishments on LGBTQIA+ individuals.

Paradoxically, the tragedy of the HIV/AIDS epidemic has played a huge role in this positive change over the past 25 years (Correa, Petchesky, & Parker, 2008; Epstein, 1999; Herdt, 2010a). In the mid-1980s, when the AIDS epidemic became visible, gay men had no rights. In fact, tens of thousands of men died because people in politics and the medical profession did little to prevent it (Aggleton & Parker, 2003; Diaz, 1998; Herdt, 2009b; Teunis, 2006). But because of these deaths over the years, anti-gay attitudes in medicine, science, religion, and society at large began to decline. Likewise, as LGBTQIA+ civil rights increased and provided some new protections, the AIDS epidemic began to recede, and people's lives were saved (Epstein, 1999; Levine, Nardi, & Gagnon, 1997). Now, as gay rights expand globally, there is a greater chance that effective HIV policies will extend to health and sexual well-being for all people (Aggleton & Parker, 2010).

Many places still have policies that oppose the rights of LGBTQIA+ people or criminalize them. Many African countries, for example, not only do not offer gay civil rights, they also have extremely negative laws against LGBTQIA+ people. In fact, 38 out of 53 African countries criminalize same-gender sexuality, some with the death sentence, and prominent gay

President Obama endorses sexual orientation as a human right, 2015.
VASILIS VERVERIDIS/123RF

activists have been murdered in eastern and southern Africa for being open about or supporting the rights of LGBTQIA+ people to live with dignity, marry, or have children. People are still being executed for same-gender sexual behavior, and others arrested and imprisoned, from Egypt to Nigeria to Zimbabwe and Saudi Arabia. In Malawi, for example, two gay men were imprisoned for declaring their love for each other in a marriage.

While things are improving globally, these abuses are not unique, as we have seen repeatedly in this chapter. Even in the United States and Western European countries, where LGBTQIA+ rights are visible and growing, sexual prejudice, suspicion, stigma, and homophobia exist. Unfortunately, LGBTQ rights have been challenged in more recent years, as sexually conservative policies and political appointments of the Donald Trump administration have come into play. These negative actions include efforts to reverse healthcare protection for transgender people, a ban on trans people serving in the military, and elimination of protections of trans people in certain businesses.

As President Obama affirmed, democracies should support the rights and dignity of all people, including LGBTQIA+. Then people can work together on issues rather than working against one another.

Chapter Review

SUMMARY

Understanding Sexual Orientation

- There is a diverse range of sexual orientations and gender identities in the United States today: lesbian, gay, bisexual, transgender, queer, questioning, intersex, asexual, and others (LGBTQIA+).
- Sexual orientation is a person's sexual or romantic attractions for people of the same or opposite sex, or for people of both sexes.
- A gap can exist between attraction and behavior for some individuals when it comes to sexual expression.
- Sexual socialization and learning may influence the expression of romantic and sexual attractions in many cultures.
- Four main sources explain the development of sexual orientation: genetic, prenatal, postnatal, and interactive.
- Compulsory heterosexuality is the condition of being socially compelled to have sexual relationships with the other gender, be married and have children, regardless of sexual orientation.
- Sexual individuality is a factor in the expression of variations in sexual orientation.

Variations in Sexual Orientation Across Time and Cultures

- Same-gender variations occur across cultures through age differences, gender differences, and social role differences.
- There is a difference between engaging in same-gender behavior and having a same-gender orientation; being openly LGBTQ is relatively recent in history.
- Sexual identity was formulated in the late 19th century as a form of sexual individuality to support social and political rights for people.
- Bisexuality is attraction to both genders; it has been a controversial orientation historically, and culturally is disregarded in society in the United States.
- Men who have sex with other men (MSM) may live in societies that require heterosexual marriage and make it very hard to come out or to express their sexual or romantic attractions for other men.

- "Being on the down low" (BODL) may involve African American married men having secretive sex with other men.
- Sexual fluidity appears to occur among women more frequently than among men.
- Individuals who question their sexual position in society refer to themselves as queer and questioning.

LGBTQ Identity Discrimination and Stigma

- Sexual prejudice is the form of disapproval related to sexual orientation.
- Homophobia is the fear and hatred of LGBTQIA+ individuals. Homonegativity is a subtler form of prejudice toward LGBTQIA+ people.
- Bullying in the context of sexual orientation can have terrible consequences, including suicide for LGBTQIA+ people.
- Internalized homophobia is a feeling that a person may absorb from society's hostility toward LGBTQIA+ people.
- Minority stress, resulting from long-term stigma and discrimination, creates negative physical and mental health effects, such as high blood pressure, depression, suicide, and shortened life.

Coming Out and Sexual Well-Being

- People may express their sexual orientation in a variety of ways and live openly with dignity and respect.
- Being out and finding social acceptance in community can increase one's self-esteem and life satisfaction.
- Pressures from culture, parents, and peers may restrain some people from coming out or being open until later in life.
- In the United States, large cities offer the most supportive environment for open expression of sexual orientation.

Coming Out, Sexual Well-Being, and Sexual Rights

- Recognition by the United Nations that LGBTQIA+ rights are human rights is a measure of progress for LGBTQIA+ individuals throughout the world.
- However, sexual prejudice and homophobia still exist, and in some parts of the world, such as certain African countries, LGBTQIA+ individuals are still jailed or even executed.

What's Your Position?

1. **How did you come to realize your sexual orientation?**
   - What do your best friends think of your sexual orientation?
   - Are people born with a sexual orientation, or can they learn it?
   - Have you thought about being gay, lesbian, bisexual, or transgender?
   - If you are currently questioning your sexual orientation, what questions are you asking yourself? If you are not questioning your own, is anyone you know questioning his or hers?

2. **What has culture taught you about different sexual orientations?**
   - What is your position about sexual orientation, and how is it similar to or different from that of your culture?
   - How do you reconcile any messages you may have been taught about someone being gay when you were younger with your current position?
   - Have you ever wondered if one of your friends is gay or lesbian? How did you respond?
   - What is your position about sexual orientation being learned or changed?

3. **Have you ever experienced or witnessed homophobia?**
   - Has anyone ever said you were gay or a fag or queer?
   - What was it like for you to be at school with your sexuality?

4. **Do you have a view about sexual orientation as a human right?**
   - Should people have the dignity and right to express their sexuality even when it goes against the sexual norm of their culture? Why or why not?

Design elements: Controversies in Sexuality: HBRH/Shutterstock; Research and Sexual Well Being: verity jane smith/Getty Images; Healthy Sexuality: Sergey Furtaev/Shutterstock; Communication Matters: PeopleImages/Getty Images; Know Yourself: Plush Studios/Blend Images LLC; What's Your Position: Luis Molinero/Shutterstock; Healthy Sexuality: A. Minde/PhotoAlto; Did You Know icon: McGraw-Hill Education; Page corner icon: McGraw-Hill Education.

Sexuality in Childhood and Adolescence

11

Sexual Development in Childhood and Adolescence
- Describe the role of the family in teaching children about sexuality.
- Compare normative and nonnormative sexual behaviors of children and adolescents.

Sexuality in Childhood
- Recall at what point in the life span we humans are considered to be sexual.
- Describe the common sexual behaviors of children and their role in healthy sexual development.

Sexuality in Adolescence
- Describe the common sexual curiosities, interests, and behaviors of adolescence.
- Identify and describe the processes of puberty for both boys and girls.

Sexuality in Context: The Role of Institutions
- Describe the major sources of sexual socialization for children and explain how each of them influences an individual's sexual development.
- Identify the best programs available for sex education in schools.

Young People's Rights and Sexual Well-Being
- Evaluate how to protect young people's well-being while protecting their right to have sexual relationships.

● **Learning**
● **Objectives**

Jupiterimages/Stockbyte/Getty Images

Developing Your Position

1. At what age do you believe we become sexual beings?
2. What role do parents play in developing a positive sexual identity in children and adolescents?
3. How were you taught about sexuality early in your life?
4. What was your pubertal development like?

Self, Society, and Culture: Children Are Sexual Beings, Too

Several years ago I (Nicole) had the chance to help dear friends with their then 18-month-old daughter. Much to their chagrin, they noticed that their daughter loved to touch her genital region when she was naked. Knowing that I teach human sexuality, they asked me how to "deal" with her behavior. I assured them that this behavior was normal—their daughter had simply discovered that touching this area of her body made her feel really good. I encouraged them to refrain from punishing this behavior or labeling it a "no-no." To do that would instill in this child the idea that parts of her body were off-limits to her.

We often do not realize how powerful our early messages can be for our kids. To help children develop a healthy view of their own bodies and an age-appropriate understanding of their sexuality, we have to begin looking at sexual development in new ways. Instead of classifying childhood sexual behaviors as bad or inappropriate, we need to accept the fact that children are sexual beings, just like adults. Our children's healthy sexual development relies on how comfortable we adults are with our own sexuality and our own level of sexual literacy. These factors may then translate into how we communicate positive messages about sexuality to children from the start.

As you read this chapter, you may reflect upon your own sexual development up to this point and look forward to the role that you might take one day as a parent, aunt, uncle, godparent, or friend. This is the challenge and promise of becoming sexually literate.

SEXUAL DEVELOPMENT IN CHILDHOOD AND ADOLESCENCE

It is no secret that many people are uncomfortable talking about young people's sexuality. The truth is, our culture teaches children about gender, and adolescents about sex, because that is what feels safer or more comfortable to adults. Our culture believes that children need to learn gender roles, boundaries, and rules—but not sex—because they are not ready for that. Puberty is often the milestone that many people believe is necessary to achieve before the discussion of sexuality should begin. **Puberty** is a period of rapid bodily and sexual maturation that occurs mainly in early adolescence. After puberty, which may be long after some young people have started exploring their sexuality in behaviors, parents and caretakers then

puberty
A period of rapid bodily and sexual maturation that occurs mainly in early adolescence.

turn their attention to teaching sexuality education, but it is often too little and too late. Perhaps this is because our culture continues to treat young people as if they have no sexual interest and experience or their sexuality is dangerous to themselves, their family, and society. The real risks to young people, old and new, don't really get the attention they deserve.

In our view, nothing is more important than finding a positive, constructive way to help young people understand their own sexual well-being and how it changes as they mature. Research suggests that it is time to provide new models that go beyond risk and danger to include pleasure, self-affirmation, and well-being in childhood and adolescence (Kirby, 2008; Santelli et al., 2006; Tolman & Diamond, 2002). Parents and families want to do their best to protect young people from danger such as sexual predation, but we should not go so far as to threaten young people's development to such an extent that they are unable to truly enjoy their sexual relationships in life. This is where resilience comes in. **Resilience** is the process that allows individuals to grow and thrive in physical and mental health in spite of the risk and challenges they encounter. Children and adolescents are amazingly resilient, and it's important to help people understand how to encourage and support resilience and sexual well-being in youth.

Children watch and imitate their parents closely. By providing positive examples, parents can teach children about healthy sexuality.
Ty Milford/Getty Images

resilience
The process that allows individuals to grow and thrive in physical and mental health in spite of the risk and challenges they encounter.

In this chapter, we discuss sexuality and sexual development over the first 18 years of the life cycle, during childhood and adolescence. In the next chapter, we discover the changes that occur in sexuality during adulthood and the aging process.

Biology, Family, and Culture

What reaction do you have when you hear the words *sexuality* and *childhood* together? Your reaction may be that these things just don't belong together—with good reason. Our culture today largely avoids coupling the topics of sexuality and childhood. When they do come together, it is often shocking, as seen in stories about sexual abuse. The reality is that the discussion about children and sexuality is seldom positive (Irvine, 2002). Historically and in modern times, childhood sexuality has long been a challenge to sexual science, which has found that cultures vary greatly in whether they approve or disapprove of childhood sexual play among peers (Ford & Beach, 1951; Goldman & Goldman, 1982; Money & Ehrhardt, 1972; Moore & Reynolds, 2018). Not only have we failed to address it, we have punished people who tried. For example, physician Joycelyn Elders was fired in 1994 as surgeon general of the United States for stating that masturbation could be a healthy and appropriate activity for young people in the right context. Being fired for such a statement reveals just how many people in the United States still think it's not acceptable to discuss sex or sexuality in the context of childhood and even adolescence. You can also see how this attitude continues to create controversy when it comes to teaching young people sex education.

Think back to your own childhood. How did your parents communicate with you about sex and values? Were they open minded, or embarrassed, or did they avoid the topic completely? At what age did they begin to talk with you about sex if at all? Were your parents openly affectionate to each other in front of you? Did they ever talk in positive ways about intimate relationships with

Joycelyn Elders, M.D., was fired from her position as surgeon general of the United States in a controversy over what she said are appropriate sexual behaviors.
Universal History Archive/Universal Images Group/Getty Images

Talking about sex with children is an important parental responsibility.
Chris Clinton/Getty Images

you? What were their views about masturbation, dating, and premarital sex? And finally, did those messages impact your own sexual behaviors and attitudes? Thinking about these questions as you read this chapter will help you understand your own sexual attitudes and skills as you journey toward sexual literacy.

Biology plays an important role in the immense physical changes we go through from childhood to adolescence and then in the transition to young adulthood. Biological processes cause our bodies to change shape and appearance. They are associated with new physical sensations and perhaps new desires or sexual feelings. These processes enable adults to initiate love and sexual relations, and to reproduce. They impact our images of ourselves and others, our emotions, and our interactions with other people.

Remember the little girl mentioned at the beginning of the chapter? What kind of values about her body would she have learned if her parents had condemned her natural inclination to touch her own body in a pleasurable way? How might she then grow up and communicate sexual messages and values to her own children? We often do not realize just how much our family's early teachings influence our sexual well-being through our thoughts, behaviors, and future interactions with people and the environment (Arbeit, 2014; Diamond, 2014; Impett et al., 2006; Regnerus, 2007). For example, when it comes to premarital sex and attitudes about using condoms and other contraceptives, familial teachings are powerful. The family remains the primary source of early lessons about sexuality for the majority of Americans (Bancroft, 2003; Regnerus, 2007), and in other cultures (Wright, Williamson, & Henderson, 2006). The actions and attitudes of our family members typically impact our core feelings and ideas about sex and sexuality, such as shame, pride, guilt, anticipation, excitement, or fear in response to sexual topics. For example, a long-term study of 5,041 Scottish teenagers shows how less parental attention predicts early sexual activity for both sexes; and for females, also predicts that they will have more sexual partners and less condom use to protect themselves—showing the correlation with family interaction (Wright et al., 2006).

Like family, culture and community are also important in shaping our sexual attitudes and behavior. By community, we mean your own particular culture and its positive or negative valuation of sex, as explained in Chapter 2. In the larger community, the messages your family has instilled are either reinforced or contradicted. In addition, friends, peers, religious community, school, and media have all imparted sexual messages from the start of life, as discussed in previous chapters. Do you remember what those messages were and how they combined with what you learned from your family?

Healthy Sexuality and Values in Childhood and Adolescence

Encouraging healthy sexuality and sexual well-being in childhood and adolescence involves accepting the fact that we humans are sexual beings from the beginning moments of life. Like all humans, children want to understand what is going on around them. We cannot shut that curiosity down without doing great harm to our children, their

Children learn by observing how their parents and other important people in their lives behave toward each other, especially in expressing love and affection.
sarahwolfephotography/Getty Images

bodies, and their emotional ability to handle their future sexuality. Once we accept this, we can begin to instill healthy, positive, and age-appropriate teaching and messages about sexual well-being from very early on in children's lives. Approaching communication in this way helps to ensure that children grow up with a positive attitude about their own sexuality and to understand how to make healthy decisions that allow them to enjoy their own sexual development.

We *can* develop values that provide healthy sexuality from the start. Take a moment to explore your own beliefs about sexuality and sexual feelings and how you might communicate your values to young people in your life, in "Know Yourself: Are My Child's Sexual Needs Being Met?"

Emotional Literacy in Young People

How do we communicate the importance of self-expression in relation to sexuality for children and adolescents? Learning to use terms such as *love* and *sex* at the right time and in the proper context can make a huge difference in how intimacy and love are achieved. Young people especially learn by observing how their parents and other important people in their lives behave toward each other (Moore & Reynolds, 2018). Affection and love, the appropriate expression of sexual feelings, and dignity and respect are all critical components that children seem to home in on in their observations of parental and familial interaction. It is easy to see evidence of their intense observations by watching children play "house," as they will often mimic characteristics of their parents' roles and relationships with one another. Learning early on how to express positive feelings about sexual love is very important for children.

To understand how to communicate age-appropriate sexual teaching to young people, you need to know what kinds of sexual curiosities and behaviors are normal and appropriate for various age groups (Flanagan, 2014). Discovering what is normative for sexual behaviors in children and adolescents is not an easy task because of the variation between individuals, families, and cultures (Bancroft, 2003; De Graaf & Rademakers, 2006; Kinsey et al., 1948; Laumann et al., 1994; Russell, Crockett, Shen, & Lee, 2008; Savin-Williams, 2005; Moore & Reynolds, 2018; Tolman, 2006). Researchers typically rely on reports from parents or caregivers or they use self-report data from adults—years after those adults experienced sexual behaviors or feelings as children (Bancroft, 2003).

Children and adolescents learn values, including ideas about what is and is not acceptable sexual behavior, from their parents, peers, and society.
SW Productions/Getty Images

WHAT'S ON YOUR MIND?

Q: What words should I use when describing sexual body parts to my children? I think that words like "penis" and "vagina" sound so formal but I don't like some of the more common terms either.

ANSWER: We don't have an easy answer. It is true that many people don't use the medical terms for sexual body parts; so using them when talking to your kids may sound unusual. It is problematic, though, to use words that can have other meanings. One friend referred to her vagina as her "cookie." You might imagine the confusion and humor this term causes. Teaching your children the formal terms for their sexual body parts can help them avoid miscommunication when it's important. Also, teaching them some of the slang terms could help identify what they hear from the media or from their friends.

Know Yourself

Are My Child's Sexual Needs Being Met?

Many people will find even the asking of this question to be challenging if not offensive. The sexual culture in the United States is one that disregards the *lifelong* development of our sexual selves. But for those thoughtful parents who are open to the ideas expressed in this book, the question is easy to imagine in a straightforward manner. All children have physical, emotional, and intellectual needs, and we have no problem considering these—why not face our child's needs for sexual safety and age-appropriate sexual information in the same way? In order to help families find a reasonable way to assess their treatment of their child's sexual development, the following statements are offered. A range of numbers (from 1 to 5) follows each of these statements; 1 indicates "poorly" and 5 indicates "superior." Obviously, an answer like 5 indicates it is time for a pat on the parental back, just as a lesser answer indicates there's room for improvement. If you do not have children, consider whether your needs as a child were met, and think about how you might approach these issues when and if you decide to have children one day.

1. When asking their immediate caregivers questions about the human body and sexual activities, my child feels safe and is safe from inappropriate shame or ridicule.

    1 2 3 4 5

2. My child is protected from information that would be above and beyond their ability to process in an emotionally comfortable manner.

    1 2 3 4 5

3. My child is allowed to access age-appropriate information that satisfies their curiosity and prepares them for the next stage of learning.

    1 2 3 4 5

4. My child is not shamed, ridiculed, or exploited for expressing thoughts about sexuality, feelings that are sexual, or behaviors that do no harm to others.

    1 2 3 4 5

5. My child's statements of discomfort with how they are treated in sexual matters are taken seriously and respectfully, and I make sure of this.

    1 2 3 4 5

6. My child has been informed regarding the need of and right to privacy so that they can begin to observe the privacy needs of others.

    1 2 3 4 5

7. My child is allowed and encouraged to talk about and otherwise intellectually ponder human sexuality.

    1 2 3 4 5

8. When it comes to sexuality, my child is allowed to laugh, make jokes, and engage in age-appropriate sexual play with peers, and conversation with peers and safe adults such as parents.

    1 2 3 4 5

9. My child may get mocked about sexual matters because no one can be protected at all times from all people, but to the degree that a parent can, I have guarded my child's sexual dignity, including remarks about their body, their questions, their play, and so forth.

    1 2 3 4 5

Source: Ing, S. (2015). *We're all like this: Learning to talk about or human sexual needs.* Tuscon, AZ: Giant Publishing.

SEXUALITY IN CHILDHOOD

As we have established, sexual development begins with the first breath of life and does not end until we draw our last breath (Coleman & Coleman, 2002; Freud, 1905; Friedrich, Fisher, Broughton, Houston, & Shafran, 1998). Sexuality is developmental, meaning it grows and changes throughout our life span. Childhood sexuality is especially sensitive to context and may vary significantly by culture (Ford & Beach, 1951; Herdt, 2009b, 2010b; Jordan-Young, 2010; Moore & Reynolds, 2018). In this section, we discuss the biological development of sexuality during childhood. We will also learn more about the social influences on our sexual development and the role that context may play in young people's sexual behaviors.

Infants as Sensual Beings

For infants, the parent–child attachment creates the dynamics of what experts have called "tender, careful holding" practices (Ainsworth, 1967; Bowlby, 1999), which in turn create the capacity for affection and emotional response and lay the foundation for the sensual and sexual responses that occur in adolescence (Chopra & Tanzji, 2018; Hrdy, 2010). And so for infants, sexuality begins with sensuality. Infants recognize when something feels good. They nuzzle up to a caregiver whose touch nurtures and comforts them; this type of touch is part of the foundation of future sexual behavior.

Within the first year of life, there is a surprising range of sexual responsiveness. Penile erections in young infants are common, and orgasm has been reported in boys as young as 5 months and girls as young as 7 months, although ejaculation doesn't occur in boys until puberty (Calderone, 1985; Kinsey et al., 1948). Alfred Kinsey (1948) and his colleagues reported that infant boys experienced orgasm from masturbatory activities that created rhythmic movements of the infants' body with distinct thrusts of the penis. Following the thrusts was muscle tension, and a release marked by convulsions or rhythmic contractions was observed. Though boys are incapable of ejaculation in infancy, it seems that all the necessary mechanisms for sexual response are present from birth. Kinsey and colleagues (1953) also noted comparable orgasmic experiences in infant girls.

As children move into toddlerhood, their sexual behaviors often become much more purposeful. Toddlers still perceive those physical sensations as sensual rather than sexual, but parents may worry that these are **sexualized behaviors,** meaning the behaviors are sexual in nature. In turn, parents begin to transmit value messages to their children with regard to these behaviors. These **value messages,** which can come from parents, teachers, or other authorities, communicate a value or moral statement about a particular behavior, issue, or event.

Sexualized behaviors during toddlerhood are mostly **autoerotic,** or self-stimulated. Toddlers find that stimulation of the genitals feels good to them. Driven by positive reinforcement, young children continue in these behaviors unless parents or other caregivers prohibit them from doing so. Parents often assign sexual motivation to these behaviors, which is the main reason they intervene when they notice their toddlers touching themselves or behaving in sexually curious ways. Inadvertently, parents' reactions send powerful negative sexual messages that children are not supposed to touch their own bodies. These messages often stay with children for many years, creating in them a sense of fear regarding the most intimate areas of their bodies. During toddlerhood, **sexual socialization** is taking hold. How a parent communicates sexual messages, in terms of the meaning and emotion, whether consciously or subconsciously, is critical in a child's current and future perception of sexuality. It is highly appropriate to teach children concepts about boundaries and privacy because they will carry forward these subjective senses for the rest of their lives. However, discouraging children from

Infants are wired for physical touch and intimacy from the first moments of life.
LWA/Getty Images

sexualized behaviors
Human behaviors that are sexual in nature.

value messages
Moral statements regarding a particular behavior, issue, or event.

autoerotic
Behaviors that are self-stimulating.

sexual socialization
The process of learning values and norms of sexual behaviors.

touching their own bodies can often lead to later discomfort with the physical and sexual parts of oneself (Haffner, 2008).

Childhood Curiosity, Masturbation, and Sexual Play

Many influences affect children's sexual attitudes and behavior, including parents, siblings, peers, culture, and exposure to media, so it isn't surprising that there are variations in their sexual development (Montemayor, 2019). Nonetheless, children and adolescents do exhibit some common behaviors in particular age ranges. For example, children naturally express curiosity about many things between 2 and 4 years of age, and pediatricians now consider young children's interest in sex just another form of the "why" stage of development (Spock & Needleman, 2004). For example, many children express curiosity about where babies come from. They also show a lot of curiosity about the bodies of other children and adults, and this interest may lead them to engage in sexual exploration. By about age 4 or 5, the influence of culture becomes obvious, as children begin to have a sense of learned modesty and recognize the distinction between acceptable private and public behaviors, such as using the toilet, touching themselves, and being nude (Calderone, 1985; Goldman & Goldman, 1982; Herdt, 2009b; Weiss, 2004).

Playing doctor is one way that children express typical and normative curiosity about their and others' bodies.
mangostar/123RF

Children may also display age-inappropriate behaviors or sexual behaviors that appear to be too mature for their age. Professionals may link atypical behaviors to sexual abuse or to an inappropriate level of exposure to sexual material, media, and information, although this is not always the case. Tables 11.1 to 11.3 summarize normative sexual behaviors as well

Table 11.1 Sexual behaviors in 2- to 4-year-olds

NORMATIVE BEHAVIORS	ATYPICAL BEHAVIORS
Touches or rubs own genitals when going to sleep, when tense, excited, or afraid.	Touches or rubs self in public or in private to the exclusion of normal childhood activities.
Explores differences between boys and girls.	Plays male or female role in an angry or aggressive manner. Hates own/other sex.
Touches the genitals or breasts of familiar adults and children.	Sneakily touches adults. Makes others allow touching, or demands touching of self.
Looks at nude people.	Tries to forcibly undress people.
Asks about genitals, breasts, and intercourse.	Asks strangers about genitals, breasts, and intercourse after parent has answered. Displays a sexual knowledge too great for age.
Experiences erections.	Experiences painful erections.
Likes to be naked. May show others his/her genitals.	Refuses to put on clothing. Secretly shows nude self in public even after warnings.
Is interested in watching people doing bathroom functions.	Refuses to leave people alone in the bathroom.
Is interested in having/birthing a baby.	Displays fear or anger about babies, birthing, or intercourse.
Is interested in own urine or feces.	Repeatedly smears feces.
Plays "doctor" and inspects others' bodies, including the same sex.	Forces other children to play "doctor."
Puts something in the genitals or rectum of self or others for curiosity or exploration.	Coerces or forces to the point of causing pain when putting something in genitals or rectum of self or other child.
Plays "house" and acts out roles of mommy and/or daddy.	Simulates real intercourse or oral sex without clothes on.

Table 11.2 Sexual behaviors in 5- to 8-year-olds

NORMATIVE BEHAVIORS	ATYPICAL BEHAVIORS
All behaviors for 2- to 4-year-olds plus:	*All behaviors for 2- to 4-year-olds plus:*
Thinks children of the opposite sex are "gross" or have "cooties." Chases them.	Uses excessively bad language against another child or deliberately hurts children of the opposite sex.
Talks about sex with friends. Talks about having a boy/girlfriend.	Talks about sex and sexual acts habitually. Is repeatedly in trouble with regard to sexual behaviors.
Wants privacy when in the bathroom or changing clothes.	Acts aggressive or tearful in demand for privacy.
Likes to tell and hear "dirty" jokes.	Tells "dirty" jokes even after exclusion from school and other activities.
Looks at nude pictures.	Wants to masturbate while looking at nude pictures or display them.
Plays games with same-aged children related to sex and sexuality.	Forces others to play sexual games.
Draws genitals on human figures.	Draws intercourse or group sex.

Table 11.3 Sexual behaviors in 9- to 11-year-olds

NORMATIVE BEHAVIORS	ATYPICAL BEHAVIORS
Shows decreased interest in sexual play and sex games. May have intense or passionate friendships with same gender.	Forces younger children to participate in sexual games.
Shows curiosity and interest in sex.	Engages in sexual contact with children. Touches the genitals of others without permission (e.g., grabbing) even when told to stop.
Shows interest in sexual jokes and obscenities within the cultural norm.	Humiliates self or others with sexual themes.
Shows interest in nude pictures of same and opposite sex. Draws genitals on human figures.	Shows chronic preoccupation with nudity of same/opposite sex to exclusion of normal activities.
Engages in solitary masturbation.	Engages in compulsive masturbation (especially chronic or in public).
Shows some interest in hugging, kissing, holding hands.	Attempts to expose other's genitals; exhibitionism.
Shows some interest in dressing up/pretending to be opposite sex.	Forces peers to dress in sexually explicit manner.

as atypical ones for various age groups in childhood. Keep in mind that not all children experience these normative behaviors, because each person's sexual development is unique.

Professionals consider childhood masturbation a natural, common, and harmless behavior. Childhood masturbation typically occurs among one third of children from infancy through preschool (Steele, 2002). If children are not made to feel ashamed or guilty about their sexual feelings and masturbation, it is likely that they will be better able to enjoy their sexuality as adults (Leung & Robson, 1993). Masturbation does not cause any kind of physical injury to the body nor does it lead a child to become sexually promiscuous later in life. It is completely normal and is a wonderful way for children to learn about the sensations the body can produce.

By age 6, most children have learned cultural rules about touching themselves sexually. For example, in a study of 1,114 children aged 2–12, familial, cultural, and contextual influences regarding such issues as nudity, peer sexual interaction, and sexual behavior were present early in life but these factors became increasingly influential by adolescence (Friedrich et al., 1998). Many children in this age group become increasingly aware of how it is inappropriate to touch themselves in public places and that it should be done in privacy. If a child masturbates during naptimes and bedtimes, a healthy parental response is to ignore the behavior because it can be highly self-soothing and the child is doing it privately. However, the more open and honest parents are, the greater the comfort level of sexual

HEALTHY Sexuality

Children and Masturbation

It may seem peculiar today, but in the late 1700s, masturbation was widely viewed by doctors as a serious mental illness, and it was suspected of being spread like a disease from one person to the next, requiring isolation, restraints such as straitjackets, and other severe treatments. According to psychiatrist Thomas Szasz (2000), doctors believed that masturbation was the cause of blindness, sexually transmitted diseases, constipation, nymphomania, acne, painful menstruation, suicide, depression, and untreatable madness. There was no objective evidence for any of these claims, but countless children who were found to be masturbating were shackled and mistreated at the hands of parents, teachers, and doctors whose actions, by today's standards, would be called "child abuse" (Hunt, 1998). These beliefs were highly sex-negative and especially oppressive of childhood sexuality right up to the mid-20th century (Herdt, 2009b). Nevertheless, medical researchers published hundreds of papers into the 20th century about masturbation as a disease, calling for circumcision for males and cauterization of the clitoris for girls to prevent masturbation. In the 20th century, progressive baby doctors such as Benjamin Spock (Spock & Needleman, 2004), whose work was read by as many as 50 million people, helped to change these attitudes.

expression in appropriate ways (Friedrich et al., 1998). Some children may tend to fondle themselves when they are tired or cranky, too (American Academy of Pediatrics, 2005; Hagan, Shaw, & Duncan, 2008).

As you might be aware, masturbation has historically carried a bad reputation. Many parents still regard masturbation in childhood as abnormal, though research has long shown that it is normal in human development (Calderone, 1985; Coleman & Coleman, 2001; Goldman & Goldman, 1982; Weiss, 2004). See "Healthy Sexuality: Children and Masturbation" for a discussion of the history of masturbation and some of the myths that have surrounded solo sexual activity.

According to many psychologists and developmental experts, children begin to engage in sex play during the 3- to 7-year age range. Kinsey and colleagues (1948) reported that by age 5, 10% of all boys and 13% of all girls had experienced childhood sexual exploration and play. As children advance in their own cognitive development, they become aware of the physical differences between boys and girls (Lamb, 2006). This awareness also sparks curiosity about the bodies of others, so they may incorporate those individuals into their own sexual exploration.

Typically these experiences will be with same-age peers with whom they spend the most time, either of the same or opposite gender (Fitzpatrick, Deehan, & Jennings, 1995). Children this age may engage in sex play with children of the same sex, but it does not usually reflect sexual orientation. The reality of these play situations is that a 3-year-old who is touching another 3-year-old is not having "sex" with that child. They are most likely expressing natural curiosities about each other's bodies (Spock & Needleman, 2004). They are discovering that touching each other feels good. Despite the positive feelings they are getting from these interactions, it is unlikely that these behaviors will progress to anything further than enjoying their own interactions and sensations. Ultimately, according to several pieces of research, it appears that sexual play in childhood has much more to do with curiosity than with sexuality as adults think about it, while emerging adult sexuality is more strongly influenced by biological and psychosocial factors that are directly linked to a sexual response (Montemayor, 2019).

Children begin developing marriage scripts, ideas about how married couples interact, by about age 5.
Lisa B./Corbis/Getty Images

Appropriate sexual expression with peers has been found to support and lead to normative development in 2- to 12-year-olds (Friedrich et al., 1998). The challenges of studying sexual behavior in childhood and adolescence make it difficult to predict the later significance of sexual expression with peers, but the normative effects make sense when we recognize that such learning actually may lead to important life and survival skills (Hrdy, 2010). In some primate species, for example, early sexual play lays the foundation for later successful male–female reproduction (Haffner, 2008; Martin, 2013). Primates that are raised in isolation and do not have the same opportunities for sexual play as those who live in the wild may have problems mating even when they are paired with an experienced mate (de Waal, 1995). The finding suggests the possible importance of early sexual curiosity and play interactions for intimate interactions later on, for human and nonhuman primates alike (Fitzpatrick, Deehan, & Jennings, 1995).

Children begin to enact **marriage scripts** by about age 5. The scripts include their ideas about how married couples interact intimately. They also help instill messages about the value of reproduction and having children. Having spent time learning about the relationships of their parents, children begin to emulate these relationships. For example, if a child has parents who are openly affectionate, children may mimic these actions. Conversely, a couple who refrains from public displays of affection may see little physical interaction in their children's scripts. Children might "catch" their parents in a sexual act that they may later imitate in their own play. Parents might talk to their children about what they saw and explain the behavior in a positive context rather than condemning their children's natural inclination to imitate what they have seen. Having a positive attitude about such issues appears to be significant for developing resilience (Ford & Beach, 1951; Herdt, 2010b).

As with masturbation, some parents and caregivers exhibit concern, anger, or worry if they see their children engaging in sexual play. We know that these concerns often center on emotional, psychological, or sexual effects that might result from this behavior. However, there is no evidence to suggest that child-to-child sex play causes any lasting negative consequences for later sexual development (Okami, Olmstead, & Abramson, 1997).

One aspect of growing up is learning to negotiate crushes and new romances. Some may consider age 9 or 10 too young to dive into these conversations with children, but parents know that some young people are talking about these issues more openly than ever. In fact, children are now writing books to offer advice on negotiating love interests. One boy who offers advice on how to approach the opposite sex is Alec Greven, a bright 9-year-old who is actively interested in the opposite sex. In his book *How to Talk to Girls,* he writes about the formation of crushes and the way that boys try to win girls in the "disease of love." Alec describes how to interact with girls for the first time and has even written a script for what to say to them. He talks about giving them small gifts and relating to them on their own terms. He also tells kids what to do when they are noticed and how to "be nice and friendly."

As children move into adolescence, their sexual curiosities and desires deepen and change as they begin to consider romantic and sexual relationships (Ing, 2015; Montemayor, 2019). In addition to these exciting possibilities, they find themselves in a whirlwind of change as their bodies enter puberty. Just as desirable as an environment that encourages sexual literacy in childhood is one that allows adolescents to flourish during this period of sexual development.

marriage scripts
Mental or cognitive representations of marriage including ideas about how married couples interact.

WHAT'S ON YOUR MIND?

Q: My 5-year-old nephew is constantly touching himself and his mom is really getting scared that he is going to be constantly masturbating when he grows up. Is this behavior normal and how should she deal with it?

ANSWER: Your nephew's behavior is quite common. Like most of us, he has learned that when you touch your genitals, it feels good. We would caution you to approach the subject positively. Tell him that you know it feels good and he is welcome to explore his own body but that it is something that should be done in privacy.

SEXUALITY IN ADOLESCENCE

Do you recall any awkward memories about middle school? Many people exclaim that this time in their life, the beginning of adolescence, was uncomfortable. Researchers struggle with the age parameters for this part of the life cycle (Diamond, 2014; Lerner & Steinberg, 2004; Tolman, 2006). Some researchers who study biological development say that adolescence encompasses the ages when adolescent maturation occurs, roughly 10 to 18 years old, though other perspectives on adolescence that emphasize identity development and emotional maturation view this phase as stretching from age 10 or 11 to the late 20s. Many professionals divide adolescence into early, middle, and late stages to more fully discuss the differences and nuances of development during the adolescent years.

The Magical Age of 10: Development of Desire

Around the age of 10, children display more purposeful sexual behaviors than younger children do. For example, they may become nervous as their bodies begin to change and they begin avoiding the opposite sex. They may seek out more privacy in their daily lives. They may or may not show romantic interests in others, but as puberty takes form, children may show an increase in sexual desire. Generally, in early adolescence, sexual desire begins with self-exploration, and then, romantic and sexual expression, typically with other peers (Bancroft, 2003; Friedrich et al., 1998; Laumann et al., 1994; Moore & Reynolds, 2018).

Adolescents spend a lot of time juggling pleasure and risk. While they learn that sexual activities bring intense physical pleasure, they also learn that sexual activities come with an element of risk that they must negotiate. During this time, adults can help adolescents understand the pleasures of sexuality as well as help them deal with the risks of sexual activity.

We saw earlier how 9-year-old Alec Greven expressed his interest in attracting girls. Here we can see the magical age of 10 at work. Alec's book is a window into the mind of a real boy who is figuring out how to act on his attractions. For anyone who thought that 9 or 10 was too young to start expressing sexual desire, Alec actually wrote the book when he was 8! You may be surprised to learn that a sample of heterosexual males shows clearly that many boys who are physically active and aware of their bodies may have awareness of their sexual feelings and attractions toward the opposite sex by age 9 (Bailey & Oberschneider, 1997).

The Biological Changes of Adolescence: Pubertal Development

Puberty is a word that often provokes a strong reaction. People tend to remember puberty as a time of physical change and strong emotions. It's no wonder, given all the changes that do occur. But puberty is a process, one that includes physical, mental, and behavioral changes and takes a few years to complete.

The primary change of puberty is the maturation of the reproductive system. Though you might think that puberty starts at about age 12, the process actually begins at around age 6 to 7 and continues into the early teens (McClintock & Herdt, 1996). Between the ages of 6 and 8, the adrenal glands begin to mature in a process called **adrenarche.** They secrete *DHEA,* a hormone that converts to testosterone in boys and estrogen in girls. In addition, between the ages of 8 and 14, the hypothalamus increases secretions that cause the pituitary gland to release **gonadotropins,** specifically follicle stimulating hormone (FSH) and luteinizing hormone (LH), which stimulate activity and growth in the gonads of both boys and girls. This process is called **gonadarche.** In boys, gonadotropins spur development of the testes and production of testosterone. In girls, gonadotropins increase estrogen levels in

---

adrenarche
The process of maturation of the adrenal glands; often thought of as one of the first markers of pubertal development.

gonadotropins
Chemicals that stimulate activity and growth in the gonads of both boys and girls.

gonadarche
Refers to the earliest gonadal changes of puberty; in response to gonadotropins, the ovaries in girls and the testes in boys begin to grow.

Sexuality in Childhood and Adolescence

the ovaries. Levels of these sex hormones continue to increase throughout pubertal development into the midteens, and sometimes longer.

A wealth of research shows how the pubertal process is associated with the development of sexuality, and especially with sexual feelings and attractions. *Attraction* here means really liking someone or wanting to be close or intimate with them, though not necessarily with genital sexual arousal. These feelings seem to emerge after adrenarche begins and take wings around ages 9 or 10 for boys and girls, typically around fourth grade in the United States. This occurs among boys and girls, both heterosexual and homosexual, in the United States and in other cultures (Herdt, 2006; Herdt & McClintock, 2000; Martin, 2013).

In addition to the maturation of the reproductive system, the development of secondary sex characteristics occurs during puberty. **Secondary sex characteristics** are physical characteristics other than genital development that are signs of maturation. A growth spurt, body hair growth, changes in body contours, breast development, and enlargement of the external genitals are all a result of increasing levels of sex hormones in the pubescent individual. Figure 11.1 shows the secondary sex characteristics in females and males.

A curious fact surrounding pubertal events for boys and girls is that the internal and external signs of puberty seem to happen on opposite spectra. For example, external anatomical changes are often the first sign of puberty in girls, while boys tend to undergo internal hormonal changes that produce physical changes in their genitals before the world sees any outward evidence of pubertal development (Worthman, 1998). Let's explore these differences.

secondary sex characteristics
Physical characteristics that indicate pubertal development other than genital development.

Male — Facial hair, Enlarged Adam's apple, Broad shoulders, Increased body hair, Pubic hair, Mature genital organs, Body more muscular

Female — Mature breasts, Broader hips, Pubic hair

Figure **11.1**
Secondary sex characteristics in males and females.

Puberty for Girls Besides adrenarche, we often see the growth spurt as the first marker of female pubertal development. Between the ages of 10 and 12, girls usually experience a noticeable change in height. This growth continues throughout pubertal development and concludes between the ages of 14 and 16 when sex hormones send messages to close the long ends of the bones, which prevent our bodies from growing any taller. In addition to changes in height, breast development and growth in pubic and underarm hair begin. An adolescent girl will also notice her body contours changing, as her hips widen to facilitate easier childbirth in the future.

Menarche, the first menstrual period, typically occurs at 12–14 years of age (Brooks-Gunn & Reiter, 1990; Coleman & Coleman, 2002; Martin, 2013). In the United States, the average age at menarche is approximately 12 years. The age of menarche is determined by a collection of factors including heredity, ethnicity, nutrition, and body fat. The age of menarche dropped dramatically in the 20th century, though the range seems to have remained relatively stable in the last 40 years or so. We refer to this decline in age as the **secular trend.** Figure 11.2 shows the secular trend for several societies in the last two centuries. Figure 11.3 lists pubertal events in girls and the average ages at which these changes occur.

It is important to understand the associated theories about the earlier age at menarche. Some of these theories are unsettling because they reflect social and environmental changes that have major implications for health and well-being (Herman-Giddens, 2007). One of the known contributors to earlier menarche appears to be the epidemic of schoolchildren who are overweight or obese. Other factors more recently established in the research include certain endocrine disruptors, being born small for gestational age, diets high in protein and low in fiber, decreased physical activity, and interestingly, being raised in a home without a biological father (Herman-Giddens, 2007). Potential factors that are still being researched include exogenous hormones (hormones coming from an external source rather than produced within the body), the use of soy formulas in infancy, and the hypersexualization of our culture.

Girls generally react well to the changes of puberty if they are well prepared for them. Research shows that parents who are open and honest about sexuality tend to produce children who are themselves more comfortable with and express sexual behavior in appropriate

secular trend
The decline in the age of menarche during the 20th century.

Figure 11.2

Graph of the secular trend in the United States and other Western countries. Researchers attribute the downward trend in the age of menarche to such factors as improved childhood nutrition and stress due to parental divorce and other family problems.

Source: Bellis, M. A., Downing, J., & Ashton, J. R. (2006). Adults at 12? Trends in puberty and their public health consequences. *Journal of Epidemiology of Community Health, 60,* 910–911.

Average Age Ranges in Years of Pubertal Events

Pubertal Event	8–10	10–12	12–14	14–16	16–20
Onset of Puberty	Typical period of time in which genital, skeletal, and secondary sexual characteristics and development occur (≈8–15)				
Skeletal Growth	Growth spurt begins (≈8–12)		Growth spurt ends: after menarche, girls gain 3–4 inches in height at most, often less (≈12–15)		
Weight Gain			Body fat increases at a normal rate (≈12–15)		
Acne			Oil glands often overproduce and cause acne (≈12–15)		
Breast Development	Pre-pubertal appearance: No glandular tissue (≈8–11)		Growth of breast tissue, areola, and nipple (≈11–15)	Attainment of adult breast size (≈15–17)	
Underarm Hair			Underarm hair develops (≈13–16)		
Pubic Hair	No pubic hair visible (≈8–11)	Soft, long, pubic hair begins growing in (≈11–13)	Hair increases in thickness and coarseness (≈13–15)	Hair reaches adult levels (≈14–16)	
Menarche		Menstrual period begins (≈11–14)			

Figure 11.3
Pubertal events in girls.
Source: Coleman, L., & Coleman, J. (2002). The measurement of puberty: A review. *Journal of Adolescence, 25,* 535–550; Feldman, S., & Elliott, G. R., (Eds.). (1990). *At the threshold: The developing adolescent.* Harvard University Press, 16–53; Lee, 1980.

ways (Friedrich et al., 1998). Conversely, adolescents who have not been prepared for puberty may find it difficult to deal with these changes, as noted in the large Scottish study cited earlier (Wright et al., 2006).

Some girls experience **precocious puberty,** which is puberty that occurs several years before the average age in a given society; this was discussed in Chapter 4. In most developed nations, precocious puberty begins at age 9 or before (Aksglaede et al., 2009). When a girl experiences menarche this young, she often looks much older than her peers. This apparent maturity can attract the attention of older adolescents, which places her at risk for engagement in early sexual activity (Ge, Conger, & Elder, 1996). It also places her at a higher risk for earlier related sexual issues, including an increased chance of unintended pregnancy (Curtis & Schuler, 2008). In addition, she may experience emotional states like depression, low self-esteem, and anxiety associated with pubertal development as a result of an increasingly complex environment that exposes adolescents to a variety of stressors and challenges (Aksglaede et al., 2009; Brooks-Gunn & Reiter, 1990; Ge et al., 2001; Russell et al., 2008; Worthman, 1998). Some of these traits, such as depression, appear to be more common in some cultures than in others (Russell et al., 2008), and may occur disproportionately more to girls than boys (Worthman, 1998).

precocious puberty
Puberty that occurs several years before the average age in a given society.

Puberty for Boys For boys, pubertal development often starts with events not typically visible to the public. Testes growth begins to occur around the age of 12 for most boys in the United States (Brooks-Gunn & Reiter, 1990; Coleman & Coleman, 2002). The penis, prostate, and seminal vesicles begin to grow and mature at this time. Approximately 1 year after the penis begins to grow, boys become capable of ejaculation. **Spermarche,** the first ejaculation, often occurs when boys are asleep. This kind of ejaculation is also known as *nocturnal emission.* Pubic hair growth begins and the voice starts to deepen. By about age 14, boys

spermarche
First ejaculation; occurs during male pubertal development.

WHAT'S ON YOUR MIND?

Q: My girlfriend, who is African American, says that she developed sexually at a very young age because of her early pubertal development. She feels that this has allowed her to become more aware of her sexuality and how people respond to her sexually. Is this normal?

ANSWER: Studies show that many African Americans may develop pubertal characteristics, such as breasts for girls, earlier than in other ethnic groups. Sometimes earlier development may be associated with other issues, such as weight or diet, but it may also be linked with the earlier onset of sexual relationships, though not necessarily. Your girlfriend may be one of the fortunate individuals who are resilient, able to adapt to early pubertal changes, and achieve sexual well-being and relational success.

begin to experience their growth spurt, which usually lasts well into the latter part of their teenage years. Underarm and facial hair develops later in puberty. Figure 11.4 lists the pubertal events in boys and the average ages at which these changes occur.

As with girls, how well adults prepare adolescent boys for pubertal development is critical in his comfort with the bodily changes. For example, a boy who experiences a nocturnal emission and is unaware of what it is may feel embarrassed or ashamed (Kinsey et al., 1948). Conversely, a boy who is informed about it will usually approach it with positive feelings and possibly a sense of pride regarding the maturation of his body (American Pediatrics Association, 2005).

Figure 11.4
Pubertal events in boys.
Source: Coleman, L., & Coleman, J. (2002). The measurement of puberty: A review. *Journal of Adolescence, 25,* 535–550; Feldman, S., & Elliott, G. R., eds. (1990). *At the threshold: The developing adolescent.* Harvard University Press, 16–53; Lee, 1980.

Average Age Ranges in Years of Pubertal Events

Pubertal Event	Description
Onset of Puberty	Typical period of time in which genital, skeletal, and secondary sexual characteristics and development occur (8–20)
Skeletal Growth	Growth spurt begins (~10–13); Growth spurt ends: bones lengthen due to increased testosterone which gives men longer arms and legs and a heavier bone structure than women (~13–17)
Muscle Mass	Lean muscle mass increases, giving men a more muscular appearance
Acne	Oil glands often overproduce and cause acne
Voice Changes	Experience of voice deepening and "voice cracking" occur. This change is a result of growth of the vocal cords as a result of increased testosterone.
Body Hair	Hair growth increases on various parts of the body, including underarm, legs, chest, and face
Pubic Hair	No pubic hair visible; Pubic hair begins growing in; Hair increases in thickness and coarseness; Hair reaches adult levels
External Genital Growth	External genital growth begins about age 12 with the increase in size of the testicles. Penile growth begins about 13 years of age. Adult size is usually reached 2–3 years after penile growth has started.
Nocturnal Emissions	Nocturnal emissions or "wet dreams" occur, signaling ability to ejaculate

With regard to timing, delayed puberty may be problematic for boys. They may experience some internal distress, such as insecure feelings, over the delay. Additionally, research has confirmed that precocious puberty can be problematic for boys (Ge et al., 2001). They may display high levels of externalized hostility and internalized distress.

Ethnic Diversity in Pubertal Changes There are some known ethnic differences in pubertal timing, although these are difficult to study due to restrictions on research involving minors in the United States (Friedrich et al., 1998b). However, pediatric studies have tended to reveal evidence of significant ethnic variation in menarche for girls (Aksglaede et al., 2009; Chumlea et al., 2003; Herdt & McClintock, 2000). For example, the population of African American girls typically reaches menarche at an earlier age than the populations of White American and Hispanic American girls in the United States.

Similar variations occur worldwide. Due to the considerable differences in diet and health around the world, we see quite a difference in age at menarche. Generally, the average age of menarche is higher in countries where individuals are more likely to be malnourished or to suffer from diseases. For example, in the United States and Western Europe, the average age of menarche ranges from 12 to 13 years, whereas in Africa the range is from 13 to 17 years (Worthman, 1998). The wider variability in Africa is due to the range of health and living conditions that exist on that continent (Hrdy, 2010).

Romantic Relationships

As they mature, boys and girls want to develop their flourishing sexual feelings. As recently as 10 years ago, research on adolescent relationships focused mainly on peers and parents. In the past decade, though, researchers began looking at romantic interests and relationships in adolescence (Meier & Allen, 2009). As a result, we are beginning to understand how adolescent romantic relationships impact human sexual development.

Despite the media stereotypes of sex-crazed teenagers driven by hormone surges, adolescents show an increased interest in romantic relationships as they explore the wide world of sexual behaviors (Schalet, 2000). For them, it is not necessarily all about "sex." Young people are quite interested in developing lasting romantic relationships; and dating and romantic relationships are of paramount importance, even early in adolescence, as we saw with Alec Greven. Teenagers make some of the most important developmental and interpersonal connections of their lives (Furman, 2002). Over 50% of all adolescents report having been in a romantic relationship within the previous 1.5 years, and by their 16th birthday most report spending more time with romantic partners than they do with family or friends (Furman, 2002). For boys especially, but also for girls, these intense intimacies tend to move them away from their parents and families (Tolman, 2006).

Teenage romantic relationships also contribute to their emotional literacy and provide a context in which to understand their sexual behaviors, motivations, and intentions. Many theorists believe that adolescent romance is an integral part of learning how to engage in adult romantic relationships. In the United States, because we now delay marriage significantly, most individuals do not enter marriage as blank romantic slates. Rather, they often have extensive and progressive experience with romantic relationships (Meier & Allen, 2009).

People often wonder if adolescents who identify with a particular faith tradition and those who do not follow a particular faith have similar experiences with relationships and sexual behaviors. For a discussion of religion and its impact on adolescent sexuality, see "Healthy Sexuality: Religion and Adolescent Sexual Relationships."

Fluidity in Adolescent Sexual Expression

Research over the past few years has revealed a pattern of flexibility or "fluidity" in the expression of sexual feelings and behaviors consistent with long-standing notions of

HEALTHY Sexuality

Religion and Adolescent Sexual Relationships

Few researchers have examined the effect that religious belief has on sexual health, but a few important studies shed light on how much religion or deeply held spiritual beliefs affect teens' sexual relationships (Baltazar, McBride, Vanderwaal, & Conopio, 2016; Regnerus, 2007). Here are the key findings:

- **Religiousity does not appear to have a major impact on reducing sexual activity among young people.** In fact, studies have shown that approximately 80% of unmarried 18- to 29-year-old evangelical Christians participate in sexual activity (Albert, 2009).

- **The degree of religious devotion is more important than religious affiliation in youths' sexual decision making.** For religion to make a difference, however, young people need additional reinforcement from authorities like parents, friends, and other family members who teach religious perspectives about sexuality in order to compete with the more sexually permissive scripts that exist outside religious circles.

- **Parental conversations around sexuality lack content and do not occur often enough.** Religiously devout parents talk less about birth control and sex and talk more about sexual morality. African American parents who are religious tend to talk with greater ease about sex and contraception. Religious parents struggle with conversations about sexuality, in part because they do not understand it in the context of religious teachings and texts. Their adolescents, then, have a limited understanding of sexuality, pregnancy, and other sexual health issues.

- **Religion has a great impact on sexual attitudes.** Youths who are devoutly religious anticipate guilt from engaging in sexual activity and are less likely to believe that sex can be pleasurable. In addition, they may think that engaging in sexual intercourse will damage their future education and financial status. This notion may contribute to the trend of Protestant and Jewish adolescents replacing vaginal intercourse with oral sex and pornography.

- **"Emotional readiness for sex" is a slippery phrase.** The phrase "being emotionally ready for sex" resonates with religious youth, but they can only really understand it after they have engaged in sex. If an adolescent has sex and later regrets it, it might be said that the individual was not "emotionally ready." If the person doesn't regret it, the deduction would be that he or she was ready. Religious adolescents talk about sexual norms that have little to do with religion. These norms are (1) don't allow yourself to be pressured or to pressure someone else into having sex; (2) sleeping around harms your reputation; (3) you are the only person who has the authority to decide if a sexual relationship is OK; and (4) sex should occur within the framework of a "long-term relationship," which is defined as one that has lasted at least 3 months.

- **The success of abstinence pledging is mixed.** The more religious an adolescent is, the more likely he or she is to pledge abstinence before marriage. Pledgers, particularly the girls, tend to have great expectations about marital sex. Most pledgers break their promise, and in 7 out of 10 cases, the lapse in abstinence does *not* happen with their future spouse. Most pledgers do significantly delay their first experience of intercourse. They also tend to have fewer and more faithful sexual partners. While these outcomes seem positive, a darker side is that many pledgers do not use contraception when they engage in sex for the first time.

- **Despite mass media's representation, American teenagers are not oversexed.** The way the media represent adolescent sexuality generally gives the impression that adolescents today are excessively focused on sex. This picture does not match what adolescents reveal in research. Though most teenagers engage in sexual activity, many have not had sex as early as people may think.

- **Evangelical Protestant youths may have less permissive attitudes about sex than other religious youths, but they are not the last to lose their virginity.** Evangelical Protestant teens living in the United States, which prizes individualism and self-focused pleasure, also abide by a religious tradition that teaches values such as family and abstinence. These kids try to honor both, a difficult task, indeed. What results is a tension of "sexual-conservatism-with-sexual-activity, a combination that breeds instability and the persistent suffering of consequences like elevated teen pregnancy rates" (Regnerus, 2007, p. 206).

- **U.S. youths believe in contraception but use it inconsistently.** Although 92% of religious teenagers, including Catholics, Mormons, and Protestants, agree with the use of contraception, 30–40% of them fail to use it in their first experience of intercourse. According to these teenagers, being prepared to use contraception looks like they wanted to have sex, which is a clear violation of religious teaching.
- **Technical virginity may not be as common as media reports claim it is.** Technical virginity is a belief that one can engage in sexual behaviors, including oral and anal sex, and still maintain the state of virginity by abstaining from vaginal intercourse. This term presents problems because of differing opinions about what constitutes virginity. It also excludes gays and lesbians because some people describe the loss of virginity as penile–vaginal penetration.
- **The practice of anal sex is increasing among heterosexual teenagers.** Although some may think that anal sex is another way to maintain technical virginity, more religious teenagers stay away from this practice. It is increasing among teenagers who are not religious. So while it seems that many teenagers are remaining fairly traditional in their sexual practices, this landscape may be changing.
- **Few adolescents are able to understand the religious tension between the appreciation of sex and apprehension about it.** Despite the fact that religious texts suggest that sex is an important part of life, most religious youth are simply told, "Don't do it." They do not get to discuss their budding sexuality in any context other than avoidance. This failure to provide the knowledge and skills to protect oneself and also form positive intimate relationships puts adolescents at risk, rather than encouraging healthy sexuality and sex-positive dialogue.

adolescent development, as for example in the early writing of Erickson (1969) on youth and identity development. The work of Diamond in studying sexual fluidity and development, as seen in Chapter 10, has helped researchers and educators to place this variability and change in context. Current research has found that young men and women in the United States are identifying with various labels that may appear to be unconventional; however, these new identities are bringing more awareness to how gender affects sexuality. Explorations of self and sexuality are developmental milestones for present-day adolescents in the United States. Being curious and exploring their curiosities help with establishing their romantic strivings and sexual identity. Looking past gender norms and commonly used sexual identities, we can start to understand that sexuality is based not just on biological events but also on various experiences and situational opportunities for expression (Diamond, 2014; Van Anders, 2015). We are learning from youth who do not exclusively identify as heterosexual or who may identify sometimes as bisexual or queer, that individuals who identify as mostly straight can "assist others to understand previously unrecognized feelings and a range of sexual and romantic possibilities . . . [and be able to] 'come out' of their heterosexual straightjacket" (Kaufman & Powell, 2014, p. 15). Therefore many youth report an interest in enhancing "personal freedom and the normalization of homoeroticism among all teenagers" (Kaufman & Powell, 2014, p. 18).

As young people begin to avoid the use of labels and as this becomes culturally approved, there can be a shift in how families and communities think about sexuality and orienting ourselves. Sexual identity becomes less straightforward and less constructed, more changeable over the life span (Bailey et al., 2016; Diamond, 2008, 2014). The implications of sexual fluidity then are to modify and sometimes challenge the ideas of fixed or stable adolescent sexual identities or orientations that were previously assumed (Erickson, 1969; Herdt & Boxer, 1993). Yet given the cultural differences across communities (Moore & Reynolds, 2018), we need to keep in mind that whether fluid or fixed, the "contextual, environmental, historic, socio-cultural, socio-economic, political, and geographical differences . . . as well as

technical virginity
A belief that one can engage in sexual behaviors, including oral and anal sex, and still maintain the state of virginity by abstaining from vaginal intercourse.

other factors including age and ethnicity, may result in variations in the process by which an individual identifies" or expresses sexual identity (McInroy & Craig, 2012, p. 139).

Sexual Identity

Adolescents also begin the process of forming a sexual identity and coming to understand their own desires, needs, and hopes for sexual fulfillment. As explained in Chapter 10, sexual identity seems to have its seeds in childhood, shaped by both biology and environment. For some people, fluidity of romantic and sexual feelings and behaviors shapes this period of their lives (Bailey et al., 2016; Diamond, 2014). Thus identity continues to form throughout adulthood for some individuals, while other people tend to consolidate their sense of sexual identity during their late teens and early 20s (Diamond, 2008; Katchadourian, 1990; Rosario, Schrimshaw, Hunter, & Braun, 2006).

Society's assumption has long been that all individuals begin life under the heterosexual umbrella. If they do not find comfort there, they relocate to a smaller umbrella. This smaller umbrella may not provide as much protection from the elements, but it might fit their sexual identity. This transition can be critical in adolescence. Men and women, boys and girls alike may experience a time of questioning, exploration, and fluidity as they make important decisions about their own sexual identity. For example, a young woman who identifies herself as heterosexual may question this identity if she becomes sexually aroused after viewing a sexually explicit photograph of another woman. Many adolescents often try to assign meaning to or question their sexual identity in response to these kinds of occurrences.

Discussing sexual identity, particularly an LGBTQ identity, can be emotional for adolescents and their parents (Levkoff, 2007). Because our culture still discriminates against gays, lesbians, bisexuals, and transgender individuals, parents would seek to shelter their children from these harsh realities, whether or not they support their child's sexual identity. Common questions that youths ask about sexual identity and orientation help to anticipate such discussions (Levkoff, 2007):

- Do gay men want to be women? Do lesbians want to be men?
- What is it called if someone has two moms or two dads?
- How do gay people have sex?
- What makes someone LGBTQ?
- What do I do if I think I am gay?
- Would you be disappointed in me if I were LGBTQ?
- What is homophobia, and why are some people prejudiced like that?
- How many people are gay or lesbian?
- Do gay people want to turn other people gay?
- What do you do if you find out one of your friends is gay?

Questions such as these may or may not reflect a young person's own sexual identity. The point is that when they are answered with a positive attitude, young people feel more accepted and comfortable in their own skin regardless of their sexual orientation.

Sexual identity development can be a daunting task for adolescents grappling with same-sex attractions, particularly if they believe that these attractions are not "heterosexual." As we studied in Chapter 10, the term *heterosexuality* has been the norm in reference to sexual orientation, perhaps because heterosexual individuals make up a majority of the population. In the research literature

Teenagers may try on different sexual identities as they try to find one that fits their needs and desires.
Greg Ceo/The Image Bank/Getty Images

about sexual identity formation for sexual minority men and women, we find some common threads (Bailey et al., 2016; Diamond, 2014; Rosario & Scrimshaw, 2014). One common thread involves signs of a same-gender sexual orientation, such as feelings of being different as a child (Herdt & Boxer, 1993; Savin-Williams, 2005). Another thread is that adolescents report same-sex attractions or a lack of attraction for the opposite sex, and subsequently engage in same-sex experimentation that might lead to self-identification as lesbian, gay, or bisexual (Diamond & Savin-Williams, 2000; Diamond, 2008). For bisexual, lesbian, and questioning women, however, sexual identity development seems to differ in several ways from the sexual identity development for men:

- Some women have no childhood or adolescent recollections of same-sex attraction.
- Many sexual minority women experience same-sex attractions for the first time in adulthood as a result of exposure to lesbian, gay, or bisexual ideas or people.
- Sexual minority women may develop an emotionally intense attachment to one particular woman.
- Sexual minority women may experience multiple abrupt changes in sexual attractions over time.

These variations in women's sexual attractions, behaviors, and relationships suggest a lot more variation and richness and fluidity than researchers once perceived (Diamond, 2008, 2014). And so it may be that the process of sexual identity formation for women is quite different and may continue longer in the life span than it does for some men (Diamond, 2008; Diamond & Savin-Williams, 2000; Van Anders, 2015).

Sexual Behaviors in Adolescence

Adolescents may approach sexual behaviors with curiousity, anxiety, elation, and excitement. Their attitudes about romantic relationships and sexual behaviors reflect the messages they have recieved from those closest to them as well as from the larger social context. They begin to make decisions based on those messages. If they have received positive messages, their decisions may reflect emotional maturity and readiness, as well as an intention to protect themselves and their partners from unintended events such as pregnancy or STIs. Table 11.4 characterizes normal and atypical sexual expression of adolescents.

Masturbation   Masturbation is an important milestone in adolescent sexual development. Research shows that by the end of adolescence nearly all males and many females have masturbated (Friedrich et al., 1998; Laumann et al., 1994; Montemayor, 2019). Just as autoerotic behaviors serve a sensual purpose in infancy and early childhood, masturbation serves an important sexual purpose in adolescence. Not only does it provide an avenue for the release of sexual tension, but masturbation is also an educational experience for many individuals. It is a positive and safe way for people to learn about their bodies and begin to understand what feels good to them. Equipped with this knowledge, individuals can later communicate that knowledge to sexual partners and enjoy a more satisfying sexual life.

Touching, Making Out, and Other Sexual Behaviors   Do you remember the first time you made out with someone? Did it stir intense feelings within you? As individuals progress through their teenage years, they naturally desire to experience sexual pleasure. These feelings are present early in life (Levkoff, 2007). In addition to continued exploration and curiosity about their own bodies, adolescents begin to want to connect intimately with another person.

Noncoital sexual behaviors, erotic sexual behaviors that exclude intercourse, are another milestone in the sexual development of adolescents. To maintain their technical virginity, adolescents often feel free to engage in noncoital sexual expression to connect with one

Table 11.4 Sexual behaviors in 12- to 18-year-olds

NORMATIVE BEHAVIORS	ATYPICAL BEHAVIORS
Has intense sexual curiosity and sexually explicit conversations with peers.	Has sexually explicit conversations with significantly younger children.
Uses sexual obscenities and jokes within cultural norms.	Humiliates self or others with sexual themes.
Displays strong sexual attraction to the same or opposite sex, or both.	Engages in obscene phone calls, voyeurism, and sexual harassment.
Engages in sexual innuendo, flirting, or petting. May have intense brief romances.	Makes sexually explicit threats either verbal or written.
Engages in solitary masturbation.	Engages in compulsive masturbation (especially chronic or in public).
Shows interest in erotica and pornography and may seek this out on the Internet.	Shows chronic preoccupation with sexually aggressive pornography.
Participates in hugging, kissing, holding hands, and bodily closeness.	Attempts to expose other's genitals; exhibitionism.
Engages in foreplay (petting, making out, fondling) and mutual masturbation. Moral, social, or family rules may restrict these behaviors but they are developmentally normal, and are not illegal when private, consensual, equal, and noncoercive.	Has sexual contact with minors/children with a significant age difference (child sexual abuse). Touches the genitals of others without permission (e.g., grabbing) even when told to stop.
Engages in sexual intercourse with a partner over time, probably monogamous. Stable monogamy is defined as a single partner throughout adolescence. Serial monogamy indicates involvement of several months or years that ends and is followed by another. Sexual involvement may also be casual and include sexual encounters with a variety of individuals.	Forces sexual contact with peers, adults, or minors (sexual assault). Forces sexual penetration (rape). Engages in sexual contact with animals.

another. Necking, petting, mutual masturbation, and making out are all ways in which adolescents begin to express their sexuality and erotic feelings while maintaining some safety with regard to pregnancy.

Extensive research shows that oral sex is increasing in adolescence (Regnerus, 2007), as it is in the general population (Sanders & Reinisch, 1999). Some researchers think that adolescents consider oral sex a safer activity than intercourse in terms of social, emotional, and health consequences. Consequently, adolescents often do not use protection, which puts them at risk for STIs that are easily transmitted through oral–genital activity.

Sexual Intercourse Engaging in intercourse for the first time can be one of the most exhilarating experiences in an adolescent's life, especially if the teen enters into it equipped with accurate knowledge and is emotionally prepared to accept the responsibilities of an intimate relationship. A variety of motivations and emotions surround an individual's decision to have sex for the first time. It is common today for adolescents in long-term relationships to say they engage in intercourse because they feel a close connection to their romantic partner and desire a deeper connection or further intimacy with that individual (Overbeek et al., 2003). In fact, one study showed that among sexually experienced adolescents aged 15–19 years, 73% of females and 58% of males reported that their first sexual experience was with a partner that they had been dating steadily, was living with, or was engaged or married to. Only 16% of females and 28% of males reported engaging in sex with someone they had just met (Martinez, Copen, & Abma, 2011). Some adolescents, however, want to engage in adult sexual behavior or satisfy their sexual curiosity, both of which may result in casual sexual relationships rather than intimate ones (Overbeek et al., 2003).

Research shows somewhat consistently that early sexual activity (engagement by age 15) is related to negative physical and psychological symptoms such as headaches, difficulty

Figure 11.5
Sexual intercourse among teenagers. Sexual intercourse is rare among very young teens but becomes more common in the later teenage years.
Source: NCHS, National Survey of Family Growth, 2011–2015.

sleeping, depressive symptoms, irritability etc., for girls, but not for boys (Madkour, Farhat, Halpern, Godeau, & Gabhainn, 2010). Young men, in contrast, tend to report their first sexual intercourse experience as quite positive. Girls have a different response. A significant proportion of teenage girls report that they really did not want it (Thompson, 1995). They weren't necessarily forced into having sex, but girls may feel external pressure either from partners or peers that led them to make a decision they were not totally comfortable with. In addition, young women feel a wide range of emotions regarding their first experience of sexual intercourse. The reactions most often reported by women after having sex for the first time are feelings of pleasure/romance, anxiety, and guilt (Guggino & Ponzetti, 1997). With regard to painful first sexual intercourse experiences, a significant proportion of women feel some physical pain, usually because they are nervous or unprepared for the actual physical act of penetration; about one third report no pain at all (Thompson, 1995). Figure 11.5 shows the percentage of teenagers who have had intercourse.

STIs, Pregnancy, and Contraception

Why does the United States have one of the highest rates of teenage pregnancy and STIs in the world? For one thing, teenagers are not using contraceptives effectively (CDC National Center for Health Statistics, 2010). Even more disconcerting is that most teenagers do not use contraception during the first several times they engage in sexual intercourse. What is encouraging, though, is that the teenage pregnancy rate seems to be slowly declining (Hamilton & Ventura, 2012). In fact, as illustrated in Figure 11.6, the birth rate among teens is currently only 50% of what it was in 1990 (National Campaign, 2012). Some polls show that today's teenagers are more likely to use contraception than teenagers 10 to 20 years ago (CDC National Center for Health Statistics, 2011h).

Because teens may feel overwhelmed when gathering information about contraceptive methods, they have some misconceptions about them. These misconceptions often relate to how a particular device works. For example, many individuals are unaware that a diaphragm must be left in place for at least 8 hours after intercourse to maximize its effectiveness. Confidentiality is another major concern. Teenagers may feel anxious about talking to their family physician about contraception. Even college students worry that their parents will receive a statement if they seek contraception from their campus health center.

DID YOU KNOW

- Most teenage births are to girls ages 18 and 19 (Martin et al., 2009; National Campaign to Prevent Teen and Unplanned Pregnancy [National Campaign], 2012).
- The rate of teen pregnancy in the United States has declined by 50% since 1990 (National Campaign, 2012).
- More than 730,000 teenagers become pregnant every year, and about 430,000 give birth (National Campaign, 2012).
- Approximately 3 in 20 teenage girls become pregnant at least once before the age of 20 (National Campaign to Prevent Teen Pregnancy, 2009).
- The birth rate for U.S. teenagers fell 9% from 2009 to 2010, to 34.3 per 1,000 women aged 15–19, the lowest level ever reported in the seven decades for which consistent data are available (Hamilton & Ventura, 2012).
- Fewer babies were born to teenagers in 2010 than in any year since 1946 (Hamilton & Ventura, 2012).

Figure 11.6
Teen pregnancy 50% lower than 1990

Although the rate of teen pregnancy may be declining in the United States, it is still a significant issue.
Katarzyna Białasiewicz/123RF

Societal and economic changes have combined to delay the onset of living with intimate partners and marrying. A sluggish economy forced more young people in their 20s and 30s to continue living at home with their parents. These changes are critical because people may experience a much longer period of sexual needs and engage in sexual behaviors prior to committing to one person, if they choose to do that. As a result, the need for sexual education may continue into adulthood, so that people can benefit from new information about contraception and STI transmission.

SEXUALITY IN CONTEXT: THE ROLE OF INSTITUTIONS

How much of the sexual information you acquired in childhood came from friends or peers? Peers are the second most common source of information for reproductive sexual information. Schools are the first (Somers & Gleason, 2001). Even as adults, we continue to learn about sex from a variety of sources to be sure. Parents, siblings, friends, romantic partners, spouses, television, movies, magazines, books, and the Internet are just a few of these sources.

Our culture, history, and religion, part of the Sexual Triangle described in Chapter 2, all impact our sexual development. Now let's examine the role of key institutions in our culture—families, peers, media, and schools—in children's sexual development.

Families

The family remains the most important and most consistent factor in sexual socialization, according to researchers. A large study of 1,343 middle and high school students examined the effects of several institutions on their sexual knowledge, attitudes, and behaviors (Moore et al., 2002). The study considered the roles that parents, peers, and mass media play in sexual socialization. Although these institutions and influences made a difference, the study revealed that parents are the most consistent influence and sexual socialization agent across all different age groupings. Perhaps this should not surprise us, because parents are mainly responsible for their children's sexual well-being (Santelli et al., 2006). It is important to note that even within the family, parents are not the only ones to discuss the topic of sexuality with children. These discussions often can come from others in the family such as older siblings, uncles, aunts, or even cousins. Although parents play a significant role sometimes children don't seek out knowledge from their parents.

When you ask people who should be the primary source of sexual information for children, most answer, "parents." Most people assume that parents are or should be able to provide the most timely, accurate, positive, and complete information about sex to meet the needs of their children. Often, the reality is far different (Sanders & Reinisch, 1999), because people don't even agree about what constitutes a sexual act. In fact, many parents lack the knowledge or language to discuss sex with their children, they feel emotionally ill-equipped, or they think others, such as their church or school, should take this responsibility (Irvine, 2002; Regnerus, 2007). Yet these institutions typically are also unable to meet the challenge.

Peers are commonly providers of sexual information to their friends.
Fuse/Getty Images

If parents do not talk about sex, their silence teaches their children that talking about sex is taboo. This lack of sexual teaching may result in the following:

1. Children fail to learn the appropriate sexual language, such as the words to describe body parts and core sexual behaviors. Instead they may learn sexual vocabulary that is slang and sexual knowledge that is incorrect.

2. Children do not learn how to discuss sex in a manner that is socially acceptable. Their casual conversation may be negative or demeaning to others.

3. Although adolescents may not have learned to talk about sex, it does not prevent them from engaging in it, sometimes frequently (Tolman, 2006).

4. Without an honest discussion about sex, adolescents who become sexually active may hide this fact from their families, adding guilt and a sense that they are lying to their parents to their confusion (Regnerus, 2007).

5. When they become parents, people who grew up without learning to talk about sex may be unable to teach their own children about sexuality. In effect, they continue the cycle by stifling their own children's healthy development.

Researchers have concluded that when parents balance the positive aspects of sex with the necessary cautions when talking with their children, those children tend to become sexually active at a later age, when they feel more emotionally ready for the experience (Ayres, 1987; D. Kelly, 2008). Talking to children about sex is one of the most important things a parent can do. Ideally, these conversations should start very early in life. If parents can make sexuality a normal topic in their homes, it is likely their children will grow up with a natural comfort that fosters their own growth and sexual well-being. See "Communication Matters: Guidelines for Talking to Children About Sex" for suggestions about how to conduct these conversations.

Parental monitoring of their adolescents has also shown well-established benefits. Studies have consistently shown that parental monitoring is related to decreased sexual initiation, increases in condom use, and decreases in STIs and unplanned pregnancy (Ethier, Harper, Hoo, & Dittus, 2016). Effective monitoring is considered to be an active process within a family that includes setting appropriate boundaries and providing an open exchange of information (Ethier, Harper, Hoo, & Dittus, 2016).

COMMUNICATION Matters

Guidelines for Talking to Children About Sex

Discussing sex with your own children, or children who are close to you, can be difficult. Talking with children and adolescents about sexuality means knowing what is typical sexual curiosity for any given age. Try to remember your own curiosities when you were their age and have fun engaging in conversations that may help them to enjoy their bodies and make healthy decisions in their future. These tips may make sexuality a normal part of family discussion:

1. *Start early:* As you begin to teach your children names for body parts such as nose and mouth, teach them the words for their own penis or vagina. As they grow, it may feel more natural for you and comfortable for children to talk about age-appropriate sexual topics.

2. *Be kind, patient, and understanding:* Remember that children gauge your comfort level with this subject by watching your interactions with others. Create an open environment and be patient as they ask questions, even if their questions evoke a strong emotion from you.

3. *Take the initiative:* If you see an opportunity to discuss sexuality, start a conversation with your child. For example, when you see someone who is pregnant, talk with your child about pregnancy, childbirth, and new siblings.

4. *Talk about more than reproduction:* Teach children that sexual relationships involve caring, concern, and responsibility for others. With preteens and teenagers, discuss the responsibilities of sexual activity and possible consequences using positive messages rather than fear-based ones. For example, parents may want to discuss contraceptive options. Discussing the potential outcomes of engaging in sexual activity is a positive thing. Talk about the possibilities of STIs and pregnancy and the emotions that can result from sexual relationships, but also try to approach the subject in a positive way.

5. *Give accurate, age-appropriate information:* If a 3-year-old asks about how babies are made, you can correctly answer them without giving too much explicit information. If a 9-year-old asks that question, describe conception more explicitly, because a child this age can process a more complicated response.

6. *Anticipate the next stage of development:* To curb children's anxiety about their bodily changes, discuss their current stage of development and prepare them for what is coming next.

7. *Communicate your values:* Communicate your own values about sex, but remember that children will develop their own set of values, based on messages they receive from the Internet, books, television, movies, and video games. Your values will certainly contribute to your children's values, but there may be some differences. When there is a clash in values, it is important for parents to continue exercising tolerance and understanding. This doesn't mean you have to change your values but it may mean that a positive relationship with your children requires listening to and understanding their perspective. As children figure out for themselves how to approach sex, they will know what your values are.

8. *Relax:* If you approach these discussions with openness, your children may learn that you are a great resource, and they may learn that sex is an interesting, fascinating topic.

Source: Information adapted from www.talkwithkids.org/sex.html.

Peers

I (Nicole) was 10 years old when I first heard where babies come from. Once my best friend learned about it, she couldn't wait to tell me all the details. Our families were together at a local pizza restaurant when she asked if we could both be excused to go to the restroom. As soon as we were behind closed doors, she exclaimed, "I just found out how babies are made! Do you know how that happens?" I told her that I didn't know and she gave me the details about sex right then and there. A few months later, I feigned ignorance when my mother asked me if I knew how babies were made. I still appreciate her openness with me in that conversation, and I've never had the heart to tell her that she wasn't the first to explain it.

Evidence indicates that both parents and peers are particularly important sources of social and sexual norms (Coley, Lombardi, Lynch, Mahalik, & Sims, 2013). Peer behaviors have been linked to both sexual debut and condom use (Huebner, Neilands, Rebchook, & Kregeles, 2011). With regard to information about sex, it appears that children and adolescents prefer their parents to be the source of sexual information (Somers & Surmann, 2004), although the majority of parents fail to engage in meaningful conversations about sex with their children. It is understandable, then, that children and adolescents turn to their friends for answers to their questions about sex. They may communicate inaccurate or incomplete information on which young people then base their decisions and sexual values (Sanders & Reinisch, 1999).

Media Exposure: Television, Movies, Music, and the Internet

To understand how a person's sexuality develops, we must consider all of the contexts that impact that development, including the media, as noted in Chapter 3. Researchers have long known that young people's sexual identity development is influenced by the media (Plummer, 1995). Further, we understand that many of those influences on sexuality from media are positive. Some of these potential benefits include topics not often discussed, such as sexual health information regarding STIs and AIDS disseminated with youth in mind, portraying sexually responsible females, providing healthy models of gay and lesbian relationships, and fostering transparent conversations about other taboo topics (Watson & McKee, 2013).

Social media today certainly shape people's thinking and conversations, but do they affect how we view ourselves and how we develop sexually? Every form of media and technology may sexualize us as a society (American Psychological Association [APA], 2010). Not all of it is necessarily bad or even unwanted. After all, media do appeal to our interests and desires (e.g., money, beauty, fame, power). Media also contribute to healthy sexuality by making accurate information about sexual health available through web-based resources and texting (Pascoe, 2011). Consider the critical information pertaining to social media presented in Chapter 3. We know that young people employ the Internet, social media sites, and even text messaging to acquire sexuality-related information. Today's young people, essentially, are naturally inclined to use these technologies to explore sexual issues (Montemayor, 2019).

Public and Private Spaces Adolescents—and adults—saturate social networking spaces such as Instagram, Facebook, and other websites or blogs with sexual themes as they publicly negotiate their own sexual identity formation. These once personal but now public narratives are transforming the sexual landscape of our society. With the sexualization of the media, individuals feel free to express their stories to individuals they do not know. They use status updates, video postings, personal writings, and pictures to communicate aspects of their personal identity. As public and private boundaries have become blurred, we make intimate storytelling an active part of our own development rather than the private retrospective that it once was.

It is not yet obvious how this public intimate sharing will affect us as a society. Perhaps it will make sexual conversations easier—seemingly a move in the right direction toward more open communication within communities and families. Will this kind of openness help us in our pursuit of emotional literacy surrounding sexuality? Is there a downside to this kind of transparency? These are questions for researchers to continue to tackle as technology moves us in new directions every day.

Research findings on the relationship between sexual content in the media and adolescent sexual attitudes, values, and beliefs are fairly consistent. The more adolescents report engaging with sexual content, whether on TV, in movies, music, or the Internet, the more permissive attitudes about sex they tend to have (Koletic, 2017). A few explanations have been offered about this relationship between exposure to media sex and adolescent behavior. One explanation posits that sexual material in the media helps to inform our sexual scripts—our ideas about how males and females are supposed to interact with one another in romantic and/or sexual situations (Montemayor, 2019). Another possible explanation is an increase in sexual sensation-seeking. We know from studies in cognitive development that sensation-seeking behavior is typical of adolescent cognitive development. Finally, adolescents may be seeking out sexual information in media to better understand what they believe their peers are doing. Specifically, the more adolescents are exposed to sexuality in the media, the more they come to believe that their peers are engaging in sexual behavior (van Oosten, Peter, & Vandenbosch, 2017).

Several years ago, the American Psychological Association (2010) convened a group of scientists to discuss the sexualization of young children, particularly girls. **Sexualization** is the process of being treated as a sex object. The objectification becomes so intense that the person may feel worthless as a human being beyond his or her sex appeal. The APA's findings have important implications for young women's development. Take time to consider this topic in more detail in "Research and Sexual Well-Being: Media and the Sexualization of Girls."

sexualization
The process of someone being treated as a sex object, and the objectification becomes so intense that the person may feel worthless as a human being beyond his or her sex appeal.

Media and Body Image As we have seen, the barrage of information in the media dictates much of what we deem beautiful or sexy. It is no wonder, then, that the rates of disordered eating patterns are skyrocketing. Additionally, body image is no longer an issue just for teenagers, as increasingly younger children report they are dieting. Just as sexual behavior changes during the life cycle, our self-image changes as well. Talking with young children can build the foundation for positive body image and self-esteem. The Sexuality Information and Education Council of the United States (SIECUS) publishes materials regarding sexuality that outline developmentally appropriate guidelines for talking to children and adolescents about body image. For some of these guidelines, see "Communication Matters: Talking with Children and Adolescents About Bodies."

Children and adolescents often form ideas about what is beautiful or sexy based on media images of celebrities such as Selena Gomez.
Jason Merritt/Getty Images

Sexuality Education in Schools

Over the past several decades there has been a debate about how best to educate U.S. children about sexuality. In other chapters we have noted that government officials are conservative on the issue of sexuality education. The current reality around sexuality education in the United States is interesting in that in recent years we have actually seen a decrease in the percentage of U.S. adolescents who are receiving formalized, school-based sexuality education (Lindberg, Maddow-Zimet, & Boonstra, 2016). The decline is particularly apparent for adolescents living in rural areas. We are not yet completely certain what the consequences of this decline may be. One interesting fact is that during the same time we have seen decreases in formalized sexuality education, we have also experienced a decline in teen pregnancy rates. The reality is that there may be multiple ways to examine the relationship between access to sexuality education and pregnancy rates (Montemayor, 2019).

Three important new perspectives help us to understand how unsuccessful the abstinence-only model has been. First, the scientific evidence is now overwhelming that abstinence-only education is ineffective in delaying the onset of sexual behavior and in preventing STIs and unintended pregnancies (Kirby, 2008; Santelli et al., 2006). This disease and prevention model is based on false assumptions about sexual behavior, including the notions that young people will be promiscuous if taught about sexuality and that condoms are ineffective at preventing unintended pregnancy and STIs (Impett et al., 2011; Santelli et al., 2006; Tolman, 2011).

RESEARCH and Sexual Well-Being

Media and the Sexualization of Girls

In 2007, an American Psychological Association (APA) task force released a report on the impact of media on girls. The report asserted that the sexualization of girls occurs when four conditions are present:

1. A person's value comes primarily from her sex appeal or behavior, to the exclusion of other characteristics.
2. A person is held to a standard that equates physical attractiveness with being sexy.
3. A person is sexually objectified, or made into a thing for another's sexual use, rather than being seen as a whole person with the capacity for independent action and decision-making.
4. Sexuality is inappropriately imposed upon an individual.

The task force determined that it is unnecessary for all four conditions to be present to create sexualization. The inappropriate imposition of sexuality is most problematic and damaging to children.

Evidence of the sexualization of children, and girls in particular, has been found in virtually every form of media that researchers have studied (Burns, Futch, & Tolman, 2011). Examples of this kind of sexual portrayal include being dressed in revealing clothing with facial expressions or bodily postures that indicate sexual readiness. Other evidence communicates the sexual objectification of women and the unrealistic standards of physical beauty and attractiveness that the media heavily promote. These models of beauty and femininity are rampant in our culture and provide young girls and women with unrealistic expectations to imitate. How are young girls affected by sexualization? The task force identified five areas in which it has an impact:

1. *Cognitive and emotional consequences:* It appears that the concentration and thought devoted to thinking about one's body disrupts mental capacity. For example, girls are unable to focus on important tasks such as academics when they are focused on their appearance and how others view them. Regarding emotions, objectification and sexualization undermine how comfortable girls are with themselves, and especially with their bodies. The possible emotional consequences of a negative body image include shame, anxiety, and self-disgust in girls as young as 12 years old (Slater & Tiggemann, 2002).

2. *Mental and physical health:* Eating disorders, low self-esteem, and depression are three of the most common mental health problems of girls and women. These challenges are associated with sexualization. In some individuals, the correlation of sexualization to mental disorders may be very high. In addition, girls' physical health may be indirectly affected in a negative way. Eating disorders, for example, can cause significant negative health effects and may lead to suicide.

3. *Sexuality:* When girls are bombarded by unrealistic physical and sexual expectations, sexualization may strongly impact their sexual well-being and development. For example, sexualization and objectification have been associated with poorer sexual health among adolescents, including decreased condom use and decreased sexual assertiveness (Impett, Schooler, & Tolman, 2006).

4. *Attitudes and beliefs:* Exposure to ideals of sexuality, beauty, and femininity in the media can change how women and girls conceptualize these issues. The more often girls consume this kind of media material, the more they tend to support the sexual stereotypes that depict the objectification of women.

5. *Impact on society:* Women are not the only ones who can fall prey to unrealistic expectations of attractiveness or physical intimacy. False ideals can affect heterosexual men in their search to find partners or in their abilities to enjoy intimacy with a woman as their expectations may be shaped by the unrealistic images media portray.

This APA report presents a gloomy view of the media effect on sexualization. The silver lining, though, is that if we become aware of how sexualization occurs, we can collectively move away from its negative influences toward a more wholesome and healthy sexuality.

COMMUNICATION Matters

Talking with Children and Adolescents About Bodies

Messages about body image for children ages 5–8:

- Bodies come in different size, shapes, and colors.
- Male and female bodies are different. Both are special.
- Differences are what make us unique.
- All bodies are special, including those who are disabled.
- Good health habits like eating nutritiously and exercising can improve the way a person looks and feels.
- Each person can be proud of the special qualities of their body.

Messages about body image for children ages 9–12:

- Heredity, environment, and health habits determine a person's appearance.
- Bodies grow and change during puberty.
- Television, movies, and magazines portray "beautiful" people but most people do not fit these images.
- Standards of beauty change over time and differ from culture to culture.
- A person's value is not determined by their appearance.
- Poor body image can lead to eating disorders.

Messages about body image for young people ages 12–15:

- The size and shape of the penis or breasts does not affect reproductive ability or the ability to be a good sexual partner.
- The size and shape of a person's body may affect how others feel about and behave toward that person.
- People with physical disabilities have the same feelings, needs, and desires as people without disabilities.

Messages about body image for young people ages 15–18:

- Physical appearance is only one factor that attracts one person to another.
- A person who accepts and feels good about their body will seem more likable and attractive to others.
- People are attracted to different physical qualities.

For messages about other sexuality-related topics, download the "Guidelines for Comprehensive Sexuality Education: Kindergarten–12th Grade" at www.siecus.org/pubs/guidelines/guidelines.pdf.

ericsphotography/iStockphoto.com

In addition, this model uses scare tactics emphasizing fear, shame, danger, and the risk of diseases and unintended pregnancy (Irvine, 2002, 2009)—and this approach has not been successful (Santelli et al., 2006).

Second, the abstinence-only model rarely teaches adolescents what they need to know to be sexually healthy. For example, it doesn't prepare young people to make informed decisions about when and how to engage in sexual relations or how to protect themselves while also expressing their own sexual feelings (Tolman, 2006). Instead, this model reinforces negative attitudes about sexuality that lead to a lack of comprehensive and accurate sexual knowledge. Because of this lack of awareness, adolescents are left unprepared to deal with their own sexual feelings and desires. When faced with confusing choices, such as a boyfriend's demand to either engage in sex or else end the relationship, young people are especially vulnerable to risky behavior (Carpenter, 2005; Santelli et al., 2006).

Finally, and most important, the abstinence-only model in no way prepares young people to develop healthy relationships across the life span, but especially in adolescence (Coleman & Coleman, 2002). Adolescents lack the life skills, knowledge, and ability to talk with their parents or loved ones about their sexual feelings and well-being. The lack of open, honest, and caring discussions may carry over into later life, and in turn influence how they treat their own children's sexual development (Ing, 2015; Moore, Raymond, Mittelstaedt, & Tanner, 2002).

Data from the Youth Risk Behavior Surveillance System (YRBSS) give us a clearer picture of sexual activity in adolescence in the United States. Nationwide, 41% of high school students had had sexual intercourse at least once (Kost, & Maddow-Zimet, 2016). In fact, between 1991 and 2015, the proportion of high school students who ever had sexual intercourse decreased from 54% to its current 41%. In addition, we have seen contraception use increase since the 1990s. It is believed that the decrease in sexual activity in this age group, coupled with increased contraceptive use among young people engaging in sex, are major contributors to the lowest rate of teen pregnancy seen in the United States in many years (Kost & Maddow-Zimet, 2016).

What is also interesting and important is that adolescent sexual activity may include behaviors other than vaginal intercourse. Between 2007 and 2010, about half of adolescents aged 15–19 reported ever having oral sex with an opposite-sex partner, and about one in 10 reported ever having anal sex with an opposite-sex partner. It is important to have a clear understanding of what one defines as "sex" in order to get a clearer picture of the kinds of behaviors that young people are engaging in so we can best educate them and provide resources to enhance their sexual health, well-being, and even enjoyment. Looking at sex with multiple partners in adolescence, the YRBSS showed that 11% of heterosexual students had sex with four or more partners, 29% of gay/lesbian youth reported sexual contact with four or more partners, and bisexual students followed closely behind (28%). Compared with heterosexual students, a disproportionate number of sexual minority students engaged in high levels of sexual activity (CDC, 2011f). These issues highlight the disparity in access to resources and education. One of the common issues heard from some of my (Nicole) students is that sexual education, when provided in high school, does not address same-sex relationships, behaviors, and safety considerations for these young people. Often sex education is still presented in the context of heterosexual relationships without any accommodation for those who are LGBTQ (Montemayor, 2019).

Figure 11.7 presents some of this youth sexual behavior data visually. These data indicate part of what it means to mature sexually during adolescence. Children experience sexual curiosities and desires, but adolescents experience desires in response to hormonal changes, as discussed earlier in this chapter, and cultural shifts that promote adolescent sexuality. Adolescents' desires can be sexual, but often surround the need for intimacy and relationships. These desires are healthy, though some adolescents have not had the right to experience this intimacy with someone of their own choosing.

Because sexual behaviors and relationships are a common part of what it means to be an adolescent in the United States, young people need sexual education that effectively furthers their sense of sexual health and well-being, and enables them to protect themselves against STIs, pregnancy, and sexual violence.

Figure **11.7**
Young people's sexual behavior by age and across time.
Source: www.guttmacher.org

Teens have indicated that they want to talk about sex and would like to have a say in the sexuality education curriculum.
Peter Dazeley/Getty Images

Student Perspectives About Sexuality Education Sexuality education is a hot topic for diverse groups around the globe. In New Zealand, for example, sexuality education is a target for competing social and political interests. Parents, teachers, school administrators, policymakers, civil liberties organizations, conservatives, and liberals have all made their preferences clear regarding the content to include in sexuality education. Until recently, though, young people have been left out of the conversation. To get a student perspective, Louisa Allen (2008) looked at the preferences of 16- to 19-year-olds for improving the content of sexuality education. She based her analysis on information gathered from 10 focus groups and 1,180 surveys from youths in New Zealand.

Allen's study revealed that young people in New Zealand want content about emotions in relationships, teenage parenthood, abortion, and how to make sexual activity pleasurable. In addition, their responses indicate a desire to make their own decisions, to have a voice in their own sexual development and behavior, and to have access to information that will help them find more pleasure in their relationships. These results are important because they give adults a glimpse of the kind of information that interests teenagers. They want to be informed. They want to talk about sex. Interestingly, there has been some conversation about creating a more provocative curriculum for sexuality education and including the topic of sexual pleasure. For a discussion on teaching sexual pleasure, see "Controversies in Sexuality: To Teach or Not to Teach Sexual Pleasure?"

Categories of Sexuality Education Programs Today, three major categories of programs address childhood and adolescent sexuality: (1) abstinence-only programs, (2) comprehensive sexuality education programs, and (3) youth development programs.

We have seen that abstinence-only programs are highly ineffective in their goal of delaying the onset of sexual intercourse. In addition, these programs provide little to no information for LGBTQ youth—a dangerous omission for sexual minorities that may be exposed to harrassment and bullying, HIV, and suicide risk.

The second category, comprehensive sexuality education, has four primary goals (SIECUS, 2004):

1. To provide youth with accurate information regarding sexuality
2. To provide youth with opportunities to explore, question, and assess their sexual attitudes and values
3. To help youth develop healthy and effective interpersonal skills, including communication, decision-making, and assertiveness
4. To encourage sexual responsibility among youth regarding sexual relationships; this includes addressing abstinence, resisting pressures to engage in unwanted or early sexual activity, and encouraging safe-sex practices, including contraception and other sexual health measures

Reviews of effective comprehensive sexuality education programs have found that they produce desirable effects with regard both to delaying the onset of intercourse and to preventing pregnancy and disease transmission (Kirby, Laris, & Rolleri, 2006; Kohler et al., 2008). Based on a theoretical model of behavioral change, effective comprehensive sexuality education programs achieve the following results:

- An increase in knowledge regarding the risks of unprotected intercourse and options for reducing risk

CONTROVERSIES in Sexuality

To Teach or Not to Teach Sexual Pleasure?

It is clear that comprehensive sexuality education is critical for every child and citizen in the United States. But should the topic of sexual pleasure also be part of the curriculum? In recent news, there has been some controversy surrounding a Pennsylvania sex-ed teacher, Al Vernacchio, who has abandoned the usual "sex is dangerous, don't do it, but if you must, use a condom approach." Instead, Vernacchio aims for candor, telling his students in grades 9 and 12 that sex can be pleasurable. In fact, one of his homework assignments requires that students interview their parents about how *they* learned about sex. Some professionals have begun to inquire about whether teaching young people about the pleasures of sex would be beneficial to their sexual well-being. While many cultures may not accept that teaching young people how to achieve sexual pleasure is valuable, research supports that positive and healthy sexuality education may benefit from a greater focus on positive sexual experiences (Ingham, 2005).

Should the topic of sexual pleasure also be part of a sexuality education curriculum?

Yes:

- If young people feel more relaxed about natural bodily pleasures, they may feel less pressure to engage in sexual activity against their will or engage in sexual activity in ways that make them feel uncomfortable.
- Allowing students to discuss sexual pleasure can help them discern their own desires for sexual fulfillment and prepare them for experiences that can happen when they are alone (i.e., masturbation) or with a partner.
- Arranging small group discussions, moderated by an adult, may allow individuals at the same stage of sexual development and experience to discuss deeper and personally relevant issues (Ingham, 2005).

No:

- Teaching children about sexual pleasure may be more than most parents can handle or desire to communicate with their children about.
- For educators, sexual pleasure can be a touchy subject. Many professional educators have significant fears about saying something that could be harmful to a child (especially a child who has previous experience with sexual abuse), jeopardize a sexuality education program, or cost them a job and a career (Fay, 2002).

What's Your Perspective?

1. Do you believe that sexual pleasure should be part of comprehensive sexuality education? Why or why not?
2. Who do you believe is responsible for teaching the topic of sexual pleasure to young people?
3. What kind of outcomes do you see as a result of the inclusion of sexual pleasure into sexuality education curriculum?

- Clarification of sexual values
- An increase in communication between parent and child
- Delay in onset of sexual intercourse (for programs targeted at young adolescents)
- An increase in use of contraception (particularly condoms)
- Discussion of specific risky sexual behaviors
- Opportunity for students to practice interpersonal skills and discuss situations that are meaningful and realistic, including opportunities to practice communication and negotiation skills
- A decrease in the influence of media, peers, and culture on sexual decision-making
- Development or reinforcement of students' values that support their decisions regarding abstinence or contraception use (Kirby, 2001)

The third category, youth development programs, is gaining popularity. These programs use a holistic approach. They rarely address sexuality at all. Their primary goal is to provide mechanisms for children and adolescents to fulfill their basic needs, including a sense of structure and safety. These programs seek to develop youths' sense of belonging, group membership, self-worth, independence, and social competence with peers and nurturing adults. Supporters of this type of program suggest that once these needs have been met, adolescents can effectively build competencies necessary to become successful and productive adults, which, in turn, may make them more motivated to avoid early sexual behavior and childbearing (Kirby & Coyle, 1997). Youth development programs are often targeted to populations in the 9- to 13-year-old range (Tepper & Betts, 2009). Most people agree it is developmentally inappropriate for young people age 9 to 13 to engage in intercourse or other types of sexual behavior (National Campaign to Prevent Teen Pregnancy, 2002). While youth development programs do not directly address issues of sex, abstinence, or even protection, they do help young people develop a positive orientation toward the future (Brindis & Davis, 1998). They also foster increased involvement with and attachment to critical youth institutions such as school, youth clubs, and organizations (Kirby, Lezin, Afriye, & Gallucci, 2002). Essentially, youth development programs work toward the goal of helping youth be healthy and successful in their lives by building a foundation for a strong future. The ability of youth development approaches to impact many risk and protective factors provides strong support for the use of youth development as a means of reducing young people's engagement in early sexual activity (Tepper & Betts, 2009).

Sexual Health in Europe and the United States

Young people enjoy better sexual health and well-being in Western Europe, compared to many regions of the United States (Schalet, 2000, 2011). In the Netherlands, for example, sociologist Amy Schalet has shown that sexuality education begins years earlier, involves better health care, offers free access to information, provides contraceptives, and has much broader societal and government support than in the United States, all of which may explain why Dutch youths are healthier than U.S. youths when it comes to STIs, unintended pregnancy, and related sexual issues (Schalet, 2011).

In general, the rates of sexual health are better in Western Europe than in the United States today. This includes the rates of STIs, the rate of unintended pregnancy, and the rate of sexual violence. Perhaps one of the reasons for these differences is that the sexual cultures in these countries, including the Netherlands, Denmark, France, Germany, and the United Kingdom, are more positive or approving of sexuality, including acceptance of premarital and living-together situations as well as same-gender marriage rights as expressed in their media and government policies (Badgett, 2009). For example, in 2001 the Netherlands became the first country to make gay marriage legal, and since that time, several other

WHAT'S ON YOUR MIND?

Q: I work in a high school and the student body is asking that our nurse's office provide condoms for students to purchase or obtain. We are worried that if we make condoms available, we are sending the message that we support sexual activity and that we will see an increase in early sexual activity and maybe even pregnancy and STIs. Do you think we should comply with the students' request?

ANSWER: We understand what a difficult position this request puts you in. But consider this, your students are asking you to help them pursue healthy decisions regarding sexuality. Research shows that schools that provide condoms to students do not see an increase in sexual activity. If you decide to comply with this request, couple it with an educational program designed to give students comprehensive sexual information so that they are fully informed. We believe this will help you to avoid the outcomes that are of concern to you.

Western European nations have done so (Badgett, 2009; Herdt, 2009b). Sexuality education is more comprehensive from an early age on and is regarded as a normal part of family and school life (Schalet, 2011). Denmark, Sweden, the Netherlands, France, and similar Western European countries not only have legalized abortion when appropriate and made contraceptives available to teens without parental consent (Schalet, 2011), but they also do something that is controversial in the United States: They begin sexuality education in kindergarten. This is something that most professionals in sexuality recommend (Haffner, 2008; Irvine, 2002; Kantor, Rolleri, & Kolios, 2014). However, political barriers stand in the way of making it a reality in the United States.

As we have seen, it appears that Western European countries have consistently had a better report card when it comes to sexual health. Why? Some critics say that it is because these countries are more homogeneous, while others argue that sexuality education in the United States starts too late.

When comparing statistics for the United States and the European countries of France, Germany, and the Netherlands, we find that the rates of unintended pregnancy and STIs are much higher in the United States than in these European countries. In the United States, the rate of teen pregnancy is 9 times higher than in the Netherlands, and 5 times higher than in France and Sweden (Stobbe, 2010). In addition, our estimated rates of HIV and other STIs for youths ages 15-24 is considerably greater than for these European countries. On just about every measure of sexual health and well-being, Western European countries outperform the United States. Europeans are more willing to invest in their young people's education and well-being to ensure a positive future. Their children have greater latitude in sexual exploration and are able to have comfortable and open conversations with their parents about sex. In short, Western Europe has greater sexual literacy than the United States (Moore & Reynolds, 2018).

Beginning in 1998, Advocates for Youth and the University of North Carolina at Charlotte began to sponsor annual trips to European countries to explore why European youth sexual outcomes are so much more positive than in the United States. After reviewing media, public policy, and educational messages, they found that these nations have an unwritten social contract with their youth that says: "We'll respect your right to act responsibly and give you the tools you need to avoid pregnancy and sexually transmitted infections, including HIV" (Berne & Huberman, 2001). In addition to this valuable message, other values appear to set them apart from the United States:

- Very significantly, adults in France, Germany, and the Netherlands view their youth as important assets who deserve respect, and they expect youth to behave responsibly.
- Government supports comprehensive sexuality education beginning at an early age through public schooling and utilizing television, the Internet, film, radio, and other public venues.
- Research rather than moral debates or personal opinions drives public policy and the goal to reduce unintended pregnancy, abortion, and sexually transmitted infections.
- Youth have access to free or low-cost sexual and pregnancy planning and prevention resources and contraceptive care and technology.
- Sexuality is built into curriculum and school settings. Educators are free to answer students' questions.
- It is more common for families to have open and honest conversations about sexuality, responsibility, and decision-making.
- Adults see sexual development and intimate relationships as normative for adolescents. Similarly, sexually active adolescents view unprotected sexual interactions as "stupid and irresponsible" and believe that if one is not going to engage in "safe sex" they should have "no sex."

- Despite the huge controversy surrounding immigrants in Europe today, these countries diligently work to include cultural diversity and immigrant populations (Advocates for Youth, 2001).

Sex education may be the key to understanding these differences in sexual literacy. Today Western European countries teach sexuality education as a mandatory course, often spanning kindergarten through high school. Additionally, researchers have discovered that many but not all parents in these countries are more willing and ready to discuss sexuality with their children (Schalet, 2011). Many Western European parents regard their children as needing comprehensive early sexuality education that is respectful and teaches that each person is responsible when it comes to learning this information (Schalet, 2000). All these factors combine to enhance people's potential for sexual well-being.

YOUNG PEOPLE'S RIGHTS AND SEXUAL WELL-BEING

age of consent
The age at which an individual can legally agree to have sex.

You might be surprised to know that within the United States and around the world, there are greatly divergent and varying ages of consent for sexual behavior. The **age of consent** is the age at which an individual can legally agree to have sex. Heterosexuals are routinely treated more carefully and fairly than nonheterosexuals when it comes to issues of consent (Bailey et al., 2016; Moore & Reynolds, 2018). In most countries, until a person reaches this age, it is against the law to have sex with anyone, even with someone who's older than the age of consent. In many countries it is the law that girls may begin sexual intercourse at an earlier age than boys, often because they marry younger. Sometimes the law is slightly different when both partners are the same age, but usually a minimum legal age exists below which sex is illegal. The age of consent depends on where you live in the world.

If a girl is even 1 day younger than the age of consent, her partner is in violation of the law. There are sound reasons for such laws, but the discrepancies create weird, unfortunate, and discriminatory situations that may take away people's rights. For example, consider a boy who was arrested for having sex with his girlfriend and sentenced to time in jail, because he was 6 months older than she was. In many states this kind of conviction results in mandatory reporting and registration as a sex offender. Such cases are also reported in the media.

statutory rape
Sexual intercourse with an underage minor, regardless if it is consensual and regardless of the age difference between partners.

When someone breaks the law by having sex with an underage minor, he or she can be charged with **statutory rape,** regardless of whether this was a consensual act or not, and regardless of whether there is 1 day or 10 years' age difference. Age of consent laws vary so widely across the different states within the United States that they sow confusion and mayhem for individuals and authorities alike. This is a challenge to young people's sexuality and well-being because many of these laws are quite old and do not take into account how our views of sexuality have changed (Abramson et al., 2003; Klein, 2006).

Several conditions create disparity with regard to the age of consent. Poverty, ethnicity, and sexual orientation all have an impact on how the law applies these ages of consent: Being poor makes people vulnerable, as does racism, and homophobia—completely changing what it means to give consent when you are pushed around. Immigrants also are not recognized by the authorities in some states as having legal rights and may be more vulnerable to arrest. Table 11.5 shows the age of consent for the states within the United States.

Sexual well-being requires protecting young people from abuse, molestation, or rape, but it also necessitates respect for individuals acting responsibly and for couples as they aspire to engage in intimate relationships and proceed through life together. Finding justice in such situations requires recognition of the importance of inequality and social protection as well as sexual literacy and sexual well-being in young people's development.

Table **11.5** The age of consent across the United States

STATE	MALE-FEMALE SEX	MALE-MALE SEX	FEMALE-FEMALE SEX
Arkansas, Indiana, Iowa	14/16	14/16	14/16
Colorado	15/17	15/17	15/17
Alabama, Alaska, Connecticut, District of Columbia, Georgia, Hawaii, Kansas, Kentucky, Maine, Maryland, Massachusetts, Michigan, Minnesota, Mississippi, Montana, North Carolina, Nevada, New Hampshire, New Jersey, North Carolina, Ohio, Oklahoma, Pennsylvania, Rhode Island, South Carolina, South Dakota, Vermont, West Virginia	16	16	16
Delaware, Florida, Utah, Washington, Wyoming	16/18	16/18	16/18
Illinois, Louisiana, Missouri, Nebraska, New Mexico, New York, Texas	17	17	17
Arizona, California, Idaho, North Dakota, Oregon, Tennessee, Virginia, Wisconsin	18	18	18

Notes: If more than one age is given, the law within the state varies according to region or circumstances. Male-female sex is vaginal or anal sex, and male-male sex is anal sex. Other sexual activities may be legal at a lower age.

Chapter Review

SUMMARY

Sexual Development in Childhood and Adolescence

- In childhood and adolescent sexual development, biology, family, and community interact to help determine how we view sexuality as we move through the life span.
- Families are the primary source of sexual socialization. The actions and attitudes of our family members directly impact our early feelings about sex and sexuality.
- Our communities, which include friends, peers, church, school, and media, communicate sexual messages and impact our sexual socialization. Peer influence, in particular, increases during adolescence.
- Current models need to examine healthy and positive sexuality so that children can grow up and safely pursue sexual well-being.
- Sexuality begins at birth.
- Encouraging healthy sexuality in childhood and adolescence means accepting our sexual nature and teaching children about sexuality in age-appropriate ways.

Sexuality in Childhood

- Children can display both age-appropriate and age-inappropriate sexual behaviors. Age-inappropriate sexual behaviors may signal sexual abuse or an inappropriate level of exposure to sexual material, media, and information.
- Masturbation is a common sexual behavior in childhood and is now thought to be completely harmless and possibly beneficial to children's sexual development.
- Sex play begins at about age 3 as children become more curious about their own bodies and the bodies of the opposite sex.
- Children begin to enact marriage scripts by the age of 5.

Sexuality in Adolescence

- The body begins preparing for puberty between 6 and 8 years of age. Pubertal development may become evident any time from age 8 to 15 years in the United States.
- Health and diet are significant in determining the age at which pubertal development occurs.
- More teenagers today seek romantic relationships and view these relationships as important in their lives.
- Most teenagers experience intercourse by the time they leave high school.
- Teen sex is not limited to intercourse. It can include masturbation, mutual masturbation, oral sex, and other sexual behaviors.
- Teenage pregnancy and STI rates among adolescents in the United States indicate a need for better resources and education around sexuality.

Sexuality in Context: The Role of Institutions

- People often assume that parents should be the main source of sexual information for kids, but parents often fail to meet this expectation.
- Failing to teach age-appropriate sexuality can result in children failing to learn sexual language, being unable to discuss sex in a socially acceptable manner, and being unable to teach their own children about sexuality.
- Peers are important sources of sexual information for kids. Many children and adolescents will consult their friends on a variety of sexual issues.
- Media have a big impact on our sexual socialization, especially as more and more teens are sharing private aspects of their sexual lives in public spaces such as Facebook.
- Media also influence body image. It is important to have conversations with children of all ages regarding the impact media can have on their own body image.
- Abstinence-only education is not an effective means of preventing pregnancy, preventing STIs, or delaying onset of intercourse.
- Studies are beginning to show that adolescents want a role in selecting the content of their own sexuality education, including how to further their own sexual pleasure.
- Comprehensive sexuality education programs appear to produce desirable effects with regard both to delaying the onset of intercourse and to preventing pregnancy and disease transmission.
- Western European models of sexuality education may provide a good model for the United States because teen pregnancy and STI rates are lower there than in the United States.

Young People's Rights and Sexual Well-Being

- Age of consent laws are intended to protect young people from sexual violence and abuse, but they are inconsistent, unequal, and create havoc across different states and countries.
- In the United States, the age of consent varies from state to state.
- Young people's sexual well-being requires respect for couples and for their rights as individuals to engage in intimate relationships, as well as protection from sexual violence and abuse.

What's Your Position?

1. **At what age do you believe we become sexual beings in our lifetime?**
   - At what age were you when you experienced your first sexual feelings? What were they and what did you do or think in response to them?
   - How old do you believe children should be when we begin talking with them about sex?

2. **How were you taught about sexuality early in your life?**
   - What early messages did your parents or caregivers pass on to you about sexual behaviors like masturbation and sexual play?
   - Do you remember your first experiences with sexual play or masturbation? What feelings do you associate with those first experiences?
   - How did you feel about the sexual parts of your body when you were a child?
   - At what age did you first see or read something that was sexually explicit? What was it and how did it affect your own sexual develoment?
   - Did your parents or teachers ever talk to you about sexual abuse or dating violence?

3. **What was your pubertal development like?**
   - Did you experience puberty early, on time, or late? How did the timing of your own pubertal development affect you?
   - How did you prepare for puberty? Did you talk to parents or friends, or seek information from other sources?
   - What do you remember most about your own pubertal development?
   - What do you believe is the ideal way to teach children and adolescents about puberty?

Design elements: Controversies in Sexuality: HBRH/Shutterstock; Research and Sexual Well Being: verity jane smith/Getty Images; Healthy Sexuality: Sergey Furtaev/Shutterstock; Communication Matters: PeopleImages/Getty Images; Know Yourself: Plush Studios/Blend Images LLC; What's Your Position: Luis Molinero/Shutterstock; Healthy Sexuality: A. Minde/PhotoAlto; Did You Know icon: McGraw-Hill Education; Page corner icon: McGraw-Hill Education.

Sexuality in Adulthood and Later Life

12

Ariel Skelley/Blend Images/Alamy Stock Photo

Early Adulthood
- Identify the factors that lead people to stay single.
- Describe cohabitation and the influence it might have on our subsequent experiences and behaviors.
- Recognize the difference between living apart together and friends with benefits.

Integrating Marriage and Sexual Well-Being
- List the reasons why people are marrying later in life in the United States.
- Identify key differences in the institution of marriage across cultures.
- Describe the factors involved in sexual satisfaction after marriage.
- Identify the recent legal changes creating same-sex marriage equality.
- Describe divorce trends in the United States and the effect of divorce on families.

Sexualtiy in Midlife and Aging
- Identify the myths and taboos pertaining to sex in midlife.
- Explain how caring for your body and keeping fit can contribute to positive sexuality in midlife.
- Describe issues of sexuality and sexual satisfaction in the later years.

Sexuality and Well-Being Late in Life
- Describe sexual desire in late life and challenges to the expression of sexual desire among elders.

Learning Objectives

Developing Your Position

1. How do you feel about being married in general? About being single?
2. How do you feel about having a life partner to love and with whom to share intimacy in your life?
3. If you expect to enjoy an active sexual life in your late adult years, what can you do when you're younger to remain sexually active later on?

Self, Society, and Culture: It's Never Too Late

Katherine had lived alone for a long time, and so had Laurel. Katherine's longtime partner had died some years before, and she had adapted, but never given up hope that she might find someone special again. Laurel was older and had been married and divorced, and then in a relationship for several years that had actually been hurtful to her. They were introduced to each other in an unexpected way—via email by a health care professional who knew them both and thought they might like each other. You might call it matchmaking, or just sticking your nose in someone else's life. Whatever you call it, Katherine and Laurel grudgingly met for coffee, both anticipating disappointment or worse. They took an instant shine to each other, went out on a date the next day, and have been inseparable since that time, almost 3 years ago. Oh, and what we didn't tell you is that Katherine is 74 and Laurel is 83. Recently they celebrated their anniversary together by getting legally married! Theirs is a true story, and it reveals that we are never too old to give love and sexual well-being a chance to flourish in our lives.

It is human nature to search for meaning, identity, love, and pleasure as ways to become whole and vibrant people. As populations age and more people remain single globally, there is a growing debate about the role of marriage and intimacy in defining life (Das, Waite, & Laumann, 2012). Increasingly, people in the United States live alone or continue to live with their families for longer periods and appear to be relatively happy with what this brings them in life (Klinenberg, 2012). Nevertheless, for large numbers of young adults, falling in love and finding a life partner define their transition into adulthood and contribute greatly to sexual well-being (Das, Waite, & Laumann, 2012; Laumann et al., 2006). Whatever the case, research evidence from across disciplines supports the general role of positive relationships in how people adapt, cope, and get on in life (Argyle, 2001; Diener & Diener, 2008; IOM, 2010; Taylor, 2010).

As the story of Katherine and Laurel reveals, all kinds of things can happen in life that may disrupt relationships and life itself. Researchers have found that committed happy relationships help people cope successfully with such challenges, in the United States and across cultures (Hirsch et al., 2009; Waite & Gallagher, 2000). Today economics, health, laws surrounding relationship formation, age, gender, and diversity all influence how people are able to be together and stay together in their life circumstances. Understanding this complex of factors not only will help you to achieve sexual well-being in later life but also provides insight and compassion for other people's situations.

In this chapter, we consider different phases of adulthood and human sexuality. The first phase covers **early adulthood,** the years of the early 20s to mid-30s when many people establish their full sense of self-direction in life. Sex, love, the search for mates and the expression of desire (Buss, 2016), and marriage are a critical part of this period. Adulthood extends into **midlife,** which encompasses the early 40s to mid-60s. During this time many people experience changes in their relationships and the life cycle of having children or not,

early adulthood
Early 20s to mid-30s.

midlife
Adulthood beginning in the late 40s.

just as their bodies continue to age. What it means to be sexually fulfilled may also change and mature during this time. The later phase includes **seniors,** people 65 to about 85. Of course, as people live longer and retire later, life takes on a different shape than it once had, because individuals may become grandparents or remarry or develop new pursuits, such as a hobby, or even take up a whole new career or service to society, for example, by joining the Peace Corps. **Elders** are individuals 85 and older and may themselves be the parents of seniors. Research shows that through all of these stages of life our sexual functioning and zest for sexuality and intimacy may continue right up to the end of life (Aronson, 2019; Valliant, 2002).

It's never too late to find intimacy and sexual well-being.
Caiaimage/Tom Merton/Getty Images

EARLY ADULTHOOD

The beginning of adulthood is a time of huge transition in education, careers, relationships, travel, and being part of society. The transition from late adolescence to early adulthood brings the freedom and responsibility of being increasingly independent of parents and family, beginning careers and jobs, and growing closer to friends and intimate partners. Some decisions that young adults make during this transition may affect their whole life, such as career and marriage choices. They may move to another city to pursue education or career, remain single or live with someone before marriage, and opt to have children or not. In short, this is the time when we develop a basic sense of being an autonomous adult alone or in relationship, in the world and engaged in getting a life.

To help make these decisions and achieve a positive transition into adulthood, young adults may want to consider these questions:

- Will I continue to live with my family or be on my own?
- Do I need to move to another city or another country to pursue my career?
- How will I combine my desires for sex and love with a fulfilling relationship?
- What am I willing to sacrifice to achieve pleasure or security or both?
- How will I value career and educational goals against love and sex and family formation?
- Do I want to live alone or with someone else, either as partner or friend?
- Do I expect to have a life partner and share sex with that person when I am old?

Notice that these questions concern one person in relationship to others.

All through the industrial world, including the United States, relationships are changing dramatically. Instead of entering and staying in marriage, people enter into cohabitation, and then convert to marriage, or move on to another relationship (Perelli-Harris et al., 2012). In the United States, the social landscape surrounding intimate relationships has changed radically over the last several decades to include entering into a relationship that lasts a long time, or leaving it and then forming new relationships, or staying single. The changes have altered the way we look at the transition from adolescence to adulthood. In the 1960s and 1970s, young people often graduated from high school and got married soon afterward or went traveling or became involved in social movements, but young people today often sidestep committed marital relationships in their teens, postpone leaving home, and pursue educational and occupational goals. Thus the timing, duration, and repetition of cohabiting and marital unions is very complex (Perelli-Harris & Lyongs-Amos, 2015).

seniors
Adults 65 and up.

elders
Adults 85 and up.

Figure 12.1

People are marrying later than they did 50 years ago. Since 1960, the median age at first marriage increased by nearly 6 years for men and slightly more than 6 years for women.

Marriage is being delayed longer in the United States and all other major industrial countries. Historically, as you can see from Figure 12.1, the age of first marriage has gone up by several years.

Marriage now occurs later in life on average—age 29.5 for males and 27.4 years for females (U.S. Census Bureau, 2017). However, more people live with their parents, more people live alone, and a lot more couples than ever are living together before they marry or make a life commitment (Klinenberg, 2012). Many of these trial arrangements break up quickly, and we will later discuss how divorce is changing as well. What do these changes mean for our individual sexual well-being? They imply that as society changes, individuals can benefit from having the knowledge and skills that will help them navigate life successfully for the rest of their lives.

single
Uncommitted or unmarried.

Single Living

Singles outnumber married people in America today (U.S. Census Bureau, 2017). This is a huge change, a reversal of the 1950s. The reasons are in part the economy, the changing nature of life expectancy, and how people look at relationships. For some people, living alone enhances their options—freedom, self-realization, career, and personal control, values that Americans tend to like and endorse (Klinenberg, 2012). Some 5 million people in the United States between ages 18 and 34 live alone, which is 10 times the number in 1950. As you can see from Figure 12.2, the percentage of increase in living alone gets larger the older you get. The largest number of **single** people, around 15 million between ages 35 and 64, live solo. Upwards of 40% of all households in prosperous cities including Atlanta, Denver, Seattle, San Francisco, and Minneapolis contain a single occupant, and in Manhattan, the number is about 50% (Klinenberg, 2012).

And what is even more surprising is that there is a mix of generations—Z's, millennials, and boomers—who say that they enjoy living alone and plan to stay that way. One of the reasons people may choose to be alone is that singles tend to go out more, to socialize with friends and neighbors, to take in theater, or to enter adult education classes (Klinenberg, 2012). Following a breakup or a divorce some people may choose to move in with roommates or family; however, a growing number choose to live alone because, as some would admit, there's nothing worse than living with the wrong person.

Historically, cultural and sexual norms suggested that young people who did not marry and form a family were odd, possibly abnormal, perhaps associated

Many young adults today are choosing to stay single.
Jason Homa/Getty Images

Figure 12.2

Since 1850, the percentage of American adults living alone has more than doubled (a). For adults 65 and older, the increase has been huge, in part because people are living longer and outliving their partners. Still, the United States ranks lower than many Western countries in the percentage of single-person households (b).

Source: Bill, M., & Cox, A. (2012). *The New York Times, 2/4/12.* New York Times Company, Inc.

with being less eligible as a mate (Cott, 2002). Sure, there are exceptions, such as little-known President James Buchanan or religious figures, but the historical trend was toward marriage. The belief was single individuals would not have children to provide the necessary economic and social support in late life (Cott, 2002). Now it is becoming less common for people to

DID YOU KNOW

Some Facts About Being Single From the U.S. Census (2017)

- 110.6 million—the number of unmarried Americans in 2016. This group comprised 45.2% of all U.S. residents age 18 and older.
- 19.5 million—those who are unmarried and single age 65 and older. These older Americans comprise 17.7% of all unmarried and single people.
- 53.2%—unmarried and single who are women.
- 63.5%—unmarried and single who have never been married. Another 23.1% are divorced and 13.4% are widowed.
- 88—number of unmarried men age 18 and older for every 100 unmarried women in the United States.
- 59.8 million—number of "unmarried households" (men or women) in the U.S. census; these comprise 47.6% of all households nationwide.
- 35.4 million—number of people who live alone. These persons comprise 28.1% of all households, up from 17% in 1970.
- 37.5%—the percentage of opposite-sex, unmarried-partner couples in 2016 that lived with at least one biological child of either partner.
- 7.3 million—number of unmarried-partner households in 2015. Of this number, 433,539 were same-sex households.

Source: Unmarried and Single Americans Week: Sept. 17–23, 2017, https://www.census.gov/content/dam/Census/newsroom/facts-for-features/2017/cb17-ff16.pdf

celibacy
The condition of remaining single, often by choice.

marry and have children as young adults, though plenty still do (Waite & Gallagher, 2000). Love tops the reasons that people want to get married; 88% said love was more important than commitment (Pew, 2019). Whether or not to remain single, what that will mean, and whether one should live with someone before getting married are core issues for a young adult.

Of course, there are many options when it comes to being a single adult, or living alone, or being in a relationship. Adults can choose to live with a romantic partner, get married, or pursue an active dating and sex life including multiple partners, and may or may not actually live together. As we saw, people are delaying marriage, especially among the middle class and the educated (Goldstein & Kenney, 2001). All of these changes probably reflect changing demographics, economic uncertainty, and how societal attitudes over time have come to stress the need for greater preparation for life decisions, such as whether or not to live with someone, marry, and have children.

Culturally there are several different sexual conditions associated with being single. One is being sexually active in a search for sexual satisfaction. Another sexual condition is **celibacy,** intentionally not having sex, a choice typically associated with being single. Involuntary celibacy is when someone wants to have sex but cannot find a partner (Delamater & Carpenter, 2012, p. 13). Celibacy occurs across many cultures, whether it is elected or imposed and whether temporary or permanent (Bell & Sobo, 2001). In some cultures the religious celibate, such as a priest or nun, a permanent condition, exchanges the right to engage in sex for the privilege of sacred status. Abstinence is a choice for some people through their lives, though not necessarily permanent. Celibacy and abstinence in many people's minds preclude all bodily intimacy, including masturbation. As discussed in Chapter 11, many young people who make a commitment to sexual abstinence before marriage apply different meanings to this term in their intimate relationships (Carpenter, 2005), including the temporary notion of "saving themselves" as "virgins" for marriage. Yet "abstinence until marriage" is a hard standard to live by, given that more people are delaying marriage till their late 20s, or even later, and people are more tolerant of breaking up or ending relationships.

Many traditional cultures stress abstinence until marriage and having children, but since World War II, western Europe has experienced a long-term trend toward remaining single and having fewer children or none at all (Badgett, 2009; Ryser, 2018). This difference is reflected partly in the age of marriage. For example, in Germany and France, the average age of first marriage is approximately 33 years, whereas in the United States it is approximately 4 years younger—a significant difference. In Sweden, there is a longer tradition of people remaining single or marrying later or being a couple but living apart, as we will explore later. Additionally, in Sweden and northern European countries, there is a growing cultural tradition of not marrying and having children outside of marriage. There are various economic, cultural, and legal reasons for these differences, including state policies of socialized medicine and support for childcare that enables single women to rear children apart from men and to pursue careers (Badgett, 2009; Koontz, 2005). But whether in the

HEALTHY Sexuality

Who Has More Sex: Singles or Couples?

The answer may surprise you, and depending on your answer, it may give you an opportunity to reflect upon your attitudes about being single. There appear to be two camps of opinion surrounding whether marriage brings more or less opportunity to have sex, in part because of the demands of raising children. However, a widespread belief says that singles have the most sex and married couples' sex lives become dull or even dead with time. In fact, on average, married couples continue to have sex more steadily over the years compared to singles, but let's consider some distinctions. First, men and women who are live-in partners tend to have more sex than men and women who are married (Laumann et al., 2006).

Second, married couples over the past generation tend to have significantly more sexual satisfaction and more frequent sex compared to singles who do not live together. Indeed, 47% of the men and 41% of the women in married relationships describe sex with their spouse as "extremely physically pleasurable" (Laumann et al., 1994, p. 118). Additionally, singles found sex to be more "exciting" on average by comparison with their matched married peers, which might mean that single sex is perceived to be novel, risky, and more pleasurable. Research suggests that having children may influence the experience of having sexual pleasure for couples, whether they are married or not.

United States or Europe, being single allows people to explore and get to know who they are and what they want in life, and it appears to be most satisfying for people who are intentionally single, especially in middle age (Klinenberg, 2012; Schwartz, 2007b). Allowing for the fact that some singles choose an abstinent lifestyle, does being single mean having more sex than married couples do? Find out by reading "Healthy Sexuality: Who Has More Sex: Singles or Couples?"

Casual Sex and What It Means

Casual sex, also known as *hooking up,* is sex with people to whom you are not in love or committed (Bogle, 2008; Wade & Heldman, 2012). Once regarded as taboo, even to talk about, an increasing number of people living alone are changing the meaning of being single and having casual sex, into middle age or beyond (Klinenberg, 2012). Although premarital sex was especially controversial in U.S. society at the time of Kinsey's groundbreaking study (1948), especially for females, it has grown to be much less so and is prevalent among many age groups today (Regnerus & Uecker, 2011; Wade & Heldman, 2012). Dating and engaging in casual sex may precede falling in love and finding a mate. Some people prefer to engage for some period of time in casual sex, and define this as a sexual relationship with no "emotional strings" attached (Bernstein, 2008; Perel, 2006). At some point, however, the cultural expectation that people should "settle down" kicks in, and this appears to be especially true for women compared to men (Bernstein, 2008; Regnerus & Uecker, 2011). For example, families may exert increasing pressure on their offspring to make commitments, marry, and have children, as the biological clock ticks on, especially for women (Bogle, 2008; Gagnon, 2004).

In recent years, casual sex has become a normative part of the cultural landscape of adolescents and young adults—particularly on college campuses (Reiber & Garcia, 2010). According to one study, 81% of study participants reported engaging in sexual behavior of some sort during a hookup (Reiber & Garcia, 2010). Research suggests that hooking up is associated with people being highly dissatisfied with sex on campus (Wade & Heldman, 2012, p. 129). So the term *hooking up* has quite a range of meanings and emotional attitudes

casual sex
Sex with people with whom you are not in love or committed.

Table **12.1** Sexual Behaviors Common in Hookup Interactions

BEHAVIOR	% OF MALES	% OF FEMALES
Sexual touching above the waist	58%	58%
Sexual touching below the waist	54%	53%
Oral sex, performer	31%	40%
Oral sex, recipient	36%	34%
Intercourse	35%	32%

Source: Adapted from Reiber, C., & Garcia, J.R. (2010). Hooking up: Gender differences, evolution, and pluralistic ignorance. *Evolutionary Psychology, 8*(3), 390–404.

associated with such an interaction. Table 12.1 gives a look at one study's findings regarding the kinds of behaviors that are most common during hookups.

Note the similarity in responses by males and females. Men and women hook up at similar rates (Owens, Behund, Manning, & Reid, 2012), and some of both genders are enthusiastic about hooking up. Where we do see differences is in reports by men and women of their level of comfort with the behaviors they engage in. This particular study (and in many others) revealed that men were more comfortable with all sexual behaviors than women and that men tend to overestimate women's comfort levels with higher-risk behaviors such as oral sex and intercourse (Lambert, Kahn, & Apple, 2003; Reiber & Garcia, 2010). This is an important point because when you pair men's higher comfort levels with these behaviors and their overestimation of their partner's comfort level, there may be unintended and unfortunate consequences, such as when men unintentionally pressure women and women give in to the pressure despite their discomfort. Another study has found that students sought one of three things in these hookups: meaningfulness, empowerment, or pleasure, and most students, women especially, found it difficult to achieve any of these things (Wade & Heldman, 2012).

The reality of young adulthood and singlehood is that those who are single today have a wide range of sexual and social possibilities (Manning, Brown & Payne, 2014), in part because of social media and all the societal changes outlined earlier. One possibility is **serial monogamy,** in which individuals have an exclusive relationship with one person, break up with that person, and then go on to an exclusive relationship with a different person. Another possibility is that some singles may be involved sexually with a friend or acquaintance for some benefit, such as shared rent, but without commitment, an arrangement also known as **friends with benefits (FWB).** Research suggests that cross-sex friendships are complicated, however, because many friends are past or potential partners (Wade & Heldman, 2012). People may relocate to certain neighborhoods in part because of the kind of prospective mates they will encounter in the local coffee shop, grocery, or mall (Laumann et al., 2004). Some singles choose to work in certain industries, where they think they have a better chance of meeting Ms. or Mr. Right (Pincott, 2008). Movies and popular television shows, such as *How I Met Your Mother, Modern Family,* or *Brooklyn 99,* depict complex arrangements for sharing space, expenses, companionship, and love and intimacy. These shows, however, generally portray marriage as the best situation in which to find true happiness.

In the United States, as norms and attitudes about sexual relations and casual sex change and incorporate having sexual relationships without being married, we will discover that new forms are evolving of living together without being married. All of these changes imply greater societal acceptance of casual sex relationships (Badgett & Herman, 2011; Laumann et al., 2004; Manning, Brown, & Payne, 2014) in general, which has probably contributed to the increase in unmarried couples living together before marriage.

serial monogamy
The practice of having an exclusive relationship with one person, breaking up, and going on to another exclusive relationship.

friends with benefits (FWB)
Singles involved sexually with a friend or acquaintance for some mutual benefit, such as shared rent, but without commitment.

Polyamory

Sexual science has focused considerable attention on consensual nonmonogamous (CNM) relationships since the time of Kinsey et al. (1948), a construct that includes "open relationships" (vaguely defined), "swinging," a practice that is generally understood to mean "wife or husband swapping" in an earlier generation, and more recently polyamory (Balzarini et al., 2017), which we will focus on here.

Polyamory is a nonmonogamous practice that consists of having more than one intimate relationship at a time with the consent of all the partners involved. The key is for everyone to accept both the desire and the expression of the relationship. Polyamory is much more common now than a generation ago. The words that have been used to describe the openness of polyamory are consensual, ethical, responsible, transparent, and authentic. Polyamorous relationships seemed more frequent among younger LGBT adults (LaSala, 2010) until recently, but new research suggests that heterosexual polyamorous relationships are on the rise (Balzarini et al., 2019). A recent major study in the United States found that approximately 21% of all Americans had engaged in a CNM relationship at some point in their lives (Haupert et al., 2017).

Polyamory should not be confused with "cheating" or having an affair outside of a committed relationship because all the partners consent to the relationships. Supporters of CNM relationships, including polyamory, like to remind us that "while more than 90% of all Americans marry, at least 50% of these men and women have affairs" (Stone, Goetz, & Shackelford, 2005, p. 269). Many of these affairs probably fall under the guise of "cheating," that is, secret sexual relations hidden from spouses. In other words, we must be mindful not to create a binary opposition between monogamy and polyamory, since the reality of monogamy does not always hold, and polyamorous partners aspire to be open and responsible in their intimate relations (Emens, 2004). The length of time in a relationship also should not be the main defining characteristic of polyamorous relationships, because some are short-term and others can last for years (Haupert et al., 2017). Polyamorous partners may or may not live together, for short or longer periods of time, in ethical, respectful, meaningful, and satisfying relationships (Kleese, 2006). Unlike polygamy, however, polyamory does not necessarily involve marriage, and it may involve two men and one woman, rather than one man with more than one wife. These understandings require negotiation; as researchers have noted when it comes to CNM, "exclusive" sexual and emotional commitment are also not that easy to negotiate, and they may be subject to all kinds of cultural conditions, such as polygamy (Hirsch et al., 2009).

Religious authorities object to polyamory as a violation of morals and monogamy in many faiths (Regnerus, 2007). However, the same objection applies to adultery, studied below. Some people wonder what happens when children are involved in polyamorous relationships, an area of research still lacking. Children are affected by such relationships and may be influenced by partners outside of the primary couple. This could be confusing to some children (Shernoff, 2006).

One study has found that in some rural areas, relationships outside of marriage are regarded as suspect and carry the risk of stigma for the individual partners in CNM (Kirkman, Dickson-Swift, & Fox, 2015).

Some proponents of polyamory consider love and a spiritual connection to be as important as sexual relations. In fact, some people in polyamory relationships start off with sexual intimacy but may drift into complex arrangements of companionship and household security (Haupert al., 2017). Thus, proponents of polyamory embrace the following values:

- Love and intimacy: Key attributes describing many of these relationships. Fidelity and loyalty: Polyamorists define fidelity as being faithful to the promises and agreements they have made, rather than only to sexual exclusivity.

- Trust, honesty, dignity, and respect: Polyamorists emphasize respect, trust, and honesty. Secrecy or deception violates the trust.

polyamory
The intentional acceptance of one's partner having sexual relations with someone else, typically for a significant period of time.

- Mutual support: The idea is that partners support the others in the relationship and avoid harm to any involved in the relationship.
- Communication and negotiation: Staying open to discussing changes and being creative about how to communicate in triadic relationships are keys to successful polyamorous relationships. When people break the rules or make mistakes, the partners stress that communication is important to repair any breaches (Shernoff, 2006).

Have you ever wondered what kind of personality traits may go along with polyamory? To find out more, read "Healthy Sexuality: The Polyamorist: Is There a Personality Type that Fits?"

Cohabitation

As we have seen, people today tend to enter into relationships and stay in them or exit and go on to another one, rather than marrying and staying on in the marriage (Perelli et al., 2012). Such relationships can occur for any adult and any stage of life in adulthood, but the social pressures differ for heterosexual and same-sex couples (Gates & Newport, 2015). Although the number of people cohabiting before marriage has increased significantly in recent years, as noted below, and the percentage of same-sex couples getting married has dramatically increased since gay marriage became legal in America in 2015, it is hard to figure out how many same-sex couples cohabit because of continuing legal and social barriers and the lack of good evidence and census information.

There were 18 million adults cohabiting in 2016, 29% more than in 2007 (Pew, 2017). More than half of them were under the age of 35, but the number of older adults 50 and up cohabiting had increased hugely and keeps rising. These couples generally are assumed to be heterosexual.

There is an untold number of same-sex couples who live together but are not counted as partners in the census, but thanks to changes in the law allowing same-sex marriage since 2015, we have a better idea than before. Of course it is more difficult to estimate the true numbers of same-sex couples living together, because as we saw in Chapter 10, many of them do not disclose their identities; however, a reported 2 million Americans cohabit as same-sex couples, and 780,000 of them were married in 2015 (Gates & Newport, 2015).

Unmarried couples who live together are said to be cohabiting, and historically they have been counted as heterosexual, though today we know that some of them are LGBTQ (Gates, 2012). **Cohabitation** is defined as the state of living together or sharing the same space as if the couple were married but without being legally married. Cohabitation has three components:

1. Living arrangements
2. Meaning of cohabitation to both partners
3. Level of commitment between partners

Let's consider each component individually.

Cohabitation Living Arrangements Many different kinds of living arrangements qualify as cohabitation in the United States. Different living arrangements may create a different set of social networks for the couple, depending on the geographic locale, cultural meanings of the arrangements, and neighborhood identity (Laumann et al., 2004; Perelli-Harris & Lyons-Amos, 2015). The arrangements may include one of the following:

- Sharing an apartment or house and having regular sex as a couple
- Living together occasionally, while maintaining separate households
- Living together without necessarily having sex, to share living expenses or possibly to pool resources to buy property together
- Maintaining separate residences and referring to yourselves as a couple

cohabitation
The state of living together or sharing the same space as a couple without being legally married.

Cohabitation may or may not include sexual intimacy. For gay couples, there are legal barriers to cohabitation in some states.
Rawpixel.com/Shutterstock

HEALTHY Sexuality

The Polyamorist: Is There a Personality Type that Fits?

As we have seen, consensual nonmonogamy, better known as polyamory, is an intentional open state of mind to have multiple partners who all agree to be in a relationship openly. There is no way to know how frequent or common polyamory is due to how new this kind of relationship is and the complexity of factors, but one significant study has suggested that perhaps 5% of people may be involved (Balzarini et al., 2017). Based upon a fairly reasonable sample of 1,308 self-identified polyamorous individuals, the authors reported fairly high levels of satisfaction and less stigma than would have been expected. It is interesting that the authors reported that the participants reported greater sexual and romantic involvement with the secondary partner than with the primary partner. All of this raises some very interesting questions, and among them is the one you may have thought of: Is there a personality type more likely to be a polyamorist? In earlier studies, such qualities as fidelity, trust, and loyalty have been reported (Shernoff, 2006). But we suspect that as a new generation takes on polyamorous relationships, other things will become apparent. Here are some of the personality traits that are reported from online writers about the polyamorist today.

- **Openness and honesty.** The polyamorist feels that it is very important to be open and honest with the self and with all partners about how they are feeling. Openness to new experiences helps quite a bit, too!
- **Flexibility and adaptability.** The polyamorists have to learn to accept the needs of multiple partners and to make space for them. The "making space" part may require flexibility.
- **Nonconformance to tradition.** The polyamorist identified this trait as being pretty common among poly people. They tend to question the norms and not care as much about rules and traditions.
- **Empathy.** Being empathetic to others' needs is crucial in any relationship. With polyamory, since more people are involved, there are more needs and feelings to consider. Having said that, a sense of worth and knowing our own boundaries are also very important because it's hard to sustain a relationship while consistently deprioritizing your own needs.
- **Patience.** The polyamorist needs to be patient because the pace in relationships (and generally in life) in the sense of the degree of change expected may be faster or slower; they need to give space and time to getting used to things on multiple occasions.
- **You have to be an engineer.** *Just kidding*. But it does seem to be true that a disproportionately greater number of engineers are among people who self-identified as poly. They report a sense of "geekiness" and creativity mentioned online that helps provide enough quality time for all the partners to meet at least some of their needs!

Among the various barriers heterosexual and nonheterosexual people may experience are legal barriers to renting or owning in the housing market (Badgett, 2009). While people have worked around these barriers by creating many types of living arrangements, many social policies and laws pose barriers to same-sex cohabitation and couple's rights. The laws vary by state (Badgett, 2009; Gates, 2012; West, 2007). These policies and laws overlap and sometimes are even contradictory. Some of the legal definitions regarding cohabitation are presented in "Communication Matters: The Evolving Terminology of Living Together."

The Meaning of Cohabitation The meanings of cohabitation have changed dramatically in the last few years across the industrial world (Perelli-Harris et al., 2012). These meanings for couples can include things about their personal lives, including their race and faith, and things about their life circumstances, such as their finances,

COMMUNICATION Matters

The Evolving Terminology of Living Together

The increasing number of straight couples living together before marriage and the challenges posed by same-sex couples who aspire to have marriage rights have led to new terminology and laws in the United States (U.S. Census, 2012). To avoid any legal wrangling, you might want to research the laws in your state before you move in with someone. Consider these terms and what they mean:

1. **Common law marriage**—a status that involves two people of the opposite sex living together, typically for at least 1 or 2 years, and regarding each other publicly as spouses even though they are not legally married. People in a common law marriage usually have a claim on each other's property and incomes, and may be entitled to child care support or alimony if the relationship breaks up; however, there are laws that may completely deprive the common law partner of any inheritance even after years and favor the original biological parents or siblings, as for example, in Sweden today. Many common law couples do not know that if they break up, they may have to file for a legal divorce just as if they had been legally married.

2. **Domestic partnership**—a defined legal and social relationship in some states, and in the private corporate sphere for some companies, that provides some benefits, such as health care, to one's registered domestic partner. This is a lesser legal status than common law marriage, which may or may not be recognized by local or state law.

3. **Civil union**—a legally recognized union similar to marriage in some states, though not performed in a church. Denmark was the first country to recognize civil unions in 1989.

4. **Same-sex marriage**—a legal marriage between two people of the same biological sex; now legal in the United States and in 27 countries.

5. **Registered partnership**—Any couple regardless of sexual orientation can officially register their partnership in some states in the United States and other countries. This status has almost all the rights as marriage, including the right to a church wedding in 10 countries.

---

common law marriage
An interpersonal status involving two people who live together and regard each other publicly as spouses even though no marriage or civil ceremony has occurred.

domestic partnership
A defined legal and social status in some states, and in the corporate sphere for some companies, that provides some benefits, such as health care, to registered domestic partners.

civil union
A legally recognized union similar to marriage but not having all the same protections and rights.

job opportunities, shared values, and a common core of interests. However, implicit in different living arrangements are love, sexual intimacy, and some level of emotional commitment. But if a couple sees their relationship as a domestic partnership, for example, it may not be recognized by the state or local authorities, or by religious groups. When issues arise, such as visiting the cohabiting partner in the hospital, the cohabiting couple may find themselves without rights. There is a broad range of economic, social, and health care rights denied to cohabiting couples, and especially LGBTQ people, such as employment discrimination, adoption rights, and housing discrimination in some states (Badgett & Herman, 2011; IOM Report, 2012). This denial of rights occurs even though living and sleeping together identifies a deep emotional bond between the couple.

Level of Commitment The third component of cohabitation is emotional commitment. Cohabitation often creates emotional bonds about being open, truthful, and sharing. Exploring the level of trust and commitment is common to couples at this stage of a relationship, and it may involve faithfulness (Perel, 2006). Trust is especially important among minority youth in developing relationships (Laborde, van Dommelin-Gonzales, & Minnis, 2014). As people's commitment deepens they may begin to plan for the future. Additionally, many individuals want to know someone intimately before they make a long-term commitment. This makes sense for a variety of reasons, including economic commitments and emotional comfort.

CONTROVERSIES in Sexuality

Cohabitation Before Marriage

Does living together make it easier or harder to get married later on? For several decades researchers have studied this question, but the research remains inconclusive and suggestive but controversial (Dush et al., 2003; Perelli-Harris & Lyons-Amos, 2015; Regnerus & Uecker, 2011). Evidence does suggest that cohabitation may be *either* bad or good for relationships, but the outcome is dependent upon the quality of the couple's relationship while living together. The reasons appear to be that each couple's situation is unique because their personalities are different, and they may have different aspirations for having a long-term relationship, including whether they want to have children, and how much their sense of living together is temporary or permanent (Perelli-Harris & Styrc, 2018).

Historically, half of all cohabitations in the United States ended within a year through a breakup, and about 40% ended in a formal marriage (Laumann et al., 1994). That was from a national sample from the early 1990s, but another, more recent study found that cohabitation is associated with less interpersonal commitment and satisfaction between partners (Stanley, Whitton, & Markman, 2004). Experts are not sure just why. Some studies suggest that cohabiting may contribute to a sense of dissatisfaction or unhappiness later in marriage (Dush et al., 2003). The reason for that may be that some individuals who move in prior to marriage may not have been the best candidates for happy marriages down the road (Schwartz, 2007a; Smock, 2000).

Gender also appears to be a factor in the likelihood of marriage after cohabitation (Perelli-Harris & Styrc, 2018). Studies have found that for males, cohabitation is associated with being less religious and less committed, factors that link to lower levels of well-being and more negative interactions (Stanley et al., 2004). Another study found that males cohabited with female partners more frequently to "test" the relationship, and later some of them changed their attitudes toward their mates. This attitude change was associated with some negative outcomes, such as poor communication with partners, less confidence, and less dedication to making the relationship work (Rhoades et al., 2009).

The implication of cohabitation studies, then, is that postponement of marriage is changing many things in relationships, including creating cohabitation as its own unique class that is not the same as being married (Perelli-Harris & Styrc, 2018). Still, the results are inconclusive because every relationship is unique, and the controversy lingers.

Does living together first make it harder to get married later on?

Yes:

- Plenty of studies give some support to the idea that cohabitation does not necessarily lend itself to a happier marriage later on.
- Some social, familial, and religious groups continue to be opposed to living together before marriage, and this may make it harder for the couple.
- Societal attitudes appear to influence how people feel about cohabitation, and some women still feel that it's shameful to live together before marriage (Laumann et al., 2004).

No:

- There are studies that suggest cohabiting before marriage contributes to a better relationship down the line, if the couple like each other and are happy.
- Every couple is different, and just because cohabitation doesn't "work" for everyone doesn't mean that it is a bad idea before marriage.
- Research suggests that young men, who previously may have been less inclined to marry a woman if they cohabited first, are different today and are more committed to this outcome (Mastekaasa, 2006; Perelli-Harris & Styrc, 2018).

Because every couple's situation is unique, it is nearly impossible to determine how cohabitation contributes to the success or failure of a long-term relationship in the abstract.

What Is Your Perspective?

1. What do you think about the gender difference that suggests men may be reluctant to marry if they cohabit first?
2. What do you think about the societal perception that a "good girl" should not cohabit before marriage? Does this perception affect your thinking about the possibility of cohabiting before marriage?
3. What could you do to determine if cohabitation is the right arrangement for you and your partner?

same-sex marriage
A term used to describe a legal marriage and formal status between two people of the same biological sex.

registered partnership
Legal status granted in some states allowing same-sex or opposite-sex couples to receive tax benefits and other benefits granted to married couples.

contraceptive switch
Phase of cohabitation when couples develop reproductive plans.

Determining whether a partner shares the same values, such as truthfulness and providing mutual support for life aspirations, and is a good prospective parent or life companion, are among the most frequently mentioned reasons for cohabitation (Perel, 2006).

It's still unclear whether or not cohabitation is entirely positive for a couple's relationship in the long term. To find out what the research says, read "Controversies in Sexuality: Cohabitation Before Marriage."

Whether or not cohabitation is beneficial in the long term for a couple's relationship, all the research says that the decision to live together is very important in people's lives and futures (Perelli-Harris & Lyons-Amos, 2015; Smock, 2000). For example, it appears that couples may measure their degree of commitment by whether they use condoms or switch to a more long-term contraception method, such as birth control pills or an IUD. This phase in the relationship, when couples develop reproductive plans, is now known as the **contraceptive switch** (Civic, 2000). Research suggests that it is, however, difficult to predict young men's decision making without knowing their experiences and values (Raine et al., 2010). College students are increasingly using the contraceptive switch when they think about live-in relationships.

To help you determine if cohabitation is right for you and your partner, consider some key factors and the questions in "Know Yourself: Is Cohabitation Right for Me?"

Research suggests that allowance for more mutual expectations regarding gender roles and heterosexual expectations of living together are making cohabitation more successful and acceptable, at least for some couples in some communities (Laumann et al., 2004; Perelli-Harris & Amos-Lyons, 2015). A study in Norway found that young women were less distressed when they lived with someone before marrying them, especially when their expectations were similar about living together, compared to the past. Additionally, young men are more positive about their relationships, at age 23 and older (Mastekaasa, 2006). In short, cohabitation today leads to more positive future commitments and marriages in such contexts (Perelli-Harris et al., 2012). Note that the rate of marriage in the U.S. population among people who cohabited is going up.

A study of recent college graduates aged 18–40 found that 60% of 125 people had experienced a friends-with-benefits relationship (Bisson & Levine, 2009). Other studies have found a similar result (Afifi & Faulkner, 2000), which suggests that among the culture of college students, this practice is increasing (Perelli-Harris & Lyons-Amos, 2015). The friends in these intimate relationships tend not to discuss commitment or boundaries regarding their friendship and having sex. Some 85% reported not talking about these relationship questions, and nearly 66% of the friends had no ground rules or boundaries. A minority of the sample who had not experienced FWB relationships found them to be morally unacceptable because they felt that friendship and sex do not mix (Bisson & Levine, 2009).

In western Europe, a much older relationship trend has solidified a cultural pattern. **Living apart together (LAT)** is the expression the Dutch use to explain their version of FWB. LAT is about having one's own individual space and life, separate from a lover or partner, but still being part of a couple (de Vries and van Veen, 2010; Perelli-Harris & Lyons-Amos, 2015). The term comes from the 1978 film *Eva and Frank: Living Apart Together*. It gives new meaning to the idea of cohabiting. Some gay men and lesbians have experienced LAT relationships for years because they have been denied the right to legal marriage (Badgett, 2009; Herdt & Kertzner, 2006). But these are heterosexual relationships and they appear to be widespread in Holland and other European countries, such as Italy, France, and Great Britain. Researchers have found that the concept has now spread to nearly 50% of all younger couples 30 and under in Europe (de Vries and van Veen, 2010). According to John Haskey at Oxford University in Great Britain, 1 million couples were living in similar relationships. Additionally, LAT relationships are on the rise in the United States (Brooke, 2006). A new large-scale study of 5,253 people from seven European

living apart together (LAT)
The cultural idea that two people can be a couple but live apart in separate households.

Is Cohabitation Right for Me?

Know Yourself

People who are considering cohabitation might want to take into account three key issues:

1. **Short- and long-term commitment.** Cohabitation is rarely a permanent relationship status, although cohabitation is becoming more common and lasting longer than before (Perelli-Harris & Amos-Lyons, 2015). Relationships will usually progress to the commitment of marriage or dissolve. The majority of cohabitation arrangements end after 6 months in early adulthood (Dush et al., 2003; Laumann et al., 1994; Regnerus & Uecker, 2011). Reflecting on the length of the commitment may help you make a decision about whether living together is right for you.

2. **Fidelity in the relationship.** Research shows that couples who cohabit have slightly higher risks of relationship infidelity (Regnerus & Uecker, 2011). Because infidelity is a common reason that couples break up, discussing faithfulness and being clear about your definitions of commitment before you move in together can be helpful.

3. **Cohabitation leading to marriage later.** Even though a couple may not be thinking about marriage as a possibility at the outset, it can come up in the future. Communication can really help you to develop your ideas on the short- and long-term commitment issue.

People considering cohabitation and couples negotiating new relationships may want to discuss the following questions (Bisson & Levine, 2009). Communicating as a couple about these questions can help people achieve sexual well-being because they can better understand their own and their partner's needs, emotions, and sexual behaviors. Also, a couple's responses to these questions may provide important clues about the stability of the relationship and the potential for a shared future.

1. Is your relationship primarily for sex? If so, is it necessary to live together?
2. Is your relationship primarily motivated by love and wanting to be with the other person exclusively?
3. What will change in your relationship dynamics if you and your partner live together?
4. Is the decision to live together primarily about economics? If so, is living together really going to make a financial difference?
5. Will each individual take responsibility for his or her own share of the household expenses and chores, and the emotional work of living together?
6. Are you and your partner as individuals committed to being with the person only under certain conditions, such as each one pays a share of the rent, or each one can have a personal space within the relationship?

The key to making an informed decision about cohabitation is to understand how your own sexual individuality fits the whole situation with a prospective life partner, including your own values, options about cohabitation, and what the research reveals about trends before making a decision to cohabit.

countries shows that LAT relationships are determined by the nature of the family, age, and especially social pressures exerted on people to live together (Ayuso, 2018). One final observation about LAT: In Holland, when LAT couples decide to have children, they tend to get married and move in together. This is as much for legal and financial clarity as it is for the fact that the children would have both parents living with them (de Vries and van Veen, 2010).

DID YOU KNOW

After a lifetime of working on the psychology of sex and love, when he was asked at the end of a long life what most mattered, Freud said three words: "Love and work."

Early Cohabitation and Sexual Well-Being

Cohabitation, relationships, and sexual well-being all fit together (Adams & Jones, 1999; Perelli-Harris & Styrc, 2018). The key is to know how "commitment" fits different kinds of relationships. Three characteristics of commitment stand out in cohabitation research:

1. *Attraction:* People want the relationship to continue because of its high reward value.

2. *Moral-normative perception:* Cultural and emotional expectations compel people to stay in the relationship, often supported by moral and religious views.

3. *External constraints:* Real-world factors such as finances, family and/or religious pressure, and shared experiences make it harder to leave the relationship (Adams & Jones, 1999).

With the first characteristic, *attraction,* couples living together tend to share social, emotional, romantic, and even political values, as well as a sexual attraction (Blackwell & Lichter, 2005; Regnerus & Uecker, 2011). Their shared values may also include the perceived degree of honesty, faithfulness, and commitment to each other. Partners who are personally committed tend to identify with each other, further strengthening the relationship.

Some evidence suggests that being attracted to someone makes the pair want to stay together, regardless of what happens. *Congruence* means how well suited the couple is in terms of their physical, educational, and other traits. Here are several of the significant qualities many people associate with congruence:

- Sincerity and authenticity in what you say and do with your partner
- Honesty with yourself about how you feel about you and your partner
- Openness to each other initiating sexual intimacy
- Faithfulness to your commitments, feelings, and relationships
- The ability to communicate and express your feelings in constructive ways
- Flexibility and willingness to negotiate your goals

Many couples' therapists particularly emphasize respect for a partner's needs, identities, values, goals, family, and friendship networks (Perel, 2006).

The second characteristic, a *moral-normative perception,* is often supported by moral and religious views, including the traditional idea that divorce is a sin. As explained in Chapter 2, religion is an important influence on people's attitudes about commitment and marriage. Traditionally, many cultures have perceived the moral values surrounding marriage as being very important and even "sacred," as an arrangement for life (Regnerus, 2007; Smith, 1991). In fact, a culture may saturate the meaning of cohabitation with marriage so as to make it clear that living together without marriage is stigmatized (Carpenter, 2005; Kirkman, Dickson-Swift, & Fox, 2015). The moral-normative perception thus serves primarily to promote family formation and child rearing in a moral and normative religious way, and consequently makes marital separation and divorce difficult and especially hard on children. Although the norms may be changing in certain communities, many of these beliefs endure.

With the third characteristic, *external constraints,* social and economic factors may be especially important today. More people are cohabiting before marriage and fewer people are marrying today because of the Great Recession that left many people poorer and some homeless (Regnerus & Uecker, 2011). Economic trends now reveal the gender pay gap more than ever. But there is also a marriage and single gap. Specifically, married men have tended to earn as much as 27% more than single men (Antonovics & Town, 2004). Women still receive less than men, on average–18%, according to the U.S. government (U.S. Labor Department, 2014). The majority of women work outside of the home, and some of them support their husbands and families while the father is at home with the children (Laumann et al., 1993). On the other hand, women are gaining in earning power compared to a generation ago; they also have more opportunities in terms of high-paying careers, which generally stop short of being the CEO–the so-called glass ceiling that remains prominent in the United States as well as Japan and other countries (World Economic Forum, 2018).

Clearly, many factors are involved in the decision about living together before marriage, the norms are changing, and no single recipe will be successful for everyone. Sexual well-being and happiness require careful reflection on the needs of both people and their feelings about each other and commitment as they get to know each other.

INTEGRATING MARRIAGE AND SEXUAL WELL-BEING

Integrating love, work, and emotional commitment through marriage or long-term cohabitation is one of the truly great challenges and joys in life. It is entirely possible to do so when respect, mutual regard, sexual well-being, and shared values and goals help define this unique partnership. Viewed historically, marriage and family have become more important than other social institutions, particularly friendship, which was once on par with marriage in connecting people (Bray, 2003). Today many people regard marriage as a "God-given but also a civilized practice, a natural right" (Cott, 2002, p. 9). Experts cite the following reasons why marriage contributes to mental health and sexual well-being:

1. Marriage is a long-term contract that enables people to plan, sacrifice, and build together.
2. Commitment allows people to pool resources against the tough times in life.
3. Commitment allows for specialization, division of labor, and economic scale for the couple.
4. Commitment enables each partner to affirm their support of the value of these other factors in their lives as individuals and as a couple (Waite, 1995; West, 2007).

As we consider the topic of marriage, think about these questions: At what age, if any, do you hope you'll marry, and why then? If you are married, how old were you when you wed and do you think you were too young, too old, or just the right age? How long should two people know each other before marrying? Should they share the same religion, be of the same race and social class, live in the same city, and even be of the same political persuasion?

Some researchers characterize the transition from cohabitation to marriage as a winnowing or mate selection process that leads to increasingly more careful selectivity in dating, mating, cohabiting, and marriage (Blackwell & Lichter, 2005). The **winnowing hypothesis** suggests that people select mates based on such shared factors as education, race, age, religion, and shared values, even political attitudes. These patterns are known as *heterogamy* and *homogamy*. **Heterogamy** refers to a marriage between two individuals of different ethnicities, income, social class, or religion. **Homogamy** refers to marriage between individuals who are culturally similar (Blackwell & Lichter, 2005).

In the United States, the biggest sources of heterogamy in recent generations have been race and religion. In the United Kingdom, social class differences, race, and religion have been the greatest differences. It appears that homogamy increases slightly with respect to race or religion, as relationships progress from dating to cohabitation to marriage—that

winnowing hypothesis
The idea that people become increasingly selective and more careful during the process of dating, mating, cohabiting, and marriage.

heterogamy
Marriage between two individuals of different ethnicities, income, social class, or religion.

homogamy
Marriage between individuals who are culturally similar.

dual income, no sex (DINS) couples

Partners who are so busy that they cannot cope with intimacy or they omit sex from the relationship.

is, people may stop dating or living together because of their differences, and want to marry people with whom they have the most values in common (Cott, 2002). Overall, men and women use the same factors of race, religion, education, age, and social class in selecting a marital partner (Blackwell & Lichter, 2005). However, income differentials do make a difference.

The phenomenon of **dual income, no sex (DINS) couples** has been reported in the media as a pattern in which partners are so busy that they cannot cope with intimacy or they omit sex from the relationship (Hyde et al., 1998, 2001). These factors definitely reduce sexual satisfaction in the relationship, while on the other hand, research shows that when men and women participate in traditional housework, they report having more sex (Kornrich, Brines, & Leupp, 2013). They influence all couples, including same-sex couples (Carrington, 2000).

Although it is true that all emotionally supportive relationships support physical health and well-being (Chopra & Tanzji, 2018; House et al., 1988; Waite & Gallagher, 2000), marriage appears to have the greatest positive potential for individual well-being. A large number of studies report that, on average, married individuals have better mental health, more emotional support, less psychological distress, and lower rates of psychiatric disorder than unmarried ones (Ross et al., 1990; Umberson & Williams, 1999; Waite & Gallagher, 2000). Additionally, research shows that mental health improves when people transition into marriage (Marks & Lambert, 1998; Simon & Marcussen, 1999; Williams, 2003; Williams & Umberson, 2004).

In the United States, people today are generally marrying later in life than in previous generations, as you saw in Figure 12.1. People delay marriage for many reasons today. One has to do with key economic changes in society, including the shift from full-time to temporary work, lack of affordable housing, loss of benefits, and the lack of policies supporting families (Mills et al., 2011). Additionally, many women postpone marriage to go to college and pursue careers, and they may choose to postpone having children (Mills et al., 2011). Another is waiting to have children due to life goals and career aspirations (Berrington, Perelli-Harris, & Trevena, 2015). The increase in cohabitation among couples may also be a factor in delaying marriage, as we have seen. Avoiding divorce is yet another factor. A whole generation of today's young adults comes from divorced and blended families (Laumann et al., 1994; Regnerus, 2007). People who grew up in a divorced home may fear that they will repeat the "mistakes" that their parents made. These fears, however, may mean an individual never gives a relationship a chance to flower. We can see how these changes are reflected in people's attitudes toward marriage. According to the survey shown in Figure 12.3, 75% of 18- to 30-year-olds say that they would "rather be alone than marry the wrong person." Yet 82% say that they plan to marry, and even expect to be married for life.

WHAT'S ON YOUR MIND?

Q: Some of my friends talk about the ideal or good marriage, but I really wonder if that is possible?

ANSWER: With such a varying degree of commitment and happiness among couples it may seem as if there is no ideal marriage. Nevertheless, marital experts and researchers agree that these characteristics help create solid marriages:

- Commitment to the relationship
- Intimacy and unity with autonomy
- Mutual management of stressful events
- Imaginative and pleasurable sex life
- Emotional nourishment provided to each other
- Honesty and respect for each other's needs

Attitude	Percent
Expect to be married for life	82
I'd rather be alone than marry the wrong person	75
I have skills to make relationship last forever	70
Important to live with partner before marriage	56
Divorce never an option for me	36
There's only one perfect marriage partner for everyone	28
Lifelong commitment scares me	22

Figure 12.3
Attitudes toward marriage according to a survey of 18- to 30-year-olds.
Source: Gadlasky, A. (2008). Changing attitudes toward marriage. *USA Today.*

Variations in Marriage

Marriage is a universal concept in human societies (Buss, 2016; Ford & Beach, 1951; Martin, 2013; Mead, 1949; West, 2007). Yet the variations in marriage across cultures are enormous, and we should not equate marriage with the binary concepts of monogamy or polygamy (Schippers, 2016) defined below. For example, polygamy, or having multiple wives, is acceptable in some cultures, including numerous societies in Africa, many indigenous South American societies, and virtually all Pacific Island societies (Ford & Beach, 1951; Herdt & Leavitt, 1988; West, 2007). In these traditional societies, marriage was arranged, often by extended families, rather than being organized by individuals (Jolly, 1997; Martin, 2013). These arrangements definitely changed the meaning of marriage. A man who is always considering taking a second wife (or more) is married in a very different way than his monogamous counterpart in the United States and other Western countries. Likewise today, younger urban generations in many cities consider nonmonogamous relationships a choice that they can make in beginning adulthood (Manley, Diamond, & Van Anders, 2015). Nevertheless, the fact that marriage is universal testifies to some enduring realities about human nature and sexuality combined in marriage. Many societies explicitly equate marriage to procreation, and people without children are thought to be socially immature (Ford & Beach, 1951; Herdt, 1997a; Mead, 1961). Marriage also meets the cultural expectations of families, peers, community, and religious institutions, especially in the following areas:

- Love—We associate being in love with a desire for lifelong marriage.
- Security—With marriage, we expect the social support, income, and household security of a lifetime mate who will be with us "through sickness and health, till death do us part."
- Mutual pleasure—A significant part of being an adult is to seek a stable life with someone whose emotions and behaviors are relatively predictable, and who desires to be with you, and no one else.
- Family formation—We perceive marriage to be the best environment in which to rear children and happy marriages as the source of contented children.
- Long-term companionship—One of the most neglected elements of attraction, love, and marriage, companionship is one of the most compelling and enduring reasons to be and stay married in the long run.

As a human institution, marriage is defined quite differently across cultures, sometimes involving elaborate, years-long ceremonies and rituals, but sometimes little more than the social recognition of the family and community that two people are now a married couple (Mead, 1949). For example, in some non-Western and premodern societies, as previously noted, the community arranges marriage, and romance does not play a part. Virginity is often prized in many of these groups, although it is really more of a male-enforced taboo (Buss, 2016). On the other hand, in societies such as the Trobriand Islands in the South Pacific, the spouses are expected to be sexually experienced and practiced in giving pleasure to their mates, before they get married (Lepani, 2008, 2012).

In India and South Asia, where marriage is extremely important and the focus of enormous resources and ceremony, it is considered very wrong for people to marry above or below their **caste**—that is, the social and religious status group of their family. Marriage arrangements may also be made for people of greatly different ages, as much as a generation apart, as it is among Aboriginal Australians. Even in contemporary America there are expectations and norms regarding who people do not marry, especially if they are outside of their social class (Strieb, 2015). In all of these cases, marriage and parenting are widely viewed as the means for achieving social esteem, power, knowledge, and most social privileges, including economic support and sometimes religious status (Badgett, 2009; Cott, 2002; Friedl, 1994). In many societies, for example, marriage gives structure to the transition to adulthood (Mead, 1949). In the Pacific Islands, the passage from childhood, to adolescence, to adulthood requires marriage (along with sexual relations and reproduction) to attain full status as an adult (Herdt & Leavitt, 1998; Mead, 1961). Historically, in many countries including the United States (Coontz, 2016), marriage created social inequalities and a power imbalance between men and women (Cott, 2002), as for example, in how men controlled the household finances or were able to control when and how to have sex.

caste
Hereditary social status of Hindu families in India and South Asia.

Throughout the world, two forms of marriage exist: **monogamous marriage,** in which one man and one woman are legally married, usually having moral and religious meanings, and **nonmonogamous marriage**, in which a person has more than one spouse. The most common form of nonmonogamous marriage is polygamy, in which a man has more than one wife. In 84% of 185 societies, men were found to have multiple wives (Ford & Beach, 1951; Hirsch et al., 2009; Martin, 2013, p. 58). In the Muslim world, for example, such as in Saudi Arabia or Indonesia, it is acceptable for a man to have two and sometimes three wives. Around the world, the historical trend is toward monogamy, however. In the United States in the 19th century, polygamy was the norm for a few religious faiths, including the Church of Jesus Christ of Latter Day Saints (Mormons). Polygamy has long been illegal in the United States, although some people still practice it in secret. One reality show on cable TV, *Sister Wives,* follows real-life polygamous relationships in the United States.

monogamous marriage
Legal union between one man and one woman.

nonmonogamous marriage
Practice of one person having more than one spouse.

Another historical trend in marriage in the United States has to do with interracial marriage and changing attitudes toward it. Until 1967, it was illegal for people of different races

WHAT'S ON YOUR MIND?

Q: I am a college student here in the United States from India. In my family, marriages have historically been arranged. My parents have already chosen my husband but I do not know him very well. Do you think that someone can fall in love in an arranged marriage?

ANSWER: The answer is yes, but your experience may or may not match the cultural expectations of your family. Over the course of time, we humans have evolved these kinds of sexual cultures and we need to recognize that they are part of the cycle of life. We know from studies that people do create wonderful and fulfilling marriages that are arranged for them, but sometimes the arranged match between two individuals doesn't work. Follow your intuition, but also seek the guidance of your friends and family, as you find your way toward sexual well-being.

to marry in most places in the United States. Here are some relevant facts surrounding this taboo (Ontario Consultants on Religious Tolerance, 2011):

- 1948—90% of adults in the United States opposed interracial marriage when California became the first state to legalize it. The ruling was hugely controversial.
- 1967—about 72% opposed interracial marriage when the U.S. Supreme Court struck down laws against it everywhere in the United States.
- 1991—adults opposed to interracial marriage became a minority for the first time.

Today interracial marriage is widely supported in the United States, and research indicates 39% of all Americans say different races intermarrying is good for society (Pew, 2017). This is far more than only a few years ago, and it includes people saying they are more open to a close family member marrying someone of another race. Among multiracial family members is Barack Obama, the child of an interracial marriage, who became the 44th president of the United States.

Sex and Marriage

What makes sex in marriage satisfying? Does it change with age? A myth in our culture is that older married or cohabiting couples get bored with each other and stop having sex. At the beginning of a sexual relationship the excitement and joy may be indescribable and sex may enhance that feeling. Dr. Ruth Westheimer, a noted psychologist and sex therapist, likes to say that people continue to want to have physical relationships and sex as they age. "It is just plain wrong," she says, "to think that romantic love occurs only among young adults" (Westheimer & Lopater, 2002, p. 469).

The frequency of sex does typically decline as we age, but not for everyone, and not at the same pace. But the primary reason people do not have sex later in life is the lack of a partner. Older adults continue to enjoy sexual activity, and even the very elderly enjoy sex (Mahan Buttaro, Koeniger-Donohue, & Hawkins, 2014). First, as noted, people who are married have more sex than singles, even older married couples (Das, Waite, & Laumann, 2012; Laumann et al., 1994). Second, after the birth of children, many couples report a drop in sexual relations and sex drive or energy. This seems to be relatively normal and common, transitory, and widely enough recognized that traditional societies had a postpartum taboo on certain aspects of sexual intimacy (Mead, 1949). Thus, a variety of factors may enter into the situation, including desire, gender, and the quality of the relationship between the spouses. Husbands often report less sexual satisfaction than wives, which may relate to their role as a father: The father's role may not be as intense in the early years of a child's life as the role of mother. A full-time stay-at-home mother may have the challenge of maintaining a balance between being autonomous and true to herself, while the needs of parenting may overwhelm her ability to surrender sexually (Perel, 2006). Finally, data from a sample of 3,005 adults aged 57–85 suggest that among sexually active individuals in the 75–85 age range, 54% have sex two or three times per month, and 23% report having sex at least once a week or more (Lindau et al., 2007). Much of this reported sex occurs among married couples or long-term cohabiting partners.

Some key factors seem to enhance the cognitive and emotional appreciation of sexuality within marriage in general, and especially for heterosexual

President Barack Obama and First Lady Michele Obama share an affectionate moment.
Jewel Samad/AFP/Getty Images

couples. One factor that appears to be important for heterosexual couples is their ability to find mutual satisfaction and initiate sex with each other in a supportive way (Waite & Gallagher, 2000). The frequency of sex is also a significant factor regarding marital sexual relations (Das, Waite, & Laumann, 2012; Laumann et al., 1994). Some factors that may lower satisfaction include physical and mental stress, loss of self-esteem, the lack of an intimate space that is private to the couple, and differential income factors. Since same-sex marriage has been legal since 2015 in the United States, same-sex partners when they are compared to heterosexuals, in general, appear to do well (Badgett, 2009; Badgett & Herman, 2011; Herdt & Kertzner, 2006; Schippers, 2016; Shepler et al., 2018). As noted in Chapter 10, however, same-sex couples may experience minority stress, which influences their cognitive and emotional appreciation of marriage, and may create challenges to sexual well-being (Frost, Lehavot, & Meyer, 2013; Meyer, 1995).

There is some controversy about whether men or women experience more sexual satisfaction in marriage. The research results may surprise you. According to a significant clinical study conducted in 29 countries with 27,500 people, there is significant variation by gender and culture (Laumann et al., 2006). Intuitively, we would expect that the countries where men have the greatest degree of control over women would have greater sexual satisfaction for men. It turns out, though, that countries having the greatest power imbalance between men and women in marriage have the lowest levels of sexual satisfaction. For example, in Islamic countries today, as noted in Chapter 2, such as Iran, Saudi Arabia, and others, marriage is arranged and women are limited in how they may dress and act in public, having to wear the veil and perhaps never looking a man in the eyes. In countries with greater equality, research has shown that both women and men say that they have more sexual satisfaction in their relationships (Laumann et al., 2006). The United States, which is such a large, complex country with many diverse sexual cultures within it, generally reveals a higher level of mutual sexual satisfaction for both genders, suggesting that gender equality may be relatively high for many Americans (Das, Waite, & Laumann, 2012; Laumann et al., 1994; Regnerus & Uecker, 2011). It appears, then, that sexual satisfaction is more likely to occur in countries where there is a closer match in the gender power of men and women, and where the couple can be on more intimate, affectionate terms in all areas of their lives (Laumann et al., 2006).

Extramarital Relationships

There are two kinds of extramarital relationships: consensual and nonconsensual. Previously in this chapter we studied CNM, and in particular we noted the importance in polyamorous relationships of all the partners being aware and giving consent. Consensual extramarital relationships occur when couples decide to leave themselves open for emotional and/or sexual interactions with other people outside of marriage and do so with their spouse's consent. One or both members of the marriage may engage in these kinds of relationships. In fact, the majority of men and women in marriages have affairs at some point in their life cycle (Balzarini et al., 2017).

Going outside a marriage to have sex secretly with another person, commonly known as cheating, is one of the most scorned behaviors in U.S. society. In a poll by the Pew Research Center (2006), 88% of Americans disapproved of **adultery,** in which a married person has an extramarital relationship. Both genders may engage in adultery, though it is more common among men than among women (Laumann et al., 1994). Adultery is more strongly condemned than capital punishment in the United States. In fact, adulterous affairs that involve elected officials, including former president Bill Clinton, often have terrible consequences, such as disgrace and the loss of political office or, at the very least, intense public humiliation. However, the public reaction in the United States is not as extreme as in countries where adultery is punished by imprisonment or even death, but it is far more extreme than in western Europe, where adultery seems to be more accepted.

adultery

An act of sexual intercourse between a married person and someone other than the person's spouse; also called "cheating."

Why is U.S. society's attitude about adultery so intense? Is it just that we had a Puritan history? Surely the morality of attitudes about chastity and fidelity have played a key role (D'Emilio & Freedman, 1998). Secrecy about sex is part of the answer as well, because it raises anxiety and fear, including fear of disease and infection (Hirsch et al., 2009). Mistrust is another factor, because by definition, some people in our culture define adultery as "cheating," which means violating trust on some level. Some experts see infidelity as a "private lie" that breaks trust, betrays a relationship, and breaches a life agreement (Pittman, 1989). But critics of monogamous relationships point to the frequency of affairs in marriage by men and women and suggest that marriage does not always provide the ethical and responsible attitude of the ideal (Kleese, 2006). Finally, religion treats adultery as infidelity, and the implications for morality are almost always very negative.

With whom does infidelity usually occur? For men, a new lover is often a friend or co-worker. Sociologists have discovered that infidelities in the workplace are not that rare. People strike up relationships where they spend the most time during the day. One striking study did find, however, that some single women who are career oriented prefer to have a secret affair with a married man because it has "no strings attached" (Bernstein, 2008; Richardson, 1985). Few men appear to engage in sex the first time that they meet another woman who may interest them. Clinical studies in the United States show that if a man has a good friend who has cheated, that man's likelihood of cheating increases, because it sends the message that infidelity is "normal" (Neuman, 2002).

The relationship rules that couples set with respect to what is or is not cheating vary to some extent, but they distinguish between nonconsensual and consensual extramarital relationships. Nonconsensual cheating occurs when one marriage partner does not know of or agree to an outside relationship. In consensual extramarital relations, the couple agrees that sex with people outside the marriage is acceptable. For example, some couples may agree that the husband may have safe sex with a female sex worker when he is away from home and not consider that "cheating." In an older generation, this form of consensual infidelity was called **swinging,** as we have noted, and it was associated primarily with open heterosexual relationships (Gagnon, 2004). Swinging should not be confused with polyamory, because the swingers were married heterosexuals who engaged in sexual exchange for brief periods and often in secretive "party" contexts.

A generational change appears to be occurring in the pattern of extramarital relationships. Younger people tend to have more affairs than older people, although there is a gender difference, with older men having more extramarital relationships, including visiting sex workers, than their female peers (Hirsch et al., 2009; Laumann et al., 2004). The increase in women's economic independence has allowed for having extramarital relationships for both genders; not only do women have opportunities where they work, but men seem more likely to exploit opportunities without always fully thinking through the consequences of their decisions (Neuman, 2002; Regnerus & Uecker, 2011).

These affairs occur because of less satisfaction in marriages and midlife changes, as noted below (Das, Waite, & Laumann, 2012; Laumann et al., 1994). As social norms and laws have changed, infidelity has apparently increased, and the effect seems to have increased the dissolution of marriages, with greater numbers of divorces in the United States.

Divorce and Subsequent Marriages

Divorce, the legal termination of a marriage, has become more common in our society over past generations. There are actually several different kinds of divorce that vary by the laws of each country. Divorce is widely perceived to have increased in western Europe and the United States, though since 1980, it has decreased. The current divorce rate is 17.7 per 1,000 married women, down from 22.6 in 1980. About 3.2 divorces occur for every 1,000 people today, according to the Centers for Disease Control and Prevention (2018). The increase in

swinging
The idea that married heterosexuals can have casual sex with other heterosexuals outside the relationship, generally with the spouse's consent.

divorce
The legal termination of a marriage.

cohabitation, resulting in fewer marriages among young adults, may have contributed to the decline in the divorce rate over about 30 years. However, to put the statistics in perspective, approximately 40% of all marriages in the United States end in divorce.

Divorcing can be a huge shock for some people and may include depression for some and relief for others. The most common reason people divorce is problems in communication or a sense of feeling unhappy or unloved in a relationship (Defrain & Olson, 1999; Perel, 2006). Some couples cite "incompatibility," which may refer to psychological and emotional differences that result from any number of things, including sex, money, and children (Defrain & Olson, 1999). Younger people are more likely to divorce than older people, which is why some people recommend delaying marriage until later in life. People with less education and less income, as well as women who attain graduate degrees and career success, have higher rates of divorce. Additionally, the so-called "4-year" or "7-year" itch is not just a myth but refers to higher divorce rates around these milestones in the cycle of marriage and commitment—which may suggest a gradual awakening to the level of dissatisfaction with one's partner.

Adding to the stress of divorce on the partners is concern about the effects of the breakup on their children. The effect of divorce or separation on children has been widely studied (Gottman, 2011). The older and more emotionally stable the children are, the better they adjust. At whatever age, though, divorce is disruptive and children may have many reactions, including anger, depression, sadness, and grief. Boys and girls differ somewhat in their reactions to the divorce of their parents. Strong emotional support, communication, and parents keeping clear boundaries by respecting the roles of being mother and father no matter what happens in the divorce are important to help the children and family cope with divorce (Gottman, 2011; Perel, 2006). For example, allowing visitation rights to both parents after divorce, assuming that there are no other issues involved, recognizes the roles of each parent in the lives of their children.

The initial reaction to divorce varies among individuals. Some may lose interest in sexual activity for some time; others may be more interested in casual sex and sexual experimentation. However, most divorced people resume sexual activity, and many remarry. Getting a second chance to find fulfillment and sexual joy are part of being in a new relationship and possibly remarrying later in life, but this is not the whole story. As people age, they reassess their personal circumstances and growth, desires, and sexual expression (Gottman, 2011; Schwartz, 2007a). For some people, the search for an ideal mate in midlife includes finding someone who shares the same interests and is a great companion, not just a lover.

Second marriages in the United States are more likely to fail than first marriages, but that does not mean that people cannot find fulfillment in a relationship later on (Gottman, 2011). A growing tendency among many older lovers is to cohabit or live apart rather than to marry and cohabit (Burgess, 2004; Klinenberg, 2012; Perelli-Harris & Lyons-Amos, 2015). When the marriage is successful, however, individuals who remarry are actually more satisfied and happier (Waite & Gallagher, 2000). These experiences support the importance of becoming sexually literate early in life to make the decisions that give you the best chance for success and happiness.

Michael Kemp/Alamy Stock Photo

Same-Sex Marriage Equality

In 2015, the U.S. Supreme Court ruled that lesbian and gay people have the fundamental right to marry just like heterosexual people, a landmark ruling that has changed our society. How far Western civilization has come! In 1961, a Dutch comedian commented that the only people in The Netherlands who wanted to marry were homosexuals and former priests! Exactly 40 years later in 2001, The Netherlands became the first country in the world to legalize same-sex marriage. Since then, 27 countries have enacted laws that bestow the legal right of marriage to same-sex couples. Between the 1960s and 2001, attitudes toward homosexuality and same-sex marriage evolved dramatically, and today are far more positive (Badgett & Herman, 2011; Pew Foundation, 2017).

Today a broad and diverse group of LGBTQ people desire to live in legal marriages and long-term committed relationships, form families, and express feelings of love, trust, and emotional connection (Badgett, 2009; Soloman et al., 2004). A new study suggests that just as the traditional attitudes against homosexuality held support back, the new laws and government support actually increase people's personal support of same-sex marriage (Ofosu et al., 2019). The challenge facing the U.S. Supreme Court was to figure out what role marriage rights played in the basic life cycle and well-being of people. The majority opinion in the case of *Obergefell v. Hodges,* written by Justice Anthony Kennedy, stated how this fundamental right to marry could alter the lives of LGBTQ people. He stated:

> No union is more profound than marriage, for it embodies the highest ideals of love, fidelity, devotion, sacrifice, and family. In forming a marital union, two people become something greater than once they were. As some of the petitioners in these cases demonstrate, marriage embodies a love that may endure even past death. It would misunderstand these men and women to say they disrespect the idea of marriage. Their plea is that they do respect it, respect it so deeply that they seek to find its fulfillment for themselves. Their hope is not to be condemned to live in loneliness, excluded from one of civilization's oldest institutions. They ask for equal dignity in the eyes of the law. The Constitution grants them that right.

Since the Court's ruling, upwards of 1 million LGBTQ couples have opted to marry and assert their equality in the eyes of their families, friends, and society.

Remarkably, 67% of all Americans now support marriage equality, according to a recent *USA Today* poll. As recently as 1996, when Congress passed the Defense of Marriage Act barring the federal government from recognizing same-sex marriage, only about a quarter of all Americans supported marriage equality (Figure 12.4). Between 2004 and 2012, eight states and the District of Columbia legalized same-sex marriage. However, the federal government had still not recognized same-sex unions, while 31 states amended their constitutions to prohibit same-sex couples from marrying—and one state, California, changed its mind. San Francisco's mayor began allowing same-sex marriage in 2004, but in 2008, California voters passed Proposition 8 to ban it.

During this time many same-sex couples expressed concern, anxiety, and even fear that they would not be able to live together or support their relationship in the face of a health emergency or discrimination due to the lack of societal acceptance and benefits (Badgett & Herman, 2011). For example, they were not able to access health or long-term care insurance (De Vries & Herdt, 2012). Without the same laws that protected marriages of heterosexual couples, the surviving partner of a same-sex couple did not have legal access to

Figure 12.4
Polls show support is rising for same-sex marriage in the United States. For the first time, the majority of Americans now favor making same-sex marriage legal.

benefits that could be crucial to the well-being of the survivor. Social Security benefits, for example, were denied to gay partners when one of them died even though they had lived with their partner for decades (Badgett, 2009). Without these legal protections, same-sex couples faced the possibility that their loved one would be viewed as a complete stranger in the eyes of the law.

SEXUALITY IN MIDLIFE AND AGING

No matter what your sexual orientation, the transition from young adulthood into midlife is filled with important changes surrounding love, romance, marriage, career, and other life events. And the reality is that today's older adults are living much longer and healthier lives than ever before. The baby boomers are pushing into new territory, some of them proudly asserting 60 is the "new 40" and 80 is the "new 60." As we shall see, advances in sexual health and medicine back up their claim, at least to some extent. In addition, people in midlife are postponing retirement, and starting a second or sometimes a third act in their lives, founding businesses, starting families later in life, taking on new challenges in helping to improve society, and so on. The notion of falling in love and starting all over again is just part of this story of how human sexual nature continues to evolve. However, all of these changes in aging populations in the United States, Europe, Japan, and even China have typically failed to give due consideration to how to maintain health, as well as love and how to achieve sexual well-being as people age (Chopra & Tanzi, 2018). In this section, we focus on the challenges and joys of maintaining healthy sexuality and some of the advances in holistic medicine as well as technology and other ways of supporting sexual well-being in middle adulthood and elderhood.

Love seems the swiftest, but it is the slowest of all growths. No man or woman really knows what perfect love is until they have been married a quarter of a century.

—MARK TWAIN'S NOTEBOOK

Sex and Well-Being at Midlife

In our younger years, we look ahead to a limitless future. This is because in our late teens and 20s there is so much new raw experience and so many things to do in starting educational, professional, and personal goals, not to mention the incredible excitement of falling in love and beginning relationships.

In our late 30s and 40s there is a maturing, sometimes inertia, a sense of some of the challenges already overcome or a sense of defeat and lack of energy to grow and continue new things. Thus, our sense of companionship may change, and the need to share with others or reconnect with friends, including childhood friends and companions. This form of reappraisal of the quality of life can lead to some of the most wonderful experiences and new avenues of mature creativity and social connection (Herdt & DeVries, 2003; Chopra & Tazine, 2018). In the second half of life, we tend to look back on what happened and why, and how we feel about it. Our established patterns of midlife often set in, including our work and home lifestyles, patterns of communication and expressions of needs, emotions, and commitments. Separation, divorce, romance, and new relationships have a different significance, especially for women who pursue new careers and aspirations in this phase of life.

Adults in midlife today are more aware of and concerned with healthy lifestyles and extending their sense of well-being than previous generations. Longevity and advances in preventive care—which include regular exercise, walking, and workouts—are an important part not only of maintaining health, but of having a satisfactory sexual life. Research by famed Harvard doctor George Valliant (2002) almost a generation ago revealed that healthy lifestyles featuring exercise, rest, and abstention from smoking and excessive alcohol use actually make a big difference in our relationship satisfaction as we age. By the time of the late 30s to the mid-60s, sexual health and relationships are adapting to the consequences of advancing

WHAT'S ON YOUR MIND?

Q: My husband of 27 years has recently begun to avoid sexual contact with me. It is so unlike him, as we have always had a great intimate relationship, and having sex was important to him. He seems to be too embarrassed to talk about it. Could he be having some kind of "midlife crisis" or be involved with another woman, or could it be something medical?

ANSWER: So many men of the baby boom generation were brought up to feel that sexual arousal was natural and that if something went "wrong" with their erection, something must be wrong with them. It is common for men heading into their 50s to begin to have declining desire and arousal, for a variety of reasons. The media tends to think of the Viagra solution as a matter of taking a pill. Supportively raise the issue of seeing a physician or seeing a family therapist together; this may help to provide answers for your husband. If the cause is medical, he may be able to discuss it with a doctor. If the cause is interpersonal and part of your relationship, a skilled therapist will be able to help. Masculinity for men in midlife can sometimes be a challenge, and we encourage a positive approach.

in years, which may include a natural decline in sexual desire. People who have driven themselves too hard, smoked and drank and partied too much begin to see the effects in declining health, relationships, and sexual satisfaction (Chopra & Tanzi, 2018). Of course, the nature of these changes today is quite a bit different due to longevity and medical changes, as mentioned above. Americans now are living about 31 years longer on average than they did in 1900 (Santrock, 2011). In fact, babies born in the United States today have an expected life span of 78.3 years, and individuals who are 65 now can expect to live another 18.7 years (U.S. Census, 2012). However, the most significant part of the story of how midlife and elderhood is changing with longer lives is the way that love, romance, sex, and erotic passion continue to thrive well into our later years due to these advances in health and well being.

A host of long term research and carefully designed studies have greatly expanded our knowledge of sexual feelings and relationships in midlife up to the 80s. Time and again we are discovering that when someone has good health, sex can flourish, and when their sexual life ebbs, it is sometimes a warning of physical or medical changes that are already occurring (Das et al., 2012). In short, sex is a major sign of how the body and mind are doing in general. Such studies provide strong evidence that sexual satisfaction and relationship satisfaction can increase with time, even into our 60s and beyond, and for many older men and women, sex continues to be of real importance and meaning and excitement to them as they age (Perelli-Harris & Styrc, 2018). For example, a large important clinical sample that used survey methodology and interviews surrounding sexual activity among older adults reported that sexual activity is not uncommon in older people (Laumann et al., 2006). Another study found that unless they have a health problem or lack a partner, older adults enjoy having sex (Kingsberg, 2002). Two additional studies revealed that 62% of men and 51% of women believed sexual activity was important for a good relationship (AARP, 2005). One survey of 1,300 adults over age 60 found an even higher percentage of people who said that sex was important: 74% of the men and 70% of the women (National Council on Aging, 1998).

Baby boomers, those individuals born between 1946 and the mid-1960s, are more open and progressive in their sexual beliefs and experiences than adults from the previous generation, who tend to express more conservative or traditional values about sexuality (Laumann et al., 1994). One study of midlife adults ages 45–59 reported that they are more likely than elders in their 70s and up to approve of and experiment with different sexual techniques, such as oral sex and masturbation (Burgess, 2004). Other studies have found that about 50% of all older adults were satisfied or very satisfied with relatively low levels of sexual activity. These results suggest that the quality of the intimacy and sexual experience may be just as important if not more so than the absolute quantity of sex (Das, Waite, & Laurmann, 2012). In short, a large body of research reveals that sex in midlife and aging is far more relevant and common than it was even a generation ago.

Empty nest couples whose children have grown up and left home may seize the opportunity to explore new interests and find sexual fulfillment.
Fuse/Getty Images

In the social sphere, midlife may bring a variety of changes, such as starting a second career, illness and loss of family and friends, divorcing, or remarrying. Research shows that some people may experience a resurgence or renewal of sexual interest, expression and purpose that folds intimacy and love into well-being as they enter the second half of their lives. This is often associated with new relationships or remarriage, with being single again after 20 years, with taking on new life skills and finding joy in a new kind of sex (Delamater & Sill, 2005; Lindau et al., 2007). According to one classic study, "empty nesters"—couples whose children are grown and no longer living at home—may experience significant improvements in marital happiness (White & Edwards, 1990). For example, some women who were full-time mothers may start second careers, and couples may actually enjoy rediscovering and exploring their sexuality (Schwartz, 2007a). There are also numerous examples of the empty nest leading to extramarital relationships, separation, and divorce, although research suggests that the empty nest is more of an excuse than anything else (White & Edwards, 1990). In general, the empty nest brings new opportunities for growth and change in love and sexual well-being, too.

We want to emphasize that part of sexual literacy is understanding how important healthy lifestyles are to good sex and satisfying sexual relationships. Healthy lifestyles mean keeping mentally healthy and fit, which includes keeping your mind active and also unstressed, and following best physical exercise practices appropriate to your age and situation. Some basic guidelines for well-being at any age are obvious: Keep a healthy body weight, exercise regularly, don't smoke or drink too much alcohol, and eat plenty of fresh fruits and vegetables (Chopra & Tanzi, 2018). The general idea is that if you want to know what kind of older person you want to be, consider the kind of love and sexual life that you currently have and how you will want to live in 20 or 30 or 40 years. Think about how you would like to look and feel in the second half of your life and build your physical, emotional, and intimate sexual health now around that image. The pressures of modern life that come from feeling busy, successful, and connected via social media have all conspired to make American lifestyles extremely stressful today, and this is a challenge to maintaining healthy sexuality. Staying healthy overall allows the body to continue to respond sexually to a partner, in fact, to actually adapt to your partner's physical and emotional well-being, perhaps not at the same level, but with the deepening sense of enjoyment that sometimes characterizes this later stage of maturation. To read more about how mental and physical health in midlife and aging contribute to our sexual well-being, see "Healthy Sexuality: Stressful Lives for Older Americans and How This Impacts Sex."

Sexual performance can serve as a barometer of our physical and mental health. For example, erection issues for men may be an early warning sign of high blood pressure, diabetes, or a decline in testosterone (Das, Waite, & Laumann, 2012; Lindau et al., 2007). Females may experience vaginal dryness, some loss of desire, decline in androgens, or high blood pressure and diabetes. Medication for some medical conditions can also cause sexual dysfunction (Carpenter et al., 2006). With respect to mental health, a common symptom of hormonal changes is depression, which may also be associated with a decline in sexual desire (Laumann et al., 2006). Previous generations of aging adults may have felt embarrassed to discuss these issues with anyone, even with a physician, who also may not have been prepared to discuss them. In one important study of 3,005 adults (aged 57–85), 38% of men and 22% of women reported having discussed sex with a physician since the age of 50

HEALTHY Sexuality

Stressful Lives for Older Americans and How This Impacts Sex

American society is now one of the most productive in the world, but success comes with a price—stress. In a new Gallup poll of 150,000 people, Americans reported the highest level of stress in a decade (Chokshi, 2019). Americans reported feeling stress, anger, and worry in their everyday lives, which was disturbing but not surprising to those of us living at this fast pace. The pollsters discovered how people reported a "lot of worry"—in fact, a level of worry that makes the United States comparable to Greece, where people have been living in an economic and political crisis for years. When they were asked about experiencing positive or negative feelings the day before they were interviewed, the pollsters were astounded that 55% of the people stated that they experienced high levels of stress "a lot of the day." It does not take a Freud or a Kinsey to realize that high daily stress like this is going to affect the quality of our lives and especially our relationships and sex.

For decades, psychologists have known that stress can influence our personal lives and our work. We have also known that when people are chronically stressed, it creates an accumulating sense of dread, of emotional instability, and a questioning of trust in our intimate lives (Mayer, 1997). This is doubly true of minority stress. And as we have seen, abundant evidence links good mental and physical health with sexual satisfaction and the continuance of positive and rewarding intimate relationships at all stages in life, but especially in midlife and beyond. When people feel that their self-worth depends on increasing the time they commit to work, this surely increases stress. It also squeezes out quality time for personal relationships—the time they need to develop deep and respectful mental and emotional connections required for intimacy. Finally, there is no doubt that handheld devices and smartphones have made our lives much more connected but also much busier. As we discussed in Chapter 3, social media is marvelous, but our attachment to technology is stressing us out! Too much time on phones causes adults to refrain from spending quality time together. Before you know it, the relationship is suffering and the sexual intimacy is in decline.

Stress reduction is an absolute priority in keeping a healthy and happy sexual life going. The influential doctor and healer Deepak Chopra and R. Tanzi (2018: pp. 191–193) have discussed some of the dos and undo's of stress reduction. Here we offer some tips in addition to theirs for your own sexual literacy.

DO

- Meditate.
- Go to a yoga class.
- Practice mindful breathing.
- Schedule downtime and quiet time.
- Put away your devices for an hour.
- Practice being centered.
- Recognize your own stressors.
- Spend a little time listening to beautiful music every day.
- Walk your dog.
- Play with your children.
- Take a moment to smell the flowers.
- Hold your friend's hand.
- Smile at your partner or friend.

UNDO

- Stop adding to a stressful situation.
- Refrain from ignoring stressful events.
- Don't automatically agree to take on an extra work assignment.
- Resolve a repeated stress.
- Walk away from stress as soon as you can.
- Don't use a friend or partner as a punching bag for your stress.
- Turn irregular habits into a regular routine.
- Don't make your sex life the victim of your stress.
- Examine a problem you have been putting up with out of frustration.
- Don't ignore the signs of stress: irritability, fatigue, mental dullness.
- Get rid of the myth that you can thrive on stress!

We live in stressful times, but it is important to highlight how American culture in particular sets the stage for decreased and diminished sexual happiness by feeding on stress. We must stop equating productivity with self-worth, and give more time and quality attention to our hearts and loved ones every day. This is going to immensely lower your stress level and ultimately provide for better mental and physical health, and sexual well-being.

(Lindau et al., 2007). The current trend toward sexual literacy and the recognition that sexual functioning is a sign of good health and well-being in general affords both doctors and patients the sense that talking about sexual functioning is healthy and vital to well-being in the second half of life (Chopra & Tanzi, 2018; Lindau et al., 2007).

How Sex Shapes Men and Women as They Age

Myth or fact: "Older people do not have sexual desires, older people are not able to make love even if they wanted to, older people are too fragile and might hurt themselves if they attempt to engage in sexual relations, older people are physically unattractive and therefore undesirable, the whole notion of older people engaging in sex is shameful and perverse" (Henry & McNab, 2003, p. 61). This is how two leading specialists on aging have summarized the collective myth about sex and aging in the United States.

We have seen that sexual desire is not extinguished as people age, but what about the other notions: that sexual activity declines with age, because sex becomes more physically difficult, and that people abandon it because they associate it with youthful vigor (Gott & Hinchliff, 2003; Potts et al., 2003)? It is worth noting that such traditional stereotyping is **ageist**—that is, it expresses prejudicial attitudes about being older. However, there are a variety of conditions, including the internal decline of sexual desire for women and men, and difficulty with erections for men, that create issues for sexuality in later life. We will examine these in depth in Chapter 15.

The fact is that many older adults continue to enjoy intimacy, physical closeness, hugging, and touching, which may or may not involve bodily penetration (DeVries & Herdt, 2012; Lindau et al., 2007; Schwartz, 2007a). Humans naturally enjoy intimacy and touching at all ages, when they occur with respect, dignity, and emotional regard. In fact, friendly (not sexual) hugs with others definitely supports mental and physical well-being (Chopra & Tanzi, 2018; Valliant, 2002). It is in this context that we consider sexuality for men and women in later life. While sex may decline in terms of actual penetration or orgasm, its quality may actually increase in terms of overall satisfaction, as older adults may experience a greater focus and ability to enjoy their partner than when they were younger (Delamater & Sill, 2005).

Elderhood and Healthy Sexuality

Have you ever observed interactions between two people who have been together for decades and still care about each other? The joy and love on display in these interactions are remarkable because we associate them with "being in love." That couple may still be enjoying their intimate sexual relationship in their old age, much as we saw that an elder couple fell in love in the opening story.

Older adults who continue to enjoy sexual relations often express positive and energetic ideas, values, and connections to the world in other areas, such as work and friendships (Delamater & Sill, 2005). It appears that people who continue to enjoy sexual relations are not only healthier, but also are more engaged in the world (Chopra & Tanzi, 2018; Valliant, 2002). Physical health, positive mental attitudes, and social engagement are critical elements of continued sexual well-being later in life (Das, Waite, & Laumann, 2012). When their sexual relations decline, other things may be occurring, such as physical challenges or disability, which will be examined in Chapter 15. Sex, in short, is an excellent sign and predictor that people are doing well.

The challenges to gay and lesbian people as they age are equal to many of the earlier challenges in life of LGBTQ people, except that they are now placed on top of aging (De Vries & Herdt, 2012). There are approximately 2.4 million LGBT older adults over the age of 50 in the United States (Choi & Meyer, 2016). Research suggests that this population has a higher frequency of mental health problems, disability, and disease limitations compared to the

ageist
Treating older adults in a discriminatory way.

older heterosexual population (Choi & Meyer, 2016). For example, many older LGBTQ people who have lost a partner may not have the social and health care support necessary to maintain a good quality of life compared to their heterosexual peers. Also, many older gay men and lesbians who were "out" during their lives enter care facilities or nursing homes that do not recognize sexual minorities and assume that everyone is heterosexual (DeVries & Herdt, 2012). Exclusion of this kind late in life may add to the burdens of earlier losses, such as the loss of a loved one. The fact that many LGBTQ people do continue to thrive in old age and are resilient is a testimony to how they have been able to address all of the issues of aging and societal exclusion as well. Researchers refer to this sense of resilience as "crisis competence" because the challenges and stigma of being gay earlier in their lives seems to have prepared three-fourths of them for the challenges of elderhood (DeVries, 2011).

In social terms, trends in the United States suggest that at age 55, men are more likely to be married than women, by a 75% to 66% ratio. By age 75, however, the reasons for this have to do with the tendency of heterosexual men to marry, remarry, and stay married, sometimes to younger women (Burgess, 2004). By age 75, roughly two-thirds of men are married, compared to one-third of women (U.S. Census, 2010). This drop occurs because, on average, women outlive men by about 7 years today, which means husbands have died during the 20-year period between ages 55 and 75 (Das, Waite, & Laumann, 2012). Let's explore the implications of these changes among elders.

Elderhood, which starts at about age 85, is often overlooked in people's thinking about sexual experience and relationships. Studies reveal, however, that a significant number of people age 75 and older continue to have sexual relations on a regular basis (Laumann et al., 2006). Physical and mental health are very important to the context of their sexual expression, more so than in younger years, because of the importance of physical exercise, social engagement, staying active, and enjoying hobbies, family, and friends. Gender differences remain significant in the elder years, however, because research shows that older women are more likely than men to say that love is necessary for sex, and religious faith influences their sexual feelings (Das, Waite, & Laumann, 2012, p. 254). Together with good medical care, a healthy diet, and a positive attitude toward life, elders can expect to continue having positive sexual relations (Das, Waite, & Laumann, 2012; Lindau et al., 2007).

The choices we make earlier in life may influence what happens later. Even though we cannot predict the quality of life when we are 60 or 80, sexual fulfillment in late life is both possible and probable for many people. A study of sex and aging in Finland reviewed two large surveys that examined more than 5,000 people age 18–74 and found that the high number of years a couple lived together had no impact on how they assessed their relationship. Remarkably, young and old saw their relationships as happy, and even those couples who had been together 40 years or more continued to value touching and physical closeness. A gradual drop in sexual relations did occur. Detailed large-scale studies in the United States reveal in general that the challenges to sexuality in aging are more physical for men, and more social and psychological for women (Das, Waite, & Laumann, 2012, p. 258). However, one-third of the couples who had been together for 40 years or more continued to enjoy sexual intercourse once a week (Kontula & Haavio-Mannila, 2009).

In the United States, as people age, they may need to relocate to retirement facilities, nursing homes, or assisted-living centers that provide medical and care support. What happens to their sexual life in these facilities? It is a controversial area of study, but we are learning that elders in assisted living often want and even demand the right to have a sexual life.

elderhood
The period of life that starts at about age 85, and is often overlooked in people's thinking about sexual experience and relationships.

Contrary to a popular myth, many people continue to enjoy physical and emotional intimacy well into old age.
Digital Vision/Getty Images

SEXUALITY AND WELL-BEING LATE IN LIFE

Following the death of a partner, people typically go through a period of grief, a cycle that helps them to cope with such profound loss of someone with whom they may have shared decades of experiences. On average due to age differences, women are more likely than men to experience such loss (Das, Waite, & Laumann, 2012). The decline of sexual energy during such periods is to be expected and may vary in duration. Being with friends and family members may replace sexual intimacy during this time, although people who lose a life partner may withdraw socially for a time. When they have finished grieving, they may be ready for a new social life. They may want to date, which brings new challenges, although being single during late adulthood may also bring opportunities for romance, love, and sexual intimacy.

Across large studies of older men and women, there are two important challenges that stand out. First, men's physical and physiological changes suggest that men's sexuality is significantly more responsive to these changes than women's, and women's sexual expressions are significantly more responsive to social and psychological changes than men's. Also, the reliance on family members for caretaking as people age and health declines can significantly constrain their sexual expression, particularly for older women (Das, Waite, & Laumann, 2012).

Another challenge is the settings in which the elderly may meet new people. They may find intimate partners in senior centers, assisted-living facilities, and retirement homes. The staff and younger adults may regard these facilities as "desexualized" because they may harbor the attitude that sex is for young people and not for elders. Nothing could be further from the truth.

Almost 1 million older persons are in assisted-living programs, according to the National Center for Assisted Living (Hauser, Ujvari, & Mollica, 2012). They might include your grandparents or family friends. All the taboos and myths that surround sex among elders have resulted in some negative attitudes that have generally denied these citizens their rights in retirement settings. Yet, as we have seen, people aged 57–85 think of sexuality as an important part of life, and the frequency of sexual activity, for those who are active, declines only slightly from the 50s to the early 70s (Lindau, 2007). In fact, leading experts suggest that love, intimate sex, and also very close bonds of friendship are vital to our well-being as we enter elderhood (Chopra & Tanzji, 2012; Chopra & Tanzji, 2018).

The issues related to decline in desire and arousal also affect this population. For women, having a partner in centers of assisted living may be related to their level of sexual desire, because the presence of prospective sexual and romantic partners may increase a person's interest in sexuality in such circumstances. The more they desire sex, the more likely they are to marry. Men seem to be less influenced by the presence of a partner and sexual desire, but they wish to find privacy and engage in sexual pleasure with someone in these settings (Das, Waite, & Laumann, 2012). Also, women report that having a partner may create greater desire for sex—a finding that differs for men (Delamater & Sill, 2005).

Imagine the awful situation of a longtime married couple who move into assisted living and who are forbidden by the staff to continue having intimate relations. Part of the reason that this situation is so challenging is that there is generally little to no privacy in some of these centers. For singles, due to the gender disparity among elders with more women than men, a variety of issues emerge when two people desire to find privacy and engage in sexual relations. Imagine how difficult it may be for a gay person to enter one of these facilities, and after having been out. He may have to hide his sexual orientation (Orel, 2004). Caretakers often do not know how to handle these issues and may embarrass people, due to the absence of sexual literacy and the persistence of negative attitudes about gays and lesbians and about sexual activity in old age (De Vries & Herdt, 2012). The least society can provide for all people in their elderhood is dignity and respect for their rights. Sex can be fulfilling during this part of the life span, too, because as the story at the beginning of the chapter suggests, it's never too late for love.

SUMMARY

Early Adulthood

- Single living may be the context for our first major adult attractions and relationships.
- Cohabitation is living together, but it is a highly variable experience that may influence our enjoyment of marriage and attachments to people later on.
- Living apart together (LAT) and friends with benefits (FWB) are relatively new ways of people being a couple in the United States and western Europe that may or may not include actual cohabitation.

Integrating Marriage and Sexual Well-Being

- Marriage occurs in almost all human societies and is diverse in its meanings and practices.
- Couples now tend to wait till their late 20s to marry, due to a variety of factors, including gender role changes and cohabitation.
- Diversity is a major factor of marriage today, including the acceptance of interracial marriage, which was once stigmatized and illegal.
- Some therapists see love and surrender as the major issues of how marriage succeeds or fails.
- Polyamory is a relatively new kind of intimate relationship based upon having more than one loving, intimate relationship at a time, with the consent and full knowledge of everyone involved.
- Gay marriage is the expression of love and desire for two people of the same gender, and remains controversial in many states and countries, but is legal in the United States.
- Choosing to be married without children is increasingly common in our society but remains stigmatized among traditional communities.
- Divorce has actually declined in frequency in the United States, although it is common and has left its mark on many families and perhaps contributed to the cohabitation trend.

Sexualtiy in Midlife and Aging

- A variety of illnesses in later life, including cardiovascular disease, diabetes, and cancer, may influence sexual functioning at any point in the life span, although these are more prevalent in older adulthood.
- Sex definitely shapes men and women as they age, in part because there are more women than men in midlife, but also due to issues involving menopause.
- Being widowed or retiring to an assisted-living facility may bring real challenges to sexual expression, as taboos may prevent the expression of sexual desire among elders and the achievement of sexual fulfillment.

Sexuality and Well-Being Late in Life

- Regardless of the physical and mental challenges of aging, elders should expect caretakers to respect their right to love and intimate sexual expression.
- Midlife is that phase of older adulthood associated with myths and taboos, including the complete absence of sex.

What's Your Position?

1. **How do you feel about being married in general? About being single?**
   - What are some reasons that you might choose to live as single?
   - What does casual sex mean to you and to your friends? In your culture?
   - Why might you consider cohabiting with someone before making a life commitment to this person?
   - How do you feel that cohabitation may help or hinder your own process of finding sexual happiness?
   - Is polyamory something you might choose in your own life? Why or why not?
   - What concerns about divorce do you have in thinking about sharing a life with someone?

2. **How do you feel about having a life partner to love and with whom to live out your life?**
   - What is the relationship between love and sex in your key relationships?
   - What do you think about remaining abstinent prior to being married?
   - How do you understand love in your search for a life partner?
   - How do you think about the relationship between love and surrender in your most intimate relationship?
   - What are your views of same-sex marriage?
   - Why do some same-sex couples want to marry?
   - How do you regard extramarital relationships?

3. **If you expect to enjoy an active sexual life in your late adult years, what can you do when you're younger to remain sexually active later on?**
   - How do men and women differ in their search for an active and satisfying sexual life?
   - Do singles or married couples have more sex? How and why?
   - If you can picture yourself at midlife with a sexual partner, how might it be different from now?
   - How do you think elders manage their love and sexual relationships?

Design elements: Controversies in Sexuality: HBRH/Shutterstock; Research and Sexual Well Being: verity jane smith/Getty Images; Healthy Sexuality: Sergey Furtaev/Shutterstock; Communication Matters: PeopleImages/Getty Images; Know Yourself: Plush Studios/Blend Images LLC; What's Your Position: Luis Molinero/Shutterstock; Healthy Sexuality: A. Minde/PhotoAlto; Did You Know icon: McGraw-Hill Education; Page corner icon: McGraw-Hill Education.

Attraction, Love, and Communication

Sexual Attraction
- Describe the cultural influence on the standards of physical attractiveness.
- Identify the main theories of physical and psychological attraction.
- Describe variability in physical attractiveness across cultures.
- Explain forms of sexual interest across cultures.

Love
- Describe the main theories of love.
- Identify different ways love can shape sexual expression in personal relationships.

Communication
- Explain how emotional literacy affects your sexual and intimate communication.
- Describe the importance of the connection between sexual health, positive decision-making, and communication skills.
- Describe how the concept of emotional literacy contributes to sexual literacy and sexual well-being.
- Identify the characteristics of effective and ineffective communication in relationships.
- List ways that communication skills can be enhanced in healthy relationships.

Communication and Sexual Well-Being
- Identify effective ways to say no to a partner's request.

- **Learning**
- **Objectives**

Diane Macdonald/Getty Images

Developing Your Position

1. What kinds of traits or attributes are important to you in your pursuit of sexual and/or romantic relationships?
2. What is love to you and what characteristics of love are important to you in relationships?
3. How comfortable are you discussing sex with romantic and intimate partners?
4. Have you ever discussed your sexual history with a partner?

Self, Society, and Culture: Understanding How Love Changes

My husband and I (Nicole) met, fell in love very quickly, and were engaged about 2 months later. About 5 months into our engagement, I panicked because my early passionate feelings had begun to change. The butterflies in my stomach had begun to lessen, and I found myself less consumed with amorous daydreams. I started to worry that maybe I wasn't in love and that I should rethink my decision to get married so soon. I thought about what I loved most about my fiance and what I desired for my future, reaching the conclusion that I had unrealistic expectations of what love is because my own feelings did not mirror what I saw on television and the Internet or read in magazines. I had expected that the early, powerful feelings of attraction and infatuation would last forever. I was disillusioned when those feelings began to fade. Wanting to understand my own story, I researched the topic of love. What I found were countless stories of people who turned away from their relationships, marriages, and partnerships in search of greener pastures when love failed to meet what they expected based on popular culture. Other people's stories reflected the reality that early feelings of infatuation were replaced by a deeper sense of friendship, companionship, intimacy, and commitment. These are traits of love and life that last, and we do not always see these depicted in media. I found that my experience resonates with the narrative that understands that early lust and fireworks in relationships may fade, but they are replaced by a more solid and enduring love characterized by joy, fulfillment, and hard work. I am happy to report my husband and I are still very much in love and just passed 10-year anniversary!

Consider some ways that love can be misrepresented in popular culture. We are given messages that we should look like a sexy model or behave like a porn star to have a lasting love relationship that is passionate and fulfilling. Furthermore, love may be represented as unending passion and infatuation that exist in a relationship free of the stresses of real life. Most adults understand that these beliefs and messages do not represent reality, but we often do not acknowledge the degree to which our expectations have been influenced by these unrealistic ideas of love. The reality is that a lasting love relationship goes through stages and is built on mutual trust and sustained by effective communication. We invite you to join us in this chapter to discover your own reality related to love and lasting relationships.

SEXUAL ATTRACTION

The reality around love relationships is that they all start from attraction—attraction that happens in a variety of ways. Two people meet in a coffee shop and a spark ignites; they talk and the seeds of a relationship are planted. It can happen slowly, too, when two old friends start to see each other in a different way—they are attracted to something that perhaps they had never paid attention to before. The strong emotion of attraction can often catch us off-guard. Have you ever felt irresistibly attracted to someone? The feeling appears to be so common that anthropologist Helen Fisher believes that each of us may instantly "size up" a potential mate, which she claims is an intuitive skill that likely developed millions of years ago as our ancestors evolved to separate friend from foe (Fisher, 2009a). In fact, it may take only a second or two to intuitively feel whether you are attracted to someone or not—whether that person is too short or tall, young or old, has the right body type, and so on. Decades of research explain a great deal of how we gauge attraction based on the biology of human sexual nature as well as on the culture in which we grow up (Fisher, 2004). The experiences of moving from being attracted to someone to falling in love are very much individual; however, objective factors are at work as well (Jankowiak, 2008). For example, cultural gender roles provide people with expectations and behaviors about attraction, flirting, romance, courtship, sex, and lovemaking (Diamond, 2008; Gagnon, 2004; Hirsch et al., 2009; Stoller, 1979).

Theories of Sexual Desire and Attraction

People are attracted to each other through a combination of what is exciting or different and what is familiar and comfortable. They may even equate attraction to what is risky or dangerous (Stoller, 1979). Poets and philosophers have pondered why people experience that intense chemistry of sexual attraction, sometimes known as "love at first sight." It doesn't happen to all of us, though the concept appears to be widely known across cultures (Twamley, 2013). In fact, one study found that only 11% of the 493 respondents said their long-term relationships started with love at first sight (Malach-Pines, 2005). To learn more about this phenomenon, read "Controversies in Sexuality: Does Love at First Sight Truly Exist?"

The great mystery of sexual attraction is how and why people are attracted to each other at all, given all the possible barriers that we may experience: language and cultural difference, race, gender, sexual orientation, and differences attributable to tastes and interests (Stoller, 1979). Just how does a person's sexual excitement emerge from all these differences to create the sexual attraction that can be identified through nuances of interaction, such as the way someone smiles or arches an eyebrow or moves across a room? Lust, the raw form of desire and attraction, is not the same as love (Stoller, 1979). Pure lust is based solely on physical attraction and fantasy—it often dissipates when the "real person" surfaces and imperfections and flaws become known. Being in love doesn't exclude lust. In fact, lust can lead to love. However, real love, not based on idealization, requires time to get to know each other (Orloff, 2011).

Compare your standards of facial beauty in women to the images here. What is similar, and what is different, from your own perspective?
David Malan/Getty Images; Travelasia/Getty Images; Dimitri Vervitsiotis/Getty Images; Wasif Hassan/Getty Images

CONTROVERSIES in Sexuality

Does Love at First Sight Truly Exist?

Movies are made of this idea: Two people see one another from across a crowded room and BAM! They are in love and live happily ever after. In fact, media and movie stars have generated billions of dollars from selling the plot of "love-at-first-sight" to eager moviegoers. Even Shakespeare noted in his play *Twelfth Night* that "whoever loves, loves at first sight." Many people truly want to believe in such a concept yet feel hesitant in allowing themselves to be swept off their feet because the concept seems either too good to be true or something about it rubs against what we know about lasting love relationships.

Therefore, we ask this question: Does love at first sight truly exist?

YES:

- Experience can be a powerful piece of evidence when trends begin to erupt. An Israeli poll of 240 males and 253 females found that 56% believed in love at first sight. Another earlier survey of men and women showed that 30% reported they had fallen in love the moment they laid eyes on their partner (Fulbright, 2008).
- Many people who report love at first sight in their relationships perceive themselves to be relatively similar in personality to their partner, which is a consistent factor in studies looking at attraction. Studies show that relationship success may be more strongly related to people's perception of similarity than to their actual degree of similarity to their partner (Barelds & Barelds-Dijkstra, 2007).
- Physical attractiveness often plays a role in the phenomenon of love at first sight. In love at first sight, the high value of someone's physical attractiveness is often projected onto other characteristics (i.e., what is attractive or beautiful is seen as good or positive). In some cases, love at first sight can be the basis for long-term love and relationship success provided that the characteristics revealed in later communication and interactions enhance (rather than oppose) the characteristics revealed at first sight (Ben-Zeév, 2008).

NO:

- If romantic love consists of evaluating the other person as attractive and as having positive characteristics, how are people truly able to make these assessments at first glance? Some characteristics such as honesty, compassion, and responsibility cannot be revealed at first glance. Knowledge of critical characteristics requires familiarity and shared history and are absent in the first meeting of someone (Ben-Zeév, 2008).
- Individuals who report that they fell in love at first sight often become intimate very quickly. In these cases, physical chemistry lures people into a relationship before getting to know their partner's true personality. What may have been perceived early as personality similarity may be a misperception and personality dissimilarity gets revealed later, which can lead to lower relationship satisfaction (Barelds & Barelds-Dijkstra, 2007). This means, then, that people who fall in love quickly really do not know their partners well, which can be a risk factor for longevity of the relationship. If the relationship ends, was it truly love at first sight?

CONSIDER THIS:

What many perceive to be love at first sight may simply be a very strong initial attraction that we perceive as love at first sight. One study found that individuals' experiences of love at first sight were not necessarily correlated to high levels of passion, intimacy, or commitment, suggesting that love at first sight may be much more an experience of intense initial attraction than something indicative of actual "love" (Zsok, Huacke, De Wit, & Barelds, 2017).

What's Your Perspective?

1. Have you experienced love at first sight?
2. What do your instincts tell you about whether or not it exists?
3. If you do believe that it exists, do you also believe that relationships started in this way have hope for existing in the long term? Why or why not?

People may find each other sexually attractive, but not to the same degree and not because of the same characteristics. For example, a man may be very excited over the combination of his girlfriend's figure and her energetic, warm smile, whereas she may be most attracted to his muscular build and the combination of his ambition and many friendships.

Or a woman may be attracted to a smart, aggressive, good-looking man, but may not think he would make a very good father, and thus thwart a long-term commitment.

Essentially, men and women may complement each other in their differences (Fisher, 2004, 2009b; Jankowiak, 2008; Stoller, 1979). In the short term, sexual attraction and lust may suffice, but in the long term, the differences that create mystery and excitement need to be balanced out by the sense of shared interests and, of course, love (Jankowiak, 2008). Same-sex couples may also start out with desire but move into the sphere of mutual interests and family planning (Diamond, 2008). Couples may be drawn together by their shared values and interests and their longer term goals, social class, education, ethnicity, faith, hobbies, and planning a family or having a dog and enjoying life, which may increase as time goes on, but not at the loss of desire (Schwartz, 2007a). Theories regarding how and why we find others attractive are rooted in the concepts of physical, psychological, and biological attraction, all of which we consider.

Physical Attractiveness

The physical attractiveness of another person as the foundation or primary motivation for the initiation of intimate relationships does not sit well with many people (Erber & Erber, 2011). Many people want to deny that we base romantic attraction on the physical appearance of others, but it is hard to deny this fact in the face of research (Erber & Erber, 2011). One reason we seem to be so drawn to people who are physically attractive is because we often make inferences about what physically attractive and unattractive people might be like or how they might behave. Essentially, whether we like to admit to it or not, we often tend to "judge a book by its cover."

Research about this behavior and attitude has led to a theory based on a "what is beautiful is good" stereotype, called the **halo effect**—that is, the tendency to think of someone we perceive to be attractive or beautiful in positive terms (Morrow et al., 1990). Stated differently, this applies to the tendency to attribute positive characteristics to attractive people and negative characteristics to unattractive people (Dion, Berscheid, & Walster, 1972). Attractive people are thought to be more sensitive, kind, interesting, strong, and sociable than unattractive people and are even perceived to have better lives. Attractiveness is a benefit in other areas of life as well. Consider these research findings about physical attractiveness:

halo effect
A positive perception of someone based on physical attractiveness.

- It is indicative of intelligence (Zebrowitz & Rhodes, 2004).
- Attractive people are promoted more often in the workplace than unattractive people (Morrow et al., 1990).
- Attractive people have a higher social status than others (Kalick, 1988).
- Even infants as young as 6 months prefer looking at more attractive faces (Ramsey, Langlois, Hoss, Rubenstein, & Griffin, 2004).

Beauty and Sexiness

Standards of sexiness change with culture and also appear to change over time (D'Emilio & Freedman, 1988; Foucault, 1980). In fact, beauty and attractiveness standards have come and gone and come again throughout history. For example, in the 19th century until about World War I, being round or plump was considered sexy for a woman. Women thought men who were stout and well padded were the most sexually attractive. To be thin was regarded as ugly, unhealthy, and unsexy. Weight differences definitely reflected social class standards because upper- and middle-class people ate better and worked less and were considered prosperous and healthy by being plump, while poor people had less food and worked more and tended to be thin and even skeletal.

DID YOU KNOW

In 2019, Barbie turned 60 years old, which is quite a remarkable milestone for a doll. There has been much debate around Barbie's body and whether or not she is an unrealistic representation of the "ideal woman." If Barbie's body proportions were applied to a woman who is 5 feet 6 inches tall, she would have a 20-inch waist, a 27-inch bust, and 29-inch hip measurements (Winterman, 2009). In the United States, White women ages 18 to 25 have measurements, on average, of 38-32-41; White women ages 36 to 45 have measurements of 41-34-43. In that same age group, Black women measure, on average, 43-37-46, Hispanic women 42.5-36-44, and women categorized as "other," which researchers said meant mostly Asian, 41-35-43 (Zernike, 2004). Do you believe that Barbie is a realistic ideal that women should compare themselves to?

Today the opposite seems to be true: The thinner and the more athletic one is, the more sexually appealing, as you can see in fashion magazines. Some researchers suggest that fat was associated with wealth and higher class in the 19th century, which is similar to how we now associate fat with poor health and lower class (Bledsoe, 2002). With the privilege of middle- and upper-class life, people have better-quality food and more time for exercise, leisure, and rest (Bledsoe, 2002).

Many sexual stereotypes surround heterosexual men and women across cultures (Hirsch et al., 2009; Jankowiak, 2008). Heterosexual men appear to be attracted to women who more closely match the ideals of their society in terms of height, weight, and facial looks (Fisher, 2004). They also respond to the size of a woman's bust and hips (Bledsoe, 2002). Heterosexual women are the focus of stereotypes in cultures regarding sexual attraction, such as the focus on breast size. Yet, as standards of beauty change, it appears that some female celebrities can diverge from such norms and still be considered highly sexy to some men. For example, some men may say that Marilyn Monroe was too "fat" to be attractive to them, while some men think actress Christina Hendricks is too much like a "bean pole."

While physical attraction stereotypes also apply to LGBTQ people, some evidence suggests that the same standards of beauty and sexiness may not apply, as for example, in the use of makeup, the choice of hairstyles, and clothes that some lesbians and bisexual women reveal in the expression of their sexual individuality (Diamond, 2008).

Historical standards of desire, beauty, and sexiness also apply to ethnic minorities in the United States, including differences that have been found in patterns of attraction within Latino, Asian American, and African American communities (Collins, 2005; Gonzales-Lopez, 2005). For example, historically African Americans have judged beauty on the basis of the color of skin tones, form of noses, stature, and weight of males and females (Collins, 2005). They thought that fairer skin tones with a slight reddish chocolate hue were more "beautiful" than deeper black or dark brown hues, and they much preferred a long nose to a blunt nose.

Marilyn Monroe, a movie star in the mid-20th century, and actress Christina Hendricks, known for her role on the TV series *Mad Men,* are well known for their body proportions.
Time & Life Pictures/Getty Images; Charles Eshelman/FilmMagic/Getty Images

WHAT'S ON YOUR MIND?

Q: I am 21 years old and am becoming increasingly frustrated with the images of women and men in the media. I am so tired of going to the movies only to see female characters who are rail-thin with large breasts, not to mention the typical sexy male character of virile masculinity. The more I watch movies and read magazines, the more inadequate I feel and I am afraid my insecurity about my own body is affecting my relationship with my partner. What do I do?

ANSWER: It is understandable that you are frustrated with media images of celebrities. Many people share your frustrations but that does not mean that you should feel the need to compare yourself to these individuals or that to be happy, you must be an exact replica of the images portrayed in media. Instead, think about characteristics of your body you love. If you have a difficult time with this, ask your partner what is attractive about your body and write it down or take a picture of that part of your body and keep it somewhere to remind yourself that we are all beautiful in different ways. If you continue to feel insecure and it causes you severe anxiety or depression, consider professional help to sort through the difficulty.

Standards of sexiness and beauty also vary greatly across cultures (Mead, 1949; Stoller, 1985). What is considered beautiful or disgusting is a part of the cultural standards and sexual norms as expressed through body types and intimate behaviors (Stoller, 1985). Such standards are part of the cultural expressions that seem to go into creating sexual excitement and attraction in many societies (Herdt & McClintock, 2000).

Consider how forms of sexual attraction were expressed as stereotypes for gay men in the 19th century. Then, many people saw homosexual men as effeminate in appearance and believed that they could only be attracted to heterosexual men, who were thought to be masculine (Hekma, 1994). This social stereotype changed over time, right up to the portrayal of gay men as being hypermasculine in appearance (Levine, 1998). Nevertheless, the earlier stereotypes continued to be used in 1960s and 1970s Hollywood films that portrayed gay men as hairdressers and florists who wore frilly clothes and had flamboyant hairdos, such as in the film *Boys in the Band*. After the Stonewall Riots in 1969, gay men were portrayed as much more masculine looking, even similar to the "Marlboro man," with his muscles and mustache and rough and tumble cowboy look (Levine, 1998). It was as if gay men reacted to the stereotypes of effeminacy with which they had grown up and wanted to be portrayed as hypermasculine to be set apart from the old stereotype. Today many types of gay sexiness are portrayed in media: the muscled look; the "clean cut" college prep look; the "ordinary guy next door" look; and the queer who fits no stereotype and just wants to be himself look (Savin-Williams, 2005). Who did the portraying? Both society and individual gay men who were socialized into these stereotypes, and then reacted to them by creating a new sexual culture of attraction specific to gay men (Halperin, 2007; Levine et al., 1997).

Chemistry and Attraction

When a strong match occurs, it may be that a person has found someone who is similar in terms of physical attractiveness. This **matching hypothesis** suggests that people select romantic and sexual partners based on the other person's attractiveness (Feingold, 1988). When couples have similar interests, they feel "matched" in terms of their self-esteem and sense of emotional security. They may also feel they have found someone who will not reject them (Tucker & O'Grady, 1991).

matching hypothesis
The hypothesis that people select romantic and sexual partners based upon the other person's attractiveness.

Gay men are portrayed in a variety of different ways in media and popular culture today. In *Modern Family*, the characters Mitchell and Cameron are a family-oriented couple.
ABC/Photofest

HEALTHY Sexuality

Why Him, Why Her?

Is chemistry part of sexual attraction? Some researchers seem to think so, including Helen Fisher. Her research is about how genes, brain patterns, and other hereditary factors may influence sexual attraction.

In her book, *Why Him? Why Her? How to Find and Keep Lasting Love* (2010), Fisher describes four "love" personalities that she says are based on brain chemistry. She believes that each one of us expresses a dominant love personality:

- The *Explorer* is a person driven by the brain chemical dopamine and seeks novelty, adventure, and spontaneity.
- The *Builder* is a person who responds to the effects of the "soothing" brain chemical serotonin and appears calm, social, and orderly.
- The *Director* is a person motivated by the "male" hormone testosterone and who appears to be logical, intensely focused, and who practices tough love.
- The *Negotiator* is a person guided by the "female" hormone estrogen and who appears to be creative, highly verbal, and compassionate.

Are people with similar brain chemistry attracted to each other? Not always, in Fisher's view. Builders are compatible with other Builders, and two Explorers may make a great couple. But Directors tend to seek out Negotiators and vice versa. Fisher suggests that the reasons for these pairings are evolutionary in nature. Simply put, they may do a better job of producing viable offspring (Martin, 2013).

Consider these characteristics about attraction to help you to think about what happens when you meet someone for the first time:

- Body image: Fat or thin? Tall or short? Muscular or not?
- Facial features: Beautiful or handsome? Pretty or rugged?
- Sex: Female or male? Intersexual? Transgender? Other?
- Age: Older, younger, or same age? How much difference in age—2, 5, 10, or more years?
- Personality: Outgoing? Introverted? Focused on you?
- Education: High school? College degree? More or less education than you?
- Faith: Same religion or beliefs?
- Ethnicity: Same or different?
- Social class: Similar income? Social status? Family prestige? Community standing?

Is chemistry also part of attraction? As you can read in "Healthy Sexuality: Why Him, Why Her?" researcher Helen Fischer believes that a lot of the mystery of attraction depends on brain chemistry.

While physical attractiveness plays a role in the formation of romantic relationships, psychological factors are important as well.

Psychological Attraction

Anyone who has been on the website eHarmony.com will note that the way individuals are matched is not based on physical attractiveness but on 29 dimensions of compatibility. The people of eHarmony.com claim that these dimensions lead to successful, long-lasting romantic relationships. In many ways, similarity is seen as an indicator of relationship satisfaction and success (Erber & Erber, 2011). In fact, the **similarity-attraction hypothesis** suggests that the more similar two individuals are, the greater the attraction between them will be (Byrne, 1971). In addition, the theory of homogamy states that we tend to be more attracted to people

similarity-attraction hypothesis
The more similar two individuals are, the greater the attraction between them will be.

who share characteristics such as attachment style, political and religious attitudes, socioeconomic status, level of education, and intelligence (Klohnen & Luo, 2003; Luo & Klohnen, 2005). Research also shows that when given the time and opportunity, individuals prefer to select partners with personality traits similar to themselves (Barelds & Barelds-Dijkstra, 2007).

When two people have similar beliefs, values, and attitudes and share interests in hobbies or occupation, they can reinforce one another's ideals and experiences. This reinforcement can cause a strong bond to form and to be maintained. It is hard to disagree with the notion that, all else being equal, we will be more attracted to people who agree with us than to people who disagree with us (Erber & Erber, 2011).

Is the adage "opposites attract" true? This difference, or opposite, is referred to as **complementarity.** One could argue that complementarity is important when it comes to personality traits, but it may not be important when discussing values or attitudes in relationships. For example, a person whose personality is shy and reserved may find great benefit in forming a relationship with someone who is outgoing because they complement each other's needs for social interaction. With characteristics such as performance and expertise, partners may benefit from complementarity because they will not compete against one another in an occupation, for example, and so they can enjoy the success of their partner rather than perceive the other's success as a threat (Erber & Tesser, 1994).

Complementarity in other dimensions, however, may pose a threat. Consider the traits of dominance and submission. These traits are often driven by culture and may be assigned to genders. For example, research has shown that verbally outspoken and expressive women who are paired with retiring and verbally inhibited men make for a precarious couple, and the couple is unlikely to experience high levels of relationship satisfaction (Swann, Rentfrow, & Gossling, 2003).

In summary, based on the available research, similarity appears to be a more important, powerful force than complementarity in successful, long-term relationships.

complementarity
The idea that opposites attract, that individuals are attracted to what's different in others.

Biological Attraction

Many of the above studies actually imply that there are powerful but hidden biological differences in sexual attraction, which may be influenced by genes, hormones, and other factors of sexual individuality (Diamond, 2008). The biology of sexual attraction suggests that such innate differences may be at the heart of some heterosexual male and female responses when it comes to arousal, attraction, and sexual behavior (Bailey & Oberschneider, 1997; Fisher, 2004, 2009). For example, a person may experience sexual arousal in response to another person's smell (Buss, 2008). Sexual attraction to others of the same gender may arise from genetic, brain, or hormonal or other differences that provoke attraction and later, arousal and sexual response, for boys to other boys by age 9.5 years, for example, and for girls to other girls by age 10 years, on average (Herdt & McClintock, 2000; McClintock & Herdt, 1996). Some women say that they had early attractions to other women that were beyond their conscious control and seemed so natural to them that they must have a biological basis (Diamond, 2008).

Same-Sex Attraction

What are theories about attraction for gay men and lesbian women? Some people think there is a contradiction between attraction and being attracted to the same sex. Other people think that bisexuals have the capacity to be attracted to both genders but not necessarily at the same time (Diamond, 2008; Klein, 1978). If people are of the same sex and if attraction depends upon physical differences, then how can they be attracted to each other? Answering this question may yield some answers about how and why people become attracted to someone.

The **exotic becomes erotic (EBE) theory** of sexual orientation created by psychologist Daryl Bem is a controversial answer to this question. Bem's theory states that people are

exotic becomes erotic (EBE) theory
A theory that states people are attracted to what is unusual or exotic to them.

attracted to what is unusual or exotic to them. He goes on to say that for heterosexuals, it is the difference of anatomy wrapped up with the cultural stereotype that men and women come from two different worlds. With gay men and lesbian women, he states that people are attracted to something in the other person's body or personality that excites them because it is different from their own body or personality. For example, temperamental and personality differences are considered sexual and sufficiently different to arouse some individual women to be attracted to some other women (Diamond, 2008). Critics have been negative about this theory because it explains only part of the picture of attraction (Peplau et al., 1998).

The "difference" is thus in the eye of the beholder to some extent. Whether it is skin color, social class, gender behavior, personality, and so on, when one person thinks that some trait is sufficiently different from the self, it may lead to arousal and excitement (Stoller, 1979). It might be that when people become aroused because of a difference in a partner, they emphasize that difference when they imagine that person and the group to which he or she belongs (Bem, 2000). For example, more than 70% of the gay men and lesbian women in one study felt that they were different from their same-sex peers in childhood when they were growing up (Bem, 2000). Many of the gay men, for example, said that they didn't really like team sports growing up, which separated them from many straight boys. Lesbian women also felt that they were more masculine in growing up than straight girls. These feelings were long-lasting and not fleeting or temporary. The gay men were also more likely to have girls as best friends growing up, which is a very different experience for straight men (Bell et al., 1981).

Bem hypothesizes that as people experience differences, both heterosexual and homosexual, they associate them with being aroused cognitively and emotionally. The theory thus attempts to integrate biological and experiential but not so much the cultural factors to explain how some children's experiences may lead them to feel that they are different from opposite-sex or same-sex peers and perceive them as exotic. However, when same-gender people do express this new kind of desire, it can become positively associated with attraction, intense interest, and it can even have an impact on love and commitments throughout life (Halperin, 2007; Herdt & Koff, 2000).

Sexual Scripts

Individual tastes, desires, arousal, and expressions in sex and love have been termed "love maps" (Money, 1986). When constructed into something that guides our actions internally and interpersonally, these sexual characteristics have been referred to as "sexual scripts" (Gagnon & Simon, 1973). Sexual scripts connect personalities and bodies to what culture has taught people to perceive and respond to as sexy (Gagnon, 2004). For example, a heterosexual couple may experience this attraction in terms of differences in and the fit between their physical sizes and ages. Facial and bodily features, personality, and sexual signals may likewise arouse same-sex couples to be highly attracted to each other (Diamond, 2008; Savin-Williams, 2005). This attraction also occurs within a frame of seeking affection, attachment, and perhaps love, either long term or short term (Blumstein & Schwartz, 1983). Much of this kind of sexual communication and attraction may be cued to culture, depending on the individuals and couples. So much so that we can think about the interplay of how each person learns a script and expresses it, or possibly several scripts at the same time (Gagnon, 2004; Laumann et al., 1994). Consider this story:

> Kimberly sees John across the room at a party and their eyes meet. Instantly Kim feels a spark, and John seems to respond with wide-open eyes and a growing smile. The chemistry has begun. One of them fantasizes kissing and the other going further. Before they are even introduced by a mutual friend, they are moving toward each other, and the feeling of intimacy grows so quickly that the friend bows out. Within minutes they are touching, still surrounded by people talking and dancing. In less time than it takes to do a morning jog, this couple's scripts are off and running. But how did it happen?

Individuals and cultures interact in complicated ways when it comes to sexuality, both in terms of what they positively value and by how they assign risk taking (Halperin, 2007). Sociologists and psychologists have long believed that sexual feelings and sexual excitement are not purely spontaneous. The story of Kim and John immediately "hitting it off" with eye contact followed by intimate talk and then touching so quickly illustrates how people learn a set of sexual rules. As they focus on each other, certain rules kick in: rules about what to say, how much to flatter, when to smile back, and how far to go in touching a stranger at a party. One way to understand how people learn this psychosocial process is with **sexual script theory,** the idea that individuals learn the sexual rules and roles to play, just as actors learn lines from scripts that determine their roles and actions (Gagnon & Simon, 1973). Sexual scripts, then, help people to understand information about sexual nature, fantasies, sexual motivations, and physical attraction.

What is interesting and important to note is how traditional gender roles and traditional heterosexual scripts outline sexual roles for many women. Some researchers have found that when young women are exposed to television (and thus, active illustrations of sexual scripts) and perceive television to be a real reflection of life and relationships, these women are more likely to endorse gendered sexual scripts and exhibit lower levels of sexual agency. This is identified as less sexual assertiveness, less condom use, and higher levels of sexual shame (Seabrook, Ward, Cortina, Giaccardi, & Lipman, 2017). This is important to be aware of so that we can practice sexual literacy by being critical and aware of the various influences on the development of our sexual scripts, and so that we can dismantle gender-stereotypic heterosexual scripts when they appear to have a negative impact on our sexual agency, particularly for women (Seabrook, Ward, Cortina, et al., 2017).

A powerful tool of sexual scripts is sexual fantasy as people imagine erotic and romantic experiences with other people before they occur. This sort of sexual rehearsing and role-playing is consistent with sexual script theory. Through sexual fantasy and scripts, people can adjust to a situation as it changes and can prepare for how to adapt to the interpersonal situation and to the culture. Sexual scripts even affect how we behave and represent ourselves in the world. For a deeper discussion on the importance of sexual scripts, see "Research and Sexual Well-Being: African American Girls and Online Sexual Scripts."

sexual script theory
A theory that individuals develop scripts for sexual roles and behavior that incorporate the sexual rules of their culture.

LOVE

For centuries, people have attempted to define the word *love,* describe the emotions that accompany the experience of falling in love, and understand how love is manifested in the variety of human relationships. If we could look into the hearts and minds of many people we might find that love comes in a variety of flavors. One group of researchers views the actions fitting a description of a loving relationship as physical and emotional expressions of

Finding love is, arguably, one of the most important goals in the lives of many people.
William Manning/Corbis Documentary/Getty Images

RESEARCH and Sexual Well-Being

African American Girls and Online Sexual Scripts

People create and adapt sexual scripts according to how they live and what their culture expects of them. We can see this clearly in the research of Dr. Carla Stokes. In 2000, she began to research the online profiles of African American girls on social networking websites because they were constructing their identity and attracting romantic partners. She examined 216 home pages of African American adolescent girls residing in southern U.S. states. Dr. Stokes reported that girls in her study constructed their profiles similar to stereotypical sexual and relationship roles of hip-hop culture. She discovered that African American girls were creating different types of sexual scripts. Her analysis revealed five scripts with roots in controlling images of African American female sexuality (Stokes, 2007):

1. Freaks: This script closely aligns with a modern-day version of the sexually insatiable "Jezebel" image. Girls in this study defined a "freak" as a person who is sexually adventurous and willing to do anything with a person they are intimately involved with.

2. Virgins: This sexual script can be best defined as the "good girl" image that African American girls have been historically encouraged to adopt by parents and other adults. These girls typically place a higher emphasis on their intelligence, positive personality characteristics, and life goals.

3. Down-Ass Chicks/Bitches: This sexual script defines girls as fiercely loyal girlfriends who are "down for their man" and willing to engage in destructive behaviors, including committing or being an accomplice to crimes for their boyfriend's benefit.

4. Pimpettes: This sexual script defines girls as "female pimps" who are able to manipulate a relationship for sexual and economic gain while maintaining a romantic and sexual network consisting of more than one romantic or intimate partner.

5. Resisters: These were girls who disrupted stereotypical sexual scripts. The distinguishing factor among these girls is that they had begun a process of creating independent self-definitions. They were similar to the Virgins in that they rejected the Freak script and defined themselves as well-rounded, personable, and sweet, but none of them were explicit in declaring that they were "virgins."

To help younger African American girls get beyond these stereotypes, Dr. Stokes has become an activist whose website encourages exploration of a broader range of healthy sexual attitudes and behaviors. According to Dr. Stokes, "the study provides evidence that sexual images of women and girls in the media and American culture affect black girls' self-image and sexual development."

---

affection; a desire to offer pleasure and satisfaction to one's partner; compassion, tenderness, and sensitivity to the needs of the other; a desire to share in activities and pursuits; an appropriate level of sharing possessions; an ongoing and honest exchange of personal feelings; and the process of offering concern, comfort, and encouragement of a partner's goals and aspirations (Firestone, Firestone, & Catlett, 2006).

Love is also essential to sexual well-being. Media stories today may focus on either sex or love, but the package of sex and love is what distinguishes many people's search for positive and fulfilling relationships. In short, true and lasting sexual pleasure often is wrapped up with love. Finding the right combination of sexual pleasure, commitment, and emotional connection can take time, energy, and exploration.

Theories of Love

What are some social and psychological factors that are part of falling in love? When we look at how people fall in love we realize that culture plays a big role in "telling" us who we can and cannot fall in love with, typically with taboos and stereotypes. Another factor, at least in the United States, is age difference.

DID YOU KNOW

When is the right time to say, "I love you," when you are getting to know someone who feels truly special? Dr. Gail Saltz suggests that if someone says the "L" word too soon, it can sour the whole relationship. She says that it can be humiliating to blurt out "I love you" at a passionate moment and then watch the other person retreat.

Source: Saltz, 2006.

Society responds differently to younger men being with older women than to younger women being with older men. Gender stereotypes play a role in considering whether we ought to fall in love with someone of a different ethnic background, someone with a different faith or religion, or someone of a very different nationality. Another factor, social class, can also play a significant role in terms of falling in love. In countries with monarchies, for example, royalty usually do not marry commoners. Even wealthy families in the United States tend to marry into other wealthy families, because these families may wish to conserve their wealth, and one way to ensure that is to arrange marriages among families of similar wealth (Gilding, 2005). These are just some factors that may shape someone's journey toward love.

One of the difficulties in understanding a concept of love is that it seems every person has a different idea of what love is or means. These different ideas make it an even more difficult concept to measure and study. Consider the number of books dedicated to the topic of love. A recent search of the book section on Amazon.com on the topic "What is love?" yielded more than 250,000 matches. A few theorists, however, have successfully researched and written on the concept of love. Two of the most popular love theorists are Robert Sternberg and John Alan Lee.

Sternberg's Theory of Love Psychologist Robert Sternberg (1988) defines his research as the **triangular theory of love.** The theory suggests that people can have varying degrees of intimacy, passion, and commitment at any one moment in time. Finding a balance that works for the sex plus love needs of each individual is the key. Its core components include the following:

1. **Intimacy**—the feelings of closeness, connectedness, and bondedness
2. **Passion**—the feelings and desires that lead to romance, physical attraction, and sexual consummation
3. **Commitment**—the feelings leading one to remain with another, and in the long term, the shared achievements and plans made with that other

As shown in Figure 13.1, these three components interact with each other and with the actions they produce. In all, seven kinds of love experiences may occur, plus the experience of "liking." The shape of the triangle functions to represent the "type" of love, which may vary over the course of the relationship:

- *Infatuation* is pure passion. Romantic relationships often start out as infatuated love and become stronger and longer-lasting as intimacy develops. Without the development of intimacy or commitment, infatuated love may disappear quickly.

triangular theory of love
Suggests that people can have varying degrees of intimacy, passion, and commitment at any one time in their romantic relationships.

intimacy
One component of the triangular theory of love that includes feelings of closeness, connectedness, and bondedness.

passion
One component of the triangular theory of love that consists of the feelings and desires that lead to romance, physical attraction, and sexual consummation.

commitment
One component of the triangular theory of love that consists of the feelings leading one person to remain with another, and in the long term, the shared achievements and plans made with that partner.

Figure 13.1

In Sternberg's triangular theory of love, seven different kinds of love—plus liking—interact. People typically experience more than one type over the course of a relationship.
Source: Sternberg, J. R., & Barnes, M. L. (1988). *The psychology of love.* Yale University Press.

Liking (intimacy)
Romantic love (intimacy + passion)
Companionate love (intimacy + decision/commitment)
Consummate love (intimacy + passion + decision/commitment)
Infatuation (passion)
Fatuous love (passion + decision/commitment)
Empty love (decision/commitment)

- *Empty love* is characterized by commitment without intimacy or passion. Sometimes, a stronger love deteriorates into empty love. In arranged marriages, by contrast, relationships often begin as empty love and develop into one of the other forms with the passing of time.
- *Romantic love* bonds individuals emotionally through intimacy and physically through passionate arousal. In this relationship, partners have great conversations that are deep and that allow them to get to know a lot of intimate details about each other. They also enjoy great physical passion. What may lack here are discussions surrounding commitment and long-term plans for their relationship with one another.
- *Companionate love* is an intimate, nonpassionate type of love that is stronger than friendship because of the element of long-term commitment. Sexual desire is not an element of companionate love. This type of love is often found in marriages in which the passion has gone out of the relationship but a deep affection and commitment remain. The love ideally shared between family members is a form of companionate love, as is the love between close friends who have a platonic but strong friendship.
- *Fatuous love* can be exemplified by a whirlwind courtship and marriage in which passion motivates a commitment without the stabilizing influence of intimacy. A relationship, however, in which one person agrees to engage in sex purely out of commitment or is pressured into sexual acts does not comprise fatuous love. That type of relationship tends toward empty love.
- *Consummate love* is the complete form of love and represents an ideal relationship. It is theorized to be the type of love associated with the "perfect couple." According to Sternberg, such couples often continue to have great sex several years into the relationship, as they cannot imagine themselves happy over the long term with anyone else. They overcome difficulties gracefully and delight in the relationship with one another. Sternberg cautions that maintaining a consummate love may be even harder than achieving it. He stresses the importance of translating the components of love into action. "Without expression," he warns, "even the greatest of loves can die" (1988, p. 341). Thus, consummate love, without action, may not be permanent. If passion is lost over time, it may change into companionate love.
- *Nonlove* is the absence of all three of Sternberg's components of love, so it is not represented in the triangle. Many daily relationships represent nonlove, such as those developed with store clerks and so on.

Lee's Styles of Love John Alan Lee developed another theory about the concept of love in personal relationships. It centers on the idea that people have a style of how they approach love in romantic relationships. He refers to these love styles as "colors of love" (Lee, 1973). He color-coded these love styles into six major categories and named them using terms from

> ### WHAT'S ON YOUR MIND?
>
> *Q: I have been dating my girlfriend for over a year and I love her very much but I am not really sexually attracted to her. Can a relationship last without that kind of physical attraction?*
>
> **ANSWER:** What you have is a really great friendship. According to Sternberg's triangular theory of love you have *companionate love*, which means you have intimacy and commitment but the relationship lacks *passion*. Your relationship may be successful if you and your partner are on the same page and you both are happy without sexual passion. But if either of you has a need for this element, it may be difficult to sustain a happy and healthy relationship. We recommend some serious thought and communication in order to decide how you want to progress with this relationship.

Greek mythology. Figure 13.2 summarizes these brief descriptions of the six love styles and their corresponding color.

- *Eros (Beauty and Sexuality):* The eros lovers focus on physical beauty, attraction, and passionate love. They place great value on sexual desire and sexual interaction in their relationships. In fact, sexual intimacy is sought out in very early stages of a relationship. They often see marriage as a lasting honeymoon. The eros lovers have an idealized image of beauty that cannot be attained in reality and are highly sensitive to the imperfections of their partner. Those who possess other love styles perceive eros lovers as trapped in a fantasy world. Due to the high sexual charge and extreme passion, these relationships tend to burn out quickly because the passion and sexuality cannot be maintained. Consequently, the eros lovers often feel empty.

Figure 13.2

Lee's colors of love include three primary love styles, which are combined in different ways in the other three styles.
Source: Lee, A. J. (1976). *Colours of love.* Prentice-Hall.

STYLE	BASED ON	COMBINATION	DESCRIPTION
Eros (IR-os)	Beauty and Sexuality	Primary Style	This love style is the one most commonly portrayed in media (movies, TV, etc.). It is based off of physical chemistry and a strong physical or emotional attraction.
Ludus (LOO-dos)	Entertainment and Excitement	Primary Style	Ludus lovers are those who see love as a game and are more interested in quantity than quality of relationships. The focus is on having fun in the moment.
Storge (STORE-gaye)	Peace and Friendship	Primary Style	Storge love is a style of love that grows slowly out of friendship and is based more on similar interests and commitment. Passion is often lacking.
Pragma (PRAG-ma)	Practicality and Tradition	Ludos + Storge	This love style is based on practicality and compatibility. Pragma lovers approach their relationships in a businesslike fashion and look for partners with whom they can share common goals.
Mania (MANE-ee-ah)	Elation and Depression	Eros + Ludos	Mania lovers are characterized by having extreme highs and lows. This style usually results from low self-esteem and a need to be loved by one's partner. Possessiveness and jealousy are common issues in this love style.
Agape (aw-GAW-pay)	Selflessness and Compassion	Eros + Storge	This style of love is characterized by compassion, selflessness, and sacrifice. It is considered to be a spiritual love, offered without concern for personal reward or gain.

Mania lovers often cling to their partners as they fear losing love.
Joos Mind/Stone/Getty Images

- *Ludus (Entertainment and Excitement):* Ludus lovers might be called "players" and tend to have more than one lover at a time. They tend to be more interested in quantity than in quality of romantic relationships. They choose their partners by playing the field and they tend to recover very quickly from breakups. For them, love should not be taken too seriously and emotions should be kept in check. They are also known to have a partner only for as long as that person is interesting or amusing.

- *Storge (Peace and Friendship):* Storge (pronounced STOR-gay) lovers thrive on relationships born out of deep friendship. Their relationships often lack passion and intensity and grow from a gradual process of unfolding feelings and emotions. Sex in storge love comes later in the relationship and when it does, it usually assumes no great importance. While passion is not a central feature of storge love, these relationships do tend to be peaceful, secure, and stable, which are valuable characteristics of any romantic relationship.

- *Pragma (Practicality and Tradition):* Pragma lovers seek compatibility and choose partners who are similar to themselves. They are more concerned with social qualities than personal ones and they tend to rely on logic rather than feelings. Family and personal background are important and when choosing a potential partner they ask questions such as:

    "Will this person earn a good living?"

    "Can this person cook?"

    "Will my family like this person?"

    "Will this person be a good parent to future children?"

    Pragma relationships are often long lasting because they tend to choose partners carefully. The major downside to this love style is that pragma lovers tend to place too little importance on the emotional bond in a romantic relationship, which means it may be lacking in mutual satisfaction and attachment.

- *Mania (Elation and Depression):* Mania lovers experience extreme highs and extreme lows. Mania love can be possessive, dependent, and controlling. Mania lovers love intensely, and can be insecure about the loss of the love, which means they may experience fear that prevents them from enjoying relationships. Partners of mania lovers often feel much loved in the beginning of the relationship but often find that the feelings of being intensely loved change into feelings of being smothered by a clingy partner. Mania lovers tend to feel that their insecurities and poor self-esteem will improve with more intense love. Mania lovers may exhibit danger signs such as stalking and threats of suicide and violence, if they think the relationship may be ending.

- *Agape (Selflessness and Compassion):* Agape (pronounced, ah-GAH-pay) love is tolerant and gentle, compassionate, and self-giving. Many spiritual leaders including Jesus, Buddha, and Gandhi practiced and preached this unconditional love. Agape love is also known as a spiritual love, offered without concern for personal reward or gain. These lovers love without expecting to receive anything in return. While it may sound like the perfect kind of love, in reality, agape does not provide a romantic foundation for love between two adults. Romantic love requires a balance of giving and receiving, and agape love is all about giving. In one sense, agape is more a philosophical kind of love than a love that most people have the strength to achieve.

Research about these love styles has shown that men tend to associate more with ludus style and women tend to associate more with the storge and pragma love styles. Mania is often found in young adolescent or teenage relationships. Additionally, relationships based on similar love styles are found to last longer (Hendrick & Hendrick, 1986).

Types of Attachment

In addition to understanding the theories of love, it is important to examine how attachment contributes to our romantic relationships. **Attachment theory** helps to explain how we attach to caregivers during infancy. These infant attachment styles may have strong implications for attachment to romantic partners (Ainsworth, 1989; Ainsworth et al., 1978; Hazan & Shaver, 1987).

Infants attach to their caregivers in three distinct styles: secure, anxious, and avoidant (Ainsworth et al., 1978). The secure attachment style is associated with a wide variety of positive relationship characteristics including trust, commitment, intimacy, self-confidence, and a willingness to self-disclose. The latter two are insecure attachment styles and are associated with poorer relationship outcomes. For example, the anxious attachment styles may leave someone with ineffective coping techniques, which can result in greater conflict in relationships. In addition, the tendency for anxious people to be more self-focused can combine with worries that others will not be available when needed, and this can be an interference in a couple's ability to care for one another (Shaver, Mikulincer, & Cassidy, 2019). Individuals with avoidant attachment styles are more likely to be emotionally distant in relationships and have a more difficult time trusting their partner or providing sensitive and responsive caregiving to their partners (Shaver, Mikulincer, & Cassidy, 2019).

Researchers conceptualize attachment in adult relationships in different ways. Some classify adult attachment as close-independent and secure-insecure (Madey & Rodgers, 2009). Others have developed a three-dimensional model of secure, anxious, and avoidant adult attachment (Hazan & Shaver, 1987). Still others have proposed a four-dimensional structure of secure, preoccupied, fearful-avoidant, and dismissively avoidant attachment (Bartholomew & Horowitz, 1991).

The preoccupied attachment style is characterized by a person who has a negative view of self and a positive view of others. These individuals feel anxious in their relationships, are highly dependent on others, and invest a significant amount of energy in relationships that are not necessarily in their best interest to maintain (Bartholomew & Horowitz, 1991).

The fearful attachment style is characterized by a person who has highly negative views of both self and others. Observation suggests that these persons are socially avoidant because they are fearful of the level of vulnerability often required in intimate relationships. In contrast, people with a dismissing attachment style tend to have a positive view of self and a negative view of others. They place very little value in intimacy and often choose independence and autonomy over relational interdependence (Bartholomew & Horowitz, 1991).

Regardless of how researchers conceptualize attachment, their findings are fairly consistent: A strong association exists between attachment styles and relationship variables such as commitment, intimacy, communication, coping, and disclosure (Madey & Rodgers, 2009).

We also know that attachment has an impact on how we experience sexual intimacy. For example, research has shown that those individuals who are securely attached tend to be self-assured in their approach to sexual intimacy and experience increased enjoyment in mutual sexual interactions

attachment theory
A theory developed by Ainsworth that helps to explain how we bond with caregivers during infancy and childhood.

How we attach to caregivers early in life impacts our style of attachment in romantic relationships in adulthood.
Ariel Skelley/Blend Images LLC

within relationships (Birnbaum, 2016). Overall, the confident approach to sex exhibited in people who are securely attached promotes pleasurable engagement in highly affectionate relationships, which tends to foster relationship quality and longevity (Birnbaum, 2016).

Contrast this with those individuals who are insecure in attachment, whether avoidant or anxious. Individuals who are highly anxious tend to fear that they will lose their partners. This fear can lead them to consent to their partner's wishes and engage in unwanted or risky sexual activities, such as unwanted sexual intercourse (Davis, Shaver, Widaman, et al., 2006).

Individuals who are avoidant in their attachments tend to have other issues that may present sexual barriers in their relationships. These include a preference for less affectionate sexual interactions, masturbating rather than engaging in sex with their intimate partner(s), and a higher likelihood of engaging in emotionless and uncommitted sexual activities (Birnbaum & Reis, 2019).

Understanding attachment styles can help people to overcome potential obstacles in their relationship and to work on creating greater trust, intimacy, and communication. When people increase these factors, it may allow them to enjoy their intimate experiences more.

When Love Ends: The Dissolution of Relationships

It is an unfortunate fact of life that relationships end. As wonderful and exciting as relationships can be, they are highly complicated and many end after a period of time due to a variety of factors. While the reasons for the dissolution of relationships can vary, the reality is that this issue has not been well studied in scientific and academic research. Several articles, books, and blogs, however, have been dedicated to the subject of why relationships fail. The following points explain some of the most common reasons (Cottinger, 2003).

- *Selfishness:* Healthy romantic relationships require a balance between giving and taking. The more this balance is skewed in either direction, the greater the feeling that something is not right. When people are selfish, they fail to consider the needs or desires of their partner, most likely leading to a negative outcome for the relationship.

- *Inequality:* Healthy relationships are characterized by equality on many levels, and typically, equality means trust and respect. Important decisions about finances, children, family, friends, career, and so on, should be handled by both partners so that they truly feel heard and respected. When a relationship is marked by an imbalance of power, trust is hard, perhaps impossible; it generally means that one person is making most or all the decisions that affect both people and perhaps an entire family. Inequality in relationships can lead to feelings of resentment from the partner who is not given the opportunity to contribute to the decision making.

- *Intolerance:* Healthy relationships require partners to focus on each other's strengths, rather than on their weaknesses. Everyone has annoying habits and shortcomings that can easily irritate partners. When looking at your partner, you need to decide if those habits are deal breakers. If they are not, begin to look for the positives in your partner and focus on those.

- *Incompatibility:* Finding some similarity in such areas as moral values, sexual needs, hobbies, intellectual abilities, and spirituality is important for a relationship to feel enjoyable and comfortable. Some couples start relationships that are so far out of alignment that the initial attraction fizzles quickly. Unless two people are exceptionally fluid and changeable, a relationship may suffer from too much difference.

Breaking up can be a painful, but valuable, experience if both parties learn and grow from it.
Peter Dazeley/Photographer's Choice RF/Getty Images

- *Deception:* Honesty is the foundation of any healthy relationship. Lying, cheating (i.e., infidelity), and purposely hurting a partner are blatant betrayals of trust. Once trust is eroded through these various behaviors, it is unlikely to come back. Even subtle forms of deception can tear apart a relationship.
- *Poor communication:* Good communication is critical to sexual literacy, and it is a marker of the start of a good relationship. It requires intentional listening, respect between the partners, and an attempt to understand and respond to needs effectively. It also involves thinking about what to say and expressing it respectfully. Communication also involves gentleness and patience, and not always needing to be right. It also means having the courage to confront potential conflicts. If relationship problems grow without attempts to resolve them by communication, people may engage in behaviors such as deception that can erode the relationship even further.

The end of a relationship, though possibly painful, can be a valuable learning experience. Learning about why a relationship ends can help people understand themselves better to avoid similar pitfalls in the next relationship. Loving, successful relationships take a lifetime of care, which means there is room to improve. In the next section, we continue the discussion about communication because it is critical to ensure sexual well-being and positive relationships.

COMMUNICATION

Communication within the context of personal, romantic relationships can be a daunting task. So much of the conversation between romantic partners is deeply personal and increases vulnerability within individuals. If people have difficulties discussing sex, whether from a lack of vocabulary, discomfort, or differences in communication styles, their sexual well-being may be compromised. The better people can communicate within sexual and romantic relationships, the better they can avoid potential risks related to sexual health and the better they can deepen their understanding of their partner's desires and needs.

The biggest complicating issue in learning to communicate well is the subject matter—sex. Many people find themselves at a loss when it comes to communicating about sexuality. Parents may ignore the issue completely or "beat around the bush" when discussing sexuality with their children. Partners will stay in a sexual relationship with hidden needs and desires because they don't have the words to best communicate with their partners. Patients are uneasy to disclose information to their doctors about their sexual issues, function, or performance because they are nervous about talking about sexuality. This lack of sexual literacy has stifled people's abilities to discuss sex. It is time to acknowledge this difficulty and work toward being comfortable discussing sexuality.

Emotional Literacy: Communicating Your Needs

Sexuality includes dealing with all of our feelings, including our deepest feelings, which means emotions play a large role when communicating about it. In learning how to express these emotions, people develop emotional literacy, which is the capacity to perceive and to express feelings (Mayer, Salovey, & Caruso, 2000). The ability to explore and process feelings is basic to emotional literacy, and this is especially important in intimate relationships because people often need to share personal information.

When parents talk openly about sex with their kids, it helps increase effective communication for the child's future intimate relationships.
SW Productions/Photodisc/Getty Images

To understand how well you can talk about sexuality and your feelings about it, ask yourself the following questions:

- Do I know how to communicate my feelings to the person I care about?
- Would I like to learn some new ways of communicating?
- Do my sexual attitudes reflect who I am and who I would like to be in my sexual relationships?
- Would I like to learn more about how to bring my feelings more in line with my actual sexual expressions?

Answering these questions and others like them is important because learning to talk about emotions in relation to sexual intimacy can help or hinder sexual pleasure, a sense of sexual well-being, and enjoyment of life. Some people may be afraid of feelings; others may be hindered because they are stubborn or proud; and others may push their friends or partners away by withholding their feelings, even though they may yearn to be emotionally and intimately connected.

The area of emotional skills in relation to sexual communication is mostly undeveloped in research and in education (McCafferty, 2007). Reasons for this may include the negative approach taken toward sexuality education, and because some consider it unacceptable to express certain emotions, especially those about sexual desire and intimate needs. Here is where the achievement of sexual literacy can really make a difference in life (Moore & Reynolds, 2018).

Research does show that learning to develop keener emotional expression can heighten people's emotional intelligence (Salovey & Sluyter, 1997). To help develop emotional intelligence, Steve Hein of Eqi.org advises to start with three-word declarative sentences such as, "I feel respected," "I feel excited," "I feel happy," and then write the reverse of these statements. Using as many words related to emotions and feeling as possible may increase an understanding of how to express feelings and to talk about perceptions of situations.

emotion work

Individuals' attempts to try and change in degree or quality and emotion or feeling.

Other research indicates that intimate communication relies on **emotion work,** which is the attempt to change an emotion or feeling (Hochschild, 2001). Offering encouragement, showing appreciation, listening closely to what someone has to say, and expressing empathy with another person's feelings (even when they are not shared) are all examples of emotion work in relationships (Erickson, 2005). When people search for the right words to say to connect with their intimate partner, they may fall back on what they have heard or learned, often unconsciously. Additionally, they may use information they have heard on television or from other media. This may work but sometimes people can get into trouble because they do not fully communicate what they want to say. Emotion work helps people connect with their partner(s) in a positive way and further to develop caring and intimacy between them (Erickson, 2005).

Developing emotional literacy and the skills to communicate it may be hard to do in societies that frown on sexual pleasure (Moore & Reynolds, 2018). For example, in many societies, including the United States, women more than men are expected to be cautious and reserved when it comes to talking about sex. Thus, culturally-patterned gender differences in sexual expression may make it harder to develop communication skills about sexuality (Sanders & Robinson, 1979; Tannen, 1990). In fact, in one study, women more than men seemed to prefer a more narrow set of sexual terms for communication. The women used terms such as "penis," "vagina," and "make love" as well as pet names for the genitals, such as calling the penis "Oscar." Men tended to have a wider collection of terms to use for sexual communication (Levine, 1995, p. 114).

When people feel unsure about how to communicate feelings, they may feel vulnerable and fear rejection or failure as they try to express themselves. Consider the following situations:

- People may not know how to express their desires or their sexual needs when they are in a new relationship or unfamiliar with someone else's body and needs.

- In new relationships, people may not know what makes their partner feel good. This uncertainty may create shyness, avoidance, or even fear of offending the other.
- Developing the ability to trust exposes people to vulnerability, but trust is important for people to express their emotions freely.
- Because of cultural prohibitions, people may only indirectly express themselves through actions or body language. People may feel shame or fear and then lie about how they really feel.
- People may mask their feelings and substitute one thing for another; for example, rather than expressing their need, they may express dislikes, disgust, or hate.
- A person's voice and body language may convey inconsistency, as when they feel one thing but say or do another. This may cause people to disguise how they feel in intimate situations.
- Some feeling terms, such as love, may be used too often, or people may exaggerate their feelings, perhaps to get attention.

Emotional literacy can help people learn about the importance of honest and clear communication, which can help to improve relationships and society. As people develop greater emotional literacy, they can become more comfortable with sexual vocabulary, our next topic.

Sexual Language

On an internet blog about love, sex, health, and well-being, an individual wrote the following:

> It is a little embarrassing to admit that I don't know how to talk about what I want sexually from my partner. I can't get any of the words that they use in porn movies out of my mouth and I feel weird using medical words in the middle of pleasurable acts. We don't talk much during our intimacy anyway, I think because we both don't know what words to use to convey what we want without grossing each other out. Any ideas? (Strgar, 2010. http://www.care2.com/greenliving/loveologist-sexual-vocabulary.html.)

It is interesting how much the Internet and other media are flooded with explicit and titillating sexual talk and, yet, when it comes to having an everyday conversation about improving our intimate lives or sharing sexual health information, many people are silenced. The good news is that becoming a good sexual communicator is definitely a skill that can be acquired. The following are some obstacles that may block having easy and meaningful conversations about sexuality (Strgar, 2010):

- *Sex myths:* To be good in bed, do you have to be a mind reader? The reality is that people feel they should "just know" what arouses their partner without communicating. This reality presents a great disservice for many people. Learning to feel comfortable with anatomically correct information is a great start to being a better communicator about sex because talking about it is more reliable than trying to read the minds of others.
- *Sexual fear:* Many individuals walk around with a lot of fear about sexuality. Common fears include sexual performance, sexual rejection, or making a fool of oneself. Sex can bring many people to their most vulnerable point and this means that fear can arise quite easily. Fearing sexuality can cut people off from others and can make communicating nearly impossible.
- *Negative beliefs about sex:* Many people are from families, cultures, or communities that express negative sex beliefs. For some, these beliefs relate to their bodies and the idea that the sexual parts of the body are ugly, dirty, and a source of shame.

WHAT'S ON YOUR MIND?

Q: *I don't think dick and pussy are respectful names for penis and vagina. What are some respectful names for genitalia that are also "hot"?*

ANSWER: People differ in what vocabulary they think is respectful (and hot). It's up to you and your partner to decide what you're comfortable saying. Luckily, many terms can be used to describe genitalia.

For an international flavor, you can try some foreign slang terms. Nicknames for the penis include *chinchin* in Japanese, *badajo* in Spanish, *verga* in Portuguese, *uccello* in Italian and *schwanz* in German. When it comes to the vagina, the Spanish *almeja*, Hindi *bhosdo*, Portuguese *cona*, or the Japanese *manko* are slang names.

If these terms are still leaving you hungry and not yet satisfied, think about your own relationship for memorable experiences, inside jokes, pet names, and so on for some inspiration. People have been known to come up with all kinds of names. Most of all, remember to have fun when you're finding new, beautiful-sounding names. After all, there's nothing sexier than a great sense of humor.

Others were raised with universal or religious-based sanctions against sexual pleasure. These beliefs can hinder people from engaging in positive conversations about sexuality.

- *Lack of sex information:* It is difficult to have a conversation about sex when there is no sexual information to draw from. A lack of sexual education may cause some sexual communication problems in the United States. A lack of basic knowledge of sexual organs and their function, contraceptives, and STIs makes a real conversation difficult.

- *Privacy and boundaries:* People tend to be private about sexuality. As they age, they usually become more private with sexual information rather than more open about it. People's sense of privacy affects their ability not only to communicate but also to purchase contraception or to purchase items that may enhance their sexual experience. Privacy is important to be comfortable about their sexuality, but it should also enhance their ability to communicate about it. Also, a clear sense of personal boundaries is critical because feeling confident in their ability to stretch within their boundaries may ultimately build their ability to communicate.

Nonverbal Sexual Communication and Flirting

There's a language in her eye, her cheek, her lip; Nay, her foot speaks. Her wanton spirit looks out at every joint and motive of her body.

—SHAKESPEARE, *TROILUS AND CRESSIDA,* ACT IV, SCENE 5, LINE 55

Notice the nonverbal cues in this quote that communicate romantic interest.

Even when words are not being said, people can communicate volumes through silence, facial expressions, proximity, sounds, and body movements. Nonverbal messages, though, may not be clear. For example, does a smile communicate being happy or nervous? Does silence communicate thoughtfulness or does it express distance, disapproval, or hostility?

The difficulty with nonverbal communication comes when we don't have a cross-cultural understanding. For example, in the United States, it is considered a sign of respect and courtesy to maintain eye contact with someone while they are speaking. In many other cultures, eye contact is considered to be abrasive or a sign of disrespect. For example, in Latino cultures, looking someone in the eye is a way of challenging authority, while looking down communicates respect. Even when it comes to the distance between people when speaking, people from various European countries tend to stand quite close to the person with whom they are speaking while Americans tend to step away—offering personal space. Interestingly, Americans often convey sexual or romantic interest when they step close to someone with whom they are speaking.

People use nonverbal communication to express their feelings and emotions. While the value of this may be increased in some cultures, the ability to interpret nonverbal communication is critical for successful relationships in most cultures. Common methods of nonverbal communication used in relationships can include all the following:

- Touch
- Glances
- Eye contact (gaze)
- Vocal nuance
- Vocal volume
- Proximity
- Gestures
- Facial expressions
- Intonation
- Dress
- Posture
- Smell
- Sounds

Flirting happens through a variety of communication cues—many of them nonverbal and associated with body language.
Ingram Publishing

Nonverbal communication can serve the following functions:

- To repeat a verbal message (e.g., pointing in a specific direction while stating driving or walking directions).
- To accent a verbal message (e.g., verbal tone can indicate the meaning of some words). This is why writing can also create misunderstanding. When people are reading words, they can often misunderstand meaning because they are speaking in a different tone than what the author intended.
- To complement or to contradict a verbal message (e.g., a nod can reinforce a positive message and a wink can contradict a stated message).
- To offer cues to convey when another person should speak or not speak.
- To substitute a verbal message (e.g., gestures such as putting a finger to a closed mouth to indicate "be quiet" or nodding in place of saying "yes").

Nonverbal behaviors are also important in how people express romantic or sexual interest (Moore, 2010). One of these behaviors is flirting, which easily can be misinterpreted because it is often inherently vague. Though people can flirt verbally, nonverbal flirting plays a significant role. Flirtatious behaviors convey initial interest in potential partners. They can also be used effectively to pace a dating relationship. Additionally, people in established relationships can use flirting to interject some fun (Moore, 2010).

Research shows that women often initiate the first flirtatious behaviors. One study estimated that in approximately two-thirds of cases, women made the first move. Neither gender, however, dominates in flirting behavior during dating or courtship (Perper, 1985). Further research is needed to develop a true understanding of the specific behaviors that are used in flirting and how these differ among individuals from different cultures and sexual orientations.

Sexual Self-Disclosure: To Reveal or Not to Reveal?

I (Nicole) had an experience during college with my roommate and her boyfriend. Over a bottle of wine we were discussing our personal histories with dating and significant others when my roommate looked at her boyfriend and asked, "So, how many women have you had sex with?" I knew that now I was part of a highly personal conversation but given that the conversational tone was light, I stuck around. My roommate's boyfriend was hesitant to admit his "number" and when she continued to press him, he finally revealed it. My roommate was instantly moved to tears and anger and what had been a friendly, fun conversation among friends instantly became a source of pain and jealousy.

This conversation and its outcome may be what some may call "TMI" (too much information). Many people think that romantic partners should disclose everything—innermost desires and feelings as well as details about past sexual relationships. Research shows that knowing what to disclose or how much to disclose is a subtle art that individuals must learn to negotiate. The same research shows that though self-disclosure is important, too much sharing can potentially hinder relationship development (Anderson, Kunkel, & Dennis, 2011).

When it comes to disclosure about past sexual histories, a theory called **communication privacy management theory** suggests that the revelation of private information in a relationship has the potential to leave individuals feeling vulnerable or resentful regarding the shared information (Petronio, 2002). When disclosing information relating to past sexual experiences there may be a stigma of "too much experience" or "too little experience" associated with that disclosure.

As is true with most issues with at least two sides, some believe that sexual self-disclosure is a critical part of establishing and maintaining intimate relationships. Research has shown that when partners reciprocate in sharing their sexual histories, greater sexual and relational satisfaction tends to follow (Byers & Demmons, 1999; MacNeil & Byers, 2009; Sprecher & Cate, 2004). For years, health practitioners in sexuality have asserted that sexual disclosure is a critical part in the prevention of STIs, including HIV. The assumption is that partners need to assess their risk of infection by discussing each other's sexual pasts. Disclosures of this nature can also help partners discuss what protection or contraception to use.

Sexual self-disclosure mainly concerns verbal aspects of communication, but interpretation of that information is also important. How a couple interprets each other's disclosure and relationship-related behaviors can have a significant impact on the quality of the relationship, which is part of communicating effectively.

communication privacy management theory
Idea that the revelation of private information in a relationship has the potential to leave individuals feeling vulnerable or resentful regarding the shared information.

Characteristics of Effective Communication

Just as with books about love, a plethora of titles are published that relate to communication in intimate relationships. Many authors believe that improving communication between partners is the most critical aspect of ensuring a mutually rewarding relationship (Erber & Erber, 2011). For more information on how one kind of conversation can contribute to love and connection between partners, see "Communication Matters: The One Daily Talk that Will Benefit Your Relationship."

When it comes to sexual communication, many people may be surprised to learn that talking about sex is just one aspect of good sexual communication. The ability to listen and comprehend what someone is saying is often one of the most difficult skills to master in communication, including sexual communication. An active listener is someone who both listens to and is genuinely interested in what the other person is saying. The following are some important skills and tips for improving listening skills generally as well as between partners.

COMMUNICATION Matters

The One Daily Talk that Will Benefit Your Relationship

In today's faced-paced world, where people are struggling to maintain presence in their workplace or school, at home with family and friends, and even in online social spaces, connecting with partners can end up being a source of frustration when we unload on one another at the end of a busy day.

If you want to connect with your partner at the end of the day but don't want these conversations to escalate into a stressful conversation filled with tension and anger, therapist Kyle Benson (2016) offers up what he calls The 4 Agreements of Love to guide couples in their end-of-day connecting conversations.

Agreement #1: Agree on Timing

As we have learned throughout this text, people are quite different in the ways in which they express themselves and how they like to communicate. Some people like to connect with partners the moment they walk in the door. Others may need some time to decompress or be quiet before they are ready to debrief their day. Agreeing on timing for your reconnecting conversation at the end of the day can help avoid tension that might be created when needs for either conversation or quiet are not being met. Agree on a time that meets both your needs. This can be at 8:00 P.M. every night or it can be 15 minutes after both of you get home at the end of the school or workday.

Agreement #2: Dedicate Your Presence for 20–30 Minutes

Once you make an agreement about when to connect, make a commitment to truly connect and spend some time with one another. Twenty to 30 minutes without distractions such as cell phones, social media, or television can provide a space for quality interaction and deeper connection to each other.

Agreement #3: Don't Discuss Your Relationship

This daily talk is really an opportunity to share about your day and support one another in other areas of your life outside your relationship. This conversation should be a place where each of you can vent frustrations about the day if needed and respond to one another in a way that exercises empathy and curiosity rather than judgment. When you aren't combining this with relationship issues, it is much easier to express support and understanding to your partner.

Agreement #4: All Emotions Are Welcome

This conversation is an opportunity to share feelings whether they are positive, celebratory, and joyful or negative, angry, irritated, or sad. Relationships are about sharing our victories as well as our hardest challenges. Opening up a space where partners can be free to share any and all emotions can make life and your relationship all that much more meaningful and connected.

Source: Adapted from Benson, K. (2016). The one daily talk that will benefit your marriage. Retrieved November 30, 2016, from https://www.gottman.com/blog/the-one-daily-talk-that-will-benefit-your-marriage/

- Use nonverbal body language, such as looking at the other person, nodding the head, and using sympathetic facial expressions.
- Ask questions, making brief comments about what the other person says, and share personal experiences to encourage your partner to continue.
- Engage to hear the other person. Listening is not waiting for the other person to stop talking. Fully listen by dropping defenses to hear what the other person is saying.
- Paraphrase the other person's message. Summarizing what is said helps the listener to understand what the other person means. The paraphrase allows the person the opportunity to correct any misunderstandings. Paraphrasing may slow down the conversation, which may also make a difficult discussion feel safer.
- Create ground rules for important discussions. Examples for these rules might be do not interrupt the other person and the listener needs to paraphrase what the other person has said before beginning to talk.

- Make eye contact. In the United States and in some other cultures, eye contact is a vital aspect of face-to-face communication. If a person is from another culture, be aware that eye contact may be invasive, disrespectful, or intimidating.
- Be supportive. Comments that are supportive may lessen the other person's fear of talking about sex. These comments create mutual empathy and can increase the love that flows between partners.
- Express positive regard for the other person. Conveying care and respect may encourage a person to talk about difficult or painful topics.

Ultimately, let your partner know you will continue to care, even when you may disagree about an issue.

Styles of Communication

It is important to understand how we tend to communicate. John Gottman's research in relationships and communication shows that it is not how much a couple fights but rather how they fight that determines the success of their relationship. Gottman believes that to grow in relationships, people must reconcile their differences. In fact, he believes that fighting, when it airs grievances and complaints, can be one of the healthiest things a couple can do for their relationship (Gottman, 1994).

Gottman's research has largely centered around heterosexual married couples. To categorize marriages, he noted such factors as the frequency of fights, facial expressions, tone of voice, content of speech, and physiological responses (such as pulse rate and amount of sweating) of both partners during confrontations. He found three different styles of problem solving into which healthy marriages tend to settle: *validating, volatile,* and *conflict-avoiding.* All three styles are equally stable and bode equally well for the future success of a relationship (Gottman, 1994).

Validating couples let each other know in the midst of disagreement that they each consider the emotions of the other as valid even if they don't agree with the emotions. This mutual respect has the tendency to limit the number of arguments they have. For validating couples, conflicts are resolved through calm discussion and compromise. Both partners listen and try to understand the other's feelings, problems, and points of view.

Volatile couples are those who appear to thrive on constant conflict. These couples fight on a large scale but also make up on just as large a scale if not larger. More than any other type of couple, volatile couples see themselves as equals. They are both usually independent people who believe that marriage should strengthen and protect their individuality. Partners tend to be very open with each other about both positive and negative feelings.

Conflict-avoiding couples appear to be the complete opposite of volatile couples because these couples avoid conflict. They tend to make light of their differences rather than try to resolve them. They find their happiness in their shared perception of the similarities between them. Essentially this couple thrives on the mantra "let it go" and they seem truly happy with their lack of conflict resolution.

What, then, is the key for the success of relationships when it comes to communication? For Gottman, it is the balance between negativity and positivity in

Couples who are considered "volatile" experience a high level of conflict in their relationship.
Howard Kingsnorth/Cultura/StockImage/Getty Images

COMMUNICATION Matters

Do Gay and Lesbian Couples Communicate Better?

Though research about gay and lesbian relationships is more lacking than it is for heterosexual couples, researchers have found some interesting differences in interactions between heterosexual and same-gender couples in commit-ted relationships (Gottman et al., 2003). The research showed that when discussing areas of conflict in romantic relationships, same-gender couples began the interaction much more positively and far less negatively than heterosexual couples. Additionally, same-sex couples were much more positive in the ways they received issues of concern from their partners (Gottman et al., 2003; Kurdek, 2005). They also work to continue that positive interaction.

There are a variety of theories regarding these seemingly positive and protective differences note in communication between same-sex couples and heterosexual couples. These include the ideas that:

Same-gender couples tend to value equality more than heterosexual couples (Garanzini, Yee, Gottman et al., 2017). Gender differences and status hierarchy in heterosexual relationships has the potential to breed hostility in their interactions, particularly from women who tend to have less power than men.

ericsphotography/iStockphoto.com

---

any relationship. To be exact, the ratio between positive and negative interactions should be 5:1. As long as there is five times as much positive feeling and interaction between the couple as there is negative, the relationship is likely to be stable over time.

Some research indicates that gay and lesbian couples may communicate better than heterosexual couples. See "Communication Matters: Do Gay and Lesbian Couples Communicate Better?" to read more on this topic.

Characteristics of Ineffective Communication

While romantic partners can provide a host of wonderful things for each other such as warmth, comfort, support, and satisfaction, they are also capable of inflicting the deepest kinds of hurts such as criticism, insults, and rejection (Theiss et al., 2009). Few things can be as damaging to a relationship as poor, abusive, and manipulating communication between partners.

Four disastrous modes of communication can sabotage a couple's attempts to salvage a disintegrating relationship. Over time, these modes become entrenched and the couple increasingly focuses on the escalating sense of negativity and tension (Gottman, 1994). Gottman refers to these four modes as the four horsemen. Each horseman paves the way for the next one to arrive, and eventually a relationship that was once loving and passionate may be on its way to death. These horsemen are criticism, contempt, defensiveness, and stonewalling.

Criticism This behavior can begin when one partner complains about the habits of the other. The difference between complaining and criticism may seem minimal, but there are important differences. Complaining can be a healthy factor in a relationship because each partner can express needs and possibly get them met (Gottman, 1994). If those needs are not met, frustration can build and the complaints can become criticism. Criticizing involves attacking someone's personality or character rather than a specific behavior or event. In reality, few couples are able to refrain from criticizing each other once in a while. So even in healthy long-term relationships and marriages this horseman may permanently reside. The problem occurs when partners are critical of the other's personality rather than of a specific action or behavior. The following are verbal examples of a complaint and a criticism:

Complaint: "We don't spend as much quality time alone anymore."

Criticism: "You never want to spend time with me."

Know Yourself

How Do Your Relationships Compare to Those of Other Couples?

Whether or not you are in a relationship, consider completing the following four steps because they might help you to improve communication. If you are not currently in a relationship, these steps may be more difficult to complete, but thinking about them may still be helpful for a future relationship.

1. Each partner writes down the names of four different couples that you both know. Two couples should be examples of "bad" relationships and two couples should be examples of "good" relationships.

2. Share the names with one another and discuss why you feel the good relationships work and the bad relationships don't.

3. Talk about your own relationship as it relates to these good and bad relationships you've identified. Compare and discuss the way you and your partner manage to get through difficult challenges with the way the other couples handle their trials and difficulties. Identify behaviors you would like to imitate and behaviors you would like to avoid.

4. As a couple discuss how you would be able to overcome hardship. Have you already been through a challenge successfully that you are proud of? If so, what elements helped you reach a successful resolution? Write them down and try to use those skills again when obstacles present themselves.

Being critical becomes destructive when it is so pervasive that the relationship begins to corrode. When that happens, the road is paved for the next horseman to arrive. Before reading about this next horseman, consider the communication patterns in your relationship or possibly those of other people you know. See "Know Yourself: How Do Your Relationships Compare to Those of Other Couples?" for an exercise that may help you ultimately improve your own communication.

Contempt Contempt is the intention to insult and psychologically abuse someone. People may use both words and nonverbal communication to lodge insults right at a partner's sense of self. Partners may fuel these cruel actions with negative thoughts about their partner (e.g., their partner is incompetent, stupid, or incapable of change). When this happens, the memory of how the couple fell in love fades dramatically. As a consequence, compliments, admiration, loving exclamations, and affection are withheld and the focal point of the relationship becomes abusiveness. In fact, this relational amnesia results in not even being able to remember a single positive attribute or act that the partner possesses or has done. Signs of contempt in a relationship are fairly easy to recognize and can include:

- Insults and name-calling
- Hostile humor
- Mockery
- Body language that includes rolling the eyes, sneering, curling the upper lip, among other things

The reality is that most of us state our criticisms in a contemptuous manner at some point. However, if the relationship is heading toward abusiveness, the best thing partners can do to neutralize the interaction is to stop using arguments as a way to retaliate or exhibit one's superior stance over the other. Refraining from attacking personality and character is also a great way to keep this dangerous horseman at bay (Gottman, 1994). If this is not done, the third horseman of defensiveness may arrive.

Defensiveness Defensiveness is a likely outcome when someone disrespects another person. When partners act defensively toward one another it is usually because each feels victimized by the other. This act of defending oneself is understandable, but using defensive phrases and the attitude behind those phrases may escalate conflict rather than resolve it. The following are some signs of defensiveness in interactions:

- Denying responsibility: Partners may insist that they are not to blame, regardless of the accusations against them.
- Making excuses: One partner may claim that external forces caused a behavior or action that upset the other partner.
- Disagreeing with a partner's attempts to attribute negativity in thoughts: One partner may attribute negative thoughts to the other partner or make assumptions about that partner's private thoughts, feelings, motives, or behaviors. When this kind of "mind reading" is delivered back to the partner, it can often trigger defensiveness.
- Cross-complaining: Instead of hearing one another's complaints, one partner may simply complain in response to the other's complaint and completely ignore the concern that the other partner just stated.
- Repeating yourself: Partners often restate their position without hearing or considering the opinion of the other person.

Stonewalling is a behavior that can be detrimental to a relationship.
Image Source/Getty Images

Stonewalling The fourth horseman is stonewalling, because in a relationship marred with arguing, strife, and bitter words, silence may be a welcome change. Stonewalling often happens while a couple is trying to talk about issues and one partner turns into a "stone wall." This person disengages from the interaction both verbally and nonverbally and becomes silent. Stonewalling displays disapproval, smugness, and cold distance. It can be very upsetting for the partner who is trying to talk with the stonewaller. Research shows that when a man stonewalls a woman, her heart rate increases dramatically, which indicates a heightened state of physiological arousal and distress (Gottman, 1994). For Gottman, stonewalling is the final event in a deteriorating relationship because it can lead to one or both partners deciding that the relationship is broken beyond repair.

After this fourth horseman arrives, is all lost? Absolutely not. Once partners can recognize what may be leading to the deterioration of their relationship, they can still develop or improve the necessary skills to get their relationship back on track.

Improving Communication Skills

When learning how to improve communication, a few tips can help improve sexual communication with partners. These suggestions may be useful not just at the beginning of a relationship but throughout its life in order to avoid needing to repair damage caused by ineffective communication.

- **Pick a neutral time and place:** Oftentimes, people tend to choose an inopportune time or place to bring up concerns or complaints with their partners. Carefully select the time and place for such discussions, such as when both partners are relaxed and open to one another. Additionally, consider not discussing sexual issues in the bedroom or in places of regular sex.
- **Read and discuss:** Media are full of resources pertaining to sexuality and relationships. Oftentimes, people find it easier to read about sex than to talk about it. One way to open up communication about sex or relationship difficulties is to read a book or magazine article together or separately and then discuss it.

- **Engage in active listening:** As mentioned previously in the chapter, be a good listener. Engage in active listening to encourage the other person to open up or to continue expressing needs or concerns about the relationship.
- **Validate and support your partner's efforts to communicate:** When one partner supports the other's efforts to communicate, it can alleviate anxiety associated with beginning a sensitive conversation and encourage the other to continue to talk. Supportive comments can help to foster understanding for one another and help to encourage future caring communication.

Repairing damage done by ineffective communication is also an important part of improving our communication skills. Gottman (1994) calls these techniques *repair mechanisms*. Repair mechanisms are needed most when people are frustrated and angry. The following are some gestures that can act as a glue to help hold a relationship together during tense times (Gottman, 1994).

1. Comment on the communication process itself, using statements such as "Please let me finish," or "That hurt my feelings."
2. Comment on what is happening in the here and now. Don't save the comments for a later time, rather discuss it while it is taking place.
3. Remind your partner that you admire, respect, and empathize with him or her even though you may not agree with your partner's perspective.
4. Use active listening phrases such as "I see" or "Go on" to show that you are paying attention and hearing the other person.

These repair mechanisms can help to stabilize a couple during a disagreement and repair damage from negative interactions.

COMMUNICATION AND SEXUAL WELL-BEING

People often find it difficult to say "no" to a partner. They may even hesitate doing this with people they barely know. Consider the neighbor who asks for a favor at an inconvenient time or the adorable child who asks for just one more piece of candy. Saying *no* to people they love is even more difficult at times and saying *no* to a romantic partner can cause increased feelings of anxiety and guilt. Nevertheless, for a healthy relationship, saying *no* is a critical skill to learn.

When a romantic partner asks for sexual intimacy or to engage in a role play or fantasy or to try a new position that makes the other person uncomfortable, it is important to have the necessary skills to politely refuse without alienating the other partner and causing a barrier to future requests. Being honest is the best way to proceed in a situation like this. It is important in relationships for both partners to feel comfortable in expressing feelings and needs. The way someone says *no* depends on the partner's nature and state of mind (Yadavar, n.d.). How to say no also depends on the reason for saying it. Divulging the reason is not necessary; however, it can be easier for the partner and may help to avoid hurt.

So, how should you say "no"? You should say it with an assertive and firm tone but not aggressively. Be clear that you are not consenting to whatever the request is. Saying no to sex or to a new position or to a fantasy does not mean you are saying no to your partner. In fact, there are ways to make up or offer suggestions for alternative activities including the following:

- *Say no with affection:* When saying no, make sure you do so with some affection. Snuggle, cuddle, say "I love you," and spend time with your partner. These actions show your partner that you care and that it is not the person but the specific request that you are saying no to.
- *Suggest alternatives:* Don't just say no and leave the subject at that. It most likely took your partner a great deal of courage to approach you with the request. As you say no

to that request, offer an alternative that is more acceptable to you. Whether it is another time or place or playing out an alternative fantasy, give your partner suggestions that you may both be comfortable with.

- *Be open:* If your partner has a request that you are too uncomfortable with, even though your tendency is to say no, ask why that activity is appealing. Listen to the reasons offered and try to be open to the idea. If you can understand what it is your partner wants to experience with you, you may find a middle path where you go ahead with the idea but with limits. In time, you may find that the request is something you enjoy as well.

These suggestions can help you in the art of negotiation and assertiveness in your relationships. Sexual well-being and communication are two closely related concepts. With increased awareness and new insights into love and relationships, you can enhance your life overall.

Chapter Review

SUMMARY

Sexual Attraction

- How humans gauge sexual attraction depends on both our sexual nature and the culture in which we grow up.
- While culture has an impact on attraction, experiences beyond attraction, including falling in love, are much more individual.
- Cultural standards of what is beautiful and sexy have changed dramatically throughout history.
- While people may complement each other in their differences, we are often most attracted to those who are similar in terms of social class, education, ethnicity, faith, and interests.
- Bem's exotic becomes erotic (EBE) theory of sexual orientation states that people are attracted to what is unusual or exotic to them.
- The matching hypothesis states that people select romantic and sexual partners based upon the other person's attractiveness.
- Sexual script theory states that individuals learn internal sexual rules and roles to play just as actors learn lines and actions from scripts.

Love

- The combination of sex and love is essential to sexual well-being and is distinctive of many people's search for positive and fulfilling relationships.
- Sternberg's triangular theory of love suggests that people can have varying degrees of intimacy, passion, and commitment at any one moment in time.
- According to Sternberg, "consummate love" is the complete form of love and represents the ideal relationship, which includes high levels of intimacy, passion, and commitment.
- Lee developed six love styles that can help us to understand how we behave in love relationships: eros, ludus, storge, pragma, mania, and agape.
- Adults' attachment to their romantic partners often mirrors childhood attachment to primary caregivers.

Communication

- Emotional literacy involves being aware of emotions in intimate relationships and having the necessary skills to communicate with partners.
- It is important for individuals to be comfortable with sexual vocabulary so they can effectively communicate with partners.

- Sexual self-disclosure helps to build intimacy in relationships as well as to ensure safety about potential STI risks. Knowing what to disclose or the degree of disclosure is a subtle art that individuals must learn.
- The ability to listen and comprehend what someone is saying is often one of the most difficult communication skills to master. An active listener is someone who communicates that she or he is both listening to and interested in what the other person is saying.
- Methods to improve the quality of communication in relationships include picking a neutral time and place for a discussion; choosing a literary resource about the sexual or intimate topic and discussing it together; engaging in active listening; and validating the efforts of partner(s) to communicate.
- Ineffective methods of communication include criticism, contempt, defensiveness, and stonewalling. Recognizing and avoiding these ineffective tactics in a relationship can help couples to communicate better.

Communication and Sexual Well-Being

- Learning to say no to a partner is an important skill in being assertive in your relationship and communicating your needs.

What's Your Position?

1. **How important is physical attraction in your pursuit of romantic relationships?**
   - What kind of physical attributes do you find attractive in potential romantic and sexual partners?
   - How do these attributes reflect what society sees as sexy or beautiful?

2. **What is love to you and what characteristics of love are important to you in relationships?**
   - Have you ever been in love?
   - What does it mean to you to be in love?
   - Which of Lee's love styles do you most identify with?

3. **How comfortable are you discussing sex with romantic and intimate partners?**
   - How have you talked about sex with partners?
   - What kinds of communication skills do you use to talk about sex in your relationships?
   - Have you ever had to say "no" to a partner's request for sex or intimate behavior? How would you do this in a way that maintains your position, yet preserves the dignity of your partner?

4. **Have you ever discussed your sexual history with a partner?**
   - How did that process make you feel?
   - What can you do to make this process more comfortable if necessary?

Design elements: Controversies in Sexuality: HBRH/Shutterstock; Research and Sexual Well Being: verity jane smith/Getty Images; Healthy Sexuality: Sergey Furtaev/Shutterstock; Communication Matters: PeopleImages/Getty Images; Know Yourself: Plush Studios/Blend Images LLC; What's Your Position: Luis Molinero/Shutterstock; Healthy Sexuality: A. Minde/PhotoAlto; Did You Know icon: McGraw-Hill Education; Page corner icon: McGraw-Hill Education.

Sexual Coercion and Resiliency

14

Sexual Coercion
- Differentiate sexually coercive behaviors from typical sexual behavior.
- Describe the two core concepts central to sexual coercion—molestation and sexual exploitation.

Rape
- Compare and contrast the different forms of rape, including date rape, marital rape, and prisoner rape.
- Describe cultural differences in sexual norms as they relate to coercive behaviors.
- Identify commonly understood characteristics of perpetrators of sexual coercion.
- Describe differences between rape-prone and less rape-prone societies and groups.
- Explain the impact of rape on its survivors, including suggestions on supporting survivors.

Childhood Sexual Coercion
- Identify the forms of child sexual abuse and characteristics of children at risk.
- Identify signs of childhood sexual abuse, behaviors of children who have been abused sexually, and consequences of childhood sexual abuse experienced by survivors.
- Recall how child pornography contributes to the sexual victimization of children.

Teen and Adult Sexual Coercion
- Identify behaviors that are part of sexual harassment and explain how to respond to them.
- Identify behaviors associated with teen dating abuse and sexual bullying.

Sex Work and Sex Trafficking
- Explain the link between sex work and sex trafficking.

Recovery, Resiliency, and Sexual Well-Being
- Describe resiliency research, and discuss its importance in understanding sexual coercion.

● Learning
● Objectives

Vassiliy Kochetkov/123RF

Developing Your Position

1. In your mind, what constitutes rape?
2. In what ways have you witnessed sexual violence in your life, your family, or your community?
3. In what ways have you experienced sexual harassment or seen it in school or in the workplace?
4. What can you do to help victims of sexual violence?

Self, Society, and Culture: Sexual Violence and Its Aftermath

Olivia comes to human sexuality class every day. Like many of my (Nicole) students, she is intelligent, asks questions, and often contributes comments during discussions. The day I lectured about sexual coercion issues, I noticed her unease as I flashed through PowerPoint slides of statistics. It was after she completed her personal reflection paper for the course that I got confirmation that she was indeed a victim of sexual coercion.

Many "Olivias," and some "Olivers," take my human sexuality class. They are Black, White, Asian, Hispanic, and Middle Eastern and come from every corner of the earth. They are mostly—though not always—female. They are all shapes and sizes: thin or overweight; blue, green, or brown eyes; short or long hair. They sit in class and wonder when I will bring up the subject. One day my lecture floods their minds with painful memories. *Rape, molestation, incest, sexual harassment,* and *abuse*—all words that are a lot more than just course material; they are traumatic pieces of their life experience. For some, the experiences started when they were toddlers, young children, preadolescents, or teenagers, but for others the trauma might have occurred just a week ago in a dorm room or at a party. The cause of their pain stems from the actions of a cousin, uncle, brother, grandfather, father, boyfriend, neighbor, or basketball coach.

They hold it together so that the others around them won't know the hell and torment they are reliving during this lecture. They hurt for the part of them that was violently taken. They wish for the day that they could have a relationship that is honest, mutual, loving, and respectful. That hope and dream causes my Olivias and Olivers to get up every day, get dressed, go to class and work, meet with friends, and look for that special person. They begin to work through their pain with the help of family, friends, therapists, and teachers. They begin to heal and one day, while the pain is still there, the wonderful things in life begin to dull it and they realize that they have the power. They become a support to others who have traveled their road; they become an advocate for sexuality free of violence. They post their #MeToo stories on social media, giving others the knowledge that they aren't alone. They are no longer victims or even survivors—they are conquerors. They become heroes in their own lives and heroes to others. These Olivias and Olivers are the thousands of individuals who experience sexual coercion and live to tell the story of hurt and pain that can turn into strength, hope, and sexual well-being.

In this chapter, you will read about various types of sexual coercion, including rape, childhood sexual abuse, sexual exploitation, and sexual harassment. You will also learn about prevention, recovery, and resiliency. Let's begin by defining sexual coercion.

SEXUAL COERCION

The two words, *sexual coercion,* illustrate the darkest side of human sexual nature. When the beautiful, amazing, and powerful world of human intimacy is turned into rape, conquest, abuse, and harassment, there are devastating, life-altering consequences for victims and perpetrators alike.

Sexual coercion is an umbrella term that includes the threat of sexual force or aggression, in addition to other forms of assault on the self, especially rape, incest, childhood sexual abuse, marital or partner rape, sexual exploitation, and harassment. An act of sexual coercion is not motivated primarily by sexual desire but by someone's intent to control, humiliate, or harm another person (National Sexual Violence Resource Center, 2010). It is especially important to this definition of sexual coercion whether an individual is unable to give consent due to age, illness, disability, or under the influence of drugs and alcohol (National Sexual Violence Resource Center, 2010). Central to this approach are two core concepts: **molestation,** considered to be any sexual act performed with a child by an adult or an older child; and **sexual exploitation,** the sexual abuse of children and adults through the exchange of sex or sexual acts for drugs, food, shelter, protection, other basics of life, and/or money.

In 2006, Tarana Burke, a Black social activist and community organizer, began using the phrase "Me Too" in order to help survivors of sexual violence (particularly Black women and girls) find a pathway to healing. In October 2017, because of the viral #MeToo hashtag tweeted out by Alyssa Milano and followed by a number of famous individuals such as Gwyneth Paltrow, Ashley Judd, and Jennifer Lawrence, the topic of sexual violence was suddenly thrust into national discourse. Women all over the world began to engage in sharing their experiences of sexual violence and recovery through social media. Suddenly, it was no longer considered acceptable to ignore these stories or to allow this kind of violence to continue unchecked. On Facebook alone, the hashtag was used by more than 4.7 million people in 12 million posts during the first 24 hours. In the days, weeks, and months to follow, powerful men in the public eye, whether in Hollywood, major news organizations, professional sports, or government, began to experience the social and legal consequences of their choice to sexually coerce, harass, or rape. It is incredibly powerful to have seen this kind of social movement gather traction so quickly and produce such an instant shift in public discourse. We can only hope that #Me-Too continues to gather strength as women and men feel empowered to tell their stories and create a unified call to alter the sexual norms in our culture that have allowed sexual violence to go unchecked for so many years.

While sexual coercion can have short- and long-term detrimental effects on its victims, it may or may not be illegal and/or criminal. We first turn to the topic of rape and discuss its various forms, in addition to ways in which we can be proactive in preventing rape and understanding how best to respond to its occurrence.

sexual coercion
Acts of sexual violence committed against an unwilling or incapacitated individual.

molestation
Any sexual act performed with a child by an adult or an older child.

sexual exploitation
Sexual abuse of children and adults through the exchange of sex or sexual acts for drugs, food, shelter, protection, other basics of life, and/or money.

The original #MeToo campaign was started by Tarana Burke in 2007 hopes to reach women of color who were victims of sexual assault.
Jordan Strauss/January Images/Shutterstock

RAPE

Like many other words related to human sexuality, *rape* is difficult to define. Traditionally, rape was viewed as the forcible penetration of a woman's vagina by a man's penis. Now the definition of rape includes other forcible sex acts in a variety of circumstances. The meaning and impact of the violent act changes with the nature of

WHAT'S ON YOUR MIND?

Q: I was raped by my best friend a few years ago. I was a virgin then, and still, years later, I can't seem to "go all the way" with anyone. How can I stop freaking out and messing up relationships?

ANSWER: Before being too hard on yourself about "messing up relationships," try to remember that being raped may make it hard for anyone to have an emotionally or sexually intimate relationship. Perhaps it was your lover or best friend, someone you trusted, who assaulted you, and of course you feel betrayed. Some rape survivors who were virgins at the time of the assault also confuse being raped with having had sex. Rapists use sex as a vehicle for gaining power and control over someone. This is not consensual sex, let alone love. If you feel pressure to move faster than you're comfortable with in your relationship(s), consider cutting yourself some slack and allowing things to progress as slowly as feels natural for you. Healthy sexual relations rely on clear and assertive communication and respect. You may need more time, understanding, the right partner, or even counseling before you feel more comfortable and ready to take this step.

rape
Sexual penetration of the body using physical force, the threat of bodily harm, or oral penetration by a sex organ of another person, without consent.

the assault, the relationship between the two people, and to some extent how it is experienced. Also, the definition of rape varies from one state to another in the United States and around the world. For the purposes of this discussion, we define **rape** as sexual penetration of the body using physical force, the threat of bodily harm, or oral penetration by a sex organ of another person, without consent.

Living with the experience of rape can define a person's life. The U.S. government reports 17.6% of women have been raped at some point in their lifetime (Tjaden & Thoennes, 2006). While not as severe, the reality is that rape not only affects the victim but also the victim's loved ones, family, friends, and communities. In fact, rape continues to be a serious social problem in American society today.

Figure 14.1 provides some positive news regarding rates of sexual assault in the population, noting that the rate of sexual assault and rape has fallen 63% since 1993. While this is encouraging, there is still much room for improvement as other statistics confirm that sexual violence is all too common an occurrence. According to a variety of studies, rape affects as many as one in four college women in the United States (Crisis Connection, 2012). Increasingly, men are also victims of rape. It is estimated that 1 in 71 men has been raped in his

Figure 14.1

The rate of sexual assault and rape has fallen 63% since 1993, from a rate of 4.3 assaults per 1,000 people in 1993 to 1.2 per 1,000 in 2016.

Source: Department of Justice, Office of Justice Programs, Bureau of Justice Statistics, National Crime Victimization Survey, 2013–2017 (2018).

Figure 14.2

If we think of the relationship between various sources of data on sexual coercion and reality as an iceberg floating in water, the tip of the iceberg represents the cases reported to law enforcement. Beneath the surface remains a substantial set of gestures, intimidation, propositioning, bullying, and many other issues.

Source: Adapted from World Report on Violence and Health. Geneva: World Health Organization, 2002.

lifetime (Black, Basile, Breiding et al., 2011); and in 2012, the FBI changed its definition to include males, to acknowledge this fact. Many assaults are not reported to authorities, particularly if the perpetrator is a boyfriend or the husband of the victim (Figure 14.2). In addition, rape victims incur significant cost and risk in order to report the assault to authorities (Allen, 2007). Examples of these losses and risks that come as a result of reporting are the loss of anonymity, the risk of retribution by the offender, stigmatization from other people, and the harsh legal process that can unfold as a result of any investigation or trial (Allen, 2007). As you will learn, the United States continues to have a higher rate of rape than some other countries around the world.

Myths about rape abound. Although stranger rape is believed to be the most common form of rape, female victims are more likely to know their perpetrators (U.S. Department of Justice, 2005). To understand rape better, read "Know Yourself: Myths About Rape."

Consider this scenario, which plays out in countless movies and television shows. A woman is walking alone on a vacant street at night or in a park and a man with a mask jumps out and attacks her. He throws her to the ground and forces her to engage in sexual intercourse with him. While this kind of rape does occur, it certainly does not represent the typical scenario of sexual violence in the United States. That's because many rape victims actually know the rapist, and sexual violence is not limited to vaginal penetration. Certainly, rape can include the forcible penetration of a woman's vagina by a man's penis, but it also includes forcible sexual penetration of the mouth or anus with a penis or foreign object, such as a broomstick.

In recent years rape has been categorized according to the relationship of the victim to the perpetrator. This leads to two major categories of rape, date rape and marital rape (Sanday, 2007). We discuss both types next.

Date Rape

Date rape is now a significant problem in the United States: Over 1 in 3 (36.4% or 43.6 million) women experience sexual violence, physical violence, and/or stalking by an intimate partner during their lifetime (Smith, Zhang, Basile et al., 2018).

Date rape results in a variety of negative outcomes (Teten et al., 2009). Perhaps most importantly they include major depression, substance use as a coping mechanism to deal with the pain and memories, suicidal ideation and suicide attempts, disordered eating and weight management problems, and other symptoms of extreme stress (Banyard & Cross, 2008; Silverman et al., 2001).

date rape
Forcible sex from someone a victim knows socially or is dating.

Know Yourself

Myths About Rape

Read each statement and indicate whether you think it is true or false.

1. Any woman could prevent rape if she really wanted to. No woman can be raped against her will.
2. It is impossible to rape a man.
3. Rapists are easy to spot because they are abnormal perverts.
4. Rape is an impulsive, uncontrollable act of sexual gratification.
5. If a woman has consented to sexual relations in the past with a man, that man cannot rape her in the future.
6. A man has to show a woman who is boss right from the start.
7. Some women deserve to be raped because of their actions or dress.
8. Women say "No" when they really mean "Yes."
9. Rape is no big deal if the woman has had sex previously.
10. It is not rape if a woman consents to sex under the influence of drugs or alcohol.
11. A husband cannot rape his wife because they are married.

Answers can be found on p. 481.

Given this level of impact on the self, it is clear that the effects of date rape are truly serious. Survivors of date rape not only suffer damage to their self-concept, but also have to deal with the lingering memories of the trauma, the possibility of pregnancy, the fear of the next assault, or the inability to create and sustain intimate sexual relationships, as well as performance problems at school and work (Banyard & Cross, 2008; Silverman et al., 2001). Because of the serious nature of sexual assault during adolescence, experts now recognize that it poses a greater risk for post-traumatic stress disorder (PTSD) than does victimization later, during adulthood (Masho & Ahmed, 2007).

The high incidence of date rape on college campuses may be due to the use of alcohol and recreational drugs (Abbey, Zawacki, Buck et al., 2001). While alcohol and drug use do not cause sexual assault, it contributes to the higher frequency of assault in a couple of key ways. For example, the desire to commit sexual violence may actually lead to alcohol consumption by a male perpetrator before committing a sexual assault in order to justify his behavior. In addition, among college-age males, fraternities often encourage both heavy drinking and the sexual exploitation of women (Abbey, Zawacki, Buck et al., 2001; Sanday, 2007). The high incidence of date rape among college students can also be attributed to the culture of the college campus, which may not have protection built into it, as we will explore later in the chapter.

Date Rape Drugs A popular film, *The Hangover,* tells the story of four men who go to Las Vegas for a bachelor party and wake up the next morning with no recollection of what happened the night before. They had accidentally taken the drug Rohypnol. Sexual predators use this powerful drug and other similar substances to overcome their victims and leave them with no memory of the events under its influence. Rohypnol is one of the substances that are referred to as **date rape drugs.**

Date rape drugs are fast-acting sedatives that are virtually undetectable because they are tasteless, odorless, and colorless. They are easily slipped into drinks and food causing people

date rape drugs
Substances used by predators to overcome their victims in order to commit nonconsensual sexual acts with them.

ANSWERS to Myths About Rape *(p. 480)*

All of the statements are false. Understanding the common myths about rape and other forms of sexual coercion is critical to preventing such acts.

Know Yourself

to lose consciousness but remain sexually responsive with little or no memory of what happens (Victim Witness Assistance Program, 2017). Without any memory of events, victims are often unaware that they have even been raped, and if they are aware or have suspicions about it, they are unreliable witnesses because of their memory loss.

The three most common date rape drugs are Rohypnol, GHB, and Ketamine. Table 14.1 lists different names for these drugs. Rohypnol, a pill with the chemical name *flunitrazepam,* dissolves in liquids. Some pills are small, round, and white. Others are green-gray and oval. The green-gray ones have a dye in them that turns clear liquids bright blue and darker drinks cloudy, but these changes may be difficult to see in dark rooms. The effects of this substance can be felt within 30 minutes after being drugged and can last for several hours. Rohypnol is not legal in the United States, but it is legal in Mexico and Europe, where it is often prescribed for sleep problems and to assist with anesthesia before surgery (U.S. Department of Health and Human Services, 2008).

GHB is short for *gamma hydroxybutyric acid* and comes in three forms: a liquid with no odor or color, a white powder, and a pill. It may give drinks a slightly salty taste, although mixing it with a sweet drink such as fruit juice can mask the saltiness. GHB takes effect in about 15 minutes and can last 3 or 4 hours. It is very potent, so it is easy to overdose. It is legal in the United States as a treatment for the sleep disorder narcolepsy (U.S. Department of Health and Human Services, 2008).

Ketamine is a fast-acting liquid or white powder normally used as an anesthetic. People under its influence might be aware of what is happening to them but may be unable to move. People may not remember what happened to them while under its influence (U.S. Department of Health and Human Services, 2008).

It is difficult but not impossible to know if you have been given a date rape drug. Short of being told that you were given one of these drugs, medical testing is the only way to verify. To learn more about what people may experience if they've been given a date rape drug, read "Know Yourself: Am I a Victim of a Date Rape Drug?"

Date Rape Prevention and Intervention Dating violence has been recognized as a public health problem, given its prevalence, potential for injury, and other negative health outcomes. Date rape prevention efforts are most effective when approached from different

WHAT'S ON YOUR MIND?

Q: Last weekend I was drunk at a party. I woke up the next morning next to this guy who said we had sex. I don't ever remember saying that I wanted to have sex and now I don't know how to feel. Even though I may have said "yes," I really did not want to have sex with him. Was this rape?

ANSWER: What you experienced can be considered forcible sex—yes, rape—because you were under the influence of alcohol. Most state laws suggest that people cannot legally consent to sexual activity if they are under the influence of any drug or alcohol. We encourage you to speak with a counselor for some guidance on how to proceed legally and to talk through your experience and the feelings you have now.

Know Yourself

Am I a Victim of a Date Rape Drug?

If you think you have been given a date rape drug, ask yourself the following questions:

- Are you sore or bruised in the genital area, in the anal area, on the inner or outer thighs or both, or on the wrists and forearms? Do you see any bruising or scratching that might occur during a struggle?
- Do you see used condoms near you or in garbage containers or traces of semen or vaginal fluids on clothes, body, or furniture?
- Have people told you that you seemed very intoxicated the night before?
- Are you aware that you did not drink much alcohol the night before but feel hung over?

Aside from indications of sexual activity, other clues about ingesting date rape drugs include a feeling of having had hallucinations or very "real" dreams; fleeting memories of feeling or acting intoxicated despite having taken no drugs or drinking no alcohol; and having no clear memory of events during an 8- to 24-hour period with no known reason for the memory lapse.

If your answers to these questions indicate that you were raped after being given a date rape drug, see the information provided later in the chapter in "Healthy Sexuality: Steps to Take if You Are Raped." *Remember: If you had sex but cannot remember giving consent, you have been raped under the law, whether or not you were drugged.*

Table 14.1 Common names for date rape drugs

ROHYPNOL	GHB	KETAMINE
Circles	Bedtime Scoop	Black Hole
Forget Pill	Cherry Meth	Bump
LA Rochas	Easy Lay	Cat Valium
Lunch Money	Energy Drink	Green
Mexican Valium	G	Jet
Mind Erasers	G Juice	K
Poor Man's Quaalude	Gamma 10	K-Hole
R-2	Georgia Home Boy	Kit Kat
Rib	Gook	Psychedelic Heroin
Roach	Goop	Purple
Roach-2	Great Hormones	Special K
Roches	Grievous Bodily Harm	Super Acid
Roofies	Liquid E	
Roopies	Liquid Ecstacy	
Rope	Liquid X	
Ropies	PM	
Ruffles	Salt Water	
Trip-and-Fall	Soap	
Whiteys	Somotomax	
	Vita-G	

Source: U.S. Department of Health and Human Services, Office on Women's Health. (2008). *Date rape drugs.* Retrieved from http://www.womenshealth.gov/faq/daterape-drugs.pdf

levels (Teten et al., 2009). For example, prevention programs that educate the broad national population about the prevalence of date rape are critical to changing the perception that date rape is not a serious problem. These programs are just as important as efforts to empower young people to protect themselves and to educate them about the sexual rights of their peers (Teten et al., 2009).

These tips may help to protect you from being a victim of date rape drugs (U.S. Department of Health and Human Services, 2008; Victim Witness Assistance Program, 2017).

- Don't accept drinks from other people, even if you know the person. It is safer to get your own drink from a bar or make it yourself.
- If someone offers to get you a drink, go with that person to order it. Watch the drink being poured and carry it yourself.
- Open your own containers.
- Keep your drink with you at all times, even when you go to the bathroom.
- Don't share drinks.
- Don't drink from punch bowls or other common containers because they may have drugs in them.
- Don't drink anything that tastes or smells strange.
- Have a nondrinking friend with you to make sure nothing happens.
- If you leave your drink unattended, pour it out.
- If you feel drunk and haven't drunk any alcohol or if you feel like the effects of drinking alcohol are stronger than usual, get help right away.

Taking precautions to prevent sexual violence is important, but sometimes victimization can occur even when safety measures are followed. Experiencing a forced sexual act can be one of the most frightening and traumatizing events that anyone can imagine. However, there are specific steps that a victim of a forced sexual act can take to pursue justice as well as to help ensure that they quickly get on the road to healing and sexual well-being. The good news is that it is possible to recover from sexual coercion and go on to enjoy respectful and loving sexual encounters with trusted individuals.

Marital Rape

Marital rape is intercourse forced on one spouse by the other spouse, almost always a husband forcing his wife into having sex. Only in recent years have people realized how offensive and cruel marital rape can be for the victims. Our society tends to think of marriage vows as a contract that automatically gives consent to have sex—under any circumstances at any time (e.g., even when someone feels ill or is recuperating from a stressful event). Here we can see how the victim perceives marital rape as a catch-22, between being required to have sex in marriage and having choice and control over your own body, especially when one is feeling out of sorts or not particularly "sexual" on occasion. So marital rape is not just a minor bedroom argument: He wants sex, she is not in the mood—but he forces her anyway, and he wins the argument. Despite the statistic that reports 80% of the general U.S. population believes husbands use force to have sex with their wives, marital rape is not often considered to be "real rape" (Bennice & Resick, 2003; Lynch, Jewell, Golding & Kembel, 2017). We can see how marital rape is so much a part of who has power and choice, and who does not (Basile, 2002). Whenever another factor, such as a language or cultural difference is inserted into the marriage, as when one of the spouses is an immigrant, it may actually compound the issue of power and control within marriage (Merry, 2006).

marital rape
Forcible sex from one's spouse.

Despite differences in state laws and attitudes that vary by culture and region of the country, and other factors, there is widespread recognition that marital rape is a significant and continuing social problem. In fact, in one study, almost three-fourth of victims agreed that husbands sometimes use force (Basile, 2002). Research has shown that marital rape is highly prevalent among battered women and that the types of force used include hitting, holding their wives down, or threatening them with a weapon (Bennice & Resick, 2003). A husband might force sex with his wife because he thinks she is leading him on or because she continually refuses to have sex with him. A majority agreed that if a husband forces his wife to have sex, he has raped her (Basile, 2002).

Marital rape is a crime in all 50 states in the United States; however, in many states marital rape is considered to be less of an offense than other forms of rape and is treated more leniently (Hines & Malley-Morrison, 2005). Despite laws that prohibit spouses from forcing their partners to engage in sexual activity, there is still some controversy about whether or not there is such a thing as marital rape. See "Know Yourself: Marital Rape" to assess your own views regarding this issue.

As with other forms of sexual violence, we know that there is a critical intersection of sexual behavior norms and subsequent beliefs about what is acceptable or constitutes rape and sexual violence in marital relationships. It is critical that research continue to better reveal how gendered social norms contribute to how people decide what is "real" and "not real" in intimate partner rape so that survivors of this kind of violence can see a cultural shift whereby validation, justice, and healing can occur (Lynch, Jewell, Golding, & Kembel, 2016).

Prisoner Rape

Sexual violence behind bars is an issue of national attention in part due to the statistics showing rape, torture, and sexual assault of inmates by other inmates and even prison staff as part of prison life (Anderson, 2005). But another very important reason has to do with the racial disparity in our nation's prisons: so many inmates are men of color (Alexander, 2010). According to the Federal Bureau of Justice Statistics, American prisons and jails were the site of 24,661 formal allegations of sexual assault in 2015 (Bauman, 2018). Some researchers believe that the real figure is much higher, due to the shame and fear of male prisoners reporting rape. More than half (approximately 58%) of the allegations in 2015 were claims that prison staff sexually assaulted inmates, while the remaining 42% were incidences between inmates (Bauman, 2018). In addition, because condoms are rarely available in prisons, the incidence of HIV/AIDS and other STIs is quite high (Jurgens, Nowak, & Day, 2011).

One thing is certain: Sexual assault has risen as the prison population has increased, with the emphasis on confinement creating harsh conditions for the management of inmates (Anderson, 2005). One study of male prisoners reported that sexual assault victims in prison are typically younger, more vulnerable, weaker outcasts who cannot defend themselves (Man & Cronan, 2002). They are also more likely to be homosexual or transgender. Some researchers have documented that sexual assault was 13 times more common for transgender women in prisons for men (Jenness & Fenstermaker, 2016). See Table 14.2.

Female prisoners also experience sexual coercion and assaults, generally by male prison officers, but also by female inmates. Male prison officers have vaginally, anally, and orally assaulted female prisoners. Prison guards and other officials have abused their positions of power through coercion and using sex in exchange for privileges and material items. Male corrections officers are often allowed to watch female inmates while dressing, showering, or using the toilet. Many also engage in verbal sexual harassment of female prisoners (Man & Cronan, 2002).

Know Yourself

Marital Rape

Read the following statements and decide how much you agree or disagree with each statement according to the following scale:

1 – Completely disagree   2 – Disagree   3 – Neutral   4 – Agree
5 – Completely agree

_____ 1. When you get married you are supposedly in love and you shouldn't even think of lovemaking as rape under any circumstances.

_____ 2. Sexual relations are a part of marriage and both members should realize this before they make a commitment.

_____ 3. If the wife did not want to have sex for many months, the husband may force her to have sex instead of seeking sexual pleasure with someone else.

_____ 4. If the wife doesn't want to have sex for a long time and has no reason for it, the husband should just have sex with her.

The degree to which you agree or disagree with these statements reveals how much you believe there is such a thing as marital rape. For example, if you completely disagree with every statement and score 4, you believe marital rape is a form of sexual coercion. If you score 20, you are more inclined to believe that marital rape is not a form of sexual coercion.

Source: Based on Finkelhor & Yllo, 1983.

In addition to being tolerated, prison rape is often approached with indifference. Some critics believe that the main reason is the racial inequality in the prisons (Alexander, 2010). Reporting procedures, if they exist, are often ineffective and even ignored by prison staff and government authorities (Anderson, 2005). In addition, authority figures are not held accountable for their actions, and victims are threatened, shamed, and discouraged from reporting sexual assault (Anderson, 2005). As mentioned, virtually no precautions are taken to prevent the spread of STIs, even when authorities know that sexual contact and rape occur in prisons.

Federal lawmakers have passed legislation to end prisoner rape, but they have not effectively funded it. The Prison Rape Elimination Act of 2003 calls for the development of

Table **14.2** Difference in the percentage of sexual assaults against the total population and transgender people in California prisons

VARIABLE	RANDOM SAMPLE	TRANSGENDER SAMPLE
Prevalence of sexual assault	4.4	59.0
Prevalence of undesirable sexual acts	1.3	48.3
Weapon used if involved	20.0	75.0
Officer aware of the incident	60.6	29.3
Provision of medical attention (if needed)	70.0	35.7
Racial composition (% of incidents interracial)	17.2	63.9
Relational distance	Evenly distributed	Skewed toward familiarity

Source: Jenness et al., 2007.

national standards to address prisoner rape and for funding programs to address this widespread problem at the state level.

Victim-Blame

Avoiding sexual violence requires understanding not only what precipitates it in a given society but also how the community and society respond to sexual violence (Jurgens, Nowak, & Day, 2011). As an example of a community's response, consider what you just read about prison rape: It continues because authorities in the prison community ignore it and the community in general is hostile toward the victims. Research indicates that, in general, the response to sexual violence in the United States is hostility toward the victims (Wang & Rowley, 2007).

Blaming the victim is not unique to the United States. **Victim-blame,** the formal term for hostility toward crime victims, is a cross-cultural phenomenon. One cross–cultural study tested the level of acceptance of the belief that a healthy woman can fight off a rape. It found that 20% of students surveyed in the United States held this belief, compared with 45% of those surveyed in Turkey, 50% in India, and 56% in Malaysia (Wang & Rowley, 2007). Just as troubling was the result that 64% of the U.S. students in the sample agreed that women provoke rape and that they place themselves at risk for rape when they go out alone.

How do these attitudes impact victims of rape? The psychological effects are devastating. Victims who are made to feel blame for an assault experience self-devaluation, have higher levels of psychological distress, and recover poorly (Wang & Rowley, 2007). Conversely, in societies where rape victims are not blamed, the psychological outcomes are much better (Merry, 2006; Sanday, 2007). Societies where victims of rape are not blamed legally and culturally define sexual coercion and assault as a crime and a violation of personal rights; support freely disclosing the crime after being victimized; believe the victim; provide understanding for the victim; and offer empathy, psychological support, and counseling (Wang & Rowley, 2007). In societies with positive outcomes, advocacy for victims of sexual violence can have positive results and help to promote respect for the sexual rights of all individuals.

victim-blame
The tendency of victims of abuse to place the blame for the abusive actions of others onto themselves.

Cultural Differences in Rape

Sexual coercion occurs throughout the world, and there are no industrial countries that are "rape free." However, rape takes different forms and has different meanings in different cultures. For example, the rate of rape in Japan is 1.78 per 100,000 people, whereas the United States has twice as many rapes. By comparison, the rate is .078 per 100,000 in Canada, and perhaps as high as 119 per 100,000 in South Africa today (NationMaster.com, 2011). War-torn or conflict-ridden countries typically have much higher rates of sexual violence. Countries with huge poverty and income differences also tend to have more violence and more rape than others, due to the lack of stability and a culture of victimization in such places (Farmer, 2003). But poverty and war do not fully explain high rates of sexual coercion. For example, Sweden, regarded in many respects as progressive and supportive of sexual literacy, has a rate of rape twice as high as the United States. Why would this be true?

The reasons are complex but probably have to do with gender and the ability of women, men, and children to protect themselves against the threat of rape (Sanday, 2007). Societies vary greatly in their tolerance of sexual aggression, and when it comes to rape, they also vary with regard to enforcement and prosecution of offenders (Correa et al., 2008; Sanday, 2007). As with all behaviors, however, culture influences not only the context but also whether people actually talk about these crimes or report them to the authorities. In a society that silences discussion of rape, the shame may be so great that the crime is actually hidden or covered up, especially by the family (Levinson, 1989; Sanday, 1981a, 1981b, 2007). For example, in some communities, attitudes surrounding rape may blame the victim or not take seriously rape or sexual coercion attempts, as researchers found in a study of 90 different countries (Levinson, 1989). In cases of child abuse, the attitudes of the family play a key role in how people perceive and respond to victims across cultures (Korbin, 1981, 1987).

In many war-prone societies or those with military regimes, such as Vietnam in 1960–1970, Bosnia-Herzegovina (Correa et al., 2008; Long, 1997) in the 1990s, or in Central Africa today, women, children, and men who have been raped fear stigma, retaliation such as subsequent rape, or even murder, if they speak out about their experience (Correa et al., 2008). Having to keep rape a secret thus implies the extent to which a society takes victims' reports seriously (Sanday, 2007). But let's be clear: Cultures rarely tolerate rape and most regard it as obscene or abnormal, as an extreme sexual behavior or a horrible act of violence. This terrible treatment tends to make people regard sexual abuse victims as the "throwaways" of society (Correa et al., 2008; Petchesky, 2003). When sex is connected to daily survival and conditions like violence or war, it is not surprising that the most vulnerable members of society will suffer (Farmer, 2003).

Sexual violence occurs throughout the world, a disturbing reality that is not often acknowledged.
Simon Maina/AFP/Getty Images

Societies Prone to Rape

It is also important to consider whether a culture is prone to rape due to its social, economic, political, or sexual characteristics. War has historically been one of the most important sources of sexual violence (Merry, 2006; Sanday, 2007; Wardlow, 2006). We know that societies differ dramatically in the incidence of rape due to how conditions may change when it comes to war, for example, or very negative attitudes toward women (Merry, 2006; Sanday, 1981b). For example, every 20 minutes a girl is raped in India—though the country is not at war and has a religious and cultural tradition that would seem to make rape unlikely (Kandar et al., 2017). Researchers suggest that the lack of respect toward women in public combined with false beliefs and negative attitudes explains why. In societies where men have great power and make decisions about marriage and sex, women may be more vulnerable to sexual coercion (Sanday, 2007). Generally, the status of sexual and gender rights in a society helps to explain the broad societal context of coercion in the 21st century (Merry, 2006). In particular, how women are treated in a society may determine their vulnerability to rape (Sanday, 2007; Wardlow, 2006).

A **rape-prone society** is one in which women's desires are unimportant and physical sexual coercion is normative. Advanced industrial societies such as the United States, Japan, and Germany reveal contexts in which sexual coercion of women may be implicitly tolerated (Merry, 2006). Recent laws and policies have tried to address these abuses, often through creation of laws that protect against rape, even in the context of marriage, although this right is by no means universal or enforceable (Correa et al., 2008).

Increasingly, however, researchers have learned that these same conditions may apply to men and children as rape victims, an issue that has been made clear in the context of the Afghanistan and Iraqi wars through such novels as *The Kite Runner* by Khaled Hosseini, and

rape-prone society
A society or cultural group in which women's desires are considered to be unimportant and physical sexual coercion is normative.

Women in universities across the United States come together in an event called "Take Back the Night," which is designed to raise awareness of the problem of sexual coercion on college campuses.

John Wagner/ZUMApress/Newscom

by recognition that anyone can be a target for sexual violence and rape (Correa et al., 2008). However, male rape is such a shameful silent issue in many countries that it can be totally hidden or covered up, even more so than rape of females (Sanday, 2007). When shamed or silenced by their families or peers or by an institution such as their church, male rape victims, especially men raped as children, have to bear these horrible experiences alone their whole lives, even keeping them secret from their adult sexual partners (Korbin, 1990; Sanday, 1981b).

So this saying about sexual relations has an element of truth in it: *"No doesn't mean no; it's just the beginning of negotiations."* Here are some common characteristics of rape-prone societies (Sanday, 2007; Stotzer & MacCartney, 2016):

- Rape myths are accepted.
- Consumption of pornography is significant.
- Attitudes toward women are more gender stereotyped.
- Women do not have equal power.
- Male violence is tolerated and even promoted.
- Violence is often sexualized with high sexual arousal to depictions of rape and/or sexual violence.
- Aggressiveness and competition are encouraged in male behavior.
- Male physical force is viewed as both a natural behavior and an appropriate reflection of masculinity.

As you can see, these traits are mostly about unequal power between men and women, and of course between adults and children, and U.S. society's overall acceptance of aggressive behavior in men.

College campuses in the United States, unfortunately, are part of this rape-prone society. Some concerning research findings have shown that one out of three college-aged men reported some likelihood to rape if they could be assured they would not get caught (Stotzer & MacCartney, 2016). Though it may sound disheartening, some campus organizations are working on prevention programs to turn this trend around, as discussed in "Research and Sexual Well-Being: Sexual Abuse and Prevention on College Campuses."

Societies less prone to rape are cultures that have more respect for gender relations, less use of physical force and violence, and better quality of life overall for women and men (Merry, 2006). Consider by contrast to the United States the rather low incidence of rape in Japan, mentioned earlier.

In addition, some areas of the non-Western world reveal sexual cultures that are reported to be free from rape, such as the Mbuti Pygmies of Central Africa and the Ashanti of West Africa (Benderly, 1987; Sanday, 1981a, 2007). What is distinctive about these societies when it comes to rape? They are noted to promote gender equality, respect, and peace, rather than aggression and violence. For example, there is a group from South Africa, the !Kung of the Kalahari, where rape is practically unknown in spite of very active sexual aggression by boys when they are young (Shostak, 1980). Researchers have speculated that when it comes to the difference between these cultures and those with high rates of rape that are not the result of war, gender equality that begins early in social life may be a key (Merry, 2006). Also, intolerance for the use of violence in sexual contexts appears to link these groups. What else do they have in common?

- They face no immediate danger from human predatory enemies.
- They harmoniously occupy ancestral natural surroundings that neither need nor condone such violence.

RESEARCH and Sexual Well-Being

Sexual Abuse and Prevention on College Campuses

The U.S. Department of Justice estimates that between one-fifth and one-quarter of all college women are the victims of completed or attempted rape while in college (Fisher, Cullen, & Turner, 2000; Department of Justice, 2014). In fact, some estimate that a rape occurs every 20 hours on American college and university campuses, and many of them probably go unreported. How does it happen?

It is an all too common phenomenon on college campuses: A young woman goes to a fraternity party and is handed an alcoholic beverage. Over the course of the evening, she consumes more alcohol. As free-flowing alcohol silences her inhibitions, she decides to head into a room with a guy. They engage in physically intimate activity and the next morning she wakes up with a fuzzy recollection of the previous night's activities and begins to feel the blunt force of fear and regret as she tries to recall what happened. When asked whether this constitutes as rape, the majority of college students say *no* because despite her level of intoxication, she consented (Sanday, 2007). The reality is that in most states, a person who is under the influence of drugs or alcohol is not legally capable of consenting to sex.

In 2007, anthropologist Peggy Reeves Sanday published an important study called *Fraternity Gang Rape: Sex, Brotherhood, and Privilege on Campus* (2007). This research built upon a prior study by Sanday (1981a) that showed how important male power was to explaining sexual coercion. In her 2007 study, Sanday found some disturbing trends that support the idea that rape-prone attitudes exist in the United States. She researched both acquaintance rape and gang rape on college campuses, first to understand the hidden sexual culture that exists, and second to expose it to fuel positive social change on college campuses.

Sanday examined the history of rape and sexual bullying at some fraternities across the United States. She found that the composition of fraternities, including sexually suggestive hazing rituals that initiate males into their ranks, perpetuate attitudes and rituals that seemingly bond them together. But they do so at the expense of sexualizing women and, to some extent, younger or more vulnerable males, including gay males, as sexual targets. Their rituals of initiation have underlying themes of sexism, which continue to manifest even after initiation rituals have been completed (Sanday, 2007). Many fraternity brothers admit that the goal of their parties is to get women drunk enough to compromise their inhibitions (Sanday, 2007). They rationalize or justify their sexual urges as a sort of natural male sex drive that is more animal than cultural in its nature. A woman who allows herself to go to these parties or gets drunk or high is said to be "asking for it." When a woman is particularly vulnerable and drunk, acquaintance rape may turn into gang rape (Sanday, 2007, p. 2).

Sanday's work prompted many college campuses to forge new rape-prevention education programs in which students are taught that sexual behavior and safe sex practices are to be negotiated between consenting sexual partners (Sanday, 2007). "Safe spaces" on campus are now critical to helping teach and pass on respectful attitudes regarding consent and sexual initiation. Accordingly, some colleges now have clear-cut policies that define the issue of "consent" for students. Antioch College's sexual offense policy, for example, includes these guidelines:

- The person(s) who initiate(s) the sexual activity is responsible for asking for consent.
- Each new level of sexual activity requires consent.
- Consent is required regardless of the parties' relationship, prior sexual history, or current activity (e.g., grinding on the dance floor is not consent for further sexual activity).
- Silence is not consent.
- Body movements and nonverbal responses such as moans are not consent.

In another hopeful sign, many fraternities in the United States are trying to create a rape-free environment. The anti-rape discourse is associated with a new sexual revolution that promotes respect and equality and is as much about women's desires as men's. It is important to recognize that there are many males on campus who totally repudiate these kinds of actions, but may not until recently felt empowered to speak out against their male peers' sexual aggression. These are positive signs of a new culture of respect, tolerance, and prevention, but it is important not to be complacent and continue to promote sexual literacy on these matters.

- Their food supplies usually fluctuate little from season to season or year to year.
- Females and males share power and authority.
- The culture glorifies female traits such as nurturance and fertility, and values some other feminine qualities.
- They enjoy a stability that diminishes the need for male physical prowess.

Gender violence leading to sexual coercion in cultures more prone to rape is now documented (Merry, 2006; Petchesky, 2003). Countries vary considerably in their treatment of perpetrators of sexual coercion (Korbin, 1990; Seto, 2008). Also, there is a basic difference when it comes to how public the whole issue is, that is, whether people feel free or fearful of talking about sexual coercion and whether perpetrators are regarded sympathetically, or not (Merry, 2006). Returning to the issue of campus rape in the United States, there are striking differences in how some American colleges tolerate sexual coercion and others express an attitude of "zero tolerance" (Fisher, Cullen, & Turner, 2000).

Perpetrators of Sexual Coercion

Of course, the public may really demand to know the characteristics of potential sex offenders; and again, these characteristics vary by context and culture (Seto, 2008). The public may also feel a deep need to identify stereotyped and even false beliefs about sex offenders because of the overall need to feel separate from these kinds of criminals (Herdt, 2009b; Kamdar et al., 2017). For this reason, people may picture what sex offenders look like and define them only in terms of their abusive and harmful acts (Marshall, 1996). For example, one belief is that the person who sexually molests children is an old man who lures young children with candy or some other enticement. Researchers have learned that in fact there is no simple or typical age for someone who sexually abuses children (Seto, 2008). People of all ages and social classes commit sex offenses. This also applies to ethnicity, national origin, and other social traits that characterize who may perpetrate rape (Tjaden & Thoennes, 2006).

To protect themselves from perpetrators of sexual violence, people want to understand whether there are factors, such as personality or demographics, such as race or national origin, that perpetrators may share. In this context, it is important to remember that, historically, many people in the United States targeted Black men as the perpetrators of rape, but today we understand that such notions were largely the result of racism and continuing segregation of the Black community (Collins, 2004). Despite attempts to identify a specific set of characteristics that apply to sex offenders, researchers continue to find that they are a diverse population of individuals without a single profile (Chaffin, Letourneau, & Silvosky, 2002).

You might wonder if *any* characteristics are common among perpetrators. The answer is "yes." The main characteristic they share is gender: The vast majority of all sex offenders are heterosexual males (Seto, 2008). Women are their primary but not exclusive target (Correa et al., 2008). By comparison, males between the ages of 18 and 22 may be more aggressive with sexual partners than are older men. Researchers have found that certain men use coercive tactics that may involve alcohol or other substances to go further sexually, and will become more aggressive when a woman says "no," possibly using physical force (Sanday, 2007). This tendency appears to decline as men mature into their late 20s (Teten et al., 2009).

Men and boys, especially in contexts of war, are the victims of rape and sexual violence as well, though they may feel so ashamed of what happened that it goes unreported, even to parents (Kristof & WuDunn, 2009; Long, 1997). Children are especially vulnerable due to power, force, and other inequities involved in child sexual assault (Kristof & WuDunn, 2009).

Research shows that 80% of the people who molest a child know the child—whether as family member, friend, or neighbor. Consider these other common characteristics of rapists and child molesters (Center for Sex Offender Management, 2007):

Sex offenders have often been found to:

- Have low self-esteem
- Harbor hostile attitudes toward women
- Tend to be very conservative and moralistic
- Have sex-negative attitudes about intimacy
- Associate with peer groups that accept rape
- May grow up feeling guilty about sex and see sex and nudity as foul and shameful

Although the vast majority of attention on sex crimes focuses on men as the offenders, awareness of females as sex offenders has increased (Seto, 2008). Until recently, females as perpetrators of sex offenses have been largely ignored in the research because societal stereotypes persist that only men are abusers (Anderson & Struckman-Johnson, 1998). Highly publicized cases that involve inappropriate, illegal sexual contact between female high school teachers and their male students are a primary source of this growing attention. These cases are not representative of the full nature or scope of sexual abuse that females commit, however. In fact, such cases can potentially promote myths and misconceptions about the broader issue of female-perpetrated sex crimes (Center for Sex Offender Management, 2007; Levine, 2002).

Keeping in mind the limited amount of research done as well as the diversity of the population, some preliminary findings about adult women who commit sex offenses suggest that they may have the following characteristics:

- Histories of childhood maltreatment, including sexual victimization
- Mental health symptoms, personality disorders, and substance abuse problems
- Difficulties in intimate relationships or an absence of intimate relationships
- A tendency to primarily victimize children and adolescents (rarely adults)
- A tendency to commit offenses against persons who are related or otherwise well known to them
- An increased likelihood of perpetrating sex offenses in concert with a male intimate partner

Recent attention to female offenders should not detract from understanding the diverse experiences of survivors of rape and other forms of sexual coercion.

Survivors of Rape and Other Forms of Coercion

Survivors of sexual coercion are young and old; gay and straight; wealthy and poor; male and female—as studies have repeatedly shown. Ultimately, each survivor reacts to sexual violence in a unique way, which may have lifelong consequences for their sexual well-being. Personal coping methods, culture, and the context of the survivor's life may have a critical impact on these reactions (National Sexual Violence Resource Center, 2010). For example, some people express their emotions, while others hide their feelings. Some people tell others right away while others wait days, weeks, months, or even years before talking about their experience with anyone—or maybe they never do. To be aware of the steps to take immediately after a rape attack, read "Healthy Sexuality: Steps to Take If You Are Raped."

Sexual violence and abuse can significantly affect a survivor's life and potentially the ability to function. Table 14.3 lists some of the most common physical, emotional, and psychological reactions. Perhaps the most far-reaching effect of rape and sexual abuse is a general psychiatric condition known as PTSD (post-traumatic stress disorder), as previously

HEALTHY Sexuality

Steps to Take If You Are Raped

1. Immediately seek a safe place to ensure that no further assault can occur.
2. Notify the police immediately. Reporting the crime right away can help you regain a sense of personal power and control.
3. You can insist on an officer of the appropriate gender to help you complete the police report.
4. Immediately contact a trusted individual who can stay with you to provide emotional and physical support.
5. Try to preserve all physical evidence of the assault. Do not shower, bathe, douche, eat, drink, wash your hands, or brush your teeth until after you have had a medical examination. Save all of the clothing you were wearing at the time of the assault. Place each item of clothing in a separate paper bag. Do not use plastic bags. Do not clean or disturb anything in the area where the assault occurred.
6. Seek medical care as soon as possible. Go to a hospital emergency room or a specialized forensic clinic that provides treatment for sexual assault victims. Even if you think that you do not have any physical injuries, you should have a medical examination to talk with a health care provider about the risk of exposure to STIs and the possibility of pregnancy. Having a medical exam is also a way to preserve physical evidence of the rape.
7. If you suspect that you have been given a rape drug, ask the hospital or clinic to take a urine or blood sample.
8. Write down as much as you can remember about the circumstances of the assault, including a description of the assailant.
9. Ask questions whenever you have concerns. There are rape centers and also police rape specialists who may be of help. After a sexual assault, you have a lot of choices and decisions to make about getting medical care, making a police report, and telling other people. You may have concerns about the impact of the assault and the reactions of friends and family members. You can get information by calling a rape crisis center, a rape hotline, or other victim assistance agencies.
10. Longer term, seek the help of a trained rape counselor or another professional who can provide counsel. Counseling can provide genuine support for how to cope with the emotional and physical impacts of the assault. You can find a counselor by contacting a local rape crisis center, a rape hotline, a counseling service, or other victim assistance agencies.
11. Remember that being raped is not your fault.

Source: National Sexual Violence Resource Center, 2010.

mentioned. PTSD is a severe anxiety disorder that may result from many kinds of psychological trauma, but violence and violent sexual assault are perhaps the most common factors leading to PTSD (APA, 2000).

Sexual coercion is a life-changing event with far-reaching effects, as we have seen, but the impact can reach into the family, friends, and community as well. Research has shown that sexual coercion can have continuing effects on parents, friends, partners, children, spouses, and even co-workers of the survivor (National Sexual Violence Resource Center, 2010). As they try to make sense of what happened, significant others may experience reactions similar to those of the survivor. Fear, guilt, self-blame, and anger are just a few of the common reactions that significant others may face (National Sexual Violence Resource Center, 2010).

In communities prone to a high incidence of rape, such as some communities in South Africa and South Asia, women and families have tremendous difficulty coping, and the quality of life suffers (Correa et al., 2008; Kamdar et al, 2017; Merry, 2006). People in schools, workplaces, neighborhoods, and cultural and religious communities may feel fear, anger, or shock if an act of sexual violence occurred in their community (Pascoe, 2007). In addition, acts of sexual violence have an economic impact on communities. One study estimated the lifetime income loss for an individual who experiences sexual violence during adolescence to be $241,600 (MacMillan, 2000).

Table **14.3** Common reactions to sexual coercion

COMMON PHYSICAL REACTIONS	
• Changes or disturbances in eating and sleeping patterns	
• Increased startle response and hypervigilance—that is, looking out for danger and being in a "fight or flight" mode	
• Concerns about physical safety	
• Concerns about becoming pregnant or contracting an STI	
COMMON EMOTIONAL REACTIONS	
• Guilt, shame, or self-blame	• Embarrassment
• Sadness	• Fear and distrust
• Increased vulnerability	• Numbness
• Isolation	• Confusion
• Lack of control	• Shock and disbelief
• Anger	• Denial
COMMON PSYCHOLOGICAL REACTIONS	
• Nightmares	• Anxiety
• Flashbacks of the event or abuse	• Eating disorders
• Depression	• Substance use or abuse
• Difficulty focusing or concentrating	• Phobias
• Post-traumatic stress disorder (PTSD)	• Low self-esteem

Sources: Based on Ellis, E. M., Atkeson, B. M., & Calhoun, K. S. (1982). An assessment of long-term reaction to rape. *Journal of Abnormal Psychology, 90,* 263–266; Ullman, S. E., & Filipas, H. H. (2001). Predictors of PTSD symptom severity and social reactions in sexual assault victims. *Journal of Traumatic Stress, 14,* 369–389.

Even college sports must now deal with the issue of sexual abuse. In one case involving the revered coach and football team at Penn State, a former assistant football coach, Jerry Sandusky, was convicted in 2012 of having sexually assaulted as many as eight or more young men over a period of decades, allegedly raping boys in the showers at the university. Though the authorities knew about them, these crimes were systematically covered up until a grand jury exposed how the university and athletics department had engaged in a conspiracy of silence—in part to avoid the bad publicity to the coach and team (NPR, 2012). The victims' rights were totally ignored. Some of the young male victims had complained or tried to bring the abuse to the attention of police and public authorities. Others were so ashamed that they hid what happened, with the effect that the abuse continued far longer than it might have if the community had been more sensitive to the rape of males. This shocking story brings us to the topic of childhood sexual coercion.

CHILDHOOD SEXUAL COERCION

She was 6 years old when it happened. The daughter of one of my (Nicole's) friends experienced sexual abuse at the hands of her juvenile cousin for at least 6 months. Her parents were at a loss over how to help their innocent daughter recover from the hurt she had experienced from a trusted family member. They did what many parents would have done; they sought counseling and they cried on each other's shoulders, mourning the hurt their daughter experienced. And they waited.... They waited to see how this abuse would affect their little girl in the long run. As the years began to pass, they noticed that their daughter seemed to be fine. There were no major behavioral outbursts, no terror-filled nightmares, no problems in school or with academic achievement; they saw none of the negative effects that they had expected to see. What they saw instead was that their daughter appeared to be dealing with the situation very well. She was open about what had happened to her, understood it as well as her young mind could, and went on with her life. Now she is a young adult, and while she has dealt with her trauma at various different stages in her life, she is strong and resilient and has even walked with others who have gone through similar experiences.

This story is still unfolding as it will continue to impact her life in different ways at different times. While she seems to be faring well now, there are many uncertainties in this young woman's future. In fact, research paints a fairly grim picture of the future for victims of childhood sexual abuse. Part of our discussion as a society needs to figure out how we can help restore victims' psychological, social, and physical well-being, as well as their sexual well-being after the trauma of sexual abuse (Sanday, 2007).

Childhood sexual abuse (CSA) is arguably one of the most difficult topics to understand as it represents the extreme end of disturbing acts of sexual violence against a vulnerable population. As we have seen, CSA is characterized by acts of sexual assault, molestation, or sexual exploitation perpetrated by older individuals on minors. The offender can be an older adolescent who has not reached legal age or someone decades older (Seto, 2008).

Accurate statistics regarding rates of childhood sexual abuse are difficult to gather because so many instances are not reported, but some experts believe that one in nine girls and 1 in 53 boys under the age of 18 experience sexual abuse at the hands of an adult (Finkelhor, Shattuck, Turner, & Hamby, 2014). Today, many mental health professionals, including psychologists, believe that childhood sexual abuse is a common problem in the United States (APA, 2010). In one study, for example, researchers found that among female rape victims surveyed, more than half were younger than 18. In this study, some 32% of the victims were between the ages of 12 and 17, while 21% of victims were actually under the age of 12 (Siegel & Williams, 2001). In short, victims vary tremendously by age.

Every year, approximately 63,000 sexual cases are substantiated by Child Protective Services (CPS). Of these cases, 80% of perpetrators were a parent, 6% were other relatives, 4% were unmarried partners of a parent, and 5% were classified as "other" (U.S. Department of Health and Human Services, 2018). Psychologists have long suspected that not only are many perpetrators close to the child, whether friend of the family or extended family, but they also may be a member of the nuclear family (Barnitz, 2001). For example, incest appears to occur more often between fathers and daughters, especially stepfathers and daughters, and between older and younger siblings (Seto, 2008). Figure 14.3 shows the relationship of perpetrators to victims of childhood sexual abuse.

childhood sexual abuse (CSA)

Sexual abuse committed against a minor child, including adult acts of sexual assault, molestation, and sexual exploitation.

Figure 14.3

Relationship of perpetrators to victims of childhood sexual abuse.

Sources: Based on data from Snyder, H. N., & Sickmund, M. (2006). Juvenile offenders and victims: 2006 national report. *Office of Juvenile Justice and Delinquency Prevention.* Washington: National Center for Juvenile Justice.

What are the signs of child sexual abuse? How a child acts may indicate abuse is going on somewhere in the background. For example, a child who behaves in inappropriate, unusual, or sexually aggressive ways with peers or toys may have experienced sexual abuse. Table 14.4 provides a full list of such behaviors.

What kind of behavior constitutes sexual abuse? Abusive acts include touching the sexual or other intimate parts of a child's body for the purpose of satisfying the adult's sexual desire (that includes touching children through their clothing); inappropriately exposing an adult's sexual organs to a child; encouraging a child to engage in any sexually explicit activity or conduct; forcing or encouraging a child to engage in child pornography activities; and encouraging a child to watch the sexual activities of others.

It is critical to understand the potential negative consequences of sexual victimization at a young age for normal adjustment. Research has long shown a strong link between experiences of early sexual abuse in childhood or adolescence and later use of alcohol or other potentially self-destructive coping mechanisms in young adults (Gibson & Leitenberg, 2001; Tjaden & Thoennes, 2000). For example, 600 participants who experienced childhood sexual abuse reported greater psychological stress and post-traumatic stress symptoms compared to those who had not experienced it (Marx & Sloan, 2003). The National Sexual Violence Resource Center (2010) found that U.S. women who were raped before the age of 18 were twice as likely to become victims again as adults.

If we understood what causes sexual abuse of children and the behavioral symptoms pointing to abuse going on, we could consider how we might prevent such abuse before it happens. In reality, however, there is no foolproof way of predicting whether a child's behavior means abuse is going on. This raises the question of how far child welfare agencies or psychologists and parents or teachers should go in efforts to prevent childhood sexual abuse. Intervention and prevention programs, which are fairly new in the United States, are not without controversy. We explore the issues concerning these programs in "Controversies in Sexuality: Are Child Sexual Abuse Prevention Programs Appropriate for Children?"

Oprah Winfrey, shown here at her school in South Africa, has tirelessly advocated for child victims of sexual abuse. She acknowledged great disappointment about a "not guilty" verdict rendered by a South African court in the wake of a trial surrounding sexual abuse at her school.
Ludbrook/EPA/Shutterstock

Table **14.4** Characteristics and signs of child sexual abuse

1. Child reports sexual activities to a trusted person.
2. Child has a detailed and age-inappropriate understanding of sexual behavior.
3. Child wears torn, stained, or bloody underclothing.
4. Child is a victim of other forms of abuse.
5. Child has a sexually transmitted infection.
6. Child compulsively masturbates.
7. Child engages in unusually seductive behaviors.
8. Child engages in sexual activity that is inappropriate for the developmental age.
9. Child engages in inappropriate, unusual, or aggressive sexual behavior with peers or toys.
10. Child exhibits school problems or significant change in academic performance.
11. Child regularly soils the bed with urine or feces.
12. Child suddenly experiences speech disorders without logical cause.

CONTROVERSIES in Sexuality

Are Child Sexual Abuse Prevention Programs Appropriate for Children?

All U.S. states have laws against child sexual abuse (CSA). Unfortunately for many child victims of sexual abuse, these laws are not enough to deter potential perpetrators, who are sometimes clever and cunning. For this reason, many professionals and advocacy groups support prevention programs for young children. This may seem like a logical idea, but controversies have surfaced about both the aim and the content of these programs (Hines & Malley-Morrison, 2005).

Prevention programs all have similar goals: educating children about what sexual abuse is; broadening awareness of possible perpetrators to include people they know; teaching children that they have the right to control access to their body; and describing touches that are "OK" and "not OK." Other issues addressed include teaching young children that some secrets should not be kept; assuring children that they are never at fault for sexual abuse; and learning to say *no* and run to a trusted adult. In theory, these all seem like great goals, but the controversy stems from the fact that many of them are modeled after sexual assault programs aimed at educating grown women about sexual assault and protecting themselves against assault. The controversy is this: Are children developmentally mature enough to understand the curriculum of these programs and to become responsible for their own bodily protection?

Yes:

- Child sexual abuse prevention programs have had a positive influence on the prevention of child sexual abuse (Plummer, 1993; Seto, 2008). Participation also opens up a sexual literacy process that can flourish later in teen years.
- As a result of these programs, millions of people, including children, have become better educated about the extent and nature of child sexual abuse and children are now more willing to disclose if they have been sexually abused (Plummer, 1993).

No:

- Given that many of these programs were adapted from adult programs, much of the material is not suitable for children, particularly young children before puberty, who are at most risk for sexual abuse (Repucci & Haugaard, 1993).
- Even if older children are mature enough to understand the intricacies of sexual abuse, they should not be responsible for protecting themselves.
- If children become victims of sexual abuse even after they have completed a prevention program, they may react with a greater degree of self-blame following an abusive experience, because they were supposed to have protected themselves (Hines & Malley-Morrison, 2005).

People on both sides of this controversy do agree that parents should be included in these programs as the primary protectors of their children (Plummer, 1993; Repucci & Haugaard, 1993). Unfortunately, parents do not often attend these programs, and so they remain unaware of the risks and outcomes of child sexual abuse.

What's Your Perspective?

1. How do you feel about child sexual abuse prevention programs for children?
2. Do you feel that these programs put too much emphasis and responsibility on young children to protect themselves?
3. How do you think these programs can be improved to help children protect themselves without giving them explicit sexual knowledge?

Online Sexual Abuse Thus far we have only considered issues related to the actual world, but what about the virtual world that children inhabit today? With so much focus on sexuality on the Internet, as discussed in Chapter 3, it is not surprising that online protection against sexual predators has become a subject of societal concern.

Stories about the dangers of the Internet, for children and teenagers especially, thrive in the media. Some of these stories describe real-world concerns, such as the ease with which a sexual predator can contact a child and begin a relationship that could end up hurting the child significantly. Some studies, though limited in scope, have worked to examine how adult predators get involved with children in online spaces and develop relationships that essentially groom them into sexual situations (de Santisteban, del Hoyo, Alcazar-Corcoles, & Gamez-Guadix, 2018). *Online grooming* is the process by which an adult using means offered through online technologies enters into the dynamic of persuading and sexually victimizing a child (Kloess et al., 2014). It appears that online predators go through a process where they attempt to gain access to a large number of potential victims and initiate persuasion strategies to begin contact with children more easily. Then they begin to study the children's environment and vulnerabilities, and then develop strategies specifically adapted to each child's needs that then gains the children's involvement in the abuse (de Santisteban, del Hoyo, Alcazar-Corcoles, & Gamez-Guadix, 2018). The reality is that online spaces, while positive in so many ways as we learned in Chapter 3, can be dangerous places as well and certainly pose a threat to children's sexual safety and well-being if their activity is not being monitored by a trusted adult.

Incest

Since the beginning of civilization, as described in Chapter 2, human groups have had taboos surrounding sex with biological family members. This behavior is referred to as **incest.** Research suggests that the incest taboo, which prohibits sex between relatives, is universal and is a uniquely human trait (Seto, 2008).

The theme of incest, especially mother–son sexual relations and father–son sexual rivalry, is also the premise of many ancient Greek tragedies, such as *Oedipus Rex* by Sophocles, first performed in 429 BCE. The play reveals the scope of lust and seduction within human groups and the power of incest to destroy the family. In today's world, connecting the facts of incest to early childhood sexual abuse and later sexual violence are critical to helping prevent greater abuse in society (Seto, 2008).

Incest taboos vary across cultures and the reason is that the definition of "relatedness" or kinship varies by how it is defined in a particular society. There are two dimensions of relatedness: whether one is related by blood or marriage and how closely related one is to someone else within a larger family. In many societies, sexual relations are forbidden between all family members, whether they are related by blood or marriage. **Biological kin** are directly related by blood, and **social kin,** or in-laws, are relatives through marriage. People who are most closely related are members of the **nuclear family,** including the biological father, mother, and siblings. The **extended family** is a larger group that includes grandparents, aunts, and uncles who are related to the biological parents by blood, and cousins, as well as the children of siblings, nieces, and nephews. In some societies, sexual relationships between first cousins are allowed. In fact, a number of U.S. states permit first cousins to marry.

incest
Sex between relatives.

biological kin
People directly related by blood.

social kin
People who become relatives through marriage.

nuclear family
A family system that includes the biological mother, father, and siblings.

extended family
A family system that includes grandparents, aunts, and uncles who are related to the biological parents by blood and cousins as well as the children of siblings, nieces, and nephews.

Princess Leia and Luke Skywalker fall in love. Incest has fascinated the great thinkers from ancient Greek philosophers to Shakespeare to Freud, and some would say, to George Lucas. Lucas created the *Star Wars* movies, which depict a life-and-death struggle between two men who, unknown to each other, are father (Darth Vader) and son (Luke Skywalker). Luke falls in love with Princess Leia, whom he later discovers is his sister.
RGR Collection/Lucasfilm/Alamy Stock Photo

Most of the time people have no sexual interest in their close relatives. One theory about avoiding incest explains why: People living together from very early in life lack any kind of sexual desire for each other. Also, scientific consensus suggests that inbreeding due to incest creates undesirable birth defects in offspring. Incest avoidance, therefore, is a healthy sign of normality for families (Seto, 2008).

Nevertheless, some individuals violate the taboos and commit incest (Seto, 2008). Much of the incest reported from other cultures is with social kin, not with biological kin. In this case, someone may be attracted to another person with whom they did not grow up within the nuclear family, and yet that type of relationship is forbidden in the culture. In the United States, however, research shows that incest within the nuclear family occurs more frequently than once thought. As noted earlier in the discussion of childhood sexual abuse, most of the incest reported is between fathers and daughters and between older brothers and younger sisters (Seto, 2008). Some evidence suggests that incest between a stepfather (an unrelated man living in a household) and a stepdaughter is occurring more frequently in the United States, though it is very difficult to statistically measure because these abuses are widely hidden; however, this behavior is still considered incest (Hines & Malley-Morrison, 2005).

Incest often occurs behind closed doors, causing pain and shame for its victims. Because incest is illegal and considered vile, perpetrators go to great lengths to hide their actions and keep the abuse hidden, which further compounds the victimization and injustice, sometimes for years. This is one of the effects of growing up in a society that does not teach sexual literacy or the importance of sexual socialization (Seto, 2008).

Child Pornography

Another disturbing form of sexual coercion involving children is the production and distribution of child pornography. The Internet allows images and movies to be reproduced and disseminated to tens of thousands of individuals at the click of a button. The distribution and receipt of such images can be done almost anonymously. As a result, pornography that uses children is readily available through websites, e-mail, instant messaging/ICQ, Internet Relay Chat (IRC), newsgroups, bulletin boards, and peer-to-peer file sharing. All of these developments have led to an explosion of child pornography.

The law in the United States (18 U.S.C. §2256) is very precise about **child pornography,** which is defined as any visual depiction, including any photograph, film, video, or computer-generated image, of sexually explicit images that

- Involve an actual minor engaging in sexually explicit conduct
- Is a digital image, computer image, or computer-generated image that is, or is indistinguishable from, that of a minor engaging in sexually explicit conduct
- Has been created, adapted, or modified to appear that an identifiable minor is engaging in sexually explicit conduct

Other laws criminalize knowingly producing, distributing, receiving, or possessing child pornography (Abramson et al., 2003). It doesn't matter whether it is a cartoon, picture, or video. If it is sexually explicit or sufficiently suggestive of sexual intercourse and appears to show a minor engaging in graphic sexual intercourse of any kind, it is illegal.

These laws have not actually stopped the production of child pornography (Elliott, Beech, Mandeville-Norden, & Hayes, 2009). Ironically, however, it appears that increased surveillance online has resulted in greater prosecution of first-time ("amateur") offenders who might never have been caught unless they had tried to contact victims through the Internet (Bourke & Hernandez, 2009).

child pornography
Any visual depiction, including photographs, films, videos, or computer-generated images, of sexually explicit conduct involving children.

TEEN AND ADULT SEXUAL COERCION

Common acts of sexual coercion that usually occur with teens and adults include sexual harassment, and dating violence among teens. Here we will discuss both of these forms of sexual coercion.

Sexual Harassment

Sexual harassment has been an important topic of discussion in the U.S. media since at least 1991, when no less than three high-profile individuals were accused of this crime, including Supreme Court Justice Clarence Thomas. While the Senate was debating the appointment of Thomas to the Supreme Court, Anita Hill, an attorney who reported to Thomas, accused him of making sexually provocative statements to her when he was the chairman of the U.S. Equal Employment Opportunity Commission (EEOC). There have been many highly publicized cases of sexual harassment in the news since that time, some involving male movie stars and male politicians accused of harassment by other males, typically younger staff members. Even a contender for the Republican nomination for president in 2012, Herman Cain, a former pizza company executive, was accused by five women of harassment.

What is harassment anyway? **Sexual harassment** is any unwelcome verbal, physical, or sexual conduct that has the effect of creating an intimidating, hostile, or offensive environment. Notice that this definition says nothing about the person's gender—harassment can and is directed toward both males and females, and toward the same gender, too, although traditionally female harassment is more common.

Generally, there are two types of sexual harassment. The first type is referred to as ***quid pro quo,*** a Latin phrase meaning "this for that." Quid pro quo sexual harassment occurs when submission to unwelcome sexual conduct becomes either a condition of employment or something to exchange for a promotion or raise (Stoddard, 2000). The second type involves the creation of a **hostile environment** where the harassment interferes with a person's ability to work. As the term implies, when sexual harassment is present, it is often felt throughout the environment (Stoddard, 2000).

Many behaviors can be considered sexual harassment. These behaviors, in particular, are considered unwelcome, hostile, and harassing:

- Actual or attempting rape or sexual assault
- Pressuring for sexual favors or for dates
- Deliberate touching, leaning over, cornering, or pinching
- Sending letters, telephone calls, or material of a sexual nature
- Making sexual looks, gestures, jokes, remarks, innuendos, or asking sexual questions
- Calling an adult a *girl, hunk, doll, babe,* or *honey*
- Turning work discussion to sexual topics
- Asking personal questions about social life, sexual life, preferences, sexual fantasies, or histories
- Making kissing sounds, whistling, howling, or smacking lips
- Touching or rubbing oneself sexually around another person
- Looking a person up and down (sometimes referred to as using "elevator eyes")
- Sending or requesting nude pictures through text or social media

When it comes down to it, *unwelcome behavior* is the critical term. *Unwelcome* does not mean *involuntary.* A victim may consent or agree to certain conduct and actively participate

DID YOU KNOW

In 2010, there were **11,717 complaints** of sexual harassment reported. This number was down from 12,696 in 2009, which may speak to the fact that employers now require regular sexual harassment training (EEOC, 2010). In 2010, men filed 16.4% of the complaints and women filed 83.6%. The percentage has increased over the years for men—that is, in 1997, men filed 11.6% of complaints (EEOC, 2010).

sexual harassment
Any unwelcome verbal, physical, or sexual conduct that has the effect of creating an intimidating, hostile, or offensive environment.

quid pro quo
A form of sexual harassment in which submission to unwelcome sexual conduct becomes either a condition of employment or personnel action.

hostile environment
A form of sexual harassment in which the harassment of an individual interferes with his or her ability to be productive and work.

Sexual harassment can make a work and/or school environment uncomfortable and hostile.
Wavebreak Media Ltd/123RF

in it even though it is offensive and objectionable. Therefore, sexual conduct is unwelcome whenever the person subjected to it considers it unwelcome. To understand what constitutes harassment, consider these questions:

- Was the behavior unwelcome, unsolicited, or offensive?
- Was the behavior repeated, despite notification that the behavior was unwelcome or perceived as offensive?
- Did the behavior involve a relationship in which one individual had power over another?
- Was the behavior verbal, physical, hostile, disruptive, continuous, pervasive, or provoking?
- Was preferential treatment given to individuals based on their sexual behavior, and if so, did it have a negative impact on the working environment?
- Would a "reasonable person" (a legal definition) be substantially negatively affected if that person were in a similar circumstance?

As these questions suggest, an individual does not file sexual harassment charges because of an occasional sexual joke or flirtation. A co-worker who tells you how fashionable your clothing is or how good your cologne smells may simply be offering a compliment with no further intention.

Remember that sexual harassment is imposed, unwanted sexual attention. No matter how complicated the situation, the harasser is responsible for the abuse. You may wonder if you encouraged the behavior by smiling or offering a compliment to a co-worker, but being kind to someone is not an invitation for unwanted sexual behavior or advances. In fact, you can tell the offender specifically what you find offensive. You can specifically say what you want or don't want to happen, such as "Please call me by my name, not Honey," or "Please don't tell that kind of joke in front of me." Also, do not try to handle any severe or recurring harassment problem by yourself. Rather, ask someone for help. People bring charges because of blatant sexually harassing behaviors that do not stop, even after they have told the offender that the behavior is causing them significant levels of discomfort and distress.

Knowing what constitutes sexual harassment is essential for sexual health and well-being, and thinking about how to handle a situation can help to deflect unwanted behaviors in the future. Whether you choose to complain can depend on many factors, including whether you feel you can get support from colleagues and friends as well as other people who are part of the complaint process, such as human resource representatives or union representatives. Race and class differences may also affect your decision to file, partly because these differences in a workplace can isolate workers from each other. If you do file a complaint, some of the possible outcomes include loss of employment, status, and resources in addition to the psychological and emotional stress. Before you file a complaint, you may want to discuss the behavior that you find offensive with another person as well as take some other actions, as explained in "Communication Matters: Protecting Yourself When Confronting Sexual Harassment."

Same-Sex Sexual Harassment Several different social factors, such as the role of power and inequality mentioned previously, may play a role in sexual harassment. A man can harass another man, for sexual reasons, and a woman can harass a woman, again for sexual or other reasons. As noted in Chapter 10, there have been a variety of well-known examples of same-sex harassment in the media in recent years, including those involving notable politicians. Additionally, society has been witness to many cases of same-sex harassment between peers in schools, and the strong connection between harassment and homophobia in these environments (Pascoe, 2007).

COMMUNICATION Matters

Protecting Yourself When Confronting Sexual Harassment

Filing a sexual harassment complaint can have unwanted consequences. To help protect yourself, here are some things to discuss, some things to think about, and some things to do before you file a sexual harassment complaint:

- Document what happens. Keep a detailed diary including dates, times, and places of unwanted sexual behavior. Keep a record of anyone who witnessed the harassment.
- Let the harasser know as explicitly as possible that you are not interested in this type of attention. If you do this in writing, keep a copy of your letter.
- Save any notes or pictures from the harasser—don't throw them away in anger.
- Investigate the policy and grievance procedure of your workplace or school for sexual harassment cases. Know the overall record of sexual harassment complaints where you work or are in school before you act.
- Talk with others to generate support for yourself before you take action.
- Talk with others who have been harassed who can act with you. Collective action and joint complaints strengthen everyone's position.
- Ask for help in working out a complaint. Try to use organizations that already exist, such as a union, an employee organization, or an advocacy organization.

ericsphotography/iStockphoto.com

But when it comes to adults and the law, the issue of same-sex sexual harassment has a complicated history in the United States. On March 4, 1998, a case decided by the U.S. Supreme Court involved a male employee working on an off-shore oil rig, who claimed he was the victim of sexual harassment from other male workers (*Oncale v. Sundowner Offshore Services*, 523 U.S. 75, 1998). The Supreme Court justices unanimously said that federal law prohibits same-sex sexual harassment. In addition, the Court said that the sexual orientation of the individual is not important. For example, a heterosexual man or woman can sexually harass another heterosexual man or woman, or a gay man or lesbian can sexually harass a heterosexual man or woman, and so on. In fact, the parties involved do not even need to be sexually interested in each other for sexual harassment to occur, although that is usually assumed to be the case. The key ingredients that constitute sexual harassment are some form of sexual content and some form of discrimination occurring in the workplace regardless of the gender of the person.

Sexual Harassment in Educational Settings Sexual harassment is not limited to the workplace. It is all too common on college campuses as well. The majority of cases reported are between peers, usually with male harassers and female victims (Sanday, 2007). One case that made headlines concerns Yale University. *The Yale Daily News* cited an incident that occurred in 2008 in which fraternity pledges were photographed holding a sign referring to female Yale students in sexually degrading language. Following a federal investigation of a harassment complaint filed by several Yale women, Yale acknowledged failing to take appropriate action in response to harassment complaints over the years and agreed to improve reporting of harassment incidents and take steps to prevent further incidents (Ariosto & Remizowski, 2012). But many other campuses face similar issues (Sanday, 2007). While most colleges have specific policies prohibiting sexual harassment, it is often hidden. When such behavior is out of sight, it can make it extremely difficult to prove.

While sexual harassment is more common on a peer-to-peer basis, it also occurs between faculty, researchers, and students. In fact, most college students are adults and can legally consent to sexual activity with an adult. Relationships between professors and students can and do grow from a mutual attraction toward one another. Although a minority of faculty members prey on vulnerable students, that is not as common as the mutual romantic relationship that sometimes develops between two people who happen to be professor and student. While many universities prohibit such romantic relationships, many individuals believe that it is not the business of academic administration to govern the personal relationships of their faculty or their adult students. The real issue is whether or not students are really free to say *no* in these relationships. Because a mismatch in authority exists between students and teacher, students may feel pressured to engage in that relationship.

Teen Dating Violence

In the United States, it is now well reported that there are four kinds of teen dating violence: physical violence, sexual violence, psychological aggression, and stalking (CDC, 2019). In fact, millions of teens suffer from one of these forms of abuse regularly. While that statistic is alarming, some researchers believe it is an underrepresentation of the amount of people who experience abuse at the hands of their intimate partners (Sanday, 2007). A large study in 2006 surveyed 1,043 children age 11–14 and 626 teens age 15–18 about the issue of **teen dating violence** (TRU, 2008). Its purpose was twofold: to gauge the degree to which teens have been involved in abusive and controlling relationships and to understand how teens perceive what is and is not acceptable behavior in a relationship. For teens who have been in relationships, the study found the following statistics:

- 1 in 5 teens reports being hit, slapped, or pushed by a partner.
- 1 in 3 girls reports concern about being physically hurt by her partner.
- 1 in 4 teens reports a boyfriend or girlfriend has tried to prevent him or her from spending some time with friends or family; the same number have been pressured to spend time only with the partner.
- 1 in 3 girls between the ages of 16 and 18 says sex is expected for people their age if they're in a relationship; half of teen girls who have experienced sexual pressure report they are afraid their relationship would break up if they did not have sex.
- Nearly 1 in 4 girls (23%) reports going further sexually than desired as a result of pressure from the partner (TRU, 2008).

The damage to teenagers from intimate partner violence can be extensive and can occur in different ways. Research shows that being a survivor of teen dating violence is associated with mental health concerns, such as depression and substance abuse, as well as negative educational outcomes such as dropping out of school (Banyard & Cross, 2008). In addition, teen victims of dating violence in high school are at greater risk for victimization in college (CDC, 2006). Despite these negative effects, research also shows that having good social supports in places such as school and neighborhoods can help victims cope with their experiences of violence (TRU, 2008).

Early teens age 11–14 also experience dating violence, as previously noted. Although research and education rarely focus on the middle school age group (Fredland, 2008), children this age often experience different forms of bullying, one of which is **sexual bullying**. This involves the use of sexual threats to intentionally hurt someone. Sexual bullying and homophobia go together in some schools where the culture supports this practice, implicitly or even explicitly (Pascoe, 2007). But whether it is a boy or a girl who is being bullied sexually, the intent is usually malicious. The victims usually suffer repeated unpleasant sexual teasing, taunting, or harassing threats. Developmentally, this type of bullying may occur after nonsexual bullying in early adolescence and before dating violence, which can occur among later teens. For behaviors to be identified as sexual bullying, at least one party must

teen dating violence
A pattern of abusive behaviors used to gain power and control over a current or former dating partner.

sexual bullying
Any bullying behavior, whether physical or nonphysical, based on a person's sexuality or gender; involves using sexuality as a weapon and can be carried out in person, behind someone's back, or via technology.

have a sexual interest in the other (Fredland, 2008). You might recognize some of these examples of sexual bullying behaviors as being similar to sexual harassment behaviors:

- Directing sexual comments and sexual jokes at a person
- Writing sexual messages or graffiti about a person in school restrooms
- Calling a person names (e.g., slut, gay, dyke)
- Flashing or mooning a person
- Being shown sexual doodles, pictures, or photographs
- Being touched, grabbed, rubbed against, or pinched
- Being trapped and subjected to sexual advances
- Having clothing altered in a sexual way (e.g., being given a "wedgy")
- Being the subject of sexual rumors spread by telephone, e-mail, Internet postings, or text messages
- Being forced to do something sexual, such as kissing or other oral sexual behaviors

There is nothing natural about sexually bullying—it is implicitly learned and reinforced in certain sexual cultures, including college campuses (Pascoe, 2007; Sanday, 2007). Programs to prevent this kind of behavior are becoming more visible in some schools and online, too (Pascoe, 2011). Teaching about teen dating violence in sexual education programs may help to lower these statistics.

SEX WORK AND SEX TRAFFICKING

Here we turn to a discussion of sex work (historically called prostitution) and sex trafficking, which may involve actually moving people across borders to sell or enslave them, because people in sex work are often exploited and victimized. Often, though not always, the most inhumane and severe forms of sexual exploitation and trafficking like this arise out of conditions of extreme poverty. And while other factors, such as the need to escape from abuse or incest or political or religious discrimination may also lead to people becoming sex workers, in general, poverty and dire need are key (Correa et al., 2008). Some people consider sex work to be yet another form of male dominance over women and children and a result of social power differences, which are critically important here (Bernstein, 2008). Some critics have suggested that prostitution may be the oldest profession in the world but it has become a huge global business, and sex workers deserve the same rights as other workers (Correa et al., 2008). Historically, researchers have certainly found that sex workers lack social and economic power and suffer the inequalities of societies that are riddled with poverty, unemployment, food and housing shortages, and lack of social and economic opportunity (Padilla, 2008).

Sex work, or **prostitution,** is as old as civilization and war, and we can find many examples of sex work dating from the times of the ancient Greeks and Roman Empire right up to the present. Sex work is paid-for sex, whether payment is in money or goods or a roof over one's head or the receipt of some other resource, such as a meal, a pair of shoes, or a diamond necklace, in exchange for sex. The word *prostitution* is a moral concept, largely negative in meaning, and is explicitly associated with women (not men or boys). Some people use even more negative terms, such as *hooker* or *whore,* in reference to female sex workers. Researchers and medical doctors long ago created the term *sex work* to indicate that either gender can engage in sex work and to reduce the stigma attached to this work, because in some places, sex work may be the only way to make a living. Sex work does not discriminate by age or gender or race, and it may include the spectrum of people (Bernstein, 2008; Correa et al., 2008). Male sex workers are also called *gigolos* or *rent boys.*

sex work or **prostitution**
Exchanging sex for money or gifts.

No one knows for sure, but sex work globally and with social media applications is believed to be a growing multibillion dollar industry (Kristof & WuDunn, 2009). Since the 1960s, the ways in which sex is bought and sold and linked to the exploitation of people in sexual cultures has become a greater international concern. Part of the reason is that sex work is related to the trafficking of women, girls, and boys into sexual slavery, which continues to be a danger in Africa and Asia and even on the margins of Europe. In 2012, for example, more than 4.5 million people were believed to have been forced into sex work or slavery (International Labour Organization, 2012). The Vietnam War, which began in the 1960s, was a backdrop for a 20th century mass sexual pattern of sex work in southeastern Asia. Cities such as Bangkok (Thailand) and Saigon (Vietnam) developed into places for soldiers and civilians to find sex workers when they were on leave from military duty. Additionally, governments of these countries tacitly accepted "sex for sale" (Trouong, 1990). Over time, sex work has expanded in these countries, bringing tourists who come just to buy sex (Estes & Weiner, 2002). Some people believe that Bangkok today is the sex capital of the world. Sexual exploitation of girls occurs in major cities of the United States, such as in the San Francisco Bay area (Ferguson et al., 2009).

Different Types of Sex Work

All over the world, sex workers may be victims of powerful social forces, such as poverty, disease, corruption, and exploitation by government officials including the police. For example, police may abuse sex workers by blackmailing them or extracting sexual favors in return for not arresting them (Bernstein, 2008). Additionally, these public figures may expose sex workers to STIs such as HIV/AIDS (Correa et al., 2008; Farmer, 2003; Herdt, 1997b). In fact, sex workers in countries such as Cambodia, Thailand, or South Africa are many times more likely to contract HIV than other people, especially if they work in the tourist industry, such as hotels or massage parlors (Gazi, 2009). The concept of **survival sex,** meaning people who sell their bodies for basic needs such as food, clothing, and shelter, is evident in a growing number of countries around the world (Correa et al., 2008; Greene et al., 1999; International Labour Organization, 2012). For example, in South Africa, poor women face the grim reality of selling their bodies or having their children go hungry, and so they sell their bodies to survive (Correa et al., 2008; Preston-Whyte, 2000). To some extent this is also happening with men and boys who turn to sex work to survive (Padilla, 2007). Whenever war or armed conflict occur in impoverished areas, survival sex also increases, and sexual violence and abuse soon follow (Long, 1997). Refugee women and children, in particular, may engage in survival sex, as was reported among the 1.5 million Iraqis who fled to Syria when the United States invaded in 2003 (Harper, 2008).

survival sex

Sex engaged in by people who sell their bodies for basic needs such as food, clothing, and shelter.

Sex Work and Rights

Countries differ dramatically in how they handle sex work and the rights of sex workers. Historically, sex work was regarded not only as sinful and immoral but also as illegal, and sex workers were routinely arrested, jailed, and blackmailed, and generally had no rights at all (Bernstein, 2008). Many countries still criminalize prostitution and sex work. Sex workers are randomly arrested, beaten, or sexually abused—in short, denied the most basic of all human rights, to survive with dignity (Correa et al., 2008). Even in the United States, all states except in the rural counties of Nevada generally regard all sex work as illegal and prosecute people who are caught either providing sex for sale or partaking in it. The laws in Nevada about sex work are complex, but they do allow some of it.

In some places, people are sex workers of their own free choice; in other places, people are forcibly abducted and made to practice sex work (Bernstein, 2008; International Labour Organization, 2012). In places where the latter occurs, the rights of sex workers may be very diminished or nonexistent. War and refugee insecurity may contribute to the increase in sex work through exploitation of refugees and migrants. Today the immigration crisis in Europe, primarily focused on illegal refugees coming from Africa, is the cause of major trafficking and sexual slavery issues, as widely reported in the media (UN Refugee Agency, 2018). Even the September 11, 2001, terrorist attacks on the United States, which made it much more difficult to secure legal immigration status in this and other countries, may be contributing to this increase (Correa et al., 2008).

One place where sex work is legal but is being curtailed is The Netherlands. In The Netherlands sex work has been legal within certain boundaries since the 17th century, when the Dutch government began to control the business by protecting sex workers and their patrons. Their desire to control sex work developed from at least three factors in Dutch culture: (1) an attitude toward sex that moved it away from being sinful with a religious foundation to handling it as a social issue; (2) the attitude that sex is normal and natural and that it's difficult to eliminate people's natural tendencies; and (3) the creation of "safe zones," known as "red light districts," in certain areas of cities and at certain times.

The Dutch believed the profession should be treated with respect but also regulated by medical doctors and police. With sex work confined to specific areas of cities, the authorities could monitor it easily to ensure that drugs and violence were not involved, and that sex workers did not spread disease. As a result of this centuries-old policy, Dutch sex workers have a successful union and a pension plan secured by decades of stock market investments. As the "Dutch solution" caught on, other countries copied it (Bernstein, 2008; Van der Meer, 1994).

In red light districts in Amsterdam and elsewhere in The Netherlands, sex work is legal but regulated to ensure the well-being of sex workers and their clients.
Anna Belkina Spb/Shutterstock

WHAT'S ON YOUR MIND?

Q: This is embarrassing to me but I suspect that my roommate may be selling sex for money when she goes out on weekends. We have known each other for years and I am shocked that she could even consider this. Although she does not earn a lot of money at her job in a cell phone store, she seems to have a lot more money lately. I don't even know if I should bring this up but I am worried about her getting infections or being physically hurt if this is true. What should I do?

ANSWER: It sounds like you are worried that your roommate could be harmed, either physically or from an STI. You might also be worried whether you have the "right" to ask her questions about her sexual relationships. Maybe ask yourself how you feel about her doing sex work. Do you approve or disapprove of it? Would your friendship change if she were involved in sex work? Consider asking her what she thinks about sex work in general and see if that leads to an open conversation.

Sex Trafficking

sex trafficking
Human trafficking for the purpose of commercial sexual exploitation; the U.S. legal definition of sex trafficking includes the exploitation of anyone under 18 involved in commercial sex.

Sex trafficking is the commercial exploitation of people, including selling them into sexual slavery, sometimes across continents. It occurs in many regions, including Eastern Europe, South America, and Africa. Trafficking women and children for sex has been widely documented (Estes & Weiner, 2002, 2007; Ferguson et al., 2009; International Labour Organization, 2012). In many countries people enslave women, girls, and boys to become lifelong involuntary sex workers by taking them from their homes and transporting them to other cities or countries, sometimes confining them to brothels that function like "sweat houses" with no possible escape. This kind of large-scale sexual exploitation also has been found to occur in Mexico, Canada, and the United States (Estes & Weiner, 2007), and increasingly on the margins of Europe (UN Agency for Refugees, 2018).

Literally thousands of young women, some of them children, may be kidnapped and sold into global sexual slavery by their community, family, or strangers. In some countries, child sex workers have been estimated to service between 100 and 1,500 clients per year (Harvey & Roberson, 2015, p. 197). Parents may even sell children to sex traffickers to get funds for their own survival (Long, 1997). These children may be as young as 4 or 5 but under the age of 13. Learning that people are willing to sell their own children as sex workers to provide for their own survival illustrates the connection between sex trafficking and issues of poverty, education, public health, and justice. Among the underage children who have been trafficked, there is good reason to believe that they have not given their consent because they do not have a concept of what choice means when it comes to protecting their own bodies. Child sex work is a growing menace to global sexual health (U.S. State Department, 2008).

Historically, even in a liberal country such as The Netherlands, sex trafficking has been discovered. It may be that as many as 75% (8,000) of Amsterdam's 11,000 prostitutes are from Eastern Europe, Africa, and Asia, according to a former prostitute who produced a report about the sex trade in Amsterdam, and many of these people do not have immigration papers, making them more vulnerable to abuse and violation of their rights (United Nations, 1998).

New York Times journalist Nicholas D. Kristof has become an expert on sex trafficking through exposure of "seduction, slavery, and sex" as a package of practices with little or no prosecution or protection of human rights in Nepal, Cambodia, and the Philippines (Kristof, 2015; Kristof & WuDunn, 2009). This kind of trafficking is associated with tourists who visit countries to have sex, a topic examined in Chapter 15. People who travel to have sex with those who must engage in survival sex may see it as a game that meets their expected collective fantasy (Padilla, 2007). After a few days they return home not thinking much about these survivors. To the victims of survival sex, it is often a grim reality and the chance for sexual well-being may be out of reach (Correa et al., 2008).

RECOVERY, RESILIENCY, AND SEXUAL WELL-BEING

After reading the array of short- and long-term effects that sexual coercion can have on victims, you might think the prospects for recovery appear bleak. However, we know beyond a shadow of doubt that people can heal from even the most violent acts of sexual coercion (Seto, 2008). That healing process is often difficult and may take a long time, but with adequate support healing is possible (Carnes, 2001). One reason healing is complicated is because the coping mechanisms used by victims of sexual violence may help to prolong the trauma. A study of 106 participants who had recently experienced sexual violence found that they tended to use **disengagement coping,** a psychological response that involves disengagement from reality, such as denial, self-blame, wishful thinking, and avoidance of their real feelings (Gibson & Leitenberg, 2001). Helping people to understand that

disengagement coping
Mental methods of coping with abuse that result in disengagement from reality, such as denial, self-blame, wishful thinking, and avoidance of real feelings.

HEALTHY Sexuality

Being an Advocate for Victims of Sexual Coercion

Part of recovery through resilience involves having a supportive friend who can provide a safe space when the need arises. Such a friend can help in these ways:

- Listen without judging. Accept the person's version of the facts and be supportive. Victims do not need to prove their story.
- Offer shelter. If it is at all possible, the friend should stay with the person, at one or the other's residence, for the night. This is not the time for the victim to be alone.
- Be available. Victims may need to talk at strange hours, or may need help running errands or screening calls.
- Let the victim know he or she is not to blame.
- Be patient and understanding.
- Encourage the victim to act. Suggest calling a hotline, going to a hospital or health center, or calling the police. Respect the victim's decision about whether or not to file charges.
- Encourage the victim to make decisions, to gain better control of his or her own life.
- Accept the victim's choice of solution to the rape or abuse as final. It is more important for the victim to make decisions and have them respected by others than it is to impose one's own views upon them.
- The friend should deal with personal feelings about this situation away from the victim. Although it is supportive for sexual abuse survivors to know that others are equally upset with what happened, it does them no good if they also have to deal with a friend's feelings of rage and anger.

In addition, be a champion for human rights. It is the responsibility of all community members to create a society where sexual abuses are not welcome. Think about how you can best be an advocate for healthy and positive sexuality for all people including yourself.

---

disengagement does not help them heal is one way to support the recovery and resiliency of the victims. This is a critical part of sexual literacy support.

Resiliency is the positive capacity of people to cope with stress and adversity. People vary greatly in their ability to be resilient in the face of adversity. Researcher George Valliant describes resilience as the "self-righting tendencies" of the person, "both the capacity to be bent without breaking and the capacity, once bent, to spring back" (Valliant, 1993).

How does someone spring back from the trauma of sexual violence and coercion? Many factors are involved, including care of the self and deep, strong support from friends (Chopra & Tanzi, 2018). Recovery after sexual coercion can take a variety of paths. For some individuals, the path is survival. They may have to take it one day at a time. They may not be able to face their family or friends, or even their intimate partner, just when they may need their support the most. Resiliency in the context of sexual coercion means being able to get up every day and do one's best to move on with life. It means having loved ones reach out to help with recovery. Some conquer their tragedy. These individuals also get up every day, but they seek out the help they need to recover from the experience. They look to people and resources to help them confront what happened to them; they retrain any thought processes that foster self-blame; and they actively seek positive ways to cope.

The study of resilience in mental health has expanded significantly in the last 25 years. In its early history, resiliency research was reserved for high-risk populations, mainly youth who demonstrated the ability to overcome the emotional, developmental, economic, and environmental challenges they faced growing up (Goldstein & Brooks, 2006). For victims of childhood sexual abuse, we have seen the risks associated with functioning later on in life. Depression, post-traumatic stress disorder, substance abuse, low self-esteem, interpersonal issues, and risk of revictimization have all been documented as long- and short-term effects of sexual abuse

resiliency
The positive capacity of people to cope with stress and adversity.

(Walsh et al., 2007). The key in understanding resiliency is to determine what kinds of individual characteristics, prevention, and intervention efforts can bring about the best outcomes.

Some encouraging research notes that not all victims of sexual coercion resort to personal denial or disengagement coping methods (Gibson & Leitenberg, 2001) or suffer from depression, substance abuse, extreme risk-taking, and other psychological effects. Many studies suggest that good coping skills can predict better emotional adjustment and decrease the risk for future revictimization (Gibson & Leitenberg, 2001). Positive coping skills victims can use include disclosing and discussing the abuse, and refusing to dwell on the experience. Along with seeking support from family, friends, and health care professionals if needed, these strategies may lead to more positive emotional adjustment later on (Walsh et al., 2007). Victims who use social support systems, such as college counseling, health centers, and rape and trauma abuse resources, have lower levels of psychological distress and revictimization. Lastly, those who do not blame themselves for the abuse also have reduced levels of psychological distress and revictimization (Arata, 2000).

Refocusing energy into other aspects of life is another positive way to help the healing and recovery process (Bogar & Hulse-Killacky, 2006). Some ways to refocus and define new purpose in life are to pursue educational goals, become involved in family, take up a sport, and develop an understanding of religion or spirituality. Additionally, strategies such as mentally processing the trauma and violence, practicing meditation and yoga or exercise, setting limits and boundaries, keeping busy with projects of interest, writing, and praying have all helped victims survive and cope both in childhood, if the abuse occurred during that time in the life span, and in adulthood (Bogar & Hulse-Killacky, 2006; Chopra & Tanzi, 2018). All of these are ways to build sexual well-being.

Health and healing are not just the responsibility of those who have experienced sexual coercion. After a rape or other experience of sexual coercion, survivors may need help with their immediate needs. In addition to the guidelines noted, consider how important it is to communicate "believing" the victims. With date rape especially, victims need to be believed that rape occurred. Many victims also feel that the sexual coercion was their fault. Helping them know that it was not their fault is critical. As victims continue to work through their recovery process, and their needs may not be as immediate, we can help in small and large ways. Read more in "Healthy Sexuality: Being an Advocate for Victims of Sexual Coercion."

Chapter Review — SUMMARY

Sexual Coercion

- Sexual coercion represents the darkest side of human sexual nature.
- In sexual coercion, perpetrators force their victims to participate in sexual activity against their will once or many times over a longer period.
- Molestation and sexual exploitation are two core concepts of sexual coercion.

Rape

- There are many myths about rape, including the belief that the perpetrators are most often strangers to their victims, the notion that a woman can't be raped against her will, and the idea that a man can't be raped.
- Date rape and the use of date rape drugs remain significant challenges to protecting the rights of individuals, particularly on college campuses.
- The three most common date rape drugs are Rohypnol, GHB, and Ketamine.
- Marital and prison rape are among the types of rape that society often dismisses.

- Research indicates that U.S. society is hostile toward victims, which creates a culture where it is common for victims to blame themselves for the violence they suffered and may deter victims from reporting sex crimes to the authorities.
- Culture influences almost every facet of sexual violence, including the prevalence of acts committed, as well as how communities and groups respond to victims and perpetrators.
- The United States is considered a rape-prone society due to the normative occurrence of sexual violence as well as widely held beliefs that women's desires are unimportant.
- Less rape-prone societies have much lower rates of sexual violence than other parts of the world and cultures that value and promote respect and peace.
- While there are some common characteristics of perpetrators of sexual violence, such as most likely being male, they are highly diverse as individuals.
- Experiencing sexual coercion can significantly affect one's life and potentially impair daily functioning.
- Sexual coercion not only affects the victim but can also have profound effects on the people close to the survivor.

Childhood Sexual Coercion

- Sexual abuse of children is a significant problem in the United States.
- Most victims of childhood sexual abuse are related to the perpetrator or know them in some way.
- There are significant long- and short-term effects on children who are victims of childhood sexual abuse including later alcohol use, post-traumatic stress disorder, and further victimization.
- The Internet has made childhood sexual abuse somewhat easier to identify as well as to perpetrate.
- Victims of childhood sexual abuse may be too young, naive, or lacking in social and psychological support to get the help they need to cope with the trauma.
- The creation and distribution of child pornography has become much more pronounced with the advent of the Internet.
- Strict U.S. laws prohibit the creation, dissemination, and possession of child pornography.

Teen and Adult Sexual Coercion

- There are two types of sexual harassment commonly found in educational and occupational settings in the United States: quid pro quo harassment and the creation of a hostile environment.
- Filing a sexual harassment claim is an important step in combating sexually harassing behaviors, but one that takes careful consideration.
- Over the last 10–15 years, the EEOC has seen a significant increase in the proportion of sexual harassment claims that involve same-sex harassment.
- Teen dating abuse affects one in four teens every year, leaving victims at risk for mental health problems and further victimization later on in life.
- Sexual bullying, sometimes with homophobic overtones, affects middle school students as well as older teens and college students.

Sex Work and Sex Trafficking

- Sex trafficking has become a critical issue across the globe, but particularly in the regions of Southeast Asia and Africa, and the refugee crisis in Europe has made trafficking an issue there, too.
- Sex work is sex for payment in money or goods or some kind of favor.
- People are often pushed into sex work by societal forces, such as poverty, disease, corrupt officials, forced migration, and war.

HUMAN SEXUALITY

- In the United States, all states except Nevada generally regard all sex work as illegal and prosecute people who are caught providing sex for sale or partaking in it.
- Sex trafficking, the enslavement of women and children as sex workers, has been widely documented in many countries.

Recovery, Resiliency, and Sexual Well-Being

- Focusing on resiliency rather than on risk allows people to focus on better prevention and intervention techniques.
- The study of resiliency helps us to see the problem of sexual coercion from a more positive standpoint, looking at how individuals can cope positively with emotional, developmental, economic, and environmental challenges.
- Positive coping styles can help survivors of sexual abuse adjust and prevent revictimization.

What's Your Position?

1. **In your mind, what constitutes rape?**
   - Do you believe that rape victims contribute to their own victimization? If so, how?

2. **In what ways have you witnessed sexual coercion in your life, your family, or your community?**
   - What kinds of media representation of sexual coercion have you seen?
   - In what ways should media alter their interpretation of sexual coercion?
   - How does your community contribute to or reject rape-prone attitudes?

3. **In what ways have you experienced sexual harassment or seen it occur in school or the workplace?**
   - How did the sexual harassment change the learning or work environment?
   - What were the consequences of the harassment for the harasser or the victim?
   - In what ways do you believe our society contributes to sexually harassing behaviors?

4. **How can you respond to sexual coercion?**
   - How can you become an advocate for victims of sexual abuse?
   - How would you respond if a close friend or family member confided in you about being a victim of sexual coercion?

Design elements: Controversies in Sexuality: HBRH/Shutterstock; Research and Sexual Well Being: verity jane smith/Getty Images; Healthy Sexuality: Sergey Furtaev/Shutterstock; Communication Matters: PeopleImages/Getty Images; Know Yourself: Plush Studios/Blend Images LLC; What's Your Position: Luis Molinero/Shutterstock; Healthy Sexuality: A. Minde/PhotoAlto; Did You Know icon: McGraw-Hill Education; Page corner icon: McGraw-Hill Education.

Sexual Diagnoses: Sexual Dysfunction to Stigmatized & Normative Sexual Variations

15

Victor Moussa/Shutterstock

Understanding and Challenging Diagnostic Models of Human Sexuality
- Explain how sexual norms and behaviors may increase in acceptance over time.

Medical and Physical Challenges to Normative Sexual Response
- Differentiate between the difference between male and female issues of sexual arousal and dysfunction.
- Describe how a variety of illnesses in later life may affect sexual functioning, especially later in life.

Diagnoses of Sexual Dysfunction and Behavior: The *DSM-5* and Paraphilic Disorders
- Describe the Diagnostic and Statistical Manual of Psychiatry (*DSM-5*) criteria for diagnosis.
- Differentiate between impulsive and compulsive disorders.
- Differentiate amongst types of paraphilias.
- Compare the theories of the origins of paraphilias.
- Describe treatments for paraphilic disorders.

From Normative to Extreme Sexual Behaviors
- Explain how cultures may provide a context for ESB.
- Define extreme sexual behaviors (ESBs).
- Describe kinky sex.
- Describe sex tourism as a distinct human activity.

Sexual Novelty and Healthy Sexuality
- Identify how sexual novelty in pleasure is normative.

Achieving Sexual Well-Being: Accepting Your Own Enjoyment
- Describe the meaning of normative variations in the context of healthy sexuality.

● Learning
● Objectives

Developing Your Position

1. What do you believe are the major contributors to the provision of freedoms of sexual expression during the past century? Do you believe these freedoms are the result of changes in society as a whole or as a result of changing fields such as medicine?
2. To what degree have sexual values shifted in the United States and how do these changing values impact our understanding of what is considered typical, atypical, or extreme sexual behavior?
3. Should medical doctors, scientists, or other people in positions of authority have a large say in defining what is normal or abnormal in sexuality? Why or why not?

Self, Society, and Culture: How Societal Norms Have Changed

The Folsom Street Fair in the city of San Francisco is famously known for a variety of kinky sex and fetish gear, and it attracts tens of thousands of local people and sexual tourists from all over the world. In 1984, it started as a celebration of sexual liberation for gay men. Over the years, it has expanded to include far more heterosexuals who participate in a range of sexual behaviors that some would label extreme but have become more common as a reflection of changing sexual norms online and in society. I (Gil) attended the first one and was both amused and shocked by the raw public sexual behaviors actually expressed in the street. The adults who engaged in these acts did so voluntarily and for pleasure. At the time this clearly was considered extreme behavior, and many people considered it to be unacceptable. In subsequent years, however, some of these behaviors became more common online, and they evolved into new sexual cultures. Still, this was San Francisco, a place known for its tolerance of sexuality. I moved to Chicago and did not visit the event again for years.

In 1998, I returned to visit the Fair once again and observed that it had become far bigger, much more touristy—like a spectacle, more heterosexual, but also more mainstream, with local news coverage of the exotic things being done in public. By the late 1990s, the participating heterosexuals outwardly showed that they were interested in sexual behaviors that many of their peers in other parts of the country or in their own cities might label as kinky, bizarre, or worse. In reality, many of these practices are fairly common in the BDSM (bondage and discipline; dominance and submission; and sadism and masochism) community and are popularized in the books and film called *Fifty Shades of Grey*. For example, fetishism associated with men being aroused by women all dressed in rubber clothes and boots appeared to be quite common, and some couples liked to inflict low-impact consensual pain on each other for pleasure. Clothing was optional; some men wore pants that exposed their buttocks, and some women walked around without tops. Today it feels more like a 21st-century version of Carnival in Rio de Janeiro or Mardi Gras in New Orleans. This microcosm is not representative of the United States as a whole, of course, but it does provide an indication of a growing trend in "mainstream sexuality" when it comes to sexual norms.

UNDERSTANDING AND CHALLENGING DIAGNOSTIC MODELS OF HUMAN SEXUALITY

Today the expansion of our concept of human sexual nature through sexual literacy enables us to understand the Folsom Street Fair sexual behaviors not as abnormal but rather as normative variations in lifestyle or extreme variations in human behavior. Culture and societal change play a role in this process. Pathologizing sexual activities that many consider a lifestyle has come under fire (Yakeley & Wood, 2014). This is a controversial area in sexual science and society that raises questions about how government, medicine, and culture (including religion) have intersected historically, and not necessarily to the betterment of individuals. Understanding these cultural differences and understanding why difference has been treated as a disease or a norm is critical to your own sexual individuality and sexual literacy.

From the time of the ancient Greeks and Romans thousands of years ago right up to the present day, cultures have long struggled to define what is normal and natural or abnormal or just "different" in human sexual expression (Foucault, 1986; Institute of Medicine, 2012; Money, 1986; Rubin, 1984; Stoller, 1985b). This is not only because each sexual culture creates a moral blueprint for how people should behave and what kind of sexual behavior they should exhibit. Historically, societies enacted sexual control through their institutions such as the family, morals, laws, social attitudes, and various controls and punishments. This does not mean, however, that everyone has followed those blueprints and sexual norms mindlessly. Individual sexual expression is a significant factor in human adaptation. People will go to extraordinary lengths under difficult circumstances to express their romantic and sexual feelings, nurture emotional attachments, and pursue sexual behaviors and relationships. In response, societies have invested resources to retain control not just over a preferred definition of human sexual nature, but also over individuals and their sexual behaviors, especially as these influence the general population.

Western society over the past century and more has witnessed an explosion in sexual variations, and probably the expansion of individual sexuality in terms of attraction, romance, and love, especially in large, complex industrial countries such as the United States (Kinsey et al., 1948). Many scholars believe that this expansion of sexual variability is part of the inherent change that accompanies progress in modern society (Giddens, 1992). Sexual individuality has thus expanded to include a broader spectrum of moral and social and erotic variations than has ever been seen before, creating controversy about what is normal and abnormal in mainstream media, law, religion, and medical science (Bailey et al., 2016; Diamond, 2014; Herbenick et al., 2017; Irvine, 2000; Oosterhuis, 2000; Yakeley & Wood, 2014).

The very nature of these societal changes enables individuals to experiment with and "test out" what they like or enjoy, what makes them "feel good," and what the effects are upon their sexual selves, bodies, relationships, and communities. This is one of the explanations for how the Folsom Street Fair, and the huge variety of online forms of sexual exploration discussed in Chapter 3, may have come about. And with all these new sexual developments there came renewed focus on the "traditional" clinical and medical views of what is or is not human nature, and what ought to be treated as abnormal came under fire. Eventually science and psychiatry began to challenge the existing paradigms for normative human sexuality (Bayer, 1987; Irvine, 2000; Institute of Medicine, 2012; Oosterhuis, 2000; Stoller, 1985; Yakeley & Wood, 2014).

This transformation in psychiatry was in part a change in the perception of how the clinician was controlling what people do in sexual intimacy. Two generations ago, in the time of Kinsey et al. (1948), traditional morals were not considered controversial, even if people violated them more often than should have been the case (Gagnon & Simon, 2005). Psychiatric models of "perversion and deviancy," primarily created by the dominant class of White men, were beginning to be challenged by women, by people of color, by LGBTQ people, and by researchers whose work suggested the need for improvement in the models (Stoller, 1985). These critics suggested that if a sexual behavior labeled as perversion was not problematic and was not causing distress to people, then it should not be considered abnormal. Better to think of it as a "natural" reflection of normative population sexual variation. Here is a simple example of a rather common difference. John and Mary (Couple A), typically have sex once a week and feel positive about it. George and Joan, Couple B, also typically have sex once a week but feel this is inadequate and want more. They have sought and found medical treatment to increase their sexual expression and performance. In terms of the current diagnostic criteria, one or both couples might get a diagnosis of "low sexual desire." But Couple A appears to feel fully satisfied in their sexual relationship, and indeed they appear happy to society. Why should society worry about them? Which is abnormal, Couple A or Couple B? The clinical answer is neither. But the thing is, this is about perception, about social comparisons (Couple A compared to Couple B). And as in many other areas of human life, perception is also reality. If one of the couples feels discontent, society and clinicians are going to consider helping them to relieve their anxiety or distress. But from the strict perspective of clinical science, it is not correct to interfere in these relationships unless the individuals or couples feel distress or the sense that this is interfering with their lives. There are no other people involved in these issues, and if the couple are consenting adults, there is no victim and therefore, from the perspective of sexual science, no problem.

Consider one huge example of how human sexual behavior moved from being clinically defined as abnormal and illegal, with cruel forms of clinical treatment to eradicate it, to being widely regarded as normal and natural: the amazing history of homosexuality in modern Western society. Like masturbation in the 19th century, homosexuality was regarded as perversion, inversion, and was believed to be sinful, abnormal, disgusting, and illegal for centuries. In Europe, people, including children, were being executed for homosexuality until 1811. Well into the late 19th century the treatments for homosexuality were nothing short of cruel and inhumane. The whole clinical approach began to change in European countries in the 20th century, and in the 1950s homosexuality became legal in the United Kingdom. In the United States, Kinsey's core work in the late 1940s and 1950s paved the way for rethinking homosexuality as being more normative. By the time of the 1960s sexual revolution, many norms had radically begun to change, especially perceptions and attitudes toward premarital sex, masturbation, and homosexuality. The women's movement and the gay movement put more force behind these changes. Nonetheless, the mainstream laws and controls on homosexuality did not change until well into the 1980s, when social activism was very strong due to the AIDS epidemic. Eventually all laws against homosexuality between consenting adults were struck down, and same-sex marriage became the law of the land. Nevertheless in some ways, the traditional punitive attitudes are still present in some corners of society (Regnerus, 2007; PEW, 2017), as we have seen in previous chapters.

All of this history is in part the result of the fact that psychiatry treated homosexuality as a mental disorder (a psychiatric category), classified by all clinicians as a paraphilia. **Paraphilia** is a psychiatric category to replace the term *perversion* that doctors created in the 1920s to describe abnormal, difficult-to-understand sexual arousal from individuals, objects, or situations that radically departed from typical mainstream behavior, and which caused personal distress or serious problems. Why was something once labeled a perversion, and then paraphilia, treated by such severe means as electric shock, even into the 1970s, then treated as normal behavior (Cohler & Galatzer-Levy, 2000)? The obvious answer is that society, culture, and attitudes about what constitutes mental health changed.

Many forms of research conducted by medical doctors and clinicians have indicated that homosexuality is as normal as heterosexuality. As this fact gained acceptance, LGBTQ people began to come out and were accepted by family, friends, and communities, and negative attitudes began to reverse (Herek, 2004). By this time the controversies in psychiatry

paraphilia

Sexual behavior characterized by sexual arousal to individuals, objects, or situations that departs from mainstream normative or typical behavior that does not necessarily or automatically require psychiatric treatment.

had changed completely: Society now regards it as ethically or morally wrong to express prejudice toward gay and lesbian people. People who express strong homophobia may be referred for treatment if their own actions cause distress to victims. Even more importantly, harmful clinical practices to remove homosexual desires became illegal. It became illegal to use electric shock against LGBTQ people. A whole range of so-called reparative therapy treatments, not just shock but also ice pick lobotomies, chemical castration, aversive therapies that make people take nausea-inducing drugs, and others became ethically suspect.

Today, these "conversion therapy" or "reparative therapy" practices are unethical and illegal in the states of California, New Jersey, Illinois, and Oregon. Sadly, however they continue to be part of standard psychiatry in Asia, Africa, Oceania, and parts of the Americas. It is estimated that as many as 700,000 people have been and continue to be treated clinically to eliminate their homosexuality through these cruel practices, inflicting trauma and lifelong damage to their mental health (Trevor Project, 2019).

There are now many other areas of human sexual expression in which the definition of normal human sexual nature has expanded greatly in our society. To take a very popular example: By the time *Fifty Shades of Grey* became a successful book and then a movie in 2015, jolting viewers into a different understanding of how playful pain is part of sexual pleasure, vibrators had already become part of mass consumer culture, easily one of the more widely ordered items on Amazon.com, and today available from Walmart.

You will begin to realize that the very nature of what is deemed normal and natural sexuality is changing in our time. Think about the following list of sexual behaviors. Once deemed unmentionable and unacceptable in the 1950s through the 1990s, these behaviors and practices were treated as abnormal. Some behaviors were even illegal and, if caught, people were prosecuted for engaging in them, including a penalty of death (Cott, 2002; Foucault, 1980; Gagnon & Simon, 1973; Irvine, 2000).

Fifty Shades of Grey brought the practice of BDSM into popular culture and illustrates how quickly a set of extreme sexual behaviors can move from being viewed as strange and atypical to accepted and mainstream over time and in the right context.
Entertainment Pictures/Alamy Stock Photo

- Mild consensual adult bondage, dominance, sadism, and masochism (BDSM, which is explained in a later section)—as popularized in *Fifty Shades of Grey*
- Same-sex behaviors between same-aged adolescents
- Possession of hard-core heterosexual pornography
- Premarital sexual behavior as an adult
- Masturbation as an adolescent or adult
- Mixed-race marriage
- Consensual oral sex between adults
- Consensual anal sex between adults
- The use of contraceptives correlated with the increase in women's sexual pleasure

The list could go on (Bailey et al., 2016; Bullough, 1995; Irvine, 2000; Jordan-Young, 2010; Herbenick et al., 2017; Laumann et al., 1994; Regnerus, 2007; Regnerus & Uecker, 2011; Stoller, 1986). In short, over time sexual behaviors once seen as truly diseased and abnormal shifted into the mainstream to become part of ordinary intimate relationships (Gagnon, 2004; Irvine, 2000; Jordan-Young, 2010). Sexual behaviors labeled as "paraphilias" in past decades were typically perceived to be sinful, immoral, illegal, and dangerous to society, and thus the treatment that was directed toward controlling these sexual expressions included being isolated, medicated, incarcerated, tortured, or worse (Nussbaum, 1999;

Oosterhuis, 2000; Szasz, 1988). Consider that each of the following was once considered to be a paraphilia or a symptom of disease:

- Female orgasm, especially clitoral
- Adult and adolescent homosexuality
- Masturbation
- Pornography

Are you surprised? The behaviors did not change; rather, society changed its attitude and then its norms toward each category of experience (Herdt, 2009b; Northrup, Schwartz & Witte, 2014; Regnerus & Uecker, 2011). The societal changes were not simply capricious; again, the changes came about largely because medicine and psychiatry confirmed through research the normality of the practices.

Later in this chapter, we will examine the controversies surrounding the most extreme sexual variations in pleasure and arousal, which do differ widely across cultures. However, clinicians agree that there are still a few minimal behaviors that cause distress, risk, and disruption and are thus diagnosed, as we will study below. These behaviors have long been associated with coercion and distress and are treated as harmful to the self and/or others. Contemporary treatments for these conditions have been refined to help the individuals and families suffering from them.

For now, let us first turn to more typical problems associated with sexual functioning that are not directly the result of disease and indeed may occur in many people's lifetimes.

MEDICAL AND PHYSICAL CHALLENGES TO NORMATIVE SEXUAL RESPONSE

There are several sexual variations that arise from normal processes of aging and disability, and which may in some cases reduce or hinder normative sexual expression. These different kinds of essential physical problems are not regarded as psychiatric diseases but are instead treated as challenges to basic sexual function in the general population. We begin with challenges to desire and sexual arousal that are related to complete sexual response, and other issues related to aging and disability faced by both men and women. We will then discuss problems having to do with disability and aging that, while not in themselves disease, may result in reduced sexual function, drive, desire, response, and other consequences.

Desire Issues for Women

Although men and women alike continue to find satisfaction in sex as they grow older, and a not insignificant number of elders really enjoy sex, it is also true that aging definitely affects the sexual lives of people. In particular, individual heterosexual women may experience challenges to expressing sexual desire earlier and more adversely than is the case with heterosexual men (Carpenter et al., 2006; Das et al., 2012). In part, this is because women outnumber men in the aging population, and a higher and earlier male mortality rate limits the availability of sexual partners for women. Also, older women tend to be more sexually conservative than younger women (Carpenter et al., 2006). Cultural taboos may discourage many older single or widowed women from having active sexual relationships, especially if they experience problems with desire.

Female sexual arousal disorder (FSAD) is the inability to attain or maintain sexual excitement, expressed as a lack of subjective excitement or as a lack of genital lubrication or swelling or other physical responses. Another disorder, hypoactive female sexual desire disorder (HSDD), is the persistent inability to achieve fulfilling sexual activity, or to maintain

female sexual arousal disorder (FSAD)
The inability to attain or maintain sexual excitement due to subjective or physical factors and responses.

a level of sexual desire that the woman feels comfortable with. Typically, FSAD occurs after age 25, but the symptoms vary greatly among individuals. In the *DSM-5*, three of the following symptoms must be expressed to diagnose this:

1. Little interest in sex
2. Few thoughts about sex
3. Decreased start or rejecting sex
4. Little pleasure experienced in sex
5. Lack of arousal, even using external erotic stimuli
6. Little genital sensation during sex

In part FSAD is a function of biology, and in part it stems from psychosocial and cultural beliefs and practices. Many women who experience FSAD for 6 months or more may benefit from medical and therapeutic support (APA, 2000). Some researchers think that the medical establishment has overrated the significance of FSAD and is medicating and treating people who have psychological, not biological, problems (Tiefer, 2006). Dr. Lenore Tiefer, a psychologist, launched a "pink campaign" to oppose medicalizing women's sexuality, especially when it seemed that large pharmaceutical companies would benefit from doctors' prescribing unneeded medications for women, as stated in her "New View Campaign" (2016). In some women, a decline in desire affects their response to partners, their ability to have orgasms, and their sexual well-being (Huang et al., 2009). This lack of interest is not universal, however. Research points out some similarities among women of different ethnicities in sexual desire, vitality, and aging. One important study of 876 White, 388 Black, 347 Latina, and 351 Asian women showed these results (Huang et al., 2009):

- 43% of these women, ages 45–80, reported at least moderate sexual desire.
- 60% had been sexually active in the previous 3 months.
- About half of these women described their overall sexual satisfaction as moderate to high.

The same research found that among sexually inactive women, the most common resons for inactivity were:

- Lack of interest in sex (39%)
- Lack of a partner (36%)
- Physical problem of partner (23%)

These results indicate that a large number of ethnically diverse women are interested and engaged in sexual activity into older age. Any lack of interest in sex seems to be associated to a significant degree with not having a partner. The issue of loss of sexual desire can relate to menopause in women. As described in Chapter 4, in menopause the ovaries stop releasing eggs and producing hormones. Some women may experience certain cognitive and psychosocial changes, including mood swings. Psychologically, they may also experience a sense of loss or even depression with the knowledge that they are no longer fertile. These changes vary widely among women, and even among groups of women. Japanese women, for example, report very limited experiences with menopausal changes. Furthermore, 20–50% of women may never experience the hot flashes and other symptoms that result from hormonal changes (Breast Cancer.org, 2019). Behavioral changes do not affect all women, either. Such changes may or may not interrupt the ability to work, and may not be noticeable to others (Burgess, 2004).

Some women may experience vulvo-vaginal atrophy, generally as a consequence of menopause and the body's declining level of estrogen. If intercourse hurts because of this atrophy, women's interest in intercourse may decline (Levine, Williams, & Hartman, 2008). Vaginal dryness, another consequence of menopause and lack of estrogen production, may cause a decline in sexual desire, but is treatable with lubricants (Maurice, 1999). Aftercare is vital to ensure that the holistic effect is positive.

Several diseases are associated with menopause and the drop in hormone production, including cardiovascular disease, cancer, and osteoporosis (Delamater & Sill, 2005). Beginning in the 1960s, doctors prescribed hormone replacement therapy (HRT), also known as estrogen replacement therapy (ERT), to treat menopausal symptoms. While many women do find that ERT helps them get through hot flashes, there may be side effects that include moodiness, depression, sore breasts, weight gain, and severe headaches, among other issues. It is important to recognize, though, that midlife is when some women experience the ability to have sexual pleasure and love, filled with intimacy and excitement. Some people refer to this period as a woman's "prime" (Schwartz, 2007a).

Arousal Issues for Men

The possibility of lifelong sexual expression for men now exists not only due to changing positive attitudes surrounding sex among elders but also because of sexual enhancement medications such as Viagra, Cialis, and other pharmaceuticals aimed toward helping men achieve and maintain erections.

erectile dysfunction (ED)
The inability to have or maintain an erection for sexual expression.

Erectile dysfunction (ED) is increasingly common as men live longer and health issues may influence their sexual performance (Das et al., 2012). Some 30 million men in the United States and 100 million men globally suffer from ED, though this estimate is probably very low due to lack of access to health care and other issues (Anderson, 2019). Sexual well-being and performance from midlife until old age is associated with a variety of issues, including a decline in arousal and the use of pharmaceutical medications to enhance arousal (Everaerd & Laan, 2000). For example, such medications as antidepressants, blood pressure drugs, HIV medications, and antipsychotics are known to contribute to ED in some cases (Anderson, 2019). While there is nothing comparable in men to the menopause of women, a variety of changes surrounding the nature and perceptions of declining virility as portrayed in media may contribute to the popular idea that there is a "male menopause."

Viagra and many other medications have been introduced to help men deal with ED. Since 1996, when Viagra was patented, men may seek a doctor's advice about using Viagra or another pharmaceutical product, each costing about $10 to $25 per pill. So far, approximately 65 million men globally have taken several billion Viagra pills. The drugs are more easily prescribed than ever, and because some of the stigma of using such medications has decreased as they became more common, more men use them.

No doubt the baby boomers' attitudes about sex has contributed to this multimillion-dollar industry. Not just men but women are also interested in sexual enhancement drugs such as Levitra or others, although the medical effectiveness of these drugs is less than that of the medications created for men and still seems uncertain (Tiefer, 2006; New View Campaign, 2016). Other experts believe that pharmaceutical companies have actively promoted a new emphasis on youthful masculinity and sexuality that Viagra makes possible, even for men of very advanced age (Potts et al., 2003). This new sexual script challenges the old myth about men's naturally diminishing sexual capacity as they enter old age. Advertising campaigns now promote "sex for life," and implicitly motivate aging men to pursue youthful masculinity by purchasing sexual enhancements to remain sexually active. Even teenagers have been found to take Viagra, and it has become more popular among college-aged men, too. Because of these campaigns and men's fears about declining arousability, it is easy to understand the commercial success of Viagra. However, Viagra's success was made possible by an increase in the prevalence of erectile dysfunction as the population of men grew older and expected to have sex later in life. How much are these expectations fueled by culture and how much stems from biology? "Healthy Sexuality: Viagra: Do or Die" examines both sides of this question.

HEALTHY Sexuality

Viagra: Do or Die

Some experts believe that the pharmaceutical companies have made a molehill into a mountain in order to make lots of money. When these companies label age-related arousal problems as ED, we must critically consider what they are trying to sell (Potts et al., 2003). Some research suggests that pharmaceutical companies have engaged in "disease mongering" by promoting the idea of a "disorder" that didn't exist 20 years ago (Tiefer, 2006). Before Viagra became available, people considered the decline in erectile function a normal part of aging. Was it good or bad to challenge this normal aging function by inventing and then advertising a pharmaceutical to help with sexual arousal?

Also, news reports are filled with stories about how younger men, even college-age guys who want to be "super-performers," are taking Viagra and similar "party" drugs—a sign that the college culture is changing in ways that are challenging the legitimate use of such medications (Carrington, 2006).

Certainly, sexual enhancement drugs have given men greater choice in treating arousal problems, but they may encourage younger men who have no problems with arousal to pop a pill thinking that it may make them into sexual supermen (Carrington, 2006). Following the release of Viagra, biomedical writers made erectile dysfunction into more of a condition than it is and included alarming statistics to suggest that this new disorder affected at least a third of the men over 40.

At the time Viagra went on the market, sexual dysfunction, or difficulty at any stage of sexual activity that prevents enjoyment, was considered more common in men than in women (Laumann et al., 2006). This is changing today, as one can see from many advertisements in the media geared toward women's arousal issues and medications for them. The science and effectiveness of those drugs is less certain than those for men (Tiefer, 2006), but there is no question that a sea change is occurring in the use of medicine to enhance many people's sexual performance in later life.

Erectile difficulties tend to be the most significant sexuality-related issue for many middle-aged and older men. The Viagra-popping 64-year-old whom Jack Nicholson portrays is the humorous side of this issue in the movie, *Something's Gotta Give*. On a serious note, older men report having not only ED but also difficulty with premature ejaculation (Laumann et al., 2006). All of these ED conditions may be influenced by other medical conditions, such as heart disease or diabetes, and medications taken for them (Das et al., 2012).

Although more research is needed on the ways in which midlife men experience sexuality (Potts et al., 2003), recent large national survey studies have revealed a better picture of ED among men who continue to engage in sexual intercourse after age 50 (NSSHB, 2010). Overall, approximately 17% of all men (ages 50–80) reported taking medication for ED. The percentage of ED peaks in the 60s, when about 30% of all men have acknowledged using medication for ED problems, but then it declines, probably in part because the frequency of sex declines and the number of men engaging in sex declines as these men age. As we explore the emergence of disability in later life, we will find that, in spite of the challenges to desire and arousal, people are finding new and creative ways to continue sexual happiness in the second half of life.

The Challenges of Disability: Embracing New Possibilities

Disability may occur at any time in life to all genders, races, social classes, and orientations, and it may come in the form of a mental or physical challenge to one's basic abilities. In general, people with disabilities report greater issues surrounding sexual satisfaction than the general population (Tepper & Owens, 2007). In addition, as people age, it is more common for disabilities to influence their sexual well-being, for example, due to heart or cardiovascular problems. It is notable that the new view of sex continuing until old age is occurring as the baby boomers have come into middle age. This generation is living longer because they take better care of their physical and mental health, and many of them expect to continue having sexual relations (Laumann et al., 2006; Schwartz, 2007a).

Among the many changes that occur along the road toward elderhood, the emergence of disabilities may be a part of the human experience. In fact, as our society develops ways to prolong life, the number of people who develop mental or physical disabilities or both may increase (Oliver, 1990). Impairments in our abilities are often looked upon with pity or scorn, or stigma, or all of these (Oliver, 1990). Disabilities that involve sexuality, in particular, are generally not discussed openly and honestly (Shakespeare et al., 1996). In the United States, people often think of those living with disabilities and chronic conditions as incapable of experiencing sexual feeling or sexual identity, and so they rarely receive sex education. This gap leaves them vulnerable to exploitation, at risk for STIs and HIV, and without the knowledge and tools that they need to develop appropriate sexual relationships (Shildrick, 2007). The risk of sexual exploitation, coercion, and assault among people living with disabilities is high, especially those with developmental disabilities. Many people living with disabilities and chronic illnesses may experience some form of coercion or assault in their lifetimes (Shuttleworth, 2006). For the most part, the perpetrators are their caretakers and family members, as is typically the case for others who are sexually assaulted or raped. Vulnerability to assault reveals how important sexual literacy is for people with disabilities. Like everyone else, people with disabilities need the sexual knowledge and skills to navigate their lives, to protect themselves, and to flourish in terms of sexual well-being.

Some people who are disabled cannot meet their own sexual needs (Tepper & Owens, 2007). Men who have degenerative diseases of the central nervous system may not be able to use their hands to touch their own genitals or those of their partners. One detailed study revealed that some men with this type of disability had not received sexual education or experienced sexual relations of any kind (Shuttleworth, 2006). They sometimes had an acute need for human touch and a sense of being loved. To help them meet this need, sometimes caretakers masturbated them to orgasm, bringing them sexual pleasure for the first time in their lives. A caretaker performing this service is controversial due to ethical concerns, but this study calls attention to the fact that people with disabilities are sexual beings with a need for sexual fulfillment.

As previously noted, there is a variety of medical conditions that may influence the experience of sexual desire and the expression of sexuality and well-being as we age, especially when people live into their 80s (Das et al., 2012; Delamater & Sill, 2005). Illness, especially chronic, long-lasting conditions, such as cardiovascular disease, diabetes, arthritis, and cancer, produce sexual side effects (Maurice, 1999; Schiavi, 1999).

WHAT'S ON YOUR MIND?

Q: My friend was just in a major car accident, and he is now permanently paralyzed from his shoulders down. Will he be able to engage in an active sex life?

ANSWER: Many people with disabilities, including those with severe paralysis, have created very active sexual lives through the love and commitment of their intimate partners. His options are unique to his condition, of course, and he can discuss them with his doctor, physical therapist, and lover. But the short answer to your question is yes, he will be able to engage in a wide variety of sexual activities that may or may not include penile penetration. Think beyond vaginal penetration to oral sex as possibilities. Think about the whole range of human interactions to expand his possibilities, and give this man hope about his situation. The need for hugging, touching, and kissing is hugely important for all humans.

- Cardiovascular disease—the cause of many issues related to loss of arousal and potentially of sexual desire in men and women. High blood pressure, related to heart disease, may inhibit erection for men, and if it goes untreated, it may cause irreparable damage to the person, including permanent sexual dysfunction.
- Diabetes—a chronic disease marked by high levels of sugar in the blood. High blood levels of glucose can cause several problems, including vision and hearing problems, and among the results of these conditions may be disruption of sexual arousal.
- Arthritis—inflammation of one or more joints, which results in pain, swelling, stiffness, and limited movement. These factors may inhibit sexual functioning. Chronic pelvic pain appears to be more notable among older women and is associated with loss of sexual desire.
- Prostate cancer—increasingly found in older men in the United States, in the prostate gland. The prostate is a small, walnut-sized structure that wraps around the urethra, the tube that carries urine out of the body. The prostate is also associated with seminal discharge when men become aroused.
- Breast cancer—among women (95%) and men (5%) starts in the tissues of the breast, and appears to be increasingly common. There are two main types of breast cancer: The most common is ductal carcinoma, which starts in the ducts that move milk from the breast to the nipple; lobular carcinoma starts in the breast lobules, which produce milk.

The treatments for these diseases are often controversial, especially when it comes to the effect on sexuality, because they can hinder or even eliminate sexual expression. As we have seen, however, there are some new treatments and more innovative ways of coping with these ailments. Not all these diseases are fatal, but rather they become chronic conditions that result in people learning how to handle and sometimes overcome the restrictions. Good medical treatment, combined with positive social support and continued engagement in life, go together to create the best possible outcomes.

Now let us examine the more psychological issues that surround the paraphilias and the treatment of sexual distress today.

DIAGNOSES OF SEXUAL DYSFUNCTION AND BEHAVIOR: THE *DSM-5* AND PARAPHILIC DISORDERS

Of all the controversies and changes in sexual science in recent decades, none is more important, exciting, and potentially confusing than the whole area of diagnosing paraphilias. In this section we provide you with a road map through this complex maze.

The *DSM* and Sexual Diagnosis

In sexual science, the most widely regarded clinical tool is the *Diagnostic and Statistical Manual of Mental Disorders* of the American Psychiatric Association, typically referred to as the *DSM*. It is now in its fifth edition. This tool is designed for psychiatrists and psychologists trying to help people who are suffering. Numerous changes in the *DSM* have followed the trends in society regarding the expansion of the definition of what is normal and natural in human sexual nature. In the latest *DSM-5*, a new distinction was made between *paraphilias* and *paraphilic disorders* that can guide your understanding in this section. According to the *DSM-*, paraphilias do not require or necessitate psychiatric treatment as such. Some of these behaviors seem more mainstream today. However, a more serious condition is the paraphilic disorder, which the *DSM-5* (2013, pp. 685–686) defines as "a paraphilia that is currently causing distress or impairment to the individual or a paraphilia whose satisfaction has entailed personal harm, or risk of harm, to others." This distinction separates paraphilias that reveal benign interests and behavior (normal variations of sexual behavior) from the paraphilic disorders.

Difference is not illness. It is important to be accurate when distress, harm, and suffering come from society or from within a person, independent of society. Consider the following key points regarding how to apply the sexual diagnoses of the *DSM-5*.

1. There are people who are distressed significantly by their sexual impulses and behaviors; this includes people feeling out of control and sometimes doing things that harm others or harm themselves.
2. The *DSM-5* is meant to help bring consistency to how people are treated. Diagnosing the nature of the suffering, in a consistent and accurate way, means that the care people receive will be more effective, and there will be agreement and coordination among health care providers.
3. We have to be careful not to diagnose someone as ill or sick just because they are different or because they have a different sexuality than another.
4. The *DSM* distinction between a paraphilia (a difference in sexuality) and a paraphilic disorder suggests that people have a paraphilic disorder when they are distressed and will express it through their sexuality. So the difference of having a paraphilia is not automatically indicative of illness; but when there is harm, distress, and suffering, the diagnosis of paraphilic disorder indicates treatment.

But what about compulsions?

Impulsive or Compulsive Sexual Behavior

One of the most widely discussed areas of psychiatric symptoms today is known as impulsive or compulsive behavior. Impulsive behavior is any behavior that lacks cognitive control through executive functioning (Grant & Potenza, 2011). Compulsive behavior is any behavior that one cannot control even though he or she has repeatedly tried to do so, and it is a function of underlying anxiety or is a means of regulating emotions (Hollander & Wong, 1995). Whether it has to do with eating or drinking, shopping, talking, lying, or stealing, these impulsive or compulsive behaviors are difficult to treat or change. Not everyone who expresses compulsive behavior engages in **extreme sexual behavior** or behavior that involves risk taking. Compulsive sexual behavior disorder is distinguished from paraphilic disorders in that the former involves culturally normative sexual behaviors that are lacking in control and are sometimes taken to compulsive extremes. Paraphilic disorders involve unusual sexual behaviors that lack impulse control and can be compulsive (Coleman, 2015). Not everyone who behaves impulsively or compulsively, however, engages in extreme sexual risk taking. Some seem to be quite focused and in apparent control of their sexuality.

When compulsive behavior is applied to extreme sexual behavior, it can resemble what some therapists call **compulsive sexual behavior,** which indicates a person's inability to control sexual urges, and leads to negative consequences (Coleman, 1991; Kafka, 2010). The actions of people who spend hundreds of hours watching pornography or who pay thousands of dollars for sex suggest compulsive sexual behavior. Other clinicians use the term **hypersexuality** or hypersexual disorder to refer to similar behaviors (Kafka, 2010; Reid et al., 2012). Hypersexual disorder was proposed as a distinct sexual disorder in the American Psychiatric Association's classification of psychiatric disorders but was not

extreme sexual behaviors
Risky, noncoercive behaviors between consenting adults that test the limits of what a culture tolerates within its spectrum of sexual behavior.

compulsive sexual behavior
Behavior that individuals are unable to control even though they have repeatedly tried to do so.

hypersexuality
Frequent or sudden expression of sexual urges; not a paraphilia.

accepted due to continued controversy over criteria, nomenclature, and lack of substantial research (Kafka, 2014). However, recently the World Health Organization created a new category of impulse control disorders called *compulsive sexual behavior disorder* (Kraus et al., 2018; World Health Organization, 2019). In the APA's *DSM*, clinicians could classify this disorder as *otherwise specified sexual dysfunction* (Krueger, 2016).

No matter how you define it, recent research has indicated that a sizable number of people in the United States feel that their sexual behavior is out of control, and they are distressed by it (10% of men and 7% of women). This may not represent all that could be considered to have a compulsive sexual behavior disorder, but it certainly indicates that this is a widespread concern (Dickenson et al., 2018).

Notably, research is showing that an attitude and emotion known as sexual shame is the best predictor of sexual compulsion and addiction (Grubbs et al., 2015). **Sexual shame** refers to overwhelming and grave feelings of shame, guilt, and remorse having to do with sexual memories, feelings, and fantasies that impede sexual satisfaction. Grubbs and colleagues have found that in certain people, moral disapproval of sexuality and deep religiosity are highly correlated with sexual addiction (Grubbs et al., 2015; Grubbs & Perry, 2018).

Consider this case study of compulsive sexual behavior. Brian is a high-profile banker in his 40s, a man respected in his profession. He has engaged in compulsive masturbation since he was a child. He currently spends huge amounts of money and time visiting female sex workers and engaging in phone sex. Some days Brian is online for 10 hours a day looking at Internet porn. At the beginning he could balance his banking work with the porn, but recently it has been getting out of control. All of his sexual activity is disrupting his life and work. He has sought treatment but keeps falling back into **sexual compulsivity** (Derogatis et al., 2010). Some people like Brian may find 12-step programs or other forms of treatment, but they may not seek or find help, and they may go through profound disruptions and even catastrophes in their lives, such as losing their families and jobs. Brian's story suggests the following common features of compulsive sexual behavior (or hypersexuality):

- Excessive time consumed by sexual fantasies, sexual urges, and planning for or engaging in sexual behaviors
- Repeatedly engaging in compulsive sexual behavior as a way to deal with emotional states such as depression and anxiety
- Repeatedly returning to compulsive sexual behavior during stressful life events
- Repeatedly but unsuccessfully trying to control or reduce this sexual behavior
- Typically disregarding or denying the physical risk and emotional harm of these compulsive sexual behaviors

In other words, compulsive sexual behavior disorder is characterized by a persistent pattern of failure to control intense, repetitive, sexual impulses or urges resulting in repeated sexual behavior. Symptoms may include (a) repetitive sexual activities becoming a central focus of the person's life to the point of neglecting health and personal care or other interests, activities, and responsibilities; (b) many unsuccessful efforts to significantly reduce repetitive sexual behavior; and (c) continued repetitive sexual behavior despite adverse consequences or despite deriving little or no satisfaction from it. The pattern of failure to control intense sexual impulses or urges, and the resulting repetitive sexual behavior, is manifested over an extended period of time (e.g., 6 months or more), and it causes marked distress or significant impairment in personal, familial, social, educational, occupational, or other important areas of functioning. (Distress that is entirely related to moral judgments and disapproval about sexual impulses, urges, or behaviors is not sufficient to meet this requirement.)

sexual shame
overwhelming and grave feelings of shame, guilt, and remorse having to do with sexual memories, feelings, and fantasies that impede sexual satisfaction.

sexual compulsivity
A person's inability to control sexual urges; not a paraphilia.

sexual addiction
A controversial disorder of intimacy; not a paraphilia.

One of the terms for compulsive sexual behavior that is found mostly in media reports, in popular culture, and to some extent in research, is the term **sexual addiction.** This controversial condition includes sexual urges, feelings, and behaviors that appear so extreme in frequency or intensity as to be out of one's control (Carnes, 2001). Specific behaviors related to sexual addiction include the following: frequent or compulsive masturbation; having compulsive phone or Internet sex; compulsively watching pornography; having numerous sex partners, including anonymous partners; engaging in risky and unsafe sex practices often; engaging in sexual molestation, voyeurism, or exhibitionism; and a combination of some or all of these behaviors. Essentially, this definition of sexual addiction is very similar to compulsive sexual behavior disorder or hypersexual disorder, except that this term assumes a particular cause of the behavior, and it approaches treatment in a manner similar to treating substance use disorders. Further, it does not make a distinction between paraphilic behavior and compulsive sexual behavior that is normative.

Some therapists use the following criteria to define sexual addiction: recurrent inability to resist impulses to engage in acts of sex; frequently engaging in those behaviors to a greater extent over time; making unsuccessful efforts to stop, reduce, or control those sexual behaviors; spending an inordinate amount of time trying to obtain sex, being sexual, or recovering from sexual experiences; preoccupation with preparing or getting ready for sex; and being so caught up in sexual activities that social, financial, psychological, or physical problems may result (Carnes, 2001). Not all of these traits apply to the broader range of extreme sexual behaviors that we will study below, and not everyone who engages in extreme sexual behaviors manifests all of these behaviors. Note that the term *sexual addiction* refers to the sexual behavior being out of control and less focused on what has been observed of culturally patterned extreme sexual behaviors.

The controversy about sexual addiction extends to research, education, and treatment because many doctors and therapists disagree on the criteria for diagnosing it, how to treat it, and if it is a real condition—that is, they do not consider sexual addiction a paraphilia or any kind of sexual disorder. Sexual addiction therapists believe that the best treatment focuses on underlying trauma, and they often refer clients to 12-step programs called *Sexual Addicts Anonymous* (SAA).

Understanding why people's sexual behavior is impulsive, compulsive, or addictive can make all the difference in helping them—if they want help (Perel, 2006). To learn more about this complex topic, read "Research and Sexual Well-Being: Sexual Addiction—Reality or Myth?"

In summary, many different conditions explain sexual variations across society, some of which are extreme and some of which are considered paraphilias, which we discuss next.

Paraphilias

As noted earlier, some sexual behaviors are extreme and potentially distressful, and clinicians classify them as paraphilias. The term comes from the Greek language: *para,* meaning abnormal, and *philia,* referring to love or attraction. Since the 1920s this psychiatric category was synonymous with perversion in a highly negative way, but it has evolved along with the growth of our understanding of psychiatry and sexual science (Bullough, 1995; Groneman, 2001; Krueger & Kaplan, 2001; Money, 1986; Stoller, 1985). The actual use of the term in the *DSM* came much later, about 1980, and by then it was being used differently by clinicians. Today, paraphilia means sexual urges and behaviors connected to persons or objects that are different from normative variations but do not necessarily require psychiatric treatment. However, the more extreme form of paraphilic disorder does suggest serious distress in social, occupational, or other important arenas of the person's life and may even result in trauma to someone. In general, if we focus on the issue of distress, and especially coercion, we can make better sense of the complexity of the paraphilias, which are such a complex area of human sexuality.

RESEARCH and Sexual Well-Being

Sexual Addiction—Reality or Myth?

Researchers probe issues surrounding sexual compulsivity and sexual addiction, but there is no consensus about these issues yet (Bancroft & Vukadinovic, 2004). Sexual addiction is apparently not confined to sport celebrities such as golfer Tiger Woods or actors like Michael Douglas, Eric Benét, and Charlie Sheen. Consider the story about Greg, a 28-year-old married man in the retail industry. He states that he has been "addicted" to masturbating and porn for years. Recently his wife discovered messages he was posting on social media looking for women to sexually hook up with. She became furious and threatened to leave him and take their children. He still sits for hours watching online porn, as if he can't get enough of it. He is shy around women and says that this addiction is taking over his life. He feels powerless to stop it, but even when thinking of seeking help, he also feels an urge to view porn online.

Some critics may say that sexual addiction is an easy excuse for people to do what they want, but people like Greg seem to be in distress. Researchers also suggest that the logic of the condition and its diagnosis may be circular: (1) Individuals may be diagnosed with sexual addiction; (2) this diagnosis relates to extreme sexual behaviors that are not inherently diseased or do not have signs of addiction; (3) once diagnosed this way, these people tend to think of themselves as "sex addicts," and so do their friends and partners; and (4) they repeat these learned behaviors, and dominant societal institutions such as family and church stigmatize them because they are not living up to the sexual norms and values of those institutions (Bancroft & Vukadinovic, 2004; Levine & Troiden, 1988).

1. What seems problematic about the definition of addiction is that it alludes to a physical and psychological dependence and increased tolerance. Sexual addiction does not fit this definition of addiction. There are no known mechanisms in the brain that operate similarly to substance use. Many of the behaviors associated with sexual addiction are considered within the spectrum of sexual variations, albeit extreme (Coleman, 1986; Levine & Troiden, 1988).
2. If viewed as an addiction, there is a tendency to treat the condition like alcohol or drug addiction and employ 12-step groups that emphasize a program of spiritual recovery. The goal is often to achieve immediate and long-term abstinence from a variety of sexual behaviors (Coleman, 1986).
3. There is often a myriad of coexisting mental health conditions, which can be overlooked if one is simply looking at the behavior through an addiction lens. For example, the behavior may be associated with high rates of anxiety and depression that are better treated with medications and various forms of psychotherapy (Miner, Dickenson, & Coleman, 2019; Raymond, Coleman, & Miner, 2003).
4. The notion of sexual addiction is best understood today as an identity or intimacy disorder that may be caused by inhibiting factors of psychosexual development, such as sexual shame associated with intense religiosity (Grubbs et al., 2015), and not a paraphilia (Coleman et al., 2018). In fact, some people with this condition express their compulsive sexual behavior because they do not feel good about themselves and they actually fear intimacy. They engage in compulsive sexual behavior as a way to build up self-esteem or to avoid intimacy, as in online compulsive pornography viewing or compulsive anonymous sexual behavior (Braun-Harvey & Vigorito, 2015).
5. The concept of sexual addiction tends to be sex-negative and is based on degeneracy theory—that somehow one negative behavior will lead to another one in a never-ending downward spiral (Coleman, 1986).
6. There is a risk of viewing anything that is extreme or nonnormative as an "addiction." This can have severe consequences for sexual and gender minority groups through racial profiling and other forms of sexual prejudice (Herek, 2004). It also does not take into account sociocultural factors that prejudge what is "normal" for other groups (Coleman, 1986). Although heterosexual men may participate in sex tourism and other extreme sexual behaviors, gay men may engage in anonymous sexual contacts and take sexual risks. If they engage in such risky behavior often enough, the behavior may look like compulsive sexual behavior (Diaz, 1998; Halkitis & Parsons, 2002; Stall, McKusick, Wiley,

Coates, & Ostrow, 1986). Thus, there is a risk of over-pathologizing nonnormative or extreme sexual behaviors simply because they deviate from the norm.

7. Because of a general sex-negative culture in the United States, many people pathologize their own sexual behavior out of their guilt and shame around sexuality. A single young man who has grown up in a religious background might view his masturbation as a sexual addiction and attempt to stop it through going to 12-step groups (Braun-Harvey & Vigorito, 2015; Coleman, 1986).

Thus, sexual addiction may be a myth, but compulsive sexual behavior is not. What we call it, how we classify it, and how we treat it are all part of an ongoing debate. Certainly, it is important to get a thorough clinical assessment by someone who is experienced in working with sexual disorders, who understands the wide range of sexual behaviors, and who can evaluate and treat the variety of coexisting conditions. But first ask clinicians about their model of compulsive sexual behavior and their approach to treatment.

DID YOU KNOW

What Is a Paraphilia?

[A]ny intense and persistent sexual interest other than sexual interest in genital stimulation or preparatory fondling with phenotypically normal, physically mature, consenting human partners (American Psychiatric Association 2013: p. 685). For example, zoophilia—sexual arousal with animals, such as cows or sheep or dogs, which is clinically not rare—is a more frequent form of paraphilia. Kinsey and his colleagues (1948) famously reported that for young men living on farms in rural areas in the mid-20th century, it was not uncommon for them to have experienced sex with farm animals. Today zoophilia if not causing distress or serious problems for an individual does not indicate psychiatric treatment.

coercive paraphilia
A sexual practice that involves the use of force against a sexual partner.

noncoercive paraphilia
A sexual practice that involves only one person or involves consent between adults to engage in a sexual practice that may involve pain, humiliation, pleasure, and other emotions.

transvestic fetishism
A form of fetishism in which a man becomes aroused by wearing women's clothes.

Categories of Sexual Paraphilic Disorders As previously noted, psychiatrists, medical doctors, psychologists, sexologists, and other clinicians use the standard diagnostic criteria of *DSM-5* (2013), which distinguishes the range of paraphilias from the more serious paraphilic disorders. *DSM-5* also distinguishes between paraphilic behaviors that do not cause personal distress or impairment or harm to others, and those that do (First, 2014). In discussions of the proposed new changes to the *DSM* several years ago, some experts suggested that a paraphilia could be classified depending on the kinds of sexual urges, fantasies, and behaviors it expressed, but the diagnosis of a paraphilic disorder depended upon distress and potential harm. In general, there is greater consensus among experts when there is acute distress or harm to the self or others. Thus, clinicians can distinguish between a healthy person with a paraphilia (nonnormative sexual behavior)—such as sexual urges directed toward animals, raincoats and shoes, or dead bodies—and a person whose nonnormative sexual urges cause distress, impair daily functioning at home, work, or school, or harm others.

Paraphilic disorders can be divided generally into those that involve coercion and those that do not, as previously noted. Clinicians tend to have more consensus on diagnosis and treatment when it comes to issues of coercion. **Coercive paraphilias** involve the use of force or power against another person. **Noncoercive paraphilias** are those that involve consent or agreement between adults to engage in a variety of practices that may involve pain, humiliation, shame, pleasure, or other powerful emotions. It is interesting that, at the global level of psychiatric treatment, these changes in thinking about paraphilic disorders are now recognized by a revision of the World Health Organization's "International Classification of Diseases." The new WHO classification has eliminated some paraphilic disorders such as sexual masochism, sexual sadism, fetishism, and **transvestic fetishism,** which previously were viewed as noncoercive paraphilias. Also, WHO now limits the categories of paraphilias that require treatment to actions that "involve others whose age or status renders them unwilling or unable to consent and on which the person has acted or by which he or she is markedly distressed" (WHO, 2019). This coercive form of paraphilia in the WHO system is like the *DSM-5* paraphilic disorder.

WHAT'S ON YOUR MIND?

Q: *My boyfriend showed me this rough anal sex pornography on the Internet between a man and a woman and he said he wanted me to try it out with him. I haven't ever done that, and I could be open to it, but I am worried about whether it could damage me, and yet I don't want to seem like a prude to him because I love him.*

ANSWER: The Internet is filled with all kinds of sexual behavior and porn, and some of it looks very glossy and slick. It looks this way because it is commercially produced using professional sex stars who know how to protect themselves from bodily injury. For example, they know how to stretch a rectum to keep from damaging tissue and they know to hide a condom from the camera. Follow your intuition and best judgment, and don't do what you think someone else would do because they are not you. It is your desires, feelings, and body that count, not someone else's. If you decide to go ahead, please read about anal sex, and see what your options are in having intimacy. A good lubricant is necessary to prevent torn muscles or tissue damage. Also, have your boyfriend use a condom. It can be a positive experience if you want to do it for your own reasons and if you are confident about protecting yourself.

To summarize, there are two main criteria for paraphilic disorders. Depending on the paraphilia, there are sometimes additional and very specific criteria (American Psychiatric Association, 2013):

1. Over a period of at least 6 months, recurrent and intense sexual arousal from [the specific paraphilia], as manifested by fantasies, urges, or behaviors.
2. The individual has acted on these sexual urges with a nonconsenting person (such as a minor), or the sexual urges or fantasies cause clinically significant distress or impairment in social, occupational, or other important areas of functioning.

These traits apply to many different cases and require that people who exhibit them see a doctor or clinician. This may be problematic if their sexual fantasies or urges are against the law (Stoller, 1991). That is because in most places, clinicians whose clients report such behaviors are required by law to report them to the authorities. Such individuals may fear the legal repercussions and hide their behaviors to act out their urges. For example, some authorities have long believed that sex tourism, as noted above, actually caters to pedophilia, and is thus enabling pedophilic disorder with children or underaged minors, as one way of evading detection in one's own society (Gagnon, 1997).

However, there is one other confusing exception to the coercive/noncoercive or paraphilia/paraphilic disorder distinction that involves a *DSM-5* category called "Other Specified Paraphilic Disorder." This is the default diagnosis in which the symptoms being presented look like a paraphilic disorder that causes distress or harm, but the case does not meet the full criteria mentioned above as required to make a correct diagnosis. For example, in certain instances of obscene phone calls or zoophilia, among other types of paraphilias, the clinician may choose to communicate the diagnosis differently by indicating "Other Specified Paraphilic Disorder," followed by the particular reason (e.g., "zoophilia"). Notice that in this example the issue of coercion may not be present, and the issue of distress to the client remains ambiguous. This is sometimes due to a lack of information or a reluctance on the part of the clinician to go beyond the known facts. At any rate, this sort of complexity reveals the difficulty of dealing with the diagnostic criteria, but in the following discussion we will ignore this other designation.

Coercive Paraphilias This category of paraphilias poses a risk to victims who may be unaware of what is going on or are unable to give consent to a sexual interaction.

Voyeuristic Disorder The "peeping Tom," as commonly described in popular culture and the media, is different from the paraphilic disorder of **voyeurism.** Someone can engage in voyeurism as extreme sexual behavior for a variety of reasons, one of which may include being dared to do it. This behavior is not the same as someone who is diagnosed with

voyeurism
The act of secretly watching someone undress or engage in some kind of intimate or sexual behavior.

"Exhibitionism or "flashing" by exposing the genitals is a form of paraphilia best responded to by being underwhelmed, that is, unless the exhibitionist is physically aggressive (rare), ignored."
Martin Lee/Alamy Stock Photo

voyeurism as a paraphilic disorder. In fact, this practice may be more common than once thought, even though it is probably an ancient one (Bullough, 1995).

The clinical condition of voyeuristic disorder, however, can cause those who practice it pain, humiliation, distress, and the possibility of being arrested. This paraphilia refers to the act of secretly watching someone undress or engage in some kind of intimate or sexual behavior. There are no reliable statistics, but this disorder may begin at around age 15 and is typically experienced by males (APA, 2013). Sometimes the voyeur appears to become more sexually aroused the more he believes that he is "stealing" the intimate privacy of the person he is watching. Webcams have made voyeurism much more widespread, and some of the pornography that appears on the Internet is advertised as being voyeuristic in selling it.

exhibitionism
The act of exposing genitals to unsuspecting victims for the purpose of sexual arousal.

Exhibitionistic Disorder This paraphilia is the act of a person becoming sexually aroused by exposing his or her genitals to unsuspecting victims, **exhibitionism.** "Flashers" typically are men in their mid-teens to middle age (APA, 2000; Kuzma & Black, 2008). The reactions of shock, stun, and surprise from the victim appear to create more sexual arousal in the exhibitionist. Research reveals that exhibitionists tend to engage in other types of sexual offenses, including making obscene calls (Krueger & Kaplan, 2016). The Internet has made it possible for anyone, anytime, anywhere to expose themselves, which has connected this paraphilia to online extreme sexual behavior (Carnes, 2001).

frotteurism
The act of rubbing one's genitals against another person.

Frotteuristic Disorder This is the act of a person rubbing his or her genitals against another person, typically a man against a woman (APA, 2000). For example, a clothed man may rub his penis against a woman on a crowded bus or subway. For some men, **frotteurism** is their most desired form of sexual expression, and they may spend hours riding around in public transportation in order to achieve multiple orgasms inside their pants.

pedophilia
Sexual urges and gratification related to minors, especially prepubertal females and males.

Pedophilic Disorder Of all the coercive paraphilic disorders, this one may inflict lifelong trauma on children, and it is universally condemned. **Pedophilia** is the sexual urge and gratification related to under-age minors, especially prepubertal boys and girls. Pedophilia is the most reviled of the coercive paraphilias. It involves sexual attraction to and abusive exploitation of children. It can be distinguished from hebophilia (or ephebophilia), which is the sexual attraction to peripubescent or adolescent males or females. In the popular media, these distinctions are rarely made, but they are important psychologically. While pedophilia and hebophilia are both typically illegal activities (depending upon age of consent in any given area), clinicians make a clearer distinction and address treatment differently. Someone may be attracted sexually to children and even have intense sexual urges but control them and never express them. Pedophilic disorder occurs only in those cases where the urge is acted out against a child. There are many different conditions associated with this paraphilia, including the expression of power over immature children (Payne et al., 2014; Seto, 2007).

In most societies, pedophilic disorder, even when not recognized in local psychiatric practice, is considered immoral and taboo, or it may be so extreme that people do not even recognize it as a subject. That is, the

DID YOU KNOW

What do you do when a man exposes himself to you? Feign boredom, act disinterested, give him the cold shoulder, and walk away. Then report it to the local police. An unadvisable response is to laugh at the exhibitionist and say, "Is that all you've got?"

subject may be hidden and avoided in public sex education and even medical training, as it was until very recently in Western countries like the United States. This is a very unfortunate loophole in sexual literacy that creates greater risk and vulnerability among young people. However, as people are speaking out openly about their childhood sexual abuse, as for example in the context of the #Me-Too Movement and in the sexual abuse scandals involving the Catholic Church, there is growing recognition of how widespread some of these abuses are (Moore & Reynolds, 2018). Even critics of categorizing the paraphilias as mental disorders still accept that societies dislike the expression of power and force over children in this way and view sexual assault against children as a heinous crime (Moser & Kleinplatz, 2005, 2006).

Why would someone find children sexually arousing in the first place? The answer is not obvious, and it is psychologically complex because people diagnosed with paraphilic disorder have few things in common except that most of them are men, the vast majority identify themselves as heterosexual, many were sexually victimized as children, and they may live in very lonely or alienated circumstances (Howells, 1994; Lee et al., 2001). Other research shows some similar findings and some additional ones (Finkelhor, 1984; Seto, 2007):

- Incarcerated sex offenders have higher rates of psychopathology than the general population.
- Increased psychopathology is associated with a greater number of paraphilias.
- Some of these individuals appear to have arrested emotional development.
- They are more likely to have been victims of sexual child abuse.
- They may be inclined to view child pornography online.

Additionally, some factors may also fail to inhibit sexual assault on children, including poor impulse control, multiple life stressors, alcohol and drug abuse, and psychosis (Seto, 2007).

There are several things to keep in mind when understanding pedophilic disorder. First, there is the basic distinction between having the desire and engaging in the behavior. It is not a crime to have the desire to have sex with children, but it is a despised crime if acted out. Someone may have intense sexual urges but control them and never express them, as argued by the organization known as "Virtuous Pedophiles," virped.org—an online group that accepts the desire but condemns the action, and does not seek to make it legal or socially accepted. There are various distinct traits associated with this paraphilia, including the wish to express power over children (Payne et al., 2014; Seto, 2007).

Second, it is important to keep in mind the age of the minor. In federal and state laws, minors cannot by definition consent to a sexual act with an adult, so all sexual interaction involves coercion of some kind (Seto, 2007). Keep in mind that minors are cognitively and emotionally unprepared to know what having sex means or how it might affect them (Herdt & McClintock, 2000; Seto, 2007). Thus, sexual interaction with an 18-year-old is very different than sex with an 8-year-old, if they are cognitively and emotionally normative. When they are victims of sexual coercion, the resulting trauma is great in both cases, but it is more difficult to treat when the victim is younger, and indeed it can become a focus of lifelong trauma. The majority of pedophilic or hebophilic victims are girls, typically in late childhood, and 90% know the molester (Kuzma & Black, 2008). As noted in Chapter 11, reform in the laws of the age of consent may actually help to focus resources on who needs to be protected most.

Third, childhood sexual abuse, especially from a family member or close friend of the family, reveals the influence of context on the trauma. This is the result of the child's sense of betrayal of trust, exploitation, lack of respect from the natural protector, and feelings of rage, anger, and shame that are far too common in these instances. It is terribly sad and noteworthy that many of the young people who were abused and later recovered have stated how they felt that they were somehow deserving of their sexual assault or abuse. Victims express feelings of shame or guilt as well as characteristics that are typical of posttraumatic stress syndrome (Seto, 2007), the sense of sexual shame previously noted. For example, research on three different ethnic groups (Blacks, Latinos, and non-Latino Whites) of men reveals how the culture may deeply influence the expression of trauma suffered from childhood sexual abuse. In a study of 150 adult men who survived childhood sexual abuse, researchers found major emotional and cognitive differences. Black men often denied or downplayed that they were abused. Latino men expressed anger, anxiety, hypervigilance, flashbacks, and problems in communication. Whites tended to experience more low self-esteem, loneliness, and isolation, and they suppressed their guilt and shame more than Black and Latino men (Payne et al., 2014).

These cultural differences also reveal different perspectives on social justice and inequality linked to trauma in the broader society. Much work is needed in this area to support survivors and to increase sexual literacy. Seeking help and support to recover and heal from such horrible experiences is critical to the victim's return to sexual well-being.

sadism
The act of inflicting pain on one's sexual partner, to create sexual pleasure for the person inflicting the pain.

masochism
The act of inflicting pain on oneself for the purpose of pleasure.

Noncoercive Paraphilias In this category of paraphilias, coercion is not involved. Because of this difference, the burden of diagnosis is based upon the paraphiliac person feeling distress and other signs of internal conflict that disrupt typical functioning at home, work, school, or other important places.

Consider the case of Carl, a 23-year-old graduate student whose raincoat fetish sexually arouses him. Carl does enjoy sex with his girlfriend, but he also enjoys a secret sexual thing he does alone, with raincoats, which leads him to masturbate to orgasm. He keeps this behavior secret because he fears people in general and his girlfriend in particular will think he is weird. But he is not impaired psychologically and does not feel distressed by his behavior. According to the *DSM-5,* this type of behavior is a normal variation of human sexuality for some people. The day arrived when Carl's girlfriend did discover him in the act of being aroused by a raincoat, and she reacted with disgust and horror. She ranted about it, so much so that Carl felt guilty, then depressed. Eventually he accepted her opinion that he is weird and diseased. He now feels he has a mental illness, and he suffers from acute distress. Examples of this kind are common and have prompted psychiatrists to consider whether to remove this type of sexual behavior from the *DSM* and categorize it as normal (Derogatis et al., 2010; Moser, 2016).

Sadism, Masochism, and Sexual Sadism Disorder The term "S and M" refers to sadism (S) and masochism (M), which are sexual practices that involve giving and receiving pain (or intense sensations that can be perceived as pain), suffering, or humiliation. **Sadism** is inflicting pain on one's sexual partner in order to create sexual pleasure for the person inflicting the pain. Its counterpart is **masochism,** which is receiving painful stimulation for the purpose of pleasure. Sadism and masochism together create a complex system of sexual practices (Stoller, 1991). In fact, S and M behaviors are difficult to categorize as either coercive or noncoercive because they may or may not involve distress to the individual or pose a problem of consent, because some adults willingly consent to these sexual practices.

Sexual sadism disorder occurs alongside many different paraphilias because the impulse to inflict pain and humiliation is a recurrent urge, and the act sexually excites the person inflicting the pain. Also, some sadists may not be able to completely control

The Marquis de Sade, for whom sadism is named, was an 18th century French aristocrat whose erotic writings and nonnormative sexual behavior landed him in prison and an insane asylum. In this illustration, he is surrounded by horned demons and a satyr having sex with a mermaid.
The Art Gallery Collection/Alamy Stock Photo

their behaviors with their partners, creating a gray area when it comes to paraphilia, because inflicting suffering on someone else against his or her will fits the most important *DSM* criteria.

Sexual masochism disorder can involve a wide variety of behaviors, from seemingly mild behaviors such as spanking, whipping, or pulling hair to more extreme situations such as tying people up, cutting the body, sticking objects such as light bulbs or carrots up the rectum, or having sex long enough to experience acute pain in the genital area. Many an emergency room doctor can tell stories about retrieving all manner of things from people's rectums, such as pool balls that were being used to create pain and pleasure in the heat of passion. These examples illustrate the extreme edges of sexual compulsivity and behaviors that clearly involve risk even when consent occurs.

As previously noted, the whole area of **BDSM**—bondage/discipline (BD) and sadism/masochism (SM)—is problematic when we think about paraphilic disorders, due to what is now more mainstream and consensual and what can be pushing the boundary. BDSM, as a more general practice, is like Kink because it does not necessarily involve sexual arousal for all people on all occasions. BDSM involves power plays and role playing, such as pretending to be a police officer and convict, or a teacher and student. These roles may or may not move into more extreme sexual behaviors involving BD or SM. BDSM thus qualifies as a form of more general kinky sex because it is typically consensual. It is no longer classified as a paraphilic disorder, and it has been removed from the *DSM*. Importantly, BDSM also does not appear typically to cause distress for people engaging in these behaviors. BDSM now seems more common because many online venues, periodicals, and associations help people to locate partners who prefer BDSM to other forms of sexual activity (Moser, 2006). Leather clothes and other paraphernalia identified with BDSM are available in shops and online, as is BDSM pornography.

Consensual sado-masochism among adults was removed from the *DSM-5* as a sexual disorder, even though the connection to mental illness remains significant for some mental health providers. This example of change in labeling a sexual behavior as a disorder and then later changing that label is the issue discussed in "Controversies in Sexuality: Are Kinky Behaviors Abnormal or Just a Variation of Human Sexuality?"

Transvestic Disorder In transvestic disorder, men get sexually aroused by wearing women's clothes. Typically, transvestic disorder involves heterosexual men from an older generation (Money, 1986; Stoller, 1986). It is not the act of cross-dressing itself that is a paraphilia; that is very common. Rather, it's how they may be distressed by being aroused in that context. Some of these fetishists are aroused by the feel of the soft clothes, such as nylons, against the skin, sometimes combined with the smells and sensations of dressing and applying makeup. Notice that there is no coercion involved here; the object is the clothing, not a person. Also note that this kind of fetishism should not be confused with being transgender or transsexual, which is a gender identity, not a paraphilia.

Fetishistic Disorder In fetishistic disorder, individuals are aroused from either the use of nonliving objects or a highly specific focus on nongenital body part(s). The fetish objects are not limited to articles of clothing used in cross-dressing (as in transvestic disorder) or devices specifically designed for the purpose of tactile genital stimulation (e.g., vibrators).

Autoerotic Asphyxiophilia One of the most peculiar noncoercive paraphilias is **autoerotic asphyxiophilia,** which is sexual arousal by near suffocation. Individuals who engage in this practice choke or suffocate themselves to get sexually aroused; when oxygen is cut off

Today BDSM is not considered a psychiatric disorder as long as it is consensual between adult partners.
Howard Kingsnorth/Getty Images

BDSM
Refers to bondage/discipline (BD) and sadism/masochism (SM); power plays and role acting that is not necessarily sexual.

autoerotic asphyxiophilia
A form of fetishistic arousal from near suffocation.

CONTROVERSIES in Sexuality

Are Kinky Behaviors Abnormal or Just a Variation of Human Sexuality?

Would it be better to say that Kink, or kinky sex, is just a lifestyle that is not for everyone, rather than label it as a paraphilic disorder? If it's considered just a sexual variation, then engaging in kinky becomes a matter of individual choice and pleasure rather than a disease or mental illness. As we read earlier, many clinicians and researchers now question whether it is accurate to label everyone who has a paraphilia as if they were in need of treatment (Derogatis et al., 2010).

The question, then, is this: Is it better for society to allow individual sexual variation and sexual freedom than to label it as disorder and mental illness?

Yes:

- It would be better to totally drop outdated psychiatric models and stereotypes because they belong to another era when everyone was expected to conform to one mode of sexual behavior in Western societies—namely, face-to-face sex between a man and a woman only within legal marriage.
- It's the classic problem of victimless crimes—that is, consenting adults doing what they want in their own bedroom with no one being hurt against their will.
- The controversy continues to erupt in the basic issues of how therapists provide treatment (Kolmes, Stock, & Moser, 2006).
- Experts say that many people who have paraphilias don't harm anyone, are not psychologically impaired, and might find partners who enjoy the same pleasures, such as rough anal sex.

No:

- Society needs to set boundaries between what is normal and abnormal in sexual behavior because some people are not capable of setting such boundaries for themselves.
- Evidence shows that paraphilic disorders continue to be a serious problem for certain people, and people can get out of control with them.
- People can be hurt or can kill themselves, even if by accident, with some forms of BDSM if they don't realize what they are getting into.
- Some doctors say society needs the category of paraphilic disorder because labeling some sexual behaviors may help prevent some people from sexually acting out against others or from coming into conflict with the law, even being imprisoned. Sexual freedom has limits.

What's Your Perspective?

1. What does the concept of paraphilic disorder mean to you? Can you distinguish between a paraphilia that does not cause distress or harm, and a paraphilic disorder?
2. If it is better to let people exercise extreme sexual behavior, what should they do to protect themselves from unplanned harm?
3. Do you know people who engage in paraphilic sexual behaviors, and if you do, how do you relate to them, or do you just avoid them?

---

suddenly people may experience feelings of giddiness and pleasure not unlike the feelings experienced during masturbation. This behavior can lead to accidental death (Janssen, Koops, Anders, Kuhn, & Püschel, 2005). Actor David Carradine and Michael Hutchence, the lead singer of the band INXS, may have accidentally killed themselves while engaged in this risky form of sexual behavior.

AB/DL These initials stand for the paraphilia of adult baby and diaper lover fetishism, also known as paraphilic infantilism. **AB/DL** is expressed when an adult dresses and acts as a baby and wants the adult partner to treat him or her as a baby. Being spanked, being wrapped in diapers, and being cuddled but also being humiliated as a baby is part of this paraphilia. Most AB/DL are heterosexual men (APA, 2000). This paraphilia is not to be confused with pedophilia (Seto, 2008).

Mass media and popular culture may contribute to many people knowing about paraphilias, including some of the rarest ones. For example, websites exist for a paraphilia that

AB/DL

A type of fetishism in which an adult dresses as a baby and the adult partner treats him or her like a baby; also called *paraphilic infantilism*.

was once unknown to the general public: **abasiophilia,** which is the sexual attraction to people who use leg braces. Another fetishism popularized by media is **robot fetishism,** which is sexual arousal brought on by a robot or androidlike being. The TV series *Futurama* refers to robot-lovers as "robosexuals." The media can make an unusual sexual behavior seem less threatening, even quaint. Perhaps one day some of these behaviors considered paraphilias will be considered normal. Let's consider how paraphilic behaviors begin. At least three theories can help explain this answer, which we discuss next.

abasiophilia
Sexual attraction to *people* who use leg braces.

robot fetishism
Arousal to a robot or androidlike being.

Theories of Origins of Paraphilias

Many factors contribute to someone expressing a paraphilia. Even in the most studied paraphilias, such as pedophilia, not much is known about the causes or why they develop in one person and not in another (Finkelhor, 1984; Howells, 1994; Klein, 2003; Seto, 2008). Psychoanalytic, behavioral, and sociobiological theories, however, have emerged to explain how individuals may develop paraphilias.

Psychoanalytic Theory Psychoanalytic theory focuses on inner conflict and unresolved incestuous fantasies and how these may lead to paraphilias. It also focuses on obsessions, such as the unconscious male fear of castration. Freud (1905) suggested that paraphilias result from the unsuccessful negotiation of conflicts that begin in childhood. If a person's psychosexual development did not progress normally from these childhood conflicts, the person may develop sexual urges that are expressed at a later time as a paraphilia. Few researchers and practitioners take a strict psychoanalytic approach in the study of human behavior; however, when sexuality professionals and educators discuss the possible origins of paraphilias, many argue that these behaviors are rooted in early childhood experiences (Stoller, 1986, 1991).

Another theory traces the early development of paraphilias to courtship behavior between males and females, with the purpose of mating (Brannon, 2010). Courtship behavior usually begins during adolescence and progresses for a few years. For some, it may involve sexual intercourse at a younger age of sexual development and for others at an older age. Four sequential phases make up this behavior:

1. Attraction to a potential partner
2. Initial sexual interaction that includes behaviors such as talking or flirting but not touching
3. Sexual interaction that is tactile, such as hugging, kissing, and hand-holding
4. Sexual intercourse

Although most people engage in these four courtship phases appropriately, some people may not adhere to these socially acceptable norms. Thus, others may view any extreme sexual practices as exaggerations of any one of the four phases of courtship or all of them (Freund, 1990; Brannon, 2010).

According to psychoanalytic theory, distortions of the courtship sequence are associated only with the first three phases, leading up to the actual sexual expression or gratification. One example of this distortion in the first phase is voyeurism (Stoller, 1985, 1986). The theory suggests that voyeurism may be manifest in boys who witness many episodes of their parents engaged in sexual intercourse. These experiences may hinder their development of social and sexual skills, which may then develop into voyeurism as an outlet for sexual pleasure as an alternative to sexual interaction. Ultimately such a mechanism may fail to protect them from anxiety or fear of discovery and loss of their masculinity (Stoller, 1986).

The concept of love maps is based in psychoanalytic theory (Money, 1986). **Love maps,** which are brain templates for attraction and sexual expression, emerge around the

love map
A cognitive template for attraction and sexual expression believed to develop in childhood.

age of 8 or 9 years and are usually well developed by puberty. A love map may combine both the image of an idealized lover and the script and technique for sexual action. Such abnormal love maps might be the result of any number of factors or stressors during this developmental period, such as restrictive attitudes around sexuality, punishment for sexual rehearsal play, a lack of close attachment and love from parents, traumatic experiences that leave lifelong scars, or desires that children are afraid to express. Ultimately, paraphilias might be abnormal love maps that develop in childhood (Money, 1986).

Behavioral Theory   Behavioral theory and the process of conditioning may be how certain paraphilias develop. Paraphilias are a result of conditioning in which a stimulus and a response become accidentally "hardwired" for sexual pleasure in a person (Brannon, 2010). If a nonsexual object is repeatedly associated with a pleasurable sexual activity, the object becomes sexually arousing. In fact, it may become so powerful that a person may not be able to control the sexual urge. For example, consider a young boy who hides in his mother's closet to masturbate. Several pairs of high-heeled shoes are also in the closet. He masturbates to orgasm with all the shoes in his field of vision. If he continues this behavior regularly, he might become conditioned to become sexually aroused just looking at a pair of high-heeled shoes. Just touching the shoes may give him an erection. That positive reinforcement can set off a chain reaction in sexual development that may lead to extreme sexual behaviors as the outcome.

If a person experiences unpleasant consequences with normal sexual activity, such as profound guilt and shame, an aversion to sex may occur, resulting in different kinds of potentially negative outcomes. Such negative reinforcement can be a powerful barrier to optimal sexual development and perhaps even lead to the avoidance of intimacy, which as mentioned earlier, is a component of certain paraphilias. An example of this would be a young boy whose parents humiliate and punish him for proudly displaying his erect penis. If he learns to associate an erection with guilt and shame, later he may be unable to sustain erection during sex, creating sexual dysfunction. If, in turn, he attempts to counter this shame by inflicting humiliation or pain on someone else in order to feel an erection, that behavior may result in a paraphilic disorder.

Sociobiological Theory   Sociobiology is the study of the biological aspects of behavior. In the treatment of paraphilias, a genetic theory has emerged that in a very general way connects genetic variations to the extremes of human sexual behavior (Dawkins, 1989). These extreme variations, perhaps even paraphilias, are seen as indirectly related to the survival of the species (Gardner, 1993). According to this view, different paraphilias may enhance an individual's level of sexual excitation through a process of adaptation that results in increased procreation, and thus survival of the species (Buss, 2008). That is, with greater sexual excitation, even when forced, there is more reproduction.

Treatment of Paraphilic Disorders

There are in sexual science a few types of treatments that suggest the potential to help people deal with their paraphilic disorders. Some of these treatments help many types of problems, such as 12-step programs that are applied to alcoholism and other addictions. Those who do seek treatment vary according to several factors, including the following:

1. *Self-distress and sexual dysfunction:* People may seek treatment because they cannot continue to feel distressed all the time. Their distress may also involve sexual dysfunction because they may not be able to respond to intimacy or other typical sexual cues and pleasures.
2. *Court-ordered treatment:* Convicted sex offenders are sometimes ordered to undergo therapy so they are no longer threats to society.

3. *Couples therapy and relationship distress:* These people seek resources to cope with a variety of issues related to their sexuality. The issues may involve paraphilias or extreme sexual behaviors.

People suffering from sexual problems may find help by using one or more of the following types of structured clinical treatments:

- Cognitive-behavioral therapy, which may help people to recondition their sexual behaviors. This approach has proven to be increasingly popular and successful.
- Social skills training, which may be applied to how people handle intimacy, and thus help them relate to sexual partners better.
- Twelve-step programs, historically modeled on Alcoholics Anonymous (AA), may help people when they think they cannot control their sexual urges, including the challenge of compulsive sexual behavior. These programs are available around the globe.
- Group psycho- and sexual therapy, which may help people to overcome shame and guilt, and, perhaps, overcome past trauma.
- Individual supportive psychotherapy, which can support a person's desire and need to change.
- Medications, such as anti-androgens, psychiatric drugs, prescribed by a psychiatrist or physician, which may enable people to address coexisting conditions which might be responsible for the lack of impulse control or compulsive behavior.

Now we will move on to consider the more general issue of what is extreme cultural variation and individual sexual expression.

FROM NORMATIVE TO EXTREME SEXUAL BEHAVIORS

As we have observed, cultures vary greatly in terms of being more sex-positive and approving of sexual variations or more sex-negative and disapproving of sexual behaviors. In general, sex-positive societies allow greater variations in sexual expression and make some allowances for what we will call extreme sexual behavior. But it is important to compare how cultures also vary greatly in what they define or label as normative or extreme when it comes to human sexual behavior. Extreme does not necessarily mean pathological or diseased in another culture; it means that it goes further than the norm and may even be regarded within the community as extreme enough that most people would never do it. See the discussion in "Healthy Sexuality: How the Vibrator Went from Extreme Sexual Behavior to Walmart Merchandise."

Now let's apply this knowledge of sexual literacy to detail how cultures handle normative or acceptable and kinky or extreme and unacceptable sexual behaviors. Specifically, how do they link the definition of extreme sexuality to their own perceptions and values? In addition, let's include our own Western diagnostic criteria of psychiatry to make the evaluation.

1. All cultures have sexual norms that serve as a blueprint for how to behave sexually and moral rules and laws to enforce these norms.
2. The vast majority of people in a society conform to these sexual norms in their private sexual relationships—the sexual mainstream of the society, though that mainstream may include harmless variations such as mild pain for pleasure between consenting adults (Laumann et al., 1994).
3. However, a small number of people do not conform to these mainstream sexual norms, at least not all of the time. Instead, they express their sexual individuality in terms of sexual novelty, romantic creativity, and sexual experimentation online or virtually; this

HEALTHY Sexuality

How the Vibrator Went from Extreme Sexual Behavior to Walmart Merchandise

Vibrators are mechanical devices designed to stimulate the skin, body, and genitals. They may be inserted in the vagina or rectum to arouse people sexually to create pleasure. There are many myths surrounding them, and they have a very strange history.

The use of vibrators was once considered so extreme, kinky, and abnormal that the mere possession of a vibratory device was illegal and cause for being arrested, imprisoned, and stigmatized. In fact, vibrators were illegal or implicitly so everywhere at one time. Why? In part it is because vibrators are associated with masturbation, which was once regarded as abnormal in Western society, and in part it is because vibrators are associated with female sexual liberation and pleasure (Maines, 1999). Thus, vibrators were regarded as sinful, immoral, and way out of the mainstream of what the culture would tolerate within the spectrum of sexual behavior.

Consider the strange parallel mythology of "hysteria"—one of the most commonly diagnosed sexual conditions of the 19th century. In the late 19th century, in major Western capitals such as London, New York, Vienna, and Boston, women were routinely diagnosed with a psychiatric disorder then known as *hysteria,* a gendered sexual dysfunction historically believed to be associated with the uterus from centuries ago. In that era, it was medically treated by pelvic massages that were much like masturbation (Maines, 1999). The funny, ironic film, *Hysteria* (2011), tells how a young British doctor invented and used the electric vibrator in that era to treat upwards of half the upper-class women in London because they were suffering hysteria. In reality, hysteria was tied to their sexuality and was characterized by symptoms of irritability, intense emotional reactions, and sexual frustration—aka, feeling "horny" or sexually repressed, as well described in European history (Foucault, 1980). Only decades later, as primitive vibrators became available in the mid-20th century, couples would sneak to "adult bookstores," often located on the edges of towns, to purchase vibrators and other sex toys. Way into the 1990s and beyond, vibrators were still regarded as indecent, shameful, or banned.

Today, vibrators are clearly part of the mainstream. In fact, today 50% of women and 33% of men use vibrator/dildos (Herbenick et al., 2017). Vibrators are available from numerous online stores and Amazon and are sold not only in urban shopping mall stores but recently at Walmart!

includes certain extreme sexual behaviors that may be perceived as outside of the mainstream that are suppressed or hidden because they create risk but are generally harmless to the consenting adults involved.

4. Then, there is an even smaller number of people who engage in sexual variations that are defined by the cultures as abnormal and classified as paraphilias because they involve sexual arousal to individuals, objects, or situations who cannot or do not give consent and are regarded by definition in the community as inappropriate and unacceptable.

5. In Western society, then, we can regard an extreme sexual behavior as needing a diagnosis if and only if it results from any of three conditions: (1) a lack of consent for practicing a certain sexual act in a relationship; (2) it makes someone into a victim and causes them distress; or, (3) the sexual behavior distresses the person doing it to such an extent that it interferes with daily functioning.

Cultural Extremes of Sexuality

Just because a sexual behavior occurs in one society does not mean that it is common in other societies and certainly does not mean that it is universal. What this means is that there are, even across different societies, some behaviors that we can consider cultural extremes.

For example, historically, oral sex was regarded as strange or foreign, and it was seldom practiced in the United States, but in the previous generation it came to be a majority sexual pattern (Laumann et al., 1994; Herbenick et al., 2017). Today among Western societies, oral sex is fairly common, if not in fact normative. However, there are a variety of contemporary non-Western societies in which oral sex is considered rare or so extreme as to never be practiced.

But now let's examine one non-Western society in which the opposite seems true. Among the Sambia of Papua New Guinea, oral sex in which an older guy was fellated or sucked, was once the universal form of sexual debut for all boys and girls. This is because it was part of their ritual initiations and normative cycle of how heterosexual relations began. Since the introduction of Christianity there, oral sex has all but vanished as a sexual practice, and societal changes have made vaginal sex the very strong normative practice (Herdt, 2019). In other words, after social change, the Sambia have altered their view of what was culturally normative and culturally extreme, and they now resemble a Western culture in their sexual expression.

Cross-culturally there are many sexual behaviors that at first glance might seem bizarre or even abnormal compared to what might be considered risky sex in Western societies. When we look closer, however, these sexual practices often have meaning, integrity, and broad acceptance in their own context (Foucault, 1980; Greenberg, 1988; Herdt, 1997a, 2009; Herdt & Stoller, 1990; Lyons & Lyons, 2011; Money & Ehrhardt, 1972; Stoller, 1991).

Some sexual behaviors that would be considered extreme in U.S. society are normative and may be associated with social or religious ceremonies and rituals in cultures such as the Sambia of Papua New Guinea, among many others (Hirsch et al., 2009). Cultural practices that might seem risky in the United States include combining sex with practices such as harsh sexual taboos, cutting the skin, ritual beatings, fasting, and special food taboos (Herdt, 2006). In some societies, people also use substances, such as alcoholic beverages or mood-altering substances or plants, in the context of sexual behavior (Diaz, 1998; Gregor, 1985; Herdt, 2009a; Mead, 1961).

By the same token, sexual behavior initiated at a young age is considered extreme or abnormal in the United States. Consider how the Kung people allow casual sexual exploration and even sexual aggression by young boys toward young girls (Shostak, 1980). Another example is found among the Trobriand Islanders of the South Seas, who encourage casual and pleasurable sexual exploration in childhood as well as extensive teenage sexual partnering before marriage—and the more the better (Lepani, 2012). At the peak of orgasm, Trobriand lovers, who are facing each other in the unusual sexual position of a woman's thighs resting on top of her partner's while he has penetrated her vaginally, are roused to such passion that they may bite each other's eyelashes (Lepani, 2012; Malinowski, 1929).

Many cultures have extreme sanctions against extramarital sex, including the United States, and some societies even punish it with death (Hirsch et al., 2009). But the Mehinaku people of Brazil have multiple continuous extramarital relationships that are a subject of village life. In fact, they believe that having plenty of sex is good and natural, including sex with other people's spouses (Gregor, 1985, 1996). Mehinaku children grow up knowing that adult men and women have lovers other than their spouses. They take pride in it, as can be seen from the fact that children can name their parents' extramarital lovers. This notion that people are not monogamous and it is normal to desire other people's sexual partners is extreme compared to prescribed sexual norms in the United States.

There are a variety of cultures in which sexual aggression is so extreme that rape and sexual violence are daily hazards for women (Sanday, 2007). These cultures train warriors to express their masculinity through sexual intimidation and even rape (Herdt, 2006; Hirsch et al., 2009; Mead, 1961). Many cultures that

In the Pacific Islands, traditional body tattoos are considered sexually attractive.
Anders Ryman/Corbis NX/Getty Images

emphasize patriarchy and male dominance, as well as close emotional bonds between males, allow men to be sexually aggressive toward women, even using rape as a means of controlling women (Sanday, 1981b, 2007; Shostak, 1981). Increasingly, however, experts argue that rape as an extreme sexual behavior is found in cultures that have suffered a disruption of positive relationships between the genders due to natural disasters or wars or the breakdown of society due to globalization and issues of refugee survival (Correa, Petchesky, & Parker, 2008; Sanday, 1981a; UN Refugee Agency, 2018).

It can be difficult to determine what a culture's norms are about sexual behavior. At first it may seem like certain sexual behaviors are spontaneous, but after close observation, the sexual norms of a culture may create a pattern. One example relates to cunnilingus. In the mid-1950s, it was discovered that about 45% of men engaged in cunnilingus (Kinsey et al., 1948). Nevertheless, many American men continued to dislike cunnilingus and treated it as an extreme sexual behavior to avoid; some even felt it was repugnant (Laumann et al., 1994). By the 1980s, however, 93% of heterosexual couples had engaged in cunnilingus (Blumstein & Schwartz, 1983). By comparison, whole cultural areas of the world, such as the southwestern Pacific Islands, where cunnilingus was unknown as a sexual behavior, still treat it as abnormal (Herdt, 1993, 2019).

Another example of a harmless sexual behavior that one culture considers typical and another culture thinks is extreme is French kissing, placing the tongue in a partner's mouth, or vice versa. In the United States and many western European cultures, French kissing is considered completely normal. But in South Pacific island countries, such as Papua New Guinea, French kissing was totally unknown in traditional times, and until recently was repugnant because kissing and mixing bodily fluids, especially saliva, is tabooed (Herdt, 2019). In short, what the people of one culture think are extreme sexual behaviors another group may not.

Extreme Sexual Behaviors in Contemporary Society

What does the range of variation in extreme sexual behavior (ESB) look like in American society? Extreme sexual behaviors such as "bondage and sadism," where people appear to be craving a release and may risk pain or bodily damage to indulge themselves, seem to challenge the limits of pain tolerance and are apparently more common than in the past (Stoller, 1985). Before answering the question, let's compare how extreme sexual behaviors are like or unlike extreme sports that have either potential risk or inherent danger if pushed far enough.

There is something about pushing oneself to the limits in extreme sports, and especially among young men, but increasingly in young women, too, that goes far beyond what many in the mainstream would do or want to do. Not only that: The practitioners of extreme sports, such as certain kinds of rock climbing or surfing, are very proud of it. To be sure, extreme sports have very real elements of life-threatening daredevil risk and may result in injury and even death. They include activities such as free-falling while skydiving, certain types of extreme snowboarding or skateboarding, caving and, especially under the threat of landslide, ice climbing, mountain climbing the most dangerous peaks (such as Mt. Everest, where climbers routinely die), bull-fighting, reckless motor racing, and so on. Notice that many of these sports are mostly done by men, although there is growing interest among some women, too (Wallace, 2009). Extreme sports can be very intense and exhilarating, in part, because people know they are risky, and because men may associate them with feelings of high achievement, honor, and pride, that is, extreme masculinity. Many athletes who participate in extreme sports say that they love the adrenaline rush that comes from the risk (Wallace, 2009). It is a rush not unlike the feeling that some report when they experience extreme sexual expression.

In fact, some experts have suggested that historically at least, adult **sado-masochism relationships,** or S/M, are examples of extreme sexual behaviors because they featured pain and pleasure, bondage, and practices such as spanking and whipping. The physicality of these sexual experiences, whipping, spanking, and others described below, lends itself to

sado-masochism relationships (S/M)
Relationships that may involve pain and pleasure, bondage, and other practices, such as spanking and whipping.

a sense of risk that things will get out of control. In fact, perhaps control is a key to understanding the rush.

For example, it is well reported that people who engage in the rituals of bondage and sado-masochism for pleasure are highly concerned about control and risk. These are sexual practices that occur between consenting adults, and due to the very detailed negotiated rules and routines, the ESBs have been likened to a ritual, with precise behavioral rules, boundaries, and pain limits that partners impose and must observe or else lose their sexual partners (Stoller, 1986). People in ongoing S/M relationships are able to control themselves, or at least they try to in order to maintain work and a regular social life, and they have perspective on the risk-taking involved. This is different from those who have such strong compulsions that they get out of control and threaten their livelihood, families, and even life itself.

Contemporary examples of extreme sexual behaviors include engaging in frequent online sex, combining drugs with sex at parties, toying with being infected with an STI, having anonymous sex, and engaging in numerous casual relationships, including with partners who are married or as an extramarital relationship. As long as the individual maintains boundaries and is not distressed by these activities and no one else is harmed, there may not be an issue as far as society is concerned. In other words, extreme—not normative, but not a disease.

Yet ESBs are risky or unusual enough or both to be perceived as being outside the mainstream and thus open to more surveillance or scrutiny than society usually applies to individual sexual expression.

Extreme behaviors like rock climbing are an adrenaline rush to some people.
Ingram Publishing

As long as the laws are not broken, society is generally not drawn into these issues. But when the risks mount, and people get hurt—not unlike what happens when too many people are injured or killed in an extreme sport, and new policies and laws are passed to protect people from themselves—then there is a red flag. The risk can be physical, mental, or social. In the case of a social risk from practicing an ESB such as BDSM, it may be in the form of disapproval with a stigma that harms their reputation, if it becomes known in a community that someone is into kinky sex. Or the risk may arise from social avoidance: When someone abuses alcohol or drugs or both and then has intense sexual interactions, people will avoid them as sexual partners out of fear of disease or pregnancy. Nevertheless, these examples make them extreme sexual behaviors rather than paraphilias because the risk is somewhat controlled, involves consenting adults, and does not necessarily cause distress or impair someone's daily functioning, at least not at first. The point will be obvious: Extreme sexual behaviors are not for everyone, and for a lot of people they can be a total turn-off.

But please note: When something is so extreme, and friends or family get involved, and the person does not connect their risk taking to distress or suffering, or they pretend that what they are doing is not risky or harmful to themselves or others, then something is amiss. In short, they may be in **denial,** which is a form of coping with fear or anxiety that involves distortion of reality. ESB denial can have very negative consequences for life and well-being. Consider some statements that you might hear from people who use denial as a way to cope with situations that may be risky or that others might condemn for not meeting societal expectations in "Communication Matters: Listening for Denial about Sexual Risk."

denial
A form of coping with fear or anxiety that involves distortion of reality and its perception.

Kinky Sex

One of the more frequently practiced forms of ESB, already mentioned, has to do with what is called kinky sex or just Kink. It may include a variety of sexual interests that are serious or playful, creative or ritualized, and it may include extreme sexual behaviors such as role playing,

COMMUNICATION Matters

Listening for Denial About Sexual Risk

Some people cope with risk by not facing it, and they even go to great lengths to try to pretend or imagine that they are invulnerable. In addition, they may not realize that they are in denial of reality. Learning to listen for friends' and lovers' statements of denial can help to ensure that their participating in extreme sexual behaviors does not go too far. Consider these possible scenarios:

- A close friend repeatedly engages in hooking up online with total strangers and agrees to meet with them for sex in person. Yet your friend claims there is no risk.
- Denial of the risk of unintended pregnancy or protection from an STI may sound something like this: "I take the pill but sometimes I forget," or "I expect my partner to use a condom, but I'm not sure it always happens."
- A close friend who has been the victim of abuse appears to be avoiding dealing with the pain and trauma. Listening for statements of denial about ordeals like these may provide opportunities for you to suggest resources to help.
- You have friends who occasionally engage in risky sex after becoming intoxicated at parties. They remark casually, "Oh, we only spent the night together once, so I didn't need protection."
- Your friend appears to be having a passionate relationship but may not be taking care due to the demands of the intimate partner. That denial may sound something like this: "In a moment of passion, I just lost it and got carried away."

Encountering situations in which people appear to use denial as a way to cope can be a challenge if you care about them. Sometimes the most helpful thing is just to listen to let them know that you care. Other times you can reflect back to your loved ones what they have said, which may make their denial more apparent. That may lead them to seek support, guidance, or additional resources to take care of themselves and their sexual well-being.

---

dominance and submission, spanking, and tickling. Note that the practitioners of Kink are in general very careful to practice among consenting adults. Kink can involve practices known today as BDSM, which stands for *bondage/discipline, dominance/submission, sadism/masochism*. Obviously, Kink contains practices, such as whipping or pinching, that are present in some sexual cultures around the world. While it is not normative in America, it does not have the clinical characteristics of a paraphilia. BDSM is now regarded by psychologists as paraphilia, due to the fact that some adults engage in this practice voluntarily and without distress (Yakeley & Wood, 2014). For individuals engaging in BDSM, who "declare no distress, exemplified by anxiety, obsessions, guilt, or shame, about these paraphilic impulses, and are not hampered by them in pursuing other personal goals, they could be ascertained as having masochistic sexual interest but should not be diagnosed with sexual masochism disorder." (DSM-5, p. 694)

WHAT'S ON YOUR MIND?

Q: I read an article in a popular women's magazine the other day that detailed stories about people's sexual encounters. Some of the things being discussed just seemed kind of weird to me. Will people think I'm a prude if I don't want to engage in these kinds of behaviors?

ANSWER: The realm of sexual experiences that people have today is vast. What seems odd to you may seem completely normal to someone else. Of course, you get to decide what kinds of experiences you want to have and which ones cross your boundaries. Your responsibility is to communicate openly your desires and needs. Just as you hope people will not judge you for the kinds of behaviors you do not want to engage in, you'll need to refrain from judging people who enjoy different experiences. As long as people aren't forcing others to do something they don't want to do, there is an incredible variation of sexual activity to engage in and enjoy.

One of the characteristics of kinky sex is sexual fetishism. **Sexual fetishism** is when an object or body part, whether a raincoat or buttocks, arouses intense sexual interest and urges. Sexual fetishes might include practices such as sniffing people's underwear or sucking on people's toes. Generally, these are totally noncoercive and may be playful or harmless. In fact, some individuals and couples believe that kinky sexual practices increase their sense of intimacy and love together (Stoller, 1991; Sagarin, Cutler, Cutler, Lawler-Sagarin, & Matuszewich, 2009). For example, research reveals that across studies, both bottoms (sexual receptors) and tops (active sexual insertors) experienced increases in relationship closeness (Sagarin et al., 2009, p. 196). These practices may occur among all orientations, whether heterosexual, gay, and lesbian couples or people who are single. Traditionally Kink was more common among men than women, but the gender ratio is changing rapidly, as a recent study of 1,580 female participants in the Kink community reveals (Rehor, 2015).

A Furry couple enjoys a romantic moment.
nullplus/Getty Images

One of the relatively new and seemingly harmless ESBs is called *Furries*, people who are interested in dressing up to look like certain animals, such as playing the role of tiger or bear, and sometimes engaging in sexual relationships in costume. It is not clear how much kinky sex actually goes on in the Furry community, when they kiss, hug, play at sex, or just hang out together (Evans, 2008). What makes this more of an ESB is that some individual Furries go to such lengths as having surgery on their faces or bodies to actually look like the animal they play—for example, having artificial facial whiskers implanted in their own face to resemble a tiger's face. Approximately one-third of the people who are Furries are sexually attracted to other Furries. Supposedly the mega-hit movie *Avatar* led to many Furry imitations of its imaginary planetary characters (Handy, 2009). Sexual interest in creatures seems to have increased as media and technology have projected their image into society (Padva, 2005).

In these gray areas of kinky sex and mild pain and sexual pleasure, individuals vary in what they will do to achieve arousal and gratification. Before we go further in thinking about the meaning of these behaviors, ask this: Do you enjoy a playful bite on your neck or some other mild form of pain, such as spanking, while having sex? How far do you let yourself go with this potential—in fantasy or reality—when it comes to kinky sexual practices? To think more about these questions in relation to your own sexual individuality, read "Know Yourself: What Do You Consider Pleasurable Sex?"

sexual fetishism
An object or body part that arouses intense sexual interest and urges, and may launch a person into an uncontrollable episode alone or with another person, typically leading to sexual gratification.

Sex Tourism and Extreme Sexuality

For centuries, people have traveled to other lands in search of food, land, wealth, and sex (Gagnon, 1997). Whether it was ancient Greeks as told in the classics more than 2,000 years ago, or Captain Cook and the voyages he and his crew took through the South Seas in the 18th century, or sexual activity taken by many GIs in Thailand and Southeast Asia during the Vietnam War in the 1960s and 1970s, sex was always part of this adventuring (Jolly, 1997). This sexual adventuring is sometimes viewed as extreme sexual behavior, and it may move into sex work or sexual exploitation of adults and adolescents (Padilla, 2008). Sexual explorers may have encountered sexual practices that are now considered kinky sex because they most likely found sexual norms in other cultures that were different from their own, which are far more open and sex-positive than Western societies (Jolly, 1997).

In the 21st century, however, we are more aware of the challenge to basic human rights and sexual rights that comes from tourists' sexual adventuring and exploitation of the bodies of women, men, and children. Experts often refer to **sex tourism** as prostitution tourism, which means traveling for the purpose of having sex in return for the security of food,

sex tourism
Traveling for the purpose of having sex in return for money or goods.

Know Yourself

What Do You Consider Pleasurable Sex?

Test your own feelings about what is pleasurable and kinky by taking the following quick self-assessment. To help determine how you feel about each question, answer using this scale:

1 – Never   2 – Almost never   3 – Sometimes   4 – Often   5 – Always

1. Anal sex is enjoyable to me.
2. To struggle but eventually be taken by my partner in a passionate manner is enjoyable to me.
3. I enjoy being tied up with a scarf or some restraint that I can get out of easily because it feels exciting to me.
4. I enjoy being spanked sometimes, but not too hard.
5. I enjoy wearing sexy clothes that are so revealing that some people might say I am exposing myself.
6. I like my intimate partner to handle me roughly.
7. Oral sex is very pleasurable to me and I can't get enough of it.
8. Watching porn with my partner to get aroused is very exciting to me.
9. I can get turned on easily watching other people have sex.
10. I like seeing two people of the same sex make out because it arouses me.
11. I like my partner to play with my genitals to the extent that sometimes I feel sore afterward.
12. I like to act out my fantasies of being treated like a naughty schoolchild by my partner who then gets aroused to have sex with me.
13. I really like sex toys and want to use them to get aroused when I make love.
14. The idea of my partner bringing home a stranger to have sex with us in a three-way is exciting.
15. I like dressing up in the clothes of the opposite gender and pretending that I am like that when I have sex with my partner.

Now score yourself. If you answer with all "1s," meaning all "never," you would score 15 points and may find plain vanilla sex pleasurable. If you answer with all 5s (all "always"), you would score 75 points and may find very kinky sex pleasurable.

Points	
61—75 points	Very kinky sex
46—60 points	
32—45 points	Moderately kinky sex
16—30 points	
0—15 points	Vanilla sex

money, housing, or luxuries like cell phones (Puccia, 2009). This form of sex work is strongly related to poverty, the absence of household security for youths who migrate to cities, and the inability to find other gainful employment (Correa et al., 2008).

The Internet revolutionized sex tourism, enabling people from different cultures to connect virtually first. Then, after viewing a video or photo of a sex worker online, the person can arrange to visit to have sex in reality (Padilla, 2008). Platforms such as Facebook, GRINDR, online dating services, and adult sexual entertainment websites are all potential springboards for the collective fantasy of virtual romance and real-life sexual encounters (Boellstorff, 2008).

Men are the most frequent sexual tourists, either as individuals or groups, often seeking sex with prostitutes or sex workers, but more women are having such experiences as well. There also appears to be a growing market for women who may seek sex with locals once they arrive at popular destinations, such as Machu Picchu, Peru (Bauer, 2008).

Sex tourism employs women and girls and sometimes boys. In the countries of El Salvador, Guatemala, and Honduras, the U.S. government estimates that between 8% and 26% of all females have been victims of sexual crimes, including rape and sexual tourism (Speizera, Goodwin, Whittle, Clyde, & Rogers, 2008). In other parts of the world, including Africa, Asia, eastern Europe, Central America, and South America, sex tourism as an industry is large and also folds into sex trafficking. Sex tourism is a billion-dollar global business associated with organized crime (Padilla, 2008; Puccia, 2009). Sadly, some of the countries in which these practices are most prominent either have no laws or lax enforcement to prevent abuses.

Sex tourists go in search of sexual adventure for several reasons. One reason is that they may regard the skin color of some people as a kind of sexual fetish, which they can more easily pursue abroad (Padilla, 2008). Another reason is that their own society may forbid ESB and especially sexual interaction with a younger generation, such as sex with minors, whether male or female. Societies have laws that cover these sexual predatory behaviors, but sadly, they are often ignored or the individuals involved are clever enough to evade the law (Kristof & WuDunn, 2009). Sometimes law enforcement has difficulty keeping up with changes in society, as is currently the case with the Internet (Klein, 2006). As stated in Chapter 14, the minimum age restrictions on consensual sex vary across nations, cultures, and communities, which means that there is no universal law to enforce, making it more difficult to effectively deal with the sexual use and abuse of children (Kristof & WuDunn, 2009). In an effort to stop sex tourism, the U.S. State Department now has posted signs at most airports and customs points warning Americans that if they engage in sex with minors abroad, they can be arrested and imprisoned in the United States if convicted. The fact that sex tourism is flourishing around the world suggests that there are no international standards when it comes to enforcing laws against certain extreme sexual behaviors (Correa et al., 2008).

The most dreadful correlation with sex tourism is sex trafficking, that is, enslaving people, especially women and children, for sexual purposes (Long, 1997; Petchesky, 2003). Sex trafficking of children has attracted more attention in recent years. Much of the research surrounding these issues has been done in underdeveloped countries in Africa and Asia, but in fact, trafficking of children occurs in North America and has recently been highlighted in Miami, Florida (Rani, 2019). There a treatment and research center has focused on how to help homeless children and trafficked children recover from the trauma of their exploitation. This behavior of seeking sex with enslaved people may also connect to some types of paraphilias.

Sex tourism and sex slaves also thrive in the havoc that war creates when families and communities are disrupted and cannot take care of their own (Speizera et al., 2008). During World War II, for example, when the Japanese invaded Korea and China, they forced women in those countries to serve as sex slaves, whom they referred to as comfort women (Soh, 2009). During the Vietnam War, American soldiers on leave traveled to neighboring countries, such as Thailand, for sexual pleasure, and this created a market for sex tourism that was eventually associated with the trafficking of women and children. Thailand, Cambodia, and the Philippines have all relaxed laws governing prostitution and are well known for their sex tourism trade (Trouong, 1990). Thus, mass commercial sex tourism began in Southeast

DID YOU KNOW

Since 1993, vending machines in public places such as train stations throughout Japan sell kinky items, including used underpants of schoolgirls (for about $50). Schoolgirls appear to be a popular sexual fantasy of some Japanese men who, for example, may pay sex workers to dress and act like schoolgirls. This is a kind of sexual fetishism. Also, a woman's flight attendant uniform from Japan Airlines sold for as high as $17,000 because female flight attendants also figure prominently in the sexual fantasies of some other Japanese men.

Asia, but it can now be found in China, the Middle East, South America, and as noted earlier, in the United States.

Much of the early research on sex tourism was conducted in underdeveloped countries, but in recent years, mass sophisticated markets such as China, and closer to home, the United States, have gotten more scrutiny for sex trafficking. Miami is one of the 13 cities in the United States that the FBI monitors for sex trafficking (Rani, 2019). Healing the deep wounds inflicted by this horrible aspect of trafficking is one of the aims of the research, sexual literacy, and treatment surrounding the work highlighted in Miami.

In the next section, we discuss sexual novelty, which may enhance sexual well-being.

SEXUAL NOVELTY AND HEALTHY SEXUALITY

sexual novelty

Creative exploration of what is sexually arousing and satisfying to one or both partners.

Sexual novelty in a very general way means creative exploration of what is sexually arousing and satisfying. This is a basic part of learning to practice sexual literacy to enhance your own sexual experience, whether it is mainstream "vanilla" sex and/or kinky sex, involving imagination and fantasy and employing all kinds of everyday enhancement props, such as music, candles, scented oils, fragrant baths, and the more unusual enhancements of dildos and sex toys. Sexual novelty might include changing the place of sexual intercourse, such as from a bedroom to the kitchen table, the garage, the great outdoors, or the backseat of a car. Partners may rent a hotel room for the night or take a vacation to renew their sexual fun and joy.

The use of sexual novelty appears to be on the increase in the United States. In a 2009 study, researchers found that 21% of men and women said they were extremely satisfied with the sex in their relationship, while most people felt that their level of satisfaction was just average (Herbenick et al., 2009). The majority of women and almost the majority of men in these large surveys say that they are using vibrators and other sex toys or trying out enhancements and considering other novel ways, such as massage, to enhance their sexual well-being (Herbenick et al., 2009). In the same survey, 83% said they firmly believe good sex is an important part of overall health and well-being. Another 76% told researchers that they are looking for ways to make their sex lives more exciting.

However, a more recent, cross-sectional study of more than 2,000 adults found the following: 80% of the sample had lifetime masturbation and oral sex; lifetime anal sex was reported at 43% of the men (insertive) and 37% of the women (receptive). Common lifetime themes included wearing sexy underwear (women 75%, men 2%), sending nude or seminude pictures digitally (54% of the women, 65% of the men), reading erotic stories (57% of all), public sex (43%), role playing (20%), being tied up (20%), being whipped (8%), having a three-way (10% of women, 18% of men), going to sex parties (8%), BDSM (8%), and many other forms of expression (Herbenick et al., 2017). The researchers concluded that there is a lot more diversity of sexual experience than ever before.

Consent is an important concept in understanding any of these areas of sexual novelty, including extreme sexual behavior. Both people need to give full conscious consent. Fundamental to mutual consent is that both parties must be adults and sober or free of drug influence, as defined by their culture. There is more to it than that, as you can read in "Healthy Sexuality: Mutual Consent: When to Say 'Yes,' 'No,' or 'Maybe'?"

Sexual novelty can include other sexual behaviors, such as using new sexual techniques or delaying orgasm long enough to build to a sexual climax. It can include play acting, like playing doctor or playing other roles that are sexually exciting for couples. For some gay and straight couples, that could mean playing the fantasy of cops and robbers, of being arrested, and then of being sexually roughed up by a partner playing the part of a cop. Or for a straight couple it could mean that the woman plays the charming southern belle, and her gentleman partner seduces her. In short, imagination is a great source of sexual novelty in relationships.

HEALTHY Sexuality

Mutual Consent: When to Say "Yes," "No," or "Maybe"?

Consent means agreeing to something, even in the area of sexual novelty between longtime partners. Giving consent to be bound and gagged for sex, however, seems more complicated than how people usually talk about giving consent. Possibly that's because such a behavior seems more extreme, and it's unknown how willing the partner may be to go along with this request, let alone find it sexually arousing. Giving mutual consent to engage in a sexual interaction that involves pain, punishment, and humiliation thus raises issues about how people agree to engage in any behavior that goes beyond the mainstream sexual norms. When people have powerful sexual urges and are not able to control them, at least not entirely, the question arises as to whether we should think of consent differently, not as a yes-or-no choice, but as a spectrum of possible willingness that could include "maybe" or "yes, but be careful," or "we have to have a ritual that you have to do exactly as I say or else I won't agree" (Stoller, 1991). In fact, many couples who engage in S and M create signals to communicate "that's enough" or "stop" or "do it but in this way." These ritual rules of S and M can help the masochist feel in control of the sexual interaction and may actually have power over the sadist, whether in reality or in a mental fantasy script (Stoller, 1986).

Sometimes novelty in relationships is correlated with the frequency or, more often, the lack of having sex often. Some people are concerned about the frequency of their sexual activity, and it is helpful to look at it in the context of normative variations in sexuality.

Can people have too much sex? The answer for most people is probably no. However, at one time in the United States and western Europe, having sex too often was believed to be morally and physically unhealthy (Money, 1986). Sex was not supposed to be fun or satisfying, and if it was, something was wrong. Today, attitudes about healthy sexuality tend toward the other end of the spectrum (Herbenick et al., 2009).

Many people in the United States feel that having sex in certain contexts is natural, normal, and healthy. In fact, it appears to be common to think that sex should occur fairly often or else something is wrong (Herbenick et al., 2009). Yet research has shown that the frequency of having sex is highly variable across individuals and populations. For more information about this, read "Healthy Sexuality: Frequency of Sex—Has It Changed, and Are We Having More Fun?"

As mentioned at the beginning of this chapter, vibrators and sex toys were once diagnostic of abnormality, but today, their use has expanded to become part of the larger culture of sexual pleasure. They come in an endless assortment of shapes, sizes, forms, and colors and can do everything imaginable to enhance sexual pleasure (Tepper & Owens, 2007). Here is a list of some items that people buy or make:

- Plastic or rubber dildos can stimulate various parts of the body.
- Penis-shaped vibrators, some of which are very long.
- Vibrators simulate a massage for the vagina or anus or another bodily orifice.
- Artificial vaginas allow for penile insertion.
- Cock rings clamp around the base of the penis to increase arousal and prolong sex.
- Penile extensions are short dildos that increase penis size.
- Nipple clamps can put gentle pressure on nipples and breasts to create pleasure.

These types of toys should be made from nontoxic material, they should be sold only to adults, and they should be used in ways that do not inflict harm on someone.

HEALTHY Sexuality

Frequency of Sex—Has It Changed, and Are We Having More Fun?

Has the frequency of sexual intercourse changed over time? Are people enjoying it more or less? There are no simple answers to such complex questions, but it would appear that the answer to the first question is yes, at least for some segments of the general population, and not necessarily, to the second question. In the United States, having sex with a partner once a month is satisfying for some people; others want sex with their partners very frequently, such as 2 or 3 times a day, though not necessarily every day (Laumann et al., 1994). Another study of 1,000 adult men and women found that the average American has sex 84 times a year or 7 times per month (Herbenick et al., 2009). The people surveyed rated their sexual satisfaction as average. They also stated that they were constantly looking for all kinds of ways to enhance pleasure in the bedroom, including sex toys or other aids. In other words, people in the United States may be seeking more fun and satisfaction in their sexual relations, but not necessarily attaining it.

Perhaps the real change is that people combine sex with extremely busy, complex lives, and still find fun and satisfaction and are increasingly willing to try new ways of pleasing themselves and their partners (Herbenick et al., 2009; Schwartz, 2007a).

As previously noted, electric vibrators are becoming very common among U.S. adults (Herbenick et al., 2009; Reece et al., 2009). Many women use vibrators effectively for orgasm all the time. The research was done on nationally representative samples of adult men and women ages 18 to 60: 53% of women and 45% of men say that they use them. Women report that vibrators enhance their overall sexual experience, including desire, arousal, lubrication, and orgasm. Among heterosexual men, a large number of males reported using vibrators sometimes in their relationships with women and feeling positive about their use. There was some variation among survey respondents in how they used vibrators to enhance their sexual experience. Some used them only with their intimate partner. Others used them when they were alone, as for example, women who experimented with them on their own (Herbenick et al., 2009).

Another study examined how normal heterosexual women might use sex toys and vibrators, oral and anal sex, lubricants, and pornography to increase their sexual pleasure (Shafer, 2009). The women who had never used sex toys expressed concerns that these toys were an artificial source of pleasure. Some also worried that a sex toy, such as a dildo or a vibrator, could produce orgasms that their own partners could not, and that this might result in dissatisfaction with their male partners. Also, they worried that they would become dependent on sex toys and that this would affect their relationships (Shafer, 2009).

WHAT'S ON YOUR MIND?

Q: My girlfriend has started using a vibrator and she wants me to use it on her when we have sex, too. It makes me feel like I am not enough for her, and while she says that's not it, I still find it weird.

ANSWER: Communication is important in such situations. People vary so much in what turns them on, how lubricated they are, and how easily or quickly they are aroused, and being able to communicate this at the right time can make a difference in the quality of relationships. Vibrators may help some people relax and feel a bit more at ease when having vaginal or anal sex, and communicating that helps a lot. Your response to your girlfriend's request is totally understandable, but see if she can help you also feel comfortable with using it by telling you more about how it helps her feel pleasure and intimacy with you—that might bring the two of you closer.

Women who used a dildo and vibrator for masturbation or with a partner also reassured their partner that these toys wouldn't decrease or change the sexual desire they felt for that partner. Others reported that sex toys lost their novelty and that they preferred their partner because the body contact caused their arousal, which made them feel more connection with the other person. Some women felt that using sex toys exclusively was abnormal (Herbenick et al., 2009).

The increasing popularity of lubricants, a dildo, massage, fragrant oils, feathers, and all kinds of other things to make sex more pleasurable speaks to a significant change that has been occurring in recreational sex among adults over the past generation (Das et al., 2012; Herbenick et al., 2009, 2017; Laumann et al., 1994; Northrup, Schwartz, & Witte, 2014). People seem willing to experiment to find novel ways of achieving greater pleasure for themselves and their partners than in the past. In fact, according to a recent study, the greatest measure of this motivation is occurring not in cities, such as San Francisco, which is known for embracing sexual novelty, but in the more conservative regions of the country (Herbenick et al., 2009).

ACHIEVING SEXUAL WELL BEING: ACCEPTING YOUR OWN ENJOYMENT

Shops selling dildos and other sex toys are common.
Sean Gallup/Getty Images

As we near the end of our journey toward sexual literacy, it is fitting to recognize both how much our sexual pleasure and behavior is conventionalized by society, and how much variation there is out there. We have come to understand that much of our judgment about what is normative or acceptable, "good" or "bad," is based on our societal standards and cultural trends. These trends clearly change over time, as we have seen so vividly in the change from paraphilia to acceptance and the diagnosis of the more serious paraphilic disorders. Keeping an open mind to consider new things is really important for your own journey toward sexual well-being and happiness. Ask yourself this question: If I were to advise someone who cared for me, such as a friend or younger sibling, about setting the limits of their sexual experience, what could I apply from this chapter's knowledge and skills to enable them to better achieve their own sexual literacy and well-being? Then apply that understanding to your own way of putting your learning about all these sexual variations into practice.

There is never going to be one truly "right" or correct way to perform sexuality or engage in sexual intimacy or achieve sexual pleasure and satisfaction—that is so much a part of your own unique sexual nature. Sexual individuality means in part our own realization of what we find satisfying and pleasurable in our lives. When that leads to inner conflict, distress at work or home, the infliction of suffering on others, or out-of-control behavior that leads to social trouble, then we know that it has crossed a line. Understanding what separates normative variations from the paraphilias is not that difficult. You will be able to create your own understanding of these issues in your life and with the people you love. But in the great range of normative variation, there is an almost infinite range of behaviors and things to do, a great big world of sexual pleasure that is yours to initialize and make unique to your own being.

When you understand and accept your own personal sexual enjoyment and find the skills to express that in your own life, you know that you have, at least for this stage in your own life cycle, found sexual literacy. It will never end, of course, because as we adapt to life cycle changes, our own journey toward discovery and adaptation continues. For the moment, however, we hope that you will take this newfound knowledge and skill set and also apply it to help support others and improve the world around us.

Chapter Review

SUMMARY

Understanding and Challenging Diagnostic Models of Human Sexuality

- From the beginning of civilization, cultures have struggled to define norms concerning sexual behavior.
- Individuals choose to follow or not follow the sexual blueprints of their society and/or culture depending on their own specific desires and feelings.
- In the last century, Western society has seen an explosion in sexual variations, which has led to criticism of the historical pathologizing of individual sexual desires and behaviors that are neither coercive nor stressful.
- Sexual diagnoses have changed over time, expanding the definition of human sexual nature, and allowing greater sexual individuality.
- Currently, "conversion" or "reparative" therapies and practices are considered unethical and illegal in many parts of the United States, but they continue to be a part of standard psychiatric care in other parts of the world.

Medical and Physical Challenges to Normative Sexual Response

- Physical and medical challenges to sexual dysfunction may increase with aging and in later adulthood.
- A variety of illnesses in later life, such as cardiovascular diseases and diabetes, may create disabilities that influence sexual functioning.
- Women may experience decreases in sexual desire due to a lack of partners in older age or due to the impacts of sexual norms and taboos around aging and sexual activity.
- Female sexual arousal disorder (FSAD) is characterized as the inability to attain or maintain sexual excitement or physical arousal.
- Hypoactive female sexual desire disorder (HSDD) is the persistent inability to achieve fulfilling sexual activity.
- Menopause may be a significant factor in reducing desire and physical comfort in women.
- For some women, midlife is a time of increasing sexual freedom and pleasure.
- Erectile dysfunction (ED) is increasingly more common as men live longer and health issues have the potential to affect sexual performance.
- Several common medications used to treat depression, high blood pressure, HIV, and other conditions can also contribute to ED.
- There are medications (such as Viagra) available to help treat ED. These medications are more commonly prescribed today due to a reduction of stigma surrounding their use.
- In general, people with disabilities report more issues with sexual satisfaction than the general population.
- Sex education in the United States is rarely directed to those with disabilities due to the myth that people who have disabilities and chronic health conditions are incapable or uninterested in experiencing sexual feelings, desires, and activity. This lack of education can contribute to higher risks of sexual abuse and exploitation.

Diagnoses of Sexual Dysfunction and Behavior: The *DSM-5* and Paraphilic Disorders

- What is regarded as extreme sexual behavior or the sexual norm has changed significantly over time.
- What was once regarded as characteristic of the paraphilias has also changed in the view of psychiatry.
- The *DSM-5* helps to advance our understanding of the difference between paraphilia and paraphilic disorder.
- When sexual behavior creates coercion, chronic distress, and disruption of social, occupational, and other important spaces are involved, paraphilic disorder is the indicated sexual diagnosis.
- Extreme sexual behaviors are risky sexual behaviors between consenting adults that test the limit of what a culture tolerates within its sexual spectrum. Men more than women engage in extreme sexual behaviors.
- When compulsive behavior is applied to extreme sexual behavior, it can resemble compulsive sexual behavior, which is indicative of a person's inability to control sexual urges.
- Kink or kinky sex is an expanding area of sexual culture that is about extreme sexual behavior and not about paraphilias.
- Sexual addiction is a controversial concept that points toward compulsive sexuality.
- Paraphilias are a medical category created in the 1920s to describe perversion and abnormal sexual arousal to individuals, objects, or situations that depart from mainstream normative or typical behavior in a community and cause distress or serious problems.
- Paraphilic disorder is not the same as a paraphilia.
- The paraphilias are categorized as either coercive or noncoercive.
- S and M stands for sadism and masochism, one of the paraphilic disorders.
- Theories about the origins of paraphilia include psychoanalytic, behavioral, and sociobiological ones.

From Normative to Extreme Sexual Behaviors

- Sex-positive societies tend to allow greater variations in sexual expression and make some allowances for sexual behavior that could be classified as "extreme sexual behavior."
- Just because a sexual behavior occurs in one society does not necessarily mean that it is a common behavior in other societies. Conversely, some sexual behaviors that are seen as extreme in U.S. society are normative and may be associated with social or religious ceremonies in other cultures.
- Kinky sex or "Kink" may include a variety of sexual interests that are serious or playful, creative or ritualized, and it may include extreme sexual behaviors such as role playing, dominance and submission, spanking, and tickling.
- BDSM is considered a paraphilic disorder, not a paraphilia, because some people engage in the behavior in noncoercive and consensual ways.
- Sexual fetishism is another characteristic of kinky sex and is when an object or body part arouses intense sexual interest and urges.
- Sexual tourism is a practice that is centuries old and is a form of extreme sexual behavior that may move into sex work or sexual exploitation of adults and children.
- Men are the most frequent sexual tourists though there appears to be a growing market for women who seek sex with locals once they arrive at popular destinations.

- The most dangerous correlation with sex tourism is sex trafficking or enslaving people (especially women and children) for sexual purposes. This often occurs in areas where there are high levels of poverty and in underdeveloped countries.

Sexual Novelty and Healthy Sexuality

- Sexual novelty in people's relationships is on the increase and is normative.
- Vibrators and other sexual enhancements are now accepted as mainstream.
- People may use sex toys and other sorts of gadgets or things to enhance pleasure in their sexual experience.
- Consent and respect are a critical part of all normative sexual relationships.

Achieving Sexual Well-Being: Accepting Your Own Enjoyment

- It is important to realize how much our sexual pleasure and behavior is conventionalized by society, and how much variation exists.
- Keeping an open mind to consider new things is critical for our journeys toward sexual well-being and happiness.
- When we understand and accept our own personal sexual enjoyments and find the skills to express that in our lives, we have, at least in this moment, found sexual literacy. Of course, the journey continues as we move onward to acquire new knowledge, develop skills and practice them in our efforts to maintain and further sexual literacy, for ourselves and each other.

What's Your Position?

1. **What do you believe are the major contributors to the provision of freedoms of sexual expression during the past century? Do you believe these freedoms are a result of changes in society as a whole or as a result of changing fields such as medicine?**
   - When you hear the term extreme sexual behavior, what do you feel and think?
   - How does your own community react to reports of extreme sexual behavior(s)?

2. **To what degree have sexual values shifted in the United States and how do these changing values impact our understanding of what is considered typical, atypical, or extreme sexual behavior?**
   - How have the media represented sexual behaviors such as S and M and fetishism?

3. **Should medical doctors, scientists, or other people in positions of authority have a large say in defining what is normal or abnormal in sexuality? Why or why not?**

Design elements: Controversies in Sexuality: HBRH/Shutterstock; Research and Sexual Well Being: verity jane smith/Getty Images; Healthy Sexuality: Sergey Furtaev/Shutterstock; Communication Matters: PeopleImages/Getty Images; Know Yourself: Plush Studios/Blend Images LLC; What's Your Position: Luis Molinero/Shutterstock; Healthy Sexuality: A. Minde/PhotoAlto; Did You Know icon: McGraw-Hill Education; Page corner icon: McGraw-Hill Education.

Glossary

A

abasiophilia The love of or sexual attraction to people who use leg braces. *(p. 533)*

AB/DL A type of fetishism in which an adult dresses as a baby and the adult partner treats him or her like a baby; also called paraphilic infantilism. *(p. 532)*

abortifacients Medications utilized to prevent the progression of pregnancy and induce uterine contractions to remove embryonic or fetal tissue. *(p. 290)*

abortion Elective termination of a pregnancy before 37 weeks of gestation. *(p. 289)*

acquired immunodeficiency syndrome (AIDS) A late-stage infection with HIV. *(p. 188)*

adrenarche The process of maturation of the adrenal glands; often thought of as one of the first markers of pubertal development. *(p. 380)*

adultery When a married person has an extramarital relationship, also called "cheating." *(p. 430)*

ageist Discrimination or attitudes based upon prejudice toward older adults. *(p. 438)*

age of consent The age at which an individual can legally agree to have sex. *(p. 404)*

amenorrhea The absence of menstrual periods. *(p. 118)*

amniocentesis A procedure done usually between 16 and 20 months of gestation where a doctor removes a small amount of amniotic fluid via a needle in the abdomen to test for genetic abnormalities. *(p. 272)*

amniotic sac (amnion) The sac of membranes in which the fetus develops in utero. *(p. 260)*

anal intercourse A form of sexual expression where the anus is penetrated by a penis. *(p. 158)*

anatomy The study of the physical structure of our bodies and the intricate design of the systems that live within the structures. *(p. 100)*

androgyny Characteristics of a male or female who has a high degree of both feminine (expressive) and masculine (instrumental) characteristics. *(p. 317)*

andropause A process similar to menopause that occurs in some men. *(p. 128)*

anilingus Oral-anal stimulation. *(p. 158)*

anus The opening of the digestive tract for the expulsion of feces. *(p. 104)*

areola The dark visible center of the breast. *(p. 108)*

artificial insemination (AI) The deliberate introduction of semen into a female for the purpose of fertilization, by means other than ejaculation directly into the vagina or uterus. *(p. 286)*

aspiration An abortive procedure where suction is used to remove an embryo or fetus from the uterus. *(p. 290)*

asexuality Asexual people do not feel any noteworthy sexual attraction to other people, but some might have romantic relationships. *(p. 335)*

assisted reproductive technique A variety of fertility technologies that assist people in their efforts to conceive. *(p. 284)*

atrophic vaginitis This type of vaginitis is due to reduced estrogen levels resulting from menopause and can cause vaginal tissues to become thinner and drier. *(p. 178)*

attachment theory A theory developed by Ainsworth that helps to explain how we attach and the degree of attachment to caregivers during infancy and childhood. *(p. 459)*

autoerotic Behaviors that are self-stimulating. *(p. 375)*

autoerotic asphyxiophilia A form of fetishistic arousal related to asphyxiation; sexual arousal from suffocating. *(p. 531)*

avatar An online representation or alter ego for someone playing a computer game. *(p. 89)*

B

bacterial vaginosis A type of vaginitis that results from overgrowth of one or more of several organisms typically present in the vagina; upsets the natural balance of vaginal bacteria. *(p. 178)*

Bartholin's glands Glands located on each side of the vaginal opening. *(p. 104)*

basal body temperature (BBT) The lowest temperature attained by the body during rest (usually during sleep). *(p. 243)*

BDSM Refers to bondage/discipline (BD) and sadism/masochism (SM); power plays and role acting that is not necessarily sexual. *(p. 531)*

being on the down low (BODL) An African American term that refers to a man who hides his sexual orientation. *(p. 350)*

bimanual exam An exam that requires that the doctor insert two fingers in the vagina while placing the other hand on top of the lower part of the abdomen in order to feel for any abnormalities and to check the size, shape, and mobility of the uterus. *(p. 176)*

biological bisexuality The idea that people may be naturally attracted to both sexes. *(p. 11)*

biological kin People directly related by blood. *(p. 497)*

bisexual A person who is sometimes attracted to men or women or both, although not necessarily to the same degree or at the same point in time. *(p. 332)*

blastocyst The developing zygote with cells surrounding a fluid-filled core, upon entering the uterus but prior to implantation in the uterine wall. *(p. 260)*

bodily integrity The idea of the inviolability of the physical body and the importance of personal autonomy and the self-determination of individuals over their own bodies. *(p. 128)*

breech Position of a fetus that is emerging with buttocks or legs first rather than head first. *(p. 267)*

C

case study A research method that professionals in clinical psychology, medicine, and sexuality use to study a single individual or very small group in depth. *(p. 22)*

caste The social and religious status group of Hindu families. *(p. 428)*

casual sex Sex with people with whom you are not in love or committed. *(p. 415)*

celibacy The condition of remaining single, often by choice. *(p. 414)*

cervical cancer A gynecologic cancer that begins in the cervix. *(p. 178)*

cervix The neck of the uterus, connecting the uterus with the vagina. *(p. 104)*

cesarean (C-section) birth Removal of a fetus from the mother's uterus surgically, through an incision in the abdomen. *(p. 267)*

chancre A sore that typically appears at the site of infection with syphilis. *(p. 202)*

childhood sexual abuse (CSA) Sexual abuse committed against a minor child, which includes adult acts of sexual assault, molestation, or sexual exploitation. *(p. 494)*

child pornography Any visual depiction, including photographs, films, videos, or computer-generated images, of sexually explicit conduct. *(p. 498)*

chivalry A code of Christian knights that focused on purity of heart and body, chastity for females, and honor in war. *(p. 44)*

chlamydia An STI caused by the bacterium *Chlamydia trachomatis*. *(p. 200)*

chorion A membrane that exists during pregnancy between the fetus and the mother. *(p. 260)*

chorionic villus sampling (CVS) A screening procedure in which a small amount of tissue from the placenta is obtained and analyzed for chromosomal disorders and specific genetic diseases. *(p. 272)*

cisgender A person whose behaviors and identity are congruent with more traditional gender roles, and which may include a man with a masculine gender identity or a woman with a feminine identity. *(p. 300)*

civil union A legally recognized union similar to marriage but not having all the same protections and rights. *(p. 420)*

clitoral crura The internal portion of the clitoris. *(p. 103)*

clitoral glans The small external portion of the clitoris. *(p. 103)*

clitoral hood The fold of skin that surrounds and protects the clitoral glans. *(p. 103)*

clitoris A highly sensitive structure of the female external genitals. *(p. 103)*

coercive paraphilia A sexual practice that involves the use of force against a sexual partner. *(p. 526)*

cohabitation The state of living together or sharing the same space as if the couple were married but without legal marriage. *(p. 418)*

coital positions The placement of bodies during sexual intercourse involving penile-vaginal penetration. *(p. 150)*

coitus Penile-vaginal intercourse. *(p. 159)*

coitus interruptus Withdrawal of the penis from the vagina before ejaculation. *(p. 217)*

coitus obstructus The general category of putting pressure on the testicles, which was thought to cause sperm to be ejaculated into the bladder. *(p. 217)*

commitment One component of the triangular theory of love that consists of the feelings leading one person to remain with another, and in the long term, the shared achievements and plans made with that partner. *(p. 455)*

common law marriage An interpersonal status that involves living together and regarding each other publicly as spouses even though no marriage or civil ceremony has occurred. *(p. 420)*

communication privacy management theory States that the revelation of private information in a relationship has the potential to leave individuals feeling vulnerable or resentful regarding the shared information. *(p. 466)*

companionate marriage The cultural idea that a man and woman are not just sex partners but also social and intellectual companions and equals for life. *(p. 47)*

complementarity The idea that opposites attract, that individuals are attracted to what's different in others. *(p. 451)*

compulsive sexual behavior Behavior that individuals are unable to control even though they have repeatedly tried to do so. *(p. 522)*

compulsory heterosexuality The condition of being socially compelled to have sexual relationships with the other gender, be married, and have children, regardless of sexual orientation. *(p. 341)*

condom Popular barrier contraceptive device worn externally over an erect penis or internally within a vagina. *(p. 218)*

continuous abstinence A form of contraception that involves completely refraining from sexual intercourse. *(p. 231)*

contraception Any process or method used to prevent conception or pregnancy. Some contraceptive methods may also prevent the transmission of STIs. *(p. 216)*

contraceptive switch Phase of cohabitation when couples develop reproductive plans. *(p. 422)*

contractions Muscular movement during labor that causes the upper part of the uterus (fundus) to tighten and thicken while the cervix and lower portion of the uterus stretch and relax, helping the baby pass from inside the uterus and into the birth canal for delivery; also referred to as the pain of childbirth. *(p. 273)*

corona The rounded area at the base of the penile glans. *(p. 121)*

corpus cavernosa Two paired tubular cylinders in the penis that during sexual arousal will be filled with blood causing an erection. *(p. 121)*

corpus luteum The tissue formed from a ruptured ovarian follicle. *(p. 116)*

corpus spongiosum The underlying spongy tissue in a tubular structure located below the corpora cavernosa containing the urethra. *(p. 121)*

correlation The statistical measurement of the strength of a relationship between variables, such as dating and marriage. *(p. 22)*

couvade A syndrome in which male partners experience pregnancy symptoms similar to the symptoms experienced by their pregnant partners. *(p. 265)*

Cowper's gland During sexual arousal this structure secretes a clear mucus-like fluid; also called the *bulbourethral gland*. *(p. 123)*

cremaster muscle A muscle in the scrotum that helps to create the ideal temperature for sperm production no matter the climate. *(p. 122)*

cryptorchidism A condition that occurs in infancy where one or both of the testicles may not descend. *(p. 180)*

cultural chauvinism The belief that one's cultural norms are superior to the norms of another's group. *(p. 49)*

cultural relativism The viewing of people's attitudes and behavior in the context of their own culture. *(p. 49)*

cunnilingus Oral sex performed on a woman. *(p. 155)*

D

date rape Forcible sex from an individual whom a victim knows socially or is dating. *(p. 479)*

date rape drugs Substances used by predators to overcome their victims in order to commit nonconsensual sexual acts with them. *(p. 480)*

denial A form of coping with fear or anxiety that involves distortion of reality and its perception. *(p. 539)*

dependent variable The variable that is being measured in a research study. *(p. 22)*

detumescence The soft state of penis after the semen has been ejaculated. *(p. 125)*

digital rectal exam An exam during which the physician inserts the fingers into the rectum in order to feel the size of the prostate gland. *(p. 183)*

dilation Where the cervical opening expands to approximately 10 cm in width, in preparation for birth. *(p. 273)*

dilation and evacuation (D&E) An abortive procedure when a pregnancy has passed the first trimester. This involves medication given to ensure fetal death. Scraping the uterine walls and suctioning out the contents removes fetal tissue. *(p. 290)*

direct observation A data collection method that provides the researcher an opportunity to observe natural behaviors in context as they occur. *(p. 23)*

disengagement coping Mental methods of coping with abuse that result in disengagement from reality, such as denial, self-blame, wishful thinking, and avoidance of real feelings. *(p. 506)*

divorce The legal termination of a marriage whether sanctified by church or common law. *(p. 431)*

domestic partnership A defined legal and social status in some states, and in the private corporate sphere for some companies, that provides some benefits, such as health care, to one's registered domestic partner. *(p. 420)*

douching A method of washing out the vagina or washing the penis. *(p. 217)*

doula A person trained in the process of labor and delivery and assists a midwife in childbirth. *(p. 277)*

DSD An identity label used by some transgender people to refer to "differences in sex development" rather than the old-fashioned and negative language of "disorders of disease." *(p. 326)*

double stigma Experienced by individuals when they are excluded from their own community as well as from the larger society. *(p. 63)*

dual income, no sex (DINS) People who are so busy that they cannot cope with intimacy or they omit sex from the relationship, as reported in media. *(p. 426)*

dysmenorrhea Severe uterine pain during menstruation. *(p. 118)*

E

early adulthood Early 20s to mid-30s. *(p. 410)*

ectopic pregnancy A pregnancy complication in which a fertilized ovum attaches and begins to grow outside of the uterus, most commonly in the fallopian tubes. *(p. 270)*

effacement Thinning of cervical tissue that occurs in preparation for birth. *(p. 273)*

ejaculation The ejection of semen (usually carrying sperm) from the male reproductive tract, and is usually accompanied by orgasm. *(p. 123)*

ejaculatory ducts Two short ducts located within the prostate gland that transport sperm to the urethra prior to ejaculation. *(p. 125)*

ejaculatory inevitability Semen prepares to secrete and a male feels that he is "about to come." *(p. 125)*

elderhood The period of life that starts at about age 85, and is often overlooked in people's thinking about sexual experience and relationships. *(p. 439)*

elders Adults 85 and up. *(p. 411)*

embryo A blastocyst that has implanted in the uterine wall. *(p. 260)*

embryonic period In pregnancy, this period encompasses day 14 through day 56. *(p. 259)*

emergency contraception (EC) Concentrated hormonal pills that can interrupt a woman's normal hormonal patterns to protect against an unplanned pregnancy in the event of unprotected intercourse. *(p. 239)*

emission phase The first of two stages of the ejaculation process. *(p. 125)*

emotional literacy Knowing the words and meanings to use to express yourself emotionally in sexual experiences and relationships. *(p. 8)*

emotion work Individuals' attempts to try and change in degree or quality and emotion or feeling. *(p. 462)*

endocrine system The system of glands that regulates body functions and processes, including puberty, metabolism, and mood, by releasing hormones. *(p. 112)*

endometriosis A potentially painful and dangerous medical condition caused when endometrial cells grow outside of the uterus into the abdominal cavity. *(p. 256)*

endometrium The inner membrane of the uterus; the lining of which is shed during menstruation. *(p. 106)*

endorphins Chemicals produced in the brain during strenuous exercise, excitement, pain, and orgasm that may alter our emotions in the period after orgasm; work as "natural pain relievers" to produce a sense of well-being. *(p. 148)*

epididymis A tightly coiled tubular structure that is located on top of each testicle. *(p. 122)*

epidural A common form of pain management where a doctor passes pain medication through a small tube that has been inserted at the base of a woman's spine. *(p. 278)*

episiotomy An intervention where an incision is made at the base of the vaginal opening and extends to the perineum to assist in providing a larger space to birth an infant. *(p. 279)*

EPOR model Four stages of the human sexual response, including excitement, plateau, orgasm, and resolution. *(p. 147)*

erectile dysfunction The inability to gain or sustain an erection. *(p. 126)*

erectile dysfunction (ED) The inability to gain or sustain an erection. *(p. 518)*

erectile tissues *See* penile columns. *(p. 122)*

erection The firm and enlarged condition of a body organ or part when the erectile tissue surrounding it becomes filled with blood. *(p. 120)*

erogenous zones Major areas of the body, especially the mouth, genitals, and anus, that are highly sensitive to sexual stimulation and excitement. *(p. 11)*

estriol A chemical found in women's saliva that may indicate possible preterm birth. *(p. 271)*

estrogen Hormones that produce female reproductive and secondary sex characteristics and impact the functioning of the menstrual cycle. *(p. 109)*

estrus The recurring time when a female ovulates and is most receptive to becoming pregnant. *(p. 34)*

evolution The general idea that change occurs in all life forms over time. *(p. 10)*

excitement phase The first stage of the body's sexual response, marked by vasocongestion and erection in the clitoris and the penis. *(p. 147)*

exhibitionism The act of exposing genitals to unsuspecting victims for the purpose of sexual arousal. *(p. 528)*

exotic becomes erotic (EBE) theory A theory that states people are attracted to what is unusual or exotic to them. *(p. 451)*

experimental research A data collection method that involves researchers putting more limitations into place, to examine or predict how changes in independent variables influence dependent variables. *(p. 25)*

expulsion phase The second stage of the ejaculation process. *(p. 125)*

extended family A family system that includes grandparents, aunts, and uncles who are related to the biological parents by blood and cousins as well as the children of siblings, nieces, and nephews. *(p. 497)*

external condom A thin sheath made of latex, natural animal membrane, polyurethane, silicone, or other synthetic material that fits over the erect penis prior to intercourse. *(p. 231)*

extreme sexual behaviors Risky, noncoercive behaviors between consenting adults that test the limits of what a culture tolerates within its spectrum of sexual behavior. *(p. 522)*

F

failure rate The number of women out of 100 who will become pregnant within the first year of using a particular method of contraception. *(p. 223)*

fallopian tubes Oviducts that connect the ovaries to the uterus. *(p. 104)*

family leave The amount of paid or unpaid leave allowed for the parents of a new child. *(p. 252)*

family of choice A group composed of those intimate partners or legally married spouses, close friends, and neighbors who feel so close to each other that they celebrate holidays and birthdays. *(p. 363)*

fantasy system Groupings of sexual fantasies that express individuals' deepest sexual motivations, pleasures, fears, and yearnings for emotional connections with others. *(p. 145)*

fellatio Oral sex performed on a man. *(p. 155)*

female circumcision The removal or shortening of the clitoris. It may include sewing the labia together to prevent sexual intercourse or the rupture of the hymen. *(p. 111)*

female genital mutilation (FGM) Performing female circumcision without antiseptic or anesthesia. *(p. 111)*

fertility awareness methods Contraceptive methods based on ovulation prediction and the viability of sperm; intercourse is timed to avoid fertile days in a woman's reproductive cycle. *(p. 242)*

fetal alcohol spectrum disorders (FASDs) A group of conditions (including FAS) that can occur in a person whose mother ingested alcohol during pregnancy. *(p. 516)*

fetal alcohol syndrome (FAS) Condition of infant born to a mother who ingested high levels of alcohol during her pregnancy; the infant displays certain physical characteristics. *(p. 254)*

fetal period In pregnancy, this period encompasses the ninth week through birth. *(p. 259)*

fetishism The attraction to physical objects such as boots or to human appendages. *(p. 10)*

fetus A developing baby from the eighth week of pregnancy until birth. *(p. 260)*

field study A research method in which the researcher observes behavior outside a clinical setting in its own cultural and linguistic context. *(p. 12)*

fimbria The fringe tissue near the ovary leading to the fallopian tube. *(p. 108)*

fissure Small breaks in the anal tissue often caused by anal penetration without proper lubrication. *(p. 159)*

flaccid The state of a penis being limp or soft. *(p. 125)*

fluid-free sexual behavior Sexual behaviors that avoid the sharing or mixing of bodily fluids including unprotected vaginal, anal, or oral intercourse. *(p. 231)*

follicle Part of the ovary; each contains a hollow ball of cells with an immature egg in the center. *(p. 108)*

follicle stimulating hormone (FSH) A hormone secreted by the pituitary gland in a female during the menstrual cycle which helps stimulate the development of ovarian follicles. In males, it stimulates sperm production. *(p. 117)*

forceps Metal instruments placed around the baby's head inside the birth canal to aid in the birth of the child. *(p. 278)*

foreskin A thin, sensitive layer of skin that covers part of the shaft, the corona, and the glans of the penis. *(p. 121)*

frenulum Sensitive tissue on the backside of the penis which connects the penile glans with the shaft and the foreskin of the penis. *(p. 122)*

friends with benefits (FWB) Singles involved sexually with a friend or acquaintance for some mutual benefit, such as shared rent, but without commitment. *(p. 416)*

frotteurism The act of rubbing one's genitals against another person. *(p. 528)*

G

G-spot orgasm An orgasm achieved during intercourse that occurs from stimulation to the G-spot rather than the clitoris. *(p. 107)*

gamete intrafallopian transfer (GIFT) A procedure where the sperm and egg are placed directly into the fallopian tube in hopes that their near proximity will aid in the process of fertilization. *(p. 285)*

gay/homosexual An individual who is attracted only or primarily to other individuals of the same sex and/or gender. *(p. 332)*

gender The social assignment of people to one sex or the other in a historical culture. *(p. 299)*

gender binary The illusionary but common perception that sex and gender are either male or female. In actuality, sex and gender exist on a spectrum. *(p. 308)*

gender dysphoria Refers to discomfort or distress that is caused by a discrepancy between a person's gender identity and that person's sex assigned at birth (and the associated gender role and/or primary and secondary sex characteristics). *(p. 314)*

gender expression The way people express their gender by behavior, clothes, hair, voice, or gait. *(p. 309)*

gender identity The sense of being male (maleness) or female (femaleness). *(p. 299)*

genderism The belief that people need to be cisgender and that all gender nonconformity is bad or unacceptable. *(p. 322)*

gender nonconforming Those who manifest gender behaviors that go beyond or against the norm of their community. *(p. 325)*

gender role The socialization of people in masculinity and femininity in society. *(p. 299)*

gender stereotypes Traditional notions about being masculine or feminine. *(p. 317)*

gender variance Nonconforming gender behavior that may be the result of the interaction of biology, culture, and individual characteristics such as personality and temperament. *(p. 325)*

generalizability The extent to which research findings and conclusions from a study conducted on a sample population can be applied, or *generalized,* to the population at large. *(p. 21)*

genital integrity The idea that someone's genitals ought to be left intact and not be interfered with by anyone. *(p. 129)*

germ cells Cells in the testicles that produce immature sperm. *(p. 180)*

germinal period In pregnancy, this period encompasses the moment of conception through day 14. *(p. 259)*

gestation The period of time between conception and birth; it is usually referred to in terms of weeks. *(p. 259)*

gestational diabetes A condition of glucose intolerance that commonly occurs during pregnancy. *(p. 271)*

global pandemic Worldwide epidemic. *(p. 189)*

gonad Glands that make sex hormones and reproductive cells; called testes in the male, ovaries in the female. *(p. 113)*

gonadarche Refers to the earliest gonadal changes of puberty; in response to gonadotropins, the ovaries in girls and the testes in boys begin to grow. *(p. 380)*

gonadotropin-releasing hormone (GnRH) Pituitary hormone that stimulates activity in the gonads (testes and ovaries). *(p. 117)*

gonadotropins Chemicals that stimulate activity and growth in the gonads of both boys and girls. *(p. 380)*

gonorrhea A common STI caused by the bacteria *Neisseria gonorrhea*. *(p. 198)*

G-spot The Grafenberg spot, a controversial area of the vagina that is potentially erogenous and may produce powerful orgasms. *(p. 107)*

G-spot orgasm An orgasm achieved during intercourse that occurs from stimulation to the G-spot rather than the clitoris. *(p. 107)*

great world religions Religions that have huge followings around the world, have roots in traditional holy texts and moral principles, and have changed the course of history. *(p. 40)*

gynecologic cancer A group of five different cancers affecting a woman's reproductive system. Includes vaginal, vulvar, uterine, ovarian, and cervical cancers. *(p. 178)*

H

habitualization Actions repeated frequently enough to be cast into a pattern and seem natural. *(p. 334)*

halo effect A positive perception of someone based on physical attractiveness. *(p. 447)*

hard-core pornography Nude images that depict penetrative sex and aggressive, raw sexual interactions between adults. *(p. 93)*

hate crime An act of aggression or hatred targeted toward someone because of religion, race, or sexual orientation. *(p. 357)*

hepatitis A chronic viral infection of the liver. *(p. 209)*

herpes A recurrent skin condition characterized by sores on the mouth or genitals; caused by the herpes simplex virus. *(p. 207)*

heterogamy Refers to a marriage between two individuals of different ethnicities, income, social class, or religion. *(p. 425)*

heterosexual/straight People who are attracted to the other sex. *(p. 332)*

holistic sexuality The integration of body, mind, feelings, and social life through your sexuality. *(p. 3)*

homogamy Marriage between individuals who are culturally similar. *(p. 425)*

homonegativity Subtle negative social perceptions and behaviors against LGBTQIA+ people or those suspected of same-gender sexuality. *(p. 354)*

homophobia Irrational fear, aversion to, or discrimination against homosexuality or homosexuals. *(p. 354)*

hooking up Meeting a partner online or in a physical setting for a casual sexual encounter outside of a romantic or committed relationship. *(p. 88)*

hormonal implants Small tubes that contain progestin, which is inserted under the skin of a woman's upper arm. These can provide continuous protection against pregnancy. *(p. 237)*

hormone A chemical substance produced in the body that controls and regulates the activity of certain cells or organs. *(p. 112)*

hormone replacement therapy (HRT) Treatment that can offset some of the effects of decreased natural levels of hormones associated with menopause. *(p. 119)*

hostile environment A form of sexual harassment where the harassment of an individual interferes with his or her ability to be productive and work. *(p. 499)*

human immunodeficiency virus (HIV) A virus that leads to the destruction of the immune system through a variety of illnesses known as AIDS. *(p. 188)*

human papillomavirus (HPV) A sexually transmitted infection; known to be one of the main causes of cervical cancer. *(p. 179)*

human sexual nature The combination of human culture and human nature working together to produce sexual behavior. *(p. 35)*

hydrotherapy The use of hot tubs or water in the birth process in order to encourage relaxation. *(p. 277)*

hymen The fold of tissue that partially covers the introitus. *(p. 104)*

hypersexuality Frequent or sudden expression of sexual urges; not a paraphilia. *(p. 522)*

hypothalamus The area of the brain that secretes substances that influence pituitary and other gland function and is involved in the control of body temperature, hunger, thirst, and other processes that regulate body equilibrium. *(p. 112)*

hypothesis A proposition set forth to explain some observation, method, or data analysis. *(p. 21)*

I

imperforate hymen Occurs when the tissue of the hymen completely closes the vaginal opening causing menstrual fluid to accumulate. *(p. 106)*

imprinting A rapid early learning process by which a newborn establishes a behavior pattern of recognition and attraction to another animal of its own kind or to an object identified as the parent. *(p. 340)*

incest Sex between relatives. *(p. 497)*

incest taboo Social or cultural prohibition against sex between close family members. *(p. 37)*

independent variable A variable that is manipulated to test its effect on other variables in a research study. *(p. 21)*

interactive biopsychosocial approach A theory that suggests that biological, psychological, and social factors work together to produce sexual attractions and feelings, and perhaps sexual orientation. *(p. 340)*

interdisciplinary perspective The holistic integration of research in different disciplines to describe and explain all of human sexuality. *(p. 19)*

internal condom A thin sheath made of latex or polyurethane that is worn internally in the vagina during intercourse. The sheath has a closed flexible ring on one end and an open-ended ring on the other and is coated inside and out with a silicone-based lubricant. *(p. 234)*

internalized homophobia A feeling that a person may absorb from societal hostility toward LGBTQ people. *(p. 355)*

intersectionality Research methodology that addresses social identities and social inequality. *(p. 20)*

intersexuality The condition of someone being biologically between a male and female. *(p. 302)*

intimacy One component of the triangular theory of love that includes feelings of closeness, connectedness, and bondedness. *(p. 455)*

intrauterine device (IUD) A small T-shaped plastic device equipped with hormones or copper that is placed in the uterus to prevent pregnancy. *(p. 239)*

introitus The opening of the vagina. *(p. 104)*

in-vitro fertilization (IVF) A procedure in which mature eggs are removed from a woman's ovaries and are fertilized by sperm in a laboratory dish. *(p. 285)*

K

Kegel exercises The contraction and relaxation of pelvic floor muscles. *(p. 283)*

kink or kinky sex A form of sexual interaction that may involve pain and ritual rules, pushing sexuality to the extreme. *(p. 91)*

L

labia majora The outer lips of the vulva which extend from the mons veneris to the perineum. *(p. 103)*

labia minora The inner lips of the vulva, one on each side of the vaginal opening. *(p. 103)*

lanugo A fine, soft hair that covers a fetus's body in prenatal development. *(p. 265)*

laparoscopy A surgical procedure whereby small incisions are made in the abdomen in which a viewing scope and surgical instruments are inserted to perform surgery. *(p. 242)*

lesbian A woman who is attracted to other women. *(p. 332)*

LGBTQIA+ (lesbian, gay, bisexual, transgender, queer, questioning, intersex, and asexual) The collective name adopted for the social movement of sexual minority rights in the United States and similar Western nations. *(p. 332)*

living apart together (LAT) The cultural idea that two people can be a couple but live apart in separate households. *(p. 422)*

lochia Fluid that is expelled following the birth of a child. *(p. 283)*

love map A cognitive template for attraction and sexual expression believed to develop in childhood. *(p. 533)*

lumpectomy Removal of the cancerous tumor in the breast while leaving the breast intact. *(p. 174)*

luteinizing hormone (LH) A hormone secreted by the pituitary gland that stimulates ovulation in the female. In males it stimulates the production of androgens in the testes. *(p. 117)*

M

male circumcision A common genital modification in the United States and other places in which the foreskin is removed from the penis. *(p. 125)*

malformed sperm Sperm that are abnormally formed in some way; usually die quickly. *(p. 284)*

mammary glands Internal breast; its principal function is to produce milk to nourish an infant after childbirth. *(p. 108)*

mammogram Low-dose X-ray of the breast used to detect growths and cancer in breast tissue. *(p. 174)*

marital rape Forcible sex from one's spouse. *(p. 483)*

marriage scripts Mental or cognitive representations of marriage including ideas about how married couples interact. *(p. 379)*

masochism The act of inflicting pain on oneself for the purpose of pleasure. *(p. 530)*

mastectomy Removal of one or both breasts, and possibly other tissue around the breast, to eradicate cancer from that area. *(p. 174)*

matching hypothesis A hypothesis regarding attraction that states that people select romantic and sexual partners based upon the other person's attractiveness. *(p. 449)*

matriarchal Type of social system in which females are dominant. *(p. 34)*

matrilineal society A society in which descent and inheritance come through the mother's kinship line. *(p. 258)*

menarche A female's first menstrual period. *(p. 109)*

menopause The time in a woman's life when her periods (menstruation) eventually stop and the body goes through changes that no longer allow her to get pregnant. It is a natural event that normally occurs in women age 45 to 55. *(p. 119)*

menstrual phase The third and final phase of ovulation. *(p. 116)*

menstrual synchrony A phenomenon wherein the menstrual cycles of women who live together (such as in homes, prisons, convents, bordellos, dormitories, or barracks) reportedly become synchronized over time. *(p. 114)*

menstruation The shedding of the uterine lining. *(p. 114)*

men who have sex with men (MSM) Men who are married or date women and also have sex with other men. *(p. 350)*

microcelebrities A term coined by Theresa Senft to describe Internet users who gain a cult or mainstream following online. *(p. 80)*

midlife Adulthood beginning in the late 40s. *(p. 410)*

midwife A person who has been trained in most aspects of pregnancy, labor, and delivery but who is not a physician. *(p. 275)*

minority stress Chronic health effects of homophobia such as high blood pressure and depression. *(p. 354)*

miscarriage The unintentional loss of an embryo or fetus during the first 20 weeks of pregnancy. *(p. 270)*

missionary position Position in which the man lies on top of the woman during sexual intercourse. *(p. 160)*

molestation Any sexual act performed with a child by an adult or an older child. *(p. 477)*

monogamous marriage One man and one woman are legally married, usually having moral and religious meanings. *(p. 428)*

monotheism Belief in one God. *(p. 56)*

mons pubis Also called the *mons veneris,* the female pubic mound; the fatty tissue that covers the pubic bone. *(p. 102)*

motility Ability of sperm to move when ejaculated. *(p. 284)*

mucous membrane The inner wall of the vagina made up of moist, soft tissue. *(p. 104)*

myometrium The middle layer of the uterus which comprises smooth muscle and vascular tissue. *(p. 106)*

N

natural methods *See* fertility awareness methods *(p. 242)*

neurotransmitters Chemical messengers in the brain. *(p. 118)*

nipple The raised bud at the center of the areola. *(p. 108)*

noncoercive paraphilia A sexual practice that involves only one person or involves consent between adults to engage in a sexual practice that may involve pain, humiliation, pleasure, and other emotions. *(p. 526)*

noncoital behaviors Sexual behaviors that do not involve penetration of a vagina by a penis. *(p. 150)*

nonmonogamous marriage Practice of one person having more than one spouse. *(p. 428)*

norms Cultural rules about acceptable behavior. *(p. 34)*

nuclear family A family system that includes the biological mother, father, and siblings. *(p. 497)*

O

objectivity A researcher not inserting personal bias into the research question. *(p. 21)*

open adoption A form of adoption where birth parents remain tied to the adoptive family through periodic updates and other communication. *(p. 286)*

opportunistic infections A group of infections that establish themselves in the human body as a result of a weakened immune system due to HIV infection. *(p. 196)*

oral contraceptives Pills containing female hormones that are taken every day by women to prevent pregnancy; also known as birth control pills. *(p. 236)*

oral sex The stimulation of a partner's genitals by mouth. *(p. 155)*

organized religion Sharing practices of worship with others and belonging to a group that is based on shared beliefs and practices. *(p. 56)*

orgasm The peak of sexual excitement, characterized by strong feelings of pleasure and by a series of involuntary contractions of the muscles of the genitals and other areas of the body; the third phase of the human sexual response. *(p. 107)*

osteoporosis Abnormal bone loss. *(p. 119)*

ovarian cancer A gynecologic cancer that begins in one of the two ovaries. *(p. 178)*

ovarian follicle *See* follicle *(p. 108)*

ovary Houses both gonads and endocrine glands; attaches to the fimbria of each fallopian tube to allow release of ovum into the uterus. *(p. 108)*

ovulation The phase of a woman's menstrual cycle in which an egg is released. *(p. 108)*

oxytocin Produced in the hypothalamus, is one of the most important neuropeptides. *(p. 114)*

P

pair bonding The sexual and romantic association between two individuals. *(p. 35)*

paraphilia A medical category created in the 1920s to describe sexual urges and behaviors connected to persons or objects that are not part of normative variations and may cause serious distress or even trauma to others. *(p. 514)*

participatory action research (PAR) Collecting information that honors, centers, and reflects the experiences of people most directly affected by issues in their communities. *(p. 25)*

passion One component of the triangular theory of love that consists of the feelings and desires that lead to romance, physical attraction, and sexual consummation. *(p. 455)*

patriarchal society A society where descent and inheritance come through the father's kinship line. *(p. 258)*

pedophilia Sexual urges and gratification related to minors, especially prepubertal females and males. *(p. 528)*

pelvic inflammatory disease (PID) A painful condition in women marked by inflammation of the uterus, fallopian tubes, and ovaries; typically caused by the presence of one or more untreated STIs. *(p. 185)*

penile columns Spongy tissue within the penis that becomes engorged with blood during an erection. *(p. 122)*

penile glans A sexually sensitive area at the very top of the penis that contains numerous nerve endings. *(p. 121)*

penile implants Objects or substances inserted into the penis to increase size and pleasure. *(p. 126)*

penile shaft The part between the penile glans and the body. *(p. 121)*

penis The primary male organ of sexual pleasure that transports semen as well as urine. *(p. 120)*

perfect-use failure rate The failure rate of a contraceptive method used by people who utilize it regularly and correctly. *(p. 223)*

perimenopause The time when the female body is undergoing changes associated with menopause. *(p. 119)*

perimetrium The outer layer of the uterus. *(p. 106)*

perineum A sexually sensitive and arousing area in both men and women. In women it extends from the vulva to anus and in men between the scrotum and anus. *(p. 123)*

perversions Sexual urges or acts considered unusual or extreme in that culture. *(p. 10)*

pheromones Chemical signals or odors that bodies release to affect a behavioral or psychological response in another body. *(p. 114)*

physiology The study of how all these systems and structures function. *(p. 100)*

pituitary gland A small oval endocrine gland that lies at the base of the brain. It is sometimes called the master gland of the body because all the other endocrine glands depend on its secretions for stimulation. *(p. 113)*

placenta An organ that is attached to the uterine wall during pregnancy that joins the embryo to the mother's bodily systems in order to transfer nutrients, oxygen, and waste products between the developing fetus and the mother. *(p. 261)*

plateau phase The second stage of the human sexual response, according to the EPOR model, in which sensitivity to touch increases and becomes more pleasurable. *(p. 147)*

polyamory The intentional acceptance of one's partner having sexual relations with someone else, typically for a significant period of time. *(p. 417)*

polygamy Marriage between one man and more than one woman at the same time. *(p. 49)*

polytheism Belief in multiple gods and spirits. *(p. 55)*

pornification Turning popular culture sexual images into porn even when they are not pornographic. *(p. 94)*

pornography Involves sexual images being sold for personal titillation; any form of media used to create sexual arousal, especially for commercial purposes. *(p. 92)*

postpartum depression A common psychological depressive disorder that typically begins within 4 weeks following the birth of a child. *(p. 282)*

postpartum period Literally meaning "following birth," this typically refers to the months or first year following the birth of a child. *(p. 281)*

precocious puberty Puberty that occurs several years before the average age in a given society. *(p. 383)*

premature *See* preterm. *(p. 270)*

premenstrual dysphoric disorder (PMDD) A condition in which a woman has severe depression symptoms, irritability, and tension before menstruation. The symptoms of PMDD are more severe than those seen with premenstrual syndrome (PMS). *(p. 118)*

premenstrual syndrome (PMS) An uncomplimentary catchall phrase for a woman identified as grouchy or moody. *(p. 117)*

preterm Birth of an infant less than 37 weeks after conception. *(p. 270)*

primary erogenous zones Areas of the body that are most commonly associated with sexual touch and pleasure, including the genitals, butt, anus, perineum, breasts, inner surface of the thighs, armpits, navel, neck, ears, and mouth. *(p. 141)*

procreation Conception of offspring. *(p. 33)*

progesterone A steroid hormone produced in the ovary; prepares and maintains the uterus for pregnancy. *(p. 116)*

proliferative phase The first phase of ovulation. *(p. 115)*

pronatalism A belief system that promotes childbearing. *(p. 251)*

prostate gland An exocrine gland that produces prostatic secretions. *(p. 123)*

prostate-specific antigen (PSA) test A routine screening used to detect prostate cancer. *(p. 183)*

prostitution Receiving money or gifts in exchange for sex. *(p. 503)*

psychoanalysis Treatment approach, known as talking therapy, developed by Freud to uncover feelings and memories hidden in the unconscious mind. *(p. 11)*

puberty A period of rapid bodily and sexual maturation that occurs mainly in early adolescence. *(p. 370)*

pubic bone Part of the pelvis, the pubic bone is covered by a layer of fat (mons veneris). *(p. 102)*

pubic lice (crabs) Very small parasitic insects that attach themselves to hair shafts and cause itching. *(p. 206)*

puritanism The morally upright and socially strict beliefs and practices of the Puritans. *(p. 61)*

Q

qualitative research method A type of study that focuses on meaning and context, with small or nonrandom samples, or both. *(p. 21)*

quantitative research method A type of study that focuses on sample design and on large representative or random samples. *(p. 21)*

queer or questioning A person who does not wish to be classified as heterosexual and who may be questioning attractions to people of the same sex. *(p. 332)*

quid pro quo A form of sexual harassment where submission to unwelcome sexual conduct becomes either a condition of employment or personnel action. *(p. 499)*

R

random sample A sample in which every element in the population has an equal chance of being selected. *(p. 15)*

rape Sexual penetration of the body using physical force, the threat of bodily harm, or oral penetration by a sex organ of another person, without the consent of the victim. *(p. 478)*

rape-prone society A society or cultural group where women's desires are considered to be unimportant and physical sexual coercion is normative. *(p. 487)*

refractory period The normal response immediately after ejaculation, when a man cannot get another erection. *(p. 15)*

registered partnership An official state policy that allows a same-sex or opposite-sex couple to register as partners for tax and other purposes. *(p. 422)*

reliability The consistency of measures by testing them in repeated experiments. *(p. 21)*

religious identity The social expression of an individual's faith in the context of community and nation. *(p. 56)*

representative samples Components of the natural population that represent diverse segments of the population of interest. *(p. 13)*

repress In Freudian terms, to suppress upsetting sexual feelings or memories to keep them from causing mental distress or motivating unacceptable behavior. *(p. 11)*

research designs Scientific models that lay out the aims, methods, and analysis of data utilized in sexual science. *(p. 21)*

resilience The process(es) that allows individuals to grow and thrive in physical and mental health in spite of the risk and challenges they encounter. *(p. 371)*

resiliency The positive capacity of people to cope with stress and adversity. *(p. 507)*

resolution The fourth phase of the human sexual response, involving the relaxation of the body and a feeling of psychological wellness, as the extra blood in the genitals that caused erection drains out and the genitals return to their normal state. *(p. 148)*

retrospective bias The tendency for people to not remember certain aspects of their lives clearly or to misremember certain aspects. *(p. 22)*

retrospective self-report An account of a memory of an event in one's life. *(p. 22)*

retrovirus A virus that survives and multiplies by invading and destroying the DNA of normal body cells and then replicating its own DNA into the host cell's chromosomes. *(p. 195)*

robot fetishism Arousal to a robot or androidlike being. *(p. 533)*

root The base of the penis. *(p. 120)*

S

sadism The act of inflicting pain on one's sexual partner, to create sexual pleasure for the person inflicting the pain. *(p. 530)*

sado-masochism relationships (S/M) Relationships that may involve pain and pleasure, bondage, and other practices such as spanking and whipping. *(p. 538)*

same-sex marriage A term used to describe a legal marriage and formal status between two people of the same biological sex. *(p. 422)*

scabies A skin infestation caused by a microscopic mite that burrows under the skin and causes a very itchy rash. *(p. 205)*

scrotal sac Holds the testicles. *(p. 122)*

scrotum Located between the penis and the anus and is an extension of the abdomen. *(p. 122)*

sebaceous glands Glands that produce oil. *(p. 103)*

sebum Oil produced by sebaceous glands that coats and protects the surface tissue the glands are on. *(p. 103)*

secondary erogenous zones Other areas of the body where we feel sexual sensation. Due to individual variation in people's preferences for touch, virtually any other area of the body can be a secondary erogenous zone. *(p. 141)*

secondary sex characteristics Physical characteristics that indicate pubertal development other than genital development. *(p. 381)*

secretory phase The next phase of ovulation. *(p. 115)*

secular trend The decline in the age of menarche during the 20th century. *(p. 382)*

selective abstinence A form of contraception where individuals engage in safe sexual behaviors by avoiding behaviors such as vaginal, anal, or oral intercourse. *(p. 231)*

semen Sexual fluid ejaculated through the penis that contains sperm and fluid from the prostate gland, seminal vesicles, and Cowper's glands. *(p. 123)*

seminal vesicles A paired set of tubular glands that produces seminal fluid which makes up the majority of semen. *(p. 123)*

seminiferous tubule A thin, coiled structure in the testes where sperm is produced. *(p. 122)*

seniors Adults 60 and up. *(p. 411)*

serial monogamy The practice of having an exclusive relationship with one person, breaking up, and going on to another exclusive relationship. *(p. 416)*

sex The genes and biological development that determines whether we are male or female. *(p. 299)*

sex-approving Culturally supportive of positive attitudes toward sexual expression and behavior. *(p. 51)*

sex-disapproving Generally negative cultural attitudes toward sexual expression and behavior. *(p. 51)*

sex flush During the plateau phase, as the genitals are stimulated more, the chest area flushes to pink or red. *(p. 147)*

sexism The prejudice directed toward women as equals in society. *(p. 323)*

sexology Systematic study of sexual interests, functions, and behaviors. *(p. 8)*

sexting Sharing highly explicit sexual images of oneself through the Internet, to express sexual individuality. *(p. 81)*

sex tourism Traveling for the purpose of having sex in return for money or goods. *(p. 541)*

sex trafficking Human trafficking for the purpose of commercial sexual exploitation; the U.S. legal definition of sex trafficking includes the exploitation of anyone under 18 involved in commercial sex. *(p. 506)*

sexual addiction A controversial disorder of intimacy; not a paraphilia. *(p. 524)*

sexual bullying Any bullying behavior, whether physical or nonphysical, based on a person's sexuality or gender; involves using sexuality as a weapon and can be carried out in person, behind someone's back, or via technology. *(p. 502)*

sexual chauvinism The belief that one's sexual culture is superior to others. *(p. 49)*

sexual coercion Acts of sexual violence committed against an unwilling or incapacitated individual. *(p. 477)*

sexual compulsivity A person's inability to control sexual urges; not a paraphilia. *(p. 523)*

sexual consumerism The use of sexuality to market and sell products to consumers *(p. 70)*

sexual culture Distinct shared sexual meanings and sexual practices of a group. *(p. 39)*

sexual degeneracy Impairment or decline of sexual function. *(p. 9)*

sexual differentiation The process of developing into a male or female that begins before conception and continues during fetal development. *(p. 300)*

sexual dimorphism Being either female or male. *(p. 302)*

sexual dysfunction When people cannot enjoy sexual intercourse or orgasm. *(p. 15)*

sexual empowerment Taking responsibility for one's own sexuality, making one's own choices, and respecting one's own needs, desires, and values. *(p. 3)*

sexual excitement The subjective experience of sexual arousal. *(p. 144)*

sexual exploitation Sexual abuse of children and adults through the exchange of sex or sexual acts for drugs, food, shelter, protection, other basics of life, and/or money. *(p. 477)*

sexual fantasy Private mental imagery associated with explicitly erotic feelings, possibly accompanied by sexual arousal. *(p. 144)*

sexual fetishism An object or body part that arouses intense sexual interest and urges, and may launch a person into an uncontrollable episode alone or with another person, typically leading to sexual gratification. *(p. 541)*

sexual fluidity A form of sexual expression that is more situation-dependent and perhaps more open to the characteristics of the individual, rather than focusing so much on the anatomy. *(p. 351)*

sexual geography Cities and neighborhoods where sexual minorities migrate to, as safe places to live. *(p. 348)*

sexual harassment Any unwelcome verbal, physical, or sexual conduct that has the effect of creating an intimidating, hostile, or offensive environment. *(p. 499)*

sexual identity Self-identification as heterosexual, bisexual, or homosexual. *(p. 46)*

sexual individuality The unique expression of an individual's most basic sexual needs and attractions, based on the individual's body and anatomy, DNA, hormones, orientations, fantasies, feelings, behaviors, and relationships. *(p. 52)*

sexualization The process of someone being treated as a sex object, and the objectification becomes so intense that the person may feel worthless as a human being beyond his or her sex appeal. *(p. 396)*

sexualized behaviors Human behaviors that are sexual in nature. *(p. 375)*

sexual literacy The knowledge and skills needed to promote and protect sexual well-being; a defined social and political position in society, which implies an underlying sexual orientation. *(p. 3)*

sexual negotiation Discussion and interaction that lead to agreement about sexual relationships. *(p. 3)*

sexual norm A cultural standard of sexual behavior expected of people in a particular role, relationship, and situation. *(p. 49)*

sexual novelty Creative exploration of what is sexually arousing and satisfying to one or both partners. *(p. 544)*

sexual orientation The structure of a person's sexual or romantic attractions or both in people of the same or other sex, or toward both sexes. *(p. 332)*

sexual prejudice Irrational hatred directed toward people because of their sexual orientation or sexual behavior. *(p. 354)*

sexual science The study of sexual behavior across the human species, all cultures and individuals. *(p. 8)*

sexual script theory A theory that individuals develop scripts for sexual roles and behavior that incorporate the sexual rules of their culture. *(p. 453)*

sexual selfhood The totality of oneself as a sexual being, including positive and negative feelings. *(p. 3)*

sexual shame Overwhelming and grave feelings of shame, guilt, and remorse having to do with sexual memories, feelings, and fantasies that impede sexual satisfaction. *(p. 523)*

sexual socialization The application of a culture's blueprints to sexual feelings, thoughts, and behaviors; the process of learning values and norms of sexual behaviors. *(p. 49)*

sexual unlearning The process of unlearning something about sexuality that may have been learned at a very young age. *(p. 52)*

sexual well-being The condition of experiencing good health, pleasure, and satisfaction in intimate relationships. *(p. 3)*

sex work Receiving money or gifts in exchange for sex. *(p. 503)*

shared sexual images Content that contains explicit or hidden sexual messages, whether real or imagined, visual or auditory. *(p. 71)*

similarity-attraction hypothesis The more similar two individuals are, the greater the attraction between them will be. *(p. 450)*

single Uncommitted or unmarried. *(p. 412)*

smegma Smelly, cheesy substance formed by penis secretions that accumulate beneath the foreskin. *(p. 121)*

social construction The social, cultural, political, economic, and other institutional forces that shape sexual behavior. *(p. 18)*

social justice The fair distribution of wealth, opportunities, and privileges in society that imply respect, dignity, and the application of human rights in the daily lives of people. *(p. 17)*

social kin People who become relatives through marriage. *(p. 497)*

social media A collective term referring to online communication channels devoted to user-based input, interaction, collaboration, and sharing of content. *(p. 80)*

social networking sites (SNSs) Sites that allow people to form online relationships, for business and pleasure, extending networks that encompass friends and sexual and romantic interests. *(p. 80)*

soft pornography Nude images that do not depict penetrative sex scenes. *(p. 92)*

speculum An instrument used to open the vagina during vaginal exams performed by a physician. *(p. 175)*

spermarche First ejaculation; occurs during male pubertal development. *(p. 383)*

spermatogenesis The process of sperm production. *(p. 122)*

spermicides Substances that kill sperm cells. Usually used alone or together with a barrier method of contraception. *(p. 236)*

spirituality An individual's inner sense of having deeper values, a spiritual path, or belief in an ultimate reality. *(p. 38)*

spontaneous abortion The unintentional loss of an embryo or fetus during the first 20 weeks of pregnancy. *(p. 270)*

statutory rape Sexual activity with an individual who is too young to legally consent to sex. *(p. 404)*

sterilization A surgical alteration of the internal reproductive system of either male or female that permanently blocks sperm cells from fertilizing an ovum. *(p. 241)*

steroid hormones A group of hormones that include androgens and estrogens. *(p. 113)*

stig The capacity for some individuals to have context-dependent changes in their erotic response, in Lisa Diamond's research. *(p. 351)*

stigma Extreme disapproval attached to someone who deviates from socially and culturally acceptable standards of behavior, spoiling the person's identity and turning the person into an outcast in society. *(p. 354)*

stillbirth The unintentional loss of a pregnancy after 20 weeks of gestation. *(p. 270)*

strange familiarity A person's ability to feel like they know someone intimately without the other person knowing who they are. *(p. 80)*

surrogacy A situation where a woman becomes pregnant for another individual or couple and then surrenders the child after birth. *(p. 286)*

survey study Investigations of different kinds of sexuality employing representative samples of people from different populations to establish norms of some kind, such as sexual health norms. *(p. 13)*

survival sex Sex engaged in by people who sell their bodies for basic needs such as food, clothing, and shelter. *(p. 504)*

swinging The idea that married heterosexuals can have casual sex with other heterosexuals outside the relationship. *(p. 431)*

symbolic boundary Divides people according to their religious beliefs about what are "good" and "bad" sexual behaviors. *(p. 62)*

syphilis An STI caused by a bacterium and characterized by a chancre, or sore, at the point of infection. *(p. 202)*

T

technical virginity A belief that one can engage in sexual behaviors, including oral and anal sex, and still maintain the state of virginity by abstaining from vaginal intercourse. *(p. 387)*

teen dating violence A pattern of abusive behaviors used to gain power and control over a current or former dating partner. *(p. 502)*

tenting effect The vaginal wall's increase in size during sexual arousal. *(p. 104)*

testicles Also known as testes or male gonads, is part of the reproductive system and produces sperm and the sex hormone testosterone. *(p. 122)*

testicular cancer A cancer that begins in one of the testicles; tends to occur among younger men. *(p. 180)*

testosterone A steroid hormone that helps organize male reproduction and produces secondary sex characteristics in males, and impacts sexual functioning in both sexes. *(p. 113)*

thelarche The first stage of breast development. *(p. 109)*

toxic shock syndrome (TSS) A severe disease that involves fever, shock, and problems with the function of several body organs. *(p. 118)*

transgender A person who expresses gender behaviors that vary from the norm; self-identification as woman, man, neither sex, or both sexes does not match their assigned sex, which was identified by others as XY male or XX female. *(p. 97)*

transphobia The fear and hatred of transgender people. *(p. 313)*

transvestic fetishism A condition of a man who becomes aroused by wearing women's clothes. *(p. 526)*

transvestite Someone with an interest in wearing clothing typical of the other gender. *(p. 345)*

triangular theory of love Suggests that people can have varying degrees of intimacy, passion, and commitment at any one time in their romantic relationships. *(p. 455)*

trichomoniasis A common sexually transmitted protozoan parasite causing symptoms in women, including genital irritation, burning or pain during urination, and a foul-smelling vaginal discharge; infected men typically do not have symptoms but are contagious. *(p. 178)*

trimester One of three periods of approximately 3 months each that make up the phases of a full-term pregnancy. *(p. 259)*

tubal ligation A form of permanent, surgical contraception where egg and sperm are prevented from joining together by tying, cutting, clipping, or blocking the fallopian tubes. *(p. 223)*

tumescence The state of being swollen or engorged with blood. *(p. 103)*

tunica albuginea The capsule that holds the tightly coiled seminiferous tubules. *(p. 122)*

twin studies Research that compares twins to determine what part of nature or nurture may have influenced behavior. *(p. 338)*

typical failure rate The typical number of people who become pregnant accidentally utilizing a particular contraceptive method. *(p. 223)*

U

ultrasound A common form of screening used often to monitor development of the fetus throughout a pregnancy. *(p. 262)*

umbilical cord A long structure consisting of two large arteries and one large vein that transports oxygen, waste, and nutrients between the fetus and the placenta. *(p. 261)*

universal human rights Freedoms to which all humans are entitled, such as the freedoms of speech and religion, and the most basic right of all, to life. *(p. 26)*

urethral opening Located between the clitoris and the vaginal opening, it allows urine to be expelled from the bladder. *(p. 104)*

urinary tract infection (UTI) An infection of the urethra, bladder, or other urinary structure, usually caused by bacteria. *(p. 177)*

uterine cancer A gynecologic cancer that begins in the uterus. *(p. 178)*

uterus Also called the womb, the structure connected at one end to the cervix and at both sides to the fallopian tubes. *(p. 104)*

V

vacuum extraction An intervention where a plastic or metal suction cup is placed on the baby's head. The doctor then uses that suction to deliver the baby's head and body. *(p. 279)*

vagina An elastic, muscular canal that extends from the vulva inward to the cervix. *(p. 104)*

vaginal cancer A gynecologic cancer that begins in the vagina. *(p. 178)*

vaginal lubrication Fluid produced by glands in the vagina to aid in penetration during sexual activity. *(p. 104)*

vaginal opening Located between the urethral opening and the perineum; a tubular tract that leads to the uterus. *(p. 104)*

vaginitis Inflammation of the vagina that can result in some unpleasant symptoms including discharge, itching, and pain. *(p. 177)*

validity The extent to which a test measures what it claims to measure. *(p. 21)*

value messages Moral statements regarding a particular behavior, issue, or event. *(p. 375)*

variable Something that can be changed, such as a characteristic or value. *(p. 21)*

vas deferens Ducts that help to move sperm from the epididymis to the ejaculatory ducts. *(p. 122)*

vasectomy A form of permanent, surgical contraception where sperm are prevented from mixing with semen in ejaculate by cutting or tying off the vas deferens. *(p. 223)*

vasocongestion Increasing blood flow to erectile tissues in the genitals. *(p. 105)*

vernix A protective waxy substance on a fetus's body in prenatal development. *(p. 265)*

victim-blame The tendency of victims of abuse to place the blame for the abusive actions of others onto themselves. *(p. 486)*

virilization The masculinization of the human body and genital structures. *(p. 302)*

virtual sex Sexual activity through online communication. *(p. 78)*

voluntary surgical contraception (VSC) A surgical alteration of the internal reproductive system of either male or female that permanently blocks sperm cells from fertilizing an ovum. *(p. 241)*

voyeurism The act of secretly watching someone undress or engage in some kind of intimate or sexual behavior. *(p. 527)*

vulva The external female genitals; often incorrectly referred to as the vagina. *(p. 102)*

vulvar cancer A gynecologic cancer that forms in the vulva. *(p. 178)*

W

winnowing hypothesis People become increasingly selective and more careful during the process of dating, mating, cohabitating, and marriage. *(p. 425)*

withdrawal method An unreliable method of contraception involving removing the penis from the vagina just prior to ejaculation. *(p. 222)*

Y

yeast infections Type of vaginitis that occurs when a naturally occurring fungus changes the normal environment in the vagina, mouth, skinfolds, or fingernail beds. *(p. 178)*

Z

zona pellucida The thick, protective layer on the outer part of the ovum. *(p. 259)*

zygote A fertilized ovum. *(p. 260)*

zygote intrafallopian transfer (ZIFT) A procedure where an ovum is fertilized in a laboratory dish and then placed in the fallopian tube in order to make a more natural progression down to the uterus for implantation. *(p. 286)*

References

Abbey, A., Zawacki, T., Buck, P. O., Clinton, A. M., & McAuslan, P. (2001). Alcohol and sexual assault. *Alcohol Research & Health, 25*(1), 43-51.

Abdullaeva, M. (2008). *Abortion around the world: Overview*. Retrieved November 16, 2008, from NOW Foundation website: http://www.nowfoundation.org/issues/ reproductive/050808-abortion_worldwide.html

Abrams, N. (Ed.). (2008). *Jews and sex*. Nottingham, UK: Five Leaves.

Abramson, P. R. (1996). *Sarah-A sexual biography*. Albany, NY: State University of New York Press.

Abramson, P. R., & Pinkerton, S. D. (1995). *Pleasure: Thoughts on the nature of human sexuality*. New York, NY: Oxford University Press.

Abramson, P. R., Pinkerton, S. D., & Huppin, M. (2003). *Sexual rights in America: The Ninth Amendment and the pursuit of happiness*. New York, NY: New York University Press.

Adams, J. M., & Jones, W. H. (1999). Introduction: Interpersonal commitment in historical perspective. In J. M. Adams & W. H. Jones (Eds.), *Handbook of interpersonal commitment and relationship stability* (pp. 3-37). New York, NY: Springer.

Addiego, F., Belzer, E. G., Comolli, J., Moger, W., Perry, J. D., & Whipple, B. (1981). Female "ejaculation." *Journal of Sex Research, 17,* 13-21.

Afifi, W. A., & Faulkern, S. L. (2000). On being 'just friends': The frequency and impact of sexual activity in cross-sex friendship. *Journal of Social and Personal Relationships, 17,* 205-222.

Aggleton, P., & Parker, R. (2002). *HIV/AIDS-related stigma and discrimination: A conceptual framework and an agenda for action*. Birmingham, AL: The Population Council, Inc.

Aggleton, P., & Parker, R. (2003). HIV and AIDS-related stigma and discrimination: A conceptual framework and implications for action. *Social Science & Medicine 57,* 13-24.

Aggleton, P., & Parker, R. (Eds.). (2010). *Routledge handbook of sexuality, health and Rights*. New York, NY: Routledge.

Aggleton, P., Wood, K., Malcolm, A., & Parker, R. (2005). *HIV-related stigma, discrimination, and human rights violations: Case studies of successful programmes*. New York, NY: UN AIDS.

Ahmed, L. (1992). *Women and gender in Islam: Historical roots of a modern debate*. New Haven, CT: Yale University Press.

Ainsworth, M. D. S. (1967). *Infancy in Uganda: Infant care and the growth of love*. Baltimore, MD: Johns Hopkins University Press.

Ainsworth, M. D. S. (1989). Attachments beyond infancy. *American Psychologist, 44,* 709-716.

Ainsworth, M. D. S., Blehar, M. C., Waters, E., & Wall, S. (1978). *Patterns of attachment: A psychological study of the Strange Situation*. Hillsdale, NJ: Erlbaum.

Aksglaede, L., Juul, A., Olsen, L. W., & Thorkild, I. A. (2009). Age at puberty and the emerging obesity epidemic. *PloS One, 4*(12), e8450.

Albert, B. (2009). With one voice. *The national campaign to prevent teen and unplanned pregnancy*. Retrieved from TheNationalCampaign.org

Alexander, B. (2012). *Final word: Expert panel rejects routine PSA tests for men*. Retrieved October 25, 2012, from Men's health on NBC News.com website: http://www.msnbc.msn. com/id/47505948/ns/health-mens_health/t/ final-word-expert-panel-rejects-routine-psa-tests-men/

Alexander, M. (2010). *The new Jim Crow: Mass incarceration in the age of color blindness*. New York, NY: The New Press.

Allen, L. (2008). They think you shouldn't be having sex anyway: Young people's suggestions for improving sexuality education content. *Sexualities, 11*(5), 573-594.

Allen, W. D. (2007). The reporting and under-reporting of rape. *Southern Economic Journal, 73*(3), 623-641.

Altman, D. (2001). *Global sex*. Chicago, IL: University of Chicago Press.

Alzate, H., & Hoch, Z. (1986). The 'G spot' and 'female ejaculation': A current appraisal. *Journal of Sexual & Marital Therapy, 12,* 211-220.

Amati, V., Meggiolaro, S., Rivellini, G., & Zaccarin, S. (2018, May 4). Social relations and life satisfaction: The role of friends. *Genus, 74*(1). Published online. DOI: 10.1186/s41118-018-0032-z

American Academy of Child and Adolescent Psychiatry (AACAP). (2011, August). *Children with lesbian, gay, bisexual and transgender parents* (Report No. 92). Washington, DC: Author.

American Academy of Pediatrics (AAP). (2001). Care of the adolescent sexual assault victim. *Pediatrics, 107*(6), 1476-1479.

American Academy of Pediatrics (AAP). (2005). *Sexual behaviors in children*. Retrieved February 15, 2009, from http://www2.aap.org/ pubserv/PSVpreview/pages/behaviorchart.html

American Academy of Pediatrics. (2012). *Newborn male circumcision*. Technical Report. 8/27/12. Retrieved July 5, 2019, from https://www.aap.org/en-us/about-the-aap/aap-press-room/Pages/Newborn-Male-Circumcision.aspx

American Academy of Pediatrics (AAP). (2011). *Breast feeding as a form of contraception*. Retrieved October 25, 2012, from http://www. healthychildren.org/English/ages-stages/baby/ breastfeeding/pages/Breastfeeding-as-a-Form-of-Contraception.aspx?

American Association of Retired Persons (AARP). (2005). *Sexuality and midlife and beyond: 2004 update of attitudes and behaviors*. Washington, DC: Author.

American Cancer Society. (2008). *How to perform a breast self-exam*. Retrieved October 25, 2012, from http://www.cancer. org/docroot/CRI/content/CRI_2_6x_How_ to_perform_a_breast_self_exam_5.asp)

American Cancer Society. (2015). *Breast cancer screening guidelines*. Retrieved July 13, 2019, from https://www.cancer.org/health-care-professionals/american-cancer-society-prevention-early-detection-guidelines/breast-cancer-screening-guidelines.html

American Cancer Society. (2019). *How common is breast cancer?* Retrieved July 13, 2019, from https://www.cancer.org/cancer/breast-cancer/about/how-common-is-breast-cancer.html

American College of Obstetricians and Gynecologists (ACOG). (2019). *Cervical cancer screening*. Retrieved July 13, 2019, from https://www.acog.org/Patients/FAQs/Cervical-Cancer-Screening?IsMobileSet=false

American Pregnancy Association. (2007). *Human chorionic gonadotropin (hCG): The pregnancy hormone*. Retrieved July 18, 2012, from http://www.americanpregnancy.org/ duringpregnancy/hcglevels.html/

American Pregnancy Association. (2009). *Exercise guidelines during pregnancy*. Retrieved September 17, 2009, from http://www. americanpregnancy.org/pregnancyhealth/ exerciseguidelines.html

American Pregnancy Association. (2018). *Oral sex & anal sex during pregnancy*. Retrieved from https://americanpregnancy.org/is-it-safe/oral-sex-anal-sex/

American Pregnancy Association. (n.d.). *Pregnancy Symptoms-Early Signs of Pregnancy*. Retrieved October 24, 2008, from http://www. americanpregnancy.org/gettingpregnant/ earlypregnancysymptoms.html

American Pregnancy Association. (n.d.). *Statistics. Factsheet*. Retrieved July 20, 2012, from http://www.americanpregnancy.org/ main/statistics.html

American Psychiatric Association. (2000). *Diagnostic and statistical manual of mental disorders (DSM-IV-TR)* (Rev. ed.). Arlington, VA: Author.

American Psychiatric Association. (2013). *Diagnostic and statistical manual of mental disorders (DSM-5®)*. Washington, DC: American Psychiatric Association.

American Psychological Association (APA). (2004). *Sexual orientation, parents, and children*. Washington, DC: Author.

American Psychological Association (APA). (2010). *Report on the APA Task Force on the Sexualization of Girls*. Washington, DC: Author.

American Sexual Health Association. (2019). *Statistics*. Retrieved March 19, 2019, from at http://www.ashasexualhealth.org/stdsstis/statistics/

Amnesty International. (2010). *Deadly delivery: The maternal health care crisis in the USA*. London, UK: Amnesty International Secretariat.

Anderson, J. (2005). Prison rape and sexual coercion behind bars. *Research & Advocacy Digest, 7*(3), 1-2.

Anderson, L. (2019). Viagra: How a little blue pill changed the world. *Drugs.com*. Retrieved July 1, 2019, from https://www.drugs.com/slideshow/viagra-little-blue-pill-1043

Anderson, M., Kunkel, A., & Dennis, M. R. (2011). Let's (not) talk about that: Bridging the past sexual experiences taboo to build healthy romantic relationships. *Journal of Sex Research, 48,* 381-391.

Anderson, P. B., & Struckman-Johnson, C. (Eds.). (1998). *Sexually aggressive women: Current perspectives and controversies*. New York, NY: Guilford.

Andre, T., Whigham, M., Hendrickson, A., & Chambers, S. (1999). Competency beliefs, positive affect, and gender stereotypes of elementary students and their parents about science versus other school subjects. *Journal of Research in Science Teaching, 36*(6), 719-747.

Antonovics, K., & Town, R. (2004). Are all the good men married? Uncovering the sources of the marital wage premium. *American Economic Review, 94,* 317-321.

Arata, C. (2000). From child victim to adult victim: A model for predicting sexual victimization. *Child Maltreatment, 5,* 28-38.

Arbeit, M. R. (2014). What does healthy sex look like among youth? *Towards Human Development, 57*(5), 259-286. DOI:10.1159/000367856

Argyle, M. (2001). *The psychology of happiness.* New York, NY: Routledge.

Ariosto, D., & Remizowski, L. (2012, June 15). *Yale settles sexual harassment complaint.* Retrieved September 24, 2012, from CNN Justice website: http://articles.cnn.com/2012-06-15/justice/justice_connecticut-yale-settlement_1_sexual-harassment-sexual-misconduct-sexually-hostile-environment?_s5PM:JUSTICE

Armstrong, K. (1999). *A History of God.* New York, NY: Vintage Books.

Armstrong, K. (2001a). *Buddha.* New York, NY: Penguin Books.

Armstrong, K. (2001b). *Islam: A Short History.* London, UK: Pheonix Phoenix Books.

Armstrong, K. (2015). *St. Paul: The Misunderstood Apostle.* London, UK: Atlantic Books.

Aronson, L. (2019) *Elderhood: Redefining aging, transforming medicine, and reimagining life.* New York: Bloomsbury Publishing.

Ashton, S., McDonald, K., and Kirkman, M. (2018). Women's experiences of pornography: A systematic review of research using qualitative methods. *The Journal of Sex Research, 55*(3), 334–347. DOI: https://DOI.org/10.1080/00224499.2017.1364337

AVERT. (2009). *The origin of AIDS and HIV and the first cases of AIDS.* Retrieved October 25, 2012, from: http://www.avert.org/origin- aids-hiv.htm

AVERT. (2011a). *Worldwide HIV & AIDS statistics commentary.* Retrieved September 29, 2012, from http://www.avert.org/worlstatinfo.htm

AVERT. (2011b). *New antiretroviral AIDS drugs.* Retrieved October 25, 2012 from http://www.avert.org/new-aids-drugs.htm

AVERT. (2019). *Global information and education on HIV and AIDS.* Retrieved from https://www.avert.org/professionals/hiv-programming/prevention/overview

AVERT. (n.d.). *HIV & AIDS in the United States of America.* Retrieved July 17, 2012, from http://www.avert.org/america.htm

Ayres, T. (1987). Scared sexless. *American Health,* 83–91.

Ayuso, L. (2018). What future awaits couples living apart together (LAT)? *Sociological Review, 67*(1), 226–244.

Badgett, M. V. L. (2009). *When gay people get married.* New York, NY: New York University Press.

Badgett, M. V. L., & Herman, J. L. (2011). *Patterns of relationship recognition by same-sex couples in the United States.* Los Angeles, CA: UCLA, Williams Institute.

Bahn, P. G. (1998). *The Cambridge illustrated history of prehistoric art.* Cambridge, UK: Cambridge University Press.

Bailey, J. M. (2003). *The man who would be queen: The science of gender-bending and transsexualism.* Washington, DC: Joseph Henry Press.

Bailey, J. M., & Oberschneider, M. (1997). Sexual orientation and professional dance. *Archives of Sexual Behavior, 26,* 433–444.

Bailey, J. M., & Pillard, R. D. (1991). A genetic study of male sexual orientation. *Archives of General Psychiatry, 48,* 1089–1096.

Bailey, J. M., Vasey, P. L., Diamond, L. M., Breedlove, S. M., Vilain, E., & Epprecht, M. (2016). Sexual orientation, controversy, and science. *Psychological Science in the Public Interest, 17*(2), 45–101. DOI:10.1177/1529100616637616

Baker, J. H. (2011). *Margaret Sanger: A life of passion.* New York, NY: Macmillan.

Ball, T. (2008). Female genital mutilation. *Nursing Standard, 23*(5), 43–47.

Baltazar, A. McBride, D., Vanderwaal, C., & Conopio, K. (2016). Sex, drugs, and alcohol: What Adventist college students say about the role of parents and religion. *Faculty Publications, 145.* Retrieved from http://digitalcommons.andrews.edu/pubs/145

Balzarini, R. N., et al. (2017, May 18). Perceptions of primary and secondary relationships in polyamory. *PloS One.* Retrieved from https://journals.plos.org/plosone/article?id=10.1371/journal.pone.0177841

Balzarini, R. N., et al. (2019). Demographic comparison of American individuals in polyamorous and monogamous relationships. *Journal of Sex Research, 56*(6), 681–694.

Bamforth, N. (Ed.). (2014). *Sexual orientation and rights.* London: Routledge. DOI:10.4324/978131 5243375

Bancroft, J. (2003). *Sexual development in childhood.* Indianapolis, IN: Indiana University Press.

Bancroft, J., Graham, C. A., Janssen, E., et al. (2009). The dual control model: Current status and future directions. *Journal of Sex Research, J Sex Res.* 2009; *46,* 121–142.

Bancroft, J., & Vukadinovic, Z. (2004). Sexual addiction, sexual compulsivity, or what? Toward a theoretical model. *Journal of Sex Research, 41,* 225–234.

Banner, L. W. (1984). *Women in America: A brief history.* San Diego, CA: Harcourt Brace Jovanovich.

Banyard, V. L., & Cross, C. (2008). Consequences of teen dating violence: Understanding intervening variables in ecological context. *Violence Against Women, 14*(9), 998–1013.

Barak, A., & King, S. A. (2000). The two faces of the Internet: Introduction to the special issues on the Internet and sexuality. *Cyberpsychology and Behavior, 3*(4), 517–520. DOI: 10.1089/109493100420133

Barclay, T. (2017). Labia minora—female reproductive system. *Innerbody.* Retrieved from https://www.innerbody.com/image_repfov/repo20-new.html

Bardzell, S. (2006). The submissive speaks: The semiotics of visuality in virtual BDSM fantasy play. *Proceedings of the 2006 ACM SIGGRAPH symposium on Videogames,* 99–102. New York, NY: ACM Press.

Barelds, D. P. H., & Barelds-Dijkstra, P. (2007). Love at first sight or friends first? Ties among partner personality trait similarity, relationship onset, relationship quality, and love. *Journal of Social and Personal Relationships, 24,* 479–496.

Bargh, J. A., McKenna, K. Y. A., & Fitzsimons, G. M. (2002). Can you see the real me? Activation and expression of the 'true self' on the Internet. *Journal of Social Issues, 58,* 33–48.

Barker, J. C., Herdt, G., & DeVries, B. (2006). Social support in the lives of lesbians and gay men at midlife and later. *Sexuality Research & Social Policy, 3,* 1–23.

Barnitz, L. (2001). Effectively responding to the commercial sexual exploitation of children: A comprehensive approach to prevention, protection, and reintegration services. *Child Welfare, 80,* 597–610.

Barrell, A. (2018, November 14). Do penis enlargement methods work? *Medical News Today.* Retrieved July 5, 2019, from https://www.medicalnewstoday.com/articles/323688.php

Barth, F. (1974). *Cosmologies in the making.* New Haven, CT: Yale University Press.

Bartholomew, K., & Horowitz, L. M. (1991). Attachment styles among young adults: A test of a four-category model. *Journal of Personality and Social Psychology, 61*(2), 226–244.

Basham, A. L. (1999). *A cultural history of India.* New Delhi, India: Oxford University Press.

Basile, K. C. (2002). Prevalence of wife rape and other intimate partner sexual coercion in a nationally representative sample of women. *Violence and Victims, 17,* 511–524.

Basson, R. (2000). The female sexual response: A different model. *Journal of Sex and Marital Therapy,* *26*(1), 51–65. DOI: https://DOI.org/10.1080/00926 2300278641

Basson, R. (2001). Human sex-response cycles. *Journal of Sex and Marital Therapy, 27,* 33–43.

Bauer, I. (2008). 'They don't just come for Machu Picchu': Locals' views of tourist-local sexual relationships in Cuzco, Peru. *Culture, Health, and Sexuality, 10,* 611–624.

Bauman, V. (2018). The forgotten voices of #metoo: Prison rape in America—perpetrated by both inmates and staff—remains pervasive and under-reported 15 years after the passage of a law intended to end crisis. Retrieved from https://justdetention.org/the-forgotten-voices-of-metoo-prison-rape-in-america-perpetrated-by-both-inmates-and-staff-remains-pervasive-and-under-reported-15-years-after-the-passage-of-a-law-intended-to-end-crisis/

Baumeister, R. F. (2000). Gender differences in erotic plasticity: The female sex drive as socially flexible and responsive. *Psychological Bulletin, 126*(3), 347–374.

Bayer, R. (1987). *Homosexuality and American psychiatry.* Princeton, NJ: Princeton University Press.

BBC. (2015) Where is it illegal to be gay? Citing International Gay Lesbian Bi Trans Association. Retrieved May 27, 2019, from https://www.bbc.com/news/world-25927595

Becker, E. (1973). *The denial of death.* New York, NY: Simon & Schuster.

Becker, L. G. (2018) Advancing global health and strengthening the HIV response in the era of sustainable goals: The International AIDS Society and the Lancet Commission. *Lancet, 392,* 312–358.

Beckstead, A. L. (2012). Can we change sexual orientation? *Archives of Sexual Behavior, 41*(1), 121–134. DOI:10.1007/s10508-012-9922-x

Beisel, N. (1997). *Imperiled innocents: Anthony Comstock and family reproduction in Victorian America.* Princeton, NJ: Princeton University Press.

Bell, A., Weinberg, M., & Hammersmith, S. (1981). *Sexual preference: Its development in men and women.* Bloomington, IN: Indiana University Press.

Bell, S., & Sobo, E. (2001). Celibacy in cross-cultural perspective. In E. Sobo & S. Bell (Eds.), *Celibacy, culture, and society* (pp. 3–26). Madison, WI: University of Wisconsin Press.

Bellah, R. (2006). *The Robert Bellah reader.* Durham, NC: Duke University Press.

Bellah, R., Madisen, R., Sullivan, W. M., Swindler, A., & Tipton, S. M. (1985). *Habits of the heart: Individualism and commitment in American life.* Berkeley, CA: University of California Press.

Belous, C. K., & Bauman, M. L. (2017). What's in a name? Exploring pansexuality online. *Journal of Bisexuality, 17*(1), 58–72. DOI:10.1080/15299716.2 016.1224212

Belzer, E. G., Whipple, B., & Mosher, W. (1984). On female ejaculation. *Journal of Sex Research, 20*(4), 304–306.

Bem, D. J. (1996). Exotic becomes erotic: A developmental theory of sexual orientation. *Psychological Review, 103,* 320–335.

Bem, D. J. (2000). Exotic becomes erotic: Interpreting the biological correlates of sexual orientation. *Archives of Sexual Behavior, 29,* 531–548.

Bem, S. L. (1974). The measurement of psychological androgyny. *Journal of Consulting and Clinical Psychology, 42,* 155–162.

Bem, S. L. (1993). *The lenses of gender: Transforming the debate on sexual inequality.* New Haven, CT: Yale University Press.

Benderly, B. L. (1987). *The myth of two minds: What gender means and doesn't mean.* New York, NY: Doubleday.

Benedict, R. (1938). Continuities and discontinuities in cultural conditioning. *Psychiatry 1,* 161–167.

Bennice, J. A., & Resick, P. A. (2003). Marital rape: History, research, and practice. *Trauma, Violence, & Abuse, 4*(3), 228-246. https://DOI.org/10.1177/1524 838003004003003

Benson, K. (2016). The one daily talk that will benefit your marriage. Retrieved November 30, 2016, from https://www.gottman.com/blog/the-one-daily-talk-that-will-benefit-yourmarriage/

Benwell, B. (2003). *Masculinity and men's lifestyle magazines.* Oxford, United Kingdom: Blackwell.

Ben-Zeév, A. (2008, May 24). Love at first sight (and first chat). Retrieved April 18, 2011, from *Psychology Today* website: http://www.psychologytoday.com/blog/in-the-name-love/200805/ love-first-sight-and-first-chat

Berenbaum, S. A., & Resnick, S. M. (1997). Early androgen effects on aggression in children and adults with congenital adrenal hyperplasia. *Psychoneuroendocrinology, 22,* 505-515.

Berne, L., & Huberman, B. (2001). European approaches to adolescent sexual behavior and responsibility. Washington, DC: Advocates for Youth. Retrieved October 36, 2012, from www.advocatesforyouth.org/storage/advfy/ documents/european.pdf

Bernstein, E. (2008). *Temporarily yours: Intimacy, authenticity, and the commerce of sex.* Chicago, IL: University of Chicago Press.

Berrington, A., Perelli-Harris, B., & Trevena, P. (2015). Commitment and the changing sequence of cohabitation, childbearing, and marriage: Insights from qualitative research in the UK. *Demographic Research, 33*(12), 327-362.

Berube, A. (1990). *Coming out under fire.* New York, NY: Free Press.

Bhana, D. (2013). Kiss and tell: Boys, girls and sexualities in the early years. *Agenda, 27*(3), 57-66.

Bhana, D. (2016). *Gender and childhood sexuality in primary school* (3). DOI:10.1007/978-981-10-2239-5

Binson, D., Michaels, S., Stall, R., Coates, T. J., Gagnon, J. J., & Catania, J. A. (1995). Prevalence and social distribution of men who have sex with men: United States and its urban centers. *Journal of Sex Research, 32,* 245-254.

Birdsong, W. M. (1998). The placenta and cultural values. *Western Journal of Medicine, 168*(3), 190-192.

Birkhead, T. (2000). *Promiscuity: An evolutionary history of sperm competition.* Cambridge, MA: Harvard University Press.

Birnbaum, G. E. (2016). Attachment and sexual mating: The joint operation of separate motivational systems. In J. Cassidy & P. R. Shaver (Eds.), *Handbook of attachment: Theory, research, and clinical applications* (3rd ed.) (pp. 464-483). New York, NY: Guilford.

Birnbaum, G. E., & Reis, H. T. (2019). Evolved to be connected: The dynamics of attachment and sex over the course of romantic relationships. *Current Opinion in Psychology, 25,* 11-15.

Bisson, M., & Levine, T. R. (2009). Negotiating friends with benefits relationships. *Archives of Sexual Behavior, 38,* 66-73.

Black, M. C., Basile, K. C., Breiding, M. J., Smith, S .G., Walters, M. L., Merrick, M. T., & Stevens, M. R. (2011). The National Intimate Partner and Sexual Violence Survey (NISVS): 2010 summary report. Retrieved from the Centers for Disease Control and Prevention, National Center for Injury Prevention and Control: http://www.cdc.gov/ViolencePrevention/pdf/NISVS_Report2010-a.pdf

Blackwell, D. L., & Lichter, D. T. (2005). Homogamy among dating, cohabiting, and married couples. *The Sociological Quarterly, 45,* 719-737.

Blair, E. (2019, March 26). A male contraceptive pill has just been successfully tested. *Totum.* Retrieved July 21, 2019, from https://www.totum.com/stories/a-male-contraceptive-pill-has-been-successfully-tested-on-humans

Blanchard, J., & Bogaert, A. F. (2001). Proportion of homosexual men who owe their sexual orientation to fraternal birth order: An estimate based on two national probability samples. *American Journal of Human Biology, 16,* 151-157.

Blanchard, R. (2018). Fraternal birth order, family size, and male homosexuality: Meta-analysis of studies spanning 25 years. *Archives of Sexual Behavior, 47*(1), 1-15. DOI: 10.1007/s10508-017-1007-4.

Blanchard, R., Zucker, K. J., Siegelman, M., Dickey, R., & Klassen, P. (1998). The relation of birth order to sexual orientation in men and women. *Journal of Biosocial Science, 30,* 511-519.

Blank, H. (2007). *Virgin: The untouched history.* New York, NY: Bloomsbury.

Bledsoe, C. (2002). *Contingent lives: Time, fertility, and aging in West Africa.* Chicago, IL: Chicago University Press.

Bloom, J., & Blair, S. (2002). *Islam: A thousand years of faith and power.* New Haven, CT: Yale University Press.

Blount, D. (2005). Growing a baby: Diet and nutrition in pregnancy. *The Birthkit, 46.*

Blumstein, P., & Schwartz, P. (1983). *American couples: Money, work, sex.* New York, NY: William Morrow.

Boellstorff, T. (2008). *Coming of age in second life.* Princeton, NJ: Princeton University Press.

Bogaert, A. F. (2012). *Understanding asexuality.* Lanham, MD: Rowman & Littlefield Publishers.

Bogaert, A. F. (2015). Asexuality: What it is and why it matters. *The Journal of Sex Research, 52*(4), 362-379. DOI:10.1080/00224499.2015.1015713

Bogaert, A. F. (2017). What asexuality tells US about sexuality. *Archives of Sexual Behavior, 46*(3), 629-630. DOI:10.1007/s10508-016-0892-2

Bogar, C. B., & Hulse-Killacky, D. (2006). Resiliency determinants and resiliency processes among female adult survivors of childhood sexual abuse. *Journal of Counseling and Development, 84,* 318-327.

Bogle, K. (2008). *Hooking up: Sex, dating, and relationships on campus.* New York, NY: New York University Press.

Boog, G. (2010). Cerebral palsy and perinatal asphyxia. *Gynecologie, Obstetrique, & Fertilite, 38*(4), 261-277.

Bos, H., & Sandfort, T. (2015). Gender nonconformity, sexual orientation, and Dutch adolescents' relationship with peers. *Archives of Sexual Behavior, 44*(5), 1269-1279. DOI:10.1007/s10508-014-0461-5

Bos, H. M. W., van Balen, F., & van den Boom, D. C. (2007). Adjustment and parenting in lesbian-parent families. *American Journal of Orthopsychiatry, 77,* 38-48.

Boswell, J. (1980). *Christianity and intolerance of homosexuality.* New Haven, CT: Yale University Press.

Bourke, M. L., & Hernandez, A. E. (2009). The 'Butner Redux': A report of the incidence of hands-on child victimization by child pornography offenders. *Journal of Family Violence, 24,* 183-191.

Bowker, J. (1998). *World religions: The great faiths explored and explained.* New York, NY: DK Publishing.

Bowker, J. H., & Holm, J. (1994). *Women in religion.* London, United Kingdom: Continuum.

Bowlby, J. (1973). *Separation: Anxiety and anger. Attachment and loss: Vol. II.* London, United Kingdom: Hogarth.

Bowlby, J. (1999). *Attachment. Attachment and Loss: Vol. I* (2nd ed.). New York, NY: Basic Books.

Bowleg, L. (2008). When black+ lesbian + woman does not equal black lesbian woman: The methodological challenges of qualitative and quantitative intersectionality research. *Sex Roles, 59,* 312-325. Retrieved from https://DOI.org/10.1007/s11199-008-9400-z

Boxer, S., & Cohler, B. (1989). The life course of gay and lesbian youth: An immodest proposal. In G. Herdt (Ed.), *Gay and lesbian youth* (pp. 315-355). New York, NY: Haworth.

Boyarin, D. (1994). *A radical Jew: Paul and the politics of identity.* Berkeley, CA: University of California Press.

Boyd, D. (2008). Social networking sites: Definitions, history, and scholarship. *Journal of Computer-Mediated Communication, 13*(2), 210-230. DOI:10.1111/j.10836101.2007.00393.x

Boyd, D. (2014). *It's complicated: The social lives of networked teens.* New Haven, CT: Yale University Press.

Boykin, K. (2005). *Beyond the down low: Sex, lies, and denial in black America.* New York: Carroll & Graf.

Bradburn, N. (1969). *The structure of psychological well-being.* Chicago, IL: Aldine.

Braman, S. (2011). The framing years: Policy fundamentals in the Internet design process, 1969-1979. *The Information Society, 27*(5), 295-310.

Brand, M., Young, K., Laier, C., Wölfling, K., & Potenza, M. N. (2016). Integrating psychological and neurobiological considerations regarding the development and maintenance of specific Internet-use disorders: An interaction of person-affect-cognition-execution (I-PACE) model. *Neuroscience & Biobehavioral Reviews, 71,* 252-266.

Brannon, G. E. (2010). *Paraphilias.* Retrieved October 24, 2012, from Medscape Reference website: http://emedicine.medscape.com/ article/291419-overview#aw2aab6b2b3

Brathwaite, B. (2006). *Sex in video games.* New York, NY: Charles River Media.

Braun-Harvey, D., & Vigorito, M. A. (2015). *Treating out of control sexual behavior: Rethinking sex addiction.* New York: Springer.

Bray, A. (2003). *The friend.* Chicago, IL: University of Chicago Press.

BreastCancer.Org. (2019). *Online therapy helps ease effects of hot flashes and night sweats caused by breast cancer treatment.* Retrieved September 17, 2019, from https://www.breastcancer.org/research-news/online-tx-eases-hot-flashes-and-night-sweats

Breedlove, S. M. (2017). Prenatal influences on human sexual orientation: Expectations versus data. *Archives of Sexual Behavior, 46*(6), 1583-1592.1-10. DOI:10.1007/s10508-016-0904-2

Brettell, C., & Sargent, C. F. (Eds.). (2017). *Gender in cross-cultural perspective.* (7th ed.). New York, NY: Routledge.

Brill, S., & Pepper, R. (2008). *The transgender child: A handbook for families and professionals.* San Francisco, CA: Cleiss Press.

Brindis, C., & Davis, L. (1998). Linking pregnancy prevention to youth development. (Vol. 5). In S. Alford & S. Pagliaro (Series Eds.), *Communities responding to the challenge of adolescent pregnancy prevention.* Washington, DC: Advocates For Youth.

Brooke, J. (2006, May 4). Home alone together. Retrieved October 26, 2012, from *The New York Times* website: http://www.nytimes.com/2006/05/04/garden/04lat.html?_r51

Brooks-Gunn, J., & Reiter, E. O. (1990). The role of pubertal processes. In S. Feldman & G. Eillott (Eds.), *At the threshold: The developing adolescent* (pp. 16-53). Cambridge, MA: Harvard University Press.

Brott, A. A., & Ash, J. A. (2001). *The expectant father: Facts, tips, and advice for dads-to-be.* New York, NY: Abbeville.

Brotto, L. A., & Yule, M. (2017). Asexuality: Sexual orientation, paraphilia, sexual dysfunction, or none of the above? *Archives of Sexual Behavior, 46*(3), 619-627. DOI:10.1007/s10508-016-0802-7

Brown, P. (1988). *The body and society: Men, women, and sexual renunciation in early Christianity.* New York, NY: Columbia University Press.

Broyde, M. J., & Ausubel, M. (2005). *Marriage, sex, and family in Judaism.* Lanham, MD: Rowman & Littlefield.

Buchanan, E. A., & Ess, C. (2009). Internet research ethics: The field and its critical issues. In K. E. Himma & H. T. Tavani (Eds.), *The handbook of information and computer ethics* (pp. 273-292). New York, NY: Wiley-Blackwell.

Bui, Q., & Miller, C. C. (2018, August 4). The age that women have babies: How a gap divides America. *The New York Times.* Retrieved from https://www.nytimes.com/interactive/2018/08/04/upshot/up-birth-age-gap.html

Buisson, O., & Jannini, E. A. (2013). Pilot echographic study of the difference in clitoral involvement following clitoral or vaginal sexual stimulation. *Journal of Sexual Medicine, 10,* p 2734-2740.

Bulcroft, R. A., & Bulcroft, K. A. (1991). The nature and functions of dating in later life. *Research on Aging, 13,* 244-260.

Bullough, V. L. (1995) *Science in the bedroom: A history of sex research.* New York, NY: Basic Books.

Burgess, E. O. (2004). Sexuality in midlife and later life couples. In J. H. Harvey, A. Wenzel, & S. Sprecher (Eds.), *Handbook of sexuality in close relationships* (pp. 437-454). San Francisco, CA: Lawrence Earlbaum.

Burns, A., Futch, V., & Tolman, D. (2011). "It's like doing homework": Academic achievement discourse in adolescent girls' fellation narratives. *Sexual Research and Social Policy, 8,* 239-251.

Burri, A. V., Cherkas, L., & Spector, T. D. (2010). Genetic and environmental influences on self-reported G-spots in women: A twin study. *The Journal of Sexual Medicine, 7,* 1842-1852.

Buss, D. (1994). *Evolution of desire.* New York, NY: Basic Books.

Buss, D. (2008). *Evolutionary psychology.* New York, NY: Pearson.

Buss, D. M. (2016). *The evolution of desire: Strategies of human mating* (Revised and updated ed.). New York, NY: Basic Books.

Butler, J. (1990). *Gender trouble: Feminism and the subversion of identity.* New York, NY: Routledge.

Byers, E. S., & Demmons, S. (1999). Sexual satisfaction and sexual self-disclosure within dating relationships. *Journal of Sex Research, 36,* 180-189.

Byers, E. S., & Rehman, U. S. (2014). Sexual well-being. In D. L. Tolman, L. M. Diamond, J. A. Bauermeister, W. H. George, J. G. Pfaus, & L. M. Ward (Eds.), *APA handbook of sexuality and psychology,* Vol. 1: *Person-based approaches* (pp. 317-337). Washington, DC: American Psychological Association. DOI:10.1037/14193-011

Byrne, D. (1971). *The attraction paradigm.* New York: Academic.

Byrne, W., & Parsons, B. (1993). Human sexual orientation: The biologic theories reappraised. *Archives of General Psychiatry, 50,* 228-239.

Caceres, C. F., & Race, K. (2010). Knowledge, power and HIV/AIDS. In P. Aggleton & R. Parker (Eds.), *Routledge handbook of sexuality, health and rights* (pp. 175-183). New York, NY: Routledge.

Calderone, M. (1985). Adolescent sexuality: Elements and genesis. *Pediatrics, 76*(4), 699-703.

Califia, P. (2002). *Sensous magic: A guide to s/m for adventurous couples.* San Francisco, CA: Cleis Press.

Calzo, J. P., Antonucci, T. C., Mays, V. M., & Cochran, S. D. (2011). Retrospective recall of sexual orientation identity development among gay, lesbian, and bisexual adults. *Developmental Psychology, 47*(6), 1658-1673. DOI:10.1037/a0025508

Carey, B. (2012, May 19). Psychiatry giant sorry for backing gay "cure." Retrieved May 18, 2012, from *The New York Times* website: http://www.nytimes.com/2012/05/19/health/dr-robert-l-spitzer-noted-psychiatrist-apologizes-for-study-on-gay-cure.html?pagewanted5all

Carlsson, U. (2006). *Regulation, awareness, and empowerment: Young people and harmful media content in the digital age.* Goteberg, Sweden: Nordicom and Goteberg University.

Carnes, P. (2001). *Out of the shadows: Understanding sexual addiction.* Center City, MN: Hazelden Publishing.

Carpenter, L. (2005). *Virginity lost: An intimate portrait of first sexual experiences.* New York, NY: New York University Press.

Carpenter, L. M., Nathanson, C. A., & Kim, Y. J. (2006). Sex after 40? Gender, ageism, and sexual partnering in midlife. *Journal of Aging Studies, 20,* 93-106.

Carpenter, L., & DeLamater, J. (Eds.). (2012). *Sex for life: From virginity to Viagra.* New York, NY: NYU Press.

Carrier, J. (1995). *De los otros: Intimacy and homosexuality among Mexican men.* New York, NY: Columbia University Press.

Carrillo, H. (2007). Imagining modernity: Sexuality, policy and social change in Mexico. *Sexuality Research and Social Policy, 4,* 74-91.

Carrillo, H., & Hoffman, A. (2016). From MSM to heteroflexibilities: Non-exclusive straight male identities and their implications for HIV prevention and health promotion. *Global Public Health, 11*(7-8), 923-936. DOI:10.1080/17441692.2015.1134272

Carrillo, H., & Hoffman, A. (2018). 'Straight with a pinch of bi': The construction of heterosexuality as an elastic category among adult US men. *Sexualities, 21*(1-2), 90-108. DOI:10.1177/1363460716678561

Carrington, C. (2000). *No place like home: Relationships and family life among lesbians and gay men.* Chicago, IL: University of Chicago Press.

Carrington, C. (2006). Circuit culture: Ethnographic reflections on inequality, sexuality, and life on the party circuit. In N. Teunis (Ed.), *Sexual inequalities* (pp. 123-147). Berkeley, CA: University of California Press.

Carver, P. R., Egan, S. K., & Perry, D. G. (2004). Children who question their heterosexuality. *Developmental Psychology, 40*(1), 43-53. DOI:10.1037/0012-1649.40.1.43

Casey, M. B., Nuttall, R. L., & Pezaris, E. (2001). Spatial-mechanical reasoning skills versus mathematics self-confidence as mediators of gender differences on mathematics subtests using cross-national gender-based items. *Journal for Research in Mathematics Education, 32,* 28-57.

Castells, M. (2001). *The rise of the network society.* London, United Kingdom: Blackwell.

Catania, J. A., Binson, D., van der Straten, A., & Stone, V. (1995). Methodological research on sexual behavior in the AIDS era. In R. Rosen, C. Davis, & H. Ruppel (Eds.), *Annual review of sex research* (pp. 77-125). Mount Vernon, IA: Society for the Scientific Study of Sexuality.

CBS News. 60 Minutes. (2007, December 5). *Porn in the USA.* Retrieved September 12, 2012, from http://www.cbsnews.com/stories/2003/11/21/60minutes/main585049.shtml

CDC Fact Sheet. (2017). HIV in the United States and dependent areas. Atlanta, GA: Centers for Disease Control and Prevention. Retrieved May 5, 2019, from https://www.cdc.gov/hiv/statistics/overview/ataglance.html

Center for Sex Offender Management. (2007). *Female sex offenders.* Silver Spring, MD: Author, U.S. Department of Justice.

Center of Excellence for Transgender Health, Department of Family and Community Medicine, University of California. (2011) *Primary care protocol for transgender patient care.* San Francisco, CA: Author.

Centers for Disease Control (CDC). (1981). *Kaposi's sarcoma and pneumocystis pneumonia among homosexual men—New York City and California.* Retrieved November 6, 2012, from http://www.cdc.gov/hiv/resources/reports/mmwr/pdf/mmwr04jul81.pdf

Centers for Disease Control (CDC). (2004). *Sexual violence as a public health problem.* Atlanta, GA: Author.

Centers for Disease Control (CDC). (2006). Physical dating violence among high school students—United States, 2003. *Morbidity and Mortality Weekly Report (MMWR), 55,* 532-535.

Centers for Disease Control (CDC). (n.d.). *Get the facts about gynecologic cancer.* Retrieved November 6, 2012, from http://www.cdc.gov/cancer/knowledge/print_materials.htm

Centers for Disease Control and Prevention (CDC). (2010a, June 4). Youth Risk Behavior Surveillance System—United States, 2009. *Morbidity and Mortality Weekly (MMRW) Report, 59*(5), 20-21. Retrieved November 1, 2012, from http://www.cdc.gov/mmwr/pdf/ss/ss5905.pdf

Centers for Disease Control and Prevention (CDC). (2010b, April 16). Congenital syphilis—United States, 2003-2008. *Morbidity and Mortality Weekly Report (MMWR), 59*(14), 413-417. Retrieved September 29, 2012, from http://www.cdc.gov/mmwr/preview/mmwrhtml/mm5914a1.htm

Centers for Disease Control and Prevention (CDC). (2010c). *HIV transmission.* Retrieved October 26, 2012, from http://www.cdc.gov/hiv/resources/qa/transmission.htm

Centers for Disease Control and Prevention (CDC). (2010d). *Ovarian cancer* (Publication No.99-9124) CDC Publication #99-9124. Retrieved October 26, 2012, from http://www.cdc.gov/cancer/ovarian/pdf/ovarian_facts.pdf

Centers for Disease Control and Prevention (CDC). (2010e). *Parasites-Lice-Pubic "Crab" Lice. General Information. Frequently Asked Questions.* Retrieved September 29, 2012, from http://www.cdc.gov/parasites/lice/pubic/gen_info/faqs.html

Centers for Disease Control and Prevention (CDC). (2010f). *Parasites-scabies. Epidemiology & risk factors.* Retrieved September 29, 2012, from http://www.cdc.gov/parasites/scabies/epi.html

Centers for Disease Control and Prevention (CDC). (2011a). *Annual survey of family life.* Atlanta, GA: Author, National Center for Health Statistics.

Centers for Disease Control and Prevention (CDC). (2011b). *Fetal alcohol spectrum disorders (FASDs).* Facts about FASDs. Retrieved July 18, 2012, from www.cdc.gov/ncbddd/fasd/facts.html

Centers for Disease Control and Prevention (CDC). (2011c). *HIV Among African Americans.* Retrieved November 6, 2012, from http://www.cdc.gov/hiv/topics/aa/PDF/aa.pdf

Centers for Disease Control and Prevention (CDC). (2011d). *Vaccines & Immunizations-Vaccines & Preventable Diseases-HPV Vaccine-Questions & Answers.* Retrieved November 6, 2012, from http://www.cdc.gov/vaccines/vpd-vac/hpv/vac-faqs.htm

Centers for Disease Control and Prevention (CDC). (2011e). *Sexual health.* Retrieved from http://www.cdc.gov/sexualhealth/

Centers for Disease Control and Prevention (CDC). (2011f). *Sexually transmitted diseases. Pelvic inflammatory disease (PID)-CDC fact sheet.* Retrieved September 29, 2012, from http://www.cdc.gov/std/PID/STDFact-PID.htm

Centers for Disease Control and Prevention (CDC). (2011g). *Sexually transmitted diseases surveillance 2010.* Atlanta, GA: Department of Health and Human Services.

Centers for Disease Control and Prevention (CDC). (2011h). Vital signs: Teen pregnancy—United States, 1991-2009. *Morbidity and Mortality Weekly Report (MMWR), 60*(13), 414-420.

Centers for Disease Control and Prevention (CDC). (2012a). *The ABCs of Hepatitis.* Retrieved November 6, 2012, from http://www.cdc.gov/hepatitis/Resources/Professionals/ PDFs/ABCTable.pdf

Centers for Disease Control and Prevention (CDC). (2012b). *Gynecologic cancers-cervical cancer.* Retrieved November 6, 2012, from http://www.cdc.gov/cancer/cervical/index.htm

Centers for Disease Control and Prevention (CDC). (2012c). *Gynecologic cancers-uterine cancer.* Retrieved November 6, 2012, from http://www.cdc.gov/cancer/uterine/index.htm

Centers for Disease Control and Prevention (CDC). (2012d). *Gynecologic cancers-vaginal and vulvar cancers.* Retrieved November 6, 2012, from http://www.cdc.gov/cancer/ vagvulv/

Centers for Disease Control and Prevention (CDC). (2012e). *Preconception care and health care. Planning for pregnancy.* Retrieved October 25, 2012, from http://www.cdc.gov/ncbddd/ pregnancy_gateway/before.htm

Centers for Disease Control and Prevention (CDC). (2012f). *Prostate cancer rates by race and ethnicity. Prostate cancer.* Retrieved September 6, 2012, from http://www.cdc.gov/cancer/prostate/statistics/race.htm

Centers for Disease Control and Prevention (CDC). (2012g). *Reproductive health. Pregnancy complications.* Retrieved July 20, 2012, from http://www.cdc.gov/reproduc- tivehealth/maternalinfanthealth/Preg-Complications.htm

Centers for Disease Control and Prevention (CDC). (2012h). *Sexually transmitted disease. Gonnorhea-CDC fact sheet.* Retrieved October 2, 2012, from http://www.cdc.gov/std/ Gonorrhea/STDFact-gonorrhea.htm

Centers for Disease Control and Prevention (CDC). (2012i). *Sexually transmitted diseases (STDs). Chlamydia-CDC fact sheet.* Retrieved October 20, 2012, from http://www.cdc.gov/ std/chlamydia/stdfact-chlamydia.htm

Centers for Disease Control and Prevention (CDC). (2012j). *Sexually transmitted diseases (STDs). Genital herpes-CDC fact sheet.* Retrieved October 2, 2012, from http://www.cdc.gov/ STD/Herpes/STDFact-Herpes-detailed.htm

Centers for Disease Control and Prevention (CDC). (2012k). *Sexually transmitted diseases (STDs). Syphilis-CDC fact sheet.* Retrieved September 29, 2012, from http://www.cdc.gov/ std/syphilis/stdfact-syphilis.htm

Centers for Disease Control and Prevention (CDC). (2012l). *Reproductive health. Infertility FAQs.* Retrieved November 14, 2012, from http://www.cdc.gov/reproductivehealth/ infertility/index.htm

Centers for Disease Control and Prevention (CDC). (2015a). *Breast cancer screening guidelines for women.* Retrieved July 12, 2019, from https://www.cdc.gov/cancer/breast/pdf/BreastCancerScreening-Guidelines.pdf

Centers for Disease Control and Prevention (CDC). (2015b). *Pelvic inflammatory disease (PID)—CDC fact sheet.* Retrieved July 12, 2019, from https://www.cdc.gov/std/PID/STDFact-PID.htm

Centers for Disease Control and Prevention (CDC). (2015c). *What is breast cancer screening?* Retrieved July 14, 2019, from https://www.cdc.gov/cancer/breast/basic_info/screening.htm

Centers for Disease Control and Prevention (CDC). (2017a). *HIV in the United States and dependent areas—CDC fact sheet.* Retrieved May 5, 2019, from https://www.cdc.gov/hiv/statistics/overview/ataglance.html

Centers for Disease Control and Prevention (CDC). (2017b). *STIs at record high, indicate need for prevention.* Retrieved May 5, 2019, from https://www.cdc.gov/media/releases/2017/p0926-std-prevention.html

Centers for Disease Control and Prevention (CDC). (2018a). *Hepatitis B questions and answers for health professionals.* Retrieved from https://www.cdc.gov/hepatitis/hbv/hbvfaq.htm#overview

Centers for Disease Control and Prevention (CDC). (2018b). Marriage and divorce data. Retrieved from https://www.cdc.gov/nchs/fastats/marriage-divorce.htm

Centers for Disease Control and Prevention (CDC). (2018c). *Planning for pregnancy.* Retrieved from: https://www.cdc.gov/preconception/planning.html

Centers for Disease Control and Prevention (CDC). (2019a). *Gestational diabetes.* Retrieved from https://www.cdc.gov/diabetes/basics/gestational.html

Centers for Disease Control and Prevention (CDC). (2019b). *Hepatitis A questions and answers for health professionals.* Retrieved from https://www.cdc.gov/hepatitis/hav/havfaq.htm#general

Centers for Disease Control and Prevention (CDC). (2019c). *Hepatitis C questions and answers for health professionals.* Retrieved from https://www.cdc.gov/hepatitis/hcv/hcvfaq.htm#section1

Centers for Disease Control and Prevention (CDC). (2019d). *HIV and African American Gay and Bisexual Men.* Retrieved May 9, 2019, from https://www.cdc.gov/hiv/group/msm/bmsm.html

Centers for Disease Control and Prevention (CDC). (2019e). *HIV and African Americans.* Retrieved July 14, 2019, from https://www.cdc.gov/hiv/group/racialethnic/africanamericans/index.html

Centers for Disease Control and Prevention (CDC). (2019f). *Preventing teen dating violence.* Retrieved from https://www.cdc.gov/violenceprevention/intimatepartnerviolence/teendatingviolence/fastfact.html

Central Intelligence Agency (CIA). (2010). *The world fact book.* Nov. 19, 2010. Retrieved December 22, 2010, from https://www.cia.gov/library/ publications/the-world-factbook/geos/xx.html

Chaffin, M., Letrourneau, E., & Silvosky, J. F. (2002). Adults, adolescents, and children who sexually abuse children: A developmental perspective. In J. E. B. Myers, L. Berliner, J. Briere, C. T. Hendrix, C. Jenny, & T. A. Reid (Eds.), *The APSAC handbook on child maltreatment* (2nd ed.) (pp. 205-232). Thousand Oaks, CA: Sage.

Chamie, J. & Mirkin, B. (2019, June 11). *Sex, gender and identity revolution.* Yale Global Online. Retrieved June 14, 2019, from https://yaleglobal.yale.edu/content/sex-gender-and-identity-revolution

Chandra, A., Mosher, W. D., Copen, C., & Sionean, C. (2011). Sexual behavior, sexual attraction, and sexual identity in the United States: Data from the 2006-2008 National Survey of Family Growth. *National Health Statistics Reports, 36,* 1-36.

Chauncey, G., Jr. (1995). *Gay New York: Gender, urban culture, and the making of the gay male world, 1890-1940.* New York, NY: Basic Books.

Cheng, G., Gerlach, S., Libuda, L., Kranz, S. Günther, A. L., Karaolis-Danckert, N., . . . & Buyken, A. E. (2010). Diet quality in childhood is prospectively associated with the timing of puberty but not with body composition at puberty onset. *Journal of Nutrition, 140,* 95-102.

Chesson, H. W., Dunne, E., Hariri, S., & L. Markowitz, L. (2014, November). The estimated lifetime probability of acquiring human papillomavirus in the United States. *Sexually Transmitted Diseases, 41*(11), 660-664.

Child, B. (2011, June 13). Russell Crowe apologises for Twitter circumcision comments. Retrieved September 12, 2012, from *The Guardian* website: http:// www.guardian.co.uk/film/2011/jun/13/russell-crowe-twitter-comments-circumcision

Chivers, M. L. (2017). The specificity of women's sexual response and its relationship with sexual orientations: A review and ten hypotheses. *Archives of Sexual Behavior, 46*(5), 1161-1179. DOI:10.1007/s10508-016-0897-x

Chodorow, N. (1978). *The reproduction of mothering.* Berkeley, CA: University of California Press.

Choi, N. (2004). Sex role group differences in specific, academic, and general self-efficacy. *Journal of Psychology, 138,* 149-159.

Choi, S., & Meyer, I. (2016). LGBT aging: A review of research findings, needs, and policy implications. The Williams Institute Report, UCLA School of Law, August. Retrieved April 24, 2019, from https://williamsinstitute.law.ucla.edu/research/lgbt-older-adults-highlighting-isolation-discrimination/

Chokshi, N. (2019). Americans are among the most stressed people in the world, poll finds. *New York Times,* April 25, 2019. https://www.nytimes.com/2019/04/25/us/americans-stressful.html Retrieved August 20, 2019

Chopra, D., & Tanzi, R. (2018). *The healing self.* New York, NY: Penguin Random House.

Chumlea, W., Schubert, C., Kulin, H., Lee, P., Himes, J., & Sun, S. (2003). Age at menarche and racial comparisons in U.S. girls. *Pediatrics, 111,* 110-113.

Cianciotto, J., & Cahill, S. (2010). *Lesbian, gay, bisexual and transgender youth in America's schools: Research, policy, and practice.* Ann Arbor, MI: University of Michigan Press.

Civic, D. (2000). College students' reasons for nonuse of condoms within dating relationships. *Journal of Sex & Marital Therapy, 26,* 95-105.

Cocks, H. G. (2009). *Classified: The secret history of the personal column.* New York, NY: Random House.

Cohen, C. (2009). Black sexuality, indigenous moral panics, and respectability: From Bill Cosby to the down low. In G. Herdt, *Moral panics, sex panics* (pp. 104-129). New York, NY: NYU Press.

Cohen, C. (2010). *Democracy remixed.* New York, NY: Oxford.

Cohen, C. J. (1999). *The boundaries of Blackness: AIDS and the breakdown of Black politics.* Chicago, IL: University of Chicago Press.

Cohler, B., & Galatzer-Levy, R. M. (2000). *The course of gay and lesbian lives: Social and psychoanalytic perspectives.* Chicago, IL: University of Chicago Press.

Colapinto, J. (2000). *As nature made him: The boy who was raised as a girl.* New York, NY: HarperCollins.

Coleman, E. (1986, July). Sexual compulsion vs. sexual addiction: The debate continues. *SIECUS Reports, 14*(6), 7-11. Retrieved October 23, 2012, from http://www.siecus. org/_data/global/images/14-6.pdf

Coleman, E. (1991). Compulsive sexual behavior: New concepts and treatments. *Journal of Psychology and Human Sexuality, 4,* 37-52.

Coleman, E. (2010). From sexology to sexual health. In P. Aggleton & R. Parker (Eds.), *Routledge handbook of sexuality, health and rights* (pp. 135-145). New York, NY: Routledge.

Coleman, E. (2015). Impulsive/compulsive sexual behavior. In K. Wylie (Ed.), *ABC of sexual health* (3rd ed.) (pp. 93-95). London: John Wiley & Sons.

Coleman, E., Dickenson, J. A., Girard, A., Rider, G. N., Candelario-Pérez, L. E., Becker-Warner, R., Kovic, A. G., & Munns, R. (2018). An integrative biopsychosocial and sex positive model of understanding and treatment of impulsive/compulsive sexual behavior. *Sexual Addiction & Compulsivity, 25*(2-3), 125-152. DOI:10.1080/10720162.2018.1515050

Coleman, L., & Coleman, J. (2002). The measurement of puberty: A review. *Journal of Adolescence, 25,* 535-550.

Coley, R. L., Lombardi, C. M., Lynch, A. D., Mahalik, J. R., & Sims, J. (2013). Sexual partner accumulation from adolescence through early adulthood: The role of family, peer, and school social norms. *Journal of Adolescent Health, 53,* 91-97. DOI: 10.1016/j.jadohealth.2013.01.005

Collins, P. H. (1998). It's all in the family: Intersections of gender, race, and nation. *Hypatia, 13,* 62-82.

Collins, P. H. (2005). *Black sexual politics: African Americans, gender, and the new racism.* New York, NY: Routledge.

Connell, R. M. (1995). *Masculinities.* Cambridge, United Kingdom: Polity Press.

Coolidge, F. L., & Wynn, T. (2009). *The rise of Homo sapiens: The evolution of modern thinking.* New York, NY: Wiley-Blackwell.

Coontz, S. (2016). *The way we never were: American families and the nostalgia trap* (Revised and updated ed.). New York, NY: Basic Books.

Cooper, A., Putnam, D. E., Planchon, L. A., & Boies, S. C. (1999). Online sexual compulsivity: Getting tangled in the Net. *Sexual Addiction and Compulsivity, 6*(2), 79-104.

Copen C. E., Chandra, A., & Martinez, G. (2012). Prevalence and timing of oral sex with opposite-sex partners among females and males aged 15-24 years: United States, 2007-2010. National Health Statistics Reports, No. 56. Retrieved from https://www.cdc.gov/nchs/data/nhsr/nhsr056.pdf

Corber, R. (1997). *Homosexuality in cold war America.* Durham, NC: Duke University Press.

Corey, L., & Handsfield, H. (2000). Genital herpes and public health: Addressing a global problem. *JAMA, 283*(6), 791-794.

Cornforth, T. (2009). *Going to the gynecologist 101: When to see your OB/GYN.* Retrieved October 26, 2012, from About.com Women's Health website: http://womenshealth.about.com/od/gynecologicalhealthissues/a/gyn101.htm?p51

Correa, S., Mcintyre, P., Rodriguez, C., Paiva, A., & Marks, C. (2005). The Population and Reproductive Health Programme in Brazil 1990-2002: Lessons learned. *Reproductive Health Matters, 13*(25), 72-80.

Correa, S., Petchesky, R., & Parker, R. (2008). *Sexuality, health, and human rights.* New York, NY: Routledge.

Cott, N. (2002). *Public vows: A history of marriage and the nation.* Cambridge, MA: Harvard University Press.

Cottinger, W. S. (2003, March 4). *Why relationships fail.* Retrieved October 10, 2012, from authorsden.com website: http://www.authorsden.com/visit/viewArticle.asp?id56885

Cover, R. (2018). The proliferation of gender and sexual identities, categories and labels among young people. In P. Aggleton, R. Cover, D. Leahy, D. Marshall, & M. Lou Rasmussen (Eds.), *Youth, sexuality and sexual citizenship* (pp. 278-290). New York, NY: Routledge. DOI:10.4324/9781351214742

Coxon, A. P. M. (1988). Something sensational . . . : The sexual diary as a tool for mapping detailed sexual behavior. *Sociological Review, 36,* 353-367.

Cozzarelli, C., Sumer, N., & Major, B. (1998). Mental models of attachment and coping with abortion. *Journal of Personality and Social Psychology, 74*(2), 453-467.

Cranney, S. (2017). Does asexuality meet the stability criterion for a sexual orientation? *Archives of Sexual Behavior, 46*(3), 637-638. DOI:10.1007/s10508-016-0887-z

Crenshaw, T. L., & Goldberg, P. J. (1996). Testosterone in men. In T. L. Crenshaw & P. J. Goldberg (Eds.), *Sexual pharmacology* (pp. 115-128). New York, NY: Norton.

Crisis Connection. (2012). *College campuses and rape.* Retrieved September 24, 2012, from http://www.crisisconnectioninc.org/sexualassault/college_campuses_and_rape.htm

Cromwell, J. (1999). *Transmen & FTMs: Identities, bodies, genders, and sexualities.* Urbana, IL: University of Illinois Press.

Csikszentmihalyi, M. (1998). *Finding flow: The psychology of engagement with everyday life.* New York, NY: Basic.

Currah, P., Juang, R. M., & Minter, S. P. (Eds.). (2006). *Transgender rights.* Minneapolis, MN: Minnesota University Press.

Curtis, G. B., & Schuler, J. (2008). *Your pregnancy: Week by Week.* Philadelphia, PA: DaCapo Press.

Cusick, L., & Rhodes, T. (2000). Sustaining sexual safety in relationships: HIV positive people and their sexual partners. *Culture, Health, and Sexuality, 2,* 473-487.

D'Augelli, A. R., Hershberger, S. L., & Pilkington, N. W. (1998). Lesbian, gay, and bisexual youths and their families: Disclosure of sexual orientation and its consequences. *American Journal of Orthopsychiatry, 68,* 361-371.

D'Emilio, J. (1998). *Sexual politics, sexual communities.* Chicago, IL: University of Chicago Press.

D'Emilio, J. D., & Freedman, E. B. (1988). *Intimate matters: A history of sexuality in America.* New York, NY: Harper & Row.

D'Emilio, J., & Freedman, E. (1998). *Intimate matters: A history of sexuality in America.* Chicago, IL: University of Chicago Press.

Dailard, C. (2006). The public health promise and potential pitfalls of the world's first cervical cancer vaccine. *Guttmacher Policy Review, 9*(1).

Dailard, C., & Richardson, C. T. (2005). Teenagers' access to confidential reproductive health services. *Guttmacher Report on Public Policy, 8*(4).

Dake, J. A., Price, J. H., Maziarz, L., & Ward, B. (2012). Prevalence and correlates of sexting behavior in adolescents. *American Journal of Sexuality Education, 7*(1), 1-15. DOI:10.1080/15546128.2012.650959

Daniélou, A. (1994). *The complete kama sutra.* Rochester, VT: Park Street Press.

Darwin, C. (1879). *The descent of man.* London, United Kingdom: John Murray.

Das, A., Waite, L., & Laumann, E. (2012). Sexual expression over the life course: Results from three landmark surveys. In L. M. Carpenter & J. DeLamater (Eds.), *Sex for life: From virginity to Viagra* (pp. 236-259). New York, NY: NYU Press.

Davidson, D., Thill, A. D. W., & Lash, D. (2002). Male and female body shape preferences of young children in the United States, Mainland China, and Turkey. *Child Study Journal, 32*(3), 131-143.

Davidson, M. (2007). Seeking refuge under the umbrella: Inclusion, exclusion, and organizing within the category transgender. *Sexuality Research and Social Policy, 4*(4), 60-80.

Davis, D., Shaver, P. R., Widaman, K. F., Vernon, M. L., Follette, W. C., & Beitz, K. (2006). "I can't get no satisfaction": Insecure attachment, inhibited sexual communication, and sexual dissatisfaction. *Personal Relationships, 13,* 465-483.

Davis, S., Howell, S., Wilson, R., Tanda, T., Ross, J., Zeitler, P., Tartaglia, N. Advances in the Interdisciplinary Care of Children with Klinefelter Syndrome. Adv Pediatr. 2016 Aug;63(1):15-46. DOI: 10.1016/j.yapd.2016.04.020. Review.

Dawkins, R. (1989). *The selfish gene* (2nd ed.). Oxford, United Kingdom: Oxford University Press.

Dawkins, R. (2006). *The God delusion.* Boston, MA: Houghton Mifflin.

de Santisteban, P., del Hoyo, J., Alcázar-Córcoles, M., & Gámez-Guadix, M. (2018). Progression, maintenance, and feedback of online child sexual grooming: A qualitative analysis of online predators. *Child Abuse & Neglect, 80.* Retrieved from http://search.proquest.com/docview/2077580672/

de Vries, H., & van Veen, E. (2010, October). Living apart together? On the difficult linkage between DDR and SSR in post-conflict environments. *Conflict Research Unit (CRU) Policy Brief, 15.* The Hague, Netherlands: Netherlands Institute of International Relations.

de Waal, F. (1987). Tension regulation and non-reproductive functions of sex in captive Bonobos. *National Geographic Research 3,* 318-338.

de Waal, F. (1995). Bonobo sex and society. *Scientific American, 272,* 82-88.

de Waal, F., & Landing, F. (1998). *Bonobo: The forgotten ape.* Berkeley, CA: University of California Press.

DeAngelis, T. (2008). The pregnant brain: How pregnancy and motherhood change a woman's brain for good. *Monitor on Psychology, 39*(8), 29-31.

DeCuypere, G., T'Sjoen, G., Beerten, R., Selvaggi, G., De Sutter, P., Hoebeke, P., . . . Rubens, R. (2005). Sexual and physical health after sex reassignment surgery. *Archives of Sexual Behavior, 34,* 679-690.

DeFrain, J., & Olson, D. H. (1999). Contemporary family patterns and relationships. In M. B. Sussman, S. K. Steinmetz, & G. W. Peterson (Eds.), *Handbook of marriage and the family* (pp. 309-327). New York, NY: Plenum.

Dekker, R. M., & van de Pol, L. C. (1989). *The tradition of female transvestitism in early modern Europe.* London, United Kingdom: Macmillan Press.

DeLamater, J., & Carpenter, L. (2012). Sexualities over the lifecourse: The development of a perspective. In L. Carpenter & J. DeLamater (Eds.), *Sex for life: From virginity to Viagra* (pp. 3-22). New York, NY: NYU Press.

DeLamater, J., & Sill, M. (2005). Sexual desire in later life. *Journal of Sex Research, 42,* 138-149.

DeMeo, J. (1986, March). *The geography of genital mutilations.* Presented at The First International Symposium on Circumcision, Anaheim, California.

Department of Justice (U.S.). (2014). *Rape and sexual victimization among college-aged females, 1995-2013.* Office of Justice Programs, Bureau of Justice Statistics, Washington, DC.

Department of Justice (U.S.). (2018). *National crime victimization survey, 2013-2017.* Office of Justice Programs, Bureau of Justice Statistics., Washington, DC.

Derogatis, L. R., Laan, E., Brauer, M., Van Lunsen, R. H. W., Jannini, E. A., Davis, S., . . . Goldstein, I. (2010). Responses to the proposed DSM-V changes. *Journal of Sexual Medicine, 7,* 1998-2014.

Deschner, A., & Cohen, S. A. (2003). Contraception use is key to reducing abortion worldwide. *Guttmacher Report on Public Policy, 6*(4).

DeVries, B. (2011). LGBT aging comes of age and holds lessons for all elders. *Aging Today.* Retrieved April 24, 2019, from https://www.asaging.org/blog/lgbt-aging-comes-age-and-holds-lessons-all-elders

DeVries, B., & Herdt, G. (2012). Aging in the gay community. In T. Witten & A. Eyler (Eds.), *Gay, lesbian, bisexual, and transgender aging: Challenges in research, practice, and policy* (pp. 84-129). Baltimore, MD: John Hopkins University Press.

DeVries, J. (1967). *Perspectives in the history of religion* (K. W. Bole, Trans.). Berkeley, CA: University of California Press.

Di Pietro, G., Chomokur, G., Kumar, N., Davis, C., & Park, J. (2016). Racial differences in the diagnosis and treatment of prostate cancer. *International Neurourology Journal, 20*(Supplement 2), S112-119.

Diamond, J. (1997). *Why is sex fun?* New York, NY: Basic Books.

Diamond, L. M. (2005). 'I'm straight, but I kissed a girl': The trouble with American media representations of female-female sexuality. *Feminism and Psychology, 15,* 104-110.

Diamond, L. M. (2008). *Sexual fluidity.* Cambridge, MA: Harvard University Press.

Diamond, L. M. (2012). The desire disorder in research on sexual orientation in women: Contributions of dynamical systems theory. *Archives of Sexual Behavior, 41*(1), 73-83. DOI:10.1007/s10508-012-9909-7

Diamond, L. M. (2014). Gender and same-sex sexuality. In D. L. Tolman, L. M. Diamond, J. A. Bauermeister, W. H. George, J. G. Pfaus, & L. M. Ward (Eds.), *APA handbook of sexuality and psychology, vol. 1: Person-based approaches* (pp. 629-652). Washington, DC: American Psychological Association. DOI:10.1037/14193-020

Diamond, L. M. (2016). Sexual fluidity in males and females. *Current Sexual Health Reports, 8*(4), 249-256. DOI:10.1007/s11930-016-0092-z

Diamond, L. M. (2018). The dynamic expression of sexual-minority and gender-minority experience during childhood and adolescence. In J. Gilbert & S. Lamb (Eds.), *The Cambridge handbook of sexual development* (pp. 94-112). Cambridge: Cambridge University Press. DOI:10.1017/9781108116121.006

Diamond, L. M., Dickenson, J. A., & Blair, K. L. (2017). Stability of sexual attractions across different timescales: The roles of bisexuality and gender. *Archives of Sexual Behavior, 46*(1), 193-204. DOI:10.1007/s10508-016-0860-x

Diamond, L. M., & Rosky, C. J. (2016). Scrutinizing immutability: Research on sexual orientation and U.S. legal advocacy for sexual minorities. *Journal of Sex Research, 53*(4-5), 363-391. DOI:10.1080/00224499.2016.1139665

Diamond, L. M., & Savin-Williams, R. (2000). Explaining diversity in the development of same sex sexuality among women. *Journal of Social Issues, 56*(2), 297-313.

Diaz, R. M. (1998). *Latino gay men and HIV*. New York, NY: Routledge.

Dickenson, J. A., Gleason, N., Coleman, E., & Miner, Michael H. (2018). Prevalence of distress associated with difficulty controlling sexual urges, feelings, and behaviors in the United States. *JAMA Network Open, 1*(7), e184468-e184468. DOI:10.1001/jamanetworkopen.2018.4468

Diener, E., & Diener, R. B. (2008). *Happiness: Unlocking the mysteries of psychology*. Malden, MA: Blackwell.

Diener, E., & Seligman, M. (2004). Beyond money: Toward an economy of well-being. *Psychological Science in the Public Interest, 5,* 1-31.

Dillier, L., Mitchell, K. J., & Ybarra, M. L. (2012). The Internet as a safety net: Findings from a series of online focus groups with LGB and non-LGB young people in the United States. *Journal of LGBT Youth, 9*(3), 225-246.

Dillon, B. E., Chama, N. B., & Honig, S. C. (2008). Penile size and penile enlargement surgery: A review. *International Journal of Impotence Research, 20,* 519-529.

DiMaggio, P., Hargittai, E., Celeste, C., & Shafer, S. (2004). From unequal access to differential use: A literature review and agenda for research on digital inequality. In K. Neckerman (Ed.), *Social inequality* (pp. 355-400). New York, NY: Russell Sage Foundation.

DiMauro, D., & Joffe, C. (2009). The religious right and the reshaping of sexual policy: Reproductive rights and sexuality education during the Bush years. In G. Herdt (Ed.), *Moral panics/sex panics* (pp. 47-103). New York, NY: New York University Press.

Dion, K. K., Berscheid, E., & Walster, E. (1972). What is beautiful is good. *Journal of Personality and Social Psychology, 24,* 285-290.

Dixon, Alan. (2015) "Primate sexuality." *International Encyclopedia of Human Sexuality*. New York, NY: Wiley and Sons.

Dodge, B., Herbenick, D., Friedman, M. R., et al. (2016, October 26). Attitudes toward bisexual men and women among a nationally representative probability sample of adults in the United States. *PLoS One, 11*(10), e0164430. DOI:10.1371/journal.pone.0164430

Dougherty, C. (2010, September 29). New vow: I don't take thee: Young single adults surpass married peers amid high divorce, cohabitation rates. Retrieved October 25, 2012, from *The Wall Streeet Journal* website: http://online. wsj.com/article/SB10001424052748703882404575519871444705214.html

Dover, K. J. (1978). *Greek homosexuality*. Cambridge, MA: Harvard University Press.

Dreger, A. D. (1998). *Hermaphrodites and the medical invention of sex*. Cambridge, MA: Harvard University Press.

Dreger, A. D. (1999). *Intersex in the age of ethics*. University Publishing Group.

Drescher, J. (2014). Controversies in gender diagnoses. *LGBT Health, 1*(1), 10-14. DOI:10.1089/lgbt.2013.1500

Drescher, J., & Pula, J. (2014). Ethical issues raised by the treatment of gender-variant prepubescent children. *Hastings Center Report, 44*(5), S17-S22. DOI:10.1002/hast.365

Duberman, M. (1993). *Stonewall*. New York, NY: Penguin.

Duggan, S. J., & McCreary, D. R. (2004). Body image, eating disorders, and the drive for masculinity in gay and heterosexual men: The influence of media images. In T. G. Morrison (Ed.), *Pornucopia: Eclectic views of gay male pornography* (pp. 45-58). New York, NY: Harrington Park Press.

Dunham, C., Myers, F., McDougall, A., & Barnden, N. (1992). *Mamamoto: A celebration of birth*. New York, NY: Penguin.

Dunson, D. B., Colombo, B., & Baird, D. D. (2002). Changes with age in the level of duration of fertility in the menstrual cycle. *Human Reproduction, 17*(5), 1399-1403.

Durex. (2007/2008). *Sexual Wellbeing Global Survey*. Retrieved September 17, 2012, from http://www.durex.com/en-US/ SexualWellbeingSurvey/pages/default.aspx

Durkheim, E. (1915). *Elementary forms of the religious life* (K. E. Fields, Trans.). New York, NY: Free Press.

Dush, C., Cohan, C. L., & Amato, P. R. (2003). The relationship between cohabitation and marital quality and stability: Change across cohorts? *Journal of Marriage and Family, 65,* 539-549.

Edelman, B. (2009). Markets: Red light states: Who buys online adult entertainment? *Journal of Behavioral Economics, 23,* 209-220.

Edgerton, R. B. (1964). Pokot intersexuality: An East African example of sexual incongruity. *American Anthropologist, 66,* 1288-1299.

Edleman, K. A., Fergal, D. M., Sullivan, L., Dukes, K., Berkowitz, R. L., Kharbutli, Y., . . . D'Alton, M. E. (2006). Pregnancy loss rates after midtrimester amniocentesis. *Obstetrics & Gynecology, 108*(5), 1067-1072.

Efstathiou, G. (2006). *Species other than humans that have sex for pleasure*. Retrieved May 23, 2011, from Helium website: http://www. helium.com/items/104268-species-other-than-humans-that-have-sex-for-pleasure

Ehrensaft, D. (2011). *Gender born, gender made: Raising healthy gender-nonconforming children*. New York, NY: Workman Publishing.

Ehrensaft, D. (2016). *The gender creative child: Pathways for nurturing and supporting children who live outside gender boxes*. New York, NY: The Experiment.

Ehrman, B. D. (2008). *The New Testament: A historical introduction to the early Christian writings*. New York, NY: Oxford University Press.

El-Bassel, N., Witte, S. S., Gilbert, L., Wu, E., Chang, M., Hill, J., & Steinglass, P. (2003). The efficacy of a relationship-based HIV/STD prevention program for heterosexual couples. *American Journal of Public Health, 93*(6), 963-969.

Elders, M. J. (2008, Summer). Sexual healing. *Ms. Magazine, 18*(3), 79.

Eleuteri, S., Saladino, V., & Verrastro, V. (2017). Identity, relationships, sexuality, and risky behaviors of adolescents in the context of social media. *Sexual and Relationship Therapy, 32*(3-4), 354-365. https://DOI.org/10.1080/14681994.2017.1397953

Eliason, M. J. (1997). The prevalence and nature of biphobia in heterosexual undergraduate students. *Archives of Sexual Behavior, 26,* 317-326.

Ellington, S. (2004). Constructing casual stories and moral boundaries: Institutional approaches to sexual problems. In E. O. Laumann, S. Ellington, J. Mahay, Paik, & Y. Youm (Eds.), *The sexual organization of the city* (pp. 283-308). Chicago, IL: University of Chicago Press.

Elliott, I. A., Beech, A. R., Mandeville-Norden, R., & Hayes, E. (2009). Psychological profiles of Internet sexual offenders: Comparisons with contact sexual offenders. *Sexual Abuse: A Journal of Research and Treatment, 21,* 76-92.

Ellis, E. M., Atkeson, B. M., & Calhoun, K. S. (1981). An assessment of long-term reaction to rape. *Journal of Abnormal Psychology, 90,* 263-266.

Ellis, L., & Blanchard, R. (2001). Birth order, sibling sex ratio, and maternal miscarriages in homosexual and heterosexual men and women. *Personality and Individual Differences, 30,* 543-552.

El-Rouayher, K. (2005). *Before homosexuality in the Arab-Islamic world, 1500-1800*. Chicago, IL: University of Chicago Press.

Elton, C. (2009, March 31). *As egg donations mount, so do health concerns*. Retrieved July 20, 2012, from Time, Health & Family website: http://www.time.com/time/health/ article/0,8599,1888459,00.html

Emarketer Round-Up. (2016). *Media usage around the world*. March, 2016. Retrieved July 9, 2019, from http://www.looooker.com/wp-content/uploads/2016/04/eMarketer_Roundup_Media_Usage_Around_The_World.pdf

Emens, E. F. (2004). Monogamy's law: Compulsory monogamy and polyamorous existence. University of Chicago, Public Law Working Paper No. 58; *New York University Review of Law & Social Change, 29,* 277.

Engeleman, P. (2011) *A history of the birth control movement in America*. Santa Barbara, CA: Praeger.

Ensler, E. (2001). *The vagina monologues*. Cambridge, MA: Harvard University Press.

Epstein, R., Klinkenberg, W., Wiley, D., & McKinley, L. (2001). Ensuring sample equivalents across Internet and paper-and-pencil assessments. *Computers in Human Behavior, 17,* 339-346.

Epstein, S. (1996). *Impure science*. Berkeley, CA: University of California Press.

Epstein, S. (1999). Gay and lesbian movements in the United States: Dilemmas of identity, diversity and political strategy. In D. Adam, J. W. Duyvendak, & A. Krouwel (Eds.), *The global emergence of gay and lesbian politics* (pp. 30-90). Philadelphia, PA: Temple University Press.

Epstein, S. (2003). *Inclusion: The politics of difference in medical research*. Chicago, IL: University of Chicago Press.

Epstein, S. (2007). *Inclusion: The politics of differences in medical research*. Chicago, IL: University of Chicago Press.

Erber, R., & Erber, M. W. (2011). *Intimate relationships: Issues, theories, and research* (2nd Ed.). Boston, MA: Allyn & Bacon.

Erber, R., & Tesser, A. (1994). Self evaluation maintenance: A social psychological approach to interpersonal relationships. In R. Erber & R. Gilmour (Eds.), *Theoretical frameworks for personal relationships* (pp. 211-234). Hillsdale, NJ: Erlbaum.

Erickson, R. J. (2005). Why emotion work matters: Sex, gender, and the division of household labor. *Journal of Marriage and the Family, 67,* 337-351.

Erzen, T. (2006). *Straight to Jesus.* Berkeley, CA: University of California Press.

Espey, D. K., Wu, X., Swan, J., Wiggins, Jim, M., Ward, E., . . . Edwards, B. K. (2007). Annual report to the nation on the status of cancer, 1975-2004, featuring cancer in American Indians and Alaska natives. *Cancer, 110*(Suppl. 2), 2371-2490.

Espiritu, Y. (2012). US colonialism, migration, and sexualities: The Filipino American case. In L. M. Carpenter and J. DeLamater, *Sex for life: From virginity to Viagra* (pp. 163-197). New York, NY: NYU Press.

Esposito, L. (2011, November 6). *Teen 'sexting' common and linked to psychological woes.* Retrieved June 16, 2012, from the USA Today website: http://usatoday30.usatoday.com/news/health/wellness/teen-ya/story/2011-11-05/Teen-sexting-common-and-linked-to-psychological-woes/51073214/1

Estes, R. J., & Weiner, N. A. (2002). *The commercial sexual exploitation of children in the U. S., Canada, and Mexico: Full report of the US national study.* Philadelphia, PA: University of Pennsylvania, Center for the Study of Youth Policy.

Estes, R. J., & Weiner, N. A. (2007). The commercial sexual exploitation of children in the United States. In S. W. Cooper, R. J. Estes, A. P. Giardino, N. D. Kellogg, & V. I. Vieth (Eds.), *Medical, legal, and social science aspects of child sexual exploitation* (pp. 95-128). St. Louis, MO: GW Medical.

Ethier, K. A., Harper, C. R., Hoo, E., & Dittus, P. J. (2016). The longitudinal impact of perceptions of parental monitoring on adolescent initiation of sexual activity. *Journal of Adolescent Health, 59,* 570-576. DOI: 10.1016/j.jadohealth.2016.06.011

Eunice Kennedy Shriver National Institute of Child Health and Human Development, NIH, DHHS. (1997). *Understanding Klinefelter Syndrome: A guide for XXY males and their families* (Report No. 97-3202). Washington, DC: U.S. Government Printing Office.

Eunice Kennedy Shriver National Institute of Child Health and Human Development, NIH, DHHS. (2007). *Klinefelter syndrome.* Retrieved from October 27, 2012, http://www.nichd.nih.gov/health/topics/klinefelter_syndrome.cfm

Evans, K. (2008). *The Furry Sociological Survey.* Retrieved September 1, 2012, from http://cannedgeek.com/images/sharedfiles/fss_report_finaldraft.PDF

Everaerd, W., & Laan, E. (2000). Drug treatments for women's sexual disorders. *Journal of Sex Research, 37,* 195-213.

Fahs, B., Plante, R., & McClelland, S. (2018). Working at the crossroads of pleasure and danger: Feminist perspectives on doing critical sexuality studies. *Sexualities 21*(4), 503-519.

Farmer, P. (2003). *Pathologies of power: Health, human rights, and the new war on the poor.* Berkeley, CA: University of California Press.

Farmer, P. (2006). Social inequalities and emerging infectious diseases. *Emerging Infectious Diseases, 2*(4), 259-269.

Farmer, P. (2008). *Pathologies of power.* Berkeley, CA: University of California Press.

Farr, R. H., Diamond, L. M., & Boker, S. M. (2014). Female same-sex sexuality from a dynamical systems perspective: Sexual desire, motivation, and behavior. *Archives of Sexual Behavior, 43*(8), 1477-1490. DOI:10.1007/s10508-014-0378-z

Fausto-Sterling, A. (2000). *Sexing the body: Gender politics and the construction of sexuality.* New York, NY: Basic Books.

Fausto-Sterling, A., Crews, D., Sung, J., Garcia-Coll, C., & Seifer, R. (2015). Multimodal sex-related differences in infant and in infant-directed maternal behaviors during months three through twelve of development. *Dev Psychol, 51*(10), 1351-1366. DOI:10.1037/dev0000033

Fay, J. (2002). Teaching teens about sexual pleasure. *Siecus Report, 30*(4), 12-18.

Feinberg, L. (1992). *Trans gender liberation: A movement whose time has come.* New York, NY: World View Forum.

Feingold, A. (1988). Matching for attractiveness in romantic partners and same-sex friends: A meta-analysis and theoretical critique. *Psychological Bulletin, 104,* 226-235.

Fenwick, H., & Kerrigan, K. (2011). *Civil liberties and human rights.* New York, NY: Routledge.

Ferguson, K. M., Soydan, H., Lee, S., Yamanaka, A., Freer, A. S., & Xie, B. (2009). Evaluation of the CSEC Community Intervention Project (CCIP) in five U.S. cities. *Evaluation Review, 33,* 568-597.

Fields, J. (2008). *Risky lessons: Sex education and social inequality.* Rutgers, NJ: Rutgers University Press.

Fine, M., & McClelland, S. I. (2007). The politics of teen women's sexuality: Public policy and the adolescent female body. *Emory Law Journal, 56,* 993-1038.

Finkelhor, D. (1984). *Child sexual abuse.* New York, NY: Free Press.

Finkelhor, D., Shattuck, A., Turner, H. A., & Hamby, S. L. (2014). The lifetime prevalence of child sexual abuse and sexual assault assessed in late adolescence. *Journal of Adolescent Health, 55*(3), 329-333.

Finkelhor, D., & Yllo, K. (1983). Rape in marriage: A sociological view. In D. Finkelhor, R. J. Gelles, G. T. Hotaling, & M. A. Straus (Eds.), *The dark side of families* (pp. 119-130). Beverly Hills, CA: Sage.

Firestone, R. W., Firestone, L., & Catlett, J. (2006). *Sex and love in intimate relationships.* Washington, DC: American Psychological Association.

First, M. B. (2014). DSM-5 and paraphilic disorders. *Journal of the American Academy of Psychiatry and the Law Online, 42*(2), 191-201.

Fischer, N., Hauser, S., Brede, O., Fisang, C., & Müller, M. D. (2010). Implantation of artificial penile nodules—A review of literature. *Journal of Sexual Medicine, 7,* 3565-3571.

Fisher, B. S., Cullen, F. T., & Turner, M. G. (2000). *The sexual victimization of college women.* Washington, DC: U.S. Department of Justice, Office of Justice Programs.

Fisher, H. (2004). *Why we love: The nature and chemistry of romantic love.* New York, NY: Henry Holt.

Fisher, H. (2009a). *Why him? Why her? How to find and keep lasting love.* New York, NY: Holt Publishing.

Fisher, H. (2009b). *Why him? Why her? Finding real love by understanding your personality type.* New York, NY: Henry Holt.

Fisher, H. F. (2009a, November). *The realities of love at first sight.* Retrieved October 27, 2012, from Oprah.com website: http://www.oprah.com/relationships/Love-at-First-Sight-Helen-Fisher-Love-Column

Fisher, S. (1989). *Sexual images of the self: The psychology of erotic sensations and illusions* (1st ed.). Hillsdale, NJ: Erlbaum.

Fisher, W. A. (1986). A psychological approach to human sexual behavior: The sexual behavior sequence. In D. Byrne & K. Kelley (Eds.), *Alternative approaches to the study of sexual behavior* (pp. 131-172). Hillsdale, NJ: Lawrence Erlbaum.

Fisher, W. A., & Barak, A. (2001a). Internet pornography: A social psychological perspective on Internet sexuality. *Journal of Sex Research, 38*(4), 312-323.

Fisher, W. A., & Barak, A. (2001b). Online sex shops. Phenomenological, psychological, and ideological perspectives on Internet sexuality. *Cyberpsychology and Behavior, 3*(4), 579-590. DOI: 10.1089/10949310042018

Fitzpatrick, C., Deehan, A., & Jennings, S. (1995). Children's sexual behavior and knowledge: A community study. *Irish Journal of Psychological Medicine, 12*(3), 87-91.

Floyd, D., & Sargent, C. F. (Eds.). (1997). *Childbirth and authoritative knowledge: Cross-cultural perspectives.* Berkeley and Los Angeles, CA: University of California Press.

Floyd, F. J., & Bakeman, R. (2006). Coming-out across the life course: Implications of age and historical context. *Archives of Sexual Behavior, 35,* 287-296.

Ford, C. S., & Beach, F. A. (1951). *Patterns of sexual behavior.* New York, NY: Harper & Brothers.

Forgeard, M. J. C., Jayawickreme, E., Kern, M., & Seligman, M. E. P. (2011). Doing the right thing: Measuring wellbeing for public policy. *International Journal of Wellbeing, 1,* 79-106.

Foucault, M. (1973). *Birth of the clinic.* New York, NY: Pantheon.

Foucault, M. (1980). *The history of sexuality* (R. Hurley, Trans.). New York, NY: Viking.

Foucault, M. (1986). *The use of pleasure.* (R. Hurley, Trans.). New York, NY: Vintage Books.

Foucault, M., & Barbin, H. (1980). *Herculine Barbin—Being the recently discovered memoirs of a nineteenth century hermaphrodite.* New York, NY: Random.

Fox, J., & Ralston, R. (2016). Queer identity online: Informal learning and teaching experiences of LGBTQ individuals on social media. *Computers in Human Behavior,* 1-8. https://DOI.org/DOI:10.1016/j.chb.2016.06.009

Francis, L. J. (1997). The psychology of gender differences in religion: A review of empirical research. *Religion, 27,* 81-96.

Franek, J. (2006). *Penis health care.* Retrieved October 27, 2012, from AskMen.com website: http://www.askmen.com/feeder/askmenRSS_article_print_2006.php?ID5http://askmen.com/sports/health_150/186_mens_health.html

Frederick, D. A., Lever, J., & Peplau, L. A. (2007). Interest in cosmetic surgery and body image: Views of men and women across the lifespan. *Plastic & Reconstructive Surgery, 120*(5), 1407-1415.

Fredland, N. M. (2008). Sexual bullying: Addressing the gap between bullying and dating violence. *Advances in Nursing Science, 31*(2), 95-105.

Free, C. (2019, January 4). This woman offered to be the 'mom' at any gay wedding. *Washington Post* Retrieved February 15, 2019, from https://www.washingtonpost.com/lifestyle/2019/01/04/this-woman-offered-be-mom-any-gay-wedding-her-post-went-viral/?utm_term=.ac974fde0d2f

Freeman-Longo, R. E., & Blanchard, G. T. (1998). *Sexual abuse in America: Epidemic of the 21st century.* Brandon, VT: Safer Society Press.

Freitas, D. (2017). *The happiness effect: How social media is driving a generation to appear perfect at any cost.* New York, NY: Oxford University Press.

Freud, S. (1905). *Three essays on the theory of sexuality.* New York, NY: Basic. 4, and additional chapter, 11, 10, 15

Freund, K. (1990). Courtship disorder. In *Handbook of sexual assault* (pp. 195-207). Boston, MA: Springer.

Friedl, E. (1975). *Women and men.* New York, NY: Waveland.

Friedl, E. (1994). Sex the invisible. *American Anthropologist, 96,* 833-844.

Friedman, T. (2005). *The world is flat.* New York, NY: Farrar, Strauss and Giroux.

Friedrich, W., Fisher, N. J., Roughton, D., Houston, M., & Shafran, C. R. (1998). Normative sexual behavior in children: A contemporary sample. *Pediatrics, 101*(4), 1-9.

Frost, D., Lehavot, K., & Meyer, I. (2013). Minority stress and physical health among sexual minority individuals. *Journal of Behavioral Medicine, 38,* 1-8.

Frost, J. J., & Lindberg, L. D. (2012). Reasons for using contraception: Perspectives of U.S. women seeking care at specialized planning clinics. Retrieved corrected proof on October 27, 2012, from *Contraception* website: http:// www.contraceptionjournal.org/article/ S0010-7824(12)00739-1/abstract

Fuhrman, J. (2011, May 6). *Girls' early puberty: What causes it, and how to avoid it.* Retrieved Oct. 22, 2012, from *Huffington Post* website: http://www.huffingtonpost.com/joel- fuhrman-md/girls-early-puberty_b_857167. html

Fulbright, Y. (2008, July 14). *FOXsexpert: Is love at first sight the real deal?* Retrieved October 3, 2012, from Fox News. com website: http://www.foxnews.com/ story/0,2933,382283,00.html

Fuller, C. J. (2004). *The camphor flame: Popular Hinduism and society in India.* Princeton, NJ: Princeton University Press.

Fullilove, R. E. (2006). *African Americans, health disparities and HIV/AIDS: Recommendations for confronting the epidemic in Black America.* Washington, DC: National Minority AIDS Council.

Furman, W. (2002). The emerging field of adolescent romantic relationships. *Current Directions in Psychological Science, 11,* 177–180.

Gaetano, P. (2017). Davide Reimer and John Money gender reassignment controversy: The John/Joan case. *The Mebryo Project Encyclopedia.* Retrieved June 2, 2019, from https://embryo.asu.edu/pages/david-reimer-and-john-money-gender-reassignment-controversy-johnjoan-case

Gagnon, J. (1997). Others have sex with others: Captain Cook and the penetration of the Pacific. In G. Herdt (Ed.), *Sexual cultures and migration in the era of AIDS* (pp. 23–40). New York, NY: Oxford University Press.

Gagnon, J. (2004). *An interpretation of desire.* Chicago, IL: University of Chicago Press.

Gagnon, J., & Simon, W. (1973). *Sexual conduct: The social sources of human sexuality.* Chicago, IL: Aldine.

Gagnon, J. H., & Simon, W. (2005). *Sexual conduct: The social sources of human sexuality* (Rev. ed.). London, UK: Hutchinson.

Galambos, C. M. (2005). Health care disparities among rural populations: A neglected frontier. *Health and Social Work, 30*(3), 179–181.

Galey, P. (2018, November 6,). Study finds 'significant decline' in genital mutilation rates in girls. *Yahoo News.* Retrieved from https://news.yahoo.com/study-finds-significant-decline-genital-mutilation-rates-girls-004501245.html

Gallup, G. G., Hughes, S. M., & Harrison, M. A. (2007). Sex differences in romantic kissing among college students: An evolutionary perspective. *Evolutionary Psychology, 5(3),* 612–631.

Gallup Poll. (May 20, 2011). *For first time, majority of Americans favor legal gay marriage.* Retrieved October 27, 2012, from www. gallup.com/poll/147662/First-Time-Majority-Americans-Favor-Legal-Gay-Marriage.aspx

Gamson, J. (1998). *Freaks talk back.* Chicago, IL: University of Chicago Press.

Garanzini, S., Yee, A., Gottman, J., Gottman, J., Cole, C., Preciado, M., & Jascula, C. (2017). Results of Gottman couples therapy with gay and lesbian couples. *Journal of Marital and Family Therapy, 43*(4), 674–684. DOI: 10.1111/jmft.12276

Gardner, H. (1993). *Frames of mind.* New York, NY: Basic Books.

Garofalo, R., Wolf, R., Wissow, L., Woods, E., & Goodman, E. (1999). Sexual orientation and risk of suicide attempts among a representative sample of youth. *Archives of Pediatrics and Adolescent Medicine, 153,* 487–493.

Garretson, J., & Suhay, E. (2016). Scientific communication about biological influences on homosexuality and the politics of gay rights. *Political Research Quarterly, 69*(1), 17–29. DOI:10.1177/1065912915620050

Gates, G. (2012). LGBT identity: A demographer's perspective. *Loyola of Los Angeles Law Review, 45*(3).

Gates, G., & Newport, F. (2015, April 24) An estimated 780,000 Americans in same-sex marriage. *Gallup Social and Policy Issues.* Retrieved April 19, 2019, from https://news.gallup.com/poll/182837/estimated-780-000-americans-sex-marriages.aspx

Gazi, R. (2009). Young clients of hotel-based sex workers in Bangladesh: Vulnerability to HIV, risk perceptions, and expressed needs for interventions. *International Journal of Sexual Health, 21,* 167–182.

Ge, X., Conger, R. D., & Elder, G. H., Jr. (1996). Coming of age too early: Pubertal influences on girls' vulnerability to psychological distress. *Child Development, 67,* 3386–3400.

Ge, X., Conger, R., & Elder, G. H., Jr. (2001). The relation between puberty and psychological distress in adolescent boys. *Journal of Research on Adolescence, 11,* 49–70.

Geertz, C. (1966). Religion as a cultural system. In M. Banton (Ed.), *Anthropological approaches to the study of religion* (pp. 1–46). London, United Kingdom: Tavistock Publications.

Geertz, C. (1968). *Islam observed: Religious development in Morocco and Indonesia.* Chicago, IL: University of Chicago Press.

Geertz, C. (1973). *The interpretation of cultures.* New York, NY: Basic Books.

Gelman, S., Collman, P., & Maccoby, E. E. (1986). Inferring properties from categories versus inferring categories from properties: The case of gender. *Journal of Child Development, 57,* 396–404.

Gerber, P., & J. Gory, J. (2014). The UN Human Rights Committee and LGBT rights: What is it doing? What could it be doing? *Human Rights Law Review, 14* (3), 403–439.

Germon, J. (2009). *Gender: A genealogy of an idea.* London: Palgrave Macmillan.

Gerrard, M. (1987). Sex, sex guilt, and contraceptive use revisited: The 1980's. *Journal of Personality and Social Psychology, 52(5),* 975–980.

Gershon, I. (2010). *The breakup 2.0: Disconnecting over new media.* Ithaca, NY: Cornell University Press.

Ghavami, N., & Peplau, L. A. (2018). Urban middle school students' stereotypes at the intersection of sexual orientation, ethnicity, and gender. *Child Development, 89*(3), 881–896. DOI:10.1111/cdev.12763

Ghoncheh, M., Pournamdar, Z., & Salehiniya, H. (2016). Incidence and mortality and epidemiology of breast cancer in the world. *Asian Pacific Journal of Cancer Prevention, 17*(S3), 3–46.

Gibson L., & Leitenberg, H. (2001). The impact of child sexual abuse and stigma on methods of coping with sexual assault among undergraduate women. *Child Abuse & Neglect, 25,* 1343–1361.

Gibson, P. (1989). *Suicide risk and prevention for gay, lesbian, bisexual and transgender youth.* Newton, MA: Suicide Prevention Center.

Giddens, A. (1992). *The transformation of intimacy: Sex, love, eroticism.* Palo Alto, CA: Stanford University Press.

Giddons, A. (1992). *Sex and the social order: The transformation of intimacy.* Oxford, UK: Blackwell.

Gilbert, M. R., Masucci, M., Homko, C., & Bove, A. A. (2008). Theorizing the digital divide: Information and communication technology use frameworks among poor women using a telemedicine system. *Geoforum, 39*(2), 912–925.

Gilding, M. (2005). Families and fortunes: Accumulation, management succession, and inheritance in wealthy families. *Journal of Sociology, 41*(1), 29–45.

Global Cancer Observatory. (2012). *Cancer today.* World Health Organization. Retrieved April 5, 2019, from http://gco.iarc.fr/today/online-analysis-dual-bars-2?v=2018&mode=cancer&mode_population=regions&population=250&populations=250&key=asr&sex=0&cancer=39&type=0&statistic=5&prevalence=0&population_group=0&ages_group%5B%5D=0&ages_group%5B%5D=17&nb_items=10&group_cancer=1&include_nmsc=1&include_nmsc_other=1&dual_distribution=1&population1=250&population2=554&show_values=false&type_multiple=%257B%2522inc%2522%253Atrue%252C%2522mort%2522%253Atrue%252C%2522prev%2522%253Afalse%257D&population_group_globocan_id=&type_sort=0

Gmeiner, M., Price, J., & Worley, M. (2015). A review of pornography use research: Methodology and results from four sources. *Cyberpsychology: Journal of Psychosocial Research on Cyberspace, 9*(4), article 4. http://dx.DOI.org/10.5817/CP2015-4-4

Godelier, M. (1985). *The making of great men.* New York, NY: Cambridge.

Goldman, R., & Goldman, J. (1982). *Children's sexual thinking.* Boston, MA: Routledge and Kegan Paul.

Goldstein, J. R., & Kenney, C. T. (2001). Marriage delayed or marriage forgone? New cohort forecasts of first marriage for U.S. women. *American Sociological Review, 66,* 506–519.

Goldstein, S., & Brooks, R. B. (2006). *Handbook of resilience in children.* New York, NY: Springer.

Gonzaga, G. C., Turner, R. A., Keltner, D., Campos, B., & Altemus, M. (2006). Romantic love and sexual desire in close relationships. *Emotion, 6*(2), 163–179.

Gonzales-Lopez, G. (2005). *Erotic journeys: Mexican immigrants and their sex lives.* Berkeley, CA: University of California Press.

Goodwin, M. (2019, July 1). Alabama isn't the only state that punishes pregnant women. *New York Times.* Retrieved July 19, 2019, from https://www.nytimes.com/2019/07/01/opinion/alabama-pregnant-woman-shot.html

Gordon, L. (1976). *Woman's body, woman's right: A social history of birth control in America.* New York, NY: Penguin Books.

Gott, M., & Hinchliff, S. (2003). How important is sex in later life? The views of older people. *Social Science and Medicine, 56,* 1617–1628.

Gottman, J. M. (1994). *What predicts divorce?* Hillsdale, NJ: Lawrence Erlbaum Associates.

Gottman, J. M. (2011). *The science of trust: Emotional attunement for couples.* New York, NY: Norton.

Gottman, J. M., Levenson, R. W., Gross, J., Fredrickson, B., McCoy, K., Rosentahl, L., Ruel, A., & Yoshimoto, D. (2003). Correlates of gay and lesbian couples' relationship satisfaction and relationship dissolution. *Journal of Homosexuality, 45*(1), 23–43.

Grant, J. E., & Potenza, M. N. (Eds.). (2011). *The Oxford handbook of impulse control disorders.* Oxford: Oxford University Press.

Grauvogl, A., Peters, M. L., Evers, S. M., & van Lankveld, J. J. (2015). A new instrument to measure sexual competence and interaction competence in youth: Psychometric properties in female adolescents. *Journal of Sex & Marital Therapy, 41*(5), 544–556.

Gray, N. J., & Klein, J. D. (2006). Adolescents and the Internet: Health and sexuality information. *Current Opinion in Obstetrics & Gynecology, 18*(5), 519–524.

Gray, N. J., Klein, J. D., Noyce, P. R., Sesselberg, T. S., & Cantrill, J. A. (2005). The Internet: A window on adolescent health literacy. *Journal of Adolescent Health, 37*(3), 243.e1–243.e7.

Grce, M., & Davies, P. (2008). Human papilloma virus testing for primary cervical cancer screening. *Expert Review of Molecular Diagnosis, 8*(5), 599–605.

Greaves, L. M., Sibley, C. G., Fraser, G., & Barlow, F. K. (2019, February 6). Comparing pansexual- and bisexual-identified participants on demographics, psychological well-being, and political ideology in a New Zealand national sample. *Journal of Sex Research*, 1-8. DOI:10.1080/00224499.2019.1568376

Greenberg, D. (1986). *The construction of homosexuality*. Chicago, IL: University of Chicago Press.

Greenberg, D. (1988). *The construction of homosexuality*. Chicago, IL: University of Chicago Press.

Greene, J. M., Ennett, S. T., & Ringwalt, C. L. (1999). Prevalence and correlates of survival sex among runaway and homeless youth. *American Journal of Public Health, 89*, 1406-1409.

Gregoire, A. (1999). Male sexual problems. *British Medical Journal, 318*(7178), 245-247.

Gregor, T. (1985). *Anxious pleasures.* Chicago, IL: University of Chicago Press.

Gregor, T. (1996). Sexuality and the experience of love. In P. Abramson & S. D. Pinkerton (Eds.), *Sexual nature, sexual culture* (pp. 330-352). Chicago, IL: University of Chicago Press.

Gressgård, R. (2013). Asexuality: From pathology to identity and beyond. *Psychology and Sexuality, 4*(2), 179-192. DOI:10.1080/19419899.2013.774146

Greven, A. (2008). *How to talk to girls*. New York, NY: Harper.

Grogan, S. (2006). Body image and health: Contemporary perspectives. *Journal of Health Psychology, 11*(4), 523-530.

Groneman, C. (2001). *Nympho-mania: A history*. New York, NY: Norton.

Gross, L. (2001). *Up from invisibility: Lesbians, gay men, and the media in America.* New York, NY: Columbia University Press.

Grossman, A. H., D'Augelli, A. R., Howell, T. J., & Hubbard, S. (2006). Parents' reactions to transgender youths' gender nonconforming expression and identity. *Journal of Gay & Lesbian Social Services, 18*(1), 3-16.

Grossman, A. H., D'Augelli, A. R., Salter, N. P., & Hubbard, S. M. (2006). Comparing gender expression, gender nonconformity, and parents' responses of female-to-male and male-to-female transgender youth: Implications for counseling. *Journal of LGBT Issues in Counseling, 1*(1), 41-59.

Grubbs, J. B.; Volk, F.; Exline, J. J.; and Pargament, K. I. Internet Pornography Use: Perceived Addiction, Psychological Distress, and the Validation of a Brief Measure. *Journal of sex & marital therapy*, 41(1): 83-106. 2015.

Grubbs, J. B. & Perry, S. L. (2019) Moral Incongruence and Pornography Use: A Critical Review and Integration, *The Journal of Sex Research*, 56:1, 29-37, DOI: 10.1080/00224499.2018.1427204

Guggino, J. M., & Ponzetti, Jr., J. J. (1997). Gender differences in affective reactions to first coitus. *Journal of Adolescence, 20*, 189-200.

Günther, A. L., Karaolis-Danckert, N., Kroke, A., Remer, T., & Buyken, A. E. (2010). Dietary protein intake throughout childhood is associated with the timing of puberty. *Journal of Nutrition, 140*, 565-571.

Guttmacher Institute. (2009). *Facts on sexually transmitted infections in the United States. In Brief: Fact Sheet.* Retrieved October 27, 2012, from http://www.guttmacher.org/pubs/ FIB_STI_US.html

Guttmacher Institute. (2011). *Facts on induced abortion in the United States.* Retrieved October 27, 2012, from http://www.guttmacher.org/ pubs/fb_induced_abortion.html

Guttmacher Institute. (2018). *Induced abortion in the United States—fact sheet.* Retrieved from https://www.guttmacher.org/sites/default/files/factsheet/fb_induced_abortion.pdf

Guttmacher Institute. (2019a). *An overview of abortion laws*. Retrieved from https://www.guttmacher.org/state-policy/explore/overview-abortion-laws

Guttmacher Institute. (2019b). *Sex and HIV education*. New York, NY: Guttmacher Institute. Retrieved on April 3, 2019, from https://www.guttmacher.org/state-policy/explore/sex-and-hiv-education

Guzman, B. L., Schlehofer-Sutton, M. M., Villanueva, C. M., Stritto, M. E. D., Casad, B. J., & Feria, A. (2003). Let's talk about sex: How comfortable discussions about sex impact teen sexual behavior. *Journal of Health Communication, 8*, 583-598.

Haffner, D. W. (2008). *From diapers to dating: A parent's guide to raising sexually healthy children from infancy to middle school.* New York, NY: Newmarket Press.

Hagan, J. F., Shaw, J. S., & Duncan, P. (Eds.). (2008). Theme 8: Promoting healthy sexual development and sexuality. In *Bright futures: Guidelines for health supervision of infants, children, and adolescents* (3rd ed.) (pp. 169-176). Elk Grove Village, IL: American Academy of Pediatrics.

Hald, G. M. (2006). Gender differences in pornography consumption among young Danish adults. *Archives of Sexual Behavior, 35*, 577-585.

Halkitis, P. N., & Parsons, J. T. (2002). Recreational drug use and HIV-risk sexual behavior among men frequenting gay social venues. *Journal of Gay and Lesbian Social Services, 14*, 19-39.

Hall, P. C., West, J. H., & Hills, S. (2012). Sexualization in lyrics of popular music from 1959-2009: Implications for sexuality educators. *Sexuality & Culture, 16*, 103-117.

Halley, J. E. (2014). Sexual orientation and the politics of biology: A critique of the argument from immutability. In N. Bamforth (Ed.), *Sexual orientation and rights*. London: Routledge. DOI:10.4324/9781315243375

Halperin, D. (1995). *Saint Foucault.* New York, NY: Oxford University Press.

Halperin, D. (20072008) *What do gay men want?* Ann Arbor, MI: University of Michigan Press.

Hamilton, B. E., & Ventura, S. J. (2012). Birth rates for U.S. teenagers reach historic lows for all age and ethnic groups. *NCHS Data Brief, 89.* Hyattsville, MD: National Center for Health Statistics.

Hammack, P. L. (2005). The life course development of human sexual orientation: An integrative paradigm. *Human Development, 48*(5), 267-290. DOI:10.1159/000086872

Hammack, P., & Cohler, B. J. (2009). *The story of sexual identity.* New York, NY: Oxford.

Hammar, L. (2011). *Me, my intimate partner, and HIV: Fijian self-assessments of transmission risks.* Suva, Fifji Islands: United Nations Development Programme Pacific Center. Retrieved October 27, 2012, from Me_My_Intimate_ Partner_web.pdf

Handy, B. (2009, October). Avatar's *unexpected influences: Psychedelic cover art, Disney, and . . . Furries?* Retrieved October 27, 2012, from *Vanity Fair* website: http://www. vanityfair.com/online/oscars/2009/10/avatars-unexpected-influences-psychedelic-cover-art-disney-and-furries

Harawa, N. T., Wilton, L., Wang, L., Mao, C., Kuo, I., Penniman, T., & Koblin, B. (2014). Types of female partners reported by black men who have sex with men and women (MSMW) and associations with intercourse frequency, unprotected sex and HIV and STI prevalence. *AIDS and Behavior, 18*(8), 1548-1559. DOI: 10.1007/s10461-014-0704-4.

Hargittai, E. (2007). Whose space: Differences among users and non-users of social network sites. *Journal of Computer-Mediated Communication, 13*(1), article 14. Retrieved October 22, 2012, from http://jcmc.indiana.edu/vol13/ issue1/hargittai.html

Harper, A. (2008). Iraq's refugees: Ignored and unwanted. *International Review of the Red Cross, 90*(869), 169-190.

Harvey, P., & Roberson, C. (2015). *Family and relationships.* New York, NY: Routlege.

Hatcher, R. A., Trussell, J., Stewart, F., Nelson, A. L., Cates, W., Guest, F., & Kowal, D. (Eds.). (2008). *Contraceptive technology* (19th rev. ed.). New York, NY: Ardent Media.

Haupert, M., Gesselman, A., Moors, A., Fisher, H., & Garcia, J. (2017). Prevalence of experiences with consensual nonmonogamous relationships: Findings from two nationally representative samples of single Americans. *Journal of Sex & Marital Therapy, 43*(5), 424-440.

Hauser, A., Ujvari, K., & Mollica, R. (2012, July). *Assisted living and residential care in the States in 2010. Insight on the Issues.* Retrieved October 22, 2012, from AARP Public Policy Institute website: http://www.aarp.org/home-family/ caregiving/info-07-2012/assisted-living-and-residential-care-in-the-states-AARP-ppi-ltc.html

Hazan, C., & Shaver, P. (1987). Romantic love conceptualized as an attachment process. *Journal of Personality and Social Psychology, 52*(3), 511-524.

Health, Empowerment, Rights and Accountability (HERA). (1995). *Sexual rights. Action sheet.* Retrieved October 5, 2012, from http:// www.iwhc.org/docUploads/HERAAction- Sheets.PDF

Heap, C. (2009*). Slumming: Sexual and racial encounters in American nightlife, 1885-1940.* Chicago, IL: University of Chicago Press.

Hebernick, D., et al. (2015). Sexual diversity in the United States: Results from a national probability sample of adult women and men. *PLoS ONE, 12*(7), e0181198. https://DOI.org/10.1371/journal.pone.0181198

Hedges, L., & Nowell, A. (1995). Sex differences in mental test scores, variability, and numbers of high-scoring individuals. *Science, 269,* 41-45.

Hekma, G. (1994). A female soul in a male body: Sexual inversion as gender inversion in nineteenth-century sexology. In G. Herdt (Ed.), *Third sex, third gender: Beyond sexual dimorphism in culture and history* (pp. 213-239). New York, NY: Zone Books.

Hendrick, C., & Hendrick, S. S. (1986). A theory and method of love. *Journal of Personality and Social Psychology, 50*(2), 392-402. DOI:10.1037/0022-3514.50.2.392. http://psycnet.apa.org/journals/psp/50/2/392.html

Hendrick, C., Hendrick, S. S., & Dicke, A. (1998). The love attitudes scale: Short form. *Journal of Social and Personal Relationships, 15*(2), 147-159.

Henry, J., & McNab, W. (2003). Forever young: A health promotion focus on sexuality and aging. *Gerontology and Geriatrics Education, 23*, 57-74.

Hensel, D. J., & Fortenberry, J. D. (2014). Life-span sexuality through a sexual health perspective. In D. L. Tolman, L. M. Diamond, J. A. Bauermeister, W. F. George, J. G. Pfaus, & L. M. Ward (Eds.), *APA handbook of sexuality and psychology*, Vol. 1: *Person-based approaches* (pp. 385-413). Washington, DC: American Psychological Association. DOI:10.1037/14193-013

Herbenick, D., Bowling, J., Fu, T-C. (Jane), Dodge, B., Guerra-Reyes, L., & Sanders, S. (2017). Sexual diversity in the United States: Results from a nationally representative probability sample of adult women and men. *PLoS ONE, 12*(7), e0181198. https://DOI.org/10.1371/journal.pone.0181198

Herbenick, D., Fu, T-C (Jane), Arter, J, Sanders, S. A., & Dodge, B. (2018). Women's experiences with genital touching, sexual pleasure, and orgasm: Results from a U.S. probability sample of women ages 18 to 94. *Journal of Sex & Marital Therapy, 44*(2), 201-212, DOI: 10.1080/0092623X. 2017.1346530

Herbenick, D., Reece, M., Sanders, S. A., Dodge, B., Ghassemi, A., & Fortenberry, J. D. (2009). Prevalence and characteristics of vibrator use by women in the United States: Results from a nationally representative study. *Journal of Sexual Medicine, 6,* 1857-1866.

Herdt, G. (1981). *Guardians of the flutes.* New York, NY: McGraw-Hill.

Herdt, G. (1982). Sambia nose-bleeding rites and male proximity to women. *Ethos, 10,* 189-231. 2

Herdt, G. (1984). *Ritualized homosexuality in Melanesia.* Berkeley, CA: University of California Press.

Herdt, G. (1990). Developmental continuity as a dimension of sexual orientation across cultures. In D. McWhirter, J. Reinisch, & S. Sanders (Eds.), *Homosexuality and heterosexuality: The Kinsey Scale and current research* (pp. 208-238). New York NY: Oxford University Press.

Herdt, G. (1991). Representations of homosexuality in traditional societies: An essay on cultural ontology and historical comparison. *Journal of the History of Sexuality, 1,* 603-632.

Herdt, G. (Ed.). (1993). *Third sex, third gender: Beyond sexual dimorphism in culture and history.* New York, NY: Zone Books.

Herdt, G. (Ed.). (1994). *Third sex, third gender: Beyond sexual dimorphism in culture and history.* New York, NY: Zone Books.

Herdt, G. (1997a). *Same sex, different cultures: Perspectives on gay and lesbian lives.* New York, NY: Westview Press. Chapters 1, 2, 9, 10, 12, 8, 15.

Herdt, G. (1997b). Sexual cultures and population movement: Implications for HIV/STDs. In G. Herdt (Ed.), *Sexual cultures and migration in the era of AIDS: Anthropological and demographic perspectives* (pp. 3-22). New York, NY: Oxford University Press.

Herdt, G. (1999a). *Sambia sexual culture.* Chicago, IL: University of Chicago Press.

Herdt, G. (1999b). Sexing anthropology: Rethinking participant observation in sexual study. In D. Suggs & A. Miracle (Eds.), *Culture, biology, and sexuality* (pp. 17-32). Athens, GA: University of Georgia Press.

Herdt, G. (2000). Social change, sexual diversity, and tolerance for bisexuality in the United States. In A. D'Augelli & C. Patterson (Eds.), *Gay, lesbian and bisexual youth: Research and intervention* (pp. 267-283). New York, NY: Oxford University Press.

Herdt, G. (2004). Sexual development, social oppression, and local culture. *Sexuality Research and Social Policy, 1,* 1-24.

Herdt, G. (2006). *The Sambia: Ritual, sexuality and gender* (Rev. 2nd ed.). New York, NY: Wadsworth/Thompson Learning.

Herdt, G. (2009a). Cultural and historical factors—Childhood sexuality. In R. Schweder (Ed.), *The child: An encyclopedic companion* (pp. 895-897). Chicago, IL: University of Chicago Press.

Herdt, G. (Ed.). (2009b). *Moral panics, sex panics: Fear and the fight over sexual rights.* New York, NY: New York University Press.

Herdt, G. (2010a). Anthropological foundations of sexual Rights and health. In P. Aggleton & R. Parker (Eds.), *Routledge handbook of sexual health* (pp. 19-27). New York, NY: Routledge.

Herdt, G. (2010b). Sex/gender, culture, and development: Issues in the emergence of puberty and attraction. In C. Worthman, P. M. Plotsky, D. S. Schechter, & C. A. Cummings (Eds.), *Formative experiences: The interaction of caregiving, culture, and developmental psychobiology* (pp. 356-374). New York, NY: Cambridge University Press.

Herdt, G. (2019) Intimate consumption and new sexual subjects among the Sambia of Papua New Guinea. *Oceania* 89(1), 1-33.

Herdt, G., Beeler, J., & Rawls, T. (1997). Life course diversity among older lesbians and gay men: A study in Chicago. *Journal of Gay, Lesbian, and Bisexual Identity, 2,* 231-247. 10

Herdt, G., & Boxer, A. (1993). *Children of horizons.* Boston, MA: Beacon.

Herdt, G., & Davidson, J. (1988). The Sambia "turnim-man": Sociocultural and clinical aspects of gender formation in male pseudohermaphrodites with 5-alpha-reductase deficiency in Papau Guinea. *Archives of Sexual Behavior, 17*(1), 33-56. DOI: 10.1007/ BF01542051

Herdt, G., & DeVries, B. (Eds.). (2003). *Gay and lesbian aging: A research agenda for the 21st century.* New York, NY: Springer.

Herdt, G., & Howe, C. (Eds.). (2007). *21st century sexualities: Contemporary issues in health, education, and rights.* London, United Kingdom: Routledge.

Herdt, G., & Kertzner, R. (2006). I do, but I can't: The impact of marriage denial on the mental health and sexual citizenship of lesbians and gay men in the United States. *Sexuality Research and Social Policy, 3*(1), 33-49.

Herdt, G., & Koff, B. (2000). *Something to tell you: The road families travel when a child is gay.* New York, NY: Columbia University Press.

Herdt, G., & Leavitt, S. C. (Eds.). (1998). *Adolescence in the Pacific Island societies.* Pittsburgh, PA: University of Pittsburgh Press.

Herdt, G., & McClintock, M. (2000). The magical age of 10. *Archives of Sexual Behavior, 29*(6), 587-606.

Herd., G., Russell, S., Sweat, J., & Marzullo, M. (2006). Sexual inequality, youth empowerment, and the GSA: A community study in California. In N. Teunis (Ed.), *Sexual inequalities and social justice* (pp. 233-251). Berkeley, CA: University of California Press.

Herdt, G., & Stoller, R. J. (1990). *Intimate communications.* New York, NY: Columbia University Press.

Herek, G. M. (2004). Beyond "homophobia": Thinking about sexual stigma and prejudice in the twenty-first century. *Sexuality Research and Social Policy, 1*(2), 6-24.

Herek, G. M. (2009). Sexual stigma and sexual prejudice in the United States: A conceptual framework. In D. A. Hope (Ed.), *Contemporary perspectives on lesbian, gay, and bisexual identities: The 54th Nebraska Symposium on Motivation* (pp. 65-111). New York;, NY: Springer.

Herek, G. M. (2015). Beyond "homophobia": Thinking more clearly about stigma, prejudice, and sexual orientation. *American Journal of Orthopsychiatry, 85*(5, Suppl), S29-S37. DOI:10.1037/ort0000092

Herek, G. M., Gillis, J. R., Cogan, J. C., & Glunt, E. K. (1997). Hate crime victimization among lesbian, gay, and bisexual adults: Prevalence, psychological correlates, and methodological issues. *Journal of Interpersonal Violence, 12,* 195-215.

Herman, D. (1997). *The antigay agenda: Orthodox vision and the Christian right.* Chicago, IL: University of Chicago Press.

Herman, J. L., Flores, A. R., Brown, T. N. T., Wilson, B. D. M., & Conron, K. J. (2017). Age of individuals who identify as transgender in the United States. Retrieved from https://williamsinstitute.law.ucla.edu/wp-content/uploads/TransAgeReport.pdf

Herman-Giddens, M. E. (2007). The decline in the age of menarche in the United States: Should we be concerned? *Journal of Adolescent Health, 40,* 201-203. DOI: 10.1016/j.adohealth.2006.12.019

Herrell, R., Golberg, J., True, W. R., Ramakrishnan, V., Lyons, M., Eisen, S., & Tsuang, M. T. (1999). Sexual orientation and suicidology: A co-twin control study in adult men. *General Archives of Psychiatry, 56,* 867-874.

Hess, E. (2008). *Nim Chimpsky: The chimp who would be human.* New York, NY: Bantam Books.

Hess, K. L., DiNenno, E., Sionean, C., Ivy, W., & Paz-Bailey, G., & NHBS Study Group. (2016). Prevalence and correlates of heterosexual anal intercourse among men and women, 20 U.S. cities. *AIDS Behavior, 20*(12), 2966-2975. DOI 10.1007/s10461-016-1295-z

Hickey, M. T. (2009). Female college students' knowledge, perceptions, and use of emergency contraception. *Journal of Obstetric, Gynecologic, & Neonatal Nursing, 38,* 399-405.

Higdon, M. J. (2011). To lynch a child: Bullying and gender nonconformity in our nation's schools. *Indiana Law Journal, 86*(3), 827-878.

Hill, D. B., & Willoughby, B. L. B. (2005). The development and validation of the genderism and transphobia scale. *Sex Roles, 53*(7/8), 531-544. DOI: 10.1007/s11199-005-7140-x

Hillier, L., & Harrison, L. (2007). Building realities less limited than their own: Young people practicing same-sex attraction on the Internet. *Sexualities, 10*(1), 82-100.

Himmerick, K. (2005). Enhancing contraception: A comprehensive review. *Journal of the American Academy of Physicians Assistants, 18,* 26-33.

Hine, C. (2000). *Virtual ethnography.* London, United Kingdom: Sage.

Hines, D. A., & Malley-Morrison, K. (2005). *Family violence in the United States: Defining, understanding, and combating abuse.* Thousand Oaks, CA: Sage.

Hines, M., & Kaufman, F. R. (1994). Androgens and the development of human sex-typical behaviour. Rough-and-tumble play and sex of preferred playmates in children with congenital adrenal hyperplasia (CAH). *Child Development, 65,* 1042-1053.

Hirsch, A. (1998). *Scentsational sex: The secret to using aroma for arousal.* Boston, MA: Element.

Hirsch, J., Wardlow, H., Smith, D., Phinney, H., Parikh, S., & Nathanson, C. (2009). *The secret: Love, marriage, and HIV.* Nashville, TN: Vanderbilt University Press.

Hochschild, A. (2001). Emotion work, feeling rules, and social structure. In A. Branahan (Ed.), *Self and society* (pp. 138-155). New York, NY: Blackwell.

Hoff, C., Beoughers, S., Deepalika, D. M., Chakravarty, M., Darbes, L., & T. Neilands, T. (2010, July 22). Relationship characteristics and motivations behind agreements among gay male couples: Differences by agreement type and couple serostatus. *AIDS CARE,* 827-835.

Hoffman, J. (2011, March 26). *A girl's nude photo, and altered lives.* Retrieved September 12, 2012, from *The New York Times* website: http://www.nytimes.com/2011/03/27/ us/27sexting.html?pagewanted5all

Hollander, D. (2003). Even after having an STD, many teenagers do not adopt safer-sex practices. *Perspectives on Sexual and Reproductive Health, 35,* 103-104.

Hollander, E., & Wong, C. M. (1995). Obsessive-compulsive spectrum disorders. *The Journal of Clinical Psychiatry, 56*(Supplement 4: 3-6), discussion 53-55.

Holloway, S. L., & Valentine, G. (2003). *Cyberkids.* New York, NY: Routledge Falmer.

Hook, E. B. (1981). Rates of chromosome abnormalities at different maternal ages. *Obstetrics & Gynecology, 58*(3), 282-285.

Hooker, E. (1957). The adjustment of the male overt homosexual. *Journal of Projective Techniques, 21,* 18-31.

Hopkins, J. (2006, March 15). Egg-donor business booms on campuses. Retrieved October 27, 2012, from *USA Today* website: http:// usatoday30.usatoday.com/money/industries/ health/2006-03-15-egg-donors-usat_x.htm

Horn, S. S. (2007). Adolescents' acceptance of same-sex peers based on sexual orientation and gender expression. *Journal of Youth and Adolescence, 36,* 363-371.

Horowitz, A., & Gomez, C. (2018). Identity override: How sexual orientation reduces the rigidity of racial boundaries. *Sociological Science, 5,* 669-693. DOI:10.15195/v5.a28 https://www.pewresearch.org/fact-tank/2017/06/13/5-key-findings-about-lgbt-americans/

Horowitz, H. L. (2002). *Rereading sex: Battles over sexual knowledge and suppression in nineteenth-century America.* New York, NY: Knopf.

House, J. S., Landis, K. R., & Umberson, D. (1988). Social relationships and health. *Science, 241,* 540–545.

Howell, E. A., Mora, P., & Leventhal, H. (2006). Correlates of early postpartum depressive symptoms. *Maternal and Child Health Journal, 10*(2), 149–157.

Howells, K. (1994). Child sexual abuse: Finkelhor's Precondition Model revisited. *Psychology, Crime, & Law, 1,* 201–214.

Hrdy, S. (2010). Myths, monkeys and motherhood: A compromising life. In L. Drickamer & D. Dewsbury (Eds.), *Leaders of animal behavior: The next generation* (pp. 343–374). Cambridge, United Kingdom: Cambridge University Press.

Hrdy, S. B. (2009). *Mothers and others: The evolutionary origins of mutual understanding.* Cambridge, MA: Harvard University Press.

Hsu, B., Kling, A., Kessler, C., Knapke, K., Diefenbach, P., & Elias, J. E. (1994). Gender differences in sexual fantasy and behavior in a college population: A ten-year replication. *Journal of Sex and Marital Therapy, 20,* 103–118.

Huang, A. J., Subak, L. L., Thom, D. H., Van Den Eeden, S. K., Ragin, A. I., Kuppermann, M., . . . Brown, J. S. (2009). Sexual function and aging in racially and ethnically diverse women. *Journal of the American Geriatrics Society, 57,* 1362–1368.

Hubbard, T. K. (2014). *A companion to Greek and roman sexualities.* Chichester, UK; Malden, MA: Wiley Blackwell.

Huebner, D. M., Neilands, T. B., Rebchook, G. M., Kregeles, S. M. (2011). Sorting through chicken and eggs: A longitudinal examination of the assoications between attitudes, norms, and sexual risk behavior. *Health Psychology, 30,* 110–118.

Huebner, D. M., Rebchook, G. M., & Kegeles, S. M. (2004). Experiences of harassment, discrimination, and physical violence among young gay and bisexual men. *American Journal of Public Health, 94,* 1200–1203. http://dx.DOI.org.ezp2.lib.umn.edu/10.2105/AJPH.94.7.1200

Hughes, I. A., Houk, C. P., Ahmed, S., et al. (2006). Consensus statement on management of intersex disorders. *Archives of Disease in Childhood, 91*(7), 554–563.

Hull, I. (1997). *Sexuality, state, and civil society in Germany, 1700–1815.* Ithaca, NY: Cornell University Press.

Hull, T. H., & Budiharsana, M. (2001). Male circumcision and penis enhancement in Southeast Asia: Matters of pain and pleasure. *Reproductive Health Matters, 9,* 60–67.

Human Dignity Trust. (2019). Map of countries that criminalise LGBT people. Retrieved August 6, 2019, from https://www.humandignitytrust.org/lgbt-the-law/map-of-criminalisation/

Human Rights Campaign. (2019). *Violence against the transgender community in 2019.* Retrieved July 29, 2019, from https://www.hrc.org/resources/violence-against-the-transgender-community-in-2019

Human Rights Watch. (2017). I want to be like nature made me: Medically unnecessary surgeries on intersex children in the US. Retrieved May 31, 2019, from https://www.hrw.org/report/2017/07/25/i-want-be-nature-made-me/medically-unnecessary-surgeries-intersex-children-us

Human Rights Watch. (2018a). A national epidemic: Fatal anti-transgender violence in America in 2018. Retrieved from https://assets2.hrc.org/files/assets/resources/AntiTransViolence-2018Report-Final.pdf

Human Rights Watch. (2018b). *World report, China events of 2018.* Retrieved April 11, 2019, from https://www.hrw.org/world-report/2019/country-chapters/china-and-tibet.

Hunt, A. (1998). Great masturbation panic and the discourses of moral regulation in nineteenth and early twentieth century Britain. *Journal of the History of Sexuality 8,* 575–616.

Hunt, L. (2007). *Inventing human rights: A history.* New York, NY: Norton.

Hyde, J. S. (2005). The gender similarities hypothesis. *American Psychologist, 60,* 581–592.

Hyde, J. S., Delamater, J., & Durik, A. (2001). Sexuality and the dual-earner couple, Part II: Beyond the baby years. *Journal of Sex Research, 38* 10–23.

Hyde, J. S., DeLamater, J., & Hewitt, E. (1998). Sexuality and the dual-earner couple: Multiple roles and sexual functioning. *Journal of Family Psychology, 12,* 354–368.

Hyde, J. S., Krajnik, M., & Skuldt-Niederberger, K. (1991). Androgyny across the life span: A replication and longitudinal follow-up. *Developmental Psychology, 27*(3), 516–519.

Hydy, S. (2009). *Mothers and others: The evolutionary origins of mutual understanding.* Cambridge, MA: Harvard University Press.

Ilkkaracan, P., & Seral, G. (2000). Sexual pleasure as a woman's human right: Experiences from a grassroots training program in Turkey. In P. Ilkkaracan (Ed.), *Women and sexuality in Muslim societies* (pp. 187–196). Istanbul, Turkey: Women for Women's Human Rights (WWHR).

Imperato-McGinley, J., Peterson, R. E., Gautier, T., & Sturla, E. (1979). Male pseudohermaphroditism secondary to 5 alpha-reductase deficiency—a model for the role of androgens in both the development of the male phenotype and the evolution of a male gender identity. *Journal of Steroid Biochemistry, 11*(1B), 637–645.

Imperato-McGinley, J., Peterson, R. E., Gautier, R., & Sturla, E. (1981). The impact of androgens on the evolution of male gender identity. In S. J. Kogan & E. S. E. Hafez (Eds.), *Pediatric Andrology* (pp. 125–140). Hingham, MA: Kluwer.

Impett, E. A., Henson, J. M., Breines, J., Schooler, D., & Tolman, D. L. (2011). Embodiment feels better: Girls' body objectification and well-being across adolescence. *Psychology of Women Quarterly, 35,* 46–58.

Impett, E. A., Schooler, D., & Tolman, D. L. (2006). To be seen and not heard: Femininity ideology and adolescent girls' sexual health. *Archives of Sexual Behavior, 21,* 628–646.

Ing, S. (2015). *We're all like this: Learning to talk about our human sexual needs.* Tucson, AZ: Giant Publishing.

Ingham, R. (2005). We didn't cover that at school: Education against pleasure or education for pleasure. *Sex Education, 5(4),* 375–388.

Ingraham, N. (2009, February 17). *Do certain foods affect the taste of semen or other bodily fluids?* Retrieved October 27, 2012, from the Kinsey Confidential: Sexual Health Information from the Kinsey Institute website: http://kinseyconfidential.org/taste-bodily-fluids/

Institute for Reproductive Health. (2019). *Two day method.* Georgetown University. Retrieved July 21, 2019, from http://irh.org/twoday-method/

Institute of Medicine (IOM). (2000). *No time to lose: Getting more from HIV prevention.* Washington, DC: The National Academies Press.

Institute of Medicine (IOM). (2011). *The health of lesbian, gay, bisexual, and transgender people: Building a foundation for better understanding.* Washington, DC: The National Academies Press.

Institute of Medicine (IOM). (2012). *The health of lesbian, gay, bisexual and transgender people.* Washington, DC: The National Academies Press.

International Labour Organization. (2012). *Global estimate of forced labour.* United Nations. Retrieved August 7, 2019, from http://www.ilo.org/wcmsp5/groups/public/—ed_norm/—declaration/documents/publication/wcms_181953.pdf

IOM Report. (2011). *The health of lesbian, gay, bisexual, and transgender people.* Washington, DC: The National Academies Press.

Irvine, J. (2000). *Disorders of desire: Sexuality and gender in modern American sexology.* Philadelphia, PA: Temple University Press.

Irvine, J. (2002). *Talk about sex.* Berkeley, CA: University of California Press.

Jacob, B. A. (2002). Where the boys aren't: Noncognitive skills, returns to school, and the gender gap in higher education. *Economics of Education Review, 21,* 589–598.

Jacobs, S. E., Thomas, W., & Lang, S. (1997). *Two spirit people.* Urbana, IL: University of Illinois Press.

Jacobson, T. (2011). *Perspectives on gender in early childhood* (1st ed.). St. Paul, MN: Redleaf Press.

James, S. E., Herman, J. L., Rankin, S., Keisling, M., Mottet, L., & Anafi, M. (2016). *The report of the 2015 U.S. transgender survey.* Washington, DC: National Center for Transgender Equality. Available at https://www.transequality.org/sit

Jankowiak, W. (2008). *Intimacies: Love and sex across cultures.* New York, NY: Columbia University Press.

Jansen, K. L. (2000). *The making of the Magdalen: Preaching and popular devotion in the later Middle Ages.* Princeton, NJ: Princeton University Press.

Janssen, W., Koops, E., Anders, S., Kuhn, S., & Püschel, K. (2005). Forensic aspects of 40 accidental autoerotic deaths in Northern Germany. *Forensic Science International,* 147(Suppl.), S61–S64.

Jenness, V., & Fenstermaker, S. (2016). Forty years after Brownmiller: Prisons for men, transgender inmates, and the rape of the feminine. *Gender & Society, 30*(1), 14–29. DOI:10.1177/0891243215611856

Jenness, V., Maxson, C. L., Matsuda, K. N., & Sumner, J. M. (2007). *Violence in California correctional facilities: An empirical examination of sexual assault.* Report to the California Department of Corrections and Rehabilitation, Center for Evidence-Based Corrections, Department of Criminology, Law and Society, University of California, Irvine.

Jensen, J. T. (2011). The future of contraception: Innovations in contraceptive agents: Tomorrow's hormonal contraceptive agents and their clinical implications. *American Journal of Obstetrics and Gynecology, 205*(4), S21-S25. 7

Joffe, C. (2006). *The regulation of sexuality.* Philadelphia, PA: Temple University Press.

Joffe, C. (2009). *Dispatches from the abortion wars.* Boston, MA: Beacon.

Johns, M., Liddon, N., Jayne, P., Beltran, O., Steiner, R., & Morris, E. (2017, January). Systematic mapping of relationships-level protective factors and sexual health outcomes among sexual minority youth: The role of peers, parents, partners and providers. *LGBT Health, 5* (Jan1), 1:5–32.

Johnson, C. K. (2019, March 4). Second man seems to be free of AIDS virus after stem cell transplant. *Chicago Tribune.* Retrieved from https://www.chicagotribune.com/lifestyles/health/ct-aids-virus-stem-cell-transplant-20190304-story.html

Johnson, E. P. (2008). *Sweet tea: Black gay men of the South.* Durham, NC: University of North Carolina Press.

Johnson, T. M., & Grim, B. J. (2013). *The world's religions in figures: An introduction to international religious demography.* Hoboken, NJ: Wiley.

Johnston, J. (2017). Subscribing to sex edutainment: Sex education, online video, and the YouTube star. *Television & New Media, 18*(1), 76–92. https://DOI.org/10.1177/1527476416644977

Jolly, M. (1997). From Point Venus to Bali Ha'i: Eroticism and exoticism in representations of the

Pacific. In L. Manderson & M. Jolly (Eds.), *Sites of desire, economies of pleasure: Sexualities in Asia and the Pacific* (pp. 99-122). Chicago, IL: University of Chicago Press.

Jolly, M., Stewart, C., & Brewer, C. (2012). *Engendering violence in Papua New Guinea*. Canberra: ANU Press.

Jones, J. (1998). *Alfred Kinsey: A public/private life*. New York, NY: Norton.

Jones, M. (2019). What teenagers are learning from online porn. In E. O. Burgess (Ed.), *Sex matters: The sexuality & society reader (5th edition)* (pp. 128-138). New York, NY: W.W. Norton & Company

Jones, R. K., & Biddlecom, A. E. (2011). Is the Internet filling the sexual health information gap for teens? An exploratory study. *Journal of Health Communication: International Perspectives, 16*, 112-123.

Jones, R. K., Frohwirth, L. F., & Moore, A. M. (2008). "I would want to give my child, like, everything in the world": How issues of motherhood influence women who have abortions. *Journal of Family Issues, 29*, 79-99. 8

Jordan-Young, R. (2010). *Brainstorm: The flaws in the science of sex differences*. Cambridge, MA: Harvard University Press.

Joseph, H. A., Pan, Y., Mendoza, M., et al. (2018). HIV Acquisition and transmission potential among African American men who have sex with men and women in three U.S. cities. *Archives of Sexual Behavior, 47*, 183-194. https://DOI.org/10.1007/s10508-017-1052-z

Josephs, L. (2015). How children learn about sex: A cross-species and cross-cultural analysis. *Archives of Sexual Behavior, 44*(4), 1059-1069. DOI:10.1007/s10508-015-0498-0

Josephy, A., Jr. (1991). *The Indian heritage of America*. Boston, MA: Houghton Mifflin.

Judaism 101. (2010). *Kosher sex*. Retrieved on December 22, 2010, from http://www.jewfaq.org/sex.htm

Jurgens, R., Nowak, M., & Day, M. (2011). HIV and incarceration: Prisons and detention. *Journal of the International AIDS Society, 14*, 14-26.

Kafka, M. P. (2010). Hypersexual disorder: A proposed diagnosis for DSM-V. *Archives of Sexual Behavior, 39*(2), 377-400.

Kafka, M. P. (2014). What happened to hypersexual disorder? *Archives of Sexual Behavior, 43*(7), 1259-1261.

Kaiser Family Foundation. (2009). *Randomized controlled trial shows circumcision does not prevent male-to-female HIV transmission*. Retrieved September 13, 2012, from http://globalhealth.kff.org/Daily-Reports/2009/July/17/GH-071709-HIV-Circumcision.aspx

Kaiser Family Foundation. (2019). *Black Americans and HIV*. Retrieved March 19, 2019, fromat https://www.kff.org/hivaids/fact-sheet/black-americans-and-hivaids-the-basics/

Kaiser Permanente. (2009, July 14). *Kaiser Permanente Survey shows seniors embrace Internet to manage their health* [Press release]. Retrieved from October 27, 2012, from http://www.hr.com/en/communities/kaiser-permanente-survey-shows-seniors-embrace-int_fxgc3wuk.html

Kalick, S. M. (1988). Physical attractiveness as a status cue. *Journal of Experimental Social Psychology, 24*, 469-489.

Kamdar, Z., Kosambiya, J. K., Chawada, B. L., Verma, M., & Kadia, A. (2017). Rape: Is it a lifestyle or a behavioral problem? *Indian Journal of Psychiatry, 59*, 77-82.

Kane, E. W. (2013). *Rethinking gender and sexuality in childhood*. London/New York, NY: Bloomsbury Academic.

Kantor, L., Rolleri, L., & Kolios, K. (2014). Doug Kirby's contribution to the field of sex education. *Sex Education 14*, 473-480.

Kaplan, H. (1979). *Disorders of sexual desire*. New York, NY: Brunner/Mazel.

Kapumba, B. & S. King, S. (2019, February 27). Perceived HIV-protectiove benefits of male circumcision: Risk compensation behavior among women in Malawi. *Plos/One*. Retrieved May 19, 2019, from https://journals.plos.org/plosone/article?id=10.1371/journal.pone.0211015

Karim, Q. A., Karim, S. S. A., Frolich, J. A., Grobler, A. C., Baxter, C., Mansor, L. E., . . . Taylor, D. (2010). Effectiveness and safety of tenofvir gel, an antiretroviral microbicide, for the prevention of HIV infection in women. *Science, 329*, 1168-1174.

Karkazis, K. (2008). *Fixing sex: Intersex, medical authority, and lived experience*. Durham, NC: Duke University Press Books.

Karraker, K. H., Vogel, D. A., & Lake, M. A. (1995). Parents' gender-stereotyped perceptions of newborns: The eye of the beholder revisited. *Sex Roles: A Journal of Research, 33*, 687-701.

Katchadourian, H. (1990). Sexuality. The role of pubertal processes. In S. S. Feldman & G. R. Elliott (Eds.), *At the threshold: The developing adolescent* (pp. 330-351). Cambridge, MA: Harvard University Press.

Katz, J. N. (2007). *The invention of heterosexuality*. Chicago, IL: University of Chicago Press.

Katz-Wise, S. L. (2015). Sexual fluidity in young adult women and men: Associations with sexual orientation and sexual identity development. *Psychology & Sexuality, 6*(2), 189-208. DOI:10.1080/19419899.2013.876445

Katz-Wise, S. L., & Hyde, J. S. (2014). Sexuality and gender: The interplay. In D. L. Tolman, L. M. Diamond, J. A. Bauermeister, W. H. George, J. G. Pfaus, & L. M. Ward (Eds.), *APA handbook of sexuality and psychology*, Vol. 1: *Person-based approaches* (pp. 29-62). Washington, DC: American Psychological Association. DOI:10.1037/14193-002

Katz-Wise, S. L., & Hyde, J. S. (2015). Sexual fluidity and related attitudes and beliefs among young adults with a same-gender orientation. *Archives of Sexual Behavior, 44*(5), 1459-1470. DOI:10.1007/s10508-014-0420-1

Katz-Wise, S. L., Rosario, M., Calzo, J. P., Scherer, E. A., Sarda, V., & Austin, S. B. (2017). Endorsement and timing of sexual orientation developmental milestones among sexual minority young adults in the Growing Up Today study. *Journal of Sex Research, 54*(2), 172-185. DOI:10.1080/00224499.2016.1170757

Kaufman, J. & Powell, D. (2014). *The meaning of sexual identity in the twenty-first century*. Newcastle-upon-Tyne, UK: Cambridge Scholars Publishing.

Kendrick, K. M. (2004). The neurobiology of social bonds. *Journal of Neuroendocrinology, 16*(12), 1007-1008.

Kessler, S. J. (1998). *Lessons from the intersexed*. New Brunswick, NJ: Rutgers University Press.

Khattak, S. (2016, October 14). *Internet censorship: Making the hidden visible*. Cambridge, England: University of Cambridge. Retrieved April 11, 2019, from https://www.cam.ac.uk/research/features/internet-censorship-making-the-hidden-visible.

Killermann, S. (2017). *Social justice advocate's guide to gender* (2nd ed.). Austin, TX: Impetus Books. Retrieved from http://www.guidetogender.com/get/

Kimmel, M., & Mahler, M. (2003). Adolescent masculinity, homophobia, and violence: Random school shootings, 1982-2001. *American Behavioral Scientist, 46*, 1439-1458.

King, M., Semlyen, J., Tai, S. S., Killaspy, H., Osborn, D., Popelyuk, D., & Nazareth, I. (2008). A systematic review of mental disorder, suicide, and deliberate self harm in lesbian, gay, and bisexual people. *BMC Psychiatry, 8*. DOI: 10.1186/1471-244X-8-70

King, R., & Belsky, J. (2012). A typological approach to testing the evolutionary functions of human female orgasm. *Archives of Sexual Behavior, 41*(5), 1145-1160. DOI: https://DOI.org/10.1007/s10508-012-0001-0

Kingsberg, S. A. (2002). The impact of aging on sexual function in women and their partners. *Archives of Sexual Behavior, 31*(5), 431-437.

Kinnish, K. K., Strassberg, D. S., & Turner, C. W. (2005). Six differences in the flexibility of sexual orientation: A multidi-mensional retrospective assessment. *Archives of Sexual Behavior, 34*, 173-183.

Kinsey, A., Pomeroy, W., & Martin, C. (1948). *Sexual behavior in the human male*. Philadelphia, PA: W. B. Saunders.

Kinsey, A., Pomeroy, W., Martin, C., & Gebhard, P. (1953). *Sexual behavior in the human female*. Philadelphia, PA: W. B. Saunders.

Kirby, D. (2001). *Emerging answers: Research findings on programs to reduce teen pregnancy*. Washington, DC: National Campaign to Prevent Teen Pregnancy.

Kirby, D. (2007). *Emerging answers 2007: Research findings on programs to reduce teen pregnancy and sexually transmitted diseases*. Washington DC: The National Campaign to Prevent Teen and Unplanned Pregnancy.

Kirby, D. (2008). The impact of abstinence and comprehensive sex and STD/HIV education programs on adolescent sexual behavior. *Sexuality Research and Social Policy, 5*, 18-27.

Kirby, D. (2012). *Reducing sexual risk behavior among young people: A training toolkit for curriculum developers*. Scotts Valley, CA: ETR Associates. Cited in Kantor et al., 2014.

Kirby, D., & Coyle, K. (1997). School-based programs to reduce sexual risk taking behavior. *Children and Youth Services, 19*(5/6), 415-436.

Kirby, D., Laris, B. A., & Rolleri, L. (2006). *Sex and HIV education programs for youth: Their impact and important characteristics*. Scotts Valley, CA: ETR Associates.

Kirby, D., Lezin, N., Afriye, R. A., & Gallucci, G. (2002). *Preventing teen pregnancy: Youth development and after-school programs*. Scotts Valley, CA: ETR.

Kirk, K. M., Bailey, J. M., Dunne, M. P., & Martin, N. G. (2000). Measurement models for sexual orientation in a community twin sample. *Behavioral Genetics, 3*, 345-356.

Kirkman, L., Dickson-Swift, V., & Fox, C. (2015). Midlife relationship diversity, sexual fluidity, well-being and sexual health from a rural perspective. *Rural Society, 24*(3), 266-281. https://dx.DOI.org/10.1080/10371656.2015.1099272

Kleese, C. (2006). Polyamory and its 'others': Contesting the terms of non-monogamy. *Sexualities, 9*(5), 565-583. Chokshi

Klein, F. (1978). *The bisexual option: A concept of one hundred percent intimacy*. New York, NY: Arbor House.

Klein, L. K. (2018). *Pure; inside the evangelical movement that shamed a generation of young women and how i broke free*. New York, NY: Atria Books.

Klein, M. (2003). *Why there is no such thing as sexual addiction—and why it really matters: Part 2*. Retrieved October 27, 2012, from EmpowHER website: http://www.empowher.com/sexual-well-being/content/why-theres-no-such-thing-sexual-addiction-and-why-it-really-matters-part-.

Klein, M. (2006). *America's war on sex: The attack on law, lust, and liberty*. New York, NY: Praeger.

Klernan, K. (2004). Redrawing the boundaries of marriage. *Journal of Marriage and Family, 66*, 980-87.

Klettke, B., Hallford, B. J., & Mellor, D. J. (2014). Sexting prevalence and correlates: A systematic literature review. *Clinical Psychology Review, 34*(1), 44-53.

Klinenberg, E. (2012). *Going solo: The extraordinary rise and surprising appeal of living alone.* New York, NY: Penguin.

Kloess, J. A., Beech, A. R., & Harkins, L. (2014). Online child sexual exploitation prevalence, process, and offender characteristics. *Trauma, Violence, & Abuse, 15,* 126-139. http://dx.DOI.org/10.1177/1524838013511543.

Klohnen, E. C., & Luo, S. (2003). Interpersonal attraction and personality: What is attractive-self similarity, ideal similarity, complementarity, or attachment security? *Journal of Personality and Social Psychology, 85*(4), 709-722.

Kohler, P. K., Manhart, L. W., & Lafferty, W. E. (2008). Abstinence-only and comprehensive sex education and the initiation of sexual activity and teen pregnancy. *Journal of Adolescent Health, 42*(4), 344-351.

Koletic, G. (2017). Longitudinal associations between the use of sexually explicit material and adolescents' attitudes and behaviors: A narrative review of studies. *Journal of Adolescence, 57,* 119-133.

Kolmes, K., Stock, K., & Moser, C. (2006). Investigating bias in psychotherapy with BDSM clients. *Journal of Homosexuality, 50:* 301-24.

Kon, I. (1995). *The sexual revolution in Russia.* New York, NY: Free Press.

Kontula, O., & Haavio-Mannila, E. (2009). The impact of aging on human sexual activity and sexual desire. *Journal of Sex Research, 46,* 46-56.

Koontz, S. (2005). *Marriage, a history: From obedience to intimacy or how love conquered marriage.* New York, NY: Viking.

Kornrich, S., Brines, J., & Leupp, K. (2013). Egalitarianism, housework and sexual frequency in marriage. *American Sociological Review, 78,* 26-50.

Kost, K., & Maddow-Zimet, I. (2016). U.S. teenage pregnancies, births and abortions, 2011: National trends by age, race and ethnicity. Guttmacher Institute. Retrieved from https://www.guttmacher.org/sites/default/files/report_pdf/us-teen-pregnancy-trends-2011_0.pdf

Koukounas, E., & McCabe, M. P. (1997). Sexual and emotional variables influencing sexual response to erotica. *Behaviour Research and Therapy, 35,* 221-231.

Krafft-Ebing, R. von (1886). *Psychopathia sexualis.* Burbank, CA: Reprinted by Bloat Books, 1999.

Kraus, S., Voon, V., & Potenza, M. (2016). Should compulsive sexual behavior be considered an addiction? *Journal of Addiction, 111,* 2097-2106.

Kraus, S. W., Krueger, R. B., Briken, P., First, M. B., Stein, D. J., Kaplan, M. S., et al. (2018). Compulsive sexual behaviour disorder in the ICD-11. *World Psychiatry, 17*(1), 109-110.

Kreider, R. M., & Ellis, R. (2011, May). Number, timing, and duration of marriages and divorces: 2009. *Current Population Reports* (P70-125). Washington, DC: U.S. Census Bureau. Retrieved October 22, 2012, from http://www.census.gov/prod/2011pubs/p70-125.pdf.

Kristof, N. (2015, Oct. 24). Meet a 21st century sex slave. *The New York Times.* Retrieved August 7, 2019, from https://www.nytimes.com/2015/10/25/opinion/sunday/meet-a-21st-century-slave.html

Kristof, N., & WuDunn, S. (2009). *Half the sky: Turning oppression into opportunity for women worldwide.* New York, NY: Knauft.

Krueger, R. B. (2016). Diagnosis of hypersexual or compulsive sexual behavior can be made using ICD-10 and DSM-5 despite rejection of this diagnosis by the American Psychiatric Association. *Addiction, 111*(12), 2110-2111.

Krueger, R. B., & Kaplan, M. S. (2001). The paraphilic and hypersexual disorders: An overview. *Journal of Psychiatric Practice, 7*(6), 391-403.

Krueger, R. B., & Kaplan, M. S. (2016). Noncontact paraphilic sexual offenses. In A. Phenix & H. Hoberman, (Eds.), *Sexual offending* (pp. 79-102). New York, NY: Springer.

Krueger, R. B., Reed, G. M., First, M. B., Marais, A., Kismodi, E., & Briken, P. (2017). Proposals for paraphilic disorders in the International Classification of Diseases and Related Health Problems, eleventh revision (ICD-11). *Archives of Sexual Behavior, 46*(5), 1529-1545.

Kuhn, T. (1970). *The structure of scientific revolutions.* Chicago, IL: University of Chicago Press.

Kumari, R. (2019). Baby brain or pregnancy brain or momnesia. *International Journal of Nursing Education and Research, 7*(1), 2454-2660.

Kurdek, L. A. (2005). What do we know about gay and lesbian couples? *Current Directions in Psychological Science, 14,* 251-254.

Kuzma, J. M., & Black, D. W. (2008). Epidemiology, prevalence, and natural history of compulsive sexual behavior. *Psychiatric Clinics of North America, 31,* 603-611.

Laborde, N. D., vanDommelen-Gonzalez, E., & Minnis, A. M. (2014). Trust—that's a big one: Intimate partnership values among urban Latino youth. *Culture, Health & Sexuality, 16*(9), 1009-1022.

Lacquer, T. (2003). *Solitary sex: A cultural history of masturbation.* New York, NY: Zone Books.

Ladas, A., Whipple, B., & Perry, J. (2005). *The G Spot: And other discoveries about human sexuality.* New York, NY: Holt.

LaHood, G. (director), & Keir, J. (producer). (2012). *Intersexion: Gender ambiguity unveiled* [Documentary film]. Ponsonby Productions: New Zealand.

Lamb, S. (2006). *Sex therapy and kids: Addressing their concerns through talk and play.* New York, NY: Norton.

Lamb, S., & Gilbert, J. (Eds.). (2018). *The Cambridge handbook of sexual development: Childhood and adolescence.* Cambridge, UK: Cambridge University Press. DOI:10.1017/9781108116121

Lambert, T. A., Kahn, A. S., & Apple, K. J. (2003). Pluralistic ignorance and hooking up. *Journal of Sex Research, 40*(2), 129-135.

Lamptey, P., Johnson, J., & Khan, M. (2006). The global challenge of HIV and AIDS. *Population Bulletin, 6,* 1-24.

Lance, L. M. (1987). The effects of interaction with gay persons on attitudes toward homosexuality. *Human Relations, 40,* 329-336.

Landolt, M. A., Bartholomew, K., Saffrey, C., Oram, D., & Perlman, D. (2004). Gender nonconformity, childhood rejection, and adult attachment. *Archives of Sexual Behavior, 33,* 117-28.

Lang, S., & Vantine, J. L. (1998). *Men as women, women as men: Changing gender in Native American cultures.* Austin, TX: University of Texas Press.

Langer, S. J. (2019). *Theorizing transgender identity for clinical practice: A new model for understanding gender.* London: Jessica Kingsley Publishers.

Langley, L. L. (Ed.). (1973). *Contraception.* Springfield, MA: G & C Company.

Laqueur, T. (1992). *Making sex: Body and gender from the Greeks to Freud.* Revised ed. Cambridge, MA: Harvard University Press.

LaSala, M. (2010). *Coming out, coming home.* New York, NY: Columbia University Press.

Laumann, E. O., Ellington, S., Mahay, J., Paik, A., & Youm, Y. (2004). *The sexual organization of the city.* Chicago, IL: University of Chicago Press.

Laumann, E. O., Gagnon, J. H., Michael, R. T., & Michaels, S. (1994). *Social organization of sexuality: Sexual practices in the United States.* Chicago, IL: University of Chicago Press.

Laumann, E. O., Paik, A., Glasser, D. B., Kang, J. H., Wang, T., Levinson, B., . . . Gingell, C. (2006). A cross-national study of subjective sexual well-being among older women and men: Findings from the Global Study of Sexual Attitudes and Behaviors. *Archives of Sexual Behavior, 35* 143-159.

Laumann, E. O., Paik, A., & Rosen, R. (1999). Sexual dysfunction in the United States. *Journal of the American Medical Association (JAMA), 10*(281), 537-544.

Lawrence, E., Rothman, A. D., Cobb, R. J., Rothman, M. T., & Bradbury, T. N. (2008). Marital satisfaction across the transition to parenthood. *Journal of Family Psychology, 22*(1), 41-50.

Lee, J. A. (1973). *Colours of love: An exploration of the ways of loving.* Toronto, ON: New Press.

Lee, J. A. (1988). Love styles. In M. H. Barnes & R. J. Sternberg (Eds.), *The psychology of love* (pp. 38-67). New Haven, CT: Yale University Press.

Lee, J. K. P., Pattison, P., Jackson, H. J., & Ward, T. (2001). The general, common, and specific features of psychopathology for different types of paraphilias. *Criminal Justice and Behavior, 28,* 227-256. DOI:10.1177/0093854801028002005

Lee, J. Y., & Lee, S. J. (2018). Caring is masculine: Stay-at-home fathers and masculine identity. *Psychology of Men & Masculinities, 19*(1), 47-58. DOI:10.1037/men0000079

Leitenberg, H., & Henning, K. (1995). Sexual fantasy. *Psychological Bulletin, 117*(3), 469-496.

Lenhart, A., & Madden, M. (2007). *Social networking websites and teens: An overview.* Washington, DC: Pew Internet & American Life Project.

Lenhart, A., Madden, M., & Hitlin, P. (2005). *Teens and technology.* Washington, DC: Pew Internet & American Life Project.

Lenhart, A. (2009). Teens and sexting: How and why minor teens are sending sexually suggestive nude or nearly nude images via text messaging. Pew Internet & American Life Project. Retrieved from http://www.pewinternet.org/Reports/2009/Teens-and-Sexting.aspx

Lepani, K. (2008). Fitting condoms on culture: Rethinking approaches to HIV prevention in the Trobriand Islands of Papua New Guinea. In R. Eves & L. Butt (Eds.), *Making sense of AIDS: Culture, sexuality, and power in Melanesia* (pp. 246-266). Honolulu, HI: University of Hawaii Press.

Lepani, K. (2012) *Islands of love, islands of risk.* Nashville, TN: Vanderbilt University Press.

Lepani, K. (2012). *Islands of risk/islands of love: HIV and culture in the Trobriands.* Nashville, TN: Vanderbilt University Press.

Lerner, R., & Steinberg, L. D. (2004). *Handbook of adolescent psychology.* New York, NY: Wiley.

Lester, T. (2002). Introduction. In T. Lester (Ed.), *Gender nonconformity, race, and sexuality* (pp. 3-17). Madison, WI: University of Wisconsin Press.

Leung, A., & Robson, L. (1993). Childhood masturbation. *Clinical Pediatrics, 32,* 238-241.

Leung, A. W., Mak, J., Cheung, P. S., & Epstein, R. J. (2008). Evidence for a programming effect of early menarche on the rise of breast cancer incidence in Hong Kong. *Cancer Detection and Prevention, 32,* 156-161.

LeVay, S. (1991). A difference in hypothalamic structure between heterosexual and homosexual men. *Science, 253,* 1034-1037.

LeVay, S. (2016). *Gay, straight, and the reason why: The science of sexual orientation.* Oxford, UK: Oxford University Press.

LeVay, S. (2017). Proceed with caution: Interpreting evidence for prenatal influences on sexual orientation. *Archives of Sexual Behavior, 46*(6), 1607-1608.

Levin, D. (2019, February 21). As Colorado moves to bar abstinence-only sex education, teenagers take the lead. Retrieved April 2, 2019, from https://www.nytimes.com/2019/02/21/us/colorado-sex-education-in-schools.html

Levin, R. (2004). Smells and tastes—their putative influence on sexual activity in humans. *Sexual and Relationship Therapy, 19*(4), 451-462.

Levin, R. J. (2002). The physiology of sexual arousal in the human female: A recreational and procreational synthesis. *Archives of Sexual Behavior, 31*(5), 405-411.

Levin, R. J. (2015). Recreation and procreation: A critical view of sex in the human female. *Clinical Anatomy, 28*, p. 339-354. DOI: 10.1002/ca.22495

Levin, S. (2019, July 3). I shouldn't be forced to give birth to a baby that won't live. *New York Times.* Retrieved July 19, 2019, from https://www.nytimes.com/2019/07/03/opinion/abortion-hyde-amendment.html

Levine, A., & Heller, R. (2010). *Attached: The new science of adult attachment.* New York, NY: Penguin.

Levine, D. (1998). *The joy of cybersex.* New York, NY: Ballantine Books.

Levine, D. (2011). Using technology, new media, and mobile for sexual and reproductive health. *Sexuality Research and Social Policy, 8*, 18-26.

Levine, E. (2007). *Wallowing in sex: The new sexual culture of the 1970s American television.* Durham, NC: Duke University Press.

Levine, J. (2002). *Harmful to minors.* Minneapolis, MN: University of Minnesota Press.

Levine, J. M. (1995). *Sexuality education across cultures.* San Francisco, CA: Jossey-Bass.

Levine, K. B., Williams, R. E., & Hartmann K. E. (2008). Vulvovaginal atrophy is strongly associated with female sexual dysfunction among sexually active postmenopausal women. *Menopause, 15*(4 Pt 1), 661-666.

Levine, M. P., Nardi, P. M., & Gagnon, J. H. (1997). *In changing times: Gay men and lesbians encounter HIV/AIDS.* Chicago, IL: University of Chicago Press.

Levine, M. P., & Troiden, R. R. (1988). The myth of sexual compulsivity. *Journal of Sex Research, 25*, 347-363.

Levinson, D. (1989). Family violence in cross-cultural perspective. In H. R. Bernard (Series Ed.), *Frontiers of Anthropology: Vol. 1.* Thousand Oaks, CA: Sage.

Levi-Strauss, C. (1971). *Mythologiques.* New York, NY: Harper Torchbooks.

Levkoff, L. (2007). *Third base ain't what it used to be: What your kids are learning about sex today–and how to teach to become sexually healthy adults.* New York, NY: New American Library.

Lewin, E. (1999). *Recognizing ourselves.* New York, NY: Columbia University Press.

Lewin, E. (2009). *Gay fatherhood: Narratives of family and citizenship in America.* Chicago, IL: University of Chicago Press.

Lewis, M. (2000). A brief history of condoms. In A. Mindel (Ed.), *Condoms* (pp. 1-18). Malden, MA: BMJ Books.

Li, G., & Hines, M. (2016). In search of emerging same-sex sexuality: Romantic attractions at age 13 years. *Archives of Sexual Behavior, 45*(7), 1839-1849. DOI:10.1007/s10508-016-0726-2

Liamputtong, P. (2007). *Researching the vulnerable.* London, United Kingdom: Sage.

Lieberman, H. (2017, May 12). Was Christine Jorgensen the Caitlyn Jenner of the 1950s? *Jestor Daily.* Retrieved June 2, 2019, from https://daily.jstor.org/christine-jorgensen-caitlyn-jenner/

Lindau, S. T., Schumm, L. P., Laumann, E. O., Levinson, W., O'Muircheartaigh, C. A., & Waite, L. J. (2007). A study of sexuality and health among older adults in the United States. *New England Journal of Medicine, 357*, 762-774.

Lindberg, L. D., Maddow-Zimet, I., & Boonstra, H. (2016). Changes in adolescents' receipt of sex education, 2006-2013. *Journal of Adolescent Health, 58*(6), 621-627.

Lippa, R. A. (2017). Category specificity of self-reported sexual attraction and viewing times to male and female models in a large U.S. sample: Sex, sexual orientation, and demographic effects. *Archives of Sexual Behavior, 46*(1), 167-178. DOI:10.1007/s10508-016-0844-x

Livingston, G. (2014). *Growing number of dads home with the kids.* Retrieved from https://www.pewsocialtrends.org/2014/06/05/growing-number-of-dads-home-with-the-kids/st-2014-06-05-stay-at-home-dads-04/

Livingstone, S. (2002). *Young people and new media: Childhood and the changing media environment.* London, United Kingdom: Sage.

Long, L. (1997). Refugee women, violence, and HIV. In G. Herdt (Ed.), *Sexual cultures and migration in the era of AIDS* (pp. 87-106). New York, NY: Oxford University Press.

Luker, K. (2006). *When sex goes to school.* New York, NY: Norton.

Luo, S., & Klohnen, E. C. (2005). Assortative mating and marital quality in newlyweds: A coupled-centered approach. *Journal of Personality and Social Psychology, 88*, 304-326.

Luoto, S., Krams, I., & Rantala, M. J. (2018). A life history approach to the female sexual orientation spectrum: Evolution, development, causal mechanisms, and health. *Archives of Sexual Behavior.* DOI:10.1007/s10508-018-1261-0

Lynch, K. R., Jewell, J. A., Golding, J. M., & Kembel, H. B. (2017). Associations between sexual behavior norm beliefs in relationships and intimate partner rape judgments. *Violence Against Women, 23*(4), 426-451. https://DOI.org/10.1177/107780 1216642871

Lyons, A. P., & Lyons, H. D. (2011). *Sexualities in anthropology: A reader.* New York, NY: Wiley-Blackwell.

Mabilia, M. (2006). *Breast feeding and sexuality behavior: Beliefs and taboos among the Gogo mothers of Tanzania.* New York, NY: Berghan Books.

Maccoby, E. E. (1998). *The two sexes: Growing up apart, coming together.* Cambridge, MA: Harvard University Press.

Maccoby, E. E. (2002). Gender and group process: A developmental perspective. *Current Directions in Psychological Science, 11*, 54-58.

Maccoby, E. E., & Jacklin, C. N. (Eds.). (1974). *The psychology of sex differences.* Stanford, CA: Stanford University Press.

Machacek, D. W., & Wilcox, M. M. (2003). *Sexuality and world religions.* Santa Barbara, CA: ABC-Clio.

MacMillan, R. (2000). Adolescent victimization and income deficits in adulthood: Rethinking the costs of criminal violence from a life-course perspective. *Criminology, 38*, 553-577.

MacNeil, S., & Byers, E. S. (2009). Role of sexual self-disclosure in the sexual satisfaction of long-term heterosexual couples. *Journal of Sex Research, 46*, 1-12.

MacPhee, M. (1992). Deodorized culture: Anthropology of smell in America. *Arizona Anthropologist, 8*, 89-102.

Madey, S. F., & Rodgers, L. (2009). The effect of attachment and Sternberg's Triangular Theory of Love on relationship satisfaction. *Individual Differences Research, 7*, 76-84.

Madkour, A. S., Farhat, T., Halpern, C. T., Godeau, E., & Gabhain, S. N. (2010). Early adolescent sexual initiationand physical/psychological symptoms: A comparative analysis of five nations. *Journal of Youth and Adolescence, 39*(10), 1211-1225. DOI:10.1007/s10964-010-9521-x

Mahan Buttaro, T. M., Koeniger-Donohue, R., Hawkins, J. (2014). Sexuality and quality of life in aging: Implications for practice. *Journal for Nurse Practitioners, 10*(7), 480-485.

Mahdavi, P. (1978). *Passionate uprisings: Iran's sexual revolution.* Stanford, CA: Stanford University Press.

Maier, T. (2009). *Masters of sex: The life and times of William Masters and Virginia Johnson, the couple who taught America how to love.* New York, NY: Basic.

Maines, R. P. (1999). *The technology of orgasm: "Hysteria," the vibrator, and women's sexual satisfaction.* Baltimore, MD: Johns Hopkins University Press.

Makadon, H., Mayer, K., Potter, J., & Goldhammer, H. (Eds.). (2008). *Fenway guide to lesbian, gay, bisexual, and transgender health.* Philadelphia, PA: American College of Physicians.

Malach-Pines, A. (2005). *Falling in love: Why we choose the lovers we choose* (2nd ed.). New York, NY: Routledge.

Malinowski, B. (1929). *Sexual life of savages.* New York, NY: Dutton.

Malinowski, B. (1948). *Magic, science, and religion.* London, United Kingdom: Robert Redfield.

Man, C. D., & Corman, J. P. (2002). Forecasting sexual abuse in prison: The prison subculture of masculinity as a backdrop for "deliberate indifference." *Journal of Criminal Law and Criminology, 92*(127), 1-38.

Manley, M. H., Diamond, L. M., & van Anders, S. M. (2015). Polyamory, monoamory, and sexual fluidity: A longitudinal study of identity and sexual trajectories. *Psychology of Sexual Orientation and Gender Diversity, 2*(2), 168-180. DOI:10.1037/sgd0000098

Manning, W. D., Brown, S. L., & Payne, K. K. (2014). Two decades of stability and change in age at first union formation. *Journal of Marriage and Family, 76*(2), 247-260.

March of Dimes. (2018). *Preterm labor and premature birth: Are you at risk?* Retrieved from https://www.marchofdimes.org/complications/preterm-labor-and-premature-birth-are-you-at-risk.aspx

Marin County, Department of Health and Human Services, Division of Public Health. (2010). *STD Risk Assessment Questionnaire.* Retrieved September 29, 2012, from http://www.co.marin.ca.us/depts/HH/Main/forms/ hhsclinics/STD%20Risk%20Assessment%20 Questionnaire.pdf.

Mark, K. P., & Lasslo, J. P. (2018). Maintaining sexual desire in long-term relationships: A systematic review and conceptual model. *Journal of Sex Research, 55*, 563-581.

Marks, N., & Lambert, J. D. (1998). Marital status continuity and change among young and midlife adults: Longitudinal effects on psychological well being. *Journal of Family Issues, 19*, 652-686.

Marshall, W. L. (1996). Assessment, treatment and theorising about sex offenders: Developments during the past twenty years and future directions. *Criminal Justice and Behaviour, 23(1)*, 162-199.

Martin, C. L., & Ruble, D. (2004). Children's search for gender cues. *Current Directions in Psychological Science, 13*(2), 67-70. DOI:10.1111/j.0963-7214. 2004.00276.x

Martin, J. (2013). *How we do it: Evolution and future of human reproduction.* New York, NY: Basic Books.

Martin, J. A., Hamilton, B. E., Osterman, M. J. K., Driscoll, A. K., & Mathews, T. J. (2015). Births: Final data for 2013. *National Vital Statistic Reports, 64*(1), 1-68.

Martin, J. A., Hamilton, B. E., Osterman, M. J. K., Driscoll, A. K., & Mathews, T. J. (2017). Births: Final data for 2015. *National Vital Statistic Reports, 66*(1), 1-70.

Martin, J. A., Hamilton, B. E., Sutton, P. D., Ventura, S. J., Menacker, F., Kirmeyer, S., & Mathews, T. J. (2009). Births: Final data for 2006. *National Vital Statistics Reports, 57*(7).

Martin, R. (2013) *How we do it: The evolution and future of human reproduction*. New York, NY: Basic Books.

Martinez, G., Copen, C. E., & Abma, J. C. (2011). Teenagers in the United States: sexual activity, contraceptive use, and childbearing, 2006-2010. National Survey of Family Growth, Vital and Health Statistics, Series 23, No. 31, https://www.cdc.gov/nchs/data/series/sr_23/sr23_031.pdf.

Marwick, A., & Boyd, D. (2011). To see and be seen: Celebrity practice on Twitter. *Convergence: The International Journal of Research into New Media Technologies, 17*(2), 139-158.

Marx, B. P., & Sloan, D. M. (2003). The effects of trauma history, gender, and race on alcohol use and posttraumatic stress symptoms in a college student sample. *Addictive Behaviors, 28*(9), 1631-1647.

Marzullo, M., & Herdt, G. (2011). Marriage rights and LGBT youth: The present and future impact of sexuality policy changes. *Ethos, 39,* 526-552.

Mashburn, J. (2006). Etiology, diagnosis, and management of vaginitis. *Journal of Midwifery and Women's Health, 51,* 423-430.

Masho, S. W., & Ahmed, G. A. (2007). Age at sexual assault and post-traumatic stress disorder among women: Prevalence, correlates, and implications for prevention. *Journal of Women's Health, 16,* 262-271.

Mastekaasa, A. (2006). Is marriage/cohabitation beneficial for young people? *Journal of Community and Applied Psychology, 16,* 149-165.

Masters, W. H., & Johnson, V. E. (1966). *Human sexual response.* Boston, MA: Little, Brown.

Matthews, B. (2006). *Engaging education. Developing emotional literacy, equity and co-education.* Buckingham, UK: McGraw-Hill/Open University Press.

Maurice, W. L. (1999). *Sexual medicine in primary care.* St. Louis, MO: Mosby.

Mayer, J. D., Salovey, P., & Caruso, D. (2000). Models of emotional intelligence. In R. J. Sternberg (Ed.), *The handbook of intelligence* (pp. 396-420). New York, NY: Cambridge University Press.

Mayo Clinic. (2011a). *Pelvic inflammatory disease (PID). Prevention.* Retrieved October 27, 2012, from http://www.mayoclinic.com/health/pelvic-inflammatory-disease/DS00402/ DSECTION5prevention.

Mayo Clinic. (2011b). *Pelvic inflammatory disease (PID). Risk factors.* Retrieved October 27, 2012, from http://www.mayoclinic.com/health/pelvic-inflammatory-disease/ds00402/ dsection5risk-factors

Mayo Clinic. (2011c). *Testicular cancer: Risk factors.* Retrieved October 27, 2012, from http://www.mayoclinic.com/health/testicular-cancer/DS00046/DSECTION5risk-factors

Mayo Clinic. (2012). *Sexually transmitted diseases (STDs). Risk factors.* Retrieved October 27, 2012, from http://www.mayoclinic.com/health/sexually-transmitted-diseases-stds/ DS01123/DSECTION5risk-factors

Mayo Clinic. (2017). *Toxic shock syndrome.* Retrieved from https://www.mayoclinic.org/diseases-conditions/toxic-shock-syndrome/symptoms-causes/syc-20355384

Mayo Clinic. (2018a). *Infertility.* Retrieved from https://www.mayoclinic.org/diseases-conditions/infertility/symptoms-causes/syc-20354317

Mayo Clinic. (2018b). *Postpartum depression.* Retrieved from https://www.mayoclinic.org/diseases-conditions/postpartum-depression/symptoms-causes/syc-20376617

Mayo Clinic. (2019). *Vaginal atrophy, diagnosis and treatment.* Retrieved July 13, 2019, from https://www.acog.org/Patients/FAQs/Cervical-Cancer-Screening?IsMobileSet=false

Mays, V. M., & Cochran, S. D. (1994). Depressive distress among homosexually active African American men and women. *American Journal of Psychiatry, 151,* 524-529.

Mays, V. M., & Cochran, S. D. (2001). Mental health correlates of perceived discrimination among lesbian, gay, and bisexual adults in the United States. *American Journal of Public Health, 91,* 1869-1876.

McBride, K. R., & Fortenberry, J. D. (2010). Heterosexual anal sexuality and anal sex behaviors: A review. *Journal of Sex Research, 47*(2-3), 123-136.

McCafferty, C. (2007, November). *Experiential learning: Emotional literacy, too!* Presented at the 2007 Annual Sexuality Education Conference "SEX ED 101" by The Center for Family Life Education, Greater Northern New Jersey, Somerset, New Jersey.

McCann, C. (2010). Women as leaders in the contraceptive movement. In K. O'Connor (Ed.), *Gender and women's leadership: A reference handbook*, p. 749. Thousand Oaks, CA: SAGE.

McClelland, S., Swank, E., & Fahs, B. (2017). Sexuality, pleasure, power, and danger: Points of tension, contradiction, and conflict. *APA Handbook of the Psychology of Women, Vol. 1* (pp. 229-247). Washington, DC: American Psychological Association.

McClintock, M. K. (1971). Menstrual synchrony and suppression. *Nature 229*(5282), 244-245.

McClintock, M. K., & Herdt, G. (1996). Rethinking puberty: The development of sexual attraction. *Psychological Sciences, 5,* 178-183.

McCulloch, S. (2018). *Why only 3-5% of babies are born on their 'due date'.* Retrieved from https://www.bellybelly.com.au/pregnancy/why-only-3-5-percent-babies-born-on-due-date/

McInroy, L., & Craig, S. L. (2012). Articulating identities: Language and practice with multiethnic sexual minority youth. *Counseling Psychology Quarterly, 25*(2), 137-149.

McKenna, K. Y. A., Gree, A. S., & Gleason, M. J. (2002). Relationship formation on the Internet: What's the big attraction? *Journal of Social Issues, 58,* 9-31.

McQuillan, J., Greil, A. L., Shreffler, K. M., & Tichenor, V. (2008). The importance of motherhood among women in the contemporary United States. *Gender and Society, 22*(4), 477-496.

Mead, M. (1927). *Coming of age in Samoa.* New York, NY: Dutton.

Mead, M. (1935). *Sex and temperament in three primitive societies.* New York, NY: Dutton.

Mead, M. (1949). *Male and female.* New York, NY: Dutton.

Mead, M. (1961). Cultural determinants of sexual behavior. In W. C. Young (Ed.), *Sex and internal secretions* (pp. 1433-1479). Baltimore, MD: Williams and Wilkins.

Medline Plus. (2010). Androgen insensitivity syndrome. Retrieved from http://www.nlm.nih.gov/medlineplus/ency/article/001180.htm

Meerwijk, E. & Sevelius, J. (2017). Transgender population size in the United States: A meta-regression of population-based probability samples. *American Journal of Public Health, 107,* e1-e8.

Megge, S. (2006). *Men dealing with women's menopause symptoms.* Retrieved October 27, 2012, from Ezine Articles website: http://ezinearticles.com/?Men-Dealing-With-Womens-Menopause-Symptoms&id5336056

Meier, A., & Allen, G. (2009). Romantic relationships from adolescence to young adulthood: Evidence from the national longitudinal study of adolescent health. *Sociological Quarterly, 50,* 308-335.

Merelli, A. (2018). Women's sexual rights include the right to pleasure. Retrieved June 12, 2019, from https://qz.com/1470374/womens-sexual-rights-include-the-right-to-pleasure/

Merry, S. E. (2006). *Human rights and gender violence.* Chicago, IL: University of Chicago Press.

Meston, C. M., & Buss, D. (2009). *Why women have sex.* New York, NY: Times Books.

Meston, C. M., Hull, E., Levin, R. J., & Sipski, M. (2004a). Disorders of orgasm in women. *Journal of Sexual Medicine, 1,* 66-68.

Meston, C. M., Hull, E., Levin, R. J., & Sipski, M. (2004b). Women's orgasm. In T. F. Lue, R. Basson, R. Rosen, F. Giuliano, S. Khoury, & F. Montorsi (Eds.), *Sexual medicine: Sexual dysfunctions in men and women* (pp. 783-850). Paris, France: Health Publications.

Meyer, I. H. (1995). Minority stress and mental health in gay men. *Journal of Health and Social Behavior, 36,* 38-56.

Meyer, I. H. (2007). Prejudice and discrimination as social stressors. In I. H. Meyer & M. E. Northridge (Eds.), *The health of sexual minorities: Public health perspectives on lesbian, gay, bisexual, and transgender populations* (pp. 242-267). New York, NY: Springer Science 1 Business Media.

Meyer, I. H., Schwartz, S., & Frost, D. M. (2008). Social patterning of stress and coping: Does disadvantaged social status confer more stress and fewer coping resources? *Social Science and Medicine, 67* (3), 368-379.

Meyer-Bahlburg, H. F. L. (1984). Psychoendocrine research on sexual orientation. Current status and future options. *Progress in Brain Research, 61,* 375-398.

Meyer-Bahlburg, H. F. L., Dolezal, C., Baker, S. W., & New, M. I. (2008). Sexual orientation in women with classical or non-classical congenital adrenal hyperplasia as a function of degree of prenatal androgen excess. *Archives of Sexual Behavior, 37,* 85-99. DOI: 10.1007/s10508-007-9265-1.

Meyerowitz, J. (1993). Beyond the feminine mystique: A reassessment of postwar mass culture, 1946-1958. *Journal of American History, 79*(4), 1455-1482.

Meyerowitz, J. (2006). Transforming sex: Christine Jorgensen in the postwar U.S. *Magazine of History, 20,* 16-20.

Meyers, D. T. (2001). The rush to motherhood: Pronatalist discourse and women's autonomy. *Signs, 26*(3), 735-773.

Michael, R. T., Gagnon, J. H., Laumann, E. O., & Kolata, G. (1994). *Sex in America: A definitive survey.* Boston: Little Brown.

Michaels, S. (1996). The prevalence of homosexuality in the United States. In R. P. Sabaj & T. S. Stein (Eds.), *The textbook of homosexuality and mental health* (pp. 43-63). Washington, DC: American Psychiatric Press.

Miller, A. (2000). Sexual but not reproductive: Exploring the junction and disjunction of sexual and reproductive rights. *Health and Human Rights, 4,* 68-109.

Mills, M., Rindfuss, R. R., McDonald, P., & Velde, E., and on behalf of the ESHRE Reproduction and Society Task Force. (2011). Why do people postpone parenthood? Reasons and social policy incentives. *Human Reproduction Update, 17*(6), 848-860.

Miner, M. H., Dickenson, J., & Coleman, E. (2019). Effects of emotions on sexual behavior in men with and without hypersexuality. *Sexual Addiction & Compulsivity,* DOI:10.1080/10720162.2018.1564408

Mkandawire-Valhmu, L., Lathen, L., Baisch, M. J., Cotton, Q., Dresel, A., Antilla, J., Olukotun, O., Washington, R., Jordan, L., & Hess, A. (2018). Enhancing birth outcomes by creating supportive spaces for pregnant African American women living in Milwaukee. *Maternal and Child Health Journal, 22,* 1797-1804. DOI: https://DOI.org/10.1007/s10995-018-2580-4

MMWR Weekly. (1982). Epidemiologic notes and reports possible transfusion-associated Acquired Immune Deficiency Syndrome, AIDS-California. *MMWR (Morbidity and Mortality Weekly Report Weekly, 31*(48), 652-654.

Money, J. (1985). *The destroying angel.* Buffalo, NY: Prometheus.

Money, J. (1986). *Love maps: Clinical concepts of sexual/erotic health and pathology, paraphilia, and gender transpostition in childhood, adolescence, and maturity.* New York, NY: Prometheus Books.

Money, J. (1988). *Gay, straight, and in-between: The sexology of erotic orientation.* Oxford, UK: Oxford University Press.

Money, J. (1991). *Biographies of gender and hermaphroditism in paired comparisons: Clinical supplement to the handbook of sexology.* Amsterdam, Netherlands: Elsevier.

Money, J. (1998). *Gay, straight, and in-between: The sexology of erotic orientation.* New York, NY: Oxford University Press.

Money, J., & Ehrhardt, E. (1972). *Man, woman, boy, girl.* Baltimore, MD: John Hopkins University Press.

Money, J., Hampson, J. G., & Hampson, J. L. (1957). Imprinting and the establishment of gender role. *Archives of Neurology and Psychiatry, 77* (3), 333-336.

Money, J., & Lewis, V. G. (1990). Puberty: Precocious, delayed, and incongruous. In M. E. Perry (Ed.), *Handbook of sexology, Vol, 7: Childhood and adolescence* (pp. 236-262). Amsterdam, Netherlands: Elsevier.

Montemayor, R. (2019). *Sexuality in adolescence and emerging adulthood.* New York, NY: The Guilford Press.

Moore, A., & Reynolds, P. (2018a). The age of consent. In *Childhood and sexuality: Contemporary issues and debates* (pp. 79-98). London, UK: Palgrave Macmillan.

Moore, A., & Reynolds, P. (2018b). *Childhood and sexuality: Contemporary issues and debates.* London, UK: Palgrave Macmillan.

Moore, J. N., Raymond, M. A., Mittelstaedt, J. D., & Tanner, J. D., Jr. (2002). Age and consumer socialization agent influences on adolescents' sexual knowledge, attitudes, and behavior: Implications for social marketing initiatives and public policy. *Journal of Public Policy & Marketing, 21,* 37-52.

Moore, M. M. (2010). Human nonverbal courtship behavior–a brief historical review. *Journal of Sex Research, 47*(2), 171-180.

Moran, D., Butcher, K., Curtis, D., & Laurence, C. (2003). *Commissioned desk-based research literature review on HIV/AIDS and governance.* London, United Kingdom: Department for International Development.

Morandini, J. S., Blaszczynski, A., & Dar-Nimrod, I. (2017). Who adopts queer and pansexual sexual identities? *Journal of Sex Research, 54*(7), 911-922. DOI:10.1080/00224499.2016.1249332

Morgan, T. (2007). Turner Syndrome: Diagnosis and management. *American Family Physician, 76*(3), 405-417.

Morin, J. (1995). *The erotic mind: Unlocking the inner sources of sexual passion and fulfillment* (1st ed.). New York, NY: HarperCollins.

Morris, N. M. (1975). The frequency of sexual intercourse during pregnancy. *Archives of Sexual Behavior, 4*(5), 501-507.

Morrison, S. D., Perez, M. G., Nedelman, M., & Crane, C. N. (2015). Current state of female-to-male gender confirming surgery. *Current Sexual Health Reports, 7*(1), 38-48. DOI:10.1007/s11930-014-0038-2

Morrow, P. C., McElroy, J. C., Stamper, B. G., & Wilson, M. A. (1990). The effects of physical attractiveness and other demographic characteristics on promotion decisions. *Journal of Management, 16,* 723-736.

Moser, C. (2006). Demystifying alternative sexual behaviors. *Sexuality, Reproduction, and Menopause, 4,* 86-90.

Moser, C. (2016a). Defining sexual orientation. *Archives of Sexual Behavior, 45*(3), 505-508. DOI:10.1007/s10508-015-0625-y

Moser, C. (2016b). DSM-5 and the paraphilic disorders: Conceptual issues. *Archives of Sexual Behavior, 45*(8), 2181-2186.

Moser, C., & Kleinplatz, P. J. (2005). DSM-IV-TR and the paraphilias: An argument for removal. *Journal of Psychology and Human Sexuality, 17*(3/4), 91-109.

Moser, C., & Kleinplatz, P. J. (2006). *Sado-masochism: Powerful pleasures.* New York, NY: Routledge.

Moses, A. E., & Hawkins, R. O., Jr. (1986). *Counseling lesbian women and gay men: A life-issues approach.* St. Louis, MO: Merrill.

Mosher, W. D., Chandra, A., & Jones, J. (2005). Sexual behavior and selected health measures; men and women 15-44 years of age, United, States, 2002. *Advanced Data from Vital Health Statistics, 362.* Hyattsville, MD: National Center for Health Statistics.

Moynihan, T. J. (2009). Testicular cancer. Retrieved October 28, 2012, from the Mayo Clinic website: http://www.mayoclinic.com/health/testicular-cancer/DS00046/ METHOD5print

Muise, A., Maxwell, J. A., & Impett, E. (2018). What theories and methods from relationship research can contribute to sex research. *Journal of Sex Research, 55,* 540-562.

Muñoz-Laboy, M. (2004). Beyond 'MSM': Sexual desire among bisexually-active Latino men in New York City. *Sexualities, 7,* 55-80.

Munoz-Laboy, M. (2008). Familism and sexual regulation among bisexual Latino men. *Archives of Sexual Behavior, 37,* 773-782.

Murdock, G. P. (1949). *Social structure.* New York, NY: Macmillan.

Murdock, G. P. (1981). *Atlas of world cultures.* Pittsburgh, PA: University of Pittsburgh Press.

Murphy, T. (1997). *Gay science: The ethics of sexual orientation research.* New York, NY: Columbia University Press.

Mustanski, B., Kuper, L., & Greene, G. J. (2014). Development of sexual orientation and identity. In D. L. Tolman, L. M. Diamond, J. A. Bauermeister, W. H. George, J. G. Pfaus, & L. M. Ward (Eds.), *APA handbook of sexuality and psychology,* Vol. 1: *Person-based approaches* (pp. 597-628). Washington, DC: American Psychological Association, American Psychological Association, Washington, DC. DOI:10.1037/14193-019

Mustanski, B. S., Chivers, M. L., & Bailey, J. M. (2002). A critical review of recent biological research on human sexual orientation. *Annual Review of Sex Research, 13,* 89-140.

Nadal, K. L., Whitman, C. N., Davis, L. S., Erazo, T., & Davidoff, K. C. (2016). Microaggressions toward lesbian, gay, bisexual, transgender, queer, and genderqueer people: A review of the literature. *Journal of Sex Research, 53*(4-5), 488-508. DOI:10.1080/00224499.2016.1142495

Nash, E. (2019, June 19). Abortion rights in peril—What clinicians need to know. *The New England Journal of Medicine.* DOI: 10.1056/NEJMp1906972

Nasr, V. (2009). *Forces of fortune: The rise of the new Muslim middle class and what it will mean to our world.* New York, NY: Free Press.

National Abortion Federation. (2009). I'm pregnant. What are my options? Retrieved from http://www.prochoice.org/pregnant/options/abortion.html

National Campaign to Prevent Teen Pregnancy. (2002, December). With one voice 2002: America's adults and teens sound off about teen pregnancy. Retrieved October 2, 2003, from http://www.teenpregnancy.org/ resources/data/pdf/WOV2002_full-text.pdf

National Campaign to Prevent Teen Pregnancy. (2009). *Why it matters.* Retrieved October 27, 2012, from http://www.thenationalcampaign.org/why-it-matters

National Campaign to Prevent Teen and Unplanned Pregnancy. (2012). *Fast facts: Teen pregnancy in the United States.* Retrieved April 23, 2012, from http://www.thenationalcampaign.org/resources/pdf/FastFacts_TeenPregnancyinUS.pdf

National Center for Educational Statistics. (2003). *The condition of education 2003.* Retrieved February 1, 2012, from http://nces. ed.gov/pubsearch/pubsinfo.asp?pubid52003067

National Council on Aging. (1998). *Healthy sexuality and vital again: Executive summary.* Washington, DC: Author.

National Organization for Rare Disorders (NORD). (2019). *XYY syndrome.* Retrieved May 31, 2019, from https://rarediseases.org/rare-diseases/xyy-syndrome/

National Sexual Violence Resource Center. (2010). *Impact of sexual violence.* Retrieved October 28, 2012, from http://www.nsvrc. org/sites/default/files/NSVRC_Publicication_ Factsheet_Impact-of-sexual-violence.pdf

National Survey of Sexual Health and Behavior (NSSHB). (2010). Findings from the National Survey of Sexual Health and Behavior, Center for Sexual Health Promotion, Indiana University. *Journal of Sexual Medicine, 7*(Suppl. 5), 243-373.

National Women's Health Information Center. (2010). *Birth control myths.* Retrieved October 20, 2012, from *Web*MD website: http://www.webmd.com/sex-relationships/ guide/birth-control-contraceptive-myths

NationMaster.com. (2011). Crime statistics—Rapes (per capita) (most recent) by country. Retrieved May 23, 2011, from http://www. nationmaster.com/graph/cri_rap_percap-crime-rapes-per-capita

Nehm, R. H., & Young, R. (2008). Sex hormones in secondary school biology textbooks. *Science and Education, 17*(10), 1175-1190.

Neuman, G. (2002). *Emotional infidelity.* New York, NY: Random.

Newell, M., & Bärnighausen, T. (2009). Male circumcision to cut HIV risk in the general population. *The Lancet, 369*(9562), 617-619.

Newton, E. (1993). *Cherry Grove, Fire Island.* Boston, MA: Beacon Press.

New View Campaign. (2016). *Challenging the Medicalization of Sex.* Retrieved July 1, 2019, from http://www.newviewcampaign.org/

Ngun, T. C., & Vilain, E. (2014). The biological basis of human sexual orientation: Is there a role for epigenetics.? In D. Yamamoto (Ed.), *Epigenetic shaping of sociosexual interactions: From plants to humans* (Vol. 86, pp. 167-184). New York, NY: Academic Press.

NIH National Library of Medicine (NIH). (2019). Triple X syndrome. Genetics Home Library. Retrieved May 31, 2019, from https://ghr.nlm.nih.gov/condition/triple-x-syndrome

Northrup, C., P. Schwartz, P., & J. Witte, J. (2014) *The normal bar.* New York, NY: Harmony Books.

NPR. (2012, June 21). *Penn State abuse scandal: A guide and timeline.* Retrieved October 28, 2012, from *NPR* website: http://www.npr.org/2011/11/08/142111804/penn-state-abuse-scandal-a-guide-and-timeline

Nussbaum, M. (1999). *Sex and social justice.* Oxford, UK: Oxford University Press.

O'Callaghan, T. (2009, August 31). *How useful are breast exams in screening for cancer?* Retrieved October 28, 2012, from *Time* website: http://healthland.time.com/2009/08/31/how-useful-are-breast-exams-in-screening-for-cancer/

O'Callaghan, T. (2011, January 6). *The future of birth control.* Retrieved October 28, 2012, from *Time* website: http://healthland.time.com/2011/01/06/the-future-of-birth-control/

O'Donnell, M. D. S. (2015). *A history of Greek art.* Malden, MA: Wiley-Blackwell.

Odem, M. E., & Clay-Warner, J. (1998). *Confronting rape and sexual assault.* Wilmington, DE: Scholarly Resources.

Odibo, A. O., Gray, D. L., Dicke, J. M., Stamilio, D. M., Macones, G. A., & Crane, J. P. (2008). Revisiting the fetal loss rate after second-trimester genetic amniocentesis. *Obstetrics & Gynecology, 111*(3), 589–595.

Office on Women's Health. (2017). Birth control methods. Fact sheet. Retrieved from https://www.womenshealth.gov/files/fact-sheet-birth-control-methods.pdf

Office on Women's Health. (2018). Premenstrual syndrome (PMS). US Department of Health and Human Services. Retrieved from https://www.womenshealth.gov/menstrual-cycle/premenstrual-syndrome

Ofosu, E. K., Chambers, M. K., Chen, J. M., & Hehman, E. (2019). Same-sex marriage legalization associated with reduced implicit and explicit antigay bias. *Proceedings of the National Academy of Sciences of USA, 116*(18), 8846–8851.

Okami, P., Olmstead, R., & Abramson, P. (1997). Sexual experiences in early childhood: 18 year longitudinal data from the UCLA Family Lifestyles Project. *Journal of Sex Research, 34,* 339–347.

Oliver, M. (1990). The politics of disablement. London: Macmillan.

Oloruntoba-Oju, T. (2007, September). *Body images, beauty culture and language in the Nigeria, African context.* Paper presented at Understanding Human Sexuality Seminar Series, University of Ibadan, Nigeria.

Olyslager, F., & Conway, L. (2007). *On the calculation of the prevalence of transsexualism.* Retrieved October 28, 2012, from http://ai.eecs.umich.edu/people/conway/TS/Prevalence/Reports/Prevalence%20of%20Transsexualism.pdf.

Ontario Consultants on Religious Tolerance. (2011). *Single polls concerning same-sex marriages (SSMs), civil unions, etc.* Retrieved September 24, 2012, from Religious Tolerance website: http://www.religioustolerance.org/hom_marp.htm

Oosterhuis, H. (2000). *Stepchildren of nature: Psychiatry and the making of sexual identity.* Chicago, IL: University of Chicago Press.

Orel, N. A. (2004). Gay, lesbian, and bisexual elders: Expressed needs and concerns across focus groups. *Journal of Gerontological Social Work, 43*(2/3), 57–78.

Oriel, J. (2005). Sexual pleasure as a human right: Harmful or helpful to women in the context of HIV/AIDS? *Women's Studies International Forum, 28*(5), 392–404.

Orloff, M. (2011). *Emotional freedom: Liberate yourself from negative emotions and transform your life and guide to intuitive healing.* New York, NY: Three Rivers Press.

Ortiz de Montellayano, B. (1990). *Aztec medicine, health, and nutrition.* Rutgers, NJ: Rutgers University Press.

Osgerby, B. (2004). *Youth media.* New York, NY: Routledge.

Our Bodies, Ourselves. (2005–2007). Women's health information and resource center. Retrieved October 11, 2012, from http://www.ourbodiesourselves.org/book/default.asp

Overbeek, G., Vollebergh, W., Engels, R., & Meeus, W. (2003). Parental attachment and romantic relationships: Associations with emotional disturbance during late adolescence. *Journal of Counseling Psychology, 20,* 28–39.

Owens, E. W., Behund R., Manning J., & Reid R. (2012). The impact of Internet pornography on adolescents: A review of the research. *Sexual Addiction & Compulsivity, 19,* 99–122.

Paabo, S. (2014). *Neanderthal man: In search of lost genomes.* New York, NY: Basic Books.

Padilla, M. (2007). *Caribbean pleasure industry: Tourism, sexuality, and AIDS in the Dominican Republic.* Chicago, IL: University of Chicago Press.

Padilla, M. (2008). *Caribbean pleasure industry.* Chicago, IL: University of Chicago Press.

Padva, G. (2005). Dreamboys, meatmen and werewolves: Visualizing erotic identities in All-male comic strips. *Sexualities, 8,* 587–599.

Pancer, S. M., Pratt, M., Hunsberger, B., & Gallant, M. (2000). Thinking ahead: Complexity of expectations and the transition to parenthood. *Journal of Personality, 68,* 253–280.

Parashar, A. (2008). *Redefining family law in India.* New York, NY: Routledge. 2

Parker, R. (2002). The global HIV/AIDS pandemic, structural inequalities, and the politics of international health. *American Journal of Public Health, 92*(3), 343–347.

Parker, R., & Aggleton, P. (2002). *HIV/AIDS-related stigma and discrimination: A conceptual framework and an agenda for action.* Population Council: Horizons Project. Retrieved October 28, 2012, from http://www.popcouncil.org/pdfs/horizons/sdcncptl-frmwrk.pdf

Parker, R., & Gagnon, J. (1995). *Conceiving sexuality.* New York, NY: Routledge.

Parmely, S. M. (2001). *A grounded theory of becoming a teen parent among juvenile hall females: Implications for public policy.* Unpublished doctoral dissertation, California School of Professional Psychology.

Parrinder, G. (1996). *Sexual morality in the world's religions.* Newark, NJ: Penguin.

Pascoe, C. J. (2007). *Dude, you're a fag.* Berkeley, CA: University of California Press.

Pascoe, C. J. (2011a). *Dude, you're a fag: Masculinity and sexuality in high school* (2nd ed.). Berkeley, CA: University of California Press.

Pascoe, C. J. (2011b). Resource and risk: Youth sexuality and new media use. *Sexuality Research and Social Policy, 8,* 5–17.

Passet, J. E. (2003). *Sex radicals and the quest for women's equality.* Chicago, IL: University of Illinois Press.

Patil, S. (2015, June 6). Twelve things you didn't know about adult entertainment. *The Richest.* Retrieved April 11, 2019, from https://www.therichest.com/rich-list/most-popular/12-things-you-never-knew-about-online-adult-entertainment/

Patterson, C. J. (2006). Children of lesbian and gay parents. *Directions in Psychological Science, 15,* 241–244.

Patterson, C. J., & Riskind, R. G. (2010). To be a parent: Issues in family formation among gay and lesbian adults. *Journal of GLBT Family Studies, 6*(3), 326–340. DOI:10.1080/1550428x.2010.490902

Patterson, M. J., Hill, R. P., & Maloy, K. (1995). Abortion in America: A consumer-behavior perspective. *Journal of Consumer Research, 21,* 677–694.

Paul, J. P., Catania, J., Pollack, L., Moskowitz, J., Conchola, J., & Mills, T., . . . Stall, R. (2002). Suicide attempts among gay and bisexual men: Lifetime prevalence and antecedents. *American Journal of Public Health, 98,* 1338–1345.

Paul, P. (2004, January 19). *Behavior: The porn factor.* Retrieved September 17, 2012, from *Time* website: http://www.time.com/time/magazine/article/0,9171,993158,00.html

Payne, J. S., Galvan, F., Williams, J., Prusiniski, M., Zhang, M., Wyatt, G. E., & Myers, H. F. (2014). Impact of childhood sexual abuse on the emotions and behaviors of adult men in three ethnic groups in the USA. *Culture, Health and Sexuality, 16*(3), 231–245.

Peplau, L. A., Garnets, L. D., Spalding, L. R., Conley, T. D., & Veniegas, R. C. (1998). A critique of Bem's "exotic becomes erotic" theory of sexual orientation. *Psychological Review, 105*(2), 387–394.

Perel, E. (2006). *Mating in captivity.* New York, NY: Harper.

Perelli-Harris, B., Kreyenfeld, M., Sigle-Rushton, W., Keizer, R., Lappegård, T., Jasilioniene, A., Berghammer, C., & Di Giulio, P. (2012). Changes in union status during the transition to parenthood: An examination of 11 European countries. *Population Studies, 66*(2), 167–182.

Perelli-Harris, B., & Lyons-Amos, M. (2015). Changes in partnership patterns across the lifecourse: An examination of 14 countries in Europe and the United States. *Demographic Research, 33,* 145–178.

Perelli-Harris, B., & Styrc, M. (2018, February) Mental well-being differences in cohabitation and marriage: The role of childhood selection. *Journal of Marriage and Family, 80,* 239–255.

Perper, T. (1985). *Sex signals: The biology of love.* Philadelphia, PA: ISI Press.

Perry, S. L., & Schleifer, C. (2018). Till porn do us part? A longitudinal examination of pornography use and divorce. *The Journal of Sex Research, 55*(3), 284–296. DOI: https://DOI.org/10.1080/00224499.2017.1317709

Petchesky, R. (2003). *Global prescriptions: Health and rights.* London, UK: Zed Books.

Petchesky, R., Correa, S., & Parker, R. (2010). Reaffirming pleasures in a world of dangers. In P. Aggleton & R. Parker, *Routledge handbook of sexuality, health and rights* (pp. 401–411). New York, NY: Routledge.

Peter, J., & Valkenburg, P. M. (2016). Adolescents and pornography: A review of 20 years of research. *Journal of Sex Research, 53*(4), 509–531.

Petersen, E. E., Davis, N. L., & Goodman, D., et al. (2019). Vital signs: Pregnancy-related deaths, United States, 2011–2015, and strategies for prevention, 13 states, 2013–2017. *MMWR Morbidity and Mortality Weekly Report 68*(18), 423–429. DOI: http://dx.DOI.org/10.15585/mmwr.mm6818e1

Peterson, M. M. (2005). Assisted reproductive technologies and equity of access issues. *Journal of Medical Ethics, 31,* 280–285.

Petronio, S. (2002). *Boundaries of privacy: Dialectics of disclosure.* Albany, NY: SUNY Press.

Pew Foundation. (2003). *Pew forum on religion.* November 18, 2003.

PEW Foundation. (2017a). *Changing attitudes on gay marriage.* Retrieved May 9, 2019, from https://www.pewforum.org/fact-sheet/changing-attitudes-on-gay-marriage/

PEW Foundation. (2017b). Five key findings about LGBT Americans. *FactTank.*

PEW Foundation. (2017c). Public views on intermarriage. Retrieved April 22, 2019, from https://www.pewsocialtrends.org/2017/05/18/2-public-views-on-intermarriage/

PEW Foundation. (2018). Social media use in 2018. Retrieved April 8, 2019, from https://www.pewinternet.org/2018/03/01/social-media-use-in-2018/

PEW Foundation. (2019, February 13). *Eight facts about love and marriage in America.* Retrieved April 18, 2019, from https://www.pewresearch.org/fact-tank/2019/02/13/8-facts-about-love-and-marriage/

Pew Research Center. (2006). *A barometer of modern morals: Sex, drugs, and the 1040*. Retrieved August 7, 2012, from http://pewresearch.org/pubs/307/a-barometer-of-modern-morals

Pew Research Center. (2013). A survey of LGBT Americans: Attitudes, experiences and values in changing times. Retrieved from http://www.pewsocialtrends.org/2013/06/13/a-survey-of-lgbt-americans/http://www.pewsocialtrends.org/2013/06/13/a-survey-of-lgbt-americans/

Pew Research Center. (2017). Number of U.S. adults cohabiting with a partner continues to rise, especially among those 50 and older. Retrieved April 19, 2019, from https://www.pewresearch.org/fact-tank/2017/04/06/number-of-u-s-adults-cohabiting-with-a-partner-continues-to-rise-especially-among-those-50-and-older/

Pflugfeltder, G. (1999). *Cartographies of desire: Male-male sexuality in Japanese discourse, 1600-1950*. Berkeley, CA: University of California Press.

Phipps, W. E. (1996). *The sexuality of Jesus*. Berea, OH: Pilgrim Press.

Pike, M. C., Pearce, C. L., & Wu, A. H. (2004). Prevention of cancers of the breast, endometrium and ovary. *Oncogene, 23*, 6379-6391.

Pincott, J. (2008). *Do gentlemen really prefer blondes? Bodies, behavior, and brains—The science behind sex, love, and attraction*. New York, NY: Random.

Pinker, S. (2018). *Enlightenment now: The case for reason, science, humanism and progress*. New York, NY: Viking Books.

Pinkerton, S. D., Bogart, L. M., Cecil, H., & Abramson, P. R. (2002). Factors associated with masturbation in a collegiate sample. *Journal of Psychology and Human Sexuality, 14*, (2/3), 103-121.

Pinon, R., Jr. (2002). *Biology of human reproduction*. Sausalito, CA: University Science Books.

Piot, P., & Quinn, T. C. (2013). Response to the AIDS pandemic—a global health model. *New England Journal of Medicine, 368*, 2210-2218.

Pittman, F. (1989). *Private lies*. New York, NY: Norton.

Planned Parenthood. (2008). *The abortion pill (Medication Abortion)*. Retrieved October 16, 2008, from http://www.plannedparenthood.org/health-topics/anortion/abortion-pill-medication-abortion-4354.htm

Planned Parenthood. (2019a). *IUD*. Retrieved from https://www.plannedparenthood.org/learn/birth-control/iud

Planned Parenthood. (2019b). *Which kind of emergency contraception should I use?* Retrieved from https://www.plannedparenthood.org/learn/morning-after-pill-emergency-contraception/which-kind-emergency-contraception-should-i-use

Plummer, C. A. (1993). Prevention is appropriate, prevention is successful. In R. J. Gelles & D. R. Loseke (Eds.), *Current controversies on family violence* (pp. 288-305). Newbury Park, CA: Sage.

Plummer, K. (1995). *Telling sexual stories*. New York, NY: Routledge.

Polen-Petit, N. (2016). Internet, social media and sexual literacy: Help or hindrance for LGBTQ youth? In Y. Kiuchi, Y., & F. A. Villarruel, (Eds.), *The young are making their world: Essays on the power of youth culture* (pp. 46-60). Jefferson, N.C.: McFarl& Company, Inc.

Ponterotto, J. G. (2005). Qualitative research in counseling psychology: A primer on research paradigms and philosophy of science. *Journal of Counseling Psychology, 52*(2), 126-136.

Porter, M. (1980). *Economic history of the United States*. New York, NY: Free Press.

Potts, A., Grace, V. M., Vares, T., & Gavey, N. (2003). Sex for life? Men's counter-stories on 'erectile dysfunction,' male sexuality and ageing. *Sociology of Health and Illness, 28*, 206-329.

Prakash, V. (2009). Hymenoplasty—how to do. *Indian Journal of Surgery, 71*(4), 221-223.

Preston-Whyte, E., Varga, C., Oosthuizen, H., Roberts, R., & Blose, F. (2000). Survival sex and HIV/AIDS in an African city. In R. Parker, R. Barbosa, & P. Aggleton (Eds.), *Framing the sexual subject: The politics of gender, sexuality, and power* (pp. 165-190). Berkeley, CA: University of California Press.

Price, D. (2017). *A practical guide to gender diversity and sexuality in early years*. London: Jessica Kingsley Publishers.

Price, M. (2018). Giant study links DNA variants to same-sex behavior. *Science* (October 18, 2018).

Prothero, S. (2007). *Religious literacy*. New York, NY: Harper.

Prothero, S. (2010). *God is not one: The eight rival religions that run the world*. New York, NY: Harper Collins.

Pryce, A. (2007). Constructing virtual selves: Men, risk, and the rehearsal of sexual identities and scripts in cyber chatrooms. In A. Petersen & I. Wilkinson (Eds.), *Health, risk, and vulnerability* (pp. 119-142). New York, NY: Routledge.

Puccia, E. (2009). *For neither love nor money: Gender, sexuality, and tourism in Costa Rica* (Doctoral dissertation, University of South Florida). Retrieved October 28, 2012, from http://scholarcommons.usf.edu/etd/2155

Quast, L. (2011, November). *Is there really a glass ceiling for women?* Retrieved October 28, 2012, from Forbes website: http://www.forbes.com/sites/lisaquast/2011/11/14/is-there-really-a-glass-ceiling-for-women/

Quinton, W. J., Major, B., & Richards, C. (2001). Adolescents and adjustment to abortion: Are minors at greater risk? *Psychology, Public Policy and Law, 7*(491) 1-23.

Rahman, Q., & Wilson, G. D. (2003). Born gay? The psychobiology of human sexual orientation. *Personality and Individual Differences, 34*, 1337-82.

Raine, T. R., et al. (2010). Contraceptive decision-making in sexual relationships: Young men's experiences, attitudes, and values. *Culture, Health & Sexuality, 12*(4), 373-386.

Ramsey, C. B. (2013). The exit myth: Family law, gender roles, and changing attitudes toward female victims of domestic violence. *Michigan Journal of Law and Gender, 20*, 1-32.

Ramsey, J. L., Langlois, J. H., Hoss, R. A., Rubenstein, A. J., & Griffin, A. M. (2004). Origins of a stereotype: Categorization of facial attractiveness by 6-month old infants. *Developmental Science, 7*, 201-211.

Rani, R. (2019, June 19). Homes to heal trafficked children. *New York Times*. Retrieved July 1, 2019, from https://www.nytimes.com/2019/06/19/opinion/foster-child-trafficking.html?partner=IFTTT

Raymond, N. C., Coleman, E., & Miner, M. (2003). Psychiatric comorbidity and compulsive/impulsive traits in compulsive sexual behavior. *Comprehensive Psychiatry, 44*(5), 370-380.

Redefining Love. (2019). Are some personality traits more common in polyamorous people? *Polyamory Today*. Retrieved from https://medium.com/polyamory-today/are-there-personality-traits-that-are-more-common-among-people-in-polyamorous-relationships-7864d11e2e5d

Reece, M., Herbenick, D., Sanders, S. A., Dodge, B., Ghassemi, A., & Fortenberry, J. D. (2009). Prevalence and characteristics of vibrator use by men in the United States. *Journal of Sexual Medicine, 6*, 1867-1874.

Regnerus, M. D. (2007). *Forbidden fruit: Sex and religion in the lives of American teenagers*. New York, NY: Oxford University Press.

Regnerus, M., & Uecker, J. (2011). *Premarital sex in America: How young Americans meet, mate*, and *think about marrying*. New York, NY: Oxford University Press.

Rehan, N., Sobrero, A. J., & Fertig, J. W. (1975). The semen of fertile men: Statistical analysis of 1300 men. *Fertility and Sterility, 26*(6), 492-502.

Rehor, J. E. (2015). Sensual, erotic and sexual behaviors of women from the "kink" community. *Archives of Sexual Behavior, 44*, 825-836. DOI: 10.1007/s105080-015-0524-

Reibner, C., & Garcia, J. R. (2010). Hooking up: Gender differences, evolution, and pluralistic ignorance. *Evolutionary Psychology, 8*(3), 390-404.

Reichert, T. (2002). Sex in advertising research: A review of content, effects, and functions of sexual information in consumer advertising. *Annual Review of Sex Research, 13*, 241-273.

Reichert, T. (Ed.). (2018). *Investigating the use of sex in media promotion and advertising*. New York, NY: Routledge.

Reid, R. C., Carpenter, B. N., Hook, J. N., Garos, S., Manning, J. C., Gilliland, R., et al. (2012). Report of findings in a DSM-5 field trial for hypersexual disorder. *The Journal of Sexual Medicine, 9*(11), 2868-2877.

Remafedi, G., Resnick, M., Blum, R., & Harris, L. (1992). Demography of sexual orientation in adolescents. *Pediatrics, 89*, 714-721.

Renju, J. (2017, July 24). Ending AIDS by 2030 means removing bottlenecks to care and treatment—but what causes them? Public address: July 24, 2017, at the London School of Hygiene and Tropical Medicine. Retrieved from https://www.lshtm.ac.uk/newsevents/expert-opinion/ending-aids-2030-means-removing-bottlenecks-care-and-treatment-what

Renold, E. (2005). *Girls, boys, and junior sexualities: Exploring children's gender and sexual relations in the primary school*. London; New York: Routledge.

Repucci, N. D., & Haugaard, J. J. (1993). Problems with child sexual abuse prevention programs. In R. J. Gelles & D. R. Loseke (Eds.), *Current controversies on family violence* (pp. 288-305). Newbury Park, CA: Sage.

Reuters Life! (2008, April 29). *Chinese struggle to orgasm, easier for Italians-poll*. Retrieved September 17, 2012, from http://in.reuters.com/article/2008/04/29/ idINIndia-33300720080429

Rhoades, G., Stanely, S. M., & Markman, H. J. (2009). Couples' reasons for cohabitation associations with individual well-being and relationship quality. *Journal of Family Issues, 30*, 233-258.

Rice, K. (2015). Pansexuality. In A. Bolin & P. Whelehan (Eds.), *The international encyclopedia of human sexuality*. Oxford, UK: John Wiley & Sons. DOI:10.1002/9781118896877.wbiehs328

Rich, A. (1994). *Compulsory heterosexuality and lesbian existence. Blood, bread, and poetry* (2nd ed.). New York, NY: Norton.

Richards, C., & Barret, J. (2013). The case for bilateral mastectomy and male chest contouring for the female-to-male transsexual. *Annals of the Royal College of Surgeons of England, 95*(2), 93-95. Published online 2013 Mar. DOI: 10.1308/003588413X13511 609957290

Richardson, D. (2000). Constructing sexual citizenship: Theorizing sexual rights. *Critical Social Policy, 20*, 105-135.

Richardson, E., Collins, S., Kung, T., Jones, J., Tram, J., Boggiano, V., Bekker, L., & Zolopa, A. (2014). Gender inequality and HIV transmission: A global analysis. *Journal of the International AIDS Society, 17*(1), 19035.

Richardson, L. (1985). *New other woman*. New York, NY: Free Press.

Rieger, G., Chivers, M. L., & Bailey, J. M. (2005). Sexual arousal patterns of bisexual men. *Psychological Science, 16,* 579-584.

Rivers, I., & D'Augelli, A. (2001). The victimization of lesbian, gay, and bisexual youth. In A. D'Augelli & C. J. Patterson (Eds.), *Lesbian, gay and bisexual identities and youth: Psychological perspectives* (pp. 199-223). New York, NY: Oxford.

Robinson, K. H. (2005). "Queerying" gender: Heteronormativity in early childhood education. *Australian Journal of Early Childhood, 30*(2), 19.

Robinson, K. H., & Davies, C. (2015). Children's gendered and sexual cultures: Desiring and regulating recognition through life markers of marriage, love and relationships. In E. Renold, J. Ringrose, & R. D. Egan (Eds.), *Children, sexuality and sexualization* (pp. 174-190). Houndmills, Basingstoke, Hampshire; New York, NY: Palgrave Macmillan UK. DOI:10.1057/9781137353399_11

Robinson, P. (1976). *The modernization of sex.* New York, NY: Harper & Row.

Robinson, P. (2000). *Gay lives.* Chicago, IL: University of Chicago Press.

Ropelato, J. *Internet Pornography Statistics.* Retrieved November 1, 2012, from http://internet-filter-review.toptenreviews.com/internet-pornography-statistics.html

Rosaldo, M., & Lamphere, L. (1974). *Women, culture, and society.* Stanford, CA: Stanford University Press.

Rosario, M., & Schrimshaw, E. W. (2014). Theories and etiologies of sexual orientation. In D. L. Tolman, L. M. Diamond, J. A. Bauermeister, W. H. George, J. G. Pfaus, & L. M. Ward (Eds.), *APA handbook of sexuality and psychology,* Vol. 1: *Person-based approaches* (pp. 555-596). Washington, DC: American Psychological Association, American Psychological Association, Washington, DC. DOI:10.1037/14193-018

Rosario, M., Schrimshaw, E. W., Hunter, J., & Braun, L. (2006). Sexual identity development among lesbian, gay, and bisexual youths: Consistency and change over time. *Journal of Sex Research, 43,* 46-58.

Roscoe, W. (1991). *The Zuni man-woman.* Albuquerque, NM: University of New Mexico Press.

Ross, C. E., Mirowsky, J., & Goldsteen, K. (1990). The impact of family on health: The decade in review. *Journal of Marriage and the Family, 52,* 1059-1078.

Rossano, M. (2010). *Supernatural selection: How religion evolved.* New York, NY: Oxford University Press.

Rothman, B. K. (2007). A lifetime's labor: Women and power in the birthplace. *Laboring on: Birth in transition in the United States* (pp. xi-xxii). New York, NY: Routledge.

Roughgarden, J. (2004). *Evolution's rainbow: Why Darwin was wrong about sexual selection.* Berkeley, CA: University of California Press.

Roy, J. R., Chakraborty, S., & Chakraborty, T. R. (2009). Estrogen-like endocrine disrupting chemicals affecting puberty in humans—a review. *Medical Science Monitor, 15,* RA137-145.

Rubin, G. (1984). Thinking sex: Notes for a radical theory of the politics of sexuality. In C.S. Vance (Ed.), *Pleasure and danger: Exploring female sexuality.* London: Routledge and Kegan Paul.

Rubin, J. Z., Provenzano, F. J., & Luria, Z. (1974). The eye of the beholder: Parents' views on sex of newborns. *American Journal of Orthopsychiatry, 44,* 512-519.

Ruble, D. N., Martin, C. L., & Berenbaum, S. A. (2007). Gender development. In *Handbook of child psychology.* New York, NY: John Wiley & Sons, Inc. DOI:10.1002/9780470147658.chpsy0314

Ruble, T. L. (1983). Sex stereotypes: Issues of change in the 1970s. *Sex Roles, 9,* 397-402.

Russell, A., & Thompson, M. S. (2000). Introduction: Contraception across cultures. In A. Russell, E. Sobo, & M. Thompson (Eds.), *Contraception across cultures: Technologies, choices, constraints* (pp. 3-26). New York, NY: Oxford University Press.

Russell, S. T., Crockett, L. J., Shen, Y., & Lee, S. (2008). Cross-ethnic equivalence of self-esteem and depression for Chinese, Filipino, and European American adolescents. *Journal of Youth and Adolescence, 37,* 50-61.

Russell, S. T., & Joyner, K. (2001). Adolescent sexual orientation and suicide risk: Evidence from a national study. *American Journal of Public Health, 91,* 1276-1281.

Russo, N. F., & Dabul, A. J. (1997). The relationship of abortion to well-being: Do race and religion make a difference? *Professional Psychology: Research and Practice, 28*(1), 23-31.

Ruttenberg, D. (2009). *The passionate Torah: Sex and Judaism.* New York, NY: New York University Press.

Ryan, C., Huebern, D., Diaz, R., & Sanchez, J. (2009). Family rejection as a predictor of negative outcomes in White and Latino lesbian, gay, and bisexual young adults. *Pediatrics, 123,* 346-352.

Ryan, C., & Jetha, C. (2010). *Sex at dawn: The prehistoric origins of sexuality.* New York, NY: Harper Collins.

Ryan, T., Allen, K. A., DeLeon, G. L., & McInerney, D. M. (2017). How social are social media? A review of online social behaviour and connectedness. *Journal of Relationship Research, 8*(e8), 1-8. https://DOI.org/10.1017/jrr.2017.13

Ryser, V. A. (2018). The transition to marriage for cohabiting couples: Does it shape subjective well-being and opinions or attitudes toward family? In R. Tillman, M. Voorpostel, & P. Farago (Eds.), *Social dynamics in Swiss society* (pp. 47-59). New York, NY: Spring.

Saario, T. N., Jacklin, C. N., & Tittle, C. K. (1973). Sex-role stereotyping in the public schools. *Harvard Educational Review, 43,* 386-416.

Sadker, M., & Sadker, D. (1994). *Failing at fairness: How America's schools cheat girls.* New York, NY: Simon & Schuster.

Saewyc, E. M. (2011). Research on adolescent sexual orientation: Development, health disparities, stigma, and resilience. *Journal of Research on Adolescence, 21*(1), 256-272.

Safarinejad, M. R., Kolahi, A. A., & Hosseini, L. (2009). The effect of mode of delivery on the quality of life, sexual function, and sexual satisfaction in primparous women and their husbands. *Journal of Sexual Medicine, 6*(6), 1645-1667.

Safe Schools Coalition. (1999). *Understanding anti-gay harassment and violence in schools.* Seattle, WA: Author.

Sagarin, B. J., Cutler, B., Cutler, N., Lawler-Sagarin, K. A., & Matuszewich, L. (2009). Hormonal changes and couple bonding in consensual sadomasochistic activity. *Archives of Sexual Behavior, 38,* 186-200. DOI 10.1007/s10508-008-9374-5

Salam, M. (2018, October 26). For transgender Americans, the political gets even more personal. *New York Times,* October 26, 2018. Retrieved July 31, 2019, from. https://www.nytimes.com/2018/10/26/us/transgender-lgbt-rights-trump.html

Salovey, P., & Sluyter, D. J. (1997). *Emotional development and emotional intelligence: Educational implications.* New York, NY: Basic Books.

Saltz, G. (2006, July 3). *The right time to say the "l" word: Love.* Retrieved October 28, 2012, from NBCNews.Com *Today* website: http://today.msnbc.msn.com/id/13145511/

Sanday, P. R. (1981a). *Female power and male dominance: On the origins of sexual inequality.* New York, NY: Cambridge University Press.

Sanday, P. R. (1981b). The socio-cultural context of rape: A cross-cultural study. *Journal of Social Issues, 37,* 5-27.

Sanday, P. R. (2007). *Fraternity gang rape: Sex, brotherhood, and privilege on campus* (2nd ed.). New York, NY: University Press.

Sanders, A. R., Martin, E. R., Beecham, G. W., Guo, S., Dawood, K., Rieger, G., .& Bailey, J. M. (2015). Genome-wide scan demonstrates significant linkage for male sexual orientation. *Psychological Medicine, 45*(7), 1379-1388. DOI:10.1017/S0033291714002451

Sanders, J. S., & Robinson, W. (1979). Talking and not talking about sex: Male and female vocabularies. *Journal of Communication, 29*(2), 22-30.

Sanders, S., & Reinisch, J. (1999). What would you say if . . . ? *Journal of the American Medical Association, 281*(3), 275-277.

Santelli, J., Ott, M. A., Lyon, M., Rogers, J., Summers, D., & Schleifer, R. (2006). Abstinence and abstinence-only education: A review of U.S. policies and programs. *Journal of Adolescent Health, 38,* 72-81.

Santrock, J. (2011). Life expectancy. In *A topical approach to life-span development* (pp. 128-132). New York, NY: McGraw-Hill.

Saunders, S. A., Hill, B., Yarber, W., Graham, C., Crosby, R., & Milhausen, R. (2010). Misclassification bias: Diversity in conceptualisations about having 'had sex.' *Sexual Health, 7,* 31-34.

Saunders, S. A., & Reinisch, J. M. (1999). Would you say you "had sex" if? *Journal of the American Medical Association, 28,* 275-277.

Savin-Williams, R. (2005). *The new gay teenager.* Boston, MA: Beacon.

Savin-Williams, R. C. (2016). Sexual orientation: Categories or continuum? Commentary on Bailey et al. (2016). *Psychological Science in the Public Interest, 17*(2), 37-44. DOI:10.1177/1529100616637618

Savin-Williams, R. C., Cash, B. M., McCormack, M., & Rieger, G. (2017). Gay, mostly gay, or bisexual leaning gay? An exploratory study distinguishing gay sexual orientations among young men. *Archives of Sexual Behavior, 46*(1), 265-272. DOI:10.1007/s10508-016-0848-6

Savin-Williams, R. C., & Ream, G. L. (2007). Prevalence and stability of sexual orientation components during adolescence and young adulthood. *Archives of Sexual Behavior, 36,* 385-394.

Scarleteen. (2009). *And more with the popping of cherries.* Retrieved October 28, 2012, from http://www.scarleteen.com/article/advice/and_more_with_the_popping_of_cherries

Schaffir, J. (2006). Sexual intercourse at term and onset of labor. *Obstetrics and Gynecology, 107*(6), 1310-1314.

Schalet, A. (2000). Raging hormones, regulated love: Adolescent sexuality and the constitution of the modern individual in the United States and the Netherlands. *Body & Society, 6*(1), 75-105.

Schalet, A. T. (2011). *Not under my roof: Parents, teens, and the culture of sex.* Chicago, IL: University of Chicago Press.

Schiavi, R. C. (1999). *Aging and male sexuality.* Cambridge, UK: Cambridge University Press.

Schippers, M. (2016). *Beyond monogamy: Polyamory and the future of polyqueer sexualities.* New York, NY: NYU Press.

Schneider, J., & Weiss, R. (2001). *Cybersex exposed: Simple fantasy or obsession?* Center City, MN: Hazelden.

Schroeder, E., & Kuriansky, J. (2009). *Sexuality education: Past, present, and future* [4 volumes]. Westport CT: Praeger Publishers.

Schroeder, L. (2011). *Is there really a glass ceiling? Women of HR.* Retrieved February 10, 2012, from the Women of HR website: http:// womenofhr.com/is-there-really-a-glass-ceiling-2/

Schwartz, P. (2007a). *Prime.* New York, NY: Collins.

Schwartz, P. (2007b). The social construction of heterosexuality. In M. Kimmel (Ed.), *The sexual self* (pp. 80-92). Nashville, TN: Vanderbilt University Press.

Seabrook, R. A., Ward, L. M., Cortina, L. M., Giaccardi, S., & Lippman, J. R. (2017). Girl power or powerless girl? Television, sexual scripts, and sexual agency in sexually active young women. *Psychology of Women Quarterly, 41*(2), 240-253. DOI:10.1177/0361684316677028

Sears, J. (1990). *Growing up gay in the South.* Downers Grove, IL: Sebastian Enterprises.

Seligman, M. (2002). *Authentic happiness.* New York, NY: Free Press.

Seligman, M. (2011). *Flourish.* New York, NY: Simon & Schuster.

Seligson, F. J. (1989). *Oriental birth dreams.* Elizabeth, NJ: Hollym International Corp.

Seligson, F. J. (2002). *Queen Jin's handbook of pregnancy.* Berkeley, CA: North Atlantic.

Senft, T. (2013). Microcelebrity and the branded self. In J. Hartley, J. Burgess, & A. Bruns (Eds.), *A companion to new media dynamics.* Hoboken, NJ: John Wiley & Sons.

Setel, P. (2000). *A plague of paradoxes: AIDS, culture, and demography in Northern Tanzania.* Chicago, IL: University of Chicago Press.

Seto, M. C. (2007). Treatment of pedophilia. In G. O. Gabbard (Ed.), *Gabbard's treatments of psychiatric disorders* (4th ed., pp. 657-669). Arlington, VA: American Psychiatric Publishing.

Seto, M. C. (2008). *Pedophilia and sexual offending against children.* Washington, DC: American Psychological Association.

Sexual Exploitation and Other Abuse of Children (§ 2251-2260A), Definitions for Chapter, 18 U.S.C. §2256 (2008).

Sexuality Information and Education Council of the United States (SIECUS). (2003). *The truth about STDs.* New York, NY: Author.

Sexuality Information and Education Council of the United States (SIECUS). (2004). *Guidelines for comprehensive sexuality education.* Washington, DC: Author.

Shafer, E. (2009). *Beyond heterosexuality: Sexual subjectivity, personal attitudes, and partner negotiations* (Master's thesis). San Francisco State University, San Francisco, CA.

Shakespeare, T., Gillespie-Sells, K., & Davies, D. (1996). *The sexual politics of disability: Untold desires.* London, United Kingdom: Cassell.

Shanker, T. (2011, November 3). *U.S. report accuses China and Russia of Internet spying.* Retrieved October 28, 2012, from the Herald Tribune website: http://www.heraldtribune.com/article/20111103/ZNYT05/111033033/1/news?Title5U-S-Report-Accuses-China-and-Russia-of-Internet-Spying&tc5ar

Shapiro, J. L. (1992). *The measure of a man.* New York, NY: Delta.

Shaver, P. R., Mikulincer, M., & Cassidy, J. (2019). Attachment, caregiving in couple relationships, and prosocial behavior in the wider world. *Current Opinion in Psychology, 25,* 16-20. DOI:10.1016/j.copsy.2018.02.009

Sheeder, J., Tocce, K., & Sturns-Simon, C. (2009). Reasons for the ineffective contraceptive use antedating adolescent pregnancies, Part I: An indicator in gaps of family planning services. *Maternal and Child Health Journal, 13*(3), 295-305.

Sheldrake, P. (2007). *A brief history of spirituality.* New York, NY: Wiley-Blackwell.

Shepler, D. K., Smendik, J. M., Cusick, K. M., & Tucker, D. R. (2018). Predictors of sexual satisfaction for partnered lesbian, gay, and bisexual adults. *Psychology of Sexual Orientation and Gender Diversity, 5*(1), 25-35. http://dx.DOI.org/10.1037/sgd0000252

Sherman, P. W. (1988). The levels of analysis. *Animal Behavior, 36,* 616-619.

Shernoff, M. (2006). Negotiated nonmonogamy and male couples. *Family Processes, 45,* 407-418.

Sherwood, C. C., F. Subiaul, F., & Zawidzki, T. W. (2008). A natural history of the human mind: Tracing evolutionary changes in brain and cognition. *Anatomy,* April 212(4), 426-454.

Shildrick, M. (2007). Contested pleasures: The sociopolitical economy of disability and sexuality. *Sexuality Research and Social Policy, 1*(55), 53-66.

Short, M., Black, L., Smith., A., & Wetterneck, C. (2012). A review of Internet pornography use research: Methodology and content from the past 10 years. *Cyberpsychology, Behavior and Social Networking 15*(1), 13-23.

Shostak, M. (1980). *Nisa: The life and words of a !Kung woman.* New York, NY: Vintage Books.

Shostak, M. (1981). *Nisa: The life and words of a !Kung woman.* Cambridge, MA: Harvard University Press.

Shostak, M. (1991). *Nisa* (2nd ed.). New York, NY: Free Press.

Shuttleworth, R. (2006). Disability and sexuality: Toward a constructionist focus on access and the inclusion of disabled people in the sexual rights movement. In N.Teunis & G. Herdt (Eds.), *Sexual inequalities and social justice* (pp. 174-207). Berkeley, CA: University of California Press.

Siegel, J. A., & Williams, L. M. (2001). *Risk factors for violent victimization of women: A prospective study, final report.* Rockville, MD: U.S. Department of Justice.

Silva, R. R., Koch, M., Rickers, K., Kreuzer, G., & Topolinski, S. (2019). The Tinder stamp: Perceived trustworthiness of online daters and its persistence in neutral contexts. *Computers in Human Behavior, 94,* 45-55. https://DOI.org/10.1016/j.chb.2018.12.041

Silverman, J. G., Raj, A., Mucci, L. A., & Hathaway, J. E. (2001). Dating violence against adolescent girls and associated substance use, unhealthy weight control, sexual risk behavior, pregnancy, and suicidality. *Journal of the American Medical Association, 286,* 572-579.

Simkin, P., Whalley, J., & Keppler, A. (2001). *Pregnancy, childbirth and the newborn: The complete guide.* New York, NY: Meadowbrook Press.

Simon, R. W., & Marcussen, K. (1999). Marital transitions, marital beliefs, and mental health. *Journal of Health and Social Behavior, 40,* 111-125.

Simonds, W. (2007). Birth matters: Practicing midwifery. In W. Simonds, B. K. Rothman, & B. M. Norman (Eds.), *Laboring on: Birth in transition in the United* States (pp. 55-206). New York, NY: Routledge.

Simonds, W., Rothman, B. K., & Norman, B. M. (Eds.). (2007). *Laboring on: Birth in transition in the United States.* New York, NY: Routledge.

Slater, A., & Tiggemann, M. (2002). A test of objectification theory in adolescent girls. *Sex Roles, 46*(9-10), 343-349.

Slater, R., & Uniat, L. (2019, March 28). Paid family leave policies and population health. *Health Affairs.* Retrieved July 21, 2019, from https://www.healthaffairs.org/do/10.1377/hpb20190301.484936/full/

Smith, C., Emerson, M., Gallagher, S., Kennedy, P., & Sikkink, D. (1998). *American evangelicalism: Embattled and thriving.* Chicago, IL: University of Chicago Press.

Smith, H. (1991). *The world's religions.* New York, NY: Harper Collins.

Smith, S. G., Zhang, X., Basile, K. C., Merrick, M. T., Wang, J., Kresnov, M., & Chen, J. (2018). *The National Intimate Partner and Sexual Violence Survey (NISVS): 2015 data brief–updated release.* Atlanta, GA: National Center for Injury Prevention and Control, Centers for Disease Control and Prevention.

Smock, P. J. (2000). Cohabitation in the United States: An appraisal of research themes, findings, and implications. *Annual Review of Sociology, 26,* 1-20.

Snowdon, G. (2011, February 20). *Women still face a glass ceiling.* Retrieved October 28, 2012, from The Guardian website: http:// www.guardian.co.uk/society/2011/feb/21/ women-glass-ceiling-still-exists-top-jobs

Soble, A. (2002). Correcting some misconceptions about St. Augustine's sex life. *Journal of the History of Sexuality, 11,* 545-569.

Soh, S. (2009). *The comfort women.* Chicago, IL: University of Chicago Press.

Soloman, S. E., Rothblum, E. D., & Balsam, K. F. (2004). Pioneers in partnership: Lesbian and gay male couples in civil unions compared with those not in civil unions and married heterosexual siblings. *Journal of Family Psychology, 18,* 275-286.

Somers, C. L., & Gleason, J. (2001). Does source of sex education proedict adolescents' sexual knowledge, attitudes, and behaviors? *Education, 121,* 674-681.

Somers, C. L., & Surmann, A. T. (2004). Adolescents' preferences for source of sex education. *Child Study Journal, 34*(1), 47-59.

Sonfield, A. (2007). Popularity disparity: Attitudes about the IUD in Europe and the United States. *Guttmacher Policy Review, 10*(4).

Soriano, C. (2014). Constructing collectivity in diversity: Online political mobilization of a national LGBT political party. *Media Culture & Society 36*(1), 20-36.

Sosis, R., & Alcorta, C. (2003). Signaling, solidarity, and the sacred: The evolution of religious behavior. *Evolutionary Anthropology, 12,* 264-274.

Sowadsky, R. (2009). *How do you talk to your partners about HIV/AIDS and other sexually transmitted diseases?* Retrieved October 28, 2012, from the The body: The complete HIV/AIDS resource website: http://www.thebody.com/content/art2299.html

Speizera, I. S., Goodwin, M., Whittle, L., Clyde, M., & Rogers, J. (2008). Dimensions of child sexual abuse before age 15 in three Central American countries: Honduras, El Salvador, and Guatemala. *Child Abuse and Neglect, 32,* 455-462.

Speroff, L., & Fritz, M. A. (2005). *Clinical gynecologic endocrinology and infertility* (7th ed.). Philadelphia, PA: Lippincott, Williams and Wilkins.

Spock, B., & Needleman, R. (2004). *Dr. Spock's baby and child care: Updated and revised by R. Needleman.* New York, NY: Pocket Books.

Sprecher, S., & Cate, R. M. (2004). Sexual satisfaction and sexual expression as predictors of relationship satisfaction and stability. In J. H. Harvey, A. Wenzel, & S. Sprecher (Eds.), *The handbook of sexuality in close relationships* (pp. 235-256). Mahwah, NJ: Lawrence Erlbaum.

Sprott, R. A., & Benoit Hadcock, B. (2018). Bisexuality, pansexuality, queer identity, and kink identity. *Sexual and Relationship Therapy, 33*(1-2), 214-232. DOI:10.1080/14681994.2017.1347616

Squire, C. (2003). *The social context of birth.* Oxon, UK: Racliffe.

Stacey, J., & Biblarz, T. J. (2001). How does the sexual orientation of parents matter? *American Sociological Review, 66,* 159-183.

Stall, R. D., McKusick, L., Wiley, J., Coates, T. J., & Ostrow, D. G. (1986). Alcohol and drug use during sexual activity and compliance with safe sex guidelines for AIDS: The AIDS behavioral research project. *Health Education Quarterly, 4,* 359-371.

Stanford, A. (2013). *Homophobia in the black church: How faith, politics, and fear divide the black community.* Santa Barbara, CA: Praeger.

Stanley, S., Whitton, S. W., & Markman, H. J. (2004). Maybe I do: Interpersonal commitment and premarital or nonmarital cohabitation. *Journal of Family Issues, 25,* 496-519.

STD Test Express. (2011). *Top 10 myths about STDs.* Retrieved from http://www.stdtestexpress.com/std-myths/

Steele, R. (2002). *Masturbation: Is this normal for preschoolers?* Retrieved September 25, 2012, from the iVillage webiste: http://www.ivillage.com/masturbation-normal-preschoolers/ 6-n-146002.

Steingraber, S. (2007). *The falling age of puberty in U.S. girls: What we know, what we need to know.* San Francisco, CA: Breast Cancer Fund.

Sterling, A. F. (2001). *Sexing the body.* New York, NY: Basic Books.

Sternberg, R. J. (1988). *The triangle of love: Intimacy, passion, commitment.* New York, NY: Basic Books.

Stevens, J. (1990). *Lust for enlightenment: Buddhism and sex.* New York, NY: Random House.

Stewart, C. (2014). *Name, shame, and blame: Criminalising consensual sex in Papua New Guinea.* Canberra: ANU Press.

Stief, M. (2017). The sexual orientation and gender presentation of Hijra, Kothi, and Panthi in Mumbai, India. *Archives of Sexual Behavior, 46*(1), 73-85. DOI:10.1007/s10508-016-0886-0

Stimpson, C. & Herdt, G. Herdt (2014)). *Critical terms for the study of gender.* Chicago, IL: University of Chicago Press.

Stobbe, M. (2010, December 30). Even at lowest, U.S. teen birth rate far higher than W. Europe. Retrieved October 28, 2012, from the *Huffington Post* website: http://www.huffingtonpost.com/2010/12/30/teen-pregnancy-us-_n_802854.html

Stoddard, J. J., Anderson, M. R., Berkowitz, D., Britton, C., Nordgren, R., Pan, R. J., ... Woodhead, J. C. (2000). Prevention of sexual harassment in the workplace and educational settings. *Pediatrics, 106,* 1498-1499.

Stoker, B. (1897). *Dracula.* London, United Kingdom: Constable.

Stokes, C. E. (2007). Representin' in cyberspace: Sexual scripts, self-definition, and hip hop culture in black American adolescent girls' home pages. *Culture, Health and Sexuality, 9,* 169-184.

Stoller, R. J. (1974). *Sex and gender. Vol. 2.* London, UK: International Universities Press.

Stoller, R. J. (1975). *Sex and gender: Vol. 2.* New York, NY: International Universities Press.

Stoller, R. J. (1979). *Sexual excitement.* New York, NY: Pantheon.

Stoller, R. J. (1985a). *Observing the erotic imagination.* New Haven, CT: Yale University.

Stoller, R. J. (1985b). *Perversion: The erotic form of hatred.* New York, NY: Pantheon Books.

Stoller, R. J. (1986). *Observing the erotic imagination.* New Haven, CT: Yale University Press.

Stoller, R. J. (1991). *Pain and passion: A psychoanalyst explores the world of s and m.* New York, NY: Plenum.

Stombler, M., Baunach, D. M., Burgess, E. O., Simonds, W., & Windsor, E. J. (Eds.). (2019). What teenagers are learning from online porn. In *Sex matters: The sexuality & society reader (5th Edition)* (pp. 128-138). New York, NY: W.W. Norton & Company.

Stone, E. A., Goetz, A. T., & Shackelford, T. K. (2005). Sex differences and similarities in preferred mating arrangements. *Sexualities Evolution and Gender, 7*(3), 269-276.

Stotzer, R. L., & MacCartney, D. (2016). The role of institutional factors on on-campus reported rape prevalence. *Journal of Interpersonal Violence, 31*(16), 2687-2707.

Strgar, W. (2010). *Ask the loveologist: Five barriers to a sexual vocabulary.* Retrieved July 27, 2012 from the Care2 website: http://www.care2.com/greenliving/loveologist-sexual-vocabulary.html

Strieb, J. (2015). *The power of the past: Understanding cross-class marriages.* New York, NY: Oxford University Press.

Striepe, M., & Tolman, D. (2003). Mom, Dad, I'm straight: The coming out of gender ideologies in adolescent sexual-identity development. *Journal of Clinical Child & Adolescent Psychology, 32*(4), 523-530.

Stryker, S., & Buskirk, J. (1996). *Gay by the bay.* San Francisco, CA: Chronicle Books.

Surgeon General's Report. (2001). *The Surgeon General's call to action to promote sexual health and responsible sexual behavior.* Washington, DC: Government Printing Office.

Sutter Health. (n.d.). *Partners and pregnancy.* Retrieved November 12, 2008, from http:// www.babies.sutterhealth.org/during/preg_part- ners.html

Sutton, M. Y., Jones, R. L., Wolitski, R. J., Cleveland, J. C., Dean, H. D., & Fenton, K. A. (2009). A review of the Centers for Disease Control and Prevention's response to the HIV/AIDS crisis among blacks in the United States, 1981-2009. *American Journal of Public Health, 99*(Suppl 2), S351-359.

Swank, E., Faulkner, C., & Hesterberg, L. (2008). Comfort with gays and lesbians after a class discussion on homophobia. *American Journal of Sexuality Education, 3,* 255-276.

Swann, W. B., Jr., Rentfrow, P. J., & Gosling, S. D. (2003). The precarious couple effect: Verbally inhibited men 1critical, disinhibited women 5 bad chemistry. *Journal of Personality and Social Psychology, 85,* 1095-1106.

Swanson, K. M., Connor, S., Jolley, S. N., Pettinato, M., & Wang, T-J. (2007). Contexts and evolution of women's responses to miscarriage during the first year after loss. *Research in Nursing & Health, 30,* 2-16.

Symonds, D. (1979). *The evolution of human sexuality.* New York, NY: Oxford.

Symonds, D. (1987). An evolutionary approach: Can Darwin's views of life shed light on human sexuality? In J. H. Geer & W. T. O'Donoue (Eds.), *Theories of human sexuality* (pp. 9-26). New York, NY: Plenum.

Szasz, T. (1988). *Pain and pleasure* (2nd ed.). New York, NY: Basic Books.

Szasz, T. (2000). Remembering Krafft-Ebing. *Ideas on Liberty, 50,* 31-32.

Tannen, D. (1990). *You just don't understand.* New York, NY: Harper Collins.

Tannen, D. (2001). *Talking from 9 to 5.* New York, NY: Harper Collins.

Taylor, S. E. (2010). Social support: A review. In H. S. Friedman (Ed.), *Oxford handbook of health psychology.* New York, NY: Oxford University Press.

Taylor, T. (1997). *The prehistory of sex.* New York, NY: Bantam Books.

Tepper, K. H., & Betts, S. C. (2009). *A youth development approach to abstinence education for 9 to 13 year olds: Support from the literature.* Retrieved October 29, 2012, from the Building Partnerships for Youth website: http://cals-cf.calsnet.arizona.edu/fcs/bpy/content.cfm?content5ydAbstinence

Tepper, M., & Owens, A. (Eds.). (2007). *Sexual health, Vol. 2: Physical foundations.* Westport, CT: Praeger.

Terry, J. (1999). *An American obsession: Science, medicine, and homosexuality in modern America.* Chicago, IL: University of Chicago Press.

Terry, K. (2011). *The causes and context of sexual abuse of minors by Catholic priests in the United States, 1950-2010.* Washington, DC: U.S. Conference of Catholic Bishops.

Teten, A. L., Ball, B., Valle, L. A., Noonan, R., & Rosenbluth, B. (2009). Considerations for the definition, measurement, consequences, and prevention of dating violence victimization among adolescent girls. *Journal of Women's Health, 18*(7), 923-927.

Teten, A. L., Hall, G. C., & Capaldi, D. M. (2009). Use of coercive sexual tactics across 10 years in at-risk young men: Developmental patterns and co-occurring problematic dating behaviors. *Archives of Sexual Behavior, 38,* 574-582.

Teunis, N. (2006). *Sexual inequalities and social justice.* Berkeley, CA: University of California Press.

Teunis, N. F., & Herdt, G. (2006). Sexual inequalities: Agency and social change: An introduction. In N. Teunis (Ed.), *Sexuality inequalities and social justice* (pp. 1-39). Berkeley, CA: University of California Press.

Theiss, J. A., et al. (2009). Relationship characteristics associated with the experience of hurt in romantic relationships: A test of the relational turbulence model. *Human Communication Research, 35,* 588-615.

Thompson, S. (1995). *Going all the way: Teenage girls' tales of sex, romance, and pregnancy.* New York, NY: Hill and Wang.

Thoreson, R. (2018, February 19). "All we want is equality": Religious exemptions and discrimination against LGBT people in the United States. *Human Rights Watch.* Retrieved from https://www.hrw.org/report/2018/02/19/all-we-want-equality/religious-exemptions-and-discrimination-against-lgbt-people

Thornhill, R., & Gangestad, S. W. (1999). The scent of symmetry: A human sex pheromone that signals fitness? *Evolution and Human Behavior, 20*(3), 175-201.

Thornhill, R., & Gangestad, S. W. (2008). *The evolutionary biology of human female sexuality.* New York, NY: Oxford.

Thurlow, C., & McKay, S. (2003). Profiling "new" communication technologies in adolescence. *Journal of Language and Social Psychology, 22*(1), 94-103.

Tiefer, L. (1986). In pursuit of the perfect penis: The medicalization of male sexuality. *American Behavioral Scientists, 29,* 579-599.

Tiefer, L. (2004). *Sex is not a natural act and other essays.* Boulder, CO: Westview Press.

Tiefer, L. (2006). Female sexual dysfunction: A case study of disease mongering and activist resistance. *PLoS Medicine, 3*(4), e178. DOI:10.1371/journal.pmed.0030178.

Tjaden, P., & Thoennes, N. (2000a). Extent, nature, and consequences of intimate partner violence. Retrieved from https://www.ncjrs.gov/pdffiles1/nij/181867.pdf.

Tjaden, P., & Thoennes, N. (2000b). *Full report of the prevalence, incidence and consequences of violence against women: Findings from the National Violence Against Women Survey.* Washington, DC: National Institute of Justice.

Tjaden, P., & Thoennes, N. (2006). *Extent, nature, and consequences of rape victimization: Findings from the National Violence Against Women Survey.* Washington, DC: National Institute of Justice.

Tolman, D. (2005). *Dilemmas of desire.* Cambridge, MA: Harvard University Press.

Tolman, D. (2006). *Dilemmas of desire.* Cambridge, MA: Harvard University Press.

Tolman, D. (2011). Adolescent girls' sexuality: The more things change, the more they stay the same. In S. Seidman, N. Fischer, & C. Meeks (Eds.), *Introducing the New Sexuality Studies, Second Edition.* New York: Routledge.

Tolman, D., & Diamond, L. (2002). Desegregating sexuality research: Cultural and biological perspectives on gender and desire. *Annual Review Sex Research, 12,* 33-74.

Tone, A. (2001). *Devices and desires: A history of contraceptives in America.* New York, NY: Hill and Wang.

Tovar, V. (2012). *Hot and heavy: Fierce fat girls on life, love, and fashion.* Berkeley, CA: Seal Press.

Trevor Project. (2019a). *About conversion therapy.* Retrieved August 9, 2019, from https://www.thetrevorproject.org/get-involved/trevor-advocacy/50-bills-50-states/ about-conversion-therapy/

Trevor Project. (2019b). *Facts about suicide.* Retrieved May 9, 2019, from https://www.thetrevorproject.org/resources/preventing-suicide/facts-about-suicide/

Trouong, T. (1990). *Sex, money, and morality: Prostitution and tourism in South-East Asia.* London: Zed Books.

TRU. (2008). *Teen and tween dating violence and abuse study.* Retrieved April 26, 2012, from the National Domestic Violence Hotline webiste: http://www.google.com/url?sa5t&r ct5j&q5&esrc5s&source5web&cd51&v ed50CCkQFjAA&url5http%3A%2F%2F www.loveisrespect.org%2Fwp-content%2Fu ploads%2F2008%2F07%2Ftru-tween-teen-study-feb-081.pdf&ei5pNaZT7anEqiI2gW2 gsWsBw&usg5A FQjCNGYWEhE8jWetv06z HlC_UBD4pwcrw

Trumbach, R. (1977). London's sodomites: Homosexual behavior and Western culture in the eighteenth century. *Journal of Social History, 11,* 1–33.

Trumbach, R. (1994). London's sapphists: From three sexes to four genders in the making of modern culture. In G. Herdt (Ed.), *Third sex, third gender: Beyond sexual dimorphism in culture and history* (pp. 111–136). New York, NY: Zone Books.

Trumbach, R. (1998). *Sex and the gender revolution: Vol. 1. Heterosexuality and the third gender in Enlightenment London.* Chicago, IL: University of Chicago Press.

Trussell, J. (2004). The essentials of contraception: Efficacy, safety, and personal considerations. In R. A. Hatcher (Ed.), *Contraceptive technology* (18th ed.). New York, NY: Ardent Media.

Trussell, J. (2007). Choosing a contraceptive: Efficacy, safety, and personal considerations. In R. A. Hatcher, J. Trussell, A. L. Nelson, W. Cates, F. H. Stewart, & D. Kowal (Eds.), *Contraceptive technology* (19th rev. ed., pp. 19–47). New York, NY: Ardent Media.

Trussell, J., Aiken, A. R. A., Micks, E., & Guthrie, K. A. (2018). Efficacy, safety, and personal considerations. In R. A. Hatcher et al. (Eds.), *Contraceptive technology.* 21st ed. New York, NY: Ayer Company Publishers, Inc.

Tschann, J. M., & Adler, N. E. (1997). Sexual self-acceptance, communication with partner and contraceptive use among adolescent females: A longitudinal study. *Journal of Research in Adolescence, 7(4),* 413–430.

Tucker, M. W., & O'Grady, K. E. (1991). Effect of physical attractiveness, intelligence, age at marriage, and cohabitation on the perception of marital satisfaction. *Journal of Social Psychology, 131,* 253–269.

Turkle, S. (1996). *Life on the screen: Identity in the age of the Internet.* New York, NY: Simon & Schuster.

Turkle, S. (2006). A nascent robotics culture: New complicities for companionship. MIT Technical Report. Retrieved July 9, 2019, from http://web.mit.edu/sturkle/OldFiles/www/nascentroboticsculture.pdf

Turnbull, D., Holmes, A., Shields, N., Cheyne, H., Twaddle, S., Gilmour, W. H., . . . Lunan, C. B. (1996). Randomised, controlled trial of efficacy of midwife-managed care. *Lancet, 347,* 213–218.

Turner, A. M., Osterhage, K., Taylor, J. O., Hartzler, A., & Demiris G. (2018). A closer look at health information seeking by older adults and involved family and friends: Design considerations for health information technologies. *AMIA Annual Symposium Proceedings 2018,* 1036–1045.

Turner, V. (1967). *Forest of symbols.* Ithaca, NY: Cornell University Press.

Twamley, K. (2013). Love and desire amongst middle-class Gujarati Indians in the UK and India. *Culture, Health & Sexuality, 15,* 327–340. DOI: 10.1080/13691058.20121.754945

Twenge, J. M., Sherman, R. A., & Wells, B. E., (2017). Declines in sexual frequency among American adults, 1989–2014. *Archives of Sexual Behavior, 46,* 2389–2401. DOI: https://DOI.org/10.1007/s10508-017-0953-1

Ullman, S. E., & Filipas, H. H. (2001). Predictors of PTSD symptom severity and social reactions in sexual assault victims. *Journal of Traumatic Stress, 14,* 369–389.

Umberson, D., & Williams, K. (1999). Family status and mental health. In C. Aneshensel & J. Phelan (Eds.), *Handbook of the sociology of mental health* (pp. 225–253). New York, NY: Klewer Academic/Plenum.

UN Refugee Agency. (2018). *Desperate journeys: Refugees and migrants arriving in Europe and at Europe's borders.* Retrieved August 7, 2019, from https://www.unhcr.org/desperatejourneys/

UNAIDS. (2009). *HIV transmission in intimate partner relationships in Asia.* Geneva, Switzerland: United Nations.

UNICEF. (2005). *Changing a harmful social convention: Female genital mutilation/cutting.* New York, NY: Author.

United Nations. (2007). *Male circumcision: Global trends and determinants of prevalence, safety, and acceptability.* Geneva, Switzerland: Author.

United States Department of Health and Human Services. (2018). *Child maltreatment survey, 2016.* Administration for Children and Families, Administration on Children, Youth and Families, Children's Bureau.

Urban Justice Center. (2005). *Behind closed doors: An analysis of indoor sex work in New York City.* New York, NY: Author.

Urrutia, R. P., Polis, C. B., Jensen, E. T., Greene, M. E., Kennedy, E., & Stanford, J. B. (2018). Effectiveness of fertility awareness–based methods for pregnancy prevention: A systematic review. *Obstetrics and Gynecology, 132,* 591–604.

U.S. Bureau of Labor Statistics. (2016). Economic news release: Employment characteristics of families summary. Retrieved from http://www.bls.gov/news.release/famee.nr0.htm

U.S. Cancer Statistics Working Group. (2009). *United States cancer statistics (USCS): 1999–2005 incidence and mortality data.* Atlanta, GA: Centers for Disease Control and Prevention and National Cancer Institute.

U.S. Cancer Statistics Working Group. (2012). *United States cancer statistics (USCS): 1999–2008 cancer incidence and mortality data.* Retrieved October 25, 2012, from the Centers for Disease Control and Prevention website: http://apps.nccd.cdc.gov/uscs/

U.S. Census Bureau. (2010). *2010 American Community Survey of 1-Year Estimates. Unmarried partner households by sex of partner. Table B11009.* Retrieved October 19, 2012, from http://factfinder2. census.gov/faces/tableservices/jsf/pages/ productview.xhtml?pid5ACS_10_1YR_ B11009&prodType5table

U.S. Census Bureau. (2012a). *Table 104: Expectation of life at birth, 1970 to 2008, and projections, 2010 to 2020. Table 105: Life expectancy by sex, age, and race: 2008. Statistical abstract of the United States: 2012.* Retrieved October 28, 2012, from http://www.census.gov/compendia/ statab/2012/tables/12s0104.pdf

U.S. Census Bureau. (2012b, November 15). American householders are getting older, Census Bureau reports. Retrieved August 18, 2019, from https://www.census.gov/newsroom/releases/archives/families_households/cb12-216.html

U.S. Census Bureau. (2017, Sept. 17–23). Unmarried and single Americans week. Retrieved from https://www.census.gov/content/dam/Census/newsroom/facts-for-features/2017/cb17-ff16.pdf

U.S. Department of Health and Human Services (USDHHS), Office on Women's Health. (2009). *Pap test: Frequently asked questions.* Retrieved October 28, 2012, from http://womenshealth.gov/publications/our-publications/fact-sheet/pap-test.pdf

U.S. Department of Health and Human Services, Office on Women's Health. (2008). *Date rape drugs.* Retrieved October 28, 2012, from http://www.womenshealth.gov/faq/date- rape-drugs.pdf

U.S. Department of Justice. (2005). *National Crime Victimization Study, 2005.* Washington, DC: Author.

U.S. Department of Labor. (2014 December). *Women in the labor force: A databook.* U.S. Bureau of Labor Statistics, Report 1052.

U.S. Department of State. (2008). The facts about child sex tourism. Fact Sheet. U.S. Dept. of State Office to Monitor and Combat Trafficking in Persons. February 29, 2008. Retrieved December 7, 2010, from http://www.state.gov/g/tip/rls/fs/08/112090.htm.

U.S. Equal Employment Opportunity Commission (EEOC). (2010). Sexual harassment charges. Retrieved November 16, 2012, from http://www.eeoc.gov/eeoc/statistics/ enforcement/sexual_harassment.cfm

U.S. Preventive Services Task Force. (2009). *Screening for breast cancer. Recommendation statement.* Retrieved October 28, 2012, from http://www.uspreventiveservicestaskforce.org/ uspstf09/breastcancer/brcanrs.htm

USA Today. (2018, May 23). Poll: Approval of same sex marriage in US reaches new high. Retrieved April 22, 2019, from https://www.usatoday.com/story/news/nation/2018/05/23/same-sex-marriage-poll-americans/638587002/

Ussher, J. M. (2017). Unraveling the mystery of "the specificity of women's sexual response and its relationship with sexual orientations": The social construction of sex and sexual identities. *Archives of Sexual Behavior, 1-46*(5), 1207–1211. DOI:10.1007/s10508-017-0957-x

Vahratian, A., Patel, D., Wolff, K., & Xu, X. (2008). College students' perceptions of emergency contraception provision. *Journal of Women's Health, 17*(1), 103–111.

Valentine, D. (2007). *Imagining transgender: An ethnography of a category.* Durham, NC: Duke University Press.

Valliant, G. (1993). *The wisdom of the ego.* Cambridge, MA: Harvard University Press.

Valliant, G. (2002). *Aging well.* Boston, MA: Little, Brown.

van Anders, S. M. (2015). Beyond sexual orientation: Integrating gender/sex and diverse sexualities via sexual configurations theory. *Archives of Sexual Behaviour, 44*(5), 1177–1213. DOI:10.1007/s10508-015-0490-8

van Oosten, J., Peter, J., & Vandenbosch, L. (2016). Adolescents' sexual media use and willingness to engage in casual sex: Differential relations and underlying processes: Sexual media use and casual sex. *Human Communication Research, 43.* 10.1111/hcre.12098

Van der Meer, T. (1994). Sodomy and the pursuit of a third sex in the early modern period. In G. Herdt (Ed.), *Third sex/third gender: Beyond sexual dimorphism in culture and history* (pp. 137–212). New York, NY: Zone Books.

van Gelderen, L., Bos, H., Gartrell, N., Hermanns, J., & Perrin, E. (2012). *Journal of Developmental and Behavioral Pediatrics, 33*(1), 1-7.

Van Houdenhove, E., Gijs, L., T'Sjoen, G., & Enzlin, P. (2014). Asexuality: Few facts, many questions. *Journal of Sex & Marital Therapy, 40*(3), 175-192. DOI:10.1080/0092623X.2012.751073

Van Rossem, R., & Gage, A. J. (2009). The effects of genital mutilation on the onset of sexual activity and marriage in Guinea. *Archives of Sexual Behavior, 38*(2), 178-185.

Vandenbosch, L., Vervloessem, D., & Eggermont, S. (2013). "I might get your heart racing in my skin-tight jeans": Sexualization on music entertainment television. *Communication Studies, (64)*, 178-194.

Vanita, R., & Kidwai, S. (2001). *Same-sex love in India: Readings from literature and history*. New York, NY: Palgrave Macmillan.

Vansintejan, J., Vandevoorde, J., & Devroey, D. (2013). The Gay Men Seks Studies: Anodyspareunia among Belgian gay men. *Sexual Medicine, 1*(2), 87-94.

Vasey, P. L. (2017). Introduction to the special section: The puzzle of sexual orientation: What is it and how does it work? *Archives of Sexual Behavior, 46*(1), 59-61. DOI:10.1007/s10508-016-0913-1

Vasey, P. L., & Bartlett, N. H. (2007). What can the Samoan "fa'afafine" teach US about the Western concept of gender identity disorder in childhood? *Perspectives in Biology and Medicine, 50*(4), 481-490.

Vázquez, E. (2008). A transgender therapy primer: Basic information for hormonal treatment and drug interactions. *Positively Aware, 19*(4), 46-48.

Veale, J. F., Lomax, T., & Clarke, D. (2010). Identity-defense model of gender-variant development. *International Journal of Transgenderism, 12*(3), 125-138. DOI:10.1080/15532739.2010.514217

Verhaeghe, J., Gheysen, R., & Enzlin, P. (2013). Pheromones and their effect on women's mood and sexuality. *Facts, Views, & Vision in Obgyn., 5*(3), 189-195.

Victim Witness Assistance Program. (2017). *Drug-facilitated sexual assault*. Washington, DC: U.S. Department of Justice, Drug Enforcement Administration.

Villanti, A. C., Johnson, A. L., Llakkuvan, V., Jacobs, M. A., Graham, A. L., & Rath, J. M. (2017). Social media use and access to digital technology in US young adults in 2016. *Journal of Medical Internet Research, 19*(6), e196.

Viloria, H. (2016). "What's in a name: Intersex and identity." In J. Schneiderman (Ed.), *Queer: A reader for writers* (pp. 213-217). New York, NY: Oxford University Press.

Vincent, L. (2008). 'Boys will be boys': Traditional Xhosa male circumcision, HIV, and sexual socialisation in contemporary South Africa. *Culture, Health & Sexuality: An International Journal for Research, Intervention and Cure, 10*(5), 431-446. DOI: 10.1080/13691050701861447.

Vogel, V. (1977). *American Indian medicine*. Norman, OK: University of Oklahoma.

Vogel, V. (1990). *American Indian medicine*. Norman, OK: University of Oklahoma.

Voyer, D., Voyer, S., & Bryden, M. P. (1995). Magnitude of sex differences in spatial abilities: A meta-analysis and consideration of critical variables. *Psychological Bulletin, 117*(2), 250-270.

Vrangalova, Z., & Savin-Williams, R. C. (2010). Correlates of same-sex sexuality in heterosexually identified young adults. *Journal of Sex Research, 47*(1), 92-102.

Vrangalova, Z., & Savin-Williams, R. C. (2012). Mostly heterosexual and mostly gay/lesbian: Evidence for new sexual orientation identities. *Archives of Sexual Behavior, 41*(1), 85-101. DOI:10.1007/s10508-012-9921-y

Vrouenraets, L. J., Fredriks, A. M., Hannema, S. E., Cohen-Kettenis, P. T., & de Vries, M. C. (2015). Early medical treatment of children and adolescents with gender dysphoria: An empirical ethical study. *Journal of Adolescent Health, 57*(4), 367-373. DOI:10.1016/j.jadohealth.2015.04.004

Waal, F. de (2018). *Mama's last hug: Animal emotions and what they tell us about ourselves*. New York, NY: W.W. Norton & Co.

Wade, L., & Heldman, C. (2012). Hooking up and opting out: Negotiating sex in the first year of college. In L. Carpenter & J. DeLamater (Eds.), *Sex for life* (pp. 128-145). New York, NY: NYU Press.

Waite, L., & Gallagher, M. (2000). *The case for marriage*. New York, NY: Doubleday.

Waite, L. J. (1995). Does marriage matter? *Demography, 32*(4), 483-507.

Waite, L. J., & Joyner, K. (2001). Emotional and physical satisfaction with sex in married, cohabiting, and dating sexual unions: Do men and women differ? In E. O. Laumann & R. T. Michael (Eds.), *Sex, love, and health in America: Private choices and public policies* (pp. 239-269). Chicago, IL: University of Chicago Press.

Waites, M. (2005). *The age of consent: Young people, sexuality and citizenship*. Houndmills, Basingstoke, Hampshire; New York; London, UK: Palgrave Macmillan.

Walker, A. (1982). *The color purple*. Orlando, FL: Orlando.

Wallace, L. (2009, March 29). *Adrenaline rush: Adventure, stress, and extreme sports*. Retrieved October 28, 2012, from no map. no guide. no limits website: http://www.nomapnoguideno-limits.com/2009/03/

Wallen, K. (1995). The evolution of female sexual desire. In R. Abramson & S. D. Pinkerton (Eds.), *Sexual nature, sexual culture* (pp. 57-79). Chicago, IL: University of Chicago Press.

Wallen, K., & Parsons, W. A. (1997). Sexual behavior in same-sexed nonhuman primates: Is it relevant to understanding human homosexuality? *Annual Review of Sex Research, 8*, 195-223.

Walling, A. D. (2002). Women's regret after sterilization procedures. *American Family Physician, 66*, 1326.

Walsh, K., Blaustein, M., Knight, W. G., Spinazzola, J., van der Kolk, B. A. (2007). Resiliency factors in the relation between childhood sexual abuse and adulthood sexual assault in college-age women. *Journal of Child Sexual Abuse, 16*(1), 1-16.

Walter, C. (2008). Affairs of the lips. *Scientific American Mind, 19*(1), 24-29.

Walton, M. T., Lykins, A. D., & Bhullar, N. (2016). Beyond heterosexual, bisexual, and homosexual: A diversity in sexual identity expression. *Archives of Sexual Behavior, 45*(7), 1591-1597. DOI:10.1007/s10508-016-0778-3

Wang, S. K., & Rowley, E. (2007). Rape: How women, the community and the health sector respond. *Initiative of the Global Forum for Health Research commissioned by the World Health Organization for the Sexual Violence Research Initiative*. Geneva, Switzerland: World Health Organization (WHO).

Wardlow, H. (2006). *Wayward women*. Berkeley, CA: University of California Press.

Warf, B. (2011, February). Geographies of global Internet censorship. *GeoJournal 76*(1), 1-23, February.

Watson, A. F., & McKee, A. (2013). Masturbation and the media. *Sexuality and Culture, 17*, 449-475.

Webb, D. A., & Culhane, J. (2002). Time of day variation in rates of obstetric intervention to assist in vaginal delivery. *Journal of Epidemiology and Community Health, 56*, 577-578.

Weber, M. (2002). *The Protestant ethic and spirit of capitalism* (G. C. Wells, Trans.). New York, NY: Penguin. (Original work published 1905.)

WebMD. (2017). *How effective is Depo-Provera for birth control?* Retrieved July 8, 2019, from https://www.webmd.com/sex/birth-control/birth-control-depo-provera#1

Weeks, J. (2010). The importance of being historical: Understanding the making of sexualities. In P. Aggleton & R. Parker, *Routledge handbook of sexuality, health and rights* (pp. 28-36). New York, NY: Routledge.

Weinberg, M. S., Williams, C. J., & Pryor, W. (1995). *Dual attraction: Understanding bisexuality*. New York, NY: Oxford.

Weir, K. (2016) The risks of earlier puberty. *American Psychological Association Newsletter, 47*(3), 40. Retrieved from https://www.apa.org/monitor/2016/03/puberty

Weisman, A. (2012). *Justin Bieber by the numbers*. Retrieved March 21, 2012, from Business Insider website: http://www.businessinsider.com/justin-bieber-by-the-numbers-600-girls-scream-his-name-as-he-wears-900-sneakers-2012-3

Weisner, T. S. (2009). Parenting. In A. Shweder, T. R. Bidell, A. C. Dailey, D. Dixon, P. J. Miller, & J. Modell (Eds.), *The child: An encyclopedic companion*. Chicago, IL: University of Chicago Press.

Weisner, T. S., Bradley, C., & Kilbride, P. (Eds.). (1997). *African families and the crisis of social change*. Westport, CT: Greenwood Press/ Bergin & Garvey.

Weiss, D. (2004). United States interpersonal heterosexual behavior: Childhood sexuality. In R. T. Francoeur & R. J. Nooran (Eds.), *The Continuum complete international encyclopedia of sexuality* (pp. 1180-1188). New York, NY: Continuum Press.

Weisskirch, R. S., Drouin, M., & Delevi, R. (2017). Relational anxiety and sexting. *The Journal of Sex Research, 54*(6), 685-693.

Wellings, K. (1994). *Sexual behaviour in Britain: The National Survey of Sexual Attitudes and Lifestyles*. New York, NY: Penguin Books.

Welti, K., Wildsmith, E., & Manlove, J. (2011, August). Trends and recent estimates: Contraceptive use among U.S. teens and young adults. *Child Trends* (Research Brief No. 2011-23). Washington, DC: Child Trends.

West, R. (2007). *Marriage, sexuality, and gender*. Boulder, CO: Paradigm.

Westheimer, R., & Lopater, S. (2002). *Human sexuality*. Philadelphia, PA: Lippincott, Williams and Wilkins.

White, L., & Edwards, J. N. (1990). Emptying the nest and parental well-being: An analysis of national panel data. *American Sociological Review, 55*, 235-42.

White, M. (1995). *Stranger at the gate*. New York, NY: Plume.

White, P. C. (2011). Congenital adrenal hyperplasia due to 17-hydroxylase deficiency. In R. M. Kliegman, B. F. Stanton, J. St. Geme, N. Schor, & R. E. Behrman (Eds.), *Nelson Textbook of Pediatrics* (19th ed.). Philadelphia, PA: Saunders Elsevier.

Whiting, B., & Edwards, C. (1988). *Children of different worlds*. Cambridge, MA: Harvard University Press.

Whiting, J. (1941). *The Kwoma*. New Haven, CT: Yale University Press.

Whitley, R. J., & Roizman, B. (2001). Herpes simplex virus infections. *Lancet, 357*(9267), 1513-1518.

Whittle, S. (2002). *Respect and equality: Transsexual and transgender rights*. Oxford, UK: Routledge-Cavendish.

Wholeslagle, B. (2006). *Pixilated propriety* (Unpublished master's thesis). Department of Sexuality Studies, San Francisco State University, San Francisco, CA.

Widom, C. S., & Kuhns, J. B. (1996). Childhood victimization and subsequent risk for promiscuity, prostitution, and teenage pregnancy: A prospective study. *American Journal of Public Health, 86*, 1607-1612.

Wigfield, A., Battle, A., Keller, L., & Eccles, J. S. (2002). Sex differences in motivation, self-concept, career aspirations, and career choice: Implications for cognitive development. In A. McGillicuddy-DeLisi & R. DeLisi (Eds.), *Biology, society, and behavior: The development of sex differences in cognition* (pp. 93-124). Greenwich, CT: Ablex.

Williams, D. N., Yee, N., & Caplan, S. E. (2008). Who plays, how much, and why? Debunking the stereotypical gamer profile. *Journal of Computer-Mediated Communication, 13*(4), 993-1018. DOI: 10.1111/j.1083-6101.2008.00428.x

Williams, J. E., Satterwhite, R. C., & Best, D. L. (1999). Pancultural gender stereotypes revisited: The Five Factor Model. *Sex Roles, 40*, 513-525.

Williams, K. (2003). Has the future of marriage arrived? A contemporary examination of gender, marriage, and psychological well being. *Journal of Health and Social Behavior, 44*, 470-487.

Williams, K., & Umberson, D. (2004). Marital status, marital transitions, and health: A gendered life course perspective. *Journal of Health and Social Behavior, 45*, 81-98.

Williams, T. J., Pepitone, M. E., Christenson, S. E., Cooke, B. M., Huberman, A. D., Breedlove, N., . . . Breddlove, M. (2000). Finger length ratios and sexual orientation. *Nature 404*, 455-456.

Williams, W. (1992). *The spirit and the flesh: Sexual diversity in American Indian culture.* Boston, MA: Beacon Press.

Wilson, B. D. M., Choi, S. K., Herman, J. L., Becker, T., & Conron, K. J. (2017). Characteristics and mental health of gender nonconforming adolescents in California. Retrieved from http://healthpolicy.ucla.edu/publications/Documents/PDF/2017/gncadolescents-factsheet-dec2017.pdf

Wilson, G. D. (1978). *The secrets of sexual fantasy* (1st ed.). London, United Kingdom: Dent.

Winterman, D. (2009, March 6). *What would a real life Barbie look like?* Retrieved July 21, 2012, from *BBC News Magazine* website: http://news.bbc.co.uk/2/hi/uk_news/maga-zine/7920962.stm

Wolak, J., Finkelhor, D., Mitchell, K., & Ybarra, M. (2008). Online "predators" and their victims: Myths, realities, and implications for prevention and treatment. *American Psychologist, 63*, 111-128.

Wolfson, E. (2005). *Why marriage matters.* New York, NY: Simon and Shuster.

Wong, W. I., & Hines, M. (2015). Preferences for pink and blue: The development of color preferences as a distinct gender-typed behavior in toddlers. *Archives of Sexual Behavior, 44*(5), 1243-1254. DOI:10.1007/s10508-015-0489-1

Wood, A., & Kilvington, J. (2016). *Gender, sex and children's play.* London; New York, NY: Bloomsbury Academic.

Woodhead, L. (2004)). *Christianity: A very short introduction.* Oxford: Oxford University Press.

Woodruff, L., & Woodruff, B. (2007). *In an instant.* New York, NY: Random House.

World Economic Forum. (2018). Global gender gap report, 2018. Retrieved April 22, 2019, from http://reports.weforum.org/global-gender-gap-report-2018/

World Health Organization (WHO). (1975). *Education and treatment in human sexuality: The training of health professionals.* Geneva, Switzerland: Author.

World Health Organization (WHO). (2017). *HIV/AIDS*—Global Health Observatory data. Retrieved July 13, 2019, from https://www.who.int/gho/hiv/en/

World Health Organization (WHO). (2018a). *Delivering quality health services: A global imperative for universal health coverage.* Geneva: World Health Organization, Organisation for Economic Co-operation and Development, and The World Bank. Licence: CC BY-NC-SA 3.0 I.

World Health Organization (WHO). (2018b, February 8). *Emergency contraception.—key facts.* Retrieved July 8, 2019, from https://www.who.int/news-room/fact-sheets/detail/emergency-contraception

World Health Organization (WHO). (2018c). WHO to develop new guidelines on male circumcision. Retrieved from https://www.who.int/hiv/mediacentre/news/gdg-male-circumcision/en/

World Health Organization (WHO). (2019a). *Female genital mutilation.* Retrieved May 19, 2019, from https://www.who.int/reproductivehealth/topics/fgm/prevalence/en/

World Health Organization (WHO). (2019b, January 24). *Human papillomavirus (HPV) and cervical cancer.* Retrieved from https://www.who.int/news-room/fact-sheets/detail/human-papillomavirus-(hpv)-and-cervical-cancer

World Health Organization (WHO). (2019c). *International classification of diseases-11 for mortality and morbidity statistics.* Retrieved June 16, 2019, from https://icd.who.int/browse11/l-m/en

World Health Organization (WHO). (2019d). *Nonoxynol-9 ineffective in preventing HIV.* Retrieved July 8, 2019, from https://www.who.int/mediacentre/news/notes/release55/en/

World Health Organization (WHO). (2019e). *Sexual and reproductive health.* Retrieved from https://www.who.int/reproductivehealth/topics/sexual_health/sh_definitions/en/

Worobey, M., Gemmel, M., Teuwen, D. E. Haselkorn, T., Kuntsman, K., Bunce, M., Muyembe, J-J., Kabongo, J-M., Kalengayi, M., Van Marck, E., Gilbert, T. P., & Wolinsky, S. M. (2008). Direct evidence of extensive diversity of HIV-1 in Kinshasa by 1960. *Nature, 455*, 661-664.

Worthman, C. (1998). Adolescence in the Pacific: A biosocial view. In G. Herdt & C. Leavitt (Eds.), *Adolescence in Pacific Island societies* (pp. 27-55). Pittsburgh, PA: University of Pittsburgh Press.

W-PATH (World Professional Association for Transgender Health). (2012). Standards of care for the health of transsexual, transgender, and gender-nonconforming people, 7th version. *International Journal of Transgenderism, 13*(4), 165-232. DOI: 10.1080/15532739.2011.700873

Wright, D., Williamson, L., & Henderson, M. (2006). Parental influences on young people's sexual behaviour: A longitudinal analysis. *Journal of Adolescence, 29*, 473-494.

Wyatt, G. E., Peters, S., & Guthrie, D. (1988). Kinsey revisited, part II: Comparisons of sexual socialization and sexual behavior of black women over 33 years. *Archives of Sexual Behavior, 17*, 289-332.

Yadavar, S. (n.d.). *How to say "no" to your partner for sex.* Retrieved October 12, 2012, from medimanage.com website: http://www.medimanage.com/my-sex-life/articles/how-to-say-no-to-your-partner-for-sexaspx.aspx.

Yakeley, J. & Wood, H. (2014) Paraphilias and paraphilic disorders: Diagnosis, assessment and management. *Advances in Psychiatric Treatment, 20*, 202-213.

Yalom, M. (2002). *A history of the wife.* New York, NY: Harper.

Yang, Z., & Schank, J. C. (2006). Women do not synchronize their menstrual cycles. *Human Nature, 17*(4), 434-447.

Ybarra, M., & Mitchell, K. J. (2005). Exposure to Internet pornography among children and adolescents: A national survey. *CyberPsychology & Behavior, 8*(5), 473-486. DOI:10.1089/cpb.2005.8.473.

Ybarra, M. L., & Mitchell, K. J. (2014). "Sexting" and its relation to sexual activity and sexual risk behavior in a national survey of adolescents. *Journal of Adolescent Health, 55*(6), 757-764.

Yockey, R. A., King, K. A., Vidourek, R., Burbage, A. M., & Merianos, A. (2019). The depiction of sexuality among university students on Snapchat. *Sexuality & Culture, 23*, 132-131. https://DOI.org/10.1007/s12119-018-9546-y

Yule, M. A., Brotto, L. A., & Gorzalka, B. B. (2017). Sexual fantasy and masturbation among asexual individuals: An in-depth exploration. *Archives of Sexual Behavior, 46*(1), 311-328. DOI:10.1007/s10508-016-0870-8

Zebrowitz, L. A., & Rhodes, G. (2004). Sensitivity to "bad genes" and the anomalous face overgeneralization effect: Cue validity, cue utilization, and accuracy in judging intelligence and health. *Journal of Nonverbal Behavior, 28*, 167-185.

Zernike, K. (2004, March 1). *Sizing up America: Signs of expansion from head to toe.* Retrieved July 21, 2012, from the New York Times website: http://www.nytimes.com/2004/03/01/us/sizing-up-america-signs-of-expansion-from-head-to-toe.html?pagewanted5all&src5pm

Zsok, F., Haucke, M., De Wit, C. Y., & Barelds, D. P. H. (2017). What kind of love is love at first sight? An empirical investigation. *Personal Relationships, 24*, 869-885. DOI: 10.1111/pere.12218

Zucker, K. J., & Bradley, S. J. (1995). *Gender identity disorder and psychosexual problems in children and adolescents.* New York, NY: Guilford Press.

Name Index

A

Abbey, A., 480
Abdullaeva, M., 291
Abma, J. C., 390
Abrams, N., 59
Abramson, P., 379
Abramson, P. R., 93, 135, 140, 150, 404, 498
Adams, J. M., 424
Addiego, F., 105
Adler, N. E., 230
Afifi, W. A., 422
Afriye, R. A., 402
Aggleton, P., 26, 27, 101, 129, 163, 343, 351, 354, 365
Ahmed, G. A., 480
Ahmed, L., 60
Ahmed, S., 303
Ainsworth, M. D. S., 375, 459
Aksglaede, L., 116, 383, 385
Albert, B., 386
Alcázar-Córcoles, M., 497
Alcorta, C., 37, 38
Alexander, M., 322, 484, 485
Allen, G., 385
Allen, K. A., 80, 89, 91
Allen, L., 400
Allen, W. D., 479
Altemus, M., 135
Altman, D., 71, 96
Alzate, H., 105
Amati, V., 7, 8
Amato, P. R., 421, 423
Anafi, M., 316
Anderson, J., 484, 485
Anderson, L., 518
Anderson, M., 466
Anderson, P. B., 491
Andre, T., 322
Antilla, J., 269
Antonovics, K., 425
Antonucci, T. C., 333
Apple, K. J., 416
Arata, C., 508
Arbeit, M. R., 3, 8, 372
Argyle, M., 8, 410
Ariosto, D., 501
Armstrong, K., 36, 39, 40, 43, 44, 55, 56, 58, 59, 60
Aronson, L., 411
Arter, J., 149, 150, 515
Ash, J. A., 257, 264, 265, 282
Ashton, S., 142
Austin, S. B., 333
Ausubel, M., 59
Ayres, T., 393
Ayuso, L., 423

B

Badgett, M. V. L., 18, 19, 341, 343, 348, 354, 363, 402, 403, 416, 419, 420, 422, 428, 430, 433, 434
Bahn, P. G., 37, 38
Bailey, J. M., 16, 18, 129, 142, 299, 308, 314, 325, 333, 334, 337, 338, 341, 349, 380, 387, 388, 389, 404, 451, 513, 515
Baird, D. D., 256
Baisch, M. J., 269
Bakeman, R., 17, 325, 333, 334, 340, 342, 349, 352
Baker, J. H., 219
Baker, S. W., 339
Ball, B., 483
Ball, T., 129
Balsam, K. F., 433
Baltazar, A., 386
Balzarini, R. N., 416, 417, 419, 430
Bancroft, J., 144, 372, 373, 380, 525
Banner, L. W., 319
Banyard, V. L., 479, 480, 502
Barak, A., 93, 94
Barbin, H., 307
Barclay, T., 102
Bardzell, S., 89
Barelds, D. P. H., 446, 451
Barelds-Dijkstra, P., 446, 451
Bargh, J. A., 89
Barker, J. C., 357
Barlow, F. K., 334
Barnden, N., 257, 273
Bärnighausen, T., 127
Barnitz, L., 494
Barrell, A., 126
Barth, F., 318
Bartholomew, K., 325, 459
Basham, A. L., 40, 57
Basile, K. C., 479, 483, 484
Basson, R., 148, 149
Battle, A., 322
Bauer, I., 543
Baumeister, R. F., 351
Baxter, C., 212
Bayer, R., 346, 347, 513
Beach, F. A., 49, 51, 52, 251, 299, 323, 335, 371, 375, 379, 427, 428
Becker, E., 39, 71
Becker, L. G., 39, 197
Becker, T., 327
Becker-Warner, R., 525
Beech, A. R., 497, 498
Beeler, J., 342, 349
Beerten, R., 316
Behund R., 84, 93, 95, 416
Beisel, N., 219
Beitz, K., 460
Bekker, L., 189
Bell, A., 452
Bell, S., 414
Bellah, R., 55, 56
Beltran, O., 185, 188
Belzer, E. G., 105
Bem, D. J., 340, 452
Bem, S. L., 317, 319
Benderly, B. L., 488
Benedict, R., 52, 54
Bennice, J. A., 483, 484
Benson, K., 467
Benwell, B., 92, 93
Ben-Zeév, A., 446
Beoughers, S., 188, 189
Berenbaum, S. A., 299, 302, 319
Berghammer, C., 411, 418, 419, 422
Berkowitz, R. L., 272
Berne, L., 403
Bernstein, E., 415, 431, 503, 504, 505
Berrington, A., 426
Berscheid, E., 447
Berube, A., 348
Betts, S. C., 402
Bhana, D., 319, 333, 341
Bhullar, N., 335
Biblarz, T. J., 343, 364
Biddlecom, A. E., 86, 91
Binson, D., 23, 336, 348, 351
Birdsong, W. M., 274
Birkhead, T., 35
Birnbaum, G. E., 460
Bisson, M., 422, 423
Black, D. W., 528, 529
Black, L., 94
Black, M. C., 479
Blackwell, D. L., 424, 425, 426
Blair, E., 245
Blair, K. L., 352
Blair, S., 60
Blanchard, G. T., 94
Blanchard, J., 338
Blanchard, R., 337, 339
Blank, H., 111
Blaszczynski, A., 334
Blaustein, M., 508
Bledsoe, C., 251, 263, 448
Blehar, M. C., 459
Bloom, J., 60
Blose, F., 504
Blount, D., 255
Blum, R., 353
Blumstein, P., 452, 538
Boellstorff, T., 71, 78, 89, 91, 96, 543
Bogaert, A. F., 335, 338
Bogar, C. B., 508
Boggiano, V., 189
Bogle, K., 84, 88, 89, 90, 415
Boies, S. C., 94
Boog, G., 279
Boonstra, H., 396
Bos, H., 364
Boswell, J., 354
Bourke, M. L., 498
Bove, A. A., 96
Bowker, J., 58, 59
Bowlby, J., 340, 375
Bowleg. L., 20
Bowling, J., 13, 188, 536, 544
Boxer, A., 18, 54, 326, 332, 333, 349, 350, 352, 353, 358, 361, 387, 389
Boxer, S., 11, 22
Boyarin, D., 59
Boyd, D., 77, 80, 82, 84, 85, 96
Bradburn, N., 8
Bradbury, T. N., 253
Bradley, C., 251, 258
Bradley, S. J., 308
Braman, S., 96
Brannon, G. E., 533, 534
Brathwaite, B., 89

588

Brauer, M., 523, 530, 532
Braun, L., 334, 388
Braun-Harvey, D., 525, 526
Bray, A., 425
Brede, O., 126
Breedlove, M., 339
Breedlove, N., 339
Breedlove, S. M., 16, 18, 129, 299, 314, 325, 333, 334, 337, 338, 387, 388, 389, 404, 513, 515
Breiding, M. J., 479
Breines, J., 396
Brettell, C., 299
Brewer, C., 323
Briken, P., 146
Brill, S., 312
Brindis, C., 402
Brines, J., 426
Brooke, J., 422
Brooks, R. B., 507
Brooks-Gunn, J., 382, 383
Brott, A. A., 257, 264, 265, 282
Brotto, L. A., 335
Brown, J. S., 517
Brown, P., 60
Brown, S. L., 416
Brown, T. N. T., 327
Broyde, M. J., 59
Bryden, M. P., 322
Buchanan, E. A., 21, 23
Buck, P. O., 480
Budiharsana, M., 126
Bui, Q., 250
Buisson, O., 103
Bullough, V. L., 515, 524, 528
Bunce, M., 193
Burbage, A. M., 80
Burgess, E. O., 432, 435, 439, 517
Burns, A., 251, 397
Burri, A. V., 105
Buskirk, J., 346
Buss, D., 33, 34, 35, 37, 119, 144, 337, 338, 428, 451, 534
Buss, D. M., 410, 427
Butcher, K., 212
Butler, J., 342
Buttaro, M., 429
Buyken, A. E., 116
Byers, E. S., 466
Byrne, D., 450
Byrne, W., 338

C

Caceres, C. F., 351
Cahill, S., 326, 353, 359, 360, 361, 362, 363, 364
Calderone, M., 375, 376, 378
Califia, P., 84
Calzo, J. P., 333
Campos, B., 135
Candelario-Pérez, L. E., 525
Cantrill, J. A., 84
Caplan, S. E., 89
Carey, B., 347
Carillo, H., 52, 54, 351
Carlsson, U., 82, 84
Carnes, P., 506, 524, 528
Carpenter, B. N., 522
Carpenter, L., 136, 398, 414, 424
Carpenter, L. M., 436, 516
Carrier, J., 349
Carrington, C., 426, 519
Caruso, D., 8, 461
Carver, P. R., 341
Casad, B. J., 5
Casey, M. B., 322
Cassidy, J., 459

Castells, M., 76
Catania, J. A., 23, 336, 348, 357, 358
Cate, R. M., 466
Cates, W., 231, 232
Catlett, J., 454
Cecil, H., 150
Celeste, C., 78
Chaffin, M., 490
Chakraborty, S., 116
Chakraborty, T. R., 116
Chakravarty, M., 188, 189
Chama, N. B., 124
Chambers, M. K., 433
Chambers, S., 322
Chamie, J., 298, 299, 302, 326, 327
Chandra, A., 159, 349
Chang, M., 189
Chauncey, G., Jr., 346, 348
Chawada, B. L., 490, 492
Chen, J., 479
Chen, J. M., 433
Cheng, G., 116
Cherkas, L., 105
Chesson, H. W., 184
Cheung, P. S., 116
Cheyne, H., 277
Child, B., 81
Chivers, M. L., 142, 337
Chodorow, N., 318, 319
Choi, N., 317
Choi, S., 438, 439
Choi, S. K., 327
Chokshi, N., 437
Chopra, D., 375, 426, 434, 435, 436, 437, 438, 440, 507, 508
Christenson, S. E., 339
Chumlea, W., 385
Cianciotto, J., 353, 359, 360, 361, 362, 363, 364
Civic, D., 422
Clay-Warner, J., 323
Cleveland, J. C., 194
Clinton, A. M., 480
Clyde, M., 543
Coates, T. J., 336, 348, 351, 526
Cobb, R. J., 253
Cochran, S., 351
Cochran, S. D., 333
Cocks, H. G., 69
Cogan, J. C., 357
Cohan, C. L., 421, 423
Cohen, C., 322, 350
Cohen, S. A., 221
Cohler, B., 11, 22, 346, 514
Cohler, B. J., 138
Colapinto, J., 311
Cole, C., 469
Coleman, E., 19, 26, 27, 163, 522, 523, 525, 526
Coleman, J., 375, 378, 382, 383
Coleman, L., 375, 378, 382, 383, 398
Coley, R. L., 395
Collins, P. H., 9, 20, 322, 448, 490
Collins, S., 189
Collman, P., 320, 321
Colombo, B., 256
Comolli, J., 105
Conchola, J., 357, 358
Conger, R. D., 116, 383, 385
Conley, T. D., 340, 453
Connell, R. M., 299, 318, 319, 326
Connor, S., 270
Conopio, K., 386
Conron, K. J., 327
Conway, L., 309, 314
Cooke, B. M., 339
Coolidge, F. L., 33, 35, 37, 38
Coontz, S., 428
Cooper, A., 94
Copen, C., 159

Copen, C. E., 390
Corber, R., 76, 310, 346
Corey, L., 208
Corman, J. P., 484
Cornforth, T., 176
Correa, S., 19, 26, 27, 128, 136, 163, 164, 365, 486, 487, 488, 490, 492, 503, 504, 505, 506, 538, 542, 543
Cortina, L. M., 453
Cott, N., 12, 17, 319, 413, 425, 426, 428, 515
Cottinger, W. S., 460
Cotton, Q., 269
Cover, R., 312, 334, 353
Coyle, K., 402
Craig, S. L., 388
Crane, C. N., 315
Crane, J. P., 272
Crenshaw, T. L., 113
Crews, D., 307, 319
Crockett, L. J., 250, 373, 383
Cromwell, J., 312, 314
Cross, C., 479, 480, 502
Csikszentmihalyi, M., 5
Culhane, J., 280
Cullen, F. T., 489, 490
Currah, P., 97
Curtis, D., 212
Curtis, G. B., 267, 268, 270, 271, 276, 279, 383
Cusick, L., 188
Cutler, B., 541
Cutler, N., 541

D

Dabul, A. J., 291
Dailard, C., 209, 232
Dake, J. A., 81
D'Alton, M. E., 272
Daniélou, A., 57
Darbes, L., 188, 189
Dar-Nimrod, I., 334
Darwin, C., 34
Das, A., 8, 11, 13, 136, 154, 318, 410, 429, 430, 431, 435, 436, 438, 439, 440, 516, 518, 519, 520, 547
D'Augelli, A., 354, 358
Davidoff, K. C., 313, 357
Davidson, D., 125
Davidson, J., 306
Davidson, M., 308, 312
Davies, C., 333
Davies, D., 520
Davies, P., 208
Davis, D., 460
Davis, L., 402
Davis, L. S., 313, 357
Davis, N. L., 269
Davis, S., 523, 530, 532
Dawkins, R., 55, 534
Day, M., 484, 486
Dean, H. D., 194
DeAngelis, T., 264
DeCuypere, G., 316
Deehan, A., 378, 379
Deepalika, D. M., 188, 189
DeFrain, J., 432
Dekker, R. M., 345
DeLamater, J., 136, 414, 426, 436, 438, 440, 518, 520
DeLeon, G. L., 80, 89
Delevi, R., 82
del Hoyo, J., 497
DeMeo, J., 111, 126, 129
D'Emilio, J. D., 8, 45, 50, 61, 310, 341, 346, 348, 363, 431, 447
Demmons, S., 466
Dennis, M. R., 466

Derogatis, L. R., 523, 530, 532
de Santisteban, P., 497
Deschner, A., 221
De Sutter, P., 316
DeVries, B., 342, 349, 357, 433, 434, 438, 439, 440
de Vries, H., 422, 423
DeVries, J., 39
Devroey, D., 159
de Waal, F., 33, 379
De Wit, C. Y., 446
Diamond, J., 19, 33
Diamond, L. M., 16, 18, 21, 129, 136, 141, 145, 299, 308, 314, 320, 333, 334, 335, 336, 337, 338, 340, 341, 342, 348, 349, 351, 352, 353, 354, 371, 372, 380, 387, 388, 389, 404, 427, 445, 447, 448, 451, 452, 513, 515
Diaz, R., 358, 363
Diaz, R. M., 349, 351, 365, 525, 537
Dicke, J. M., 272
Dickenson, J. A., 352, 523, 525
Dickey, R., 339
Dickson-Swift, V., 417, 424
Diefenbach, P., 154
Diener, E., 8, 17, 410
Diener, R. B., 8, 410
Di Giulio, P., 411, 418, 419, 422
Dillon, B. E., 124
DiMaggio, P., 78
DiMauro, D., 17, 19, 244, 289, 292, 293
DiNenno, E., 159
Dion, K. K., 447
Dittus, P. J., 393
Dixon, A., 34
Dodge, B., 13, 149, 150, 172, 188, 356, 360, 515, 536, 544, 545, 546, 547
Dolezal, C., 339
Dover, K. J., 344
Dreger, A. D., 302, 307, 308, 311
Dresel, A., 269
Driscoll, A. K., 278
Drouin, M., 82
Duberman, M., 346
Duggan, S. J., 125
Dukes, K., 272
Duncan, P., 378
Dunham, C., 257, 273
Dunne, E., 184
Dunne, M. P., 341, 349
Dunson, D. B., 256
Durik, A., 426
Durkheim, E., 56
Dush, C., 421, 423

E

Eccles, J. S., 322
Edelman, B., 96
Edgerton, R. B., 307
Edleman, K. A., 272
Edwards, B. K., 181
Edwards, C., 319, 320
Edwards, J. N., 436
Efstathiou, G., 33
Egan, S. K., 341
Eggermont, S., 75
Ehrensaft, D., 312
Ehrhardt, E., 145, 299, 302, 325, 337, 340, 341, 371, 537
Ehrman, B. D., 43
Eisen, S., 358
El-Bassel, N., 189
Elder, G. H., Jr., 116, 383, 385
Elders, M. J., 168, 169
Eleuteri, S., 80
Elias, J. E., 154
Eliason, M. J., 348
Ellington, S., 23, 55, 56, 348, 418, 421, 422, 431

Elliott, I. A., 498
Ellis, L., 337
El-Rouayher, K., 60
Elton, C., 285
Emens, E. F., 417
Emerson, M., 62
Engelman, P., 217, 218, 219, 237, 244, 288
Engels, R., 390
Ennett, S. T., 504
Ensler, E., 319
Enzlin, P., 144, 335
Epprecht, M., 16, 18, 129, 299, 314, 325, 333, 334, 337, 338, 387, 388, 389, 404, 513, 515
Epstein, R. J., 21, 116
Epstein, S., 17, 21, 354, 365
Erazo, T., 313, 357
Erber, M. W., 154, 155, 447, 450, 451, 466
Erber, R., 154, 155, 447, 450, 451, 466
Erickson, R. J., 462
Erzen, T., 343, 354
Espey, D. K., 181
Espiritu, Y., 9
Esposito, L., 81, 85, 96
Ess, C., 23
Estes, R. J., 504, 506
Ethier, K. A., 393
Evans, K., 541
Everaerd, W., 518
Evers, S. M., 49

F

Fahs, B., 168
Farhat, T., 391
Farmer, P., 26, 189, 212, 486, 487, 504
Faulkner, C., 361
Faulkner, S. L., 422
Fausto-Sterling, A., 101, 128, 299, 307, 319, 340
Fay, J., 401
Feinberg, L., 312
Feingold, A., 449
Fenstermaker, S., 484
Fenton, K. A., 194
Fenwick, H., 128
Fergal, D. M., 272
Ferguson, K. M., 504, 506
Feria, A., 5
Fertig, J. W., 123
Fields, J., 17, 20, 23, 25
Fine, M., 350
Finkelhor, D., 84, 85, 494, 529, 533
Firestone, L., 454
Firestone, R. W., 454
First, M. B., 146
Fisang, C., 126
Fischer, N., 126
Fisher, B. S., 489, 490
Fisher, H., 35, 37, 49, 136, 417, 445, 447, 448, 451
Fisher, N. J., 375, 377, 378, 379, 380
Fisher, S., 145
Fisher, W. A., 56, 93
Fitzpatrick, C., 378, 379
Fitzsimons, G. M., 89
Flores, A. R., 327
Floyd, D., 275
Floyd, F. J., 17, 325, 333, 334, 340, 342, 349, 352
Follette, W. C., 460
Ford, C. S., 49, 51, 52, 251, 299, 323, 335, 371, 375, 379, 427
Forgeard, M. J. C., 8, 17
Fortenberry, J. D., 158, 172, 343, 544, 545, 546, 547
Foucault, M., 9, 11, 15, 45, 46, 50, 307, 345, 447, 513, 515, 536, 537
Fox, C., 417, 424
Fox, J., 77
Francis, L. J., 322

Franek, J., 180
Fraser, G., 334
Frederick, D. A., 111
Fredland, N. M., 502, 503
Fredrickson, B., 469
Free, C., 65
Freedman, E. B., 8, 45, 50, 61, 310, 341, 431, 447
Freeman-Longo, R. E., 94
Freer, A. S., 504, 506
Freitas, D., 84, 96
Freud, S., 11, 22, 134, 145, 299, 345, 375, 533
Freund, K., 533
Friedl, E., 318, 319, 428
Friedman, M. R., 356, 360
Friedman, T., 96
Friedrich, W., 375, 377, 378, 379, 380, 382, 385
Fritz, M. A., 119, 223, 241
Frohwirth, L. F., 289
Frolich, J. A., 212
Frost, D. M., 354, 355, 361, 430
Frost, J. J., 244
Fu, T-C, 13, 188, 536, 544
Fu, T-C (Jane), 149, 150, 515
Fuhrman, J., 115, 116
Fulbright, Y., 446
Fuller, C. J., 40, 57
Fullilove, R. E., 194
Furman, W., 385
Futch, V., 251, 397

G

Gabhain, S. N., 391
Gaetano, P., 311
Gage, A. J., 112
Gagnon, J., 11, 12, 13, 14, 52, 82, 136, 140, 150, 335, 353, 415, 431, 445, 452, 453, 515, 527, 541
Gagnon, J. H., 9, 13, 16, 17, 22, 23, 48, 52, 56, 62, 63, 136, 299, 334, 336, 337, 342, 348, 349, 352, 365, 373, 380, 389, 415, 421, 423, 426, 429, 430, 435, 449, 513, 515, 535, 537, 538, 546, 547
Gagnon, J. J., 336, 348, 351
Galambos, C. M., 292
Galatzer-Levy, R. M., 346, 514
Galey, P., 111
Gallagher, M., 410, 414, 426, 430
Gallant, M., 252
Gallegher, S., 62
Gallucci, G., 402
Gallup, G. G., 154
Galvan, F., 528, 529, 530
Gámez-Guadix, M., 497
Gamson, J., 70
Gangestad, S. W., 33, 37, 114
Garanzini, S., 469
Garcia, J., 417
Garcia, J. R., 415
Garcia-Coll, C., 307, 319
Gardner, H., 534
Garnets, L. D., 340, 453
Garofalo, R., 349, 353
Garos, S., 522
Gartrell, N., 364
Gates, G., 418, 419
Gautier, R., 306
Gautier, T., 305
Gavey, N., 438, 518, 519
Gazi, R., 504
Ge, X., 116, 383, 385
Gebhard, P., 13, 51, 134, 375
Geertz, C., 33, 40, 73
Geertz, G., 60
Gelman, S., 221, 320, 321
Gemmel, M., 193
Gerlach, S., 116

Germon, J., 298
Gerrard, M., 221
Gershon, I., 78, 82, 83
Gesselman, A., 417
Ghassemi, A., 172, 544, 545, 546, 547
Gheysen, R., 144
Ghoncheh, M., 172
Giaccardi, S., 453
Gibson, P., 358
Gibson L., 20, 495, 506, 508
Giddens, A., 49, 78, 319, 513
Gijs, L., 335
Gilbert, L., 189
Gilbert, M. R., 96
Gilbert, T. P., 193
Gilding, M., 455
Gillespie-Sells, K., 520
Gilliland, R., 522
Gillis, J. R., 357
Gingell, C., 3, 8, 154, 155, 410, 415, 430, 435, 436, 439, 519, 520
Girard, A., 525
Glasser, D. B., 3, 8, 154, 155, 410, 415, 430, 435, 436, 439, 519, 520
Gleason, J., 392
Gleason, M. J., 89
Gleason, N., 523
Glunt, E. K., 357
Gmeiner, M., 96
Godeau, E., 391
Godelier, M., 318
Goetz, H. T., 417
Goldberg, J., 358
Goldberg, P. J., 113
Goldhammer, H., 357
Golding, J. M., 483, 484, 490
Goldman, J., 52, 371, 376, 378
Goldman, R., 52, 371, 376, 378
Goldsteen, K., 426
Goldstein, I., 523, 530, 532
Goldstein, J. R., 414
Goldstein, S., 507
Gonzaga, G. C., 135
Gonzales-Lopez, G., 293, 448
Goodman, D., 269
Goodman, E., 349, 353
Goodwin, M., 244, 543
Gordon, L., 217, 218, 219
Gorzalka, B. B., 335
Gosling, S. D., 136, 451
Gott, M., 438
Gottman, J. M., 432, 468, 469, 470, 471, 472
Grace, V. M., 438, 518, 519
Graham, A. L., 77
Graham C. A., 144
Grant, J. E., 522
Grauvogl, A., 49
Gray, D. L., 272
Gray, N. J., 78, 84
Grce, M., 208
Greaves, L. M., 334
Gree, A. S., 89
Greenberg, D., 45, 60, 127, 343, 344, 354, 537
Greene, G. J., 333, 334, 336, 337
Greene, J. M., 504
Gregoire, A., 180
Gregor, T., 537
Greil, A. L., 251, 252
Gressgård, R., 335
Grim, B. J., 60
Grobler, A. C., 212
Grogan, S., 125
Groneman, C., 9, 524
Gross, L., 354
Grubbs, J. B., 523
Guerra-Reyes, L., 13, 188, 536, 544
Guest, F., 231, 232
Guggino, J. M., 391

Günther, A. L., 116
Guthrie, D., 22
Guzman, B. L., 5

H

Haavio-Mannila, E., 439
Haffner, D. W., 376, 379, 403
Hagan, J. F., 378
Hald, G. M., 141
Halkitis, P. N., 525
Hall, P. C., 75
Hallford, B. J., 81
Halperin, D., 342, 449, 452, 453
Halpern, C. T., 391
Hamby, S. L., 494
Hamilton, B. E., 278, 391
Hammack, P., 138, 333, 342
Hammar, L., 351
Hammersmith, S., 452
Hampson, J. G., 340
Hampson, J. L., 340
Handsfield, H., 208
Handy, B., 541
Hargittai, E., 78, 96
Hariri, S., 184
Harkins, L., 497
Harper, A., 504
Harper, C. R., 393
Harris, L., 353
Harrison, L., 81, 84
Harrison, M. A., 154
Harvey, P., 506
Haselkorn, T., 193
Hatcher, R. A., 231, 232, 238
Hathaway, J. E., 479, 480
Haucke, M., 446
Haugaard, J. J., 496
Haupert, M., 417
Hauser, A., 440
Hauser, S., 126
Hawkins, J., 429
Hayes, E., 498
Hazan, C., 459
Heap, C., 47
Hedges, L., 322
Hehman, E., 433
Hekma, G., 449
Heldman, C., 415, 416
Henderson, M., 372, 383
Hendrick, C., 459
Hendrick, S. S., 459
Hendrickson, A., 322
Henning, K., 145
Henry, J., 438
Hensel, D. J., 343
Henson, J. M., 396
Herbenick, D., 13, 17, 149, 150, 172, 188, 356, 360, 513, 515, 536, 537, 544, 545, 546, 547
Herdt, G., 3, 9, 12, 13, 15, 17, 18, 19, 21, 25, 33, 35, 37, 39, 49, 51, 52, 53, 54, 55, 58, 62, 70, 96, 134, 135, 138, 140, 145, 156, 163, 218, 251, 258, 275, 284, 299, 306, 307, 318, 320, 321, 323, 326, 332, 333, 334, 336, 337, 341, 342, 343, 344, 345, 349, 350, 352, 353, 354, 356, 357, 358, 361, 362, 363, 365, 375, 376, 378, 379, 380, 381, 385, 387, 389, 403, 422, 427, 428, 433, 434, 438, 439, 440, 449, 451, 490, 504, 516, 529, 537, 538
Herek, G. M., 17, 326, 353, 354, 355, 357, 358, 361, 364, 514, 525
Herman, D., 310
Herman, J. L., 312, 316, 327, 348, 354, 363, 416, 420, 430, 433
Herman-Giddens, M. E., 382
Hermanns, J., 364
Hernandez, A. E., 498

Herrell, R., 358
Hershberger, S. L., 358
Hess, A., 269
Hess, E., 34
Hess, K. L., 159
Hesterberg, L., 361
Hewitt, E., 426
Hickey, M. T., 240
Higdon, M. J., 312
Hill, D. B., 322
Hill, J., 189
Hill, R. P., 289
Hillier, L., 81, 84
Hills, S., 75
Himes, J., 385
Himmerick, K., 242
Hinchliff, S., 438
Hine, C., 77
Hines, D. A., 484, 496, 498
Hines, M., 302, 320
Hirsch, A., 141
Hirsch, J., 18, 23, 39, 49, 51, 135, 318, 351, 410, 417, 428, 431, 445, 537
Hitlin, P., 78
Hoch, Z., 105
Hochschild, A., 462
Hoebeke, P., 316
Hoff, C., 188, 189
Hoffman, A., 351
Hoffman, J., 82
Hollander, E., 522
Holloway, S. L., 80, 84
Holm, J., 58
Holmes, A., 277
Homko, C., 96
Honig, S. C., 124
Hoo, E., 393
Hook, E. B., 256
Hook, J. N., 522
Hooker, E., 347
Hopkins, J., 285
Horn, S. S., 326
Horowitz, H. L., 346
Horowitz, L. M., 459
Hoss, R. A., 447
Hosseini, L., 283
Houk, C. P., 303
House, J. S., 426
Houston, M., 375, 378, 380
Howe, C., 3, 17, 19
Howell, E. A., 282
Howells, K., 529, 533
Hrdy, S. B., 249, 251, 375, 379, 385
Hsu, B., 154
Huang, A. J., 517
Huberman, A. D., 339
Huberman, B., 403
Huebner, D. M., 358, 363, 395
Hughes, I. A., 303
Hughes, S. M., 154
Hull, E., 148, 350
Hull, I., 43
Hull, T. H., 126
Hulse-Killacky, D., 508
Hunsberger, B., 252
Hunt, A., 378
Hunt, L., 26, 27
Hunter, J., 334, 388
Huppin, M., 93, 404, 498
Hyde, J. S., 318, 321, 426
Hydy, S., 34

I

Ilkkaracan, P., 164
Imperato-McGinley, J., 305, 306
Impett, E. A., 49, 372, 396, 397

Ing, S., 137, 138, 141, 145, 379, 399
Ingham, R., 401
Ingraham, N., 143
Irvine, J., 8, 9, 10, 12, 14, 18, 82, 169, 299, 364, 371, 393, 398, 403, 513, 515
Ivy, W., 159

J

Jacklin, C. N., 319, 322
Jackson, H. J., 529
Jacob, B. A., 321
Jacobs, M. A., 77
Jacobs, S. E., 344
Jacobson, T., 319
James, S. E., 312, 316
Jankowiak, W., 52, 135, 136, 445, 447, 448
Jannini, E. A., 103, 523, 530, 532
Jansen, K. L., 61
Janssen, E., 144
Jasilioniene, A., 411, 418, 419, 422
Jayawickreme, E., 8, 17
Jayne, P., 185, 188
Jenness, V., 484
Jennings, S., 378, 379
Jensen, J. T., 245
Jetha, C., 140, 144
Jewell, J. A., 483, 484, 490
Joffe, C., 17, 19, 27, 217, 219, 244, 289, 292, 293
Johns, M., 185, 188
Johnson, A. L., 77
Johnson, E. P., 196, 349, 350
Johnson, J., 212
Johnson, T. M., 60
Johnson, V. E., 138, 141, 146, 148, 283
Johnston, J., 80
Jolley, S. N., 270
Jolly, M., 323, 427, 541
Jones, J., 12, 86, 91, 189, 349
Jones, R. K., 82, 289
Jones, R. L., 194
Jones, W. H., 424
Jordan, L., 269
Jordan-Young, R., 8, 19, 339, 340, 375, 515
Josephy, A., Jr., 218, 219
Juang, R. M., 97
Jurgens, R., 484, 486
Juul, A., 116, 383, 385

K

Kabongo, J-M., 193
Kadia, A., 490, 492
Kafka, M. P., 522, 523
Kahn, A. S., 416
Kalengayi, M., 193
Kalick, S. M., 447
Kamdar, Z., 490, 492
Kang, J. H., 3, 8, 154, 155, 410, 415, 430, 435, 436, 439, 519, 520
Kantor, L., 91, 403
Kaplan, H., 148
Kaplan, M. S., 146, 524, 528
Kapumba, B., 127
Karaolis-Danckert, N., 116
Karim, Q. A., 212
Karim, S. S. A., 212
Karkazis, K., 302, 307, 311
Karraker, K. H., 320
Katchadourian, H., 388
Katz, J. N., 341
Katz-Wise, S. L., 333, 334
Kaufman, F. R., 302
Kaufman, J., 353, 387
Kegeles, S. M., 358

Keir, J., 327
Keisling, M., 312, 316
Keizer, R., 411, 418, 419, 422
Keller, L., 322
Keltner, D., 135
Kembel, H. B., 483, 484, 490
Kendrick, K. M., 114
Kennedy, P., 62
Kenney, C. T., 414
Keppler, A., 281
Kern, M., 8, 17
Kerrigan, K., 128
Kertzner, R., 343, 422
Kessler, C., 154
Kessler, S. J., 311, 312
Khan, M., 212
Kharbutli, Y., 272
Khattak, S., 96
Kidwai, S., 58
Kilbride, P., 251, 258
Killaspy, H., 358
Killermann, S., 311, 312
Kim, Y. J., 436, 516
Kimmel, M., 356
King, K. A., 77, 80
King, M., 358
King, R., 142
King, S., 127
King, S. A., 94
Kingsberg, S. A., 114, 435
Kinnish, K. K., 334
Kinsey, A., 92
Kinsey, A., 11, 13, 51, 52, 56, 82, 125, 134, 136, 141, 145, 299, 319, 334, 335, 349, 373, 375, 378, 384, 417, 513, 526, 538
Kirby, D., 3, 17, 85, 185, 244, 288, 371, 396, 400, 401, 402
Kirk, K. M., 341, 349
Kirkman, L., 417, 424
Kirkman, M., 142
Kirmeyer, S., 391
Klassen, P., 339
Kleese, C., 417, 431
Klein, F., 334, 335, 349, 451
Klein, J. D., 78, 84
Klein, L. K., 63
Klein, M., 19, 84, 404, 533, 543
Kleinplatz, P. J., 529
Klernan, K., 253
Klettke, B., 81
Klinenberg, E., 410, 412, 415, 432
Kling, A., 154
Klinkenberg, W., 21
Kloess, J. A., 497
Klohnen, E. C., 451
Knapke, K., 154
Knight, W. G., 508
Koch, M., 88
Koeniger-Donohue, R., 429
Koff, B., 356, 358, 361, 362, 363
Kohler, P. K., 400
Kolahi, A. A., 283
Kolata, G., 430
Koletic, G., 396
Kolios, K., 91, 403
Kolmes, K., 532
Kon, I., 221
Kontula, O., 439
Koontz, S., 414
Korbin, J., 487, 488, 490
Kornrich, S., 426
Kosambiya, J. K., 490, 492
Kost, K., 399
Koukounas, E., 141
Kovic, A. G., 525
Kowal, D., 231, 232
Krajnik, M., 318
Kranz, S., 116

Kraus, S. W., 146
Kregeles, S. M., 395
Kresnow, M., 479
Kreuzer, G., 88
Kreyenfeld, M., 411, 418, 419, 422
Kristof, N., 490, 504, 506, 543
Kroke, A., 116
Krueger, R. B., 146, 523, 524, 528
Kuhn, T., 45
Kuhns, J. B., 20
Kulin, H., 385
Kumari, R., 264
Kung, T., 189
Kunkel, A., 466
Kuntsman, K., 193
Kuper, L., 333, 334, 336, 337
Kuppermann, M., 517
Kurdek, L. A., 469
Kuzma, J. M., 528, 529

L

Laan, E., 518, 523, 530, 532
Lacquer, T., 151
Ladas, A., 105
Lafferty, W. E., 400
LaHood, G., 327
Lake, M. A., 320
Lamb, S., 378
Lambert, J. D., 426
Lambert, T. A., 416
Lamphere, L., 319
Lamptey, P., 212
Lance, L. M., 361
Landing, F., 34
Landis, K. R., 426
Landolt, M. A., 325
Lang, S., 265, 344
Langley, L. L., 219
Langlois, J. H., 447
Lappegård, T., 411, 418, 419, 422
Laris, B. A., 400
LaSala, M., 356, 358, 360, 362, 363, 417
Lash, D., 125
Lathen, L., 269
Laumann, E. O., 3, 8, 9, 11, 13, 16, 17, 22, 23, 48, 52, 56, 62, 63, 136, 154, 155, 173, 299, 318, 334, 336, 337, 342, 348, 349, 352, 373, 380, 389, 410, 415, 418, 421, 422, 423, 426, 429, 430, 431, 435, 436, 438, 439, 440, 452, 515, 516, 518, 519, 520, 535, 537, 538, 546, 547
Laurence, C., 212
Lawler-Sagarin, K. A., 541
Lawrence, E., 253
Leavitt, S. C., 12, 427, 428
Lee, J. A., 456
Lee, J. K. P., 529
Lee, J. Y., 252
Lee, P., 385
Lee, S., 250, 373, 383, 504, 506
Lee, S. J., 252
Lehavot, K., 430
Leitenberg, H., 20, 145, 495, 506, 508
Lenhart, A., 78, 81, 83
Lepani, K., 135, 257, 258, 428, 537
Lerner, R., 249, 380
Lester, T., 325
Letrourneau, E., 490
Leung, A., 377
Leupp, K., 426
LeVay, S., 337, 340
Levenson, R. W., 469
Leventhal, H., 282
Lever, J., 111
Levin, D., 244
Levin, R., 114
Levin, R. J., 103, 148, 350

Levine, D., 78, 80, 84, 96, 449
Levine, E., 76
Levine, J., 491
Levine, M. P., 365, 449, 525
Levine, T. R., 422, 423
Levinson, B., 3, 8, 154, 155, 410, 415, 430, 435, 436, 439, 519, 520
Levinson, D., 487
Levinson, W., 429, 436, 438, 439, 440
Levi-Strauss, C., 71, 73
Levkoff, L., 388, 389
Lewin, E., 363
Lewis, M., 217, 218
Lewis, V. G., 301
Lezin, N., 402
Liamputtong, P., 257
Libuda, L., 116
Lichter, D. T., 424, 425, 426
Liddon, N., 185, 188
Lieberman, H., 309
Lindau, S. T., 429, 436, 438, 439, 440
Lindberg, L. D., 244, 396
Lippman, J. R., 453
Livingston, G., 252
Livingstone, S., 80, 84
Llakkuvan, V., 77
Lombardi, C. M., 395
Long, L., 487, 490, 504, 506, 543
Lopater, S., 429
Luker, K., 55
Lunan, C. B., 277
Luo, S., 451
Luria, Z., 320
Lykins, A. D., 335
Lynch, A. D., 395
Lynch, K. R., 483, 484, 490
Lyon, M., 49, 371, 393, 396, 398
Lyon-Amos, M., 432
Lyons, A. P., 35, 49, 51, 537
Lyons, H. D., 35, 49, 537
Lyons-Amos, M., 411, 418, 421, 422, 423

M

Mabilia, M., 284
MacCartney, D., 488
Maccoby, E. E., 319, 320, 321
Machacek, D. W., 40, 55, 56
MacMillan, R., 492
MacNeil, S., 466
Macones, G. A., 272
MacPhee, M., 139, 140
Madden, M., 78, 83
Maddow-Zimet, I., 396, 399
Madey, S. F., 459
Madisen, R., 56
Madkour, A. S., 391
Mahalik, J. R., 395
Mahan Buttaro, T. M., 429
Mahay, J., 23, 56, 348, 416, 418, 421, 422, 431
Mahdavi, P., 60
Mahler, M., 356
Maier, T., 8, 14, 15
Maines, R. P., 536
Major, B., 289, 292
Mak, J., 116
Makadon, H., 357
Malach-Pines, A., 445
Malcolm, A., 101, 351
Malinowski, B., 258, 537
Malley-Morrison, K., 484, 496, 498
Maloy, K., 289
Man, C. D., 484
Mandeville-Norden, R., 498
Manhart, L. W., 400
Manley, M. H., 427
Manning, J. C., 522

Manning, W. D., 416
Manning J., 84, 93, 95, 416
Mansor, L. E., 212
Marcussen, K., 426
Markman, H. J., 421
Markowitz, L., 184
Marks, C., 26, 163
Marks, N., 426
Marshall, W. L., 490
Martin, C., 11, 13, 51, 52, 56, 82, 92, 125, 134, 136, 145, 299, 319, 320, 334, 335, 349, 373, 375, 378, 384, 415, 417, 513, 526, 538
Martin, J., 114, 115, 118, 119, 123, 134, 135, 136, 282, 337, 379, 381, 382, 427, 428, 449, 450
Martin, J. A., 278, 391
Martin, N. G., 341, 349
Martin, R., 109, 257
Martinez, G., 390
Marx, B. P., 20, 495
Marzullo, M., 17, 62, 341, 354, 361
Mashburn, J., 178
Masho, S. W., 480
Mastekaasa, A., 421, 422
Masters, W. H., 138, 141, 146, 148, 283
Masucci, M., 96
Mathews, T. J., 278, 391
Matthews, B., 8
Matuszewich, L., 541
Maurice, W. L., 518, 520
Mayer, J. D., 8, 461
Mayer, K., 357
Mays, V., 351
Mays, V. M., 333
Maziarz, L., 81
McAuslan, P., 480
McBride, D., 386
McBride, K. R., 158
McCabe, M. P., 141
McCafferty, C., 462
McCann, C., 219, 220
McClelland, S., 168
McClelland, S. I., 350
McClintock, M., 18, 114, 134, 144, 156, 299, 321, 332, 333, 334, 337, 343, 380, 381, 385, 449, 451, 529
McCoy, K., 469
McCreary, D. R., 125
McCulloch, S., 273
McDonald, K., 142
McDonald, P., 426
McDougall, A., 257, 273
McElroy, J. C., 447
McInerney, D. M., 80, 89
McInroy, L., 388
Mcintyre, P., 26, 163
McKay, S., 80, 84
McKee, A., 395
McKenna, K. Y. A., 89
McKinley, L., 21
McKusick, L., 525
McNab, W., 438
McQuillan, J., 251, 252
Mead, M., 12, 35, 37, 40, 47, 51, 251, 318, 319, 427, 428, 429, 449, 537
Meerwijk, E., 311
Meeus, W., 390
Megge, S., 120
Meggiolaro, S., 7, 8
Meier, A., 385
Mellor, D. J., 81
Menacker, F., 391
Merelli, A., 163, 164
Merianos, A., 77, 80
Merrick, M. T., 479
Merry, S. E., 27, 293, 483, 486, 487, 488, 490, 492
Meston, C. M., 34, 35, 37, 119, 148, 350
Meyer, I. H., 20, 353, 354, 355, 358, 361, 430, 438, 439

Meyer-Bahlburg, H., 301
Meyer-Bahlburg, H. F. L., 339
Meyerowitz, J., 309
Meyers, D. T., 251
Michael, H., 523
Michael, R. T., 9, 13, 16, 17, 22, 23, 48, 52, 56, 62, 63, 136, 155, 299, 334, 336, 337, 342, 348, 349, 352, 373, 380, 389, 415, 421, 423, 426, 430, 431, 435, 452, 515, 535, 537, 538, 546, 547
Michael, S., 535, 537
Michaels, S., 9, 13, 16, 17, 22, 23, 48, 52, 56, 62, 63, 136, 155, 299, 334, 336, 337, 342, 348, 349, 351, 352, 373, 380, 389, 415, 421, 423, 426, 429, 431, 435, 452, 515, 538, 546
Mikulincer, M., 459
Miller, A., 26, 27, 163
Miller, C. C., 250
Mills, M., 426
Mills, T., 357, 358
Miner, 523
Miner, M., 523, 525
Minnis, A. M., 420
Minter, S. P., 97
Mirkin, B., 298, 299, 302, 326, 327
Mirowsky, J., 426
Mitchell, K., 84, 85
Mitchell, K. J., 81, 84
Mittelstaedt, J. D., 392, 399
Mkandawire-Valhmu, L., 269
Moger, W., 105
Mollica, R., 440
Money, J., 9, 145, 168, 299, 301, 302, 306, 325, 333, 334, 337, 340, 341, 371, 513, 524, 531, 534, 537, 544, 545
Montemayor, R., 75, 376, 378, 379, 389, 395, 396, 399
Moore, A., 3, 8, 17, 49, 51, 52, 56, 289, 319, 320, 371, 373, 375, 380, 387, 403, 404, 462, 529
Moore, J. N., 392, 399
Moore, M. M., 465
Moors, A., 417
Mora, P., 282
Moran, D., 212
Morandini, J. S., 334
Morgan, T., 304
Morin, J., 333
Morris, E., 185, 188
Morris, N. M., 257
Morrison, S. D., 315
Morrow, P. C., 447
Moser, C., 529, 530, 532
Mosher, W., 105
Mosher, W. D., 159, 221
Moskowitz, J., 357, 358
Mottet, L., 312, 316
Moynihan, T. J., 180
Mucci, L. A., 479, 480
Müller, M. D., 126
Munns, R., 525
Munoz-Laboy, 351
Munoz-Laboy, M., 349, 351, 363
Murdock, G. P., 127, 284
Murphy, T., 338, 346
Mustanski, B., 333, 334, 336, 337
Muyembe, J-J., 193
Myers, F., 257, 273
Myers, H. F., 528, 529, 530

N

Nadal, K. L., 313, 357
Nardi, P. M., 365, 449
Nash, E., 287, 288
Nasr, V., 59
Nathanson, C., 18, 23, 39, 49, 51, 135, 318, 351, 410, 417, 428, 431, 445, 448, 537

Name Index

Nathanson, C. A., 436, 516
Nazareth, I., 358
Nedelman, M., 315
Needleman, R., 249, 376, 378
Nehm, R. H., 113
Neilands, T., 188, 189
Neilands, T. B., 395
Nelson, A. L., 231, 232
Neuman, G., 431
New, M. I., 339
Newell, M., 127
Newport, F., 418
Newton, E., 345
Ngun, T. C., 337
Noonan, R., 483
Norman, B. M., 276, 278, 279
Northrup, C., 516, 547
Nowak, M., 484, 486
Nowell, A., 322
Noyce, P. R., 84
Nussbaum, M., 515
Nuttall, R. L., 322

O

Oberschneider, M., 18, 333, 380, 451
O'Callaghan, T., 175, 245
Odem, M. E., 323
Odibo, A. O., 272
O'Donnell, M. D. S., 43
Ofosu, E. K., 433
O'Grady, K. E., 449
Okami, P., 379
Oliver, M., 520
Olmstead, R., 379
Oloruntoba-Oju, T., 109
Olsen, L. W., 116, 383, 385
Olson, D. H., 432
Olukotun, O., 269
Olyslager, F., 309, 314
O'Muircheartaigh, C. A., 429, 436, 438, 440
Oosterhuis, H., 8, 9, 10, 314, 345, 513, 516
Oosthuizen, H., 504
Oram, D., 325
Orel, N. A., 440
Oriel, J., 164
Orloff, M., 445
Ortiz de Montellayano, B., 218, 219
Osborn, D., 358
Osgerby, B., 84
Osterman, M. J. K., 278
Ostrow, D. G., 526
Ott, M. A., 49, 371, 393, 396, 398
Overbeek, G., 390
Owens, A., 101, 520, 545
Owens, E. W., 84, 93, 95, 416, 520

P

Paabo, S., 35
Padilla, M., 344, 351, 503, 504, 506, 541, 542, 543
Padva, G., 541
Paik, A., 3, 8, 23, 154, 155, 173, 348, 410, 415, 416, 421, 422, 430, 431, 435, 436, 439, 519, 520
Paiva, A., 26, 163
Pancer, S. M., 252
Parashar, A., 58
Parikh, S., 18, 23, 39, 49, 51, 135, 318, 351, 410, 417, 428, 431, 445, 448, 537
Parker, R., 10, 14, 19, 26, 27, 101, 128, 129, 136, 163, 164, 189, 343, 351, 354, 365, 486, 487, 488, 490, 492, 503, 504, 505, 506, 538, 542, 543

Parmely, S. M., 251
Parrinder, G., 55, 56
Parsons, B., 338
Parsons, J. T., 525
Parsons, W. A., 34
Pascoe, C. J., 20, 22, 23, 78, 80, 81, 84, 85, 86, 89, 96, 97, 169, 321, 326, 360, 395, 492, 500, 502, 503
Passet, J. E., 217
Patel, D., 240
Patil, S., 95
Patterson, C. J., 343
Patterson, M. J., 289
Pattison, P., 529
Paul, J. P., 357, 358
Paul, P., 146
Payne, J. S., 528, 529, 530
Payne, K. K., 416
Paz-Bailey, G., 159
Pearce, C. L., 116
Pepitone, M. E., 339
Peplau, L. A., 111, 340, 453
Pepper, R., 312
Perel, E., 125, 340, 415, 420, 422, 424, 429, 432, 524
Perelli-Harris, B., 411, 418, 419, 421, 422, 423, 424, 426, 432, 435
Perez, M. G., 315
Perlman, D., 325
Perper, T., 465
Perrin, E., 364
Perry, D. G., 341
Perry, J. D., 105
Perry, S. L., 146, 525
Petchesky, R., 19, 26, 27, 128, 129, 136, 163, 164, 292, 365, 486, 487, 488, 490, 503, 504, 505, 506, 538, 542, 543
Peter, J., 85, 93, 94, 95, 396
Peters, M. L., 49
Petersen, E. E., 269
Peterson, M. M., 284
Peterson, R. E., 305, 306
Petronio, S., 466
Pettinato, M., 270
Pezaris, E., 322
Pflugfeltder, G., 344
Phinney, H., 18, 23, 39, 49, 51, 135, 318, 410, 417, 428, 431, 445, 537
Phipps, W. E., 61
Pike, M. C., 116
Pilkington, N. W., 358
Pillard, R. D., 338
Pincott, J., 416
Pinker, S., 10
Pinkerton, S. D., 93, 140, 150, 404, 498
Pinon, R., Jr., 259
Pittman, F., 431
Planchon, L. A., 94
Plummer, C. A., 496
Plummer, K., 138, 395
Polen-Petit, N., 77
Pollack, L., 357, 358
Pomeroy, W., 11, 13, 51, 52, 56, 82, 92, 125, 134, 136, 145, 299, 319, 334, 335, 349, 373, 375, 378, 384, 415, 417, 513, 526, 538
Ponterotto, J. G., 21
Ponzetti, J. J., Jr., 391
Potenza, M. N., 522
Potter, J., 357
Potts, A., 438, 518, 519
Pournamdar, Z., 172
Powell, D., 353, 387
Prakash, V., 107
Pratt, M., 252
Preciado, M., 469
Preston-Whyte, E., 504
Price, D., 325

Price, J., 96
Price, J. H., 81
Prothero, S., 40, 54, 55, 56, 61, 62, 322
Provenzano, F. J., 320
Prusiniski, M., 528, 529, 530
Pryce, A., 84
Pryor, W., 348, 349
Puccia, E., 542, 543
Putnam, D. E., 94

Q

Quast, L., 324
Quinton, W. J., 292

R

Race, K., 351
Ragin, A. I., 517
Rahman, Q., 341
Raine, T. R., 422
Raj, A., 479, 480
Ralston, R., 77
Ramakrishnan, V., 358
Ramsey, C. B., 47, 51
Ramsey, J. L., 447
Rani, R., 543, 544
Rankin, S., 312, 316
Rath, J. M., 77
Rawls, T., 342, 349
Raymond, M. A., 392, 399
Raymond, N. C., 525
Ream, G. L., 335, 339, 340, 349
Rebchook, G. M., 358, 395
Reece, M., 172, 544, 545, 546, 547
Regnerus, M. D., 53, 54, 55, 56, 61, 62, 63, 85, 322, 357, 372, 386, 390, 393, 415, 417, 421, 423, 424, 426, 430, 431, 514, 515, 516
Rehan, N., 123
Rehor, J. E., 541
Reibner, C., 415, 416
Reicher, R., 73
Reichert, T., 70
Reid, R., 84, 93, 95, 416, 522
Reinisch, J., 390, 393, 395
Reis, H. T., 460
Reiter, E. O., 382, 383
Remafedi, G., 353
Remer, T., 116
Remizowski, L., 501
Renju, J., 212
Renold, E., 333
Rentfrow, P. J., 451
Repucci, N. D., 251
Resick, P. A., 483, 484
Resnick, M., 353
Resnick, S. M., 302
Reynolds, P., 3, 8, 17, 49, 51, 52, 56, 319, 320, 371, 373, 375, 380, 387, 403, 404, 462, 529
Rhoades, G., 421
Rhodes, G., 447
Rhodes, T., 188
Rice, K., 334
Rich, A., 341
Richards, C., 292
Richardson, C. T., 232
Richardson, D., 56
Richardson, E., 189
Richardson, L., 431
Rickers, K., 88
Rider, G. N., 525
Rieger, G., 142
Rindfuss, R. R., 426

Ringwalt, C. L., 504
Riskind, R. G., 343
Rivellini, G., 7, 8
Rivers, I., 354, 358
Roberson, C., 506
Roberts, R., 504
Robinson, K. H., 333
Robinson, P., 8, 9, 10, 11, 12, 13, 14, 18, 345
Robinson, W., 462
Robson, L., 377
Rodgers, L., 459
Rodriguez, C., 26, 163
Rogers, J., 49, 371, 393, 396, 398, 543
Roizman, B., 208
Rolleri, L., 91, 400, 403
Ropelato, J., 93
Rosario, M., 333, 334, 348, 388, 389
Roscoe, W., 345
Rosenbluth, B., 483
Rosentahl, L., 469
Ross, C. E., 426
Rossano, M., 39, 56
Rothblum, E. D., 433
Rothman, A. D., 253
Rothman, B. K., 276, 278, 279
Rothman, M. T., 253
Roughgarden, J., 340
Roughton, D., 375, 377, 378, 379, 380
Rowley, E., 486
Roy, J. R., 116
Rubens, R., 316
Rubenstein, A. J., 447
Rubin, G., 513
Rubin, J. Z., 320
Ruble, D., 319, 320
Ruble, D. N., 299, 319
Ruel, A., 469
Russell, A., 217
Russell, S. T., 250, 373, 383
Russo, N. F., 291
Ruttenberg, D., 59
Ryan, C., 140, 144, 358, 363
Ryan, T., 80, 89, 91

S

Saario, T. N., 322
Sadker, D., 322
Sadker, M., 322
Saewyc, E. M., 334
Sagarin, B. J., 541
Saladino, V., 80
Salam, M., 313
Salehiniya, H., 172
Salovey, P., 8, 461, 462
Saltz, G., 454
Sanchez, J., 358, 363
Sanday, P. R., 258, 479, 480, 486, 487, 488, 489, 494, 501, 502, 503, 537, 538
Sanders, J. S., 462
Sanders, S. A., 13, 149, 150, 172, 188, 390, 393, 395, 515, 536, 544, 545, 546, 547
Santelli, J., 49, 371, 393, 396, 398
Santrock, J., 435
Sarda, V., 333
Sargent, C. F., 275, 299
Savin-Williams, R., 333, 334, 335, 337, 338, 339, 340, 343, 348, 349, 353, 358, 363, 373, 389, 449, 452
Schaffir, J., 257
Schalet, A. T., 52, 54, 169, 385, 402, 403, 404
Scherer, E. A., 333
Schiavi, R. C., 520
Schippers, M., 49, 427
Schlehofer-Sutton, M. M., 5
Schleifer, C., 146

Schleifer, R., 49, 371, 396, 398
Schooler, D., 49, 372, 396, 397
Schrimshaw, E. W., 333, 334, 348, 388, 389
Schubert, C., 385
Schuler, J., 267, 268, 270, 271, 276, 279, 383
Schumm, L. P., 429, 436, 438, 439, 440
Schwartz, P., 119, 141, 415, 421, 436, 438, 447, 452, 516, 518, 520, 538, 546, 547
Schwartz, S., 354, 355, 361
Seabrook, R. A., 453
Sears, J., 348
Seifer, R., 307, 319
Seligman, M., 5, 8, 17
Seligson, F. J., 258
Selvaggi, G., 316
Semlyen, J., 358
Senft, T., 80
Sesselberg, T. S., 84
Setel, P., 195
Seto, M. C., 490, 491, 494, 496, 497, 498, 506, 528, 529, 530, 532, 533
Sevelius, J., 311
Shafer, E., 546
Shafer, S., 78
Shafran, C. R., 375, 377, 378, 379, 380
Shakelford, T. K., 417
Shakespeare, T., 520
Shanker, T., 97
Shapiro, J. L., 264
Shattuck, A., 494
Shaver, P. R., 459, 460
Shaw, J. S., 378
Sheeder, J., 221
Sheldrake, P., 39
Shen, Y., 250, 383
Sherman, P. W., 19
Sherman, R. A., 155, 418
Shernoff, M., 417, 419
Sherwood, C. C., 33
Shields, N., 277
Shildrick, M., 520
Short, M., 94
Shostak, M., 35, 218, 537, 538
Shreffler, K. M., 251, 252
Shuttleworth, R., 520
Sibley, C. G., 334
Siegel, J. A., 494
Siegelman, M., 339
Sigle-Rushton, W., 411, 418, 419, 422
Sikkink, D., 62
Sill, M., 436, 438, 440, 518, 520
Silva, R. R., 88
Silverman, J. G., 479, 480
Silvosky, J. F., 490
Simkin, P., 281
Simon, R. W., 426
Simon, W., 11, 453, 513, 515
Simonds, W., 271, 278, 279
Sims, J., 395
Sionean, C., 159
Sipski, M., 148, 350
Skuldt-Niederberger, K., 318
Slater, A., 252, 397
Slater, R., 252
Sloan, D. M., 20, 495
Sluyter, D. J., 462
Smith, A., 94
Smith, C., 62
Smith, D., 18, 23, 39, 49, 51, 135, 318, 351, 410, 417, 428, 431, 445, 448, 537
Smith, H., 40, 41, 44, 54, 55, 57, 58, 60, 71, 424
Smith, S. G., 479
Smock, P. J., 421, 422
Snowdon, G., 324
Soble, A., 61
Sobo, E., 414

Sobrero, A. J., 123
Soh, S., 543
Soloman, S. E., 433
Somers, C., 392
Somers, C. L., 395
Sonfield, A., 239
Soriano, C., 97
Sosis, R., 37, 38
Sowadsky, R., 188
Soydan, H., 504, 506
Spalding, L. R., 340, 453
Spector, T. D., 105
Speizera, I. S., 543
Speroff, L., 119, 223, 241
Spinazzola, J., 508
Spock, B., 249, 376, 378
Sprecher, S., 466
Squire, C., 258
Stacey, J., 343, 364
Stall, R., 336, 348, 351, 357, 358
Stall, R. D., 525
Stamilio, D. M., 272
Stanely, S. M., 421
Stanley, S., 421
Steele, R., 377
Stein, D. J., 146
Steinberg, L. D., 249, 380
Steiner, R., 185, 188
Steinglass, P., 189
Steingraber, S., 115, 116
Sterling, A. F., 299, 306
Sternberg, R. J., 455, 456
Stevens, J., 58
Stevens, M. R., 479
Stewart, C., 323, 341, 351
Stewart, F., 231, 232
Stimpson, C., 318
Stobbe, M., 403
Stock, K., 532
Stoddard, J. J., 499
Stokes, C. E., 454
Stoller, R. J., 2, 9, 50, 53, 92, 129, 138, 140, 144, 145, 168, 301, 302, 306, 308, 309, 311, 325, 445, 447, 449, 452, 513, 514, 524, 527, 530, 531, 533, 537, 538, 539, 541, 544
Stone, E. A., 417
Stone, V., 23
Stotzer, R. L., 488
Strassberg, D. S., 334
Strgar, W., 463, 464
Strieb, J., 428
Striepe, M., 342
Stritto, M. E. D., 5
Struckman-Johnson, C., 491
Stryker, S., 346
Sturla, E., 305, 306
Sturns-Simon, C., 221
Styrc, M., 421, 424, 435
Subak, L. L., 517
Subiaul, F., 33
Sullivan, L., 272
Sullivan, W. M., 56
Sumer, N., 289
Summers, D., 49, 371, 393, 396, 398
Sun, S., 385
Sung, J., 307, 319
Surmann, A. T., 395
Sutton, M. Y., 194
Sutton, P. D., 391
Swan, J., 181
Swank, E., 168, 361
Swann, W. B., Jr., 451
Swanson, K. M., 270
Swindler, A., 56
Symonds, D., 33
Szasz, T., 378, 516

T

Tai, S. S., 358
Tannen, D., 252, 462
Tanner, J. D., Jr., 392, 399
Tanzi, R., 375, 426, 434, 435, 436, 437, 438, 440, 507, 508
Taylor, D., 212, 410
Taylor, T., 39
Tepper, K. H., 402
Tepper, M., 101, 520, 545
Terry, J., 346
Terry, K., 85
Teten, A. L., 479, 483, 490
Teunis, N., 25, 363, 365
Teuwen, D. E., 193
Theiss, J. A., 469
Thill, A. D. W., 125
Thoennes, N., 323, 478, 490
Thom, D. H., 517
Thomas, W., 344
Thompson, M. S., 217
Thompson, S., 391
Thorkild, I. A., 116, 383
Thornhill, R., 33, 37, 114
Thurlow, C., 80, 84
Tichenor, V., 251, 252
Tiefer, L., 125, 126, 517, 518, 519
Tiggemann, M., 252, 397
Tipton, S. M., 56
Tittle, C. K., 322
Tjaden, P., 323, 478, 490
Tolman, D., 5, 8, 21, 25, 49, 136, 172, 173, 251, 299, 319, 320, 337, 341, 342, 350, 371, 372, 373, 380, 385, 393, 396, 397, 398
Tone, A., 219, 244
Topolinski, S., 88
Tovar, V., 101
Town, R., 425
Tram, J., 189
Trevena, P., 426
Troiden, R. R., 525
Trouong, T., 504, 543
True, W. R., 358
Trumbach, R., 45, 344, 345
Trussell, J., 223, 231
Trussell, R., 232
Tschann, J. M., 230
T'Sjoen, G., 316, 335
Tsuang, M. T., 358
Tucker, M. W., 449
Turkle, S., 80, 91
Turnbull, D., 277
Turner, C. W., 334
Turner, H. A., 494
Turner, M. G., 489, 490
Turner, R. A., 135
Turner, V., 55
Twamley, K., 445
Twenge, J. M., 155

U

Uecker, J., 415, 421, 423, 424, 430, 431, 515, 516
Ujvari, K., 440
Umberson, D., 426
Uniat, L., 252

V

Vahratian, A., 240
Valentine, D., 313
Valentine, G., 80, 84
Valkenburg, P. M., 85, 93, 94, 95
Valle, L. A., 483
Valliant, G., 11, 411, 434, 438, 507
van Anders, S. M., 138, 333, 341, 344, 387, 389, 427
van Balen, F., 364
van den Boom, D. C., 364
Vandenbosch, L., 75, 396
Van Den Eeden, S. K., 517
van de Pol, L. C., 345
van der Kolk, B. A., 508
Van der Meer, T., 45, 505
van der Straten, A., 23
Vanderwaal, C., 386
Vandevoorde, J., 159
vanDommelen-Gonzalez, E., 420
van Gelderen, L., 364
Van Houdenhove, E., 335
Vanita, R., 58
van Lankveld, J. J., 49
Van Lunsen, R. H. W., 523, 530, 532
Van Marck, E., 193
van Oosten, J., 396
Van Rossem, R., 112
Vansintejan, J., 159
Vantine, J. L., 265
van Veen, E., 422, 423
Vares, T., 438, 518, 519
Varga, C., 504
Vasey, P. L., 16, 18, 129, 299, 314, 325, 333, 334, 337, 338, 387, 388, 389, 404, 513, 515
Vázquez, E., 314, 315
Velde, E., 426
Veniegas, R. C., 340, 453
Ventura, S. J., 391
Verhaeghe, J., 144
Verma, M., 490, 492
Vernon, M. L., 460
Verrastro, V., 80
Vervloessem, D., 75
Vidourek, R., 77, 80
Vigorito, M. A., 525, 526
Vilain, E., 16, 18, 129, 299, 314, 333, 334, 337, 338, 387, 388, 389, 404, 513, 515
Villanti, A. C., 77
Villanueva, C. M., 5
Viloria, H., 307, 308, 312, 327
Vincent, L., 127
Vogel, D. A., 320
Vogel, V., 218, 219
Vollebergh, W., 390
Voyer, D., 322
Voyer, S., 322
Vrangalova, Z., 334, 343, 348, 349, 353
Vukadinovic, Z., 525

W

Waal, F. de, 37
Wade, L., 415, 416
Waite, L., 8, 11, 13, 136, 154, 318, 410, 414, 426, 429, 430, 431, 435, 436, 438, 439, 440, 516, 518, 519, 520, 547
Waite, L. J., 425, 429, 432, 436, 438, 439, 440
Waites, M., 52
Wall, S., 459
Wallace, L., 538
Wallen, K., 34
Walling, A. D., 241
Walsh, K., 508
Walster, E., 447
Walter, C., 153, 154
Walters, M. L., 479
Walton, M. T., 335
Wang, J., 479
Wang, S. K., 486
Wang, T., 3, 8, 154, 155, 410, 415, 430, 435, 436, 439, 519, 520
Wang, T-J., 270
Ward, B., 81
Ward, E., 181
Ward, L. M., 453
Ward, T., 529
Wardlow, H., 18, 23, 39, 49, 51, 135, 318, 351, 410, 417, 428, 431, 445, 448, 487, 537
Warf, B., 96
Washington, R., 269
Waters, E., 459
Watson, A. F., 395
Webb, D. A., 280
Weber, M., 40
Weeks, J., 9
Weinberg, M. S., 348, 349
Weiner, N. A., 504, 506
Weir, K., 116
Weisman, A., 72
Weisner, T. S., 249, 251, 258
Weiss, D., 52, 56, 376, 378
Weisskirch, R. S., 82
Wellings, K., 335
Wells, B. E., 155
Welti, K., 221
West, J. H., 75
West, R., 419, 425, 427
Westheimer, R., 429
Wetterneck, C., 94
Whalley, J., 281
Whigham, M., 322
Whipple, B., 105
White, L., 436
White, M., 351
Whiting, B., 319, 320
Whiting, J., 51
Whitley, R. J., 208
Whitman, C. N., 313, 357
Whittle, L., 543
Whitton, S. W., 421
Wholeslagle, B., 89
Widaman, K. F., 460
Widom, C. S., 20
Wigfield, A., 322
Wiggins, J. M., 181
Wilcox, M. M., 40, 55, 56
Wildsmith, E., 221
Wiley, D., 21
Wiley, J., 525
Williams, C. J., 348, 349
Williams, D. N., 89
Williams, J., 528, 529, 530
Williams, K., 426
Williams, L. M., 494
Williams, T. J., 339
Williams, W., 344, 345
Williamson, L., 372, 383
Willoughby, B. L. B., 322
Wilson, B. D. M., 327
Wilson, G. D., 145, 341
Wilson, M. A., 447
Winterman, D., 448
Wissow, L., 349, 353
Witte, J., 516, 547
Witte, S. S., 189
Wolak, J., 84, 85
Wolf, R., 349, 353
Wolff, K., 240
Wolinsky, S. M., 193
Wolitski, R. J., 194
Wong, C. M., 522
Wong, W. I., 320
Wood, H., 513, 540
Wood, K., 101, 351
Woodhead, J. C., 319
Woods, E., 349, 353
Worley, M., 96

Worobey, M., 193
Worthman, C., 383, 385
Wright, D., 372, 383
Wu, A. H., 116
Wu, E., 189
Wu, X., 181
WuDunn, S., 490, 504, 506, 543
Wyatt, G. E., 22, 528, 529, 530
Wynn, T., 33, 35, 37, 38

X

Xie, B., 504, 506
Xu, X., 240

Y

Yadavar, S., 472
Yakeley, J., 513, 540
Yalom, M., 107
Yamanaka, A., 504, 506
Yang, Z., 114
Ybarra, M., 81, 84, 85
Yee, N., 89
Yockey, R. A., 77, 80
Yoshimoto, D., 469
Youm, Y., 23, 56, 348, 416, 421, 422, 431
Young, R., 113
Yule, M., 335
Yule, M. A., 335

Z

Zaccarin, S., 7, 8
Zawacki, T., 480
Zawidzki, T. W., 33
Zebrowitz, L. A., 447
Zernike, K., 448
Zhang, M., 528, 529, 530
Zhang, X., 479
Zolopa, A., 189
Zsok, F., 446
Zucker, K. J., 308, 339
Zuckerberg, M., 84

Subject Index

Note: Page numbers in bold refer to definitions. Page numbers followed by f refer to figures, and those followed by t refer to tables.

A

abasiophilia, **533**
AB/DL, **532**-533
abnormal behavior, **49**-51, 513-516. *See also* paraphilias
abortifacients, **290**-291
abortion
  contraception versus, 217
  efforts to ban, 244, 287-288, 288f, 293
  methods, 289-291
  religions' views, 57t, 58, 59
  spontaneous, 270
  teens' access debated, 232
  U.S. overview, **289**
abstinence
  as contraceptive method, 225t, 231
  before marriage, 61
  pledges, 386
  singleness and, 414
abstinence-only sex education, 41f, 396-399
Achilles, 43f
acquired immunodeficiency syndrome. *See* AIDS (acquired immunodeficiency syndrome)
active listening, 466-468, 472
Adams, Abigail, 45
Adams, John, 45
addiction, sexual, 524, 525-526
adolescents
  contraceptive and abortion access, 232, 292
  development of sexual identity, 385-389
  exposure to porn, 84
  gender stereotypes, 321
  media aimed at, 76-77
  physical sexual development, 380-385. *See also* puberty
  pregnancy, 386, 391-392, 392f, 396, 399, 402, 403
  romantic relationships, 385
  sexting by, 81-82
  sexual behaviors, 386-387, 389-392
  sexual bullying, 502-503
  STI risk, 169
  suicide risk, 357, 358
  technology access, 77
  Viagra use by, 518
adoption, 286-287
adrenal glands, 113, 302, 380
adrenarche, **380**
adult entertainers, 94, 95-96
adultery, 417, **430**-431. *See also* extramarital relationships; infidelity
adult sexual content, 92-96. *See also* pornography
advertising, sexual imagery in, 69, 70, 73
advocates for victims of sexual coercion, 507
Advocates for Youth, 355
AdvocatesforYouth.org, 362
Africa
  cultures without sexual violence, 488-490
  female genital mutilation, 111-112, 113f
  HIV risk, 189, 195, 212-213
  opposition to same-sex relationships in, 365-366
  sex tourism in, 504, 543
  sexual violence in, 486, 487, 495f
African Americans. *See also* race
  attractiveness standards, 448
  gender stereotypes, 322
  HIV infection among, 192, 194
  same-sex orientation among, 350
  sexual scripts, 454
agape, 457f, 458
age, pregnancy and, 256
age-defined same-sex relationships, 344
ageism, 438
age of consent, **404**, 405t, 529, 543
Age of Enlightenment, 38f
age of first marriage, 414, 426
age of sex offenders, 490
aggression, gender stereotypes, 320-321, 537-538. *See also* violence
aging, sexual activity and, 428, 434-440, 517-521
AIDS (acquired immunodeficiency syndrome)
  defined, **188**
  diagnosing, 197
  history, 193-196
  impact on positive sexuality movement, 15
  impact on sexual rights, 365
  initial responses to, 48
  key dates, 41f
  risks, 188-193, 212-213
  in sex workers, 504
  treatment, 197-198
alcohol use
  by abuse victims, 495
  date rape and, 480, 481, 483, 489
  during pregnancy, 253, 254, 260, 267
  STI risk and, 184-185
5-alpha-reductase deficiency, 305-306, 307t
AmbienteJoven. org, 362
amenorrhea, **118**
American Psychiatric Association, 40f, 347, 521-522
American Psychological Association, 347
American Revolution, 45
amniocentesis, 272f, **272**
amniotic sac, 260f, **260**
amphetamines, 254t
anal intercourse
  NHSLS findings, 16
  penalties for, 515
  in pornography, 527
  during pregnancy, 257-258
  as sexual technique, 158f, **158**-159
  STI risk from, 201
anatomy
  defined, **100**
  female genitals, 101-108, 102f, 104f, 105f, 106f, 111-112
  knowledge of, 101
  male genitals, 120-125
  variability, 109-111, 125
androgen insensitivity syndrome, 303, 307t
androgens, 113-114, 339
androgyny, **317**-318
andropause, **128**
androstadienone, 144
anilingus, **158**
animals, arousal by, 526

animated pornography, 93
anthropology, 12
antibiotics, 200, 202, 203, 204
antiretroviral therapy, 197-198, 212
anus, **104**
anxious attachment, 459, 460
Araujo, Gwen, 313
areola, **108**, 109f
arousal. *See also* pleasure
  by animals, 526
  motivations, 139-140
  penile response, 122-125
  physical challenges to, 516-521
  physical senses and, 140-144
  psychological stimuli, 144-145
  sexual response cycles, 146-150
  vaginal response, 104, 105
arranged marriages, 135, 427, 428
art, 38-39, 38f, 41f
arthritis, 521
artificial insemination, **286**
asexuality, 333, **335**
Ashanti people, 489
Asia, sex tourism in, 504, 543-544
Asian civilizations, sexuality in, 40-42
aspiration method, **290**
assisted-living centers, 439, 440
assisted reproductive techniques, **284**-286
asymptomatic shedding, 170
atrophic vaginitis, **178**
attachment theory, **459**-460
attraction, sexual
  behavior versus, 335-337, 349
  elements of, 444-453
  odors and, 114
  pubertal changes, 381
  role in commitment, 424
  same-gender, 335-337, 448, 449, 451-452
Augustine, Saint, 61
autoerotic asphyxiophilia, **531**-532
autoerotic behaviors, **375**. *See also* masturbation
Avatar (film), 541
avatars, 89, 91
avoidance of intimacy, 534
avoidant attachment, 459, 460
Ayre spatula, 177f
azithromycin, 202

B

baby boomers, 47-48, 435, 518
baby brain phenomenon, 264
backup contraception, 222, 237, 238
bacterial STIs, 190t, 198-205
bacterial vaginosis, **178**
Baird v. Eisenstadt, 220
Bangkok, 504
Barbie doll, 448
Barbin, Herculine, 307
barbiturate use in pregnancy, 254t
bar mitzvah, 59
barrier methods of contraception, 217, 225t-226t, 231-235. *See also* condoms
Bartholin's glands, 102f, **104**
basal body temperature, **243**

598

Subject Index

Basal Body Temperature Method, 229t, 242, 243, 244f
Basson, Rosemary, 148–149, 149f
bat mitzvah, 59
BDSM
  common behaviors, 512, **531**, 540
  defined, **531**
  laws against, 515
  percent engaging in, 544
  risk in, 532, 539
beauty standards, 447–449
behavioral approach to paraphilias, 534
being on the down low, **350**
Bem, Daryl, 451–452
Bem Inventory, 317, 318
Benedict, Ruth, 54
Bhagavad-Gita, 57
bias, 22, 24, 25
bimanual exams, **176**, 177f
biological attraction, 451
biological bisexuality, **11**
biological kin, **497**
biphasic pill, 237
biphobia, 356
birth. *See* childbirth
birth control. *See* contraception
birth control pill
  introduction, 40f, 220, 237
  for men, 216
  STI risk and, 185
  types, 226t–227t
  using, 237, 238
birth order, sexual orientation and, 339
birth plans, 280–281
birth weight, 267, 268
bisexuality
  anal sex and, 159
  defined, **332**
  early views, 9, 348–349
  Freud's view, 11
  gender differences in expression, 340
  growing acceptance, 349–350
blastocysts, **259**, 260
blood tests
  for AIDS, 197
  for hepatitis, 209
  for herpes, 208
  for prostate cancer, 183
  for syphilis, 203
bodily integrity, **128**–129
body image, 396, 397, 398
body knowledge
  in children, 370, 372, 373
  importance, 168–169
  men's sexual health concerns and, 180–184
  taking responsibility for, 169–171
  women's sexual health concerns and, 171–179
body odors, 114, 140. *See also* odors
body shape, beauty standards and, 447–449
bondage. *See* BDSM
Bono, Chaz, 316, 316f
bonobos, 33–34
boundaries, online, 86
BPA, 116
brain (human), 35, 339–340
brain chemistry, attraction and, 450
Braxton-Hicks contractions, 267
breast augmentation, 315
breast cancer
  effects on sexuality, 521
  frequency of occurrence, 171, 172
  risk factors, 172–173
  screening for, 110, 173–175, 176f
breastfeeding, 218, 222
breasts, female
  anatomy, 108–109, 109f
  pregnancy's effects on, 263
  self-exams, 110, 175

  surgical alteration, 112, 112f
  variability, 111f
breathing, Lamaze, 277
breech position, **267**, 268f
Brown, Timothy Ray, 198
Buddha, Gautama, 40–42
Buddhism
  origins and tenets, 38f, 40–42
  sexual norms, 57t, 58
Builders, in Fisher's model, 450
bullying
  for gender nonconformity, 326, 360
  homophobia and hate crimes, 356–359
  sexual harassment, 499–502
  teen dating abuse, 502–503
Burke, Tarana, 477
burqas, 60
Bush, George W., 41f
Buttigieg, Pete, 347

C

cable TV, 76
Cain, Herman, 499
Calderone, Mary, 14
calendar method, 229t
Call to Action to Promote Sexual Health and Responsible Sexual Behavior, 18–19
Canada, rape in, 486
cancer
  breast, 110, 172–175, 173f, 176f, 521
  men's reproductive organs, 124, 180–183, 181f, 182f, 521
  self-exams for, 110, 124, 175
  women's reproductive organs, 178–179, 179t, 208, 209
cardiovascular disease, 521
careers, parenthood and, 251–252
caregivers, sexual assault by, 520
caregivers' influence on gender roles, 319–320
Carville, James, 50
case studies, **22**
caste, **428**
castration, 60
casual sex, 138, **415**–416
cave paintings, 38–39, 38f
celebrities
  media impact on, 69
  micro-level, 80
  as sex symbols, 72, 73–75
  Twitter postings, 81
celibacy, 60, **414**
cell phones, 90
censorship
  of movies and TV, 76
  online sexuality, 96–97
  pornography, 93
Central America, sex tourism in, 543
Cervarix, 209
cervical barrier methods of contraception, 225t–226t, 235, 235f, 236f
cervical cancer, **178**–179, 179t, 208, 209
cervical caps, 226t, 235, 235f, 236f
cervical mucus method, 229t
cervical secretions, 243
cervix
  defined, **104**, 105f
  dilation, 273
  during pregnancy, 257
  STI symptoms, 200f
cesarean birth
  defined, **267**, 268f
  impact on sexual dysfunction, 283
  when performed, 276, 279
chancres, **202**–203
Changing Our Minds (film), 347

Chapman, Tracy, 346
Chauvet-Pont-d'Arc Cave, 38, 38f
cheating. *See* infidelity
chemical exposure, 116
chemistry, attractional, 449–450
chest reconstruction, 315
childbirth
  approaches, 274–281
  mortality rates, 20, 269
  process, 273–274, 274f
childhood sexual abuse, 494f, **494**–498. *See also* children, sexual coercion of
child pornography, 82, 94, 95, **498**
child rearing, 319–323
children
  abortion access, 232
  awareness of sexual orientation, 332, 333
  divorce's effect, 432
  exposure to porn, 84
  influences on sexual orientation in, 340
  marriage and, 427
  parental age trends, 426
  parental talks with about sex, 62, 371–372, 393, 394
  of same-sex parents, 343, 364–365
  sex trafficking of, 506
  sexual coercion of, 490–491, 493–498, 494f, 507–508, 527, 528–530
  sexual development, 370–374
  sexuality in, 375–379, 537
  teaching gender roles, 319–323
chimpanzees, 33–34
China, 42, 96–97
chivalry, **44**
chlamydia, 190t, **200**–202, 201f
chlorine, 170
chorion, 260f, **260**
chorionic villus sampling, **272**
Christianity. *See also* religion
  early influence on sexuality, 43
  origins, 38f, 43
  sexual norms, 57t, 60–62
  in U.S. sexual culture, 61–63, 64
chromosomal abnormalities, 270, 302–307, 307t
chronic conditions, sexual function and, 519–521
circumcision
  bodily integrity debates, 128–129
  female, 111–112, 128–129
  male, 125–128, 127f, 129
cisgender, **299**, **300**, 311. *See also* heterosexuality
cities, LGBTQ acceptance in, 348
civilizations, development of sexuality in, 39–48. *See also* cultures
civil unions, **420**
Clementi, Tyler, 356, 358
clinically asymptomatic stage (HIV), 196
Clinton, Bill, 41f, 70, 430
Clinton, Hillary, 41f, 324, 365
clitoral crura, **103**
clitoral glans, **103**
clitoral hood, **103**
clitoris
  anatomy, 102f, **103**–104
  origins debated, 19
  removal, 111
  role in orgasm, 149–150
cocaine use in pregnancy, 254t
cock rings, 545
coercive paraphilias, **526**, 527–530
cognitive-behavioral therapy, 535
cognitive effects of pregnancy, 264
cohabitation, 51t, **418**–425
coitus. *See also* intercourse
  defined, **159**
  positions, 159–163, 160f, 161f, 162f, 163f
  during pregnancy, 257
coitus interruptus, 217
coitus obstructus, 217

coitus reservatus, 217
cold sores, 207–208
collectivist cultures, 155
college students. *See also* schools
    polyamory among, 422
    rape risk, 478, 480, 488, 489
    sexual harassment, 501–502
The Color Purple (Walker), 350
combination pills, 226t–227t, 237
comfort women, 543
Coming of Age in Samoa (Mead), 12
Coming of Age in Second Life (Boellstorff), 91
coming out, 360–365
commitment
    of cohabiting partners, 420–423, 424–425
    to daily communication, 467
    influence on sexual well-being, 138
    in Sternberg's theory, 455
common law marriage, **420**
communication
    about contraception, 230
    about parenthood, 253
    about sexual pleasure, 143
    effectiveness, 466–468, 469–471
    emotional literacy and, 8, 461–463
    within families about sex, 62, 371–372, 373, 392–394
    improving, 471–472
    loss in relationships, 461
    during menopause, 120
    nonverbal, 464–465
    in online dating, 90
    respect for sexual cultures, 50
    self-disclosure, 170, 230, 466
    sexual language, 462, 463–464
    sexual well-being and, 472–473
    styles, 468–469
communication privacy management theory, **466**
communities, general influence on sexuality, 372
companionate love, in Sternberg's theory, 456
companionate marriage, **47**, 427
compatibility, attraction and, 450–451
complaining, criticism versus, 469–470
complaints, harassment, 500, 501
complementarity, **451**
compulsive sexual behavior, **522**–524
compulsive sexual behavior disorder, 523
compulsory heterosexuality, 341–342
computers, 77
Comstock, Anthony, 219
Comstock Act, 39f, 40f, 64, 219, 220
conception, 258, 260f
conditioning, 534
condoms
    advantages and disadvantages, 225t
    early forms, 218
    proper use, 170
    in schools, 402
    for STI prevention, 184, 198, 200, 202
    storage and use, 231–233, 233f
confidentiality. *See* privacy
conflict-avoiding couples, 468
congenital adrenal hyperplasia, 302, 307t, 339
Congress, LGBTQ persons in, 347
congruence, 424
consensual nonmonogamous relationships, 417–418, 419, 430
consent
    age of, 404, 405t, 529, 543
    campus policies, 489
    to nonmonogamous relationships, 417–418, 419, 430
    to sexual novelty, 544, 545
Conservative Judaism, 59
consummate love, in Sternberg's theory, 456
contempt in relationships, 470
continuous abstinence, **231**
contraception

adolescents' use, 387, 391, 399
attitudes about, 36
choosing methods, 221–224
cross-cultural variations, 217–219
defined, **216**
discussing with partners, 230
history, 219–220
impact on sexual culture, 47–48
insurance coverage debate, 64
myths, 221, 222, 391
overview of methods, 225t–229t
pill introduced, 40f, 220, 237
religions' views, 57t, 58, 59, 63
in schools, 402
sexual well-being and, 244–245
surgical methods, 222–223
withholding information on, 14
Contraceptive Clinical Trial Network, 245
contraceptive switch, **422**
contractions, **273**–274
conversion therapies, 515
Cooper, Anderson, 346
coping mechanisms, 506–508
copper IUDs, 239, 240
corona, 121f, **121**
corpus cavernosa, 121f, **121**
corpus luteum, 115f, **116**
corpus spongiosum, 121f, **121**
correlations, **22**, 25
correlation studies, 25
corruption, 504
Cosmopolitan magazine surveys, 24
counseling for abortion, 293
counseling for rape victims, 492
couples therapy, 535
court-ordered treatment, 534
courtship behavior, 533
couvade, **265**
cowgirl position, 160–161, 161f
Cowper's glands, 121f, **123**
crabs, 206f, **206**–207
Craig, Daniel, 347
Crandall, Rachel, 313
cremaster muscle, 122f, **122**
crisis competence, 439
criticism in relationships, 469–470
cross-complaining, 471
cross-dressing, **345**
Crowe, Russell, 81
crusades, 44
cryptorchidism, **180**
cultural chauvinism, **49**
cultural relativism, **49**
cultures. *See also* sexual cultures
    androgyny in, 317
    attractiveness standards, 449
    beauty standards, 109, 125
    beliefs about conception, 258
    bodily integrity debates, 128–129
    childbirth practices, 274–275
    circumcision in, 111–112, 126–127
    compulsory heterosexuality in, 341
    gender roles in, 319, 320
    general influence on sexuality, 12, 18, 32, 34–37, 372, 377
    historic evolution of sexuality within, 39–48
    impact on contraception, 217–219
    influence on sexual pleasure, 135–136, 140
    intersex conditions within, 306, 307
    nonverbal communication in, 464–465
    sexual norms in, 48–51, 513–516, 535–538
    sexual satisfaction and, 154–155
    variations in marriage, 135, 427–429
    variations regarding sexuality, 50
    varied sexual orientations within, 343–353
    views of rape, 486–490, 537–538
cunnilingus. *See also* oral sex
    acceptance among religious groups, 63

in sexual cultures, 538
as sexual technique, **155**, 157, 157f
Cunningham, Sara, 64–65
CVS (chorionic villus sampling), 272
cyberbullying, 357, 358, 360
cybersex. *See* virtual sex

D

Dalkon Shield, 220
dance halls, 47
danger, 168. *See also* risk taking
Darwin, Charles, 10
date rape, 479–483
date rape drugs, **480**–481, 482, 482t, 483
death penalty
    for extramarital relationships, 537
    for same-sex relationships, 341, 365–366, 514
    for stigmatized behaviors, 515
deception in relationships, 461
deep orgasms, 142
Defense of Marriage Act (U.S.), 433
defensiveness in relationships, 471
degeneracy, 9, 525
DeGeneres, Ellen, 346
denial, **539**, 540
Denmark, civil unions in, 420
dependent variables, **21**, **22**
Depo-Provera, 227t, 238, 239f
depression. *See also* emotional health; mental health
    in abuse victims, 502, 507
    with divorce, 432
    with gender identity struggles, 311
    in menopause, 119, 517
    with minority stress, 354, 355, 358
    post-abortion, 291–292
    postpartum, 282
    premenstrual, 118
    in rape victims, 479
    sexual desire and, 436, 517
    sexualization's impact, 397
desire for sex
    aging and, 435, 440
    development in children, 380
    hormonal influences, 114, 517–518
    individual differences, 37
    in Kaplan's sexual response model, 148
    men versus women, 17
    19th century views, 9, 46
    physical challenges to, 516–521
    during pregnancy, 257
    theories, 445–447
detumescence, **125**
DHEA, 380
diabetes (gestational), 271
diabetes, effects on sexuality, 521
Diagnostic and Statistical Manual of Mental Disorders
    on BDSM, 531
    paraphilia categories, 526–533
    paraphilias vs. paraphilic disorders in, 521–522, 526
Diamond, Lisa, 352
diaphragms, 225t, 235, 235f, 236t
digital rectal exams, 183f, **183**
dilation, **273**
dilation and evacuation, **290**
dildos, 545, 546–547
direct observation, **23**–25
Directors, in Fisher's model, 450
disability, sexual function and, 519–521
disclosure, sexual histories, 170, 230, 466
discrimination
    ageism, 438
    against gender nonconformity, 327
    against LGBTQ persons, 353–359, 433–434
    racism, 20
    against transgender people, 312–313

disease, sexuality as, 9
disengagement coping, **506**-507, 508
dismissing attachment, 459
distress, as mark of sexual disorder, 522, 523, 524
divorce
    changing attitudes about, 62
    cohabitation as avoidance, 426
    current rates, 431-432
    defined, **431**
    pornography's impact, 146
    religions' views, 57t, 58, 60, 62
    remarriage and, 432
dizygotic twins, 338-339
documenting harassment, 501
dogbane, 218
doggy style, 162-163
domestic partnerships, **420**
domestic violence, 323. *See also* sexual coercion; violence
dominance trait, 451
double stigma, **63**
douching, 204, **217**, 222
doulas, **277**
Down-Ass Chicks/Bitches, in Stokes's model, 454
doxycycline, 202
Dracula (Stoker), 72
dreams, conception, 258
Dr. Jekyll and Mr. Hyde (Stevenson), 46
drug use
    by abuse victims, 495
    date rape and, 480-481, 482, 483
    during pregnancy, 254, 254t, 260, 267, 270
    STI risk and, 184-185
DSD, **326**-327
DSM-5, 521-522, 526-533
dual income, no sex couples, **426**
ductal carcinoma, 521
due dates, 262
dysmenorrhea, **118**

E

early adulthood
    cohabitation during, 418-425
    defined, **410**
    major life decisions of, 411-412
    polyamory in, 417-418, 419
    single living during, 412-415
eating disorders, 397
ectoderm, 260-261
ectopic pregnancy, **270**
"Education and Treatment in Human Sexuality" (WHO), 27
effacement, **273**
egg donation, 285-286
ejaculation, **123**-125, 217
ejaculatory ducts, **124**, **125**
ejaculatory inevitability, **124**, **125**
Elbe, Lilli, 310
elderhood, **439**
Elders, Joycelyn, 371
elders
    defined, **411**
    sexual activity, 428, 438-440
Ella, 239
Ellis, Havelock, 11
email accounts, 90
embryonic period, **259**
embryos, **259**, **260**, 285
emergency contraceptive pills, 228t, **239**, 240
emergency health information, 171
emission phase, **124**, **125**
emotional commitment. *See* commitment
emotional health. *See also* mental health
    after abortion, 291-292
    dating abuse victims, 502
    with early puberty, 383
    marriage and, 425, 426
    rape's impact, 479-480, 486, 491-492, 493t
emotional intelligence, 462
emotional literacy
    in childhood and adolescence, 373
    defined, **7**
    in intimate relationships, 8, 461-463
emotional readiness, 386
emotional satisfaction, 37
emotion work, **462**
empathy, polyamory and, 419
empowerment, sexual. *See* sexual empowerment
empty love, in Sternberg's theory, 456
empty nesters, 436
endocrine-disrupting chemicals, 116
endocrine system, **112**, 113-114
endoderm, 260-261
endometrial cancer, 178
endometriosis, **256**, 284
endometrium, **106**-108, 108f, 259
endorphins, **148**
engineers, 419
Enlightenment, 38f, 45
Enovid, 220
epididymis, 121f, **122**, 123f
epididymitis, 200
epidurals, **278**, 280
epigenetics, 337-338
episiotomy, **279**, 280
EPOR model, 147f, **147**
Equal Pay Act (U.S.), 323
erectile dysfunction, **126**, 518-519
erectile tissues, **122**, **125**
erections
    in childhood, 375
    of clitoris, 103, 105
    of penis, **120**, **121**, 122-125
erogenous zones, **11**, 140f, **141**
eros, 457, 457f
erotic art, 41f
ESSURE, 241
estradiol, 115f
estriol, **271**
estrogen
    body's production, 113-114
    defined, **109**, **110**
    gender confirmation use, 314
    in hormonal contraceptives, 237, 238
    replacement therapy, 518
    role in maturation and menstruation, 116, 117t
estrogen replacement therapy, 305
estrus, **34**
ethics in sexual research, 21
ethnicity
    abortion and, 289
    attractiveness standards and, 448
    breast cancer occurrence and, 173f
    childhood sexual abuse and, 530
    impact on mortality rates, 20
    influence on sexual practices, 16, 16t
    problem pregnancies and, 20, 269
    pubertal changes and, 385
    sexual orientation and, 349-350
    transphobia and, 313
Europe, sexual health in, 402-404
evangelical Christianity, 32, 386
EverQuest, 89
evolution, **10**, 33, 34-37
excitement phase, **147**
excuses, 471
exercise, 255-257, 434-435
exhibitionism, **528**
exotic becomes erotic theory, **451**-452
experimental research, **25**
Explorers, in Fisher's model, 450
expulsion phase, **124**, **125**
extended families, 35, **497**
external constraints, role in commitment, 424-425
extramarital relationships
    attitudes about, 430-431
    cohabitation's impact on, 423
    cultural views, 537
    polyamory versus, 417
    religions' views, 57t, 58, 60, 61
extreme sexual behavior
    contemporary views, 538-539
    defined, **522**
    kinky sex, 91, 532, 539-541
    normative versus, 535-536
    in other cultures, 536-538
    over-pathologizing, 526
    sex tourism as, 525, 527, 541-544
extreme sports, 538
eye contact, 464, 468

F

Facebook, 84
facial feminization, 315
faculty-student relationships, 501-502
Fafafina role, 344
"fag" behavior, 326
failure rates of contraceptives, **223**, 224f
fallopian tubes
    anatomy, **104**, 108, 108f
    fertilization in, 259, 260f
    implantation in, 270
    problems with, 284
    STI symptoms, 201
    surgical contraceptive procedure, 241, 241f
false positives, 272
families
    childhood sexual abuse in, 494, 497-498
    communication about sex, 62, 371-372, 373, 386, 392-394
    of LGBTQ persons, 363-365
    rape's impact, 492
families of choice, **363**
Family and Medical Leave Act (1993), 252
family histories, 171
family leave, **252**
fan clubs, 75
Fans of Adult Media and Entertainment Awards, 96
fantasies, **144**-145, 452, 453. *See also* extreme sexual behavior
fantasy systems, **145**
Farmer, Paul, 212
fathers, 282, 320. *See also* sexual partners
fatuous love, in Sternberg's theory, 456
fear about sexuality, 464
fearful attachment, 459
fellatio, 63, **155**-156, 156f. *See also* oral sex
female circumcision, **111**-112, 128-129
female condoms, 225t, **234**-235
female genital mutilation, **111**-**112**, 113f, 129
female sexual arousal disorder, **516**-517
female-to-male procedures, 315-316
FemCap, 235, 235f, 236t
feminine hygiene products, 114
femininity, 317. *See also* gender roles
feminism. *See also* gender roles; women
    first wave, 39f, 47
    second wave, 40f, 47-48
fertility
    age and, 256
    breastfeeding and, 218, 222
    interventions for, 284-287
fertility awareness methods, 229t, **242**-244
fertilization, 259, 260f
fetal alcohol spectrum disorders, 254
fetal alcohol syndrome, **254**, 255f

fetal monitoring, 275f, 278
fetal period, **259**
fetishism. *See also* paraphilias
　defined, **10**, 541
　robot, 533
　transvestic, 526, 527
fetishistic disorder, 531
fetus
　chances for survival, 259
　defined, **259**, 260
　development stages, 259-267, 262f
　potential problems, 254-255, 254t, 259, 267-273
fidelity, 16, 16f, 82. *See also* extramarital relationships; infidelity
field studies, **12**
Fifty Shades of Grey (James), 75, 515
fimbriae, **108**
first-time mothers, age of, 250f
first trimester, 259-264, 262f
first wave feminism, 39f, 47
Fisher, Helen, 450
fissures, **159**, 170
fitness, sexual health and, 434-435
5-alpha-reductase deficiency, 305-306, 307t
five senses, 140-143
flaccid penis, **125**
flashers, 528
flirting, 465
fluid-free sexual behavior, 225t, **231**
fluidity, 351-352, 385-388
Flunder, Yvette, 64
flunitrazepam, 481
focus, role in sexual well-being, 5-7
folic acid, 253
follicles, 108f, **108**
follicle stimulating hormone, 115f, 117t, **117**, 119, 380
Folsom Street Fair, 512, 513
food tastes, 342-343
forceps deliveries, **278**-279, 279f
foreign slang, 463
foreskin. *See also* circumcision
　defined, 121f
　hygiene, **121**-122
　removal, 125-128, 127f
foster adoption, 287
Foucault, Michel, 15, 18
4 Agreements of Love, 467
four horsemen, 469-471
France, marriage in, 414
Franklin, Benjamin, 45
fraternal twins, 338-339
fraternities, 489, 501
Fraternity Gang Rape (Sanday), 489
Freaks, in Stokes's model, 454
free love movement, 39f
French kissing, 170, 538
French Revolution, 45
frenulum, 121f, **122**
frequency of sexual activity, 154-155, 415, 429-430, 545, 546
Freud, Sigmund
　methods, 11, 22
　overview of contributions, 11-12, 39f, 46
　on paraphilias, 533
friends with benefits, **416**, 422
frotteurism, **528**
Furries, 541

G

Galilei, Galileo, 45
gamete intrafallopian transfer, **285**-286
gaming, 89, 91
gamma hydroxybutyric acid, 481
Gardasil, 209

gay, **332**, 333. *See also* homosexuality; sexual orientation
gay liberation movement, 48
gay marriage. *See* same-sex marriage
Gay Straight Alliances, 355
gender, **299**
gender binary, **308**
gender confirmation surgery. *See* sex reassignment procedures
The Gender Creative Child (Ehrensaft), 312-313
gender differences
　in expressing sexual orientation, 336-337, 340, 350
　in fantasies, 145
　in first intercourse experience, 390-391
　in pubertal changes, 381-385
　refractory periods, 148
　sexuality in elder years, 439, 440
　sexual satisfaction in marriage, 430
　visual arousal, 141, 142
gender dysphoria, **314**
gender expression, **308**, 309
gender identity
　androgyny, 317-318
　biological effects on, 309-311
　defined, **299**, 307-308
　history, 308-309
　with intersex conditions, 302, 303
　social justice and, 326-327
　transgender challenges, 311-313
genderism, **322**
gender nonconformity, 314, 317, **325**-326
genderqueer, 317
gender roles
　20th century evolution, 47-48
　androgyny and, 317
　defined, **299**, 318
　historical development, 42
　inequality in, 323-324
　nonconformity to, 325-326
　in same-sex relationships, 344-345
　sexual scripts and, 453
　social expectations, 319-323
　Victorian era, 45-46
Gender Spectrum, 313
gender stereotypes, **317**
gender variance, **325**
generalizability, **21**
genetics, 337-339, 450
genital integrity, **129**
genitals
　desirable features, 100
　female, 101-108, 102f, 104f, 105f, 106f, 111-112
　with intersex conditions, 302-303, 302f, 305-306
　male, 120-125, 121f, 122f, 123f, 127f
　personal feelings about, 172, 173
　prenatal development, 301, 301f
　STI symptoms, 200f, 201f, 203f, 207f, 208f
　surgical reassignment, 315-316
　terms for describing, 462, 463
genital warts, 191t, 208-209, 208f
Germany, marriage in, 414
germ cells, **180**
germinal period, **259**
gestation, **259**
gestational diabetes, 271
gestational limits for abortion, 293
GHB, 481
Gibson Girls, 70f, 72f
gigolos, 503
Girl (film), 311
glass ceiling, 323, 324
global pandemics, **189**
Global Study of Sexual Attitudes and Behaviors, 154
Gold, Ari, 347
gonadotropin-releasing hormone, 116, 117t, **117**
gonadotropins, **380**-381
gonads, 113

gonarche, **380**
gonorrhea, 190t, 198-200, 200f
Gottman, John, 468, 469, 471, 472
government corruption, 504
government policies, 20, 27. *See also* laws
great world religions, **40**, 54-61. *See also* religion
Greece (ancient), 38f, 42-43, 344
Green, Laci, 80
Greven, Alec, 332, 379, 380
Griswold v. Connecticut, 220
grooming, online, 497
group therapy, 535
growth spurts, 382
G-spot, 105f, **105**
G-spot orgasm, **107**
Guardians of the Flutes (film), 53
guevedoche, 306
gynecologic cancers, **178**
gynecologic exams, 176, 177f

H

habitualization, **334**
halo effect, **447**
The Hangover (film), 480
harassment, 499-502
hard-core pornography, **93**
hate crimes, **357**-359
health. *See also* sexual health
　physical, 253-258, 519-521
　public measures, 39f, 45
　role of sexual rights in, 26
Health, Empowerment, Rights and Accountability, 164
health care buddies, 171
healthy lifestyles, 436
hebophilia, 528
Hefner, Hugh, 71f, 92
hemorrhoids, 257
Hendricks, Christina, 448
hepatitis, 192t, **209**, 210t-211t
heredity, attraction and, 450
hermaphrodites, 308
herpes simplex virus, 191t, 207f, **207**-208
heterogamy, **425**-426
heteronormativity, 342
heterosexuality
　anal sex and, 158-159
　defined, **332**
　in history, 39f, 46
　nature vs. nurture debate, 16-17, 18
　socialization, 333, 341-342, 388
　variations, 341, 353
hijabs, 59f, 60
Hill, Anita, 499
Hinduism
　origins, 38f, 40
　sexual norms, 57-58, 57t
　spread, 42
hip-hop music, 75
Hirschfeld, Magnus, 10
Hispanic communities, bisexuality in, 349-350
history of sexuality
　20th century, 47-48
　ancient Greece and Rome, 42-43
　Asian civilizations, 40-42
　Christianity's influence, 43
　depictions of sexual pleasure, 134-135
　Islamic civilization, 43-44
　major influences, 37, 38f-42f
　Middle Ages to Enlightenment, 44-45
　Victorian era, 45-47
HIV (human immunodeficiency virus)
　among African Americans, 350-351
　defined, **188**
　effects of circumcision on transmission, 127-128

history, 193–196
impact on sexual rights, 365
risks, 188–193, 200, 212–213
in sex workers, 504
symptoms, 192t, 196–197
transmission, 192t, 195, 195f, 196, 208
treatment and prevention, 192t, 197–198, 199, 212–213
Hmong people, 275
holistic sexuality, **3**
Holy Inquisition, 38f, 44–45
home births, 276
homogamy, **425**–426, 450–451
homonegativity, **354**
homophobia, **354**–359
Homo sapiens, 33
homosexuality. *See also* LGBTQ persons; same-sex relationships; sexual orientation
anal sex and, 159
attractiveness standards, 448, 449
changing attitudes about, 62, 514–515
cultural relativism and, 51
defined, **332**
early views, 9, 44, 45
evolving views of, 514–515
family formation and, 363–365
gay liberation movement, 48
in history, 42, 43, 46, 47
Kinsey's studies, 13, 16, 18
lack of acceptance, 136, 341, 365–366, 514
NHSLS findings, 16
as paraphilia, 516
religions' views, 57t, 58, 59, 60, 61, 62
honesty, polyamory and, 417, 419
Hooker, Evelyn, 346, 347
hooking up, **88**, 415–416, 416t
hormonal contraceptives
effectiveness, 223, 224f
health issues, 223
history, 220
for men, 216, 245
methods compared, 226t–228t, 236–239
hormonal implants, **237**–238
hormone replacement therapy, **119**, 518
hormones
basic functions, **112**, **113**–114
effect on gender identity, 309
gender confirmation use, 314, 315
influence on sexual desire, 517–518
menopause and, 119, 120, 517
in menstruation, 115f, 116–118
during pregnancy, 259–260, 261, 264
prenatal effects on sexual orientation, 339
pubertal changes, 380
hospital births, 275, 276, 280, 281
hospital requirements for abortion, 293
hostile environment, **499**
hot flashes, 119
How to Talk to Girls (Greven), 332, 379
Huffman, Felicity, 316
human chorionic gonadotropin, 117t, 259, 260
human immunodeficiency virus. *See* HIV (human immunodeficiency virus)
human papillomavirus, **178**–**179**, 191t, 208–209, 208f
human rights of sex workers, 504–505
human sexuality, unique traits, 33, 34. *See also* sexuality
human sexual nature, **35**, 36, 37–48
human sexual rights, 26–27, 163–164
Hustler magazine, 93
hydrotherapy, **277**–278
hygiene, 204–205
hymen, **104**–106, 106f
hypersexuality, **522**–523
hypnosis, 11
hypoactive female sexual desire disorder, 516–517

hypothalamus, **112**, **113**, 339–340
hypotheses, **21**
hysterectomies, 315
hysteria, 536

I

Ibo people, 274
identical twins, 338–339
IGF-1, 116
imperforate hymen, 106f, **106**
Implanon, 237, 238f
implantation of blastocyst, 259, 260f
implants, contraceptive, 227t
imprinting, **340**
impulsive sexual behavior, 522–524
incest, **497**
incest taboo, **37**, 497–498
incompatibility in relationships, 460
independent variables, **21**
India, rape in, 487
individuality. *See* sexual individuality
individual supportive psychotherapy, 535
inequality in relationships, 460
infant mortality, 20, 269f
infants
attachment, 459
gender expectations of, 320
influences on sexual orientation in, 340
intersex conditions in, 302–303, 304
sex reassignment procedures on, 311
sexual development, 375
STI risks to, 200, 201, 203, 208, 209
infatuation, in Sternberg's theory, 455
infections, during pregnancy, 270
infertility, 258, 284–287
infidelity
attitudes about, 430–431
cohabitation's impact on, 423
polyamory versus, 417
religions' views, 57t, 58, 60, 61
U.S. statistics, 16, 16f
injectable contraceptives, 227t, 238
Inquisition, 38f, 44–45
insecure attachment, 459, 460
Institute for Sexual Research, 10
institutional review boards, 22
instrumentality, 36
insurance coverage for abortion, 293
insurance coverage for contraceptives, 64
interactive biopsychosocial approach, **340**
intercourse. *See also* sexual activity
in adolescence, 390–391
following childbirth, 282–283
frequency, 154–155, 415, 429–430, 545, 546
gender differences in desire, 17
interdisciplinary perspective, **19**–20
internalized homophobia, **355**, 356, 358
International Classification of Diseases, 526
International Coalition for Genital Integrity, 129
Internet. *See also* pornography; social media
adult sexual content, 92–96
exhibitionism via, 528
extent of influence, 76–80
impact on private sexual expression, 69
impact on sex tourism, 542–543
impact on sexual socialization, 82–85
sexual contexts, 86–91
social media growth, 80–82
social support via, 76–80, 96–97
Internet surveys, 23
interracial marriage, 428–429
intersectionality in research, **20**
Intersexion (film), 307
intersexuality
causes, **302**–307
discrimination against, 327

labeling, 308
interviews, 23
intimacy, in Sternberg's theory, 455
intimate partner violence, 502–503. *See also* rape; sexual coercion
intolerance in relationships, 460
intrauterine devices, 220, 228t, **239**–241, 240f
introitus, **104**
intuition, 90
in-vitro fertilization, **285**
involuntary celibacy, 414
Islam
early influence on sexuality, 44
marriage traditions, 428
origins, 38f, 43–44
sexual norms, 57t, 59–60
It Gets Better, 361

J

James, William, 345
Jameson, Jenna, 95
Japan
erotic art, 41f
rape in, 486, 489
sex fantasies in, 543
sexuality in, 42
Tokugawa era, 39f
Jefferson, Thomas, 45
jelqing, 126
Jesus Christ, 43, 61. *See also* Christianity
Johnson, E. Patrick, 350
Johnson, Virginia, 14–15, 146–147
Jorgensen, Christine, 309
journaling, 138–139
Judaism
origins, 38f
sexual norms, 57t, 58–59, 63
Judd, Ashley, 477

K

Kama Sutra, 57, 135
Kaplan, Helen Singer, 148
Kardashian, Kim, 86f
Kaurma position, 135, 135f
Kavanaugh, Brett, 42f
Kegel exercises, **283**
Kellogg, John Harvey, 9
Kennedy, Anthony, 433
Ketamine, 481
kidnapping, 506
kinky sex, **91**, 532, 539–541
Kinsey, Alfred
on childhood sexual development, 375, 378
on homosexuality, 13, 16, 18
overview of contributions, 12–14, 40f, 70f, 71f
sexual orientation scale, 334–335, 335f
Kinsey scale, 334, 335f
kinship, 497
kinship adoption, 287
kissing
arousal and, 143
French kissing, 170, 538
herpes transmission via, 208
as sexual technique, 153–154
Klein Scale, 335
Klinefelter syndrome, 303, 304f, 307t
Krafft-Ebing, Richard von, 10, 39f
Kristof, Nicholas D., 506
Kshudgaga position, 135
!Kung people, 218, 489
kwolu-aatwul, 306
Kwoma culture, 51
Kyleena, 239, 240

L

labeling, gender, 308
labia majora, 102, 102f, **103**, 111
labia minora, 102f, **102**, **103**, 111
labor, 273-274, 274f. *See also* childbirth
Lamaze method, 275, 277
lanugo, **265**
Lao Tsu, 42
laparoscopy, 204, 241f, **241**, **242**
The Laramie Project (film/play), 359
last menstrual period calculation, 262
latent and late stage syphilis, 203
latex allergies, 223
Laumann, Edward O., 15
Lawrence, Jennifer, 477
Lawrence v. Texas, 41f
laws
    age of consent, 404, 405t, 529, 543
    banning contraception education, 39f, 40f, 64
    cohabitation and, 419-420
    hate crime, 359
    legalizing same-sex marriage, 41f, 42f
    rape, 487
    research goals to influence, 20
    same-sex harassment under, 501
    against same-sex relationships, 41f, 44, 353-354, 365-366, 514
    on sex work, 504-505
    sodomy, 41f, 353-354
Lea's Shield, 226t, 235, 236t
Lee, John Allen, 456
Lee's styles of love, 456-459
lesbians. *See also* LGBTQ persons; same-sex relationships
    defined, **332**
    family formation, 343, 363, 364
Levitra, 518
levonorgestrel, 239
LGBTQIA+, **332**-**333**
LGBTQ movement, 345-347
LGBTQ persons. *See also* same-sex marriage; same-sex relationships
    acceptance among religious groups, 64-65
    adoption barriers, 287
    anal sex and, 159
    attractiveness standards, 335-337, 448, 449, 451-452
    coming out, 360-363
    communication skills, 469
    defined, **332**-**333**
    family formation, 363-365
    growing acceptance, 346-347, 360-361
    lack of acceptance, 136, 341, 346, 353-359, 365-366, 514
    online communities, 77, 81
    as percentage of population, 334, 336-337, 347, 348
    sexual identities among, 348-353
    sexuality in elder years, 438-439, 440
lice, 206-207, 206f
life expectancy, 435
Lightfoot, Lori, 347
Liletta, 239, 240
Lindane, 206-207
listening skills, 466-468, 472
literacy, sexual. *See* sexual literacy
living apart together, **422**-**423**
lobular carcinoma, 521
lochia, **283**
locker-room syndrome, 125
long-acting PrEP, 199
love
    in adolescence, 385
    loss of, 460-461
    marriage and, 135, 427
    popular conceptions, 444, 453-454
    sexual desire versus, 136
    theories, 454-459
love at first sight, 445, 446
love maps, 340, **533**-**534**
love personalities, 450
low birth weight, 267, 268
lubricants, 234
lubricated condoms, 231
ludus, 457f, 458, 459
lumpectomies, **174**, **175**
lust, love versus, 445
luteinizing hormone, 115f, 117t, **117**, 119, 380

M

machismo, 349
magazine surveys, 24
making out, 389-390
male circumcision, **125**-**128**, 127f. *See also* circumcision
male condoms, **231**-**233**, 233f. *See also* condoms
male-to-female procedures, 314-315
malformed sperm, **284**
Malinowski, Bronislaw, 12
mammary glands, **108**, 109f
mammograms, 174f, **174**-**175**, 176f
mania love, 457f, 458, 459
Marditaka position, 135
marijuana use in pregnancy, 254t
marital rape, **483**-**484**, 485
Markata position, 135
marriage. *See also* same-sex marriage
    abstinence before, 61
    age of first, 414, 426
    changing attitudes about, 427f
    cohabitation's impact on, 421, 422
    cohabitation versus, 418-425
    common law, 420
    conflict in, 468-469
    contemporary approaches, 411-412, 414
    cultural variations, 135, 427-429
    divorce and remarriage, **431**-**432**
    frequency of sexual activity, 155, 415
    history of sexuality in, 43, 44, 46-47
    moral perceptions, 424
    parenthood's impact, 252-253
    rape in, 483-484, 485
    same-gender, 41f, 42f, 346, 360, 422, 432-434
    sexual activity in, 415, 429-430
    sexual well-being and, 425-426
    single living versus, 412-415
marriage scripts, **379**
Martin, Clyde, 13
Martin, Ricky, 346
masculinity. *See also* gender roles
    19th century movements, 46
    androgyny and, 317
    gender stereotypes, 320, 325, 326
    in Hispanic communities, 349
    rituals to develop, 32, 52f, 53, 344
    sexual aggression and, 537-538
masochism, **530**. *See also* BDSM
mastectomies, **174**, **175**, 315
Masters, William, 14-15, 146-147
Masters and Johnson studies, 14-15, 146-147
masturbation
    in adolescence, 389
    by caregivers, 520
    in children, 375, 377, 378
    cultural influences, 136
    early views, 9, 10, 378
    Elders' comments, 371
    as paraphilia, 516
    penalties for, 515
    religions' views, 57t, 59, 63
    as sexual technique, 150-153, 152f, 153f
    in virtual sex, 68
matching hypothesis, **449**

maternal mortality, 20
matriarchal groups, **34**
matrilineal societies, **258**
Matthew Shepard and James Byrd, Jr., Hate Crimes Prevention Act, 359
Maxim magazine surveys, 24
Mbuti Pygmies, 489
McClintock, Martha, 144
McClintock effect, 144
McGreevey, Jim, 83
Mead, Margaret, 12
media. *See also* social media
    acceptance of same-gender relationships, 346-347
    attractiveness standards in, 448, 449
    censorship, 76
    depictions of romantic relationships, 416, 446
    history of sexuality in, 70f-72f
    impact of sexual expression in, 68-71
    influence on gender roles, 322
    as information source about sexuality, 395-396, 397
    music and sexual expression, 73-75
    shared sexual images, 71-73
    soft pornography in, 94
    video's evolution, 75-76, 93-94
medical community
    approaches to desire and performance issues, 517, 518, 519
    early views of LGBTQ persons, 346, 347
    LGBTQ acceptance, 514-515
    views of abnormal sexual behavior, 513
medical interventions during childbirth, 267, 276, 278-280
medical model of sexual science, 8-9
medications. *See also* drug use
    abortion, 290-291
    during childbirth, 278
    impact on sexual function, 436, 518
    for paraphilic disorders, 535
    during pregnancy, 254, 254t
    for sexual dysfunctions, 41f, 518, 519
medroxyprogesterone acetate, 238
Mehinaku people, 537
memory, pregnancy's effects on, 264
men
    breast cancer in, 110
    causes of infertility, 284
    challenges to sexual arousal, 518
    circumcision, 125-128
    desire for sex, 17
    hormonal contraceptives for, 216, 245
    masturbation techniques, 152, 152f
    postpartum depression, 282
    pubertal changes, 381f, 383-385
    as rape victims, 478-479, 488
    same-sex attraction, 336-337, 340, 452
    sexual anatomy, 120-122, 121f, 122f
    sexual health concerns, 180-184
    sexual response, 122-125
    as sexual tourists, 543
menarche, **109**, **110**, 115, 382, 385
menopause, **119**, 120, 517
menstrual phase, **116**
menstrual synchrony, **114**, 144
menstruation
    complications, 117-119
    defined, **114**
    overview of cycle, 114-117, 115f
    as taboo, 52, 53
    timing, 114
mental health. *See also* depression; emotional health
    aging and, 436, 438-439
    child sexual abuse and, 530
    dating abuse victims, 502
    with early puberty, 383
    with gender identity struggles, 311, 327
    LGBTQ persons, 327, 355-356, 358
    marriage and, 425, 426

paraphilias and, 521–522, 526–533, 531
resiliency, 371, 439, **507–508**
of sex offenders, 491
sexual addiction and, 525
sexualization's impact, 397
mental health profession
changing views of sexual norms, 513–516
early views of LGBTQ persons, 346, 347
men who have sex with men, **350–351**
mesoderm, 260–261
metoidioplasty, 315
#Me-Too Movement
in China, 97
key dates, 42f, 72f
origins, 477
social impact, 17
metrosexuals, 317
Miami, sex trafficking in, 543, 544
microaggressions, 356–357
microcelebrities, **80**
microperforate hymen, 106f
Middle Ages, sexuality in, 44
Middle East, female genital mutilation, 111–112, 113f
midlife, **410**, 434–438
midwives, **275–277**
mifepristone, 240, 290–291
Milano, Alyssa, 477
Milk, Harvey, 346
Millennials, 155
minipills, 227t, 237
minorities, infant and maternal mortality rates, 20
minority stress, **354**, 355–356
minors. *See* adolescents; children
Mirena, 239, 240
miscarriage, **270**
misoprostol, 290
missionary position, 160, 160f
Mitcham, Matthew, 346
mixed-race marriage, 515
Modern Family, 449f
Mohave culture, 344
molestation, **477**
Mollys, 345
Money, John, 310–311
monogamous marriage, **428**
monogamy, 416, 417
monophasic pill, 237
monotheism, **56**
monozygotic twins, 338–339
Monroe, Marilyn, 448
mons pubis, 102f, **102**
moral-normative perceptions, 424
morning sickness, 261–262
mortality rates, 20
mosaicism, 304
motherhood, careers and, 251–252
motility, **284**
movies, 75t
mucous membrane, **104**
Muhammad, 38f, 44
Müllerian ducts, 301
music, 73–75
music videos, 75
mutual consent, 544, 545
myometrium, **106**, 108f

N

National At-Home Dad Network, 252
National Football League, 173f
National Health and Social Life Survey, 15–17
National Minority AIDS Council, 194
natural contraception methods, **242–244**
natural selection, 10
Negotiators, in Fisher's model, 450
Neisseria gonorrhea, 198

nesting, 37
Netherlands
family leave in, 252
same-sex marriage in, 432–433
sexual health in, 402
sex work in, 505, 506
neuropeptide hormones, 114
neurotransmitters, **118**
Nevada, sex work in, 504
newborns, STI risks to, 200, 201, 203, 208, 209
New Testament, 61
New View Campaign, 517
New Zealand, sex education in, 400
Nicholson, Jack, 519
nicotine, 254t
19th Amendment (U.S.), 46–47
90-day pills, 227t
nipple clamps, 545
nipples, **108**, 109f
nits, 206
nocturnal emission, 383, 384
noncoercive paraphilias, **526**, 530
noncoital sexual behaviors, 389–390
nonconsensual cheating, 431
nongonococcal urethritis, 190t
nonlove, in Sternberg's theory, 456
nonmonogamous marriage, **428**
nonoxynol-9, 236
nonverbal communication, 464–465
normative behaviors, extreme versus, 535–536
norms, **34**. *See also* sexual norms
novelty, sexual, 544–547
nuclear families, 35, 46–47, **497**. *See also* families
nursing homes, 439, 440
nutrition, 116, 255
NuvaRing, 228t, 239, 241f

O

Obama, Barack, 77, 365, 429
Obergefell v. Hodges, 42f, 433
obesity, 116
objectivity, **21**
Ocean, Frank, 361f
odors
arousal and, 141–142, 144
attraction and, 114
cultural views, 140
Oedipus Rex (Sophocles), 497
oil-based lubricants, 234
Oncale v. Sundowner Offshore Services, 501
online bullying, 357, 358, 360
online communities, 77, 81, 84, 96–97
online dating
advantages, 81
attitudes about, 88f
growing participation, 77, 86–89
guidelines, 90
online grooming, 497
online sex. *See* virtual sex
online sexual abuse, 496–497
online sexual entertainment, 95–96
online sexual scripts, 454
online surveys, 23
oophorectomy, 315
open adoption, **286–287**
opportunistic infections, **196–197**
oral contraceptives, **236**, **237**. *See also* birth control pill
oral sex
acceptance among religious groups, 63
in adolescence, 390, 399
cultural views, 537
NHSLS findings, 15–16
penalties for, 515
during pregnancy, 257
as sexual technique, 155–157, 156f, 157f

STI risk from, 169, 201
orchiectomy, 315
organized religion, 56. *See also* religion
orgasm
in childhood, 375
defined, **107**, 148
difficulties, 107
G-spot role, 105
influence of smell, 142
Masters and Johnson studies, 14–15, 146–147
as paraphilia, 516
physical manifestations, 147–148, 149–150
Orthodox Judaism, 59
Ortho Evra, 227t–228t, 238
osteoporosis, **119**
Other Specified Paraphilic Disorder, 527
ova, 259, 260f
ovarian cancer, **178**, 179t
ovarian follicles, 108f, **108**
ovaries, 108f, **108**
ovulation, **108**, 242, 260f, 284
oxytocin, **114**, 117t

P

pain management during childbirth, 277–278
pair bonding, **35**
Palin, Sarah, 324
Paltrow, Gwyneth, 477
pandemics, 189
pansexuality, **334**
Pap smears, 176, 177f
paralysis, sexual activity and, 520
paraphilias. *See also* extreme sexual behavior
changing views of behaviors as, 515–516
defined, **514**, 526
evolution of term, 524
origin theories, 533–534
paraphilic disorders versus, 521–522, 526
types, 526–533
paraphilic disorders. *See also* extreme sexual behavior
defined, 522, 527, **540**
paraphilias versus, 521–522, 526
treatment, 534–535
types, 526–533
paraphrasing, 467
parasitic STIs, 191t, 205–207
Paravartita position, 135
parental monitoring, 393
parental notification laws, 292, 293
parenthood
impact on sexual activity, 429
reproductive decisions, 248–253, 426
parents
consent for contraception and abortion, 232
discussion with children about sexuality, 62, 371–372, 386, 393, 394
effects of sexual orientation on children, 343
influence on gender roles, 319–320, 322, 325
same-sex, 363–365
sexual abuse by, 494, 498
Parents, Families, and Friends of Lesbians and Gays, 362
Paris Is Burning (film), 333
"partial birth" abortion, 293
participatory action research, **25–26**
partners. *See* sexual partners
passion, in Sternberg's theory, 455
patches, contraceptive, 227t–228t, 238–239, 239f
patriarchal societies, **258**
peak hours deliveries, 280
pediculicides, 206–207
pedophilia, 527, **528–530**
peers
communication about sex with, 394–395
influence on gender roles, 320–321, 326

pelvic exams, 176, 177f
pelvic inflammatory disease, **185**, 190t, 200, 203–205
pelvic pain, 283
penicillin, 203
penile columns, **122**
penile enhancement, 126
penile extensions, 545
penile glans, 121f, **121**
penile implants, **126**
penile shaft, 121f, **121**
penis
    anatomy, 120–122, 121f
    circumcision, 125–128, 127f
    defined, **120**, 121
    desirable features, 100, 123, 124, 125, 126
    health care, 180
    prenatal development, 301f
    pubertal changes, 383
    STI symptoms, 200f, 201, 203f, 207f
    surgical construction, 315
Penn, Sean, 346
Penn State sex scandal, 493
pennyroyal tea, 218–219
perfect-use failure rate, **223**
perimenopause, **119**
perimetrium, **106**, 108f
perineum, **123**
permissiveness, 36
personal ads, 69
personal computers, 77
personal information, sharing online, 77, 79, 90
personal needs for pleasure, 136–139
personal safety, online, 85, 90
personal space, 464–465
perversions, **10**, 46
pessaries, 217
phalloplasty, 315
Phat Girlz (film), 109
pheromones, **114**, 142, 144
photos, sharing, 90
physical attractiveness, 447–449. *See also* attraction, sexual
physical health, 253–258, 434–435, 519–521
physician requirements for abortion, 293
physicians. *See also* medical community
    discussing sexual health with, 436–438
    early views of LGBTQ persons, 346
physiology, **100**, 112–119, 128
Pimpettes, in Stokes's model, 454
Pinsky, Drew, 76
pinup girls, 70f, 72f
Pitocin, 280
pituitary gland, **112**, **113**
placenta, 260f, **260**, **261**, 274–275
Plan B, 239
Planned Parenthood, 14, 40f, 70f
plastic surgery, 111, 112
plateau phase, **147**
play, gender stereotypes, 320–321, 325
play acting, 544
Playboy magazine, 71f, 92–93
pleasure. *See also* arousal
    adding to sex education curricula, 400, 401
    contraception and, 230
    culture and, 135–136
    danger and, 168
    depictions in history, 134–135
    evolution in humans, 35
    as human right, 163–164
    penis size and, 125
    personal needs, 136–139
    role in sexual well-being, 5
    Victorian era views, 46
Pneumocystis carinii pneumonia, 197
police corruption, 504
police officers, 324
Polis, Jared, 347

politics
    impact on sexual well-being, 17–19
    LGBTQ persons in, 347
    sex scandals in, 70, 83, 430
    women in, 324
polyamory, **417**–**418**, 419, 422
polycystic ovary syndrome, 64
polygamy, **49**, 427, 428
polytheism, **55**–**56**
Pomeroy, Wardell, 13, 14
pop culture, 68–71. *See also* cultures; sexual cultures
popular music, 73–75
pornification, **94**–**95**
pornography
    arousal and, 141, 142, 145
    children in, 82, 94, 95, 498
    defined, **92**
    evolution, 92–96
    financial rewards, 93
    growth in pop culture, 69, 94–95
    impact on relationships, 146
    increased access, 78, 84, 93–95
    influence on sexual behavior, 527
    as paraphilia, 516
    sexting versus, 81–82
    social effects, 94–95
    teens' exposure to, 84
positions. *See* sexual techniques
positive regard, 468
positive sexuality, AIDS impact on, 15
postpartum depression, **282**
postpartum period, **281**–**284**
post-traumatic stress disorder, 480, 491–492
poverty
    HIV infection and, 189–192, 194, 212–213
    reproductive rights and, 292
    sex trafficking and, 503
    sexual violence and, 486
    sex work and, 504, 506, 542
pragma, 457f, 458, 459
precancerous lesions, 209
precocious puberty, 116, **383**, 385
pre-exposure prophylaxis, 199
pregnancy
    in adolescence, 391–392
    assisted methods of achieving, 284–286
    childbirth approaches, 273–281
    conception, 258
    drug use during, 254, 254t, 260
    good health for, 253–258
    myths, 249, 250
    physical symptoms, 261–262, 263f, 265, 267
    postpartum period, 281–284
    potential problems, 254–255, 254t, 259, 268–273
    stages and progression, 259–268
prehistoric sexuality, 38–39
premarital sex
    changing attitudes about, 63
    religions' views, 57t, 58, 60, 61
premature ejaculation, 519
premenstrual dysphoric disorder, **118**
premenstrual syndrome, **117**
prenatal classes, 266
prenatal development, 259–267, 339–340. *See also* pregnancy
preoccupied attachment, 459
PrEP, 199
Presley, Elvis, 71f, 76
preterm birth, **270**–271
prevention programs, child sexual abuse, 496
Priapus, 120, 121f
primary care physicians, 171
primary erogenous zones, **141**
primary HIV infection, 196, 197f
primary stage syphilis, 202
primate sexuality, 34, 379
prisoner rape, 484–486
Prison Rape Elimination Act, 485–486

privacy
    communication versus, 464, 466
    media impact on, 69
    protections in sexuality studies, 22
private adoption, 287
private sexual images, 69, 82
procreation, 33
progesterone, 115f, **116**, 117t, 259–260, 290
progestin
    in birth control pills, 226t–227t, 237
    in injections, implants, and patches, 237–239
    in IUDs, 228t, 239–240
    virilization from, 302–303, 307t
progestin-only pill, 227t, 237
prolactin, 117t
proliferative phase, 115f, **115**
pronatalism, **251**–**252**
prostaglandins, 117t, 118
prostate cancer, 182f, 521
prostate gland, 121f, **123**
prostate-specific antigen (PSA) test, 182, **183**–**184**
prostitution, **503**–**505**
protection, 5. *See also* sexually transmitted infections
Protestant Reformation, 38f
PSA test, 182, 183–184
psychiatry, 40f, 347, 513–516
psychoanalysis, **11**
psychoanalytic approach to paraphilias, 533–534
psychological attraction, 450–451
Psychopathia Sexualis (Krafft-Ebing), 10
psychotherapy, 535
puberty
    defined, **370**
    early occurrence in girls, 116, 383
    physical changes, 108–109, 380–385
puberty blockers, 314
pubic bone, **102**
pubic lice, 191t, 206f, **206**–**207**
public adoption, 287
public funding for abortion, 293
public health, 39f, 45
Puritanism, **61**
purpose in life, 7

Q

qualitative research, **21**
quantitative research, **21**
queer persons, **332**, 352–353
questioning, **332**, 353
questionnaires, 13, 23
quid pro quo harassment, **499**
Quran, 44, 60

R

race
    abortion and, 289
    attractiveness standards and, 448
    breast cancer occurrence and, 173f
    gender stereotypes and, 322
    HIV infection and, 192, 193f, 194
    marriage and, 428–429, 515
    problem pregnancies and, 269
    sexual orientation and, 350–351
    transphobia and, 313
racism, 20
radical inclusion, 64
random samples, **15**
rape
    of children, 494, 495. *See also* childhood sexual abuse
    cultural and social influences, 486–490, 537–538
    date rape, 479–483
    defined, **478**

in marriage, 483–484
myths, 479, 480, 486
occurrence in U.S., 478–479, 478f
overview, 477–479
perpetrators, 490–491
in prisons, 484–486
recovering from, 491–493
rape-prone societies, **487**–488, 490
rapists, 490–491
rap music, 75
Ravi, Dhuran, 356
reality TV, 76
rear entry position, 162–163, 162f, 163f
red light districts, 505
reduction thyroid chrondroplasty, 315
Reform Judaism, 59
refractory periods, **15**, **125**, **148**
refugees, 504, 505
registered partnerships, **420**, 422
Reimer, David, 311
relationships, pornography's impact, 146
reliability, **21**
religion
  adolescent sexual relationships and, 386–387
  celibacy in, 414
  gender roles and, 319, 322–323
  historic influence on sexuality, 40–45, 47, 48
  impact on sexual well-being, 63–65
  influence on mate selection, 425–426
  key dates, 38f
  sexual orientation and, 350–351
  strength of influence on sexuality, 32, 54–61
  views of marriage, 421, 424
religious identity, **56**
remarriage, 432
Renaissance, 45
rent boys, 503
repair mechanisms, 472
reparative therapies, 515
representative samples, **13**
repression, **11**
reproduction, as sole rationale for intercourse, 9
reproductive decisions, 248–253, 426
reproductive system
  cancer of, 178–179, 179t, 180–183, 181f, 182f
  female external organs, 101–104, 102f, 104f
  female internal organs, 104–108, 105f, 106f, 108f
  male, 120–125, 121f, 122f, 123f
  prenatal development, 301, 301f
  STI symptoms, 199–209, 200f, 201f, 203f, 207f, 208f
research designs, **21**, 22–26
resilience, **371**
resiliency, 371, 439, **507**–508
Resisters, in Stokes's model, 454
resolution phase, **148**
retrospective bias, **22**
retrospective self-reports, **22**
retroviruses, **195**
rhythm method, 229t
rings, contraceptive, 228t, 239
risk taking
  as key to extreme behaviors, 538–539, 540
  in online sexual behavior, 82, 83, 85
  over-pathologizing, 525–526
  pleasure and, 168
rituals. *See also* taboos
  in Judaism, 59
  masculinity, 32, 53
  prehistoric, 38–39
robot fetishism, **533**
Roe v. Wade, 40f, 42f, 293
Rohypnol, 480, 481
Roman Catholic Church, 38f, 43, 44
Roman Empire, 43
romantic love. *See* love
romantic relationships in childhood and adolescence, 379, 385

root of penis, **120**, **121**
Rosie the Riveter, 47f
RU486, 290–291
rural areas, gay people in, 348

S

sadism, **530**
sado-masochism relationships, **538**–539, 545. *See also* BDSM
Sakulambei, 306
Saltz, Gail, 454
Sambia culture
  childbirth practices, 275
  contraception, 218
  intersex conditions in, 306
  masculinity rituals, 32, 52f, 53, 344, 537
  postpartum taboos, 284
  sexual socialization in, 53
same-sex attraction in adolescence, 388–389
same-sex marriage. *See also* marriage
  defined, **420**, 422
  frequency of sexual activity, 430
  growing acceptance, 346, 360, 432–434
  key dates, 41f, 42f
same-sex relationships. *See also* homosexuality; LGBTQ persons
  anal sex in, 159
  attraction in, 335–337, 448, 449, 451–452
  cohabitation in, 418
  communication in, 469
  cultural relativism and, 51, 53, 344–346
  family formation and, 363–365
  frequency of sexual activity, 430
  in history, 42, 43, 44, 45, 47, 48
  lack of acceptance, 136, 341, 346, 365–366, 514
same-sex sexual harassment, 500–501
Samoa, Mead's studies in, 12
Sanday, Peggy Reeves, 489
Sandusky, Jerry, 493
Sanford, Mark, 83
San Francisco, 512
Sanger, Margaret, 39f, 219–220
sanitation systems, 45
Sapphists, **345**
Satcher, David, 17–19
Savage, Dan, 361
scabicides, 206
scabies, 191t, 205f, **205**–206
schoolgirls, in sex fantasies, 543
schools. *See also* college students
  influence on gender roles, 321–322
  sexual harassment in, 501–502
  sexuality education approaches, 396–402
scripts, sexual, 452–453, 454
scrotal sac, **122**
scrotoplasty, 316
scrotum
  anatomy, 121f, 122f
  defined, **122**
  sensitivity, 152
  surgical construction, 316
Seasonale, 227t
sea sponges, 218
sebaceous glands, **102**, **103**
sebum, **102**, **103**
secondary erogenous zones, **141**
secondary sex characteristics, 381f, **381**
secondary stage syphilis, 202–203
Second Life, 89, 91
second marriages, 432
second trimester, 262f, 264–265
second wave feminism, 40f, 47–48
secretory phase, 115f, **115**–116
secular trend, 382f, **382**
secure attachment, 459–460
security, marriage and, 427

selective abstinence, **231**
self-assessment
  anatomy knowledge, 101, 103
  attitudes about sex, 36
  birth planning, 281
  cohabitation, 423
  communicating with children about sexuality, 374
  communication in relationships, 470
  gender identity, 310
  homophobia, 355
  music and sexual expression, 75
  pleasurable sex, 542
  rape myths, 480, 481
  reproduction knowledge, 249, 250
  sexual literacy, 6, 7
  sexual needs, 137–138
  sexual orientation, 336
  STI risk, 186–187
self-castration, 60
self-disclosure, 170, 230, 466
self-exams
  breast, 110, 175
  testicular, 124, 180–181
selfishness, 460
self-reports, 22
self-selection bias, 24, 25
semen
  defined, **123**
  ingesting, 155–156
  rituals involving, 53
seminal vesicles, 121f, **123**
seminiferous tubules, **122**, 123f
seniors, **411**, 413f, 428
sensation-seeking behavior, 396
senses, pleasure and, 140–143
septate hymen, 106f
serial monogamy, **416**
sex (biological)
  defined, **299**
  determinants, 300–301, 300t
  gender versus, 299
  variations, 270, 302–307, 307t
  visual arousal and, 141
sex-approving cultures, **51**–52
sex chromosomes, 300, 300f, 302–304, 307t
sex-disapproving cultures, **51**–52
sex drive. *See* desire for sex
sex education
  approaches, 396–402
  cultural influences, 52
  current prevalence in U.S., 2
  for disabled persons, 520
  early efforts, 14
  Internet versus, 82
  Kirby's model, 3
  when to begin, 371
sex flush, **147**
sex-for-sale websites, 95–96
sexiness standards, 447–449
sexism, **323**–324, 489
sex myths, 464
sex-negative cultures
  beliefs, 464
  emotional literacy in, 462
  pleasure and, 136
  sexual shame and, 525, 526
sex offenders, 490–491
sexology, **8**
sex-positive cultures, 136, 535
sex reassignment procedures, 309, 311, 314–316
sex scandals, 70, 83, 493, 529
sex symbols, 71–72, 73–75
sexting, **81**–82, 83
sex tourism
  development of, 504, **541**–544
  for extreme behavior, 525, 527
  to Folsom Street Fair, 512
  relation to trafficking, 506, 543–544

sex toys, 536, 545-547
sex trafficking, 504, 505, **506**, 543-544
sexual activity. *See also* sexual techniques
    casual, 415-416
    coital positions, 159-163, 160f, 161f, 162f, 163f
    following childbirth, 282-283
    frequency, 154-155, 415, 429-430, 545, 546
    in marriage, 415, 429-430
    in midlife, 434-438
    physical disability and, 519-521
    polyamory, 417-418, 419
    during pregnancy, 257-258
    religions' impact, 386-387
    of single vs. married people, 415
sexual addiction, **524**, 525-526
Sexual Addicts Anonymous, 524
sexual assault. *See* rape; sexual coercion
sexual behaviors
    in adolescence, 386-387, 389-392, 390t
    attraction versus, 335-337
    causes of paraphilias, 533-534
    in children, 375-379, 376t, 377t
    diagnostic models, 513-516
    impulsive or compulsive, 522-524
    normative to extreme, 535-544
    novelty in, 544-547
    paraphilias vs. paraphilic disorders, 521-522
    predicting, 20
    in primates, 34
    public displays, 512
    social construction, 18
    treatment of paraphilic disorders, 534-535
    types of paraphilias, 524-533
sexual bullying, **502**-503. *See also* bullying
sexual chauvinism, **49**-50
sexual coercion. *See also* rape
    cultural and social influences, 486-490, 537-538
    date rape, 479-483
    defined, **477**
    with extreme sexual behavior, 526, 527-530
    in marriage, 483-484
    overview, 477-479
    perpetrators, 490-491
    in prisons, 484-486
    recovering from, 491-493, 506-508
    teen dating abuse, 502-503
    in workplaces and schools, 499-502
sexual communion, 36
sexual compulsivity, **523**
sexual consumerism, **70**
sexual cultures
    approving and disapproving, 51-52
    defined, **39**
    Europe versus United States, 402-404
    historic development, 40-48
    norms in, 48-51, 513-516, 535-538
    in United States, 61-63, 345-346, 349
    unlearning in, 52-54
sexual degeneracy, **9**, 46
sexual differentiation, **300**
sexual dimorphism, **302**
sexual dysfunctions, **15**
sexual empowerment, 3, 8
sexual excitement, **144**-145
sexual exploitation, **477**
sexual fantasies, **144**-145
sexual fetishism, **541**. *See also* fetishism
sexual fidelity, 16, 16f, 82. *See also* infidelity
sexual fluidity, **351**-352, 385-388
sexual geography, **348**
sexual harassment, **499**-502
sexual health
    aging and, 434-440
    leading concerns for men, 180-184
    leading concerns for women, 171-179
    Surgeon General's study, 17-19

    taking responsibility for, 169-171
sexual histories, sharing, 170, 230, 466
sexual identity. *See also* sexual orientation
    adolescent development, 385-389
    defined, **46**
    modern Western development, 345-346
sexual imagery, 69-70, **71**-73
sexual individuality
    boundaries and, 86
    defined, **52**
    Internet's impact, 77, 80, 81, 84, 87
    pornography's impact, 95
    sexual orientation and, 342-343
    unlearning and, 54
sexual intercourse. *See* intercourse
sexuality
    in children, 375-379, 537
    in chimpanzees, 33-34
    diagnostic models, 513-516
    discussing, 461-464. *See also* communication
    gender differences, 17
    historical development, 37-48
    in human cultural evolution, 34-37
    nature vs. nurture debate, 16-17, 18
    physical disability and, 519-521
    unique human traits, 33, 34
    in United States, 61-63
Sexuality Information and Education Council of the United States, 14, 396
Sexuality in the Human Female (Kinsey), 71f
Sexuality in the Human Male (Kinsey), 70f
sexualization, **396**, 397
sexualized behaviors, **375**
sexual journals, 138-139
sexual literacy
    achieving, 3-5
    defined, **3**
    goals, 4-5
    Internet's impact, 80, 87, 96
    self-assessment, 6, 7
    younger generation's pursuit, 2
sexually transmitted infections. *See also* AIDS (acquired immunodeficiency syndrome); HIV (human immunodeficiency virus)
    in adolescence, 391-392
    common misconceptions, 169, 170
    contraceptive methods and, 223
    effects of circumcision, 127-128
    Europe versus United States, 402-403
    HIV/AIDS, 188-198
    from oral sex, 169
    poverty and, 189-192, 194, 212-213
    during pregnancy, 255
    prevalence, 184
    in prisons, 484, 485
    reduced prevention education, 2
    risks and protective factors, 184-188
    sexual self-disclosure and, 466
    in sex work, 504
    summary of, 190t-192t
sexual negotiation, **3**, 8
sexual norms
    defined, **49**
    of great world religions, 57-61, 57t
    variation among sexual cultures, 48-51, 513-516, 535-538
sexual novelty, **544**-547
sexual offense policies, 489
sexual orientation. *See also* homosexuality; LGBTQ persons
    across cultures, 343-346
    behavior versus, 335-337
    coming out, 360-365
    defined, **332**
    development, 333, 337-341
    discrimination and aggression against, 353-359
    early views, 9
    fluidity, 352

    gender identity versus, 312
    HIV infection and, 193f
    individuality and, 342-343
    nature vs. nurture debate, 16-17, 18
    overview, 332-334
    socialization, 341-342
    spectrum, 334-335, 335f
sexual partners
    coital positions, 159-163
    coping with menopause, 120
    discussing contraception with, 230
    discussing STIs with, 187-188, 189
    fidelity to, 82
    multiple in adolescence, 399
    pregnancy's effects on, 264, 265, 268, 282
    rape by, 483-484
    saying no to, 472-473
    tastes and smells, 142-144
sexual pleasure. *See* pleasure
sexual prejudice, **354**
sexual renunciation, 60
sexual research
    evaluating, 24
    historical developments, 10-17
    human rights impact, 27
    methodologies, 21-26
    perspectives on, 19-21
sexual response cycles, 146-150
sexual rights, 26-27, 365-366
sexual sadism disorder, 530-531
sexual satisfaction
    global research findings, 154-155
    in marriage, 415, 429-430
    penis size and, 125
sexual science
    defined, **8**
    development of research methods, 10-17
    medical model, 8-9
    perspectives on, 19-21
    research methodologies, 21-26
    social justice emphasis, 17-19
sexual script theory, 452-**453**, 454
sexual selfhood, **3**
sexual shame, **523**, 525, 526
sexual socialization
    during childhood, 375, 392-396
    defined, **49**
    heterosexual, 333, 341-342
    online, 82-85
sexual techniques
    anal sex, 158-159, 158f
    coital positions, 159-163, 160f, 161f, 162f, 163f
    masturbation, 150-153
    oral sex, 155-157, 156f, 157f
sexual terms, 462, 463-464
sexual unlearning, **52**-54
sexual well-being
    of children and adolescents, 404
    cohabitation and, 424-425
    coming out, 360-365
    communication's role, 472-473
    contraception and, 244-245
    defined, **3**
    dimensions, 5-7, 6f
    in marriage, 425-426
    personal enjoyment and, 547
    pleasure and, 135-139, 547
    politics and, 17-19
    religion and, 63-65
    reproductive rights and, 292-293
    sexual orientation and, 365-366
    STI prevention and, 212-213
sex work, **503**-505, 541-542
shame, sexual, **523**, 525, 526
shame of rape, 487
shared sexual images, **71**-73
Shepard, Matthew, 359

side lying position, 161–162, 162f
SIECUS, 396
sight, arousal and, 141
silicone-based lubricants, 234
similarity-attraction hypothesis, **450**–**451**
Sinatra, Frank, 70f, 74
single living, 412–415
Sister Wives (TV show), 428
sitcoms, 76
sizes of condoms, 233
Skyla, 239, 240
slang terms, 463
slavery, sexual, 504, 505, 506, 543–544
smartphones, 77
smegma, **121**
smell sense, 141–142, 144
Smith, Bessie, 70f
smoking, 223, 253, 254t
Snapchat, 68, 72f
social avoidance, 539
social class, love and, 455
social construction of sexual behavior, **18**
socialization, heterosexual, 333, 341–342, 388
social justice, **17**–**19**
social kin, **497**, 498
social media. *See also* Internet
    cyberbullying, 357
    elements of, **80**–81
    growth, 80–82
    as information source about sexuality, 395–396
    lack of boundaries, 86
    sexual scripts on, 454
    user statistics, 76–77, 78f
social networking sites, **80**–**81**
social skills training, 535
sociobiological approach to paraphilias, 534
sodomy
    early Christian views, 43
    laws against, 41f, 44, 353–354
soft pornography, **92**, 94
Something's Gotta Give (film), 519
sound, arousal and, 143
South Africa
    rape in, 486, 492
    sex work, 504
    STI study, 212–213
special needs children, adopting, 287
speculums, **175**, **176**, 177f
sperm, 242, 259, 284
spermarche, **383**
spermatogenesis, **122**
sperm banks, 286
sperm count, 284
spermicides, 226t, 235, **236**
spirituality, **38**–**39**, 56, 61–63. *See also* religion
Spitzer, Robert L., 347
sponge, contraceptive, 226t
spontaneous abortion, **270**
sports, extreme, 538
Standard Days Method, 242–243
Star Wars, 497f
statutory rape, **404**
stay-at-home parents, 252
Stephenson, Neal, 89
stereotypes
    attractiveness, 448, 449
    gender, **317**, 319, 320, 322
    LGBTQ persons, 354
    romantic love, 455
sterilization, 222–223, 228t–229t, 241–242, 241f, 242f
Sternberg, Robert, 455
Sternberg's love theory, 455–456, 455f
steroid hormones, **112**, **113**, 114
stig, **351**
stigma, **354**. *See also* discrimination
stillbirth, **270**

Stokes, Carla, 454
stoneseed, 219
stonewalling, 471
Stonewall riots, 40f, 346
storge, 457f, 458, 459
straight, **332**. *See also* heterosexuality
strange familiarity, **80**
stress
    of divorce, 432
    elder sexuality and, 436, 437
    minority, 354, 355–356
    sexual satisfaction and, 430, 437
student-faculty relationships, 501–502
submission trait, 451
substance use. *See* drug use
suffocation, autoerotic, 531–532
Sufi dancers, 44
suicide, 356, 357, 358
support groups, 355, 362, 507, 508
supportive comments, 468, 472
Supreme Court (U.S.)
    same-sex harassment decision, 501
    same-sex marriage ruling, 346, 360, 433
surface orgasms, 142
surgical contraceptive methods, 222–223, 228t–229t, 241–242
surrogacy, **286**
survey studies, **13**, 15–17, 23, 24
survival sex, **504**, 505
suspensory ligaments, 109f, 126
Sweden, marriage in, 414
Sweden, rape in, 486
Sweet Tea (Johnson), 350
swingers, 69, **431**
Swinton, Tilda, 317f
symbolic boundaries, **62**
symptomatic HIV infection, 196–197
syphilis, 190t, **202**–**203**

T

taboos
    changing attitudes about, 53–54
    incest, 37, 497–498
    marriage, 428, 429
    media impact on, 72, 75
    methods of conveying, 54
    postpartum period, 284
    during pregnancy, 257
    religious influence, 55
    in sexual cultures, 53, 344, 349, 537
    in United States, 62
tampons, 118
Tanzania, HIV risk, 195
tape analogy, 2
tastes, changing, 342–343
taste sense, 142–143
T-cells, 196
teachers, influence of, 322
technical virginity, **387**
techniques. *See* sexual techniques
Teena, Brandon, 313
teenagers. *See* adolescents
teen dating abuse, **502**–**503**
teen pregnancy, 386, 391–392, 392f, 396, 399, 402, 403
telephone service, 90
television, 75–76, 346–347. *See also* media
tenting effect, **104**
testicles (testes), 122f, **122**, 201f
testicular cancer, 124, **180**–181, 181f
testicular self-exams, 124
testosterone
    defined, **113**, 117t
    gender confirmation use, 315
    increased production, 128
    insensitivity to, 303

    reduced production, 119, 128
    therapies, 303
tests for fetal abnormalities, 271–273
tests for pregnancy, 260
theatre, 345
thelarche, **109**, **110**
therapies. *See* treatment
third trimester, 262f, 265–267
Thirteen Reasons Why (TV show), 76
Thomas, Clarence, 499
Tiefer, Lenore, 517
timing of communications, 467
Tinder, 72f
Tiresias, 306
tobacco use, 223, 253, 254t
Tokugawa era, 39f
Torah, 59
torrents, 93
touch, arousal and, 140–141
toxic shock syndrome, **118**
toxoplasmosis, 270
toys, gender expectations and, 320, 325
traditional medicine, contraception in, 218–219
tranquilizers, 254t
Transamerica (film), 316
The Transgender Child (Brill & Pepper), 312–313
Transgender Day of Visibility, 313
transgender persons
    defined, **312**
    Internet's impact, **97**
    key dates, 41f, 42f
    as sexual assault victims, 484
    social challenges, 311–313
    societal expectations, 308
transphobia, **313**
transvestic disorder, 531
transvestic fetishism, **526**, **527**
transvestites, 345
trauma during pregnancy, 270
treatment
    compulsive sexual behavior, 524, 525, 526
    early medical approaches, 10–12
    gender affirmation, 315
    HIV/AIDS, 192t, 197–198, 199, 212–213
    of menstrual disorders, 118
    paraphilic disorders, 534–535
    postpartum depression, 282
    premature labor, 271
    to promote sexual health, 27
    for same-sex attraction, 346, 515
    sexually transmitted infections, 200, 202, 203, 204
Treponema pallidum, 202
triangular theory of love, 455f, **455**–**456**
trichomoniasis, **178**, 191t
trimesters
    defined, **259**
    first, 259–264, 262f
    second, 262f, 264–265
    third, 262f, 265–267
triphasic pill, 237
triple X syndrome, 303, 307t
trisomy X, 303, 307t
Trobriand Islanders, 537
Trump, Donald, 42f, 77, 83
trust, violating, 461
tubal ligation, **222**–**223**, 228t–229t, 241, 241f
tumescence, **103**, 123
tunica albuginea, **122**, 123f
turnem men, 306
Turner syndrome, 304–305, 305f, 307t
12-step programs, 524, 525, 535
Twilight series, 72–73
twin studies, **338**–**339**
Twitter, celebrities' use, 81
TwoDay Method, 242, 243
two-spirit role, 344
typical failure rate, **223**

U

ulipristal acetate, 239
ultrasound
   to diagnose PID, 204
   fetal screening, 262, 272-273, 273f
umbilical cord, 260f, **260**, **261**
unconscious, in Freud's approach, 11, 12
United Nations, 26, 40f
United States, sex trafficking in, 543, 544
Universal Declaration of Human Rights (United Nations), 26, 40f
universal human rights, **26**
unlearning, sexual, 52-54
unmarried households, 412, 414. *See also* single living
unsafe abortions, 291
unwelcome behavior, harassment as, 499-500
urethral opening, 102f, **104**
urethroplasty, 316
urinary tract infections, **176-177**
urine tests, 260, 271-272
uterine cancer, **178**, 179t
uterus. *See also* pregnancy
   anatomy, **104**, 105f, 106-108
   growth during pregnancy, 266f
   implantation of blastocyst, 259, 260f
   IUD placement, 240f
   labor and childbirth, 273-274, 274f
   menstruation, 114-117
   structural problems, 270

V

vaccines, 209, 211t
vacuum aspiration, 290, 290f
vacuum extraction during childbirth, 279f, **279**
vagina
   anatomy, **104-106**, 105f
   artificial, 545
   cervical cap insertion, 236f
   female condom insertion, 234-235, 234f
   following childbirth, 283
   penis size and, 125
   physical exams, 176, 177f
   prenatal development, 301f
   STI symptoms, 201f
vaginal cancer, **178**, 179t
vaginal dryness, 517-518
vaginal lubrication, **104**
vaginal opening, 102f, **104**
vaginal ring, 239
vaginal spermicides, 235, 236
vaginectomy, 316
vaginitis, **177-178**
vaginoplasty, 303, 315
validating comments, 472
validating couples, 468
validity, **21**
value messages, **375**, 394
values, shared, 451
vampires, 72-73
variables, **21-22**, 25

vas deferens, 121f, **122**, 123f, 242
vasectomies, 182, **222-223**, 229t, 241, 242, 242f
vasocongestion, **105**
veils, 44
Venus of Willendorf, 39f
Vernacchio, Al, 401
vernix, **265**
Viagra, 41f, 518, 519
vibrators, 536, 545, 546-547
victim-blame, **486**, 487
Victorian era sexuality, 39f, 45-47
videos, self-produced, 92, 93-94
Vietnam War, sex tourism during, 504, 543
violence. *See also* rape
   cultural and social influences, 537-538
   domestic, 323
   homophobia and, 356, 357-359
   against LGBTQ persons, 354
   teen dating abuse, **502-503**
   against transgender people, 312, 313
viral STIs, 191t-192t, 207-209, 210t-211t. *See also* HIV (human immunodeficiency virus)
virginity, 106, 107
Virgins, in Stokes's model, 454
virilization, **302**-303, 307t
virtual identities, 78
virtual sex
   defined, **78**
   experimenting with, 78
   fidelity and, 82
   games and avatars, 89-91
   gender impersonation in, 88
   methods, 68
Virtuous Pedophiles, 529
visual stimulation, 140, 141
vocabulary, 462, 463-464
voice surgery, 315
volatile couples, 468
voluntary surgical contraception, 241f, **241-242**, 242f
voyeurism, **527-528**, 533
vulva, 102f, **102**, 104f
vulvar cancer, **178**, 179t
vulvo-vaginal atrophy, 517

W

waiting periods, 293
Walker, Alice, 350
wars
   sex trafficking during, 543
   sexual violence and, 486, 487
   survival sex during, 504, 505
water-based lubricants, 234
websites. *See* Internet
weight gain during pregnancy, 265, 267
weight training, 257
Weiner, Anthony, 83
well-being, sexual. *See* sexual well-being
Western society, sexual evolution, 513-516, 536
Why Him? Why Her? (Fisher), 450
Wilde, Oscar, 70f
Wilson, Clark, 2

Winfrey, Oprah, 495f
winnowing hypothesis, **425**
withdrawal method, **222**
Wolffian ducts, 301
The Woman Rebel (magazine), 219
women. *See also* feminism; gender roles
   causes of infertility, 284
   challenges to sexual desire, 516-518
   desire for sex, 9, 17
   early views of sexual role, 9, 42, 43, 44, 46
   image in sexual cultures, 53, 58, 60, 62
   Kinsey's studies, 13
   masturbation techniques, 152-153, 153f
   pubertal changes, 381f, 382-383, 383f
   religiosity, 322-323
   same-sex attraction, 336-337, 340, 452
   as sex offenders, 491
   sexual anatomy, 101-112
   sexual fluidity, **351-352**
   sexual health concerns, 171-179
   sexual physiology, 112-119
   sexual subordination, 164
   as sexual tourists, 543
   stimuli needed for orgasm, 149-150
workplace
   infidelities in, 431
   sexism in, 323, 324
   sexual harassment, 499-501
World Health Organization
   on compulsive sexual behavior, 523, 526
   HIV statistics, 189
   sexual rights position, 27, 163
World War II, influence on LGBTQ movement, 348
world wars, impact on sexual culture, 47
W-PATH, 314

X

X chromosomes, 300, 300f, 302-304, 307t
XYY syndrome, 303, 307t

Y

Yale University harassment incident, 501
Y chromosomes, 300, 300f, 302
yeast infections, **178**
young adults. *See* early adulthood
youth development programs, 401-402
YouthResource.com, 362
Youth Risk Behavior Surveillance System, 399
YouTube microcelebrities, 80

Z

Zeus, 42-43
zona pellucida, **259**
zoophilia, 526
Zuckerberg, Mark, 84
zygote intrafallopian transfer, **286**
zygotes, **259**, 260